good housekeeping

WORLD COOKERY

This edition first published 1972 by
Octopus Books Limited
67 Fleet Street, London EC4
© The National Magazine Company Limited, England 1962
ISBN 7064 0012 7

PRODUCED BY MANDARIN PUBLISHERS LIMITED AND PRINTED IN HONG KONG

good housekeeping
WORLD COOKERY

Compiled by Good Housekeeping Institute
with Foreword by André L. Simon,
Late President of the Wine and Food Society

Octopus Books

LONDON · NEW YORK · SYDNEY · HONG KONG

Contents

Foreword

FOOD and drink there must be where there is life : the beasts of farm and jungle ; the fishes in salt and fresh waters ; the birds that fly through the air and the worms that hide in the earth ; and all that grows in garden, field, forests and everywhere else, they all must have the food that suits them, and no other. But all are quite content to share the same drink : water. Not so man, the omnivorous lord of creation : he can eat and drink almost anything. Although there has always been enough water for all to drink since the Flood, when there was too much, man has always spent and he is still spending some of his hard-earned income for all kinds of drinks other than water. Both in food and in drink, man craves for variety : oats and hay, day after day, may be right for his horse, but not for him. How could it be otherwise ? Every one of us has different finger-prints which we can see for ourselves, and because we cannot see our taste buds we must not imagine that they are all alike : they are not. All our senses are tuned up and geared differently, and so are all our inner works. Which is why personal likes and dislikes are by no means necessarily due to fancies and prejudices but to some differences in the gearbox below the belt which are usually called allergies. There is also, of course, a very great variety of conditions and circumstances which are responsible for the choice and suitability of many foods and their culinary preparation : the climate of the country, the season of the year, available supplies, financial and transport facilities, or the lack of them, must necessarily make all the difference to the food habits of all the world's peoples. This is what this book so clearly shows : it is a guide to the kitchens of the world and should stimulate our gastronomic curiosity whilst giving us the opportunity to introduce a greater measure of variety into our daily fare.

ANDRE L. SIMON.

Introduction

THE WORLD'S FOOD

WHEN the hunters of pre-history took to agriculture they started food habits which still endure, closely bound up with our everyday life. The plants they and their successors cultivated became our staple foods, simply because it is cheaper to produce food from plants than from animals.

As a general rule these staples are cereal foods, but they can be roots or tubers, depending on soil, climate and chance. A bird's-eye view of the world's main crops would show them distributed roughly in this way, wheat and rice being the most widespread.

First the cereals :

Wheat : Generally in dry, temperate climates.

Rice : Generally in damp, tropical climates.

Maize : In parts of America, Africa and India.

Millet : In dry, hot climates, e.g., in Africa, Asia and Latin America.

Rye : In cold climates, e.g., in North East Europe.

Oats : Northern climates.

All these cereals can be ground into flour to make some sort of cake or porridge, but only wheat and rye flour can be made into true bread.

Now for the roots and tubers :

Potato : In South America, whence it spread to Europe and other parts.

Cassava : In parts of South America, Africa, Asia.

Sweet Potato : In America.

Yam : In the Pacific Islands.

Taro : In the Pacific Islands.

Although in any one territory several of these foods may be obtainable, one of them will generally form the staple food of a particular country or district and it is almost impossible to change the tradition. Rice-eaters do not take kindly to wheat, for example, so it is pointless trying to relieve a rice famine by sending surplus wheat in from elsewhere.

Throughout the world hundreds of vegetables and fruits (including the leaves, flowers, seeds, stems and roots of trees, shrubs and herbs of all kinds) add variety of flavour and texture to the main food. Particularly important types of vegetable are those known as the pulses, for these have high food value.

Meat and fish are used as available—that is, comparatively freely in the Western world, but carefully in other parts. Often, they are little more than an occasional addition—scraps of meat in rice or fish in soup—and many are the recipes for eking them out, from haggis (which incidentally uses the Scotsman's staple food, oats) to stuffed vine leaves. Domestic fowls are used all over the world, although some of the scraggy, tough birds are a far cry from our own plump, tender chicken.

Eggs, milk and other dairy foods are pretty generally used, though the quality varies considerably. Fermented milk not surprisingly crops up in various forms all over the world; because fresh milk will not keep, man has perforce acquired a taste for the soured or souring form and has even endowed it with imaginary virtues over and above the qualities it naturally shares with fresh milk.

In the old days spices were extremely important, although hardly to be classed as true foods. During the winter meals became very monotonous, depending as they did on the storable foods such as cereals; sometimes they were actually unpleasant if the carefully hoarded meat decayed too quickly. Spices were therefore essential to make food palatable. Trade routes followed these precious products all over the globe and hastened the progress of exploration and civilisation.

One of the odd contradictions about man is that while as a species he is quite the most omnivorous of animals the individual tends to get hide-bound ideas about food and would literally sooner starve than eat a food which is to him not acceptable. Man has spread over the whole world, eating anything from moth grubs, locusts, monkeys, rats and blubber to seaweed, fungi, moulds and moss. Any food instincts he may once have had (and most animals have an innate desire for the foods they need) were lost at a very primitive stage of development and " trial and error " has since been man's main guide. But once a group of men develops a social framework, its food habits become very rigid.

The movements of history have of course tended to break down some of these barriers and food habits have spread or been modified from time to time. For example, Greek slaves cooking for their Roman masters brought their own methods with them. The Norman conquerors introduced their ideas (and their culinary language) into English kitchens. French émigrés to the States took with them their liking for salads, sauces and dressings and ice cream.

Prestige is also an important factor. For at least two thousand years white bread has been considered more aristocratic and desirable than brown or wholemeal. In fact, many highly refined foods, nutritionally of less value than the more natural ones, are highly esteemed; they are a sign of civilisation and are usually more expensive and therefore add status to the consumer. This may not be a terribly important point for those who get plenty of varied foods, but it is frequently disastrous for poorer classes or countries aping the better-fed.

Nowadays shrinking distances and widespread travel, not to mention the technological food revolution, are introducing many unfamiliar foodstuffs and recipes to the man in the street and there is among Western peoples a growing interest in foreign cookery.

In this book we have slightly adapted most of the recipes according to whether the original ingredients are available or suitable for people in this country (believing that bees and slugs, for instance, might not appeal). But we have left in one or two rather surprising ones because they are so interesting. We think, however, that this collection amply demonstrates the enormous variety of dishes and cooking methods and the fascinating diversity of the world's food.

Europe

Austria has stood for hundreds of years at the centre of Europe and her close contact with other countries, both as friend and enemy, has strongly influenced her cuisine. But the Austrian cook has a lightness of touch, a gaiety of approach to that fascinating subject, food—and all Austrians are absorbedly interested in food— which has transformed the dishes that she has adopted. From Germany she has taken many recipes and by adding perhaps a trace of different seasoning, a teaspoonful of a different ingredient, she has changed them almost beyond recognition. Hungary has contributed much to Austrian cuisine, for the Slav element in Austria is strong, and through Hungary we can also trace Turkish influence ; it is interesting to remember that the delicious crescent rolls served for breakfast in Vienna owe their shape to the victory gained over the Turks by Sobieski in the seventeenth century— a victory which saved Vienna from Turkish domination. Until 1914, Vienna was the centre of the great Austro-Hungarian Empire, whose inhabitants also comprised Czechs, Slovaks, Poles, Italians, Croats and Serbs, so it is not surprising that Austrian cuisine is varied and often exotic. The wide use of pasta derives from Italy's close connection with Austria, though here again Austria has added her own touches, and Austria Nudeln and Nockerln are subtly different from Italian pasta.

Austrian pastrycooks are, of course, among the best in the world and their rich pastries and luscious tortes are unsurpassed anywhere.

But in spite of this varied culinary heritage, the average Austrian midday meal will consist of soup, often served with dumplings or noodles, meat—veal is a great favourite—with potatoes and salad and a fruity pudding or torte to finish with. Goose fat is extensively used for cooking, which adds considerably to the richness of stews and soups.

Austria does not produce any really great wine, but there are many pleasing red and white wines made from the vineyards of Niederösterreich, Steiermark and Burgenland.

Austria

CARAWAY SEED SOUP

2 oz. butter	1 tbsp. caraway seeds
2 oz. flour	2 pints chicken stock

Make a brown roux with the flour and butter, stir in the caraway seeds and the stock and allow to simmer for half an hour. Adjust the seasoning and serve with fried croûtons.

CHEESE SOUP

2 oz. butter	2 oz. cooked noodles
1 oz. flour	1 tbsp. chopped chives
3 pints chicken stock	Salt and pepper
3 oz. grated cheese	

Make a roux with the butter and flour and stir in the stock. Simmer for 30 minutes and add grated cheese. Cook for another 5 minutes and stir in the noodles, cut small. Heat through and serve with some chives in each plate.

PIKE WITH VEGETABLES

2 lb. pike	1 onion
1 lb. veal bones	Juice of a lemon
3 oz. butter	Salt
2 carrots	2 tbsps. flour
1 head celery	

Cut the fish into slices. Brown the veal bones in 2 oz. of butter, add the chopped vegetables and lemon juice, 1 pint of water and salt to taste. Simmer all together for 30 minutes, until vegetables are tender. Add the fish and cook very slowly until it is done. Remove fish and keep hot. Strain the liquid and thicken with a roux of 1 oz. butter and the flour. Boil up this sauce and pour over the fish.

FISH GOULASH

1 lb. onions	2 lb. carp
3 oz. butter	1 cup sour cream
1 tsp. paprika	2 tbsps. flour
1 pint stock	

Slice the onions and fry till golden. Add paprika and stock and cook for 10 minutes. Put in the fish, reduce the heat and simmer very gently until done. Mix the flour with the cream and stir into the fish liquid. Boil up gently and simmer for 5 minutes. Serve with boiled potatoes.

BAKED TROUT

2 trout	½ lb. tomatoes
¼ lb. mushrooms	Juice of 1 lemon
3 oz. butter	Parsley

Make incisions along the back of the fish and insert some slices of mushroom. Fry the trout on both sides and season. Place in a baking pan with the rest of the sliced mushrooms, the sliced tomatoes, lemon juice and butter. Bake in a hot oven (450° F., mark 8) for 30 minutes, basting frequently. Garnish with parsley.

VEAL RAGOÛT

1 lb. veal	½ pint milk
2 oz. butter	2 oz. flour
4 oz. carrots	Parsley
4 oz. mushrooms	Nutmeg
A small cauliflower	Yolk of 1 egg
4 oz. green peas	

Cube the veal and fry in half the butter. Add diced carrots and mushrooms, fry lightly and cover with water. Bring to the boil and add cauliflower in sprigs and the peas. Season and simmer till the veal is tender. Add the milk, thicken with the flour and the remaining butter and boil up again. At the last minute before serving, stir in the parsley and the egg yolk, previously mixed with a little of the liquid.

STUFFED BREAST OF VEAL

Medium onion, chopped	1 egg
2 oz. mushrooms, chopped	Salt and pepper
2 oz. butter	Parsley
2 white rolls	Nutmeg
2 tbsp. milk	2 lb. breast of veal

Fry onion and mushrooms lightly in the butter. Dice the rolls and soak in the milk. Add onions and mushrooms, with the butter, the egg, seasoning, parsley and a pinch of nutmeg. With a sharp knife, make a pocket in the meat, just above the bones. Insert the stuffing, skewer and roast very slowly (300° F., mark 1, allowing 25 minutes per lb. plus 25 minutes), basting frequently with a little more butter. Serve with rice and salad.

WIENER SCHNITZEL

8–10 cutlets of veal or pork	A pinch of salt
	Breadcrumbs
1 egg	Oil or fat for frying
1½–2 tbsps. milk	

Wipe the cutlets. Break the egg into a basin, add the milk and salt, and mix well. Sprinkle salt on both sides of each cutlet, and beat with a rolling pin or knife handle to make the meat tender. Dip the cutlets into the egg mixture and then into breadcrumbs, coating both sides. Fry in hot oil or fat until crisp and golden-brown—about 3 minutes on each side.

This popular Sunday dinner dish is usually garnished with a slice of lemon, and served with green salad and sauté potatoes.

POTATO GOULASH

2 large onions — Salt and paprika
Lard, cooking fat or oil — 8 oz. firm ham sausage
  for frying   or luncheon meat
2½ lb. potatoes

Peel and slice the onions and fry till golden-brown. Add the potatoes, peeled and cut into ½-inch cubes, with half a cup of water, and salt and paprika to taste. Turn the heat low, cover the pan with a well-fitting lid and simmer for 15 minutes, then add the cubed sausage or meat, and simmer for a further 5 minutes.

VEAL WITH CREAM SAUCE

4 escalopes of veal — 1 tbsp. capers
Salt — ½ tsp. paprika
Pepper — 1 tsp. French mustard
Flour — ¼ pint cream
2 oz. butter — 1 dessertsp. lemon
4 tbsps. water   juice

Trim the veal escalopes and beat them well, season and dip in flour. Melt the butter in a pan and fry the meat until golden, then keep hot. Pour the water into the pan and add the chopped capers, paprika, and other seasonings, then simmer. Remove from the heat, add the cream, and lastly the lemon juice. Add a little more seasoning if necessary, pour over the meat and serve immediately.

BEEF WITH BACON

3 lb. topside of beef — 10 peppercorns
4 oz. bacon — 1 bay leaf
Pepper and salt — Sprig of thyme
1 carrot — Pinch of nutmeg
1 onion — 1 slice rye bread
Stock — ½ cup red wine

Cut the bacon into strips and push the strips into holes in the beef. Rub the meat with pepper and salt and put into the roasting pan with the diced vegetables. Add a little water and roast slowly, basting all the time and adding more stock if necessary (325° F., mark 2). When the meat is done (about 2 hours) skim the gravy and add all the other ingredients, including the bread which has been soaked in the wine. Return to the oven until thoroughly hot, dish up the meat, strain the gravy and pour over.

ROAST PORK

2 lb. lean pork — 1 tsp. chopped parlsey
1 onion — Paprika
2 carrots — Caraway seeds
1 tbsp. lard — Salt and pepper
1 tsp. capers — 1 cup sour cream

Rub the meat with salt, pepper and paprika,

and sprinkle with caraway seeds. Dice the vegetables and fry in the fat. Transfer to a roasting pan with a lid and add the meat and a little water. Cover the pan and cook slowly for 1½ hours at 340° F., mark 3. Remove the lid and let the meat brown a little, remove, slice and keep hot. Add capers and parsley to the liquid and vegetables in the pan, pour in the cream, bring to the boil and pour over the meat.

MEAT WITH RICE

1½ lb. veal — 3 tbsps. oil
2 medium onions — Salt and pepper
1 tsp. paprika — ½ lb. rice

Slice the onions and fry golden-brown in the oil. Cube the meat and add to the onions, with the paprika and salt. Pour in half a cup of water, cover and simmer very gently until the meat is nearly done. Add the washed rice and cover rice and meat with water. Bring to the boil and simmer until the water is absorbed and the rice and meat are tender. Add a little more hot water from time to time if necessary. Dish up and serve with grated cheese and salad.

VIENNESE BEEFSTEAKS

4 fillet steaks, ½ inch — 4 tbsps. chopped onion
  thick — 1 tbsp. butter
1 tbsp. lard — 1 cup beef broth

Beat the steaks well and fry quickly in the lard on both sides. Add the onions and continue cooking on a lower heat until the meat is done. Remove the meat and keep it hot, continuing to fry the onions until golden, adding butter to the pan. Pour in the broth and bring to the boil. Pour over the meat and serve with boiled potatoes.

MEAT LOAF

1 lb. minced lean beef — 1 egg
1 lb. minced pork — Salt and pepper
3 white rolls — 2 tbsps. breadcrumbs
1 cup milk and water — 2 oz. lard
2 oz. bacon — ½ cup good stock
2 tbsps. chopped parsley — 1 cup sour cream
1 chopped onion

Mix the meats and add the rolls, which have been soaked in the milk and water, squeezed well and put through the mincer. Add the chopped bacon, parsley, onion previously fried, egg, salt and pepper and mix very thoroughly. Put the mixture into a loaf tin which has been greased and sprinkled with breadcrumbs. Pour over 2 oz. of melted lard and bake in a moderate oven (350° F., mark 4) for 1½ hours. After the first ten minutes, pour over the stock and baste the loaf frequently. When cooked, skim off the fat from the gravy, add the cream, boil it up and pour over the loaf.

MUTTON WITH RUNNER BEANS

3 lb. mutton	2 onions
2 lb. potatoes	Pepper and salt
2 lb. runner beans	2 oz. butter

Dice the meat, peel the potatoes and cut into thick slices, string the beans and break into 2-inch lengths, peel and slice the onions. Spread some of the butter on the bottom of a heavy, lidded saucepan and fill the pan with layers of onion, meat, beans and potatoes, seasoning each layer and adding dabs of butter. The top layer should be of potatoes. Pour in half a cup of water and cover the pan closely. Simmer very slowly for about 1½ hours.

TYROLEAN LIVER

2 lb. liver	1½ cups stock
1 oz. flour	3 tbsps. sour cream
3 oz. lard	1 tsp. capers
4 tbsps. chopped onion	1 tbsp. vinegar

Slice the liver, toss in flour and fry on both sides. Remove from pan and keep hot. Fry onions golden, stir in flour, stock and cream, chopped capers and vinegar. Bring to the boil and simmer for 5 minutes. Just before serving add the liver and season with salt. Serve with rice.

LIVER DUMPLINGS

½ lb. calf's liver	1 egg
1 roll or large slice of bread	Chopped parsley
	Salt and pepper
1 oz butter	4 oz breadcrumbs

Mince (or " liquidise ") the liver. Soak the roll in water, and when it is soft, squeeze out the surplus moisture, and then mince it. Cream the butter with the other ingredients, finally adding sufficient breadcrumbs to make the mixture firm enough to be formed into small dumplings (less than 1 inch in diameter). If the dumplings are to be served with a soup or stew, simmer them in this for 5 minutes. They may also be cooked in stock and served with meat and gravy.

KIDNEY WITH ONIONS

1 lb. sheep's kidneys	Seasoning
1 large onion	A pinch of caraway seeds
2 oz. dripping	¼ pint water
2 tsps. flour	1 tbsp. vinegar

Soak the kidneys in warm water to remove the skins, cut in half and remove the cores. Slice the onion and fry until brown in a pan in a little melted dripping, then fry the kidneys until they are well browned. Add the flour and seasoning and lastly the caraway seeds. Gradually pour in the water and vinegar, and simmer gently for 5 minutes ; serve at once.

GEDÜNSTETES RINDFLEISCH
(BRAISED BEEF)

1–2 onions	French mustard
Fat for frying	A small tin of tomato
2 lb. beef	purée
Salt	A little cream or top of
A slice of bread	the milk

Peel and slice the onions, and fry till golden-brown. Brown the meat in the fat, then add just enough water to cover the meat ; season, put on the lid, and braise slowly for 1½ hours. Add the bread to the gravy, then sieve (or " liquidise ") and add a little French mustard, the tomato purée and a dash of cream.

BRÖSELKNÖDEL
(PARSLEY DUMPLINGS)

2 oz. butter or margarine	1 roll or large slice of bread
2 eggs	Salt
Chopped parsley	4 oz. breadcrumbs

Cream the butter and add the eggs and plenty of chopped parsley. Soak the roll in water, then squeeze out the surplus liquid, and add the roll to the butter, with a little salt, and as many breadcrumbs as required. The mixture should be stiff enough to be formed into little balls (about 1 inch in diameter) in the hands ; if the mixture is too dry, add a little milk. Simmer the dumplings in water for 5 minutes, and serve in place of potatoes, or in soup.

BRAINS WITH EGG

2 sets of brains	2–4 eggs
2 oz. butter	Salt and pepper
Parsley	

Fry the brains in the butter with some finely chopped parsley until they look white and stiff, and no longer red. Pour the beaten eggs over, add salt and pepper to taste, and let the eggs set. Serve immediately.

FRIED LIVER

1 lb. calf's liver	Flour
1 small onion	Lemon juice
Fat for frying	Salt

Have the liver sliced by the butcher, and then cut it into small pieces. Peel and slice the onion and fry till golden-brown. Add the liver and its juice, turning the pieces over as soon as they are brown on one side. Sprinkle some flour over the liver and stir vigorously while adding a little water, so as to obtain a smooth gravy. Add 1 tbsp. lemon juice, and salt to taste. Serve immediately.

BEEF GOULASH WITH NOCKERLN

2 lb. beef	Salt
1½ lb. onions	2 tbsps. vinegar
2 oz. dripping	A pinch of marjoram
1 tbsp. paprika	A pinch of caraway
¼ pint tomato purée	seeds

Cut the beef into neat cubes, and slice the onions. Melt the fat in a pan and fry the onions until just brown, then add the paprika and 2 tbsps. water. Put the meat into the pan and stir well until all the liquor has disappeared, then add the tomato purée, salt, vinegar, marjoram and caraway seeds, cover the pan with a lid and simmer gently for 2 hours, or until the meat is quite tender ; if the goulash gets very dry, add a little liquor. Serve with the little savoury dumplings called Nockerln. (See next recipe).

NOCKERLN
(DUMPLINGS)

Put 1 oz. of butter into ¼ pint milk and without boiling, heat gently until the fat has melted. Remove from the heat, add a well-beaten egg and season well. Put 6 oz. self-raising flour into a basin and work into a stiff paste with the milk. Drop the mixture in spoonfuls into a pan of boiling water, cook for 3 minutes, then drain well. Melt 2 oz. butter in a frying pan and lightly toss the Nockerln in the heated butter.

GEFÜLLTE PAPRIKA
(STUFFED PEPPERS)

Allow 2 peppers each, choosing green ones (the red and yellow ones are supposed to be hotter). Cut off the stalk end to form a " lid," and remove all pips. Pour boiling water over the peppers and let them stand for ½ hour. Drain (the liquor can be used in soup-making), and fill with a mixture of boiled rice, cooked minced meat, a little parsley and chopped onion. Lay with the " lids " on a fireproof dish, cover with tomato sauce and bake in a moderate oven (350° F., mark 4) for 1 hour.

For the tomato sauce, melt 1 oz. of butter, stir in 1 oz. flour, add a small tin of tomato purée, pour in some water gradually, keeping the sauce fairly thick and stirring all the time ; add salt and sugar to taste.

SCHINKENFLECKERL
(HAM AND NOODLES)

1 lb. " fleckerl " (noodle pieces)	6 oz. butter or margarine
Salt	4 eggs
10 oz. ham	

Three-quarters fill a 3-pint saucepan with water, bring to boiling point and add a pinch of salt, then put in the " fleckerl." Allow to boil for 10-15 minutes, then turn them into a colander to drain, and pour cold water through until cool.

Cut the ham into small squares. Cream the butter till smooth, add the eggs and a little salt, and mix. Put in the ham and the " fleckerl " and mix well. Transfer the mixture to a baking tin and bake in a moderate oven (350° F., mark 4) for ½-1 hour, until the top is light brown. Serve with green salad.

TYROLEAN DUMPLINGS

6 slices of day-old white bread	½ pint milk
	½ lb. diced ham
2 oz. bacon fat	Flour as needed
2 eggs	Salt and pepper

Cube the bread and fry in the bacon fat. Mix the eggs and milk, salt and pepper and pour over the bread cubes. Leave for 20 minutes and then add diced ham. Stir in enough flour to make a workable dough, form into balls and poach in boiling salted water for 10 minutes. These dumplings may also be cooked in soup and served with the soup or with a plain lettuce salad.

CHEESE DUMPLINGS

3 white rolls	2 eggs
¼ pint milk and water	2 oz. butter
½ lb. cream cheese	1 tbsp. semolina
Salt	Fried breadcrumbs

Soak the rolls in the milk and water, squeeze well and sieve. Add the cheese, salt, beaten eggs and softened butter. Mix well and stir in the semolina. Leave the mixture in a covered bowl for 1 hour. Form into small balls and poach in boiling salted water for 5 or 6 minutes. Drain, roll in fried breadcrumbs. Serve as an accompaniment to meat or stewed fruit.

PAPRIKA CHICKEN

3-4 lb. chicken	3 tsp. tomato purée
6 oz. butter	Salt
1 lb. onions	1 oz. flour
1 tsp. paprika	½ pint sour cream

Joint the chicken. Fry onions until golden, add chicken and paprika. Fry the chicken on all sides until nicely coloured. Add the tomato purée, thinned with a little water and salt to taste. Cover and simmer till the meat is tender. Stir flour into cream and pour over the chicken. Boil up and simmer for 5 minutes. Serve with noodles.

MARINATED RABBIT
For the Marinade

2 pints water	Sprig of thyme
3 oz. parsley	1 cup vinegar
10 peppercorns	3 oz. carrot
10 juniper berries	2 oz. celery
4 bay leaves	Salt

For the Sauce

2 tbsps. flour	1 cup sour cream
½ oz. butter	

Boil up all the ingredients of the marinade for about 10 minutes. Cool, pour over the jointed rabbit, cover and let stand for 12 hours. The next day, simmer all together until the meat is tender. Remove the meat and keep hot, strain the liquid and add to it the flour mixed with the cream and butter. Boil up again, pour over the meat and serve with dumplings.

STUFFED CUCUMBERS
3 large cucumbers Meat Loaf mixture (see p. 13)

For the Sauce

3 oz. butter	2 tbsps. chopped parsley
2 tbsps. chopped onion	2 tbsps. chopped dill
2 oz. flour	1½ tbsps. vinegar
Salt and paprika	½ cup sour cream

Cut off both ends of the cucumbers and remove the seeds with a sharp-pointed knife and the handle of a wooden spoon. Fill the cucumbers with meat mixture. Melt the butter and let the onion get soft, but not brown. Stir in the flour, seasonings, parsley and 1 pint of water. Bring to the boil and add the remaining ingredients. Cover the cucumbers with the sauce and simmer until soft.

EGGS IN SOUR CREAM

8 eggs	1 tbsp. breadcrumbs
1 tbsp. chopped chives	2 tbsps. melted butter
1 tbsp. chopped parsley	Salt and pepper
1 cup sour cream	

Pour the cream into a flat oven dish and break in the eggs one by one. Season lightly, sprinkle with chives, parsley and breadcrumbs and pour the melted butter over the top. Bake in a hot oven (450° F., mark 8) until the eggs are set and the top is browned.

LETTUCE AND BACON SALAD

2 firm heads of lettuce	2 tbsps. vinegar
2 oz. fat bacon	Salt and pepper

Wash lettuce and shake dry. Cube the bacon and let it fry gently until it is golden-brown and much of the fat has been extracted. Toss the lettuce with the vinegar, season to taste and mix in the bacon and bacon fat when it is cool but not solidified.

EGG SALAD

4 hard-boiled eggs	Salt and pepper
4 tbsps. oil	Lettuce
2 tbsps. vinegar	Freshly grated horseradish

Quarter the eggs and turn them gently in a mixture of the oil, vinegar and seasonings. Serve on a bed of lettuce, sprinkled with plenty of horseradish.

PALATSCHINKEN
(PANCAKES)

½ lb. flour	1 pint milk
Pinch of salt	Oil for frying
2 eggs	Apricot jam

Sieve flour and salt together, beat in one egg and half the milk, then add the other egg and the rest of the milk. Let the batter stand for a few minutes. Heat a little oil in a frying pan and pour in some batter, tipping the pan so that the batter is evenly distributed. When the pancake is done on one side, turn over. Tip out of the pan, put a spoonful of jam in the middle and roll up. Cook all the batter in this way, rolling up each pancake separately around a spoonful of jam and placing side by side on a hot dish. When all the batter is used up, sprinkle the rolled pancakes with sugar and grill for a moment before serving.

GEFÜLLTE ORANGEN
(STUFFED ORANGES)

1 tbsp. cornflour	A little grated orange
¼ pint orange juice	peel
Juice of 1 lemon	½ pint cream
2 oz. sugar	8 orange " cups "

Put the cornflour into a small saucepan, blend to a smooth paste with a little of the orange juice, then stir in the rest of the fruit juices, the sugar and the peel, and keep stirring while bringing to the boil. Take off the heat, and when cool, fold in the whipped cream, retaining a small amount for the final decoration. Now pour the mixture into the neatly cut empty halves of the oranges, or into individual glasses. Either meringues or little orange sticks (see below) make a delicious accompaniment to this sweet.

ORANGENSTANGERLN
(LITTLE ORANGE STICKS)

2 eggs	2 oz. coarsely chopped
5 oz. sugar	nuts
3½ oz. flour	Grated peel of 3 oranges

Beat the whole eggs with the sugar, then fold in the other ingredients. Spread the mixture in a greased Swiss roll tin, and bake in a moderately hot oven (400° F., mark 6) for at least ½ hour, then test in the usual way. Cut into narrow " sticks " while still hot. When the biscuits are cold, remove them from the tin.

REISAUFLAUF
(AUSTRIAN RICE PUDDING)

2 oz. rice	4 oz. sugar
1 pint milk	A little grated lemon
A little salt	peel
2 oz. butter or mar-	3 eggs
garine	

Simmer the rice in the milk with a pinch of salt till soft. Cream the butter, sugar, grated lemon peel and egg yolks, and mix with the cooled rice. Gently fold in the stiffly beaten egg whites, put into a fireproof dish, and bake for ¾ hour in a slow oven (325° F., mark 2).

KAISERSCHMARREN
(BROKEN PANCAKES)

3 oz. flour	¼ pint milk
1½ oz. sugar	2 eggs
1 oz. butter	1 oz. sultanas

Put the flour and sugar in a basin, and add the melted butter, milk and egg yolks. Fold in the stiffly beaten egg whites and the sultanas. Pour into a well-buttered hot frying pan, and let the mixture set and brown on the underside, but be careful not to let it burn. When it is golden-brown underneath, turn it over, and when again brown underneath, tear it into irregularly shaped pieces (the so-called Schmarren) with two forks. These pieces can then continue to cook very gently until you are ready ; sprinkle caster sugar on top before serving.

This is the story they tell to explain the origin of these pancakes. One day, when the old Emperor Joseph was out hunting in the Tyrol, he went into a mountain peasant's house and asked for a meal to be served. But the girl making the sweet was so nervous at cooking for the Emperor that she broke the pancake in the pan, and burst into tears. To cover up the mistake, her mistress broke the whole pancake

into small pieces, and served it as a " special dish." The Emperor graciously declared himself very pleased with the dish, which was henceforward known as " Kaiserschmarren," or—literally—Emperor's fragments !

VIENNESE ORANGE CAKE

4 eggs	1 juicy orange
5½ oz. caster sugar	2 tsps. fresh white
5½ oz. ground almonds	breadcrumbs

Separate the eggs, put the yolks and sugar into a basin over hot water and beat until creamy. Fold the ground almonds into the mixture, and add the orange juice. Beat the egg whites stiffly and fold in, sprinkling in the breadcrumbs at the same time. Bake in a shallow lined and greased cake tin for ½–¾ hour in a moderate oven (350° F., mark 4). Turn out carefully, as this cake is of a very rich, moist consistency.

SALZBURGER NOCKERL

3 oz. butter	1 tbsp. flour
5 egg whites	Icing sugar
4 egg yolks	

Pre-heat the oven to 450° F. (mark 8). Melt the butter in a flat fireproof dish over a low flame. Whip the whites very stiffly and stir in the yolks very carefully, with the flour. Turn up the flame so that the butter in the dish foams, but do not let it get brown. Carefully drop the egg mixture into the butter in large, pointed mounds. The bottom of the mixture will begin to set in a minute ; then transfer the whole dish to the hot oven until the tops of the Nockerl are browned—about 3 minutes. Dust with icing sugar and serve at once.

APFEL STRUDEL

10 oz. flour	3 lb. apples
1 level tsp. salt	¼ lb. seedless raisins
1 egg, beaten	3 oz. chopped almonds
A little melted butter	Grated rind of ½ a lemon
Fine breadcrumbs	8 oz. sugar

Put the flour on a board and make a hollow in the centre. Mix salt, egg, ¼ pint water and 1 tbsp. melted butter, and pour carefully into the flour. Gradually work in the flour to form a sticky dough, then knead lightly on a well-floured board, keeping hands floured. Stretch the dough out, re-knead and leave to " rest " for ½ hour, with a warm dish over the top. Cover a table with an old table-cloth, and sprinkle well with flour. Place the dough in the centre and roll it slightly, then pull it out, using the backs of the hands, with thumbs tucked in. Pull until the dough is paper thin—when one part becomes transparent, leave it and start on another area. Any thick pieces left around the edges should be trimmed off. Sprinkle half the pastry lightly with fine breadcrumbs.

Combine the thinly sliced apples, chopped raisins and remaining ingredients, and cover the dough with this mixture to within an inch of the edge. Roll up like a Swiss roll and pinch together at the edges. Place on a baking sheet, brush with melted butter, bake for $\frac{1}{2}$ hour in a moderately hot oven (400° F., mark 6), and reduce to moderate (350° F., mark 4) for a further $\frac{1}{2}$ hour; baste occasionally. Serve hot or cold, sprinkled with icing sugar.

MARILLENKUCHEN
(APRICOT CAKE)

4 eggs	Weight of 3 eggs in flour
Weight of 4 eggs in butter and in sugar	$\frac{1}{2}$ lb. fresh apricots (or other fruit)

Separate the eggs. Cream the butter well, add the egg yolks and sugar, then fold in the stiffly beaten egg whites and the flour. Spread the mixture about $\frac{1}{2}$ inch thick on to a greased baking tin, and over it lay halved stoned apricots at regular intervals. Bake in a hot oven (450° F., mark 8) for $\frac{1}{2}$ hour till set and golden-brown.

NUSSTORTE
(NUTCAKE)

2 oz. fine breadcrumbs	5 oz. grated walnuts or hazelnuts
A little rum (or rum essence to flavour)	A little sieved apricot jam
5 oz. sugar	
5 eggs	

For the Filling

2 oz. chocolate	1 egg yolk
1 oz. butter	

For the Icing and Decoration

6 oz. sugar	Halved walnuts
Juice of 1 lemon	

Sprinkle the breadcrumbs with a little rum. Whisk the sugar and egg yolks, fold in the stiffly beaten egg whites, the breadcrumbs and nuts. Put in a greased and floured cake tin and bake it in a moderate oven (375° F., mark 5) for about $\frac{3}{4}$–1 hour. Test it by sticking a steel knitting needle into the middle—if it is dry on withdrawing, the cake is ready; when it is quite cold, turn it out of the tin. Halve, and sandwich together with a filling made by melting the chocolate and stirring in the other ingredients. Turn the cake upside down (so that there is a

completely flat surface on top) and cover with a very thin layer of sieved jam.

To make the icing, stir the sugar with the lemon juice and add a little water, stirring carefully, until you have a very thick liquid. Gently heat this mixture, continuing to stir, until it becomes quite runny, then pour it quickly over the cake. Decorate with halved walnuts. Mark the surface into sections before the icing has time to set, in order to make the cutting easier.

MOHR IM HEMD
For the Pudding

3 oz. butter	3 oz. plain chocolate
3 oz. caster sugar	3 oz. ground almonds
5 eggs	2 tbsps. sponge cake crumbs

For the Sauce

3 oz. plain chocolate	$\frac{1}{2}$ oz. butter
3 oz. caster sugar	1 gill water

Cream butter and sugar and add egg yolks and melted chocolate. Stir in almonds, crumbs and stiffly beaten whites. Pour the mixture into a buttered and sugared pudding basin; cover and steam for 1 hour. For the sauce, melt together the chocolate, sugar and butter in a double boiler. Add the water and pour over the pudding when cooked. Serve with whipped cream.

SACHERTORTE
(CHOCOLATE CAKE)

8 oz. plain chocolate	3 oz. ground almonds or other nuts
4 oz. unsalted butter	
$6\frac{1}{2}$ oz. sugar	$1\frac{1}{2}$ oz. self-raising flour
5 eggs	Jam for filling

For the Icing

5 oz. chocolate	$2\frac{1}{2}$ oz. butter

This most famous of Viennese cakes takes its name from the restaurant in Vienna where it was first served. There are many slightly varying recipes for it, each claiming to be the original one. Though no such claim is made here, this cake is certainly delicious, and will keep exceptionally well.

Melt the chocolate over a low heat; when it is soft, cream it with the butter, sugar and egg yolks, then fold in the stiffly beaten egg whites, the almonds and flour. Put in a greased and lined cake tin and bake in a moderate oven (350° F., mark 4) for at least 45 minutes, then test with a steel knitting needle—this cake should remain very slightly moist in the centre.

Cut the cake in half when quite cold, fill with a layer of jam, and coat with chocolate icing;

melt the chocolate over low heat, mix it with the melted butter, leave for 20–30 minutes, to cool to a coating consistency, and pour over the cake. Decorate with cream.

This cake may also be baked in a flat tin, in which case retain a small amount of ground almonds to sprinkle on the top before it is baked.

AUSTRIAN HONEY CAKES

¼ lb. honey	1 level tsp. baking
2 oz. sugar	powder
1 level tsp. powdered	1 beaten egg
cinnamon	Egg white
A pinch ground cloves	Halved or flaked
½ lb. plain flour	blanched almonds

For the Filling

2 oz. ground hazel-	1 oz. chopped mixed
nuts	peel
2 oz. sugar	1 small egg

Heat honey, then add sugar, cinnamon and cloves. Stir, cool slightly. Stir in the sifted flour and baking powder with the beaten egg. Knead well and leave overnight in a plastic bag. Mix together the filling. Roll the dough out thinly. Cut in fancy shapes. Join in pairs with a little filling in each, seal edges with egg white. Brush tops with egg white and decorate with almonds. Bake on a greased tray at 350° F. (mark 4), for about 20 minutes. (Makes about 30.)

VIENNESE STRAWBERRY CAKE
For the Cake

8 oz. Vienna flour or	3 oz. butter
6 oz. fine flour and	4 eggs
2 oz. cornflour	8 oz. caster sugar
2 heaped tsps. baking	¾ gill cream
powder	

For the Filling and Decoration

Strawberries	Cream
Sherry	

Mix and sieve the flour and baking powder. Melt the butter, taking care not to overheat it. Put the eggs and sugar into a bowl and whisk over a pan of hot water until thick and light; remove from the heat, and continue whisking for a few minutes. Add the cream, then quickly fold in the flour, and lastly add the melted butter. Pour the mixture into a buttered 8-inch cake tin or into 2 buttered sandwich tins, and bake in a moderate oven (350° F., mark 4) for 40–50 minutes, until firm and golden-brown, then cool. When the cake is quite cold, cut in half, and fill with a thick layer of sliced strawberries soaked in sherry, and a layer of whipped cream. Join the cake together again firmly, spread the top with whipped cream, and decorate with whole strawberries.

SCHLAGOBERS SKARNITZELN
(WHIPPED CREAM CORNETS)

3 eggs	Whipped cream
3 oz. sugar	Caster sugar
3 oz. flour	Small strawberries

Beat the eggs and sugar and fold in the flour. Grease and flour a baking tin very thoroughly. Using a tablespoon, put small heaps of the mixture on the tin, and spread them out thinly. Bake for about 10 minutes in a moderately hot oven (400° F., mark 6) and while they are still hot, take them off the tin with a butter knife, and gently fold each over to form an open-ended cornet or cone. When cool, fill with slightly sweetened whipped cream and decorate with strawberries. (Wild or " Baron Solemacher " type are best.)

If the cream is rather rich and thick, a better result is often obtained by mixing some " top of the milk " with it before whipping.

MALAKOFF TORTE

6 oz. butter	2 tbsps. rum (or rum
6 oz. caster sugar	essence to flavour)
1 egg yolk	20–30 sponge biscuits
3 oz. melted chocolate	

Mix fat, sugar, egg yolk and chocolate to a smooth cream. Almost fill a cup with cold water and add the rum, and pour into a bowl; put in the biscuits and let them soak up some of the liquid, but do not saturate.

Take an oblong or square cake tin, line with paper, and put in one layer of sponge biscuits, followed by a layer of the cream mixture. Continue to fill the tin alternately with sponge biscuits and cream mixture until all is used up, then place a lid on the tin and a weight on this to hold it down. Put in the refrigerator or a very cool place for 2–3 hours.

TOPFENKUCHEN
(CHEESECAKE)

5 oz. sour milk cheese	5 oz. sugar
5 oz. butter or mar-	5 eggs
garine	Juice and grated rind of
5 oz. ground almonds,	1 lemon
walnuts or hazelnuts	1 oz. flour

Cream together the cheese, butter, nuts, sugar, egg yolks, lemon juice and grated rind. Carefully fold in the stiffly beaten egg whites and the flour. Pour the mixture into a greased and lined

8-inch baking tin, and bake for $\frac{1}{4}$ hour in a hot oven (450° F., mark 8), then for a further $\frac{1}{2}$ hour in a moderate oven (350° F., mark 4), until the mixture is dry inside when tested with a skewer.

AUSTRIAN GLACÉ RING CAKE

$\frac{1}{2}$ oz. baker's yeast
8 oz. plain bread flour
A pinch of salt
1 oz. melted butter
1 level dessertsp. caster sugar

1 egg yolk
Approximately $\frac{1}{4}$ pint milk
5 oz. butter
1 oz. flour

For the Filling

1 oz. ground almonds
4 oz. seedless raisins
1 oz. grated chocolate
2 level tbsps. cake or biscuit crumbs
2 level tbsps. caster sugar

$\frac{1}{4}$ level tsp. ground cinnamon
1 tbsp. melted butter
Rum
Glacé icing, plain or lemon

Rub the yeast into the flour and salt. Make a well in the centre and add the butter, sugar and egg yolk beaten together with enough milk to give a pliable dough. Beat well. Put to rise in a warm place in a covered plastic container, plastic bag or covered bowl for 15–20 minutes. Meanwhile knead the 5 oz. butter with the 1 oz. flour till pliable. Knead dough on a floured board, roll out to an oblong, place tablet of butter in the centre and fold as for flaky pastry. Roll and fold four times as for flaky pastry. If dough gets sticky put to rest in a cool place for 20 minutes between rolls. Meanwhile, mix together the ground almonds, raisins, chocolate, biscuit crumbs, caster sugar and ground cinnamon. Roll yeast pastry out to an oblong about 21 inches long. Brush with melted butter, cover with filling, sprinkle with rum and roll up as for a Swiss roll. Twist into a circle to fit in a greased 7–8 inch cake tin. Make sure ends are firmly joined. Make a few slashes along the top. Cover with a cloth and put to prove for about 20 minutes. Bake at 425° F. (mark 7), for about 45 minutes or until well risen, golden-brown and just firm to the touch. Turn out carefully. While still hot, top with glacé icing. Serve fresh.

LINZER TORTE

5 oz. caster sugar
5 oz. plain flour
5 oz. finely chopped almonds

5 oz. butter
1 egg yolk
$\frac{3}{4}$ lb. raspberries
Sugar

Mix together the sugar, flour and almonds. Rub butter into the dry ingredients. Add the egg yolk and work to a dough. Chill to a man-ageable consistency. Roll out two-thirds and line an 8-inch fluted flan ring. Spread with a layer of roughly chopped raspberries and sugar. Roll out rest of the dough, cut into wide strips, and closely lattice the flan. Bake at 350° F. (mark 4), for $1\frac{1}{4}$–$1\frac{1}{2}$ hours. Leave to cool slightly before removing ring. Serve cold, dusted with icing sugar.

AUSTRIAN VANILLA KIPFEL

5 oz. plain flour
2 oz. ground almonds

$1\frac{1}{2}$ oz. vanilla sugar
$3\frac{1}{2}$ oz. butter

Sieve the flour and ground almonds on to a pastry board, add the sugar and mix carefully. Make a well in the centre, place the pat of butter in it, and knead together until a stiff paste is formed. Roll out to about $\frac{1}{4}$ inch in thickness, and cut into rounds, using a floured plain or fluted cutter. Place on a greased and floured baking tin and bake in a slow oven (325° F., mark 3) till a very pale straw colour. Allow to cool for 5 minutes, then very gently lift the biscuits on to a sheet of greaseproof paper sprinkled with vanilla icing sugar (icing sugar in which a vanilla stick has been stored). Sprinkle liberally with sugar and allow to cool. Store in an airtight tin.

MARCHEGGER STANGERL

2 small egg whites
6 oz. ground almonds

4 oz. caster sugar
Royal icing for coating

Whisk egg whites stiffly. Stir in the ground almonds (the Viennese use unblanched almonds) and sugar. Turn on to a board or table top dusted with icing sugar. Knead lightly and roll out to the thickness of a wafer. Cut into strips, about 1 inch by 3–4 inches. Coat the top of each strip with royal icing. This is most easily done by using a forcing bag fitted with a $\frac{1}{4}$-inch plain vegetable pipe. Line a baking tin with a sheet of silicone paper. Put the strips on this and dry them out in a cool oven (200° F., or under mark $\frac{1}{4}$) for about 2 hours.

STREUSEL CAKE (AUSTRIAN)

8 oz. plain flour
2 oz. fine semolina
2 oz. sugar
3 oz. butter
1 oz. baker's yeast

$\frac{1}{2}$ an orange
2 eggs
5 tbsps. milk
3–4 oz. cleaned currants
Raspberry jam

Streusel Topping

$1\frac{1}{2}$ oz. butter
$1\frac{1}{2}$ oz. flour

2 oz. brown sugar
Pinch of cinnamon

Sift together the flour, semolina and sugar. Rub in the fat and then the yeast. Add the beaten eggs and milk. Mix to give a soft dough. Squeeze the orange. Remove the pith from the peel, mince the rest and add with currants to the dough. Spread evenly in a greased shallow baking tin approximately 8½ inches by 5½ inches. Cover with a layer of raspberry jam. Put to rise, until double the size, in a warm place. Cover with Streusel topping. Bake at 400° F. (mark 6), for about 30–40 minutes. Turn out and cool on a wire tray. For the Streusel topping rub together butter, flour, sugar and cinnamon, and sprinkle the topping evenly over the surface.

GUGLHUPF

9 oz. flour	1 tbsp. flour or ground
1 level tsp. salt	almonds
½ oz. yeast	4 oz. butter
2 oz. caster sugar	3 standard eggs
¼ pint tepid milk	4 oz. washed and dried
1–1½ oz. blanched	raisins
almonds	Grated rind of 1 lemon

Sift the flour and salt into a warmed bowl. Mix yeast with a teaspoonful of the sugar and the milk. Make a well in the centre of the flour and pour in the yeast mixture. Sprinkle with a little flour, cover with a cloth and set in a warm place to " prove." Butter a guglhupf mould (a fluted mould), generously sprinkle with the blanched almonds cut into strips, then sprinkle with flour or ground almonds. Melt the butter gently in a warm place. When the yeast mixture begins to bubble, mix well with the flour, adding remaining sugar and the lightly beaten eggs. Beat well with a wooden spoon or the hand, gradually adding the tepid melted butter. Beat until the mixture leaves spoon and sides of the bowl clean. Stir in the raisins and the grated lemon rind. Place mixture in prepared mould, which should be about two-thirds full. Set in a warm place to rise. When the mixture has risen to within ½ inch of the top of the tin, put the cake on a baking tray and place in a hot oven (425° F., mark 7), turning the heat down to mark 5 after 5 minutes. Bake for about 40 minutes in all until the cake feels firm on top when pressed and is a good golden-brown colour. Turn out on to a wire cooling tray and dust thickly with icing sugar while the cake is still warm.

APRICOT-CHEESE PASTRY HEARTS

Into bowl sift 1 cup flour, ⅛ tsp. salt. Add ½ cup butter or margarine, ¼ lb. cream cheese, in small pieces.

With pastry blender or two knives, scissor fashion, cut butter and cheese into flour mixture till they are well blended. Lightly shape into ball ; wrap in waxed paper or foil ; refrigerate till well chilled.

Heat oven to 400° F. (mark 6). Lightly grease two baking sheets. On floured surface, roll out dough ⅛ inch thick. Then cut with 3¼-inch by 2½-inch heart-shaped biscuit cutter. In centre of each of half of cut-out pastry hearts, place 1 tsp. of apricot preserves. Now brush their edges with beaten egg, cover each with another cut-out heart, then, with fork, lightly press edges together. Arrange on baking sheets. Brush top of each with beaten egg, sprinkle with sugar. Bake 10–12 minutes or till golden ; cool on rack. Makes about 24.

ALMOND-CHEESE PASTRY CRESCENTS

Make up Cheese Pastry as above. In bowl, with mixer at high speed, beat 2 egg whites, till stiff ; then beat in ¼ cup sugar, 1 tbsp. lemon juice, 1 tbsp. grated lemon rind, ½ tsp. almond extract, fold in 1 cup ground blanched almonds. Heat oven to 400° F. (mark 6). Lightly grease two baking sheets. On floured surface, roll out one-third Cheese Pastry ⅛ inch thick. Cut into 10-inch circle ; cut circle into 8 wedges. In centre of wide end of each wedge, place rounded teaspoonful almond mixture. Starting at wide edge, lightly roll up each wedge ; place, centre point down, on baking sheet ; curve ends in crescent. Repeat with remainder.

Brush crescents with beaten egg ; sprinkle with almonds. Bake 10–12 minutes, cool. Makes about 28.

VIENNA ALMOND TORTE

¾ cup butter	2 tbsps. single cream
1 cup granulated sugar	½ cup slivered almonds
2 eggs	1 tbsp. all-purpose
¾ cup sifted cake flour	flour

Start heating oven to 375° F. (mark 5). Grease bottom and sides of 8-inch by 2-inch pan.

Mix ½ cup butter and ¾ cup sugar till creamy and light. Add eggs, one at a time, beating well ; fold in ¾ cup flour. Pour batter into pan ; bake for 25 minutes.

Meanwhile, in saucepan, combine ¼ cup butter, ¼ cup sugar, cream and one-third of almonds ; over medium heat, warm till creamy. Add 1 tbsp. flour ; simmer ½ minute, remove from the heat.

When cake has baked for 25 minutes remove from the oven. Spread nut mixture over the top ; sprinkle with rest of nuts. Bake for 20 minutes more. Cool slightly ; remove from pan.

BELGIUM is rightly famous for the richness and variety of her cooking which, influenced as it is by both Germany and France, combines hearty solidity with originality and refinement.

Practically every foodstuff is available to the Belgian housewife, whose long tradition of skilled and careful housekeeping enables her to make the very best and most economical use of all ingredients. Fish and shell fish abound along the coastline; Belgian vegetables are famous for flavour and tenderness, and both chicory and asparagus are particularly good. Poultry is raised for the table on a grain diet and eaten, deliciously tender, while still quite small. Crisp, golden waffles are served everywhere as a snack, while Belgian pastries are succulent and delicious, rich with chocolate and cream.

The Ardennes country, that charming link between Belgium and Luxembourg, provides both countries with the famous smoked Ardennes hams, trout and fresh-water fish. Luxembourg produces quite a large quantity of light, dry and refreshing white wine from the vineyards bordering the Moselle, while Belgian beer needs no recommendation and has a reputation that stretches far beyond the actual frontiers of the country.

Belgium
and Luxembourg

Belgium

CHERVIL SOUP

2 leeks	1 quart boiling stock
1 medium-sized onion	or water
2 large potatoes	Seasoning
Butter or margarine	1 bunch of chervil

Clean and wash the leeks, peel the onion and potatoes and cut all up roughly. Melt a little fat in a saucepan and gently fry the vegetables, stirring till they change colour. Add the liquid, with seasoning to taste, bring to the boil and simmer slowly for at least ½ hour. Meanwhile wash, clean and chop the chervil, and keep covered till required. Sieve the vegetables, return them to the pan and boil for 5 minutes, then add the chervil and a knob of butter.

ECREVISSES À LA LIÉGEOISE
(CRAYFISH)

Crayfish	2 shallots
½ pint white wine	1 carrot
½ pint water	Parsley, thyme, bay leaf
12 small onions	Seasoning

Boil the crayfish for about 7 minutes in a court-bouillon of wine, water, onions, shallots, finely chopped and shredded carrot. When they have boiled for 30 minutes, with a few sprigs of herbs and a seasoning of salt, pepper and a little cayenne, remove from the stock, and keep hot; reduce stock by one-half, add little butter and parsley and pour over the crayfish.

WATERZOOI
(POACHED FISH WITH VEGETABLES)

3 lb. fish (filleted	A few mushrooms
hake, brill, halibut	½ oz. butter or margarine
or sole)	Pepper and salt
1 leek	½ a lemon
½ a head of celery	½ lb. eels or 1 pint
1 carrot	mussels
Several parsley roots	1 egg yolk
2 bay leaves	About 1½ tbsps. milk
A sprig of thyme	A little flour

Prepare the fish, scaling and filleting it as required, and wash it in cold water. Prepare the vegetables and cut up finely, as for a Julienne garnish. Butter a fireproof dish or a saucepan, put in the vegetables, and cover with greaseproof paper and the lid. Put in a hot oven (450° F., mark 8) for 2 minutes and then turn the heat to very low; allow the vegetables 15 minutes in all, or until they change colour, but do not let them become brown; stir occasionally.

Wash the parsley roots and put them in cold water with the fishbones; add the bay leaves and thyme, bring to the boil, and simmer 5–10 minutes. Cut the fish in 2-inch pieces, grease a fairly deep fireproof dish, put in the fish, add the mushrooms, sprinkle with seasoning, add the lemon juice, and poach in a moderately hot oven (400° F., mark 6) until the fish starts to boil— 7–10 minutes.

If the vegetables are in a dish, transfer to a saucepan. Strain the fishbone liquor over them. If eels are used, cut into 2-inch pieces, put into 1 cup of boiling salted water and simmer 10–15 minutes. If mussels are used, wash and clean them, put in a pan with a stick of celery and a sliced onion, and toss over a brisk heat until the shells open. Add the eel or mussel liquor to the vegetables and boil gently, uncovered, until the vegetables are tender—15–20 minutes. Meanwhile take the mussels from their shells and remove the beard and "core."

As soon as the fish is cooked, take it from the oven, add the cooked eels or prepared mussels and keep hot. Beat the egg yolk, add the milk and sufficient flour to bind, pour over the vegetables, stir in well and bring to the boil; pour this sauce over the fish and serve at once.

CROQUETTES AUX CREVETTES
(SHRIMP CROQUETTES)

1½ oz. butter	6–8 oz. peeled shrimps
1½ oz. flour	Flour, beaten egg and
¼ pint milk	browned breadcrumbs
A little grated cheese	for coating
Salt and pepper	Fat for frying
A little lemon juice	

Make a white sauce with the butter, flour and milk, add the cheese, and season well with salt, pepper and lemon juice. Stir in the shrimps, put the mixture into a refrigerator or a very cold larder, and allow it to stiffen. Flour the hands, and roll the mixture into 8 croquettes. Dip these in flour, brush with beaten egg, and roll in breadcrumbs. Fry in hot fat until brown all over.

If you peel the shrimps yourself, boil the heads in water and use this stock instead of the milk.

BELGIAN-STYLE EELS

1 lb. small eels	1 tbsp. mixed herbs
2 oz. butter	(sage, chervil, mint,
1 small onion	parsley, sorrel, water-
¾ pint white wine	cress)
Seasoning	3 egg yolks
1 lb. fresh spinach,	Juice of 1 lemon
washed and trimmed	

Remove the heads of the eels, skin the fish and cut into 2–3-inch lengths. Melt the butter, put the eels in this with the sliced onion and add the seasoning, spinach and the chopped mixed herbs. Add the wine, and simmer gently for 15–20 minutes until the fish and spinach are cooked.

Remove the pan from the heat and stir in the egg yolks, previously mixed with the lemon juice. Reheat gently, but do not boil; serve either hot or cold.

ŒUFS MEULEMEESTER
(BRUGES EGG SAVOURY)

4 eggs	½ pint cream
A little butter	Salt and pepper
A little chopped chervil and parsley	2 oz. grated Gruyère cheese and a little butter for topping
French mustard	
A few shelled prawns	

Boil the eggs for 6–7 minutes, put them in cold water for 1–2 minutes, then shell and slice them into a saucepan. Add the rest of the ingredients, mix well and pour into a greased fireproof dish.

Sprinkle with the cheese, dot with a little butter, put into a hot oven (450° F., mark 8) and cook till the top browns. Garnish with prawns and sliced hard-boiled egg, or as desired.

ROGNON DE VEAU À LA LIÉGEOISE
(VEAL KIDNEY)

Veal kidney	2 tbsps. white wine
Butter	1 tsp. juniper berries

Put well-seasoned kidney, with fat, in very hot butter. When it begins to brown, cover pan and put on slow fire for 4 or 5 minutes. Add 1 tbsp. of white wine; cook till the kidney is tender, sprinkle with 1 heaped tsp. of juniper berries, previously pounded to a powder in a mortar, add another tbsp. white wine, 1 heaped tsp. of butter, divided in small pieces. The kidney should take about 10 minutes to cook.

BELGIAN BEEF STEW

1½ lb. stewing beef	Pepper
Butter or margarine	A bunch mixed herbs
6 oz. chopped onion	or 1 small tsp. dried
1¼ pints beer	mixed herbs
Salt	Flour

Cut the beef into ¾-inch cubes, fry in a little butter until brown, and put it in a casserole. Fry the onion until brown and add this to the casserole. Pour the beer over, season and add the herbs.

Cover and simmer in a slow oven (325° F., mark 3) for 4 hours, until the meat is tender. Remove the herbs (if whole) and thicken the stew with a little flour mixed to a smooth paste with water.

FLEMISH STEAKS

4 pieces chuck steak	4–8 oz. button mushrooms
3 tbsps. oil	
Salt and pepper	Flour
3 sliced medium-sized onions	1 bottle lager
	1 oz. Demerara sugar
Butter	1 clove of garlic

Marinade the meat overnight in the oil with a little seasoning. Sauté the onions in a little butter until slightly coloured and place in a casserole with the washed mushrooms. Dip the steaks in flour and fry lightly in the pan in which the onions were sautéed, adding any remaining marinading oil. Put the steaks on top of the vegetables in the casserole. Mix together the lager, sugar, finely chopped garlic, salt and pepper and pour over the meat. Cover with a lid and cook in a slow oven (300° F., mark 2) for 3½–4 hours.

When available, use 12 small pickling onions in place of the large onions—left whole, they are delicious and look attractive when the dish is served.

BELGIAN CARBONNADES

2 lb. chuck steak	½ pint stock or water
Salt and pepper	1 lb. chopped onions
2 oz. dripping	1 clove of garlic
3 oz. lean bacon	1 oz. sugar
1½ oz. flour	A bouquet garni
½ pint beer	2–3 tbsps. vinegar

Cut the meat into neat pieces, season with salt and pepper, and brown in the dripping. Add the diced bacon and continue cooking for a few minutes. Remove the meat and bacon from the pan, stir in the flour, and brown lightly over very gentle heat. Gradually add the beer and stock, stirring continuously. Fill a casserole with layers of meat, bacon, chopped onion, garlic and a sprinkling of sugar. Pour the sauce over and add the bouquet garni. Cook very gently for 3½–4 hours in a slow oven (325° F., mark 2). Add a little more beer while cooking, if necessary. Just before serving, remove the bouquet garni and stir in the vinegar. Serve with plain boiled potatoes.

ROULADES
(BEEF OLIVES)

1½ lb. thinly cut beefsteak	Lard or bacon fat
Streaky bacon	2 onions, sliced
Chopped parsley	½ pint stock or water
Salt and pepper	1 tbsp. vinegar

Cut the meat into small oblongs and lay a rasher of streaky bacon on each. Sprinkle with parsley, salt and pepper, and roll up. Tie these rolls with fine string and fry them on all sides in a little hot lard or bacon fat. Add the sliced onions and fry, then add the stock or water and vinegar. (A little dry red wine may be added instead of vinegar, if preferred.) Simmer for about $1\frac{1}{2}$–2 hours, remove the strings and serve on a dish, with the slightly thickened liquor poured round.

POULETS SANS TÊTE
(MOCK CHICKENS)

$1\frac{1}{2}$ lb. thinly sliced beefsteak	$\frac{1}{2}$ pint stock
	1 onion
$\frac{3}{4}$ lb. minced pork or veal	A sprig of thyme
	$\frac{1}{2}$ oz. flour
1 tbsp. breadcrumbs	1 small bay leaf
1 egg	Juice of 1 lemon
Seasoning	A few cooked mushrooms
Butter for frying	1 tsp. chopped parsley

Cut the steak into pieces 5 inches long and 3 inches wide. Mix the minced pork or veal with the breadcrumbs and egg; season and spread this mixture on the beef slices, also seasoned. Roll up the mock chickens (thinner at the ends than the middle), tie and brown them in butter. Add the stock, sliced onion, thyme and bay leaf, cover and simmer for 2 hours. Thicken the liquid with the blended flour, and add the lemon juice, mushrooms, and chopped parsley.

Serve in a flat dish and pour the sauce over them.

LE HOCHEPOT

$1\frac{1}{2}$ lb. brisket beef	3 oz. carrots
$1\frac{1}{2}$ lb. shoulder and breast of mutton	4 leeks
	1 or 2 turnips
$1\frac{1}{2}$ lb. veal	3 or 4 sticks celery
$1\frac{1}{2}$ lb. pigs' feet	1 doz. small onions
$\frac{3}{4}$ lb. pigs' ears	1 doz. chipolata sausages
$\frac{1}{2}$ lb. pigs' tails	A bouquet of mixed herbs
1 cabbage	Salt and pepper

Put all the meat in a large glazed earthenware casserole, cover with water, bring slowly to the boil, and skim thoroughly. When the scum has ceased to rise, add the vegetables, sliced or coarsely chopped and the cabbage cut in quarters, the outer leaves having been removed. Season, cover and simmer for about 3 hours. Add the sausages and simmer for another $\frac{3}{4}$–1 hour. When ready, put the meat on a hot dish, drain the vegetables, chop and garnish the dish with them and pour a little stock over the whole. Serve the stock in the soup tureen and serve the meat afterwards as a separate course.

LES CHŒSELS
(MEAT WITH SWEETBREADS)

1 ox tail	1 bottle of beer
1 lb. breast of mutton	1 glass of Madeira
1 lb. breast of veal	1 lb. of onions
6 sheep's feet	Mixed herbs
5 sweetbreads	2–3 cloves
$\frac{1}{2}$ an ox kidney	Grated nutmeg
1 lb. cooked mushrooms	Salt and pepper
A few fricadelles (see p. 28)	

Slice the onions and brown in a large earthenware casserole in a little butter. When lightly browned, add the ox tail, cut into joints, season with salt, pepper and nutmeg, add a bouquet of mixed herbs, the cloves and cover with beer. Bring to the boil and simmer for 1 hour. Then add the breast of mutton, cut in small pieces, and simmer for another $\frac{1}{2}$ an hour. Now put in the 5 sweetbreads, the breast of veal, also cut in small pieces, the sheep's feet, divided in four and blanched and boiled till nearly done, the sliced ox kidney, and simmer for another $1\frac{1}{2}$ hours. Ten minutes before serving add the previously cooked fricadelles, the cooked mushrooms, more salt and pepper and the glass of Madeira.

BLANQUETTE DE VEAU
(RICH VEAL STEW)

2 lb. neck or breast of veal	1 sprig of parsley
	1 oz. butter
1 quart water	1 oz. flour
1 large onion stuck with 6 cloves	The juice of lemon
	Seasoning
2 bay leaves	1 egg
2 sprigs of thyme	

Cut the meat up into fairly small pieces. Bring the water and flavourings to the boil and add the meat, cover the saucepan and cook until the meat is almost tender (about 2 hours). Remove the veal, and pass the liquid through a sieve. Melt the butter in a saucepan, blend the flour with it, and add some of the meat liquor, lemon juice, seasoning and beaten egg yolk; the sauce should be quite thick. Add the meat, and place in a dish. Serve with boiled or mashed potatoes —no other vegetable is needed.

To make a good soup from the liquid, season it to taste, and add some tapioca or sago ($\frac{1}{2}$ oz. to 1 pint); cook until the cereal is transparent, and serve with small fried croûtons.

HARE—FLANDERS STYLE

Cut a hare into joints and fry in butter in a saucepan. Stir a little flour into the fat. Fill the pan to the half-way level with half-and-half stock and white wine and add pepper, salt, spices, etc. Then add ½ cupful of stoneless dried raisins and a similar amount of stoned prunes. Roast chestnuts can also be added if desired. Stir gently until tender. Finish with a glass of red wine and the hare's blood poured in a moment or two before serving.

A variety of other flavours, notably pears and even anchovies, are sometimes added. The blood of the hare is sometimes made into omelettes, particularly when the hare is an old stager, needing long hanging or marinading and the blood will not keep until the hare is ready for cooking as above.

SADDLE OF HARE WITH
HORSERADISH SAUCE

1 saddle of hare	¼ pint port
Strips of fat pork or bacon	A pinch of nutmeg or cinnamon
1 clove of garlic	1 tbsp. redcurrant jelly
Seasoning	1 dessertsp. shredded
2 oz. dripping	horseradish
½ lb. mixed root vegetables (cut up)	Sliced oranges
	Boiled potatoes
½ pint stock	Salad

Wash and dry the hare, and lard it well with the strips of fat pork or bacon. Put the meat with the garlic and season well. Melt the fat in a pan and fry the meat all over, then remove it from the pan and fry the mixed vegetables. Arrange the vegetables in a casserole, put the meat on top, pour in about ½ pint stock, and cook gently for 30 minutes. Pour in the wine, grated nutmeg and powdered cinnamon, and cook for a further 30 minutes. Drain off half the liquor, and add the redcurrant jelly and the horseradish. Pour this sauce over the hare, garnish with sliced oranges, and serve with plain boiled potatoes and a green salad.

ROAST HARE—FLEMISH STYLE

For this dish you need all the blood of the hare, and the liver. Put the cleaned hare in a baking tin and cover the back with about ¼ lb. butter and lard mixed, smearing it on thickly. Sprinkle with salt and pepper, pour ¼ pint vinegar over and put in a moderately hot oven (400° F., mark 6).

Pound the liver with the blood, place over a low heat, add about ⅓ lb. butter and lard mixed, and stir until the fat is completely melted. Boil 1 pint creamy milk and add the liver mixture and seasoning. Pour this over the hare, and continue to cook (basting often to keep the flesh moist) for 1½–2 hours, lowering the heat towards the end of the time. Before serving, taste the sauce,

and if necessary add the juice of ½ a lemon to sharpen the flavour, and a pinch of pepper.

RABBIT WITH PRUNES

1 rabbit, jointed	2 oz. butter
About ½ bottle of red wine	2 oz. flour
2 tbsps. vinegar	Salt and pepper
4 peppercorns	1 lb. prunes
2 bay leaves	1 tbsp. redcurrant
1 tsp. thyme	jelly

Marinate the rabbit in the wine and vinegar with peppercorns and herbs for 24 hours. Drain, and fry lightly on all sides in the butter, then stir in the flour. Add enough water to cover and season well. Add the prunes (soaked if necessary). Cover the pan and simmer for 1 hour, or until tender. Stir in the redcurrant jelly before serving.

POULARDE À LA WALLONE
(CHICKEN)

1 chicken or capon	1–2 sticks celery
2–3 lb. knuckle of veal	1 bay leaf
1 calf's sweetbread	A bouquet of mixed
4 carrots	herbs
1 large onion stuck with 1–2 cloves	Salt
	Pepper

For the Sauce

4 tbsps. butter	Chicken stock
3 tbsps. flour	Mushroom stock
5 yolks of eggs	Salt
2 tbsps. Madeira	Pepper

For the Garnish

6 large mushrooms, cooked in a little water	The juice of 1 lemon
	1 tbsp. butter

Put the knuckle of veal in a large earthenware casserole and cover with cold water. Bring to the boil, skim thoroughly and add the sliced carrots, celery, onion, herbs and seasoning. Simmer for about ¾ hour. Then add the chicken or capon and the sweetbread, previously blanched. Bring to the boil and simmer for ¾ hour or longer according to the size of the bird. The sweetbread should be removed as soon as tender, drained, cut in large cubes and kept warm till required.

Make a sauce with the butter, flour and hot chicken stock, stirring continuously, and simmer on a very slow fire for about 30 minutes. Mix the 5 yolks of eggs in a basin with cream, butter, Madeira and a little of the mushroom liquid, seasoning with salt and pepper. Beat all this thoroughly and add to the sauce, and keep on beating till the sauce comes to the boil. Strain it, put it in a clean saucepan and add the mush-rooms and sweetbread.

Put the chicken or capon on a hot dish, pour the sauce over it and garnish with the mushrooms and sweetbread.

L'OIE DE VISE
(GOOSE AS PREPARED AT VISE)

1 goose	4 rusks
2–3 onions	½ pint cream
2–3 carrots	Mixed herbs
12 cloves garlic	2–3 cloves
1½ pints of milk	Salt
6 yolks of eggs	Peppercorns

Put the goose in a large saucepan with the giblets, cover with slightly salted warm water, bring to the boil, and skim. Add the sliced vegetables, the herbs and spices. Simmer till tender. Remove from the saucepan and carve into neat pieces. Put a little goose fat in a frying pan and lightly brown the pieces of goose in this.

Put the milk in a saucepan with the skinned garlic and simmer till the garlic is quite tender. Remove the garlic from the milk. Add 4 rusks, broken up, stir, and when quite dissolved, strain the sauce. Beat the egg yolks with the cream and a few tbsps. of the hot milk. Add this mixture to the milk and stir for a few minutes over a slow fire. Pour this over the goose and garnish with the cloves of garlic.

CHICKEN WATERZOOI

4 leeks	Seasoning
1 head celery	4 egg yolks
1 head white cabbage	¼ pint cream
1 boiling fowl	

Finely shred the leeks, celery and cabbage. Boil or steam the chicken with some seasoning until tender. Add the vegetables and simmer until cooked. Remove the chicken, cut in two portions and place in a casserole. Mix the egg yolks with the cream. Bring the stock to the boil, reduce by half, then remove from the heat and stir in the egg yolks and cream and mix in the vegetables. Do not re-boil. Pour over the chicken.

GUINEA FOWL AND RED CABBAGE

Truss a guinea fowl and brown it in butter or dripping, in a flameproof casserole. Remove, then fry 1 small red cabbage, finely shredded. Add 1 lb. peeled chestnuts and 1 lb. apples, sliced, peeled and cored. Place the bird on top, add 1 glass of red wine, 1 glass of stock and seasoning to taste. Cover, and cook for 1½–2 hours, until the cabbage and chestnuts are cooked.

LE PÂTÉ DE BRUXELLES

3–4 lb. chicken	2 wineglasses brandy
2 lb. fat bacon	Rashers of fat bacon
1½ lb. lean pork	Bay leaves
Salt and pepper	Thyme
Allspice	Melted pork fat

Bone the chicken, fillet the breast and mince all the remaining meat with bacon and pork. Pound thoroughly in a mortar, seasoning highly with salt and pepper, a little allspice and the brandy. Line a high rectangular earthenware terrine with wide, thick rashers of fat bacon, put in 1 or 2 bay leaves, 1 or 2 sprigs of thyme, cover with half the forcemeat, then with the pieces of chicken breast, a thin rasher of bacon and the remaining forcemeat. Top this with more bacon, press well down, cover with the lid, put in a meat tin with a little water, and cook in a slow oven (325° F., mark 2) for 3 hours, replacing the water in the pan as it evaporates. When done, remove the lid, cover the pâté with a plate or board and weigh down. Let it stand in a cool place for 12 hours. Cover with a layer of melted pork fat and use as required.

FRICADELLES

3 tbsps. butter	2 lb. minced pork
2 shallots, chopped	shoulder
1½ qt. fresh breadcrumbs	Flour
(6 cups)	⅓ cup drained cocktail
1 cup milk	onions
¾ cup white wine	1¾ cups canned beef
3 eggs, slightly beaten	broth
3½ tsps. salt	1 tsp. dried orégano
1¼ tsps. pepper	¼ tsp. paprika
¾ tsp. grated nutmeg	Chopped parsley

Melt 1 tbsp. butter in a large frying pan and sauté the shallots till golden; set aside. Put the breadcrumbs in a large bowl and soften with the milk, 6 tbsps. white wine and the eggs. Then add the sautéed shallots, 3 tsps. salt, 1 tsp. pepper, ½ tsp. nutmeg and the minced pork; stir till well blended. Shape into about 20 balls; and roll in ½ cup flour till well coated. Heat 2 tbsps. butter in the same frying pan over a medium heat and brown half of the meat balls well on all sides. Remove from the pan and set aside. Brown the remaining meat balls, then return the first lot to the pan.

Add the cocktail onions, beef broth and remaining white wine. Sprinkle with ½ tsp. salt, ¼ tsp. pepper, ¼ tsp. grated nutmeg, the orégano and paprika. Cover and simmer for 30 minutes, then add 2 tbsps. flour made into a smooth paste with 2 tbsps. cold water; cook, stirring till thickened. Serve on a heated platter, with boiled potatoes sprinkled with parsley. (Makes 6 servings.)

CHICORY MONTMORENCY

Butter	½ cup grated Swiss cheese
2 whole chicken	½ cup fresh breadcrumbs
breasts	2 tbsps. capers
⅓ cup lemon juice	¼ tsp. celery seeds
4 heads of chicory	2 tbsps. chopped parsley
1 tbsp. flour	

Cut each chicken breast in half. Heat ½ cup water and 2 tbsps. butter in a large pan and slowly simmer the chicken (covered) for 45 minutes, or till tender. Drain, reserving the broth. Meanwhile, heat 2 tbsps. butter and the lemon juice in another saucepan and slowly simmer the chicory (covered) for 30 minutes or till tender; drain. Melt 1 tbsp. butter in a saucepan, remove from the heat, stir in the flour and then the chicken broth (about ¾ cup). Bring to the boil, stirring and simmer till it thickens, then add the cheese. Now start heating the oven to moderate (350° F., mark 4). Toss the breadcrumbs with 3 tbsps. melted butter and set aside. Remove the bones from the chicken breasts and arrange the flesh in a buttered baking dish; top each with a head of chicory and sprinkle with capers and celery seeds. Pour the sauce over all, top with breadcrumbs and bake for 20 minutes; sprinkle with parsley.

CHICORY AU GRATIN ET JAMBON
(CHICORY WITH CHEESE AND HAM)

5

1 lb. Brussels chicory	Nutmeg
1 oz. butter	2 oz. Gruyère cheese
1 tsp. plain flour	(grated)
Seasoning	8 slices cooked ham
1 cup of milk	Toasted breadcrumbs

Select some short, well-developed heads of chicory, wash and clean them, put in boiling salted water to which a little lemon juice has been added (to keep them white) and boil slowly for 25 minutes.

Pour into a colander (keeping back about 1 teacupful of the liquid) and drain for about 5 minutes. Make the sauce; melt the butter in a small saucepan, add the flour, pepper and salt, stirring all the time, then add the liquid and milk, a little nutmeg (according to taste) and three-quarters of the cheese, and bring to the boil.

Wrap each head of chicory in a slice of ham and put in a fireproof dish, pour the sauce over, top with breadcrumbs and the remaining cheese, dot with a few pieces of butter, and put under the grill until golden-brown.

FLEMISH ASPARAGUS

Trim 2 lb. of asparagus and cut it into even-sized lengths. Wash it very thoroughly, then plunge it into slightly salted boiling water and cook for 12–15 minutes. Prepare a sauce; sieve the yolks of 3 hard-boiled eggs, add 4 oz. melted butter gradually and season with salt and pepper. Serve with the sauce poured over the asparagus.

CUCUMBER COOKED THE BELGIAN WAY

Peel 4 medium-sized cucumbers and cut them into rounds about 2 inches thick. Cook in fast-boiling salted water until tender (about 10 minutes). Drain well, and arrange in a fireproof dish. Beat 2 egg yolks, mix with ½ pint of yoghourt and ¼ pint of mayonnaise and warm gently, but do not boil. Pour this mixture over the cucumber, sprinkle with chopped dill, and serve with thin brown bread and butter.

BELGIAN TART

6

8 oz. butter	1 lb. flour
2 oz. caster sugar	1 tsp. baking powder
2 tbsps. olive oil	¼ tsp. salt
A few drops of vanilla	Apricot or raspberry
essence	jam
1 egg	Icing sugar

Soften the butter and cream in the sugar. Beat well, and add the oil and vanilla essence. Add the beaten egg and stir in the flour, baking powder and salt, sieved together. Mix all well together, and knead to a shortbreadlike dough. Grease an 8-inch cake tin. Using a coarse grater, grate half of the mixture into the tin, covering the bottom completely. Spread with some slightly warmed jam, and then in turn cover this with the rest of the mixture, grated as before. Bake in a moderate oven (350° F., mark 4) for about 1¼ hours. When the tart is done, sprinkle sieved icing sugar over the top while it is still hot, and turn it out of the tin when cold.

BEIGNETS DE POMMES
(APPLE FRITTERS)

4 oz. plain flour	A little light beer
1 egg	Cooking apples
½ tbsp. brandy	Fat for frying
(optional)	Caster sugar

Sieve the flour into a basin and make a well in the centre; into this break the egg, and add brandy. Gradually work flour into the liquids, and finally add enough beer to make the batter of a coating consistency, then allow it to stand for 1–2 hours. Peel and core the apples, and cut them into rings crossways. Dip these into the batter, removing them with a skewer, and fry in smoking-hot fat until brown on both sides. Drain. Serve drenched with caster sugar.

PRUNE TART

½ lb. prunes	Salt
2 oz. sugar	1½ oz. margarine
½ a stick of cinnamon	1 oz. cooking fat
¼ lb. plain flour	1 oz. icing sugar

Soak the prunes overnight. Stew them with the sugar and cinnamon until very tender; towards the end of the cooking time remove the lid and allow almost all the liquid to evaporate. Sieve the prunes and return them to the pan. Blend 2 tsps. flour with 1 tbsp. cold water, add to the mixture, and boil for 2 minutes. Make some shortcrust pastry with the flour, salt, fats and enough water to give a fairly stiff dough. Roll out, line a pie plate or tin, prick and fill with baking beans. Bake for ¼ hour in a moderately hot oven (425° F., mark 7); remove beans, fill with prune mixture and bake for another 10 minutes. When cold, dust with icing sugar.

GAUFRES À LA FLAMANDE
(FLEMISH WAFFLES)

1 lb. flour	½ glass brandy
8 whole eggs	½ oz. yeast
½ pint cream	A pinch of salt
2 oz. butter	A pinch of sugar

Mix ¼ lb. flour with the yeast, dissolved in a little warm water, and set to rise. Then work in the rest of the flour, with the salt and sugar, the eggs, slightly beaten, and the cream, which should have been boiled and to which the butter is added. Knead well and let stand for 2½ hours in a warm place. Heat and grease the waffle irons. The batter should be sufficiently liquid to spread of itself over the waffle irons. When evenly browned on both sides, sprinkle with sugar and serve very hot.

GALETTES DE NOUVEL-AN
(NEW YEAR'S WAFFLES)

1 lb. plain flour	½ lb. fresh butter
10 oz. caster sugar	1 fresh egg
A pinch of salt	Brandy or rum (optional)

The dough should be made the day before the wafers are cooked, and the wafers themselves are best eaten a week or so later. Store them in an air-tight tin.

Put the flour, sugar and salt into a bowl, add the butter (or margarine) and mix together, working the butter into the other ingredients. Add the well-beaten egg and mix well. To improve the flavour half a small wineglass of either brandy or rum may be added. Leave the dough in the bowl in a cool place until the next day.

Heat the waffle iron. Shape the dough into oblong pieces, rolling them lightly, put in the hot iron, press well down, and bake for 2 minutes on each side, or until golden-brown. Take out with a flat knife or spatula, put on to a wire tray and let them become quite cold before storing.

CRAMIQUE
(TEA-TIME BREAD)

2 lb. flour	1 oz. lard
1 lump of sugar	A large pinch of salt
1 wineglassful of luke-warm water	6 oz. caster sugar
2 oz. yeast	4 oz. sultanas
½ pint milk	2 eggs
1 oz. butter	Egg yolk to glaze

Sieve the flour. Dissolve the lump of sugar in the water, break up and add the yeast, cover the basin with paper and put near the stove to warm. Warm the milk, butter and lard in a pan. Put the flour into a bowl, with the salt, caster sugar and sultanas. Mix well, add the egg yolks, and then the egg whites, beaten up separately. Slowly mix the eggs with the dry ingredients, a little at a time, add some of the warmed milk, and lastly mix in the yeast and add the rest of the milk. Knead well, and add a little flour, until the side of the bowl is quite clean. Cover with a cloth and leave in a warm place to rise for 1 hour. Knead the dough lightly, put in round or oblong tins and bake for 1–1½ hours in a moderately hot oven (400° F., mark 6). When almost cooked, glaze with beaten egg yolk, or, more simply, with cold water, and return the cake to the oven to finish cooking.

Luxembourg

BO'NESCHLUPP
(PEASANT BEAN SOUP)

String 1 lb. beans and cut them into ½-inch pieces, pour boiling water over them, repeat two or three times and then strain. Put them into about 3 pints tepid water and bring to the boil, adding salt to taste. An hour before serving, add 1½–2 lb. raw potatoes, peeled and cut into small cubes.

Brown 2 tbsps. or about 1½ oz. flour with 1¼ oz. cooking fat in a saucepan and stir until thoroughly blended. Add a little of the liquid from the soup and season to taste with pepper, salt and 1 tbsp. vinegar. Add this mixture to the soup a few minutes before serving and stir thoroughly. If desired, a cupful of sour cream may also be added.

ONNENZOPP
(ONION SOUP WITH CHEESE)

6–8 onions	Salt
2 oz. butter or margarine	3–4 oz. cheese
2–3 pints water	Paprika

Peel and mince the onions and brown them lightly in the hot butter in the saucepan, add the water and salt and allow to simmer until the onions are quite clear. Put the grated cheese in a warmed soup tureen and, just before serving, pour the boiling soup over it, stirring constantly. Add paprika to taste and serve at once.

PORRETTENZOPP
(LEEK SOUP)

5 leeks	4 lb. potatoes
2 oz. lard or margarine	1 cup cream or sour
3 pints water	milk
Salt	

Wash and chop the leeks and brown lightly in the fat. Add the water and salt and boil for 30 minutes. Add the raw potatoes, peeled and cut in cubes, and boil 20–30 minutes till cooked. Rub the soup through a sieve, reheat, and just before serving add the cupful of cream. (If you use sour milk, beat it with a fork so that the curd is broken up and well blended.)

LENZENZOPP MAT SPECI
(LENTIL AND BACON SOUP)

1 pint lentils	A small bunch of parsley
2 pints water	Salt
Garlic to taste	½ lb. bacon
1 clove	1 lb. potatoes

Wash lentils and soak them overnight. Boil them in the water in which they have been soaked, adding the garlic, clove, coarsely minced parsley and the salt. Add the diced bacon and allow the mixture to simmer until both the lentils and bacon are cooked. Then add the potatoes, peeled and cut into very small dice, and cook for a further 20 minutes. If a thicker soup is required, brown some butter with a little flour and add to the soup just before serving.

REISSZOPP MAT TOMATEN
(RICE AND TOMATO SOUP)

2 onions	A few tomatoes
2 tbsps. cooking fat	Chopped parsley
3 pints water	1 cup cream or top of
Salt	the milk
4 oz. rice	

Chop the onions and brown them in the fat.

Add the water, salt and the well-washed rice and allow to simmer very slowly for ½ hour until it is quite cooked and soft—do not boil quickly or the rice will be starchy. Before serving, add some chopped and fried tomatoes, chopped parsley and a cup of cream or top of the milk. Serve at once.

SAUERAMPELSZOPP MAT KI'ERBEL
(SORREL AND CHERVIL SOUP)

½ lb. sorrel	Salt
Chervil to taste	2 slices of bread
2 tbsps. butter	1 cup cream
2 pints water	Pepper

Remove the stalks from the sorrel and chervil, wash the leaves thoroughly and chop finely, then fry in the butter. Add 2 pints hot salted water and allow to simmer for 30 minutes. Crumble the bread to make about 3 oz. crumbs and add to the soup. Before serving put a little more bread, the cream and pepper to taste in a hot tureen and pour the soup over.

GEME'SZOPP MAT TAPIOCA
(VEGETABLE AND TAPIOCA SOUP)

2–3 lb. vegetables (leeks, carrots, parsnips, celeriac, peas and beans)	3–4 potatoes
	3 oz. tapioca
	1–2 egg yolks
Butter, margarine or cooking fat	Cream
	Finely chopped
4 pints water	parsley
Salt and pepper	

Prepare the vegetables, chop them all very finely and fry lightly in the hot fat. Add the water and salt and after about 15 minutes the potatoes, cut into small cubes. Allow to simmer for 1½ hours, but do not boil rapidly. About 20 minutes before serving, stir in the tapioca, boil quickly for a minute and then simmer very slowly. Add the tapioca to the soup while it is gently boiling. Mix the egg yolks with the cream in a warm tureen, and then pour in the soup. Add salt, pepper and chopped parsley just before serving.

CARBONADEN VU RENDFLESCH
(BEEF CARBONADES)

1½ lb. beef	1 cup vinegar and water, mixed
2 oz. cooking fat	Salt
Carrots	1 bay leaf
1 onion	Parsley
2 tbsps. flour	A little white wine (optional)

Cut the meat in slices and fry lightly. Put alternate layers of meat, carrots and onion in a pan, sprinkle with flour and allow to brown slightly. Add a very little boiling vinegar and water and then the seasoning and herbs and allow to stew for $2\frac{1}{2}$ hours. Just before serving add a little vinegar, or white wine, and stir gently.

JUDD MAT GARDEBO'NEN
(BACON AND BROAD BEANS)

1 lb. lean bacon	2 oz. cooking fat
$1\frac{1}{4}$ pints broad beans	1 clove
Salt and pepper	1 bay leaf
2 oz. flour	Thyme

Put the bacon in sufficient tepid water to cover and bring slowly to the boil. Wash the beans, pour hot water over them and then bring to the boil. Add some salt and allow to simmer for $\frac{1}{2}$ hour. Meanwhile make a sauce : brown the flour and fat together, and when blended add some water from the bacon pot, together with the clove, spices, herbs and a little pepper. When the beans are cooked, mix with the sauce and simmer gently for $\frac{1}{2}$ hour. About 20 minutes before serving, add the bacon, cut in slices or dice, arrange on a hot dish and serve with boiled potatoes. In place of bacon, pork or pickled pork may be used.

TREIP MAT SAUERKRAUT
(BLACK PUDDING AND SAUERKRAUT)

$1\frac{1}{2}$ lb. black pudding	Garlic
2 oz. cooking fat	$\frac{1}{2}$ cup stock or broth
2 lb. sauerkraut	1 glass white wine

Slice the black pudding and fry in the hot fat. Wash the sauerkraut and squeeze to remove all water. Boil for 10 minutes in water, strain and chop finely. Brown the garlic in the hot fat, add the sauerkraut and, just before serving, the white wine. Pile the sauerkraut in a dish and place the sausage round it.

SCHWENGSBROT
(ROAST PORK)

1 neck of pork	Fat for frying
Vinegar	Salt
1 bay leaf	Cream
1 clove	1 oz. butter
Parsley, thyme and tarragon	1 oz. flour
A few onions	Mustard
A garlic clove	

This takes 3–4 days to prepare. Wipe and trim the meat. Boil 1 cup vinegar and 1 cup water together, with the spices and herbs, and pour this mixture over the meat. Cut some onions in slices and place over the meat, which should be only half covered by the liquid as it is to be turned daily for 3–4 days and basted with the liquid.

Before roasting the meat, place it in about 1 inch of boiling water to which some vinegar, a chopped onion or two and a small piece of garlic have been added, and leave for about 30 minutes. Then dry the meat, fry it lightly in hot fat, sprinkle with a little salt and just a little of the pickle mixture, cover and roast gently in a moderate oven for $1\frac{1}{2}$–2 hours. While it is cooking, baste it several times with some cream.

Make a gravy with the meat liquid, butter and flour, stir, simmer and serve together with some mustard mixed with cream.

PANE'ERT SCHENGSFE'SS
(PORK FEET IN BREADCRUMBS)

Fresh or lightly pickled pig's trotters	4 oz. breadcrumbs
	1 minced onion
Salt and pepper	Fat for frying
1 clove	Chopped parsley
1 bay leaf	A little mustard
1 leaf of celeriac	Horseradish cream

Wash the trotters, place in tepid water with the salt, pepper and celeriac leaf and spices, and boil gently for $2\frac{1}{2}$ hours. Cut each trotter in half and remove the bones. Mix the breadcrumbs, minced onion, salt and pepper. Dip the hot trotters in this mixture, then fry in deep fat. Serve sprinkled with finely chopped parsley and mustard, together with a little horseradish cream.

SCHWENGSJELLY or FIERKELCHESJELLY
(PORK JELLY)

2 lb. pork	1 bay leaf
Salt	Parsley
1 pint white wine	A few leaves of celeriac
1 clove	Thyme

Cut the meat in cubes and soak for several hours. Bring to the boil in water, with the salt and wine, and skim. Now add all the spices and herbs. Cook for about 3 hours. When the meat is tender, place it on a sieve till dry. Allow the broth to simmer a little longer, skim and put it through a strainer. Place the meat in dishes, pour the broth over and allow to set.

VULLEN ONI KAPP
(BIRDS WITHOUT A HEAD)

3 slices of beef	Flour
Salt and pepper	3 oz. cooking fat
Chopped parsley	1 carrot
Finely chopped onion	1 whole onion
3 slices of bacon	A little broth or water
3 hard-boiled eggs	

Beat the slices of beef flat with a rolling pin. Place on each slice some salt, parsley, a slice of bacon and in the centre a hard-boiled egg.

Roll up the pieces of meat and bind firmly with cotton or thin string. Roll in flour and fry slowly in an open pan, then add a sliced onion and carrot, sprinkle with a little salt, add a little hot broth or water and stew very gently for about 1½–2 hours, closely covered.

Before serving, remove the threads or pieces of string and cut the meat rolls across in halves, so that half an egg is in each part. Dish up on creamy mashed potatoes covered with chopped parsley; serve gravy separately.

KUDDELFLECK
(FRIED TRIPE)

Wash some uncooked tripe and soak for 24 hours, changing the water several times, then add some parsley, one or two bay leaves, 1 clove and a little nutmeg and boil till tender, which may take about 5 hours' cooking. The boiling should be very gentle indeed. Drain the tripe, cut it in square pieces and rub these with salt and pepper; dip in a thin batter of flour and water and then in breadcrumbs. Fry in hot cooking fat in an open frying pan and serve on a hot dish with brown or mustard sauce.

KRIBSEN À LA LUXEMBOURGEOISE
(CRAYFISH)

Buy a large crayfish, as fresh as possible, wash it well in cold water and drain in a sieve, then remove the meat and soak in milk or cream.

Meanwhile prepare a broth made with a small glass each of water and white wine, a very small glass of cognac, 1 oz. salt, 1 oz. pounded peppercorns, a little thyme, a lot of parsley and tarragon, a small piece of butter, a little paprika and 1 onion, cut in quarters. Bring this broth to the boil in a very large pan, put the crayfish in it, cover closely and boil for 5 or 6 minutes. Serve very hot on a plate on a clean napkin and decorate it with parsley.

LI'EWERKNI'EDELEN
(LIVER DUMPLINGS)

1 lb. liver	Chives
4 oz. fat bacon	2–3 eggs
Parsley	Salt and pepper
Thyme	Breadcrumbs
Onions	Soaked bread
Shallots	A little flour

Mince the liver and 2 oz. bacon and finely chop the parsley, thyme, onions, shallots and chives and mix with the eggs, salt, pepper, breadcrumbs, soaked bread and flour to a stiff dough. Form into small dumplings, using a teaspoon, drop them in boiling salted water and

W.C.B.—3

boil for about 10 minutes. Cut the remaining fat bacon in small cubes, fry it gently so that it is almost all melted; pour over the dumplings before serving.

HIERENGSZALLOT
(HERRING SALAD)

3 herrings	3 tbsps. cream
1 tsp. made mustard	Chopped parsley
3 tbsps. salad oil	1 apple, sliced or finely
4 tbsps. wine vinegar	minced
A few onions, very finely	Cream or sour milk
minced	(optional)

Wash the herrings and soak for at least 12 hours, then skin and bone them and cut the flesh into small cubes. If there are soft roes mix these with the mustard, oil and vinegar and pour this sauce over the herrings, then mix well with the onions together with the parsley and apple; add also a little cream or sour milk, if desired.

WAREM GROMPERENZALLOT
(HOT POTATO SALAD)

4 lb. potatoes	2 oz. fat bacon
Salt and pepper	3 onions
2 tbsps. olive or salad oil	2 or 3 tbsps. butter
3 tbsps. vinegar	Parsley

Boil the potatoes in their skins, peel while hot, cut in slices and mix with a sauce made of salt, pepper, oil and vinegar, beaten lightly together. Keep hot.

Cut the fat bacon in small cubes and the onions in slices, fry them lightly so that the fat runs out of the bacon—add more fat if necessary. Then pour over the hot potatoes, sprinkle with parsley and serve at once.

KLENG GROMPERENKICHELCHER
(SMALL POTATO CAKES)

2 lb. potatoes	1 pinch sugar
2 eggs	5 tbsps. flour
Salt	Fat for frying
Pepper	Chopped parsley

Boil the potatoes in their skins and peel them at once, then while still hot pass them through a sieve one at a time. Mix with the eggs, salt and pepper, a little sugar to taste and the flour. Put some more flour on a pastry board, and when the potato mixture is cold form it into small cakes, roll lightly in the flour on the board and fry in hot fat. Alternatively, make one large cake, put into a greased tin and bake in a fairly hot oven (425° F., mark 7) until brown. Sprinkle with parsley and serve hot with a little butter or with bacon.

10

11

STREISELKUCH

1 lb. flour	3 tbsps. sugar
1 oz. yeast	2 eggs
⅓ pint warm milk	1–2 oz. butter or lard
A little salt	

For the Topping

1 egg yolk	2 oz. sugar
1 oz. butter	2 oz. flour

Make a dough with 4 oz. flour, the yeast and half the warm milk, and allow to rise slowly—about 45 minutes. Now add the salt, sugar, the remainder of the milk and flour, the beaten eggs and, lastly, the creamed butter. Beat the dough till it forms bubbles and roll it on a board sprinkled with flour till it is spread out but not too thin. Put into a greased tin, allow to rise again, cover with the egg yolk, butter, sugar and flour, creamed together; spread over evenly. Bake for 10 minutes at 450° F. (mark 8) and a further 30 minutes at mark 4.

ROLLEUCH
(ROLL-CAKE)

1¼ lb. flour	5 oz. butter
1 oz. yeast	2 egg whites
1 pint milk	4 oz. sugar
A little salt	4 oz. sultanas
3 eggs	2 oz. sugar for glazing

Prepare the dough as in the recipes for Streiselkuch and as soon as it forms bubbles put it on a board sprinkled with flour and beat with the hands until it comes away from the board—add a little more flour as may be necessary. Allow to rise once more, then put in a cool place, let it rise again, then beat it down again. Repeat this two or three times, then knead the dough for a few minutes, roll to an oblong strip and cut into fingers. Mix one egg white, the sugar and sultanas, and roll together. Place these rolls in a shallow pan about 1 inch apart and allow to rise again. Before baking, brush over lightly with egg white and bake in a hot oven (450° F., mark 8) for about 45 minutes. When it is taken from the oven, cover with a thick syrup made by boiling 2 oz. sugar with a little water and replace in a slow oven until the sugar mixture is firm and white.

REISS TART
(RICE TART)

2 oz. butter	1 tbsp. cream or sour
2 oz. cooking fat	milk
½ lb. flour	1 tbsp. cold water
1 tbsp. rum, cognac	6 tbsps. sugar
or cooking sherry	Salt

12

For the Filling

5 oz. rice	2 oz. sugar
1½ pints milk	A little cinnamon
2 eggs	1 oz. chopped almonds
A pinch of salt	

Rub the butter and cooking fat into the flour and pour all the liquids into the centre, with the sugar and salt, and knead into a dough; leave in a cold place for about an hour. Roll out, place in a well-greased baking tin and cover with the filling, made as follows :
Wash the rice, put into boiling water and boil for 3 minutes, then drain and pour cold water over it; drain again. Meanwhile boil the milk, add the rice and cook slowly until it is half done. Add the egg yolks and the remaining ingredients. Add the stiffly beaten egg whites last of all and spread the mixture over the pastry. Bake in a moderate oven (350° F., mark 4) for about 45 minutes.

STERZELEN
(BUCKWHEAT CAKES)

2 pints water	1–2 oz. cooking fat
Salt	or lard
1 lb. buckwheat meal	1 cup cream or milk

Bring the water to the boil, add some salt, put in all the meal at once and stir to a smooth dough. Dip a teaspoon in hot fat, form small balls of the mixture, place these in a baking tin and put some lard and a little salt over them and then a very little hot cream or milk. Bake gently in a slow oven (300° F., mark 1) until risen and brown. Serve hot or cold.

THE phrase "English cooking" means something different to almost everybody. To the Yorkshireman it means parkin and cold tripe and Yorkshire pudding; to the Devonian it means splits and cream; to the man from the shires it means Melton Mowbray pies. But all too often, unfortunately, the foreigner thinks it still means boiled potatoes, watery cabbage and lumpy custard.

It may be that we have only ourselves to blame for this. The Englishman has never been a great frequenter of restaurants and cafés; he has found the snug warmth of his own fireside and his wife's special steak and kidney pie more to his liking than the doubtful pleasures of the local hotel or restaurant.

But now there is a return to real interest in good food and this new delight in the pleasures of the table is based on the solid foundations of excellent dairy produce, prime meat, tender and delicious fruit and vegetables and fish fresh from the rivers and the sea.

English housewives are blazing a trail for the more cautious restaurants and hotels to follow, and although we shall never, in the foreseeable future, be likely to desert our steak and kidney puddings, suet rolls and syrup tarts, we are leavening the rather starchy lump with more fish, more fruit, more vegetables and salads. The average English housewife can offer a blend of old and new that should please the most fastidious palate.

Scottish womenfolk seem to have a flair for cookery and a gift for making the best of available materials. The country is especially famed for its bannocks, baps and other breads, its scones, shortbreads and cakes. Oatmeal, that hardy cereal, has played a large part in Scottish diet and porridge and oatcakes remain everyday fare. Aberdeen Angus beef is renowned; so too are Highland honey and the late Scotch raspberries. Haggis, though the subject of so many jokes, is well worth trying, while Scotch whisky owes its world-renowned excellence to the pure, soft water of the springs and burns.

A poor country through most of its long history, Ireland inevitably reflects its character in its food. Potatoes, when introduced from the New World, suited both the soil and the native smallholder's temperament and gave rise to a number of Irish "peasant" dishes. A pig is a fairly easy animal to acquire and rear, so bacon became a staple foodstuff. Irish stew, that sublimely simple and delicious blend of mutton, potatoes and onions, makes a little meat go a long way. One Irish speciality that has made its way in the world is Irish whiskey; Irish coffee, that comforting brew, is also acquiring an international reputation.

Welsh cuisine, with its characteristic girdle cakes and fruit breads, tends to resemble plain, honest English family cooking. The basic ingredients, however, can be very, very good. Welsh mutton is excellent; Welsh salmon, too, makes good eating, and Caerphilly cheese is becoming increasingly popular outside Wales.

British Isles

England

ROAST RIBS OF BEEF

The ribs and the sirloin of beef are the best joints for roasting. They may be purchased either on the bone, or boned and rolled. Put the joint in a roasting tin with a little fat, cook it in a moderately hot oven (425° F., mark 7) for 30 minutes to seal the surface of the meat, then lower to moderate (375° F., mark 5), cover the meat and continue to cook till tender; allow 20–25 minutes per lb. and 20–25 minutes over.

Roast beef should be served slightly underdone, as it is then more succulent, especially when cold. It is usually accompanied by Yorkshire pudding, horseradish cream, thin brown gravy and roast potatoes.

YORKSHIRE PUDDING

4 oz. flour	1 egg
½ tsp. salt	½ pint milk

Sieve the flour and salt into a basin and make a well in the centre. Drop in the egg and half the milk, then mix in the flour a little at a time, using a wooden spoon and keeping the mixture smooth, until a thick creamy consistency is obtained. Beat for 5–10 minutes, till the mixture is full of bubbles, then stir in the rest of the milk. Either use at once or cover and allow to stand until required.

Heat a little dripping in a baking tin or individual deep patty tins; when it is smoking hot, pour in the batter. Bake near the top of a moderately hot oven (425° F., mark 7), allowing about 40 minutes for a large pudding, 25 minutes for small ones. Alternatively, bake the meat on a trivet over the pudding, so that it absorbs the meat juices.

HORSERADISH CREAM

1–2 tbsps. grated horseradish	Cream or " top of milk "
1 tbsp. vinegar	Salt and pepper
	Sugar

Soak the grated horseradish in the vinegar for 10–15 minutes. Stir in enough cream to give the desired consistency, and season with salt, pepper and sugar.

LANCASHIRE HOT-POT

2 lb. potatoes	1 oz. flour
2 lb. mutton (middle neck)	¾ pint stock
1 onion	Seasoning
2 kidneys	1 tsp. caster sugar
4–5 mushrooms	20 oysters (optional)
1 oz. dripping	Parsley

Peel the potatoes and slice them thickly. Cut the meat into chops. Slice the onion and the kidneys; peel and slice the mushrooms. Brown the meat in the hot dripping, then drain and put into a fairly large casserole. Lightly brown the onion, then add the flour and cook until well coloured; mix in the hot stock gradually, stirring all the time, and add the seasoning and sugar. Spread the kidney over the mutton and add a layer of mushrooms and then a layer of oysters, if used. Arrange potatoes overlapping all over the top. Strain the sauce into the casserole, cover, and cook for about 1¾ hours in a moderate oven (350° F., mark 4). Remove the lid and continue cooking for 15 minutes or so until the top is well browned. Garnish with parsley and serve with red cabbage, which is the traditional Lancashire accompaniment.

Simpler versions of this recipe use just the mutton, omitting the kidneys and oysters and often the mushrooms also.

MIXED GRILL

This consists of a selection of foods suitable for grilling, such as a chop, kidney and sausages, or a steak, liver and sausages, served with grilled halved tomatoes, mushrooms, chipped potatoes and maître d'hôtel butter.

Prepare the various items for grilling and season all meats on both sides with salt and pepper and a little lemon juice, if liked. Brush all the pieces over with melted fat, and start by grilling the foods which require the longest time, so that they are all ready at the same time.

BEEF-STEAK OR JOHN BULL'S PUDDING

Take 1–1½ lb. of the inside of a sirloin of beef, or the same quantity of rump steak. Cut off part of the fat, beat the meat until tender, then cut it into small, thin slices. Slice 2 lamb's kidneys or 1 veal kidney; beard 1 dozen oysters. Mix with pepper, salt, a minced shallot and some chopped parsley.

Grease a deep basin and line with suetcrust pastry, fill with the above ingredients, add a little water and cover with more pastry. Cover with a floured cloth or several layers of greaseproof paper and boil or steam for about 3 hours. Make some strong beef gravy, add a little mushroom ketchup, make a hole in the suetcrust top and pour it in.

The oysters and kidneys may be omitted, being replaced, if desired, by a little sliced or minced onion.

PARTRIDGE PUDDING

Line a well-greased basin with a good suet-crust (which should include fresh white bread-crumbs for added lightness). Cut a brace of well-hung partridges into neat joints and season well. Fill the basin with alternate layers of the game and mushrooms (button mushrooms are best). Cover with stock, to which a glass of claret may be added if wished. Season with salt, pepper, chopped parsley or herbs and a suggestion of powdered mace or nutmeg. Cover with suetcrust and tie over the pudding a scalded and floured cloth. Put into a deep pan of boiling water and cook for 3–3½ hours, keeping the pudding covered the whole time.

Boiling fowl or young rabbits may be substituted for the partridges; oysters were often added to the partridges in the old recipes.

Note : This is one of the oldest recorded English recipes and the pudding is said to have been made in Saxon times.

QUORN BACON ROLL

½ lb. suetcrust pastry	Parsley, potatoes, tur-
¾ lb. lean bacon	nips and carrots to
2 tsps. sage	accompany
1 large onion	

Make the suet pastry, using just enough water to moisten, and roll it out fairly thinly into an oblong. Put the bacon rashers on the pastry and sprinkle with chopped onion and sage. Roll up, tie in a pudding cloth and boil for about 2 hours. Serve very hot, sprinkled with chopped parsley, and accompanied by potatoes, carrots and turnips or other vegetables, as preferred.

MELTON MOWBRAY PORK PIE
For the Filling

3 lb. pork	1 tsp. anchovy essence
Salt and pepper	

For the Crust

¾ lb. lard	A pinch of salt
½ pint milk and water	Egg yolk and milk to
2 lb. flour	glaze

Remove the skin, bone and gristly parts from the meat, cover them with cold water and stew gently for about 1 hour. When cold, the stock will form a stiff jelly. Season and strain.

Boil the fat in the liquid, pour into the flour and salt and mix to a soft dough, using a wooden spoon. Allow to cool slightly. Set aside about a quarter of the dough in a warm place; allow the rest to cool slightly, then knead well. Grease a 7-inch cake tin with a loose bottom, and line

it with the pastry up to ½ inch above the top of the tin. Make a rose and leaves to decorate the top, using a little of the portion of pastry which was set aside.

Cut up the meat finely, season and press it firmly into the pastry case. Use the rest of the pastry to make a lid, and seal the edges well. Place the decoration in position, having made a small hole in the top. Brush over with a mixture of egg yolk and milk, and bake in a slow oven (325° F., mark 2–3) for about 3 hours. When golden-brown all over, remove from the oven, and take out the rose. Using a funnel, pour in hot stock until the pie is filled; when quite cold and beginning to set, replace the rose.

Veal and Ham Pie may be made in a similar way; use three parts veal to one part ham, and season with a little salt, pepper, grated lemon rind and chopped parsley. Cut-up hard-boiled egg may also be included.

AYLESBURY GAME PIE

Cut the flesh of a hare into finger-sized pieces. Take the equivalent weight of veal, chicken, pheasant, ham or bacon (using any or all of these ingredients), without fat or skin. Chop the liver of the hare and mix with 1–1½ lb. sausage-meat. At the bottom of a large earthenware game pie dish, place some pepper and salt, a sprig of thyme and a bay leaf; cover with a thin layer of the sausage stuffing, then with a layer of the sliced game. Repeat, using alternate layers of stuffing and meats, until there are no empty spaces; press the whole well down, and add a little more of the seasoning and herbs. Cover with slices of ham or bacon, pour on ½ pint cold water, replace lid and seal edges with a paste of flour and water. Bake in a moderate oven (350° F., mark 4) for 4–4½ hours. Serve cold.

SHROPSHIRE FIDGET PIE

1 lb. potatoes	Pepper
About ½ lb. bacon or	A little salt
ham (home-cured if	A little stock
possible)	Rich shortcrust pastry
1 lb. apples	to cover
A little sugar if needed	

Peel and slice the potatoes. Trim the bacon or ham and cut it into dice or small slices. Peel and slice the apples, and dip into sugar if of a very sour variety. Grease a pie dish and put in alternate layers of potato, bacon and apple until the dish is full, seasoning each layer. Add the stock, and cover with a layer of pastry. Bake at the bottom of a moderately hot oven (400° F., mark 6) for about 1 hour.

BUCKINGHAMSHIRE PIE

2 young rabbits	2 oz. macaroni
½ pint cream	1 tbsp. chopped onion
2 oz. grated Parmesan cheese	Pepper and salt
	Puff or flaky pastry

Stew the rabbits gently until tender—1–1½ hours. Remove all the bones and cut up the meat and place in a pie dish with the other ingredients. Cover with the pastry and bake in a moderately hot oven (400° F., mark 6) for about 1 hour.

DEVONSHIRE SQUAB PIE

6 oz. shortcrust	Salt and pepper
1½ lb. cooking apples	2 onions
8 small mutton chops	

Make the pastry. Place at the bottom of a pie dish a layer of peeled, cored and sliced apples, then a layer of mutton chops, well seasoned with salt and pepper. Then add a layer of apples, next a layer of peeled, sliced onions and another layer of apples ; follow with mutton, apples and onions. Pour on ½ pint water, cover with the pastry crust and bake in a moderately hot oven (425° F., mark 7) for 10 minutes, then in a moderate oven (375° F., mark 5) for a further ¾ hour, or until the meat is cooked.

MUTTON SAUCER PIES (CUMBERLAND)

8 oz. shortcrust pastry	1 tsp. chopped parsley
8 oz. lean cooked mutton	½ tsp. chopped thyme
1 small minced onion	A little stock or milk
2 chopped mushrooms	Seasoning

Make the pastry and use rather more than half of it to line strong saucers or small round tins. Mince the mutton, removing all fat, and mix with the remaining ingredients. Fill the pies with the mixture, and cover with another round of pastry, then bake in a moderately hot oven (450° F., mark 6) for about 45 minutes.

DURHAM BACON CAKE

½ lb. lard	Cold water to mix
1 lb. flour	Sliced cold boiled
1 tbsp. baking powder	bacon

Rub the lard into the flour till it is as fine as meal, add the baking powder and mix well ; add sufficient water to make a stiff paste, and roll it out. Cover half the pastry with sliced bacon, then cover with the remaining pastry. Roll it gently to exclude air and prevent it rising unevenly, prick all over with a fork, pinch the edges together, lay it on a baking sheet and cook in a moderate oven (370° F., mark 5) till nicely browned. Serve cut into squares.

YORKSHIRE RAREBIT

½ lb. shortcrust	2 eggs
¼ lb. ham	Pepper and salt

Line a baking plate with pastry, cut the ham up fine and spread evenly over the pastry. Beat the eggs, add the seasoning and pour over the ham. Damp the edges and cover with a round of pastry. Put into a hot oven (450° F., mark 8) for the first 10 minutes, then lower the heat to moderate (375° F., mark 5) and cook for a further 20 minutes.

The same name is also given to a Welsh rarebit (see page 52) topped with a slice of grilled ham and a poached egg.

LANCASHIRE TRIPE AND ONIONS

Take 2 lb. dressed tripe and cut it into square pieces, place it in a saucepan, cover with cold water, bring to the boil, and throw away the water. Add to the tripe 1 pint each of milk and water, 4 sliced onions, salt and pepper to season, and simmer for 3 hours. Thicken the liquid with 1 tbsp. flour mixed in a little milk and strained into the pot, re-boil and add extra seasoning if required. Serve very hot.

BELLY OF PORK

Buy a piece of belly of pork weighing about 4 lb. and rub it over first with Demerara sugar, then with coarse kitchen salt, and leave it for 5–6 days, turning and rubbing with the liquid every day. Then wash it and put in a pan with 3–4 bay leaves, 1 tbsp. sugar and about 12–14 peppercorns. Boil it in wine or water for about 6 hours and then press it between 2 plates. This pork is delicious with turkey, chicken or pheasant.

JUGGED HARE

½ a hare	Cayenne pepper
1½ oz. seasoned flour	A bouquet garni
2 oz. margarine or dripping	1 glassful of port or
1 doz. small white onions	other red wine
3–4 oz. bacon	Stock
Pepper and salt	Forcemeat balls

Cut the hare in pieces not larger than a small egg and coat them with some of the flour. Melt the fat in a saucepan, put in the onions and the bacon, cut in strips, and toss over the heat until lightly browned. Then lift these out and brown the hare in the same fat, sprinkling over it the remainder of the flour. Put all into a crock or fireproof casserole and season with pepper, salt and a little Cayenne pepper. Add the bouquet garni, wine and enough stock to cover. Cover closely and cook in a moderate oven (350° F., mark 4) until tender. It is a good plan to stand the casserole or crock in a tin and keep a little water round it. Just before serving, remove the bouquet garni and add a few forcemeat balls. Serve red-currant or cranberry jelly separately.

FORCEMEAT BALLS FOR HARE

The liver and kidneys	Seasoning
of the hare	A pinch of nutmeg
2 oz. suet	grated
1 tbsp. parsley	Egg
¼ tsp. mixed herbs	Milk or stock
6 oz. breadcrumbs	A little ham or bacon
Grated rind of ½ lemon	(optional)

Cook the liver and kidneys in a little stock, then drain and chop them finely. Chop also the suet and parsley and powder the herbs. Mix all together in a basin, with the breadcrumbs, adding the lemon rind. Season with pepper and salt and a pinch of nutmeg, and bind together with egg and milk, or egg and stock. A little chopped ham or bacon may also be added. Form the forcemeat into a roll, cut off small pieces and roll into balls. Coat them with flour, fry in hot fat and drain well.

BOILED MARROW BONES

Have long marrow bones neatly sawed into convenient-sized pieces. Cover the ends with a small piece of pastry; tie a floured cloth over each. Place the bones upright in a saucepan of boiling water, taking care there is sufficient to cover the bones, and boil for 2 hours. Remove the cloths and paste and serve them upright on a napkin, with dry toast.

Alternatively, remove the marrow from the bones, spread it on a slice of toast and add some pepper; serve at once.

FAGGOTS
(POOR MAN'S GOOSE)

¾ lb. pig's liver	1 small onion
4 oz. fat salt pork	Salt and pepper
Mixed herbs to taste	1 egg
Dash of ground nutmeg	Fresh breadcrumbs
Pig's caul	Good gravy

This substantial farmhouse dish is both nutritious and flavoursome.

Chop the liver up finely with the onion and the salt pork, place in a pan with the seasonings, cover and cook very gently for about ½ hour—do not allow the meat to colour. When done, drain off the fat and add the beaten egg, breadcrumbs and nutmeg, using just enough bread-crumbs to bind the mixture to a stiff paste. Shape into squares, rolls or oblongs and enclose each in a piece of the pig's caul. (Failing a caul, place the unwrapped faggots closely together in the dish and cover well with greaseproof paper.) Set side by side in a baking dish and add a cupful of good gravy or rich stock. Bake in a moderately hot oven (425° F., mark 7) for 35–45 minutes, until nicely browned.

Baked potatoes make a nice accompaniment to this dish. The faggots may be served hot or cold.

TOAD IN THE HOLE

Heat about ½ oz. dripping in an oblong baking tin and when smoking hot, pour in ½ pint Yorkshire pudding mixture. Over it arrange ½–¾ lb. sausages (skinned or not, as preferred), which have been rolled lightly in flour. Alternatively, arrange the required number of trimmed lamb chops over the batter. Bake in a hot oven (450° F., mark 8) for about ¾ hour.

CORNISH PASTIES

1 lb. flour	½ tsp. salt
½ lb. lard and suet	Water to mix
mixed	Filling as desired

14

Make the pastry in the usual way, roll out ¼ inch thick and cut into 6-inch rounds. Lay these on the pastry board, put in the filling, damp the edges of the pastry slightly and fold over into a neat semi-circle. Crimp the edges and stand the pasties upright on a baking sheet; brush over with a little beaten egg and bake for the first 15 minutes in a hot oven (450° F., mark 8), then lower the temperature to moderate (350° F., mark 4) and continue to bake until the filling is cooked.

A variety of different fillings, both savoury and sweet, can be used in Cornish pasties. Two popular ones are given here, the quantities being sufficient for the above amount of pastry.

Beef or Mutton : ½ lb. boneless beef or mutton, ¼ lb. potatoes, 1 carrot, 1 turnip, 1 onion. Cut up all the ingredients fairly small and mix together. Bake for a total of ¾ hour. Kidney or liver is often included with beef in these pasties; the vegetables may be varied according to taste.

Pork : 1 lb. pork, ½ lb. potatoes, 1 onion, 1 tsp. chopped or diced sage or thyme. Cut up the meat and vegetables and mix well together. Bake for 1¼ hours in all.

DOVER SOLE

Wash and dry the fish, brush it with melted butter and season. Cook it for 7–10 minutes

15

under a very hot grill, lowering the heat after the first 2–3 minutes and turning the sole to brown both sides. Garnish with lemon and parsley and serve with melted butter sauce.

SOLE BAKED WITH MUSSELS

Line a well-buttered pie dish with very thinly sliced onions; put in a thick sole which has been cleaned and skinned, season well and barely cover the fish with dry white wine or cider. Bake in a moderate oven (350° F., mark 4) for 30 minutes. Drain off the liquor and keep the fish hot. Use the liquor to make a good sauce of coating consistency. Arrange over the sole at least a dozen prepared mussels, or mussels, oysters and mushrooms. Cover with the sauce and return the dish to the oven to heat through for another 15 minutes. Garnish with croûtons of fried bread.

Crayfish, lobster or prawns, cut into suitable-sized pieces may be substituted for the mussels.

RIVER TROUT

8 small trout	Salt and pepper
2 oz. butter	Chopped parsley
A little lemon juice.	Lemon wedges

Only small trout (or grayling) should be used for this dish. Clean them and leave the heads on. Cream the softened butter with the lemon juice and seasonings, and add the parsley. Spread the sides of the fish lightly with this mixture and then wrap each in a piece of buttered greaseproof paper, twisting the ends to make a bag. Bake in a moderate oven (350° F., mark 4) for about 20 minutes. Serve the fish still in the bag to retain the flavour and liquor, or, if preferred, unwrap the fish before dishing up. Garnish with lemon wedges and serve if desired with poached mushrooms and steamed or boiled potatoes.

GRILLED SEVERN SALMON

3 salmon cutlets	4 oz. button mushrooms
Salad oil	A little butter

Dry the salmon and brush all over with oil. Put on to a hot greased grid and grill for about 10 minutes on one side, then turn carefully and cook the other side, again brushing with oil. Peel and sauté the mushrooms in a little butter. Serve the salmon on a hot dish with a small pat of maître d'hôtel butter on each cutlet, and garnish with parsley or watercress. Arrange the button mushrooms in neat groups between the cutlets.

NEWCASTLE POTTED SALMON

Scale and wipe the salmon, remove the backbone, and cut the fish to fit into a casserole. Season with salt, mace and cloves, and add a few peppercorns and 4 bay leaves. Cover with butter and bake in a moderate oven (350° F., mark 4). When done, remove and drain the fish, pound it well, put into pots and when cold, cover with melted butter.

DORSET SCALLOPED CRAB

Choose a good-sized crab. Remove the meat from the shell, add 1 anchovy and chop them together. Put into a pan with salt and cayenne pepper, 2 tbsps. vinegar, 2 tbsps. breadcrumbs and a little butter and simmer for a few minutes. Clean the crab shell, pack in the filling and bake in a moderate oven (350° F., mark 4) until lightly browned. Garnish with lemon and parsley and serve with thin brown bread and butter.

JELLIED EELS

2–2½ lb. eels	Seasoning
1 quart strong fish stock	1 tbsp. white wine vinegar
2 onions	½ oz. gelatine
1 bay leaf and a little parsley	1 tbsp. sherry (optional)

16

Clean and skin the eels and cut into pieces about 2 inches long. Put into a large pan with the fish stock, sliced onions, bay leaf, parsley, seasoning and vinegar and simmer gently for 3–3½ hours, or until the fish is tender, then lift out into a deep pie dish. Simmer the liquor in the pan to reduce it a little, remove it from the heat and add the gelatine dissolved in a little water; when slightly cooled, add the sherry. Strain this mixture over the pieces of eel and leave to set, preferably overnight.

An alternative method is as follows: Clean and skin the eels, cut into pieces of equal length and pack closely into a deep dish, the pieces of fish standing upright. Into the crevices put some chopped or sliced onion and small sprigs of parsley. Fill the dish, to cover the eel, with seasoned vinegar, diluted with 1 part in 4 of water. Cover the dish securely and bake in a slow oven (300° F., mark 1) for at least 3 hours. Leave to cool overnight.

MACKEREL WITH GOOSEBERRY SAUCE

Allow one freshly caught mackerel per person. Clean the fish and poach gently in salted water, with a bouquet garni and 1 tbsp. white vinegar, until tender—about 15–20 minutes. Lift carefully on to a hot serving dish and garnish with sprigs of parsley. Serve the sauce separately.

Gooseberry Sauce : Top and tail 1 pint green gooseberries and cook in a scant ½ pint water until soft. Pass them through a fine sieve, return the purée to the pan and add the 1 oz. butter and a pinch of powdered mace ; reheat and serve.

Some chopped sorrel, or ½ cup spinach juice or sorrel juice, improves the colour and flavour of this sauce ; if juice is used, add water to make up to the ½ pint liquid required.

CUMBERLAND SHIPPED HERRINGS

Wash the herrings and remove the backbone, tail, head and fins. Stuff each herring with forcemeat, put a small piece of butter on each and bake in a moderate oven (350° F., mark 4) for 20–30 minutes. Serve with mustard sauce.

SOUSED PILCHARDS

Clean some pilchards without splitting them open, and place a bay leaf in each. Put into an ovenproof dish and almost cover with equal quantities of vinegar and cold tea, with a little brown sugar. Cover with greaseproof paper and bake in a slow oven (325° F., mark 3) until the bones are soft. Serve cold.

Herrings and mackerel may be treated in the same way.

CORNISH STAR-GAZY PIE

17

Take enough fresh herrings or mackerel to fill a moderate-size dish. Scale and split them and remove the backbones. Lay them flat, season the inside of each with salt, pepper and chopped parsley and roll up neatly. Butter a pie dish and sprinkle in it a thick layer of fine breadcrumbs. Lay in some of the fish, then fill the dish with alternate layers of breadcrumbs and fish.

Cover the top with a few slices of fat bacon, and pour over all 6 eggs beaten up with 2 tbsps. tarragon vinegar (or, if preferred, with ¼ pint cream). Cover the dish with shortcrust pastry and arrange the heads of the fish in a hole made in the centre of the crust. Bake in a hot oven (450° F., mark 8) until the pastry is cooked. Put a piece of parsley into the mouth of each fish before serving.

If preferred, leave the heads on the fish, but clean and bone them ; put the fish with their heads towards the centre of the pie.

KEDGEREE

12 oz. cooked smoked haddock or other white fish	1 hard-boiled egg Boiled rice (4 oz. before cooking)
2 oz. butter or margarine	Salt and cayenne pepper Chopped parsley

18

Remove the bones and skin from the fish when it is hot and flake it coarsely with a fork. Chop the white and part of the yolk of the egg, reserving a little of the latter for garnishing. Melt the fat in a saucepan, add the fish, rice, chopped egg and seasonings. Stir thoroughly over a moderate heat until hot. Pile on a hot dish and garnish with lines of chopped parsley and a little sieved yolk of egg, using that which was reserved.

SALMAGUNDY

This was an old English "sallet" or salad. The main ingredients are the white meat of a cold chicken or slices of cold roast veal, 4 hard-boiled eggs, some anchovy fillets or 2 pickled herrings and a selection of the usual hors d'œuvre ingredients—gherkins, olives, sliced beetroot, pickled red cabbage, etc. If possible, use also some thin slices of cold ham or tongue. Invert a saucer on the serving dish ; using this as a base, build up a pyramid of the ingredients, placing the cold chicken or veal first. Each succeeding ring should be slightly smaller than the previous one and the colours should vary as the salad is built up. Garnish with slices of lemon and top with a small bunch of parsley.

NORTHUMBERLAND PAN HAGGERTY

1 lb. onions	8 oz. grated cheese
2 lb. potatoes	Pepper
1 tbsp. dripping	Salt

Peel the vegetables, cut them into very thin slices and remove the moisture by wrapping them in a cloth. Heat the dripping in a heavy frying pan and put in a layer of potato, a layer of grated cheese, a layer of onions and so on, seasoning each layer with pepper and salt. Fry gently until nearly cooked, then brown under the grill.

CORNISH CLOTTED CREAM

Clotted cream should be made as soon as possible after milking. Strain the milk into shallow pans, and let it stand for 24 hours in winter and 12 hours in summer. Put the pan on the stove, or into a steamer containing water, and let it heat gently until the cream begins to show a raised rim round the edge. (Ideally, a stick fire should be used for the cooking.) When the cream is sufficiently cooked, place it in a cool larder and leave for 12–24 hours. Whenever it is necessary to move the pan, do this very carefully so as to avoid breaking up the cream. When the cream is required, skim it off in layers into a glass dish, taking care to have a good " crust " on the top.

CUMBERLAND RUM BUTTER

1 lb. butter	3 tsps. allspice
3 lb. soft dark brown sugar	1½ wineglassfuls rum
	1 glass brandy
3 nutmegs	Caster sugar

Melt the butter, but do not allow it to boil. Place the sugar in a bowl, grate the nutmeg into it and add the allspice. Stir well, adding the rum and brandy. Add the melted butter, stirring slowly all the time until the mixture becomes quite stiff. Put into a china bowl, and when cold sprinkle with caster sugar.

ROSE PETAL PRESERVE

This is a very old method of making a preserve. It is rather more liquid than the usual jam, and makes an excellent accompaniment for ice cream. Pick dark red, scented roses early in the day. Strip the petals and remove the yellow tip at the base. Cover with the minimum of cold water and simmer to a pulp. To each lb. of pulp add 1 lb. sugar and boil until set. Pot in small jars.

CUMBERLAND SLOE JELLY

Prepare 3 lb. of sloes, cover with cold water, and cook until tender. Strain, and pass through a sieve. To each 1 lb. pulp allow 1½ lb. sugar; bring to the boil again and test for setting, but do not overboil. Pot as usual.

DONCASTER BUTTERSCOTCH

1 lb. brown sugar	6 oz. butter
½ pint milk	Cream of tartar

Melt the sugar over a low heat in the milk. Add the butter and a pinch of cream of tartar, and boil till a little of the mixture will harden when dropped from a spoon into cold water— about 40 minutes. Pour the mixture in a thin layer into greased tins and leave to set.

DURHAM CINDER TOFFEE

Boil 1 lb. sugar with 1 teacupful cold water for about 20 minutes. Add 1 tsp. bicarbonate of soda to the boiling sugar just as you lift it from the heat; pour the mixture immediately into a deep bowl of cold water, and when cool, remove it. Break into pieces and store in a tin.

PICKLED WALNUTS

Wipe the walnuts, prick well and put into a basin. Reject any that feel hard when pricked. Cover with brine and allow to soak for 8 days, then throw away the brine, cover with fresh brine and resoak for 14 days. Wash and dry the walnuts well and spread out, exposing them to the air until they turn black. Have ready sufficient hot spiced vinegar, put the walnuts into the pickle jars, cover with the hot vinegar and tie down when cold. Mature for 5–6 weeks before using.

SPICED VINEGAR FOR PICKLES

To 1 quart of vinegar allow :

¼ oz. blade of mace	6 peppercorns
¼ oz. allspice	¼ oz. root ginger (if a
¼ oz. cloves	hot pickle is liked)
¼ oz. stick cinnamon	

Tie the spices in muslin, place in a covered pan with the vinegar and heat slowly to boiling point. Remove from the heat, leave to stand for 2 hours and remove the spices.

PICKLED EGGS

16 eggs	½ oz. black peppercorns
1 quart vinegar	½ oz. root ginger (well
½ oz. Jamaica pepper or allspice	bruised)

Simmer the vinegar and spices for 10 minutes and leave to get quite cold. Hard-boil the eggs, shell, and cover with strained spiced vinegar in an earthenware or glass jar. The next day, cover securely to make the jar quite air-tight. The eggs will be ready for use in 4 weeks' time.

THE WASSAIL BOWL

1 rosy apple or 6 crab apples	⅛ tsp, cinnamon or ginger
3 pints beer	Peel of ½ a lemon
½ pint sherry	4 oz. brown sugar
¼ tsp. nutmeg	

Cook the apples in the oven or slice and stew. Heat together all the ingredients, cutting the lemon rind into strips; add more sugar if liked. When boiling-point is reached, pour the mixture over the apples in a punch bowl. Serve at once.

HOT ALE PUNCH

2 pints mild ale	Peel and juice of 1 lemon
1 wineglassful sherry	or 2 tbsps. lemon
1 wineglassful brandy	squash
1 tbsp. sugar	A little grated nutmeg

Mix all together, bring to the boil, strain and serve piping hot.

MULLED WINE

$\frac{1}{4}$ pint water	1 glass claret, bur-
3 tsps. sugar	gundy or other
3 cloves	red wine
A small stick of cinnamon	1 egg (optional)

Put the water, sugar and spices into a sauce-pan, bring to the boil and simmer for 10 minutes. Add the wine and bring just to the boil. Beat the egg and pour the hot mixture on to it, stirring well.

APPLE DUMPLINGS

6 oz. shortcrust or	Demerara sugar
flaky pastry	Egg white for glazing
4 good-sized cooking	(optional)
apples	Cloves (optional)

Make the pastry, peel and core the apples. Divide the pastry into 4 pieces and roll out to a size large enough to enclose an apple. Put one apple on each piece, fill the centre hole with brown sugar, add a clove, if used, and gather the pastry round the apple, damping the edges to make them stick together; press lightly. Place on a greased baking sheet, join downwards, glaze with egg white and bake in a moderately hot oven (425° F., mark 7) until the pastry is brown. Reduce the heat and continue to cook until the apples feel tender when tested with a skewer. Serve hot with custard sauce.

For boiled apple dumplings, fill the fruit as above and enclose in rolled-out suetcrust pastry. Tie each dumpling in a scalded floured cloth and boil steadily for $1-1\frac{1}{4}$ hours. Remove the cloths, place the apple dumplings on a hot dish and sprinkle with sugar; serve at once.

CHRISTMAS PUDDING

19

$1\frac{1}{4}$ lb. currants	1 tsp. salt
$1\frac{1}{4}$ lb. stoned raisins	1 tsp. grated nutmeg
2 oz. almonds	1 tsp. mixed spices
4 oz. candied peel	1 lemon
1 lb. suet	6 eggs
1 lb. white breadcrumbs	$\frac{1}{4}$ pint milk
Fat for greasing	$\frac{1}{4}$ pint brandy (or an
$\frac{1}{4}$ lb. flour	extra $\frac{1}{4}$ pint milk)
$1\frac{1}{2}$ lb. dark brown sugar	

The above quantities will make 4 puddings weighing 2 lb. each.

Wash, dry and pick over currants and raisins; blanch and chop the almonds; remove the sugar from the peel and shred it finely. Grate the suet and chop any large pieces finely, then make the breadcrumbs. Grease 4 basins, also the covering papers and pudding cloths. Place all the prepared ingredients and the flour in a large bowl, add the sugar, salt, spices, grated lemon rind and juice, and mix thoroughly. Add the beaten eggs, with the milk and brandy, so that the mixture forms a soft dropping consistency. The flavour will be improved if the mixture can be left for several hours at this stage.

Next three-quarters fill the 4 basins with the mixture; cover with greased paper or aluminium foil, and tie on pudding cloths securely, pinning or tying up the corners. Boil for 5 hours, replenishing with boiling water when necessary, or steam for $7\frac{1}{2}$ hours. Remove the basins from the pans, and take off the pudding cloths when cool enough to handle. Allow the puddings to become quite cold, and cover them with a clean ungreased cloth, then put them in a cool place.

To heat and serve the puddings, cover as usual, tie on the cloths, and boil for 4 hours, or steam for 6 hours. Turn out on a hot dish and put a sprig of holly in the centre. Serve with brandy butter, rum sauce, custard sauce or fresh cream whipped with a little caster sugar.

When a pudding is to be cooked in a pressure cooker, include black treacle, browning or coffee essence. Place in a greased basin and cover. Put $2\frac{1}{2}$ pints of boiling water in the pan, stand the basin on the rack and steam rapidly for $\frac{1}{2}$ hour, then pressure-cook at 15 lb. for $1\frac{1}{2}$ hours, reducing the pressure slowly. Before serving, pressure-cook for 25–30 minutes at 15 lb.

BAKEWELL TARTS

$\frac{1}{2}$ lb. puff pastry	4 oz. caster sugar
Jam	4 oz. butter
4 egg yolks	4 oz. ground almonds
3 egg whites	1–2 drops almond essence

Make the puff pastry and use it to line 4 small ovenglass plates. Spread a thin layer of jam over the bottom. Beat the egg yolks, egg whites and sugar together and set aside. Heat the butter in a pan and when it reaches boiling point, skim it thoroughly. While it is still boiling, stir in the eggs. Remove the mixture from the heat and beat well. Stir in ground almonds and almond essence. Spread a thick layer over the jam and bake the tarts in a moderately hot oven (400° F., mark 6) until the filling is lightly browned. Serve hot.

KENT PUDDING PIES

Boil 3 oz. ground rice in $1\frac{1}{2}$ pints milk until cooked, remove from the heat and beat in 2–3 oz. butter and 4 oz. sugar. Add some salt and a little spice or grated lemon rind, then beat in 3–4 egg yolks. Have ready some large saucers lined with a good shortcrust or thinly rolled puff pastry. When the rice mixture has cooled, fill the cases three-parts full, sprinkle with currants and bake in a moderate oven (375° F., mark 5) until the pastry is cooked.

YORKSHIRE APPLE PUDDING

½ lb. self-raising flour	1 pint milk
A pinch of salt	2 large cooking apples
2 eggs	2 oz. dripping

Sieve the flour and salt into a bowl and add the eggs and half the milk. Stir to a smooth paste and beat well. Add the remaining milk gradually, taking care to avoid lumpiness. Peel and grate the apples into the mixture. Put the dripping into a Yorkshire pudding tin and heat until very hot; pour in the batter at once and bake for 40 minutes in a hot oven (450° F., mark 8). Serve dredged with sugar.

CUMBERLAND CLIPPING-TIME PUDDING

8 oz. rice	The marrow from some
A pinch of salt	beef marrow bones
1 pint milk	1 egg
3 oz. sugar	4 oz. currants
A little cinnamon	4 oz. stoned raisins

Pour some boiling salted water over the rice to blanch it; drain, and pour the milk over it, add the sugar and spice, and simmer until the rice is cooked. Cut the marrow into small pieces, and add the beaten egg and the dried fruit, mixing well together. Add to the rice, and bake in a moderate oven (375° F., mark 5) for 20 minutes.

It was customary, when sheep-shearing (or clipping) began, to provide a bountiful spread of hearty dishes like this rich rice pudding.

BEN RHYDDING PUDDING (YORKSHIRE)

Stew 1 lb. juicy fruit with sugar to sweeten. Slice 6 sponge cakes thinly and use them to line a plain mould or basin. Put in some fruit, then a layer of cake, and so on until the mould is full, finishing with cake. Place a plate with a weight on top, and leave until cold, then turn out. Pour some whipped cream or custard over the pudding.

LANCASHIRE FIG (OR FAG) PIE

6 oz. shortcrust pastry	½ tsp. mixed spice
½ lb. figs.	1 oz. currants
A little cornflour	½ tbsp. treacle

Line a shallow pie plate with the pastry. Place the washed figs in a saucepan with just enough water to cover and stew them until

tender. Strain the liquid and thicken with cornflour. Add the figs, spice, currants and treacle, mix well and put into the dish. Bake in a moderate oven (350° F., mark 4) for about 45 minutes.

Figs used to be eaten on Palm Sunday, in commemoration of the barren fig tree, the account of which occurs in the Gospel for this season.

STEAMED CROWBERRY PUDDING (HEREFORD)

Make a suet crust and line a pudding basin with it, reserving some for the lid. Fill with either crowberries or whortleberries (also known as bilberries), adding plenty of sugar, and cover with the rest of the pastry. Cover tightly with a cloth and steam for about 2 hours.

BURNT CREAM

1 pint cream	1½ oz. sugar
Peel of ½ a lemon	4 egg yolks
A stick of cinnamon	Sugar for topping

Boil the cream with the thinly pared lemon rind and the cinnamon, cool slightly and pour over the beaten egg yolks, stirring until the mixture is almost cold. Add the sugar and stir well, strain into a dish and leave, preferably overnight. Before serving, strew the top thickly with sugar and brown under the grill.

SUMMER PUDDING

2 tbsps. water	4 oz. bread
4 oz. sugar	Whipped cream or
1 lb. raspberries and	custard sauce
red-currants	

Put the water and sugar together and bring to the boil, add the fruit and stew carefully until tender. Line a pudding basin with thin slices of bread, pour in the stewed fruit and cover with thin slices of bread : the basin should be quite full. Place a saucer with a weight on it on top of the pudding and leave for several hours. Turn out and serve with whipped cream or cold custard sauce.

JUNKET

1 pint new milk	Rennet essence
Flavouring (optional)	Nutmeg

Heat the milk to blood heat and flavour as required. Stir in the rennet essence (the amount varies with the different makes). Pour into a glass dish and put in a warm place to set. Just before serving, grate a little nutmeg over the top of the junket.

A little rum or brandy may be added to the warmed milk.

DURHAM FLUFFIN

Simmer some barley with milk until it is as smooth as velvet. Add enough grated nutmeg and sugar to taste, and a few drops of brandy.

This is traditionally eaten on Christmas Eve, and a bowl should be offered to the " stranger within the door."

SYLLABUB

20

2 oz. caster sugar	$\frac{1}{8}$ pint sherry or
Juice of $\frac{1}{2}$ a lemon	Madeira
$\frac{1}{2}$ tsp. grated lemon rind	$\frac{1}{2}$ pint double cream
	A few macaroons

Mix the sugar, lemon juice and rind with the sherry, stirring to dissolve the sugar. Add the cream and whip lightly. Place the crushed macaroons at the base of a dish, pile the syllabub on top of the biscuits and serve chilled. If liked, decorate with a few small (or crushed) macaroons and grated lemon or orange rind.

HEDGEHOG TIPSY CAKE

An oval-shaped sponge or Madeira cake	White wine, sherry or brandy
1 pint rich custard made with eggs and cream or milk (coating consistency)	Blanched and split almonds
	Whipped cream

Cut the cake to a " hedgehog " shape, tapering to form the head and tail. Pour over enough of the wine, sherry or brandy to moisten the cake without making it too damp. Cover with the custard. Insert the almonds into the cake to form the hedgehog's prickles. Place the cake on a serving dish and pipe whipped sweetened cream as a border.

WILTSHIRE LARDY CAKE

21

1 lb. flour	6 oz. lard
A pinch of salt	Granulated sugar
$\frac{1}{2}$ oz. yeast	Mixed spice
1 tsp. caster sugar	6 oz. currants or
Milk	sultanas (optional)

Grease an oblong or square baking tin. Sieve the flour and salt. Cream the yeast and caster sugar and add a little warm milk, make a well in the centre of the flour and add the yeast mixture and enough milk to make a stiff dough. Leave to rise, then roll out in a strip. Put one-third of the lard over it in pieces the size of a walnut and about $1\frac{1}{2}$ inches apart. Sprinkle with sugar and a little spice. Fold into three from the ends, and then into three from the sides ; turn to the right and roll out again. Repeat this process twice. After the three foldings and lardings,

roll out to the size of your baking tin and put it in. Score across with a knife in a diagonal pattern and bake in a moderate oven (375° F., mark 5) for $\frac{1}{2}$ hour.

If currants and sultanas are used, mix these with the flour before adding the yeast.

Lardy cake, under varying names (Lardy Johns, Shaley cake, Brotherly Love, and so on), differs from county to county. The true lardy cake was made on baking day (when the household baked its own bread), in order that the fresh loaves should not be cut on the same day. The method was to take about 2 lb. of the bread dough, roll it into a rectangular shape, add dabs of butter or lard, some sugar, spice and dried fruit, fold in three (as for puff pastry), bake and serve hot with butter.

SIMNEL CAKE

22

8 oz. flour	3 oz. mixed peel
A pinch of salt	6 oz. butter
1 tsp. grated nutmeg	6 oz. caster sugar
1 tsp. ground cinnamon	3 eggs
12 oz. currants	Milk to mix
4 oz. sultanas	

For the Almond Paste

12 oz. caster sugar	1 egg
8 oz. ground almonds	Lemon juice

Make the almond paste in usual way, take a third of it and roll it into a round the size of the tin.

Sieve the dry ingredients and add the prepared fruit and chopped peel. Cream the fat and sugar very thoroughly and beat in each egg separately. Stir the flour, fruit, etc., into the creamed mixture, adding a little milk if required to give a dropping consistency. Put half the mixture into a greased and lined cake tin, smooth the top carefully and cover with the round of almond paste. Put the remainder of the cake mixture on top and bake in a moderate oven (350° F., mark 4), for about 3 hours—the exact time depends on the thickness of cake. Cool on a rack.

Cover the top of the cake with a round of almond paste and decorate with small balls of paste placed round the edge. Brush the top with the remaining beaten egg and brown in a hot oven or under the grill.

There are many versions of this recipe and conflicting stories as to its origin ; some stories say the mixture was originally boiled and then baked. Some recipes use a yeast mixture instead of the rich fruit one given here.

The almond paste topping should be left undecorated, apart from the balls of paste round the edge ; some versions say these should be 12 in number, for the Apostles—some say 11 (omitting Judas).

Simnel cakes were originally made for Mothering Sunday, but nowadays they are frequently made for Easter.

POUND CAKE

1 lb. butter	¼ lb. shredded mixed
1 lb. caster sugar	candied peel
1 lb. fine sifted (plain)	Grated rind of 1 lemon
flour	and 1 orange
1 lb. eggs (weighed in	2 tsps. powdered mixed
their shells—8–9)	spice
1 lb. mixed dried fruit	A wineglassful of rum,
(currants, sultanas,	whisky, Irish whis-
seeded raisins)	key or brandy
1 tsp. salt	

Cream the butter until soft with the sugar. Beat in the eggs one at a time, alternating with 1 tsp. of the flour. Fold in the other ingredients. Bake in a greased tin in a slow to moderate oven (325°–350° F., mark 3 or 4) for 3–4 hours.

Pound cake was originally a yeast mixture, but nowadays the standard version is like this recipe, which has been used in the contributor's family for at least 100 years. The quantities of fruit were altered according to the occasion. For everyday use, currants only were used, but for a Christmas or birthday cake, 1 lb. mixed dried fruits was added. Irish whiskey was always used in this particular recipe.

YORKSHIRE PARKIN

¼ lb. flour	½ lb. beef dripping (or
½ lb. medium oatmeal	lard)
1 tsp. bicarbonate of	½ lb. black treacle
soda	1 egg (optional)
2 tsps. powdered ginger	Milk to mix
½ lb. Demerara sugar	

Sieve the flour, soda and ginger ; add the other dry ingredients and the fat and mix well. Make a well in the centre and pour in the warmed treacle and beaten egg. Mix and add enough milk to give a fairly stiff consistency. Put into a well-greased baking tin and bake in a moderate oven (350° F., mark 4) for about 1½ hours. Cool in the tin then cut into squares when cold.

The parkin, which will keep moist for a considerable time in an airtight tin, should not be eaten until 24 hours after baking.

Gingerbread was one of the oldest English cakes and was baked for fairs, for All Souls' Eve, New Year's Eve and later for Bonfire Night.

ANOTHER PARKIN

1 lb. flour	6 oz. butter
½ tsp. salt	¾ lb. treacle or syrup
1½ tsps. ground ginger	½ lb. brown sugar
2 tsps. baking powder	1 egg
½ tsp. bicarbonate of	½ pint milk
soda	

Mix the dry ingredients together. Put the butter, treacle and sugar in a pan and heat them ; beat the egg and warm the milk. Add all these to the dry ingredients and mix well, pour into a lined and greased tin and bake in a moderate oven (350° F., mark 4) for 1½ hours. Keep for a few days before eating.

ECCLES CAKES

½ lb. currants	¼ tsp. nutmeg
2 oz. finely chopped	4 oz. sugar
candied peel	2 oz. butter
½ tsp. allspice	½ lb. puff pastry

Put all the ingredients (except the pastry) into a pan, heat for a few minutes, then set aside to cool. Roll out the pastry about ¼ in. thick and cut it into rounds. Place 1 tbsp. of the filling on each and draw up the edges so that they meet ; turn the cakes over and press flat with a rolling pin. Make a small hole in the middle of each, then lay the cakes on a greased baking tray. Bake in a hot oven (450° F., mark 8) for 10–15 minutes, reduce heat and leave until pastry is cooked through, remove from the oven and sprinkle with caster sugar.

RICHMOND MAIDS OF HONOUR

1 pint milk	1 oz. melted butter
1 tsp. rennet	2 oz. caster sugar
4 oz. puff pastry	1 egg

Heat the milk and rennet gently until they curdle. Put a piece of muslin over a wire sieve and strain the milk through this, then leave to drain for 2 hours. Roll the pastry out ⅛–¼ inch thick and cut in 3-inch rounds. Put into patty tins, pushing the pastry out from the base towards the sides and top, so that it is paper-thin at the base and will cook through easily. Sieve the curds (there should be about 4 oz.), add the butter and sugar and beat in the egg. Put a spoonful of the mixture into each patty tin, and bake in a moderately hot oven (425° F., mark 7) for 15–20 minutes, till the pastry is well cooked and the filling set and golden-brown.

BRANDY SNAPS

4 oz. golden syrup	3½ oz. flour
4 oz. margarine	Whipped cream
3 oz. caster sugar	

Melt the syrup, margarine and sugar together, remove from the heat, stir in the flour gradually and mix well together. Drop the mixture on to a baking sheet in teaspoonfuls, giving it plenty of room to run. Bake in a moderately hot oven (375° F., mark 5) for 7–10 minutes, until brown and well-spread. Take off with a knife when beginning to get crisp, and roll up. Brandy snaps are especially good if they are filled with cream.

BATH BUNS

8 oz. flour	2 oz. caster sugar
A pinch of salt	2 oz. sultanas
3 oz. butter	1 oz. candied peel,
$\frac{1}{8}$ pint milk (approx.)	chopped finely
$\frac{1}{2}$ oz. yeast	Egg and milk to glaze
1 egg	1 oz. loaf sugar

Sieve the flour and salt and rub in the margarine. Warm the milk and cream the yeast with a little of it. Pour the milk and yeast into the middle of the flour; add the beaten egg. Beat very thoroughly, cover with a cloth, and put the dough to rise in a warm place until it doubles its size : this will take about $1\frac{1}{2}$ hours. Add the caster sugar, sultanas and peel, beat well and form into small, even-sized balls. Put on to greased tins and prove until they have doubled their size. Brush over with egg and milk and sprinkle with coarsely crushed loaf sugar. Bake in a hot oven (450° F., mark 8) for 20–30 minutes.

CHELSEA BUNS

8 oz. flour	$\frac{3}{4}$ gill warm milk and
A pinch of salt	water
3–4 oz. currants and	1 oz. butter
sultanas	1 egg
2 oz. sugar	A little melted fat
$\frac{1}{2}$ oz. yeast	2 tsps. sugar to glaze

Sieve together the flour and salt and put to warm. Clean the currants and sultanas and mix with 2 tsps. of the sugar. Cream the yeast with $\frac{1}{2}$ tsp. sugar and add it to the liquid. Add this to one-third of the flour and set it to sponge. Rub the fat into the remaining flour, add the rest of the sugar and gradually beat in the egg. Next mix in the sponge mixture. Beat all thoroughly with the hand and put in a warm place to rise.

When the dough has doubled its size, knead lightly on a floured board and then roll into an oblong strip. Brush over with melted fat and sprinkle evenly over it the mixed fruit and sugar. Roll up and cut into 12 even-sized slices. Pack lightly, cut side down, into a greased tin, which should have straight sides (e.g., a Yorkshire

pudding tin). Allow to prove for 25 minutes, then bake in a hot oven (425° F., mark 7) for 20–30 minutes. Glaze with sugar and water when almost cooked.

MADEIRA CAKE

8 oz. flour	3 eggs
A pinch of salt	A few drops of lemon
2 tsps. baking powder	essence
A little grated lemon rind	Milk to mix
5 oz. caster sugar	A slice of citron
5 oz. butter or margarine	

Prepare a cake tin. Sieve the flour, salt and baking powder together, and add the very finely grated lemon rind. Put the sugar and fat into a basin and work together until they are of a creamy consistency. Beat in the eggs, adding a little at a time to prevent curdling. Fold in the dry ingredients, and lastly add a little lemon essence, and milk if required. Put into the prepared tin, place in a moderate oven (375° F., mark 5) and bake for 1–1$\frac{1}{4}$ hours.

The slice of citron should be put on top of the cake as soon as it is set, not before, otherwise it may sink.

SEED CAKE

10 oz. flour	1 oz. caraway seeds
A pinch of salt	6 oz. sugar
2 tsps. baking powder	1–2 eggs
4 oz. margarine	4 tsps. water (approx.)

Thoroughly grease a 6-inch cake tin. Sieve together the flour, salt and baking powder and rub in the fat thoroughly. Add the caraway seeds and the sugar and then the beaten egg. Mix with sufficient water to give a soft dropping consistency and bake in a moderately hot oven (400° F., mark 6) reducing after the first hour to 375° F., mark 5) for 1$\frac{1}{2}$ hours, until golden-brown.

SHREWSBURY BISCUITS

3 oz. butter	3 oz. sugar
A few drops of vanilla	$\frac{1}{2}$ an egg
essence or a little	8 oz. self-raising flour
grated lemon rind	1 tbsp. water (approx.)

Put the fat and sugar into a bowl and cream together until soft and white, then gradually add the flavouring and egg and work in the flour, together with the water, to form a soft, pliable dough. Roll out to about $\frac{1}{8}$ inch in thickness and cut into fancy shapes with biscuit cutters. Bake in a moderate oven (350° F., mark 4) for 15–20 minutes until pale brown. This quantity makes about 16–18 biscuits.

BREAD SAUCE

½ pint milk or milk and vegetable stock mixed
2 oz. breadcrumbs (or stale bread soaked and squeezed)
1 tsp. chopped onion
1 clove
Salt and pepper
A small blade of mace
A knob of butter

Put the liquid into a pan with the onion, clove and mace, and allow to infuse for about ½ hour. Strain and add the breadcrumbs, seasoning and the knob of margarine. Leave in a warm place at the side of the stove for 15 minutes, and make very hot before serving. Serve with roast chicken, turkey, etc.

MINT SAUCE

2 tbsps. chopped mint
1 tbsp. boiling water
1 tsp. sugar
1½ tbsps. vinegar

Strip the mint from the stalks and chop it finely. Put the sugar and boiling water in a sauce-boat and stir until dissolved. Add the mint and stir in vinegar to taste. Serve with roast lamb.

APPLE SAUCE

2 lb. apples
Sugar, if required
1–2 oz. butter
Lemon juice, if required

Choose good cooking apples, peel and slice with a stainless steel knife, then cook gently to a pulp in a covered pan. Beat with a wooden spoon until smooth, and add the butter. Sugar may be added if liked ; on the other hand, if the apples are sweet, a little lemon juice may be added. Serve with roast pork, goose or duck.

HEREFORD CIDER SAUCE

Make ¾ pint thick brown sauce. Add 1 pint cider, 2 cloves and a bay leaf ; season, and mix well. Simmer, stirring occasionally, until reduced by about one-third ; then strain. Serve with boiled bacon or ham.

Wales

LEEK SOUP

5 large potatoes
Flour
4 large leeks
Salt and pepper
1 onion
½ breakfastcup fresh cream
Butter for frying
2 eggs

Peel the potatoes and partially cook in plenty of water. Carefully clean and slice the leeks ; peel and chop the onion. Heat a little butter and brown the leeks and onion. Dredge lightly with flour, then stir in enough liquid from the potatoes to make a thin sauce. Add this to the potatoes and continue to cook until all the ingredients are soft enough to rub through a coarse wire sieve. Reheat, season and add the cream. Beat the eggs until frothy and put a little into each soup plate. Pour the soup over the beaten egg, stir, and serve immediately.

LEEK AND BACON PIE

⅙ pint water
8 oz. flour
4 oz. mutton dripping
A pinch of salt

For the Filling

2 bunches of leeks
Salt and pepper
4 rashers of fat bacon, chopped
3 beaten eggs
½ pint milk

Make the filling first. Thoroughly clean the leeks, cut the white parts into thick rings and scald in boiling water. Fry the bacon in its own fat in a saucepan. Drain the leeks, add to the bacon, cover with boiling water, season and cook until the leeks are fairly soft. Now make the pastry.

Bring the water to the boil, take from the heat and quickly dissolve the dripping in it. Put the flour in a basin, make a well in the centre, add the liquid and salt and quickly work in the flour, using a wooden spoon. When the dough is firm, roll out on a floured board, cut off enough to cover the pie dish and line the sides of the dish with the remainder. Put in the filling, cover with the remaining pastry and make a large hole in the centre of the pastry. Glaze with beaten egg and bake in a hot oven (450° F., mark 8) until the pastry is light brown.

Mix remaining beaten eggs with the milk and make a custard. Take the pie from the oven and pour in the egg and milk custard through the opening. Cover the opening with a piece of pastry, return the pie to the oven to bake very slowly (300° F., mark 1) until the custard has set.

Cooked chicken may also be added to the pie filling.

I FERWI MYTN
(BOILED SHOULDER OF MUTTON)

Put a 3 lb. shoulder of mutton in a saucepan, cover with 1½ pints water, bring to the boil and add ½ lb. sliced onions, ½ lb. finely chopped celery, 1–2 sprigs of marjoram and a little lemon thyme. Simmer for 2½ hours.

HAM CYMREIG
(MUTTON HAM)

This is a fat leg of mutton, cured and smoked like a ham. When boiling Welsh ham, put a piece of fat bacon with it and serve it with the ham, which is apt to be somewhat dry and lacking in fat.

PEMBROKESHIRE MUTTON PIE

1 lb. flour	8 oz. minced lean
Salt and pepper	mutton
8 oz. lard	8 oz. currants
¼ pint water (approx.)	6 oz. sugar

Sieve the flour and salt. Heat the lard in the water and bring once to the boil. Add the flour and stir to a dough with a wooden spoon; when the dough is cool enough to handle, line a pie dish as quickly as possible (or if preferred, make several small pies). Mould into shape without rolling the dough. Add the filling, season and cover with a pastry top. Bake in a hot oven (450° F., mark 8) for the first 10 minutes, then continue to bake in a moderate oven (375° F., mark 5) until the pie is golden-brown. Serve hot.

It is essential to work quickly when shaping this pastry, for it hardens as it cools.

CAWL
(MUTTON STEW)

About 1½–2 lb. of salt beef, bacon or scrag-end of mutton	Potatoes, leeks, cabbage and carrots, as available
2 pints water	Seasoning to taste
½ cupful fine oatmeal	

With Salt Beef or Bacon : Put the meat into cold water, bring to the boil, skim and allow to simmer for 1 hour. Add the prepared vegetables, slicing leeks and carrots and leaving potatoes whole or in large pieces. Simmer for 1 hour longer. Half an hour before serving mix the oatmeal with a little cold water and add to the pan, stirring in carefully. Season to taste.

With Mutton : The meat and vegetables are put into the pan with the water at the same time, and the whole is simmered for 1½–2 hours.

To serve, lift the meat on to the hot serving dish and arrange the vegetables round it. Dish on to soup plates and pour the liquor over.

Note : Large pieces of swede are sometimes included, and in olden times the *cawl* was sprinkled with marigold petals.

This was a " two-day " dish : the meat and vegetables were eaten on the first day, and what was left was served as a soup on the second day.

ROAST WELSH LAMB

Wipe the lamb with a damp cloth, rub with salt and pepper and completely encase in a flour and water dough. Bake in a moderate oven (350° F., mark 4) for about 2 hours, basting frequently. Serve with a jelly made from the berries of mountain ash and apples.

BASTAI CIW IAR-A-CENIN
(CHICKEN AND LEEK PIE)

1 chicken	1 bunch of small leeks
1 large onion, quartered	3–4 slices of cold boiled
1 stick of celery	tongue
Mixed herbs	Parsley
Salt	3 tbsps. cream

For the Pastry

6 oz. flour	¼ pint boiling water
3 tbsps. mutton dripping	

Put the chicken in a saucepan, cover with cold water, bring to the boil and skim, then add the onion, celery, mixed herbs and salt. Simmer for 1½–2 hours, according to the size and age of the bird. When done, remove the chicken from the saucepan and strain the stock into a basin; stand this in a cool place till the stock has set in a jelly.

Remove the green part of the leeks and scald the white part in boiling water; split them and cut in 1-inch lengths. Carve the chicken in neat joints and lay in a pie dish with the slices of cold tongue, the leeks and a little chopped parsley and moisten with some of the chicken jelly.

To make the pastry, sieve the flour into a basin, make a well in centre and add the mutton dripping, previously dissolved in and mixed with the boiling water. Knead to the right consistency, roll out on a floured board and cover the pie, leaving a small hole in the centre. Bake in a hot oven (450° F., mark 8). Remove from the oven and pour the warmed cream through the opening in the pie; cover the opening with a little pastry, cut to a leaf or other fancy shape.

BOILED SALTED DUCK

1 duck	Peppercorns
1 lb. onions	1 tbsp. flour
1 pint milk	Butter

Prepare and salt the duck the day before using. Put into a large saucepan with enough water to cover and cook slowly for 1½ hours, or longer if it is still not tender. While the duck is cooking, make an onion sauce : peel and slice the onions and cook in milk, well flavoured with peppercorns, until they are tender. Add flour to thicken and boil, stirring, for 5 minutes or so to cook the flour. Stir in a good knob of butter. Take the duck from the pan, joint it and serve smothered with the onion sauce.

DRY-FRIED TROUT

This rather curious way of cooking trout is one used by the Welsh farmers, many of whom have trout streams running through their farms. The fresh trout is cleaned, wiped dry and fried on both sides in a lightly greased pan. When dealt with in this way, trout have a perfect flavour.

COCKLE CAKES

1–2 quarts freshly caught cockles	1 egg
4 oz. plain flour	$\frac{1}{4}$ pint milk
A pinch of salt	Deep fat for frying

To prepare the cockles, wash them in several waters, cover with clean cold water, add a handful of oatmeal and leave to stand overnight. The next day rinse, put into a strong pan without any liquid and heat gently until the shells open in the steam. Meanwhile make a thick coating batter with the flour, salt, egg and milk. Remove the shells and drop the cockles into the batter, then fry a tablespoonful of the cockle mixture in the deep hot fat.

TEISENNI CAWS CYMREIG
(WELSH CHEESECAKES)

Make tartlets of puff pastry, and in each put a little raspberry jam, then cover with the following mixture: Weigh 1 egg and use the same weight of butter, sugar and flour. Cream the butter and sugar, add the well-beaten egg, and lastly work in the flour; beat well with a wooden spoon, then add the juice and the finely grated rind of 1 lemon and a pinch of baking powder. Bake in a moderate oven (350° F., mark 4) till the pastry is of a light golden colour.

WELSH RAREBIT

4 oz. grated cheese	A little mustard
3 tbsps. milk	1 oz. butter
Pepper and salt	Slices of toast

Place the cheese and milk in a saucepan and melt slowly; add the pepper, salt, mustard and butter. When very hot, pour over the toast and brown under the grill. A little beer is sometimes added to the mixture.

PWDIN CYMREIG
(WELSH PUDDING)

Mix $\frac{1}{2}$ lb. finely chopped suet with 1 lb. sugar and $\frac{1}{2}$ lb. breadcrumbs and add 2 whole eggs, the juice of 2 large lemons and the finely grated rind of one. If the mixture appears too stiff, moisten with a little milk. Put into a buttered basin and steam or boil for $3\frac{1}{2}$–4 hours.

PWDIN Y WYDDFA
(SNOWDON PUDDING)

Butter	$1\frac{1}{2}$ oz. rice flour
Some good raisins	6 oz. Demerara sugar
$\frac{1}{2}$ lb. finely chopped suet	6 well-beaten eggs
$\frac{1}{2}$ lb. breadcrumbs	Grated rind of 2
6 oz. lemon or orange marmalade	lemons

Decorate the sides and bottom of a well-buttered mould with some fine raisins, split open and stoned, but not divided; press the cut side on to the butter to make them adhere. Mix the suet in a basin with the breadcrumbs, marmalade and rice flour. Then add the sugar, well-beaten eggs and the grated lemon rinds. Beat till all the ingredients are thoroughly mixed, pour into a mould, cover with buttered paper and a floured cloth and boil for $1\frac{1}{2}$ hours. Some kind of sweet sauce is usually poured over this pudding.

TEISEN CYMREIG
(WELSH TART)

Rub 2 oz. butter and 2 oz. lard into $\frac{1}{2}$ lb. flour, add a pinch of salt and mix to a paste with milk and water. Roll out half the pastry to about $\frac{1}{8}$ inch thick, cover a greased pie plate with the pastry and put over it about $\frac{1}{2}$ lb. fresh fruit (such as gooseberries, currants, rhubarb, or whatever fruit is in season). Sprinkle with sugar, cover with another layer of pastry of the same thickness, pressing the edges firmly all round to prevent the juice from running out. Bake in a moderately hot oven (400° F., mark 6) for 30 minutes or till the fruit is cooked.

CRANBERRY TART

1 quart cranberries	Vanilla essence to taste
1 lb. good quality raisins	Sweet short or flaky pastry
Sugar	Milk to glaze

Clean the cranberries and stone the raisins. Arrange in layers, each sprinkled with sugar, and leave for several hours, or overnight. The next day, put the fruit into a pan, without water, bring slowly to the boil and cook for 5 minutes; add a little vanilla. Cool before using.

Line a shallow dish or plate with the pastry, spread the mixture with fruit and cover with more pastry. Glaze very lightly with milk and bake in a hot oven (450° F., mark 8) until the pastry is golden-brown.

BARA CYMREIG
(WELSH BREAD)

2 lb. flour	1 tsp. sugar
½ oz. yeast	Sufficient milk to mix

Sieve the flour. Put the yeast and the sugar into a basin, gradually stir in a little warm milk and work till quite smooth. Stir into the flour and let it " sponge." When sufficiently risen, knead with a little warm milk, cover and set to rise in a warm place. Take about ½ lb. at a time, roll to 1 inch in thickness and put on a hot bakestone. When baked sufficiently on one side, turn over and bake until done.

BARA BRITH
(FRUIT BREAD)

4 lb. plain flour	1 lb. large raisins, stoned
A pinch of salt	A little chopped candied
1 lb. lard	peel if liked
1 lb. sugar	1 oz. yeast (barm)
1 lb. currants	3–4 eggs
1 lb. sultanas	

Sieve the flour and salt and rub in the fat. Add the sugar and cleaned, dry fruit. (It is essential that the raisins should be the large variety which need stoning, for they give the bara brith its true flavour.) Break down the yeast in ½ pint lukewarm water. Beat the eggs well. Make a hollow in the middle of the dry ingredients and pour in the eggs and yeast; mix together and knead well—the mixture should not be too stiff. Cover and leave in a warm place to rise for about 2 hours, to double its size. Knead lightly, put into well-greased tins and bake in a slow oven (300° F., mark 1) for 2–3 hours, according to the size of the loaves.

Bara brith should be 24 hours old before it is cut. It should be buttered generously and cut very thinly.

BARA CEIRCH
(OAT CAKES)

½ tbsp. bacon fat	4 tbsps. medium oatmeal
3 tbsps. water	A good pinch of salt

Melt the fat in the water and sprinkle in the oatmeal, working them together well. Roll out on a board which has been well dusted with oatmeal and cut into cakes about the size of a small plate and very thin. Cook slowly on a fairly hot griddle or a very thick frying pan for 10 minutes. Lift off carefully and leave in a warm place to harden.

As the cakes are very brittle and dry quickly, it is advisable to make the mixture in small quantities.

CREMPOG
(PANCAKES)

½ lb. plain flour	2 tsps. cream of tartar
A pinch of salt	2–3 oz. sugar
1 tsp. bicarbonate of	2 eggs
soda	Buttermilk to mix

Mix all the dry ingredients in a large bowl. Make a well in the centre and add the beaten eggs and the buttermilk alternately, to make a fairly thick batter. Beat well until bubbles rise on the surface. Crempog are fried on a greased pan the size of a small dinner plate. As each one is fried on both sides, it is placed on a hot dish, spread generously with butter and kept hot. When a pile of a dozen or more have been made, they are cut in quarters through the entire pile and served hot for tea, with jam if desired.

The same batter mixture, fried in a smaller size, makes Light or Backstone Cakes—these were originally baked on a griddle or bakestone, hence the name.

Note : If buttermilk is not available, sour milk or cream may be used; cream can be diluted with sweet milk.

WELSH PIKELETS

8 oz. self-raising flour	1 tsp. bicarbonate of
2 oz. caster sugar	soda
A pinch of salt	½ gill boiling water
¼ pint buttermilk	Lard for frying

Put the flour, sugar and salt into a basin and gradually mix to a thick batter with the buttermilk. Dissolve the soda in half a gill of boiling water and add to the mixture. Fry tablespoonfuls of the batter in hot fat as for pancakes; turn when half-cooked. Serve hot, with butter.

TEISEN FRAU GWENT A MORGANWG
(WELSH CAKES)

1 lb. flour	1 pint ewe's milk,
2 tsps. sugar	or cream or cow's
3 oz. currants	milk

Mix the flour, sugar and milk into a thick batter and stir in the currants. In the original recipe, one is told to " butter the tin of a Dutch oven and bake before the fire," but the cakes can be baked in the ordinary way in a moderately hot oven (425° F., mark 7).

BUNS CYMREIG
(WELSH BUNS)

Cream ½ lb. butter with 6 oz. sugar. Then add the yolks of 3 well-beaten eggs, mix thoroughly and beat in gradually 1 lb. flour. Add ½ lb. sultanas or currants and finally add the 3 egg whites, beaten to a stiff froth. Beat all vigorously for 20–30 minutes, shape into buns about the size of an egg, or pour the mixture in a greased tin and bake in a slow oven (320° F., mark 2) for 2½–3 hours, till lightly browned.

TEISEN 'BERFFRO
(ABERFFRAW CAKE OR SHORTBREAD)

6 oz. butter	4 oz. caster sugar
8 oz. plain flour	

Rub the butter into the flour and sugar and continue kneading without adding any moisture until you have a smooth, pliable paste. Roll out fairly thinly on a well-floured board and cut into rounds the size of a small cup. Mark each round with the impress of a scallop shell and bake in a moderate oven (375° F., mark 5). Cool on the baking tray, and when cold sprinkle lavishly with caster sugar.

The cakes were originally baked in scallop shells, hence the scallop markings. 'Berffro is short for Aberffraw, in Anglesey, the seat of the old Welsh Parliament.

TEISENAU SIWGWR
(SUGAR CAKES)

4 oz. butter	8 oz. plain flour
8 oz. caster sugar	1 egg

Cream the butter and sugar, then work in the flour and well-beaten egg to make a smooth paste. Roll out very thinly, cut into rounds and mark with a scallop shell. Bake in a moderate oven (350° F., mark 4) to a pale golden colour. When cold, dust with caster sugar.

Of this recipe, which resembles the previous one, the lady who contributed it said : " This is my own, very old family recipe. Originally it included ' as much grated rock ammonia as will go on a three-penny piece ' (that would be the old silver piece), but the recipe works quite well without it."

TEISEN GRI
(FRUIT BATCH CAKE)

8 oz. plain flour	2 oz. sugar
A pinch of salt	2 oz. currants
½ tsp. bicarbonate of soda	Buttermilk (or milk)
3 oz. lard or beef dripping	to mix

Sieve the flour, salt and soda into a bowl and rub in the fat ; add the sugar and cleaned currants. Mix to a fairly soft dough with the milk, then roll out to about ½ inch in thickness. Bake on a hot greased griddle on both sides. Serve hot and well-buttered.

LEEK PORRIDGE

Carefully clean and cut lengthwise as many leeks as required and put into a pan with cold water. Bring quickly to the boil, then cook gently until soft. Strain the leeks, cut into still thinner strips and put into porridge plates. Pour over the leeks enough of the liquid in which they have been cooked to make a porridge consistency—thick or thin to taste.

SCONS CYMREIG
(WELSH WHOLEMEAL SCONES)

Mix a pinch of salt and ½ tsp. bicarbonate of soda with 1 lb. wholemeal flour ; add a little buttermilk, roll out very thinly and bake on a hot bakestone. When done split open, butter and serve hot for tea.

LAVER BREAD

Laver, the Welsh edible seaweed, is gathered along the rocky South Wales and Gower Coast, at Marloss and in Pembrokeshire, and is much used as a breakfast dish, in salads and as an hors d'œuvre. It is a reddish-purple, rather filmy variety of seaweed, its fronds impregnated with iodine. The laver bread of Swansea Market is well known. This is made by washing the laver very thoroughly, first in sea water, then in fresh water, and wringing it absolutely dry. It is then put into a pan with sea water or salted water and simmered for several hours—in summer it takes longer to cook than in winter. When drained, the pulp can be kept for weeks, and it is in this state that it is offered for sale.

LAVER CAKES

These are made from laver pulp, sprinkled with fine oatmeal, and shaped into small cakes. These cakes are fried in bacon fat and served often with sausages as a breakfast dish. The taste for it has to be acquired, but those who eat it say that the flavour compares favourably with that of mushrooms.

Another favourite Welsh way of serving laver is as a sauce with mutton. About 1 lb. laver is mixed with 2 oz. butter, some of the thick gravy from the meat and a little strained lemon juice. It is then put into a pot and (still according to tradition), stirred with a silver spoon. The sauce must be served bubbling hot. This makes an excellent type of item to prepare at table in a chafing-dish.

NETTLE BEER

A basketful of young nettles	A handful of dande-lions
A handful of currant leaves	1 lb. sugar to each gallon of liquid
A handful of goose grass	1 oz. yeast
	1 tsp. cream of tartar

Wash and drain the nettle and currant leaves, goose grass and dandelions and put into a very large saucepan. Add enough cold water to cover, bring to the boil and cook rapidly for 10 minutes. Strain through a sieve, pressing well to obtain all the flavour from the leaves. Pour into an earthenware vessel and add the sugar. Leave until lukewarm, then add the yeast, previously dissolved in a little of the liquid, and the cream of tartar. Leave in a warm place for at least 12 hours to allow the yeast to work.

Bottle and cork lightly. After 24 hours, cork very tightly. Leave for at least 2 months before drinking.

Scotland

HOTCH-POTCH

1½–2 lb. neck or scrag-end of mutton	1 pint fresh peas and/or fresh broad beans
1 small cabbage or cauliflower	6 pints cold water
6 leeks	Salt and pepper
6 carrots	1 tsp. sugar
2 small white turnips	1 tbsp. chopped parsley

Cut the meat into pieces. Prepare the vegetables and shred or dice as necessary. Put into a large saucepan with the water and season-ing, but keeping back the peas and beans. Simmer for at least 1 hour, add the peas and beans and simmer until all the vegetables are cooked. Check the seasoning and add the sugar and chopped parsley. Lift out the meat, which is eaten separately, and serve the soup at once.

POWSOWDIE
(SHEEP'S HEAD BROTH)

1 sheep's head	2 leeks
2 oz. dried peas	1 small turnip
2 oz. barley	Salt and pepper
2 carrots	Chopped parsley

The sheep's head should be well washed and scraped and the eyes removed. Soak the dried peas and the barley overnight in cold water. Put the prepared head into a large pan, cover with cold water, bring to the boil, skim and add the peas and barley. Simmer for 2 hours, then add the diced vegetables and simmer for 1 hour longer. Season to taste. Remove the head on to the serving dish and keep hot. This is served separately as the meat course. The soup, to which the chopped parsley is added just before serving, makes either the first course or a meal in itself.

SCOTCH BROTH

1–1½ lb. lean beef, either runner or top-side	1 medium-sized onion
	2 leeks
	1½ oz. pearl barley
2 quarts water	Salt and pepper
1 carrot	2 tsps. finely chopped parsley
1 turnip	

Put the meat into a pan, add the water, bring to boiling point slowly, then simmer gently for 1½ hours. Add the vegetables, previously cut into dice, and the barley and seasonings. (If you do not want the broth to be cloudy it is advisable to blanch the barley before adding it to the stock : to do this, put the grain into cold water and bring it to boiling point, strain, and add to the soup.) After adding the barley and vegetables, continue to simmer until both are cooked—this will take about 1 hour. Serve the meat separately on a dish with a little of the broth. Put the chopped parsley into the soup tureen and pour in the broth. (If the parsley is cooked it loses its green colour.) Should any fat appear on the surface of the broth it must be removed with a spoon or by gently passing a piece of clean unglazed kitchen paper over the top.

Peas (fresh or soaked dried ones) are some-times added, and leeks may be included.

COCK-A-LEEKIE SOUP

1 boiling fowl	Pepper and salt
2 lb. neck of mutton or knuckle of veal	2 cloves
	4 leeks
3 quarts cold water	1 oz. rice

Wash the fowl carefully and put it with the meat into a saucepan, then add the water, seasonings and cloves. When it comes to the boil, add the leeks, previously prepared and cut into pieces, and simmer for 1¼ hours. Wash the rice, sprinkle it into the soup, add additional seasoning if necessary and continue to simmer for ¾ hour.

The chicken and meat can be served with the soup or separately, with a parsley sauce made with a little of the broth.

SCOTCH COLLOPS

1 lb. beef or rump-steak	1 tbsp. mushroom ketchup
1 onion	2 tbsps. breadcrumbs or 2 tbsps. oatmeal
Dripping	
Salt and pepper	Mashed potatoes
A pinch of grated nutmeg	Slices of hard-boiled eggs
Stock	Toast or fried croûtons

Mince the meat. Fry the finely chopped onion in a little dripping, then add the minced meat, season with salt and pepper, add a pinch of nutmeg, moisten with about 1 cup of stock, and simmer for 1–1½ hours, then add the ketchup and the breadcrumbs or oatmeal, mix well and cook for 5–10 minutes. Put on a hot dish, surround with a border of mashed potatoes, and garnish with sliced hard-boiled egg and the croûtons.

COLLOPS IN THE PAN

Cut thin slices from a rump steak, put them in a pan with some hot butter and a few sliced onions, then season with salt and pepper; cover the pan with a plate or dish and simmer till the meat is tender. When done, add a little oyster pickle or walnut ketchup, with a little water to thin the onion sauce.

GIGOT WITH TURNIP PURRY

A few veal chops	Sliced yolks of hard-boiled eggs
Mixed spices and chopped herbs	A few truffles or mushrooms
A few slices of lean bacon	Stock
Forcemeat balls	Pastry

Trim the meat from the bones and flavour highly with mixed spices and herbs. Put in a pie dish with the bacon, forcemeat balls, yolks of eggs and either truffles or mushrooms. Moisten with stock, cover with pastry and bake for 1½–2 hours in a moderate oven (350° F., mark 4). Serve with " turnip purry."

TURNIP PURRY

Peel some young turnips carefully, boil in salted water till quite tender, rub through a sieve, or mash with a wooden spoon through a colander. Put in a saucepan, season with salt and pepper and add a lump of butter; stir and when hot and quite smooth, put the purée in a hot dish and mark in diamond shapes.

INKY-PINKY
(BEEF HASH)

Trim the fat from a few slices of cold roast beef and cook in gravy to which a sliced onion and a few sliced cooked carrots have been added; season with a little vinegar, salt and pepper. Before serving, remove the onion, thicken the sauce and serve with fried bread croûtons.

VENISON PASTY

3 lb. breast, neck or shoulder of venison	Gravy
	A little onion-flavoured vinegar
A few fat pieces of mutton	A gill port or claret
Salt and pepper	Pastry
Mace and allspice	

Cut the venison meat into thick little squares, removing all bones and trimmings; simmer the latter to make some gravy. Place the meat in a pie dish, and if very lean, add a few fat pieces from a neck or leg of mutton. Season with salt, pepper, mace and allspice. Moisten with the gravy, add the port or claret and a little vinegar and cover the dish with a thick pie crust. Bake 3–3½ hours in a moderate oven (350° F., mark 4).

VENISON COLLOPS

Haunch, neck or loin of venison	Butter
	A glass of claret
Flour	Salt and pepper
A little lemon or orange juice	Cayenne
	Grated nutmeg

Fry oblong slices cut from the joint; make a gravy with the bones and trimmings and thicken with flour, lightly browned in a little butter. Strain into a small saucepan, add the lemon or orange juice, claret, salt, pepper, cayenne and nutmeg. Stir and simmer for a few minutes. When the collops are done, pour the sauce over them.

HAGGIS

A sheep's paunch and pluck (including the heart, liver and lights)	½ lb. minced suet
	1–2 finely chopped onions
1 breakfastcup oatmeal well browned in the oven	Salt
	Black pepper

Thoroughly clean the paunch and soak in cold water for about 12 hours; turn inside out and set aside till required. Put the pluck in cold water, bring to the boil and simmer for 1½ hours. Remove from the water and cut off the pipes and gristle. Grate half of the liver (the other half is not used) and mince the lights and the heart. Mix in a basin with the oatmeal, suet and onions, season highly with salt and black pepper and moisten with the water in which the pluck was boiled. Put the mixture in the paunch, leaving sufficient space for the oatmeal to swell, and sew up the opening. Put in a large saucepan of hot water (adding milk if liked) and boil for 3 hours, taking care to prick with a needle as soon as the haggis begins to swell.

Haggis is served without gravy or garnish and accompanied by mashed turnips (" neeps ") and mashed potatoes, and the custom is to drink neat whisky with it.

GLASGOW TRIPE

Clean and blanch the tripe, cut it into pieces, roll them up and tie. Put them in a stone or earthenware jar with a marrow bone, a knuckle of veal or some veal trimmings, and season with salt and pepper. Cover the jar, stand it in a saucepan of boiling water and cook for 8 hours, replenishing the water in the saucepan as it boils away. Let it stand till cold, when the tripe will be surrounded by jelly. It can then be dressed according to taste.

MINCE COLLOPS

Mince 2–3 lb. good venison, season with salt and pepper and fry with 1 finely chopped onion and $\frac{1}{2}$ cup venison stock. When the meat and onion have browned, reduce the heat and simmer for 2 hours.

WHITE OR MEALIE PUDDINGS

2 lb. oatmeal	Allspice
1 lb. fresh beef suet	1–2 tsps. sugar (optional)
2 onions	Tripe-skins
Salt	

Toast the oatmeal lightly in the oven or before the fire. Mince the suet and the onions finely, and add to the oatmeal, with the salt, pepper and sugar. Mix thoroughly, and fill the prepared tripe-skins, leaving room for swelling : tie the ends, drop the puddings into boiling water, and cook for 1 hour, pricking occasionally with a fork to prevent bursting.

These puddings will keep for months if hung up and kept dry, or, better still kept buried in oatmeal in the " girnel " or meal chest. When they are required, warm them through in hot water, dry, and brown the outside in hot dripping.

SCOTCH CHICKENS

Wash and dry the chickens and cut into quarters. Put into a large saucepan, just cover with water and bring to the boil. Skim before putting in some mace and a little bundle of parsley. Cover closely and stew for $\frac{1}{2}$ hour. Chop half a handful of clean washed parsley and throw in. Beat 6 eggs thoroughly, wait till the liquor returns to the boil, and pour the eggs over the boiling liquid. Put all in a deep hot dish (taking out the mace and parsley bundle) and serve at once.

ROAST GROUSE

The Scots may have learned from the French the method of putting inside the bird before it is roasted a lump of butter, worked with salt, pepper and sometimes a little lemon juice ; it is certainly a great improvement and keeps the bird moist.

The birds are then seasoned with salt and pepper and may be wrapped in fat bacon, which is removed a little before serving, so that the breast may brown, or the bacon may be dispensed with, provided the birds are constantly basted with butter. The livers are boiled, then pounded, in a mortar with a little butter, seasoned with salt and cayenne, spread on a piece of toast and moistened with a little of the dripping from the birds.

Bread or fruit sauce is sometimes served with roast grouse, but they are equally good served simply with melted butter.

HERRINGS FRIED IN OATMEAL

Prepare and bone the herrings and dry well by letting them lie in the folds of a cloth for an hour or two. Then sprinkle them with pepper and salt and dip each fish into coarse oatmeal, pressing it on to both sides. Put a small quantity of fat into a frying pan ; when it is smoking hot, put in the herrings and brown them nicely on both sides. Drain the fish on paper and serve garnished with parsley and cut lemon, or with small pat of maître d'hôtel butter on top.

FINNAN HADDIE

Wash and trim a smoked haddock (about $1\frac{1}{2}$–2 lb.) and cut in 2–4 pieces. Put 1 oz. fat and $\frac{1}{4}$ pint milk in a pan, bring to the boil and add the fish ; poach gently until cooked, then put on a hot dish. Boil the liquid for 2–3 minutes, add chopped parsley if desired, and pour over the fish. Serve if desired topped with poached eggs.

PARTAN BREE
(CRAB SOUP)

2 medium-sized crabs	½ pint cream
4 oz. rice (cooked in milk)	Salt and pepper
4 pints white (preferably fish) stock	Few drops of anchovy essence

Reserve the meat from the crab claws for garnishing. Chop the rest of the meat and pound it well in a mortar with the rice, previously boiled in milk till quite soft. Rub through a sieve, put into a saucepan and add the warmed stock gradually. Season with salt, pepper and a few drops of anchovy essence, and stir till quite hot. Remove from the heat, and stir in the warmed cream just before serving. Garnish with the meat from the claws.

PARTAN PIE
(CRAB PIE)

Pick out the crab meat, season with salt, pepper and grated nutmeg and mix with some breadcrumbs and a few small pieces of butter. Put the meat back into the cleaned shells, and pour over it a little warm vinegar, to which some mustard has been added. Alternatively substitute oil for the butter, and brown the crab meat under the grill.

PAN KAIL

Put 1 lb. or more of greens in a saucepan, cover with water, bring to the boil and simmer till quite tender. Drain thoroughly, chop finely and rub through a sieve. Put this purée back into a saucepan, thin with a little of the water in which the greens were cooked, and add a sprinkling of oatmeal. Season with salt and pepper and simmer for a few minutes. Before serving, stir in a little warmed cream. Serve with thin oatcakes.

STOVIES

Choose potatoes of good quality. Peel them, and put them on with just enough water to cover the bottom of the pan and prevent burning, sprinkle with salt, and put tiny bits of butter here and there, cover closely, and simmer very gently till soft and melted.

Dripping may be used in place of butter, and sliced onions (first tossed in the dripping) may be added, with a seasoning of pepper ; but the dish is best prepared as above.

SHORTBREAD FINGERS

4 oz. flour	2 oz. caster sugar
2 oz. rice flour	4 oz. butter

Line and grease a baking tray. Sieve both flours and the sugar together into a basin. Press all the ingredients together and mix until of a consistency of shortcrust pastry. Roll out the dough on floured board until ⅛ inch thick, prick all over with a fork, then cut into slices. Bake on a greased baking tray in a moderately hot oven (425° F., mark 7) until set, then reduce the heat and bake slowly until crisp and very slightly coloured. Allow to cool on the tray for a short time before removing.

The shortbread may also be pressed into a floured shortbread mould, turned out on to a greased baking tray and put into a hot oven (450° F., mark 8) for 5 minutes ; the heat should then be lowered to allow the shortbread to become crisp and golden-brown.

BANNOCKS

6 oz. flour	½ oz. butter
2 tsps. baking powder	2 tsps. sugar
2 oz. medium oatmeal	Milk to mix
½ tsp. salt	

Sieve the dry ingredients into a bowl. Rub in the fat, add the sugar and mix to a soft dough with milk. Roll out lightly ½ inch thick. Using a plate as a guide, cut into round bannocks, then cut across into triangular pieces. Cook on a hot lightly greased girdle for about 10 minutes, turning occasionally, until browned.

AFTERNOON TEA SCONES

1½ oz. butter	1 tsp. cream of tartar
½ lb. flour	1 tsp. sugar
½ tsp. bicarbonate of soda	A pinch of salt
	A little milk

Rub the fat into the flour. Add the dry ingredients and mix with milk to a soft dough. Roll out ½ inch thick, cut into rounds, put on to greased baking trays and bake in a hot oven (450° F., mark 8) for 7–10 minutes.

DUNDEE CAKE

10 oz. flour	Rind of 1 orange
4 oz. currants	5 eggs
4 oz. raisins	8 oz. butter or margarine
4 oz. sultanas	8 oz. sugar
4 oz. candied orange and lemon peel	3 oz. ground almonds
2 oz. whole almonds	A pinch of salt

Sieve the flour. Prepare the fruit, chop the

peel, blanch and split the almonds, grate the orange rind and beat the eggs. Cream the butter and sugar and add the eggs and flour alternately, beating well. Add the fruit, ground almonds, grated rind and salt, but not the split almonds. Turn the mixture into a tin that has been greased and lined with greased paper, cover the surface with the split almonds and bake in a slow oven (320° F., mark 2) for 3 hours. Cool on a wire tray.

Dundee cake will keep well, particularly if wrapped in greaseproof paper and stored in an airtight tin.

SCOTCH OR BLACK BUN
For the Pastry

12 oz. flour	1 oz. sugar
A pinch of salt	Cold water to mix to a
1 tsp. baking powder	stiff paste
6 oz. butter	Egg to glaze

For the Filling

2 lb. sultanas or raisins	2 tsps. allspice
2 lb. currants	2 tsps. ground ginger
4 oz. chopped orange peel	2 tsps. bicarbonate of soda
8 oz. chopped almonds	2 tsps. cream of tartar
1 lb. flour	2 eggs
8 oz. sugar	A little whisky
2 tsps. ground cinnamon	A wineglass whisky (optional)

This should be made several weeks at least before it is to be eaten (by tradition, at Hogmanay festivities).

Grease a 9-inch cake tin and make the pastry in the usual way. Roll out thinly and line the tin with it, reserving enough to cover the top. Prepare the fruit, peel and nuts for the filling, then put all the ingredients into a large bowl and mix, using just enough milk to moisten and mixing with the hands; add whisky if liked. Turn the mixture into the lined tin, damp the edge of the pastry and cover with the rest of the dough; prick all over with a fork and brush with beaten egg. Bake for 3–3½ hours in a moderate oven (350° F., mark 4). Cover with brown paper during the cooking if the pastry becomes too brown.

SEVILLE ORANGE MARMALADE

5 large or 6 small Seville oranges (about 2 lb.)	1 lemon or ½ tsp. citric or tartaric acid
4 pints water	4 lb. sugar

Wash the fruit, cut it into shreds and leave in a basin with the water overnight. Put the contents of the bowl into a deep saucepan or preserving pan, bring slowly to boiling point, add the acid (if used) and simmer gently until the peel is soft and the contents of the pan reduced almost by half; this will take about 1½ hours. Add the sugar, stir until dissolved, and then boil rapidly until a good set is obtained when a little marmalade is tested on a cold saucer. Allow to cool a little and pour into hot, sterilised jars. Cover at once with waxed circles and then tie down.

Ireland

IRISH STEW

2 lb. neck or flank of mutton	1 lb. onions
4 lb. potatoes	Salt and pepper

Cut the meat into neat pieces and slice the potatoes and onions. Put the meat into a pan with ¼ pint water and some salt, bring to the boil and skim. Add the potatoes, onions and pepper and cook slowly for 2½–3 hours, till the meat is tender. If desired, slice half the potatoes and cook the rest whole, adding them to the stew 40 minutes before serving. Arrange the whole potatoes neatly round a hot dish, pile the meat in the centre, and pour the gravy round.

Although this is usually made only with potatoes and onions, a variation especially favoured by sailors often contains large pieces of swede and/or carrots and is served with dumplings.

TIPPERARY PIE

½ lb. lean shin of beef	2 tsps. seasoning
1 onion	1 pint water
3 carrots	6 large potatoes
3 turnips	Gravy browning
A few sticks of celery	

For the Pastry

4 oz. flour	1 tsp. baking powder
2 oz. suet	⅛ pint water
½ tsp. salt	

Cut up the meat into pieces 1 inch square. Put it into a casserole and add the sliced onion, carrots, turnips and celery and the seasoning. Add the water and gravy browning; simmer for 1 hour. Add the sliced potatoes and boil a further ¼ hour. Make the pastry and roll it out to fit the casserole; cover the top of the stew, put the casserole lid on and simmer for ½ hour.

SWEDES WITH BACON

Put a layer of thinly sliced smoked bacon in the bottom of a saucepan, then add a layer of swede turnip, and so on, in alternate layers. Add 2 tbsps. cold water, place the pan at the side of the stove and simmer till cooked.

MEALIE CRENCHIE

In this country-type dish exact quantities are not important—just fry some coarse oatmeal with the breakfast bacon, including a little sliced onion if you wish. At harvest time this was sometimes served as a midday meal.

COCKLE STEW

2 quarts cockles	1 oz. butter
2 pints of the liquor	1 oz. flour
in which the cockles	Pepper and salt
were cooked	1 onion
Milk	Chopped parsley

Wash the cockles well in cold water, repeating several times. Put into clean cold water to cover, add 1 tbsp. salt and a handful of oatmeal and leave for some hours or overnight. Strain and wash. Put the cockles into a large strong pan with a very little water and heat over a low flame until the shells open. Strain off the liquor and make up to 1 quart with water if necessary. Remove the cockles from the shells.

Melt the butter in a pan and add the flour; cook for a few minutes, then gradually add cockle liquor to make a fairly thick sauce, adding milk if needed to give the right consistency. Add seasoning to taste and the very finely chopped onion, put in the cockles, bring to the boil and simmer gently for about 10 minutes. Pour into a tureen, sprinkle with chopped parsley and serve hot.

COLCANNON

Take equal quantities of boiled potatoes and boiled cabbage. Mash the potatoes and mince the cabbage. Melt a piece of butter or dripping in a saucepan, allowing about 1 oz. to 1 lb. vegetables, add the potatoes and cabbage, season and mix well. Heat thoroughly and serve at once.

The mixture may be turned into a greased pie dish, sprinkled with grated cheese, dotted with butter or margarine, and browned in a hot oven.

STELK
(ONIONS AND POTATOES)

Take 2 doz. coarse spring onions and chop them into small lengths, then simmer in milk until tender. Meanwhile, boil or steam some potatoes and mash them with a little milk. Strain the onions, add them to the potatoes, mix well and serve very hot, with a knob of butter.

CARRAGEEN MOSS BLANCMANGE

½ oz. carrageen (also called Irish) moss	Flavouring Sugar
1 pint milk	A little wine, if desired

Pick over the moss carefully before weighing it out, then wash it well in tepid water. Put into a saucepan with the milk and simmer very gently for ½ hour. (Alternatively, cook it in a double saucepan, allowing more time.) Flavour with vanilla, lemon rind or a bay leaf, or as desired, and sweeten to taste. Strain through muslin and leave until cold. A little wine may be added if wished.

To make a jelly, use 1 oz. moss, simmer in 1 pint water instead of milk, strain the liquid on to 2 oz. loaf sugar and the strained juice of 1 lemon, then leave to set.

CARRAGEEN SOUFFLÉS

½ oz. carrageen moss	1 tbsp. sherry
1 pint milk	¼ pint whipped cream
1 egg	Chopped nuts
1 oz. sugar	

Pick over the moss and remove discoloured parts, soak for 10–15 minutes in a little water, and strain. Put with the milk into a saucepan and cook until it is thick enough to coat the back of a wooden spoon. Beat up the yolk of the egg and strain the carrageen mixture on to it. Whisk well until it begins to set, then add the sugar and sherry and mix well. Fold in half the whipped cream, and the stiffly whisked egg white, pour into individual glasses and leave until set, then remove the paper carefully. Decorate with the rest of the cream and with chopped nuts.

If preferred, set in a prepared soufflé mould.

Carrageen moss is an edible seaweed which is plentiful on the rocky Irish coast and is used in most parts of the island. When bleached and dried, it will keep for years.

BOXTY PANCAKES

Peel, wash and grate some large potatoes, then drain lightly and measure. To each cupful of grated potato add 1 tsp. salt, ½ cupful flour and enough milk to make a fairly stiff batter. Leave to stand for 1 hour, then fry like pancakes in bacon dripping. Serve hot, with butter.

POTATO CAKES

Mash 6 freshly boiled potatoes, add a pinch of salt, about 2 tbsps. flour and a knob of butter. Work to a stiff dough, turn on to a floured board and roll out $\frac{1}{2}$ inch thick. Cut into squares and bake on a girdle until golden-brown on both sides.

IRISH SODA BREAD

27

1 lb. flour (white or white and wholemeal)	1 tsp. cream of tartar (2 tsps. if sweet milk is used)
1 tsp. salt	
1 tsp. bicarbonate of soda	$\frac{1}{2}$ pint (approx.) sour milk, buttermilk or sweet milk
1 oz. fat	

Sieve the dry ingredients and rub in the fat. Make a well in the centre and mix in enough liquid to give a soft, spongy dough. Turn out on to a lightly floured board and shape quickly into 1–2 round cakes, place on a floured baking sheet and score with a knife. Bake in a moderately hot oven (425° F., mark 7) for 30–40 minutes, till well-risen, lightly browned and firm underneath.

IRISH FRUIT LOAF

1 lb. mixed dried fruit	1 tsp. mixed powdered spice
$\frac{1}{2}$ lb. caster sugar	
1 cupful warm tea	1 egg
1 lb. flour	2 oz. chopped candied peel or 1 tbsp. marmalade
1 tsp. bicarbonate of soda	

Put the dried fruit and sugar in a bowl and strain the warm tea over it ; leave overnight.

Well-grease a bread tin. Sift the flour, soda and spice into a dry bowl, stir in the soaked fruit and the well-beaten egg and mix well, adding the peel or the marmalade. Put the mixture into the tin, levelling the surface, and bake in a slow oven (325° F., mark 3) for $1\frac{1}{2}$–2 hours. Cool in the tin. To serve, cut into slices and butter.

POTATO AND APPLE CAKE

Boil and mash 4 potatoes and peel and slice 4 large cooking apples. Rub 6 oz. dripping into 1 lb. of flour, then mix this with the potato to form a dough. Roll out to $\frac{1}{2}$ inch thick. Line a greased pie dish with some of the dough and cover with a layer of apple ; repeat these layers alternately, finishing with pastry. Bake in a moderate oven (350° F., mark 4) for 1 hour.

GAELIC COFFEE

Heat a goblet or claret glass and put in 2 lumps of sugar. Pour in a jigger of Irish whiskey and fill up two-thirds of the way with hot, strong black coffee. Dissolve the sugar, then carefully add some double cream, pouring it in over the back of a spoon, so that it lies on top. Do not mix, but drink the coffee and whiskey through the layer of cream.

28

CZECHOSLOVAKIA, lying in the heart of Europe, is a fertile country, rich in natural resources, grain, fruit, game and fish. For centuries trade and travel routes have met and crossed there and left an indelible imprint on Czech cooking, which is now hardly able to distinguish its own indigenous food from the variety of schnitzels, steaks, borschts and potato dishes that have slowly crept in from neighbouring countries.

In the past Czech food has tended to be over-starchy and rich with animal fats, but now the diet is more varied and contains an abundance of proteins and vitamins.

Soup is the normal beginning to a meal, always served with some addition, such as diced meat and vegetable dumplings, rice or noodles. Thick soups are popular and frequently garnished with parsley and dill. Excellent meat is available, particularly pork, as well as poultry, game and fresh-water fish in abundance. Meat dishes are frequently prepared with thick cream sauces made with vegetables and eggs. Hearty, filling bread and potato dumplings are a great favourite, made feathery light with yeast, baking powder or egg white. Eggs form the basis of many dishes and vegetables are cooked with much ingenuity, often forming a meal in themselves. The Czechs are famous for their yeast cakes and rolls, gingerbread and cream cakes and at Christmas-time the housewife bakes various kinds of biscuits.

Czechoslovakia

YEAST SOUP WITH PASTA

½ onion	Salt
3 oz. baker's yeast	3 tbsps. milk
2 oz. butter	3 oz. fine semolina
Flour	1 egg
3 pints water	Parsley
Small pieces of carrot, celeriac, parsley root	

Fry the onion and yeast in the butter; when the yeast begins to brown at the edges, sprinkle in 2 oz. flour, mix well and pour on the water. Add the finely chopped vegetables, season with salt, whisk well and cook for 20 minutes. Now prepare the pasta by mixing the milk, semolina and egg, then adding a little flour and salt. Using a teaspoon, drop small pieces of dough into the soup and cook for about 5 minutes. Garnish with parsley.

CREAMY BACON SOUP

1 oz. lard	2 egg yolks
1 oz. flour	2 slices bread
3 pints bacon or ham stock	A little fat for frying bread
¼ pint sour cream	Parsley

Make a light roux with the lard and flour, dilute with the stock and cook for about 30 minutes, then add the cream mixed with the egg yolks and reheat but do not boil. Cut the bread into small strips or cubes and quickly fry in fat to make them crisp. Place a few on each plate, together with some of the chopped parsley and pour the hot soup over. Do not salt this soup—the stock will be salty enough.

PORK SOUP

8 oz. pig's head (fresh)	A handful of dried mushrooms
3 pints water	1 oz. groats
Salt	A drop of meat extract
2 oz. root vegetables	

Wash the meat and boil in salted water together with the vegetables and mushrooms until soft. Take out the meat, remove from bone and cut into small pieces. Add the groats and meat extract and cook for a few minutes longer. Serve with a slice of bread.

PERCENA JATRA
(ROAST CALF'S LIVER)

1 calf's liver	1 lb. onions
Fat bacon	Butter

Wash the liver, put it in a greased baking tin and cover with some minced bacon, then cook in a very slow oven (275° F., mark ½). Meanwhile chop and fry the onions. Cover the liver with the onions, put some lumps of butter over the top and continue to bake slowly until onions are soft. Boiled rice and baked tomatoes are handed separately with this dish.

VEPROVA PECENE
(ROAST PORK)

This is the national dish of Czechoslovakia. Prepare a loin of pork, wiping it all over; sprinkle with caraway seeds and a little salt and roast in the usual way, basting it thoroughly with the fat. Serve with dumplings and cabbage.

BRNO SCHNITZEL
(FRIED VEAL)

4 slices of veal fillet	2 oz. ham, chopped
Salt	1 tbsp. flour
1 egg	1 tbsp. milk
2 oz. butter	1 tsp. fine breadcrumbs
Green peas	4 oz. fat for frying

Trim the meat, beat lightly and season with salt. Scramble the egg in a pan with the butter, peas and ham. Spread a little of the mixture on each piece of veal, fold the meat in half and secure with a small skewer. Carefully dip the meat in flour, milk and breadcrumbs and fry in the hot fat.

VEAL ROULADE WITH VEGETABLES

2 lb. shoulder or leg of veal	1 tbsp. green peas
	A little anchovy paste
1 small carrot, a piece of celeriac, a piece of parsley root and 1 onion	4 oz. butter
	1 pickled cucumber, chopped

Prepare the meat. Parboil the root vegetables and onion in a little salted water, then dice them, add the peas, the anchovy paste beaten with a small piece of butter and the chopped cucumber. Beat the veal well, spread with the vegetable mixture and roll up, securing it well. Pour some melted butter over it and cook in a moderate oven (350° F., mark 4) till brown, adding a little water from time to time. Cut the roll into slices and serve with mashed potatoes or rice.

STEAKS IN CAPER SAUCE

1 lb. of steak cut into 4 pieces	2 oz. bacon
	1 onion, chopped
Salt and pepper	2 tbsps. French mustard
Flour	2 tbsps. capers
1 oz. lard	¼ pint sour cream

Wipe the steaks, remove all fat, snip the edges to prevent their curling and beat lightly. Season with salt and pepper and sprinkle with flour.

Heat the lard and fry the bacon and onion, then add the meat and fry quickly on both sides. Add the mustard, capers and a little water, cover and simmer till tender. Take the meat out of the sauce and allow the latter to brown, then add the cream mixed with 1 tbsp. flour, bring to the boil and cook until thickened. Return the steaks to sauce and serve with dumplings or potatoes.

BEEF IN GINGER SAUCE

2 lb. shoulder of beef	1 onion, finely chopped
2 oz. fat bacon	2 oz. dripping
Salt	2 slices of black bread
1 tsp. ground ginger	

Wash the meat, beat well and lard with strips of bacon, then sprinkle with the salt and ginger. Fry the onion in the dripping, add the meat and quickly fry all over. Now add a little water and the dry bread, which will break up in the sauce and thus thicken it ; simmer until the meat is tender. Sieve the sauce and pour over the meat. Serve with dumplings or boiled rice.

FRIED CARP

Clean a carp (about 3 lb. in weight) and divide into portions. Wash, sprinkle with salt and leave for an hour. Dry the pieces with a cloth, dip into flour, beaten egg and breadcrumbs and fry quickly in hot butter or fat. When the fish is golden-brown on each side, lower the heat and leave to cook gently until done. Garnish with lemon and parsley and serve with potato salad.

DEVILLED CARP

3 lb. carp	1 bay leaf
Vinegar	1 cup grated ginger-
2 oz. butter	bread
1 carrot	1 pint brown ale
A piece of celeriac	Grated lemon rind
½ a small parsley root	1 tbsp. red-currant jelly
½ an onion	1 tbsp. sultanas
Salt	1 tbsp. chopped
5 peppercorns	blanched almonds
A pinch of allspice	Sugar
A pinch of dried thyme	

Keep the blood from a freshly caught carp and dilute with 2 tbsps. vinegar. Clean fish, cut into portions and fry in the butter, then remove the fish and prepare the sauce. Fry the vegetables in the butter, add the seasonings, etc., grated gingerbread, blood and vinegar, ale and lemon rind and cook all together till the sauce thickens. Sieve it, stir in the red-currant jelly, sultanas and almonds and add a little sugar,

W.C.B.—5

vinegar and salt to taste. Return the fish to this sweet-sour sauce to heat through.

FRIED SOFT-BOILED EGGS

4 eggs	1 egg
1 oz. flour	3 oz. breadcrumbs
Salt	4 oz. fat

Soft-boil the eggs until the whites are just firm, then remove the shells and allow to cool. Dip into seasoned flour, egg and breadcrumbs and fry till golden in the hot fat. Serve with raw or cooked vegetable salad.

The eggs may also be wrapped in slices of ham, salami or very thin fillets of meat, then dipped in flour, egg and breadcrumbs and fried.

CAULIFLOWER WITH EGGS

1 small cauliflower	4 eggs
1 small onion	½ tsp. salt
1 oz. butter	Pepper
1 tsp. caraway seeds	

Cook the cauliflower in salted water until just tender ; break into flowerets. Fry the sliced onion in butter until transparent but not brown, add the cauliflower and caraway seeds, mix with the onion and fry for 3 minutes. Pour the beaten and seasoned eggs into the pan and cook slowly, stirring all the time, until the eggs are set.

BRAMBOROVY GULAS
(POTATO CAKE)

A few spring onions	1 bay leaf
1 oz. fat	1 oz. flour
2 lb. potatoes	½ pint milk
1 tsp. paprika pepper	Flour and butter roux
Salt	to thicken
A pinch of pepper	Parsley

Fry the chopped onions in the fat until brown, then add the peeled and diced raw potatoes, together with the seasonings and flour. Cover the pan and cook gently until the potatoes are done. Add the milk and the roux with some chopped parsley and continue to cook until the mixture is brown and firm on the underside. Turn it out on to a hot plate and serve at once either with meat or with brown gravy and a green vegetable or with onions.

BRAMBORAK—I
(POTATO GIRDLE CAKES)

2 lb. finely grated raw	Pepper
potatoes	Chopped marjoram
Milk	(optional)
¾ tsp. salt	3 oz. flour
A clove of garlic	4–5 tbsps. oil

Leave the grated potatoes until they are

covered with their own liquid, then drain this off and add a rather smaller amount of milk. Combine with the salt mixed with the crushed garlic and add pepper to taste and the marjoram, if used. Finally mix well with the flour.

Grease a girdle or heavy frying pan with some oil and drop in spoonfuls of the potato mixture, spreading it out thinly. Fry on both sides until brown and crisp and serve very hot—if allowed to cool they lose their flavour. Lettuce or other salad makes a good accompaniment.

These potato cakes or pancakes are a Prague speciality and vast quantities are eaten in the snack bars, where they are cooked on huge girdles holding 48 at a time.

BRAMBORAK—II
(POTATO GIRDLE CAKES)

1 lb. potatoes boiled in their skins	Salt and pepper to taste
	3½ oz. flour
1 grated onion	Fat for frying

Peel and grate the potatoes as soon as possible after cooking. Mix all ingredients thoroughly to a paste and fry in the hot fat, either in one piece or in small cakes. Serve very hot.

CHLUPATE KNEDLIKY
(SHAGGY DUMPLINGS)

Use the same paste as for Bramborak. Cut off small pieces, drop into fast-boiling water and when they rise to the top, cook for another 3 minutes. Drain and serve with pork or bacon and sauerkraut, or with roast pork.

KNEDLIKY—I
(POTATO DUMPLINGS)

1 lb. potatoes, boiled in their skins	A pinch of salt
	1 egg
1 lb. flour	

These may be served as a meal in themselves, with vegetables and sauce, or as an addition to meat to " stretch " it. They can also be made into a sweet by the addition of fruit or jam and a sweet sauce.

Skin and mash the potatoes. Add the flour, salt and egg and knead into a firm dough—no extra liquid should be necessary. Shape into balls or rolls and cook in boiling water for 20 minutes.

Chopped meat added to the dough makes the dumplings into a satisfying meal; serve with vegetables (not potato) and gravy.

To serve as a sweet, add fruit or jam to the dough, or else cut the dough into squares or strips, putting some jam or fruit in centre and then rolling up. Boil as for savoury dumplings

and serve with sugar mixed with a little ground cinnamon.

KNEDLIKY—II
(POTATO DUMPLINGS)

2 lb. boiled potatoes (cooked in their skins)	1 oz. semolina
	A pinch of salt
	1–2 eggs
½ lb. wholemeal flour	

Peel the potatoes and let them cool, then put them through a potato presser or mincer. Put on a floured pastry board and sprinkle the flour, semolina and salt over the top. Make a hollow in the centre and break the eggs into it; using first a knife and then the hands, combine the ingredients to make a smooth dough. Knead a little, but do not allow it to stand for long. Form into 4 longish rolls or into dumplings the size of a large apple. Put into a large pan of boiling salted water; when the water comes back to the boil take off the saucepan lid and if necessary ease the dumplings with a wooden spoon to free them from the bottom of the pan so that they are floating freely. Cover the pan again and boil for about 15–20 minutes, until the dumplings are cooked throughout. Remove from the water, draining well, and slice, using a strong linen thread, not a knife. Put on a hot dish and brush over with a little melted lard to prevent them from sticking.

Serve with meat dishes.

SHKUBANKY
(POTATO CAKES WITH POPPY SEED)

2 lb. potatoes	Lard
Salt	2 oz. ground poppy seeds
5 oz. flour	2 oz. sugar

Peel and quarter the potatoes, cover with boiling salted water and cook till nearly soft, then drain off the water into a bowl. Mash the potatoes and make several holes in the mash with the end of a wooden spoon, going right down to the bottom of the pan. Fill these with flour and pour on about half of the boiling potato liquor. Cover and leave at the side of the stove for about 30 minutes. Pour off the excess water and beat the mixture with a wooden spoon till smooth—it should be very stiff. Using a metal spoon dipped in hot lard, place spoonfuls of the mixture on a plate and sprinkle with ground poppy seeds, sugar and lard.

Alternatives would be to sprinkle the shkubanky with grated gingerbread instead of poppy seed, or with grated cottage cheese and melted butter.

Fried shkubanky are also excellent; shape

the dough into small cakes, dip in flour, egg and breadcrumbs and fry till golden-brown.

HOUSKOVE KNEDLIKY
(BREAD DUMPLINGS)

1 lb. flour	A little butter
A pinch of salt	1 egg
4 small bread rolls	A little milk
(preferably 1 day old)	½ pint soda water

Sieve the flour and salt. Cut the rolls into thin slices and fry slowly. Beat the egg into the flour with a little milk, and then beat in the soda water. Beat for 20 minutes, then leave for 30 minutes. Now dice the fried bread and beat into the batter (which, unlike English batter, is firm enough to handle). Form into large dumplings or balls, keeping the hands wet to make it easier to handle the mixture. Cook the dumplings for 25–30 minutes in gently boiling water, drain and serve at once with roast meat or poultry, chicken in paprika or any suitable dish.

RICH DUMPLINGS

10 bread rolls (about	3 egg yolks
1 lb.)	3 tbsps. fine semolina
1 pint milk	Salt
3 tbsps. butter	

Use rolls which are a day old, cut them into cubes and sprinkle with the milk whisked together with the melted butter and eggs. Add the semolina and turn on to a floured board, knead lightly and form into small round dumplings by firmly pressing between the palms of the hand. Then throw them into boiling salted water and cook for about 20 minutes. Remove from the water and tear slightly apart with a fork to allow the steam to escape. Pour a little butter or dripping over and serve with roast or braised meat.

JABLKOVY DORT
(APPLE TART)

Butter	4 oz. sugar
Breadcrumbs	4 oz. flour
2 lb. cooking apples (or	2 tbsps. milk
1 lb. apple rings,	1 egg
soaked overnight)	

Butter a pie dish and sprinkle thickly with breadcrumbs. Arrange the sliced apples or drained rings over breadcrumbs. Make some pastry by blending the sugar, flour, milk and egg, mixing to a thick batter, and pour it over the apples in the dish. Bake for 20 minutes in a moderately hot oven (425° F., mark 7); serve hot.

If fresh apples are used stew them a little before putting into the pie dish.

APPLE STRUDEL

12 oz. flour	3 drops of vinegar
¼ pint water	1 egg
3 oz. butter or fat	Sugar to sprinkle over
A pinch of salt	cooked strudel

For the Filling

3 oz. breadcrumbs	¾ oz. chopped almonds
Butter	A pinch of ground
1¼ lb. apples	cinnamon
2 oz. sugar	½ tsp rum
1 oz. sultanas	

Put the flour on a pastry board, make a well in the middle and pour in the warm water mixed with the melted fat, salt, vinegar and beaten egg. Mix first with a knife and then with the fingers until the mixture becomes a soft dough which is shiny and malleable and does not stick to the board or the fingers. Shape into a loaf, cover with a warm baking tin and leave for ¼ hour.

Meanwhile fry the breadcrumbs in 1 oz. butter. Place the dough on a floured cloth, roll it out, brush over with about ¾ oz. melted butter and stretch it out gently with the fingers until it is quite thin. Sprinkle the dough with the cold fried crumbs, then cover half the surface with very thinly sliced apple. Add the sugar, sultanas, chopped almonds and a sprinkling of cinnamon and rum. Using the cloth to help you, roll up Swiss-roll fashion, place on a well-buttered baking tin and then bake in a moderate oven (350° F., mark 4) for about ½ hour, brushing it over from time to time with melted butter.

Sprinkle the baked strudel with sugar, and slice when cold.

CHRISTMAS APPLE GÂTEAU
For the Sponge Cake

3 eggs	3 tbsps. flour
3 tbsps. sugar	

30

For the Nut Cream

¼ pint milk (scant	2 oz. sugar
measure)	1 tbsp. strong black
2 oz. ground nuts	coffee
2 oz. butter	

For the Topping

4 apples or 3 oranges	2 tbsps. cocoa
Sugar syrup	1 egg
3 oz. butter	Chopped nuts to
4 oz. sugar	decorate

To make the sponge, whisk the egg whites to a froth, add the sugar and beat well, then add the egg yolks and the flour, mixing lightly. Put into a greased cake tin and bake in a moderate oven (375° F., mark 5) for about ¾ hour. Run a knife round the tin to loosen the cake, but leave it in the tin till cold.

Now make the nut cream. Pour the boiling milk on to the nuts. Cream the butter and sugar and add the cold nut mixture and cold coffee, mixing thoroughly. Spread this cream over the sponge, smoothing it with a palette knife, then put in a cool place.

Meanwhile peel the apples, cut into eighths and stew for a few minutes in a sugar syrup, then drain well. If oranges are used, peel and divide into segments, removing the pips.

When the cream has partly set, make regular grooves in it with the end of a wooden spoon, taking care to keep these neat and even round the edges. Place the slices of fruit neatly round the top, setting them about ¾ inch in from the outer edge.

Make an icing by beating the butter, sugar, cocoa and egg over hot water until thick and glossy. While still slightly warm, pour into the centre of the gâteau and scatter chopped nuts over the top. Keep the cake in a cool place till required.

MAKOVY DORT
(POPPY SEED CAKE)

6 oz. butter	4 oz. ground almonds
8 oz. sugar	8 oz. poppy seeds
5 eggs, separated	

Cream the butter and sugar and beat in the egg yolks one by one until the mixture is thick and creamy. Pound the ground almonds and poppy seeds together. Beat the egg whites until stiff and snowy, and blend thoroughly with the almond and poppy seed mixture. Now put the egg yolk and sugar mixture into a lightly greased tin and carefully pour the other mixture on top. Bake in a slow oven (325° F., mark 3) for about 1–1¼ hours, or until firm and spongy. Keep in the tin in a very cold place (preferably a refrigerator) until the next day.

COCOLAPOVY DORT
(CHOCOLATE MERINGUE CAKE)

½ lb. chocolate	½ lb. sugar
6 tbsps. hot water	5 egg whites

Prepare a mould for the cake by turning a round tin upside down and fastening round it a lightly buttered band of stiff kitchen paper, so that it stands up 3 or 4 inches above the tin.

Break up the chocolate, melt it in the hot water and leave for 15 minutes; it should then form a thick cream when stirred. Beat the sugar with 2 of the egg whites and add the cold chocolate. Beat the remaining 3 egg whites to a stiff, snowy froth and fold in the rest of the mixture lightly. Put into the prepared mould and bake in a very slow oven (250° F., mark ¼) for 1¼ hours. When the cake is cooked just lift the paper and cake from the tin and transfer gently to a warmed plate. This tastes rather like a marshmallow with a thin, crisp crust.

HONEY WAFER CAKE

8 oz. plain flour	1 tbsp. honey
1 egg	A little vanilla essence
3 oz. sugar	1 tsp. bicarbonate of
1 oz. fat	soda

For the Filling and Decoration

1 pint milk	1 tbsp. cocoa
1 oz. cornflour	Chopped roasted nuts or
3 oz. sugar	chocolate
2 oz. butter	

Sieve the flour. Whisk the egg, sugar, fat, honey and vanilla to a thick cream over a saucepan of boiling water, add the soda, whisk a little longer, then remove from the stove and fold in the flour; when cool turn on to a floured board. Divide into 5 parts and roll out each to wafer thinness. Put on a greased tray and bake in a moderate oven (350° F., mark 4) for 4–6 minutes. When golden remove from oven and take off the tray, using a palette knife, while still warm.

Mix a little of the milk with the cornflour, heat the remaining milk, stir in the blended cornflour and the sugar and cook, stirring, for a few minutes. Then remove from the stove; when cold add the butter and cocoa. Join the wafers together with this cream filling, cover with a weight and leave for several hours in a cool place. Decorate with the remaining filling and sprinkle the sides and top with roasted chopped nuts or grated chocolate.

CANDLE CAKES

In some parts of Czechoslovakia there is an old custom that when the Christmas cake is made, some of the mixture should be set aside to use in this way. The cake mixture is usually a rich spicy yeast dough with dried fruit and nuts, and is formed into a twist or ring shape. For each member of the family now departed a miniature twist is made; when the cakes are baked, a dab of thick glacé icing is put in the centre hollow and a candle inserted, so that as the icing sets it will hold the candle steady. At the main Christmas meal the cakes are set on the family table and their candles lit.

KOLACHE
(YEAST PASTRIES)

8 oz. butter	Salt
1 lb. flour	3 eggs
¾ oz. baker's yeast	¼ pint milk
4 tbsps. milk for yeast	Filling (see below)
1 oz. sugar	Egg to glaze

For the Poppy Seed Filling

5 oz. poppy seeds	Pinch of ground
½ pint milk	cinnamon
3 oz. sugar	Chocolate, jam or
Vanilla essence	honey (optional)
Grated lemon rind	1 oz. butter

Mix the fat with about 3 oz. flour and leave in a cool place. Mix the yeast with the milk and pour into the rest of the flour, the salt and sugar, add the eggs and the rest of the milk and work the mixture into a soft dough. Leave for about 1 hour in a warm place to rise, then roll it out and place the rolled-out fat on it. Fold over the edges like an envelope, press together and fold in half; lightly roll out, fold into three, turn and fold into three again. Leave for 1 hour, then repeat the rolling and folding. Leave for about 15 minutes, then roll out to about ½ inch thick and cut into squares. Place some thick poppy seed filling on each square and fold up the corners to the centre, pressing them well together to prevent their opening up during the baking. Brush the tops with beaten egg and bake in a moderately hot oven (425° F., mark 7) for 15 minutes.

Make the filling as follows : Grind the poppy seeds and simmer in the milk till soft; if necessary add a little water from time to time. Add the sugar and simmer for a little longer, stirring all the time. Flavour with vanilla essence, grated lemon rind and cinnamon; a little grated chocolate or 1 tbsp. of honey or jam may also be added. Mix with the butter. The filling should be thick but not dry. Apples or nuts may also be used to fill the pastries.

BEARS' PAWS

12 oz. sieved wholemeal flour	A pinch of ground cinnamon
9 oz. sugar	A pinch of ground
4 oz. walnuts or almonds, blanched and ground	cloves
	9 oz. butter
1½ oz. cocoa	Vanilla-flavoured icing sugar

Mix the flour, sugar, ground nuts, cocoa and spices and rub in the butter. Knead the dough and shape into a roll, cut off slices and press into small greased patty tins. Bake in a moderate oven (350° F., mark 4) until firm and lightly browned ; while still hot, dip into vanilla-flavoured icing sugar.

NUT ROLLS

Whisk 4 egg whites and 7 oz. caster sugar over a pan of boiling water until stiff. Sprinkle a pastry board with 4 oz. grated Brazil nuts or almonds and place spoonfuls of the egg white mixture on it. Form into small rolls, place on a greased baking tin and dry in a very slow oven (lowest possible setting) until crisp but not coloured.

VANILLA ROLLS

5 oz. flour	A tiny piece of finely
¾ oz. icing sugar	crushed vanilla pod
1½ oz. blanched and grated almonds or walnuts	or a few drops of essence
	4 oz. butter
A little grated lemon rind	1 egg yolk
	Vanilla sugar

Mix the flour, icing sugar, nuts, lemon rind and vanilla. Chop the butter into the mixture, add the egg yolk and mix to a paste. Leave in a cool place for 15 minutes. Roll the paste out, cut into small strips and make into little rolls by rolling in the hands. Put on a baking tin covered with greaseproof paper and bake in a slow oven (325° F., mark 2) until lightly browned. Dip the hot rolls into vanilla sugar.

HORSERADISH AND APPLE SAUCE

1 oz. horseradish	A pinch of sugar
2 apples	3 tbsps. cold beef stock
Vinegar or lemon juice	or water
A pinch of salt	

Wash the horseradish, scrape and grate finely ; peel and grate the apples, mix the two and at once sprinkle with a few drops of vinegar or lemon juice to prevent their turning brown. Add the salt, sugar and stock. Grated carrot may be used instead of apple, in which case the sauce should be made with lemon juice.

This condiment is served with boiled meat, particularly ribs of beef, boiled pig's head or boiled smoked meat. If it is served with boiled fish or game, 2 tbsps. thickly whipped cream may be added instead of part of the stock.

THE cooking of Denmark reflects the character of the country to a very marked degree; the hard-working Danes have hearty appetites and their meals are on a lavish scale. Dairy farming is one of Denmark's chief industries; rich pasture lands produce a plentiful supply of milk, cream, butter and cheese and although much of this is exported there remain abundant supplies for the home market. Eggs are produced in large quantities and Danish ham and bacon are world-famous. All these dairy products find their way into the Danish kitchen. Butter, eggs and cream are used lavishly and give a delicious flavour to cakes, Danish pastries and the cookies and biscuits that are so popular. Milk is used not only for drinks and in puddings, but also in soups and even in some meat dishes, such as *Frikadeller*.

The coast of Denmark yields a great harvest of fish, of which herrings are perhaps the most abundant. The herring appears on the Danish table in literally hundreds of guises; it can be salted, smoked, pickled, marinated or kippered as well as cooked and served in its fresh state. Herrings form an essential ingredient when smørrebrød are made.

Smørrebrød are, as in all Scandinavian countries, an important feature. These delicious open sandwiches may be served as a preliminary to a meal, or several of them may make a complete lunch. In one Copenhagen restaurant that specialises in smørrebrød the menu list is about a yard long and contains some 250 different kinds. In the home, the number of varieties normally depends on the occasion. For a party, all the ingredients of smørrebrød may be set out as a " cold table " so that the guests can assemble their own according to taste. This is generally the custom on festive occasions such as Christmas Eve and St. Martin's Day. There are certain well-known and traditional smørrebrød which are always available in Danish restaurants, but there is no reason why you should not prepare others to your own liking.

Puddings in the English sense of the word are not particularly popular in Denmark, but fruit or a fruit sweet is often served at the end of a meal. Currants, raspberries, bilberries and so on are all made into delicious desserts, sometimes garnished with cream and nuts.

Danish lager is, of course, world-famous and the most popular spirit is schnapps, a type of hollands gin.

Denmark

DANISH " SWEET SOUPS "

The soup course in Denmark sometimes consists of a mixture like gruel, porridge or hot blancmange, usually served with fruit, jam or a spicy flavouring and sugar. Here are some examples.

Risengrød (Rice Porridge) : Wash ¼ lb. rice, scald it with boiling water, drain and add to 1 quart boiling milk ; stir well and simmer, stirring occasionally, for 1 hour. Add a pinch of salt and some thick cream just before serving. Each person adds to the portion in his plate a knob of butter, a little sweet beer and some sugar and ground cinnamon to taste.

Fløjlsgrød (Velvet Porridge) : Melt 3 oz. butter in a saucepan, stir in 4 oz. flour and cook for a minute or two, then gradually add 1½ pints of boiling milk and a little water, stirring continuously ; add a pinch of salt, then simmer for 10 minutes. Eat with sugar, ground cinnamon (if desired) and fruit juice.

Boghvedegrød (Buckwheat Porridge) ; Cook 4 oz. buckwheat or groats slowly in 1 quart milk for 1 hour or longer. Serve in the same way as Rice Porridge, above.

Øllebrød (Beer Bread Soup) : Cut 10 oz. rye bread into dice and soak for 12 hours in a mixture of 1 pint bottled pale ale and ¼ pint water, then put in a saucepan and simmer for about 20 minutes. Sieve the mixture, put back into the saucepan, stir in another 1 pint bottle of pale ale and simmer very gently until hot and well blended. Sweeten to taste and add lemon peel to flavour. Serve with thick cream.

Hvid Sagosuppe (White Sago Soup) : Put 1–1½ oz. sago into 1½ pints boiling water, add the juice of ½ a lemon, 4 oz. sugar and 1 oz. stoned raisins, then boil for about 20 minutes, until the grain is transparent. Put 1 well-beaten egg into the soup tureen and gradually pour in the sago soup, mixing well. Add sherry to taste.

GIBLET SOUP

Clean some chicken giblets in the usual way and put in a saucepan with sufficient water to cover and a little salt ; bring gradually to the boil, skim and simmer for ½ hour. Add 2 sliced carrots, 1 stick of celery, 1 leek, 2 sliced apples and a few soaked prunes. Continue to cook until all the ingredients are tender, then add a little sugar and vinegar to taste, and serve with dumplings (see below).

MELBOLLER
(FLOUR DUMPLINGS)

Melt 2 oz. butter, stir in 3 oz. flour and cook, stirring continuously, for a few minutes. Add just over ½ pint water and stir over a good heat until the mixture will come away from the sides of the pan, then remove from the heat and " work " the mixture for about 10 minutes. Add an egg, mix this in thoroughly, then add a second egg and finally add 1 tbsp. sugar and ½ tsp. salt, mixing these in well.

Drop the mixture 1 tsp. at a time into boiling water and cook until the dumplings rise to the surface ; drain in a colander, pour cold water over them to remove the surface stickiness and serve at once in the hot soup.

HERRING ROLLS

2 gherkins	A small onion
1 eating apple	4 herrings
1 small beetroot	

Chop all the ingredients (except the fish) very finely and mix together. Cut the herrings into fillets, put a spoonful of the mixture on to each fillet, roll up, and serve with rémoulade sauce.

Rémoulade Sauce

¼ pint mayonnaise	2 tsps. chopped parsley
1 shallot, chopped	1 tsp. lemon juice
2 tsps. French mustard	1 tsp. sugar, if liked

Mix the ingredients well and serve as required.

HERRING SALAD

3 soused herrings	2 tbsps. olive oil
3–4 cooked potatoes	2 tbsps. vinegar
1 cooked beetroot	Salt and pepper
1 pickled cucumber	2–3 hard-boiled eggs
1–2 dessert apples	

Flake the fish or cut them into small pieces. Cut the potatoes, beetroot and cucumber into dice and cut up the cored apples without peeling. Blend together the oil, vinegar and seasoning in a good-sized bowl and add the salad ingredients. Mix thoroughly and serve garnished with sliced or quartered hard-boiled eggs.

Alternatively put the salad into a ring mould, chill, then turn out and garnish with the chopped egg yolk and strips of egg white.

FRIED HERRINGS

Clean and bone the herrings, rub with salt and wipe with a cloth, then arrange them to look as though they were whole. Cut 2 small slits in the skin of each herring, dip in seasoned egg and breadcrumbs ; alternatively, coat the cleaned salted herrings with made mustard and dip them in flour. Fry until light brown in butter, margarine or lard, keeping them a good shape. Garnish with fried tomatoes and onions, sprinkle with chopped parsley and serve with potato salad.

OLD-STYLE KIPPERED HERRINGS

Clean and skin some large salted herrings, slice them in 2–3 pieces (according to size), then place them together again so that they look whole, and garnish with a ribbon of finely chopped onion on one side, and one of chopped parsley on the other. Serve with hot potatoes and butter pats.

FRIED HERRINGS IN SWEET-SOUR MARINADE

Fry the herrings and arrange in a deep dish. Make a dressing by boiling 2 oz. sugar and 2 tbsps. water together, allowing it to cool, then adding ¼ pint vinegar, 1 tbsp. salad oil and pepper to taste. Cut an onion into rings or chop it, place on top of the herrings and pour dressing over. Serve cold.

THOUSAND HERRINGS

Cover some salted herring fillets with thick sour cream, and sprinkle thickly with chopped chives.

SALTED HERRINGS

Wash and scale 6–12 fish, leaving the heads on. Lay them on a layer of salt, cover with a second layer and place a weighted dish on top. Leave until all the salt dissolves—about 2–3 weeks. Soak for 24 hours before using, changing water frequently.

PICKLED HERRINGS WITH EGGS

Cut or chop the pickled herrings into small pieces, and mix with some mashed hard-boiled eggs. Add some mayonnaise, and serve on rather thick slices of buttered wholemeal or brown bread. Slices of tomato or a few capers may be used as garnish.

FETTERED HERRINGS

Clean some salted herrings carefully, remove the skin and bones and trim the fillets neatly; lay them in a shallow dish and draw them through alternate rings of onions and tomatoes. Dress with a marinade of one part vinegar to two parts salad oil.

ASTRID HERRINGS

Soak some salted herrings overnight in cold water. The next day, clean and cut into fillets; cut each fillet in three, cover with a mayonnaise sauce and garnish with a ribbon of chopped parsley, one of minced hard-boiled eggs and one of sliced tomatoes and pickles.

ROLLMOPS

Clean, skin and cut some small salted herrings into fillets. Soak for 10 hours in fresh water, then wipe dry. Place some thinly sliced onions and finely cut dill on the upper side of the fillets, and roll them firmly, spearing with a cocktail stick to prevent their unrolling. Place in a jar in layers, alternating with layers of bay leaves, cloves, allspice and mustard seeds. Boil some vinegar and salad oil together, adding sugar to taste; when the liquid is cooled slightly, pour it over the herrings, which must then stand for a couple of days before being served.

MARINATED HERRINGS

Soak some salted herrings for 8 hours in plenty of fresh water. A couple of hours before they are to be used, skin, clean, cut into fillets, and lay them in a marinade of vinegar, sugar, pepper and plenty of onions. Just before serving, remove the fillets from the marinade and place them on a platter, letting them overlap one another. Garnish with onion rings.

PRAWN MAYONNAISE

Shell the prawns and mix with a mayonnaise sauce to which some whipped cream and chopped parsley have been added. Serve in small glasses, with slices or rolls of wholemeal bread and butter.

ANCHOVY EGGS WITH MAYONNAISE

Hard-boil some eggs and when cold cut in half and remove the yolks. Pound these with chopped parsley, whipped cream and 1 fillet of anchovy to each egg yolk. Add a little olive oil, vinegar and mustard and refill the egg whites with the mixture. Serve with lettuce hearts, mayonnaise and sliced chicken (if available).

THE DANISH WAY WITH SANDWICHES

Danish open sandwiches are easy to make and interesting to eat. The Danish word for them is *smørrebrød*, which freely translated means " buttered bread." They are Denmark's national dish.

There are certain well-known and traditional smørrebrød, invariably made up of the same ingredients and prepared in the same way, which are always obtainable in Danish and Swedish restaurants. But there is no reason why you should not prepare other smørrebrød from a combination of ingredients to your own liking. Work on the simple principle of a generous portion of topping, artistically arranged on a single piece of well-buttered bread and gaily garnished. Rye bread is used in Denmark, but any firm-textured bread, white or brown, is equally suitable; crispbread can also be used. Make the sandwiches just before they are to be served.

Cut the bread into slices about 4 by 2 inches. Spread the butter thickly, leaving no bare edges —this helps to keep the topping in place as well as adding considerably to the taste. Place the slices of meat or other topping in position, folding them if possible to give the smörrebröd a little height. Add a garnish carefully chosen to give colour and bring out the flavours.

Some easy suggestions are :

Liver pâté with gherkin and a beetroot twist.
Eggs, hard-boiled and sliced, with sliced tomato.
Ham with lettuce, scrambled eggs and cress.
Pork luncheon meat, sweet pickle, cucumber.
Salami with onion rings.
Tongue with Russian salad and a tomato twist.
Bacon, crisp-grilled, with scrambled eggs.
Chopped pork, potato salad, watercress, sliced tomato.
Chopped ham, hard-boiled egg and chives.

Garnishes

These can include anything from the simple sprig of parsley to one of the following :

Radish Roses : Leave about ½ inch of green stalk. Cut the radish in sections down from the base towards the stalk. Leave in cold water until they open like flowers.

Onion Rings : Cut the onion crosswise. Use the rings in graduated sizes or singly to enclose another garnish such as chopped egg or beetroot.

Tomato Twists : Cut a firm tomato in slices across the centre. Slit each piece through the centre of the core, leaving a piece at the top holding the two halves together; turn the halves in opposite directions to make the twist. Use beetroot, lemon or cucumber similarly.

Celery Curls : Cut very thin shreds lengthwise from a stalk of celery. Soak in cold or iced water until curled—about 1 hour.

Red Pepper Julienne : Cut red or green peppers into very thin strips, cutting across the vegetable and removing any pith or seeds.

Gherkin Fans : Use long thin gherkins and cut lengthwise into thin slices, but leave them joined at one end. Spread out the strips so that they overlap slightly, like a fan.

Egg Strips : Allow 4 eggs to ½ pint milk, well beaten, strained and seasoned; cook slowly until set over warm water, then leave till cold. Cut in strips for garnishing. As a quick alternative, scramble the eggs and press them lightly while cooling.

Horseradish Salad : Grate fresh horseradish into whipped cream; flavour with lemon juice and a little sugar.

Meat Jelly : Make aspic jelly by the usual method, adding a little meat extract and gravy browning for flavour and colour.

Here is a reminder list of some of the many possible ingredients that can be included in *smørrebrød.*

Fish :	Meat and Poultry :
Salt and spiced herrings	Roast beef
Kipper fillets	Roast lamb
Anchovy fillets	Roast veal
Sliced smoked salmon	Roast pork
Smoked eel	Brisket
Sardines	Ham, sliced or diced
Sliced cod's roe	Grilled bacon rashers
Cod's roe paste	Salami
Plaice fillets	Liver sausage
Sole fillets	Liver pâté
Sliced cod	Breakfast sausage
Fresh salmon	Raw minced beef
Caviare	Tongue
Lobster	Thinly sliced fried
Crab and crab paste	liver
Crayfish	Cooked chicken
Prawns	Cooked duck
Shrimps	Cooked goose
Oysters	

Cheese :	
Cream cheese	Stilton
Danish Blue	Gruyère
Gorgonzola	Petit Suisse
Cheddar	Danish Port Salut

Other Ingredients and Accompaniments :	
Hard-boiled eggs	Sliced lemon or lemon
Scrambled egg	fans, etc.
Raw eggs	Chopped chives
Sliced cucumber	Chopped parsley
Sliced tomato	Chopped dill
Horseradish	Mayonnaise
Onion rings	Rémoulade sauce
Lettuce leaves	Béarnaise sauce
Gherkin	Chutney
Pickled beetroot	Mustard pickle

Snitter : Danish open sandwiches made about half their usual size, so that they can be easily eaten with the fingers, are called *snitter ;* they are admirable for buffet parties.

ROAST DUCK STUFFED WITH APPLES AND PRUNES

1 duck	¾ pint giblet stock
4 oz. prunes	½ oz. butter
½ lb. cooking apples	½ oz. flour
Salt and pepper	

Put the giblets into a pan with 1 pint water and simmer for 1 hour. Wash and stone the prunes and cut each into 4 ; peel the apples and cut into quarters. Wash the duck well and dry with a clean cloth, then rub inside and outside with salt and pepper. Fill the inside with the prunes and apples, using enough to fill the duck completely, and sew up with string. Truss in the usual way, place in a tin without any fat, and cook in a hot oven (450° F., mark 8) for 20 minutes. Take ¾ pint giblet stock and baste the duck, repeating every ¼ hour during the cooking. Reduce the heat to moderate (350° F., mark 4) when basting is commenced and roast in all for about 1½ hours. Remove the strings and keep the duck hot while making gravy. Serve with sweet browned potatoes.

Pour the stock from the roasting tin into a basin and carefully skim off all the fat from the top. Melt the butter in the roasting tin, mix in the flour and add the stock ; bring to the boil, stirring well, and add some seasoning, also browning if necessary.

PORK TENDERLOIN

For a simple but delicious meal it is quite sufficient to boil the meat for 20 minutes and serve with a selection of fresh vegetables. For a more sophisticated dish, the meat can be glazed and served with a wine gravy, as follows :

Place the tenderloin or fillet in a saucepan with cold water to cover. Bring to the boil, lower the heat and simmer for 20 minutes ; remove the meat from the water and dry it. Put several knobs of butter in the bottom of a meat pan, put the tenderloin in the middle and spread a thick layer of Demerara sugar (about 2 tbsps.) over it. Dot with 2–3 knobs of butter, place 4 thin slices of raw orange (unpeeled) on top, then pour a little red wine into the pan. Place in a moderately hot oven (425° F., mark 7) for 10–15 minutes, till the glazing is a pleasant brown.

Make a thick gravy to serve with the meat, using the stock from the meat, flour, gravy browning and some of the red wine left in the pan. Serve with a variety of plain boiled vegetables, young carrots, whole cauliflower (Danes remove all the green and serve only the white), small white potatoes and sugar-browned potatoes (see recipe). Arrange all on a large dish, with the thickly sliced meat in the centre. Sprinkle the cauliflower and carrots with chopped parsley.

STEGT SVINEKAM MED ÆBLER OG SVESKER (ROAST PORK WITH APPLES AND PRUNES)

5–6 lb. loin of pork	1 quart peeled and
2 tsps. salt	cored apples cut into
1 tsp. sugar	¼-inch slices
¼ tsp. pepper	1 cup water
1 cup prunes, stoned	

Partially separate the meat from the ribs of the pork loin, using a sharp knife. Mix the salt, sugar and pepper and sprinkle some on all cut surfaces of the pork, then stuff it with the apple slices and prunes ; tie securely and sprinkle the outside with the remaining seasonings.

Stand the joint on the rib ends in a shallow baking tin and roast for 1 hour in a moderate oven (350° F., mark 3), then pour on the water and roast for 1½ hours longer or till the meat is very tender, basting it often. Put it on a large hot dish and keep warm.

Make a brown gravy with the juices in the tin, after pouring off some of the fat ; include 1 cup single cream and 1 tbsp. red-currant jelly.

The Danes serve this meat with boiled or mashed potatoes, red cabbage, red-currant jelly and pickles.

BRÆNDENDE KÆRLIGHED (BACON AND POTATOES)

1 lb. mealy potatoes	½ lb. onions
⅛ pint milk	4–6 oz. diced bacon
3 oz. butter	Sliced beetroot and
Salt and pepper to taste	cooked French beans

Peel the potatoes, cut them into fingers, cook until tender in unsalted water and mash, adding the milk, 1 oz. butter, salt and pepper. Slice the onions very thinly. Heat the remaining butter and fry the onions until light brown and crisp. (If preferred, boil them in an unlidded saucepan before frying them.)

Fry the bacon until crisp. Mix potatoes, bacon and onion and garnish with beetroot and beans.

ROLLED HAM WITH CHEESE FILLING

1 oz. butter	6 oz. Samsoe cheese
1 oz. flour	8 slices ham
¼ pint milk	2 tbsps. tomato purée
2 egg yolks	mixed with 4 tbsps.
Salt and black pepper	milk

Melt the butter, gradually mix in the flour and cook for a minute ; pour in the milk slowly, stirring all the time, and cook for 3 minutes. Let the sauce cool, then mix in the egg yolks and salt and pepper to taste. Cut the cheese into cubes (first setting aside sufficient thin slices to garnish the finished dish); add the cheese cubes to the sauce and put 2 tsps. of this cheese filling on each slice of ham, roll up and place in an ovenproof dish. Cover the rolls with tomato purée and place the thin slices of cheese on the top. Cook for about 15 minutes in a moderate oven (375° F., mark 5).

BODIL'S PORK SPECIALITY

2 fillets of pork	6 sage leaves
2 oz. butter	Seasoning
2 onions	6 oz. button mush-
1½ oz. flour	rooms
¾ pint stock	8 oz. shelled peas
4 tbsps. tomato purée	12–18 asparagus tips
4 bay leaves	Boiled rice

Cut the meat into slices. Melt the fat in a pan and fry the meat until it is brown on both sides, then put it into a casserole. Slice the onions and fry them in the fat until tender and lightly coloured, then add this to the meat, draining off as much fat as possible. Add the flour to the pan and heat gently until it has browned, then gradually add the stock. Bring to the boil and put in the tomato purée, bay leaves and sage. Season well, pour over the pork and put into a moderate oven (350° F., mark 4) for ¾ hour. Peel the mushrooms and pour boiling water on to them, leave for 3 minutes, drain well and add these to the casserole. Cook the peas and asparagus tips separately and add them for garnish. Serve with boiled rice.

BAKED LIVER

4 slices of calves' liver	2 cooking apples, chop-
A little flour	ped, peeled and
Salt and pepper	coarsely grated
Butter for frying	A little cream or top of
1 large onion, chopped	the milk
8 rashers of streaky bacon	

Coat the liver with flour seasoned with salt and pepper and fry in the butter for a minute on each side; remove from the pan and fry the chopped onion in the same butter. Place the liver slices in a fireproof dish, cover with the onions, place the peeled coarsely grated apples on top and arrange the bacon rashers neatly across the whole dish. Add a little cream or top of milk to the butter in the pan, heat and pour over the dish. Put in a hot oven (450° F., mark 8) for 10 minutes, then reduce the heat to moderate (350° F., mark 4) and cook for 30 minutes. Serve with boiled potatoes.

LIVER TERRINE

1 lb. pig's liver	1 garlic clove
¼ lb. fat bacon	½ pint thick white sauce
1 small tin of anchovy	Salt and pepper
fillets	12 rashers of streaky
4 eggs	bacon

Mince the liver, fat bacon and anchovy fillets finely, then put the mixture through the mincer again, and finally sieve it to ensure a really smooth result. Mix it with the beaten eggs, pounded garlic and sauce and season to taste. Line a shallow ovenproof dish with the bacon rashers, fill with the liver mixture and place in a dish containing some cold water. Bake in a slow oven (320° F., mark 2) for 2 hours. Cover the top of the liver mixture with greaseproof paper, put a heavy plate or something similar on top and leave for 24 hours in a cold place before serving.

FORLOREN HARE
(BAKED MEAT LOAF)

7 oz. beef	Salt and pepper
7 oz. lean pork	2 oz. fat bacon or some
2 oz. breadcrumbs	olive oil
2 oz. oatmeal	1½ pints milk
3 tbsps. cream	1 oz. flour
2 eggs	Tomato ketchup

Mince the meats three times, then knead with the breadcrumbs, oatmeal, cream, eggs and seasonings. Shape the mixture like a thick sausage, place thin slices of fat bacon over it, or brush it with oil, pour the milk over and bake for about 30 minutes in a moderately hot oven (400° F., mark 6). Thicken the gravy with the flour, and season with salt, pepper and ketchup. Serve with sweet browned potatoes and raw vegetable salad. (See recipes.)

FRIKADELLER MED RØDKAAL
(MEAT BALLS WITH RED CABBAGE)

1 lb. meat without	4 oz. plain flour
bones (e.g., ½ lb.	Pepper
pork and ½ lb. veal	Chopped onion or onion
or beef)	juice
1–1½ tsps. salt	Mashed potato (optional)
1 egg	Lard for frying
½ pint milk	

Wash the meat, remove the sinews and cut the meat into small pieces; mince it 2 or 3 times, adding the salt. Whip the egg and milk together and stir into the flour, then add gradually to the minced meat. Finally add more salt, if necessary, a pinch of pepper and a little chopped onion, or onion juice to taste. If desired, add boiled mashed potato, in the proportion of 1 part potato to 2 parts meat : the mixture should be fairly thick. Heat the fat in a frying pan and spoon in the mixture in large balls. Cook them on all sides, until light brown and cooked through. Serve with red cabbage (see recipe).

ÆGGEKAGE
(EGG AND BACON CAKE)

Fry or grill a few rashers of streaky bacon and keep them hot. Put 1 tbsp. cornflour in a bowl ; break 4 eggs into it, add ¼ pint milk and salt and pepper to taste. Beat it all up with a whisk. Heat an omelette pan and melt a good knob of butter in it. Pour in the egg mixture and cook quickly until nearly set, shaking the pan from time to time. Arrange the cooked bacon on the top and turn out on to a hot dish. Garnish with chopped chives.

ÆBLESFLÆSK
(FRIED BACON WITH FRIED APPLES)

Slice thinly and rind ½ lb. bacon or pork, put it into a hot frying pan and fry over low heat till crisp. (Pour off the surplus fat during the cooking, or bacon will not become crisp.) Fry 2 lb. peeled chopped apples in the fat and add a little sugar. Place the bacon in a serving dish with the apple arranged round it.

SWEET BROWNED POTATOES

Wash, boil and peel 2 lb. potatoes ; if large, cut each into 4–8 equal-sized pieces. Melt 2 oz. sugar, add 2 oz. butter or lard and heat until lightly browned. Rinse the potatoes in cold water, put into the sugar and stir well until they are evenly golden.

SWEET BROWNED CARROTS

Clean 1½ lb. carrots and cut them in long, thin slices. Melt 1½ oz. sugar and heat until brown, then mix with 1½ oz. butter. Add the carrots and stir well, gradually adding ¼ pint water, then cook until the carrots are tender. (Alternatively, the carrots may be boiled first, then browned.) Garnish with hard-boiled eggs, cut into quarters.

RED CABBAGE

Shred the cabbage and put it in either a saucepan or a flameproof casserole, with a lump of butter and a few tablespoonfuls each of water and vinegar. Season with salt and sugar, cover, bring to the boil and simmer for 2–3 hours, till quite tender. About 10 minutes before serving, add a little red-currant jelly.

CHEESY APPLE RINGS

2 cooking apples	½ oz. finely chopped
A little sugar	roasted almonds
1 pkt. Danish cream	1 tsp. finely chopped
cheese	stem ginger

Peel and core the apples, cut in thick slices and dredge lightly with sugar, then grill until tender but still holding their shape. Blend the cream cheese with the almonds and ginger, spread on the apple slices and quickly brown under the grill. Serve as a garnish for gammon rashers.

AGURKESALAT
(CUCUMBER SALAD)

2 cucumbers	Juice of ½ a lemon
1 tbsp. salt	2–3 tbsps. sugar
¼ pint vinegar	A dash of black pepper
¼ pint water	

Do not peel the cucumbers unless the skin is tough. Wash the cucumbers well, slice very finely, sprinkle with salt, put in a bowl, with a weighted plate on top, and leave for some hours or overnight. Discard the juice, rinse off the excess salt and dry the cucumber slices in a cloth. Make a dressing of vinegar, water, lemon juice, sugar and pepper and pour it over the cucumber ; let stand for about ½ hour. Serve as a side dish with fried meats, roasts and chicken, or use to garnish open sandwiches.

PICKLED BEETROOTS

2 lb. beetroots	½ pint water
1 pint vinegar	2–4 oz. sugar

Wash the beetroots but do not peel; cook in plenty of water until tender for 1½–2 hours. Allow to cool, then peel, slice and put into a jar. Bring the vinegar, water and sugar to the boil and pour over the beets until they are completely covered.

These pickled beetroots will keep for 2–3 weeks, or longer if strips of raw horseradish are boiled with the vinegar.

Serve with any kind of roast or liver pâté, and with salads.

ASPARAGUS IN TOMATO RINGS

Choose large tomatoes, cut each into 2–3 thick slices, then take out the pulp, leaving only a ring. Thread cooked asparagus tips through these rings until each is full, and serve on lettuce, with oil and vinegar dressing to which a few finely chopped herbs have been added.

POTATO SALAD

Peel and slice 2 small onions and boil until tender in $\frac{1}{3}$ pint stock, water or milk, with 2 oz. butter. Add $\frac{1}{4}$ pint vinegar, seasonings, and a little sugar. Slice 2 lb. cooked peeled potatoes about $\frac{1}{4}$ inch thick, add to the mixture, bring to the boil and cook for a few minutes.

RAW VEGETABLE SALAD

Cut up 2 large apples and shred 2 large carrots, then mix with 1–2 tbsps. sugar, the juice of $\frac{1}{2}$ lemon and horseradish to taste. This salad must be eaten immediately.

CHEESE GÂTEAU

$\frac{1}{2}$ lb. flour	2 tbsps. water
Salt	$\frac{1}{4}$ lb. Danish Blue cheese
$\frac{3}{4}$ lb. butter	$\frac{1}{2}$ lb. cream cheese
1 lb. grated Samsoe cheese	A little cream

Sieve the flour and a pinch of salt, then rub in $\frac{1}{2}$ lb. butter with the fingertips until the mixture is like fine breadcrumbs. Add the grated cheese and the water. Knead lightly to make a smooth dough and let it rest in a cool place for at least 3 hours. Roll it out thinly and cut 3 rounds 9 inches in diameter, using a cake tin or plate as a cutting guide. Put on a baking sheet and bake in a moderately hot oven (425° F., mark 7) for 10–15 minutes. Remove the rounds carefully with a palette knife and let them cool on a rack.

Now make two separate fillings. Mix the Danish Blue cheese and the remaining butter to a soft consistency. Soften the cream cheese with a little cream and add a pinch of salt—the mixture should be soft enough to pipe.

Spread the Danish Blue mixture on one layer of pastry. Spread the second layer with half the cream cheese filling and place on the first round, then put on the third pastry round. Pour the remaining cream cheese mixture into a forcing bag fitted with a fairly large plain nozzle and decorate the top and sides of the gâteau.

QUICK APPLE FLAN

2 oz. butter	1 oz. sugar
2 oz. plain flour	A few almonds
1 tbsp. cold water	A little milk
1 cooking apple	

Rub the butter into the flour, add the cold water and mix to a dough ; roll out on a lightly floured board into an oblong about 5 by 9 inches. Peel the apple, cut into thin slices and arrange the pieces neatly along the centre of the dough, leaving 1 inch clear all round. Sprinkle the apple with half the sugar. Fold the sides of the pastry up over the apples to form a border, but do not entirely cover them. Brush the pastry edge with a little milk. Sprinkle on the remaining sugar and the chopped almonds, pressing them slightly into the dough. Place on a baking sheet and bake in a moderate oven (350° F., mark 4) for about $\frac{1}{2}$ hour.

BAKED FRUIT SALAD

Soak 1 cup dried prunes and 1 cup dried apricots in warm water for several hours (or overnight). Butter a large flat ovenproof dish and on it arrange 4 bananas, quartered, the drained prunes and apricots and a few stoned raisins. Add 3 tbsps. honey to 1 cup fresh orange juice, stir until well mixed, then pour over the fruit. Grate a little lemon rind over the dish and add a few small knobs of butter. Bake in a moderate oven (350° F., mark 4) for about $\frac{1}{2}$ hour. Serve with cream or plain, as preferred. This is a good winter sweet.

RØDGRØD
(FRUIT FOOL)

Prepare about $2\frac{1}{2}$ lb. mixed red-currants, black-currants and raspberries, cook with 1 quart water and $\frac{1}{2}$ lb. sugar until soft, then sieve. Mix about 1 oz. sago with a little of the purée, stir this into the rest of the purée and cook gently for a few minutes, until thickened. Pour into the serving dish, sprinkle with sugar (this prevents a skin forming) and leave to cool. Serve with cream or a vanilla-flavoured white sauce.

RØDGRØD MED FLØDE
(FRUIT FOOL WITH CREAM)

$1\frac{3}{4}$ lb. red-currants	Cornflour
$1\frac{3}{4}$ lb. raspberries	Vanilla essence
$1\frac{1}{2}$ pints water	Blanched almonds
Sugar to taste	Cream and sugar to serve

Wash the currants and raspberries, add the water and bring to the boil. When all the juice has boiled out, remove the berries from the heat, sieve, and put the purée back into the pan. Sweeten to taste and thicken with the cornflour, using 1 oz. to every $\frac{3}{4}$ pint of purée. Cook for a few minutes, then add a few drops of vanilla essence and while the mixture is still hot, pour it into a glass bowl. When it begins to set, decorate the surface with a pattern of blanched almonds. Serve with sugar and cream.

STRAWBERRY GÂTEAU

8 oz. flour	Vanilla essence
4–6 oz. butter	Red-currant jelly
2½ oz. icing sugar	½ lb. strawberries
2 egg yolks	Cream

Sieve the flour into a bowl and rub in the fat. Add the sugar, egg yolks and a few drops of vanilla essence and work to a smooth paste. Put in a cool place for about 30 minutes. Roll out into a large round about ¼ inch thick, prick all over and bake in a moderate oven (350° F., mark 4) for about 20 minutes, then cool. Brush the top with a thick glaze made by simmering some red-currant jelly in a small pan. Top with strawberries (halved if large) and decorate with cream.

ÆBLE PINDSVIN
(PORCUPINE APPLES)

3 large apples	½ cup shredded toasted
2½ cups water	almonds
¼ cup sugar	Whipped cream or
2 tbsps. lemon juice	custard

Peel the apples, then, starting at the blossom end, cut each in half and core it. Bring the water, sugar and lemon juice to the boil in a large shallow pan. Add the apples and simmer, covered, until tender, turning the pieces once. Arrange the apple halves, cut side down, on a deep serving dish.

Boil the syrup in which apples were cooked until it is reduced to 2 cups. Meanwhile, tuck some of the shredded almonds into the rounded side of each apple half. Pour on the syrup, cool and chill. Serve with cream or custard sauce.

BONDEPIGE MED SLØR
(PEASANT GIRL WITH VEIL)

8 oz. breadcrumbs	Lemon juice
3 oz. brown sugar	Sugar to taste
2 oz. butter or margarine	¼ pint double cream
	2 oz. grated chocolate
1½ lb. cooking apples	

Mix the crumbs and sugar together and fry in the hot fat until crisp. Peel and core the apples and cook them to pulp in a very little water with a good squeeze of lemon juice added, and with sugar to taste. Put alternate layers of the fried crumb mixture and the apple pulp into a glass dish, finishing with a layer of the crumbs. When the pudding is quite cold, spread the stiffly whipped cream on top, and sprinkle with the grated chocolate.

A variant of this recipe calls for alternate layers of the fried crumbs, hot apple purée and raspberry jam, and omits the grated chocolate.

KlEJNER
(FRIED PASTRIES)

3 oz. butter	2 oz. sugar
9 oz. flour	Grated peel of ½ a lemon
2 eggs	2 lb. lard for deep frying
1 tbsp. cream	

Rub the butter into the flour with the finger-tips until the mixture is like fine breadcrumbs. Add the eggs, cream, sugar and grated lemon peel. Mix the dough with a wooden spoon, then knead lightly to make it smooth. Roll it out very thinly and cut into diamonds. Make a slit in the centre of each and put one end of the diamond through this slit. Deep-fry in the hot lard until golden-brown—do not put too many in at a time. Drain well.

CITRONFROMAGE
(LEMON SOUFFLÉ)

2½ heaped tsps. powdered gelatine	4 oz. sugar
4 eggs	The juice of 2 lemons
The grated peel of 1½ lemons	½ pint cream or top of the milk

Soak and dissolve the gelatine in a little water. Stir the egg yolks until white with the lemon peel and the sugar, add the lemon juice, the dissolved gelatine and finally the stiffly whipped egg whites and half the whipped cream. Stir carefully until the soufflé starts to become stiff; pour it into a prepared soufflé dish, and when set decorate with the rest of the whipped cream, piping it in a decorative pattern.

DANISH PASTRIES

1 oz. baker's yeast	6 oz. butter
¼ pint milk	½ lb. almond paste
12 oz. plain bread flour	Egg to glaze
A pinch of salt	Glacé icing
2 eggs	Flaked almonds
1 oz. caster sugar	Sugar and currants

34

Cream the yeast with a little of the milk. Sieve together the flour and salt and make a well in the centre. Beat the eggs and put them with the yeast, sugar and remaining milk into the centre of the flour. Gradually work in the flour, beat the dough well, put into a lightly greased polythene bag or a greased bowl covered with polythene and leave in a warm place for 15 minutes. Lightly knead the dough on a floured board and roll it out thinly.

Knead the butter on a floured board till pliable and press out thinly. Place it on the dough and fold this over as for puff pastry; roll and fold twice, allow to stand in a cool place, then give 2 further rolls and folds, followed by another rest in a cool place. Finally, roll out the pastry to $\frac{1}{4}$ inch thick and use as required. Three typical variations are given below.

ALMOND CRESCENTS

Cut triangles of dough with a $5\frac{1}{2}$-inch base. Place on each a sausage-shaped piece of almond paste, roll up and form into crescents. Place on a greased baking tray and prove in a warm place for about 15–20 minutes, when they should be light and puffy. Brush over with beaten egg and bake in a moderately hot oven (425° F., mark 7) for 15–20 minutes, until golden-brown. While still hot, spread with glacé icing and sprinkle with flaked nuts.

ALMOND WHIRLS

Cut $3\frac{1}{2}$-inch squares of dough and snip each corner to within $\frac{1}{2}$ inch of the centre. Put a small ball of almond paste in the centre of each square and draw alternate corners to the centre, overlapping them windmill-fashion. Prove and finish as above.

CURRANT TWISTS

Cut large oblongs about 12 by 9 inches, brush over lightly with beaten egg and cover with a layer of caster sugar and cleaned currants. Roll up, cut into $\frac{1}{2}$-inch slices and prove and finish as above.

LAGKAGE

$\frac{1}{2}$ lb. butter	Vanilla cream (see
$\frac{1}{2}$ lb. caster sugar	below)
4 eggs	Fruit for filling
$\frac{1}{2}$ lb. plain flour	Lemon glacé icing

Cream the butter and sugar. Beat the eggs and add them gradually, then slowly mix in the flour. The consistency should resemble that of a sponge cake mixture. Grease 3 sponge tins, about 8 inches in diameter, and pour a third of the mixture into each. Bake in a moderate oven (350° F., mark 4) for 10 minutes; the layers should be about $\frac{1}{4}$ inch thick when cooked. Cool. Sandwich the layers together alternately with vanilla cream and some kind of soft fruit (in summer raspberries, strawberries, red-currants, etc.; in winter canned sliced apricots, peaches, etc.). Decorate the top of the cake with lemon glacé icing and a few pieces of the fruit used inside the cake.

VANILLA CREAM

2 egg yolks	$\frac{1}{2}$ pint milk
2 tbsps. caster sugar	1 vanilla pod
1 tbsp. cornflour	

Whisk together the egg yolks, sugar and corn-flour, then add a little warm milk. Boil the remainder of milk with the vanilla pod. Gradually add egg and sugar mixture to the boiled milk (removing the pod) and then return to the heat and warm till the mixture cooks and thickens. The cream should be thick enough to spread over the cake.

KRANSEKAGE
(DANISH CHRISTMAS CAKE)

$1\frac{1}{2}$ lb. ground almonds	6 egg whites
$1\frac{1}{2}$ lb. icing sugar	

Mix the ground almonds and icing sugar and heat gently for about 5–10 minutes, stirring all the time. Let the mixture cool and mix in the egg whites (which should not be whipped). Put the mixture in a forcing bag fitted with a plain $\frac{1}{2}$–$\frac{3}{4}$ inch nozzle and pipe on to a greased baking sheet in a dozen or more rings of graduated sizes (the largest about 9 inches). Bake in a moderate oven (350° F., mark 4) till pale golden-brown. Put together whilst slightly warm, joining the layers with royal icing. Decorate with piped icing flags and a Santa Claus or similar figure, as available.

CHRISTMAS BISCUITS
Basic Mixture

10 oz. butter	1 egg
16 oz. flour	6 oz. sugar

Rub the butter into the flour with the fingertips until the mixture is like fine breadcrumbs; add the egg and sugar. Mix the dough with a wooden spoon, then knead lightly to make it smooth.

Finskbrød (Finnish Bread): Use a third of the basic mixture. Roll the dough out into long " sausages " 1 inch in diameter; flatten on top with a rolling pin. Brush the " sausages " over with egg white and sprinkle with a mixture of sugar and chopped almonds. Cut into little sticks about $\frac{1}{2}$ inch wide, put on a greased baking tray and bake in a moderately hot oven (425° F., mark 7) for about 10–15 minutes, until light brown in colour.

Jødekager (Jewish Cakes): Use a third of the basic dough. Roll it out thinly and cut out biscuits, using a $1\frac{1}{2}$-inch pastry cutter. Brush the tops with beaten egg and sprinkle with a mixture of ground cinnamon, sugar and chopped almonds. Bake in a moderately hot oven (425° F., mark 7) for about 5 minutes, until light brown in colour.

Vaniliekranse (Vanilla Rings): To one-third of the basic dough add 2 oz. ground almonds

and 1 tsp. vanilla essence. Put this soft mixture into a forcing bag fitted with a large nozzle and force out on to a greased baking tray in rings about 2 inches in diameter. Bake in a moderately hot oven (425° F., mark 7) for 8–10 minutes, until light brown in colour.

CHERRY BUTTONS

5 oz. butter	Green and red pre-
6½ oz. flour	served cherries to
2½ oz. granulated sugar	decorate
2 egg yolks	

Rub the butter into the flour, then add the sugar and egg yolks. Form the dough into a " sausage " about 1 inch in diameter, cut into pieces about 1 inch long and roll into balls. Press half a cherry into each, place on a baking sheet and bake for about 10 minutes in a hot oven (450° F., mark 8) until lightly browned.

CURRANT SQUARES

4 oz. butter	4 oz. flour
2 small eggs	2 oz. currants
4 oz. granulated sugar	1 oz. chopped almonds
Grated rind of 1 lemon	

Melt the butter until liquid but not hot. Whisk the eggs and the sugar together, add the grated lemon rind and melted butter and then the sieved flour, forming a moist dough. Spread the mixture thinly on shallow baking trays. This quantity is sufficient to fill a tray measuring 12 by 10 inches 5–6 times. Sprinkle with the currants and chopped almonds and bake in a moderate oven (350° F., mark 4) for about 15 minutes. When the edges are lightly brown, remove from the oven and cut immediately into small biscuits about 2 inches by 1 inch.

BRUNE KAGER
(BROWN CAKE)

4 oz. butter	½ tsp. ground cloves
4 oz. sugar	½ tsp. ground cinnamon
2 oz. golden syrup	1 tsp. ground ginger
1 oz. finely chopped blanched almonds	½ tsp. bicarbonate of soda
1 oz. finely chopped candied peel	8 oz. flour

Put the butter, sugar and syrup into a saucepan and heat gently ; when the mixture reaches boiling point, remove it from the heat. Stir in the almonds, peel, cloves, cinnamon and ginger. Dissolve the bicarbonate of soda in a very little water and stir into the ingredients in the pan ; cool the mixture until lukewarm. Gradually stir in the sieved flour, using a wooden spoon. Turn on to a floured board and form into a roll

about 2 inches in diameter, wrap in aluminium foil or greaseproof paper and keep in the refrigerator or a cool place overnight.

Using a sharp knife, slice the dough as thinly as possible. Place the biscuits on a greased baking tray and bake in a moderately hot oven (400° F., mark 6) until they begin to brown— about 8–10 minutes. Remove carefully with a palette knife, cool on a wire rack and store in an airtight tin. These are wafer-crisp, nutty biscuits, with a subtle, spicy flavour.

WHIPPED CREAM CORNETS

2 eggs	Butter
7 oz. caster sugar	Strawberry preserve
4 oz. flour	Fresh whipped cream
5 tbsps. water	Fresh strawberries

Beat the eggs and sugar until light in colour and thick. Add the sieved flour and fold it in carefully with the water. Butter a baking sheet and drop small spoonfuls of batter in heaps, well apart. Bake these in a moderate oven (375° F., mark 5) for about 8 minutes, until pale golden-brown. Working quickly, take one at a time and form into a cornet ; to preserve the shape, let each cool in a cream horn case, or in the top of an empty milk bottle. Fill the cornets with preserve and cream and decorate with fresh fruit.

BUTTER RINGS

8 oz. butter	1 egg white
8 oz. flour	A little granulated sugar
1 tbsp. cream	

Rub the butter into the flour, add the cream and knead lightly. Let the pastry rest in a cold place for 30 minutes. Roll out into very thin " sausages," cut into 3 lengths and form into individual rings. Brush the top of each with egg white and dust with granulated sugar. Bake on a greased oven sheet for 8–10 minutes in a moderately hot oven (400° F., mark 6).

COPENHAGEN COOKIES

4 oz. butter	10 green preserved
4 oz. flour	cherries
2 oz. icing sugar	10 blanched almonds
10 red glacé cherries	

Rub the butter into the flour and add the sugar, chopped cherries and chopped almonds. Knead lightly into a smooth dough and roll into a " sausage " about 2 inches in diameter ; wrap in greaseproof paper and place in the refrigerator until firm. Cut into very thin slices, place on a baking sheet and bake for about 15 minutes in a moderately hot oven (400° F., mark 6).

FRANCE possibly owes her gastronomic leadership to her geographical position. In the centre of Europe with a coastline that stretches from the cold North Sea to the warm Mediterranean, and a climate that embraces both snowy winters and nearly tropical summers, France is uniquely able to take advantage of almost every type of cuisine. From her neighbours she has inherited touches of the rich solidity of Belgium, the teutonic sausage and sauerkraut of Alsace-Lorraine, cheeses and fondues from Switzerland, dishes " au gratin " from Italy ; and her own countryside provides the sweetest butter and cream, cheese in hundreds of varieties, fish, game, meat and poultry of every conceivable kind, fruits and vegetables, oil, herbs and wheat, as well as wines of a greater range and variety than any other country.

French " classic " cookery, the internationally famous dishes that are found in good hotels and restaurants all over the world, is based on the bourgeois or regional dishes that were brought to Paris at the end of the eighteenth century, when, following the success and esteem won by Carême, chef to Talleyrand, France began to take the place of Italy as the acknowledged leader of European gastronomy. At that time numerous regional restaurants began to spring up, each with its own speciality, its own way of serving the foods of the district. This bourgois cookery is still what is thought of as being " typically French " and has a savour and character that is often, unfortunately, missing from the international French cuisine of the restaurant in New York, London or Stockholm, relying as it does on local ingredients and local produce, and varying quite widely from province to province.

In the North of France, butter is the chief cooking agent and in the South, olive oil is used almost entirely ; the succulent shell fish of Brittany, truffles and fois gras of Bordeaux and Perigord, trout and crayfish of Alsace, Bresse poultry, Burgundy snails and fungi, andouillette and Dijon ham, give place to the salt cod, olives, saffron and tomatoes of Provence.

All over France, breakfast mainly consists of coffee with rolls, croissants, brioches, sweet butter and very often home-made jam. French bakers are among the most talented in the world and they produce wonderful crusty breads and delectable pastries. Luncheon is a meal of heroic preparations and is taken enormously seriously. It is the main meal of the day for many French families and working hours are planned accordingly. Dinner is often simpler but there are no hard and fast rules ; certainly the French approach both meals in a spirit of dedicated anticipation, which ensures a first-class standard of cooking and which other countries might do well to imitate.

France

CONSOMMÉ

35

2 lb. lean beef	2 leeks
1½ lb. beef knuckle	Stalk of celery
with bone	Small onion stuck with
Salt	a clove
2 large carrots	½ clove garlic
1 turnip	Sprig of thyme
1 small parsnip	¼ small bay leaf

Put the meat into a large stockpot with 8 pints of cold water. Bring to the boil and skim thoroughly. Add a tablespoonful of coarse salt and all vegetables and herbs. Simmer for 5 hours. Remove fat and strain through a cloth wrung out in cold water. The consommé can be served with many different garnishes (see below) and the meat and vegetables may be served separately. CHICKEN CONSOMMÉ is made as above, with the addition of a small chicken, previously browned in the oven.

CONSOMMÉ can be served cold. It should be very clear and strong enough to set into a jelly.

Garnishes for Consommés

À l'Alsacienne. Beef consommé with sauerkraut and sausages cut into small rounds.

À la Bourgeoise. Beef consommé with diced carrots, turnips and potatoes, sprinkled with chervil.

Aux cheveux d'ange. Beef consommé with very fine cooked vermicelli added.

Julienne. Beef consommé with thin strips of various vegetables.

À la madrilène. Sieved raw tomato pulp added to the consommé.

Aux œufs pochés. Garnished with a small poached egg for each person.

LOBSTER BISQUE

1 lobster weighing	⅓ cup rice
about 3 lb.	2 pints consommé
6 tbsps. butter	¾ cup fresh cream
1 cup mirepoix (see	Salt, pepper and
below)	cayenne pepper
½ cup white wine	Thyme, bay leaf and
2 tbsps. brandy	parsley

Cut the lobster into small pieces and sauté on a hot fire together with the mirepoix, salt, pepper, parsley, thyme and bay leaf. Set light to the brandy and pour over, add the wine and reduce by two-thirds. Add ½ cup consommé and cook for 10 minutes. Shell the lobster, keeping some of the tail meat for garnishing. Pound the rest of the lobster, together with the shells, in a mortar and add the rice, which has been cooked in the consommé and the lobster liquor. Rub

through a sieve into a saucepan, dilute with the rest of the consommé, boil up, strain and keep hot. Before serving, stir in the butter, cut into small pieces, and the cream. Adjust seasoning, add the cayenne pepper and garnish with the lobster meat which was reserved.

Mirepoix is a mixture of diced vegetables (carrots, onions and celery) cooked slowly in butter until extremely tender but not coloured brown. Herbs and seasoning should be added to taste.

VICHYSSOISE SOUP

4 leeks	2 pints chicken stock
2 oz. butter	2 potatoes
1 minced onion	¼ pint cream
Salt and pepper	Chives or parsley

Prepare the leeks, cut them finely and add to the hot butter with the onion and seasonings; cover and cook slowly without browning. Add the stock and the thinly cut potatoes, cook until the vegetables are tender, then sieve. Adjust the seasonings, stir in the cream and sprinkle with chives or parsley just before dishing up. Serve hot or cold.

POTAGE PRINTANIER
(SPRING SOUP)

3 tbsps. butter or	12 stalks fresh or frozen
margarine	asparagus cut into
3 leeks, finely chopped	1-inch pieces
1 small onion, minced	½ lb. raw spinach
3 potatoes, thinly sliced	leaves, chopped
1 carrot, thinly sliced	rather fine
Salt	Dash of pepper
2 quarts water	1 cup cream
¼ cup raw rice	

In hot butter in saucepan, slowly sauté leeks and onion until tender. Add potatoes, carrot, 1½ tsps. salt, water. Cover, bring to the boil; simmer for 15 minutes.

Stir in rice, asparagus; cover and simmer for 25 minutes.

Add spinach; cover and simmer for 5 minutes. Stir in 4 tsps. salt, pepper, cream. Makes 8 medium helpings.

POTAGE DUBARRY

Peel 2 lb. potatoes, slice thickly, put in a pan and cover them with water. Cut up a cauliflower, using only the flower. Reserve some nice sprigs to cook separately and use for decoration, then add the rest of the cauliflower to the pan, season, cover it with a lid and cook for about 1 hour. When it is tender, sieve, reheat, then thicken with 2 egg yolks mixed with ¼ pint cream or milk. Do not cook after adding the egg yolks, or the soup will curdle. Lastly, add the sprigs of cauliflower.

SOUPE À L'OIGNON
(ONION SOUP)

½ lb. onions	1½ pints stock or water
2 oz. butter	Pepper and salt
1 oz. flour	2 oz. French bread roll

Peel the onions, cut them into very thin slices and then cut across again. Blanch the onion for 5 minutes in boiling water. (This process is not strictly necessary, but it makes the soup more easily digested, and saves time in the later cooking.) Melt 1 oz. butter in a saucepan and fry the onion in this until it is golden-brown. Add the flour, and cook for 2 minutes, stirring frequently. Add the stock or water and season with pepper and salt. Stir over the heat until it boils, then leave to simmer slowly for 10 minutes. Put into the soup tureen the sliced bread and the remaining 1 oz. butter. Pour on the soup, stirring with a spoon to melt the butter, and serve immediately.

Alternatively, the slices of bread may be floated on the soup and covered with grated cheese, and the soup is then heated in a hot oven for a few minutes. In this case the soup must be served in a fireproof casserole.

BOUILLABAISSE
(MEDITERRANEAN FISH STEW)

2 lb. fish (see below), weighed after boning and cutting up	4 cloves
	A sprig of thyme
	A bay leaf
½ lb. tomatoes	Shredded rind of 1
½ lb. onions	orange
¾ lb. carrots	Olive oil
2 oz. sliced red peppers	1 quart water
1 large bunch of parsley	Salt and pepper
2 oz. celery	A pinch of saffron
1 clove of garlic	Chopped parsley
2 shallots	Bread slices
Peppercorns	Dublin Bay prawns

This famous Mediterranean fish soup cannot be exactly reproduced without the traditional *saint-pierres*, *chapons rouges*, *rascasses*, etc., but a similar and excellent savoury dish can be made from 2 lb. of good mixed fish such as hake, John Dory, red mullet, sole, crayfish, etc.

Prepare the fish, and put the chopped heads, tails, bones and trimmings in a large pan with ¼ lb. tomatoes, and the vegetables and flavourings (except the seasoning, saffron and chopped parsley). Moisten the mixture with olive oil, stir well, add water and cook for an hour, adding a seasoning of salt, pepper and saffron half-way through.

Strain the liquor into a clean pan, skim and bring to the boil; add the pieces of fish, with the remaining ¼ lb. tomatoes (sliced) and 1 tbsp. roughly chopped parsley, and simmer until the fish is cooked. Pour on to thick slices of crusty bread laid in soup plates. Serve the fish separately, garnished with halved Dublin Bay prawns.

SAUMON FROID A LA MAYONNAISE VERTE
(COLD SALMON WITH GREEN MAYONNAISE)

1 small salmon	Hard-boiled egg and
Court-bouillon	truffle or black olive
Parsley, cucumber and lemon	Salad

Wipe the salmon, remove only the eyes, and tie the fish in a thin cloth. Prepare the court-bouillon (see recipe below), and lower the fish carefully into it. Let it simmer very gently for 35–45 minutes, then allow the fish to cool in the bouillon. Drain thoroughly, and place on a long dish. Remove the skin carefully, decorate the fish with parsley, cucumber and lemon, and make an " eye " with the white end of a hard-boiled egg and a round of truffle or black olive. Garnish with salad, and serve with green mayonnaise. (See recipe below.)

COURT-BOUILLON

1 pint white wine	A bouquet garni
1 pint water	2 cloves
1 tsp. salt	1 sliced onion
¼ tsp. white pepper	1 sliced carrot

Place all the ingredients in a pan large enough to cook the fish, cover the pan and simmer for 45 minutes; never allow it to boil. There should be enough court-bouillon to cover the fish, so the quantity of ingredients should be varied accordingly. Simmering in court-bouillon is the most common method of preparing fish in France.

SAUCE MAYONNAISE VERTE
(GREEN MAYONNAISE)

1 egg yolk	½ pint olive oil
½ tsp. salt	1 tsp. chopped parsley
¼ tsp. white pepper	1 tsp. chopped chives
1 tsp. wine vinegar or lemon juice	Green colouring

Mix the egg yolk, salt, pepper and vinegar in a deep bowl. Add the olive oil drop by drop, beating continually, until the sauce is thick and all the oil has been used; if necessary add more vinegar. Add the chopped parsley and chives, and 1–2 drops of green colouring.

RED MULLET NIÇOISE

6 red mullet	A clove of garlic
Olive oil	4 large tomatoes
Seasoning	½ pint white wine
1 small onion	Parsley
8–12 black olives	1 orange

Clean the fish, but leave the heads on. Fry them lightly until brown in a little olive oil. Arrange the fish in a fireproof dish and season well. Mix well together the finely chopped onion, the stoned olives, clove of garlic and the peeled and sliced tomatoes. Arrange this mixture around the fish, and pour on the wine; cover with greaseproof paper and cook in a moderate oven (350° F., mark 4) for 10–15 minutes. Leave to get cold, then sprinkle with chopped parsley, and arrange slices of orange on top.

FILETS DE POISSON DUGLÉRÉ
(POACHED FISH WITH TOMATO)

1½ lb. fish fillets	¾ cup well-drained can-
1 tsp. salt	ned tomatoes
⅛ tsp. pepper	¼ cup white wine or
1 clove garlic (optional)	¼ cup water plus
1 tbsp. butter or	½ tsp. lemon juice
margarine	¼ cup cream
1 medium onion,	1 tbsp. soft butter
minced	1 tsp. flour
2 shallots, minced	Chopped parsley
(optional)	

Tear or cut circle of waxed paper to fit a large, covered pan (about 10 inches across); tear small hole in the centre and set aside. Sprinkle fish with salt and pepper. Stick toothpick in garlic.

In the pan, melt 1 tbsp. butter, add onion, shallots, garlic and top with fish, tomatoes, then 1 tbsp. chopped parsley, pour in wine. Lay paper circle over fish.

Bring to boil, cover, cook over high heat for 5–10 minutes or until fish is easily flaked with fork but still moist. Remove cover, paper and garlic.

Pour cream round fish. Mix 1 tbsp. butter with flour, stir into cream; move pan in circular motion to combine and thicken sauce. Spoon some sauce on to fish, sprinkle with parsley. Serve from pan.

SOLE MEUNIÈRE

1 large sole (whole or	Flour
filleted)	Butter
Salt and pepper	Lemon and parsley

Season the sole with pepper and salt, flour it lightly on both sides and fry it in butter until the fish is cooked and golden-brown on both sides. Serve on a hot dish, sprinkled with lemon juice, and chopped parsley, and pour over it some lightly browned melted butter.

COQUILLES ST. JACQUES

4 large scallops	Water
2 fillets of sole	Flour
½ lb. mushrooms	Butter
Mussels	Cream
White wine	Shrimps
Seasoning	Grated cheese

Sauté the mushrooms, and cook the mussels in their own steam and remove from their shells. Poach the scallops and fillets of sole in well-seasoned white wine and water for 20 minutes. Lift out, cut into small pieces, and keep hot. Make a good sauce with the liquor, adding the butter and cream, and reseasoning if necessary. Put the scallops, sole, shrimps, mussels and mushrooms into the sauce and reheat without allowing to boil. Pile the mixture into the deep halves of the scallop shells, sprinkle with grated cheese and brown under the grill.

LOBSTER PROVENÇALE

2 small boiled lobsters	A bay leaf
2 oz. butter	Thyme and parsley
2 tbsps. olive oil	A pinch of saffron
1 dessertsp. finely	4 oz. rice
chopped onion	Garlic juice (optional)
1 cup tomato purée	Quarters of lemon
Seasoning	Finely chopped chives

Remove the lobster meat from the shells and cut into pieces 1½ inches long. Heat butter and olive oil in a thick pan, add the onion and cook until soft. Then add the seasoning and herbs (garlic juice if liked). Put the meat into the pan, cover and cook over a low light for 15–20 minutes. Cook the 4 oz. rice in boiling salted water with two or three grains of saffron until tender but still crisp. Drain well, pile on the centre of a hot dish and spoon the lobster mixture over and round the rice. Garnish with quarters of lemon and chopped chives.

HOMARDS THERMIDOR
(THERMIDOR LOBSTER)

2 cooked lobsters	A little brandy
6 mushrooms	½ pint béchamel sauce
Butter	Salt and pepper
¼ pint cream	1 truffle (optional)

Remove and slice the flesh from the lobsters. Wash and slice the mushrooms, and fry in butter. Add the cream and brandy to the béchamel sauce, season and add the sliced truffle. Mix the lobster meat and mushrooms lightly in the sauce, and fill the bottom half of each lobster shell with the mixture. Put small pieces of butter on each, and brown lightly under the grill. (This dish can be prepared in advance and browned just before serving.) Serve with green salad.

SOLE À LA NORMANDE

1 quart mussels	Lemon juice
1 dozen small mush-rooms	Seasoning
	8 fillets of sole
A little butter	½ pint white wine
A few shallots	4 oz. peeled shrimps

For the Sauce

2 oz. fat	Top of the milk
2 oz. flour	2 egg yolks
Mussel liquor	1 tbsp. cream

First prepare the mussels and mushrooms for the garnish. Put a little butter in a pan, chop a few shallots and cook in the fat. Wash the mussels thoroughly, and put into the pan, cover, and cook till the shells separate. When the mussels are ready, remove them from the shells, take off the beards, and reserve the liquid. Cook the mushrooms in a little water to which a little lemon juice, butter and seasoning have been added.

Next make the sauce. Make a roux with the fat and flour, and add the mussel and mushroom liquor, made up to 1 pint with the top of the milk. Cook for 5 minutes, then thicken with the egg yolks and cream. Add a walnut-sized lump of butter, and reheat very gently without boiling.

Grease a baking dish and put the roughly chopped shallots in it. Fold each fillet in three, add to the dish, and cover with the white wine, cover with greased paper and cook in a moderate oven (350° F., mark 4) for 7–10 minutes. Garnish with the mussels, mushrooms and shrimps, and pour the hot sauce over.

MERLAN À LA SAUCE AUX CÂPRES
(WHITING WITH CAPER SAUCE)

Prepare the whiting and put them in a buttered fireproof dish, season, and add 1 gill white wine. Cover with buttered paper and cook in a moderate oven (350° F., mark 4) for 15 minutes. Have ready ½ pint thick white sauce, and add to this the liquid in which the whiting have been cooked and 2 tbsps. capers; stir, reheat, and pour over the whiting. Serve at once.

GRENOUILLES À LA MEUNIÈRE
(FROGS' LEGS À LA MEUNIÈRE)

From 2 lb. medium frogs' legs, pull off skin and cut off feet from hind legs, if not already prepared. Soak in cold water for 2 hours and then drain. Dip into ½ cup milk, then into ½ cup flour.

In ¼ inch hot salad oil, butter or margarine, sauté frogs' legs for 6–8 minutes or until brown on all sides. Remove to heated platter; sprinkle with ¾ tsp. salt, ⅛ tsp. pepper, 2 tsps. lemon juice. Pour off oil from pan; in same pan, heat 3 tbsps. butter until golden, pour over frogs' legs. Garnish with parsley. Serves 4.

BORDEAUX MUSSELS

1 quart mussels	4 peeled and chopped
2–3 bay leaves	tomatoes
1 sprig of mace	1 clove of garlic
2 oz. butter	Chopped parsley
2 oz. flour	Seasoning

Wash the mussels, bring to the boil in salted water, with the bay leaves and mace, and cook for a few minutes, until the shells open. Strain them through a sieve (reserving the liquor for stock) and remove the mussels from the shells. Melt the butter in a pan and add the flour, cook gently until the flour has browned, then add the tomatoes, chopped garlic, 1 tbsp. parsley and seasoning. Add the mussels to the pan with 1 pint of the liquor and cook gently for 15 minutes. Serve sprinkled with fresh parsley.

BRANDADE OF COD (PROVENCE)

1½ lb. cod fillet or salt cod or other white fish	Grated nutmeg
	Lemon juice
¼ pint olive oil	Quarters of lemon
2 cloves of garlic	Toast or fried bread
¼ pint milk	Hard-boiled egg
Pepper	(optional)

Soak the fish overnight; the next day, drain it, bring to the boil in fresh water and simmer for 5 minutes. Drain the fish, remove the skin and bones and return it to the saucepan. Heat the oil and add the crushed garlic. Heat the milk separately, but do not boil it. Using a wooden spoon, mask the fish and add alternate tablespoons of warm milk and warm oil, stirring constantly over the gas until all the oil and milk have been used up and a thick purée has been produced. Season with pepper, nutmeg and the juice of a lemon.

Serve hot, garnished with lemon quarters, toasted bread and sliced hard-boiled egg.

BURGUNDY SNAILS

1 tin of snails	1 onion stuck with
½ pint white wine	6 cloves
Salt and pepper	2 cloves of garlic
A bouquet garni	¼ pint brandy

Remove the snails from the tin and put them into a pan with the remaining ingredients. Cook gently for 1 hour, then let the snails cool in the liquor. Drain them, and push them into the shells. Fill up the shells with snail butter (see below), put them into a baking dish and heat through thoroughly in a hot oven (450° F., mark 8) before serving.

Note: Retailers who stock tinned snails can usually supply empty shells.

SNAIL BUTTER

4 oz. butter	1 tsp chopped
½ oz. finely chopped	parsley
shallot	Salt, pepper and
1 clove of garlic (crushed)	mixed spice

Soften the butter, add the other ingredients and mix well; use as required.

POACHED EGGS IN RED WINE SAUCE

1 small onion	½ pint red wine
1 clove of garlic	4 eggs
1 bay leaf	4 slices of fried bread
A pinch of thyme	½ oz. butter
Seasoning	½ oz. flour

Gently simmer the sliced onion, garlic, herbs, seasoning and wine for 10 minutes, then strain. Reheat the wine and poach the eggs in it, then place on fried bread. Make a sauce with the butter, flour and wine (a little reduced by boiling), then pour the sauce over the eggs and serve immediately.

OMELETTE AUX FINES HERBES

The making of omelettes is a simple process, but disregard of the few elementary rules gives lamentable results. Here is the classic French method; to make other typically French omelettes, omit the parsley and add chopped ham, cooked mushrooms, grated cheese, etc.

Break 6 eggs into a basin. Add 3 pinches of pepper, 5 pinches of salt, and 2 tsps. chopped parsley. Beat with a fork to mix the egg whites thoroughly with the egg yolks. This beating with a fork should last only about 1 minute—excessive beating quite ruins the consistency of the omelette.

The omelette pan should be scrupulously clean and should never be used for anything but omelettes. Melt in it 2 oz. butter, and as it melts stir so that the butter does not colour at all. When it is hot, pour in the eggs, and as they cook, agitate them with a fork so that they cook evenly; shake and turn the omelette pan occasionally. Fold the omelette to form an oval shape, shake lightly over the heat, and turn out on to a hot dish. Serve immediately.

FILLED OMELETTE

Butter	½ tsp. salt
6 eggs	A little pepper
1 tbsp. cold water	Filling as desired

Melt the fat over low heat in a large omelette pan, tipping the pan to grease the bottom and sides well. Make the pan really hot while you beat the eggs, water and seasonings just sufficiently to blend. Pour a third of the mixture into the pan, tipping it backwards and forwards to let the uncooked mixture flow to the bottom. Continue until the underside is set and the top still creamy. One of the following is suitable as a filling: chopped fried bacon, 2–3 oz. grated cheese, or ¼ lb. sliced and sautéed mushrooms. Put the savoury filling on to half of the omelette, fold it over and turn on to a hot plate. Repeat twice, using the rest of the mixture. Garnish, and serve immediately.

The above quantities make 3 omelettes.

BEIGNETS SOUFFLÉS
(CHEESE PUFFS)

3 oz. butter	3 eggs
¼ pint boiling water	3 oz. grated Parmesan
4 oz. flour	Deep fat for frying
A pinch of salt	Parsley

Add the butter to the water and then remove from the heat to add the sieved flour and salt. Return to the heat and cook until a smooth ball forms. Take again from the heat and beat in the eggs gradually, one at a time. Add the cheese. Take small spoonfuls of this mixture and fry in the hot deep fat until puffed up and golden-brown. Sprinkle with more cheese, and garnish with parsley.

GOUGÈRE AU FROMAGE

4 oz. fat	4 eggs
½ pint boiling water	2½ oz. finely grated
5 oz. flour	cheese
Salt	Beaten egg to glaze

Grease and lightly flour a baking tray, then mark a circle on it with the bottom of a floured flan ring (about 6 inches in diameter). Make some choux pastry as follows: Put the fat and water in a small pan and bring to the boil, remove from the heat and add the sieved flour and salt. Stir well, return pan to the heat and cook gently, stirring, for about 1 minute, until a smooth ball forms. Break the eggs into a basin and beat lightly. Allow flour mixture to cool slightly, and add the eggs a little at a time, then add 2 oz. cheese. The mixture should now be a stiff paste that will pipe easily and retain its shape. Beat thoroughly, until it is quite smooth, put it into a forcing bag fitted with a plain ¾-inch nozzle and pipe in a ring round the floured mark on the tray, making three layers. Glaze with egg and sprinkle with the remaining cheese, then bake in a moderate oven (375° F., mark 5) for ¼ hour, until well risen. Decorate with " leaves " cut from sliced cheese.

ŒUFS SOUBISE AU GRATIN

1 lb. onions	4 eggs
2½ oz. butter	1 tbsp. flour
Pepper and salt	½ pint milk
3 oz. well-flavoured grated cheese	Pinch of marjoram
	Butter for top
2 oz. fresh breadcrumbs	

Roughly slice onions and boil in salted water for 5 minutes. Drain, chop finely. Melt 2 oz. butter, add onion and cook with the lid on the pan until tender but not coloured. Season. Meanwhile mix together the cheese and breadcrumbs and place half in the base of a buttered heatproof dish. Cover with half the onion. Soft-boil the eggs (cook in boiling water for 5 minutes), then put immediately into cold water ; carefully remove shells. Place eggs on the bed of onion. Cover with a white sauce made from remaining butter, 1 tbsp. of flour and ½ pint milk, seasoned with pepper, salt and marjoram. Spoon the remainder of the onion on top of the sauce and finally the rest of the cheese and crumbs. Dot with butter. Place in a hot oven (450° F., mark 8) for 15 minutes. Serve at once.

QUICHE LORRAINE
(LORRAINE CHEESE TART)

Flaky pastry	½ tsp. salt
4–6 oz. thinly sliced Gruyère cheese	¼ tsp. pepper
	¼ lb. bacon or ham, cut into small pieces
2 eggs	
¼ pint double cream	

Line a flan tin with the pastry and crimp the edges. Slice the cheese thinly and put it at the bottom and sides of the flan. Beat the eggs lightly and mix with the cream, seasonings and bacon or ham. Pour over the cheese, and bake in a moderately hot oven (400° F., mark 6) for about 40 minutes.

This is one of the classic French regional dishes ; various alternative ingredients may be used for the filling, including leeks and spinach.

GIGOT DE MOUTON À LA BRETONNE
(BRETON ROAST LAMB)

1 leg of lamb	½ lb. (dry weight) haricot beans, soaked overnight
Salt and pepper	
1 clove of garlic	1 onion
Fat for roasting	A bouquet garni

Rub the leg of lamb with salt and pepper. Slice the clove of garlic lengthwise in 2 or 3 pieces, and insert next to the bone. Roast in a moderate oven (350° F., mark 4), allowing it 15 minutes per lb. The meat should not be overdone, but pink and juicy in the middle. Serve with a garnish of haricot beans, prepared as follows : Cook the soaked beans gently in boiling salted water with the whole onion and the bunch of herbs. When the beans are tender, drain, remove the onion and herbs, and mix the beans with some of the gravy.

NAVARIN AUX PRIMEURS
(SPRING LAMB STEW WITH VEGETABLES)

2½ lb. breast of lamb, cut into 12 pieces	2 tbsps. butter or margarine
2 tsps. salt	3 carrots, cut into ½-inch cubes
¼ tsp. pepper	
2 tbsps. fat	3 medium turnips, cut in ½-inch strips
1 clove garlic, crushed	
1 tsp. minced shallot or onion	½ tsp. sugar
	12 tiny new potatoes, peeled
2 tbsps. flour	
2½ cups water	1 cup shelled fresh peas (1 lb. unshelled)
2 large tomatoes, cut up	
1 tbsp. salt for sauce	1 cup fresh green beans, cut into 1-inch lengths (¼ lb.)
A bouquet garni	
12 small white onions	

Sprinkle lamb with 2 tsps. salt and pepper ; in hot fat in deep casserole, sauté lamb, a few pieces at a time, until brown, then remove.

Drain off all but a small amount of fat ; add garlic, shallot and flour ; cook over low heat until flour is light brown ; add water, tomatoes, 1 tbsp. salt, bouquet garni and lamb. Simmer, covered, about 45 minutes or until meat is tender. Skim fat from liquid.

In saucepan, melt butter or margarine, add carrots, turnips, onions ; sprinkle with sugar and sauté until browned ; add to casserole with potatoes ; see that the vegetables are covered by liquid. Simmer, covered, 20 minutes, add peas and beans, and continue cooking until vegetables are done, about 20 minutes. Season to taste. Makes 6 servings.

POITRINE DE MOUTON BRAISÉE
(BRAISED BREAST OF MUTTON)

1 breast of mutton	1 onion stuck with 2
3 pints water	cloves
A bouquet garni	Salt and pepper
$\frac{1}{4}$ lb. carrots	

For the Stuffing

1 onion, chopped	Seasoning
2 tsps. finely chopped	1 egg
parsley	1 tbsp. white wine
$\frac{3}{4}$–1 lb. minced pork	

Ask the butcher to bone the breast of mutton and roll it, but use the bones to enrich the liquid in which it is cooked. First prepare the filling: Mix the onion and parsley with the pork, season well, and bind with the egg and wine. Spread this mixture over the mutton, roll and tie firmly. Put the mutton in a casserole with the bones and trimmings and the remaining ingredients. Bring to the boil, and then simmer slowly for 3–3$\frac{1}{2}$ hours until the meat is cooked. Take out the meat and dust with salt and pepper. Serve with tomato or piquant sauce, and spinach.

COTELETTES DE PORC POIVRADE À LA CRÈME
(PORK CHOPS IN PEPPER SAUCE WITH CREAM)

1 carrot, thinly sliced	4–6 1-inch thick pork
1 onion, thinly sliced	chops
1 small bay leaf	$\frac{1}{2}$ cup water or stock
Pinch dried thyme	$\frac{1}{2}$ cup cream
$\frac{1}{4}$ cup Sauternes	1 tbsp. cornflour
2 tbsps. vinegar	1 tsp. salt
2 tbsps. water	$\frac{1}{8}$ tsp. pepper

Mix carrot, onion, bay leaf, thyme, Sauternes, vinegar, 2 tbsps. water; pour over chops in bowl. Leave in a cold place several hours or overnight.

About 1 hour before serving, drain chops, reserving vegetables and liquid. Dry chops well. In large pan rubbed with bit of fat cut from chops, sauté chops until golden on both sides, about 15 minutes.

Add vegetables, $\frac{1}{4}$ cup reserved liquid; cover; turn heat very low; simmer chops for 45 minutes or until tender.

Remove tender chops to heated platter; keep warm. Into pan, stir rest of reserved liquid and $\frac{1}{2}$ cup water; bring to the boil; simmer for 5 minutes. Stir in cream, then cornflour mixed with 2 tbsps. water; simmer, stirring, until thickened. Add salt and pepper. Pour over chops. Makes 4–6 servings.

COTELETTES DE PORC AUX CHAMPIGNONS
(BRAISED PORK CHOPS WITH MUSHROOMS)

4–6 1-inch thick loin	$\frac{1}{2}$ cup Sauternes
pork chops	$\frac{1}{2}$ cup water or stock
2 tbsps. butter or mar-	$\frac{1}{4}$ lb. mushrooms, sliced
garine	$\frac{1}{2}$ cup water
1 onion, thinly sliced	1 tsp. salt
1 carrot, thinly sliced	1 tbsp. flour
A bouquet garni	

In a little hot fat in large pan, brown chops on both sides; remove and drain off fat.

In 1 tbsp. butter in same pan, sauté onion and carrot 5 minutes. Add bouquet garni. Top with chops; add wine and $\frac{1}{2}$ cup water. Bring to boil; cover, simmer for 45 minutes or until chops are tender.

Meanwhile, simmer mushrooms in $\frac{1}{2}$ cup water with salt, covered, 5 minutes. Let stand.

Remove chops to serving dish; discard bouquet garni. To liquid in pan, add mushrooms and their liquid, plus flour blended with rest of butter. Cook stirring, until thickened. Pour over chops. Makes 4–6 servings.

RAGOÛT DE ROGNON DE VEAU
(VEAL KIDNEY STEW)

4 veal kidneys	1 tbsp. flour
$\frac{1}{2}$ tsp. salt	$\frac{1}{3}$ cup white wine
Dash of pepper	(optional)
2 tbsps. fat cut from	1 cup canned tomatoes
kidneys	$\frac{1}{2}$ tbsp. chopped parsley
2 tbsps. butter	$\frac{1}{2}$ tsp. salt
1 medium onion, minced	

Remove any outer membrane from kidneys; split in halves lengthwise, then, with scissors, remove fat and white veins. Cut kidneys into small pieces, sprinkle with $\frac{1}{2}$ tsp. salt and pepper.

In pan, cook kidney fat until brown, discard the bits. In it, sauté kidneys for 5–7 minutes or until browned. Drain them, discarding fat and liquid.

In hot butter in same skillet, sauté onion until tender and golden. Stir in flour, then wine, tomatoes, parsley; cook until thickened.

Add kidneys; cook until just hot. Add $\frac{1}{2}$ tsp. salt or to taste. Serve with hot fluffy rice. Enough for 4.

FILET SAUTÉ AUX CHAMPIGNONS
(FRIED FILLET STEAK WITH MUSHROOMS)

4 slices of fillet steak	$\frac{1}{2}$ pint good stock
$\frac{1}{2}$ lb. mushrooms	1 tbsp. chopped parsley
$\frac{1}{4}$ lb. butter	1 shallot, finely chopped
Salt and pepper	$\frac{1}{4}$ oz. flour

Prepare the fillets of beef by beating lightly

with a wooden spoon and trimming to an oval shape, cutting away any skin or fat. Peel and wash the mushrooms, and slice the stalks thinly. Put 3 oz. butter into a small frying pan, and when it is hot but not coloured, add the mushrooms and stalks, with 2 pinches of salt and a little pepper. Sauté the mushrooms for 4 minutes, shake on a little flour and cook for another minute. Add half the stock, the chopped parsley and shallot.

Season the fillets with salt and pepper. Melt the remaining butter in a frying pan and cook the fillets quickly for 4 minutes, turn, and cook for 4 minutes on the other side, taking care all the time that the butter does not burn. Remove the fillets and keep them hot on a dish. To the hot butter add ¼ oz. flour and cook for a minute, stirring with a wooden spoon. Add the remaining stock and the sauce strained from the mushrooms; simmer for 1 minute, add the mushrooms and reheat. Arrange the fillets on the dish, pour the mushrooms and sauce round, and serve.

FILET AUX OLIVES
(FILLET STEAK WITH OLIVES)

Prepare the fillets of beef as above, and make the sauce in the same way, but instead of mushrooms add 24 olives, prepared as follows : Stone the olives and blanch for 5 minutes in boiling water ; dry well on a cloth, put in the sauce and reheat for 2 minutes.

ÉMINCÉ DE FILET DE BŒUF À LA SAUCE PIQUANTE
(SLICED BEEF IN PIQUANT SAUCE)

This is a very good way to use up cold roast beef. Meat which has been previously roasted will be hard and tasteless if it is boiled, but gently reheated in this way, it is very good. Cut the meat in thin slices and reheat without boiling in sauce piquante (see below). The amount of sauce required depends on the quantity of meat to be used—the amount given is enough for 1 lb. meat. The same sauce is excellent served with boiled beef.

Roast leg of mutton can be reheated in the same way.

SAUCE PIQUANTE

½ oz. shallot	Seasoning
1 oz. butter	Gravy browning
2 tsps. vinegar	1 tbsp. chopped
1 oz. flour	gherkin
¾ pint stock	1 tbsp. chopped parsley

Skin, wash and chop the shallot, put it into a saucepan with the butter and vinegar and cook over gentle heat, turning with a spoon until the vinegar is entirely reduced. (The vinegar is used to acidulate the sauce, but it prevents the liaison of the roux ; it is therefore necessary to reduce it before adding the flour, by which time its flavour and acidity will be absorbed by the shallot.)

Add the flour, cook for 4 minutes, then slowly add the stock. Season and colour with a little gravy browning. Simmer gently for 15 minutes, add the gherkin and parsley, and bring quickly to the boil. As soon as it boils, remove from the heat, and reseason if necessary.

FOIE DE VEAU À LA BOURGEOISE
(CALF'S LIVER)

1½ lb. calves' liver	1 bunch of parsley
2 oz. butter	1 onion, stuck with 2 cloves
1 oz. flour	Salt and pepper
½ pint water	8 young carrots
½ pint white wine	10 small onions

Fry the calves' liver in the butter, turning it constantly to ensure even cooking. Take out the liver, add the flour, and cook for 4 minutes, stirring with a wooden spoon until the flour is dark brown but not burnt. Add the water, wine, parsley, onion with cloves, salt and pepper, then bring to the boil, stirring all the time. Put the liver back, add the sliced carrots and simmer slowly for 1½ hours, then add the onions and cook slowly for another hour. Serve the liver on a hot dish, surrounded by the onions and carrots. Remove the onion stuck with cloves, then strain the sauce and reduce it for 5 minutes on a quick heat. Pour over the liver and serve at once.

ESCALOPES DE VEAU AUX FINES HERBES
(FRIED VEAL FILLET)

1½ lb. fillet of veal	½ oz. flour
Salt and pepper	½ pint good stock
3 oz. butter	1 tbsp. chopped parsley

Cut the veal into slices about ½ inch thick, beat each slice well and season on both sides with salt and pepper. Fry the escalopes in 2 oz. of the butter, for 4 minutes on each side, then put the meat on a dish. Add the flour to the hot butter and cook for a minute, stirring well. Add the stock and cook for 5 minutes ; if any juice has come from the meat, add this to the sauce. Reheat the sauce, and when it comes to the boil add the remaining 1 oz. butter, cut into pieces, and the parsley. Stir well to melt the butter, taste, and season again if necessary. Pour the sauce over the escalopes and serve at once.

VEAL WITH SAUCE MORNAY

2½ lb. fillet of veal	Mushroom stuffing and
2 onions	Sauce Mornay (see
2 carrots	below)
Fat (preferably pork)	Grated cheese

Tie the meat and put it into a roasting tin with the sliced onion and carrot, cover with fat, put a piece of greased paper over the top, and roast for 1½ hours. When it is nearly cooked, add 1 tbsp. water to the dish. Remove the meat from the tin, and after 30 minutes cut it into slices. Meanwhile make the stuffing, spread this on the slices of meat and arrange in a fireproof dish. Make the Sauce Mornay and pour it over the meat, sprinkle the top with grated cheese and brown in the oven or under the grill.

MUSHROOM STUFFING

2 oz. butter	2 tbsps. white breadcrumbs
1 onion	Seasoning
5 oz. mushrooms	1 egg

Melt the butter and add the finely chopped onion, then the finely chopped mushrooms, and fry until they are just cooked. Add the breadcrumbs, salt and pepper ; remove from the heat, work in the egg, and use as required.

SAUCE MORNAY

¾ pint béchamel sauce   3 oz. grated cheese
Seasoning

Heat the sauce in a double pan, season if necessary, then add the grated cheese.

TOURNEDOS À LA BÉARNAISE

The best meat for this purpose is undercut or fillet, cut into 4 slices, about ¾ inch thick and weighing 3–4 oz. each. Form each fillet into neat rounds, and sauté or grill them on both sides till cooked (4–5 minutes each side). Toast slices of bread (½ inch thick) and cut into croûtes just slightly larger than the tournedos, which are placed on them. Make a border of béarnaise sauce (see below) round the edge of each, using a teaspoon, and garnish with grilled mushrooms and tomatoes.

Tournedos may be served with many other garnishes :

Tournedos à l'Estragon : Place on toast, garnish with a cross of blanched tarragon leaves, and coat with tomato sauce flavoured with chopped tarragon.

Tournedos Piémontais : Place on a bed of tomato risotto, put a grilled half-tomato on top, and coat with sauce.

Tournedos Jardinière : Pour a little tomato sauce over and surround with small heaps of different vegetables.

BÉARNAISE SAUCE

1 shallot (chopped)	3 peppercorns
2 tbsps. tarragon vinegar	2 egg yolks
6 tarragon leaves (if available)	5 oz. butter
	2 tbsps. parsley

Cook the shallot, vinegar, 3 tarragon leaves and the peppercorns for a few minutes, then strain. Boil this liquid till reduced by about half, then add 1 tbsp. water. Add the egg yolks and half of the butter to the pan, and whisk together. Heat without boiling, stirring vigorously till thick, remove from heat and beat in the remaining fat, adding it in lumps. Chop the parsley with the remaining tarragon, and add. If the sauce starts curdling, add a little cold water or vinegar, and stir the mixture well.

VEAL MARENGO

2 lb. veal	½ pint dry white wine
Flour	¼ pint water
Salt and pepper	4 tbsps. tomato purée
4 tbsps. butter	A bouquet garni
2 onions, sliced	½ lb. small mushrooms
1 clove of garlic, sliced	Parsley
	Croûtons of fried bread

Cut the meat into 1½-inch cubes and toss in seasoned flour. Heat the butter in a frying pan, add the veal and cook rather fast, turning frequently, until it turns brown. Add the onions and garlic, and cook until tender. Add 1 tbsp. flour and cook until brown, then stir in the liquid, and bring to the boil. Add the purée, seasoning and herbs, then cover the pan and simmer gently for 1 hour. Add the prepared mushrooms and cook for a further 10 minutes, until they are tender. Serve the meat piled in a dish with the sauce poured over, and garnished with parsley and fried croûtons.

TÊTE DE VEAU À LA SAUCE DITE PAUVRE HOMME
(CALF'S HEAD WITH POOR MAN'S SAUCE)

½ a calf's head	1 tbsp. vinegar
2 onions	A bouquet garni
2 carrots	Salt and pepper
1 shallot	½ a calf's tongue
1 clove of garlic	1 calf's brains

For the Sauce

1 oz. shallots	Seasoning
¼ gill vinegar	1 heaped tbsp. chopped parsley
1½ gills calf's head liquor	

Wash the calf's head well and soak it in cold water for several hours, changing the water every ½ hour. Put in a pan with the onions, carrots, shallot, garlic, vinegar and bouquet garni, season well and cover with water. Simmer slowly for 3–4 hours, until the meat comes away easily from the bones. After 2 hours, add the tongue, and just ½ hour before serving, add the brains. When all is cooked, cut up the meat, skin the tongue, cut it up, and serve on a hot dish, covered with the sauce.

To make this, chop the shallots finely, put them in a small saucepan with the vinegar and boil until the vinegar is absorbed by the shallots. Pour on to the shallots 1½ gills strained calf's head liquor, and boil for 5 minutes. Season, and add the chopped parsley.

TRIPES À LA MODE DE CAEN
(TRIPE)

2 lb. tripe	4 cloves
1–2 cow-heels	4 leeks
Salt and pepper	2 carrots
2 bay leaves	1 pint cider or dry white
2 sprigs of thyme	wine
2 sprigs of parsley	½ glass brandy (optional)
4 large onions	

Wash the tripe very thoroughly and blanch it, then cut it into small pieces; divide up the cow-heels. Put into a strong casserole with the seasonings, herbs, the onions (each with a clove stuck in it) and the sliced leeks and carrots. Add the cider or wine and the brandy. Cover closely, and stew gently for a long time—5–6 hours.

This dish may be left overnight; remove the fat from the surface and take out the bones and herbs before reheating the tripe for serving.

TERRINE DE LIÈVRE
(HARE PÂTÉ)

1 hare	A few thin slices of fat
1 lb. fat bacon	bacon
½ lb. boned veal	1 large bay leaf
Salt and pepper	Chicken fat or lard
Butter	

Skin, clean and bone the hare, keeping all the blood. Remove the shoulder and legs of the hare, carefully remove the skin and gristle, and cut up the flesh; add this meat to the bacon and veal to make the farce. Divide the body of the hare into 2 neat portions, cutting it transversely, season them well, and fry in butter for 10 minutes.

Mince and pound in a mortar the veal, boned bacon and cut-up hare flesh, adding the blood of the hare; season well with salt and pepper. Now put into the terrine first a layer about 1 inch thick of this farce, then one part of the hare, another layer of farce, the second part of the hare, and then another thick layer of farce. Cover with the thin slices of fat bacon and bay leaf. Seal closely with a lid or with 2 sheets of greased paper. Place the terrine in a large saucepan with boiling water to reach half-way up it, and simmer gently for 3 hours, testing with a skewer to see whether the hare is thoroughly cooked. Leave until it is completely cooked, and then seal with melted chicken fat or lard. Keep in a very cold place, and use as required.

SAUCISSES AU VIN BLANC
(SAUSAGES IN WHITE WINE)

1 lb. sausages	½ oz. flour
1½ gills white wine	½ pint good stock
Pepper and salt	2 egg yolks
½ oz. butter	1 tbsp. chopped parsley

Put the sausages into a frying pan with the wine and 2 pinches of pepper, cover with a lid and simmer for 8 minutes. Meanwhile make a sauce with the butter, flour and stock, cool slightly, and stir in the egg yolks. Take the sausages from the pan, drain, and keep them hot. Add the sauce to the wine in the frying pan, reheat without boiling, stir in the chopped parsley, season, and pour over the sausages. Serve the sausages accompanied by a dish or border of creamy mashed potatoes.

FOIE DE VEAU SAUTÉ AU VIN
(CALF'S LIVER SAUTÉ WITH WINE)

12 rashers of bacon	2 tbsps. butter or mar-
6 slices calf's liver,	garine
½ inch thick	1 tbsp. minced shallot
1 tsp. salt	or onion
¼ cup flour	½ cup burgundy

Fry bacon until crisp but not brittle. Remove each rasher as it browns; drain on paper towelling, keeping hot.

Meanwhile, sprinkle liver, on both sides, with salt and flour. When fat remaining in pan is very hot, use it to sauté liver quickly, turning once. Remove to heated platter. Pour off fat.

In same pan, melt butter, add shallot; cook just until tender.

Add wine, stirring in browned bits from bottom of skillet. Taste; add seasoning if needed. Pour over liver.

Top each liver slice with 2 bacon rashers. (Makes 6 servings.)

QUEUE DE BŒUF
(OXTAILS)

1 carrot, chopped	1 clove, garlic, minced
2 onions, chopped	1 cup canned tomato
8 whole black peppers	purée
1 tsp. salt	1 tbsp. salt
¼ tsp. pepper	3 cups water
⅛ tsp. mixed herbs	3 tbsps. butter
2 cups burgundy	10 small white onions
A bouquet garni	½ tsp. sugar
4 lb. oxtails, cut into	3 carrots, sliced
2-inch pieces	3 potatoes, halved
3 tbsps. fat	½ lb. mushrooms, sliced
3 tbsps. flour	Chopped parsley

Day before

In a bowl, combine chopped carrot and onions, black peppers, 1 tsp. salt, pepper, herbs and wine; add bouquet garni and oxtails; refrigerate, covered, for at least 3 hours.

From marinade, remove oxtails and dry; brown in melted fat in casserole, then remove. Next, from marinade remove carrot and onions and brown in same fat; stir in flour, add marinade (reserving bouquet garni), garlic, tomato purée, 1 tsp. salt and water; simmer for 2 or 3 minutes. Add oxtails, bouquet garni and simmer, covered, 2–2½ hours or until meat is tender.

Remove oxtails to a bowl; over them, strain liquid from casserole; return all to casserole, cool quickly; refrigerate.

About 1 hour before serving

Skim fat from surface of oxtail mixture; then heat. Remove oxtails, measure liquid—there should be about 2 cups; if necessary, simmer to reduce to 2 cups.

Meanwhile, melt butter; add whole onions and sprinkle with half of sugar, sauté until slightly browned. Remove and in same butter, sauté carrot slices, sprinkling with rest of sugar.

To liquid in casserole, add onions, carrots, potatoes and oxtails, and cook, covered, until vegetables are done—about 30 minutes.

Meanwhile, in butter left in pan, sauté mushrooms over low heat about 5 minutes, then add to oxtails, just before serving. Sprinkle with parsley. Makes 4–6 servings.

VEAL CUTLETS

1–1½ lb. best end	1 clove of garlic
of neck of veal	A sprig of chervil
4 oz. bacon	Seasoning
10 shallots	Oil

Divide the meat into cutlets and trim them to a good shape. Finely chop the bacon, shallots, garlic and chervil and mix together with the seasoning. Fry this mixture lightly and keep it hot. Brush the cutlets with a little oil and grill them under a hot grill. When they are quite cooked, arrange on a hot dish and put a spoonful of the savoury mixture on each cutlet.

BLANQUETTE D'AGNEAU

1½ lb. diced lean	1 level tsp. dried thyme
shoulder of lamb	Salt and pepper
¼ lb. carrots, sliced	¾ oz. butter
¼ lb. onions, sliced	1 oz. flour
1 oz. dripping	2 tbsps. mayonnaise
½ pint stock	Chopped parsley
2 sticks celery, sliced	Finely chopped clove of
A small bay leaf	garlic for garnish

Sauté meat, carrots and onions in a little dripping until beginning to brown. Pour over ½ pint hot stock. Add sliced celery, bay leaf, thyme, salt and pepper to season. Simmer for 1½ hours. Blend together the softened butter and flour. When thoroughly mixed, add to the stew and stir until thickened. Simmer for 10 minutes. Stir in the mayonnaise. Serve with boiled rice. Garnish with parsley and garlic.

DAUBE OF BEEF

8 slices of thinly cut	½ egg or 1 yolk
buttock steak (12 oz.)	¼ pint red wine
Salt and pepper	Crushed clove of garlic
8 rashers of lean streaky	1 oz. butter
bacon	¼ pint meat stock or
1 small onion	water
¼ lb. mushrooms	1 tsp. made mustard
Grated lemon rind	Butter and flour to
A pinch of thyme	thicken

Ask the butcher to cut 8 thin slices of beef. Flatten with a heavy flat chopper. Season with salt and pepper. Rind and trim bacon rashers, chop finely with onion and mushrooms. Add a little grated lemon rind, seasoning and thyme. Bind with egg. Spread a little over each portion of beef. Roll up and tie with fine string. Leave in a cold place overnight to marinade in the wine and garlic. Next day, well drain rolls. Brown evenly in 1 oz. butter. Place in a shallow casserole-type dish. Pour over the hot marinade and stock or water. Cook covered for 1½ hours in a moderate oven (350° F., mark 3), add mustard and cook for a further ½ hour. Thicken with 1 oz. butter and 1½ tbsps. flour. Check seasoning. Serve with peas and fried onion rings.

VEAU À LA CRÈME FLAMBÉ

4 escalopes (weight about 12 oz.)	6 mushrooms
	3 tbsps. brandy
Pepper and salt	4 tbsps. thick cream
1 tbsp. lemon juice	Parsley to garnish
1½ oz. butter	

Flatten the escalopes. Season with pepper and some of the lemon juice. Melt 1 oz. butter and fry escalopes until just brown on both sides. Remove from pan and keep warm on a serving dish. Add chopped mushroom stalks to the pan and cook stalks for 3 minutes. Add 2 tbsps. flaming brandy. When flames have died, pour in the cream and rest of lemon juice. Stir well to loosen any residue from the pan. Cook until sauce is thick. Season and strain over the escalopes. Sauté sliced mushrooms in the rest of the butter, add 1 tbsp. flaming brandy ; use to garnish escalopes. Garnish with tiny sprigs of parsley.

NAVARIN OF MUTTON

2 lb. middle neck of mutton	Salt and pepper
	A bouquet garni
¼ lb. sliced onion	½ lb. button onions
2 oz. dripping	½ lb. carrots
2 oz. flour	¼ lb. turnips
1 tbsp. tomato purée	Chopped parsley
1¼ pints stock	

Trim the meat and fry it with the onion till well browned. Add the flour and stir till browned, then the purée and the stock. Stir while bringing to the boil. Skim carefully. Add the seasoning and bouquet garni (remove latter after ½ hour). Simmer in a covered pan for 2 hours. Meanwhile fry the button onions and diced vegetables till browned and cook in the navarin for the last ½ hour. Serve very hot with the garnish round the edge of the dish, sprinkled with parsley.

VEAU EN CASSEROLE

1½ lb. boned shoulder veal	½ pint stock
	½ pint white wine
3 oz. butter	4 sliced skinned tomatoes
2 small sliced onions	
3 sliced carrots	1 sliced green pepper
2 dessertsps. flour	1 crushed clove garlic

Cut the meat into 2-inch strips and fry, a few pieces at a time, in the butter, stirring continuously so that it is browned all over. Remove and put on a plate. Put the onions in the pan and fry until soft. Toss the carrots with the onions for a few minutes then add the flour and stir well, mix the stock and the wine. Bring to the boil and add the tomatoes, pepper and crushed garlic. Simmer for 10 minutes. Stir in meat, then pour into a casserole, and bake in a moderate oven (350° F., mark 4) for about 1½ hours.

STUFFED SHOULDER OF LAMB

A shoulder of lamb	1 egg
Seasoning	1 tbsp. white wine
1 onion, chopped	Dripping
2 tsps. finely chopped parsley	1 large onion
	1 carrot
¾–1 lb. minced pork	1 clove of garlic

Bone the lamb and season well. Mix the onion and parsley with the pork, season well and bind with the egg and wine. Spread the lamb with this filling, roll up neatly from the narrow end and tie with string. Melt the fat in a roasting tin and put the meat into it, with some fat on top. Place the bones round the meat, with the sliced onion, carrot and chopped garlic. Cook in a moderate oven (350° F., mark 4) for 1½–2 hours, basting occasionally. When cooked, remove the string, but do not carve the meat for 10 minutes, so that the juices are kept in.

LEG OF MUTTON WITH MARSALA SAUCE

A leg of mutton	A few parsley stalks
2–3 sticks of celery	Rosemary, thyme, or other herbs
1 onion	
1 carrot	A few peppercorns
4 tbsps. olive oil	Olive oil for cooking
¼ pint white wine	½ pint Marsala wine
¼ pint white vinegar	2 lb. small onions
1 clove of garlic	1 lb. small sausages

Wipe and trim the meat, and prepare the marinade as follows. Fry the sliced celery, onion and carrot in the oil. Add the white wine, vinegar, crushed garlic, herbs and seasoning and simmer for 15 minutes, then leave to cool. Pour this marinade over the meat and leave for 12 hours, turning the meat occasionally. The next day, put in a deep pan with a little more oil and the Marsala wine, cover and cook for 4–5 hours in a slow oven (325° F., mark 2). Add onions and sausages after 2 hours. Serve the liquid from the pan as a sauce.

BEEF AND OLIVE CASSEROLE

3 lb. rump steak	1 clove garlic
4 tbsps. olive oil	A few peppercorns
1 carrot	8 oz. fat bacon
1 onion	¼ pint red wine
2–3 sticks celery	½ lb. black and green olives
¼ pint red wine	
¼ pint wine vinegar	4 tomatoes
A bunch of fresh herbs	

Wipe and trim the meat, then make the

marinade as follows. Heat the oil in a pan and add the sliced carrot and onion and the celery, cut into 1-inch pieces, and cook until brown. Add $\frac{1}{4}$ pint red wine, the wine vinegar, herbs, crushed garlic clove, and peppercorns, bring to the boil and simmer for 15 minutes, then leave to become quite cold. Cut the meat into thick chunks and cover with the marinade.

Fry 4 oz. bacon, remove from the pan, then fry the slices of meat on both sides and put into an earthenware casserole. Strain the marinade over the meat, add the remaining 4 oz. bacon (diced), the remaining $\frac{1}{4}$ pint wine and the olives. Cover with greased greaseproof paper, then with a lid, and cook in a slow oven (325° F., mark 2) for $2\frac{1}{2}$ hours. Before serving, add the peeled and sliced tomatoes, and remove excess fat. Serve with noodles and grated cheese.

GIGOT MARINÉ

3- or 4-lb. leg of mutton	1 quart claret
$\frac{1}{2}$ lb. onions	2 oz. salt pork
Pinch mixed spice	A bouquet garni
6 tbsps. pig's blood	Small glass cognac
	Salt and pepper

To prepare Marinade : Add to the wine, spices (as many and as varied as possible), salt, pepper and the bouquet garni. Slice the onions and add these as well. Bone—or have boned—the leg of mutton and leave it in this marinade for three whole days, turning occasionally and keeping in a cool place.

When ready to cook, dice finely the salt pork in an iron cocotte and brown the mutton in the fat on all surfaces. This operation will take some time, as it colours slowly after its immersion in the marinade. When nicely browned, add the rounds of onion and moisten with the strained marinade. Cover and cook gently for 3 hours, adding more wine as needed. When the meat is done, remove from fire and reduce the combined gravy and marinade by fast boiling, to half its original volume. Strain, then add the pig's blood. (This may be omitted, but is used to thicken and at the same time flavour the dish.) Boil for 5 minutes, then add the cognac, previously flambé. Serve the sauce separately and garnish dish with plain steamed or boiled floury potatoes.

FILETS DE BŒUF À LA MODE DU PAYS DE VAUX

Small fillet steaks	Salt and pepper
Hard-boiled eggs	Fines herbes, chopped
Lemon juice	Butter

Grill the fillets in the usual manner ; season when done, on both sides. Chop the eggs, mix with the fines herbes (chives, chervil, parsley and a tiny sprig of tarragon, if liked—and available). Moisten with lemon juice. Spread this mixture in a dish, add the fillets, place on each a nice piece of butter and, as soon as it has melted in a slow oven (325° F., mark 2) ; serve very hot.

BŒUF À LA RUSSE

1 lb. tender cut of raw beef	1 small cabbage
1 raw egg	Thin fresh tomato sauce
2 tbsps. uncooked rice	1 pinch mixed herbs
Lemon juice to taste	Sugar to taste
Flour	Salt and pepper

Chop the meat finely, mix with salt, pepper, herbs, rice and egg ; shape into small sausages. Parboil the cabbage, detach leaves and remove hard stalks. Wrap each little meat sausage in a cabbage leaf. Tie into neat shapes and place them in a deep pan, covering with tomato sauce made from fresh tomatoes. Cook slowly for 1 hour, then strain in the flour, blended with cold water or stock. Season to taste with lemon juice and sugar.

CÔTELETTES DE VEAU EN PAPILLOTES
(VEAL CHOPS EN PAPILLOTES)

8 veal chops ($\frac{1}{2}$ inch thick)	2 tbsps. chopped chives
$\frac{1}{8}$ pint olive oil	$\frac{1}{4}$ lb. mushrooms
2 tsps. chopped parsley	Butter
2 tsps. chopped onion	Salt
	Black pepper

Marinade the chops in the olive oil for 12 hours. Mix the parsley, onion, chives and thinly sliced mushrooms. Cut 8 pieces of parchment paper, large enough to envelop a chop completely, spread with butter, and sprinkle with the herb mixture. Place a chop on each paper, cover with another layer of the herb mixture, season well, and wrap up firmly. Bake in a moderately hot oven (400° F., mark 6) for 20 minutes, until tender. Serve the chops, hot, still encased in the papers.

BŒUF À LA MODE
(POT ROAST)

$1\frac{3}{4}$ lb. beef	A pinch of thyme
2 oz. pork fat, cut in squares for larding	2 bay leaves
$2\frac{1}{2}$ lb. carrots	1 calf's foot or some veal bones
2 onions	$\frac{1}{4}$ pint wine
8–10 oz. bacon	$\frac{1}{3}$ pint stock or water
2 oz. butter	Salt and pepper
2 whole cloves	

Lard the meat with the small squares of pork

1) This Austrian cheesecake, Topfen-kuchen, is made with ground almonds or hazelnuts (*top picture*).

2) Flemish Steaks (*above*) are cooked in beer and served with whole onions.

3) Blanquette de Veau, a rich Belgian veal stew, is accompanied by boiled potatoes in the picture on the right.

4) Chicken Waterzooi is a traditional Belgian dish, served in a deliciously rich and creamy sauce (*above*).

5) Belgian chicory is often served braised with ham and cheese as a light luncheon dish (*below*).

6) Belgian Tart, shown on the right, has an interesting, crumbly texture.

7) Cramique (*below*) is a Belgian tea-time bread, made rich with eggs and fruit.

8 - 10

From Luxembourg come the dishes shown on this and the facing page.

8) On the right are pig's trotters, fried in breadcrumbs with onions and herbs.

9) Birds Without Heads (*above*); for this dish hard-boiled eggs are wrapped in thin slices of meat.

10) On the left, thickly buttered Potato Cakes.

11) The top picture shows Streiselkuch, a rich yeast cake topped with a crust of egg yolk, butter and sugar.

12) Rice Tart (*below*) a creamy rice filling baked in a flaky pastry case makes a popular and delicious sweet.

13 - 15

Two pages of English specialities.

13) Steak and Kidney pudding (*top left*) is served, folded in a white napkin, in the basin in which it was cooked.

14) Cornish Pasties, with their filling of meat, onions and potato, make a popular and attractive meal (*left*).

15) Grilled Dover Sole (*shown right*) served with melted butter sauce and garnished with parsley and lemon.

16) Jellied Eels (*right*) a traditional English dish.

17) Star-gazy Pie is a Cornish speciality, made with mackerel or herring (*below*).

18) Kedgeree, an English version of an Indian dish is shown (*below*, *left*).

19) Christmas Pudding (*below*), rich, dark and decorated with the traditional sprig of holly.

20) Syllabub (*left*) deliciously frothy with cream, sherry and crushed macaroons.

21) Wiltshire Lardy Cake, made with yeast and currants, may be served hot with butter (*above*).

22) Simnel Cake (*left*) layered and iced with almond paste was originally baked for Mothering Sunday, not Easter.

23) Madeira Cake, light and buttery and topped with citron (*right*).

24) Leek and Bacon Pie, shown above, is a delicious Welsh dish, baked with eggs and milk.

25) Snowdon Pudding is steamed in a basin that has been lined with juicy stoned raisins.

26) Scotch or Black Bun (*left*) is a sipcy, rich fruit mixture, baked in a pastry case and traditionally eaten at Hogmanay.

27) Traditional Irish Soda Bread, light as a feather, is delicious with plenty of creamy butter.

28) Irish Coffee is a comforting brew of steaming black coffee, whiskey, sugar and thick cream.

29) Brno Schnitzel (*above*), a Czechoslovakian dish of fried veal, stuffed with eggs, peas and ham.

30) Apple Gâteau, spongy and rich with nut cream and fruit, is a Czechoslovakian Christmas speciality.

31) Honey Wafer Cake from Czechoslovakia is filled and decorated with a nutty chocolate cream.

32) Flaky Kolache (*shown left*), are little turnovers of rich yeast dough filled with poppy seeds or fruit. They are a Czech speciality.

33) Hearty fare from Denmark : crisp, delicious meat balls with spicy red cabbage.

34) Danish Pastries, filled with almonds and decorated with nuts and icing, are popular everywhere.

35) Consommé, a rich, clear beef or chicken stock that can be garnished in countless ways.

36) Quiche Lorraine : Gruyère cheese, eggs, ham and cream combine to make a delectable filling for a flaky pastry case.

On this and the facing page: French cooking at its best.

37) Tripe, cooked *à la mode de Caen*, is turned into a party dish with wine and herbs.

38) *Côtelettes de Veau en Papillotes*. Veal cutlets are cooked, each in its own wrapping, and served in the delicious juices.

39) Crisp, cream-filled Profiteroles, smothered in a rich chocolate sauce.

40
-
44

Five dishes from Germany :

40) Rolls of smoked salmon are stuffed with scrambled egg and decorated with olives (*left*).

41) *Right :* a typically German dish of pork, beans, sauerkraut and sausages.

42) Rum Makronenspeise (*below*), a delicious sweet made with cream, macaroons, fruit and rum.

43) Meat balls are flavoured with herbs and onion ; they are served with lightly fried spinach (*right*).

44) Kummel Kningel (*below*), golden, crisp little yeast rolls, sprinkled with caraway seeds.

fat. Prepare and slice the carrots and onions, and chop the bacon. Brown the meat in the butter. Add bacon, vegetables, cloves, herbs, calf's foot, wine and stock, and season with salt and pepper. Bring to the boil and simmer very gently for 4 hours. This pot roast is usually eaten hot, though it may be served cold; the quantities given are sufficient for 6 people.

PERDRIX BRAISÉES
(BRAISED PARTRIDGES)

2 partridges	1 pint stock
2 large carrots	Seasoning
1 turnip	A bouquet garni
2 onions	1 oz. flour
1 leek	A few cooked mush-
1 rasher of bacon	rooms
2 oz. butter	Chopped parsley

Prepare and trim the partridges. Dice some of the carrots and turnip to make a garnish, then cut up the rest of the vegetables roughly, dice the bacon and fry the vegetables and bacon until golden. Drain, place in a casserole, just cover with stock, and add the seasoning and bouquet garni. Fry the partridges until brown, place on the vegetables, cover and cook in a moderate oven (375° F., mark 5) for ½ hour. Dish up the birds and keep them hot. Thicken the gravy with the flour, bring to the boil and cook for a few minutes; season well, then strain this sauce round the birds. Garnish with the cooked diced vegetables, mushrooms and parsley.

RÔTI DE PORC À LA BOULANGÈRE

5 lb. pork loin	2 tsps. chopped parsley
1 clove garlic, cut	1 tbsp. seasoned salt
1 tsp. salt	⅛ tsp. pepper
10 cups thinly sliced potatoes	½ cup boiling water
	3 tbsps. melted butter
1 cup coarsely chopped onion	Chopped parsley

Heat oven to 425° F. (mark 7). Trim meat free of all but thin layer of fat and rub with cut garlic and salt. Place fat side up, on rack in shallow open roasting pan or large shallow casserole.

Roast pork for 1½ hours. Then, reduce oven temperature to 400° F. (mark 6); remove pork and rack from roasting pan; pour off all fat.

In roasting pan, toss potatoes with onion, 2 tsps. chopped parsley, seasoned salt, pepper; pour in boiling water; lay pork on top, then brush potatoes with butter and return pan to oven for 1 hour.

On heated platter, arrange meat; serve potatoes in vegetable dish, sprinkled with parsley.

W.C.B.—7

RÔTI D'AGNEAU À LA BOULANGÈRE
(ROAST LEG OF LAMB)

Order 7½ lb. leg of lamb, boned and rolled; rub with salt and garlic; top with a thin slice of beef suet. Heat oven to 400° F. (mark 6).

Add ¼ cup water, roast 2 hours, basting occasionally. Remove lamb and rack from pan; pour off all fat. Add potatoes as for Rôti de porc (above), roasting at 400° F. (mark 6) about 1 hour or until lamb is light pink inside. Serve as above. Makes 6 servings.

ENTRECÔTES

Béarnaise : Grilled steak served with pommes sautées, watercress and sauce béarnaise.

Bonne Femme : Steak cooked in butter in an open pan with some small onions and diced potatoes.

Bordelaise : Grilled steak with a garnish of poached marrowbone fat and served with sauce bordelaise.

Bourguignonne : Steak fried, then finished in red wine, which is used to make the accompanying gravy.

Forestière : Steak fried in butter and served with fried mushrooms.

Lyonnaise : Steak fried in butter and served with shredded fried onions.

Maître d'hôtel : Grilled steak served with a maître d'hôtel butter.

Minute : The thinnest possible piece of steak fried in very hot butter.

Mirabeau : Grilled steak garnished with anchovy fillets, chopped tarragon, stoned olives and anchovy butter.

Niçoise : Steak fried in olive oil, garnished with tomato purée, new potatoes tossed in butter, and black olives.

Vert-pré : Grilled steak served with straw potatoes, tufts of watercress and maître d'hôtel butter.

PÂTÉ DE CANARD
(DUCKLING PÂTÉ)

1 duckling	5 eggs
1 lb. pork skin, cut in ½-inch pieces	1 tsp. flour
	1 tsp. salt
1 leek	1 tsp. pepper
1 sprig of thyme	⅓ pint cognac
1 bay leaf	6 olives
1 quart stock	6 slices of fat bacon
1 lb. chicken livers	1 oz. gelatine
1 lb. lean pork	4 tbsps. cold water
A shallot	Sliced radish, olive,
3 tbsps. chopped parsley	hard-boiled egg,
1 clove of garlic	etc., to decorate

Skin the raw duckling, saving the skin. Remove the meat from the duck carcase and put aside. Place the duck bones, neck, wings and giblets in a large pan, add the pork skin, leek, thyme, bay leaf and stock, cover, and simmer for 2 hours.

Put the duck meat, duck liver, chicken livers, pork, shallot, parsley and garlic twice through a mincer, using the finest blade. Add the eggs to the mixture one at a time, beating well. Add the flour, salt and pepper, the cognac and the finely chopped olives, and mix thoroughly.

Take a baking dish of $2\frac{1}{2}$ quarts capacity, line it with the duck skin, fill with the meat mixture and cover with the bacon strips. Bake uncovered in a slow oven (325° F., mark 2) for $2\frac{1}{2}$ hours. After the stock has simmered for 2 hours, turn up the heat and reduce the liquid to $\frac{3}{4}$ pint. Meanwhile, soak the gelatine in the cold water. Strain the stock, add the soaked gelatine, and stir until it is dissolved. When the casserole is cooked turn out the pâté on to a dish and allow to cool. Decorate, then glaze with the jellied stock.

COQ AU VIN

A 3–3½ lb. chicken	Parsley
4 oz. streaky bacon	Thyme
1 oz. butter	Seasoning
3 large or 4 small onions	½ pint red wine
	Beurre manié (¾ oz.
4–6 oz. button mushrooms	flour and ¾ oz. butter)
A bay leaf	Croûtons of fried bread
	Lemon wedges

Prepare the chicken and joint into 6–8 pieces. Cut the bacon into cubes. Melt 1 oz. butter. Fry bacon and sliced onions. Take out onions. Fry the joints of chicken. Put in a casserole, adding the onions and whole washed mushrooms and herbs. Season. Cover and cook for 1–$1\frac{1}{4}$ hours at 375° F. (mark 5). Remove the joints of chicken and onions and place on a clean dish. Save the mushrooms for garnish. Skim any fat from the juice in the casserole. Add wine. Thicken sauce with beurre manié and cook for 5 minutes. Correct the seasoning. Strain sauce over the chicken. Garnish with mushrooms, croûtons and wedges of lemon.

CANARD À L'ORANGE

2 oz. lean streaky bacon	4 oz. mushrooms
2 oz. dripping	¾ pint stock
2 shallots, sliced	4 tbsps. sherry
1 small onion, sliced	1 duck, jointed
1 carrot, sliced	3 oz. butter
3 tbsps. flour	1½ oranges
2 tsps. tomato purée	Seasoning

Rind the bacon. Cut in pieces, heat in a pan to extract the fat. Drain off the fat. Add the dripping and heat. Add shallots, onion and carrot. Cook over a very low heat until vegetables are lightly browned, about 20 minutes. Add flour and continue to cook. When evenly browned, add tomato purée and sliced mushrooms (not stalked or peeled). Stir well and reheat. Gradually pour on the stock, stir meanwhile and then add the sherry. Cook slowly with the lid on the pan until the mushrooms are tender and strain. Prepare the duck. Melt the butter and fry the joints until golden-brown. Place the joints in a heavy casserole. Add the juice of $1\frac{1}{2}$ oranges to the sauce, check seasoning. Pour over the duck. Cover tightly. Cook at 350° F. (mark 4), for $1\frac{1}{4}$ hours. Meanwhile, remove rind from oranges, making sure no pith is attached. Cut in julienne strips, cook in water until tender. Drain. Add to the casseroled duck and return to the oven for a further 15 minutes. Serve with orange salad.

POULET CHASSEUR
(CHICKEN CHASSEUR)

1 chicken	Salt
1–2 shallots	Pepper
1 clove of garlic	2 tsps. flour
2 oz. butter	½ pint stock
1 tbsp. olive oil	½ gill white wine or
½ tsp. chopped fresh herbs (parsley, marjoram, chives)	sherry
	1 tbsp. tomato purée

For the Garnish

Cooked mushrooms   Fried croûtons

Cut the chicken into neat joints. Peel and chop the shallots and the garlic. Heat the butter and oil in a frying pan. Sauté the pieces of chicken until lightly browned, then add the shallot and garlic and cook a little longer. Put the chicken in a casserole and sprinkle with the herbs, salt and pepper. Stir the flour into any fat left in the pan, add the stock, wine and tomato purée, and bring to the boil, then pour over the chicken. Cover closely, and cook gently in a moderate oven (350° F., mark 4) for about $\frac{3}{4}$ hour, or until the chicken is tender. Meanwhile peel the mushrooms and fry in the 1 oz. butter. Dish up the chicken and keep hot. Reduce the sauce to a thin glazing consistency, season if necessary and pour over the chicken. Garnish with the mushrooms and croûtons.

This dish is also very good made with a boiling fowl. Cook the trussed chicken in stock or water flavoured with onion, a bunch of fresh herbs, salt and 6 peppercorns. (The liquid should be just simmering when the bird is put in.) Cover, and cook very gently until the chicken is tender; the flavour and tenderness of the flesh depend on the slow cooking. Leave the chicken to cool in the stock. When the bird is almost cold, lift it out, cut into neat joints, sauté in the oil and butter, and serve with the sauce made as above.

POULET SAUTÉ AU VIN
(CHICKEN SAUTÉ WITH WINE)

2 small frying chickens, cut-up	2 shallots, minced
	1 tsp. flour
1 tsp. salt	$\frac{1}{2}$ cup Sauternes
$\frac{1}{4}$ tsp. pepper	$\frac{1}{4}$ cup water
$\frac{1}{4}$ cup butter	2 tbsps. chopped parsley

Into chicken pieces, rub salt, pepper.

In hot butter sauté chicken, skin side down, until golden, then turn and brown other side. Cook, loosely covered, about 30 minutes or until tender.

Remove chicken to heated platter; keep warm. Into drippings in pan, stir shallots, flour; cook, stirring, until shallots are soft.

Add wine and water; then cook the sauce, stirring, until browned bits are loosened. Taste then season if necessary.

Return chicken to pan, and simmer uncovered, about 5 minutes.

Remove chicken to heated platter, pour sauce over all and sprinkle with parsley.

POMMES DE TERRE À LA BOULANGÈRE
(POTATOES AND ONIONS)

Wash and peel 1 lb. potatoes and cut them in two lengthways, then cut across into slices about $\frac{1}{2}$ inch thick. Peel and slice a large onion. Grease an earthenware dish, put a layer of potatoes at the bottom, season well, and add a layer of onions. Continue in this way, finishing with a layer of potatoes. Pour in about $\frac{1}{2}$ pint of veal stock, place small pats of butter on top, and heat the dish to boiling point, then cover with greased paper and bake in a moderate oven (350° F., mark 4) for $\frac{3}{4}$–1 hour.

DUCHESSE POTATOES

Cook 1 lb. potatoes quickly in salted water, drain, and allow to dry for a few minutes, then sieve them. Replace them in the pan and add 2 oz. butter, some pepper and salt and a little grated nutmeg.

Remove pan from the heat and add 2 egg yolks; a little milk may also be added if the potato mixture is going to be piped. Shape the duchesse potatoes or pipe them, as required, brush over with egg and bake in a hot oven (450° F., mark 8) until golden. Alternatively, shape the mixture as desired, coat with egg and breadcrumbs, and fry in deep fat.

CAROTTES VICHY

Scrub 1 lb. of carrots and scrape them, then cut into thin strips. Melt 3 oz. of butter in a pan or metal casserole and add 1 tbsp. water, 1 tbsp. sugar and the carrots. Cover closely and cook gently for about $\frac{3}{4}$–1 hour, turning them occasionally very gently. Sprinkle with a little salt and chopped parsley just before serving.

LAITUES AU JUS BRAISÉES
(BRAISED LETTUCE)

8 good firm lettuces	1 onion
$\frac{1}{2}$ pint stock	2 cloves
A bouquet garni	Fried croûtons
$\frac{1}{2}$ oz. butter	

Wash the lettuces well and remove any discoloured outer leaves. Cook for 10 minutes in boiling salted water, drain, put in a casserole, and add the stock, bouquet garni, butter and the onion stuck with the cloves. Cover with a buttered paper, and cook slowly for 2 hours. Arrange the lettuces on a hot dish, reduce by half the liquid in which they were cooked, pour this over them, and garnish with fried croûtons of bread.

MACÉDOINE DE LÉGUMES
(VEGETABLE MACÉDOINE)

4 oz. carrots	4 oz. young green peas
2 oz. turnip	4 oz. French or runner beans
4 oz. asparagus tips	

For the Sauce

1 oz. butter	$\frac{1}{2}$ tsp. sugar
$\frac{1}{2}$ oz. flour	2 egg yolks
$\frac{1}{2}$ pint stock	2 tbsps. cream
Salt and pepper	

Prepare all the vegetables and neatly cut up into small squares or slices, then cook them separately in boiling salted water, and drain carefully on a dry cloth.

Melt the butter and make a roux with the flour, then add the stock, seasoning and sugar. Cook for 10 minutes, cool a little, and then beat in the egg yolks and the cream. Put all the vegetables in the serving dish and mix them with the sauce, being very careful not to break them. Serve hot.

RATATOUILLE

4 tomatoes	½ a cucumber
2 aubergines	Oil
A small green pepper	1 oz. butter
2 onions	Seasoning
A small marrow or 3 courgettes	Clove of garlic, crushed
	Chopped parsley

Skin the tomatoes and slice. Wipe and slice the aubergines. Prepare pepper, removing pips, and slice. Skin and slice onions. Peel marrow (but not courgettes), and slice. Slice the cucumber. Place 2 tbsps. of oil and 1 oz. butter in a flame-proof casserole (enamelled iron), heat and add prepared vegetables, seasoning and crushed garlic. Stir well. Cover tightly and place in the oven at 350° F. (mark 4), for 1–1½ hours. Serve with chopped parsley.

PETITS POIS À LA FRANÇAISE
(GREEN PEAS)

1 lb. shelled young green peas	A pinch of salt
	1 oz. sugar
4 oz. butter	2 oz. butter and ½ oz. flour blended together for the liaison
½ gill water	
2 oz. small onions	

Put all the ingredients except the liaison in a well-covered casserole, and cook in a moderate oven (350° F., mark 4) for 30 minutes. Add the liaison, and shake the casserole well, cook for a few minutes and serve.

SALSIFIS SAUTÉS

Scrape the salsify carefully and cut it into pieces of even length and thickness. Wash it quickly in cold water, and then put it into boiling salted water to which 1 tbsp. vinegar has been added. Simmer slowly until it is cooked (about 30 minutes). Drain the salsify and then fry it in melted butter, stirring in at the last moment some chopped parsley.

CHOU FARCI
(STUFFED CABBAGE)

1 medium cabbage	½ tsp. salt
1 tbsp. butter	Dash of pepper
¼ cup minced onion	1 clove garlic, minced
¼ lb. pork-sausage meat	1 egg, beaten
1 cup chopped cooked lamb or beef	1 carrot, sliced
	1 onion, thinly sliced
2 tbsps. fresh bread-crumbs	2 rashers bacon
	2 cups canned tomatoes
1 cup cooked rice	

Simmer whole cabbage for 5 minutes in boiling salted water to cover. Plunge into cold water, drain well.

Meanwhile, start heating oven to 400° F. (mark 6). Also, prepare this stuffing. In hot butter in small pan, sauté minced onion until tender. Toss with meats, crumbs, rice, salt, pepper, garlic and mix in the egg.

In a 3-quart casserole, spread carrot and onion slices; on them, arrange 2 lengths of string (to be used for tying cabbage), then drained cabbage, stem end down. With knife, cut out 3-inch round centre of cabbage to about 2 inches from bottom. Press stuffing into cavity.

Top cabbage with bacon; with string, tie head together firmly, pulling up leaves over stuffing. Around it, pour tomatoes. Cover casserole, and cook until tender. Serve cut into wedges.

COURGETTES AU BEURRE TARRAGON

4 courgettes	1 tbsp. tarragon
Salted water	Salt and pepper
1½ oz. butter	1 small green pepper

Remove stem ends from the courgettes. Cook in boiling salted water for 5 minutes. Drain, cut in thick slices. Melt butter, add tarragon, season with salt and pepper. Toss sliced courgettes in the butter, cook till tender but still crisp. Just before serving fold in finely chopped green pepper.

TARTE À L'OIGNON
(ONION TART)
For the Flan Case

8 oz. flour	Salt
4 oz. fat	Cold water

For the Filling

1½–2 lb. onions	4 oz. Gruyère cheese
2 oz. butter or dripping	2 eggs, beaten
	Seasoning

Prepare some shortcrust pastry with the flour, etc., and use to line a 9- or 10-inch flan or tart case; prick the bottom carefully, to avoid rising in cooking, and leave to rest while making the filling. Prepare and slice the onions, melt the fat and cook the onions gently for 30 minutes with a lid on the pan. Remove from the heat; add 3 oz. of the grated cheese and the beaten eggs. Season well, mix, and spread in the tart case. Sprinkle with the remaining 1 oz. grated cheese and bake in a moderate oven (375° F., mark 5) for 20–30 minutes, until the pastry is cooked and the filling well browned.

SALADE DE CHOUX
(CABBAGE SALAD)

Choose a firm, young cabbage and remove the

outer leaves and the base of the stalk. Wash and cut in half across the diameter of the cabbage. Soak for 5 minutes in cold salted water, drain, and shred very finely with a sharp knife. Put into a salad bowl and dress it liberally with oil, vinegar, pepper, salt and mustard, using enough dressing to coat all the cabbage—far more than for a lettuce salad. Leave in a cool place for at least 2 hours before serving.

GLACÉ ONIONS

1 bottle of small cock-tail onions	½ gill red wine
2 tbsps. olive oil	1 tbsp. brown sugar
1 tbsp. stoned raisins	A pinch of Cayenne pepper

Strain the vinegar from the onions and rinse them in cold water (or use pre-boiled fresh onions). Place in a fireproof dish with all the other ingredients, and cook over a good heat for 10 minutes, turning the onions so that they become caramelled brown on all sides and the sauce is thick and sticky. Glacé onions are delicious with all meats.

PEA BEANS À LA BRETONNE

8 oz. dried pea beans	2 oz. butter
1 large onion	1 oz. flour
	Salt and pepper

Soak the beans in cold water overnight. Start cooking them in cold water and simmer for 2 hours until tender, then drain. Slice the onion and fry in the butter until yellow. Add the flour and let it brown, put in the beans and ¼ pint bean water, and season with salt and pepper; cover, and simmer for 15 minutes.

BÛCHE DE NOËL

3 eggs	3 oz. caster sugar
3 oz. plain flour	1 tbsp. warm water

For the Crème au Beurre Chocolat

4 oz. caster sugar	2 egg yolks
4 tbsps. water	5 oz. butter
A pinch of cream of tartar	3 oz. plain chocolate

Grease and line a 10-by-8-inch baking sheet. Whisk together the eggs and sugar until thick and creamy (this may be done over a pan of hot water); when the whisk is lifted from the mixture it should leave an impression. Lightly fold in the flour and water using a metal spoon. Pour on to prepared sheet. Spread evenly and bake at 425° F. (mark 7), for 8–12 minutes. The sponge should be golden-brown and springy to the touch. Turn out on to a sugared sheet of silicone parchment or greaseproof paper. Trim edges with a sharp knife. Roll up with paper inside and cool on a wire rack. Unroll carefully when cold. Reroll after spreading with filling and leave to set firm. Coat with the remainder of the crème au beurre and mark with a fork. If possible chill before serving. Dust lightly with icing sugar and decorate with a sprig of holly.

CROISSANTS DE PROVENCE

5½ oz. ground almonds	Vanilla or orange-flower water
5½ oz. caster sugar	
1 tsp. sieved apricot jam	Beaten egg to glaze
2 egg whites	Shredded almonds

Mix together the almonds and sugar; and add the sieved apricot jam and sufficient egg white to form a workable paste. Flavour to taste. Divide the paste into balls the size of a walnut. Flour the hands and roll each piece to form a very small sausage; brush with beaten egg, and roll it in shredded almonds. Place on a baking sheet lined with well-greased greaseproof paper, bending each in the shape of a crescent. Bake in a moderate oven (375° F., mark 5) till firm and lightly browned.

COMPOTE DE GROSEILLES À FROID

Stalk 1 lb. of ripe red-currants and wash them quickly in cold water, not letting them soak at all. Put them in a pan and add 7 oz. caster sugar and 2 tbsps. water. Shake the currants until the sugar is dissolved, and put in a glass dish. Leave for about 2–3 hours, by which time the juice should have formed a red jelly. A delicious compote to serve with brandy-flavoured crème Chantilly.

CHERRY SOUFFLÉ FLAMBE

4–6 sponge fingers	½ oz. butter
3 oz. glacé cherries	3 egg yolks
Brandy	1 tbsp. sugar
4 tbsps. milk	4 egg whites
1 level tbsp. flour	Icing sugar

Soak sponge fingers and cherries (quartered) with brandy. Warm milk. Blend flour with 1 extra tbsps. milk. Gradually add warm milk, butter, egg yolks and sugar. Cook over a low heat, stirring meanwhile till mixture thickens. Whisk egg whites until thick and fluffy, fold into the custard mixture. Pour half into a buttered and sugared 7-inch soufflé dish. Cover with sponge fingers and half the cherries. Cover with rest of the mixture. Dredge heavily with icing sugar. Bake at 350° F. (mark 4) for about 30 minutes until well risen and just set. Drain remainder of the cherries, quickly scatter over the soufflé, flambé the brandy (about 1 tbsp.) and pour immediately over the soufflé. Serve at once.

ÎLE FLOTTANTE
(MOULDED FLOATING ISLAND)
Custard Sauce

1 cup thick cream combined with 1 cup of milk	1 tbsp. flour
	⅛ tsp. salt
	4 egg yolks, beaten
½ cup granulated sugar	¼ tsp. vanilla essence

Day before:

In double boiler, heat cream.

Combine sugar, flour and salt. Add to egg yolks. Beat until well mixed.

Stir some of hot cream mixture into egg yolks; mix well. Stir egg mixture into the remaining cream mixture in double boiler.

Cook over hot water, stirring constantly for about 15 minutes or until mixture is thickened and coats spoon. Remove from heat.

Add vanilla; cover surface with waxed paper and refrigerate overnight.

Meringue

4 egg whites	⅛ tsp. cream of tartar
Granulated sugar	1 tsp. vanilla essence

Several hours before serving

Let egg whites stand at room temperature for 1 hour.

Start heating oven to 350° F. (mark 4). Butter a 1½ quart mould or 4–6 custard cups, then sprinkle lightly with a little granulated sugar.

In large bowl, beat egg whites until foamy; add salt and cream of tartar; continue beating until soft peaks form; gradually add 1 cup sugar, beating well after each addition. Continue beating until stiff peaks form.

Stir in vanilla. Turn egg white mixture into prepared mould or custard cups, set in pan of hot water. Bake mould for 30 minutes, custard cups 15 minutes.

Unmould at once on to a large serving plate or into individual serving dishes; meringue will shrink slightly. Refrigerate until ready to serve.

Caramel Syrup
Several hours before serving

In large, heavy frying pan or skillet, spread ¼ cup granulated sugar in a thin layer. Heat slowly over low heat until sugar is melted and golden in colour. Then, very slowly, stir in 3 tbsps. hot water. Continue to heat syrup until slightly thickened and all sugar lumps are dissolved. (If syrup becomes too thick to pour, reheat over hot water.)

To serve

Pour custard sauce around meringue or meringues. Top with all of caramel syrup, garnish with strawberries. Serves 6.

MELON EN SURPRISE
(SURPRISE MELON)
One or two hours before serving

From one end of cantaloupe or other small melon, cut off piece to make 4-inch or 5-inch round opening. With spoon, remove seeds, then remove flesh in small pieces.

Toss melon pieces with about 2 cups fresh raspberries or strawberries, fresh, frozen or canned pineapple chunks, or peach slices, grapes, etc. Sprinkle lightly with sugar and ¼ cup Marsala or 1 tbsp. Kirsch.

Refill melon with fruit; replace top. Refrigerate for 1–2 hours.

To serve, stand melon on plate; surround with ferns or leaves. One melon makes 3–4 servings.

CRÈME RENVERSÉE AU CARAMEL
(CARAMEL CUSTARD)

1 cup granulated sugar	¼ tsp. vanilla essence
¼ cup water	3 eggs plus 2 egg yolks
2 cups milk	

Start heating oven to 350° F. (mark 4). With ½ cup sugar and water, make Caramel Syrup (see this page). Pour into bottom of 6 custard cups.

In saucepan, scald milk, vanilla. Meanwhile, with fork, beat eggs and egg yolks with ½ cup sugar.

While stirring with fork, slowly pour hot milk into eggs. Then turn mixture into custard cups; place cups in shallow pan; pour in boiling water to come within 1 inch of tops of cups.

Bake custards 20–25 minutes or until silver knife inserted in centre comes out clean. Refrigerate.

To serve, unmould custards; caramel will run down over them as sauce. Makes 6 servings.

POIRES AU VIN ROUGE
(PEARS IN RED WINE)

4 large or 6 small pears	3 tbsps. granulated sugar
1 cup burgundy or claret	Small piece of lemon rind
1-inch stick cinnamon	

Peel pears ; leave small ones whole ; halve and core larger pears.

In pan, combine wine, sugar, cinnamon, lemon rind. Bring to boil.

Add pears ; cover and simmer for about 40 minutes or until pears are tender, turning once. Discard cinnamon, lemon rind.

Serve pears with syrup, either warm or cold. Makes 4–6 portions.

PROFITEROLES AU CHOCOLAT
(SMALL CREAM PUFFS, WITH CHOCOLATE SAUCE)

$\frac{1}{2}$ cup boiling water	Crème pâtissière (see
$\frac{1}{4}$ cup butter	below)
$\frac{1}{8}$ tsp. salt	Chocolate sauce (see
$\frac{1}{2}$ cup sifted flour	below)
2 eggs, unbeaten	

Start heating oven to 375° F. (mark 5). Bring water, butter and salt to the boil. Add flour, all at once, then beat over low heat until mixture leaves sides of pan and forms a compact ball.

Remove from heat ; continue to beat to cool slightly—about 2 minutes.

Add eggs, one at a time, beating well after each addition. After last egg has been added, beat until mixture has satinlike sheen.

On to greased baking sheet drop mixture in walnut-size balls. Bake until golden and puffy— about 30 minutes. Remove from the oven ; cut slit in side of each and bake 5–10 minutes more. Cool.

Fill puffs with Crème Pâtissière or whipped cream. Arrange in serving dish. Pour hot Chocolate Sauce over all. Serve 2 or 3 per person. (Makes 20 puffs.)

Crème Pâtissière

Make Custard Sauce (see p. 102), substituting milk for thick cream and increasing flour to $\frac{1}{3}$ cup and egg yolks to 5.

Chocolate Sauce

In saucepan, simmer 1 cup water and $1\frac{1}{2}$ cups semi-sweet chocolate until thickened and smooth. Makes 2 cups.

PETITS POTS DE CRÈME AU CHOCOLAT
(SMALL CHOCOLATE CUSTARDS)

4 squares unsweetened	$\frac{1}{4}$ cup water
chocolate	5 eggs, separated
$\frac{2}{3}$ cup granulated sugar	2 tsps. rum or cognac

Day before or early in day

In double boiler, melt chocolate ; add sugar, water ; cook, stirring until sugar is dissolved.

With egg beater, beat yolks well. Stirring vigorously, slowly pour yolks into chocolate mixture. Remove from heat, stir in rum and cool for 5 minutes.

Beat egg whites stiff. Fold in chocolate mixture. Pour into 6 custard cups. Refrigerate several hours or overnight. Serve topped with whipped cream if desired. Serves 6.

CRÈME BRÛLÉE AUX FRUITS
(CRÈME BRÛLÉE WITH FRUITS)

3 cups thick cream	1 tsp. vanilla essence
6 egg yolks	2–3 cups strawberries
6 tbsps. granulated	or cut-up pine-
sugar	apple or peaches
$\frac{1}{2}$ cup brown sugar,	or a mixture of all
sifted	three

Day before

Heat cream till scalded. In double boiler top, beat yolks with granulated sugar. Slowly stir cream into yolks.

Cook mixture over hot, not boiling, water until it coats spoon. Add vanilla. Refrigerate in casserole or flat baking dish.

Just before serving

Over custard, sprinkle brown sugar.

Set custard dish in pan ; surround with ice cubes. Grill custard till sugar caramelises— about 1 minute.

Breaking brown sugar crust by tapping with spoon, serve at once over fruit, in individual glasses. Serves 6.

POIRES À L'IMPÉRIALE
(PEARS AND RICE)

3 oz. rice	A little Cointreau
1 pint warm milk	3 pears
5 oz. sugar	Apricot jam
$\frac{1}{2}$ oz. gelatine	Glacé cherries
5 oz. cream	Angelica

Boil the rice in the warm milk, cooking it for about 20 minutes, then add the sugar and the gelatine, dissolved in a little water. Put into a basin, and stir over ice till thick. Whip the cream till stiff and add to the rice, reserving some for decoration. Add the Cointreau, put the mixture into a glass dish, and chill. Halve the pears and place on top of the mixture. Glaze with warmed jam, and place a half-cherry on each pear, with some pieces of angelica on either side to represent leaves. Pipe cream between the pears, and fill up the centre. Coat with a little mixed apricot jam and Cointreau.

ANANAS À LA CRÈME
(CREAM-FILLED PINEAPPLE)

Start heating oven to 425° F. (mark 7). Cut off top of a large ripe pineapple. With knife and spoon, cut out flesh from inside, leaving ½-inch thick shell.

Cut fruit into thin slices, discarding core ; in saucepan, simmer with ¼ cup granulated sugar for 5 minutes. Drain well.

Now, into pineapple shell, spoon Crème Pâtissière (see p. 103) and drained pineapple in layers, until shell is filled, ending with Crème Pâtissière. Toss 2 tbsps. macaroon crumbs with 2 tsps. melted butter or margarine ; sprinkle over top. Bake pineapple for 25 minutes or until golden. Serve hot. Makes 4 servings.

POMMES MERINGUÉES À L'ABRICOT
(MERINGUED APPLES)

2 lb. large cooking apples   3 oz. caster sugar
6 oz. butter   2 tbsps. apricot jam

For the Meringue
3 egg whites   6 oz. caster sugar

To prepare the apples, cut each into 4, peel, remove core and pips, and cut into sections about ¼ inch thick. Put them in a small frying pan with the butter and caster sugar and cook them for 15 minutes, shaking and turning them all the time. Add the apricot jam, and heat until this is melted over the apples, then pile up the apples to form a dome in a shallow fireproof dish. Whip the egg whites to a stiff froth, fold in the sugar and cover the apples with this meringue mixture. Dredge with caster sugar, and cook in a slow oven (300° F., mark 1) until the meringue is pale golden-brown.

SALADE D'ORANGES AUX LIQUEURS

Cut 4 oranges into thin slices, removing the pips, and arrange in the shape of a crown on a shallow dish. Sprinkle with 2 oz. of fine caster sugar, and ½ gill of rum, brandy or Kirsch.

BANANES AU CARAMEL

Use a strong, deep frying pan for this dish. Cook 4 oz. sugar and 2 tbsps. water carefully over a low heat until a caramel sauce is formed. Peel the number of bananas that you wish to serve ; these should be ripe, but unblemished by bruising. Lay them in the sauce and, using a spoon, coat them with the caramel. Cook in this way for about 10 minutes, then arrange the bananas on a hot dish. Pour remaining caramel over, and serve at once.

TARTE AUX ABRICOTS
(APRICOT TART)

8 oz. flour   2 tbsps. water
A pinch of salt   2 lb. apricots
Caster sugar   4 tbsps. apricot jam
4½ oz. butter   Pistachio nuts
1 egg yolk   Browned almonds

Sieve the flour, salt and 1 dessertsp. sugar into a bowl, then rub in the butter until the mixture resembles fine breadcrumbs. Mix to a stiff dough with the egg yolk and water, and knead into a smooth ball. Line a 9-inch plain flan ring with the pastry, prick the bottom and flute the edges with the finger and thumb. If fresh apricots are used, drop them into boiling water and skin them, halve, and arrange them in the pastry slightly overlapping one another. Sprinkle with caster sugar, and bake in a moderately hot oven (400° F., mark 6) for 25–30 minutes. Remove the flan ring when cold, and coat the top with sieved apricot jam (which has been heated gently), then sprinkle with chopped pistachio nuts and browned almonds.

PARIS-BREST
(CHOUX PASTRY GÂTEAU)

½ pint milk   2 oz. caramel (see Sans-
4 egg yolks   Gêne Cake, opposite)
2 oz. sugar   3 oz. caster sugar
1 oz. flour   2 egg whites

For the Choux Pastry
3 oz. butter   A pinch of salt
½ pint water   4–5 eggs
5 oz. flour   2 oz. flaked almonds

Grease and lightly flour a baking tray, then mark a circle in it with the bottom of a floured flan ring 6 inches in diameter. Begin by making the choux pastry. Melt the butter, add the water and bring to boil. Add flour and salt all at once and stir vigorously until a soft ball is formed in the pan. Beat in the eggs one at a time until the mixture has a soft consistency but is still firm enough to pipe. Pipe most of the pastry in a three-layer ring on the floured ring (using a ¾-inch nozzle). Sprinkle the pastry with flaked almonds. Pipe also several small balls of the paste round the edge of the tray. Bake in a hot oven (450° F., mark 8) for 15 minutes.

Heat the milk in a pan. Separate the eggs, and mix the yolks with the 2 oz. sugar in a basin. Add the flour, beat, and add half the warm milk, beat again, then add this mixture to the rest of the milk in the pan, and once more beat well. Heat the mixture until it will no longer drop from the spoon. Beat in the caramel, and cook for a few minutes over a low heat. Beat the egg whites till stiff and then add the caster sugar. Fold this meringue mixture into the caramel one, using a wooden spoon.

Split the almond ring and pipe most of the cream filling over the bottom piece. Cut each small ball in half and place rounded side upwards on the cream, then cover with the top ring, and sprinkle with icing sugar.

SAVARIN AU RHUM

10 oz. flour	3 oz. softened butter
A pinch of salt	1 oz. icing sugar
$\frac{1}{4}$ pint warm milk	6 oz. granulated sugar
$\frac{1}{2}$ oz. yeast	$\frac{1}{2}$ pint water
1 tsp. caster sugar	Rum
3 eggs	Whipped cream

Sieve the flour and salt and put to warm. Add the warmed milk to the yeast, creamed with the caster sugar. Add this mixture, and the eggs, to the flour and beat well. Leave for about 40 minutes in a warm place, covered with a damp cloth. Mix in thoroughly the butter and icing sugar and put in a greased and floured mould, filling it about one-third deep. Cover and leave to rise until it nearly fills the tin. Bake in a hot oven (450° F., mark 8) for 10 minutes, then lower the heat and bake for a further 20 minutes. Unmould and put into a basin. Boil the granulated sugar and the water for 5 minutes, remove from the heat and add some rum (reserving a little). Pour the syrup over the Savarin and leave to soak. Serve hot or cold, with the remaining rum poured over, and decorated with whipped cream.

PÊCHES MELBA

3 peaches	Raspberry sauce (see
$\frac{1}{2}$ lb. sugar	below)
1 pint water	Flaked almonds to
Ice cream	decorate

Peel the peaches (if necessary first plunge them in boiling water for a minute). Put the sugar in a pan with the water and boil for 5 minutes. Add the whole peaches, put on the lid and cook slowly for 10 minutes. Take from the heat and leave for about $\frac{1}{2}$ hour in the pan, so that the peaches absorb as much of the syrup as possible then remove them from the syrup and cool, if possible in a refrigerator. Put some ice cream in the bottom of a large glass dish or in small glass dishes, and put a whole peach on top. Pour the raspberry sauce over, and decorate with the flaked almonds.

To make the sauce, combine 3 tbsps. raspberry purée, jelly or jam, 3 tbsps. icing sugar and 1 tbsp. Cointreau.

GÂTEAU AU CHOCOLAT

6 oz. butter or margarine	Milk to mix
6 oz. sugar	Coffee butter cream
3 eggs	6 oz. chocolate
7 oz. flour	6 oz. melted butter
1 tbsp. cocoa	Walnuts, hazelnuts
1 tsp. baking powder	and icing sugar

Cream the fat and sugar and beat in the eggs gradually. Sieve the flour, cocoa and baking powder, and add to the creamed ingredients, with a little milk to give a dropping consistency. Put into two prepared 7-inch sandwich tins, and bake in a moderate oven (350° F., mark 4) for 35–40 minutes. Cool, and sandwich together with coffee butter cream. Coat the surface with a chocolate icing made with the melted chocolate and 6 oz. melted butter mixed well together. Mark round the sides with a fork, and decorate the top with some coffee butter cream and the nuts, after dusting the latter with icing sugar.

FRUIT SPONGE GÂTEAU

6 eggs	Flaked almonds
6 oz. sugar	2 small tins mandarin
6 oz. flour	oranges
4 oz. butter	Glacé cherries
Butter cream	Whipped cream

Whisk the eggs and sugar in a basin over hot water till thick and creamy. Add the sieved flour and melted butter, folding them in carefully. Put into a 10-inch prepared sandwich tin, and bake in a moderate oven (350° F., mark 4) for $\frac{1}{2}$–$\frac{3}{4}$ hour. When cool, sandwich together with butter cream, and spread this round the sides also, then decorate the sides with browned flaked almonds. Arrange well-drained mandarin slices and cherries over the surface, then coat with a little of the thickened mandarin syrup, tinted with some red colouring. Pipe whipped cream round the outside of the fruit.

SANS-GÊNE CAKE

4 oz. sugar	8 oz. praline cream (see
3 large eggs	below)
3 oz. butter	2 oz. toasted almonds
3 oz. flour	Biscuit cones (see below)

Put 1 oz. sugar into a pan with 1 tbsp. water and dissolve the sugar, bring to the boil and cook until it is a light brown colour. Pour into a greased tin and leave to get cold, then crush.

Put the eggs, caramel and remaining sugar into a basin and whisk over boiling water until thick and light ; remove from the heat and beat until cold. Melt the butter, and when it is cool, add it alternately with the flour. Bake in a greased and lined 7-inch tin for 30 minutes in a moderate oven (350° F., mark 4), then cool on a rack. Split the cake in three, then sandwich together with some of the praline cream, coat the sides of the cake and roll in split toasted almonds. Spread more cream over the top and arrange biscuit cones, piped with the cream, on top.

Praline Cream

Dissolve 4 oz. sugar in 2 tbsps. water, add 4 oz. unblanched almonds, heat until the sugar caramelises, pour into a tin and leave to cool. When cold, crush very finely. Beat the praline into 4 oz. butter creamed with 8 oz. icing sugar.

Biscuit Cones

Whisk the white of 1 egg, add 2 tbsps. caster sugar, 1 tbsp. ground almonds and 2 tsps. each of flour and melted butter. Drop small spoonfuls on to a greased baking tin and bake in a hot oven (400° F., mark 6) for 4–5 minutes. Remove and roll round cream horn tins. Place them inside the tins to cool.

PRALINE GÂTEAU

6 eggs	4 oz. butter
6 oz. caster sugar	Praline butter cream
6 oz. flour	Flaked almonds

Whisk the eggs and sugar in a bowl over hot water till thick and creamy. Lightly fold in the sieved flour and then the melted butter. Put into two greased and prepared 8-inch sandwich tins, and bake in a moderate oven (350° F., mark 4) for 20–25 minutes. Make some butter cream flavoured with praline and use some of it to sandwich the two cakes together. Spread the rest of the cream round the sides and over the top, and decorate with browned flaked almonds. Pipe some butter cream on the edges, and pipe the word " Praline " on the top.

MONT BLANC AUX MARRONS

3 eggs	Apricot purée
4 oz. sugar	Browned almonds
3 oz. butter	Chestnut purée
3 oz. flour	(see this page)

Beat the eggs and sugar together over hot water until they are thick and frothy. Melt the butter, and allow it to cool, then sieve the flour. Add the flour and melted butter alternately to the whisked mixture, and mix well. Pour the mixture into a Swiss roll tin and bake in a

moderately hot oven (400° F., mark 6) for 20–25 minutes ; cool on a rack. Cut into 2-inch rounds, using a scone cutter, and coat the sides and top of the cakes with apricot purée. Roll the sides in chopped browned almonds and pipe the chestnut purée into whirls on top of each cake.

Chestnut Purée

3 oz. granulated sugar	½ lb. cooked chestnuts,
4 tbsps. water	peeled and sieved
Vanilla essence	

Dissolve the sugar in the water and bring to the boil. Simmer gently until a hard ball is formed when a drop of the syrup is put into cold water. Mix with the sieved chestnuts, add vanilla essence, and use as required.

PROGRESS CAKE

5 egg whites	Blanched and roasted
7 oz. caster sugar	almonds
5 oz. ground almonds	Flaked chocolate to
8 oz. chocolate praline	decorate (see below)
cream (see below)	

Place the egg whites in a bowl and beat until they are very stiff. Mix together the sugar and ground almonds and add to egg mixture. Make into three 8-inch rounds, putting them on to oiled paper, and bake in a moderate oven (350° F., mark 4) for ¼ hour, then cool. Sandwich meringue rounds together with chocolate praline cream. Coat the top and sides with the same mixture, stick chopped roasted almonds round the sides and decorate the top with flaked chocolate.

Chocolate Praline Cream

Dissolve 4 oz. sugar in 2 tbsps. water, add 4 oz. unblanched almonds, heat until the sugar caramelises, pour into a tin and leave to cool. When cold, crush very finely. Beat the caramel into 4 oz. butter creamed with 8 oz. icing sugar and 2 oz. melted chocolate.

Flaked Chocolate

Melt some chocolate over a low flame, then pour it on to a cold surface (e.g. marble). Cool until the chocolate is no longer sticky when the back of the hand is put on it. Hold a large knife vertically on the chocolate and pull it along the top, which should come loose and roll into thin layers and flakes.

CHAMONIX

2 egg whites	Whipped cream
Caster sugar	Vanilla essence to
Chestnut purée (see above)	flavour

Whisk the egg whites until stiff and frothy, beat in 2 oz. sugar, and fold in a further 2 oz. Put the mixture into a forcing bag fitted with a plain nozzle, and pipe into the shape of nests. Sprinkle with caster sugar, and bake in a slow oven (250° F., mark ¼) until crisp and cooked throughout. Build up the sides of the nests with piped chestnut purée, and fill with vanilla-flavoured whipped cream.

PALMIERS

Puff pastry — Whipped cream or jam
Caster sugar — Sieved icing sugar

Roll the pastry out evenly until it is ¼ inch thick and about 20 inches long, then sprinkle it thoroughly with caster sugar. Fold the ends over to the centre until they meet and press with the rolling pin. Sprinkle thoroughly with sugar and fold the side to the centre again. Press and sprinkle with sugar. Place the two folded portions together and press, then with a sharp knife cut into ¼-inch slices. Place cut edge down on a baking sheet, allowing room to spread, sprinkle with caster sugar and bake in a hot oven (450° F., mark 8) until golden-brown. Cool on a rack, and just before serving, pipe sweetened whipped cream on to half of the slices, sandwich with the remaining ones, and dredge with icing sugar. Jam may be used, if preferred in place of cream.

GÂTEAU SAINT-HONORÉ
(SAINT-HONORÉ BIRTHDAY CAKE)

3 oz. butter — ⅛ pint water for sugar
½ pint water for choux — syrup
  pastry — ½ pint double cream
5 oz. flour — Candied or fresh soft
4–5 eggs —   fruits
5 oz. sugar

Put the fat and water into a small saucepan and bring to the boil; remove the pan from the heat and add the sieved flour, stir well, return the pan to the heat and cook gently, stirring for about a minute, or until a smooth ball is formed. Break the eggs into a basin and beat them lightly. Allow the mixture to cool slightly, and add the eggs a little at a time; use enough egg to give a stiff paste that will pipe easily and retain its shape. Beat the mixture very thoroughly until it is quite smooth. Butter and flour 2 large baking sheets. Fill a large forcing bag fitted with a plain ½-inch nozzle. Describe a circle on one baking sheet, and pipe 2 or 3 lines across the circle to make a base for the cake. Using the same pastry tube, drop about 20 small balls on the other baking sheet and bake in a

moderately hot oven (425° F., mark 7) until well risen and golden-brown—allow 20 minutes for the puffs, and 25–30 minutes for the base. Meanwhile boil the sugar and water until the syrup reaches a temperature of 238° F., or until it will form a soft ball when put in cold water. When the puffs are baked, dip each one in the syrup and place on an oiled surface to cool When the puffs and rings are cool, attach the puffs to the outer edges of the base with a little hot syrup, and build up the sides decoratively. Fill the centre of the ring with whipped cream, and decorate with fruits. Place the appropriate number of birthday candles in the puffs of the top ring.

CROISSANTS

½ oz. yeast — ¼–½ pint warm milk or
10 oz. flour —   water
½ oz. sugar — 6 oz. butter or margarine
A pinch of salt — Egg to glaze

Blend the yeast with a little cold water, and mix all the ingredients except the fat, adding sufficient liquid to give a soft elastic dough. Put in a warm place to rise for almost 1 hour; when it has about doubled its original size, put on a floured board and cool slightly. Soften the fat by beating with the hand, place it on the dough, then fold over the ends of the dough to cover it. Roll and fold as for flaky pastry, putting it in a warm place to rest after two rollings. After rolling and folding five times in all, roll out thinly, cut into wide strips, and then into large triangles; roll each into a crescent shape. Place on an ungreased tray and leave in a warm place to prove for about 20 minutes. Brush over with egg, and bake in a very hot oven (475° F., mark 9) for about 10 minutes.

DAME BLANCHE
(WHITE LADY)

4 eggs — ½ tsp. vanilla essence
5 oz. sugar — Vanilla sugar
1 pint milk — Candied fruits

Beat the egg whites very stiffly and place in a greased ovenware dish. Cover, and bake for 20 minutes in a moderate oven (375° F., mark 5); watch it carefully, and remove the cover if the whites rise too high. Beat the egg yolks with the sugar, add the warmed milk and flavour with vanilla; pour into a double saucepan and cook very slowly, as for cup custard, until the mixture has thickened. Invert the moulded whites on to a dish, and pour the sauce round. Sprinkle with vanilla-flavoured sugar and decorate with candied fruits.

GERMANY is famous for hearty eating and the rest of the world is apt to regard it mainly as the home of sausages and sauerkraut, but it is a large area and as it is only a comparatively short time since it was composed of dozens of independent states, the cookery remains strongly regional in character.

North Germany is noted for delicious sea fish, crabs and eels ; Hamburg rolls and the heather honey from the heathlands are famous. Westphalian pumpernickel is widely exported and is perfect with the local smoked hams and cheeses. The beautiful Rhineland country produces some of the best white wine in the world, as well as black bread and sausages. Franconia, the region of the Main, Neckar and Rhine rivers, is noted for delicious trout and freshwater fish. Further south, in Bavaria, there is a variety of dumplings and all kinds of sausages—in Munich, the capital, the speciality is a white sausage, served with sauerkraut and the excellent light beer which comes in enormous steins and is drunk at all times of the day, often with large radishes and twisted, salty pretzels, to make a favourite snack.

Germany produces excellent fruit and vegetables, but meat can be expensive and is not necessarily served every day. The main meal is usually eaten in the middle of the day and consists of soup and a meat dish with vegetables, dumplings and salad, followed by a light pudding or fruit. Supper is simple and often composed of cold meats and sausages, salad and a variety of breads and rolls. Puddings are not widely made, but of course the Germans are hardly to be surpassed in the art of baking breads and plain cakes and biscuits, as well as the delicious Kuchen, large round cakes filled and decorated with fruit, nuts, chocolate and cream, which are so tempting with coffee, morning, afternoon or evening.

Germany

LINSENSUPPE
(LENTIL SOUP)

1 lb. lentils	½ tsp. pepper
¼ lb. bacon, diced	½ tsp. dried thyme
2 medium onions, sliced	2 bay leaves
2 medium carrots, diced	1 large potato, peeled
2 quarts water	1 ham bone
1 cup celery, sliced	2 tbsps. lemon juice
2½–3 tsps. salt	

Wash the lentils the night before and leave to soak covered with cold water. Early next day drain them, then sauté the diced bacon till golden. Add sliced onions and diced carrots and sauté till onions are golden. Next, add lentils, water, sliced celery, salt, pepper, thyme and bay leaves. Now with medium grater, grate peeled potato into lentil mixture; add the ham bone. Simmer, covered for 3 hours, when lentils should be nice and tender. Remove the bay leaves and ham bone; cut all meat from it, and return meat to soup. Add lemon juice and serve at once.

BIERSUPPE MIT MILCH
(BEER AND MILK SOUP)

1 bottle German beer	1 pint milk
Juice of ½ lemon	2 egg yolks
A piece of cinnamon	Sugar and salt
stick	Croûtons of fried bread

Heat the beer in a pan with the lemon juice and cinnamon. Heat the milk and pour it over the egg yolks, stirring well. Add to the hot beer, and season with sugar and salt. Serve with croûtons of fried bread.

MOULDED EGGS ON TOAST

4 eggs	1 tsp. anchovy paste
¼ pint milk	1 tsp. capers
1 tbsp. lemon juice	Butter or margarine
8 oz. leftover meat	Salt and pepper

Beat or whisk the eggs well with the milk and lemon juice, and mix with the finely chopped meat, anchovy paste and capers. Taste to check the seasoning, and adjust if necessary. Put the mixture into well-greased small moulds, cover, and put into hot but not boiling water; leave until firm (about 20 minutes), then turn out on to toasted bread. Garnish as desired.

FISCHBOULETTEN VON KABELJAU
(CODFISH BALLS WITH SPINACH)

1¼ lb. cod	Breadcrumbs
1 roll soaked in milk	Butter
1 chopped onion	Spinach
1 yolk of egg	2 chopped anchovies
Flour	Salt, pepper, nutmeg

Bone and skin the fish, and chop it finely. Mix with the bread, soaked in milk and squeezed, and the finely chopped onion, lightly fried in butter but not browned, and season with salt, pepper and nutmeg. Shape the mixture in rissoles, dip in flour, brush over with yolk of egg and coat with breadcrumbs. Fry the rissoles in butter and keep hot. Pour the rest of the butter over them and garnish with chopped spinach and anchovies.

FISCH MIT SAUERKRAUT
(FISH WITH SAUERKRAUT)

2 lb. fish (any kind)	2 tbsps. flour
2 onions	½ pint fish stock
2 carrots	1 gill sour cream
2¼ lb. sauerkraut	Grated cheese
2 tbsps. chopped ham	Salt and pepper
3 tbsps. butter	

Skin and bone the fish and cut it in 2-inch lengths. Make fish stock with the bones, sliced carrots, 1 onion, salt and pepper. Boil the sauerkraut till tender, and drain thoroughly. Make a sauce with the butter and flour, 1 finely chopped cooked onion, the ham, ½ pint of fish stock, and the sour cream and simmer till slightly reduced. Put a layer of sauerkraut in the bottom of a fireproof dish, cover with fish and a little sauce; repeat the layers. Sprinkle with grated cheese, and put in a moderate oven (375° F., mark 5) for 30 minutes or longer, until the fish is cooked.

BISMARCK HERRING WITH POTATO SALAD

1 lb. new potatoes	Salt and pepper
¼ lb. small carrots	2 tbsps. white wine
2 Bismarck herrings (or	vinegar
rollmops)	Finely chopped onion
3 tbsps. olive oil	Chopped parsley

Cook the potatoes and carrots until just tender, then slice them. Add the herrings, cut up into small pieces. Thoroughly mix together the olive oil, seasonings, wine vinegar and onion, and pour over the other ingredients. Sprinkle with finely chopped parsley.

ROLLED HERRINGS IN WINE SAUCE

1½ lb. fresh herrings	¾ pint buttermilk or
Salt	sour cream or milk
Juice of 1 lemon	4–5 tbsps. white wine
1½ oz. margarine	2 rashers of bacon
1½ oz. flour	1–2 chopped gherkins

Bone the herrings, salt them and sprinkle some lemon juice over them. Make a sauce with the fat, flour, buttermilk and wine. Mix the fried bacon and gherkins, place some on each fillet and roll the fillets, securing them with cocktail sticks or fine string. Simmer them for about 20 minutes in the wine sauce, remove the cocktail sticks or string, and serve with mashed potatoes and steamed whole tomatoes.

GEFÜLLTER HECHT
(STUFFED PIKE)

1 pike	1–2 egg yolks
1 lb. uncooked white fish	Salt and pepper
1 finely chopped onion	Nutmeg
A little butter	Sliced onions
2–3 slices of bread	1 glass of white wine
Milk	A little stock

Prepare and clean the pike. Cook the white fish and chopped onion in a little butter, and rub through a sieve. Soak the bread in the milk and squeeze it, then add to the fish and onion mixture. Add the egg yolks, seasoning and a little grated nutmeg. Stuff the pike with this, skewer it, put into a fireproof dish with some sliced onions, white wine and stock ; put a little butter on top of the fish, and bake for about ¾ hour in a moderate oven (350° F., mark 4), basting frequently. Serve with béchamel sauce.

LACHSRÖLLCHEN MIT RÜHREI
(SALMON ROLLS WITH SCRAMBLED EGG)

4–6 slices of smoked salmon	A pinch of salt
	A little butter
1 egg	Olives or mayonnaise
1 tbsp. water	to garnish

Scramble the egg with the butter, water and salt and let it get cool. Cover each slice of salmon with scrambled egg and roll up carefully. Garnish with half an olive or some mayonnaise.

HERINGSALAT
(HERRING SALAD SERVED IN APPLES)

1 salted herring, soaked for 24 hours	10 small gherkins
	1 tbsp. capers
2 large cooked carrots	5 large juicy apples
3½ oz. pickled mushrooms	2 saltspoonfuls salt
	1½ gills oil
5 oz. cooked French beans	1–2 tbsps. vinegar

Remove all skin and bones from the soaked herring and shred it ; mix with the chopped carrots, mushrooms, beans, gherkins and capers. Allow to cool, and leave to stand for at least 8–10 hours. About 2 hours before serving, cut off a piece of the top from each apple (reserving it to form a lid). Scoop out part of the pulp, chop finely and mix with the salad, together with a dressing made from the last three ingredients. Fill the apples with the mixture, piling it high, and put on the " lids." Any remaining salad may be piled in small pyramids on rings of onions, and used to garnish the serving dish.

Salted cucumbers or tomatoes may be similarly stuffed.

SCHWEINSFILETS MIT SAUER SAHNE
(FILLETS OF PORK WITH SOUR CREAM)

2 lb. fillet of pork	1 tbsp. flour
Larding fat	1 tbsp. capers
Butter	2 tbsps. tomato purée
1 gill sour cream	2 tbsps. stock

Cut thin slices from the fillet, removing all fat and skin. Lard with larding fat, put them in a saucepan in hot butter, brown evenly on both sides, cover the saucepan and simmer very gently for about 10 minutes. Add cream, and simmer for another 15 minutes. Remove the fillets from the sauce, and keep hot. Stir in the flour, then add chopped capers, tomato purée and stock, cook till thickened and pour over the fillets.

SCHWEINSBRATEN MIT EINER KRUSTE
(ROAST PORK WITH CRUST)

3–4 lb. fillet of pork	1–2 egg yolks
1 onion	Breadcrumbs
1 bay leaf	1 glass of white wine
A little sage	Salt and pepper
Sweet basil	

Put the meat in a meat tin, with 1 whole onion, the herbs, and season with salt and pepper. Pour ½ a pint of hot water over the meat, and cook (375°–400° F., mark 5–6) till tender, allowing 30 minutes to the lb. plus 30 minutes and basting frequently. When done, put on a dish and let stand till cold. Then brush the top of the meat with yolk of egg, cover with breadcrumbs, moisten with a little of the liquid from the pan and continue coating the meat with breadcrumbs and liquid till a crust of about ½ inch thick is formed. Put the meat in a hot oven (450° F., mark 8) for 15 minutes, basting frequently. Place on a hot dish, add wine to the pan and boil up, scraping and stirring well. Strain liquid over the meat.

KALBSBRATEN MIT BIER
(ROAST VEAL WITH BEER)

A loin of veal	1 bay leaf
Larding fat	2 cloves
2 or 3 carrots	1 tbsp. flour
2 or 3 onions	Butter
1 glass German brown beer	Salt
	Pepper

Put the meat, which should be closely larded with larding fat, in a deep meat tin, season with salt and a little pepper, add the sliced carrots and the sliced onions, pour melted butter over it, and cook for half an hour in a moderately hot oven (425° F., mark 7) till evenly browned on all sides. Pour the beer over the meat, add the bay leaf and cloves, and cook in a moderate oven (375° F., mark 5) till the meat is tender, allowing 30 minutes per lb. and basting frequently. When done, put the meat on a hot dish. Thicken the sauce with 1 tbsp. of flour, boil up, strain and pour over the meat.

STUFFED BELLY OF PORK

2 lb. belly of pork   3 oz. sultanas
1 lb. cooking apples

Wipe the meat and slit through at one side to make a pocket. Fill this tightly with cut-up apples and sultanas, then sew up the opening with needle and thread. Bake in a moderate oven (350° F., mark 4) for 2½ hours. Remove the thread and serve with red cabbage and apple.

ROAST PORK WITH MADEIRA SAUCE

2 lb. loin of pork   Seasoning
½ pint water   1 oz. flour
½ pint white wine   ¼ bottle Madeira wine
¼ tbsp. vinegar   1 lb. apples, sliced and
4 bay leaves   cooked

Trim the pork so that it can be easily carved when cooked. Put it into a baking tin with the water, white wine, vinegar, bay leaves and seasonings, and bake in a moderate oven (350° F., mark 4), basting occasionally, until tender (1¼–1½ hours). Arrange the meat, cut into slices, down the centre of a dish and keep hot.

Make a sauce with the liquor, flour and Madeira wine, and pour over the meat. Serve with cooked apple slices.

OX TONGUE

1 ox tongue (pickled   Madeira, caper, mush-
or fresh)   room, anchovy or
A pinch of spice   raisin sauce
1 small onion   Parsley or other garnish

Wash the tongue well, and in the case of a fresh one, trim the root. Put the tongue into a pan with the spice and onion, add about 3 pints cold water, lid tightly and simmer gently for 3 hours or so, until tender when tested with a skewer. Meanwhile make the sauce, as desired. Skin the tongue, put it on a serving dish, pour the sauce over, and garnish as desired. Alternatively, slice the meat neatly and surround with an attractively arranged vegetable.

A tongue which is to be served cold is not cooked quite so soft ; let it cool in the liquor,

then place it between two plates, weight lightly, and leave until quite cold. Skin, carve neatly, trimming the slices as required, arrange on a dish, each slice overlapping the next, and garnish.

LEBERKLÖSSE
(LIVER DUMPLINGS)

½ lb. calf's liver   1 tbsp. flour
A slice of bread soaked   Salt and pepper
in milk   Grated rind of ½ a lemon
1 chopped onion   1 egg
1 heaped tbsp. chop-   Stock or salted water
ped parsley   2 oz. butter

Chop the liver very finely. Squeeze the bread dry and mix to a paste with the liver, onion, parsley and flour. Season, and add the lemon rind. Moisten with beaten egg and make into small balls. (Add the egg very cautiously—it is advisable to test the consistency of the mixture by dropping small pieces into boiling water before rolling the whole into balls.) Boil the dumplings in the stock or salted water for 15–20 minutes ; serve with melted butter poured over, and hand dry boiled rice separately as an accompaniment.

SAUERBRATEN
(BRAISED TOPSIDE)

3 lb. topside   1 onion, sliced
2 oz. lard   1 carrot, sliced
Salt   2 glasses red wine
6 peppercorns   1 tbsp. wine vinegar
1 tsp. dry mustard   1 oz. flour
1 bay leaf   ½ pint sour cream
1 sprig thyme   ¼ pint stock
4 cloves

Put the wine, vinegar, carrot, onion, spices, bay leaf, thyme, salt and mustard into a pan. Marinade the meat in this mixture for 48 hours, turning it every 12 hours. Drain the meat and fry it lightly on all sides in the lard. Pour the marinade over it and cook, covered with a lid, in a slow oven (325° F., mark 2) for 3 hours. Strain the sauce and thicken with the flour, add stock if necessary and the cream. Slice the meat and pour the sauce over it. Serve with noodles.

RINDERSCHMORBRATEN
(STEWED BEEF)

2 lb. stewing beef or   ½ oz. salt
brisket   ¾ oz. flour
1 oz. fat bacon for   1 oz. fat
larding   ¾ oz. breadcrumbs
A pinch of spice   1 small onion

Beat the meat and tie it into a good shape with string. Cut the bacon into strips 1½ inches long

and $\frac{1}{2}$ inch wide, then coat with the mixed spice and salt. Using a larding needle, insert these bacon strips into the meat at regular intervals. Meanwhile heat the fat (with any remaining bacon pieces) in a flameproof casserole until very hot, and brown the rolled meat on all sides, turning it with spoons or tongs. Now add the other ingredients and slowly pour in about $\frac{1}{2}$ pint hot water, cover tightly and simmer very slowly. After $\frac{1}{2}$ hour turn the meat, and if necessary add more hot water (or if preferred, add red wine or beer). After 3 hours—longer in the case of a large piece of meat—take it out and keep it hot while preparing the sauce.

Skim the gravy, and if necessary either thicken it with flour, or thin it down with a little more liquid, and add a little gravy browning to improve the colour; strain it, pour it back into the casserole, put in the meat, and reheat. Before serving, spoon some of the gravy over the beef, to give it an attractive glazed appearance. Garnish with sliced lemon or with vegetables as desired, and serve with roast potatoes.

The flavour may be varied by adding chopped gherkins, capers, tiny silver onions, mushrooms or olives, etc., to the brown sauce, after this has been strained, or by cooking 3–4 tomatoes with the meat.

A quickly made version of this dish may be prepared by using beef that has been previously cooked; simmer it for 1 hour only after browning it, and add gravy or pale ale instead of water.

To make *Sauerbraten* (marinaded beef), steep the beef for several days in cold spiced vinegar before cooking it in the above manner. The marinade may be added to the water used for stewing.

PORK CHOPS WITH APPLE

1 tbsp. chopped onion	Fat for frying
1 tbsp. chopped parsley	1 lb. apples
1 tsp. chopped sage	$\frac{1}{4}$ oz. butter
Salt and pepper	$\frac{1}{2}$ oz. sugar
1–2 eggs	Juice of 1 lemon
4 pork chops	1 glass wine
Fresh breadcrumbs	

Mix together the onion, parsley, sage, seasonings and eggs, beat lightly and put on to a plate. Put the trimmed chops into this mixture for about 15 minutes, turning them occasionally. Drain, and dip into fresh breadcrumbs. Fry in hot fat until brown. Meanwhile, peel and slice the apples and put into a pan with the butter, sugar, lemon juice and wine, and simmer gently until tender. Dish the pork chops on this mixture.

W.C.B.—8

MEAT CAKES WITH SAUERKRAUT SAUCE

$\frac{1}{2}$ lb. beef	$\frac{1}{2}$ pint stock
$\frac{1}{2}$ lb. pork	1 glass white wine
2 slices bread	1 tsp. capers
1 gill milk	1 tsp. French mustard
1 onion, chopped	1 dessertsp. sugar
6 anchovy fillets	Juice of $\frac{1}{2}$ lemon
1 egg	2 egg yolks
Butter	Salt
1 oz. flour	Pepper

Soak the bread in the milk, squeeze it gently and mix it with the minced meat, chopped onion and minced anchovies. Season with salt and pepper. Bind with the egg. Shape into flat cakes and fry in the butter. Keep warm.

To make the sauce, heat 1 oz. butter, cook the flour in it for 1 minute, gradually add the stock and the wine. Add the capers, mustard, sugar, lemon juice, salt and pepper. Pour the sauce over the rissoles, cook slowly for 15 minutes. Mix the beaten egg yolks with a little melted butter and stir carefully into the sauce just before serving.

PORK CHOPS WITH PLUMS

4 pork chops	4 cloves
$\frac{1}{2}$ lb. plums	1 glass red wine
1 oz. sugar	Salt
Cinnamon	Pepper

Trim the chops and fry lightly in the surplus fat. Stew the plums with the sugar in a little water. Pass through a sieve. Put the chops in a shallow fireproof dish. Mix a pinch of cinnamon and the cloves with the strained plums. Pour on top of the chops. Add the wine. Season with salt and pepper. Cover with a lid and bake in a moderate oven (350° F., mark 4) for 1 hour, adding a little water from time to time if necessary.

PORK, SAUERKRAUT AND BEANS

41

1 lb. haricot beans	Butter for frying
Ham stock	Frankfurt sausages,
1 lb. sauerkraut	previously boiled
2 oz. lard	Boiled ham, bacon or
Breadcrumbs	pork

Soak the beans overnight in cold water, and then cook in the ham stock for about 2 hours, until tender. Cook the sauerkraut until tender in salted water (if freshly made sauerkraut is available, this will take up to 2 hours; if tinned, cook for only 2–3 minutes). Drain the sauerkraut and add the lard. Sieve the beans and put them in the centre of a hot dish sprinkled with breadcrumbs fried brown in butter. Dish up the sauerkraut round the beans, and put the Frankfurt sausages and slices of ham or bacon on top.

ROLLFLEISCH
(SMALL MEAT ROLLS)

1 lb. thick steak	Fat for frying
6 rashers of bacon	A little flour
1 sliced onion	A bay leaf
Salt and pepper	

Cut the steak into small, thin slices. Spread each with ½ a rasher of bacon and 1 slice of onion, and season well; roll up and tie with cotton. Fry the rolls in the fat in a frying pan, browning them on all sides, then place them in a saucepan. Put ½ pint water into the frying pan and boil until brown, pour this over the rolls, add salt, pepper and bay leaf and simmer very gently for about 1½ hours. Thicken the gravy, and serve it with the rolls.

RINDFLEISCH IN BIER GESCHMÖRT
(BEEF STEWED IN BEER)

3–4 lb. rump steak	1 tbsp. brown syrup
Slices of fat bacon	Salt
Sliced onions	Peppercorns
Brown beer and water	2–3 cloves
½ cup of vinegar	1 bay leaf

Flatten out the beef, roll it up and tie with string. Put the bacon in the bottom of a saucepan and add the onions, then the meat. Cover with equal quantities of beer and water, add the remaining ingredients, cover, and simmer for 3 hours over a low heat.

PORK CHOPS WITH SOUR CREAM

4 pork chops	Thyme
¼ pint sour cream	Flour
Juice of ½ lemon	Salt
1 tsp. sugar	Pepper

Trim the chops and render down the surplus fat. Season the chops, and dust with flour. Fry lightly on both sides in the fat. Transfer to a casserole, add the sour cream, lemon juice, sugar and a pinch of thyme. Pour in enough water to cover the chops. Put a lid on the casserole. Cook in a moderate oven (375° F., mark 5) until tender, about an hour.

MEAT BALLS

43 Use ½ lb. minced meat, with about the same volume of stale white bread; soak the bread in a little water, then squeeze out the surplus liquid and break up the bread with a fork before adding it to the minced meat. Flavour with a little minced onion, some chopped herbs (e.g., marjoram and thyme) and a little meat extract, with some salt if required. Bind with beaten egg, form into small balls with the hands, and fry in hot fat until nicely browned.

These meat balls are particularly good served with boiled rice and fresh spinach. As a change from spinach cooked in the usual way, put the washed and well-drained leaves into a little very hot fat and cook for 10 minutes, then add a little salt, meat extract and sugar to flavour; this gives a much "drier" result.

Place the spinach in the centre of a large dish, and if desired sprinkle it with grated cheese. Arrange the meat balls round the outside.

BEEF AND BEANS

8 oz. haricot beans	3 lb. beef (salt or fresh)
2 lb. runner beans	Seasoning

Soak the haricot beans overnight. Prepare the runner beans, and put with the haricot beans in a saucepan, place the beef on top, add water until the pan is about three-quarters full, season, and cook gently till tender—about 2–3 hours. Serve with boiled potatoes.

GERMAN " BEEFSTEAK " WITH FRIED EGGS

Combine 1 lb. freshly minced fillet or rump steak with 1 large or 2 small eggs, salt and pepper. Form into 4 balls, flatten slightly, and fry in hot butter for a short time, until brown on the outside but still red inside. Fry 4 eggs, and put one on each "steak."

This makes a delicious and easily cooked meal, and is often served on Sundays. In summer it is excellent with lettuce and new potatoes, and in winter with sautéed potatoes and a green vegetable.

FALSCHER HASE
(MOCK HARE)

1 lb. beef and pork, minced	Salt
	Grated nutmeg
1 small onion	A little thyme
A little parsley	2 eggs
A little butter	2 hard-boiled eggs
¼ lb. breadcrumbs	(optional)
A little milk	

Mince the meats; chop the onion and parsley, and fry in the butter until light brown. Moisten the breadcrumbs with the milk. Put all the ingredients (except the hard-boiled eggs) in a bowl, and mix well with the hand. Put on a baking tray and form into a roll, putting the hard-boiled eggs in the centre, if used. Pour some melted butter over, and bake in a moderate oven (350° F., mark 4) for ¾ hour. Serve with a vegetable.

HUSARENBRATEN
(HUSSAR'S ROAST)

2½ lb. thick beefsteak	A few carrots or mushrooms
Filling (see recipes)	
Salt	A bouquet garni
Flour	A little bacon
Butter	½ pint stock
½ an onion	A little sour cream

Get your butcher to cut a square piece of topside, and to cut it through in ¾-inch slices, still attached at one side, so that the meat resembles a book with thick leaves. Prepare one of the following fillings :

Cheese Stuffing : Slice thinly 2 oz. Gruyère or Cheshire cheese and 4 oz. bacon ; chop 2 oz. onion and fry in a little fat ; add 3–4 oz. breadcrumbs and 1 egg yolk, and mix.

Liver Stuffing : Chop 3 oz. calf's liver and mix with 3 oz. breadcrumbs soaked in milk and squeezed fairly dry. Fry this mixture in 1½ oz. butter, allow to cool, and mix with 2 egg yolks.

Sprinkle a little salt between the meat "leaves," spread the stuffing evenly between them, then bind the meat firmly but not too tightly with string. Roll it in a little flour, and fry in very hot butter until nicely browned. Place in a casserole, add the onion, carrots (or mushrooms if liver stuffing is used), bouquet garni, shredded bacon and stock. Cover, and simmer very gently for 2–2½ hours—if boiled, the meat will be tough.

Strain the gravy and remove the grease, add the cream mixed with 1 oz. flour, and bring to the boil. Serve the meat surrounded by cooked mushrooms and whole tomatoes.

GEWÜRZIGE SCHWEINSRIPPCHEN
(SPICY SPARERIBS)

4 lb. spareribs, cracked through centre	2 tbsps. vinegar
⅓ cup flour	½ tsp. celery salt
2 tsps. salt	⅛ tsp. cayenne
¼ tsp. pepper	3 whole cloves
3 tbsps. butter	3 whole allspice
2 beef bouillon cubes	½ bay leaf
1½ cups boiling water	½ clove garlic, minced
¼ cup ketchup	1 medium onion, minced
3 tbsps. piquant sauce	¼ cup cold water
	2 tbsps. flour

Start heating oven to 350° F. about 2½ hours before serving. Wipe ribs with a clean damp cloth and cut into serving-size pieces. Combine ⅓ cup flour, salt and pepper ; use to coat ribs evenly on all sides. In large, heavy pan, melt butter ; in it, brown ribs on both sides. Meanwhile, dissolve bouillon cubes in boiling water ; then stir in ketchup, piquant sauce, vinegar, celery, salt, cayenne, cloves, allspice, bay leaf and garlic. Arrange ribs in roasting pan ; pour bouillon mixture over them ; sprinkle with minced onion. Cover with foil ; bake about 1½ hours or till ribs are tender. With a slotted spoon, remove ribs from pan to heated platter. Keep warm while preparing sauce (see below).

Spicy Sauce : Skim excess fat from liquid in roasting pan. Strain liquid into small saucepan ; then bring to a boil ; slowly stir cold water into 2 tbsps. flour until smooth. While stirring constantly, slowly pour half of flour mixture into boiling liquid ; bring back to boil ; then gradually add as much more of flour mixture as is needed to make sauce of desired thickness. Cook for 3–5 minutes until smooth and thickened. Spoon or pour about half of hot sauce over spareribs. Serve rest in gravy boat. Serves up to 6 people.

RAHMSCHNITZEL
(VEAL CUTLETS WITH CREAM)

¾ lb. minced steak	2 tbsps. packed dried breadcrumbs
¾ tsp. salt	
⅛ tsp. pepper	¼ cup melted butter
¼ tsp. nutmeg	4 pieces ½-inch thick (1½ lb.) veal cutlet
4 sprigs parsley, chopped finely	Salt and pepper
1 egg, beaten	1 tbsp. sour cream

About 1¾ hours before serving mix the steak, salt, pepper, nutmeg, parsley, beaten egg and breadcrumbs and refrigerate. Heat oven to 350° F. (mark 4). Put the butter in a pan, brown 4 pieces of veal cutlet and arrange in a 9-inch baking dish ; sprinkle with a little salt and pepper. Form steak into 4 1-inch thick cakes ; place one on each piece of veal. Pour drippings from pan over all. Bake, basting occasionally, 30–40 minutes, or till veal is tender. Turn off oven heat ; top each helping with 1 tbsp. sour cream. Let stand in oven just till cream melts.

SCHINKENTÜTCHEN MIT SAHNEMEERRETTICH
(HAM CORNETS WITH HORSERADISH CREAM)

1 tbsp. grated horseradish	A little sugar
1 tbsp. cream or tinned milk	Lemon juice
A pinch of salt	4 slices of raw ham

Mix the horseradish with the cream, add salt, sugar and lemon juice to taste. Roll the ham into tricornes and fill to the top with the horseradish mixture.

HARE IN RED WINE

1 small hare	2 cloves
6 oz. bacon	2 bay leaves
2–3 tbsps. dripping	2 peppercorns
2 oz. flour	Salt and pepper
1 pint stock or water	2 glass red wine
½ lb. small onions	

Cut the hare into small pieces, taking the flesh off the bone when practicable. Cut the bacon into thin strips and mix with the hare. Heat the dripping in a thick stewpan and fry the meat, turning it frequently until brown; then take it out and keep hot. Stir in the flour and add the stock. Add the meat, sliced onions, herbs and seasonings, simmer gently for about 3 hours and then add the red wine and continue to cook until the liquor is thick; remove any excess fat. Serve the meat in a border of potatoes, with the sauce strained over it.

ENTE MIT KASTANIEN FÜLLUNG
(CHESTNUT-STUFFED DUCKLING)

Duckling, weighing 4–5 lb.	1 egg
1 lb. chestnuts	3 tbsps. water
1 tbsp. fat	Honey
3 cups fresh bread-crumbs	2 tbsps. butter
1 tsp. salt	3 slices of apple (½ inch thick and cut in halves)
1 tsp. minced onion	Watercress
½ tsp. chopped parsley	6 cooked prunes
¼ cup melted butter	

The day before or early in the day wipe duckling inside and out with damp cloth. Wrap loosely; then refrigerate. Start heating the oven to 325° F. (mark 3) and cut gash in shell of each chestnut. Arrange them in a 10-inch pan with ovenproof handle and add fat, then bake for 15 minutes. Remove shells and inner skins and cook chestnuts in boiling water to cover until tender—about 5–10 minutes—then drain. Keep 6 whole chestnuts to use for garnish; chop rest fine and refrigerate.

Two and a half hours before serving start heating the oven to 325° F. (mark 3). Combine chopped chestnuts, breadcrumbs, salt, onion, parsley, ¼ cup butter, egg and water. Toss lightly and use to stuff neck and body of duckling; fasten neck skin to back with skewer; close body opening, and place duckling on the rack in a shallow roasting pan. Roast 1½ hours, then turn oven heat up to 425° F. (mark 7), and roast 10 minutes longer. (If you like duckling very well done, roast it 2 hours before turning up oven heat.)

Twenty minutes before duckling is done remove from oven, and brush with 3 tbsps. honey and keep warm. In 2 tbsps. butter in a small pan, sauté apple slices until tender and golden; remove. Then pour ¼ cup honey into skillet, add reserved whole chestnuts, and sauté until glazed. Heap Red Cabbage and Apples (see next page) around duckling and place glazed chestnuts and watercress on breast. Garnish cabbage with sautéed apple slices and prunes. Carve duckling at the table, or if preferred, before serving, halve duckling lengthwise, then crosswise, with poultry shears. Serves 6.

BACKHÄNDEL NACH SÜDDEUTSCHER ART
(YOUNG CHICKENS IN THE SOUTH GERMAN STYLE)

This consists of young chickens, not more than 8 weeks old, split in half, then divided in quarters. Season well with salt, sprinkle them with flour, brush over with yolk of egg, coat with breadcrumbs mixed with equal quantities of grated Parmesan cheese, and fry in butter to a light golden-brown. The sauce served with this is champignon sauce—a mushroom sauce, made with ¼ lb. of chopped mushrooms, cooked in a little butter, vinegar and lemon juice, well season with salt and pepper, mixed with 6 tbsps. of béchamel or white sauce, to which 1 glass of white wine is added and 2 yolks of egg stirred in, a few minutes before serving. Potato salad is served with this fried chicken.

BOHNEN MIT KARTOFFELN
(BEANS WITH POTATOES)

Boiling water	4 rashers bacon, diced
4 medium potatoes, pared, sliced	1 tbsp. flour
2 tsps. salt	¼ tsp. dried thyme
1 packaged frozen green beans	1¾ tsps. salt
	¼ tsp. pepper
	1½ tbsps. vinegar

About 45 minutes before serving start cooking potatoes in boiling water to cover, in covered saucepan, with 2 tsps. salt until almost tender. Then lay block of beans on top of potatoes; cover and cook all till tender; drain. Meanwhile in small pan, sauté bacon until crisp; remove bacon bits. Combine flour, thyme, 1¾ tsps. salt and pepper for the sauce, and stir the hot bacon drippings into this; cook till browned slightly and thickened. Add vinegar; stir smooth. Now pour sauce over vegetables, then sprinkle with bacon, and toss all with two forks. Serve hot, with pot roast or roulades. Makes 4 or 5 servings.

Spinat mit Kartoffeln (Spinach with Potatoes): Prepare as above, substituting 1 package frozen leaf spinach for beans. For sauce, combine

1 tbsp. flour, ½ tsp. nutmeg, ½ tsp. garlic salt, 1¼ tsps. salt, ¼ tsp. pepper. Then proceed as above, substituting water for vinegar.

BAUERNFRÜHSTÜCK
(HOT POTATO SALAD)

Slice 2 lb. cooked potatoes, and chop ¾ lb. luncheon meat or leftover cold cooked meat, etc. Beat 2 eggs in a bowl, adjusting the number according to the amount of potato and meat and the number of people to serve. Add a little chopped chives, with salt and pepper to taste, pour over the potatoes and meat, and fry in a little butter or margarine until light brown.

This is very good served with a French-dressed salad, and makes a convenient way of using up a quantity of leftover cooked potatoes.

RED CABBAGE AND APPLES

1 medium-sized red cabbage	Salt
1½ lb. apples (approx.)	Sugar

Shred the cabbage. Peel and core the apples, keeping the peel ; put this in a pan with a little water and cook until soft, then strain the liquor. Put the liquor in a saucepan with a little salt and the shredded cabbage, and bring to the boil. Put the prepared apple on top, and continue to cook gently, stirring occasionally, until the cabbage is tender—about 1 hour. Add sugar to taste, and simmer for a further 10 minutes.

If any of this cabbage is left over, it will be equally good when warmed up and served at another meal.

STUFFED CABBAGE

1 medium-sized cabbage	Paprika pepper
¾–1 lb. minced meat	Salt
1–3 tbsps. fine white breadcrumbs	4–6 oz. bacon
	Fat for frying
1–2 eggs	A little flour

Put the cabbage into warm water, so that the leaves become loose, then cook them in salted water until half-done. Mix the minced meat, breadcrumbs, eggs, seasonings and bacon, cut into small pieces and lightly fried. Remove the thick centre ribs from the cabbage leaves, put a tablespoonful of the meat filling on each leaf, and roll it up. Heat the fat in the pan and brown the rolled cabbage leaves nicely on all sides, then take them out. Add the flour to the fat and brown it, then add some water. Put in the cabbage rolls, cover, and simmer for about ½ hour.

The filling may be varied by adding some of the remaining cabbage, cooked until soft and finely chopped.

When served with potatoes, this makes an economical and filling but very appetising dish for a hungry family.

GEFÜLLTE KARTOFFELN
(STUFFED POTATOES)

5–6 potatoes	3–4 tbsps. cream
Butter or margarine	Salt, pepper, nutmeg
2 egg yolks	Grated cheese

Prick each potato, after scrubbing it well, and bake slowly until soft. Cut a hole in each and remove the inside, using a small spoon. Sieve the potato and mix with a generous amount of butter, the egg yolks and the cream. Season, add grated nutmeg, and return the mixture to the potato cases. Sprinkle with cheese, dot with shavings of butter or margarine and bake in a moderate oven (350° F., mark 4) until golden on top.

POTATO DUMPLINGS

3 lb. potatoes	3 oz. wheatmeal flour
1 tsp. salt	2 eggs
½ tsp. grated nutmeg	2 slices of bread
2 oz. semolina	Butter

Cook and sieve the potatoes, and leave to become cold. Add the salt, nutmeg, semolina, flour and eggs, and knead into a smooth dough. Cut the bread into small dice and fry light brown in the hot butter.

Flour the hands, make round dumplings about the size of a fist with the potato dough, and press a few of the fried croûtons into each. Put the dumplings into boiling salted water and cook them thoroughly—about 12–15 minutes. Place them on a flat dish and pour melted butter or margarine over them ; alternatively, chop and fry some bacon, and pour over the dumplings.

These dumplings, which are very good, are much eaten in the south of Germany, being served with fat roast meat or accompanied by tomato, herb or onion sauce. They are also served with stewed fruit.

BAVARIAN CABBAGE

Remove the outer leaves of a large white cabbage and divide it into four, then cut out the stalk and shred the cabbage finely.

Melt 1 oz. dripping in a large saucepan, and fry 1 large finely chopped onion. Add the cabbage and stir in 1 tsp. brown sugar, add 1 tbsp. wine vinegar and 2 tbsps. water (previously warmed), cover tightly, and cook until the cabbage is tender.

KARTOFFELN SALAT
(POTATO SALAD)

$1\frac{1}{2}$–2 lb. potatoes	Salt and pepper
1 tsp. finely chopped parsley	2 tbsps. olive oil
	1 tbsp. white vinegar
$\frac{1}{2}$ tsp. finely chopped onion	3–4 tbsps. hot stock
	Sliced cucumber or beetroot to garnish
$\frac{1}{2}$ tsp. finely chopped chives	

Boil the potatoes in their skins and slice them thinly while they are still hot. Put them in a salad bowl, sprinkling each layer with the parsley, onion, chives and seasoning. Mix the oil and vinegar, add the stock, and pour over the salad, mixing lightly. Garnish, and serve while still warm.

RED CABBAGE SALAD

1 lb. red cabbage	2–3 tbsps. lemon juice or vinegar
Salt	
1–2 grated apples	$\frac{1}{2}$ tsp. ground caraway seeds
2–3 tbsps. salad oil	
2–3 tbsps. water	Sugar (optional)

Wash the cabbage and shred it finely, salt it lightly and beat it for about 10 minutes, then add the grated apple. Prepare a marinade with the salad oil, water, lemon juice, caraway seeds and sugar (if used), and let the cabbage steep in it for about 1 hour. Drain well before serving.

WARMER KARTOFFELSALAT
(HOT POTATO SALAD)

2 lb. small white potatoes	$\frac{1}{4}$ tsp. pepper
	$\frac{1}{4}$–$\frac{1}{3}$ cup vinegar
1 tsp. salt	$\frac{1}{2}$ cup water
$\frac{1}{2}$ cup diced bacon	$\frac{1}{4}$ cup minced onion
$\frac{1}{2}$ cup minced onion	2 tbsps. parsley
$1\frac{1}{2}$ tsps. flour	1 tsp. celery seeds
4 tsps. sugar	$\frac{1}{2}$ cup sliced radishes
1 tbsp. salt	Celery leaves

In 1-inch boiling water in covered saucepan, cook potatoes in jackets, with 1 tsp. salt until tender—about 35 minutes. Then peel and cut into $\frac{1}{4}$-inch slices. In a small pan fry bacon until crisp. Add $\frac{1}{2}$ cup minced onion, and sauté until just tender, not brown. Meanwhile, in a bowl, mix flour, sugar, 1 tbsp. salt, and pepper. Stir in vinegar (amount depends on tartness desired) and water until smooth. Add to bacon; then simmer, stirring, until slightly thickened. Pour this hot dressing over potatoes. Add $\frac{1}{4}$ cup minced onion, parsley, celery seeds and radishes. Serve lightly tossed and garnished with celery leaves. Makes 4–6 servings.

KARTOFFELPUFFER
(POTATO PANCAKES)

5 tbsps. flour	1 egg, unbeaten
$1\frac{1}{2}$ lb. potatoes, peeled	$1\frac{1}{2}$ tsp. salt
1 small onion	$\frac{1}{8}$ tsp. pepper

To prevent darkening, plan to fry and serve pancakes as soon as batter is made.

Just before serving; measure flour into a medium bowl; over it, grate peeled potatoes and onion, using fine grater. Then quickly stir in unbeaten egg, salt and pepper. Lightly grease a heavy pan and put over medium heat. Drop heaped tablespoonfuls of potato mixture into hot pan. Fry until crisp and golden-brown on underside. Turn; brown other side. Drain on paper towels. Serve as a vegetable or with apple sauce or mixed stewed fruit at luncheon or supper. Makes about 16.

APFELSINENBISCUITTORTE
(ORANGE CAKE)

6 oz. caster sugar	4 oz. flour
3 eggs	2 oz. warmed butter
Grated rind of 1 orange	Punch icing (see this page)
1 tbsp. rum	

Put the sugar and the eggs in a basin and beat over a pan of boiling water till thick and creamy. Add the grated orange rind, with the rum, and beat thoroughly. Add the flour and the warmed butter, and mix again, then pour the mixture into a buttered and lined cake tin, about 5–6 inches in diameter. Bake in a moderate oven (350° F., mark 4) for 25–30 minutes. When the cake is cold, coat the top with punch icing. Decorate as desired.

Punschglasur
(*Punch icing*)

Mix $\frac{1}{2}$ lb. sieved icing sugar with 1 tbsp. rum and 2 tsps. strained orange juice, and stir over a very low heat, until the mixture begins to coat the back of the spoon. Use as required.

NURNBERGER LEBKUCHEN
(NUREMBERG SPICED CAKES)

2 eggs	2 oz. chopped almonds
6 oz. sugar	$1\frac{1}{2}$ oz. chopped candied lemon peel
A pinch of ground cloves	A little grated lemon peel
A pinch of ground cardamom	2 oz. ground almonds
1 tsp. ground cinnamon	6 oz. flour

Cream the beaten eggs well with the sugar, then add the spices and the remaining ingredients, stirring in the sieved flour last of all. Roll out thinly, cut into rounds, put on to pieces of rice paper and bake in a moderate oven (350° F., mark 4) for 20–25 minutes. Coat with royal or chocolate icing, and decorate with almonds, coloured sugar, etc.

SWABIAN HONEY CAKE

4–5 whole eggs	2½ oz. chopped
9 oz. sugar	candied lemon peel
A good pinch of ground	½ pint honey
cinnamon	4 oz. butter
10 ground cloves	2–3 tbsps. rum
4 grains of ground	2 tbsps. rosewater
cardamoms	1 lb. 2 oz. flour
5–6 ground peppercorns	Blanched almonds for
Grated rind of lemon	decorating.

Beat the eggs and sugar, add spices, lemon rind and peel, and beat for about ¼ hour. Heat the honey and butter, and add the rum, rosewater, and finally flour. Put in two 8-inch tins lined with greaseproof paper and bake in a moderate oven (350° F., mark 4) for 1–1¼ hours. (If baked in one large tin, the cake takes 1 hour 40 minutes.) Decorate with almonds.

MANDEL BRETZELN
(ALMOND KNOTS)

4 oz. butter	8 oz. ground almonds
2 large eggs	Almond essence
7 oz. flour	Egg to glaze

Cream the butter till soft, and beat in the eggs one at a time. Add the flour, almonds and a few drops of essence. Knead lightly, and roll out ¼ inch thick, cut into narrow strips about 6 inches long, and tie into bows or lover's knots. Place on a greased tray, brush with beaten egg and bake in a moderate oven (350° F., mark 4) or 8–10 minutes, until golden-brown.

STRIPED CAKE

4 oz. chocolate	1 egg yolk
½ pint milk	½ pint cream
3 oz. butter	8 oz. finger biscuits
4 oz. sugar	Cream to decorate

Melt the chocolate in half the milk and allow to cool for a few minutes. Cream the butter and sugar thoroughly, and beat in the egg yolk, milk, and finally the chocolate milk. Line a mould with greaseproof paper and arrange in it layers of the chocolate mixture, whipped cream and finger biscuits, the last layer being cream. Allow to cool for a few hours or overnight. Before serving, unmould, and cover or decorate with stiffly beaten dairy cream.

This dish may be served with iced fruit, especially cherries, strawberries, or red-currants; these may also be embedded in the cream.

HAZELNUT CAKES

10 oz. finely ground	Egg white to bind
hazelnuts	Vanilla essence
6 oz. ground almonds	White glacé icing
10 oz. brown sugar	Cherries or nuts to
1 tbsp. potato flour	decorate

Mix the hazelnuts, almonds, sugar and flour to a paste, using sufficient egg white to bind, and add a few drops of vanilla essence. Spread this mixture on to rice paper in circles ¼ inch thick and 5 inches in diameter, and flatten the edges with a damp knife. Bake in a moderate oven (350° F., mark 4) and when cold, coat with white icing, and decorate.

APFELKUCHEN
(APPLE CAKE)

5 oz. butter	8 oz. self-raising flour
5 oz. sugar	Grated rind of ½ a lemon
2–3 eggs	1¼ lb. cooking apples

Cream the butter and sugar and add the eggs gradually. Fold in the sieved flour (add 2 level tsps. baking powder if plain flour is used), and the lemon rind or essence. Well grease a large tin and put in the mixture, spreading it out with the spoon. Peel and core the apples, cut into slices of medium thickness, and put them over the top in a neat pattern. · Bake in a moderate oven (350° F., mark 4) for 40–50 minutes, until the apples are well cooked. Keep an eye on the cake for the last 10 minutes or so, to prevent overcooking.

CHESTNUT CREAM

1 pint milk	3 tbsps. rum
4 egg yolks	1 oz. gelatine
2 oz. sugar	½ pint whipped cream
¾ lb. chestnuts	

Boil the milk and pour it on to the beaten egg yolks. Add the sugar, return the mixture to the pan and cook very gently without boiling, stirring all the time until it has thickened. Cook the chestnuts, remove the skins and sieve. Add the chestnut purée to the mixture, with the rum. Dissolve the gelatine in a little water and add this. Add the whipped cream, and leave to set.

KIRSCHKUCHEN
(CHERRY SPONGE)

2 lb. large black	Two 8-inch sponge cakes,
cherries	1 inch thick
6 tbsps. Kirsch	Whipped cream
5 oz. caster sugar	Grated bitter chocolate

Wash the cherries, and remove the stems and stones. Mix the Kirsch and sugar, pour over the fruit in a bowl, and let it stand for at least 2 hours. Heat the mixture to boiling point, remove from the heat and cool.

Put one sponge cake on a plate. Make a border around the edge with whipped cream, and spread the cooled, thickened cherry mixture in the centre. Place the second sponge cake on top, and press down lightly, just enough to make the layers stick together. Cover the top and sides of both layers with the remaining whipped cream, and sprinkle the top with grated chocolate.

BERLIN RINGS

4 eggs	4 oz. butter
4 oz. caster sugar	8 oz. flour

Hard-boil 2 of the eggs. Sieve the yolks and mix them with the raw yolks of the remaining eggs and 3 oz. of the caster sugar. Rub the fat into the flour, combine with the first mixture and knead well. Take a portion of the dough and roll it out $\frac{1}{4}$ inch thick, then cut it into rings about 3 inches across. Brush the rings over with egg white, sprinkle with the remaining sugar and bake in a moderate oven (350° F., mark 4) until lightly coloured.

GOOSEBERRY KUCHEN

8 oz. flour	Grated rind of $\frac{1}{2}$ a lemon
$\frac{1}{2}$ tsp. baking powder	1 egg yolk
3 oz. butter	4–6 egg whites
8 oz. sugar (approx.)	4 oz. ground almonds
A pinch of powdered cinnamon	$1\frac{1}{2}$ lb. cooked gooseberries

Make a rich flan pastry with the flour, baking powder, fat, 2 oz. sugar, the flavourings, egg yolk and a little water, mixing it by hand. Grease a large round baking tin, roll out the pastry and line the tin. Mix the beaten egg whites, ground almonds and the rest of the sugar (the amount needed will vary according to the fruit used). Spread this mixture over the pastry, then cover with the well-drained gooseberries. Bake in a hot oven (450° F., mark 8) for 10 minutes, then reduce to moderate (350° F., mark 4) and cook for a further $\frac{3}{4}$ hour, until the pastry is done.

Rhubarb, grapes, red- or black-currants, plums, etc., may also be used in this type of Kuchen.

FRUIT PUDDING

$1\frac{1}{2}$ lb. fruit (preferably pears, cherries, apples or apricots)	3 eggs Vanilla essence or lemon to flavour
4 oz. margarine	$\frac{1}{2}$ lb. self-raising flour
4 oz. sugar	1 cupful milk (approx.)

Prepare the fruit as required. Mix the margarine, sugar, egg yolks and flavouring, then add the flour and milk. When well mixed, fold in the beaten egg whites. Put some of the sliced fruit at the bottom of a good-sized ovenglass dish, then add half the flour mixture, the rest of the fruit, and lastly the remaining flour mixture. Bake in a moderate oven (350° F., mark 4) for 40–50 minutes.

LINZER TORTE
(ALMOND JAM TART)

4 oz. butter	3 egg yolks
4 oz. caster sugar	12 oz. sieved flour
1 tsp. grated lemon peel (or a few drops of lemon essence)	3 oz. ground unblanched almonds Raspberry jam

Cream the butter and sugar well together, and add the lemon peel or essence. Beat in the egg yolks one at a time. Gradually add the flour and almonds, and beat until thoroughly blended and smooth. If the dough is very soft, chill it for a time. Line a flan ring with the pastry, reserving some for decoration. Crimp a decorative edge round the top. Fill the dish almost to the top with raspberry jam. Roll out the remaining dough, cut in strips about $\frac{3}{4}$ inch wide, and make a lattice over the jam. Trim the ends, and crimp them to the Torte edge. Bake in a moderate oven (350° F., mark 4) for 1 hour.

STUFFED BAKED APPLES

4–5 even-sized apples	1–2 tbsps. boiling water
2 tbsps. red jam	water
3 eggs (separated)	3 oz. grated almonds
3 oz. sugar	$1\frac{1}{2}$ oz. flour

Peel and core the apples, leaving them whole, and then fill with jam. Whisk the egg yolks, sugar and water for about 10 minutes, then sprinkle the grated almonds and sieved flour over the mixture, and blend into the other ingredients. Fold in the stiffly beaten egg whites, pile this mixture round the apples, and bake in a moderate oven (350° F., mark 4) for 30–45 minutes.

NUSSTORTE
(HAZELNUT GÂTEAU)

6 eggs	4 oz. butter
6 oz. caster sugar	1 tsp. vanilla essence
6 oz. flour	

For the Filling and Topping

1 lb. shelled hazelnuts	6 oz. caster sugar
$1\frac{1}{2}$ pints double cream, whipped	8 oz. icing sugar 3–4 tbsps. water

Whisk the eggs and sugar over hot water till thick and creamy. Fold in the sieved flour and melted butter, add the essence, and pour into a greased and lined 9- or 10-inch tin. Bake in a moderate oven (350° F., mark 4) for $\frac{3}{4}$ hour, till the cake has shrunk from the sides of the tin. Cool on a wire rack, then cut into 3 layers.

Now make the cake filling. Put the nuts into a baking tin, and toast in a moderate oven (350° F., mark 4) for 15–20 minutes, then plunge them into boiling water, drain, and rub off the skins with a towel. Grind most of the nuts medium-fine. Whip the cream till stiff, combine it with $\frac{3}{4}$ lb. of the ground nuts, and the caster sugar, and spread between the cake layers.

Mix the icing sugar and water together smoothly and spread over the top and sides of the Torte. Sprinkle any remaining ground nuts on the sides of the cake, and decorate the top with toasted nuts.

To make a more economical cake, halve the quantities, bake in a 7- or 8-inch tin, and split into 2 layers.

KUCHEN BROT
(CAKE BREAD)

1–1$\frac{1}{2}$ oz. yeast	Grated rind of $\frac{1}{2}$ a
3 oz. sugar	lemon
3–4 oz. margarine	$\frac{1}{2}$ lb. mixed raisins and
1 lb. flour	sultanas
A pinch of salt	Melted butter and icing
2 eggs	sugar to coat top of
A little warmed milk	bread

Mix the yeast with 1 tsp. of the sugar until it becomes soft. Rub the fat into the flour and salt. Beat the eggs, and mix with the warm milk, sugar and the yeast mixture. Add the lemon rind and fruit, mix well together, with the flour, and put to rise for 1 hour. Flour and grease a baking tray, put on the dough in the shape of a flat loaf, cover with a cloth, and leave in a warm place for an hour, to rise to about double its size. Put in a hot oven (450° F., mark 8) for about 10 minutes, then bake in a moderately hot oven (400° F., mark 6) for $\frac{1}{2}$ hour. Coat the top with melted butter, and sprinkle liberally with icing sugar, to keep the bread fresh.

HEIDESAND BISCUITS

9 oz. butter	1 tbsp. milk
8 oz. fine sugar	8 oz. wholemeal flour
Vanilla sugar or vanilla	$\frac{1}{4}$ tsp. baking powder
essence	

Melt the butter, heat it until it is well browned, then leave it to get cold and firm; beat it until foamy, adding gradually the sugar, vanilla sugar and milk, and beat until the mixture becomes white and foamy. Mix two-thirds of the flour with the baking powder, sieve it, and fold it in a tablespoon at a time. Knead the rest of the flour into the mixture to give a smooth dough. Make it into rolls about 1 inch in diameter, and leave in a cold place until firm, then slice into rounds about $\frac{1}{8}$–$\frac{1}{4}$ inch thick. Place on a baking tin and cook in a slow oven (325° F., mark 2) until light brown—about 15 minutes.

FRANKFÜRTER PUDDING

2 oz. butter	Powdered cinnamon
2 oz. sugar	$\frac{1}{4}$ pint red wine
4 eggs	A few almonds
2 oz. soft breadcrumbs	(blanched)
1 oz. blanched almonds	Red wine sauce

Beat together the butter and sugar, and then beat in the egg yolks very thoroughly. Soak the breadcrumbs in the wine, then add the chopped almonds and cinnamon. Beat very well, then lastly fold in the whisked egg whites.

Grease a basin and sprinkle well with sugar, fill with the pudding mixture, cover with a greased paper and steam for 1 hour. Garnish with almonds and serve with a red wine sauce.

RUM MAKRONENSPEISE
(RUM MACAROON TRIFLE)

1 cup double cream	12 almond macaroons
3 egg yolks	$\frac{1}{4}$ cup light rum
5 tbsps. sugar	1 punnet fresh straw-
1 tbsp. flour	berries
$\frac{1}{4}$ tsp. salt	2 egg whites
1 tsp. vanilla essence	

42

Heat cream until tiny bubbles appear around edge. Beat egg yolks slightly in a medium bowl, stir in 3 tbsps. sugar, flour, salt. Slowly stir in cream. Return the mixture to double boiler. Cook, stirring constantly, over hot, not boiling, water until thick enough to coat spoon with thin film of custard. Pour at once into bowl, and cool. Then add vanilla; cover and refrigerate.

At mealtime : Crumble macaroons into bottom of eight sherbert glasses; pour 1$\frac{1}{2}$ tsps. rum over each. Let stand a few minutes; then spoon berries on top. In a medium bowl, beat egg whites until frothy. Then add 2 tbsps. sugar gradually, while beating until stiff. Now fold all but $\frac{1}{2}$ cup whites into custard. Spoon $\frac{1}{2}$ cup custard over fruit in each glass; then top with reserved egg whites. Refrigerate until served. Makes 8 portions.

FRANKFURTER KRANZ
(FRANKFURT CROWN COFFEECAKE)

14 oz. sifted flour   10½ oz. granulated sugar
4 tsps. baking powder   6 eggs, separated
8 oz. butter   1½ tsp. vanilla essence

Heat the oven to 275° F. (mark ⅛). Sift flour with baking powder. Grease 8½ inch by 3½ inch Turks-head or ring mould. Cream the butter and sugar until very light and fluffy. Add the egg yolks one at a time mixing each one in well. Mix in vanilla. Fold in flour mixture just until blended, then beat egg whites until stiff, and blend thoroughly with the batter using a rubber spatula. Turn into mould, and bake 70 minutes, or until skewer comes out clean. Immediately remove from mould and cool on a rack. Split cake into 3 layers, fill them with butter cream, and sprinkle with sugar-toasted almonds. Or top whole with apricot glaze.

Butter Cream : Cream ⅓ cup soft butter, ⅛ tsp. salt, 1 cup sifted icing sugar, 1½ tsp. vanilla essence till light and fluffy. Now alternately add 2 cups sifted icing sugar and ¼ cup milk or single cream, beating till smooth.

Sugar-toasted Almonds : In saucepan cook 1 cup slivered blanched almonds with ⅓ granulated sugar, ⅓ cup butter, 1 tbsp. milk, over low heat till nuts are coated and a light caramel colour. Turn on to waxed paper ; cool ; separate into small pieces, each of one or two nut slivers. Sprinkle half of nuts over fillings ; press rest on top.

Apricot Glaze : Press ⅓ cup warm apricot jam through strainer and stir in 1 tbsp. lemon juice. Just before serving, spread over cake, letting excess drip down sides.

MANDELKUCHEN
(ALMOND YEAST BRAID)

1 oz. yeast   2½ cups sifted flour
½ cup warm (not hot)   Salad oil
   milk   1½ cups icing sugar
1 cup butter   ½ cup ground almonds
¾ cup granulated sugar   Melted butter to glaze
2 tsps. grated lemon   the braid
   rind   Boiling water
½ tsp. salt   ½ tsp. vanilla essence
1 egg, unbeaten

Crumble yeast on to warm milk in a small bowl, stir until dissolved. Cream together in a large bowl ½ cup of butter, the granulated sugar, 1½ tsps. grated lemon rind and salt, until light and fluffy. Beat in egg with a spoon till blended. Alternately stir in flour and dissolved yeast and beat with a spoon for 5 minutes. Brush the top of dough with salad oil ; cover with clean towel ;

then let rise in warm place (about 85° F.) until doubled—about 2 hours.

Mix ½ cup icing sugar with ½ cup butter, ½ tsp. grated lemon rind and ½ cup ground almonds. Set aside. When dough is doubled punch it down. On greased, lightly floured cookie sheet, roll it into a 12-inch by 9-inch by ¼-inch rectangle. Then spread the almond filling down the centre third of the dough. Along each side of the filling cut crosswise slits, 1 inch apart from edge to filling. Fold strips at an angle across filling, alternating from side to side and making sure end of preceding strip is covered. Start heating oven to 350° F. (mark 4), let braid rise until doubled, about ½ hour, brush top with melted butter and bake for about 30 minutes. Cool ; ice with 1 cup icing sugar, boiling water and vanilla essence.

KÜMMEL KNINGEL
(CARAWAY PRETZELS)

¼ cup butter   ¼ cup warm (not hot),
1¾ cups milk, scalded   or lukewarm water
5 cups sifted flour   1 tbsp. caraway seeds
1 tsp. salt   1 egg, slightly beaten
1 tbsp. sugar   2–3 tbsps. caraway seeds
1 oz. yeast   to top
1 egg, unbeaten

Melt butter in scalded milk ; let cool to lukewarm. Sift together 5 cups flour, salt and sugar. Sprinkle or crumble yeast on to warm water, stir until dissolved. Mix unbeaten egg and dissolved yeast with lukewarm milk. Next, mix in flour mixture, a little at a time, then 1 tbsp. caraway seeds ; beat until well blended. Sprinkle about 1 tbsp. flour over dough, cover with clean cloth, and let rise in warm place (about 85° F.) until doubled. Grease 2 baking sheets. When dough is doubled turn on to lightly floured surface, knead until smooth. Now with palms of hands, roll dough into 12-inch roll ; then cut it into twelve equal pieces. Roll out each piece between the palms of the hands and tie in a loose knot, tucking the ends in.

Lay two pretzels at a time in a large pan ¾ full of boiling water. Let them sink, then rise to surface of water. Then lift out with slotted spoon, place on greased baking sheet, and gently press into original shape. Brush top surfaces with beaten egg, then sprinkle with caraway seeds, about 2–3 tbsps. Put pretzels to rise in a warm place until doubled and start heating oven to 400° F. (mark 6). Bake them for 15–20 minutes or until golden-brown. Remove to cake racks and keep warm. Serve them warm, with butter, cheese, jam or salad. Makes about 12.

STRASSBURGER PLÄTZCHEN
(STRASBOURG COOKIES)

1 cup butter	2 egg yolks, unbeaten
$\frac{1}{2}$ cup granulated sugar	$2\frac{1}{4}$ cups sifted flour

Cream butter with sugar till light and fluffy, mix in egg yolks, then flour. Refrigerate $\frac{1}{2}$ an hour. Start heating oven to 375° F. (mark 5). Fill pastry bag with some of the dough. Press in 2-inch by $1\frac{1}{4}$-inch shape of "m" on to ungreased baking sheet. Refrigerate 15 minutes and bake 9–12 minutes, or until golden around edge. Cool on rack and store in tightly covered container. Makes 42–44.

KRÜMMELTORTE

$2\frac{1}{2}$ lb. cooking apples	4 oz. butter or mar-
6 oz. caster sugar	garine
Vanilla essence	1 egg
10 oz. self-raising flour	

Try to obtain a "torte" tin with loose bottom and hinged sides, measuring about 8 inches in diameter. Failing this, use a deep sandwich tin, lining it with paper and leaving a tab by which to lift the cooked cake from the tin.

Wash, peel, core and quarter the apples, and cut each quarter crossways into 5–6 pieces. Partially cook them by simmering in a saucepan without any water, and add 4 oz. of the sugar and 1 tsp. vanilla essence.

Meanwhile make some shortcrust pastry; mix the flour, the remaining 2 oz. sugar and 1 tsp. essence, rub in the butter and mix to a stiff dough with the lightly beaten egg—add a little cold water only if the dough is too stiff. Roll out half the pastry, about $\frac{1}{8}$ inch thick and cut to fit the bottom of the tin. Pile the partly cooked apples on top, but keep them $\frac{1}{2}$ inch away from the inside of the tin. Crumble the remaining pastry dough in your fingers and let it fall between the apples and the inside of the tin. Flatten the surface of the apples and cover the top with the remaining pastry crumbs. Bake at 425° F. (mark 7), for 25–30 minutes, until well browned. Remove the hinged ring, but serve the "torte" on its base. Sprinkle with caster sugar and serve it hot with whipped cream.

SPEKULATIUS

$4\frac{1}{2}$ oz. butter	$8\frac{1}{2}$ oz. plain flour
$4\frac{1}{2}$ oz. sugar	$\frac{1}{2}$ tsp. baking powder
1 egg	1 tsp. ground cinnamon

Cream together the butter and sugar. Beat in the egg. Fold in the sifted flour, baking powder and cinnamon. Knead lightly. Leave in a cool place to become firm enough to roll. Roll out thinly. Cut in fancy shapes. Bake on a greased tin at 350° F. (mark 4), for about 10–12 minutes until golden-brown. Cool. Store in an airtight tin. (Makes about 48 delicious, crisp, buttery, wafer-like biscuits.)

CHEESECAKE I

Yeast dough	Melted butter
Almonds and raisins	Vanilla sugar

For the Filling

$\frac{3}{4}$ lb. curds	$2\frac{1}{4}$ oz. melted butter
2 eggs	1–$1\frac{1}{2}$ gills milk
$2\frac{1}{2}$ oz. sugar	A pinch of salt
$\frac{1}{4}$ oz. flour	A little grated lemon
$\frac{1}{4}$ oz. cornflour	rind

Roll out the dough thinly. Mix the filling and spread it on the dough with a few thinly sliced almonds and raisins on top. Put in a greased shallow tin and bake in a moderate oven (375° F., mark 5) for 45–50 minutes. Take care not to over-bake, or the cheesecake will sink as it cools. When it is cooked, brush melted butter over the surface, and dredge with vanilla sugar.

CHEESECAKE II
For the Flan Pastry

8 oz. flour	2 tbsps. milk or water
4 oz. butter	2 oz. ground almonds
2 oz. sugar	A pinch of salt
1 egg	Egg to glaze

For the Filling

9 oz. curds	3 eggs
$1\frac{3}{4}$ oz. butter or 5 tbsps. cream	2 oz. sultanas or cur- rants
1 oz. ground almonds	1 tbsp. rum
3 oz. sugar	Egg to glaze

Make the pastry as for ordinary shortcrust, and bake blind. Mix the filling and spread over the pastry. Decorate with pastry strips, which should be brushed over with beaten egg. Put in 2 greased flan rings and bake in a moderate oven (375° F., mark 5) for 25–30 minutes. When the cakes are nearly ready, take them out of the rings, brush the whole surface over with egg and put in the oven again, to give an attractive almond-brown gloss.

GREECE, abundant in wine and olives, fruit and fish, uses the fresh and natural products of sea and country to produce a cuisine that is distinctive and delicious. The Greeks are not an extravagant people and their cooking is not unduly rich, but great care is taken over the preparation of the various dishes. Olive oil is an extremely important ingredient and the choosing of oil is a serious business, for there are many different types and qualities.

Vegetables grow abundantly and include such things as okras, aubergines and sweet peppers, as well as the more usual marrows—always eaten while small—cauliflowers, potatoes and onions. Fruit is piled high in the markets—apricots, peaches, strawberries, grapes, melons and the essential lemons which add so much piquancy to Greek cooking and are used with meat, fish and vegetables.

Fish is plentiful and of great variety ; the Greek fish stew, *caccavia*, is claimed to be the grandfather of the Provençal bouillabaisse and contains all kinds of fish, tomatoes, vegetables, seasonings and olive oil. Meat is best in the North, where the pastures are good ; there it is eaten grilled and roasted, but in the South it is often minced and made into rissoles or moussaka.

Sweet pastries and cakes are sticky and syrupy in the Turkish manner and honey is often used instead of sugar. These cakes and pastries are sometimes eaten between meals with a spoonful of the thick, sweet rose-petal or walnut preserve and a glass of water. These " spoon sweets " are offered with water and sometimes brandy as a sign of hospitality.

Coarse bread, the white, salty *feta* cheese, fruit and salad is the simplest peasant fare ; in general, meals consist of meat or fish with a vegetable, fruit or a rice sweet and thick Turkish coffee. Meals are preceded by glasses of *ouzo*, the local aniseed-flavoured spirit, and a large selection of what the Chinese call " small eats," such as olives, nuts, cheese and small pieces of fish or pickle.

Greek wines are little known outside their own country, but most of them are extremely palatable, though the famous *retsina* or resinated wine is an acquired taste and most people take a little time to become accustomed to it.

Greece

TARAMOSALATA
(TARAMA PASTE)

This is made from tarama, the dried eggs of grey mullet, which is not obtainable in this country, but smoked cod's roe makes an excellent substitute. It is a delicious hors d'œuvre, but is equally good as a cocktail canapé, or on toast.

½ lb. smoked cod's roe   1 teacup olive oil
2 slices white bread   Juice of 1–2 lemons
Milk   Salt and pepper

Cut the crusts from the bread, soak it in cold milk and squeeze almost dry. Remove the skin from the cod's roe and pound in a basin or mortar. Pound the roe and bread together, adding the olive oil drop by drop as in mayonnaise, with the lemon juice, till a soft paste is formed. Season with salt and pepper. Finish off by transferring to an electric mixer and slowly adding the rest of the oil and lemon juice, or use an egg beater. It should have the consistency of a creamy paste and be served well chilled.

MELITZANOSALATA
(AUBERGINE " CAVIAR ")

3–4 aubergines   2 tbsps. mayonnaise
1 teacupful olive oil   or whipped cream
Wine vinegar   (optional)
Salt and pepper   Black olives and tomato
Parsley   to garnish

Grill the aubergines until they are soft. It is important for them to be grilled so as to have a smoky flavour. Remove the skins whilst still hot and chop finely on a wooden board, then transfer to a basin and beat the pulp with a wooden spoon to form a thick purée. Add gradually the olive oil, vinegar, salt and pepper to taste as well as the finely chopped parsley. The mixture should be the consistency of thick cream. If desired, 1–2 tbsps. of mayonnaise or whipped cream can be added. Garnish with black olives or sliced tomatoes, sprinkle with chopped parsley and serve well chilled.

KOTTOSOUPA
(RICE AND CHICKEN SOUP)

Everyone who tastes this national soup of Greece asks for the recipe.

Boil 2 oz. rice in salted water, drain, and add to 1 quart of hot chicken stock. Simmer gently for a few minutes, then bring almost to boiling point, and pour on to 2 well-beaten egg yolks, whisking all the time. Just before serving, add the strained juice of 1 lemon.

PLAKI
(BAKED FISH)

6 finely chopped onions   Salt
Olive oil for frying   Pepper
Chopped parsley   2 lb. fish
3 or 4 tomatoes or a   Tomato and lemon to
  little tomato sauce   garnish

Fry the onions in a frying pan and add the chopped parsley. When the onions are cooked, but not brown, add the fried tomatoes or a little tomato sauce, and season the mixture. Lay the fish in a greased fireproof dish, pour the mixture over and bake in a hot oven (450° F., mark 8) for ¼ hour. Garnish and serve.

BAKALIAROS SKORDALIA
(FRIED SALT COD WITH GARLIC SAUCE)

1½ lb. salt cod   1 egg white
Flour and water for   Olive oil
  batter

Soak the cod in cold water for 12 hours. Rinse, remove skin and bones. Make a light batter by mixing the flour, white of egg and water. Dip the pieces of fish in the batter and fry in olive oil. This is served with garlic sauce, which is equally good with fresh fried fish.

For the Garlic Sauce

3–6 cloves of garlic,   2 egg yolks
  according to taste   Salt and pepper
2 slices white bread   1–2 teacups olive oil
Milk   Lemon juice or wine
2 oz. ground almonds   vinegar

Clean and pound the cloves of garlic in a mortar. Cut the crusts from the bread, soak it in cold milk, squeeze almost dry, and add to the garlic. Pound well, then add the ground almonds and mix till the whole is like a stiff paste. Meantime in another basin put the egg yolks, salt and pepper and add the oil gradually drop by drop as in mayonnaise and lastly the vinegar or lemon juice to taste. Combine with the garlic mixture and beat well together.

MIDIA YEMISTA
(STUFFED MUSSELS)

16 large mussels   1 oz. currants
4 oz. rice   1 oz. pine kernels
3 tbsps. olive oil   ½ tsp. grated nutmeg
1 teacup water   1 tsp. powdered
1 onion   cinnamon
Salt and pepper

Wash, scrape and remove the beards of the mussels. Place in a pan with water and cook for a few minutes till the shells are open. (For stuffing, the mussel should be attached to one half of its shell, the other empty half-shell being used for stuffing; the two halves must be kept together to form a whole mussel.) Mince the onion finely and cook in 1 tbsp. olive oil till soft but not brown. Add the washed rice, the currants, pine kernels, cinnamon, nutmeg, salt and pepper and 1 teacup water. Cook for about 10 minutes. Remove from the heat and fill the empty half-shell of the mussels, taking care not to overfill so that the two halves can join well together. Place the mussels in a saucepan with 2 tbsps. olive oil, cover with water and weigh the mussels down with 2-3 plates. Cook till all the water is absorbed. Serve hot or cold.

MIDIA ME TO RIZI
(MUSSELS WITH RICE)

2 pints mussels	Salt and pepper
1 large onion	1 teacup olive oil
1 wineglassful white	1 teacup Patna rice
wine	5 teacups mussel liquid

Scrape, remove beards and wash the mussels well in cold water. Put the mussels in a saucepan with the wine and cover with water and cook slowly till they are all open. Take off the heat and remove the mussels from their shells. Strain the liquid in which the mussels have cooked through a fine muslin.

Mince the onion and cook in the olive oil until soft but not brown, add the washed rice and the 5 teacups liquid from the mussels, salt and pepper. If there is not enough liquid the quantity should be made up with water. Half-cook the rice and add the mussels and continue cooking till the liquid is almost absorbed, about half an hour in all. Leave for 5 minutes in the pan and then serve.

AUBERGINE MOUSSAKA

2 aubergines	4 peeled tomatoes
3-4 tbsps. olive oil	$\frac{1}{4}$ pint stock
4-5 medium-sized	$\frac{1}{4}$ pint tomato purée
onions	2 eggs
1 lb. minced beef or	$\frac{1}{4}$ pint cream
lamb	Seasoning

Slice the aubergines and fry in some of the oil in a frying pan, then arrange them in the bottom of a fireproof dish. Slice the onions and fry till they are lightly browned. Place layers of onion and minced meat on top of the aubergine, and lastly add some fried slices of tomato. Pour in $\frac{1}{4}$ pint stock and $\frac{1}{4}$ pint tomato purée, and bake in a moderate oven (350° F., mark 3) for about 30 minutes. Beat together the eggs and cream, add salt and pepper, and pour this mixture into the casserole. Put it back into the oven for 15-20 minutes, until the sauce is set, firm and golden-brown.

MONK'S MACKEREL

2 large mackerel	1 tsp. lemon juice
1 onion	1 tsp. dried herbs
2 tbsps. olive oil	12 black olives
2 bay leaves	

Cut the fish open, wash under running cold water and remove the bone. Chop the onion finely and fry lightly in 1 tbsp. oil. Put 1 tbsp. oil in a baking dish and put the mackerel on this, cover with the fried onion, bay leaves, lemon juice and herbs, season well and put the olives over it; cover, and bake for $\frac{1}{2}$ hour in a moderate oven (350° F., mark 4). Serve with plain boiled potatoes.

RISSOLES IN TOMATO SAUCE

1 lb. finely minced lean	1 oz. finely chopped
beef	suet
$\frac{1}{4}$ pint red wine	Seasoning
1 clove of garlic	1 egg
1 tbsp. olive oil	Flour
1 onion	Oil for frying
2 oz. fine white bread-	Tomato sauce
crumbs	

Soak the beef in the wine, with the crushed garlic, for an hour. Heat the olive oil in a pan, fry the chopped onion and put into the bowl with the meat. Add the breadcrumbs, suet and seasoning, and bind together with the egg. Make the mixture into balls about the size of walnuts, and roll them in flour. Fry them in hot oil, pile into a dish and pour tomato sauce over them.

STIFADO
(BEEF RAGOÛT)

$1\frac{1}{2}$ lb. stewing steak	1-2 bay leaves
3-4 tbsps. olive oil	1-2 cloves of garlic
$1\frac{1}{2}$ lb. shallots or tiny	(optional)
onions	2-3 cloves
1 wineglassful red wine	Salt and pepper
2 teacups tomato purée	

Cut the meat into pieces and brown slightly in the oil. Add all the remaining ingredients, cover the stewpan and cook very slowly for 4-5 hours until the meat is tender and there is a very thick sauce. Serve hot.

KREAS KIDONATO
(MEAT WITH QUINCES)

$1\frac{1}{2}$ lb. stewing steak	$\frac{1}{2}$ pint water
4 oz. butter	4 oz. granulated sugar
$1\frac{1}{2}$ lb. quinces	Salt and pepper

Cut the meat into pieces and brown in the butter. Add the quinces which have been previously peeled, cored and cut into thick slices, water, sugar and seasoning. Cover and cook slowly about 3 hours until the quinces are a light red. The liquid should be absorbed and only the butter left. Serve hot.

DOLMADES
(STUFFED VINE LEAVES)

1 packet of vine leaves	Chopped parsley
3 tbsps. lard or oil	A little tomato sauce
1 lb. minced meat	Salt and pepper
1–2 thinly sliced onions	Juice of 1 lemon
2 tbsps. rice (optional)	

Dip the vine leaves in boiling water for 1–2 minutes, then leave in a colander until you have made the stuffing. Put 2 tbsps. of the lard or oil in a frying pan with meat, onions, rice, parsley, sauce and seasoning, mix well, and fry. Add the lemon juice, and stuff the vine leaves, securing with skewers or fine string. Put in a pan with a little water, the remaining lard and a little more sauce, if desired, and cook over a low heat until the gravy reduces considerably. This stuffing can also be used for aubergines, peppers, tomatoes, etc.

KREAS LEMONATO
(VEAL BRAISED IN LEMON JUICE)

2–3 lb. veal for roasting	1 teacupful lemon juice
1 lemon	$\frac{1}{2}$ pint veal stock or
$\frac{1}{2}$ lb. butter	water
1 tbsp. flour	Salt and pepper

Wash the meat and rub over with a lemon. Season. Melt the butter and brown the meat. Remove from the heat, add the flour, the lemon juice and the stock and simmer for about $2\frac{1}{2}$–3 hours with the pan covered. When the meat is tender, serve by cutting it in slices on a dish and covering it with the sauce. Serve hot with new potatoes.

MOUSSAKA À LA BOS
(MEAT AND POTATO CAKE)

$\frac{3}{4}$ lb. meat, minced	Seasoning
$\frac{1}{2}$ lb. sliced onions	$\frac{1}{2}$ oz. butter
A little chopped parsley	$\frac{1}{2}$ oz. flour
2 oz. margarine	$\frac{1}{4}$ pint milk
$\frac{1}{4}$–$\frac{1}{2}$ lb. tomatoes	1 egg
$1\frac{1}{2}$–2 lb. potatoes, peeled	1 oz. grated cheese
and thinly sliced	

Place the meat, onions and parsley in a frying pan with $\frac{1}{2}$ cup water, and simmer until all the water is absorbed. Add the margarine and cook gently, then add the skinned and sliced tomatoes,

and season well. Cook slowly for about 20 minutes longer. Grease a cake tin and place a layer of potatoes on the bottom, then a layer of the meat mixture, and repeat, finishing with potatoes. Make a white sauce with the butter, flour and milk, remove from the heat and beat in the egg and the cheese. Pour over the potatoes and bake in a moderate oven (350° F., mark 3) for about 1 hour.

Serve the moussaka on a hot dish, accompanied by a green vegetable.

PILAFF

Rice dishes are very popular in Greece, and many kinds of pilaff are served. One cup of rice is fried very slowly for 5–8 minutes in a little oil or butter. Strong beef or mutton stock is then added gradually, and the rice is simmered for 20–25 minutes. A few sliced tomatoes or sliced aubergines, a few currants, some seasoning and a little garlic are added. When cooked, the rice should be only just moist, with each grain separate.

ATZEM PILAFF

$2\frac{1}{2}$ lb. stewing lamb	A little tomato purée
5–6 tbsps. butter	$3\frac{1}{2}$ pints water
1 onion, finely chopped	4 teacups rice
Salt and pepper	

Cut the meat into pieces and sauté it in the butter in a saucepan, together with the onion. Season, add the tomato purée and simmer until brown. Add the water and cook until tender (about 40–45 minutes). Add the rice, previously washed in warm salted water. When all the water has been absorbed, stir the mixture well and put it in a moderate oven (350° F., mark 3) for 5 minutes.

STUFFED CABBAGE LEAVES

12–15 cabbage leaves	2 tbsps. olive oil
4 oz. rice	2–3 tomatoes
6 oz. onions	$\frac{1}{2}$ tsp. ground nutmeg
1 large clove of garlic	Seasoning
2 oz. sultanas	

Although vine leaves are used traditionally in this Greek recipe, cabbage leaves make an excellent substitute. Blanch the cabbage leaves to make them pliable, by dropping them into boiling water for 2–3 minutes. Fry the washed rice, finely chopped onions and garlic and sultanas in the oil until they are a golden colour, but not brown. Add the skinned and chopped tomatoes and the nutmeg, and season very well. Cut out a little of the hard stem part of each cabbage, place a good spoonful of the rice mixture in the

centre and roll up carefully, tucking in the ends to form a neat roll. Lay these rolls in rows in a saucepan, and cover them with salted water. Put on the lid and simmer for ¾–1 hour. Alternatively, cook in a covered casserole in the oven.

In this recipe, as in Dolmades, the filling can be considerably varied, to suit your taste.

ARNI SOUVLA
(MEAT ON SKEWERS)

Small squares of lamb or mutton are thoroughly seasoned with salt and pepper, threaded on skewers and grilled over an open fire or on a charcoal grill until well browned. This is always served with Salata—a salad which is distinctively Greek.

SALATA
(CABBAGE SALAD)

1 uncooked white cabbage, finely shredded	4 tbsps. vinegar
1 tbsp. cooked beans	3 tbsps. olive oil
Black olives	¼ tsp. mustard
Capers	Salt and pepper

Prepare the cabbage, and combine with the beans, olives and capers. Make a dressing of the vinegar, oil and seasonings, and when it is thoroughly well mixed, pour over the salad.

A small beetroot, sliced or chopped, may be included in this salad.

GUVETSI WITH MEAT

2 lb. middle neck of lamb	Seasoning
Fat for frying	A little tomato purée
2 large onions	¾ lb. macaroni
	Grated cheese

Fry the cut-up meat and the sliced onions. Just cover with water, add the seasoning and purée, and simmer gently for 30 minutes. Break the macaroni into pieces, add it to the stew, then simmer gently for 1 hour, stirring occasionally. If the liquid is absorbed, add more hot stock or water. Serve sprinkled with some finely grated cheese.

KEFTEPES
(CROQUETTES)

10 oz. bread (without crusts)	1½ lb. minced beef
3–4 onions	Salt and pepper
Butter or oil for frying	3–4 tsps. chopped parsley
	2 eggs
	A little flour

Soak the bread in some water. Meanwhile, divide the finely chopped onions in half; fry one half in butter or oil until brown and put the other half in a large bowl with the minced meat.

Squeeze out the bread and add to the minced meat and onions, together with the fried onions; stirring all the time, add the seasoning, parsley and eggs. Knead the paste and form it into small balls, or larger ones flattened down. Dip these into flour and fry in oil. Serve hot.

NTOMATES ME KIMA
(TOMATOES STUFFED WITH MEAT)

10–12 tomatoes	¾ lb. minced beef
Caster sugar	Parsley and dill
Salt and pepper	1 tsp. brandy (optional)
4–6 oz. butter	1 oz. rice
1 small onion	Breadcrumbs

Scoop out the tomatoes, leaving a hinged lid. Strain all the seeds for juice and chop up the cores. Place a pinch of salt in each tomato and put them upside down to drain them of excess liquid, then add a dash of pepper and sugar to each.

Fry the minced onion in the butter till soft but not brown, add the meat, chopped parsley and dill, rice and the brandy. Cook for about 10 minutes. Stuff the tomatoes with the meat and place them one by one in a baking tin or oven dish. Sprinkle the top of each tomato with breadcrumbs and a little melted butter, add the juice from the tomatoes and the other half of the butter which has been melted, and cook in a slow oven (300° F., mark 1) for 1–1½ hours, till the tomatoes are slightly shrivelled and golden.

FASOLIA YIAXNI
(HARICOT BEANS)

Soak 1 lb. dried haricot beans overnight. Fry 2 chopped onions in a little oil, then add the beans, more oil (3 oz. counting that already used), 1 tbsp. tomato purée, 1–2 sticks of celery, seasoning, and enough water to cover (this should be hot, to avoid hardening the beans). Cook until tender—about 3 hours. Serve hot or cold, sprinkled with chopped parsley.

MACARONIA TOU FOURNOU
(BAKED MACARONI)

1 lb. minced meat	1 pint milk
3 tbsps. lard	3 tbsps. flour
1 small onion, thinly sliced	4 eggs
2 tsps. tomato sauce	Salt and pepper
½ lb. macaroni	½ lb. grated cheese

Fry the meat with lard, onion and sauce. Boil the macaroni, and when it is almost cooked, put half in a greased dish; add the meat mixture, then the rest of the macaroni. Make a sauce with the milk, flour, eggs and seasoning, and pour over. Cover with cheese, and cook in a moderately hot oven (400° F., mark 6) for about 20 minutes. Serve hot.

PAPOUTSAKIA
(COURGETTES)

6–8 courgettes (boiled for 5 minutes)
1 onion
1 tbsp. olive oil
2 oz. cooked rice
4 oz. cooked minced meat
½ pint béchamel sauce
Cheese

Cut the courgettes in half, scoop out the centres and put the shells into a greased fireproof dish. Chop the onion and fry it in the oil, add the chopped fried courgette centres and mix with the meat and rice. Put the mixture back into the courgettes, and cover the tops with béchamel sauce. Sprinkle with cheese and bake for 10 minutes in a hot oven (450° F., mark 8), or brown under the grill.

BAKED COURGETTES AND AUBERGINES

2 aubergines
6–7 courgettes
6–8 shallots
1 clove of garlic
Seasoning
Sugar
3 tbsps. tomato purée or paste
¼ pint stock
2 tbsps. fine breadcrumbs
2 tbsps. olive oil
Olives to garnish

Slice the aubergines, courgettes and shallots, and chop the garlic very finely. Rub a fireproof dish with oil, put a layer of aubergine in the bottom, and sprinkle with salt and pepper ; now put in a layer of shallot and a little garlic, then one of courgettes. Continue like this until the dish has been filled. Mix together the sugar, tomato purée and stock and pour this over the vegetables. Sprinkle with the crumbs, pour on the oil, and bake in a moderate oven (350° F., mark 3) for 1 hour. Serve hot or cold, garnished with a few olives.

SOUTZOUKAKIA SMYRNEIKA
(SMYRNA SAUSAGES)

1 lb. minced beef
2 small onions
2 small slices white bread
Milk
Parsley
Mint
¼ tsp. powdered cumin or mixed spice
1 egg
3–4 tbsps. butter
3–4 tbsps. plain flour
10 tbsps. tomato purée
1 tsp. sugar
2 wineglassfuls white wine
2 wineglassfuls water
Salt and pepper

Place the meat in a basin and mix with one minced onion, the bread from which the crust has been removed and which after being soaked in a little milk has been squeezed almost dry, finely chopped parsley and mint and the cumin or mixed spice. Bind the whole with an egg and knead well.

Shape the meat into small sausage shapes about 2 inches long and fry them slightly in a little butter or oil till the meat changes colour. Place carefully in a saucepan. Meantime prepare a tomato sauce by frying the second minced onion in butter till soft but not brown, adding the flour, the wine and water, sugar, salt and pepper and tomato purée and simmer a few minutes. Pour the sauce on to the sausages in their saucepan and simmer altogether for ½–¾ hour, till the meat is cooked. Serve hot.

YOUVARLAKIA AVGOLEMONO
(MEAT BALLS WITH EGG AND LEMON SAUCE)

1 onion
1 lb. minced beef
1½ oz. rice
2 eggs
Salt and pepper
Chopped parsley
4 oz. butter
1 dessertsp. cornflour
Juice of ½–1 lemon
Walnut of butter

Mince the onion. Put the beef in a basin with the onion, the rice which has been previously washed, the whites of egg and salt and pepper. Knead all the ingredients well. Have ready the finely chopped parsley on a plate. Scoop out a tablespoonful of the meat and lightly form it into small balls. Roll these in the parsley. Melt the 4 oz. butter in a large saucepan and carefully place all the balls in one or two layers, not more as they will break. Cover with hot water and cook slowly for 1 hour. Remove the balls and keep warm on a serving dish, retaining the liquid for the sauce.

For the Sauce

Beat the yolks of the eggs, mix with the cornflour and lemon juice to taste and add the liquid in which the meat balls have cooked. Stir over a slow heat until the mixture thickens, taking care that the eggs do not curdle. Add a walnut of butter at the end. Cover the meat balls with the sauce and serve at once.

KREAS ME SELLINO AVGOLEMONO
(MEAT WITH CELERY)

4 oz. butter
8 cutlets best or middle neck of lamb or 1½ lb. stewing veal
2 onions
2–3 heads of celery
6 carrots
2 egg yolks
Juice of ½–1 lemon according to taste
1 dessertsp. cornflour
A knob butter the size of a walnut
Salt and pepper

Melt the 4 oz. butter. Gently brown the meat till it changes colour and remove. Cook the onions, cut into fine rings, in the butter till soft and not brown. Add one layer of celery which has previously been washed and scraped and cut into 3-inch lengths, then a layer of meat, the carrots cut into quarters and more meat and celery. Season and cover with water. Cook slowly till the celery and meat are tender. Remove meat and vegetables and keep warm. Strain the liquid. See the recipe opposite for lemon sauce.

BOUREKO ME MIALO
(PASTRIES FILLED WITH BRAINS)

2 sets lambs' brains	1–2 tbsps. water
1 tbsp. vinegar	4 oz. grated cheese
Salt and pepper	1 egg
3 oz. butter	$\frac{1}{2}$–1 lb. fillo (puff) pastry
$\frac{1}{2}$ lb. minced veal	

Wash the brains well in cold water and boil for about 7 minutes in water in which there is a tablespoon of vinegar, salt and pepper. Melt the butter in a frying pan, add the mince and 1–2 tbsps. water, salt and pepper and simmer till the meat is cooked. Add the brains cut in small pieces which should melt and blend with the meat. Remove from the heat, add the grated cheese and bind with the egg.

Cut the fillo with a sharp knife into long strips about 2 inches wide, covering all but a few layers with a slightly damp linen cloth as the pastry dries very quickly and can then not be folded properly. Brush the top of a double layer with melted butter and place a teaspoonful of the mixture in one corner. Fold the corner of the pastry over the filling into a triangle and continue folding to and fro, the length of the pastry strip, keeping the triangular shape. Place on a buttered baking sheet, brush the top of each triangle with butter and cook to a pale golden-brown in a moderate oven (375° F., mark 5) for about 15 minutes. Serve hot.

TIROPITA
(CHEESE PASTRY)

6 Feta cheese and fillo, which is a puff pastry, is on sale at some Cypriot grocers.

$\frac{1}{2}$ lb. Feta cheese or $\frac{1}{2}$ lb. mixture of grated cheese with some Parmesan cheese	Salt and pepper
	$\frac{1}{2}$ pint milk
	3–4 eggs
	$\frac{1}{2}$–1 lb. fillo (puff) pastry
1 oz. butter for sauce	
1 oz. plain flour	$\frac{1}{2}$ lb. butter (approx.)

If the Feta cheese is very salty, this should be first soaked in cold water before being crumbled into small pieces or grated. Make a white sauce by melting the butter, adding the flour, seasoning and the milk. Stir till thick. Remove from the heat and add the grated cheese, cool slightly and beat in the eggs one by one.

Butter well a baking tin sufficiently big enough to take each leaf of pastry without folding it. Place in it about 6 leaves of pastry, buttering each leaf with a pastry brush dipped in melted butter. Spread the cheese mixture over and then continue covering with buttered leaves of pastry till all the pastry has been used up. Butter the top layer and cut with a sharp knife into squares. Cook pastry in a moderately hot oven (400° F., mark 6) till a pale golden-brown— about $\frac{3}{4}$ hour. Serve hot.

KOUKIA LADERES
(BROAD BEANS IN OIL)

2 medium onions	Salt and pepper
1 teacup olive oil	1 tsp. sugar
1 lb. young tender broad beans	A bunch of mint
	Juice of $\frac{1}{2}$ a lemon

Mince the onions finely and cook slowly in the olive oil until soft but not brown. Add the broad beans whole in their pod, from which the strings have been removed, salt, pepper, sugar, lemon juice and mint and cover the beans with water. Cook slowly in a covered saucepan till all the water has been absorbed, about an hour. Serve cold.

NTOMATES ME RIZI
(TOMATOES STUFFED WITH RICE)

12 medium tomatoes	Sugar
$\frac{1}{2}$ gill olive oil	1 oz. currants
1 onion	1 oz. pine kernels
4 oz. Patna rice	Parsley
Salt and pepper	$\frac{3}{4}$ pint water

Choose firm round tomatoes, cut a thin slice off the top to form a hinged lid, and scoop out the seeds and fleshy core with a spoon. Once emptied, put a dash of salt, pepper and a little sugar at the bottom of each tomato. Meantime, strain all the seeds to obtain tomato juice and chop up the cores. Mince the onion and chop the parsley finely.

Heat the olive oil in a shallow pan and cook the onion slowly till soft but not brown. Add the tomato cores and cook slowly till soft and then the rice which has been previously washed and strained, the tomato juice and about $\frac{3}{4}$ pint water. Stir and add the parsley, currants and pine kernels, salt and pepper. Cook slowly, stirring occasionally to prevent the mixture sticking, till the rice is almost cooked and the liquid has been absorbed. Remove from the heat and stuff the tomatoes. Place them in a baking tin, brush the tops with olive oil and cook in a slow oven (300° F., mark 1) for about 1½ hours. They are eaten cold.

ANGINARES LADERES
(ARTICHOKES IN OIL)

47

8 large artichokes	16 shallots or button
2 onions	onions
1 teacup olive oil	8 small round new
1 dessertsp. plain flour	potatoes
2 lemons	Salt and pepper

The leaves of the artichokes must be pulled off quickly, the fuzz removed from the bottom, about an inch of stalk left on, and immediately immersed in a basin of cold water and lemon juice, to prevent them going brown.

Use a large shallow pan. Cook the minced onions in the olive oil until soft but not brown, add the flour and then put in the artichokes one by one with the stalks upwards, the lemon juice, shallots, the potatoes, salt and pepper and sufficient water to cover the artichokes. Cover with greaseproof paper and the pan lid and cook slowly till the artichokes are soft. If there is still a lot of liquid, remove the artichokes and other vegetables from the pan and simmer till all the liquid has evaporated and only the oil is left. Cover the artichokes with the oil and allow to cool. Serve cold.

SCALTSOUNIA
(ALMOND FRITTERS)

½ lb. self-raising flour	A little ground cin-
2 tbsps. lard	namon
Milk to mix	Deep fat for frying
6 oz. ground or chop-	Honey
ped almonds	Boiling water
A little sugar	A little rosewater

Make a pastry with the flour, fat and enough milk to give a dough which can be rolled out very thinly. Cut in small squares, fill with a little stuffing made by mixing the nuts, sugar and cinnamon, and damp the edges to seal. Fry for 1–2 minutes, then dip in a mixture of honey and boiling water, perfumed with rosewater.

GALATOBOUREKO
(PASTRY WITH CUSTARD FILLING)

2½ pints milk	2 pkts. vanilla powder
8 whole eggs	½ lb. butter
3 lb. sugar	1 lb. fillo (puff) pastry
4½ oz. semolina	2 pints water

Warm the milk. In another pan, mix the eggs with 1 lb. sugar and a small quantity of semolina, stirring all the time, then add the *warm* milk (it should not be hot), and the rest of the semolina and put the pan on the heat, stirring continuously with a wooden spoon till boiling point is reached. After boiling three or four times, take off the heat, adding the vanilla and 2 level tbsps. of butter. Set aside.

Meantime butter a shallow tin and place in it about 8 leaves of pastry, buttering each one before placing the next on top. Add the semolina mixture, spreading it smoothly and then the remainder of the leaves (at least 12) buttering each one. Before putting in the oven, cut the top with a sharp knife into squares, taking care not to cut into semolina. Bake for 1 hour in a moderately hot to hot oven (425–450° F., marks 7–8) so that the top is brown and crisp. Make a thick syrup with the rest of the sugar and 1 pint water and pour over whilst still warm.

MACEDONIAN ICE CREAM CUP

2 fresh peaches	1 slice of melon
2 pears	4 tbsps. icing sugar
2 apples	Cointreau
2 bananas	1 pint vanilla ice
6–8 Maraschino cherries	cream
A few seedless grapes	½ pint whipped cream

Peel, core and stone the fruits as necessary, cut into small dice-shaped pieces and put into a bowl. Sprinkle the fruit with the sugar, and add the liquor. Meanwhile make the ice cream, and whip the cream. When the ice cream is ready, divide the fruit between 6–8 glasses, put a spoonful of ice cream on each, and top with cream.

SIMIGDALENIOS HALVAS
(HALVA OF SEMOLINA)

4 oz. sugar	2 oz. ground rice
½ pint milk	1 oz. pine kernels
4 oz. butter	Powdered cinnamon
4 oz. semolina	

Dissolve the sugar in the milk and boil the milk. Melt the butter in another saucepan, add semolina, ground rice and pine kernels and cook gently over a slow heat for 15 minutes without letting the ingredients brown. Remove from the heat and add the boiling milk, stirring all the time with a wooden spoon. Cover with a linen cloth and the lid and leave it for half an hour. Remove lid and beat with a wooden spoon to make the mixture light. Place in a moulded ring and reverse on to a plate. Sprinkle the top with powdered cinnamon and eat warm.

KOURABIEDES
(GREEK SHORTBREAD)

This is traditionally offered at Christmas and

the New Year. It can be made well beforehand as it improves with keeping, provided it is stored in an airtight container.

1 lb. butter
2 lb. plain flour
⅓ coffee cup brandy
⅓ wineglass of water
2½ tsps. caster sugar
1½ tsps. baking powder
Rosewater or orange water (obtainable at most chemists)
¾ lb. icing sugar

First soften the butter and work in the flour with the hands. Gradually work in the brandy, the water, caster sugar and baking powder. Knead well for at least half an hour if not more with the fists, till the mixture comes away cleanly from the sides of the basin and in one piece. The butter in the mixture should make it all glisten. Have one or two buttered baking sheets ready, and taking about 1 tsp. of the mixture at a time, roll them into different shapes. They can be oblong, round, crescent- or heart-shaped. Bake in a moderate oven (350° F., mark 4) for ¾–1 hour and remove them before they start turning brown. Sprinkle at once with rosewater and then immerse them one by one in a deep plate filled with icing sugar so that they can be coated with as much sugar as possible and look very white. Store the shortbreads in an airtight tin with plenty of icing sugar.

KARIDOPITA
(WALNUT CAKE)

5–6 eggs
12 oz. caster sugar
12 oz. ground walnuts
1 oz. dessert chocolate
½ tsp. plain flour
½ coffee cup cornflour (small)
A little milk
½ tsp. baking powder

Beat the yolks with the sugar. Add the walnuts, melted chocolate, cornflour blended with a little milk, flour, baking powder and lastly the stiffly beaten egg whites. Pour into a cake tin lined with greaseproof paper and bake in a moderate oven (375° F., mark 5) for 1¼–1½ hours. This can be iced with chocolate if desired.

SIPHNIAC HONEY CAKE

4 oz. flour
3 oz. butter
4 oz. cream cheese
2 oz. honey
2 oz. sugar
½ tsp. powdered cinnamon
2 eggs
Sugar and cinnamon to top

Sieve the flour and chop in the butter, add 1 tbsp. water, work into a smooth paste and use to line a flat tin. Mix together the cream cheese, honey, sugar and cinnamon and add the beaten eggs. Spread this mixture over the pastry, and sprinkle the top with sugar and cinnamon. Bake ½ hour in a moderate oven (350° F., mark 3).

DUTCH cookery is very individual, combining as it does the hearty, satisfying, simple type of food evolved to combat the effects of the cold North Sea winters, and the exotic spiciness of dishes owing their origin to the Dutch colonies in the East. Dutch cuisine has, indeed, been much influenced by the spices so readily available in shops all over the country and rice has become almost a staple article of diet, appearing in various guises in many characteristic dishes.

Perhaps the Javanese *Rijstafel* is the best known of Holland's exotic imports ; this is a wonderful and often gargantuan repast of fluffy, dry boiled rice, served with countless subsidiary dishes. In hotels and on festive occasions, forty or more of these may be served, ranging from vegetable or meat soups through meat and fish in piquant sauces, chicken, eggs, pickles and dried spiced meat to fried bananas and roasted peanuts.

Holland has always been renowned for the excellence of the vegetables that grow so freely in the fertile soil. Careful and skilful market gardening means an abundance of fresh foods of first-class quality and vegetables play a large part in Dutch cooking, being added freely to soups and stews and often served on their own, dressed with butter or sauce and sometimes sprinkled with parsley or nutmeg.

Meat dishes are not necessarily served every day. Joints are often pot-roasted, and this method of cooking is also used for poultry. Dutch veal is some of the best in the world and the country is rich in fish and game. Dutch methods of salting and smoking both fish and meat are famous. Dutch dairy produce is renowned all over the world and the quality of the butter and cheese is extremely high. Cream, milk and butter find a place in many typical dishes.

Breakfast in Holland generally consists of various breads and rolls which are bought from one of the excellent bakers, with cold meats, eggs, cheese and jam. In the middle of the day a fairly light meal is eaten, often coffee or chocolate to drink, with open sandwiches and cakes. Tea with biscuits and cakes is served at four o'clock and the evening dinner is a substantial meal of rich dishes and large helpings.

Individual and interesting, the excellent quality of its ingredients ensures that Dutch food will appeal to most palates.

Holland

CREAMY VEGETABLE SOUP

2 lb. mixed vegetables (e.g., carrots, onions, celery, turnips, tomatoes)	Salt and pepper
	2 oz. barley
	¾ oz. cornflour
	Milk
2 oz. dripping	Carrot, turnip and peas
2 pints stock	(for garnish)

Cut the vegetables into neat pieces and sauté in the hot dripping until all the fat is absorbed. Add the stock, bring to the boil and season well. Cover and simmer gently for 1 hour, or until the vegetables are tender. Sieve, return to the pan with the barley and continue to cook. Blend the cornflour with a little milk and add a few minutes before the soup is ready. Meanwhile, cut strips and balls of carrot and turnip, using a Parisian potato-cutter, and cook these in boiling salted water; add the peas just before the end of the cooking time. Garnish the soup with these extra vegetables.

BONENSOEP
(BEAN SOUP)

6 oz. dried beans (any kind)	6 medium-sized potatoes
	1 oz. butter
4 pints stock or water	3 oz. raw minced beef
Pepper and salt	1 tbsp. fresh bread-crumbs
Parsley	
2 cloves	Grated nutmeg
4 leeks or large onions	A little beaten egg
2–3 carrots	

Soak the beans overnight, cook until tender in the stock or water, rub through a sieve, return them to the liquid in the saucepan, and add the seasoning, parsley and cloves. Sauté the finely chopped vegetables in the fat for about 10 minutes, add to the soup and cook until tender. Meanwhile mix the minced beef with the bread-crumbs, pepper and salt and a little nutmeg, and add egg to bind. Roll the meat into small balls the size of marbles; 10 minutes before serving, drop these carefully into the soup and allow to simmer gently.

EEL SOUP

½ lb. eel	1½ oz. butter
2 oz. capers	1½ oz. flour
Parsley	Seasoning

Clean the eel and cut into small pieces. Cover with 3 pints of salted water, bring to the boil and simmer until the fish is done. Remove the eel and add capers and a bunch of parsley. Bring the stock to the boil once more and thicken with fat and flour. Season, simmer for 10 minutes and strain into a soup tureen, adding the pieces of cooked eel.

VERMICELLISOEP MET BALLETJES
(VERMICELLI SOUP WITH MEAT BALLS)

1 quart bone or meat cube stock	Salt and pepper
	Grated nutmeg
2 blades of mace	Flour
2 oz. minced meat	2 oz. fine vermicelli

Make the stock fairly concentrated, add the mace and let it simmer. Season the meat well with salt, pepper and nutmeg, shape into about 15 balls the size of marbles and roll them in a little flour. Add to the soup, then add the vermicelli, crushing it lightly. Cover the pan and boil for 20 minutes, then remove the mace and serve.

GROENTESOEP
(VEGETABLE SOUP)

3 meat cubes	1 leek
1 quart water	½ a cauliflower
1 oz. rice	2 tbsps. finely chopped parsley
½ lb. carrots	
A few brussels sprouts	1 oz. butter
1 head of celery	Salt to taste

Dissolve the meat cubes in the water, add the washed rice and cook till tender. Clean and cut up all the vegetables, add them and cook for 20 minutes. Just before serving, add the parsley, butter and salt.

SAJOR KOOL
(CABBAGE AND SHRIMP SOUP)

A small cabbage	Salt
2 large onions	2 tsps. vinegar
1 clove of garlic	1 oz. ground peanuts or peanut butter
1 or 2 red peppers	
A little fat	1 pint shelled shrimps
1 pint stock	

Shred the cabbage and the onions, crush the garlic and slice the red peppers. Fry the onions in a little fat, add the cabbage, peppers and garlic, and stir well. Pour on the stock, add the salt, vinegar and peanuts, and cook until the cabbage is tender. Finally add the shrimps and cook until soft.

ERWTENSOEP
(PEA SOUP)

1 lb. dried or split peas	1 lb. potatoes
6 pints water	1 pint milk
1 lb. meat (ham or boiling bacon for preference)	Seasoning
	A few leeks
	A few sticks of celery
1 marrow bone	Chopped parsley

Not just a soup, but a "main meal" dish, into which almost anything is flung, Erwtensoep forms part of the staple Dutch diet in winter.

Station restaurants and cafés always have it on their menus and it is served in huge bowls, with the meat on a smaller plate; a knife, fork and spoon are provided.

Wash the peas and then soak them in 3 pints water overnight. The next day, simmer the meat and marrow bone in 3 pints boiling water; after 1 hour, add to the peas and the water in which they soaked and cook till soft—about 1 hour. Add the peeled and sliced potatoes 40 minutes before serving. Take out the marrow bone and the meat, scrape out the marrow and put this back in the soup. Sieve or mash the soup thoroughly, and add sufficient milk to thin. Season, add the leek and celery, cut up small, and cook for about 20 minutes, stirring occasionally. Stir in the parsley before serving.

BAKED EEL

2 lb. eel	Nutmeg
4 oz. butter	Pepper and salt
Breadcrumbs	2 tsps. vinegar

Clean the fish and cut into 2-inch lengths. Melt the butter in a casserole and put in the eel. Sprinkle with breadcrumbs, nutmeg, seasoning and vinegar, cover and bake in a slow oven (300° F., mark 1) for 2 hours.

MOSSELEN IN MOSTERDSAUS
(MUSSELS IN MUSTARD SAUCE)

½ lb. fresh or pickled mussels	Pepper and salt
	½ pint milk
1 oz. flour	1 oz. butter
1 tsp. sugar	1 beaten egg
1–2 tsps. dry mustard	Toasted breadcrumbs

If the mussels are fresh, cook them in plenty of salted water, then shell them; pickled mussels can be used as they are. Mix the flour, sugar and seasonings, and blend with a little cold milk to a smooth paste. Boil the rest of the milk, add to the mixture, stirring, return it to the pan and cook till it thickens, stirring well. Remove from the heat and gradually add half the butter, then carefully stir in the egg. Mix with the mussels, arrange on well-greased individual shells or in a casserole dish, and sprinkle lavishly with toasted crumbs mixed with the remaining butter, shaved finely. Bake for about 20 minutes in a moderate oven (375° F., mark 5).

STOCKFISH

1 lb. stockfish (hake or cod, split and dried but not salted)	Salt

Soak the fish in water for 12 hours, skin and bone it, slice it and make into rolls. Tie the rolls with string and simmer the fish in salted water for 45 minutes. Drain, remove string and arrange on a hot dish. Serve with boiled rice, boiled potatoes, baked onions and a good mustard sauce.

VISSCHOTEL MET MOSTERDSAUS
(FISH CASSEROLE WITH MUSTARD SAUCE)

1 lb. boiled fish	Mashed potatoes
1 oz. butter	Lemon juice
2 large sliced onions	

For the Sauce

1 pint fish stock and water mixed, or milk and water	1½ oz. flour
	1 oz. butter
	Made mustard

First make the sauce. Bring the liquid to the boil, blend the flour with a little water, add to the liquid and stir till it thickens; add the fat and mustard to taste. Divide the fish into neat pieces. Fry the onions golden-brown. Put some of the fish at the bottom of a fireproof dish and add alternate layers of potato, onion, fish and sauce, with a squeeze of lemon juice; finish with a layer of potato. Put in the oven to heat through and brown the top.

GRILLED CHICKEN

A young chicken	2 tsps. melted butter
Salt	½ cup soya sauce
Black pepper	2 red peppers

Split open the chicken, flatten it and rub well with salt and pepper. Mix the melted butter with the soya sauce and chopped red peppers, then put the chicken under the grill and brush it continually with this mixture. Cook until the chicken is browned on both sides and tender when tested—15–20 minutes. (Soya burns easily, so take care not to let the grill get too hot.)

SPEKPANNEKOEKEN
(BACON PANCAKES)

8 oz. plain flour	1 pint milk
1 tsp. salt	1 egg
½ oz. yeast	3–4 oz. bacon
1 tsp. sugar	

This is a favourite lunch-time snack. The pancakes are about the size of a large dinner plate and they are very filling, so one forms the usual serving. In snack bars they are made on a huge hotplate, but in the home a girdle or frying pan can be used.

Make a batter by mixing the flour and salt together and creaming the yeast with 1 tsp. sugar. Make a well in the flour, add the creamed yeast mixed with half of the warm milk and the beaten egg, beat well and then put to rise for

20 minutes. Work in the rest of the milk and beat well. Cover the mixture with a cloth and leave in a warm place for about 1 hour. Meanwhile cut up the bacon into strips. Pour the batter on to a hot greased girdle or into a hot greased frying pan, lay the strips of bacon on top and cook on both sides. Serve folded in halves or quarters.

This same yeast batter is often used for sweet pancakes, which are served as in England, with lemon and caster sugar.

HUTSPOT
(BOILED BEEF AND VEGETABLES)

1 lb. brisket of beef	1½ lb. potatoes
¾ pint water	½ lb. onions
1 tsp. vinegar	Salt
1½ lb. carrots	

Wash the meat and put it into the cold water, adding the vinegar, bring to the boil and simmer slowly. Peel the carrots, mince them finely and add them to the stock after the meat has been cooking for 2 hours. Half an hour later add the peeled potatoes and chopped onions, and simmer for another ½ hour, until the vegetables are thoroughly cooked. Season to taste.

HETE BLIKSEM
(PORK CHOPS WITH APPLES)

Buy 6 T-bone pork chops, 1 inch thick, and trim off the excess fat. Melt one piece of the fat in a large frying pan, then remove it. Sprinkle the chops with salt and pepper and brown well on both sides in the fat. Now add ¼ cup water, cover and simmer till the chops are well done (about 1 hour), turning often.

Meanwhile, peel 3 lb. each of potatoes and apples and cut into 1-inch cubes. Heat 2½ cups canned condensed beef broth (undiluted) in a large saucepan; add the potatoes, apples, 2 large onions (chopped), 1 tsp. salt and ¼ tsp. pepper. Cover and simmer for ½ hour, stirring often.

Meanwhile, put 12 pork sausages and ¼ cup cold water in a large pan and simmer, covered, for 5 minutes. Drain off water, then let the sausages cook till well browned. Heap the potato mixture in the centre of a heated large platter; arrange the meat and sausages on it and garnish with fresh dill (if available). (Makes 6–8 servings.)

SAUSAGE AND ONIONS

1½ lb. potatoes	1 lb. sausages
2½ lb. onions	Salt
6 oz. rice	Vinegar

Peel the potatoes and half-cover with salted water. Bring to the boil and add the onions, peeled and chopped, and the washed rice. Add a little more water, put the sausages on top and simmer till the vegetables and rice are soft and the sausages are cooked—about 30 minutes. Dish the vegetables and rice on to a hot plate and arrange the sausages round, sprinkling with vinegar to taste.

CALF'S TONGUE

1 calf's tongue	A pinch of thyme
1 tsp. salt	A little parsley
1 large carrot	1 bay leaf
1 large onion	

Heat sufficient water in a deep saucepan to cover the tongue and when it is boiling, put in the tongue and flavouring ingredients. Cover and simmer for about 1½ hours, until tender. Trim the roots of the tongue and remove the bones and skin. Slice and serve hot, covered with egg and vinegar sauce (see below) and garnished with chopped parsley.

Egg and Vinegar Sauce

5 egg yolks	¼ tsp. salt
½ gill vinegar	1 oz. butter

Beat the egg yolks and add ⅓ pint water, the vinegar and salt. Cook carefully in a double saucepan, stirring continually until the sauce thickens. Remove from the heat, and add the butter, cut into small pieces; stir well and serve.

RUNDERLAPPEN
(STEWED STEAK)

Wash and dry 2 lb. beefsteak, flatten it and season with salt and pepper. Melt 2 oz. dripping in a saucepan and brown the steak on both sides. Add 2 sliced onions, 2 bay leaves, some grated nutmeg and a little water, cover the pan and cook for 1½ hours, adding a little more water occasionally. Serve with grilled or baked tomatoes.

HACHEE
(SAVOURY BEEF AND ONION STEW)

2 large onions, sliced	3 bay leaves
1 oz. flour	5 cloves
1½ oz. lard or mar-garine	1 tbsp. vinegar
	½ lb. diced cold meat
1 pint meat or meat cube stock	Pepper
	Piquant table sauce

Brown the onions and flour in the fat in a saucepan, and add the stock gradually, stirring all the time. Add the bay leaves and cloves and simmer for 5 minutes with the lid on. Add the vinegar and meat and simmer for another hour.

Thicken if desired, then season to taste with pepper and the piquant table sauce.

GAMMON WITH SAUERKRAUT

2 lb. sauerkraut
½ pint boiling water
Salt
1½ oz. butter

4 rashers of gammon or bacon
Potato purée

Wash the sauerkraut and put it into the boiling salted water; simmer gently until all the liquor has evaporated. Melt the butter in a casserole, add the sauerkraut and mix well. Serve with grilled gammon, bacon or boiled gammon, with a border of potato purée, which may be piped in a decorative pattern.

MEAT ROLLS

1 onion
1 leek
2 oz. butter or margarine
4 oz. cooked beef
¼ pint stock flavoured with tomato purée

Seasoning
A pinch of nutmeg
1 oz. flour
2 bread rolls
Fat for frying

Peel and chop the onion, wash the leek and slice it finely, then fry both in the melted fat. Mince the beef, add it to the vegetables and fry lightly. Add the stock, seasoning and nutmeg, and simmer gently for 15 minutes. Blend the flour with a little cold water, add this to the pan and stir well until the mixture thickens and boils. Cut the rolls lengthways, scoop out the inside and fry the rolls in butter until they are golden-brown; drain well and fill the cavity in each with the beef mixture.

This is a good way of using up a small quantity of left-over cooked beef.

JACHTSCHOTEL
(HUNTER'S DISH)

½ lb. onions
2 oz. fat for frying
½–¾ lb. minced cooked meat
½ pint stock
A pinch of ground cloves

Pepper and salt
1 sour apple
1 lb. mashed potatoes
Breadcrumbs
½ oz. butter

This good, solid dish is a sort of shepherd's pie, the potato being either mixed in with the other ingredients or used to form a crust on the top.

Slice the onions and fry in the fat till light brown. Add the minced meat, stock, seasonings, peeled and chopped apple, and potatoes (if desired), and simmer gently for ¼–½ hour. Pour the mixture into a greased fireproof dish, and if the mashed potatoes were not included with the meat, spread them over the top. Smooth the surface, sprinkle with breadcrumbs, dot with butter, and brown in a hot oven (450° F., mark 8) for 10 minutes.

BLINDE VINKEN
(VEAL ESCALOPES)

Rub salt and pepper into both sides of 4 thin escalopes, and put a slice of bacon on each. Mince 4 oz. meat and blend with an egg and some breadcrumbs, giving a smooth mixture; add salt and pepper. Put some filling on each escalope, roll up and tie with thread. Fry them quickly in butter till golden-brown, then lower the heat, add some water and simmer for about ½ hour. Remove the threads and serve the escalopes very hot, garnished with piped potato purée.

CALF'S HEAD BRAWN

1 calf's head
4 lb. stewing steak
1 tsp. salt
1 nutmeg

3 tsp. ground cloves
1 tbsp. vinegar
1 tbsp. gherkins

Clean the head and boil for 5 hours in salted water. After 2 hours add the stewing steak. When the meat is falling from the bones, remove the head, take out bones and chop the meat finely. Mix the chopped meat with 3 pints of the cooking liquid, to which has been added the nutmeg, ground finely, cloves, vinegar and gherkins. Put into moulds previously rinsed with cold water and leave in a cool place to set. When cold, cover the moulds with heavy white paper and pour a little vinegar on top of this. Keep in a cool place, renewing the vinegar from time to time so that the covering paper is always damp.

SAUSAGE WITH CURLY KALE

Boil 1 lb. curly kale in salted water until tender, drain, and mix with 1 lb. mashed potatoes, a little pepper and about 1 oz. butter or dripping. Pile the mixture into a fireproof dish, and on it place some smoked sausage, fried sausages or gammon; slowly heat in the oven until the sausage or gammon is hot.

SAUCIJZEBROODJES
(TRADITIONAL NEW YEAR'S EVE DISH)

8 oz. puff pastry
2 oz. minced beef
2 oz. minced veal
2 oz. minced pork
1 small finely chopped onion

Pepper and salt
A little grated nutmeg
4–6 tbsps. fresh bread-crumbs
1 egg
Milk or egg to glaze

Prepare the pastry and roll out into a strip

about 2 inches wide. Mix the meat and other ingredients together, make into a roll of the same length as the pastry and place on it; damp one long edge, fold the pastry over lengthwise and seal as for sausage rolls. Turn the join underneath, brush the top with milk or a little beaten egg, and cut into even lengths. Bake in a moderately hot oven (425° F., mark 7) for about 30 minutes. Serve piping hot.

CABBAGE STUFFED WITH MEAT

49

1 cabbage	$\frac{1}{4}$ tsp. nutmeg
6 oz. minced pork	2 oz. breadcrumbs
6 oz. minced veal	Stock
Salt and pepper	Butter

Remove the outer leaves from the cabbage, blanch them in boiling water for 10 minutes and drain well. Mix together the minced pork and veal, salt, pepper and nutmeg, add the breadcrumbs and mix a little stock with the filling. Arrange some of the cabbage leaves on a clean cloth, then cover with a layer of filling, put another layer of cabbage on this, and continue until all the minced meat has been used up. Gather the cloth together, tie up and boil in salted water for $1\frac{1}{2}$ hours. Remove the stuffed cabbage leaves from the cloth, put into a fireproof dish, top generously with pats of butter, and brown in a hot oven.

FRIED ARTICHOKES

2 lb. artichokes	$\frac{1}{4}$ oz. gelatine
1 oz. butter	1 egg
5 oz. flour	1 tbsp. olive oil
$1\frac{1}{2}$ pints milk	Deep oil or fat for
Pepper and salt	frying
2 oz. grated cheese	Parsley to garnish

Peel and slice the artichokes, boil immediately in salted water (taking care not to over-cook), then drain. Prepare a white sauce with the butter, 1 oz. flour and 1 pint milk; add the seasoning, cheese and gelatine, dissolved in a little cold water. Arrange the artichokes on large plates, with plenty of space between the slices, cover well with sauce and allow to set. Prepare a batter by mixing the remaining 4 oz. flour with the egg, olive oil and $\frac{1}{2}$ pint milk, and beat well. Dip each artichoke slice into the batter and fry immediately in oil or fat. Drain well, serve very hot and garnish with parsley.

RED CABBAGE AND APPLE

Wash and shred a medium-sized red cabbage. Boil $\frac{3}{4}$ pint salted water and add the cabbage to it, with 4 sliced cooking apples, and a pinch of nutmeg and simmer gently until the cabbage is

cooked and most of the liquid has evaporated. Add 2 oz. butter and 1 tbsp. sugar just before serving.

RODEKOOL
(SPICED RED CABBAGE)

Remove the outer leaves of a small red cabbage, halve it, remove the core, then wash and shred very finely. Put a little butter and $\frac{1}{4}$ pint water in a saucepan, add the cabbage, 3 cloves, some salt and 2 peeled, cored and sliced cooking apples; close tightly and simmer for $\frac{3}{4}$ hour. Add a little more butter, 1 oz. sugar and 2 tbsps. vinegar and simmer for another 5 minutes before serving.

BRUSSELS LOF
(CHICORY WITH CHEESE SAUCE)

2 lb. chicory	$\frac{1}{2}$ pint milk
Salt and pepper	4 oz. grated Gouda
1 oz. butter	cheese
1 oz. flour	Piquant table sauce

Cut a very thin slice from the base of the chicory, then insert a pointed vegetable knife and remove the core, which is apt to be bitter. Wash the chicory and boil it for 20–30 minutes in plenty of salted water, until tender. Drain well, and cover with a cheese sauce made as follows:

Melt the fat, add the flour and blend into a smooth paste. Add the milk, stirring well, boil for 5 minutes, remove from the heat and add the grated cheese. Season to taste with the table sauce, salt and pepper.

SWEET CORN CAKES

1 tbsp. finely grated	Cooked corn off the
onion	cob
1 egg	Salt and pepper
$\frac{1}{4}$ pint milk	1 tsp. chopped parsley
2 oz. flour	Frying fat

Mix the onion with the egg and milk and blend the flour into the mixture. Add the sweet corn, salt, pepper and parsley. Drop spoonfuls of this mixture into hot fat and fry until golden-brown.

AARDAPPELPUREE
(MASHED POTATOES)

Cook about 2 lb. potatoes and while they are still warm, mash, mince or sieve them. Put $\frac{3}{4}$ pint milk in a saucepan, add $\frac{1}{2}$ oz. butter and a little grated nutmeg and boil. Add the potato at once and stir well; now, using a wooden spoon, whip until white and creamy. Serve at once, or put in a fireproof dish, dot with a little butter and brown under the grill or in the oven.

Do not use potatoes which have been previously cooked and allowed to become cold.

HERRING SALAD

2 large salt herrings	2 hard-boiled eggs
2 cooking apples	Pickled onions
1 lb. cooked potatoes	Gherkins
2 heads lettuce	Oil and vinegar
1 small beetroot	

Skin and bone the fish and cut into small pieces. Dice the apples, potatoes and beetroot and mix with the fish and the lettuce leaves. Garnish with the egg, onions and gherkins and serve with oil and vinegar dressing.

HUZARENSLA
(HUSSAR'S SALAD)

About $\frac{1}{2}$ lb. cold meat	Mayonnaise or salad
1–2 cooked beetroot	cream
6–8 cold potatoes	French mustard and
1 apple	seasonings
A few silver onions and	1–2 hard-boiled eggs
gherkins	

Dice the meat; chop the beetroot, potatoes, apple, onions and gherkins. Mix together with mayonnaise or salad cream and add French mustard and seasonings. Place the salad on a meat dish and garnish with mayonnaise, beetroot, egg and gherkins.

Cubed cucumber is sometimes included. The exact quantities are not important in this salad, which is a good way of serving left-overs.

NASSI GORENG
(INDONESIAN SAVOURY RICE)

1 lb. rice	$\frac{1}{2}$–1 tsp. cumin seed
2 quarts water	6 oz. cooked pork or
Salt and pepper	chicken
1 lb. onions	6 oz. cooked ham
2 cloves of garlic	6 oz. peeled shrimps
3 tbsps. salad oil	2 eggs
1–2 tsps. sweet chutney	2 tbsps. milk
1–2 tsps. ground	1 oz. butter
coriander	

Just as we borrowed curries from India, the Dutch borrowed various Oriental dishes from the Dutch East Indies, and Nassi Goreng is now served everywhere in Holland, in both homes and restaurants.

Cook the rice in the salted water, strain and dry. Chop the onion and garlic and fry in the oil in a large pan until light brown. Add the chutney and spices, also the meat, ham and two-thirds of the shrimps, then heat through. Gradually add the rice and cook over a gentle heat, turning occasionally but not stirring. Beat up the eggs into the milk with some seasoning and cook in the butter to make a dryish omelette. Cut this into strips. Dish up the savoury rice on a large flat dish and garnish it with omelette strips and the rest of the shrimps. Serve it with cucumber salad and chutney.

Alternatively, the rice may be cooked and served separately.

BITTERBALLEN
(COCKTAIL SAVOURIES)

$\frac{1}{4}$ oz. powdered gelatine	1 oz. grated Gouda
$\frac{1}{4}$ pint veal stock	cheese
1 oz. flour	1 tsp. chopped parsley
1 oz. Dutch unsalted	Pepper and salt
butter	3 oz. toasted bread-
$\frac{1}{4}$ pint milk	crumbs or finely
6 oz. cooked chopped	crushed Dutch rusks
ham and veal	Fat for frying

Dissolve the gelatine in 3 tbsps. of the boiling veal stock. Make a white sauce using the flour, butter, stock and milk, then add the dissolved gelatine, meat, cheese and parsley. Season well, turn on to a plate and allow to cool until firm. Roll into marble-sized balls, dip into bread-crumbs then into beaten egg and lastly into breadcrumbs again. Fry in hot fat until golden-brown and drain them on absorbent paper. Serve hot with mustard as a cocktail savoury.

HOT CHEESE SOUFFLÉ

3 eggs	3 oz. grated Gouda or
1 oz. butter	Edam cheese
1 oz. flour	Salt and pepper
$\frac{1}{4}$ pint milk	

Separate the eggs. Melt the fat and stir in the flour, then add the milk gradually, and bring to the boil, stirring continuously. Cool slightly, and add the cheese, seasoning and egg yolks one by one, beating well. Fold in the very stiffly beaten egg whites, and put into a large greased fireproof dish. Bake in a moderately hot oven (400° F., mark 6) for about $\frac{1}{2}$ hour, till well risen and brown. Serve immediately, piping hot.

KAASSOESJES
(CHEESE PUFFS)

$4\frac{1}{2}$ tbsps. water	1 egg
5 oz. butter or margarine	4 oz. Dutch cheese
A pinch of salt	French mustard
1 oz. flour	

Bring the water, 1 oz. of the fat and the salt to the boil. Add all the flour at once, stir for a short time till the mixture sticks together, and remove from the heat. Add the egg and beat it into the mixture. (This will take some time.)

Then with 2 teaspoons, form 25–30 small balls the size of marbles and put these in a greased baking tin 1–2 inches apart. Bake in a hot oven (450° F., mark 8) for 10–15 minutes. (Do not open the oven during first 10 minutes, or the puffs will go flat.)

Put the remaining butter or margarine in a warm place for a while, then add the shredded cheese. Flavour with French mustard to taste and stir well. Cut the puffs open at the top and fill with cheese mixture, and close them or top with grated cheese. Serve as a cocktail savoury or before a meal.

CHEESE AND HAM SAVOURY

8 thin slices of stale bread (crusts removed)
4 slices (about ½ oz. each) of Gouda or Edam cheese
4 slices of ham (about ½ oz. each)
Butter, margarine or dripping for frying

The bread, cheese and ham should be cut to the same size. Put a slice of cheese and a slice of ham between each pair of bread slices, spread the sandwiches on the outside with fat, and fry them golden-brown and crisp. They may be served as a savoury at lunch or supper, or as an entrée, after the first course of a main meal.

SPICED APPLE CAKE

6 oz. shortcrust pastry
Cooking apples
4 oz. brown sugar
2 tsps. ground cinnamon
1 tsp. grated nutmeg
3 oz. chopped almonds
Shaving of butter or margarine

Line a shallow rectangular tin (such as a Swiss roll tin) with the shortcrust pastry and crimp the edges neatly. Cover the pastry with overlapping pieces of thinly sliced apple. Mix together the brown sugar, spices and chopped nuts and sprinkle the mixture over the apples. Dot with shavings of butter and bake in a moderately hot oven (400° F., mark 6) for about 30–40 minutes, until the apples and the pastry are cooked. Leave the cake until it is cold, then cut it into fingers or squares.

LAYER BUTTER CAKE

1 lb. flour
12 oz. butter
12 oz. sugar
2 eggs

For the Filling

5 oz. ground almonds
5 oz. caster sugar
1 egg
Grated peel of 1 lemon

Rub the butter into the flour and sugar and bind with the eggs. You may not need to use both eggs, depending on the size of the eggs and the type of flour used. The mixture should form a solid ball. Divide into two and press one-half into a greased sandwich tin. Mix together the almonds, sugar, beaten egg and lemon peel and spread over the mixture in the tin. Shape the remaining dough into a round the size of the tin and press it on top of the filling. Bake in a moderate oven (350° F., mark 4) for 45 minutes. Cool on a sieve before cutting.

FLENSJES
(DUTCH PANCAKES)

4 oz. flour
Salt
3 eggs, beaten
½ pint milk
2½ oz. butter or margarine

Mix the flour, salt and eggs, and gradually add the milk. Melt the fat in a small frying pan, and pour it in, stirring well. Put an inverted saucer on a large plate and keep hot. Pour 3 tbsps. batter into the greased pan and fry brown on both sides, then put this pancake on the inverted saucer, and fry the remaining batter in the same way; stack the cooked pancakes, and serve them as hot as possible, with sugar, jam or fruit.

BESCHUIT MET BESSENSAP
(DUTCH RUSKS WITH RED-CURRANT SAUCE)

12 Dutch rusks
1 pint red-currant juice (or diluted currant jelly)
1 pint water
½ lb. sugar
1 stick of cinnamon
Rind of 1 lemon
2 tbsps. cornflour

Soak the rusks in half the red-currant juice in a large dish. Slowly heat the rest of the juice with the water, sugar, cinnamon and grated rind. Blend the cornflour with a little cold water to a pouring consistency and add this to the sauce when almost boiling. Let the sauce boil for several minutes, stirring continually, then pour over the rusks, and serve either hot or cold.

KRENTEN BOLLEN
(CURRANT ROLLS)

1½ lb. flour
1 tsp. salt
¾ oz. yeast
1 oz. sugar
2 tbsps. warm milk
1 egg
½ pint milk
3 oz. butter
½ lb. currants
1–2 oz. chopped candied lemon peel

Sieve the flour and salt into a bowl and warm. Cream the yeast with the sugar and add 2 tbsps. warm milk; make a well in the flour and pour in the yeast. Beat the egg, add the ½ pint milk and the butter and blend thoroughly. Add this to the flour, mix well and knead for 10 minutes. Add the fruits and knead again. Cover with a damp cloth and place in a warm place for 1 hour to rise. Divide into 16 small balls, knead into rounds and place on a greased baking sheet. Prove in a warm place for 15 minutes, and bake in a hot oven (450° F., mark 8) for 20 minutes. Serve cold with butter. This is a favourite item at the Dutch " Koffietafel " or cold lunch.

TULBAND MET ROZIJNEN
(SULTANA CAKE)

1 lb. plain flour	4 oz. butter
A pinch of salt	2 eggs
1 oz. yeast	6 oz. sultanas
2 tsps. sugar	2 oz. chopped candied
About $\frac{1}{4}$ pint tepid	peel
milk	2 tbsps. icing sugar

A " Tulband " is an Arab fez and this cake should be fez-shaped, so if possible use a savarin tin.

Sieve the flour and salt into a warm bowl and make a well in the centre. Cream the yeast with the sugar and pour into well; add the milk, heap the flour over, cover with a hot damp cloth and set the sponge for about $\frac{1}{2}$ hour.

Cream the butter and remaining sugar and gradually add the slightly beaten eggs, sultanas and peel. When the dough has risen well, add this mixture, beat well and " knock " it until it leaves the side of the bowl. (If the eggs are small, use a little more milk.) Cover bowl again with a hot damp cloth and leave to rise for another 45 minutes. Arrange the dough in a well-greased and crumbed savarin tin, and leave to prove until twice its original size. Bake in a moderate oven (375° F., mark 5) for about 1 hour. While the cake is still hot, sprinkle it with sieved icing sugar. Serve hot or cold; when it is eaten hot, golden syrup is often served with it.

LETTERBANKET
(ALMOND PASTRIES)

5 oz. butter or mar-garine (chilled if possible)	$\frac{1}{2}$ cupful water
	Salt
	1 egg white
5 oz. flour	

For the Filling

5 oz. ground almonds	Finely grated rind of
5 oz. sugar	1 lemon
A pinch of salt	1 egg

First make the filling. Mix the ground almonds, sugar, salt, grated lemon rind and egg and pass the mixture once through the mincer. Knead it together again and shape it into a roll about $1\frac{1}{2}$ inches in diameter.

Divide the butter into fair-sized pieces and mix with nearly all the flour. Add the water and salt and stir with a knife until the flour has absorbed the water. Roll the dough out on a floured board very lightly, then fold again and roll; repeat three times and finally roll it out to give a strip $\frac{1}{4}$ inch thick and 3 inches wide. Put the almond filling on this and fold the dough round it, sticking the edges together with water. Shape the roll into letters (e.g., the initials of the guest of honour). To make a C, seal the ends of the curved roll with some dough; for O or D, join the ends together. Brush with egg white, and bake in a moderately hot oven (425 F., mark 7) for 30–40 minutes.

CHOCOLADETAART
(CHOCOLATE LAYER CAKE)

Start heating the oven to moderate (350° F., mark 4). Grease and line 2 9-inch sandwich tins.

In a double saucepan melt 3 tbsps. butter or margarine with 3 squares of unsweetened chocolate; cool for 10 minutes. Sift $2\frac{1}{2}$ cups flour with 4 tsps. baking powder. Beat 4 eggs till thick; gradually beat in 2 cups granulated sugar, then beat again. Beat in the cooled chocolate-butter mixture and beat the mixture for a minute or two. Beat in the flour and 1 cup milk alternately, a little at a time. Pour into the tins and bake for 30 minutes, or till a fine skewer comes out clean. Cool for 10 minutes, remove from the tins on to a cake rack and carefully peel off the paper. Meanwhile in a double boiler, mix $\frac{1}{4}$ cup granulated sugar, $2\frac{1}{2}$ tbsps. cocoa, 1 tbsp. cornflour and 1 cup milk; cook, stirring, till thickened; add 1 tsp. vanilla essence and cool. Set aside $\frac{1}{3}$ cup of this filling and spread the rest between the two cake layers. Whip 2 cups double cream and fold in the remaining filling; use to ice the cake. Shred 1 square couverture chocolate over the top of cake. Chill till required.

Hungary

LIKE so many central European countries, Hungary shares many dishes with her neighbours. Even the paprika pepper, which seems so typical of Hungarian cookery, came originally from the Turkish invaders who, in their turn, had brought it from India.

The famous stew, gulyas, is one of the oldest Hungarian dishes and takes its name from the cooking pot of the nomadic shepherds. Gulyas is actually served almost as liquid as soup but pörkölt, another type of stew, is much thicker. A true Hungarian *paprikas* is always finished off by the addition of sour cream.

One unique feature of Hungarian cuisine is the roux of lard, onions and cream which is used to thicken soups and vegetable dishes. Hungarians also use freely a kind of egg and flour pasta called Tarhonya, which is made while eggs are cheap, dried in the sun and used as a substitute for potatoes or in puddings.

Soups in Hungary are good, nourishing and varied, including many made with vegetables, and they are frequently served with dumplings, noodles and other garnishes. Meat is used economically and stuffed meat dishes, minced meat and meat loaf are all popular. Veal and pork are frequently eaten, and chicken and goose are popular. Fresh-water fish and shell fish provide some very good dishes. Vegetables are cooked in a variety of ways and are often used to replace meat or fish.

Some very attractive soufflés, pancakes, fritters, pastries and cakes are also made. Almonds, hazelnuts and chestnuts figure prominently in these and brandy, rum, cinnamon and chocolate are especially popular flavourings.

The Hungarian year is full of festivals, most of which demand their own special dishes. Weddings also have their traditions as far as food is concerned and a wedding feast will consist of many hearty courses, much of the food being provided by the wedding guests. Indeed so much is generally contributed that the young couple often live on the leftovers for weeks ! In at least one Hungarian village, the wedding cake is traditionally from four to six feet long.

Hungarian wines such as Tokay and Egri Bikaver, the famous Bull's Blood, are well known all over the world, the tradition of viticulture dating back to Roman times.

Hungary

BEAN SOUP

String and slice 1 lb. of French beans (frozen beans may be used). Prepare a quart of good stock with veal or pork bones and any fresh green vegetables. Strain the liquid, add the beans with seasoning and cook until tender. Thicken with a roux made with 2 oz. of flour and 1 oz. lard. Stir into the soup and add a finely chopped onion, a little chopped parsley, a saltspoonful of red paprika and one crushed clove of garlic (optional). Cook for a few minutes. Just before serving, after removing from heat, add a gill of sour cream. Cooked pasta in small pieces may be added if liked.

CSERESNYELEVES
(SPICED CHERRY SOUP)

1 lb. sweet red cherries	3 cups water
Rind of ½ lemon	3 tbsps. quick-cooking
6 whole cloves	tapioca
A 3-inch stick cinnamon	1 cup red wine
⅓ cup granulated sugar	4–6 thin lemon slices
½ tsp. salt	Sour cream

Wash cherries ; remove stems. With vegetable peeler remove rind from lemon in strips ; stick cloves into rind.

In saucepan, combine cherries, lemon rind with cloves, cinnamon, sugar, salt, water. Simmer uncovered for 15 minutes.

Gradually stir in tapioca, bring to the boil, then remove from heat ; stir in wine, allow to cool. Remove and discard lemon rind, cloves and cinnamon, then refrigerate until serving time.

To serve, ladle ice-cold soup into individual soup bowls or plates ; top each serving with a lemon slice and spoonful of sour cream (or, if preferred, stir in cream).

PALOC SOUP

3 lb. neck of mutton (or	1 clove of garlic
1¾ lb. without bones)	1 bay leaf
1 lb. potatoes	A few caraway seeds
1 lb. French beans	Salt
½ lb. onions	2 heaped tsps. flour
2 oz. lard	⅛ pint sour cream
1 tsp. red paprika	

Cut the mutton into small cubes, and prepare the vegetables. Fry the chopped onions in the smoking hot lard until golden-brown, sprinkle with paprika, and quickly add the mutton, garlic, bay leaf, caraway seeds and salt, and cook for 15 minutes.

Meanwhile, cut the potatoes into cubes, and cook them and the beans. When both are soft, pour them with their liquor over the meat. Add the flour, blended with a little cold water, re-boil, and lastly add the cream. Do not re-boil after adding the cream.

UJHAZI CHICKEN SOUP

1 boiling fowl	1 tomato
1 carrot	Salt and pepper
1 parsnip	Water
1 onion	Vermicelli

Clean and joint the chicken and stew together with the vegetables in the seasoned water. When the meat is tender add the vermicelli and serve meat, vegetables and liquid all together in a deep dish.

RAKPAPRIKAS
(CRAYFISH WITH PAPRIKA)

2 dozen crayfish (or	4 tbsps. tomato purée
Dublin Bay prawns)	1 heaped tsp. paprika
1 tsp. cumin	Salt
Parsley	¼ pint sour cream
4 oz. butter or margarine	

Boil the crayfish or prawns in salted water flavoured with cumin and parsley. When they are cooked, strain them and remove the flesh from the tails and claws, reserving a few whole fish for garnish. Pound the shells to a paste with 2 oz. butter, and rub through a sieve. Melt the remaining butter, mix with the paste made with the shells, add the tomato purée and paprika, and season with salt. Add the pounded flesh, and stir in the cream. Garnish with the whole prawns, and serve with boiled rice.

LECSO EGGS

3 green peppers	Salt
3 tomatoes	Paprika
1 onion	1 tsp. sugar
1 oz. lard	4 eggs

Remove seeds from peppers and cut into strips. Peel and quarter tomatoes. Chop the onion finely and cook in the lard until soft but not coloured. Add peppers, sprinkle with salt and cook until the peppers are tender. Add paprika, tomatoes and sugar, cook slowly until tomatoes are soft. Beat the eggs lightly and pour over the mixture, stirring until the eggs are cooked. Serve with rice or potatoes.

VEAL CUTLETS

Allow one veal cutlet for each person. Dip in egg and breadcrumbs and fry in hot fat. Remove and keep hot. Slice and fry some mushrooms, and have ready some spinach boiled, drained and chopped. On the serving dish put a layer of the spinach, and on this place the cutlets. Cover with the mushrooms and over all pour some good béchamel sauce to which finely diced cooked ham has been added. Sprinkle with grated Parmesan cheese and brown under the grill or in a hot oven.

GOULASH

1 lb. stewing steak	Grated nutmeg
Seasoned flour	2 oz. flour
2 medium-sized onions	½ pint stock
1 green pepper	2 large tomatoes
A little dripping	A bunch of mixed herbs
3 tbsps. tomato paste	¼ pint beer
Salt	2 tsps. paprika
Pepper	

Cut the steak into small pieces and dip them in seasoned flour. Chop the onions and green pepper and sauté them lightly in a little dripping. Add the meat and fry lightly on all sides. Stir in tomato paste, seasonings and flour and add the stock, cut-up tomatoes and the herbs. Put the mixture in a casserole and cook in a slow oven (325° F., mark 2), for 1 hour. Add the beer and paprika and cook for another ½–1 hour or until the meat is tender. Remove the herbs. Serve with sauerkraut and dumplings flavoured with caraway seeds, or with a green salad.

ESTERHAZY ROSTELYOS
(BRAISED SIRLOIN ESZTERHAZY)

6 carrots	3 tbsps. flour
8–12 celery stalks	6 whole black peppers
6 sirloin steaks, about ½ lb. each, ¼ inch thick	1 tbsp. paprika
1 tbsp. salt	1 can condensed beef bouillon
1 tsp. pepper	6 bottles capers
3 tbsps. butter or margarine	1 lemon, thinly sliced
6 onions, sliced	1½ cups sour cream

Cut carrots and celery in long, thin strips. Lay meat on board; then pound in salt and pepper on both sides.

In hot butter in large pan, brown meat on both sides. Remove from pan, and set aside.

In butter left from browning meat, sauté carrots, celery, onions about 15 minutes, stirring occasionally. Stir in flour, then peppers, paprika, beef bouillon. Return meat to pan; cover, simmer for 30 minutes or till vegetables and meat are tender. Add capers, lemon. Cook uncovered about 15 minutes or until liquid is reduced by about one-third. Dilute sour cream with about 1 cup of liquid, then stir it into mixture in pan. Heat thoroughly, but do not boil. (Makes 6 servings.)

SZEKELY GULYAS
(TRANSYLVANIAN GOULASH)

2 lb. boneless pork or veal shoulder	1 tsp. caraway seeds
6 medium onions, chopped	1 tbsp. salt
¼ cup finely chopped fresh dill or 1 tsp. ground dill seed	1½ cans condensed beef bouillon, undiluted
	4 tsps. paprika
1 clove of garlic, minced	1 tin sauerkraut, drained (about 1¾ lb.)
	2 pints sour cream

Trim fat from meat; cut meat into 3-inch pieces.

In heavy pan, combine meat, onions, dill, garlic, caraway seeds, salt and bouillon. Bring to boil; simmer, covered for 1 hour.

Dissolve paprika in 1 cup hot broth from goulash; add to goulash along with sauerkraut.

Simmer, covered, 1 hour longer, or until meat is tender. Stir in sour cream.

Serve with parsley-buttered potatoes and, if desired, with more sour cream and dill (Serves 6.)

BORJU ROLADA
(VEAL ROLLS CONTINENTAL)

1¼ lb. veal, cut ¼ inch thick	1 tsp. salt
	1 tbsp. flour
1 tbsp. prepared mustard	1 tsp. paprika
¼ cup grated or shredded Parmesan cheese	¼ cup butter
	½ cup water
Chopped parsley	

Cut veal into 4 pieces; spread each with mustard, then sprinkle with cheese, 2 tbsps. parsley, salt. Roll up each piece, and tie securely with string. Combine flour and paprika, and use to coat rolls on all sides, reserving any left-over flour.

In hot butter in pan, brown rolls well on all sides. Add water, and simmer, covered for 30 minutes or until meat is tender.

Remove rolls to heated platter; thicken liquid in pan with remaining flour; heat, stirring until smooth; pour over rolls; sprinkle with parsley.

BARAMY PÖRKÖLT
(SAVOURY LAMB STEAKS)

4 leg-of-lamb steaks, 1 inch thick	2 rashers of bacon, diced
¾ cup milk	1¼ tsp. salt
1 tbsp. tarragon vinegar	⅛ tsp. pepper
¼ cup minced onion	

Trim excess fat from steaks. Let them stand in milk and vinegar about 1 hour, then remove and dry them well reserve marinade.

In pan, sauté onion, bacon, steaks until meat is well browned on both sides. Sprinkle steaks with salt, pepper; add marinade. Simmer, covered for 30 minutes or until meat is tender. To serve, pour gravy over the steaks. (Makes 4 servings.)

PÖRKÖLT À LA GUNDEL
(STEW À LA MODE)

51

1 lb. beef tenderloin, $\frac{1}{2}$ inch thick	$\frac{1}{4}$ cup butter
3 tbsps. flour	3 medium onions, thinly sliced
2 tsps. salt	$\frac{3}{4}$ cup water
$\frac{1}{2}$ tsp. dried marjoram	$\frac{1}{2}$ cup red burgundy
$\frac{1}{4}$ tsp. pepper	1 package frozen cut green beans
$\frac{1}{4}$ tsp. monosodium glutamate	1 package frozen green peas
$\frac{1}{2}$ lb. calf liver, $\frac{1}{2}$ inch thick	

Trim fat from meat. Combine flour, salt, marjoram, pepper, monosodium glutamate. Pound this flour mixture into both sides of beef; use rest of flour mixture to coat liver. Then cut both pieces of meat into 2-inch by 1-inch strips.

In hot butter in large pan, sauté onions until golden; remove and reserve.

In same butter, brown tenderloin and liver strips, turning them often. Add onions, water, wine. Simmer, uncovered, over low heat, stirring occasionally, until mixture is slightly thickened and meat is tender—about 15 minutes.

Meanwhile, cook beans and peas for 1 minute less than package labels direct; drain. Just before serving, gently stir them into stew. (Makes 4–6 servings.)

PORK CHOPS WITH GARLIC

Trim any excess fat off the chops, and season them with salt and pepper. Fry in fat, briskly at first and then more slowly, until they are cooked through—20–25 minutes, according to the thickness of the meat; drain well. Cut a clove of garlic, rub it over both sides of the meat, put the chops on a hot dish, and pour gravy round.

FILLET STEAK WITH BACON

2 pieces of fillet steak, about $1\frac{1}{2}$ lb. each	Salt and pepper
1 lb. streaky bacon	Continental mustard
	Olive oil

Choose nice lean pieces of steak, and beat slightly if necessary. Make some incisions in the meat with a knife, and insert strips of the bacon. Season the steak with salt and pepper and spread it with mustard, then marinade it in a little olive oil for 30 minutes. Now bake it in a moderately hot oven (400° F., mark 6) for 15–20 minutes, lower the temperature to slow (325° F., mark 2) and continue to cook for about the same length of time, until the meat is tender. Garnish with bacon rolls and baked tomatoes.

VEAL WITH MUSHROOMS

$1\frac{1}{2}$ lb. lean veal fillet	$\frac{1}{2}$ pint stock
Lard for frying	Salt and pepper
$\frac{1}{4}$ lb. mushrooms	Creamed potatoes or boiled rice
$\frac{1}{2}$ oz. flour	
1 tbsp. chopped parsley	

Trim the meat if required, slice it thinly, and beat to make it tender. Fry quickly on both sides in hot lard, and then keep it hot. Slice and fry the mushrooms, sprinkle in the flour and parsley, and add the stock, mixing well. Season, bring to the boil, add the meat, and cook gently until tender—about 20–30 minutes. Serve with a border of creamed potatoes or rice.

PANCAKE PUDDING WITH HAM

12–14 thin small pancakes	Seasoning
6 oz. minced ham	1 egg white
$\frac{1}{4}$ pint sour milk or cream	Grated cheese

Line a fireproof basin with one pancake, and reserve one for the top. Cut the rest into strips, mix with the minced ham, sour milk, seasoning and stiffly beaten egg white. Put into the basin and cover with the remaining pancake, sprinkle with grated cheese, and bake in a moderately hot oven (425° F., mark 7) for 10–12 minutes, then turn out.

PAPRIKA VEAL FILLETS

Beat well 4 fillets of veal and dip them in seasoned flour. Fry the meat well on both sides in 2 oz. lard, then remove it and keep it hot. Mix 1 tsp. paprika with $\frac{1}{4}$ pint sour cream and add it to the fat, stir well and put the meat back; simmer for a few minutes before serving.

TARRAGON LAMB

$2\frac{1}{2}$ lb. neck of lamb	2 tbsps. sour cream
Salt	3–4 tbsps. tarragon or wine vinegar
A sprig of tarragon (if available)	1 egg or 2 egg yolks
2 oz. flour	

Stew the meat until tender in water to cover, adding some salt and the tarragon sprig (if used). Mix the flour, half the cream, vinegar and a little water to give a thin cream, put into a saucepan, add some of the meat liquor and cook gently, stirring all the time, until it thickens. Beat the egg or egg yolks with the remaining cream, put into the serving dish and pour the sauce over, beating all the time. Cut up the meat, removing the bones, and add to the sauce.

RABBIT IN MUSTARD SAUCE

1 rabbit	1 onion
Salt and pepper	1 bay leaf
1 oz. lard	1 tbsp. flour
French mustard	1 gill sour cream
1 oz. bacon	

Soak the disjointed rabbit in cold water for several hours, changing the water once or twice. Remove, dry and rub salt and pepper, a little lard and some mustard into each piece of meat. Put the meat in a casserole with the diced bacon, sliced onion and bay leaf. Add about $\frac{1}{8}$ pint water and cook in a moderately hot oven (400° F., mark 6) for 30 minutes. Remove lid from casserole and turn up heat to crisp the bacon. Put the meat on a hot dish, make gravy from the fat remaining in the casserole, with flour and sour cream. Sieve the gravy and serve separately.

RAKOTT BURGONYA
(LAYER POTATOES)

1 cup sour cream	1 cup finely diced
$\frac{1}{2}$ cup double cream	cooked ham
$1\frac{1}{2}$ tsps. salt	1 cup fresh bread-
6 cold cooked medium	crumbs
potatoes, thinly sliced	2 tbsps. melted butter
3 hard-boiled eggs, sliced	$\frac{1}{4}$ tsp. onion salt

Start heating oven to moderate (350° F., mark 4).

Into sour cream in small bowl, stir double cream and salt until well blended.

In a greased $1\frac{1}{2}$-quart casserole, arrange one-third of potatoes; top with egg slices, then one-half of cream mixture. Add another one-third of potatoes; sprinkle with ham; pour over remaining cream mixture; then top with remaining potatoes.

Toss crumbs with butter and onion salt, and sprinkle evenly over potatoes.

Bake 30 minutes or until bubbly. (Makes 6–8 servings.)

TEJFELES COMBA
(MUSHROOMS IN SOUR CREAM)

1 lb. mushrooms	1 tsp. paprika
3 tbsps. butter	$\frac{1}{2}$ tsp. pepper
1 large onion, minced	4 tbsps. chopped
$\frac{1}{3}$ cup water	parsley
1 tsp. salt	1 cup sour cream

Wash mushrooms; trim off ends of stalks then slice lengthwise.

In hot butter in frying pan, sauté onion until golden. Add mushrooms and water; cook until tender, about 15 minutes, adding more water if needed.

Add salt, paprika, pepper and half of parsley; stir in sour cream; heat. Garnish with remainder of parsley.

TOKFOZELEK
(COURGETTES IN CREAM)

$1\frac{1}{2}$ lb. courgettes	1 tsp. paprika
1 tsp. salt	1 tbsp. fresh dill or
2 tbsps. vinegar	$\frac{1}{4}$ tsp. ground dill
2 tbsps. butter or mar-	seed
garine	$\frac{1}{2}$ cup single cream
2 tbsps. flour	

Scrub unpeeled courgettes well; cut off ends; then into bowl, cut rest in long, thin strips, about $\frac{1}{4}$ inch thick. Sprinkle with $\frac{1}{2}$ tsp. salt and vinegar; let stand 15 minutes, then drain.

In melted butter in saucepan, simmer courgettes over low heat, covered, until just tender, but not soft, about 10 minutes, stirring occasionally.

Stir in flour, paprika, $\frac{1}{2}$ tsp. salt, dill. Add cream gradually, and cook, stirring until mixture is smooth and thickened.

VOROS KAPOSZTA SALATA
(RED CABBAGE SALAD)

$\frac{1}{2}$ a medium-sized head	$\frac{1}{2}$ cup vinegar
red cabbage, finely	$\frac{1}{2}$ cup water
shredded	$\frac{1}{4}$ cup granulated sugar
1 tbsp. salt	$\frac{1}{4}$ tsp. pepper

In large bowl, sprinkle cabbage with salt; let stand for $\frac{1}{2}$ hour.

In saucepan, combine vinegar, water, sugar, pepper; bring to boil; pour over cabbage.

Refrigerate until serving time; drain. Serve with pot roast or pork.

RAKOTT SPENOT
(LAYERED SPINACH)

4 oz. medium noodles	2 tbsps. flour
($2\frac{1}{2}$ cups)	$\frac{1}{2}$ tsp. salt
2 packages frozen chop-	$\frac{1}{2}$ tsp. paprika
ped spinach or 2 cups	$\frac{1}{8}$ tsp. pepper
cooked spinach chop-	1 cup milk
ped	$\frac{1}{2}$ lb. Gruyère cheese,
3 tbsps. butter	coarsely grated

Start heating oven to moderately hot (400° F., mark 6). Cook noodles as package label directs; drain and rinse. Cook spinach and drain.

In saucepan, melt butter; stir in flour, salt, paprika, pepper, gradually stir in milk. Cook until thickened, stirring constantly, remove from heat and stir in spinach.

In greased 12-inch by 8-inch by 2-inch baking dish, arrange half of noodles, sprinkling with half of cheese; spoon spinach mixture over cheese, add layer of remaining noodles, and sprinkle remaining cheese over top. Bake for 15 minutes or until cheese is bubbly. Serve with breaded veal cutlets or grilled lamb chops. (Makes 8 servings.)

SULT HAL FEHERBORBAN
(BAKED SOLE)

½ lb. mushrooms	Paprika
4 cold cooked medium potatoes, thinly sliced	⅔ cup white wine
2 tbsps. butter	1 cup sour cream
1½ tsps. of salt	2 lb. fresh fillets of sole
½ tsp. pepper	Parsley or chives

Start heating oven to moderate (375° F., mark 5).

Wash, trim and slice mushrooms.

In buttered 12-inch by 8-inch by 2-inch baking dish, arrange potatoes; top with mushrooms; dot with butter, sprinkle with half of salt and pepper and ½ tsp. paprika; pour wine over all. Spread with half of sour cream.

Arrange pieces of fish over all, sprinkle with rest of salt and pepper and ½ tsp. paprika; top with rest of sour cream. Bake 30–40 minutes or till fish is done; sprinkle with paprika and parsley and serve. (Makes 6–8 servings.)

STUFFED SPINACH ROULADE

1 lb. spinach	2 eggs
3 oz. butter	8 oz. chopped ham
2 oz. flour	2 tbsps. sour cream
¼ pint milk	Grated cheese
Salt and pepper	

Clean the spinach, soak it in water for 10 minutes and transfer it to a pan with no water, except what clings to the leaves; lid tightly and cook until tender, drain well and sieve. Make a sauce with 2 oz. butter, flour and milk, season well, and add the spinach and the egg yolks. Finally, whisk the egg whites until stiff and fold into the mixture. Pour into a greased and lined baking tin and bake in a moderately hot oven (400° F., mark 6) for 20 minutes.

Meanwhile make a filling by heating the ham in the remaining fat, then add the cream. Turn the spinach pastry out on to a board covered with damped paper, spread it with the filling and roll up like a Swiss roll. (This must be done whilst the pastry is hot.) Cover with greased paper, and reheat in the oven. Serve sprinkled with cheese and accompanied by cheese sauce.

TÖLTÖTT PAPRIKA
(STUFFED GREEN PEPPERS)

4 oz. rice	1 egg
5 green peppers	Salt
½ lb. minced pork	Paprika pepper
1 clove of garlic	Tomato sauce
1 onion	

Boil the rice. Cut the peppers near the stalk end, removing the seeds and inner ribs, wash and drain. Mix the minced pork with the chopped garlic and onion and add the beaten egg, rice, salt and pepper. Mix well and fill the peppers with this stuffing. Put the peppers into a fire-proof dish and pour some tomato sauce over them. Bake in a moderate oven (350° F., mark 4) until the peppers are tender.

SIMPLE CUCUMBER SALAD

Peel a firm green cucumber, slice very thinly, sprinkle with salt and leave for about an hour, then squeeze well in a cloth to extract the moisture. Mix with vinegar and olive oil, add a few thin slices of onion, sprinkle with paprika or pepper and leave to stand for 2 hours before serving. A tablespoon of sour cream may be poured over the salad if pepper is not used.

CHICKEN STEW

A 4-lb. chicken	2 green peppers
2 onions	4 skinned tomatoes
Lard	¼ pint sour cream
1 tsp. paprika pepper	¼ pint milk
½ pint stock or water	1 oz. flour
Seasoning	

Cut up the chicken, reserving the liver and the gizzard, and wash the pieces in cold water. Chop the onions and fry them until golden-brown in the hot lard. Sprinkle the paprika pepper over the onions, stir, add the stock or water and bring to the boil. Add the chicken, the sliced liver, the partially cooked gizzard, cut into pieces, and a little salt. Cover the pan and simmer until the chicken is almost tender. Now add the sliced green peppers and tomatoes, and continue to cook until the chicken is quite tender. Mix the sour cream with the milk and blend in the flour; add this thickening to the chicken stew, and bring to the boil. Season to taste before serving.

TEJFELES UBORKASALATA
(CUCUMBER SALAD WITH CREAM)

2 cucumbers	½ cup sour cream
1½ tsps. salt	Paprika
2 tbsps. vinegar	

Peel cucumbers, cut into paper-thin slices;

place in bowl, toss with salt, refrigerate for 2 hours.

Drain cucumbers very well. Blend vinegar with sour cream, stir into cucumbers.

Turn cucumbers into serving dish, sprinkle with paprika, serve.

RANTOTT CSIRKE
(OVEN-FRIED CHICKEN PAPRIKA)

$\frac{1}{4}$ cup butter	1 tbsp. paprika
$\frac{1}{4}$ cup flour	$\frac{1}{4}$ tsp. onion salt
1 2–2$\frac{1}{2}$ lb. frying chicken, cut up	2 tbsps. lemon juice
2 eggs	1 cup packaged dried breadcrumbs
1$\frac{1}{2}$ tsps. salt	

Start heating oven to moderate (350° F., mark 4). In 13-inch by 9-inch by 2-inch baking dish in oven, melt butter.

Meanwhile, in flour in paper bag, shake chicken pieces, one at a time until coated; set aside.

In bowl, using fork, beat eggs with salt, paprika, onion salt and lemon juice until well blended.

Dip floured chicken pieces, one at a time, in egg mixture, then in crumbs, turning to coat evenly; then in melted butter in baking dish, arrange chicken, skin side down.

Bake about 45 minutes or until fork-tender, turning once. Serve with Tokfozelek (see p. 149).

CARAWAY DUMPLINGS

6 oz. flour	Pepper
1$\frac{1}{2}$ tsps. baking powder	1$\frac{1}{2}$ oz. fat
$\frac{1}{2}$ tsp. salt	Cold water
1 tsp. caraway seeds	

Mix the dry ingredients and rub in the fat with the fingertips. Mix to a firm, light dough with cold water, divide into 10 or 12 equal-sized portions, roll into balls, and cook in boiling water for about 25 minutes.

METELKE
(HOME-MADE NOODLES)

2 eggs	1$\frac{1}{2}$ cups sifted flour
2 tbsps. water	2 tsps. salt

In bowl, beat eggs slightly with water. Using fork, stir in flour and salt until dough is well blended.

Turn dough on to well-floured surface; knead until it is no longer sticky. Divide dough in half. Roll out one half until paper-thin. Lay it on a towel, cover with another towel. Repeat with other half. Let both stand for 30 minutes.

After the 30 minutes, transfer one of the paper-thin sheets of dough to working surface;

then cut into 6 strips of equal width. Now arrange strips one on top of the other. Then, starting at narrow end, roll up strips, like a Swiss roll, and slice off noodles of desired width. Repeat with other sheet of dough.

After lightly tossing noodles to separate them, dry thoroughly (a few hours) on towels, then store in containers until needed.

In boiling salted water to cover, cook noodles 10 minutes or until tender, drain, rinse with cold water.

KOROZOTT TURO
(CREAMY CARAWAY-CHEESE SPREAD)

An 8 oz. package soft cream cheese	1$\frac{1}{2}$ tsps. caraway seeds
$\frac{1}{4}$ cup soft butter	1$\frac{1}{2}$ tsps. chives
1 tsp. paprika	1 tsp. bottled capers, chopped
$\frac{1}{2}$ tsp. onion salt	1 tsp. prepared mustard

In bowl, thoroughly blend cream cheese with butter, add paprika, onion salt, caraway seeds, chopped chives, capers, mustard and beat until well blended.

Serve as an appetiser spread on rye bread or crispbread.

HUNGARIAN APPLES

In the evening peel and slice some apples. Make layers of the pieces on a plate and sprinkle well with sugar and cinnamon. Continue until the apples are finished. In the morning, the apples should be in a juice. Cook for about $\frac{1}{4}$ hour, adding no water, and serve with cream.

TEJFELES PITE
(SOUR CREAM PIE)

1 unbaked 9-inch pie shell	$\frac{1}{4}$ tsp. salt
3 eggs, separated	1 cup seedless raisins, chopped
$\frac{3}{4}$ cup granulated sugar	1 tsp. grated lemon rind
$\frac{1}{2}$ tsp. cinnamon	1 cup sour cream
$\frac{1}{4}$ tsp. ground cloves	

Start heating oven to moderately hot (425° F., mark 7).

Beat egg whites until stiff but not dry.

Without washing beater, beat egg yolks until thick and lemon-coloured; beat in sugar, cinnamon, cloves, salt. Fold in raisins, lemon rind, $\frac{1}{2}$ cup sour cream, and beaten whites. Pour into pie shell.

Bake for 15 minutes, then reduce oven temperature to moderate (350° F., mark 3) and bake 30 minutes longer or until a silver knife inserted into the centre of the pie comes out clean.

Let pie cool to room temperature. Top each serving with a dab of remaining sour cream.

LAYERED PANCAKES

53 Make six or eight thin pancakes with flour, eggs and milk. Keep hot until all are cooked. Put the first pancake on a buttered fireproof dish, on it spread some curd or cottage cheese mixed with egg yolk and sugar flavoured with lemon rind. Put the second pancake on top and spread with apricot jam. Cover with another pancake spread with grated nuts and chocolate. Repeat this layering until all the pancakes are used. Put into the oven while a meringue of 2 egg whites and 4 oz. of caster sugar is prepared. Cover the pile of pancakes with the meringue, return to the oven to crisp and colour a golden-brown. Sprinkle with vanilla sugar before serving. (This sweet is cut into slices like a cake, and is often served with a rich chocolate sauce.)

KOSARKAK
(LITTLE BASKETS)

54

A 3-oz. package soft cream cheese	$\frac{1}{4}$ tsp. salt
$\frac{1}{4}$ cup soft butter	1 cup sifted flour
1 tsp. granulated sugar	Filling (see below)

Start heating oven to moderately hot (400° F., mark 6).

Blend cream cheese with butter, sugar, salt; beat until smooth and creamy. Add flour, stirring until mixture is well blended. Into $1\frac{3}{4}$-inch ungreased patty pans, drop 1 tbsp. of dough; press evenly against bottom and side. Then fill each lined pan with one of fillings below.

Bake for 18–22 minutes; cool for 15–20 minutes, then carefully remove from pans. Cool before serving. (Makes 24.)

CHOCOLATE-NUT MERINGUE FILLING

3 egg whites	$\frac{1}{3}$ cup pecans, finely chopped
$\frac{1}{4}$ tsp. salt	
$\frac{1}{2}$ tsp. almond essence	$\frac{1}{3}$ cup semi-sweet chocolate, finely chopped
$\frac{1}{2}$ cup granulated sugar	

In bowl, beat egg whites until foamy; add salt and almond extract; continue beating until soft peak forms. Gradually beat in sugar and continue beating until stiff. Into this egg-white mixture, fold pecans and chocolate.

TANGY CHEESE FILLING

2 3-oz. packages soft cream cheese	1 tbsp. lemon juice
1 cup granulated sugar	$\frac{1}{2}$ cup double cream, whipped
Grated rind of 1 lemon	Toasted slivered almonds
1 egg, unbeaten	

In bowl, thoroughly blend cream cheese with sugar and lemon rind. Add egg, then, with egg beater, beat until light and fluffy. Gradually beat in lemon juice.

Just before serving, top each pastry with a bit of whipped cream and a few toasted slivered almonds.

RETES
(STRUDEL)

$1\frac{1}{2}$ tsps. salad oil	1 cup cooled melted butter
1 small egg, unbeaten	
$\frac{3}{4}$ cup lukewarm water	Icing sugar
$2\frac{1}{3}$ cups unsifted flour	

Combine oil, egg, water; using fork, beat until smooth.

Into large bowl, measure flour; make well in the centre, pour in oil mixture, stir well to form a soft dough. Turn dough out on to lightly floured surface. Knead till elastic.

Lightly brush ball of dough with melted butter, cover with large bowl and let it stand in a warm place for 30 minutes.

Meanwhile, cover a small table with a clean cloth (tablecloth or 2 pastry cloths). Rub just enough flour into cloth to cover it very well to prevent strudel dough from sticking; brush off excess flour.

Place dough in centre of cloth; with floured rolling pin (or rolling pin covered with stockinette and then floured), roll dough into large square, 16 inch by 16 inch. Using fingers, lightly spread the entire surface with more melted butter.

Stretch dough so that it hangs well over table all around and is thin enough to see through; with scissors, snip off thick edges all round. Let it dry for 15 minutes or until crisp.

Meanwhile, start heating oven to moderate (375° F., mark 5). Measure ingredients for filling.

When strudel dough is crisp, sprinkle lightly with melted butter; then proceed as in the recipe for filling (see below).

Turn overhanging sides of strudel dough over filling and over dough all the way around, to make a neat square. Roll up dough and with sharp knife, cut roll in half crosswise to make 2 strudels. Using broad spatula, lift gently on to greased baking sheet or Swiss roll pan, side by side. Brush with melted butter. Brushing several times with butter, bake for 55–60 minutes or until crisp and lightly browned. Serve warm, sprinkled generously with sifted icing sugar. If desired, serve with $\frac{1}{2}$ pint commercial sour cream mixed with 1 tsp. grated nutmeg; chill well. (Each strudel makes 8 servings.)

STRUDEL FILLINGS

CHERRY FILLING

¾ cup packaged dried breadcrumbs
¾ cup ground almonds
1 cup granulated sugar
2 tins tart red-stoned cherries, well drained
¼ tsp. almond essence
Red colouring

Combine breadcrumbs, almonds and sugar; sprinkle over the half of crisp strudel dough nearest you.

Toss cherries with almond essence and enough red colour to brighten cherries; spoon them over crumb mixture.

Proceed with rolling up strudel.

CHEESE FILLING

4 3-oz. packages cream cheese
3 egg yolks
½ cup granulated sugar
1 tbsp. grated lemon rind
½ cup light or dark raisins
⅔ cup packaged dried breadcrumbs

Combine cheese, egg yolks and sugar; beat until smooth and blended; stir in lemon rind and raisins.

Sprinkle breadcrumbs over half of strudel dough nearest you, and spread cheese filling over crumbs.

Proceed with rolling strudel as before.

APPLE FILLING

1 cup packaged dried breadcrumbs
¾ cup walnuts, finely chopped
1 cup granulated sugar
¼ tsp. nutmeg
¼ tsp. cinnamon
2 lb. sliced stewed apples, well drained
1 tbsp. grated lemon rind
½ cup light or dark raisins

Combine crumbs, walnuts, sugar, nutmeg and cinnamon; use to sprinkle over half of strudel dough nearest you.

Toss apples with lemon rind and raisins; spoon over crumb mixture.

Proceed with rolling up strudel as before.

POPPY-SEED FILLING

¼ lb. poppy seeds, ground
2 tbsps. lemon juice
1 tbsp. grated lemon rind
1 cup honey

In small saucepan, combine poppy seeds, lemon juice, rind and honey. Cook, covered over low heat for 10 minutes or until thickened. When cool, spread filling over half of strudel dough nearest you.

Proceed with rolling up strudel as before.

DOBOS TORTE
(A MANY-LAYERED CAKE)

4 8-inch sponge-cake layers (see below)
¾ lb. soft butter
2 cups sifted icing sugar
3 egg yolks, unbeaten
6 oz. semi-sweet chocolate
⅔ cup granulated sugar
⅓ cup water
¼ tsp. cream of tartar

Half-way up side of one cake layer, all the way round, insert toothpicks. Using these as a guide, with long, sharp knife, carefully split the layer. Split remaining 3 layers to make 8 thin layers in all. (The Dobos Torte may have 7 or 8 layers, as desired.)

Beat butter until fluffy, add icing sugar, gradually, then egg yolks, one at a time, beating until very fluffy. Melt the chocolate over hot, not boiling, water and cool well before blending into butter mixture.

Place round the edges of the cake plate, 4 strips of waxed paper, slightly overlapping; set 1 cake layer on top. Cover generously with butter mixture; place another layer on top and repeat until all but one layer has been used.

For caramel, in small saucepan, combine granulated sugar, water and cream of tartar. Bring the mixture to the boil, stirring, then cook, uncovered, just until golden, no longer. Stir syrup until bubbles are gone; then pour over top of last layer.

Working quickly, spread caramel, then before it hardens, using a well-buttered silver knife, mark top into 12 wedges deep enough (going over several times) to make cutting easier later. Place this layer on top of others and ice side of cake.

Refrigerate the torte until serving the next day or several days later. To serve, remove waxed paper from under the cake (cake plate is still clean) and, with sharp knife, " saw " through markings. (If wedges are too firm, let stand at room temperature for 15 minutes.)

SPONGE CAKE LAYERS

4 eggs
¾ cup sifted flour
¾ tsp. baking powder
¼ tsp. salt
¾ cup granulated sugar
1 tsp. vanilla essence

Start heating oven to moderately hot (400° F., mark 6). Then, with waxed paper, line 4 8-inch layer tins. Sift flour, baking powder and salt.

Beat eggs until thick then add sugar gradually, continuing to beat until very thick and light.

Using rubber spatula or spoon, fold in flour mixture and add vanilla. Turn into pans, spreading batter evenly. Bake 10 minutes or until light brown.

Cool slightly; carefully turn out of tins;

remove waxed paper at once ; cool completely. Wrap layers well in waxed paper or aluminium foil to keep fresh until next day. If to be used several days later, refrigerate wrapped layers.

ALMOND TORTE

5 egg whites, unbeaten	½ cup packaged dried
⅛ tsp. salt	breadcrumbs
6 egg yolks	2 tsps. grated lemon rind
1⅓ cups sifted icing	¼ tsp. cinnamon
sugar	Chocolate Glaze (see
¼ tsp. almond essence	below)
1½ cups unblanched	Blanched almonds
almonds, ground	Whipped cream

Start heating oven to moderate (350° F., mark 4). Butter a 9-inch tube pan.

Beat egg whites with salt until stiff but not dry.

Beat egg yolks until thick, gradually add sugar, beating constantly until very thick and light ; add almond essence.

Gently fold yolk mixture into egg whites, along with ground nuts, breadcrumbs, lemon rind and cinnamon. Turn into prepared pan. Bake for 35 minutes.

Cool slightly, turn cake out on to wire cake rack. When thoroughly cooled, ice with Chocolate Glaze (see below). Decorate top of cake with a circle of blanched almonds, inserting tip of each almond into cake to mark each serving.

Serve slices with chilled sweetened whipped cream. (Makes 12–16 servings.)

CHOCOLATE GLAZE

1 square unsweetened	2 tbsps. boiling water
chocolate	¾ cup sifted icing sugar
1 tsp. butter	⅛ tsp. almond essence

Over hot, not boiling, water, melt chocolate with butter.

Meanwhile add water to icing sugar, stirring until smooth ; stir into chocolate mixture to combine thoroughly ; add almond essence.

Cool well before pouring over cake.

WALNUT NOODLE PUDDING

½ lb. dried noodles (or	6 oz. coarsely ground
1 lb. freshly made)	walnuts
3 oz. butter	2 oz. sugar
3 oz. damson jam	Salt

Cook noodles in plenty of boiling salted water, drain well, then shake in a bowl, with 2 oz. of melted butter. Mix coarsely ground walnuts with sugar, add to the noodles. Butter a deep fireproof dish, put in half of the noodles, add a good thick layer of damson jam then cover with the other half of the noodles. Bake in a moderately hot oven (400° F., mark 6) for 20 minutes. Serve in the casserole, first loosening sides with a knife or spatula.

POPPY SEED NOODLE PUDDING

1 lb. freshly made (or	1 oz. caster sugar
½ lb. dried) noodles	Grated peel of ½ lemon
3 oz. butter	3 oz. sultanas
6 oz. finely ground	2 tbsps. honey
poppy seeds	

Cook the noodles in plenty of slightly salted boiling water. Heat in a saucepan, 2 oz. butter, mix in the cooked and well-drained noodles. Add ground poppy seed, 1 oz. sugar, the grated peel of ½ lemon, and the sultanas. Mix well, pour into a deep buttered fireproof dish, and bake in a moderately hot oven (400° F., mark 6) for 20 minutes. Take dish out of oven, cover and allow to stand for 4–5 minutes. Loosen the sides with a knife, turn out on to a flat warmed dish. Pour warm honey over and serve.

HUNGARIAN APPLE PIE

1 lb. apples	2 oz. sugar
6 oz. flour	Strawberry jam
4 oz. butter or mar-	1 egg white
garine	Egg white and sugar to
1 egg yolk	glaze
1–2 tbsps. sour cream	Cream and glacé
or milk	cherries to decorate
2 oz. ground almonds	

Stew the apples in the usual way. Sieve the flour and rub in the butter, mix to a dough with the egg yolk and sour cream or milk, knead, and put aside in a cool place for 30 minutes. Line a 7-inch sandwich tin with half of the pastry, and partly bake it for about 10 minutes in a moderately hot oven (400° F., mark 6). Mix the ground almonds with the sugar. Spread the pastry with strawberry jam and sprinkle half of the sugar and almond mixture on top. Fold the stiffly whisked egg white into the stewed apples and put into the pie, sprinkling the rest of the almond and sugar mixture on top. Cover with the rest of the pastry, glaze the top with egg white, sprinkle with sugar, and bake in a moderately hot oven (400° F., mark 6) for about ½ hour. Decorate with cream and glacé cherries.

SUGARED RIBBONS

4 oz. flour	1 egg yolk
A pinch of salt	Deep fat for frying
1 oz. margarine	Icing sugar
2 tbsps. sour milk or	Strawberry or cherry
cream	jam

Sieve the flour and salt together and rub in the margarine. Mix in the sour milk or cream and the egg yolk, then leave in a cool place for about ½ hour. Roll out the pastry very thinly and, using a pastry wheel, cut it into strips of even length, about 1 inch wide. Make slits in some of the ribbons and thread the ends through to make fancy knot shapes. Fry in hot fat until golden-brown and crisp, and serve sprinkled with icing sugar and accompanied by jam.

NUT TORTE

7 eggs
5 oz. caster sugar
2 oz. fine dry white breadcrumbs
3 oz. chopped walnuts and toasted almonds
A few drops of vanilla essence
Chocolate icing (see below)
A few blanched nuts to decorate

Separate the eggs and whisk the yolks with the sugar until they are thick and creamy. Whisk the egg whites stiffly. Mix together the crumbs and the nuts. Add the vanilla essence to the egg yolks and sugar, and fold in the egg whites and the nuts. Put the mixture into 3 8-inch greased layer-cake tins, and bake in a moderate oven (350° F., mark 4) for about 25 minutes, or until firm and lightly browned. Allow the cakes to cool in the tins before carefully turning them out. When cold, fill and top with the following soft chocolate icing :

Put 3 eggs and 6 oz. caster sugar into a double saucepan, and stir until the mixture thickens, taking great care that it does not overheat and curdle. Remove from the heat and stir in 2 oz. melted chocolate and a little vanilla essence. Beat until the filling is thick enough, and then spread it between the cakes and over the top. Decorate with a few nuts.

RICE SOUFFLÉ

2½ oz. rice
1 pint milk
5 oz. sugar
2 eggs
Strawberry jam
½ pint apple purée
Brandy

Cook the washed rice and the milk in a double saucepan until creamy, then cool slightly. Mix 1 oz. sugar in the egg yolks and add to the rice. Put a third of the rice in a greased fireproof dish and spread with jam. Continue with alternate layers of rice and jam, then spread the apple purée over. Top with a meringue mixture made with the egg whites and the rest of the sugar. Bake in a moderate oven (350° F., mark 4) for 20 minutes. Pour the brandy over, set alight, and serve immediately.

IT was in Italy that the so-called continental cuisine was first evolved—she is the mother of European cooking. Even the famous Brillat Savarin admitted that French cooking was inspired by that of Italy and that until the beginning of the nineteenth century, the standard of cuisine in France fell far below that of her neighbour. Perhaps this tradition of gastronomic perfection can be traced back to the days when the Roman empire was the hub of the civilised world, the mecca of all expatriate Roman citizens, who may perhaps have brought home with them after long spells of service in the outer darkness of Britain and Gaul, some new ideas in eating, some barbarian recipes for Roman cooks to amalgamate with their native dishes and even some barbarian women to cook them. Certainly since the time of the Roman Empire, Italians have been eating many foodstuffs that still play a part in Italian diet, such as red mullet, turbot, chicken livers, parsley and salads.

The pasta for which Italy is so famous is made from fine wheat and garnished or stuffed with meats, vegetables and mushrooms, sauced with tomato and cheese and sweet butter. Pasta or rice is eaten every day (though not at the same meal as soup) and makes a delicious and satisfying backbone to a meal that is often rounded off with fruit and bread and cheese, the whole washed down with a local wine.

Meat is apt to be expensive in Italy—young veal and kid are most favoured and poultry is used in many interesting and unusual ways. Fish is varied and is often served fried in a delicious egg batter, as are the vegetables which grow so freely all over the country. The perfection of Italian fruit needs no description. A dish of ripe fruit makes the perfect end to a meal and its profusion accounts for the fact that Italian cookery does not depend for its reputation to any extent upon desserts, relying mainly upon its fruit, its ice cream and graniti, its zabaglione and a few other specialities.

Italian cheeses vary from the rock-hard Parmesan that adds such flavour and individuality to so many Italian dishes, through Gorgonzola to the softer, blander Mozzarella, Bel Paese and ricotta. Italian wine is by no means confined to the straw-covered flasks of Chianti and there are now many different types of Italian wines which are exported in bulk and in bottles.

Although there are, of course, many local dishes and variations, much Italian cooking is common to the whole country. Coffee and a slice of bread makes the most usual breakfast; antipasto, those varied and fascinating hors d'œuvre, pasta or a rice dish, perhaps followed by scallopini and fruit are served for lunch; antipasto again figures on the menu with soup and chicken or fish for dinner—this is the pattern of Italian eating, and with its background of fresh salad, fruit, wine and cheese it is both satisfying and delicious.

Italy
and Malta

Italy

ANTIPASTO VARIATO
(ASSORTED HORS D'ŒUVRE)

Antipasto is a favourite from the top to toe of Italy. Many Italian housewives like to serve it particularly for special occasions and holidays, when it makes a delightful first course at the table.

Canned fish, meat and vegetables, plus crisp colourful raw vegetables, are the basis of assorted antipasto. Sometimes stuffed eggs or tomatoes or fresh cheeses are added. Choose as many or as few items from the following list as you wish, remembering to contrast flavours—spicy, sharp and bland—as well as colour :

Anchovies	Pickled mushrooms
Sardines	Olives
Tuna	Lettuce
Pimientos	Tomatoes
Pickled artichokes	Radishes
Sliced prosciutto or salami	Spring onions Ricotta cheese
Raw green peppers	Mozzarella cheese
Celery or finocchio	Bread sticks wrapped
Chick peas	in prosciutto

PROSCIUTTO CON MELLONE
(HAM WITH MELON)

56

When travelling through Italy, you may find this refreshing first course served in several ways. (Prosciutto is a delicately cured, Italian ham.)

Cut a chilled cantaloupe melon in half, remove the seeds and pare off the rind ; slice each half into thin wedges. Arrange one or more wedges on each dessert plate and top with paper-thin slices of prosciutto.

Alternatively, place a wedge of pared honey-dew melon or cantaloupe on each plate with a few paper-thin slices of prosciutto at the side. Eat with a fork and knife, cutting off a piece of melon then a piece of ham, and combining the two flavours.

SHRIMPS IN WINE SAUCE

1 lb. raw shrimps, shelled and deveined	2 tbsps. warm water $\frac{1}{2}$ tsp. salt
$\frac{1}{4}$ cup flour	$\frac{1}{4}$ tsp. pepper
$\frac{1}{4}$ cup olive or salad oil	A dash of cayenne
$\frac{1}{4}$ cup dry white wine	pepper
2 tsps. canned tomato paste	1 tbsp. chopped parsley 1 chopped shallot

Coat the shrimps with flour and sauté in hot oil in a frying pan until golden. Pour the excess oil from the frying pan into a saucepan and set aside. Add the wine to the shrimps in the frying pan and cook over a low heat for about 3 minutes. Meanwhile put into the saucepan the tomato paste, water, seasonings, parsley and shallot and cook over a low heat for 5 minutes. Combine with the shrimps and serve with lemon wedges. (Makes 2 servings.)

INSALATA D'ARINGHE O ACCIUGHE
(HERRING OR ANCHOVY TITBITS)

3 garlic cloves	$\frac{1}{4}$ cup wine vinegar
$1\frac{1}{4}$ tsps. salt	$\frac{3}{4}$ cup olive or salad oil
1 dried chilli	5 oz. herring fillets or
1 large onion, minced	1 tin of anchovies
1 large carrot, grated	Buttered slices of bread
$1\frac{1}{2}$ cups chopped parsley	(preferably Italian)

About 4 or more days before the dish is to be served put the garlic and salt in a bowl and rub them together until they form a pulp, then add the chilli and crush, next add the onion, carrot, parsley, vinegar and oil and toss all these well. Cut the herring into 1-inch cubes, put a layer in a bowl and cover with some of the sauce. Repeat until both are used up, ending with sauce on top, and leave in the refrigerator for at least 4 days. Serve on slices of bread cut into bite-sized pieces.

CUORE DI CARCIOFI
(ARTICHOKE HEARTS)

Use canned artichoke bottoms. Top each with a little canned tuna mixed with mayonnaise, then sprinkle with chopped, hard-boiled egg yolks and chopped parsley. Alternatively, use cut-up cooked shrimps mixed with mayonnaise and top with 1 cooked shrimp and chopped parsley.

MELANZANE SOTT' ACETO
(PICKLED AUBERGINE)

1 large aubergine, unpeeled	$\frac{1}{2}$ tsp. dried basil or 2 tsp. fresh basil
2 garlic cloves	$\frac{1}{2}$ tsp. dried orégano
1 tsp. salt	or 2 tsp. chopped
$\frac{1}{2}$ cup wine vinegar	fresh orégano
$\frac{1}{2}$ tsp. freshly ground pepper	$\frac{1}{4}$ cup olive or salad oil

About 12 hours or more before the salad is required cut the aubergine into large cubes and cook it for about 10 minutes in 1 inch of boiling salted water ; drain well. In a large bowl mash the garlic with the salt and add the aubergine, vinegar, pepper, basil and orégano, then put in the refrigerator overnight or longer. Just before serving stir in the oil. This will keep for about a week or more in the refrigerator. (Serves 8.)

MINESTRONE ALLA MILANESE

4 tbsps. olive oil	2–3 tomatoes
2 rashers of unsmoked bacon	2 oz. green peas or beans
2–3 potatoes	3 pints stock or water
½ a small cabbage heart	2 oz. rice
1 stick of celery	4 oz. dried beans, soaked and cooked
1 onion	Salt and pepper
1 clove of garlic	Grated Parmesan cheese

Heat the olive oil and fry the cut-up bacon, then sauté all the vegetables (which should be cut up fairly finely). Add the liquid, and when this is boiling, add the washed rice and simmer for about 15–20 minutes. Add the beans and cook for a further 10 minutes. Season to taste, and serve with Parmesan cheese.

MINESTRONE ALLA CASALINGA
(HOUSEHOLD VEGETABLE SOUP)

4 medium-sized potatoes	2 tbsps. olive oil
1 medium-sized onion	2 quarts stock or water
1 medium-sized carrot	
1 lb. cabbage	A clove of garlic (optional)
1 stalk of celery	Meat extract
A few French beans	Seasoning
A few peas	½ lb. cut macaroni
A little parsley	Grated cheese as accompaniment
A walnut-sized knob of butter	

Cut the vegetables up small, chop the parsley and part of the onion and toss in a saucepan with the fat and oil for 2 minutes. Add the other vegetables and cook for 5 minutes. Add the liquid, garlic, meat extract and seasoning, simmer for 1 hour, then add the macaroni, and cook another 20 minutes. Serve very hot, with grated Parmesan cheese. Pesto (see below) may also be served.

PESTO
(ITALIAN SAUCE)

3 tbsps. chopped parsley	¼ pint best quality olive oil
3 tbsps. chopped basil	
1 clove of garlic, crushed	Salt
3 oz. grated Parmesan	Black pepper

Blend all the ingredients, and keep in a cool place overnight. Serve with minestrone or pasta.

CONSOMMÉ ALLA STRACCIATELLA
(EGG SOUP)

6 cups chicken broth	3 tbsps. grated Parmesan cheese
3 eggs	
2 tbsps. flour	Chopped fresh chervil

Heat the chicken broth in a saucepan and bring to the boil. Using a fork, stir together the eggs, flour, cheese and 6 tbsps. chicken broth. Slowly add the egg mixture to the hot chicken broth, stirring constantly. Simmer for 5 minutes, stirring to " shred " the eggs. Serve in cups, topped with the chopped chervil. (Makes 6 servings.)

ZUPPA ALLA VENEZIANA
(VENETIAN SOUP)

4 egg yolks	½ cup double cream
6 cups undiluted beef bouillon, canned or home-made	6 slices long continental bread
	Grated Parmesan cheese

Beat the egg yolks with the cream till blended. Pour the bouillon into a medium-sized saucepan and add the cream mixture ; heat slowly, stirring constantly, until the soup almost comes to a boil but do not let it actually boil. Meanwhile toast the bread on both sides. Serve with 1 slice toast on each serving and hand Parmesan cheese separately. (Serves 6.)

ZUPPA ALLA PARVESE
(SOUP WITH POACHED EGGS)

6 cups chicken broth	Butter or margarine
1¼ cups undiluted canned consommé	6 eggs
	Grated Parmesan or Romano cheese
12 1-inch slices long continental bread	

Heat the broth and consommé in a saucepan and bring to the boil ; meanwhile sauté the bread in hot butter in a large frying pan until browned on both sides. Poach the eggs in the hot (not boiling) soup in the usual way, then place one egg in each soup plate. Pour some broth over the eggs (strain it if desired). Sprinkle the sautéed bread with cheese, place 2 slices beside each egg and hand additional cheese at table. (Makes 6 servings.)

ZUPPA SPINACE ALLA MODENESE
(SPINACH SOUP)

1 lb. fresh spinach (or 1 packet frozen chopped spinach)	1 tsp. salt
	A pinch of pepper
	Grated nutmeg
⅓ cup butter or margarine	1 tbsp. grated Parmesan cheese
4 cups chicken broth	2 eggs, slightly beaten

Cook the spinach in butter in a medium-sized covered saucepan until tender ; chop and press through a sieve. Heat the chicken broth gently. Add salt, pepper, a little nutmeg and the cheese to the spinach. Stir in the eggs and then the chicken broth, heat to the boil, then simmer for 5 minutes to " shred " the eggs and thicken the soup. (Makes 6 servings.)

SCAMPI FRITTI

Take the flesh from as many Dublin Bay prawns as you need and dip them in coating batter (see below). Fry in smoking-hot fat or in hot oil until they are crisp, pile on to a dish and garnish with parsley and lemon. This is a favourite hors d'œuvre dish.

BATTER FOR SCAMPI FRITTI

2 oz. flour	2 tsps. salad oil
A pinch of salt	1 white of egg
3 tbsps. tepid water	

Mix the flour and salt, make a well in the centre and into this put the water and oil. Mix to a smooth batter, and beat till light. Just before using the batter, add the stiffly beaten egg white.

CAPPE AI FERRI
(GRILLED SCALLOPS)

8 scallops	1 clove of garlic
Olive oil	Chopped parsley
Salt and pepper	Lemon
2 oz. butter	

Brush the scallops with oil and sprinkle with salt and pepper. Place under a hot grill, grill on both sides and put on to a very hot dish. Heat 3 tbsps. olive oil and the butter with the finely chopped garlic (and, if liked, some chopped onion). Pour this mixture over the scallops, sprinkle with the chopped parsley and serve with lemon wedges or slices.

PESCE FRITTO ALLA MARGHERITA
(MARGARET'S FRIED FISH)

¼ cup olive or salad oil	2 8-oz. cans tomato
¼ cup butter or mar-	sauce
garine	1 tsp. dried orégano
1½ lb. fillets of sole or	2 tbsps. chopped parsley
flounder	Hot cooked spaghetti

Heat the oil and butter in a large pan and slowly sauté the fish for about 5 minutes on each side; remove to a platter. Stir the tomato sauce, orégano and parsley into the fat left in the pan till blended, then return the fish to the sauce and simmer uncovered for 10 minutes, occasionally basting with the sauce. This is very good over spaghetti or mashed potatoes.

CRAB AND MUSHROOM NAPOLITANA

A fair-sized crab	Béchamel sauce
½ lb. mushrooms	Lemon juice
Butter	Macaroni

Remove the meat from the crab and flake it finely. Peel the mushrooms and cook them in a little butter. In the meantime, make a good béchamel sauce, then add the mushrooms to it, straining off the liquor; lastly, add the crabmeat and a few drops of lemon juice. Serve piled in the centre of a hot dish with a border of well-cooked macaroni.

SCAMPI ALLA MARINARA
(SHRIMPS, SAILOR-STYLE)

2 garlic cloves, minced	⅔ cup canned tomato
5 tbsps. olive or salad	paste
oil	½ tsp. garlic salt
1 can Italian tomatoes	2 lb. cooked, shelled
(undrained)	and deveined
2 tbsps. chopped parsley	shrimps
½ tsp. dried basil	Grated Parmesan
2½ tsps. salt	cheese
Pepper	Hot cooked spaghetti
¼ tsp. dried orégano	or rice (optional)

Brown the garlic in the hot oil in a frying pan, then add the tomatoes, parsley, basil, salt and pepper. Simmer uncovered for ½ hour. Stir in the orégano and tomato paste and cook uncovered for 15 minutes, then stir in the garlic salt and shrimps; heat and serve topped with the grated cheese—over spaghetti or rice if desired.

FISH FRITTO MISTO

Use a selection of small slip soles or fillets of fish, small pieces of turbot or halibut, pieces of lobster, prawns or whitebait, with parboiled and drained cauliflower flowerets or slices of marrow. Coat with egg and breadcrumbs (or a light fritter batter) and fry. Pile on a hot dish and garnish with lemon and fried parsley.

SALERNO FISH

6 fillets of hake, cod,	1 tsp. flour
bream or other soft	2–3 tbsps. bouillon
fish	¼ pint white wine
½ oz. butter	Salt and pepper
1 clove of garlic	Olive oil
6 chives	Cayenne pepper
6 mushrooms	Lemon juice
1 tbsp. chopped parsley	

Prepare the fish. Melt the butter in a saucepan, add the minced garlic, chives, mushrooms and parsley, and cook for a few minutes. Stir in the flour and cook for a further 3 minutes. Add very slowly, stirring all the time, the bouillon and wine, bring to the boil, cover and simmer gently for 10 minutes. Meanwhile, fry the seasoned fish fillets in oil, adding a dash of Cayenne and a squeeze of lemon juice to each. Drain, put into a fireproof dish, cover with the sauce, and grill until golden-brown.

MUSSELS AU GRATIN

2–3 pints mussels	4 oz. browned bread-
½ pint water	crumbs
¼ pint dry white	Parmesan cheese
wine	Chopped parsley

Scrub and beard the mussels, and put into a pan with the water and the wine. Cover and bring to the boil, leave for 2–3 minutes, then remove the pan from the heat and let it stand for 5 minutes. Drain off and reserve the liquor. Remove the " beards," and arrange the mussels in the half-shells in a heatproof dish ; sprinkle with the crumbs, and then sprinkle liberally with cheese. Pour on the liquor and bake in a moderate oven (350° F., mark 4) for 10–15 minutes. Sprinkle with parsley.

LOBSTER WITH CREAM

1 large freshly boiled	2 oz. grated Parmesan
lobster	cheese
4 oz. butter	3 egg yolks
Seasoning	¼ pint white wine or
½ pint cream	sherry
8 oz. Patna rice	Cayenne pepper
1 onion	

Remove the meat from the lobster claws and tail, and slice the pieces very thinly. Melt 2 oz. of the butter, add salt and pepper, heat gently, then fry the pieces of lobster until they are light brown. Add the cream, and simmer very gently. Meanwhile boil the rice in salted water. Chop the onion finely and fry it in the remaining butter ; add the rice and cheese, mix well and arrange in a ring on a serving dish. Place the lobster in the centre of the dish, leaving the cream in the pan. Mix together the egg yolks and wine, add to the cream, and heat gently without boiling, until the sauce has thickened slightly. Add a little Cayenne pepper and pour over the lobster. Serve immediately.

FEGATO DI VITELLO ALL' ITALIANA
(CALF LIVER, ITALIAN STYLE)

¾ lb. calf liver, thinly	¼ tsp. dried sage
sliced	2 tbsps. chopped parsley
2 tbsps. flour	¼ cup water
6 tbsps. butter or mar-	⅓ tsp. instant chicken
garine	broth
1 thin slice of cooked	2 tbsps. Marsala
ham	¼ tsp. salt
¼ cup minced onion	A dash of pepper

Coat the liver with flour and sauté it in hot butter in a frying pan until golden on both sides ; remove to a heated dish. To the butter left in the pan add the chopped ham, onion, sage and parsley ; sauté for 3–4 minutes, or till the onion

is tender. Stir in the water, broth, Marsala, salt and pepper, and simmer for 5 minutes. Return the liver to the pan and simmer just until it is warm. Serve with lemon wedges. (Makes 2 servings.)

INVOLTINI DI VITELLO CON ACCIUGHE
(ANCHOVY VEAL ROLLS)

2 lb. very thin veal cut-	Freshly ground pepper
lets (1/16 inch thick),	Salt
cut from the leg	½ cup butter or mar-
½ cup shredded Swiss	garine
cheese	⅓ cup dry white wine
12 anchovy fillets	2 tbsps. chopped parsley

Cut the veal into 12 pieces, then top each with a few slivers of cheese and 1 anchovy fillet and sprinkle with pepper. Roll up, tie with thread and sprinkle with salt. Heat the butter in a frying pan and cook the rolls uncovered for 10 minutes, turning occasionally. Add the wine, cover and cook for another 10 minutes. Remove the threads from the rolls and arrange them on a heated platter ; pour on the sauce from the pan and sprinkle with parsley. (6 servings.)

VEAL SCALOPPINE

1¼ lb. boned veal	¼ cup minced onion
shoulder	1 small can whole
¼ cup flour	mushrooms (drained)
Salt and pepper	1 cup tomato juice
¼ cup salad oil or fat	½ tsp. sugar

Start heating the oven to moderate (350° F., mark 4). Cut the veal into 1¼-inch cubes and roll these in the flour combined with ¼ tsp. salt and a dash of pepper. Heat the salad oil in a frying pan and sauté the onion until tender, then remove it to a greased 1-quart casserole. In the oil left in the pan sauté the veal until brown on all sides ; arrange it in the casserole, together with the mushrooms, tomato juice, sugar, ¾ tsp. salt and a dash of pepper. Bake uncovered for 1¼ hours, or until tender when tested with a fork. (Serves 2.)

VEAL AND MOZZARELLA ESCALOPES

6 veal escalopes	Dry white breadcrumbs
Seasoned flour	Butter for frying
1 beaten egg	Sliced Mozzarella cheese
A little milk	Sliced tomato to garnish

Beat each escalope with a heavy knife, roll in flour and then in the beaten egg and a little milk. Roll in the crumbs and fry in the butter over a moderate heat for 7–10 minutes, turning once. Keep them hot in the oven until all the pieces are cooked. Just before serving, place slices of

Mozzarella on each escalope and put under the grill. Serve at once, garnished with tomato.

BOLOGNESE ESCALOPES

57

4 veal escalopes	4 slices of ham
Seasoned flour	1 tbsp. grated Par-
1 beaten egg	mesan cheese
A little milk	Cooked mushrooms
Dry white bread-	Blanched rings of red
crumbs	pepper
Butter for frying	Green beans

Beat each escalope with a heavy knife, roll in the flour and then in the beaten egg and a little milk; coat with crumbs and fry in the butter over a moderate heat for 7–10 minutes, turning once. Place a slice of ham over each escalope and trim to the same shape. Sprinkle with the Parmesan, and spoon a little melted butter over. Cover the pan and cook for 3-4 minutes, until the cheese has melted. Garnish with cooked mushrooms and rings of red pepper and serve with green beans.

SCALOPPINE FARCITE
(STUFFED ESCALOPES)

8 veal escalopes	1 crushed garlic clove
Seasoned flour	2 rashers of chopped
8 slices of ham	streaky bacon
3 oz. thinly sliced	$\frac{3}{4}$ lb. tomatoes
Mozzarella cheese	2 tsps. tomato purée
4 oz. butter	Seasoning
1 small chopped	$\frac{1}{8}$ pint Marsala
onion	Green olives

Roll the escalopes in seasoned flour; place a slice of ham on each, then a slice of cheese, roll the escalope over and secure with a wooden cocktail stick. Melt the butter in the frying pan and brown the escalopes on all sides; reduce the heat and cook for 8–10 minutes, until the veal is cooked through. Take the meat out of the pan and keep hot. Put the onion, garlic and bacon into the pan and fry until golden-brown; chop the tomatoes and add with the purée and seasoning. Let the sauce cook gently for 10 minutes, sieve, add the Marsala and cook for a few minutes more. Arrange the veal on a plate with the olives and serve the sauce separately.

SALTIMBOCCA ALLA ROMA
(VEAL, ROMAN STYLE)

1 lb. very thin veal cut-	8 paper-thin slices of
lets ($\frac{1}{16}$-inch thick)	prosciutto or cooked
from the leg	ham
$\frac{1}{2}$ tsp. salt	5 tbsps. butter or mar-
$\frac{1}{4}$ tsp. pepper	garine
$\frac{1}{2}$ tsp. dried sage	2 tbsps. water

Cut the veal into 8 pieces and sprinkle both sides with salt, pepper and sage. On each piece of veal lay 1 slice of prosciutto and fasten with cocktail sticks. Heat 3 tbsps. butter in skillet or frying pan and sauté the meat, a few pieces at a time, for about 2 minutes on each side, or until golden. Remove to a heated platter, with the prosciutto side up, and keep warm. Add the water to the fat left in the pan, stirring to loosen the browned bits; stir in the remaining butter until melted, then pour this gravy over the veal.

SCALOPPINE AI FUNGHI
(ESCALOPES WITH MUSHROOMS)

3 tbsps. flour	2 tbsps. minced onion
$\frac{1}{2}$ tsp. salt	$\frac{1}{2}$ cup sliced mush-
A dash of freshly	rooms
ground pepper	6 tbsps. dry white wine
$\frac{1}{8}$ tsp. paprika	1 tsp. chopped parsley
1 lb. very thin veal	A pinch of chopped
cutlets ($\frac{1}{16}$ inch	fresh or dried tar-
thick) from the leg	ragon
4 tbsps. butter	

Combine the flour, salt, pepper and paprika. Cut the veal into 8 pieces and coat them with the flour mixture, then sauté in 3 tbsps. hot butter in a frying pan, a few pieces at a time, for about 8 minutes on each side, or until golden. Remove to a heated platter. Add the onion to the fat left in the pan and cook, stirring, over a medium heat for 2 minutes. Add the mushrooms and cook for 2 minutes, then add 3 tbsps. of the wine and simmer for another 2 minutes, stirring to loosen any browned bits. Add the parsley, tarragon and remaining wine, bring to the boil and stir in the rest of the butter until just melted, then pour over the veal.

VEAL CASSEROLE

$1\frac{1}{2}$ lb. leg of veal	$\frac{1}{2}$ pint tomato pulp
4 tbsps. oil or lard	$\frac{1}{2}$ pint white wine
2 garlic cloves	2 sprigs of rosemary
Salt and pepper	A strip of lemon rind

Slice the meat or cut into small pieces. Heat the oil in a casserole and cook the chopped garlic in it until slightly browned. Add the meat and seasoning and continue cooking until the meat is golden. Stir in the tomato pulp, wine, rosemary and lemon rind, cover tightly and cook gently in a moderate oven (350° F., mark 4) until the meat is tender.

BISTECCA FIORENTINA
(FLORENTINE BEEFSTEAK)

This is a speciality of Florence, but is also served throughout Italy. The steak is grilled over a charcoal fire and is served with chunky wedges of lemon.

Order 2 " porterhouse " steaks, 1½ inch thick. Brush over on both sides with olive or salad oil (in Florence they use a duck feather for this purpose), then sprinkle with salt and pepper. For very underdone steak cook over a glowing charcoal fire or grill in a pre-heated grill for about 8 minutes on each side. (If preferred less rare, increase the cooking time to 10 minutes a side.) Alternatively, sauté steaks in a frying pan over medium heat for 8–10 minutes on each side. Serve with lemon wedges and plenty of parsley. (Makes 6–8 servings.)

BISTECCA ALLA PIZZAIOLA
(BEEFSTEAK, PIZZA STYLE)

2 lb. chuck or sirloin steak, 1–1¼ inch thick	1 tbsp. minced onion
1 can of whole tomatoes (undrained)	¼ tsp. salt
	A dash of pepper
½ tsp. dried orégano	2 tbsps. olive or salad oil
1 tsp. chopped parsley	
1 garlic clove, minced	4 slices of Mozzarella cheese

Start heating the oven to moderate (350° F., mark 4). Arrange the steak in a baking dish about 10 by 6 inches and about 2 inches deep. Mash the tomatoes with a spoon and spread evenly over the steak. Sprinkle with orégano, parsley, garlic, onion, salt, pepper and oil. Bake, uncovered, for 1¼ hours, then top the steak with the cheese and bake for a further ½ hour, or until tender. (Makes 6 servings.)

BISTECCA DI MAIALE ALLA NAPOLITANA
(NEAPOLITAN PORK CHOPS)

2 tbsps. olive or salad oil	3 tbsps. white wine
1 garlic clove	3 tbsps. canned tomato paste
4 shoulder pork chops, ½ inch thick	1 medium-sized green pepper, chopped
¾ tsp. salt	½ lb. sliced mushrooms
¼ tsp. pepper	

Heat the oil in a large frying pan and brown the garlic, then discard it. In the same oil, brown the chops well on both sides ; sprinkle with salt and pepper. Add the combined wine and tomato paste, sprinkle with green pepper and mushrooms and cook covered over a low heat for about 45 minutes, or until the chops are done.

ESCALOPES OF VEAL MILANESE

Choose 4–6 escalopes of veal and season them well. Beat an egg and dip the meat into it, then toss the slices in some white breadcrumbs. Melt about 2 oz. butter in a pan and fry the escalopes for about 3 minutes on each side—they should be golden-brown in colour. Arrange the pieces of meat overlapping each other on a dish, pour the melted butter over, and serve with lemon.

VITELLO TONNATO
(VEAL WITH TUNNY FISH)

1 lb. lean veal	Olive oil
Flavouring vegetables	Home-made mayonnaise
1 bay leaf	
Seasoning	Sliced lemon, 4 gherkins, a few green olives and a few capers for garnish
4 oz. tunny fish	
6 anchovy fillets	
2 tsps. capers	
Juice of 1 lemon	

Stew the veal with a stick of celery, a carrot, a small onion, a bay leaf, salt and pepper, until tender, and allow to cool in its stock. Pass the tunny fish, anchovies and capers through a fine sieve and add the lemon juice and enough oil to make a liquid sauce. Blend with 4–5 tbsps. mayonnaise and mix well. Arrange the sliced veal on a dish, cover with sauce and garnish.

UCCELLI SCAPPATI
(" ESCAPED BIRDS "—ITALIAN BEEF OLIVES)

6 thin slices of beefsteak or veal fillet, 4 inches by 2 inches	Fresh sage
	Flour
	Butter
6 slices of streaky bacon	Salt and pepper
	White wine

Beat the meat slices with a rolling pin until they become larger and thinner. On each piece put a thin slice of streaky bacon of about the same size, with a sage leaf sandwiched between the two. Roll up the " birds," tie with thread, dust with flour and fry gently in butter. When they are half-cooked, sprinkle with salt and pepper and a little white wine and complete the cooking. Remove the threads and serve the olives with sauté potatoes and a green salad.

ITALIAN ROAST LAMB

About 5 lb. boned loin of lamb	2 tsps. ground ginger
	Salt and pepper
1 lemon	Oil or melted butter
1 lb. cooked apples	1 pint cider (or apple juice)
2 tbsps. sugar	
3 cloves	2 tbsps. cream or top of the milk
2 cloves of garlic	

Rub the lamb inside and out with the lemon peel and sprinkle with the juice. Peel and core the apples and slice thickly, then lay the slices over the meat, sprinkle with the sugar, dot with the cloves and roll up the meat, skewering or tying it firmly. Insert the garlic cloves under the skin of the meat. Rub over the outside with a mixture of ground ginger and about ½ tsp. each salt and pepper, then brush the skin over lightly with the oil or melted butter. Put into a moderately hot oven (425° F., mark 7) for 20 minutes, then lower the heat to moderate (375° F., mark 5), and cook for about 1½–1¾ hours, basting with the hot cider or apple juice every 15 minutes.

Remove the meat from the pan and keep it hot while skimming off the excess fat from the liquor and stirring in the cream.

COSTOLETTE D'AGNELLO ALLA MILANESE
(LAMB CUTLETS)

Beat 4 lamb cutlets until fairly thin, then coat with flour, egg and fresh breadcrumbs. Fry in a mixture of olive oil and butter or margarine until a nice golden-brown, and serve on a hot dish with quarters of lemon, garnished with watercress. At the last minute pour some hot foaming butter over the top.

KIDNEYS IN WHITE WINE

3 kidneys	6 mushrooms
Butter	½ glass Madeira
Bread	2 tbsps. good
Deep fat or oil	gravy
1 small truffle	Salt and pepper

Clean and prepare the kidneys, skin and cut them in half lengthwise. Sauté them in a little butter; when cooked, place on one side to keep warm. Prepare some rounds of bread and fry in deep fat or oil. Slice the truffle and peel the mushrooms; fry lightly for a few minutes in the same butter in which the kidneys were cooked. Add the Madeira and gravy, with salt and pepper to taste; simmer for 15 minutes. Dish the kidneys on the fried croûtes, pour the sauce over them and serve at once.

POLPETTONE
(STUFFED MEAT ROLL)

58

1–1½ lb. each beef, steak, veal and pork (see below)	2 chopped hard-boiled eggs
1 clove of garlic	3–4 mushrooms
Seasoning	Butter
¼ lb. lean smoked ham	1 oz. grated Parmesan cheese
A few leaves of tarragon	Olive oil
1 spring onion or a few chives	¼ pint white wine
	½ pint good stock
½ tsp. chopped rosemary	1 tsp. tomato paste

Each meat should be cut in one slice about ½ inch thick, but the beef should be slightly larger than the others. Beat all the slices. Scrape the clove of garlic over the beef, season with salt and pepper, and then cover it with thin slices of ham. Place the slice of veal over it, and scatter evenly over the surface the finely chopped tarragon leaves and onion (or chives). Put the slice of pork on top and cover it with the chopped rosemary and hard-boiled eggs. Add the chopped mushrooms, lightly fried in butter, and the grated cheese. Roll the meat tightly, and tie securely with string. Heat some olive oil in a saucepan and fry the roll in it until it is well browned. Heat together the wine and stock and add the tomato paste. Pour this liquid over the meat roll, cover the saucepan with a lid and cook gently for 2–3 hours. Serve on a hot dish, and pour over the roll all the sauce left in the pan.

FRITTO MISTO
(FRIED MEATS)

Small pieces of calves' brains, veal or sheep's kidney, calf or lamb sweetbread, liver or veal	1 aubergine or globe artichoke
	Small pieces of marrow
	Egg and breadcrumbs
	Olive oil for frying
1 small cauliflower	Lemon to garnish

Use a selection of the above ingredients, as available. Parboil the brains (the other meats do not require previous cooking). Wash the cauliflower, cut off the outer leaves and stalk, break up into flowerets, and parboil in salted water, then drain and cool. Prepare the other vegetables, and parboil and slice them. Coat all these ingredients with egg and breadcrumbs (or a light fritter batter) and fry. Pile on a hot dish and garnish.

This makes a handsome, easily served dish for a number of people if arranged on a large platter and surrounded with small boiled potatoes, which should be sprinkled with parsley.

TRIPE ROMANA

1½ lb. prepared tripe	1 oz. flour
2 tbsps. vinegar	1 can tomato purée
2 tbsps. oil	Seasoning
4 oz. mushrooms	1 cup breadcrumbs
2 small onions	A small packet of frozen
2 oz. butter	peas

Cut the tripe into narrow strips 2 inches long and soak for 30 minutes in vinegar and oil. Clean and thinly slice the mushrooms and onions. Melt 1½ oz. butter and fry the onion and mushrooms for 3–4 minutes. Remove these mushrooms and onions, stir the flour into the fat and brown slightly. Add the tomato purée and seasoning. Grease a casserole or fireproof dish and line the base with half the tripe. Add the mushrooms and onions and sprinkle on half the breadcrumbs. Place another layer of tripe on this, pour the sauce over, sprinkle the top with the remaining breadcrumbs and dot with ½ oz. butter. Bake uncovered in a moderately hot oven (400° F., mark 6) for 25-30 minutes. Garnish with cooked peas.

FRITTATA
(HAM AND MARROW)

3 slices of fat ham or bacon	Seasoning
12 spring onions	6 eggs
3-4 sprigs of parsley	2 oz. grated Parmesan cheese
4 leaves of fresh basil	A few small pieces of butter
3 small marrows or ridge cucumbers	

Cut the ham or bacon into small pieces, fry and put in a fireproof dish. Add the finely chopped onions, parsley, basil and marrows or cucumbers, season well, cover and cook slowly until the vegetables are almost done. Beat the eggs and pour over the vegetables, cook slowly for 5 minutes, then sprinkle with the grated cheese and the pieces of butter and brown quickly under a hot grill. Serve with fried potatoes. (Serves 6 people.)

POLLO ALLA CACCIATORA
(HUNTSMAN'S CHICKEN)

A small roasting chicken	Marsala wine
Flour	4 oz. mushrooms
1 onion	8 peeled tomatoes
A clove of garlic (optional)	1 tsp. tomato paste
2 oz. butter	Salt and pepper
2 tbsps. olive oil	A little stock if required
	Croûtons and parsley

Cut the chicken into pieces and rub these with flour. Chop the onion and garlic, put in a saucepan with the fat and olive oil, and fry until they are a pale golden colour. Add the chicken and fry for 5 minutes, then put in the wine, chopped mushrooms, tomatoes, tomato paste and seasoning, and cook slowly in a covered saucepan until the chicken is tender; if it becomes dry, add a little stock. Serve with fried croûtons of bread, and sprinkle a little chopped parsley over the chicken.

POLLO ALLA DIAVOLA
(DEVILLED CHICKEN)

Use a young spring chicken, either cut in half, or split, flattened out and skewered to keep it in shape. Prepare a mixture of olive oil, generous quantities of salt and pepper, a finely chopped onion and some fresh, finely chopped parsley. Turn the chicken in this mixture, leaving it in for about 10-15 minutes. (Cuts may be made in the flesh to let the seasonings penetrate.) Grill until golden-brown, and serve at once with skinned boiled tomatoes.

POLLO FRITTO ALLA FIORENTINA
(FLORENTINE FRIED CHICKEN)

¼ cup fresh, frozen or canned lemon juice	2 ready-to-cook broiler chickens, about 1½-2 lb. each, cut up
⅛ tsp. salt	
A dash of pepper	Olive or salad oil
3 tbsps. chopped parsley	½ cup flour
	3 eggs, slightly beaten

About 2½-3½ hours before the meal is required combine the lemon juice, salt, pepper and parsley; pour over the chicken pieces in a bowl and put in the refrigerator for 2-3 hours. About ½ hour before serving pour 1 inch oil into a deep pan and heat to 350° F. Drain the chicken and dip in flour, then in egg. Fry, a few pieces at a time, in the hot oil, turning often, for about 15 minutes or until golden and done. Drain on crumpled kitchen paper. Serve on a heated platter; garnish with more chopped parsley if desired.

POLLO ALLA OLIVE
(CHICKEN WITH OLIVES)

1 carrot	1 tomato
1 onion	2 tbsps. tomato purée
1 young chicken, jointed	Chicken stock
3 tbsps. oil or 1½ oz. butter	24 olives
	Seasoning

Finely chop the carrot and onion. Sauté the chicken in the oil with the carrot and onion until golden, then add the tomato and tomato purée and sufficient hot stock to cover. (A good stock can be made by covering the giblets with water and simmering gently with a slice of carrot, onion, a bay leaf and a few herbs.) Stone and chop 18 olives and add to the mixture with the 6 whole olives. Season carefully, allowing for the saltiness of the olives. Cover with a lid and cook slowly until tender—about 20 minutes. Remove the meat and thicken the gravy if necessary. Pile the chicken neatly on a hot dish and pour the gravy over.

PIGEONS ALLA TOSCANA

4 young pigeons	A small bunch of fresh sage
Salt and pepper	
¼ lb. lean smoked ham	¼ lb. mushrooms
Stale bread	Olive oil
Garlic	Butter

Carefully remove the pigeon breasts, cut them into four pieces and season well. (Put the carcasses aside to make stock for soup.) Cut the ham into thin slices, and then into squares an inch wide. Rub the stale bread well with garlic, and cut into inch cubes.

Arrange all the ingredients on small skewers, alternating a piece of pigeon with a sage leaf, a slice of ham, a bread cube and a mushroom, until skewers are full. Soak them in olive oil for 5 minutes, drain, and place on a shallow baking tin. Cook in a hot oven (450° F., mark 8), basting occasionally with melted butter, until cooked and well browned.

Serve with crisp fresh bread and green salad.

CHICKEN PUFF BALLS

Cooked fowl	Cayenne
½ tsp. salt	2 tbsps. cream
A pinch of ground cinnamon	Tinned apricots Puff pastry
A pinch of ground cloves	Oil or lard for deep frying

Mince the white meat of half a cooked fowl; mix with it the salt and cinnamon, a flavouring of ground cloves and some cayenne; moisten with the cream. Take some good canned apricots, fill the cavities with the chicken mixture and enclose in thin puff pastry. Fry in deep fat—the pan should be three-quarters full and a faint blue smoke should be rising from it before the balls are put in. Serve at once.

PHEASANT AND MACARONI

1 pheasant	6 oz. grated Parmesan
8 oz. macaroni	cheese
½ pint veal stock	Salt and pepper
4 tomatoes	

Roast a well-larded pheasant, basting it continually. Meanwhile gently simmer the macaroni in the veal stock, with the peeled and sliced tomatoes, until cooked. Add the cheese, and continue cooking for a few minutes. Season to taste. Cut up the pheasant into neat joints, then put it together again and stand it on a bed of the macaroni. Serve with fried potatoes and watercress.

FAGIOLI CON TONNO
(BEANS WITH TUNA)

1 can white or red kidney beans	¼ tsp. salt
	1 can solid-pack tuna
2 tbsps. olive or salad oil	Thin slices of onion (red onion would be used in Italy)
2 tbsps. lemon juice	
¼ tsp. pepper	

Combine the drained beans, oil, lemon juice, pepper and salt in a bowl. Add the tuna, broken into large chunks, toss lightly, then refrigerate until served. Garnish with the onion slices.

There is a popular saying about the Florentines, "*Fiorentino mangia fagioli, lecca piatti e tovaglioli*," which roughly translated, means : " Florentines eat beans, then lick their plates and napkins."

POMODORI RIPIENI ALLA CASALINGA
(STUFFED TOMATOES, HOUSEWIFE STYLE)

Allow one large tomato per person; cut them in half and scrape out the inside. Make a stuffing of finely chopped parsley, a chopped clove of garlic and a little orégano (if available), plenty of soft breadcrumbs, salt and pepper. Stuff the tomato cases, put them in a baking dish (on squares of fried bread, if you wish), dot with butter and cook for ½ hour in a moderate oven (350° F., mark 3).

MARROWS COOKED IN THE ITALIAN WAY

Small marrows about 5 inches long	Sugar
	Oil or lard for frying
Salt	

Slice the marrows finely longways, skin and all, lay the slices on a large dish or cooking board and sprinkle them with both salt and fine sugar ; leave for an hour to soak in. (The dish or board should be slightly slanting so that the liquid that comes away drains off well and the slices of marrow are left fairly dry.)

Have ready a large frying pan with boiling oil or lard and fry the slices till golden-brown. Drain well on paper to remove the grease and serve hot.

CARROTS COOKED THE ITALIAN WAY

2 large carrots	Salt and pepper
8 tbsps. cold mashed potatoes	Milk if required
	Chopped parsley
2 tbsps. butter	

Wash and scrape the carrots and boil gently in salted water till soft ; drain and mash with a fork. Mix smoothly with potatoes and butter, seasoning and adding a little milk if necessary. Butter moulds, fill them and steam for 20 minutes. Serve garnished with chopped parsley.

Young carrots are delicious if boiled whole in salted water till tender, then reheated in a pan with fried onions.

FRITELLI DI SPINACCI
(SPINACH FRITTERS)

Cook 12 oz. fresh spinach in boiling water for 5 minutes, drain, and press free of water. Chop finely, add 1 egg, salt and pepper, and 2 tbsps. grated cheese, and mix well. Divide into 6 portions and shape as desired, roll them in fresh crumbs and fry in deep olive oil. Drain well. (Frozen spinach can be used for this dish.)

RED CABBAGE AND APPLES EN CASSEROLE

1 medium-sized red cabbage	4 tbsps. vinegar and water
4 green cooking apples	Thin slices of bacon or pickled pork
Seasoning	
Sugar	

Cut the cabbage in quarters and remove the stalk and outer leaves, then chop it up finely. Peel, core and slice the apples. Take an earthenware casserole with a lid, butter it well and place a good layer of the red cabbage at the bottom; sprinkle with salt and pepper. Then put in a good layer of the prepared apples and dredge them with sugar; fill up the casserole in this fashion. Pour the vinegar and water over the whole and cover with a few slices of bacon or pickled pork. Allow to cook gently in a moderate oven (350° F., mark 4) for 3 hours.

PISELLI ALLA TOSCANA
(TUSCAN PEAS)

1 lb. shelled peas	2 tbsps. olive oil
1 slice of bacon or ham, cut up small	Salt and pepper
1 clove of garlic	A little water

Put all the ingredients in a small saucepan and cook slowly until the peas are tender. Remove the garlic before serving.

SPINACH PANCAKES

Spinach purée	Olive oil for frying
Seasoning	Butter
3 eggs	Grated Parmesan cheese

Season the spinach purée well. Beat up the eggs, season them, and mix in enough spinach to colour them green. Pour a little oil into a small omelette pan and, when it is well heated, drop in a little of the egg mixture, turning the pan about to make a thin, dry pancake; toss or turn, and cook the other side. Remove, and repeat the process with the rest of the mixture. Then lay the pancakes one on top of each other, and cut them into strips 2 inches long and $\frac{3}{4}$ inch wide. Lightly fry these strips in butter, and serve sprinkled with grated cheese.

PATATINE AL ROSMARINO
(POTATOES WITH ROSEMARY)

Cut some potatoes in small pieces, put in a frying pan with olive oil, and while they are cooking, scatter over them enough rosemary to give a good flavour, stirring it in well. Cook until well coloured and soft; serve hot.

ZUCCHINI RIPIENI
(STUFFED SMALL MARROWS)

4 marrows	2 tsps. chopped parsley
1 onion	Seasoning
4 oz. minced meat	1 tbsp. olive oil
4 sliced skinned tomatoes	Breadcrumbs
	Grated cheese

Wash the marrows and boil for 10 minutes in boiling salted water, drain, and cut in half lengthways. Chop the onion finely and mix with the meat, tomatoes, parsley and scooped-out marrow pulp; season to taste. Fry this mixture in oil, turning it frequently, for about 10 minutes. Fill the marrows with the mixture, and sprinkle the crumbs and cheese over the top. Bake in a moderate oven (350° F., mark 4) for 10–15 minutes, until hot.

STUFFED AUBERGINES

4 aubergines	4 anchovy fillets
2 oz. cold pork	2 slices of bread
1 clove of garlic	1 egg
1 small onion	Seasoning
$\frac{1}{4}$ lb. mushrooms	Lemon

Halve the aubergines lengthwise and scoop out some of the inside. Chop the pork, garlic, onion and mushrooms, and mix these with the chopped anchovies. Soak the bread, then squeeze out the surplus moisture, and mix it with the meat, vegetables and egg. Season well, and stuff the aubergines with the mixture. Place in a greased dish and bake in a moderate oven (350° F., mark 4) for 40–45 minutes. Sprinkle with a little lemon juice, and serve with sliced lemon.

COULIBIAC ALL'UOVA
(EGG AND VEGETABLE PASTY)

2 large Spanish onions	Pepper and salt
2 large tbsps. butter	6 oz. flaky pastry
2 small cabbages	4 hard-boiled eggs

Skin and mince the onions, melt the butter in a large saucepan and add the onion. Chop the cabbages very finely, season, add to the onion, cover, and simmer over a very low heat until both vegetables are tender. Roll out the pastry and divide it into two equal portions. Form into equal-sized oblongs or squares, and bake on a baking sheet in a hot oven (450° F., mark 8) for 10 minutes, until well risen and light brown. Remove from the oven, spread the vegetables and chopped eggs on one piece, cover with the second piece, reheat in the oven, and serve immediately, garnished with egg, tomato and watercress.

TORTINO DI PATATE
(SAVOURY POTATO CAKE)

Boil 1 lb. potatoes in salted water, drain and mash, adding 2 oz. butter, about 2 oz. grated Parmesan cheese, salt and pepper and a little grated nutmeg. Heat 1 tbsp. olive oil in an iron frying pan and press the potato mixture into the pan. Cook until a golden-brown crust has formed, then turn over and cook the other side. Sprinkle with grated cheese, and put under the grill to brown the cheese a little. Serve very hot.

INSALATA DI FINOCCHIO
(FENNEL SALAD)

4 small bunches of fennel	¼ cup olive or salad oil
1 tbsp. wine vinegar	Freshly ground pepper to taste
½ tsp. salt	

Trim the tops from the washed fennel, leaving the bulbous ends (hearts) intact; wash thoroughly. Make parallel cuts ½ inch apart from the top of each heart down to the root end; now make a similar set of cuts at right angles to the first, from the top of the heart to the root end, ½ inch apart. Then hold the heart firmly on the board and cut off ½-inch slices (the chopped fennel drops off as you slice). Heap the fennel in a deep salad bowl. Pour the vinegar into a large spoon, then add the salt and sprinkle over the fennel. Next drizzle oil over the fennel and sprinkle generously with pepper. Toss and serve.

Finger style : Cut the fennel stalks from the hearts; cut off the feathery tops, wash and dry the stalks. At each person's place, prop up a salad plate with a knife under the far side. On the plate, near the bottom, pour a little olive oil. At the top of the plate sprinkle a mound of salt and beside it a mound of freshly ground pepper. Each person swishes the fennel, stalk by stalk, first in salt, then in pepper, then in oil, and eats it like celery.

INSALATA DI RISO CON SCAMPI
(SHRIMP AND RICE SALAD)

½ lb. raw shrimps	½ tsp. salt
½ cup raw rice	A dash of freshly ground pepper
2 tbsps. olive or salad oil	
2 tbsps. lemon juice	¼ cup chopped parsley
A dash of cayenne pepper	½ a garlic clove, mashed
	1 tsp. prepared mustard

Shell, devein, cook, then refrigerate the shrimps. Cook the rice, drain and set aside.

Combine the oil, lemon juice, cayenne, salt, pepper, parsley, garlic and mustard and pour over the shrimps, then toss with the rice. This is good eaten with veal or chicken.

INSALATA DI CAVOLFIORE
(CAULIFLOWER SALAD)

1 medium-sized cauliflower	1 tbsp. minced shallot or onion
7 anchovy fillets, cut into small pieces	1 tbsp. bottled capers
	Freshly ground pepper
10 stoned and sliced ripe olives	3 tbsps. olive or salad oil
	1 tbsp. wine vinegar

Wash and trim the head of cauliflower and break into small flowerets. Cook in 1 inch of boiling salted water for about 10 minutes, or until tender-crisp. Drain, cool and put in the refrigerator. Place the chilled cauliflower, anchovy fillets, olives, shallot and capers in a bowl, sprinkle generously with pepper and pour oil and vinegar over all. Toss well and refrigerate for ½ hour, then serve.

PANZANELLA
(BREAD SALAD)

2 cups of stale bread, cut into small squares	2 medium-sized red, ripe tomatoes
½ cup water	1 tsp. salt
1 garlic clove, cut up	⅛ tsp. freshly ground pepper
1 sprig of fresh basil	
1 medium-sized onion, minced	2 tbsps. olive or salad oil
	1 tbsp. wine vinegar

Briefly soak the bread in the water, draining it while still firm. Meanwhile, rub the salad bowl well with garlic and fresh basil. (Or sprinkle a pinch of dried basil into the bowl.) Toss the bread in the salad bowl with the onion, cut-up tomatoes, salt and pepper. Add the oil and vinegar and mix lightly but well.

ANCHOVY SALAD

Mix some salted anchovies, finely chopped onion and green pepper, diced pickled beetroot, capers and chopped hard-boiled egg, and toss in a mixture of three parts olive oil to one of red wine and vinegar, a little sugar and freshly ground pepper.

ITALIAN RISOTTO

In the northern rice-growing provinces of Italy, in the valley of the Po, the people are likely to choose risotto or rice dishes, often yellow with saffron, for their first main course. As you travel southward, you may find risotto served with meat or tomato sauce.

Finely chop a medium-sized onion and fry gently in 2–3 oz. butter or margarine. When it is golden-brown, pour in 1 lb. rice and stir well, so that every grain is coated with fat. Add twice as much stock as rice (by volume), bring to the boil, cover tightly, reduce the heat and simmer gently for about 20 minutes, stirring occasionally so that the rice does not stick. Just before serving, add 1 heaped tbsp. grated cheese. (Cheddar, Cheshire or Lancashire cheese will serve just as well as Parmesan.)

This is a "basic" risotto. You can vary it by adding minced meat, sardines, pilchards, sliced frankfurters, small pieces of liver, kidneys, the remains of a cooked chicken—in fact, anything you have to hand. You can colour it yellow by adding a pinch of saffron, or pink by adding tomato purée; it looks very gay if peas and chopped carrots or small pieces of tomato are included.

If you add about 2 lb. peas at half-time, and about 4 oz. grated cheese before you serve it, it becomes *Risi-Bisi alla Veneziana*.

RISOTTO WITH MUSSELS

1 onion	1 oz. grated Parmesan
3 oz. butter	1½ pints mussels
8 oz. Patna rice	1 tbsp. oil
½ pint white wine	1 clove of garlic
1 quart chicken stock	1 tbsp. chopped
A pinch of saffron	parsley
Seasoning	Red pepper to garnish

Chop the onion and fry it in 2 oz. of the butter until it is pale golden—not brown. Add the washed and dried rice, stirring this in until it is covered with butter. Pour on the wine, and let the mixture cook over a low heat until all the liquid has disappeared, then add the stock, about ½ pint at a time, until the rice mixture is cooked to a creamy but not sticky consistency. Add the saffron powder, salt and pepper, and lastly the remaining 1 oz. butter and the Parmesan cheese. Meanwhile wash and scrub the mussels. Heat 1 tbsp. olive oil in a pan and add the chopped garlic and parsley. Put in the mussels and cook them until they open. Take the mussels from the shells, remove the beards and add the mussels to the risotto, with the liquid in which they were cooked. Garnish with a few mussels and some sliced red pepper, and serve immediately.

RISOTTO ALLA FIORENTINA
(RICE FLORENTINE STYLE)

4 cups chicken broth	2 cups raw rice
¼ lb. butter or margarine	2 tsps. salt
3 cups minced onions	¼ tsp. pepper

Heat the broth and start heating the oven to moderate (350° F., mark 4). Melt the butter in a frying pan and sauté the onions and rice, with salt and pepper, stirring constantly, until the rice turns golden. Add broth, turn into a 2-quart casserole and bake, covered, for 40 minutes, or until all the broth is absorbed. (Serves 6.)

RISO ALLA PIEMONTESE
(PIEDMONTESE RICE)

½ lb. rice	¼ pint tomato purée
2 quarts hot water	1 tbsp. chopped onion
¼ lb. lean diced bacon	1 tbsp. chopped
1½ pints veal or chicken stock	parsley
1 small tsp. white pepper	A few leaves of sweet basil
	Small cooked sausages

Wash and blanch the rice in the water for 5 minutes, strain and cool. Meanwhile fry the diced bacon, and when browned add the stock and pepper and simmer the rice in the stock for 20 minutes, stirring occasionally. Remove the rice from the heat and add the tomato purée, chopped onion and parsley, and the sweet basil. Mix well, pile up on a hot dish, and surround with small cooked sausages. Garnish as desired.

RISOTTO CON MELANZANE
(RICE WITH AUBERGINE)

Olive or salad oil	2 8-oz. cans of tomato sauce
1 large aubergine, pared and thinly sliced	1 cup water
⅓ cup butter or margarine	1 tsp. salt
1 thin slice of salt pork, diced	¼ tsp. pepper
1 medium-sized onion, minced	4 cups chicken broth
A 6-oz. can of tomato paste	1½ cups raw rice
	¼ lb. Mozzarella cheese, thinly sliced
	¼ cup grated Parmesan cheese
	1 tsp. dried basil

Heat the oil and sauté the aubergine slices on both sides until golden, then remove. Heat 1 tbsp. each of oil and butter and sauté the salt pork and onion until the pork is crisp. Add the tomato paste, tomato sauce, water, salt and pepper and simmer, covered, for 40 minutes. Add the chicken broth and rice, bring to the boil, then simmer, covered, for 45 minutes, stirring occasionally. Stir in the remaining butter. Start heating the oven to moderately hot (400° F., mark 6). Grease a large casserole and arrange in it half the rice, half the aubergine, then half the Mozzarella; repeat. Top with Parmesan and basil and bake, uncovered, for 25 minutes. (Makes 6 servings.)

RISOTTO ALLA MARIA
(MARIA'S RISOTTO)

½ cup butter or margarine	1½ cups raw rice
	A generous pinch of
1 medium-sized onion, minced	dried saffron
	4 cups chicken broth

Heat half the butter in a frying pan and sauté the onion and rice until golden, stirring hard. Mix the saffron with 2 tbsps. chicken broth and set aside. Add the remaining broth to the rice, bring to the boil, then simmer, covered, for 20 minutes. Just before serving stir in the remaining butter and the saffron and chicken broth. (Makes 6 servings.)

RISOTTO MILANESE

6 oz. rice	Seasoning
1 onion, minced	½ tsp. saffron
2 oz. butter	2 tbsps. grated Parmesan cheese
½ cup Marsala wine	
1½ pints meat broth	

Wash the rice through in several waters, drain and dry in a cloth. Fry the onion slowly in half the butter until golden; add the rice and fry for 5 minutes, stirring constantly. Add half the Marsala and sufficient boiling broth to cook the rice. Season, then cook rapidly until the grains swell; reduce the heat and finish cooking until nearly dry. Uncover and add the rest of butter and the Marsala, and the saffron mixed smoothly with a little broth. Cook in a very slow oven (275° F., mark ½) until the rice is dry and fluffy. When ready to serve, sprinkle with Parmesan cheese.

This is not normally regarded as a main dish, but with the addition of cooked flaked fish, cooked minced veal or pork or any canned fish or meat, it has plenty of sustenance.

PASTA

Many grocers in this country now stock an interesting range of Italian pasta, from cannelloni —rather more than ½ inch in diameter—to fine vermicelli and strips of different widths. Paste stars and letters of the alphabet are available for garnishing soups.

All these are nutritious preparations widely used in Italy, though never as a sweet dish. The preliminary cooking is the same for all of them. They are put unwashed into just enough boiling water to cover them, and cooked briskly for 8–20 minutes, until they are just tender but not at all mushy. When drained they are ready for use as required, but they must not be allowed to cool before the other ingredients are added and the dish is served.

SPAGHETTI ALLA CARBONARA

½ lb. spaghetti	Finely grated Parmesan cheese
4 eggs	
4 slices of ham, fried in oil	Black pepper

Cook the spaghetti and serve it very hot, handing each person a raw egg broken into a small dish : this is buried in a hole in the centre of the spaghetti, and covered with more spaghetti. Serve the hot ham slices in the oil in which they were fried, and mix with the spaghetti, adding a good sprinkling of cheese and a generous seasoning of freshly ground black pepper.

SPAGHETTI TURBICO

1½ lb. onions	Seasoning
1 garlic clove	1¼ lb. spaghetti
2 pieces of streaky bacon	⅓ lb. ham
4 oz. butter	½ lb. tongue
2 oz. flour	6 oz. grated cheese
4 tbsps. tomato purée	10 chipolatas
1½ pints stock	

Chop the onions and garlic, place in a pan with the bacon and 2 oz. butter, then fry lightly ; add the flour and cook for about 1 minute. Next stir in the tomato purée and stock and stir until the sauce boils, skim, season and allow to simmer for 1 hour ; remove the bacon.

Boil the spaghetti in salted water for 15 minutes, drain and toss in 2 oz. butter. Arrange the chopped ham, tongue and spaghetti in layers in a serving dish. Pour the sauce over the spaghetti, sprinkle with cheese and garnish with grilled chipolatas.

SPAGHETTI IN MUSHROOM SAUCE

¾ lb. mushrooms	½ pint stock or milk
1 medium-sized large onion	A bunch of herbs
	¼ tsp. parsley
4–5 tomatoes	Pepper and salt
2 tbsps. olive oil or 2 oz. butter	4–6 oz. spaghetti
	Grated cheese
1 oz. flour	

Chop the mushrooms and onion finely and slice the tomatoes. Put the oil or butter in a saucepan and heat gently. First cook the mushrooms for about 5 minutes, until evenly browned, remove them from the saucepan and add the chopped onion. Fry this, then remove and cook the tomatoes, adding a little more fat if necessary. Remove the tomatoes from the pan and stir the flour into the remaining oil or butter. Cook the flour slowly for a few minutes, add the ½ pint of stock or milk and bring to the boil, stirring meanwhile. Return the onions, tomatoes and mushrooms to the pan, add the bunch of herbs, the parsley, pepper and salt and simmer very slowly for 15 minutes. Remove the herbs, then add the cooked spaghetti and blend it with the sauce. Serve in a hot vegetable dish, sprinkling the top generously with grated cheese, or hand the cheese separately.

SPAGHETTI MADRAS

3 oz. butter
1 chopped onion
8 oz. shredded cabbage
Tomatoes
Salt and pepper
1 tsp. turmeric
¼ tsp. mustard powder

1 small tin tomato juice
8 oz. cooked diced chicken
8 oz. spaghetti
Seedless raisins
Parmesan cheese

Melt 1 oz. butter and gently sauté the onion till soft, without colouring. Add the cabbage and skinned and quartered tomatoes, season with salt, pepper, turmeric and mustard, then add the tomato juice and chicken and simmer gently with the lid on for 12–15 minutes. Serve poured over cooked spaghetti which has been tossed in the remaining butter. Sprinkle with the blanched raisins and a liberal amount of grated Parmesan.

SPAGHETTI ALLA BOLOGNESE

1 onion
1 small carrot
1 stick of celery
1 clove of garlic (optional)
2 tbsps. olive oil
1 oz. butter
1 bay leaf
1 glass dry Italian wine

4 oz. minced raw beef (fillet if possible)
8 peeled tomatoes
2 tbsps. tomato paste
Meat extract
Seasoning
12 oz. spaghetti
Grated Parmesan cheese

Chop the onion, carrot, celery and garlic very finely, place in a small saucepan with the oil, butter and bay leaf, and fry for 5 minutes, then add the wine, meat, tomatoes and tomato paste, with meat extract and seasoning to taste. Cook slowly for ½ hour. Meanwhile cook the spaghetti in plenty of boiling salted water for 20 minutes. Drain it, put in a hot serving dish, and add the sauce; mix well, and serve with grated cheese.

HOME-MADE CANNELLONI FILLED WITH DUCK

¾ lb. flour
1 tsp. salt
4 eggs
3 tbsps. water
6 oz. sieved cooked spinach
6 oz. finely minced cold cooked duck

Seasoning
A pinch of nutmeg
4 oz. grated Parmesan cheese
Butter
¼ pint stock (preferably chicken)

Put the flour and salt into a basin, make a

hollow in the centre, break in 2 eggs and add the water. Fold the flour into the eggs until the mixture forms into a paste. Knead very thoroughly, then divide in two. Put one half on a floured board, and roll and stretch the dough until it is very thin. Leave it, then spread on a piece of floured cloth whilst carrying out the same procedure with the rest of the paste. Prepare the filling by mixing together the spinach and the minced duck, season well and add nutmeg, 1 oz. of the cheese and remaining eggs. Cut paste into pieces about 4 inches by 3 inches, put these into boiling salted water and cook for 5 minutes. Remove them carefully from the pan, cool, spread with the filling and roll up. Arrange the rolls in layers in a fireproof dish, with butter and grated cheese. Pour on the stock, and cook in a moderate oven (350° F., mark 4) for 10–15 minutes; serve with grated cheese.

MACCHERONE ALLA NAPOLITANA

10 oz. macaroni
2 large slices of onion
2½ oz. butter
1 lb. tomatoes

Salt and pepper
A little chopped basil
1 oz. grated Parmesan cheese

Put the macaroni into just sufficient boiling water to cover, and cook briskly for 20 minutes. Meanwhile fry the onion in 1 oz. butter, and when it is lightly coloured add the peeled and sliced tomatoes, salt, pepper and basil. Cook for 5 minutes, add the remaining butter, the cheese and the cooked macaroni, and stir over the heat for 5 minutes. Serve more cheese separately.

MACARONI WITH ANCHOVIES

6 anchovies (in brine)
½ gill finest quality olive oil

2 oz. butter
2 tbsps. tomato paste
10 oz. macaroni

Wash, clean and fillet the anchovies, then cut the fillets into very small pieces. Heat but do not boil them in the olive oil; when hot, add the butter and the tomato paste, and stir over the heat until the butter melts. Meanwhile cook the macaroni, and blend it thoroughly with the anchovy mixture.

RAVIOLI

½ lb. flour
½ tsp. salt
1 whole egg
3 egg yolks

Spinach purée
Butter
Grated Parmesan cheese

Mix the flour, salt, egg and egg yolks into a paste. Roll this out on a board and leave to stand for 15 minutes; then fold it, roll out thinly and cut into rounds with a fluted pastry cutter. On the centre of each round put a little well-seasoned purée of spinach, moisten round the edge, fold over like jam puffs and pinch the edges together. Poach in boiling salted water for 15 minutes, and drain. Serve with melted butter and grated cheese; alternatively, sprinkle with grated cheese and brown in a hot oven. ·

This simple form of ravioli is quickly made, and is much more delicious than that bought ready-made or in tins.

CANNELLONI AU GRATIN

60

10 oz. cannelloni	Salt
A chunk of bread the size of an orange	Black pepper
	1 beaten egg
Milk	A little cream
1 hard-boiled egg	½ pint béchamel sauce
1 tbsp. chopped parsley	Breadcrumbs
2 oz. mushrooms	Grated Parmesan

Cook the cannelloni and drain carefully, keeping the pieces apart from each other. Meanwhile make a stuffing by dipping the bread into milk and squeezing it dry; add the finely chopped hard-boiled egg, parsley and mushrooms, season with salt and black pepper, and add the raw egg and enough cream to moisten the stuffing.

Carefully cut the cannelloni lengthwise, lay the stuffing along the centre, and fold into their original form. Lay them in a well-buttered earthenware dish, coat with béchamel sauce and sprinkle them first with dry breadcrumbs and then with grated cheese. Bake in a moderately hot oven (425° F., mark 7) for 15 minutes.

LASAGNE

¼ cup minced onion	1 8-oz. can tomato sauce
1 tbsp. salad oil	
½ lb. minced chuck steak	¼ cup grated Parmesan cheese
1 garlic clove, sliced	¼ lb. lasagne (1½-inch wide noodles)
¾ tsp. salt	
⅛ tsp. pepper	½ lb. thinly sliced Mozzarella or natural Swiss cheese
½ tsp. dried orégano	
2 tbsps. chopped parsley	
1 can tomatoes	½ lb. ricotta or cottage cheese

The day before or early in the day sauté the onion in hot oil in a frying pan. Add the meat and cook until the red colour disappears. Mash the garlic with the salt and add to the meat, with the pepper, orégano, parsley, tomatoes, tomato sauce and 1 tbsp. of the Parmesan. Simmer covered for 30 minutes, then cool and refrigerate. About 45 minutes before serving start heating the oven to moderate (350° F., mark 4). Cook the lasagne as the label directs; drain; cover

with cold water. Put one-third of the meat sauce in a baking dish, then add a single layer of drained lasagne, placed lengthwise (leave the rest in water); next a layer of Mozzarella, a layer of ricotta and 1 tbsp. Parmesan; repeat, ending with the rest of the sauce and the Parmesan. Bake for ½ hour. (Serves 3.)

PASTA E FAGIOLI
(MACARONI AND BEANS)

3–4 oz. cooked fancy Italian macaroni	3 tbsps. olive oil
	½ pint tomato sauce
1 lb. haricot beans	½ pint water
A few sprigs of thyme	Salt and pepper
2 garlic cloves	Grated cheese
2 tbsps. chopped parsley	

Choose macaroni in the form of small seashells or other shapes. Soak the beans overnight, then cook slowly in 6 pints water, adding the thyme during the last ½ hour of cooking; drain the beans. Mince together the garlic and parsley and blend with the olive oil. Add the tomato sauce and ½ pint water and simmer the beans slowly in this liquid for 10 minutes. Add the cooked and drained macaroni and continue simmering for another 10 minutes. Season well and serve very hot, with liberal amounts of grated cheese.

PIZZE

These are made with bread dough, spread on a large round tin; this is covered with such savoury titbits as fillets of anchovy, sliced tomatoes, sliced black olives, slices of Mozzarella cheese and a sprinkling of chopped marjoram, the top is coated with oil and the pizza is baked in a moderate oven (350° F., mark 4) for ½ hour.

CHEESE PIZZA

8 oz. flour	1 lb. skinned chopped tomatoes
1 tsp. salt	
½ oz. yeast	Olive oil
1 tsp. sugar	1 tbsp. mixed herbs
⅛ pint warm milk	3 oz. diced Bel Paese
2 eggs	2 oz. sliced stuffed olives
2 oz. soft butter	

Sieve and warm the flour and salt. Cream together the yeast and sugar, and add the milk and beaten eggs. Make a well in the centre of the flour, add the liquid and mix together, then add the fat and beat well. Cover and leave to rise for 40 minutes. Meanwhile, sauté the tomatoes in the oil, add the mixed herbs and cook for a few minutes. Cool and drain off the excess liquor. Spread the dough on to a well-oiled baking tin and cover it with the tomato mixture. Sprinkle with cheese and olives, then cover and leave to prove for 10 minutes. Glaze with a little oil and bake in a moderate oven (350° F., mark 4) for 20–30 minutes.

CONTADINA OMELETTE

2 large Spanish onions	4 eggs
Butter	3 tbsps. milk
2 egg yolks	Breadcrumbs
Minced parsley	Anchovy fillets
Pepper and salt	Grated Parmesan

Parboil the onions, cut in slices and fry a pale brown in butter; when soft, add the egg yolks, a little minced parsley, pepper and salt and mix over a low heat, then draw to one side. Beat up 4 eggs to a froth, and add the milk, with some salt and pepper. Make 3 small omelettes of the mixture, and as each one is cooked place a filleted anchovy on top and fold over. Sprinkle with breadcrumbs, previously sifted with a little grated Parmesan cheese, and brown for a moment in a hot oven before serving. The omelette should be lightly cooked and not too solid. (Makes 3 servings.)

POLENTA

This is made from maize flour, which can be bought at most shops supplying Italian groceries.

To 1 lb. of maize flour allow 1 quart water and 1 heaped tsp. cooking salt. Bring the salted water to the boil in a heavy saucepan and gently scatter in the flour, stirring all the time. Stir hard during the cooking, taking care not to let the polenta get too thick (you can always add more maize flour if it is too thin, but you will not be able to add more water); scrape the mixture well away from the sides of the pan, turning it over and over so that it does not stick. After about 20 minutes the polenta will start to come away from the bottom and sides of the pan, like the roux stage of a béchamel sauce. Turn it out on to a pastry board, and shape into a loaf or a ring.

Polenta may be eaten hot or cold, and should be stiff enough to cut with a knife. It can be served plain, with grated cheese, or with a meat sauce similar to that used for Spaghetti Bolognese, and it is also very good eaten plain with rich fried foods such as liver or sausages.

ITALIAN DESSERTS

Far and away the most popular of Italian desserts is *Formaggio e Frutte*—cheese and fruits. Plums, pears, peaches, apples, oranges, figs, grapes, cherries, apricots, etc., abound in

Italy, and are coupled with Gorgonzola, Bel Paese, Stracchino, or any of a number of Italian cheeses, often served with Italian bread and butter.

If just one fruit is served, it is often teamed with a cheese—pears with Bel Paese, or apples with Gorgonzola.

Most frequently, fruit is served in big luscious bowlfuls, from which each person helps himself. He then washes the fruit by swishing it in the individual bowl of water on the fruit plate before him. For small fruits, such as cherries and grapes, the serving bowl may also be partially filled with water. In Italy, such fruits as peaches and pears are pared and eaten with a knife and fork.

Sometimes on festive occasions the fruit and cheese are followed by a sweet.

PERE AL VINO
(PEARS IN WINE)

4 pears	4 whole cloves
1 cup granulated sugar	1 cup port wine
1 cup water	

Using an apple corer, core the pears from the blossom end, leaving the stems on. Simmer the sugar and water together until the sugar dissolves. Peel the pears and gently simmer them (covered) in the sugar syrup with the cloves and wine for about 30 minutes, or until tender. Refrigerate until thoroughly chilled. Before serving, remove the cloves.

FRAGOLE AL VINO
(STRAWBERRIES IN WINE)

Sprinkle 1 quart hulled strawberries with $\frac{1}{4}$ cup granulated sugar, then pour over them $\frac{1}{2}$ cup white wine. Refrigerate until very chilled.

MONTE BIANCO
(WHITE MOUNTAIN)

$\frac{1}{4}$ cup bottled chestnuts in syrup, finely chopped	$\frac{1}{4}$ cup syrup from chestnuts
2 tbsps. brandy	1 cup whipped double cream

Put into each sherbet glass a mixture of 1 tbsp. chopped chestnuts, 1 tbsp. syrup and $1\frac{1}{2}$ tsps. brandy; refrigerate until well chilled. Serve topped generously with whipped cream.

FICHI SPEZIATI
(SPICED FIGS)

1 can of figs in heavy syrup	$\frac{1}{4}$ tsp. ground ginger
2 cinnamon sticks	1 cup whipped double cream

Simmer the figs and syrup in a large pan

(uncovered) with the cinnamon sticks and ginger for about 20 minutes, or until the syrup is very thick. Leave in the refrigerator until very cold. Before serving, remove the cinnamon sticks and top with whipped cream.

ZABAGLIONE
(WINE CUSTARD)

6 egg yolks	4 half-eggshellfuls of
3 tbsps. granulated sugar	Italian Marsala

Beat the egg yolks in the top of a double boiler, gradually adding the sugar and Marsala. Cook over hot, not boiling, water, beating vigorously with a whip or egg beater until very thick. Serve hot, with sponge fingers.

Note : A half-eggshell is used to measure the Marsala so that the amount of wine will be in proportion to the amount of egg used.

PANFORTE DI SIENA
(SWEETMEAT FROM SIENNA)

61

$\frac{1}{2}$ cup granulated sugar	2 tbsps. diced citron peel
$\frac{1}{2}$ cup honey	$\frac{3}{4}$ cup toasted shelled almonds
$\frac{1}{2}$ cup sifted flour	
2 tbsps. cocoa	$1\frac{1}{4}$ cups toasted shelled filberts
1 tbsp. ground cinnamon	
8 oz. preserved mixed fruit, diced	1 tbsp. grated orange rind
	Icing sugar

Start heating the oven to very slow (275° F., mark $\frac{1}{2}$) and butter a 10-inch pie plate. Combine the sugar and honey and cook over a low heat for 15 minutes, stirring constantly. Sift the flour, cocoa and cinnamon and stir into the honey mixture. Stir in the preserved fruit, citron peel, nuts and orange rind. Quickly turn the mixture into the pie plate and bake for about 30 minutes, until firm, then cool. Dust thickly with icing sugar. Cut into pie-shaped wedges to serve. (Makes 12 servings—leftovers can be stored in aluminium foil.)

ZUPPA INGLESE
(RUM TORTE)

$\frac{1}{4}$ cup diced preserved mixed fruit	1 tbsp. vanilla essence
$1\frac{1}{2}$ tsp. brandy	$\frac{1}{2}$ cup heavy cream
2 cups milk	2 8-inch sponge cakes, each split into 2 layers
3 tbsps. cornflour	$\frac{1}{3}$ cup rum
$\frac{2}{3}$ cup granulated sugar	4 egg whites
$\frac{1}{4}$ tsp. salt	$\frac{3}{4}$ cup granulated sugar for meringue
4 egg yolks, slightly beaten	

Soak the fruit in the brandy. Heat $1\frac{1}{2}$ cups milk. Combine the cornflour, $\frac{2}{3}$ cup sugar and salt

and stir into the hot milk, then cook, stirring constantly, until thickened. Combine the egg yolks with $\frac{1}{2}$ cup milk. Slowly stir the hot mixture into the yolks and return all to the saucepan ; cook over a low heat, stirring, until thick. Add the vanilla, cool and refrigerate. Whip the cream and fold into the custard. Next heat the oven to hot (450° F., mark 8). Sprinkle the cake layers with rum, put on to a buttered baking sheet and sandwich the layers with custard ; top with fruit and secure the layers with cocktail sticks.

Beat the egg whites until they stand up in peaks. Gradually add all but 1 tbsp. of the sugar, beating constantly until the whites form stiff peaks. Spread this meringue over the top and sides of cake, covering it completely ; sprinkle top with 1 tbsp. sugar. Bake for 4–5 minutes, or until lightly browned. Cool for several hours. To serve, remove the torte to a platter with 2 broad spatulas and cut into wedges. (Makes 10 servings.)

TORTA DI RICOTTA
(CHEESE TORTE)

$1\frac{1}{2}$ cups sifted flour	About $\frac{1}{4}$–$\frac{1}{3}$ cup milk
$\frac{1}{3}$ cup granulated sugar	$2\frac{1}{2}$ tsps. vanilla essence
1 tsp. baking powder	1 lb. ricotta cheese
Salt	$1\frac{1}{2}$ cups granulated sugar for filling
$\frac{1}{4}$ cup butter or margarine	4 eggs

Start heating oven to moderate (350° F., mark 4). Sift the flour into a large bowl with $\frac{1}{3}$ cup sugar, baking powder and $\frac{1}{4}$ tsp. salt. With a pastry blender or 2 knives used scissor-fashion, cut the butter into the flour mixture until it resembles coarse meal. Make a well in the centre of the mixture and pour in most of the milk and $\frac{1}{2}$ tsp. vanilla ; with a fork, mix lightly and quickly. Add enough extra milk to form a dough just moist enough to leave the sides of the bowl. Turn on to a lightly floured surface and knead slightly—pick up the side of the dough farthest away, fold over and with the palms of the hand press down, pushing the dough away lightly. Turn the dough part-way around ; repeat 5 times, working gently. Set aside $\frac{1}{4}$ of the dough. Lightly roll the rest out from centre to edge, making a round about $1\frac{1}{2}$ inches wider than an inverted 9-inch pie plate. Line the plate, leaving the overhang. Make the filling, using a rotary beater or an electric mixer at medium speed. Beat the cheese, $1\frac{1}{2}$ cups sugar, $\frac{1}{4}$ tsp. salt, eggs and 2 tsps. vanilla until very thick and smooth ; turn into the pie shell. Roll the other dough into a round, cut into ½-inch strips and criss-cross them over the filling. Flute the edges. Bake for about 45 minutes, or until well browned. Cool on a wire rack and serve slightly warm.

PANETTONE
(CHRISTMAS FRUIT CAKE FROM MILAN)

½ cup scalded milk
½ cup granulated sugar
1¼ tsp. salt
¼ cup soft butter or margarine
2 packets of active dry, or 2 cakes compressed yeast
¼ cup warm (not hot) or lukewarm water
4¾–5½ cups sifted flour

2 eggs, beaten
½ cup raisins, light or dark
⅓ cup diced preserved mixed fruit
¼ cup chopped pecans
¼ cup chopped walnuts
2 tbsps. pine kernels (optional)
1½ tsp. aniseed
¾ tsp. vanilla essence
Beaten egg to glaze

Cool the scalded milk till lukewarm in a large bowl, then add the sugar, salt and butter. In a small bowl sprinkle the yeast into the warm water (for compressed yeast, use lukewarm water); stir till dissolved. Into the milk mixture, stir 1 cup flour, 2 eggs, the softened yeast, and no more than half of the remaining flour. Beat till smooth. Cover and leave to rise in a warm place (about 85° F.) until doubled in size—about 1½–2 hours. The batter will be light and bubbly. Combine the fruits, nuts, aniseed and vanilla; stir the batter and add to it alternately the fruit mixture and the flour, stirring until the sides of the bowl begin to be cleaned; the dough will be soft. Turn it on to a lightly floured surface and knead until smooth and elastic—about 15–20 strokes. Put in a greased bowl, cover and let rise until double the size—about 45 minutes–1 hour. Punch down the dough and turn it out on to a lightly floured surface; cut in half and leave for 10 minutes. Round it into 2 balls and place at opposite corners of a large greased baking sheet; flatten the tops slightly. Leave to rise in a warm place for 45 minutes to 1 hour to double its size; start heating the oven to moderate (350° F., mark 4). Brush the tops of the loaves with the beaten egg mixed with 1 tbsp. water. Bake for 30–40 minutes, or until done. When removed from oven, cool on a wire rack.

PEACH COMPOTE

Pare and slice some peaches and sprinkle with caster sugar. Boil together some wine, cinnamon and lemon peel for 4 or 5 minutes, then strain over the fruit. This should stand for a couple of hours before serving.

ITALIAN APPLE PIE

Rich shortcrust pastry
8 apples
4 oz. sugar
1 oz. butter
Grated rind of 1 lemon
2 egg yolks

Line a plate with pastry, brush it with egg, prick with a fork and bake blind until light brown. Bake the apples, free them from skins and cores and beat to a purée with the sugar, butter, lemon rind and egg yolks. Cook this mixture for 3 minutes, pour it on to the prepared crust, cover with strips of pastry and bake a light brown.

FLORENTINE PIE

4–5 apples
2 oz. sugar
Grated rind of a lemon
Grated nutmeg
Angelica
2 egg whites
1½ tbsps. caster sugar
Puff pastry

Pare the apples and cook with a little water, the sugar, lemon rind and a little grated nutmeg. When cooked, pour off the syrup, add as much cut-up angelica as there are apples and cook till thick. Line a dish with pastry and cook for 10 minutes. Fill with the apple mixture, cover with a meringue made of the whites of eggs and caster sugar and brown in the oven.

This is an unusual dish and it is usually liked best when eaten cold.

PESCHE RIPIENE
(STUFFED PEACHES)

Sponge cake (chocolate-flavoured if possible)
Raspberry jam
Chopped almonds
2 tinned peaches, halved
2 oz. ground almonds
2 oz. caster sugar
1 egg yolk
Liqueur to taste
A few blanched almonds
Red colouring

Cut 4 rounds of cake ¼ inch thick, spread with hot sieved jam, roll them in the chopped almonds and place a half peach on each. Mix the ground almonds, sugar, egg yolk and liqueur very thoroughly, put into a forcing bag and fill the peaches, then place a blanched almond on top; put in a moderately hot oven (400° F., mark 6) for 10 minutes. Pour over the peaches a sauce made from sieved jam diluted with a little water, flavoured with liqueur, and tinted with red colouring.

PIZZA NAPOLI

Roll out some shortcrust pastry thinly, sprinkle or brush it over with a little honey and then cover it with a mixture of chopped walnuts and hazel nuts, chopped candied peel and mixed spices. Roll up to form a long sausage, twist this into a spiral, and bake in a moderate oven (350° F., mark 4) for ½ hour, till it is of a golden colour.

SEGRETO DELLA DAMA
(LADY'S SECRET)

4 oz. vanilla wafers	6 tbsps. butter
1 egg	2 oz. roasted hazelnuts,
1 egg yolk	chopped coarsely
8 oz. caster sugar	¼ pint double cream
3 oz. cocoa	Wafers, etc., to decorate

Crumble the wafers without making them too fine. Place the eggs and sugar in a bowl and beat until smooth. Add the cocoa and mix well, then add the melted butter and stir in the nuts and the crumbled wafers. Put the mixture into a greased and lined tin and chill in the refrigerator for 2 hours. When ready to serve, unmould carefully and remove the paper. Decorate with the cream and wafers.

PIZZA ALLA NAPOLITANA

Puff or shortcrust pastry	1 egg yolk
2½ oz. sweet almonds	Lemon or vanilla
¼ pint milk	6 oz. sour cream or
2 oz. sugar	thick sour milk
1 oz. flour	Egg yolk to glaze
1 whole egg	Sugar to dredge

First make the pastry. Skin the almonds and pound them in a mortar. Put the milk, sugar, flour and the whole egg in a pan, and stir until the mixture begins to thicken. Remove from the heat, and after a few minutes add the egg yolk and flavouring, and stir in the sour cream and the almonds. Line a tart dish with thinly rolled pastry, put the mixture on it, cover with another thin sheet of pastry and decorate with small pieces of pastry cut in fancy shapes. Brush over with egg yolk and bake in a moderate oven (350° F., mark 4) for 25–30 minutes, till the pastry is a golden colour. Serve cold, sprinkled with a little sugar.

AROCE DOLCE
(RICE AND ALMOND PUDDING)

2 oz. almonds (includ-	½ lb. sugar
ing a few bitter ones)	½ pint cream
½ lb. rice	1 tsp. powdered cin-
2 pints milk	namon

Pound all the almonds together. Simmer the rice in the milk for ½ hour, then add the sugar. Continue simmering until the milk is absorbed by the rice, stirring and shaking frequently. Before the rice is completely cooked, stir in the pounded almonds, then add the cream. Turn the rice into a shallow dish, shake until the surface is smooth, and sift over it the powdered cinnamon. Serve very cold.

GRANITA DI CAFFE

A half-frozen coffee ice is made with strong essence of coffee mixed with syrup ; a flavouring of brandy or liqueur may be added, and cream can be added after the coffee has been poured into cups, but not before.

Granita di Limone is made in the same way, lemon juice being used instead of coffee. Serve in a glass jug. Better still, put some lemon or orange water ice into a jug, and fill up with champagne.

FLORENTINES

3¾ oz. butter	1 oz. cherries
4 oz. caster sugar	1 oz. candied peel
4 oz. broken walnuts	1 tbsp. cream
and almonds (mixed)	4-oz. block chocolate
1 oz. sultanas	

Melt the butter, add the sugar and boil together for 1 minute. Stir in all the other ingredients, lastly folding in the whipped cream.

Drop in small, well-spaced heaps on greased and floured trays. Bake in a moderate oven (350° F., mark 4). When golden-brown, remove from the oven and cool slightly ; press the edges to a neat shape. Remove from the tray and cool on a wire tray. Spread with melted chocolate and mark with a fork or decorating comb.

TORTA DI PASTA FROLLA
(LATTICE JAM TART)

6 oz. butter	Flavouring
8 oz. plain flour	Raspberry jam
5 oz. sugar	A little milk
1 egg, well-beaten	Icing sugar

Melt the butter without making it too hot. Mix the flour and sugar, add the melted butter and then the egg and grated lemon rind or vanilla essence. The egg should be sufficient to mix the pastry without the addition of extra liquid. Line a flan tin with the pastry, cover with the jam and then with pastry strips, making a criss-cross pattern over the jam. Brush with a little milk, and cook in a moderately hot oven (400° F., mark 6) for about 45 minutes. When the torta is cold, sprinkle with icing sugar.

Malta

The ingredients used in Maltese recipes are very similar to those used in Italy owing to the

close connections between the two countries, but it is also possible to trace a strong Arab influence in Maltese cooking. A particularly popular ingredient is Rikotta—a certain type of cheese rather similar to curd cheese. This may be bought at delicatessen shops in Soho.

TIMPANA
(SAVOURY TART)

½ lb. puff pastry	Fat for frying
1 lb. macaroni	4 eggs
6 oz. chopped chicken	Seasoning
livers	Grated Parmesan cheese
6 oz. mushrooms	Butter
2 large onions	

Line a large pie dish with the pastry. Boil the macaroni, drain and add the chopped chicken livers. Fry the mushrooms and onions and add with the well-beaten eggs to the macaroni mixture ; season and pour into the lined pie dish. Cover with grated Parmesan cheese and knobs of butter and bake in a hot oven (450° F., mark 8) for 30–40 minutes, or until the top is well browned. Serve with a good hot tomato sauce —and if wished with grated Parmesan cheese.

This is a most popular dish in Malta. The savoury ingredients can be varied according to taste and availability ; minced chicken or pork and fried aubergine or tomatoes can replace the livers and mushrooms ; sheep's brains are some-times included.

MEAT OLIVES

1½ lb. rump steak	2 eggs
½ lb. minced meat	Deep fat for frying
1 cupful breadcrumbs	Tomato sauce
2 tbsps. chopped parsley	A bay leaf
Pepper	1 tin of peas
Salt	A little wine
1 slice of ham or bacon	

Cut the steak in largish slices ; if it is not tender enough, beat it a little with a rolling pin.

Prepare the filling as follows : Fry the minced meat. Mix the breadcrumbs, parsley, pepper, salt and chopped ham or bacon together and add the fried minced meat ; bind with the eggs. Lay out the slices of steak and spread about 2 tbsps. of this mixture on each. Roll up and tie round with a piece of fibrous celery stalk or string. Fry in deep fat. Meanwhile prepare a good sauce, using onions and tomatoes or tomato paste.

When the meat olives are done, add the tomato sauce, a bay leaf, a tin of peas and a dash of wine and let simmer. These beef olives may be served

as a second dish to spaghetti—use the tomato sauce from the cooked beef olives.

FRIED RUMP STEAK

Beat the rump steak well and leave it for 2 hours soaking in olive oil. Fry in butter and serve with fried onions and melted butter with chopped parsley.

TRIPE

1 lb. tripe	1 tbsp. tomato paste
Onions	3 oz. grated cheese
Cooking oil (best	Fancy pasta
quality)	1 egg
Chopped parsley	Lemon juice

Wash the tripe thoroughly, cut into small pieces and boil in salted water.

Peel and chop the onions and fry in oil ; add the chopped parsley. Dissolve the tomato paste in a little hot water and add ; allow to simmer, then add the boiled tripe with the grated cheese and water to cover. (The water in which tripe was boiled may be used.) Simmer. Meanwhile take the rest of the water in which tripe was boiled, bring to the boil and add some fine pasta in the shape of small stars, fine rings, etc. Beat an egg and add to this " soup." Before serving soup, squeeze in some lemon juice. Serve the soup as a first dish and the cooked tripe as a second dish.

TUNNY FISH STEW

Cut the tunny fish in slices or thick pieces, roll in flour and fry in hot oil. When done, remove from the pan and keep hot.

Chop 1 onion and fry ; when tender add a clove of garlic and some peeled and sliced tomatoes and simmer. Add some olives and capers and finally add the fried pieces of tunny fish ; simmer until these are thoroughly cooked. A dash of wine added whilst the stew is simmer-ing will improve the flavour.

LAMPUKA PIE
(MEDITERRANEAN FISH PIE)

1 lampuka	1 cauliflower, cooked
Seasoned flour	and divided up
Some cooking oil	6 olives
2 onions	Shortcrust pastry
4 tomatoes	Capers
Parsley	

Cut off the head and tail of a fair-sized lampuka and cut the rest of the fish in rather thick slices ; dip in seasoned flour and fry lightly—on no account must they be overcooked. (The head and tail may be used for fish soup.) Fry the chopped onions, add the tomatoes and let simmer. Add the cooked cauliflower sprigs, parsley, olives (whole, or stoned and chopped) and capers and let simmer.

Grease a pie dish and line with pastry. Remove the fish mixture from the heat and let cool a little. Remove the backbone from the lampuka and place the fish in the pie dish, then add the vegetable mixture to cover the fish; cover with pastry. Bake in a moderate oven (350° F., mark 4) until the pastry is a pale golden colour.

IMBULJUTA
(CHESTNUT SOUP)

½ lb. peeled chestnuts	1 bar plain chocolate
Rind of 1 orange	2–3 cloves
Rind of 1 lemon	A little ground spice
1 nutmeg	A pinch of ground cin-
4 tbsps. fine chocolate	namon
powder	2 tbsps. good wine or
8 tbsps. brown sugar	1 tbsp. rum
2 tbsps. caster sugar	

Scald the peeled chestnuts overnight and remove any brownish skin left on them. Place in a pot or casserole, add all other ingredients (except the wine or rum) and simmer until the chestnuts are tender. Add the rum before removing from the heat. Before serving, remove the orange and lemon rind and cloves.

It is most important that chestnuts are well covered with water before setting to boil—this delicious juice adds much to the flavour of this recipe.

CASATELLA
(COTTAGE CHEESE SWEET)

1 large sponge cake or 4	Finely grated rind of 1
small ones	lemon
Milk	Maraschino or sherry
3 oz. ground almonds	Glacé cherries
½ lb. rikotta	Pistachio nuts

Soak the cake in milk. Add the ground almonds and rikotta and mix thoroughly. Add the lemon rind and finally the Maraschino or sherry. Decorate with glacé cherries and pistachio nuts.

TORTA TAL-BAJD UL-GOBON
(CHEESE PIE)

½ lb. rikotta (according	Peas (tinned or cooked
to size of pie)	fresh)
Milk	Grated cheese
2–3 eggs	Puff or shortcrust
Pepper and salt	pastry
Finely chopped parsley	Milk or egg to glaze

Mix the rikotta with some milk and add the beaten eggs, pepper, salt, parsley and peas. Mix thoroughly, then top with grated cheese.

Line a greased casserole with pastry, fill with the rikotta mixture, and cover with a layer of pastry. Decorate the top of the pie with the pastry trimmings. Brush top of pie with milk or beaten egg and bake in a moderately hot oven (400 F., mark 6) until the pie is a pale golden colour.

XKUNVAT
(PASTRY KNOTS)

10 oz. flour	Deep oil for frying
1 tbsp. sugar	Honey
A knob of butter	Chopped chocolate to
2 egg yolks	decorate
1 small glass anisette	

A special Maltese sweet—made of pastry dipped into or smeared with honey and spiced with anisette.

Mix thoroughly together the flour, sugar and butter; add the egg yolks and the anisette, mix into a dough and knead well. Roll out and leave to set for a few hours. Roll the pastry out very finely, cut into long strips, curl into knots and fry in deep oil until golden-brown in colour. When done remove from the pan and drain on thick kitchen paper. Finally and whilst still hot, pour honey on each strip and decorate with chopped chocolate and *kosbor* (" hundreds and thousands ").

QAGHAQ TAL-QASTANIJA BIL-CHASEL
(HONEY RINGS)
For the Pastry

1½ lb. flour	¼ lb. lard
¼ lb. margarine	Water to mix
¼ lb. sugar	¼ lb. semolina

For the Filling

2 cups honey or treacle	1 tsp. bicarbonate of
2 cups water	soda
Pulp of 2 tangerines or	1 tot anisette
1 orange	2 cups sugar
4 tsps. fine cocoa	2 tsps. ground spice
powder	

This is a special sweet for Christmas. Place in a deep pan all pastry ingredients with the exception of the semolina and bring to the boil; stir in the semolina very gently and cook, stirring once or twice. When the mixture thickens, remove from the heat and allow to cool, then prepare the Honey Rings as follows: Roll out the pastry into long strips not less than 2 inches wide, put some filling along the centre of each and roll the pastry over the filling.

Cut the filled pastry into lengths and form into rings. Slit the top of the rings at intervals. Put in a floured oven tin and bake in a moderately hot oven (425° F., mark 7). When rings are golden in colour and the filling seeps through the slits, remove from the oven.

BISKUTTINI TAR-RAHAL
(FARM BISCUITS)

3 eggs
½ lb. sugar
1 tsp. baking powder
1 lb. flour
½ tsp. ground spice

A good pinch of cinnamon and of ground cloves
Orange-flower water
Milk if necessary

Beat the eggs well, add the sugar and continue beating. Mix the baking powder with the flour, add the spices and add this mixture to the beaten eggs and sugar. Form into a dough and add the orange-flower water. If the dough is stiff, soften by adding a little milk. Form the mixture into round biscuit shapes, place on a floured tin and bake in a moderately hot oven (400° F., mark 6) until a pale golden-brown. Do not leave too long in oven as this may harden them too much.

When exposed to the air, these " Village " or " Farm Biscuits " harden and form delicious crunchy cookies.

PASTIZZI
(CHEESE CAKES)

2 eggs
¾ lb. rikotta
Salt and pepper

Milk if required
Puff pastry

Beat the eggs and mix with the rikotta. Add salt, pepper and milk (optional). If mixture is considered thin do not add any milk; 1 tbsp. cornflour would help to thicken it.

Roll the pastry into a rather wide strip and place the mixture, 1 tbsp. at a time, at intervals along it. Using a knife or pastry cutter (with a plain edge) cut into required sizes, being careful that each portion contains the necessary filling. Turn the sides of the pastry strip on to the filling, but do not cover the centre part; roll both ends into a taper by twisting the pastry at each end. Put in a greased and floured shallow tin, allowing a space between them, and bake in a moderately hot oven (400° F., mark 6).

THE sea lies all around Norway so it is hardly surprising that fish plays a very large part in Norwegian diet. There is an abundance of cod, herring and other fish and Norwegian housewives have evolved hundreds of delicious ways of serving fish hot, cold, cooked and raw. It is made not only into hearty main dishes, appetising fish puddings and soufflés, but served too in smoked or salted form; shell fish also figure prominently in the smørgaas, or hors d'œuvre, which are so typically Scandinavian. Fish is often displayed in the markets swimming in tanks of water and the housewife can choose her own fish and be sure that it is fresh. In fact, the Norwegians prefer their fish either straight from the sea or else in a state of decay: a favourite dish is trout which has been kept in salt for months until it is really " high."

The majority of Norwegians lead tough, open-air lives as fishermen, farmers or lumberjacks and to meet their needs, Norwegian food is sustaining, plain and plentiful, the housewives using large quantities of excellent home-grown produce. Most people rear their own chickens and have ample supplies of eggs, fruit and vegetables, milk, butter and cream.

Meat is not a commonplace in Norway and is rarely served more than once a week or so. Pork, reindeer and kid are all popular; smoked, salted and dried meats are all widely used. Most housewives, even in the towns, buy half a pig at Christmas-time and prepare various cold meats and brawns from it, as well as the traditional Christmas joint of roast pork. Smoked reindeer tongues are very popular and considered a great delicacy.

Norwegian dairy farms provide a large quantity of cheese, which is almost a staple food. Many different varieties are made, but the most universally popular is *Gjetost*, a hard brown cheese found everywhere in the country.

A Norwegian breakfast often consists of porridge, milk, various kinds of bread, cheese, jam, marmalade and coffee. Sometimes eggs are also served. Lunch is generally a selection of smörrebröd or open sandwiches and the evening dinner is a hearty meal, with a dessert of pancakes, rice puddings or fruit. Norwegian berries grow in great abundance and raspberries, strawberries, cranberries and blueberries are all picked during the summer and preserved for winter use.

Finland has a very similar cuisine with again the emphasis on fish, smoked, fried and salted. Reindeer meat is often served and other game, including wild duck, helps to add interest to the menus. Fruit is scarce and expensive, except for the cranberries and small yellow raspberries that grow freely. Finnish farmers make a great deal of cheese, which is eaten with the dark, heavy bread and a glass of milk or buttermilk.

Norway
and
Finland

Norway

ØLLEBRØD
(BEER BREAD SOUP)

Put 1 pint of Pilsner or light beer in a saucepan with ½ pint water, ½ gill cream, the yolks of 2 eggs and sugar to taste. Place over a low heat and whisk until very light and frothy. Remove from the heat just before it reaches boiling point and serve with diced fried bread. This is often served after salted herrings.

LAKS
(BOILED SALMON)

Clean the fish without cutting along the belly, wash and dry well. An oblong fish pan or kettle with a removable perforated rack is recommended for cooking salmon. Lower into the boiling salted water (6 oz. salt to 3 quarts water) and let it simmer gently. Allow 15 minutes for every 2 lb. for a large, thick fish. Remove it on the rack, drain and transfer carefully to a serving dish. Serve with parsley, butter and cucumber salad. Salmon may be cut in slices and cooked but is then much drier; a hollandaise sauce makes a good accompaniment.

RISTET LAKS ELLER ØRRET
(FRIED SALMON OR TROUT)

Cut salmon in finger-thick slices; small trout should be left whole. Place on a dish and sprinkle with a mixture of 2 tbsps. olive or other vegetable oil, 2 tbsps. vinegar and 1 tbsp. fish stock; leave for 2 hours. Brush over with lightly beaten egg, coat in fine breadcrumbs to which a little salt and pepper have been added and fry in smoking hot butter. Serve with parsley butter.

RAKØRRET
(FERMENTED TROUT)

This is a national dish, much appreciated in Norway. The trout are preserved in this manner at the end of August or beginning of September, when they are fat, and are ready to eat in about 3 months, when they are served cold in fillets with wholemeal bread or crispbread and butter. Use small, fresh, river trout about 1 lb. in weight. Clean them well and place in salted water (1 tsp. salt to 1 pint water) for 2–3 hours. Scrape off the scales and slime under running water with the help of a sharp knife and clean the inside of each fish well. Place the fish in a wide-mouthed stone jar or small wooden barrel so that the belly of every fish faces upwards. Sprinkle a handful of coarse salt and a little sugar between the layers. Place a few pieces of wood over the trout, with a heavy weight or stone on top and put a lid over the jar. Store in a cold place.

ØRRET
(POACHED TROUT)

Prepare trout—fresh-water or sea—in the same way as salmon. The trout fisher—an expert on the subject—never washes the fish, as it is liable to become soft. Remove the head, draw out the entrails and use a long, thin knife to loosen the tissue covering the bone and sides of the belly. Clean, then dry well with absorbent paper. Stuff a clean piece of absorbent paper in the belly and let it remain until the fish is to be cooked. Barely cover the fish with hot (not boiling) salted water and simmer gently for 10–12 minutes. Serve with parsley butter, cooked potatoes and cucumber salad.

SPICED HERRINGS

2 salted herrings	4 allspice
¼ pint tarragon vinegar	2 bay leaves
2–3 tbsps. sugar	1 pickled gherkin
¼ pint tomato juice	1 small onion
4 cloves	

Soak the herrings overnight in cold water. Mix the remaining ingredients to make a marinade and leave to stand for a few hours. The next day, clean and fillet the herrings, cut the fillets into ½-inch slices and pour the marinade over them. Leave until the next day and serve chilled. Garnish with onion, dill or chives.

BAKED PIKE WITH ANCHOVIES

2–2¼ lb. pike	Beaten egg
2 tbsps. salt	Breadcrumbs
1 tin anchovy fillets	Fish stock or milk
Butter	

Scale and clean the fish, but leave the head on. Rub the pike well with salt. Cut slits across the back of the fish about 1 inch apart and place an anchovy fillet in each cut. Coat the fish with egg and crumbs, dot with small pieces of butter and bake in a moderate oven (350° F., mark 4) for 20–30 minutes, basting frequently with a little fish stock or milk. Serve with boiled potatoes and horseradish butter (see below).

HORSERADISH BUTTER

Grate some horseradish, season with salt and pepper and cover with lemon juice. Melt some butter (about 2 oz.) and immediately before serving add the butter to the horseradish.

53

MACKEREL IN CREAM SAUCE

4 mackerel	Salt
A bunch of parsley	$\frac{1}{4}$ pint water
A little butter	$\frac{1}{4}$ pint sour cream
2 tbsps. flour	

Wash the mackerel, fillet them and then sprinkle the fillets with chopped parsley and a few flakes of butter. Roll up the fillets and tie them with string, toss them in flour and fry in a saucepan until they are brown. Add salt to taste, water and sour cream and let them simmer gently in a covered pan for 10 minutes. Remove the string from the fillets and serve them with the liquid poured over.

PICKLED SMELTS

2 lb. smelts	2 tsps. salt
Dill	1 bay leaf
$\frac{1}{2}$ pint white vinegar	$1\frac{1}{2}$ oz. gelatine
$\frac{1}{2}$ pint water	Hard-boiled egg
6 peppercorns	Tomato

Clean, bone and halve each fish, then roll up with a piece of dill in each and place the rolls in a fireproof dish. Simmer together the vinegar, water, fish bones and seasonings to make stock. Cover the fish rolls with a little water, add a bay leaf and bake in a moderate oven (350° F., mark 4) for about 15 minutes and leave to cool. Make up the strained stock to $1\frac{1}{2}$ pints and dissolve the gelatine in it. Mask a mould with a little of the jelly and arrange the rolls attractively, decorating with sliced egg, tomato, dill, etc. Fill up with stock and leave to set. Serve as hors d'œuvre.

PLUKFISK
(FISH AND POTATOES)

1 lb. cooked potatoes	$\frac{3}{4}$ pint white sauce
1 lb. boiled fish	Salt, pepper and nutmeg

Chop the potatoes and the boiled fish into small pieces and cook for a few minutes in the white sauce. Season with salt, pepper and nutmeg and serve hot, dredged with a little more nutmeg.

FISKEGRATIN
(FISH SOUFFLÉ)

Leftover cooked fish, fresh or smoked, may be used for this dish. Allow 4–6 oz. for an average-sized soufflé. Prepare a good thick white sauce with 4 oz. butter, 3 oz. flour and a little less than 1 pint milk; add a little salt (if unsalted fish is used) and a dash of pepper. Flake the fish finely and add to the sauce, together with a little powdered mace or grated nutmeg; cool. Stir in 4–5 egg yolks and the stiffly whipped egg whites. Pour into a greased fireproof dish, cover with a good layer of grated breadcrumbs (made from oven-dried bread), dot with butter and bake in a moderate oven (350° F., mark 4) for about 30 minutes. Serve at once, with melted butter or soft butter vigorously beaten; if spice is not used in the soufflé, finely chopped parsley may be added to the butter.

FISKEFARSE
(MINCED FISH)

Fresh haddock is the fish which lends itself best to made-up fish dishes. Remove all skin and bone, then pass the fish through the mincer 7 times. To 2 lb. fish allow 2 tbsps. salt and 2 tbsps. potato flour or cornflour, which should be added gradually during the mincing. Stir or beat the fish in a large earthenware bowl, adding about 2 pints milk, very gradually to begin with and increasing the amount until all is thoroughly absorbed. Place the minced fish in a greased fireproof dish, cover and steam for about 1 hour, or shape into small balls and cook carefully for a few minutes in slightly salted water. The mixture may also be shaped into flat cakes and fried in butter.

DYRESTEK
(ROAST VENISON)

Venison is usually the meat of the reindeer, but young elk is also a delicacy. Wash the meat well in tepid water. If frozen it should be immersed in cold water for 3–4 hours. Venison tends to be rather dry and should preferably be pot-roasted, which helps to keep it tender and juicy, but it may also be roasted in the oven. A 6-lb. haunch of venison requires 3–4 hours cooking. Dry the meat well, lard or stuff it with pork fat by piercing the meat and pressing in pieces of fat; rub in a little salt. Roast in a slow oven (325° F., mark 2) allowing 25 minutes per lb. A sour cream or cranberry sauce may be served with it.

RYPE
(BRAISED PTARMIGAN)

2 ptarmigans	2 tbsps. cream or top of
A 2-oz. slice of	the milk
fresh pork	Salt to taste
2 oz. butter	A slice of goat cheese
$\frac{1}{8}$ pint boiling water	(preferably Norwegian)

Clean the birds and place the pork over the breasts, securing it with skewers. Brown the birds gently in some of the fat in a saucepan, turning them till nicely browned all over and adding a little boiling water (about $\frac{1}{8}$ pint altogether) from time to time. Take care not to burn them and add 1 tsp. fat now and then—about 2 oz. in all. After 1 hour add 2 tbsps. cream and cook gently for another $\frac{1}{2}$–$\frac{3}{4}$ hour, adding the salt and cheese.

Keep the cooked birds hot while making the sauce in the same pan. Mix the remaining cream and fat and add $\frac{1}{8}$ pint boiling water, stir and cook till smooth.

Serve the birds in a dish, with vegetables.

ROAST STUFFED DUCK OR GOOSE

Singe and clean the bird and season the inside. Stuff with 1 lb. of apples, cooked, and 1 lb. of prunes, cooked and stoned. Sew up, truss and roast in the usual way. When it is almost done, baste the bird with 3–4 tbsps. cold water and leave the oven door open (this should make the skin brittle). Arrange the bird on a hot platter and serve garnished with halved baked apples stuffed with prunes. Red cabbage (see next page) and apple sauce are often served as accompaniments.

FAR I KAL
(MUTTON AND CABBAGE)

64 As soon as the autumn slaughtering of sheep takes place, Norwegian housewives prepare this popular national dish.

2 lb. lamb or mutton breast and/or shoulder	1 oz. butter Flour
4 lb. white winter cabbage	1 tbsp. peppercorns

Chop the meat into suitable serving pieces. Prepare the cabbage by removing the thick stalk and cutting it into rough cubes about an inch thick. (Allow twice as much cabbage as meat.)

Melt 1 oz. butter in a large, thick-bottomed saucepan, sprinkle with flour; add the cabbage and mutton in alternate layers, sprinkling each with salt and a little flour and adding the peppercorns here and there. Pour on boiling water until it reaches about one-third of the way up the contents of the pan. Simmer slowly for 2–3 hours, stirring occasionally to prevent burning. (About 4–6 servings.)

It is quite common to prepare sufficient for two dinners as this dish loses nothing in being heated a second time—on the contrary, many people hold that the second serving is better.

FENELAR
(CURED SMOKED LEG OF MUTTON)

This is prepared towards the end of the autumn season and is then ready for eating 7 to 8 months later.

Mix 5 handfuls of coarse salt, 1 tbsp. saltpetre and 2 tbsps. sugar. Work this mixture well into a large leg of mutton or lamb (6–8 lb.); place on a dish and as the mixture dissolves, scoop it up with a spoon and drip it over the meat at intervals during 3–4 days. Dry the meat well and have it lightly smoked, then hang in a dry and airy place until it is cured; it will shrink to about half the original weight.

When the mutton is ready, it should be cut in thin slices (remove the outer fat edge as it is sometimes slightly rancid) and served with fried eggs, or as a main dish with new spring vegetables, new potatoes and fresh butter. Alternatively it may be used after hanging for only 2 months, when it should be cooked whole and eaten hot with vegetables.

SPEKESKINKE
(CURED HAM)

In Norway this is usually prepared in November and is ready at the beginning of June.

Take a leg of pork weighing 10–16 lb. and work in a mixture of 3 tbsps. salt, 1 tbsp. sugar and 1 tsp. saltpetre. Leave for 3 days. Steep for 6 weeks in the following brine; 8 quarts water cooked with 3 lb. salt, 1 lb. syrup, 10 oz. sugar and 5 oz. saltpetre. Remove, hang to dry for 2 days and have it smoked; hang in a dry, airy place. Slice very thinly and serve with spring vegetables. It is also excellent for sandwiches. Do not be put off by the raw appearance of this meat—it is excellent food, though it does require some chewing.

CHRISTMAS HAM

10–12 lb. ham	1 egg white
2 bay leaves	2 tbsps. mustard
10 peppercorns	1 tbsp. sugar
5 allspice	Breadcrumbs
Seasoning	Butter for piping

Soak the ham overnight. Put into a pan of cold water, bring to the boil, then throw away the water. Fill up the pan again, add the herbs and seasoning and simmer for 3 hours. Remove the skin, trim and leave to cool for 1 hour. Brush the ham over with a mixture of egg white, mustard and sugar, then sprinkle with breadcrumbs. Bake in a moderate oven (350° F., mark 4) until golden-brown (about $\frac{1}{2}$ hour). When cold, decorate with piped butter.

LOIN OF PORK WITH PRUNES

Get the butcher to chine the meat and remove all the bones. Soak $\frac{1}{2}$ lb. prunes in hot water. Spread the meat flat on a board and sprinkle with salt, pepper and ground ginger. Arrange the prunes down the centre of the meat and fold over, make into a roll and tie with string. Melt some pork dripping in a pan, brown the meat on all sides, cover with stock and simmer gently over a low heat, or cook in a moderately hot oven (400° F., mark 6) for 2 hours, or until the meat is tender. When it is cooked, place it on a hot dish and serve sliced, with browned potatoes, prunes and apple sauce.

RAGOÛT OF BEEF

3 lb. beef	1 small onion, finely
Salt	chopped
Pepper	1 quart stock or water
5–6 oz. fat	1 bay leaf
1½ oz. flour	4 black peppercorns

Slice the beef across the grain, beat well, sprinkle with seasoning and brown in 3–4 oz. fat. To make a sauce, brown the remaining fat and flour slowly, fry the onion and gradually add the stock or water. Now put in the meat, with the bay leaf and peppercorns, cover, and cook slowly for 1–1½ hours. Serve with vegetables.

LIVER PÂTÉ

¾ lb. pork fat	4 oz. flour
1 lb. calf's liver	3 eggs
¼ lb. veal	½ pint cream
1 small onion	3–4 tsps. salt
8 anchovy fillets	¼ tsp. pepper

Line an oblong tin with thin slices of pork fat. Cut up the washed and dried liver, the veal, the rest of the fat, the onion and anchovies, then put all these through a mincer three times. Make a batter with the flour, eggs and cream, then slowly add the liver mixture. Season, put in the tin, cover with greased paper and place in another tin containing a little water. Bake in a moderate oven (350° F., mark 3) for 1½ hours. Unmould when cold and serve sliced.

PIG'S HEAD CHEESE

½ a pig's head (about 5 lb.)	1 small onion and
2 lb. lean pork	carrot
2 lb. veal	Salt and pepper
2 quarts stock	½–¾ lb. pork fat
1½ tbsps. mixed herbs	Spices—cinnamon,
6–8 peppercorns	allspice, ground
2 bay leaves	cloves, ginger

Wash the pig's head and singe off the hair. Wash the teeth thoroughly and remove the ears, then soak the head in cold salt water for 12 hours. Put into a large pan with the pork, veal, stock, herbs, vegetables, 2 tsps. salt and ½ tsp. pepper and bring to the boil. Simmer gently until the meats are tender—1½–2 hours. Remove the meats and cut the meat off the pig's head, then leave to get quite cold. Cut all the meats into slices. Spread a cloth wrung out in hot water in a deep bowl and line it with a thin layer of pork fat. Arrange the meat in layers of lean and fat, sprinkling each layer with salt, pepper and a few spices and cover with some more pork fat. Pull the cloth tightly together and tie securely with string, place in a pan of stock and cook for 20 minutes. Remove from the pan, drain on a plate, cover with a board and a weight and leave for 24 hours. Serve sliced for smörrebröd or with pickled beetroot.

BOILED RED CABBAGE

2 oz. butter	1 chopped onion
1 red cabbage	Juice of lemon
2 tbsps. syrup	¼ pint red wine
2 peeled and sliced apples	Salt

Melt the butter in a pan and add the shredded cabbage and the syrup; brown over a low flame, stirring constantly. Add the remaining ingredients, cover the pan and simmer gently for 1½–2 hours, stirring occasionally. Season to taste.

STUFFED CABBAGE

Plunge a large white winter cabbage (2–4 lb.) into boiling water. Remove a few of the outer leaves, then make a hole in the cabbage by removing the thick stalk and some of the heart and fill with forcemeat. Place the outer leaves over the hole and bind in place with thin string. Cook slowly in lightly salted water for about 2 hours. Serve with white sauce.

65

MELKERINGE
(NORWEGIAN " JUNKET ")

1 tbsp. sour cream	A few sweet rusks
1½ pints best quality whole milk	Caster sugar

Mix the cream gradually with the milk and put into a glass dish (or individual dishes). Leave overnight in a cool place; in the morning it should be set like English junket, with cream on top. Place on ice to get thoroughly cold. Sprinkle with rusk crumbs and caster sugar.

CHOCOLATE CREAM DESSERT

1 tbsp. caster sugar	2 oz. plain chocolate
2 tbsps. apricot jam	3 tbsps. whipped
3 eggs	cream
¾ pint milk	

Spread the apricot jam over the bottom of a

soufflé dish. Break 2 eggs and 1 extra yolk into a bowl and cream with the sugar. Pour on the hot milk, blend and strain into the soufflé dish.

Cover with a piece of greased paper or aluminium foil, put in a steamer and steam for about 1 hour until firm and set; leave to cool. Whip the remaining egg white till sufficiently stiff to stand in points and fold into the whipped cream. Grate half the chocolate over the custard, then pile the whipped cream on top and grate the remaining chocolate over it.

TYTTEBAER OG RIS
(CRANBERRIES AND RICE)

Cranberries are preserved in the autumn by stirring with sugar for a couple of hours (allow ½ lb. sugar to 1 lb. berries). Fill into jars and cover. These will keep indefinitely if sound fruit is used and the sugar is stirred until dissolved. Serve with boiled rice. Cook this in plenty of fast-boiling water for 15 minutes; drain, dry and cool. Milk and/or cream may be served separately.

EGGDOSIS
(BRANDIED EGG NOGG)

Beat for ½ hour the yolks of 4–8 eggs and 1 egg white, together with 1 level tbsp. sugar for each egg yolk used. Serve in individual glasses with 1 tsp. of brandy in each; hand small macaroons or meringues separately.

PANNEKAKER
(PANCAKES WITH RED-CURRANT JELLY)

Beat 4 eggs well with 4½ oz. plain flour, ½ pint milk and a pinch of salt and sugar; let the mixture stand for a few hours. Add 2–3 tbsps. water just before using. Heat a little butter in an iron frying pan until it smokes slightly and pour in just enough mixture to cover the surface of the pan; if necessary, add a little more butter to the pan when turning the pancake. Hand red-currant jelly or raspberry jam separately.

LINSER
(SMALL CREAM TARTS)

Make a sweet pastry with ½ lb. flour, 6½ oz. butter, 2 oz. sugar and 2 egg yolks; roll out thinly and with a pastry cutter, stamp out rounds the size of your tart tins, with slightly smaller ones for the covers. Grease the tart tins and line with the pastry rounds. Put in a little vanilla-flavoured confectioner's custard and cover with a lid of pastry. Bake in a hot oven (450° F., mark 8) until they are nicely brown. Serve lukewarm.

MOR MONSEN
(MOTHER MONSEN CAKES)

8 oz. butter	Coarsely chopped blanched
8 oz. sugar	almonds
5 eggs	Chopped stoned raisins or
8 oz. plain flour	currants

Beat the butter and sugar until white and creamy. Add the eggs one at a time and beat thoroughly; add the flour gradually. Grease a large shallow baking tin and sprinkle with flour. Pour in the mixture and smooth out with a spatula to a depth of ½ inch. Sprinkle thickly with coarsely chopped almonds and chopped stoned raisins or currants. Bake in a slow oven (300° F., mark 1) for 30–40 minutes; leave in the tin and while still warm cut into small diamonds with a sharp-pointed knife. Cool on a wire tray and store in an airtight tin.

FYRSTE KAKE
(PRINCE'S CAKE)

It is best to start preparing this early in the day. Using a very fine blade, mince 1 cup blanched almonds 3 times. Blend with ¾ cup icing sugar, ¼ cup egg whites (unbeaten), 1 egg, ¼ cup butter and 1½ tsps. almond essence. Refrigerate this paste.

Mix ½ cup butter, 3 tbsps. sugar and 1 egg (use an electric mixer, at medium speed, if available). Fold in 1½ cups sifted flour and chill for 15 minutes. Roll out two-thirds of this dough on lightly floured waxed paper into a round ⅛ inch thick. Fit into a 9-inch sandwich tin, carefully peeling off the paper, and if necessary levelling the top. Spread with ⅓ cup raspberry jam (optional), then with the almond paste. Roll out the remaining dough into an oblong ⅛ inch thick. With a pastry wheel, cut 6 strips about 8 inches by ¾ inch. Lay 3 strips 1¼ inches apart over the almond paste; lay the rest at right angles. Re-roll the pastry trimmings and cut 5 strips, 5 inches by ¾ inch. Place end to end against the inside edge of the tin; with the pastry wheel trim level with the top of the cake. Bake in a moderate oven (350° F., mark 4) for 45 minutes; cool in the tin, then lift out with a spatula and place on a cake rack until completely cold.

BIØTKAKE
(SOFT SPONGE CAKE)

Whisk 4 eggs together with ½ lb. sugar for ½ hour, or until the mixture is thick and creamy (an electric mixer will obtain this result in 5–10 minutes). Fold in 4½ oz. potato flour or cornflour and 4½ oz. plain flour, well mixed together, and finally add 1 tbsp. cold water.

Put into a round cake tin and bake in a slow oven (325° F., mark 2) for 40–50 minutes. Turn out and cool. Divide the cake into 3 layers; sprinkle each liberally with thin cream to which some sherry has been added, or use neat sherry. Sandwich the pieces together with thick layers of whipped cream and chopped almonds or walnuts, then cover the top and sides with a $\frac{1}{8}$-inch layer of marzipan.

Marzipan Icing : Whisk together 1 tsp. plain flour and 1 tbsp. milk in a small saucepan, bring to the boil, remove and cool, then stir in 5 drops of almond essence. Grind 6 oz. blanched sweet almonds, then grind them a second time with 1 lb. icing sugar. Mix well with the milk mixture until a sweet paste is formed. If desired, the marzipan may be coloured. Roll it out on a board, with the help of a little icing sugar, to a thickness of $\frac{1}{8}$ inch. Place it over the cake, allowing it to hang down over the sides and cover them completely. Decorate with flowers made from marzipan or with almonds or walnuts, according to which type of nut was used in the filling.

FØDSELSDAGSKRINGLE
(NORWEGIAN BIRTHDAY CAKE)

Mix 1 pint tepid milk with $3\frac{1}{2}$ oz. baker's yeast and stir in sufficient flour to form a light dough of a dropping consistency. Leave in a warm place until well risen. Sprinkle a handful of flour over a pastry board, tip the dough on to this and sprinkle a little flour over. Roll out very lightly and cover with $\frac{1}{2}$ lb. butter cut in thin slices (a cheese cutter or parer is admirable for this purpose). Using a palette knife, fold the dough in three so that the fat is enclosed, then roll out lightly again. Fold again in three, place in a bowl in a warm place and allow to prove for $\frac{1}{2}$ hour. Turn the dough on to the pastry board and divide in two, using the minimum of flour. Roll out one-half into a long strip about 5 inches broad and 18 inches long. Along this place a layer of thinly sliced apple rings, then sprinkle with sugar and cinnamon or a generous helping of stoned raisins and candied peel and the following filling :

Mince 4 oz. sweet almonds which have been washed and dried ; mince a second time with 4 oz. icing sugar ; add 1 egg or the stiffly beaten whites of 2 eggs.

Fold in both sides of the dough to cover the filling, giving the appearance of a long sausage. Place on a greased baking tray in a circle to form half of the kringle. Repeat the process with the other half and place it on the baking tray to complete the traditional shape of a figure eight with a straight back, the two ends crossing each other in the middle. Brush over with egg and milk and decorate. Bake in a moderately hot oven (425° F., mark 7) for about 15 minutes, then reduce to moderate (350° F., mark 4) and continue cooking for a further 20–30 minutes.

KRANSERKAKE
(RING CAKE)

1 lb. ground sweet almonds	1 lb. icing sugar
About 25 ground bitter almonds	3 egg whites
	Icing (see below)

Mix together the ground almonds and icing sugar and add 1 egg white. Set the mixture over a low heat until it is tepid, then add the other 2 egg whites, one at a time. Put the mixture in a forcing bag fitted with a fluted biscuit nozzle, the thickness of the middle finger. Pipe in rings on to greased baking trays ; the diameter of the largest should be about 10 inches and each subsequent ring must be $\frac{1}{4}$ inch less in diameter, down to the smallest of 2 inches diameter. Bake in a slow oven (300° F., mark 1) until a light golden-brown. Remove the rings and while they are still warm, mount one upon the other, the largest ring at the base and the whole forming a tower. It is customary to decorate by piping a thin line of white glacé icing in zig-zag lines all over the cake in an irregular design. (Make the icing from 3 oz. icing sugar, $\frac{1}{2}$ egg white and $\frac{1}{2}$ tsp. lemon juice.) Miniature crackers, marzipan flowers or sweets are fixed to the sides by means of lightly browned caramel. The cake is topped by a small national flag or with artificial or marzipan flowers.

JULEKAKE
(YULE BREAD)

$1\frac{1}{2}$ lb. plain flour	$1\frac{1}{2}$ oz. yeast
$4\frac{1}{2}$ oz. butter	$\frac{1}{2}$ pint milk
$3\frac{1}{2}$ oz. sugar	4 oz. seedless raisins
1 tsp. ground cardamom	4 oz. candied peel

Mix the flour, half the butter (melted), half the sugar and the cardamom in a bowl. Warm the milk slightly and add to the dry ingredients, together with the yeast. Beat the dough thoroughly with a large wooden spoon until smooth and even. Put to rise for about 20 minutes. Add the rest of the butter and sugar, the raisins and peel, then put to rise again for another 20 minutes. Divide in two and knead each portion on a lightly floured board in the shape of a long sausage. Turn in the two ends to the middle of the sausage, rounding the cake as you work so that it makes a solid, round mass. Stand it in a warm place to prove for a further

15 minutes. Brush with beaten egg and bake for 30–40 minutes in a hot oven (450° F., mark 8).

FRUIT AND NUT TWIST

1 lb. flour	2 oz. chopped nuts
2 tsps. salt	½ oz. yeast
2 oz. butter or lard	2 tsps. sugar
4 oz. dried fruit	½ pint warm milk
1 oz. chopped peel	Beaten egg

Sieve the flour and salt and rub in the fat. Add the fruit and peel and half the nuts. Cream the yeast and sugar, add half the milk and pour into the dry ingredients. Cover and leave in a warm place about ½ hour, then mix to a soft dough with the remaining milk and leave to rise for 1 hour. Knead, divide into three and form into equal length. Plait, seal the ends and prove on a greased tin till well risen. Bake for ¾ hour in a moderately hot oven (425° F., mark 7) for the first 10 minutes, then at 400° F. (mark 6). After 20 minutes, brush with egg and sugar and sprinkle with the remaining nuts.

SYRUP DIAMONDS

1 egg	8 oz. flour
2 oz. caster sugar	¾ tsp. ground ginger
2 oz. butter	½ tsp. baking powder
2 oz. syrup	Blanched almonds
2 tsps. brandy	

Whisk the egg and sugar. Warm the butter and syrup gently until the fat melts, then add to the egg and sugar and stir in the brandy. Sieve the flour, ginger and baking powder; make a well in the centre of the flour and add the egg mixture. Knead to a smooth dough, roll out thinly and cut into neat diamonds. Place half an almond in the centre of each and bake in a moderate oven (350° F., mark 4) for 20 minutes, until pale golden-brown.

BERLINERKRANSER
(COOKIE RINGS)

4 eggs	8 oz. plain flour
3½ oz. caster sugar	Egg white and granulated
8 oz. softened butter	sugar to finish

Hard-boil 2 eggs, cool and sieve the yolks. Add to the 2 whole eggs, with the sugar, and whisk together until beginning to thicken. Beat in alternately small portions of butter (not melted) and flour until the whole is a smooth paste. Put in a cool place until mixture is firm enough to handle—1–2 hours. Roll out portions lightly on a floured board into long, thin " snakes " the thickness of your little finger. Cut in lengths of 2–3 inches, join into rings, brush with egg white and dredge with granulated sugar. Bake on a greased tray in a moderate oven (350° F., mark 4) for 10–15 minutes. The cakes should remain yellowish in colour. Place on a wire rack to cool and crisp. Store in an airtight tin.

Note : A little grated orange rind gives added flavour. These are softish biscuits, perfect with coffee.

RØMMEVAFLER
(SOUR CREAM WAFFLES)

1 pint sour cream	12 oz. plain flour
½ pint milk	1½ oz. sugar
½ pint water	A pinch of salt

Beat together thoroughly and cook in a well-greased waffle iron.

FLATBRØD OG LEFSER
(FLAT BREAD AND " SOFT CAKES ")

Cook 3 lb. potatoes and mash them while still warm. Knead well with 1 lb. rye flour to a smooth paste, then leave till the following day. Roll out as thinly as possible to a round cake as large as your frying pan. Cook in the frying pan (or on an electric hot-plate) turning it over several times with a palette knife till well done. Place on paper to cool ; when ready the bread should be crisp.

To make Lefser (soft cakes) do not turn more than 2 or 3 times. Put the warm cake into a folded clean kitchen cloth. Make a paste of equal amounts of softened butter and sour cream and spread half one side of the cake ; dust with a little sugar, fold the unbuttered part over and cut into triangles. Keep the cakes in the cloth till served.

HJORTEKAK
(HARTSHORN RINGS)

4 egg yolks	½ tsp. ground cardamom
½ lb. sugar	1 lb. plain flour
2 egg whites	½ tsp. salt of hartshorn
¼ pint whipped cream	Deep fat for frying
2 oz. butter	

Beat the eggs and sugar for ½ hour and add the cream, the melted butter, cardamom and the flour, well mixed with the hartshorn salt. Leave in a cool place until the next day. Divide into workable portions and roll out into long, thin " snakes " the thickness of your little finger. Cut into lengths of 3–4 inches and tie the two ends as when beginning a granny knot. Fry carefully in boiling fat, about 6 at a time, until light brown. The fat must always be boiling or the cakes will absorb it and not become crisp as they should. Remove each batch and drain on absorbent paper. These cakes resemble small doughnut rings, but when cold they are quite firm and will keep well in an airtight tin. Two thin wooden sticks or twigs are handy for the purpose of turning the cakes in the fat and for removing them. Alternatively, use 1½ tsps. baking powder instead of salt of hartshorn, and cook the mixture at once.

TILSØRTE BONDEPIKER
(VEILED PEASANT GIRLS)

Peel, core and quarter 2 lb. apples, add sugar to taste but no water, and cook to a purée over a low heat. Melt 1 oz. butter in a frying pan, add 3 oz. oven-dried breadcrumbs, sprinkle with sugar and fry lightly to a golden-brown, taking care that the crumbs do not burn. Remove from the heat and stir well, then cool. Fill a bowl with alternate layers of breadcrumbs and apple purée and decorate with whipped cream. Alternatively, fill a greased fireproof dish with alternate layers of breadcrumbs and apple purée, sprinkle with sugar, dot with butter and bake in a moderate oven (350° F., mark 4) 40 minutes. Serve lukewarm, with whipped cream.

Note: Unlike the Danish version, this sweet is baked.

MEDALJONGER
(MEDALLIONS)

Rub ½ lb. butter into 1½ lb. flour and add ½ lb. sugar and 2 egg yolks; work well together. Roll out on a floured board ⅛ inch thick. Stamp out rounds with a wineglass or pastry-cutter and bake in a moderate oven (350° F., mark 4) until light brown. Spread a little thick vanilla cream on one biscuit of each pair and put the other on top. Decorate with glacé icing and top with a little jam or jelly.

CHRISTMAS BISCUITS

1 hard-boiled egg yolk	4 oz. unsalted butter
1 raw egg yolk	Egg white to glaze
4 oz. sugar	A few lumps of sugar
½ lb. flour	

Rub the hard-boiled egg yolk through a sieve into a basin, add the raw yolk and the sugar and stir for about 15 minutes. Add the flour and butter alternately and mix well, then divide into equal-sized portions. Form each piece into a long roll as thick as a pencil and make a circle with the ends crossed and sticking out. Beat the egg white very lightly and crush the lumps

of sugar finely. Dip the biscuits in the egg white, then in the crushed sugar, and bake them in a moderate oven (350° F., mark 4) till they are a pale golden colour.

SWEET CRANBERRY JUICE

3½ pints cranberries	Sugar
1¾ pints water	

Wash and clean the berries, put them into a preserving pan with the water, and boil until absolutely soft. Strain through a muslin bag into a basin. To each pint of juice add ¾ lb. sugar, boil for 10 minutes, skim well, fill into warm dry bottles, cork, and seal with white wax. Use to make jellies to serve as a sweet or with game, or serve the juice mixed with water, as a refreshing drink.

Finland

SILLILAATIKKO
(FISH AND POTATO CASSEROLE)

2 large salt herrings	2 tbsps. melted butter
1 lb. sliced boiled potatoes	3 eggs
	1 pint milk
1 tbsp. chopped onion or spring onion	½ tsp. pepper
	1 oz. dried breadcrumbs

Soak the fish for 6 hours, skin and bone them and cut in long strips. Butter a baking dish and put in a layer of potato, then one of herring, with a little onion; repeat, finishing with a potato layer and pour melted butter over the top. Beat the eggs, add the milk and pepper, pour into the baking dish and sprinkle with breadcrumbs. Bake in a moderate oven (350° F., mark 4) for 30–40 minutes, or until browned. (These quantities make sufficient for 6 persons.)

Tinned salmon may be used instead of salt herring to make this dish.

FINNISH HERRING PIE

3 medium-sized or 2 large herrings	4 or 5 medium-sized potatoes
2 large onions	2 oz. butter
Fat for frying	Seasoning
4 tomatoes	¼ pint milk

Several hours before the dish is to be cooked, scale and bone the herrings and put to soak in salted water. Slice the onions and fry them lightly till golden-brown. Skin and slice the tomatoes. Peel the potatoes and cut into thin lengthwise slices. Put dabs of butter over the inside of a fireproof dish, then put in a layer of sliced potato, followed by layers of onion and tomato; season, then add fish and a top layer of potato. Bake in a moderately hot oven (400° F., mark 6) for 20 minutes, until brown on top. Add just a little milk to cover and cook in a moderate oven (350° F., mark 3) for a further 1 hour.

KARJALAN PIIRAKAT
(SAVOURY PATTIES)
For the Pastry

6 oz. flour	Salt
2 oz. fine oatmeal or rye flour	3 oz. butter or margarine

For the Filling

2 oz. rice	2 chopped hard-boiled eggs
About ½ pint milk	
Seasoning	

First make the filling. Wash the rice and cook in sufficient milk to give a stiff consistency. Season well, add the chopped hard-boiled eggs and allow to cool before using.

Now make the pastry. Sieve the flour into a bowl, add the oatmeal and a little salt, rub in the fat and mix to a stiff dough with water. Roll out to ¼ inch in thickness and stamp into rounds 6 inches in diameter. Place a little of the rice mixture in the centre of each round, fold the pastry over so that it very nearly meets in the centre and press down the edges with the fingers to seal and form a decoration. Bake in a moderately hot oven (425° F., mark 7) for 20–25 minutes. Serve hot with butter.

Rye flour is always used in Finland for this dish, and if it is obtainable it should be substituted for the oatmeal.

KALLALAATIKO
(PORK CASSEROLE)

68

4 pork chops	2 eggs
2 fresh herrings	1 pint milk
4 medium-sized potatoes	1 oz. flour
4 onions	Salt and pepper to taste
Butter	

Trim the pork chops; split and bone the herrings and cut off the heads and tails; peel the potatoes and onions and slice fairly thinly. Butter an ovenproof dish, put in a layer of potatoes, a layer of onion, then 2 pork chops, next 2 herring halves and then a further layer of potato and onion. Add the remaining pork chops and herring, fill in round the sides and cover the top with the rest of the onion and potato. Put a few small knobs of butter over the top. Cook, uncovered, in a moderate oven (350° F., mark 4) for 1 hour.

Beat the eggs with the milk, add the flour and seasonings and mix well to give a smooth blend, then pour the liquid over the mixture in the casserole. Return the dish to the oven and cook for a further ½ hour, until the custard topping is set.

MAKSALAATIKKO
(LIVER PUDDING)

¾ lb. liver	3 tbsps. butter
6 oz. rice	1 large egg
½ pint water	1½ tbsp. sugar
½ pint milk	3 tsps. salt
2 oz. seeded raisins	½ tsp. pepper
1 tbsp. minced onion	

Mince and pound the liver. (It may first be parboiled, to make this easier.) Make a porridge of the well-washed rice, the water and milk and cook for about 1 hour; when it is nearly done, add the raisins and put aside to cool. Brown the onion slightly in the butter and mix with the liver, beaten egg, sugar and seasonings. Combine the two mixtures thoroughly, pour into a buttered pie dish and bake in a slow oven (325° F., mark 2) for 1 hour. Serve with cranberry sauce, if available.

LAMMASKAALI
(CABBAGE AND LAMB HOT-POT)

2 lb. white cabbage	Seasoning
1 lb. best end of neck of lamb	Tomato purée

Wash the cabbage and chop it finely. Brown the meat on both sides in a saucepan without any extra fat, then add the finely chopped cabbage, seasoning, tomato purée and a very little water and simmer until the cabbage is quite transparent. Serve like Irish stew.

CASSEROLE OF SWEDES

1 lb. boiled or mashed yellow swedes	1 tsp. salt
	Pepper
3 oz. butter	1 cup soft bread-
2 large tbsps. golden syrup	crumbs
	2 eggs, beaten

Mix the swedes with most of the butter, the syrup, salt, pepper, three-quarters of the breadcrumbs and the eggs and whip the mixture. Put into a buttered casserole, sprinkle with the remaining breadcrumbs and bake in a moderate oven (350° F., mark 4) for 20–25 minutes, until the top is brown. Dot with a little butter before browning.

This is delicious served with roast pork or cold ham.

MAUSTEKAKKU
(SPICE CAKE)

½ lb. Demerara sugar	1 tsp. ground cinnamon
½ lb. melted butter	1 tsp. ground
3 eggs	cardamoms
3 oz. chopped almonds	½ pint cream
Grated orange peel	1½ tbsp. baking powder
1 tsp. ground cloves	¾ lb. flour

Grease and flour an 8-inch square tin. Add the sugar to the melted butter and whip until the mixture is light and fluffy. Beat in the eggs a little at a time and mix in the nuts, flavourings and cream. Sieve together the baking powder and flour and stir into the cake mixture. Bake for 1 hour in a moderate oven (350° F., mark 4).

This cake is similar to gingerbread.

WIENINLEIVAT
(FILLED PASTRIES)

1 oz. yeast	6 oz. butter or margarine
¼ pint milk	Filling (see below)
A pinch of salt	Egg to glaze
1 lb. plain bread flour	Glacé icing
2 eggs	Roasted, flaked, or
1 oz. sugar	chopped almonds

Break down the yeast with a little tepid milk. Add the salt to the flour and make a well in the centre. Beat the eggs and put them with the yeast and sugar into the centre of the flour. Gradually mix in the flour and beat the dough well, then leave in a warm place for 15 minutes, covered with a cloth. Roll out the dough fairly thinly on a floured board and place the butter or margarine in the centre. Fold the dough over the butter and give two " turns," as for puff pastry. Allow to stand for 10–15 minutes, then give two further turns, followed by another rest in a cool place.

Roll out the pastry ¼ inch thick and cut it into triangles, with bases measuring about 6½ inches. Roll a little of the filling into a sausage shape and place it near the base of one of the triangles. Commencing with the base of the triangle, roll it up, bend it round to form a crescent, and place on a greased baking sheet. Prove the crescents in a warm place for 20 minutes. Brush them with egg, and bake in a hot oven (450° F., mark 8) for 15–20 minutes, until golden-brown. Whilst they are still hot, brush them over with glacé icing and sprinkle with the nuts. Alternatively, the mixture may be made into twists and rings and when baked coated with the glacé icing and nuts.

Marzipan is often used for the filling, and is very good if flavoured with orange essence or mixed with a little grated orange rind and orange juice. A popular alternative is made by stewing cranberries with sugar to make a thick syrup ; the pulp is enclosed in small rounds or squares of pastry.

Other variations in fillings for these pastries will suggest themselves to cooks in this country, for instance, jam, or confectioner's custard or stewed fruit.

PAHKINAKAKKU
(NUT CAKE)

4 eggs	3 tbsps. flour
1½ tsps. vanilla essence	½ lb. finely chopped
1 tsp. grated lemon rind	walnuts
3 oz. sugar	A little butter
¼ tsp. salt	2 tbsps. breadcrumbs

Beat the egg yolks with the vanilla essence and gradually mix in the lemon rind, sugar and salt, beating thoroughly. Sprinkle the flour over the nuts and beat into the egg yolks. Stiffly beat the egg whites and fold into the mixture. Pour into a greased and crumbed loaf tin (9½ inches by 4 inches) and then bake for 1 hour in a moderate oven (375° F., mark 5). The cake may be iced or decorated with whipped cream.

PUOLUKKALIEMI
(CRANBERRY CREAM)

Stew 1 lb. cranberries with a little water, add sugar to taste, and sufficient water to make 1 pint of fruit and juice. Mix 2 oz. cornflour with a little cold water, and add this to the cooked cranberries. Bring to the boil, and boil for about 2 minutes, stirring all the time, then pour into a wetted mould and leave to set. Turn out, and decorate with cream. Alternatively, place the mixture in individual dishes, and serve hot with cream.

In Finland this sweet is made with lingenberries, a very small type of cranberry. Redcurrants may also be used to make a similar cold sweet.

Poland

POLISH cookery has evolved slowly and is an interesting combination of Eastern, Western and native traditions and preferences. Two cuisines grew up side by side; the extravagant, rich food of court and diplomatic circles and the simple, hearty fare of the peasants. Over the years each one has lent something to the other.

The Polish aristocracy was noted for its lavish hospitality and many new and exotic fruits and vegetables were introduced by visiting diplomats and prelates who brought with them their own staffs of servants, their own preferences in food and even their own plants and seeds. Great feasts and entertainments were the order of the day and enormous quantities of food were cooked and consumed.

At the same time existed an extremely poor peasant class, who had to rely for palatable meals on ingenuity and the use of natural products, vegetables and flavourings. Dill and mushrooms (particularly dried mushrooms), were extremely popular, while fish and crayfish were often used. These typically Polish ingredients appear throughout the country and, together with Polish smoked ham and sour cream, give much individuality to the cooking.

The Polish people have always been renowned for their cordiality, courtesy, love of old traditions and spontaneous hospitality. A party is the occasion for good eating and many of the most interesting dishes are those traditionally associated with a feast day or holiday.

The countryside of Poland provides foodstuffs of excellent quality; sausages and hams are produced from grain- and milk-fattened pigs; poultry includes turkeys and fine fat geese; the lakes and rivers abound in fresh-water fish, trout and carp; mushrooms are so plentiful that they are dried and exported. The fertile fields produce vegetables of all kinds and large quantities of stone fruit, much of which is made into delicious jams and preserves that can often be bought in continental shops over here.

Poland

MUSHROOM AND BARLEY SOUP

6 cups soup stock made with bone and meat scraps
1½ tsps. butter
2–3 medium potatoes, cooked and diced
½ bouillon cube
1 tbsp. chopped parsley
6 mushrooms
6 green beans
Salt and pepper to taste
½ cup barley, cooked separately

Make some soup stock, adding ½ bouillon cube, mushrooms and green beans. Cook barley separately in covered saucepan, adding a little of the stock as necessary to separate grains. When done, add butter, stir well, pour into the stock and let it boil up. Remove bones and serve the rest without straining, adding diced potatoes and chopped parsley. Serves 6.

SAUERKRAUT SOUP

1 lb. sauerkraut
1 bay leaf (optional)
½ lb. pork meat (head or rump) marrow bone
6 peppercorns
2 strips bacon, or equivalent amount of salt pork, diced
8 cups cold water
1 medium onion (preferably baked)
½ onion, chopped
1 celery root
1 tbsp. flour, browned
1 parsley root
Salt and pepper to taste
1 parsnip
2 carrots
1 lump sugar (optional)
1–2 celery stalks
1–2 frankfurters or several slices salami, diced (optional)
4–6 dried mushrooms
A few sprigs of parsley

Cover the sauerkraut, marrow bone and meat with cold water. Boil and skim. Add browned onion, the celery, parsley, parsnip, carrots, celery, mushrooms and herbs ; let them simmer, skimming as necessary, for at least 2 hours. When the meat is soft, remove from bones and cut into small pieces ; cut mushrooms into strips. Remove marrow from the marrow bones. Strain soup or not, according to preference. Return the meat, mushrooms and marrow to the pot. In heavy skillet brown the bacon or salt pork together with chopped onion and browned flour, adding stock a little at a time until lumps are dissolved. Add to the soup and boil up once. Season to taste, adding sugar if soup is too sharp. Add diced sausage if desired. Serves 8.

CARAWAY SOUP

Heat up 3 pints beef broth with any available vegetables. Add 1 heaped tbsp. of caraway seeds to the pot at the same time. When cooked strain, thicken with paste made of browned flour and butter stirred until smooth. Serve with croûtons. For added flavour, ¾ lb. diced Polish sausage or salami may be added if desired. Serves 6.

BLACK BREAD SOUP

2 cups stale dark bread (rye, whole wheat, etc.) moistened with water
1 celery stalk
1 celery root or parsnip
2 medium onions
5 cups salted water
1–2 carrots
A dash of nutmeg
1 leek
1 cup milk
A few sprigs parsley
3 egg yolks
6 green beans or 2–3 lb. lima beans or peas
Salt and pepper to taste

Make a light broth of all the vegetables and the bread. When the vegetables are soft (30–45 minutes), put through a sieve and return to the broth. Add nutmeg and milk ; stir thoroughly and simmer but do not boil. Dilute beaten egg yolks with a few spoonfuls of the broth and blend into the soup, being careful not to curdle. Season to taste and serve with croûtons or slices of hard-boiled egg. Serves 6.

PLUM SOUP

Fruit in proportion of 1 cup to 1½ cups water
A piece of lemon rind
1 tbsp. potato flour
Sugar to taste
Sour cream for topping (optional)
A dash of lemon juice

Cook the fruit until thoroughly done (20 minutes to ½ hour). Discard stones and put the fruit through a sieve. Fruit may be stoned raw for easier handling, but the taste will be less subtle. Combine fruit pulp, sugar, lemon juice and rind, and potato flour with the water in which the fruit has boiled. Boil up and serve hot or cold, with butter croûtons.

If sour cream is added, allow ½ cup for each two servings.

This basic recipe may be used for other fruit, or several different kinds in combination. Cherries, apples and pears are all suitable. A winter variation is hot fruit soup made of soaked dried fruit. Prunes or apricots, thoroughly cooked and puréed and thickened with cornflour, are especially good. Use the same basic proportions as above. Serve hot with croûtons.

POLISH BARSZCZ
(BEETROOT SOUP)

3 cooked beetroots
Salt
5–6 cupfuls boiling water
Sugar
½ a cup of vinegar
Lemon juice
2 beef cubes (dissolved in 5–6 cupfuls of water)
Sliced Vienna sausage or other cooked meat

Slice the beetroots, pour on the boiling water and vinegar, and leave at room temperature for 2–4 days, then drain off the juice and use it as a basis for soup. Dissolve the meat cubes in 5–6 cupfuls of water and add salt, sugar and lemon to taste. Add this stock to the soup and bring to the boil (do not over-boil or it will lose its colour). Add 4 or 5 slices of Vienna sausage, pieces of bacon, ham or other cooked meat.

The above is a simple method of preparing this traditional soup, which, in various versions (and spellings) appears throughout Russia and Central Europe. In Poland, the true Barszcz is made by putting beetroots in a container with water and a piece of rye bread and leaving the mixture for several days until it becomes sour; the juice is then drained off and serves as a basis for soup.

SLEDZ MARYOWANY
(MARINATED HERRINGS)

4 herrings with their roes	A few peppercorns
¼ pint vinegar	1 bay leaf
1 clove of garlic	Salt
1 tsp. French mustard	2 onions

Clean and bone the herrings and soak them in cold water and milk for 48 hours. Now boil the vinegar with all the ingredients, except the onions and fish, for about 5 minutes. Pass the herring roes through a sieve and add them to the cooled vinegar, stirring well until thoroughly mixed. Put alternate layers of herring and thinly sliced onion into a vessel, pour the sauce over and let them stand for at least 4 or 5 days before eating them.

In this dish the herrings are not cooked, but they are preserved by the marinade and will keep for weeks. This appetising dish is to be found in every Polish home.

SALMON À LA POLONAISE
(IN WINE SAUCE)

3 lb. salmon	4 oz. red wine (dry)
Salt	3 oz. butter
4 oz. fresh bacon	1 oz. flour
Juice of 1 lemon	

Salt and lard the salmon with half the amount of fresh bacon; slice the rest of the bacon, put round the fish and roast in a hot oven for about 25 minutes. When brown sprinkle with lemon juice, add wine and put back into the oven. Before serving cream flour and butter, add wine sauce, bring to a boil and pour over the fish.

PIKE WITH HORSERADISH SAUCE

3–4 lb. pike   Salt and pepper to taste

Wash, drain and salt the fish well beforehand if possible. Simmer very slowly in court-bouillon (see below) tightly covered, for 15–20 minutes. Test to see if the fish is cooked. Drain and serve with horseradish sauce and lemon slices.

Fish may be cooked whole or cut into serving pieces, depending on convenience. A large fish served whole looks best when appearance counts. For easiest handling, cooking should be done in a large oblong pan on a rack (a roasting tin with cover can double for a fish kettle); for additional ease, the fish may be wrapped in cheesecloth.

To prepare a Court-bouillon
(using per quart water)

1 large onion	A slice of lemon
2–3 carrots	½ bay leaf (optional)
½ celery root	Salt and pepper to taste
½ parsley root	Thyme, orégano, tarragon,
2–3 celery stalks	etc. (according to prefer-
with leaves	ence)

Boil the water and vegetables until they are done, then strain. Place the fish on rack, belly down, and immerse in the liquid, of which there should be enough to cover. Simmer very slowly until done, about 5 minutes per inch of thickness. Remove with rack and drain; cut cheesecloth and remove carefully. The broth can be used for fish soups.

SOLE BAKED IN SOUR CREAM

Salt and pepper to	4 oz. grated Parmesan
taste	1 cup sour cream
2 lb. sole (or flounder)	Breadcrumbs and butter
Flour	for topping
3 tbsps. butter	

Season the fish, dust with flour and brown lightly in butter. Arrange in a shallow baking dish. Sprinkle thickly with Parmesan. Pour in the sour cream to which ½ tsp. flour has been added, sprinkle with breadcrumbs, and top with bits of butter. Bake in a hot oven (450° F., mark 8) for 20 minutes. Serve with lemon slices. Serves 6–7.

HERRING CREAM

4 large herrings	1 onion, grated
2 rolls, moistened	3 tbsps. Parmesan cheese
with milk	Salt and pepper to taste
2 tbsps. butter	A dash of nutmeg
2 eggs	Breadcrumbs
3 tbsps. sour cream	

Soak, clean and bone the herrings. Put through a mincer with the rolls. Cream the milts and roe with 1 tbsp. butter and 2 egg yolks. Add sour cream, onion and Parmesan and combine with minced fish and rolls. Season to taste and mix thoroughly. Beat egg whites until stiff and fold in last. Pour into a greased shallow baking dish, leaving the mixture in a pyramid shape. Do not flatten. Sprinkle liberally with breadcrumbs, dot with remaining butter and bake in a moderately hot oven (400° F., mark 6) for 30 minutes. Serve with melted butter. Serves 5–6.

ROAST TURKEY WITH ANCHOVIES

Turkey	10 anchovies
4 oz. fresh bacon	4 oz. butter
10 oz. veal	3 eggs
2 oz. onions	Flavouring
2 oz. roll	2 oz. butter
$\frac{1}{4}$ pint milk	

Salt the bird lightly and let stand for a short time. Cook bacon, veal and onions until tender, then cool and mince with the roll previously soaked in milk and squeezed. Skin anchovies, chop up and mash thoroughly with 4 oz. of the butter. Add egg yolks and minced meat, stirring thoroughly. Season with salt, pepper and grated lemon peel. Beat whites of eggs until frothy and add to the mixture. Stuff the bird, fasten together with wooden skewers. Roast in a hot oven (450° F., mark 8), basting with butter.

GOOSE À LA POLONAISE

1 goose	4 oz. onions
2 oz. dried mixed vegetables	8 oz. cream
	1 oz. flour
2 oz. dried mushrooms	Flavouring

Cut the bird along the backbone into halves. Pour over just sufficient water to cover the meat, add vegetables and boil until tender. Wash mushrooms and soak for about 1 hour, then boil in a quart of fresh water with onions until soft. Take out and slice. Blend together flour and cream, add to mushroom soup and bring to the boil. Carve the bird while hot and serve on a hot dish with boiled rice and some of the gravy. Serve remaining gravy separately. Ducks may be prepared in the same way.

SMOTHERED DUCK IN CAPER SAUCE

1 duckling (weighing about 5–6 lb.)	Bouillon for basting (about 1 cup)
Salt and pepper to taste	2 tsps. flour
	2 tbsps. capers
1 clove of garlic (optional)	A pinch of brown or caramelised sugar
3 tbsps. butter	Lemon juice to taste

Clean and season the duck about 2 hours beforehand and rub with mashed garlic if desired. Brown quickly in butter, reserving 2 tsps. butter. Then reduce the heat and cover tightly. Allow to simmer, basting frequently with bouillon, until well brown and tender—about 1½ hours. Blend the reserved butter with the flour, add enough juice from the pan to dissolve lumps, and add to the duck. Add capers, a pinch of brown sugar for colouring, and lemon juice to taste. Stir well and baste the duck. Continue braising for another 10–15 minutes. Serve with macaroni or noodles. Serves 5–6.

VEAL BIGOS

3 green apples	$\frac{1}{2}$ cup soup stock
2 tbsps. butter	Sugar and salt to taste
1 tbsp. flour	3 cups diced cooked veal

Core and pare the apples and just cover with water. Allow to boil up once. Blend the butter and flour without browning, dilute with $\frac{1}{2}$ cup soup stock, and combine with apples and water, add sugar to taste, and add meat to the sauce. Simmer tightly covered for about 10 minutes. Serves 6.

HUNTER'S LAMB

1 leg of lamb with bone left in (5–6 lb.)	1 large onion, sliced (optional)
2 cups vinegar	$\frac{1}{4}$ lb. salt pork for larding
20 juniper berries, pounded or ground	Salt and pepper to taste
	1 tsp. butter
1 large mashed clove of garlic	Flour for dredging
	$\frac{1}{4}$ cup sour cream

Remove excess fat from the meat, pound well and pour boiling vinegar over it. Rub well with juniper and garlic and surround with onion slices. Wrap in a cloth dipped in the vinegar and allow to stand for 4–5 days. Discard the onion, wipe meat, lard generously, rub with salt, pepper and butter and roast in a hot oven (450° F., mark 8) for about 1¼ hours, basting frequently. When nearly cooked, add sour cream. Also excellent with any sharp sauce, in which case omit the sour cream. Serves 6–8.

HAM DUMPLINGS

4 cups breadcrumbs	2 slices boiled ham, shredded
1 cup scalded milk	
2 tsps. butter	Salt to taste
3 eggs, separated	Flour for rolling
1 white roll or 2 slices bread	A few strips bacon fat

Combine breadcrumbs with scalded milk and let it stand for a few minutes to soften and cool.

Add butter and egg yolks and fold in stiffly beaten egg whites. Dice the roll or bread and fry in butter to make croûtons. Combine croûtons and shredded ham with first mixture and mix lightly. Shape into oblong croquettes, roll in flour and cook in fast-boiling salted water for about 10 minutes. Cook the bacon until crisp, drain and crumble. Use both bacon and bacon fat for topping. Serves 4–6.

LIVER MOUNDS

6 turkey or large capon livers, soaked in milk for about 2 hours
1 stale white roll, moistened in milk, and mashed, or equivalent in breadcrumbs
3 eggs, separated
1 tbsp. butter
Salt and pepper to taste
½ medium onion, grated and sautéed in butter

Chop livers, press through a sieve, and then combine with roll or breadcrumbs. Cream egg yolks and butter, add to liver mixture, season to taste and mix thoroughly. Fold in stiffly beaten egg whites and spoon the mixture into well-greased muffin tins. Cover with greased greaseproof paper and bake in a moderate oven (375° F., mark 5) for about 30 minutes. Serve as a side dish with a sharp sauce. Serves 6.

* * *

In Poland, company food is traditionally substantial (prompted by a stern winter climate). And it has an extra—a sophisticated flair exemplified by these two excellent dishes : stuffed pot roast, to star at a dinner party table, and a delicious blend of two Polish favourites—mushrooms and sour cream.

PIECZEN HAZARSKA
(HUSSAR ROAST)

⅓ cup butter or margarine
5–6 lb. boned bottom round beef
1 cup canned condensed beef broth, undiluted
1 large onion, quartered
2 tsps. salt
2 cups fresh breadcrumbs, packed
3 large onions, grated
2 tsps. salt
¼ tsp. pepper
¼ cup butter, melted
2 tbsps. flour

In ⅓ cup butter over medium heat, brown beef well on all sides. Then pour in beef broth, quartered onion and 2 tsps. salt ; simmer, covered, for 2½–3 hours, or until tender, turning now and then.

Meanwhile, in bowl, combine breadcrumbs, grated onions, 2 tsps. salt, pepper and ¼ cup melted butter.

Remove roast from the pan ; cut about ¼-inch thick crosswise slices from top of roast to about 1 inch of bottom.

Place some of breadcrumb mixture between every two slices. Then insert two wooden skewers about 3 inches into each end of the stuffed roast.

Skim all fat from the liquid ; replace meat ; sprinkle with flour ; simmer, covered, for ½ hour.

Arrange roast on heated large platter ; remove skewers. Nice served with boiled potatoes and mushrooms with sour cream (see below). Makes 6–8 servings.

GRZYBY W SMIETANIE
(MUSHROOMS WITH SOUR CREAM)

6 tbsps. butter or margarine
1 large onion, chopped
2 tbsps. flour
2 tbsps. milk
1½ cups sour cream
1¼ lb. mushrooms, sliced
¾ tsp. salt
¼ tsp. pepper
¼ tsp. paprika

In melted butter in large skillet, sauté onion till golden. Sprinkle with flour ; add milk and ¾ cup sour cream ; while stirring, bring just to a simmer.

Then add sliced mushrooms, salt, pepper and paprika. Simmer covered, for 5 minutes, stirring occasionally.

Stir in remaining ¾ cup sour cream ; heat thoroughly while stirring constantly. Serve at once. Makes 6 servings.

HUNTERS' STEW

This is a very old traditional Polish recipe and it was served at royal banquets and is still the *piéce de résistance* after hunting parties. This is best served at large parties because of the numerous ingredients and, if necessary, any left over can be put in the refrigerator for future use. The following proportions are only approximate and can be varied according to taste and availability.

Allow at least ½ lb. of each of the following cooked meats, diced :

Roast beef or pot roast   Chicken or duck
Roast lamb   Ham
Roast pork   Sausage
Venison or hare   Roast veal
together with
6–8 lb. sauerkraut   2 onions, minced
1½ oz. mushrooms, cooked   2 tbsps. flour
until soft enough to cut   Salt, pepper and
into thin strips   sugar to taste
Liquid in which mushrooms have cooked   1 cup Madeira wine (or more)
¼ lb. salt pork, diced and browned

Combine the sauerkraut and cooked mushrooms together with the liquid in which they were cooked. Brown the diced salt pork, cook the onion in this fat until limp, add flour, and stir until blended. Add to the sauerkraut. Add all the diced meats, season to taste, and simmer, tightly covered, until ready to serve.

This dish is even better reheated, so it may be prepared in the morning for use in the evening. It will keep in the refrigerator for about 3 days, if necessary.

If the meats must be prepared fresh, each piece should be pot-roasted separately, together with the following :

1 tbsp. (or less) butter	6 peppercorns
1 onion	A bay leaf (optional)
1 carrot	½ cup soup stock
1 stalk celery	(approx.) to prevent
A piece of celery root	sticking
A piece of parsley root	Salt to taste

Cook each meat until tender. Dice and combine with sauerkraut as directed above. The vegetables with which the meats have cooked may be used separately. Traditionally they are not added to the main dish. Either recipe will make 12 generous servings.

FLAKI AND PULPITY
(TRIPE AND DUMPLINGS)

1 marrow bone	Salt and pepper
1 carrot	2 sprigs of parsley
1 onion	1 tsp. marjoram
A few sticks of celery	1 tsp. ground ginger
2 lb. tripe	2 tbsps. flour

For the Dumplings

2 oz. suet	A little chopped parsley,
2 tbsps. breadcrumbs	some ground ginger
1 egg yolk	and some marjoram
1–2 tbsps. flour	to flavour

Make a stock with the marrow bone and vegetables, strain it and put aside. Wash the tripe thoroughly, pour boiling water over it, then put it into cold water and boil until soft. Cut it into strips, put it into the prepared stock and add salt and pepper. Cut the cooked vegetables into small pieces and add them, with the chopped parsley, marjoram and ginger. Blend the flour with cold water, add to the tripe stew, and cook for a few minutes until thickened.

Now make the dumplings. Chop or mince the suet, if necessary, add the breadcrumbs, egg yolk, flour, parsley, ginger and marjoram, and mix well. Form very small balls, then put them into boiling salted water and cook for 5 minutes. Strain, and add them hot to the hot stew just before serving. Serve accompanied by three small bowls of paprika, grated cheese and sieved dried marjoram for flavouring.

OZOR W SZARYM SOSIE
(TONGUE IN GREY SAUCE)

1 skinned cooked calf's tongue

For the Sauce

3 tbsps. sugar	Vinegar or lemon juice
½ cup cold water	Currants
2 oz. flour	Chopped almonds
1 pint stock	Salt and sugar
1 meat cube	½ glass red wine

Although the sauce is called " grey," it is really a lightish brown in colour. It is also served with fish, especially carp. The method of making is as follows : Put the sugar and water into a pan and heat gently, stirring continuously, until it starts to dissolve and becomes brown.

In a separate frying pan, fry the flour until it becomes brown, then gradually add the stock and the meat cube, dissolved in a little water. Add a little vinegar, or lemon juice, a few currants, some chopped almonds, and salt and sugar. Add this to the original sugar mixture, and cook over medium heat, adding the red wine.

Slice the tongue, pour the sauce over, and serve at once.

TENDERLOIN À LA KREJCIK

3 lb. tenderloin	1 small onion, chopped
Salt and pepper to taste	2 small or 1 medium
2 tbsps. French mustard	head Savoy cabbage
Butter	1 tbsp. chopped fresh
1 lb. roast veal or pork	parsley
6 mushrooms, coarsely	1 egg
chopped	6 slices bacon

Rub the meat with salt, pepper and mustard and return to the refrigerator for 2 hours. Brown in very hot butter and allow to cool. In the meantime, chop roast meat fine or put through the mincer. Sauté the mushrooms and onion in butter ; reserve outside leaves of the cabbage and shred the centres. Combine the roast meat, mushrooms, onions, and chopped cabbage, add chopped parsley and whole raw egg, season, and mix thoroughly. Spread the mixture over the meat, wrap in cabbage leaves and cover with bacon slices. Secure with cotton or string. Add any remaining butter and bake in a hot oven (450° F., mark 8) for 30–35 minutes. Remove the string, slice with very sharp knife and serve with its own juice. Serves 8.

STEAMED BEEF SLICES

2 lb. topside (thinly sliced)	1 lemon, peeled, seeded and sliced
Salt and pepper	1 tbsp. butter
¼ lb. bacon or salt pork	1 cup beer
1 large onion, minced	½ cup water
2 lb. flour	

Try to obtain thinly sliced meat. Pound even thinner and season. Line a heavy casserole with bacon or salt pork slices and arrange the meat over these, alternating with minced onion, a little flour and lemon slices. Add the butter, beer and water. Cover tightly and bake in a moderate oven (425° F., mark 7) for 1½ hours. Serve with fried potatoes or groats. Serves 6.

69

STEAK À LA NELSON

4 slices rump steak (about 6 oz. each)	¼ pint cream
	½ pint stock
4 oz. butter	1 oz. flour
1 onion	4 potatoes
¼ lb. mushrooms	Salt and pepper

Fry the chopped onion in half the butter for 5 minutes. Add the sliced mushrooms. Pour in the cream and the stock. Flour the meat. Season with salt and pepper. Fry quickly on both sides in the rest of the butter. Cook in the mushroom sauce in a covered pan for 30 minutes. Add the diced potatoes and cook for another 30 minutes.

BACON FRICASSEE

¾ lb. boiled collar bacon	¼ pint milk
	¼ pint bacon stock or water
Sauce	A few cooked mushrooms
1 oz. butter	2–3 diced cooked beetroot
1 oz. plain flour	

Cut boiled bacon into small cubes. Melt butter, blend in the flour, gradually stir in milk and stock, and cook until sauce thickens. Add the mushrooms and bacon, season to taste and heat through. Serve with hot beetroot and garnish with chopped parsley.

BAKED POLISH HAM WITH RICE AND RAISINS

70

8 thin slices Polish ham	¼ tsp. paprika
Mustard	Salt
½ cup cooked rice	Milk
⅓ cup chopped raisins	1 egg
¼ cup chopped celery	

Spread mustard on slices of Polish ham; mix rice with raisins, egg, celery, paprika and season well. Place filling on slices of ham, roll them and secure with toothpicks. Put in a baking pan, brush top of rolls with milk and bake in fairly hot oven for a short time. Serve with Cumberland sauce.

CUMBERLAND SAUCE

1 cup red-currant jelly	2 tbsps. sugar
1 egg yolk	Salt and pepper
2 tbsps. vinegar	¼ cup raisins
¾ tbsp. dry mustard	

Stir jelly over boiling water until soft. Mix yolk with vinegar, mustard, sugar, salt and pepper, add the jelly and stir the sauce until thick, about 15 minutes, add the raisins, if liked, and serve.

PORK PIE

71

1½ lb. pork rump steak	3 oz. onions
Salt and pepper	4 oz. butter
2 oz. fat	2 eggs
10 oz. brown breadcrumbs	

Salt and pepper the meat. Put into a roasting tin with fat and cook in a hot oven for about 1½–2 hours. Put breadcrumbs into a bowl, add eggs, onions, finely chopped and previously fried, and salt. Make into a paste, cover meat with mixture and put back into the oven. Bake until light brown, cut with a sharp knife and serve on a hot dish with salads to choice.

PORK VEGETABLE STEW

2¼ lb. pork loin chops	1 oz. butter
Pepper and salt	1 oz. flour
4 oz. fat	Juice and grated rind of half a lemon
4 oz. onion	
10 oz. fresh vegetables	

Remove bones, slice meat, pound lightly, add salt and pepper, and fry in hot fat until both sides are brown. Put chops in a saucepan, add sliced onions, diced vegetables and grated lemon peel. Add water and stew covered until tender. Before serving, thicken with butter creamed with flour, bring to the boil and flavour with lemon juice. Serve with potatoes or macaroni.

KULEBIAK
(SAVOURY PASTY)

½ lb. flaky pastry	Sugar
Sliced cabbage	1 beef cube, dissolved in water
Butter or lard for frying	
3 tbsps. vinegar	¼ lb. mushrooms
Salt	½ lb. onions
	2–3 hard-boiled eggs

Roll out the pastry. Put the cabbage into boiling water to soften it, then put it into a pan with the hot butter or lard, a little water, the vinegar, a little salt and sugar, and the beef cube, dissolved in water. Stew gently, adding a little more water as necessary (the less the better). Fry the mushrooms and onion in butter and add to the cooked cabbage mixture, with the hard-boiled eggs, cut into small pieces. Put the filling on the pastry, make into a roll and bake in a hot oven (450° F., mark 8) for 1 hour.

This makes an excellent family supper dish.

KOLDUNY LITEWSKIE
(POLISH-LITHUANIAN RAVIOLI)

2 medium-sized onions	Seasoning
Fat for frying	8 oz. noodle paste
1 lb. minced cooked	(see below)
lamb	Salted water
¼ cup water	Melted butter

Slice the onions and fry them, then mix with the minced lamb, water and seasoning.

Make the noodle paste, roll it out thinly and cut into 4-inch rounds. Place some of the meat mixture on each round, fold over and seal the edges. Boil in salted water for a few minutes, until they float to the top, then lift out and serve immediately with melted butter.

To make the noodle paste, mix 8 oz. flour and ½ tsp. salt, and rub in 1 oz. butter or lard. Add a beaten egg and enough milk and water (or water only) to make a very stiff dough. Knead until smooth and divide into portions for rolling out.

PURÉE OF BEETROOT AND APPLE

5–6 medium beetroots	Lemon juice to taste
2 sour apples	Sugar to taste
1 tbsp. bacon fat	2–3 tbsps. sour cream
Salt and pepper to taste	1½ tsps. flour

Peel the beetroots and apples and grate coarsely, reserving all the juices. Melt bacon fat, add grated beetroots and apples, together with all their juices. Season with salt and pepper, and add lemon juice and sugar to taste. Simmer, covered, for half an hour. Reduce liquid, add sour cream combined with flour and let it bubble. Simmer for a few more minutes. This is excellent with roast dishes. Serves 5–6.

BIGOS
(SAVOURY CABBAGE)

A large white cabbage	Leftover meat, etc.
2–3 apples	2 tbsps. vinegar
½ lb. pork, bacon or other	½ cup tomato sauce
cooked meat	or a little ketchup
4 oz. lard	½ lb. Continental
Salt	garlic sausage
1 tsp. caraway seed	

Shred the cabbage, peel and shred the apples,

and cut the meat into pieces. Heat the lard in a deep pan, and put the cabbage, apples and meat into the hot fat, together with some salt and the caraway seed. Cover, and cook over a low heat for about 2 hours, adding a little cold water from time to time and stirring frequently. Then add any leftovers, with the vinegar and sauce, and cook for another hour. Peel and dice the sausage, and put it into the pot with the *bigos* to cook for the last ¼ hour.

Bigos is very savoury when reheated the next day—in fact the more it is reheated, the better it becomes. Sauerkraut may be used instead of cabbage; in this case, omit the apples and vinegar.

Though *bigos* was a traditional hunting dish, it is now eaten everywhere. At big hunting parties it was served when the ladies joined the huntsmen for open-air lunch—usually accompanied by plenty of drink. After the meal, the serious hunting business of the day was usually considered over, and the ladies would stroll in the forest with the partners of their choice.

PLACKI KARTOFLANE
(POTATO PANCAKES)

This is the main dish of the poorer community all over Poland, and indeed in many other parts of Europe. In Poland these pancakes are eaten with sour cream, but they are equally good served at breakfast with fried bacon, or as a sweet pancake with jam or fruit.

Peel, wash and grate some large potatoes, then leave them for a short time to drain. To each cupful of grated potato add 1 level tsp. salt, some pepper, ½ cupful flour and enough milk to make a fairly stiff batter. Cut into rounds about ½ inch thick and fry in hot lard, turning the cakes when one side is browned. Serve at once.

TARTARE SAUCE WITH GHERKINS

2 eggs	1½ oz. preserved mushrooms
2 raw egg yolks	1½ oz. mustard
¼ pint olive oil	1 tbsp. grated horseradish or
1½ oz. gherkins	chopped chives, salt, sugar,
¼ pint cream	lemon

Boil 2 eggs until hard, cool and remove shells. Separate yolks from whites, put yolks in a bowl, mash with mustard and raw egg yolks into paste. Mix, adding olive oil drop by drop. Mix with finely sliced mushrooms, gherkins and hard-boiled egg whites, add 1 tbsp. grated horseradish or chopped chives. Stir in cream, season to taste with salt, sugar and lemon; note if sauce is too thick you can thin it with cold broth, vegetable extract or boiled water.

Serve with cold meat, smoked and cured meat and fish.

GHERKIN SAUCE

3 oz. gherkins	1 oz. butter
¼ pint vegetable	⅛ pint cream
extract	Salt
1 oz. flour	Sugar

Cut gherkins finely, stir flour with vegetable extract and boil. Add finely cut gherkins, salt, sugar, butter and then add cream to this sauce. Serve with meat, potato cutlets, etc.

POLISH CUCUMBER SALAD

Slice 2–3 small cucumbers, put them in a bowl with 2 tbsps. lemon juice, 2 tbsps. chopped chives and salt to taste. Cover with fresh or sour cream and chill for at least ½ hour. Serve very cold.

DRIED MUSHROOM PUDDING

2 oz. mushrooms	1 tbsp. chopped dill
1½ oz. onion	Salt and pepper
2 oz. butter or fat	¾ oz. fat for greasing
4 eggs	the baking tin
3 oz. crumbs	¾ oz. crumbs
¼ pint milk	

Clean mushrooms, boil, sieve. Soak crumbs in milk. Chop onion finely and fry in 1 oz. butter. Pass crumbs and onion through a meat grinder. Beat the egg white into stiff froth, stir egg yolks into rest of butter, adding mushroom paste, chopped dill, salt, pepper and egg white. Mix gently and fill the baking tin ¾ full, first having greased tin and sprinkled it with crumbs. Cover the tin closely and place in a pan of boiling water for about 1 hour. Serve with mushroom, tomato or dill sauce.

PANCAKES WITH MUSHROOMS
Dough

½ lb. flour	Salt
1 egg	Skin or lard or fat
½ pint milk	bacon for greasing
½ pint water	the frying pan

To prepare the dough for pancakes, pour egg into milk and beat well. Sieve flour, salt, add milk with egg and beat the batter mixture adding water sufficient to keep the batter as thick as cream. Heat the frying pan, grease with lard and pour a thin layer of the batter mixture on the frying pan, letting it run evenly over the bottom. Fry pancakes on both sides, turning over with a small shovel or a broad knife. When fried place pancakes on a plate turned bottom up. Fill with the following mixture:

For the Filling

2 oz. dried mushrooms	2 oz. cream
1 oz. butter	2 oz. crumbs
1½ oz. onion	2 oz. fat for frying
3 oz. dry roll	Salt and pepper
¼ pint milk	

Wash mushrooms, soak in lukewarm water; boil in this water, when tender drain and chop finely. Soak roll in milk, drain off, stir with a spoon into paste very thoroughly. Cut the onion thin and brown it in butter. Mix browned onion, cream, salt and pepper, stir well into paste. Spread some filling on each pancake, press edges tightly and roll. Dip pancakes in batter mixture, toss in crumbs and fry in hot fat till golden-brown.

STRINGLESS BEANS IN SPICE SAUCE

1 tin stringless beans	Salt and pepper
½ lb. tomatoes	Sugar
2 oz. butter	Green dill and green
¾ oz. flour	parsley
½ lemon	4 cloves
⅓ pint vegetable extract	

Drain beans and cut into oblique pieces. Rinse tomatoes, cut coarsely, simmer with cloves. When tender pass tomatoes through sieve, add to beans. Blend butter with flour in a frying pan and brown. Add some broth, mix with beans, bring to boil. Season to taste with salt, sugar, pepper and lemon juice. Sprinkle with dill, parsley and mix thoroughly.

RAISIN MAZUR CAKE

2 cups seedless raisins	Grated rind of
1 cup sugar	1 lemon
2 cups unpeeled almonds,	1 whole egg and 1 egg
grated or chopped very	yolk, lightly beaten
fine	Rice paper

Combine all the ingredients. Pour into a shallow cake tin lined with rice paper and bake in a very slow oven (250° F., mark ¼) until lightly done on top—20–25 minutes. This cake can be iced if desired.

BLACK BREAD PUDDING

6 eggs, separated	¼ tsp. powdered cloves
6 tbsps. sugar	Cinnamon to taste
1 cup breadcrumbs	1 tbsp. melted butter
made from black bread	Breadcrumbs and
(pumpernickel)	butter

Cream egg yolks and sugar until white. Add breadcrumbs, cinnamon, cloves and the melted butter. Mix thoroughly and fold in stiffly beaten egg whites. Line buttered pan with breadcrumbs and pour in the mixture. Bake in a moderate oven (375° F., mark 5) for 25–30 minutes. Serve with whipped cream or whipped sour cream.

FRUIT CREAM

4 cups berries	3–4 cloves
4 cups water	2 heaped tbsps.
1½ cups sugar	potato flour
1 2–3-inch piece of cinnamon	

Mash the berries, combine with water, boil for 5 minutes and press through a sieve. Reserve quarter of the liquid and allow to cool. Combine the rest with the sugar, cinnamon and cloves, and simmer another 10 minutes. Discard the cloves. Dissolve the potato flour in the cooled liquid and, when thoroughly blended, pour into the hot liquid. Stir continuously over heat for 2 minutes. Wet a mould or bowl, sprinkle with sugar and pour in the fruit cream. Chill and allow to thicken for about 2 hours.

POTATO DUMPLINGS—SAVOURY OR SWEET

1 lb. potatoes	½ tsp. salt
3 oz. flour	1 egg

Savoury Filling

1 small leek or onion, chopped	1 rasher of bacon or ham

Alternative Sweet Filling

A few prunes (soaked overnight) or bottled plums or cherries	2 oz. breadcrumbs
	1 oz. butter
	A little sugar

Boil or steam the potatoes in their skins, and peel and mash while they are still hot. Sieve together the flour and salt, add these to the potatoes when they are cold, mix with the beaten egg, and knead to a smooth dough. Shape the dumplings the size of small apples, keeping your hands wet with a little cold water while you are forming them.

If you want to serve the dumplings as a savoury, fill with a little leek and bacon, previously chopped and fried. Cook the dumplings quickly in boiling salted water; they are ready after 5 minutes of quick uncovered boiling. Take them out one by one and put them into a colander which has been rinsed in cold water. Serve in a hot dish, and pour the rest of the bacon fat and the fried onion over them. Serve with any available vegetable or with a salad.

To make sweet dumplings, fill them with the prepared fruit and follow the same method for making and boiling. Prepare 2 oz. breadcrumbs and fry them golden-brown in 1 oz. butter. Put the drained dumplings into the pan with the crumbs and a little sugar and shake it, so that the dumplings are coated with crumbs. Serve hot, accompanied by a sauce made from the fruit juice, sweetened and thickened.

HONEY CAKE

½ cup sugar	2 egg whites
3 egg yolks	2 cups honey, heated, skimmed and cooled
1 cup ground walnuts	Cinnamon, cloves and nutmeg to taste
2 cups flour	
1 tbsp. baking powder	

Cream the sugar and egg yolks until light in colour. Add nuts and sift in the flour and baking powder. Add the stiffly beaten egg whites and honey. Add spices to taste, mix thoroughly, and bake in a very slow oven (250° F., mark ¼) in a greased mould lined with breadcrumbs, for about 1 hour.

PEARS CANDIED IN HONEY

2 lb. firm pears	Sugar for rolling
2 cups honey	

Peel the pears, cut in halves and core. Simmer in water to cover until tender but not mushy. Drain and let dry while heating honey. Combine the fruit and honey and let it stand in a cool place for 2 days. Then simmer in a flat pan until honey thickens to a glaze. Allow to cool enough to handle and roll in sugar. Spread on buttered baking sheet and dry out in a slow oven (325° F., mark 2).

SERNIK
(CHEESE CAKE)
For the Topping

8 oz. cream cheese	Powdered vanilla (or vanilla essence to flavour)
6 egg yolks	
2 oz. melted butter	
8 oz. caster sugar	Glacé icing

For the Pastry

8 oz. flour	2 oz. sugar
4 oz. butter	1 egg yolk

Tie the cream cheese in muslin and squeeze out the moisture. When the cheese is dry, grate or crumble it into a mixing bowl, and add the egg yolks, melted butter, sugar and a little powdered vanilla. Beat thoroughly till the mixture is quite smooth and with no lumps (this will take about ½ hour).

Make the pastry with the flour, butter, sugar and egg yolk, and cover the bottom of a greased baking tin with it. Place the cheese mixture on top, and bake for 1 hour in a moderate oven (350° F., mark 3).

When the cake is cold, cut it into squares and coat each with a little glacé icing.

CHRUST
(VANILLA CRUNCHIES)

4 egg yolks	9 tbsps. sour cream
2 tbsps. sugar	Lard for frying
5 tbsps. clarified melted butter	Caster sugar
A pinch of ammonia carbonate	Powdered vanilla (or vanilla essence) to flavour the caster sugar
1 lb. flour	

Mix thoroughly the egg yolks, sugar and butter, and add a pinch of ammonia carbonate, then stir in gradually the flour and the sour cream. Roll the mixture out thinly into strips approximately 8 by $\frac{1}{2}$ inch. Make a slit in each strip, and twist the end through it. Have ready a pan of boiling lard and fry the pastries at an even heat. When the pastries are cooked, they should be golden-brown in colour. Remove them from the pan very carefully, as they are fragile, and while they are hot, sprinkle them with a mixture of caster sugar and powdered vanilla, or with vanilla-flavoured sugar.

STRUCLAZ MAKIEM (POLAND)
(POPPY-SEED CAKE)

A rich yeast pastry rolled out as for a Swiss roll filled with a rich poppy-seed mixture, rolled up as for a Swiss roll, baked and finished with a glacé icing.

Filling

Boiling water	1 oz. dried fruit
5 oz. poppy seeds	1 egg white
2½ oz. sugar	Almond essence
1 oz. butter	Lemon rind

Pour some boiling water over the poppy seeds and leave to stand for 3 hours. Drain overnight. Mince three times or pound in a mortar. Add the remaining ingredients, flavouring with essence and lemon rind to taste.

EXPOSED to the Atlantic Ocean yet close to the Mediterranean, formerly part of Spain and like her once dominated by the Arabs, connected by conquest and trade with both the East and the New World, Portugal has an unusually complex tradition. Inevitably this is mirrored in her cuisine, so that we find Moorish melons and stuffed cucumbers, Oriental rice dishes, Brazilian guava jelly and coconut, alongside French and Italian borrowings. But the great feature of Portuguese cookery is its emphasis on fish of every kind, fresh and salted, and on shell fish, including oysters—those delicious green " Portugaises " which are also exported to France and England and are almost as well known as the Portuguese canned sardines. The other great export is wine—port from the home country, Madeira from the island colony. Naturally enough, wine, together with Brazilian rum and home-produced brandy, figures largely at luncheon and dinner and between meals, when it will be accompanied by succulent small pasties, shrimps, titbits of cold meat, olives, radishes and so on.

The typical middle-class Portuguese menu for luncheon or dinner always includes some fish. Along the coast oysters often form the lunch-time hors d'œuvre, being replaced inland by cold meats and salads. The evening meal would start with a soup, sometimes based on shrimps or other fish ; another favourite is almond soup (the Arab influence again, probably). The actual fish course could consist of cod, fresh or salted—and salt cod, properly cooked, can be quite delicious—sole, flounder, bass, mackerel, salmon, fresh sardines or a mixture of different kinds. To follow there would be a meat dish, often beefsteak or pork, sucking pig being a particular delight, and poultry or game at a formal meal or in a restaurant. The sweet course, as in Spain, is light and often replaced by dessert fruits. Cheese concludes a hearty and flavourful meal, which would be accompanied by a variety of wines and rounded off by coffee and liqueurs. In poorer households the menu would of course be shorter and simpler and a substantial meat and vegetable stew or a fish chowder, often flavoured with bacon, might be the principal item.

Portugal

SOPA DE AMENDOAS
(ALMOND SOUP)

$\frac{1}{4}$ lb. sweet almonds
2 bitter almonds
1 quart milk, scalded
Salt
A pinch of sugar
2 tbsps. butter
Croutons

Blanch and peel the almonds, and grind to a paste, adding a little water, a few drops at a time, to keep the mass from " oiling." Add a little of the hot milk to the almond paste, mixing with a wooden spoon, then sieve well, adding more milk as necessary. Put the mixture in a double boiler and cook for 15–20 minutes, stirring constantly. Add the remaining hot milk, season with salt and then with a little sugar and add the butter. Lay the croûtons in a hot tureen and pour the soup over.

CALDO VERDE
(GREEN BROTH)

Half fill a saucepan with water and when it is boiling add about 2 tbsps. olive oil, holding the bottle over the pan and allowing the oil to run out in a very fine stream. Season, add 1–2 sliced potatoes and cook till soft, then mash roughly. Take some kale cabbage leaves, roll them up as tightly as possible and shred finely with a very sharp knife. Plunge them into the boiling broth, boil very quickly for about 2–3 minutes and then serve the soup at once.

PRINCE'S CHOWDER

2 onions, sliced
$\frac{1}{2}$ garlic clove, minced
$\frac{1}{4}$ lb. butter
$\frac{1}{4}$ lb. ham, chopped
1 large tomato
6 sorrel leaves, minced (optional)
1 small eel, skinned and sliced
8 shrimps (shelled)
1 slice each of 4 varieties of fish
2 dozen mussels
$\frac{1}{4}$ bay leaf
$\frac{1}{4}$ tsp. fresh ground pepper
Salt
8 oysters
2 tbsps. lemon juice

Slowly fry the onions and garlic in the butter in a saucepan without browning ; add the ham and fry, then the tomato. Add the sorrel, eel, shrimps and fish and turn them in the mixture, shaking the pan, until they are heated through. Meanwhile, steam the mussels open, and remove from the shells. Add sufficient boiling water to the liquid left in the mussel saucepan to make $1\frac{1}{4}$ quarts ; drop in the mussels and cook for 15 minutes. Strain the liquid and pour it over the frying fish mixture ; add the bay leaf, pepper and salt, then place over a low heat and simmer for 10 minutes. Add the oysters with their liquor, and simmer until they crinkle. Add the

lemon juice and serve, putting a little of each fish and sea food in each serving. (The mussels are discarded.)

SOPA DE TOMATE E OVOS
(TOMATO AND EGG SOUP)

2 lb. tomatoes
1 large onion
A little oil or butter
1 quart water
A little finely chopped parsley
Salt
Pepper
$\frac{1}{2}$ tsp. sugar
A knob of butter
2 hard-boiled eggs

Slice the tomatoes without peeling them ; skin and slice the onion. Put these into a pan with some oil or butter and cook for 10 minutes, crushing the tomatoes to release the juice. Add the water and parsley, cover, simmer for 1 hour, then sieve ; add the salt, pepper and a little sugar. Stir in a knob of butter just before serving, then pour the soup into a hot tureen containing the sliced hard-boiled eggs.

SOPA DE GALLINHA
(CHICKEN SOUP)

1 boiling fowl, cut up
1 tbsp. salt
$\frac{1}{2}$ a garlic clove, finely chopped
2 carrots, diced
1 onion, finely chopped
2 tomatoes, skinned, de- seeded and chopped
$\frac{1}{2}$ cup rice
Pepper

Put the fowl in a large pan with 3 quarts water, bring slowly to the boil, add the salt and skim the surface of the water. Simmer for about $2\frac{1}{2}$ hours, add the remaining ingredients and continue to cook until the chicken is done. Skim the fat off the top. In serving the soup give each person a piece of the chicken.

LUNGUADO EM MOLHO DE CAMARAO
(SOLE IN SHRIMP SAUCE)

1 medium-sized sole or flounder
$\frac{1}{2}$ lb. fresh shrimps or 1 packet frozen ones
$\frac{1}{4}$ cup butter
1 tsp. flour
2 cups shrimp liquor, if available, or light stock
Salt and pepper
A little grated nutmeg
1 tbsp. lemon juice
Buttered crumbs

Get the fishmonger to remove the fish head and dark skin. If fresh shrimps are used, shell them and cook in boiling water for 15 minutes ; drain, then reduce the liquid to 2 cups. Melt 2 tbsps. butter and fry the shrimps slowly until they begin to colour. Add the flour, shrimp liquor or light-coloured stock, seasonings and lemon juice and bring to the boil, stirring. Season the fish inside and out, put into a baking dish, skin side down, and dot with butter. Put in a moderate oven (350° F., mark 4) and cook for 10 minutes, basting it with its own juice. Add the hot shrimp sauce and continue to cook, basting with the sauce, until nearly cooked. Sprinkle the buttered crumbs over the top and allow to brown.

SOPA SECCA
(DRY SOUP)

Sprigs of sweet herbs | 2 pints good stock
(parsley, tarragon, | 2 tbsps. melted butter
thyme, bay leaf and | A little salt
plenty of mint, tied | Pepper to taste
together in a piece | Sliced stale bread, with
of muslin) | the crusts removed

Mix all together, adding sufficient bread to make a really thick mixture. Bring to the boil over a very low heat, then take out the herbs. Turn the soup into a casserole and bake in a moderate oven (350° F., mark 3) until the top is brown and crusty. Serve at once.

SARDA FRESCA GRELHADA
(GRILLED MACKEREL)

4 small mackerel | 1 tbsp. onion juice
3 tbsps. olive oil | Salt and pepper
Juice of ½ lemon | 1 tsp. chopped parsley

Split the mackerel down their entire length, remove the backbones, heads and tails, then wash and dry the fillets. Lay them in a dish and pour over them the mixed olive oil, lemon juice, onion juice, salt and pepper, covering well. Let them marinade for 2 or 3 hours, turning occasionally, then drain and grill. Serve sprinkled with parsley. The marinading liquid may be heated and poured over the fish, or they may be spread with melted butter.

BACALHAU FRESCO Á PORTUGUESA
(PORTUGUESE COD)

2 lb. cod | 4 oz. rice boiled in
¼ pint olive oil | salted water for 10
2 onions | minutes
Butter | ¼ pint white wine
1 lb. tomatoes | Salt and pepper
1 clove of garlic, finely | Chopped parsley
chopped |

If cod fillet is used, cut it into about 4 pieces (one per person), and put into a pan with the oil. Lightly brown the sliced onions in a little butter, and add these to the pan, with the skinned and sliced tomatoes, the finely chopped garlic, the rice, the wine and a little salt and pepper. Cover, and simmer gently for 15–20 minutes, then lift out the pieces of cod on to a dish and add some chopped parsley to the liquor. Stir

well and pour the mixture over the fish. Alternatively, leave out the chopped parsley from the sauce and garnish the dish with fresh herbs.

COLD FRIED FISH

4 tbsps. olive oil | 1½ lb. fish, sliced
2 tbsps. lemon juice | Butter
1 tbsp. onion juice | Breadcrumbs
½ garlic clove, crushed | 1 egg, beaten
4 peppercorns, crushed | 1 cup white wine
⅛ tsp. grated nutmeg | 1 tsp. chopped parsley
½ bay leaf | 1 tbsp. chopped onion
1 tsp. salt |

Mix the olive oil, lemon juice, onion juice, garlic, peppercorns, nutmeg, bay leaf and salt and beat well. Dip the fish slices in the mixture, lay them in a bowl and pour the remaining mixture over; marinade for 2–3 hours. Remove the fish, drain and wipe dry. Strain the marinade liquid. Brush the fish over with melted butter, dip in crumbs, then in egg, then in crumbs again. Fry in butter, drain on absorbent paper and cool. Mix the marinade with the wine and bring to the boil; add the parsley and onion. Cool, and serve in a sauce-boat.

PEIXE OPORTO
(BAKED FISH WITH PORT WINE SAUCE)

1½ lb. sea bream or any | 1 oz. butter
other suitable white | 1½ gills port wine
fish | 2 egg yolks
Salt | 1 tbsp. cream
Paprika pepper |

Prepare the fish and season with salt and paprika. Bake it with the butter in a covered fireproof dish in a moderate oven (350° F., mark 3) for 5 minutes. Add the port wine and continue cooking until the fish is tender—15–20 minutes. Strain off all the liquor from the dish and cook it quickly in a saucepan to reduce it a little. Cool, and beat in the egg yolks, add the cream and reheat very gently, but do not bring to simmering point. Pour the sauce over the fish and serve with Savoury Rice (see the recipe given below).

ARROZ REFOGADO
(SAVOURY RICE)

2 tbsps. olive oil | 1 pint boiling water
1 large onion, finely | Salt and pepper
chopped | 1 tbsp. chopped parsley
½ lb. rice |

Heat the oil in a saucepan, add the chopped onion and cook until it is just golden-brown. Add the rice, and continue cooking very slowly for 5 minutes, then pour in the boiling water and add the seasoning, stir well, cover closely and cook gently until all the liquid is absorbed and the rice tender—30–40 minutes. Stir in the chopped parsley just before serving.

PASTEIS DE BACALHAU
(SALT CODFISH CAKES)

Soak 1 lb. salt dry cod overnight, cook it the following day and shred finely. Boil 1 lb. potatoes, rub through a fine sieve and add to the cod, with 1–2 egg yolks. Beat the egg whites stiffly and add to the mixture, blending well. Fry till golden-brown in a very hot deep fat, dropping the mixture in from a tablespoon. Serve with black olives and a fresh green salad.

SALT CODFISH IN SAUCE

1 lb. salt cod	2 tomatoes, chopped
1 large onion, finely chopped	1 onion, thinly sliced
2 garlic cloves, chopped	1 sprig of parsley
2 tbsps. olive oil	1 sprig of celery
Cayenne	2 egg yolks, beaten

Soak the codfish for 24 hours, changing the water often. Parboil it for 10–15 minutes and cut into convenient pieces, removing the bones. Fry the onion and garlic in the oil until light brown and tender; add the cayenne, tomatoes, onion, parsley and celery, pour in 1½ cups boiling water and simmer for a few minutes. Put in the pieces of fish, baste with the mixture, then simmer gently. When the fish is tender, take from the heat and pour in the beaten egg yolks at several different places. Shake the pan gently to mix, then slide the contents of the pan carefully into a deep hot platter.

ESPINAFRE CON SARDINHAS
(SPINACH WITH SARDINES)

73

1 large tin of sardines	2 tbsps. onion juice
2 cups cooked spinach, chopped	1 hard-boiled egg
½ cup breadcrumbs	¼ tsp. pepper
Juice of ½ lemon	Salt
	Butter

Skin, bone and chop the sardines; mix with the spinach, breadcrumbs, lemon and onion juice, a little of the spinach liquor, the chopped egg white and half the chopped yolk; season to taste. Put in a buttered baking dish, sprinkle the remaining egg yolk over the top and dot with butter. Bake for 15 minutes in a moderate oven (350° F., mark 4).

PRAWN RISSOLES

Put a large cupful of water into a pan with 1 tbsp. butter and salt to taste; bring to the boil. Add 1 large cupful sieved flour, stirring all the time until the flour is mixed in and cooked. Turn the dough on to a floured board and roll out very thinly. Prepare a filling of prawns in a thick cream sauce flavoured with lemon. Cut the pastry into large rounds; place some filling on one half and fold over into a crescent shape. Egg and breadcrumb and fry in deep fat. Serve at once.

ARROZ DE FRANGO
(CASSEROLE OF CHICKEN WITH RICE)

Put 2 chopped onions and 2 carrots in a casserole, add some chopped parsley and seasoning, and the jointed and skinned chicken. Braise till the chicken is nicely browned, then remove it and sieve the gravy. Add enough water to give about 2 large cupfuls, and add 1 large cup washed rice; when this is cooked, put a layer of rice in a fireproof dish, then the chicken, and cover with the remaining rice. Top with sausage (preferably Portuguese paprika sausage), and brown in a moderate oven (350° F., mark 4). Garnish as desired.

PERU DE LISBOA
(ROAST STUFFED TURKEY, LISBON STYLE)

1 turkey—7–8 lb.	¼ tsp. powdered cinnamon
½ lb. fillet of pork	A pinch of powdered mace
½ lb. ham or lean bacon	A little grated nutmeg
1 onion	Paprika pepper
A little olive oil for frying	Salt
12 olives	6 oz. breadcrumbs
	3 egg yolks

Prepare the turkey for roasting; cook the giblets for 15 minutes in boiling salted water, drain and mince, together with the pork and ham. Chop the onion and fry it slowly in the olive oil, add the minced meats, stoned olives, spices and seasonings, and continue cooking for 5 minutes. Add this mixture to the breadcrumbs, stir well, and bind with the egg yolks, then leave to get quite cold. Stuff the turkey, truss for roasting, shaping it carefully, and roast in a moderate oven (350° F., mark 3) for 1½–2 hours, basting at intervals, until the flesh is tender when tested.

CASSEROLE OF DUCK WITH RICE

Braise a duck in a casserole with chopped onions, carrots, parsley and seasoning, until brown. Remove the duck from the dish and keep hot. Strain the cooking liquor into a pan and add the same quantity of water and of rice, with seasoning to taste; cook gently. When the

45) Meat and celery are here served with the favourite Greek egg and lemon sauce.

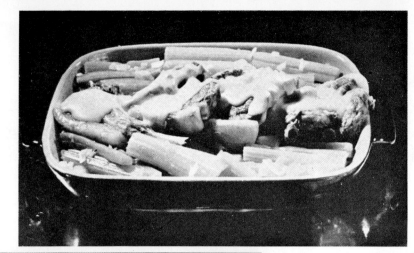

46) These flaky pastries are layered with cheese and are very popular in Greece.

47) Artichokes, cooked with onions and olive oil, that essential Greek ingredient, are served cold.

48) Crisp rolls, stuffed with savoury meat: a wonderful Dutch way of using up leftovers.

49) This satisfying dish of cabbage, layered with meat (*right*) comes from Holland.

50) A Dutch version of an Indonesian recipe, Nassi Goreng includes pork, ham, shrimps and rice (*below*).

51) Pörkölt à la Gundel is a rich stew of beef and liver, from Hungary.

52) An interesting Hungarian dish is this Spinach Roulade, stuffed with ham and served with cheese sauce (*left*).

53) Hungarian pancakes, layered with cream cheese, jam and chocolate and covered with crisp meringue.

54) These small tartlets called Little Baskets, can have different fillings and are a Hungarian speciality (*above*).

55) Dobos Torte, a rich and delicious Hungarian gâteau with a crisp caramel topping (*right*).

56) A favourite hors d'œuvre in Italy is melon served with slices of ham (*above*).

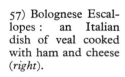

57) Bolognese Escallopes : an Italian dish of veal cooked with ham and cheese (*right*).

59) Spaghetti Madras (*left*) —an interesting dish of spaghetti and curried chicken with raisins.

60) Cannelloni, deliciously stuffed with duck and masked with butter and cheese (*below*).

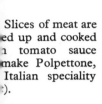

Slices of meat are
ed up and cooked
1 tomato sauce
make Polpettone,
Italian speciality
).

61) Panforte di Siena (*above*): a rich
sweet, full of nuts and fruit.

62) Xkunvat is a special
Maltese sweet, made of spicy
pastry, fried and glazed with
honey (*above*).

63) Norway is famous for fish dishes. Above is shown a dish of mackerel in sour cream sauce.

64) An autumn favourite in Norway is this combination of mutton and cabbage cooked with butter (*below*).

65) Stuffed Cabbage (*above*) is a popular Norwegian dish, both simple and satisfying.

66) Mor Monsen, a light and delicious Norwegian cake sprinkled with currants (*above*).

67) Biøtkake (*left*) is decorated with tiny marzipan flowers and is a great favourite in Norway.

68) Kallalaatiko from Finland is a casserole of pork, herring, potato and onion, topped with egg and milk (*right*).

69) Steak à la Nelson, an easy and delicious party dish from Poland (*left*).

70) Polish ham rolls (*below*) are stuffed with celery and rice and served with a savoury sauce.

71) This Polish " pork pie " has a crust of breadcrumbs, egg and onions (*below*).

72) Sernik, a Polish cheesecake on a pastry base, is decorated with glacé icing (*below*).

73) A delicious and un-usual combination of sar-dines and spinach makes this Portuguese dish (*right*).

74) Portuguese-style cutlets (*left*) are served with a sauce of tomato and onion.

76) Arroz Doce (*below*) is a lemon-flavoured rice dish, a popular sweet in Portugal.

75) Bread mountain, a Portu-guese confection made with eggs and wine and covered with meringue (*above*).

77) Sturgeon is gently steamed and served with a sauce containing diced vegetables (*right*).

78) Coulibiac (*left*) is a hot fish pie, which can be simple or very rich, as you wish.

79) Basturma, a Caucasian dish of grilled meat with tomatoes and spring onions (*right*).

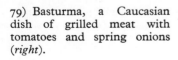

Six Russian dishes are shown on these two pages.

80) Vareniki can have either a sweet or savoury filling and is often served with melted butter (*right*).

81) Easter Bread (*above*) made from yeast dough with eggs and candied fruit.

82) Gooriefskaya Kasha, a delicious sweet made with semolina, cream, eggs, nuts and fruit (*right*).

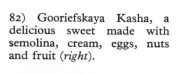

On this and the opposite page are five dishes from Spain and Gibraltar.

83 - 85

83) The Lamb Cutlets on the right are cooked in a sauce of ham, onions and tomato and served with tiny sausages.

84) Pandoras (*left*) — savoury fingers of bread and meat, fried golden-brown in batter.

85) Moreno Eggs are served on a bed of grilled tomatoes and crisp onion rings (*right*).

86) Flamenco Eggs, cooked on a macedoine of ham, sausage and mixed vegetables (*right*).

87) Spanish Apple Tart (*above*), makes a pretty party sweet with its sparkling jelly and whipped cream.

88) Fagelbo (*left*) is an attractive hors d'œuvre dish from Sweden, garnished with raw egg yolks.

89) Rabbit is cooked with chicken broth and white wine and served with browned potatoes on this Swedish main-dish (*left*).

90) Featherlight sponge, layered with vanilla cream and topped with fruit, makes this Swedish Fruit Torte (*below*).

rice is done, place half of it in a fireproof dish, lay the jointed duck on it and cover with the remainder of the rice. Garnish with slices of sausage (if possible with the Portuguese sausage known as *chourico*) which have been put into the oven for a few minutes to brown.

PORTUGUESE RISOTTO

4 tbsps. olive oil	Chopped parsley
¼ lb. rice	A pinch of saffron
½–¾ lb. cooked veal or chicken, cut up small	Salt and pepper
	½ pint stock
3 peeled tomatoes	Cooked peas
1 onion, chopped	Sliced cooked
A clove of garlic	mushrooms

Heat the oil and stir in the rice, the meat and the sliced tomatoes. Add the onion, garlic, parsley, saffron, salt and pepper and cook, stirring, for about 15 minutes, then add the stock. Cover the casserole closely and cook, gently in a moderate oven (350° F., mark 4) for 30–40 minutes, until the rice has absorbed the stock. Add the cooked peas and mushrooms (or other suitable cooked vegetables) shortly before serving.

ISCAS
(LAMB'S LIVER AND GAMMON)

1 lb. lamb's liver, cut into slices	1 clove of garlic
	1 bay leaf
½ lb. gammon rashers	Salt and pepper
¼ pint red wine	1 tbsp. chopped
1 tbsp. olive oil	parsley

Put the sliced liver and gammon rashers into a fireproof dish, add the wine, oil, garlic, bay leaf and seasoning, cover, and cook in a moderate oven (350° F., mark 3) for 30–40 minutes. Sprinkle the dish with the finely chopped parsley before serving.

PORTUGUESE COOKING SAUCE FOR MEAT

1 onion, chopped	1 tomato, chopped (optional)
2 tbsps. olive oil	
1 garlic clove, chopped	Meat broth or gravy
1 bouquet garni (parsley, celery, bay leaf, and 1 other herb, e.g., tarragon, thyme, marjoram)	½ cup white wine or 3 tbsps. Madeira (optional)

Slowly fry the onion in the oil until it begins to colour, then add the garlic and fry till golden. Add the bouquet garni and tomato and simmer; add the broth and wine and simmer again.

Meat which is to be braised or pot-roasted is browned first of all with the onion and garlic. Meats (or vegetables) which are to be boiled, are added after the broth. For roast meats, add this sauce (hot) to the tin when basting begins.

W.C.B.—14

FRIED PORK CHOPS

Trim any superfluous fat from 4–6 chops. Make a marinade of 1 tsp. salt, 4 crushed peppercorns, 1 tbsp. chopped parsley, 1 chopped bay leaf, 2 crushed cloves, some chopped pickle and sufficient tomato sauce to mix. Put the chops in this and leave for 2 days in the refrigerator, turning them over occasionally. Wipe the chops and fry (or grill). Serve with a tomato or piquant sauce and pickles.

LOMBO DE PORCO
(LOIN OF PORK)

2 lb. loin of pork	2 tomatoes
1 tbsp. butter	Chopped parsley
1 tbsp. lard	¼ pint white wine or
Salt and pepper	stock
2 onions	Cooked vegetables to
2 carrots	garnish

Prepare the meat and heat the butter and lard in a saucepan. Rub the meat well with salt and brown it on all sides. Add the sliced onions, carrots, tomatoes, a little parsley and liquid, with plenty of seasoning. Simmer gently for 2–2½ hours, until the meat is tender. Put it on a hot dish, strain the sauce over it and garnish with cooked aubergines, sweet peppers, peas, small potatoes, etc., sautéed in a little butter.

BAKED KID

4 lb. young goat in large pieces (an assortment of cuts from leg, chops and breast)	⅛ tsp. freshly ground pepper
	Salt
1 garlic clove, crushed	1 cup white wine
½ bay leaf	2 tbsps. lemon juice
3 tbsps. vinegar	¼ cup beef fat, melted
1 tbsp. minced parsley	3 cups rice, freshly cooked

Mix all the ingredients (except the rice) in a large bowl; let it stand for 2–3 hours, turning the meat over occasionally so that it will be evenly flavoured. Place the meat with the marinade liquor in a baking tin and put into a moderately hot oven (400° F., mark 6); reduce the heat and bake until tender and nicely browned, basting often. Remove the meat, pour off some of the fat from the gravy in the tin, and strain the rest; put it back in the tin, turn the rice into it and mix well; heat through and serve with the meat.

LOMBO DE VITELA Á PORTUGUESA
(PORTUGUESE LOIN OF VEAL)

Season the meat with salt and pepper and put in a deep dish with some white wine and a clove of garlic; let it stand in this marinade for several hours, turning it often. Remove the garlic, pour off half the wine, brush the joint over with melted butter and lard and roast it in a moderate oven (375° F., mark 5) until done; baste frequently with the sauce.

PORTUGUESE-STYLE CUTLETS

74

1 oz. butter	¼ pint water
1 chopped onion	Seasoning
2 tomatoes	2 tsps. vinegar
1 tbsp. tomato purée	1 tsp. sugar
1 tsp. cornflour	8 lamb cutlets
½ bouillon cube	

Melt the butter and gently sauté the onion; add the tomatoes and tomato purée, cover with a lid and cook slowly for ½ hour, then sieve. Mix in the cornflour and some stock (made with the bouillon cube and water) and thicken gently; season to taste and add the vinegar and sugar. Grill the cutlets and dish up on a large platter, overlapping each other, with the hot sauce poured round. Green vegetables may be piled in the centre.

STUFFED CUCUMBERS

Peel some small cucumbers and cut in half. Remove the seeds and fill the cavity with cooked minced meat, well seasoned and bound together with sauce. Tie the two halves together, place in a casserole or stewpan on top of some sliced onion, turnip and carrots and half-cover with stock. Season well, cover and cook gently for about 30 minutes. Remove the threads before dishing up the cucumbers.

STUFFED COURGETTES

Prepare and cook as for cucumbers, above.

OVOS DUROS Á PORTUGUESA
(PORTUGUESE HARD-BOILED EGGS)

3 large tomatoes	Tomato sauce or purée
Salt and pepper	seasoned with salt,
Oil	pepper and garlic
6 hard-boiled eggs	

Cut the tomatoes crossways in half and remove the pulp. Season lightly with salt and pepper, and cook in hot oil for a few minutes. Place a freshly shelled egg in each tomato half and pour over them a little thick tomato sauce or purée.

HAM AND GARLIC OMELETTE

4 oz. raw lean ham	Salt and pepper
1 clove of garlic	½ oz. butter
5–6 fresh eggs	

Shred the ham or cut into small dice. Chop the garlic finely and mix with the ham, put into a bowl and add the eggs. Beat lightly, add a little salt and pepper and cook the omelette lightly in the hot melted butter in the usual way.

TORRIJAS DE NATA
(FRIED CREAM)

1 cup double cream	Butter for frying
3 egg yolks	Caster sugar
1 beaten egg	Ground cinnamon

Whisk the cream; beat the egg yolks lightly and whisk into the cream. Spread the mixture about ½ inch thick in a greased frying pan, put over a very low heat and cook slowly until thick. Cook, then cut in small pieces. Using a spatula to move them, take them from the pan and brush over lightly with beaten egg. Fry in the hot butter, sprinkle with sugar and cinnamon and serve at once.

PUDIM DE MAÇÃS
(APPLE PUDDING)

8 large cooking apples	½ cup citron peel, finely chopped
1½ cups sugar	½ cup blanched and shredded pistachio nuts
½ cup seeded raisins	
½ cup seedless raisins or sultanas	
	Juice of ¼ of a lemon

Core, peel and slice 5 of the apples. Add the sugar and just enough water to cook them; stew until tender, then add the dried fruit, peel and nuts, stirring well. Core and peel the remaining apples and cut into thin rings; sprinkle the lemon juice over them and put half of them in the bottom of a buttered baking dish. Spread the cooked apples over them, then put the remaining raw slices on top. Bake for ½ hour in a moderate oven (350° F., mark 4). Serve hot.

BREAD MOUNTAIN

75

½ lb. white bread (without crusts)	½ tsp. cinnamon
½ pint red wine	3 eggs
8 oz. sugar	Fat for frying
Thinly peeled rind of ½ a lemon	Apricot jam
	6 oz. caster sugar

Cut the bread into fingers and put into a bowl. Put the wine, 8 oz. sugar, lemon peel and cinnamon into a small pan and bring slowly to the boil. Beat the egg yolks over the heat until thick, then add the wine, stirring all the time. Strain over the bread and leave for about 15 minutes. Brown the fingers of bread in hot fat and when cold, spread with the jam. Pile into a heap on a dish and cover with the whisked egg whites and caster sugar, reserving some of the sugar to sprinkle over the top. Bake in a slow oven (325 F., mark 2) till the meringue is a light golden-brown.

ARROZ DOCE
(RICE PUDDING)

Put 1 teacupful washed rice in fast-boiling water, with some lemon rind, and when it is nearly tender, drain it. Beat 2 egg yolks into enough milk to cover the rice, add 2 tbsps. sugar, and pour into the pan. Cook till soft and creamy, turn the mixture into a serving dish and decorate the top with powdered cinnamon in a pattern of criss-cross lines.

BANANA CREAM

¼ oz. gelatine	2 oz. caster sugar
¼ pint milk	½ pint double cream
6–8 bananas	

Dissolve the gelatine in the warmed milk and put aside to cool, but do not allow to set. Peel and slice the bananas and mix with the sugar. Whip the cream until thick, and fold into the sweetened bananas and the cold milk and gelatine. Turn into a glass dish or individual glasses or dishes, leave until set and serve with small cakes or biscuits.

ORANGE OMELETTE

Mix together 4 oz. sugar, a pinch of salt, the juice of 1 lemon and 1 tsp. orange-flower water, add 4 eggs, and beat lightly. Put a knob of butter into a pan and cook the mixture, stirring all the time, until just set, then serve it at once.

SUSPIROS DE FREIRA
(SIGHS OF A NUN)

6 tbsps. butter	2–3 pieces of thinly
3¾ cups granulated sugar	cut lemon rind
3½ cups hot water	Powdered cinnamon
Flour	Icing sugar
3 eggs	

Put the butter, ¾ cup of sugar and 2 cups of hot water into a saucepan and bring to the boil. Quickly stir in enough flour to hold the dough together; when it leaves the sides of the pan, remove from the heat and beat in the eggs, one at a time. Roll out the dough on a slightly floured board to about ½ inch thick and cut into small squares. Make a syrup with the remaining sugar and water and the lemon peel; boil for 2–3 minutes and cook the pastry squares in it, a few at a time. Drain and serve on a hot plate, dusted with the cinnamon and sugar. Alter-natively, flavour the cooking syrup to taste with a sweet white wine.

PUDIM DE NOSES
(COLD WALNUT PUDDING)

6 oz. shelled walnuts	5 eggs
A little powdered cinnamon	6 oz. caster sugar

Grind the walnuts and flavour with a little cinnamon. Beat up the egg yolks with the sugar until pale straw-coloured and thick, then beat in the ground nuts. Whisk the egg whites until very stiff, and then fold them into the other mixture. Grease a pudding mould, and sprinkle the inside with caster sugar. Pour in the mixture —it should come three-quarters of the way up the sides—put some greaseproof paper on top, and steam for ¾–1 hour. When it is ready, turn it out of the mould; eat cold, with whipped cream and fruit syrup.

SWEET CLOUDS

Make a custard with 3–4 egg yolks and 1 pint milk, with sugar to make it really sweet. Pour into individual glasses and leave to cool. Beat the egg whites until very stiff and poach by dropping spoonfuls into boiling milk (they cook very quickly). Lift from the milk with a draining spoon and cap the cold custard with the poached " sweet clouds."

TORTA DE AMENDOA
(ALMOND SPONGE)

6 eggs	½ tsp. cinnamon
¾ cup granulated sugar	1 tbsp. sherry
¾ cup finely ground almonds	

Beat the egg whites and yolks separately. Mix the sugar with the ground almonds, and add to the egg yolks, beating continuously until well blended; add the cinnamon and sherry and lastly fold in the beaten egg whites. Pour into an 8-inch cake tin lined with oiled paper. (The lining paper should stand about an inch above the tin, and the paper which must cover the top to prevent burning, can rest on the edge of this, so that it is not in direct contact with the mixture.) The mixture, which will rise to quite a height, is then baked in a moderate oven (350° F., mark 4) until it is golden-brown and springs back after having been pressed with the finger. It will take about an hour.

Alternatively put the mixture into dariole moulds or similar containers and steam like custards.

To many people " the Balkans " conjures up only a vision of wild, almost barbarous country, inhabited mainly by brigands and where the diet consists solely of mutton and sour milk. There is, perhaps, a remote grain of truth in this idea, but only a grain, for the Balkan peoples are friendly and volatile, the country ranges from the softly pastoral to the grandly mountainous ; the great cities of Sofia and Bucharest are of almost fairy-tale loveliness, while the food is rich, delicious and altogether excellent.

Owing to the long Turkish domination in the Balkans, many dishes are common to all the countries, though they all have individuality ; garlic is favoured in Bulgaria and dill and lovage in Rumania ; Bulgarians cook in olive oil, while Rumanians prefer lard ; the Balkans are essentially sheep countries and mutton and lamb are the chief meats in both regions, but veal and beef are served in Rumania rather more frequently than in Bulgaria. Grain and fruit grow readily and fruit is much used as a sweet course, with rich sweet pastries of the mille-feuilles type.

Eggs, cream and cheese often form part of a meat or vegetable dish—many dishes, in fact, do tend to be very rich and spicy, but can be adapted to suit the cook's own tastes and income. Good restaurants are to be found in Bucharest where the French influence has been felt, but in the countryside and in Bulgaria restaurants are infrequent and the traveller eats at small taverns or sometimes in convents and monasteries.

The daily meals of the poorer peasants consist largely of soup, bread, olives and curd cheese ; meat is something of a rarity. Beans are much eaten in soups and stews and salads are also popular. Much importance is attached to the quality of the flour used in bread-making, for bread constitutes the staple diet of the peasants. It is generally of a light brown colour, baked into flat, round loaves.

Koumis, a beverage composed of fermented cow's milk, is drunk, but ouzo, raki and slivovitz are the most widely known drinks. Dryish, rather sour wines are produced, but not exported.

Rumania
and
Bulgaria

Rumania

TRIPE SOUP

1 lb. tripe	Yolks of 2 eggs
3 onions	1 cup vinegar
2 cloves of garlic	1 cup butter
4 pimientos or chilli peppers	

Bring the tripe to the boil in cold water and drain. Cover with fresh water, the chopped onions, the garlic and 2 pimientos or peppers and the vinegar. Soak for an hour and then chop finely and add 2 more pimientos. Simmer all together until the tripe is tender and thicken the liquid with butter and egg yolks. Serve hot.

SUPA TARANEASCA
(PEASANT SOUP)

2 lb. of any vegetables in season	1 oz. sour cream or the yolk of an egg mixed with cream
1 or 2 diced onions	
1 tbsp. olive oil or butter	Salt and pepper

Cut the vegetables small and cook in the fat for a few moments. Cover with boiling water and simmer for about an hour. At the last minute beat in a little sour cream, or the yolk of an egg mixed with the cream. Add seasoning.

CHORBA TARANEASCA
(SOUP WITH MEAT)

1 small chicken, or 2 lb. veal or beef	1 large carrot
	3–4 tomatoes
Salt	A pinch of red pepper
2 sliced onions	1 tsp. chopped parsley
A few chopped celery leaves	A sprig of thyme

Cut the meat, or the chicken, into small pieces. Put in a pan with cold water and let it come to the boil. Skim well. Add salt, the vegetables, chopped small, and the red pepper. Simmer for about 2 hours, adding more water if necessary. Sprinkle on the chopped parsley and the sprig of thyme when it is ready to be served.

SOUR SOUP WITH MEAT BALLS

2–3 lb. bones	1 lb. minced beef
3 chopped onions	Salt and pepper
1 shredded carrot	A little bread
1 small finely shredded parsnip	2 tbsps. milk
	1 tbsp. plain flour
1 oz. chopped celery leaves	1 egg
	1 oz. chopped dill
1 oz. chopped parsley	½ oz. finely chopped lovage
1 sprig of thyme	

Make a broth from the bones by simmering in salted water for 3–4 hours. Strain, add 2 onions, the carrot, the parsnip, the celery, the parsley and the thyme. While these are cooking put the minced meat into a bowl, add salt, pepper and 1 grated onion, a handful of bread soaked in milk, the flour, egg and dill. Mix well, form into small balls, and drop into the boiling soup. Simmer for another 10–15 minutes. Then add the souring agent (see below) and the chopped lovage.

Souring Agent : Often, particularly during the summer, the Balkan people add a souring agent to soups. This can be citric acid, diluted with a little water, or it can be the juice of unripe green plums, grapes or rhubarb, stewed and sieved. A more complicated method is to allow cabbage and other vegetables to ferment for a short time and then pour off the juice.

BAKED STERLET

2 lb. sterlet	¼ lb. butter
1 small bunch mixed herbs	½ pint white wine
	Salt
Juice of half a lemon	Pepper

Clean and skin the fish thoroughly. Place in a large baking dish, with salt, pepper and the herbs, chopped very finely. Pour in the lemon juice and the wine. Dot with butter, and bake it for about an hour, basting frequently, until it is nicely browned (350° F., mark 4).

HARD ROE SALAD

In Rumania this is made with the roe of a carp or a pike, but if these are unobtainable, cod's or herring's roe would do as well.

As much hard roe as required for the number of people to be served	Juice of 1 lemon.
	A thick slice of crustless bread
Olive oil, equivalent amount	A little milk and water
	Salt and pepper

Take the hard roe, put it in a bowl, and mix it well with a stainless fork to get out all the fibres. To about ½ lb. of roe you will need almost a teacup of olive oil, half a lemon and a thick slice of crustless bread, soaked in milk and water. Squeeze the bread, flake it, or better still, pass it through a fairly large sieve before adding it to the roe. Season. Beat the whole mixture well. Add the oil in very small quantities at a time, as for mayonnaise. Beat with an electric-mixer if you have one, or with a fork. The mixture should come out fluffy, but stiff like whipped cream or the white of an egg. Lemon juice can be added, according to taste. This can be served as an entrée, garnished with olives, or on small croûtons for cocktails.

PIU CU CUIPERCI
(CHICKEN WITH MUSHROOMS)

1 young chicken	1 small onion
3–4 oz. butter	½ cup chopped parsley
1 tsp. flour	½ cup chopped dill
1–2 cups of stock	Small glass red or white
1 lb. mushrooms	wine

Divide the chicken into neat pieces, fry in butter until they change colour. Add the flour and let it brown, then put in the stock, stirring well to loosen the flour. See that the liquid covers the chicken, add the chopped mushrooms, the onion whole, the chopped parsley and dill, and lastly, the wine. Cover and cook until the meat is tender and the sauce reduced to the consistency of a thick gravy. Sour cream is sometimes served with this dish.

CHICKEN WITH SAUCE

1 chicken	Butter, margarine or
2 peppercorns	lard
1 onion	Flour
2 sticks celery	¾ pint water
1 tsp. chopped parsley	Salt
1 clove of garlic	Pepper
1 bay leaf	

Clean the bird, divide it into small pieces and put it to boil with sufficient water to cover. Skim, add salt, peppercorns, onion, garlic, celery, bay leaf and parsley. Simmer for 40 minutes. Remove the chicken and keep hot. Make a sauce, using 1 dessertsp. of butter or lard for each person, with 1 dessertsp. flour for each spoonful of fat. Stir over low heat, but do not brown. Gradually add the liquid from the pan, stirring well all the time. Simmer for 10–15 minutes, add salt and pepper, the pieces of chicken and a piece of butter. Serve immediately.

DUCK WITH BLACK OLIVES

1 duck cut into pieces	2–3 bay leaves
1 lb. large black olives	Salt and pepper
1 lb. small onions	Peppercorns
1 parsnip	Olive oil
2 carrots	1 tbsp. plain flour
A little chopped parsley	A little wine
1 lemon	

Make stock from the neck, giblets and bones of the duck with 1 small onion, peppercorns and a little parsley. Skim well and add the other vegetables and some salt. Fry the pieces of duck in olive oil in a deep pan and keep warm while you fry the onions whole in the same oil. Make a sauce from the oil, flour and stock with the bay leaves. Arrange the meat in the pan, put in the onions, and the sauce with the bay leaves,
season and let it all cook together for 1 hour. In the meantime, stone the olives, put them in a pan, cover with cold water and bring to the boil. Strain and tip the olives into the pan with the meat. Let them simmer together for another half-hour and add a little wine. Peel the lemon, slice it and put in a small pan with a little water and boil for 5 minutes. Take out the slices of lemon and add the juice to the meat. When the duck is done take it out, arrange it on a dish, with the onions and olives, place the slices of lemon on top, and pour over the gravy. Can be served either hot or cold.

Chicken or hare can also be cooked like this.

TOCANA
(ONION STEW)

1 lb. meat	3–4 oz. lard, butter or
1–2 lb. onions	oil
Tomatoes, or a cup	Pepper
of tomato pulp with	A little vinegar
water	Peppers (optional)
Salt	

Cut the meat into small pieces and fry in the fat, stirring all the time. When the meat has browned, add the onions, neatly sliced, and cover the pan for a minute or two until the onions get soft. Uncover and stir continually until the onions are dark brown. Season to taste and add a teaspoon of vinegar. Skin and chop the pepper and tomatoes and add them to the stew, stirring now and then so that it does not catch. It may be necessary to add a little boiling water from time to time, until the meat is really done. The stew is very rich and eaten with *mamaliga*, a thick porridge of water, salt and polenta or maize flour; and pickled cucumbers.

GUTUI CA CARNE
(QUINCES WITH MEAT)

1 lb. veal or beef or one	2 cups stock or water
small chicken	1 tsp. flour
6 large quinces	1 tbsp. sugar
½ cup butter or lard	Salt and pepper

Cut the meat into small pieces, fry them in the fat until rich brown, add a good teaspoon flour, let it brown, add stock and seasonings and simmer. Peel and quarter the quinces, dry them and fry them in fat in another pan. When the meat is nearly cooked, add the quinces. Let them simmer until tender but do not overcook.

ROASTED PEPPER SALAD

3–4, or as many as are	A little salt
required, large green	2 tbsps. olive oil
or red peppers	1 tbsp. vinegar

Roast the peppers on the top shelf in the oven (400° F., mark 6) until they are completely covered with brown blisters. As soon as one is ready, take it off, put it in a basin, sprinkle it with salt and leave it to cool with a cover on. When all the peppers are done and are cooled, dip the fingers in cold water, peel off the blistered skin and remove stalk and seeds. Arrange the peppers in a dish, cover them with oil and vinegar, and serve them with aubergine salad, or with any kind of cold meat.

EGGS WITH TOMATOES

2 onions	Salt and pepper
4 tomatoes	3½ oz. minced meat
4 eggs	(optional)
3½ oz. butter or oil	

Slice and fry the onions and tomatoes in the butter until soft. Season to taste. Break the eggs into the mixture and cook until set. Put the mixture into individual bowls. If minced meat is being used, this should be cooked with the onions and tomatoes before adding the eggs.

CIUIAMA DE CIUPERCI
(MUSHROOMS WITH CREAM SAUCE)

1–2 lb. mushrooms	1 cup sour cream
1 very small onion	½ cup butter
A little green parsley	Salt
½ tsp. dill	Pepper
2 tsps. plain flour	

Chop the onion finely and fry in the butter; add the chopped mushrooms, salt and pepper. Cook gently for about 10 minutes or until mushrooms shrink. Put in the finely chopped herbs, cover the pan. Mix the flour with the cream and pour it over the mushrooms; cook gently for another 10 minutes, stirring occasionally. Serve very hot.

Bulgaria

TRIPE SOUP

1 lb. of tripe	1 cup rice
½ oz. flour	2 cups water
1 cup butter, margarine	2–3 bay leaves
or oil	Salt and pepper
1 tsp. chopped parsley	2 eggs

Blanch the tripe in salted water, drain and cut it into strips, reserving the water. Fry the flour in the fat and add the tripe, the water, the bay leaves, the parsley and the rice. Simmer until the tripe is tender. Beat up the eggs and mix carefully with the soup. Do not allow it to boil. Sprinkle with pepper and serve. If desired, a clove of garlic and a little vinegar can also be added.

FISH SOUP

1½ lb. white fish	1 tbsp. flour
1 large onion, chopped	Pepper and salt to taste
4 tbsps. oil	A pinch of red pepper
1 egg	3 cups water
1 tbsp. chopped parsley	

Cut the fish into small pieces, wash and sprinkle with salt. Fry onion in the oil, add red pepper and flour and fry till lightly brown. Add 3 cups water and some salt, and simmer until the onion is cooked. Put the pieces of fish in the pan and let the mixture cook gently for about 20 minutes to half an hour. Beat the egg with a little of the soup and add gradually to the rest. Adjust seasoning and add parsley. Can be served hot or cold.

TARATOR
(COLD CUCUMBER SOUP)

Beat up a bottle of yoghourt, add some cucumber cut into very small cubes, some bread-crumbs and some chopped walnuts, a little olive oil, 1 pounded clove of garlic, salt, pepper and a little vinegar. Beat all together and refrigerate. Serve very cold.

BAKED FISH

1 lb. of any white fish	1 small pimiento
½ cup sliced onion	1 sliced lemon
½ lb. tomatoes	½ cup oil or butter

Slice the fish and put it into a baking tin, with the oil or butter; cover with the onions, tomatoes, sliced pimiento and sliced lemon. Cook in a moderate oven (350° F., mark 4) for about 30 minutes.

POACHED EGGS ON YOGHOURT

4 eggs	3 tbsps. butter
½ tbsp. vinegar	Salt and paprika
1 pint yoghourt	2 cloves of garlic

Beat the yoghourt well, crush the garlic and add with the salt and vinegar; pour the mixture into four little bowls. Poach the eggs in the usual way, and put one in each bowl, being careful not to break them. Melt the butter, pour over the eggs, sprinkle with salt and the paprika.

PLAKIE
(VEGETABLE MEDLEY)

1 lb. green beans	½ cup tomato purée
1 lb. tomatoes	diluted with water
1 cup chopped onions	Salt and pepper
1 cup oil	A little sugar

Fry the onions and tomatoes in the oil. Boil the beans until they are soft and then drain them carefully. Add them to the onions and tomatoes, pour in the diluted tomato purée. Add salt, pepper and a little sugar. Simmer for about half an hour to an hour. Can be eaten hot or cold. Serves 2–3 people.

STEWED BEANS

Soak 1 lb. haricot beans overnight in cold water, drain, cover with fresh water and bring to the boil. Fry about 1 lb. chopped onions and 1 lb. sliced tomatoes in 2 cups of oil. Add the beans with a little water, simmer for about half an hour, until beans are tender.

GYOVECH
(MEAT AND VEGETABLES)

2 lb. fat beef or veal	6 green peppers
2–3 tbsps. oil or butter	1 green tomato
3–4 potatoes	Salt and pepper
5 tomatoes	1 or 2 eggs
1 large aubergine	Juice of $\frac{1}{2}$ a lemon
A cup of French beans	1 spoonful of flour

Cut the vegetables in pieces. The aubergine must be sliced, salted, allowed to stand for 1 hour and then drained before being added to the other vegetables. Meanwhile, cut the meat into small pieces and put them into a pan with the butter or oil, salt and pepper. Fry gently till brown and then cover with water and simmer for about 30 minutes. Then add all the vegetables, cut into slices or diced, and more water. Stir well and simmer till the vegetables and meat are tender. Heap into a baking dish and put into a slow oven (300° F., mark 1). Beat up 1–2 eggs, add 1 tablespoonful of flour, the juice of $\frac{1}{2}$ a lemon and a little salt. Pour the egg mixture over the dish in the oven and continue cooking for a few more minutes until the egg is set. This is a national dish.

GREEN " CAVIARE "

This dish is much favoured in Bulgaria. For this aubergines (1 per person) are baked for about an hour, dipped in cold water and then skinned. The pulp is minced very finely, or sometimes pounded in a mortar. It is then mixed with grated onion, a crushed clove of garlic, the pulp of 2 tomatoes, 1 cup of oil, salt and pepper and a few drops of vinegar.

CUCUMBER SALAD

2 cucumbers	1 tsp. sugar
1 teacup sour cream	1 clove of garlic
3 tsps. lemon juice	Salt and pepper

Rub the salad bowl with garlic; peel the cucumbers and slice them very finely, sprinkle them with salt, and set aside for about 10 minutes, then drain well. Mix the lemon juice with the sour cream and sugar. Pour the mixture over the cucumbers and serve with fish or meat. Add a dash of pepper to taste.

IN a country as vast as the U.S.S.R. the food naturally varies in different districts, but there is nevertheless a national cookery which is universal and characteristically Russian. Even the simplest dishes are made exotic by the use of sharply contrasted flavours and the addition of sour cream. Dill, nettles, sorrel and green peppers give a tang to sauces and soups. Fresh, whipped cream is widely used for sweets, while *smetana* and *kephir* (varieties of sour cream) are used for both sweet and savoury dishes. *Smetana* can be bought here in some continental shops, but it can be quite easily made at home. It is only necessary to leave thick, double cream in a warm place until it is just sour, but has not become " cheesy."

Although many areas of Russia are far from the sea, the great rivers are rich in fresh-water fish and much dried and salted fish is used. The sturgeon, a migratory fish like the salmon, is in season from March to July and has firm, dry flesh of excellent flavour. The salted roe of the sturgeon gives the world-famous caviare or *ikra*. The sterlet is a fish of the same family as the sturgeon, though not often obtainable here. The eggs of the sterlet also make very fine caviare and its marrow, like that of the sturgeon, is dried and salted and used to add a rich flavour to fish dishes.

During the summer months vegetables and fruit are plentiful and freely used, but for the long winter, when the ground is deeply covered with ice and snow, much preservation of garden foods is necessary and vegetables are very cleverly salted and pickled. Instead of salad or fresh vegetables, several kinds of pickled vegetables are served together during the winter months. Sauerkraut and a delicious apple and cabbage pickle are useful preserves and pickled cucumbers and dried mushrooms of many kinds add flavour to typical Russian dishes. Of the delicious jams and conserves made in the summer, cherry jam and rose petal jam are the most notable and Povidlo the most usual. This is a thick jam of the consistency of damson cheese and is made from plums, apricots or apples. Jam is served in small individual dishes with glasses of China tea.

A Russian meal will start with Zakouski, that copious hot or cold hors d'œuvre, which is followed by soup, generally garnished with sour cream. In the summer the soup is often served cold. The main dish of fish or meat is a hearty one ; sturgeon and trout are both plentiful and delicious and meat is frequently stewed and served in a rich sauce thickened with sour cream. Sorbets or frozen fruit juices are offered between courses and sweets are very often composed of fruit in one form or another.

Tea is very much a national drink in Russia and is served at all times. The Russian taste is for China tea and it is generally sweetened very lavishly—sometimes with jam rather than sugar.

The Caucasus produces a good selection of red and white wines. *Kvass* is a pleasant, slightly alcoholic drink made usually from rye, malt, yeast, sugar and mint leaves. It is rather like cider or perry. Vodka, a white, almost tasteless spirit, which is now very popular outside Russia, is served with Zakouski.

Russia

ZAKOUSKI

These are a hearty hors d'œuvre, consisting of all kinds of small savouries. Typical zakouski include caviare of all sizes and consistencies, served with lemon juice, black pepper and rye bread and butter; mock caviare made from aubergines, onions and tomato purée; pickled mushrooms; blini pancakes; piroshki, which resemble profiteroles are filled with savoury mixtures and are served hot; smoked sausages in tomato sauce; cold meats; pickled fish and tiny cream cheese dumplings, called Tvoroinki.

BLINI
(SAVOURY PANCAKES)

¾ oz. yeast	3 eggs, separated
¾ lb. sifted flour	2 tbsp. cream
½ pint milk	A pinch of salt

Dissolve yeast in ½ pint milk and make a dough with part of the flour; leave to prove in a warm place for 2 hours. Add remaining flour, egg yolks, cream and salt to the dough and mix well to form a thickish batter. Add stiffly beaten egg whites to the mixture and leave for ½ hour. Fry pancakes in a small pan. Spread with butter, sour cream, caviare or smoked fish and pile up.

TVOROINKI
(CREAM CHEESE DUMPLINGS)

2 oz. butter	3 eggs
½ lb. firm cream cheese	14 oz. flour
A pinch of salt	

Soften butter and mix with cheese, salt, eggs and 8 oz. of the flour. When these are well mixed, rub through a sieve and add the rest of the flour. Form the mixture into small balls and cook in gently boiling water for about 15 minutes, or till they float; drain and serve with melted butter.

BORTSCH
(BEETROOT SOUP)

4 large uncooked beet-root	Pepper and salt
	1 tsp. vinegar
1 oz. butter	Sour cream
3–4 pints very rich beef or pork stock	Cooked sausages

Wash the beetroot and shred finely. Melt the butter in a saucepan and sauté the shredded beetroot for about 10 minutes, then stir in a little hot stock and cook gently. When this stock is absorbed add the remainder of the stock, season, add vinegar and simmer until the beetroot is quite tender. Strain and serve with a few thin slices of sausage as a garnish and to each plateful add 1 tbsp. very cold sour cream.

If the soup is pale in colour, put a raw beetroot into muslin and shake it in the soup to restore the scarlet colour. It should not be boiled, or it will turn a dull brown colour.

Note : With the Bortsch may be served hard-boiled eggs, small rusks or tartlets filled with cream cheese.

KEISEJ SHCHI
(SAUERKRAUT SOUP)

1 lb. sauerkraut	1 tsp. chopped parsley
4 carrots	1 oz. fat
Bone stock	2 tbsps. yoghourt or
1 lb. potatoes	sour cream
Pepper and salt	

Cut up the potatoes into dice and braise these with the sauerkraut in the fat and 1 or 2 tbsps. of stock. Add the carrots, cut up into small pieces and about 1 pint of bone stock. Add the seasoning and leave to simmer for 30–40 minutes. Just before serving add the chopped parsley and the yoghourt or sour cream.

SHCHI
(CABBAGE SOUP)

1 white-heart cabbage	Peppercorns
6 large potatoes	4 or 5 tomatoes
1 quart meat stock	Green parsley or dill
1 bay leaf	

Wash and shred the cabbage, peel and cut up the potatoes. Put the cabbage into boiling stock with the bay leaf and a few peppercorns. When the cabbage is nearly cooked add the potatoes. Skin and slice the tomatoes and add just before serving, with a little chopped parsley or dill.

OUKHA
(SOUP OF FRESH-WATER FISH)

This is one of the many excellent fish soups which are typically Russian. Though usually made of fresh-water fish, bream, halibut or turbot may be used and the addition of shelled crayfish or prawns improves the soup.

2 lb. fish	1 large bunch of parsley
4 pints water	Salt
1 onion	4 oz. chives
1 leek	Fresh fennel leaves (if available)
1 celery stalk	
1 bay leaf	

Fillet the fish and put the bones into the water with the sliced onion, leek, celery, bay leaf, parsley and salt. Bring to the boil and add 1¾ lb. of fish. Simmer slowly for 1 hour and then strain. Cut the remaining fish into small pieces and fry in butter. Serve the soup hot, adding the pieces of fried fish, prawns or crayfish and chopped chives or spring onions and chopped fennel.

CHILLED BORTSCH

1 quart good beef stock or 2 tins consommé	2 tbsps. lemon juice
¼ pint sour cream or yoghourt	A good bunch chives, finely chopped
1 lb. cooked beetroot	Sour cream
	Watercress to garnish

Beat the stock with the cream or yoghourt until smooth. Add the beetroot, skinned and cut into neat fine dice. Add the lemon juice and the chives. Chill for several hours. Serve in soup cups with a spoonful of sour cream on each cup and garnish with a tiny sprig of watercress. (If preferred, this soup may be puréed.)

KRAPIVNIE SHCHI
(YOUNG NETTLE SOUP)

1½ lb. young nettles	A few cooked sausages
1 lb. spinach	2 tbsps. yoghourt or sour cream
1 pint rich bone stock	

Blanch the nettles and mix them with the washed spinach. Pour the boiling stock over them and simmer gently for 40 minutes, adding a little more stock if necessary. Strain and serve with a garnish of small lengths of cooked sausage and add the yoghourt just before serving.

FRIED PIKE

4 lb. pike	White breadcrumbs
Salt	Fat for frying
2 eggs	Lemon and parsley

Bone the fish and cut into ¾-inch steaks. Salt them on both sides and leave overnight. Wipe off the salt; egg and breadcrumb the pieces of fish and fry in shallow fat until well browned. Garnish with lemon and parsley.

ASPASIA OF FISH

4 lb. fish (pike, perch, carp, whiting or salmon)	¼ lb. butter
	5 fresh mushrooms
3 small bread rolls	6 eggs
½ pint milk	2 truffles
Salt and pepper	¾ pint good mushroom sauce

Wash the fish and remove the skin and bones. Cut the fish into small pieces and pound in a mortar. Remove the crusts from the bread rolls and soak the white bread in the milk. Mix the soaked bread with the fish, add salt and pepper and sieve the mixture. Melt the butter in a pan and add the finely chopped mushrooms, stirring slowly for a few minutes over gentle heat. Add this to the fish mixture together with the beaten egg yolks.

Beat the whites of egg to a stiff froth and fold in; then pour the mixture into a buttered mould which is first decorated with the finely chopped truffles. Steam for 1 hour. Unmould the aspasia. Pour over it half of the mushroom sauce and serve the rest in a sauce-boat.

RED MULLETS IN SOUR CREAM

4 red mullets	¼ lb. butter
1 tbsp. flour	¼ pint sour cream
Salt	

Clean fish through gills and wash and wipe well. Coat each fish with flour, and sprinkle with salt. Melt the butter in a frying pan and fry the fish on both sides. Then pour the cream over the fish in the same frying pan and keep on the heat until the cream begins to turn deep yellow.

STURGEON (OR SALMON) À LA RUSSE

4 lb. fish	10 shallots
Salt and pepper	10 mushrooms
2 tsps. vinegar	1 oz. butter
2 stalks of celery	1 oz. flour
1 carrot	2 tbsps. tomato purée
2 leeks	1 tbsp. capers
1 onion	1 pickled gherkin
3 pickled cucumbers	5 olives

Clean and scale the fish, put it into a pan and cover with cold water to which is added 1 tsp. salt and 2 tsps. vinegar, with 1 stalk of celery, 1 carrot, 1 leek and 1 onion. Bring slowly to simmering point and cook for about 40 minutes or until the fish is cooked. Remove and drain the fish. To the stock in which it was cooked add the diced vegetables : 3 pickled cucumbers, 1 stalk of celery, 1 leek, 10 shallots and 10 mushrooms, and boil for 10 minutes. Melt the butter in a saucepan, add the flour, stir well and add some of the hot bouillon. Add this to the bouillon in which the vegetables are cooking with 2 tbsps. tomato purée, the capers, pickled gherkin, olives and salt and pepper to taste. Pour over the fish. This dish is equally good hot or cold.

STEAMED STERLET

4 lb. sterlet	2 onions
¾ pint fish stock	3 small pickled cucumbers
¼ pint white wine	
2 stalks of celery	1 tbsp. melted butter
2 carrots	½ oz. flour

Choose a sterlet with a yellow belly as these are the best kind. Clean, wash, scrape off back fins and place in a large pan or fish kettle.

Pour over the stock and white wine and bring slowly to boiling point, then cook very slowly so

77

that the fish is lightly steamed. When the fish is cooked put it on the serving dish and keep hot. Boil up the stock and add to it the finely shredded vegetables and cucumbers. Thicken the liquid with the butter and flour and pour over the fish.

ROAST CARP WITH MUSHROOM SAUCE

1 carp (4–5 lb.)	1½ oz. butter
Salt	½ pint creamy mush-
1 oz. flour	room sauce

Clean the carp and scrape it well, especially along the back. Dry with a clean cloth, rub all over with a handful of salt and coat the fish with the flour. Melt the butter and lightly fry the fish, then put it in a moderately hot oven (400° F., mark 6) to finish cooking—in all, about 25 minutes. Serve on a hot dish, the fish lying on its stomach to make it easier to help oneself from both sides. Pour the hot sauce over just before serving.

SIMPLE COULIBIAC
(FISH PIE)

78 True Coulibiac, or Hot Salmon Pie, can be a rich and elaborate dish, the filling being fresh salmon fillet with rice or semolina flavoured with mushrooms, onion, chopped parsley, hard-boiled egg and vesiga (the dried marrow of the sturgeon). Here is a simpler form :

½ lb. puff pastry	A little chopped onion
½ lb. white fish	or leek
1 oz. rice or semolina	2 tbsps. béchamel sauce
Chopped parsley	Pepper and salt

Cook the rice or semolina and mix it with the cooked, flaked fish. Add the sauce, seasoning, chopped parsley and onion. Roll the pastry into a large square. Spread the mixture in the centre of it and then fold over each of the four corners so that they meet in the centre of the square. Join the edges, leaving a small opening in the centre. Bake in a hot oven (450° F., mark 8) for 35–40 minutes.

SVINIACHI KOTIETY Z SLYUKAMY
(PORK CHOPS WITH PRUNE SAUCE)

2 lb. dried prunes	¼ cup butter
8 pork chops, 1 inch thick	1 tsp. cinnamon
3 tbsps. flour	½ tsp. powdered cloves
1 beaten egg	½ cup water
½ cup packaged dried breadcrumbs	½ cup port or sherry
	½ tsp. salt
	1 tbsp. sugar

Cook the prunes the day before without sugar, as directed on packet. De-stone and sieve coarsely, measure 1 cup and chill.

One hour before serving trim the fat from the chops ; scrape bones well. Sprinkle chops with flour ; dip in egg, then crumbs. In hot butter in a large pan over medium heat, brown chops on both sides. Lower the heat and cook, covered, 45 minutes, or until tender, turning once (add a little water if needed). Meanwhile, simmer the sieved prunes with the cinnamon, cloves, water, for 10 minutes. Add wine, salt, sugar ; boil up once ; keep warm. Fit paper frill on the end of each tender chop and group on a hot plate with favourite vegetable in centre. Spoon the prune sauce over the chops and serve with mashed potatoes. (Makes 6 to 8 servings.)

ZAVIANI BYTKY
(VEAL ROLLS)

8 veal cutlets, 5 inches by 2½ inches by ¼ inch	¼ tsp. pepper
	1 tbsp. minced onion
	3 tbsps. chopped parsley
¼ lb. minced beef	3 tbsps. butter
¼ lb. lean pork, minced	14-oz. can sliced mush-
2 tbsps. packaged dried breadcrumbs	rooms
	½ pint sour cream
¼ cup cream	1 tsp. sugar
1 egg	1 tsp. piquant table
1½ tsp. salt	sauce

Trim fat from cutlets. Mix the beef, pork, crumbs, cream, egg, 1 tsp. salt, pepper, onion and parsley well together. Then spoon 2 rounded tablespoonfuls of meat mixture on to one end of cutlet. Roll each cutlet from filled end, skewer. Heat the butter in the pan and brown veal well in it. Add the undrained mushrooms, sour cream ; simmer, covered, ¾ hour or till tender. Remove skewers from rolls ; arrange on heated platter. Season gravy with ½ tsp. salt, sugar, piquant sauce ; pour over rolls and serve with mashed potatoes or fluffy rice.

BALORINE
(SAVOURY HASH)

A favourite Russian hash of minced meat with finely chopped spring onions and boiled beetroot and a sprinkling of caraway seeds ; it is usually served with a border of either spinach or sorrel.

CAUCASIAN SHASHLICK

1½–2 lb. best loin of lamb, or leg from a very young animal	1 lemon
	Pepper and salt
	Tomatoes and
½ gill olive oil	pimientos

Cut the meat into pieces about 2 inches square and mix them with a marinade made with the olive oil, lemon juice, pepper and salt. Leave in a cold place overnight.

Then, 15 minutes before you wish to serve

the meal, put the pieces of meat on skewers, with a ripe tomato or pimiento between every 4 pieces. Place under a very hot grill, turning and basting often ; serve with rice and lemon.

Shashlick tastes best grilled as in the Caucasian mountains, on a sword turned slowly over a charcoal fire in the open air.

SELIANAKA
(SAUERKRAUT WITH PORK)

1 lb. pork	2 onions
1½ oz. fat	Pepper
2 lb. sauerkraut	1 oz. capers

Cut the pork into pieces and fry until lightly browned in the hot fat. Drain the sauerkraut through a colander, pressing out the liquid with a plate. Chop the onions and fry them, adding the sauerkraut when they are half cooked. Cook for a further 15 minutes, stirring all the time. Add pepper (not salt) to taste and stir in the capers. Put layers of sauerkraut and pork into a greased casserole and bake in a moderate oven (350° F., mark 4) for about 1 hour.

BASTURMA
(CAUCASIAN GRILLED MEAT)

1½ lb. fillet of beef	¼ lb. spring onions
1 large onion	6 small tomatoes
1 tbsp. vinegar	1 lemon
Salt and pepper	

Trim the meat but do not beat it. Cut into slices and leave in a basin with the vinegar, sliced onion and salt and pepper for 2–3 hours in a cool place, covered with a lid. Put the meat on skewers and grill for 10 minutes, turning frequently. Take the meat off the skewers and serve garnished with spring onions and slices of tomato and lemon.

OX TONGUE WITH RAISIN SAUCE

1 ox tongue	Salt and pepper
1 carrot	1 oz. butter
1 onion	1 oz. flour
Bunch of parsley	4 oz. raisins
1 bay leaf	Juice of ½ a lemon

Wash the tongue and put it in a saucepan with the carrot, onion, parsley, bay leaf, salt and pepper. Cover with tepid water, put on a lid and bring to boiling point. Simmer for 2–3 hours. When the tongue is cooked, rinse in cold water and skin immediately. Carve the tongue into slices and keep hot in a fireproof dish. Make a sauce with the butter, flour and ½ pint of the stock in which the tongue was cooked. Add the washed and stoned raisins and simmer for 10 minutes, stirring well. Add the

lemon juice, season if necessary and pour the sauce over the tongue. Serve with green peas and potato purée.

LIVER IN SOUR CREAM

1 lb. calf's liver	1 onion
¾ pint milk	½ pint sour cream, or
Salt and pepper	¼ pint sour cream
1 tbsp. flour	and ¼ pint water
2 oz. butter	

Wash the liver and put it in a china bowl with enough milk to cover it and let it soak for 1 hour. Take out the liver, wipe it and cut into thin slices. Season with salt and pepper, dip into flour and fry in the hot butter on both sides. Put the liver in a casserole, fry the chopped onion and add it with the cream. Cover and simmer slowly for about 30 minutes.

CUTLETTI

Cutletti or rissoles of various kinds are very popular in Russia. They are made from meat, fish, chicken or game. Bread soaked in milk is always added, and they are bound with egg and formed into flat rissoles in the shape of a cutlet and fried in shallow fat. Raw meat is minced at home for them and flavoured with a little onion or garlic. Fish rissoles are flavoured with nutmeg, game or poultry with mushrooms.

TOOSHONAYA GOVIADINA
(CASSEROLED BEEFSTEAK)

1½ lb. steak	6 small cabbage leaves
1 oz. flour	2 carrots
Fat for frying	6 peppercorns
2 thickly sliced raw potatoes	3 tomatoes

Wipe and beat the steak well. Cut it up into 4-inch squares, coat with flour and fry until lightly browned. Into a deep casserole put layers of steak, potato, whole cabbage leaves and sliced carrot, with the peppercorns and sliced tomato. Add 1 tbsp. water or stock and a little melted fat if necessary, but the juice of the meat and vegetables may provide enough liquid and it should be kept fairly dry. Cook covered in a moderate oven (350° F., mark 4) for 2 hours.

GROUSE WITH GRAPES (A CAUCASIAN DISH)

4 grouse	½ pint stock
1½ lb. grapes	4 ovals of toasted bread
1 oz. butter	1 wineglass red wine
Salt and pepper	Watercress

Stuff the grouse with the grapes, from which the stones have been removed. Put slices of butter on each bird and season with salt and pepper. Roast the grouse in a moderately hot oven (425° F., mark 7) for 15 minutes, then add the stock and cover with a lid. Cook for a further 20 minutes, or until the birds are cooked. Dish them on the pieces of toast, add the wine to the gravy, heat for a few minutes and pour over the grouse. Garnish with watercress.

ZAIYATS V SMETANE
(HARE WITH SOUR CREAM)

Skin and clean a hare. Cut off its head well below the neck, as the head and neck of a hare are of inferior flavour. Make small incisions in the skin and fill them with lard or fat bacon. Rub well with salt, place a few peppercorns inside the body and roast in a moderate oven (350° F., mark 4) for 2 hours, basting frequently. Hares are usually very lean, so at least 4 oz. of fat should be used for the roasting. When the hare is cooked lift it on to another dish and keep hot. Pour away the fat from the roasting tin, leaving only the brown sediment. To this add $\frac{1}{2}$ pint of sour cream and slowly stir in a dessertspoonful of flour and mix well. Blend and cook the sauce carefully and pour it over the carved hare. Serve with beetroot purée.

CHICKEN KIEV

$\frac{1}{2}$ cup butter or margarine	$\frac{1}{8}$ tsp. pepper
1 clove garlic, crushed	1 egg, slightly beaten
2 tsps. chopped chives	1 tbsp. water
2 tsps. chopped parsley	4 $\frac{1}{2}$-lb. chicken breasts, boned
1 tsp. salt	Shortening or salad oil
$\frac{1}{2}$ tsp. crumbled rosemary	$\frac{1}{4}$ cup flour

In a small bowl, combine butter, garlic, chives, parsley, salt, rosemary and pepper; blend well. Lay on sheet of waxed paper; fold paper over top; then pat into $\frac{3}{4}$-inch thick roll. Wrap in the waxed paper; freeze or refrigerate until *very hard*. In a bowl, blend egg and water well. Then with a rolling pin pound each chicken breast to $\frac{1}{4}$ inch thickness. Now cut hard roll of butter mixture into 4 equal pieces; lay one piece on chicken breast and roll it up in the chicken; secure with skewer or string. Repeat. In Dutch oven, heat $1\frac{1}{2}$ inches shortening or salad oil to 370° F. on deep-fat-frying thermometer, or until square of day-old bread browns in 60 seconds. Meanwhile dip chicken rolls in flour, then in egg mixture, then in flour. Now, with tongs, lower 2 chicken rolls into hot fat. Fry about 15 minutes, turning occasionally; then drain on paper towels. Repeat. Remove skewers or string. Serves 4.

Note : If preferred, coated chicken rolls may be pan-fried. Melt $\frac{1}{4}$ cup butter or margarine in a pan. Brown the chicken rolls on all sides; cover and cook 12 minutes; then uncover, and cook for 5 minutes or until crisp, turning once.

BEETROOT PURÉE

Boil 6 large beetroots in their skins, peel and sieve or mince them. Put into a saucepan with about 2 oz. fat, pepper and salt to taste, 1 tbsp. of vinegar and 2 tbsps. of sour cream. Heat well, stirring occasionally. This goes well with beef, hare, rabbit or game.

CABBAGE

Russians keep special choppers and little wooden troughs in the kitchen for cabbages. Shred your cabbage with a sharp cook's knife. Wash and scald it with boiling water. Strain and cook in an uncovered saucepan with half a cupful of water (which should boil away completely) and 3 oz. fat. Add salt to taste. A delicious way of cooking cabbage, but care should be taken that it does not cook too quickly or it may discolour.

BAKED CUCUMBERS AND SOUR CREAM

2 large cucumbers or 4 ridge cucumbers	Cold cooked meat, minced
$\frac{1}{2}$ oz. butter	Boiled rice
Pepper and salt	Sour cream

Peel the cucumbers and cut into 3-inch lengths. Mix together the cooked rice and minced meat, season with pepper and salt and fry them lightly in the butter. Scoop out the seeds of the cucumbers and fill with the meat and rice mixture. Lay the stuffed cucumbers in a fireproof dish, pour the sour cream over and bake in a moderate oven (350° F., mark 4) for about 20 minutes.

LAPSHA
(BAKED NOODLES)

$\frac{1}{2}$ lb. noodles	$\frac{1}{4}$ tsp. salt
1 cup sour cream	3 tbsps. grated Parmesan cheese
1 egg	
1 dessertsp. melted butter	

Cook the noodles in boiling salted water, drain and put them in a buttered fireproof dish. Pour over the cup of cream and bake in a very slow oven (lowest possible setting) until most of the cream has evaporated. Then mix in the beaten egg, melted butter and salt. Cover with the grated cheese and bake in a moderate oven (375° F., mark 5) until well browned; if preferred, brown under a grill.

SYRNIKI
(CREAM CHEESE FRITTERS)

1 lb. cream cheese	2–3 oz. butter
$\frac{1}{4}$ lb. flour	Sour cream and
1 egg	sugar

Mix the cheese with the flour and beaten egg. Shape into small round cakes, toss in flour and fry until pale golden-brown in the butter. Serve hot with sour cream and sugar.

VARENIKI
(POACHED PASTIES)

80

Vareniki make a particularly delicious and useful dish, because they can be served as a savoury or as a sweet, according to the filling. They are excellent stuffed with mashed potatoes, then served with melted butter poured over, and chopped onion or chives. When filled with fruit they can be served with a fruit syrup sauce or sour-cream yoghourt.

$\frac{1}{2}$ lb. flour	1 tbsp. melted butter
$\frac{1}{2}$ tsp. salt	Cold water
2 egg yolks	Filling

For the Filling

Sieve together the flour and salt and add the eggs and melted butter and enough water to mix to a stiff paste. Roll out very thinly and cut into rounds about 3 inches in diameter. Fill one round of the paste with mashed potatoes, cream cheese or stoned cherries, etc. (add seasoning to savoury mixtures and sugar to the fruit). Cover with another round and seal the edges, pressing them together after brushing with a little cold water. Poach in boiling water for about 15 minutes.

LENIVIYE VARENIKI
(LAZY VARENIKI)

4 oz. plain flour	1 egg yolk
4 oz. cream cheese	Water

Make a pastry of the flour and cream cheese, binding with the egg yolk and a little water if necessary. Roll out the pastry to $\frac{1}{2}$ inch thick, cut into small diamond shapes and poach in boiling water for 8–10 minutes. Test, strain and serve with hot melted butter, sour cream and sugar.

PASCHA

4 oz. butter	2 oz. stoned raisins
4 oz. sugar	4 oz. candied fruits
1 lb. cream cheese	A pinch of salt
A few drops vanilla	2 oz. crystallised cher-
1 gill sour cream	ries for decoration

Cream the butter and sugar together until the

W.C.B.—15

mixture is light and fluffy, then add the cream cheese, a little at a time, stirring vigorously. Add the vanilla essence and the sour cream, with the salt, raisins and chopped fruit. Line a basin with butter muslin, fill it with the mixture, cover with the muslin and weight it with a plate holding a heavy weight to press it down firmly. Chill overnight in a cold larder or refrigerator. Turn out and serve decorated with crystallised cherries.

Pascha, a traditional Easter dish, is usually eaten with slices of rich yeast cake called koolich.

EASTER BREAD

81

1 oz. yeast	6 oz. sugar
$\frac{1}{2}$ pint milk	2 oz. butter
1 lb. flour	$4\frac{1}{2}$ oz. candied fruit
6 egg yolks	

Dissolve the yeast in the warm milk, mix with half the flour and leave to rise. Beat the egg yolks and sugar together and, when the dough has risen, mix this in, and add the melted butter. Add the remaining flour and the chopped fruit. Beat the mixture well and leave to rise. Form into plaited loaves. Prove for 20–30 minutes and bake in a hot oven (450° F., mark 8) until well-risen and browned.

GOORIEFSKAYA KASHA
(FRUIT AND NUT SEMOLINA)

82

2 oz. semolina	2 oz. crystallised fruit
1 pint cream	2 oz. sultanas
3 oz. sugar	2 well-beaten eggs
4 oz. ground almonds	2 oz. shelled Valencia
2 oz. shelled walnuts	almonds

Make a light semolina pudding with the semolina and cream, add the sugar, ground almonds, chopped walnuts and crystallised fruit. Add the sultanas and stir in the eggs. Cover the top with chopped or sliced almonds and a little sugar. Bake in a well-buttered dish for about 35 minutes in a moderate oven (350° F., mark 4) until golden-brown.

KEESIEL
(FRUIT PURÉE)

This essentially Russian sweet is very simple and can be made from any good fruit purée, orange, apricot, apple, red-currant, raspberry. To the purée from 2 lb. fruit add 3 oz. sugar. Blend 2 tbsps. of potato flour or cornflour with cold water, add to the purée and bring to the boil. Cook gently for 2 minutes, stirring well. Serve with cream. When eaten hot the Keesiel is as thick as honey; when cold, like custard.

RICE, beans and peas, tomatoes and pimientos, eggs and chickens, garlic-flavoured sausages and salt fish, olive oil and spices, oranges and other fruits and plenty of cheap wine—that probably sums up the average Englishman's idea of Spanish food. It's a crude picture, but it includes the essential facts. Spain is a hot country, so olives, tomatoes and many fruit trees flourish, but not the lush grass of more northern countries, which means that butter, cream and tender meats tend to be lacking— not to mention the good root vegetables that we take for granted. Because the majority of people in Spain have always been poor, the typical diet contains a high proportion of the cheaper filling foods such as beans, peas and lentils, potatoes and rice and dried salt fish.

The general Mediterranean influences and the special contacts with the people of North Africa have led to the emphasis on such strong flavourings as onions and garlic, saffron and other spices, to the wide use of nuts and bright colour contrasts. Early journeys to the New World made Spain one of the first European countries to adopt chocolate as a drink and as a flavouring.

From these various elements, the good Spanish cook, both in the home and in the restaurant, can produce really excellent dishes, though perhaps more full-bodied than the typical French menu. The meals follow the general pattern of Southern Europe, beginning with a light breakfast, at which chocolate often replaces coffee. Both luncheon and dinner tend to be eaten rather late and consist of a number of courses served in somewhat leisurely fashion. The two meals are similar in style, but soup is normally reserved for the evening meal and cheese for midday.

Spain has excellent bakers and most bread, pastries and cakes are bought rather than home-made, except perhaps in large establishments. As in many continental countries, puddings in the English sense play little part and desserts tend to be custards or creams, sherbets and ices and similar light confections. Often they are replaced by cheese and fruit. As one would expect, the cheeses are not outstanding, but the fruit is superb. A Spanish speciality is *entremesas*, tiny savoury titbits to eat as appetisers or between meals; they include anchovies, pickled oysters, olives of several different kinds, shrimps, slivers of raw ham, pickles and miniature meat pies.

The different regions of Spain have of course evolved their own characteristic dishes, and the traveller should make a point of sampling Castilian game and meat, Andalusian *Gazpacho* and fried fish, Asturian or Galician bean stews and Basque fish.

Spain is the third largest wine-producing country in Europe. Malaga, Tarragona and Rioja are all well known in England and small quantities of other wines, such as Valdepeñas, are imported. The most famous of all, however, is sherry, a fortified wine made from Jerez grapes, which can be sweet, dry or medium and is an extremely popular apéritif.

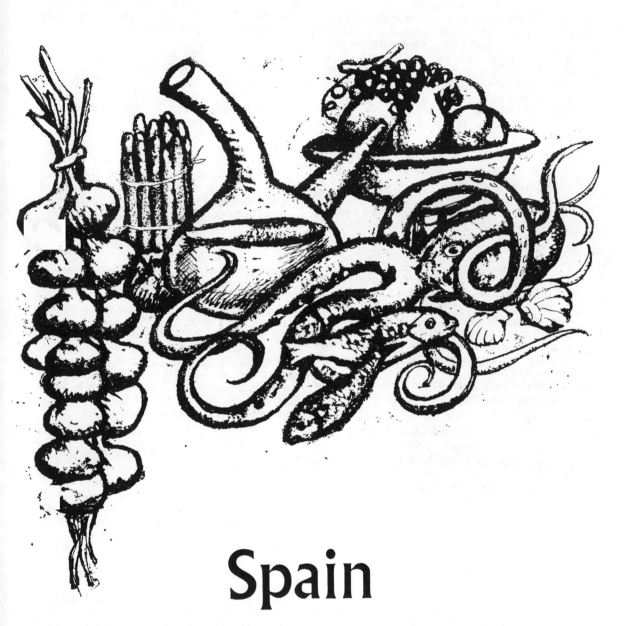

Spain

SOPA DE AJO
(GARLIC-FLAVOURED SOUP)

For each person allow 1 clove of garlic, 2 tsps. olive oil, 1 small peeled tomato, 1 tsp. finely chopped onion and ¼ pint water, also 1–2 slices of toasted bread. Fry the crushed garlic in the oil until golden, add the sliced tomato and onion and cook until tender; add the water, bring to the boil and simmer for 5 minutes, then season well with salt and pepper. Put the slices of toast in a tureen and pour the liquid over; serve at once.

GAZPACHO
(COLD UNCOOKED SOUP)

½ lb. tomatoes	A small clove of garlic
2 oz. bread	¼ cup vinegar
¼ cup olive oil	Salt, pepper and sugar
1 pint water	

For the Garnish

2 oz. diced tomatoes	2 oz. diced cucumber
2 oz. diced green pepper	2 oz. fried croûtons

Cut up the tomatoes and bread and mix with the olive oil and some of the water until creamy (use an electric mixer if available). Sieve the mixture into a bowl which has been rubbed round with garlic, then add the remaining water and the vinegar. Season to taste with salt, pepper and sugar.

Either add the garnishes to the soup, or serve them in separate bowls.

SOPA MEZCLADA
(MEDLEY SOUP)

Bring some good veal stock to the boil, then add a mixture of cut-up vegetables, such as potatoes, turnips, cabbage, celery and previously soaked and cooked haricot beans. Simmer gently until all the vegetables are well cooked. About 20 minutes before serving, add a few spoonfuls of rice and of vermicelli, with a good pinch of saffron, and continue cooking until these are done. The finished soup should be thick and satisfying.

CALDO GALLEGO
(GALICIAN SOUP)

1 lb. haricot beans	A few potatoes
A good-sized ham bone	½ oz. lard or dripping
1–2 beef bones	½ oz. flour
1 small cabbage	Salt and pepper

Soak the beans in water for some hours. Put them in a saucepan with 2 quarts water and the bones; bring to the boil and simmer gently for about 3 hours. After 2 hours add the finely shredded cabbage, the peeled and quartered potatoes and the fat and flour, mixed; season to taste and simmer for a further hour.

SOPA NAVARRA
(NAVARRE SOUP)

1 oz. butter	Salt and pepper
1 oz. flour	½ lb. vermicelli
1 pint chicken stock	Grated cheese
1 pint tomato purée	

Make a roux with the butter and flour, add the hot chicken stock and blend carefully, then add the tomato purée and season well with salt and pepper. Bring to the boil and simmer for 3 minutes. Cook the vermicelli in boiling salted water, drain and add to the soup. Serve with grated cheese handed separately.

SOPA DE ALMENDRAS
(ALMOND SOUP)

2 tbsps. olive oil	1 tsp. chopped parsley
4 oz. almonds, finely chopped	1 oz. breadcrumbs
	2 pints chicken stock
1 tbsp. chopped onion	Salt and pepper
½ tsp. chopped garlic	

Heat the olive oil and slowly cook in it the almonds, chopped onion, garlic and parsley, stirring all the time with a spoon: the mixture should be well cooked but not browned. Add the breadcrumbs and cook very slowly for a further 3 minutes. Pour on the stock, season well and simmer for 15 minutes.

PAELLA
(RICE, FISH AND CHICKEN)

8 cooked mussels	1 cup rice
4 cooked Dublin Bay prawns	½ cup frozen or tinned peas
1 small cooked lobster (optional)	2–3 globe artichokes
	3 cups chicken broth
½ a small raw chicken	Salt to taste
3 tbsps. olive oil	A little powdered saffron
1 small onion	
1 small clove of garlic	½ a tin of pimiento
2 medium-sized tomatoes	

Shell the mussels and prawns, and remove the lobster meat from the shell. Cut up the chicken. Heat some oil in the *paella* dish (a type of shallow casserole) and fry the chicken until brown, then boil it in 3 cups of water for 20 minutes.

Meanwhile cook the onion gently in the fat used for the chicken, add the finely chopped garlic, and then the tomatoes, and fry till cooked. Add the rice and mix well with the fat, without frying. Arrange the peas, mussels, lobster, prawns, chicken and artichokes attractively on top of the rice, and add 2 cups of boiling chicken broth. (Keep the remaining broth in case the rice requires more liquid.) When the rice boils, add salt to taste, and the saffron, blended with a little broth. Place the pimiento decoratively on top, and continue to cook until the rice is done— 15–20 minutes in all; the paella can be cooked in the oven for the last 5 minutes or so, if desired. Serve immediately, in the casserole.

Paella makes an excellent dish for an informal party.

ANDALUSIAN FRIED HAKE

2 lb. fillet of hake or other white fish	$\frac{3}{4}$ lb. tomatoes
Oil for frying	A bay leaf
Seasoned flour	Seasoning
1 tbsp. olive oil	Mixed herbs
1 onion	$\frac{1}{4}$ pint white wine
1 clove of garlic	1 oz. butter
1 small red pepper	1 oz. flour

Cut the fish into strips about $\frac{3}{4}$ inch wide and 3 inches in length. Heat the oil in a deep pan until smoking hot. Toss the fish in seasoned flour, put into a frying basket and fry until they are golden-brown. Drain well and pile on a hot dish in a pyramid, and serve with a sauce made as follows:

Heat 1 tbsp. olive oil and fry the chopped onion and garlic. Slice the pepper and tomatoes and put into the pan with the bay leaf, seasoning and a few herbs (including tarragon if available). Add $\frac{1}{2}$ pint water and the white wine and simmer gently for 20 minutes. Meanwhile beat together the fat and flour. Sieve the contents of the pan, then return them to the pan with the creamed flour and continue stirring until the sauce thickens; boil for 3 minutes before serving. This sauce is good with various types of fish.

PESCADO ESPAÑOL
(BAKED FISH, SPANISH STYLE)

6 slices (about 3 lb.) sea bass	6 anchovy fillets
$1\frac{1}{4}$ tsps. salt	6 thickly sliced peeled tomatoes
$\frac{3}{8}$ tsp. pepper	3 tbsps. chopped chives
$\frac{1}{4}$ tsp. red pepper	1 cup thinly sliced fresh mushrooms
$\frac{1}{4}$ tsp. grated nutmeg	
1 tbsp. olive oil	$\frac{1}{4}$ cup white wine
1 large onion, thinly sliced	$\frac{1}{2}$ cup melted butter or margarine
$1\frac{1}{2}$ tbsps. chopped pimiento	1 cup fresh bread-crumbs

Wipe the fish with a damp cloth and dry it. Sprinkle with a mixture of salt, pepper, red pepper and nutmeg. Put the olive oil into a large ovenproof dish; add the sliced onion and chopped pimiento.

Arrange the seasoned fish slices, side by side, on top of the onion slices, then place an anchovy fillet on each slice. Cover each with a tomato slice and sprinkle with chives. Scatter the mushroom slices over all; then pour on the wine. Tightly cover the dish with aluminium foil and refrigerate for a few hours.

One hour before the meal is required, heat the oven to hot (450° F., mark 8). Put· in the covered fish dish and bake for 25–30 minutes.

Meanwhile, combine the melted butter and breadcrumbs. Uncover the dish and sprinkle the top of the fish with this mixture. Continue baking, uncovered, until well browned—5–10 minutes. Serve the fish piping hot accompanied by crusty breadsticks or dry boiled rice seasoned with onion and paprika. Makes 6 servings.

LENGUADO CATALANA
(CATALAN SOLE)

4 artichoke bottoms	$\frac{1}{4}$ lb. mushrooms
4 fillets of sole (previously skinned)	2 oz. butter
Fish stock	$\frac{1}{2}$ pint béchamel sauce

Cook the artichokes and remove the leaves. Carefully curl the fillets of sole and tie with cotton to preserve their shape, then poach them for 10 minutes in boiling fish stock, drain and remove cottons. Meanwhile peel, chop and fry the mushrooms in the butter, and prepare the béchamel sauce. Fill the artichoke bottoms with the cooked mushrooms and cover them with the hot béchamel sauce. Place the curled fillets of sole on top and serve immediately.

SPANISH BREAM

Cut 2 medium-sized onions into rings, then put these with 1 tbsp. of olive oil into a fireproof dish. Clean about 2 lb. of bream and slash several times across the back. Place a slice of lemon in each slash and lay the fish over the onion. Season, pour a little more oil over and sprinkle with crumbs. Cook in a moderately hot oven (400° F., mark 6) for 30 minutes.

BAKED FISH AND BANANAS

2 lb. white fish	2 tbsps. tomato purée
Olive oil	2 tsps. sugar
Salt and pepper	2 tbsps. water
Dried mixed herbs	2 bananas

Split the fish, put in a greased ovenproof dish and brush over with a little oil, then sprinkle with seasonings and herbs. Mix the tomato purée with 2 tbsps. oil, then add the sugar and water. Pour this round the fish and trickle a little down the centre of the fish itself. Split the peeled bananas lengthwise and put round the fish. Bake in a slow oven (300° F., mark 1) for about ½ hour, basting occasionally. Serve with plain boiled rice.

TROUT

4 trout	A few cumin seeds
Olive oil	Wine or wine vinegar
1 onion, sliced	Lemon juice
1 clove of garlic	Lemon slices
A few sprigs of parsley	

Clean the trout, removing the head and the backbone if desired. Fry the fish on both sides in hot oil until they are golden-brown in colour, put into a casserole and keep hot. Fry the sliced onion golden-brown. Crush the garlic, chop the parsley finely and pound together with the cumin seeds. Put in a small pan with equal quantities of wine (or wine vinegar) and water, and a squeeze of lemon juice. Heat gently and when well blended pour on to the trout, adding the fried onion; cover and cook very gently for 10 minutes. Serve with slices of lemon.

FRESH COD WITH RED PEPPER SAUCE

2 lb. fresh cod fillet	¼ pint olive oil
2 red peppers	1 tbsp. vinegar
1 clove of garlic	Salt
½ pint fish stock or water	Chopped parsley

Skin the cod fillet and cut into 4 pieces. Halve the peppers, scoop out the seeds and cook the cases in boiling salted water for 5 minutes, then drain, and chop them finely. Skin and chop the garlic. Mix together the red peppers and garlic and crush them well, using the back of a wooden spoon.

Choose a pan of suitable size to cook the fish and put into it the pepper and garlic mixture, the liquid, oil, vinegar and salt to taste. Bring this liquid to simmering point, add the fish, cover and cook very gently until the fish is tender. Drain the fish and keep hot in the serving dish. Boil the liquid briskly until it is reduced by half and pour over the fish. Sprinkle with chopped parsley and serve at once.

BACALAO SALADO
(SALT COD)

1 lb. salt cod	½ lb. tomatoes
1 small clove of garlic	2 red peppers
2 Spanish onions	2 tbsps. olive oil
	Pepper

Cut the cod into 2-inch cubes and soak it overnight in cold water; the next day, drain and remove the skin and bones, put into a pan and just cover with tepid water, then cook very slowly until tender. (Quick cooking will cause the fish to break.) Drain the fish. Meanwhile peel and chop the garlic, peel and slice thinly the onions and tomatoes and cut the peppers into strips. Heat the olive oil and fry the fish lightly, handling the cubes carefully to avoid breaking, then drain and put in a fireproof dish to keep hot. Fry the onions with the garlic until soft and yellow, add the tomatoes and continue cooking until they are tender. Add the peppers to the sauce, season with pepper and pour over the fish.

BACALAO A LA VIZCAINA
(DRIED CODFISH, BISCAY STYLE)

1 lb. dried codfish	1 oz. bread
5 dried pimientos (peppers)	1 tbsp. flour
	2 tomatoes
½ cup olive oil	1 lump of sugar
1 chopped onion	½ cup of codfish stock
1 small clove of garlic	

Cut the fish in 2-inch squares and soak overnight, with the pimientos, in plenty of cold water. Take the fish from the water, bone it, put in a saucepan, cover with water and bring slowly to the boil. Strain the fish and place it in a pan, skin side upwards.

Now prepare the sauce. Heat the oil in a frying pan, add the onion, then the garlic, bread and flour and brown slowly. Add the peeled and seeded tomatoes. Scrape out the pimiento flesh with a spoon and add, with the sugar; add the codfish stock and cook slowly for about ½ hour, until creamy. Strain this sauce over the bacalao and stew for 15 minutes, shaking the pan from time to time to prevent sticking. (Do not add salt, as the dried fish is already salted.) Bacalao is usually served in the pan in which it has been cooked.

SCALLOPED OYSTERS À LA CRÉOLE

Butter	4 tomatoes
2 oz. white breadcrumbs	A pinch of cayenne pepper
1 tbsp. finely chopped parsley	24 small oysters
6–8 stalks of chives, finely chopped	¼–½ pint thin cream

Butter 4 fireproof dishes and put in the bottom of each a layer of breadcrumbs mixed with the chopped parsley and chives. Add the peeled and chopped tomatoes and the cayenne pepper to the mixture. Arrange 6 oysters in each dish, and put in another layer of the breadcrumb mixture. Dab the top with a few pieces of butter, and fill up the dishes with the cream and oyster liquor. Bake the dishes in a moderately hot oven (400° F., mark 6) for 10–12 minutes.

POLLO A LA CATALANA
(CHICKEN CATALONIAN STYLE)

1 chicken	2 tsps. tomato purée
1 oz. butter	Pepper and salt
1 tbsp. olive oil	12 whole chestnuts
12 small onions	Stock to cook chestnuts
Flour	$\frac{1}{2}$ lb. chipolata sausages
$\frac{1}{2}$ pint good stock	Fried bread to garnish
1 glass white wine	

Cut the chicken into 8 pieces—wings, thighs, drumsticks and breasts. Heat the butter and oil in a pan and fry the chicken and the peeled onions until lightly browned all over, then arrange them in a casserole. Sprinkle $\frac{1}{2}$ oz. flour into the fat left in the pan, stir in the stock, wine and tomato purée, season, bring to the boil and pour over the chicken. (The liquid should barely cover the joints.) Put on the lid and cook gently in a moderate oven (350° F., mark 4) for about 1 hour, or until the chicken is really tender.

Meanwhile prepare the chestnuts by cutting a small piece off the tip of each, then boil for 10 minutes, drain and peel off the shells ; cook gently in stock until tender. Fry the chipolatas until nicely browned. Fifteen minutes before serving, add the cooked chestnuts and the chipolatas to the contents of the casserole and thicken the gravy if necessary by adding 1 tsp. flour blended with a little stock. To serve, pile the chicken, etc., on a hot dish. Reseason the gravy (which should be of a thin glazing consistency) and pour it over the chicken. Garnish with squares of fried bread.

POLLO CON ARROZ
(CHICKEN WITH RICE)

1 chicken	3 tomatoes
$\frac{1}{2}$ lb. lean pork	2 red peppers
$\frac{1}{4}$ pint olive oil	$1\frac{1}{2}$ pints stock
2 large onions	A pinch of saffron
2 cloves of garlic	$\frac{1}{2}$ gill sherry
1 lb. rice	

Cut the chicken into neat joints and the pork into small pieces. Heat the olive oil in a shallow frying pan and fry the chicken and pork until they are golden-brown ; then remove them and put them in a casserole. Chop the onion and garlic and fry them in the olive oil until they are lightly browned, taking care that the fat does not become too hot. Add the rice and cook for 2 minutes, then add the sliced tomatoes and red peppers and cook for another 2 minutes. Pour

this mixture over the chicken in the casserole, add the boiling stock, saffron and sherry, and cook in a moderate oven (350° F., mark 4) or simmer over a gentle heat until the rice and chicken are cooked—about 1 hour.

PATO SEVILLA
(ROAST DUCK, SEVILLE STYLE)

1 duck	2 tsps. lemon juice
4 Seville oranges	2 tsps. sherry
2 tsps. arrowroot	Caster sugar
$\frac{3}{4}$ pint giblet stock	

Roast the duck in the usual way. Peel off the thin outer skin of 2 of the oranges, blanch it in boiling water for a few minutes, then shred it into thin strips. Blend the arrowroot with a little cold stock and add it to the boiling stock. Cook, stirring carefully, for 3 minutes. Add the lemon juice, the juice of the 2 peeled oranges and the sherry ; finally add the shredded orange peel.

Make a salad by slicing the remaining 2 oranges very thinly and sprinkling with a little caster sugar. Serve the roast duck with the Seville sauce poured over and surrounded by the orange salad.

FAISAN SIERRA MORENO
(CASSEROLED PHEASANT)

1 pheasant	2 oz. diced Spanish raw
$\frac{1}{4}$ pint red wine	ham
$\frac{1}{2}$ pint chicken or game	$\frac{1}{2}$ lb. tomatoes
stock	Salt and pepper
1 onion	Slices of fried bread

Joint the pheasant and put it in a casserole with the wine, stock, sliced onion, ham and sliced tomatoes, salt and pepper ; simmer slowly until the pheasant is cooked. Dish the joints of pheasant on the pieces of fried bread and keep hot. Reduce the sauce, sieve it, reheat and pour over the pheasant. Serve at once.

PERDICES ESTOFADAS
(STEWED PARTRIDGES)

2 young partridges	1 tbsp. vinegar
3 tbsps. olive oil	A pinch of thyme
1 medium-sized onion	Mixed herbs
2 small tomatoes	8 small onions
$\frac{1}{2}$ glass white wine	3 carrots

Fry the partridges in the oil in a saucepan until brown and place them on a plate. Chop the onion and fry it very gently in the same fat. Put the partridges back in the saucepan and continue frying for a short while. Add the sliced tomatoes and when they are cooked add the wine, vinegar, thyme and mixed herbs, then

cook for 15 minutes. Add 1 pint water and
stew until the birds are very tender (about 1
hour). Add the small whole onions and the
diced carrots; when these are cooked, remove
the partridges, divide each into 2 pieces, place
on a dish and surround with the whole onions
and carrots. Strain the sauce and pour it over
the dish.

SPANISH LAMB

A joint of lamb   Salt and pepper
2 oz. butter   1 glass white wine
1 clove of garlic   1 tbsp. chopped parsley
1 bay leaf

Any cut of lamb can be used—a small leg,
shoulder, best end of neck.

Prepare the meat and place it in a casserole
with the butter, chopped garlic, bay leaf, salt
and pepper. Cook in a moderate oven (375° F.,
mark 5), basting with the butter until the meat
is brown. Add the wine and continue cooking
until the meat is tender, basting frequently.
Remove the meat and keep it hot; strain the
gravy, adjust the seasoning, add the parsley, put
the meat back in the casserole and pour the sauce
over it.

A chopped pimiento added to the dish with
the garlic will give additional " spice."

LAMB CUTLETS NAVARRA

83

4 lamb cutlets   1 onion, chopped
Salt and pepper   1 lb. finely chopped
1 oz. lard   tomatoes
1½-lb. slice of gammon,   ½ lb. chipolata
   cut ½ inch thick, and   sausages
   diced

Season the cutlets with salt and pepper and fry
them in the fat; when cooked, transfer to a
casserole. Cook the gammon and onion in the
fat in which the cutlets were cooked. When the
onion is golden-brown, add the tomatoes, season,
and cook for 10 minutes. Pour this sauce over
the cutlets, cover the casserole and cook in a
moderate oven (350° F., mark 3) for 20–30
minutes. Fry the chipolata sausages separately.
Place the cutlets in a hot dish and garnish with
the sausages. Alternatively, serve the cutlets
with the sausages in the casserole.

FILLET STEAK WITH MADEIRA

4–6 fillet steaks   2 oz. butter
Olive oil   1 tbsp. chopped parsley
Salt   ¼ pint Madeira wine
Pepper   1 lemon

Put the meat on a board and brush over with
the oil. Beat thoroughly with a rolling pin until
the pieces are ½–¾ inch in thickness. Season well.
Heat the butter in a frying pan and put in the
steaks. When the meat juices appear on the
surface, turn the meat and cook on the other
side. Place the fillets on a hot dish, sprinkle well
with chopped parsley and keep hot. Pour the
Madeira into the pan, simmer for a few minutes,
then pour it over the steaks and garnish with
lemon.

RIÑONES CON JAMON
(KIDNEYS WITH HAM)

4 sheep's kidneys   1 wineglass sherry
1 shallot   Pepper and salt
1½ oz. butter   4 oz. lean cooked ham,
1 tbsp. olive oil   cut in 1 thick slice
⅓ pint brown sauce   Cooked peas
2 tsps. concentrated   Parsley and fried bread to
   tomato purée   garnish

Skin the kidneys and cut in small squares,
reserving any fat. Skin the shallot and chop
finely. Heat 1 oz. butter and the oil in a pan,
fry the kidney lightly, then stir in the shallot and
continue frying until this is just coloured. Add
the brown sauce, the tomato purée, sherry and
seasoning. Cover, and cook gently for about
10 minutes. Cut the ham in cubes and add to
the kidneys, with a pat of butter.

Arrange the hot peas in a border around a dish,
pour the kidney and sauce in the centre and
garnish with parsley and triangles of fried bread.

PANDORAS
(BREAD AND MEAT FRITTERS)

84

1 lb. of any cold cooked   1 egg yolk
   meat (equal quan-   1 tsp. cream or
   tities of fat and lean)   evaporated milk
Pepper and salt   Bread fingers
1–2 finely chopped   Coating batter
   shallots   Deep fat for frying

Mince or finely chop the meat, add pepper and
salt and the finely chopped shallots and mix to a
paste with the egg yolk and cream. Spread on
narrow fingers of bread, dip in coating batter
and fry in deep fat till a nice golden-brown.

COCIDO A LA MADRILENA
(MADRID STEW)

8 oz. chick peas   2 onions
1 lb. stewing steak   4 potatoes
2 oz. bacon   ¼ lb. Continental smoked
2 marrow bones   boiling sausage
3 carrots   Salt and pepper
3 leeks

Wash the chick peas and soak overnight in
1 quart of water. Cut the meat into cubes and

chop the bacon; put with the marrow bones into about 1 quart of cold salted water and bring to the boil. Skim off any scum from the top, then add the chick peas, discarding half the water covering. Boil for 30 minutes. Cut up the vegetables finely and dice the potatoes neatly, then add to the stew; cover the pan and simmer over a very low heat for about 1½ hours. Remove the marrow bones. Add the sausage, cut into small pieces, and season with salt and pepper. Cook for a further 10 minutes and serve.

It is quite permissible to add cooked leftover meats to this stew.

TORTILLA CASTELLANA
(CASTILIAN OMELETTE)

3 medium-sized potatoes	Salt
1 large onion	Olive oil for frying
½ a clove of garlic	4 eggs

Peel and wash the potatoes, cut into *very* thin slices and dry them on a cloth. Mix them with the finely chopped onion and garlic and plenty of salt, then fry them slowly in olive oil until they are well cooked, but only lightly browned; drain well. Beat the eggs and add the onion and potato mixture. Cook the omelette in a very little hot olive oil, shaking the pan occasionally. When one side is lightly and evenly browned, cover with a plate to turn the omelette, and cook the other side. Serve hot. Neither this omelette, nor the following one, is folded like a French omelette.

This omelette is also delicious when served cold, and it is a favourite picnic dish in Spain. The omelette is left to get quite cold (it can if desired be made the night before), and is packed between two plates in the picnic basket. To serve it, cut and place between slices or rolls of bread and butter, accompanied by salad.

TORTILLA ESPANOLA
(SPANISH OMELETTE)

1 tomato	Olive oil
2 cooked potatoes	2 tbsps. cooked peas
2 cooked or tinned pimientos	4 eggs
1 small onion	Salt and pepper

Peel, slice and chop the tomato, dice the potatoes, and cut up the pimientos. Chop the onion and fry it lightly in a little olive oil; add the peas, tomato, potato and pimientos, and continue cooking for a few minutes, stirring all the time with a spoon. Beat the eggs, season well, and pour them into the pan. Cook in the same way as for Tortilla Castellana. Serve hot, with tomato sauce.

SPANISH EGGS

4 large tomatoes	1 red pepper
2 oz. butter	Cayenne pepper
2 oz. flour	1 tsp. sugar
4 tbsps. white wine	Salt and pepper
4 tbsps. stock	4 eggs
1 small chopped onion	Toast or fried bread
1 clove of garlic	

Cut a small slice from the stalk end of the tomatoes and scoop out the pulp. Melt the butter, stir in the flour and let it brown lightly. Add the tomato pulp, wine and stock, stir until smooth, then add the onion, crushed garlic and chopped pepper. Season with a small pinch of cayenne pepper, 1 tsp. sugar and a little salt, then simmer for 15 minutes. Place a little of the mixture in each tomato, put in an ovenproof dish and break an egg into each tomato, sprinkle with salt and pepper and bake in a moderate oven (375° F., mark 5) until the egg is set. Serve on toast or pieces of fried bread.

MORENO FRIED EGGS

85

2 large tomatoes	Oil or fat for frying
2 large onions	4 eggs
Seasoned flour	

Halve the tomatoes and grill them. Slice the onions into rings, coat them with seasoned flour and fry in oil or fat. Fry the eggs and place one in each tomato half; arrange on a dish, with the onion rings as a garnish.

ANDALUSIAN FLAMENCO EGGS

86

2–3 slices of cooked ham	½ lb. sliced cooked potatoes
Olive oil or butter	Some strips of sweet peppers
1 tbsp. finely chopped onion	A little good stock
½ lb. tomatoes	½ lb. Continental-type sausage
½ lb. cooked peas	
A few asparagus tips	4–8 eggs

Cut the ham into small pieces and fry in the oil or butter, with the onion, until it begins to colour. Add the other vegetables and sufficient stock to moisten, then sauté gently for a few minutes, stirring carefully. Add the sliced sausage and put the mixture into an ovenproof dish; break the eggs on top and put in a hot oven (450° F., mark 8) for a few minutes, until the eggs are set.

HUEVOS CON CHORIZO
(EGGS WITH GARLIC SAUSAGE)

Into each greased individual fireproof dish drop a raw egg; add seasoning, surround each egg with pieces or thin slices of skinned Spanish garlic sausage, and bake in a moderate oven (350° F., mark 3) until the eggs are cooked.

FABADA
(BEANS AND PORK)

1 lb. butter beans	6 slices of chorizo
½ lb. lean pork	(Spanish garlic
Olive oil	sausage)
1 onion	6 slices of gutifara
1 clove of garlic	(Spanish blood
½ pint tomato purée	sausage)
Salt and pepper	

Soak the beans overnight in cold water; the next day, cook slowly in salted water until tender, then drain. Cut the pork into neat pieces and fry in the olive oil until lightly browned. Fry the sliced onion with the chopped garlic, then add the tomato purée and seasoning. Put the pork, sausages and butter beans into a casserole, pour in the tomato sauce, cover with a lid and cook in a moderate oven (350° F., mark 3) for about 40 minutes, till the meat is tender.

JUDIAS VERDES A LA ANDALUZA
(FRESH LIMA BEANS ANDALUSIAN STYLE)

Boil the beans for 5 minutes in salted water, then drain well. Fry or sauté in butter or lard with some thin strips of ham and a few chopped tomatoes; season well.

SETAS A LA PARRILLA
(GRILLED MUSHROOMS)

Marinade the mushrooms for a few hours in oil, salt and pepper. Drain (keeping the oil) and grill, then put on a hot dish. To the oil in which they were marinaded add a chopped garlic clove, with some chopped chives and parsley; fry lightly, add a little vinegar and pour over the grilled mushrooms.

ENSALADA ISABELLA

2 celery hearts	4 apples
1 lb. cooked potatoes	

For the Mayonnaise

1 clove of garlic, finely	Pepper and salt
chopped	Oil
1 egg yolk	Lemon juice

Remove the outer stalks of the celery, leaving the crisp hearts; wash, and leave in cold water until required. Slice the potatoes. Peel and slice the apples. Put the chopped garlic in a mortar and pound well. Add the egg yolk and seasoning, and stir in the oil, a few drops at a time, until the mixture is thick, then stir in a little lemon juice to taste. Cut up the celery and toss this with the apples and potatoes in the mayonnaise. Serve with cold meats.

HABICHUELAS TIERNAS AL AJO
(RUNNER BEANS WITH GARLIC)

Break the beans into short lengths and cook in the usual way. Drain well and when cold mix with a dressing made of olive oil, pounded garlic and salt.

ENSALADA DE PIMIENTOS Y TOMATE
(TOMATO AND PEPPERS IN A SALAD)

Cut some uncooked red or green peppers into strips and mix with some sliced tomatoes. Mix with a French dressing containing a little pounded garlic.

MANZANAS EN DULCE
(HONEYED APPLES)

½ cup chopped dried figs	½ cup water
	1 cup honey
⅓ cup chopped almonds (blanched)	1 tsp. melted butter
	6 medium-sized apples

Mix the figs and almonds. In another small bowl, stir together the water, honey and butter.

Twist the stems from the apples, then, starting at the blossom end, peel each apple about a third of the way down, also remove the core part-way down. Fill the apples with the fig and almond filling. Arrange them in a shallow baking dish and pour on the water and honey mixture. Put into a slow oven (325° F., mark 2) and bake, basting often with the honey syrup, until tender but still unbroken—about 1¼ hours. Refrigerate until required. Makes 6 servings.

STRAWBERRIES AND ORANGE

Wash and hull sufficient strawberries, cover with sweetened orange juice and leave for an hour. Chill, then sprinkle with a little grated orange rind. Serve in tall glasses, topped with vanilla-flavoured whipped cream, which may be decorated with grated orange rind.

COMPOTE OF CHESTNUTS

1 lb. chestnuts	1 tbsp. Maraschino
6 oz. sugar	liqueur
½ pint water	

Peel and skin the chestnuts. Dissolve the sugar in the water, and add the nuts, cover the saucepan and simmer gently until the chestnuts are quite tender. Add the Maraschino liqueur, put the nuts and syrup into a glass dish and leave them in a refrigerator or a very cold place until they are required.

DATE TART

Shortcrust pastry	2 oz. ground almonds
¼ lb. fat juicy dates	2 tbsps. cornflour
A little rum or cognac	4 oz. caster sugar
5 egg whites	Icing sugar

Line a shallow baking tin with the pastry. Stone the dates, cut them lengthwise into 4 pieces, place them in a soup plate, pour the rum or cognac over and leave them to soak as long as possible. Beat the egg whites to a stiff froth and add the almonds, cornflour and sugar and lastly the drained dates. Fill the uncooked pastry shell with this mixture and bake in a moderate oven (350° F., mark 4) for 35–40 minutes, taking care not to allow the filling to become too brown. Just before serving, sprinkle with icing sugar, and leave in the oven for a moment or two longer. Serve hot or cold.

TORRIJAS
(CHOCOLATE FRIED BREAD)

Slices of stale bread cut ½ inch thick	1 tbsp. sherry
	Olive oil for frying
1 egg yolk	Caster sugar
½ pint milk	Grated chocolate

Cut the bread into fingers about 1 inch wide. Beat the egg yolk with a fork and add the milk and sherry. Dip the fingers of bread into this mixture, drain them and fry them in olive oil until they are golden-brown. Drain, sprinkle with caster sugar and then cover with grated chocolate, pile them up in a dish and sprinkle again with grated chocolate. Serve very hot.

SPANISH APPLE TART

6 oz. shortcrust pastry	½ pint lime jelly square
4 oz. sugar	Apricot jam
¼ pint water	6 glacé cherries
A few drops of vanilla essence	Whipped cream and angelica
6 small cooking apples	

Line a flan ring with pastry, bake blind in a moderately hot oven (400° F., mark 6). Dissolve sugar in water, allow to boil for a few minutes to reduce slightly and add the vanilla essence. Gently cook the peeled and cored apples in this syrup, drain carefully and use the syrup to dissolve the jelly square. Cover the inside of the pastry with warm apricot jam and put the apples in the case, with a cherry in each hole. When the jelly is cold and beginning to set, pour over the fruit. Decorate with whipped cream and angelica.

Alternatively, pears or halved stoned plums may be used in this dish.

BIZCOCHO BORRACHO DE GUADALAJARA
(GUADALAJARA " DRUNKEN SPONGE ")

Sponge cake	6 oz. icing sugar
4 tbsps. sugar	½ pint cream
4 tbsps. water	Fresh strawberries
¼ pint brandy or rum	

Bake a sponge-cake mixture in a ring-shaped tin and cool on a wire tray. Prepare a syrup by dissolving the sugar in the water, bringing to the boil and boiling for 5 minutes. Place the sponge on a dish and pour on the hot syrup, then sprinkle with the brandy. Mix the icing sugar with a few drops of hot water to a coating consistency and ice the top of the ring. Whip the cream, add a little sugar and pile in the centre. Decorate with strawberries.

TARTA DE NUEZ
(NUT CAKE)

4 oz. crushed sweet biscuits	5 oz. ground or chopped nuts
¾ gill milk	Whipped cream to decorate
6 eggs	
9 oz. caster sugar	

For the Syrup

10 oz. sugar	The thinly peeled rind of 1 lemon
¾ pint water	

Soak the biscuits in the milk to soften them to a crumbly consistency, separate the eggs, and beat the yolks and the sugar together until creamy, add the biscuits and nuts, and stir well. Fold in the stiffly beaten egg whites, and pour into a greased and papered shallow cake tin. Bake in a moderate oven (350° F., mark 3) for 1–1¼ hours. Cool the cake, then strain over it the syrup, prepared by boiling together the sugar, water and lemon rind until slightly thick. Decorate with whipped cream, adding some glacé cherries if desired.

CHURROS

Sieve ½ lb. flour with a pinch of salt, add ½ pint hot water and mix well to form a smooth paste. Fry in long, thin pieces in fairly hot olive oil, until well browned. Churros are eaten with morning coffee.

TURRON
(ALMOND SWEETMEAT)

Blanch and brown 1 lb. almonds, add ½ lb. fine sugar and pound together. Put into a heavy saucepan with ¼ lb. honey and cook, stirring continuously, until the mixture browns and thickens. Pour into a small tin or wooden box lined with rice paper and allow to harden.

MANY people are apt to dismiss Swedish cooking as beginning and ending with "Smörgåsbord" and indeed this celestial and gargantuan hors d'œuvre is a major contribution to the world's store of good food and its popularity is steadily increasing. But the Swedes have a tradition of all-round good eating, to match a high standard of living, and their food is rich and plentiful. In the country districts particularly, meals are heavy and satisfying, suitable for the cold climate, and milk, cream and butter are freely used.

Many traditional dishes appear at festival times, and the national dish for Christmas Eve is Lutfisk—dried fish served with boiled potatoes and sauce—followed by a thick, rich rice pudding in which is concealed one whole almond—the equivalent of the ring or the sixpence in a plum pudding, for whoever gets the almond will be the first to marry.

Fish is, of course, varied and delicious as in all Scandinavian countries and the Swedish cook is fond of using fennel and dill to flavour fish dishes. Favourite meats are pork and beef; veal, lamb and reindeer are also served. Desserts are generally based on fresh fruit or fruit which has been preserved during the summer for winter use. Bread and cakes are made in great variety and much use is made of cream, butter, nuts and spices.

Although it may be either an hors d'œuvre or a full meal, the Smörgåsbord itself follows a traditional pattern : no matter how elaborate it is, it always starts with bread and butter and herring dishes with boiled potatoes, followed by one or two, small, piquant dishes. Plates are then changed and egg dishes served, with salad, cold meats, perhaps some dishes in aspic, and if the Smörgåsbord is a really elaborate one, there could be some hot dishes, such as kidneys or meat balls and then rye bread, cheese and coffee, to round off a varied and thoroughly satisfying meal.

Sweden

GUL ARTSOPPA
(YELLOW PEA SOUP)

8 oz. yellow split peas (or split peas)	1 small onion
	Salt and pepper
¼ lb. salted shoulder of pork	A sprig of marjoram

Wash the peas and soak overnight in 2 quarts salted water. The following day cook them in the water in which they have been soaked, boiling quickly at first, until the skins float on the boiling water; skim off the skins, then cook the soup very slowly with the lid on the pan. When the peas are half-cooked, add the washed pork and the sliced onion, season with pepper and salt and add the marjoram. Continue cooking slowly until the pork is cooked. Take out the pork and cut the meat into small pieces, put these back into the soup, remove the marjoram and reheat before serving.

BRYNT VITKALSSOPPA
(CABBAGE SOUP)

1 cabbage	Stock or water
2 oz. pork dripping	Salt
1 tbsp. golden syrup	¼ lb. pork sausages
3 peppercorns	

Wash, prepare and shred the cabbage, fry it lightly in the hot fat and when it is slightly coloured, add the syrup and continue frying for a few minutes. Add the peppercorns and about 3 pints stock or salted water. (The liquid in which ham or bacon has been cooked is best of all.) Simmer gently until the cabbage is almost cooked, then add the sausages and continue simmering until these are cooked. Remove the sausages, slice them, return them to the soup and serve very hot.

INLAGD SILL
(SOUSED SALT HERRING)

1 large salt herring	⅓ cup sugar
½ cup vinegar	2 tbsps. chopped onions
2 tbsps. water	5 peppercorns, crushed
10 whole allspice, crushed	Fresh dill sprigs and onion rings to garnish
2 sprigs fresh dill	

This is an indispensable smörgåsbord item.

Clean the herring, removing the head, rinse under cold running water, then soak it in cold water for 10–12 hours; change water a few times.

Cut the herring along the back, remove the big back bone and as many small ones as possible and pull off skin. (The bones come out easily after the soaking.) Drain the fillets on absorbent paper, then place them together one on top of the other, so that they look like a whole fish.

Cut into thin slices with a sharp knife, slide a spatula underneath and remove to a long, narrow dish.

Mix the remaining ingredients together in a saucepan, bring to boiling point and simmer for a few minutes; cool and strain. Pour the liquid over the herring and garnish. Chill and serve with small boiled potatoes.

FÅGELBO

4–5 chopped anchovy fillets	1–2 tbsps. diced pickled beetroot
1 tbsp. chopped onion	1 tbsp. diced cold cooked potato
1 tbsp. chopped chives	
1 tbsp. capers	2 raw egg yolks

Use a small oblong or oval dish. In the middle put two small mounds of anchovy, with a little beetroot between them. Now arrange concentric rings of the other ingredients around the two heaps; " pinch in " the rings a little at the middle of each long side, so that the whole somewhat resembles a figure-of-eight. Make a slight depression in the centre of each of the two original mounds and put a raw egg yolk in each " nest." Serve chilled.

The first person to help himself stirs all the ingredients well together to blend them completely. This is a classic Smörgåsbord dish.

ANSJOVISOGA
(ANCHOVY EYE)

This is a simpler version of the previous dish. Place a raw egg yolk in the centre of a small round plate and arrange round it a ring of about 1 tbsp. minced onion, then a ring of 8 minced anchovy fillets. Here again, the first person to help himself stirs all the ingredients together.

As an alternative, mix the ingredients, fry lightly in a little butter and serve on toast or plain biscuits.

SILLSALLAD
(HERRING SALAD)

1 salt herring	2 tbsps. water
1½ cups boiled potatoes	2 tbsps. sugar
1½ cups pickled beetroot	Pepper
¼ cup pickled gherkin	½ cup whipped cream (optional)
½ cup chopped apple	1–2 hard-boiled eggs and parsley to garnish
¼ of an onion	
4 tbsps. vinegar	

Clean the fish, removing the head, and soak overnight in cold water. Drain, skin and fillet the fish, then dice, and mix with the diced potato, beetroot, gherkin and apple and the chopped onion. Blend the vinegar, water, sugar and pepper thoroughly and add to the fish mixture, stirring gently. Add the whipped cream (if used), then put the mixture into a rinsed mould and chill. Unmould and garnish with hard-boiled egg and parsley. Serve as a Smörgåsbord dish, accompanied by sour cream, beaten stiff and coloured if desired with pickled beet juice. 6–8 servings.

JANSSON'S FRESTELSE
(JANSSON'S TEMPTATION—ANCHOVIES AU GRATIN)

8–10 medium-sized potatoes 1 oz. butter
2 tins of anchovies Salt
2 large onions ½ pint thin cream

Wash and peel the potatoes and cut them into long, thin strips about ¼ inch thick. Drain the anchovies. Slice the onions and fry them in the butter. Butter a fireproof dish or pie dish and put half the potatoes in it, add the fried onions and a little salt, then put in a layer of anchovies. Add the rest of the potatoes and cover with small dabs of butter. Bake in a moderate oven (350° F., mark 3) for 15 minutes. Pour half of the cream into the dish and bake for a further 20 minutes, then add the rest of the cream and bake for a further 45 minutes, or until the potatoes are cooked, the cream is all absorbed, and the top is golden-brown.

Jansson's Frestelse is sometimes served as one of the hot dishes for the Smörgåsbord, but it is an excellent supper dish and is often used in Sweden as a late-night snack after a dance or party.

FISK I GELE
(FISH IN ASPIC)

2–2½ lb. fish, preferably Hard-boiled eggs,
salmon, mackerel or tomato and
eel shrimps to garnish

For the Court-bouillon

1 quart water 5 allspice
1 tbsp. white vinegar 1 bay leaf
1 tbsp. salt A little dill
5 peppercorns

For the Aspic Jelly

1¼ tbsps. powdered 1 pint fish stock
gelatine Salt and pepper
2 egg whites

Clean and skin the fish; mix all the ingredients for the court-bouillon and cook for 15 minutes. Cut the fish into 1-inch slices and cook in the court-bouillon for about 10 minutes, then drain and place on a dish to cool.

Soak the gelatine in a little cold water, then beat with the egg whites and strained fish stock. Pour the mixture into a saucepan and bring slowly to boiling point, stirring constantly; cover and leave to stand for about 15 minutes. Strain the mixture, add salt and pepper to taste, then chill it.

Make an attractive pattern in the bottom of a mould with sections of hard-boiled egg, sliced tomatoes and small cooked shrimps. Pour some of the aspic jelly over slowly and chill until it sets. Arrange the cold fish carefully on top and pour the remaining aspic over. Chill until set, turn out and serve with a salad.

FISKRULADER MED CITRONSÅS
(ROLLED FISH FILLETS WITH LEMON SAUCE)

1½ lb. fillets of cod, Court-bouillon
haddock or flounder Shrimps, dill or parsley
Lemon sauce (see to garnish
below)

If the fillets are large, divide into convenient portions; roll them up and fasten with a cocktail stick, put in a shallow saucepan, cover with hot court-bouillon and cover the pan, then simmer for about 10–15 minutes. (Alternatively, instead of using court-bouillon, pour over the fish the juice of ½ a lemon mixed with 2–3 tbsps. water and dot with 1 tbsp. butter shaved into small pieces.)

Put the fish on a hot dish, removing the cocktail sticks, pour the hot sauce over and garnish. Serve with lemon wedges and boiled potatoes.

Citronsås
(Lemon Sauce)

1½ tbsps. butter ½ cup single cream
2½ tbsps. flour Salt and pepper
1 cup court-bouillon Juice of ½ a lemon
or fish stock 1 egg yolk

Melt the butter, stir in the flour, then gradually add the cream (retaining 2 tbsps.) and the court-bouillon, stirring constantly. Simmer for about 10 minutes, season to taste and add the lemon juice. Beat the egg yolk and remaining cream and add to the sauce, stirring well.

FISKFARS
(BAKED FISH MOUSSE)

Melted butter or mar- ½ lb. butter or margarine to grease tin rine, melted
¼ cup dried breadcrumbs 4 eggs
½ cup flour 1 tbsp. salt
1 tbsp. potato flour ½ tsp. white pepper
2 lb. freshly minced raw ½ tsp. ground allspice
haddock, cod or pike 2 cups milk

Butter a 9-inch tube tin, then coat generously

with breadcrumbs. Sieve together the flour and potato flour. Mix the minced fish and the melted butter; beat vigorously (using a wooden spoon), then beat in the egg yolks. Sprinkle in the sifted flour mixture, salt, pepper and allspice and stir in. Gradually add the milk, beating thoroughly until well blended. Gently fold in the stiffly beaten egg whites until well blended. Turn the mixture into the prepared tube tin and place this in a large pan of boiling water. Put into a moderate oven (350° F., mark 4) and bake for 1 hour 10 minutes, or until a cocktail stick inserted in the centre of the mixture comes out clean. (If top of mousse gets too brown before baking time is finished, cover with metal foil.) Remove the pan from the water and let it stand for 5 minutes. With a spatula carefully loosen the edges, then unmould carefully on to a heated dish.

Serve with lobster sauce (see below) and lemon wedges.

Cucumber relish and parsleyed new potatoes make good accompaniments. (6–8 servings.)

Hummersås
(Lobster Sauce)

3 tbsps. butter or mar-	2 egg yolks, slightly
garine	beaten
2 tbsps. flour	1½ cups cooked or
¾ tbsp. sugar	canned lobster, in
1½ tsps. white pepper	pieces
1½ cups single cream	1–2 tbsps. lemon
½ cup milk	juice

Melt the butter over a low heat. Using a wooden spoon, blend in the flour, sugar, salt and pepper; remove from the heat. Gradually stir in the cream, then the milk and cook over a low heat, stirring constantly, until smooth and thickened. Stir a little of this mixture into the egg yolks, then return all to saucepan and cook for about 1 minute longer. Add the lobster to sauce and heat gently until the lobster is hot; remove from heat and stir in the lemon juice. This sauce is also good served over hot boiled rice as a luncheon dish.

GRATINERSFISK MED KRABBA-STUVNING
(COD WITH CRAB STUFFING)

2 lb. cod	Milk
Salt	1 crab or 1 tin of crabmeat
Pepper	2 oz. grated cheese
1 oz. butter	2 tbsps. white breadcrumbs
1 oz. flour	Parsley to garnish

Cut the cod into pieces, season and place in a buttered fireproof dish. Cover with buttered paper and bake in a moderate oven (350° F., mark 4) 15–20 minutes. Make a roux with the fat and flour, add the fish liquor and sufficient milk to make a good white sauce. Cook the sauce slowly for 5 minutes, then add the white crabmeat to the sauce and spread the dark crab-meat on the fish. Pour the crab sauce over the fish, cover with the grated cheese and bread-crumbs and brown well either in a hot oven or under the grill. Garnish with parsley.

CRAYFISH

This small shell fish, which resembles a miniature lobster, is one of the national dishes of Sweden. The opening of the crayfish season (which starts at the end of the first week in August and continues to the end of September) is celebrated with special parties. If possible, these are held in the garden, with coloured paper lanterns hung in the trees and lighted candles on the table. The meal is served buffet fashion, and may be as simple or elaborate as you wish. Usually there would be bread, toast, butter and cheese and perhaps a herring titbit to sample before starting on the impressive pile of scarlet fish. To follow there might be something substantial like roast duck, or just a vegetable dish like globe artichokes with butter. The final course would be a cold fruit sweet or perhaps a torte and fresh fruit.

To cook crayfish, put them into boiling water, salted and flavoured with dill, cook for 6–7 minutes, cool in the liquor, and chill before serving. Dill flowerheads are the correct garnish.

POT ROAST

3 lb. whole rump steak	2 carrots
½ lb. fat pork	A bouquet garni
2 oz. butter	2 tbsps. vinegar
2 onions	2 tbsps. treacle
4 anchovies	2 tbsps. brandy
Seasoning	1½ pints stock

For the Sauce

2 oz. butter	¼ pint cream
2 oz. flour	Seasoning
1 pint stock	

Trim and wipe the meat. Cut the pork fat into ¼-inch strips and lard the steak with these, using a larding needle. Brown the meat in melted butter, then remove it from the pan. Put the other ingredients at the bottom of the pan and put the meat on top. Add the stock, and cook gently for 2–2½ hours, then remove the meat and keep hot. Make a sauce with the butter, flour and strained stock; lastly, add the cream and seasoning.

KALVRULADER
(PARSLEY-STUFFED VEAL ROLLS)

2 lb. thin veal cutlets
Salt and pepper
½ cup butter or margarine
1 cup chopped parsley
2 medium-sized carrots, cut into 1-inch chunks
2 medium-sized onions, quartered
1 can condensed beef bouillon
1 tbsp. flour
¾ cup single cream
2 tsps. sugar

Ask the butcher to flatten the veal to ¼-inch thickness. Cut the meat into suitable-sized pieces for serving and sprinkle on both sides with salt and pepper. Melt half the butter, add the parsley and spread some of this mixture on each piece of veal; roll up, tie securely and refrigerate.

Heat the remaining butter and sauté the carrots, onions and veal until the meat is well browned. Add water to the bouillon to make 2 cups liquid; add this to the meat and vegetables and simmer, covered, for 1 hour, or until the meat is tender. Remove the veal rolls, snip off the strings, then arrange on a heated dish and keep warm.

Mash the vegetables into the liquid in the cooking pan. Gradually stir the cream into the flour, then stir briskly into the vegetable mixture. Add salt and pepper to taste, with the sugar, and cook, stirring, just until heated; strain and serve as gravy. Makes 6 servings.

KÖTTBULLAR
(SWEDISH MEATBALLS)

1 lb. chuck or round steak, freshly minced
½ lb. lean pork, freshly minced
1 tbsp. butter or fat
½ cup grated or finely chopped onion
1 cup fine, dry breadcrumbs
2½ tsps. salt
1 cup cold mashed potatoes (loosely packed)
¼ tsp. pepper
½ cup single cream
¼ cup water
1 egg
Fat or oil for deep frying

To get good results it is essential to select the meats yourself and have them freshly minced. Heat the butter and sauté the onion for 5 minutes. Put it in a large mixing bowl with all the other ingredients and blend until smooth. Shape into balls, a tablespoon at a time, in the wetted palm of the hand. Fry the balls in the hot fat, shaking the pan often to keep their round shape. Remove each batch to a hot dish and keep warm while frying the rest. (If necessary, clean the pan between batches, removing the fat meantime.) Make a gravy with 1 cup single cream or milk and 1 tbsp. flour, season to taste and pour over

the meatballs. Serve with mashed potatoes, a cooked vegetable, salad or tart fruit sauce.

SMÅ KÖTTBULLAS
(SMALL MEATBALLS)

¾ lb. minced chuck or round steak
¼ lb. minced lean pork
1 tbsp. finely chopped onion
Butter
⅓ cup dry breadcrumbs
1 cup cream and water
1½ tsps. salt
¼ tsp. white pepper
½ tsp. sugar

Select the meats yourself and have them freshly minced.

Sauté the onion in 1 tbsp. butter until golden-brown. Soak the crumbs in the liquid, then add the beef, pork, onion and seasonings and mix thoroughly until smooth. Shape into very small balls, using 2 tablespoons dipped in cold water, and fry in hot butter until evenly browned, shaking the pan continuously to make the balls round. Serve hot or cold as a Smörgåsbord dish.

SJÖMANSBIFF
(SAILOR'S BEEF)

1 lb. chuck steak
1½ lb. potatoes
2 tbsps. butter
2–3 sliced onions
Salt and pepper
1–2 cups boiling water
Chopped parsley

Wipe the meat, cut into ½-inch slices and beat, with a wooden spoon or something similar. Peel the potatoes and slice thickly. Heat the butter and sauté the onions, then brown the meat slices. Put alternate layers of potatoes, meat and onions into a casserole, seasoning each layer and finishing with potatoes. Pour a little boiling water into the pan in which the meat and onions were fried, stir well and pour this liquor into the casserole, with just sufficient plain water to cover the contents. Cover and bake in a moderate oven (375° F., mark 5) for 1–1¼ hours, or until the meat is tender. Sprinkle with parsley and serve from the casserole.

PANNBIFF
(MINCED MEAT " CUTLETS ")

6 oz. finely minced pork
6 oz. finely minced steak
4–6 tbsps. breadcrumbs
About ¼ pint milk
Salt and pepper
Fat for frying
1 large onion
A little stock or water

Prepare the meats. Soak the breadcrumbs in the milk until all is absorbed, then squeeze off any surplus milk if necessary, leaving a mixture which is just moist. Season the minced meat well and add the soaked breadcrumbs. Shape into 6 thin, flat cutlet shapes, using cold water on the hands and board to help in shaping them.

Fry in smoking hot fat in a shallow frying pan until they are well browned on both sides, then remove the cutlets from the pan and keep hot. Slice the onion, fry until dark brown and put back the cutlets with the onion in the frying pan. Add 2 tbsps. boiling stock or water and let it bubble up round the cutlets and onion for a few minutes, to absorb all the juices in the pan. Serve very hot, with mashed potatoes.

BIFF À LA LINDSTRÖM
(LINDSTRÖM HAMBURGERS)

12 oz. minced beef	3 oz. diced pickled
1 finely chopped onion	beetroot
1 tsp. finely chopped	2 tbsps. chopped capers
parsley	Salt and pepper
$\frac{1}{4}$ cup single cream	2 egg yolks
6 oz. mashed potatoes	Fat for frying

Mix the very finely minced meats with the chopped onion, parsley and cream. Add the potato, beetroot, capers, pepper and salt, then bind with beaten egg yolks. Form into flat cakes, about $\frac{1}{2}$ inch thick, and fry in the smoking-hot fat until both sides are brown and crisp. Serve with fried potatoes or salad, or place on toast, and top with a fried egg.

MAKARONIPUDDING
(SAVOURY MACARONI)

8 oz. macaroni	Salt and pepper
1 pint milk	Butter
$\frac{3}{4}$ lb. raw ham	4 oz. grated cheese

Cook the macaroni in boiling salted water for 5–10 minutes, then drain in a colander and rinse it in cold water. Return it to the pan with the milk, and cook very slowly until this is absorbed. Cut the ham into small dice and fry until lightly brown. Mix the ham with the macaroni and season well, being careful not to break the macaroni. Butter a pie dish thickly and put in the macaroni mixture, cover with the grated cheese, and bake in a hot oven (450° F., mark 8) until the top is browned. Serve with baked tomatoes and accompanied by a sauce-boat of melted butter.

KALDOMAR
(STUFFED CABBAGE LEAVES)

1 large cabbage	$\frac{1}{2}$ lb. minced steak
2 oz. rice	Salt and pepper
$\frac{1}{2}$ pint milk	2 oz. butter
$\frac{1}{2}$ lb. finely minced pork	1 tbsp. brown sugar

Wash and trim the cabbage, cutting out the core, and cook for a few minutes in boiling salted water until the leaves will separate easily; drain, reserving some of the liquor, then trim the thick centre rib from each leaf. Put the washed rice into a pan with 1 cup boiling water and simmer until the water is absorbed; add the milk and cook slowly until tender, stirring occasionally. Mix the rice with the minced meats and seasonings and put some of the mixture on to each cabbage leaf; roll up and tie with string or skewer with a cocktail stick. Melt the butter in a frying pan and fry the cabbage rolls in it, turning them occasionally with a spoon. Sprinkle the sugar over them and continue frying until they are a rich brown colour. Cool slightly and then add a little of the water in which the cabbage was cooked; simmer gently with a lid over the pan for about 1 hour. Remove the strings or skewers before serving.

Make a gravy with the cooking juices, thickening them with a little flour and cream or milk; pour this over the rolls.

KROPPKAKOR
(HAM DUMPLINGS)

3 lb. potatoes	4 oz. flour
1 egg	$\frac{1}{4}$ lb. smoked raw ham
Salt and pepper	2 onions

Boil the potatoes in their skins, then peel and sieve them, or mash thoroughly. Beat in the egg, add salt and pepper, then add sufficient flour to make a mixture which is easily handled, blending it in well. Roll out this potato paste to $\frac{1}{2}$ inch in thickness and cut into rounds with a floured pastry cutter. Cut up the ham into very small pieces and chop the onion; put the ham and onion into a small frying pan and fry them slowly, turning with a metal spoon. Put a spoonful of the ham and onion mixture on to half of the potato rounds, cover with the remaining rounds, and pinch the edges together. Drop the dumplings so formed into a pan of boiling salted water and let them simmer slowly for 10 minutes. Pile on a hot dish, and serve with a lavish amount of melted butter, which should be handed in a sauce-boat; in Sweden whortleberry jam is also served as an accompaniment to this dish.

This is a dish typical of Swedish farmhouse cookery—very rich and satisfying in cold weather.

RABBIT STEW

Sprinkle 2–3 lb. cut-up rabbit with 1 tsp. salt and $\frac{1}{4}$ tsp. pepper. Then heat $\frac{1}{4}$ cup butter or margarine in a saucepan and brown the pieces well on all sides. Add 1 large onion, cut into eighths, 1 cup hot canned chicken broth, $\frac{3}{4}$ cup white wine, 1 tsp. salt and $\frac{3}{4}$ tsp. pepper and simmer (covered) for $\frac{3}{4}$–1 hour, or till tender. Remove the rabbit and onion and keep hot. Into the mixture left in the pan stir an 8 oz. can of tomato sauce, 1 tsp. sugar and 2 tbsps. flour blended with 2 tbsps. cold water. Cook till thickened. Replace the rabbit and onion, and add $\frac{1}{2}$ cup chopped parsley, then simmer, covered, till heated through. Arrange on a large hot dish and sprinkle with more parsley, if desired. Serve with Browned Potatoes.

BROWNED POTATOES

Cook 2 lb. new potatoes till tender; then peel. Toss with 2 tbsps. melted butter or margarine and $\frac{1}{4}$ cup dried breadcrumbs. Heat $\frac{1}{4}$ cup butter or margarine in a large frying pan and brown potatoes over a medium heat turning them till golden and hot.

RAGGMUNKAR
(POTATO GRIDDLE CAKES)

1 egg	Salt and pepper
2 cups milk	1 tsp. sugar
1$\frac{1}{4}$ cups flour	Bacon fat or butter for
1$\frac{1}{2}$ lb. potatoes (raw)	frying

Beat the egg with a little of the milk, then mix in the flour and the remaining milk alternately, beating well. Leave to stand for 2 hours. Peel and grate the potatoes and beat well into the batter, with the seasonings and sugar. Heat the griddle or frying pan, grease and pour in a thin layer of batter (about 1 tbsp.)—do not attempt to shape into a neat round, as the uneven edges, fried to a delicious crispness, are one of the charms of this dish. Fry until golden-brown on both sides, turning the cakes with a palette knife. Place on a hot dish and serve at once, as an accompaniment to fried pork or bacon or accompanied by a tart jam or apple sauce.

POTATISSALLAD
(POTATO SALAD)

6–8 medium-sized cold potatoes	$\frac{1}{2}$ tsp. pepper
	2 tbsps. chopped onions
2 tbsps. vinegar	2 tbsps. chopped parsley
6 tbsps. olive oil	2 tbsps. chopped chives
Salt to taste	Parsley to garnish

Slice the potatoes. Mix all the other ingredients together and lightly toss the potatoes in this dressing. Sprinkle a little parsley on top before serving.

GRÖNSAKSGRATIN
(VEGETABLES AU GRATIN)

Cook a variety of vegetables—for example, 1 small cauliflower, 2 cups sliced carrots and 2 cups green peas. Slice 4 good tomatoes. Arrange the cooked vegetables on a well-greased shallow ovenproof dish. Melt 2 tbsps. butter and stir in 3 tbsps. flour, then add 1 cup single cream and 1 cup vegetable liquor or milk, stirring them in gradually; cook gently for 10 minutes, stirring from time to time. Remove from the heat, add 2 beaten egg yolks and season to taste. Pour over the vegetables on the dish and put the slices of tomato round the edge, sprinkling them with salt and pepper. Sprinkle about 2 tbsps. grated cheese over the whole dish and grill or heat in the oven until attractively browned. Serve at once, as a separate dish or accompaniment.

GRÖNSAKSSUFFLÉ
(VEGETABLE SOUFFLÉ)

1 medium-sized cauliflower (or roughly the same quantity of broccoli, asparagus or mushrooms, as available)	3 tbsps. flour
	1$\frac{1}{4}$ cups single cream or milk and a small amount of vegetable stock
2 tbsps. butter	3 eggs, separated
	Salt and pepper

Prepare the vegetables as required and cook in slightly salted water until tender, then drain; if cauliflower is used, separate it into flowerets. Melt the butter in a saucepan and stir in the flour, then gradually add the cream and stock, stirring constantly, and cook gently for 10 minutes, stirring occasionally; remove from the heat. Add the egg yolks to the mixture and beat vigorously for 5–10 minutes, season to taste and add the vegetable. Whisk the egg whites stiffly and fold carefully into the mixture. Pour into a well-buttered and crumbed soufflé dish and bake in a moderate oven (350° F., mark 4) for 30–40 minutes. Serve as a separate dish with melted butter, or use as an accompaniment to bacon, sausages, etc.

LÖK PAJ
(ONION PIE)

1$\frac{1}{4}$ cups flour	2 cups thinly sliced onions
Salt and pepper	
$\frac{1}{4}$ cup butter or margarine	3 eggs
	1 cup sour cream
$\frac{1}{4}$ cup fat	1$\frac{1}{2}$ tsps. chopped chives
2$\frac{1}{2}$ tbsps. milk	$\frac{1}{2}$ tsp. caraway seeds
8 bacon rashers	

Sieve the flour and $\frac{3}{4}$ tsp. salt into a bowl, with a pastry-blender or 2 knives used scissor-fashion, cut in the butter and half the fat until the mixture is very fine; cut in the remaining fat until the particles are the size of peas.

Sprinkle the milk, about 1 tbsp. at a time, over the mixture, stirring with a fork until the dough clings together and leaves the bowl clean ; shape it into a smooth ball. Roll the dough out on a lightly floured surface 12-inch round and fit it into a 9-inch pie plate. Fold the surplus pastry under, making a stand-up rim ; flute the edge with a fork and prick the pastry well. Bake in a moderately hot oven (425° F., mark 7) for 10–12 minutes until golden-brown.

Meanwhile sauté the bacon until crisp and crumble it. In 3 tbsps. of the bacon fat sauté the onions till tender. Beat the eggs slightly, then stir in the sour cream, ¼ tsp. salt, a pinch of pepper, the chives, onions and bacon. Pour this mixture into the baked pie shell and sprinkle with caraway seeds ; bake in a moderate oven (350° F., mark 4) for 30 minutes. Let the pie stand a few minutes before cutting it into wedges to serve.

SKINKLÅDA
(BAKED HAM OMELETTE)

Butter a pie dish and put in 2 oz. diced bacon. Beat up 2 eggs with ½ pint milk, season with a little salt and pour the mixture over the bacon. Bake in a moderate oven (350° F., mark 4) till quite set—30 minutes.

This dish may also be made with smoked salmon or anchovies instead of bacon.

FYLLDA ÄGG
(STUFFED EGGS)

4 hard-boiled eggs	Stuffed olives, tomato,
5 tbsps. butter	and anchovy fillets
10 anchovy fillets	to garnish
Salt	Lettuce
White pepper	

Cut the eggs in half crosswise or lengthwise, remove the yolks carefully, and put the whites aside. Sieve the egg yolks, butter and anchovies, stir until smooth, and season to taste. Refill the egg whites with this mixture, forcing it through a pastry tube. Decorate each egg with a slice of stuffed olive, and place on a bed of lettuce. Garnish with slices of tomato and anchovy fillets, or as desired.

SPARRIS OMELETT
(ASPARAGUS OMELETTE)

4 eggs	Asparagus tips
Salt and pepper	¾ pint thick white sauce
½ oz. butter	¼ pint cream

Separate the eggs ; beat the yolks, and whip the whites to a stiff froth. Fold them together, and add 1 tsp. cold water and some seasoning.

Melt the butter in a heated omelette pan and cook the omelette. Mix the asparagus tips with ¼ pint of the sauce and fold this mixture into the omelette, put the omelette on a dish and leave it to get quite cold. Cool the remainder of the white sauce, sieve it and then whisk in the whipped cream. Pour this sauce over the omelette and serve cold.

PLÄTTAR
(SWEDISH PANCAKES)

1 cup flour	3 eggs
2 tbsps. sugar	3 cups milk
¼ tsp. salt	Butter or fat

Sieve the flour into a bowl and add the sugar and salt. Mix in the eggs and milk gradually, stirring until well blended, and let the batter stand for 2 hours.

In Sweden, a special iron pan (*plättpanna*) is used for cooking these pancakes, but failing this you can use a heavy frying pan or a griddle, or you can improvise a *plättpanna* ; fold some 3-inch-wide strips of metal foil lengthwise in half and then in half again, to give a stiff four-fold strip ; join the ends to make circles 3 inches in diameter, fastening with paper clips or staples. You will need 6–7 circles. Butter the inside of the pan or griddle well and put in the greased metal-foil rings.

Beat the batter again and pour a tablespoonful into each pan compartment or foil ring, then fry on both sides until nicely browned. Stack on a very hot plate and keep hot while frying the rest of the batter. Serve at once with whortleberry jam or sugar and cream.

RYSGRYNSGRÖT
(CHRISTMAS RICE PORRIDGE)

1 cup rice	½ cup single cream
2 tbsps. butter	1 tsp. salt
1 cup water	2 tbsps. sugar
4 cups milk	1 tsp. vanilla essence
A small piece of stick cinnamon	1 blanched almond

This is a traditional sweet to serve on Christmas Eve : the person who gets the almond in his or her portion will, it is said, be married before the next Christmas.

Rinse the rice under cold running water. Melt half the butter in a large saucepan, put in the rice and water and boil for about 10 minutes, or until the water is absorbed. Stir in the milk and cinnamon and cook gently for 40 minutes or until tender, stirring from time to time. Blend in the cream, salt, essence and remaining butter and stir in the almond at the last minute before serving. Extra milk, sugar and ground cinnamon are served with the pudding.

ÄPPLEMARÄNG
(APPLE MERINGUE TART)

½ lb. rich flaky pastry	2 oz. sultanas
1 lb. apples	Grated rind of 1 lemon
4 oz. sugar	2 egg whites
½ tsp. powdered cinnamon	4 oz. caster sugar for meringue

Make the pastry, line a shallow tin with it and bake " blind " in a hot oven (450° F., mark 8) for 20–30 minutes. Slice the apples and stew them with the sugar, cinnamon, sultanas and lemon rind. Spread this mixture over the pastry and decorate with a meringue mixture made by whisking the egg whites and folding in the sugar. Bake in a slow oven (300° F., mark 1) until the meringue mixture is crisp.

CITRONFROMAGE
(LEMON CHIFFON)

2 eggs, separated	2 tsps. gelatine, soaked in 2 tbsps. cold water
¾ cup sugar	
Juice of ½ a lemon	1¼ cups whipped double cream
Grated rind of ½ a lemon	

Beat the egg yolks and sugar until fluffy, then add the lemon juice, lemon rind and dissolved gelatine, stirring constantly until thick. Fold in the stiffly whisked egg whites and the whipped cream and pour the mixture into a mould which has been rinsed out with cold water ; put in the refrigerator for about 3 hours. Unmould and decorate with whipped cream and seeded grapes, or as desired. Biscuits are usually served with this pudding.

Alternatively, set in individual dishes and do not unmould. The same mixture makes a delicious filling for a flan case.

ÄPPLEKAKA
(BAKED APPLE SWEET)

6–8 medium-sized cooking apples	½ cup melted butter or margarine
½ cup fine, dry breadcrumbs	⅓ cup cherry brandy, rum, sauternes or orange juice
¾ cup brown sugar	
1½ tsps. ground cinnamon	

Peel, core and slice the apples. Mix the crumbs, sugar and cinnamon. Put a layer of apples in a buttered ovenproof dish, then sprinkle with crumb mixture and add some melted butter. Repeat, finishing with crumbs, and pour the brandy or other liquid over the top. Bake in a moderately hot oven (400° F., mark 6) for 25–30 minutes, or until the apples are cooked. Cool, turn out and serve cold with vanilla sauce (see recipe) or whipped cream. The top may be decorated with icing sugar sieved through a decorative paper doyley.

VANILJSAS
(VANILLA SAUCE)

Heat 1 cup cream with a vanilla pod (or use vanilla essence if preferred, adding this later). Beat 3 egg yolks and 2 tbsps. sugar until thick and foamy. Add a little of the cream to the eggs, then gradually pour this mixture into the cream remaining in the saucepan, stirring constantly. Simmer gently, stirring, until the sauce is thick, taking care not to let it boil. Pour it at once into a basin, remove the vanilla pod, if used, and if no pod was used, add 2 tsps. vanilla essence ; beat the sauce until it is cool and chill before serving.

TUSENBLADSTÅRTA
(THOUSAND LEAVES TORTE)

8 oz. flour	Cream
8 oz. butter or margarine	Glacé icing
	Browned chopped almonds
Iced water	
Apple pulp	Glacé cherries, etc.

Sieve the flour and cut in the fat, using a knife. Use iced water to mix and work the mixture with a wooden spoon until it is smooth ; cover and chill. Divide in 6–7 portions, roll out very thinly on waxed paper, cut into rounds and prick all over. Put on to a baking tin, brush over with iced water and bake in a hot oven (450° F., mark 8) for 6–8 minutes. Keep on the waxed paper until cold.

Spread alternate pastry rounds with apple pulp and cream, building them up like a layer cake, ice top and decorate with almonds, glacé cherries and angelica.

SAFFRANSBRÖD
(SAFFRON BREAD)

¼ tsp. saffron	10 cardamoms
1½ oz. yeast	4 oz. raisins
8 oz. sugar	Egg to glaze
4 oz. butter	3–4 tbsps. coarse sugar for topping
¾ pint milk	
2 lb. flour	

Soak the saffron overnight in a little warm water. Cream the yeast with 1 tsp. of the sugar. Melt half the butter, pour on the milk, warm to blood heat and pour on to the yeast. Sift in the flour, add half the sugar and beat to a smooth dough with the hand, adding the strained saffron while beating. Continue beating until the dough is quite smooth and leaves the sides of the basin. Cover the basin with a cloth and leave the dough to rise in a warm place. Peel the cardamoms and crush the seeds, then mix with the remaining sugar and the stoned raisins. When the dough is ready, turn it on to a floured board and divide into 2 pieces. Roll out each piece separately, spread with half the remaining butter, and sprinkle with the raisins, cardamoms and sugar. Roll up and place the rolls on a greased tin. Score with a sharp knife to show the filling, brush with beaten egg and sprinkle with coarse sugar. Prove for 15 minutes in a warm place, then bake in a hot oven (450° F., mark 8) for ½ hour, until well risen and brown on top.

This is very popular in Sweden and a batch is made every week in most households.

SEMLOR OR GETISDAGBULLAR
(SHROVE TUESDAY BUNS)

1 oz. yeast	1 egg, separated
4 oz. sugar	¼ lb. ground almonds
4 oz. butter	2 oz. icing sugar
¼ pint milk	¼ pint whipped cream
1 lb. flour	Hot milk
A pinch of salt	Ground cinnamon

Cream the yeast with 1 tsp. of the sugar. Melt the butter, add the milk and warm to blood heat. Pour the milk and butter into a mixing bowl with the creamed yeast, then add the flour, salt and sugar gradually, beating thoroughly until the dough is smooth and comes away from the sides of the basin. Leave to rise in a warm place, covered with a cloth, for 30 minutes. Shape into buns and leave to prove in a warm place for 10 minutes, then brush with beaten egg yolk and bake in a hot oven (450° F., mark 8) for 10–15 minutes. Cool on a rack.

Mix together the ground almonds, icing sugar and egg white. When the buns are cold, cut off a small circle from the top of each to make a lid, scoop out the bun mixture from the centre of the buns and stir this into the almond mixture, adding a little milk if necessary. Put this filling back into the buns, add a layer of whipped cream on the top and then cover with the lids. Dust with icing sugar. Just before serving, pour a mixture of milk, sugar and cinnamon over and round the buns.

These buns are served as a pudding in Sweden on Shrove Tuesday and on every Tuesday during Lent (the traditional first course for the same meal being fried pork and brown beans). The *Semlor* are usually made at home, but in the towns you can buy them during Lent in the shops; some Swedish housewives buy the plain buns at the baker's and fill them at home with the almond mixture and cream.

MJUK PEPPARKAKA
(SPICE CAKE)

3 eggs	2 tsps. ground ginger
9 oz. caster sugar	2 tsps. ground cinnamon
3 tbsps. sour cream	1 tsp. bicarbonate of
4 oz. butter	soda
2 rounded tbsps. orange marmalade	2 oz. chopped blanched almonds
9 oz. flour	Fresh breadcrumbs

Beat together the eggs and sugar till light and pale in colour. Fold in the cream, softened butter and marmalade and the flour sifted together with the spices and the bicarbonate of soda. Stir in the almonds. Dust with breadcrumbs a greased, loose-bottomed, spring-clip cake tin, 8–9 inches in diameter, then spoon in the cake mixture. Bake in a moderate oven (350° F., mark 4) for 1–1¼ hours. Do not open the oven door for at least 15 minutes, then test with a skewer for readiness. Cut next day.

KARDEMUMMAKAKA
(CARDAMOM CAKE)

4 oz. butter	2½ gills thin cream
12 oz. sugar	1 lb. flour
1 tbsp. ground cardamoms	1 tbsp. baking powder
	Caster sugar

Melt the butter and pour over the sugar, add the cardamoms and pour in the cream. Sieve together the flour and the baking powder and fold into the mixture. Pour into a round 8-inch cake tin which has been brushed with melted butter and dusted with flour and bake in a moderate oven (350° F., mark 4) for about 1 hour. Turn out on to a wire rack, bottom uppermost, and dredge thickly with caster sugar while the cake is still hot.

MAZARINTÅRTA
(MAZARIN CAKE)

7 oz. butter or margarine	4 oz. sugar
2 oz. icing sugar	4 oz. minced blanched almonds
1 egg yolk	2 eggs
4 oz. flour	Green colouring

Cream 4 oz. of the fat with the icing sugar until light and add the egg yolk and flour. The mixture should be worked until it is a smooth dough; if necessary, add a very little extra flour. Put in a cool place for at least 1 hour, then roll out and use to line a greased pie plate. Make a filling by creaming the remaining fat and sugar, adding the almonds and eggs and tinting carefully with a little green colouring. Put into the prepared case, spreading it evenly, and bake in a slow oven (300° F., mark 1) for ½ hour. When cold, decorate with sieved icing sugar or with glacé icing.

Small mazarins may be made in individual tartlet cases; bake in a moderate oven (375° F., mark 5) for 20 minutes.

AMBROSIAKAKA
(AMBROSIA CAKE)

2 tbsps. breadcrumbs	4 oz. caster sugar
4 oz. flour	5 oz. butter
1 tsp. baking powder	Orange-flavoured icing
2 eggs	Candied orange peel

Grease a sandwich tin and sprinkle with breadcrumbs. Sieve the flour and baking powder and whisk the eggs and sugar together until thick. Blend the egg mixture gradually into the flour and melted butter, then put in the tin and bake for ½ hour in a moderate oven (350° F., mark 4). Turn out and cool. Ice, then decorate with peel or chopped almonds.

PRINSESSTÅRTA
(PRINCESS CAKE)

2 eggs	4 oz. flour
6 oz. sugar	2 tsps. baking powder
4 oz. butter	2 oz. ground almonds
½ pint cream	

For the Vanilla Cream

3 tbsps. cornflour	2 egg yolks
½ pint milk	Vanilla essence
3 tbsps. sugar	Whipped cream

For the Marzipan

6 oz. ground almonds	1 egg white
6 oz. icing sugar	Green colouring

First make the cake. Whisk together the eggs and sugar until the mixture is thick, then pour in the melted butter and the cream. Fold in the flour, sieved with the baking powder and the almonds, pour into a round 8-inch cake tin and bake in a moderate oven (350° F., mark 4) for ¾–1 hour. Cool.

For the vanilla cream, blend the cornflour with a little cold milk and add the rest of the milk, the sugar and the egg yolks. Whisk thoroughly over gentle heat until the mixture thickens, add the vanilla essence and then whisk until cold. When it is quite cold, add a little whipped cream.

Mix all the marzipan ingredients to a paste, colour a very pale green and roll out thinly.

Cut the cake in half, sandwich it together with a layer of vanilla cream and put a layer of vanilla cream on the top. Then cover the whole cake, top and sides, with a thin layer of the pale green marzipan, smoothing this carefully on; finally, dust with icing sugar.

CHOKLADKAKA
(CHOCOLATE CAKE)

3 eggs	½ lb. flour
½ lb. sugar	3 tsps. baking powder
5 oz. butter	½ pint whipped cream
¼ pint cream	2 oz. chopped walnuts
6 tbsps. chocolate powder or cocoa	A few whole walnuts for decoration

Whisk the eggs and sugar well together, and add the melted butter, cream and chocolate powder. Fold in the flour sieved with the baking powder. Put into an 8-inch round cake tin which has been brushed with melted butter and dredged with flour and bake in a moderate oven (350° F., mark 4) for ¾–1 hour, until the cake feels firm. Cool and cut in half. Sandwich together with whipped cream mixed with chopped walnuts and cover the whole cake with cream, then decorate with whole walnuts.

POLYNÉER TARTS

3 oz. butter or margarine	2 oz. ground almonds
1 oz. sugar	3 oz. icing sugar
1 egg yolk	2 egg whites
4½ oz. flour	Green colouring (optional)

Grease some small fluted patty tins. Cream altogether the fat and sugar, add the egg yolk and flour and work them altogether till smooth. Put aside in a cool place for at least 1 hour, then roll out and use to line the prepared tins. Three-quarters fill these cases with a mixture made by beating together the ground almonds, icing sugar and egg whites; tint if desired. Cut strips from the pastry trimmings and arrange them in a cross on the top of each cake. Bake in a slow oven (325° F. mark 3) for about 20 minutes.

VALNÖTS TÅRTA
(WALNUT BARS)

6 eggs	3½ cups finely ground or minced walnuts
1¼ cups sugar	
3 tsps. almond essence	

Grease a tin about 9 inches square and 2 inches deep, line with waxed paper, then again grease the bottom. Beat the egg yolks until thick and tripled in volume. Gradually add the sugar, beating until very thick, then gradually fold in the walnuts and almond essence. Whisk the egg whites until stiff but not dry. Fold about one-quarter of the egg whites into the yolk mixture until well blended, then gradually fold in the remaining egg white. Put the mixture into the prepared tin and bake in a slow oven (325° F., mark 3) for 1 hour, or until the edges of the cake start pulling away from the sides of the tin. Cool for 10 minutes, turn out on to wire rack, remove paper and allow to cool. Wrap in foil, then store in a tightly covered container or in the refrigerator. Just before serving, cut into bars about 3 inches long and 1 inch wide; if desired, sprinkle with icing sugar.

These biscuits will keep for several weeks, if desired.

CROWN CAKE

3 eggs	5 oz. grated potatoes
3½ oz. butter	6 oz. ground almonds
11 oz. caster sugar	

Separate the eggs. Cream the butter and sugar with the egg yolks and add the finely grated potatoes, beating the mixture for about ½ hour. Add the ground almonds, mix thoroughly and finally add the egg whites, beaten to a stiff froth. Grease and line a deep 7- or 8-inch sandwich tin, pour in the mixture and bake it in a slow oven (300° F., mark 1) for about ¾ hour. Allow the cake to cool in the tin for about ¼ hour before turning it out. Split and sandwich together with lemon cream (see below).

LEMON CREAM FILLING

1 cup sugar	Grated rind and juice
⅛ pint white wine	of 1 lemon
¼ pint water	6 egg yolks

Mix all the ingredients in a saucepan and simmer the mixture, stirring continuously, till it begins to thicken. Remove the pan from the heat and continue to stir the cream until it is cool. Use as required as a cake filling or decoration, etc.

FRUIT TORTE WITH VANILLA CREAM

90

4 eggs	4 oz. caster sugar
Butter	Vanilla cream filling
Browned crumbs	(see previous recipe)
2 oz. flour	Jam
2 oz. cornflour	Glacé fruits
1½ tsps. baking powder	A little royal icing

Separate the eggs and whisk the whites until they are stiff. Grease a deep sandwich tin with butter and sprinkle well with browned crumbs. Sieve the flour, cornflour and baking powder together. Add the sugar to the egg whites, then add the yolks and the flour, etc. Stir well, until thoroughly mixed, pour into the prepared tin

and bake in a moderately hot oven (400° F., mark 6) for 30 minutes. Turn out and cool on a rack. Cut the cake into three when it is cold and spread each layer with vanilla cream. Coat the cake with a thin layer of jam, then arrange some large pieces of glacé fruit on top and decorate with piped royal icing.

PEPPARKAKOR
(GINGER SNAPS)

4 oz. butter	¾ tbsp. bicarbonate of
3½ oz. Demerara sugar	soda
7 oz. molasses	1 egg
1 tsp. ground ginger	1 lb. 2 oz. flour
1 tsp. ground cinnamon	Royal icing for
½ tsp. ground cloves	decoration

Cut up the butter roughly and put in a bowl. Heat the sugar, molasses and spices to boiling point; add the bicarbonate of soda, pour over the butter and stir until the butter has all melted. Beat in the egg and gradually blend in the sieved flour. Knead on a pastry board, using if necessary a very little flour. When of a rolling consistency, put small portions between sheets of waxed or silicone parchment paper and roll out thinly. Cut with fancy cutters (or use a small sharp knife and cut round cardboard or paper templates), making stars, hearts, animals and little human figures. (At Christmas-time include Christmas trees, Santa Claus figures, and so on.) Place on a greased baking sheet and bake in a moderate oven (325° F., mark 3) for about 10 minutes. Cool on a wire rack, then pipe with royal icing to mark the features and other details, using a fine writing nozzle.

These thin, crisp, spicy cookies may be stored (un-iced) for several weeks in an airtight tin.

SPRITSAR
(SPRITZ RINGS)

2 cups flour	⅛ tsp. salt
1 tsp. baking powder	¾ cup sugar
1 cup soft butter or	1 egg yolk, unbeaten
margarine	1 tsp. almond essence

Sieve together the flour, baking powder and salt. Cream the butter and gradually add the sugar, beating until very light and fluffy. Add the egg yolk and almond essence, beating until well blended. Gradually add the flour mixture, beating just until well mixed. Wrap the dough in waxed paper and refrigerate until easy to handle—about ½ hour. Meanwhile, start heating the oven to moderate (350° F., mark 4). Put the dough into a biscuits press fitted with a star disc, then force it on to a cold ungreased baking tray into " O," " S " and " U " shapes. Bake for 8–10 minutes or until the edges are golden-brown.

KOKOSKAKOR
(COCONUT COOKIES)

2 eggs, slightly beaten	¼ cup flour
1 cup sugar	½ tsp. almond essence
2 cups flaked coconut	

Grease and flour several baking trays. Put the eggs in a basin and add the sugar all at once ; using an egg beater, beat until smooth. Then, using a wooden spoon, stir in the coconut, flour and essence, mixing until well blended. Drop rounded teaspoons of dough about 2 inches apart on to the trays, put in a slow oven (300° F., mark 1) and bake for 12–15 minutes, or until the edges are golden-brown. Immediately remove from the trays and cool on a wire rack.

These cookies do not store very well, so it is best to make and enjoy them the same day.

KONFEKTBRÖD
(SWEDISH MACAROONS)

2 oz. caster sugar	A few drops of vanilla
2 oz. ground almonds	essence
½ oz. rice flour	Angelica
1 egg white	Crystallised cherries

Mix all the dry ingredients. Beat the egg white until just frothy, add a few drops of vanilla essence and add to the dry ingredients. The mixture should be of a stiff enough consistency to keep its shape when piped ; if necessary, moisten slightly with a little sherry. Pipe in different small shapes with a forcing bag and star nozzle on to a well-greased and floured tray or on to silicone paper. Decorate with tiny pieces of angelica and crystallised cherry, then bake in a moderate oven (350° F., mark 4) for about 15 minutes.

KLENÄTER
(CHRISTMAS CRULLERS)

4 egg yolks	1 tbsp. brandy
¼ cup caster sugar	1 tbsp. grated lemon
3 tbsps. butter	rind
1½ cups flour	Deep fat for frying

Mix all the biscuit ingredients, stirring until well blended, then chill the mixture. Put the dough on a floured board, roll out thinly and cut into strips ¾ inch wide and 3 inches long, using a pastry wheel. Cut a slit in the centre of each strip and draw one end through the slit so that the strip is twisted and looks almost like a bow. Fry the crullers in the hot fat until light brown, then drain well on absorbent paper. These are served with jam as a dessert or as an accompaniment to coffee and are popular at Christmas.

FINSKA PINNAR
(FINNISH FINGERS)

10 oz. flour	Egg white, coarse sugar
2 oz. ground almonds	and chopped almonds
2 oz. sugar	to coat biscuits
8 oz. butter	

Put the flour, ground almonds and sugar into a bowl, work in the butter with the fingers and knead to a smooth paste. Roll into small fingers, dip in beaten egg white and coat with sugar and almonds. Place on a buttered baking sheet and bake in a moderately hot oven (400° F., mark 6) until they are lightly browned and firm.

EASTER NOG

First prepare a basket of gaily coloured hens' eggs. Since they must be left uncooked, you cannot follow the traditional method of boiling them in coloured water, but you can paint the shell with vegetable food colourings, choosing strong, bright colours. When they are dry, tie them round with short lengths of narrow coloured ribbon. Allow 2 eggs per person. You will also need a decanter of cognac and some granulated sugar, and a tall glass and a long-handled spoon for each guest.

Each person cracks his eggs, transferring the egg yolks to his tall glass. (See that there is a pretty basin on the table to receive the egg whites, which you can use later for meringues.) He beats the egg yolks with the long spoon until thick and foamy, then adds 5 tsps. sugar, putting it in about ½ tsp. at a time and beating well after each addition. Finally, he adds 1–2 tbsps. cognac, drop by drop, still beating well. The Easter Nog is eaten with the long spoon.

JULGLÖGG
(CHRISTMAS PUNCH)

1 bottle Swedish aquavit	1 tbsp. cardamom seeds
or gin	½ tsp. cloves
1–2 bottles burgundy	About 1½ inches stick
or claret	cinnamon
1 cup raisins	1 small piece of lemon
½ cup sugar	or bitter orange peel

Pour half the aquavit or gin and all the red wine into a large saucepan ; add the raisins and sugar ; tie the spices and peel in a piece of muslin and add them. Cover the pan, bring very slowly to boiling point and then simmer for ½ hour. Add the remaining spirit, remove the pan from the heat and set light to the punch. Using a long-handled ladle, pour into warmed punch glasses and serve with raisins and almonds.

ALTHOUGH Switzerland is a comparatively small country, it has great variations in food from one district to another. Surrounded as it is by France, Italy and Germany, all these three languages—spoken with definite " Swiss accents "—are in common use, as well as the old Romansch tongue. The cooking, too, falls into the three categories of French, Italian and German, but the " Swiss accent " remains throughout.

In Switzerland, which is so sharply divided by its mountain ranges, each district clings to its own traditions. Everywhere the dairy produce is of excellent quality ; there are numerous delectable local cheeses, which are used in that national dish of Switzerland, the *Fondue*. Each Canton has its own recipe for the true, authentic fondue, but to a cheese-lover each is as delicious as the other.

In French-speaking Switzerland there is a plentiful supply of fresh-water fish ; pork from the Vaud is made into savoury sausages and ham ; fruit from the orchards of the Valais is combined with thick Alpine cream to make delicious gateaux and pastries. In Eastern Switzerland, sausages appear in variety and many dishes show a marked German influence ; while in the Ticino, the Italian region, the menus include ravioli, pasta, osso buco and zabaglione. The Grisons canton is a delightful mixture of all the cultures and languages and since the seventeenth century has been the cradle of many famous chefs and restaurateurs ; and the Plateau region, which stretches from Lake Geneva to Lake Constance, has its own specialities from the towns of Zürich, Basle and Berne. The Bernerplatte is composed of fresh, salt and smoked meats on a bed of sauerkraut ; hams, bacon and sausages hang in the wide chimneys of many farmhouses around Berne and are used in making this dish. Zürich is famous for its creamed veal, *Geschnetseltes*, while Basle specialises in carnival fritters and iced cakes.

There are vineyards in most of the cantons of Switzerland and some good wines are made, the best being from the cantons of Vaud, which produces Dezaley and Johannisberg ; Valais, which produces Sion from Fendant grapes ; Neuchatel and Berne.

Switzerland

VEGETABLE AND CHEESE SOUP
(UPPER VALAIS)

2 medium-sized leeks	2 oz. fancy-shaped
Sprigs of parsley	pasta
Celery leaves	2 tsps. flour
A small cauliflower	1½ oz. butter
2 onions	Salt and pepper
3 pints salted water	Valais, Bagner or
2–3 potatoes	Conches cheese
1 oz. rice	

Finely chop the leeks, parsley, celery leaves, cauliflower and onions. Cook for 30 minutes in 3 pints salted water. Add the peeled and diced potatoes, rice and pasta, and cook for another few minutes. In another saucepan brown the flour in the butter, dilute with hot water and add to the soup. Season, cook for another few minutes, then pour into a tureen lined with thin slices of Valais, Bagner or Conches cheese.

MINESTRA
(THICK VEGETABLE SOUP)

1¼–1½ lb. cut-up carrots,	1 oz. rice
leeks, celery, cabbage,	1 oz. macaroni
turnip	4 potatoes
1 onion	4 oz. lean bacon
1–2 tomatoes	Parsley
1 cup French beans	Basil
1 clove of garlic	Seasoning
1½ oz. butter or fat	2 oz. grated cheese
3½ pints water	

Fry all the cut-up vegetables in the butter for 20 minutes over a low heat. Add the liquid and cook for 2 hours. Add the rice, macaroni and potatoes, and cook for another 25 minutes. Add the diced bacon and the herbs and cook for a few minutes more. Season, dish up and serve with grated cheese.

This thick soup, together with bread and a glass of wine, often forms the Ticino peasant's main meal.

BINDENFLEISCH OR BUNDNERFLEISCH
(SLICED BEEF HORS D'ŒUVRE)

This consists of beef at its driest, cut up in very thin wafers and dressed with oil and vinegar.

KÄSSUPPE
(CHEESE SOUP)

1 lb. stale brown bread	⅓ pint dry white wine
1¼ lb. cheese	Salt
2½ pints boiling water	

Cut the bread and the cheese into small, thin slices, and arrange them in alternate layers in a tureen. Pour the boiling water over, and leave for 2–3 hours. Pour the whole into a saucepan and cook, carefully crushing the bread and cheese with a wooden spoon. Add the wine and seasoning before serving.

LAKE ZUG FISH

Clean the required number of fish and rub them with salt and pepper; make an incision in the back of each and place a sage leaf in it. Put a generous amount of fresh butter in a shallow baking dish; place the fish in the dish, together with a bouquet garni and 1 onion thickly stuck with cloves. Put knobs of butter over the top, dust with flour and put (uncovered) in a moderate oven (350° F., mark 4) for about 35 minutes. After 15 minutes, baste with the cooking juices; 10 minutes before serving add a glass of white wine.

LUCERNE FISH FILLETS

2 lb. fish fillets	Dry white wine
Court-bouillon	Flour
1 lb. potatoes	Salt, pepper, mustard
Butter	Grated cheese

Cook the fish in the court-bouillon until tender; peel and cook the potatoes at the same time. Place the fillets side by side in a buttered fireproof dish and surround by slices of potato. Make a piquant sauce with some dry white wine, butter, flour, salt, pepper and mustard and pour into the dish. Top with plenty of grated cheese and bake for about 20 minutes in a moderate oven (350° F., mark 4).

STEWED PIKE

A fresh-water pike,	1 onion, spiked with
weighing 2–3 lb.	2 cloves
Salt and pepper	1 tsp. anchovy or
3½ oz. fat bacon	lobster paste
1 medium-sized carrot	2 oz. butter
½ cup stock	1 tbsp. cream
½ cup dry white wine	Lemon juice
3–4 sage leaves	

Scale, clean and wash the fish; wipe dry and put some salt inside, then pull off the skin on either side of the dorsal fin and insert tiny strips of bacon in the flesh. Wash and peel the carrot and put it in the abdominal slit. Butter an oven-proof dish, put in the fish, back uppermost, pour in the stock and wine, add the sage leaves, onion, fish paste, pepper and a little salt, cover the fish with knobs of butter and cook in a moderate oven (350° F., mark 4), covering the dish for the first 15 minutes, then uncovering it for the next 30 minutes, till the fish turns a light gold colour and is well cooked; baste 2–3 times with stock and wine. Serve the fish whole. Dilute the cooking juice with a little water, strain, add the cream and a few drops of lemon juice and serve with the fish.

FILETS DE PERCHES " BEAU RIVAGE "
(FILLETED PERCH)

1 oz. butter	8 oz. mushrooms
4 oz. shallots	4–5 tomatoes
1½ lb. perch fillets	Parsley
Salt and pepper	⅓–½ pint white wine
Juice of 1 lemon	4 tbsps. cream

Butter an au gratin dish and sprinkle it with finely chopped shallots. Place in it a layer of perch fillets, seasoned with salt, pepper and lemon juice. Cover with the chopped mushrooms and with the tomatoes, skinned, seeded and finely chopped, and add a little chopped parsley. Put on top another layer of seasoned perch. Moisten with white wine, and cover with a buttered paper. Cook gently in a moderate oven (350° F., mark 4). When the fillets are done, pour the liquor into a saucepan, add the cream and simmer until reduced by a half. (The sauce must be very light, but well seasoned.) Cover the fish with the sauce and serve in the dish in which it was cooked.

FILETS DE PERCHES GOURMET
(GOURMET'S FRIED PERCH)

1–1½ perch fillets	Flour
Salt	2–3 oz. butter
Juice of 1 lemon	1–2 tomatoes
1 egg	⅓ pint béarnaise sauce
1 tsp. olive oil	Boiled potatoes

Salt the perch fillets and sprinkle them with lemon juice. Dip them in beaten egg mixed with a little oil, flour them, then cook in butter in a frying pan until they are of a good golden-brown. Skin, seed and dice the tomatoes. Put the béarnaise sauce in a hot dish and scatter the diced tomatoes over it. Arrange the fillets on the dish and garnish with the boiled potatoes.

FRIED PERCH·FILLETS

Soak the fillets in fresh beer for 45 minutes. Drain and coat with flour seasoned with salt and ground black pepper. Fry in very hot fat until golden-brown. Serve at once with a small piece of fresh butter and slices of lemon.

SWISS FISH À LA MEUNIÈRE

Soak and coat some fish fillets as in previous recipe. Cook them in butter in a moderate oven (350° F., mark 4), allowing each side 5 minutes. Take them out as soon as they are cooked. Leaving the cooking dish in the oven, put into it 3 knobs of butter mixed with flour and discreetly seasoned ; allow this to get light brown then dilute with ½ cup good quality white wine and serve with the fillets.

FISH COOKED IN WHITE WINE

This recipe is only suitable for biggish fillets. Place them into a saucepan, cover with salted cold water and heat until the water begins to bubble slightly. Draw the casserole to one side, cover and leave for 10 minutes for the fish to poach, then drain it. Line a fireproof dish with small knobs of butter, chopped parsley and chives, put in the fillets, season with salt and pepper and cover with white wine. Put the dish into a moderate oven (350° F., mark 4) and cook for 30–45 minutes, according to quantity.

FISH FILLETS AU GRATIN

Poach as described above, then put the fillets into a baking dish. Make a béchamel sauce, remove from the heat and beat into 2–3 egg yolks (according to quantity). Cover the fish with salted grated cheese and put into the sauce. Put into a hot oven (450° F., mark 8) to brown the top.

ROULADE DE VEAU
(VEAL ROLL)

Take some small flat pieces of veal, salt and pepper them and place a small piece of bacon in the middle of each ; roll up and secure with a cocktail stick, then fry in oil until well done. Keep hot in the oven while making the sauce as follows. Stir a little flour into the oil in the frying pan, and cook until brown, stirring all the time. Add a little water, then continue to add white wine until the mixture reaches the required consistency. Pour the sauce over the veal and serve hot.

BERNERPLATTER
(MEAT PLATTER)

1–2 onions	Ham liquor
A little fat	1¼ lb. beef flank or ribs
4½ lb. lightly salted sauerkraut	1 lb. smoked pork
	½ lb. bacon
½ pint white wine	½ lb. unsmoked sausages

Sauté the minced onions in a little fat. Cook the sauerkraut with the onions and wine. Moisten with some ham liquor to give a good smoky flavour, add the beef, smoked pork and bacon, and cook slowly. Half an hour before it is done, add 2–3 different kinds of sausage.

Place the sauerkraut on an oval dish and arrange the beef, ham, bacon and sausages on it in an attractive pattern, taking care to see that all are neatly cut and very hot. Serve with boiled potatoes. (In summer the sauerkraut is replaced by French beans.)

BRAISED MUTTON WITH WINE

1½–2 lb. thickly cut leg of mutton	1 lb. potatoes
Salt and pepper	½ lb. carrots
Cooking fat	1 small celeriac
1 glass white wine	1–2 medium-sized onions
	1 clove garlic (optional)

Beat the meat, rub with salt and pepper and fry in the fat in a flameproof casserole until lightly browned on all sides. Add the white wine (or water). Peel and chop the vegetables and place them round the meat, cover the casserole with a well-fitting lid and braise in a moderately hot oven (400° F., mark 6) for about 1¼ hours.

Pork can be cooked in the same way.

BŒUF À LA PAYSANNE
(STEAK WITH STUFFING)

Make a simple stuffing with breadcrumbs, chopped onion and chopped parsley. Salt and pepper some chunky oblongs of good stewing steak and fry lightly in oil. Meanwhile cut up some small pieces of bacon. Place each piece of steak in a casserole, on end, flanked by a mound of the breadcrumb mixture and then some chopped bacon; they should be packed fairly closely together. Cover with gravy and cook in a moderate oven (350° F., mark 4) for 1½ hours.

ZÜRICH LEBERSPIESSLI
(LIVER ON SKEWERS)

1 lb. calf's liver	Bacon strips
Pepper and salt	Butter
Sage leaves	

Skin the liver, cut it into strips about 1½ inches long and ¼ inch thick and season with pepper, salt and crushed sage leaves. Wrap the liver in the bacon strips and spear on wooden skewers; brown in a frying pan on both sides in a generous amount of butter.

ZÜRICH GESCHNETZELTES WITH RÖSCHTI
(VEAL WITH " RÖSCHTI " POTATOES)

2 lb. loin of veal	Salt and freshly ground pepper to taste
2 oz. butter	
1 medium-sized onion, finely chopped	1 cup dry white wine
3 tbsps. flour	1 cup chicken broth

Cut the veal into thin slices, melt the butter in a frying pan and fry the chopped veal for only 2–3 minutes. Remove the meat, add the chopped onion and stir over a low heat. Add the flour, seasonings, wine and broth and when lightly thickened put in the veal. Cook over a low heat stirring for 15 minutes. Garnish with finely chopped parsley and serve with " Röschti " potatoes—see page 258. Serves 6.

SKEWERED PORK IN THE TESSIN MANNER

1¼ lb. pork fillet	Sage leaves
7 oz. pig's liver	2 oz. butter
10 oz. lean bacon	Salted water

Cut the pork, liver and bacon into very thin slices. Place the slices on wooden skewers, with a sage leaf between the pieces, and fry them on all sides in a saucepan in the hot butter. When lightly browned, cover the pan and cook for 20 minutes over a moderate heat, basting every now and then with salted water.

Veal escalope and calf liver may be substituted for the pork and pig's liver but bacon must always be included.

FRICASSÉE DE PORC À LA GÉNÉVOISE
(GENEVA PORK FRICASSEE)

1¾ lb. neck of pork	A little coriander
¾–1 pint white wine	3–4 oz. lard
4 oz. small onions	1–2 tbsps. flour
A few peppercorns	Salt
A little thyme	Pig's blood
A little marjoram	Cream
A few cloves	

Cut the pork into large dice and marinade for 24 hours in the wine with the onions, herbs, etc. The next day take it out and drain it. Melt the lard in a heavy saucepan and brown the meat over a brisk heat; sprinkle with flour and let this colour. Add the strained marinade liquor and salt, then cook for 2¼ hours, stirring frequently. When the meat is cooked, add some pig's blood thinned down with fresh cream.

HOT MEAT PIE (LOWER VALAIS)

2 lb. veal	1 onion
3½ oz. fresh lean bacon	2 spoonfuls rum or brandy
3 cups dry white wine	
Salt and pepper	1½ oz. small grapes
A few cloves	Puff pastry
2–3 gherkins	Egg yolk to glaze
½ bay leaf	

Cut the veal and the bacon into small cubes. Mix the wine, seasonings, etc., spirit and grapes. Put the meat and bacon in this mixture and marinade for 2 days. Line a round, fairly deep tin with some of the pastry, pour in the pickled meat and cover with pastry, wetting the edges to make them stick together. Insert a funnel in the centre, using a piece of rolled-up cardboard. Glaze and bake in a hot oven (450° F., mark 8) until the meat is tender and the crust golden. Remove the funnel before serving.

MARINADE DE MARCASSIN
(YOUNG WILD BOAR)

Lard a shoulder of young wild boar, then marinade it in red wine for 3 days with a carrot and cut-up onion, a bay leaf, 2 cloves, some thyme and a few fir-tree shoots. Take out the meat and brown it on the outside in 4 tbsps. olive oil. Remove, then brown about 6 tbsps. flour in the oil; add the marinade liquor and the vegetables and cook the meat in this liquid, allowing 20 minutes per pound. When it is done, take it out, strain the sauce, skim off the fat, season, reduce it a little, then add ⅓ pint cream. Serve accompanied by noodles.

APPENZAL FRIED KID

1 lb. kid meat	½ lb. flour
1 leek	1 egg
1 onion	½ pint milk
Bay leaves	Oil for deep frying
Salt and pepper	

Cut the meat into small pieces and braise with the leek, onions, bay leaves and seasonings in a little salted water for about 30 minutes. Take out the meat, drain and allow to cool. Make a batter with the flour, a little salt, egg and milk. Dip the meat into the batter and fry until golden.

GRISONS MEAT DOUGHNUTS

¼ cup best olive oil	1 lb. white flour
¾ cup hot water	Salt
2 eggs	Oil or fat for frying

For the Filling

A piece of white bread (crumb)	Grated nutmeg
A little milk	Salt and pepper
½ lb. chopped veal	Chopped chives
½ lb. chopped pork	1 cup cold meat stock

First make the dough. Beat the oil with the hot water, add the well-beaten eggs and mix thoroughly. Put the flour and salt into a bowl, pour in the liquid, mix to a soft dough, cover and leave to stand for 20 minutes.

Soak the bread in the hot milk and chop it up. Add the meats, nutmeg, salt, pepper, chives and stock. Roll out the dough very thinly and divide in two. Place small portions of filling on one piece, put the other piece on top and press down; using a pastry wheel, cut into small rectangles and cook them gently in hot oil or fat. Serve with salad or whortleberries.

PIEDS DE PORC AU MADÈRE
(PIG'S TROTTERS IN MADEIRA)

3 pig's trotters	2 bay leaves
1 onion	¾–1 pint white wine
1 carrot	2 tbsps. olive oil
½ a leek	3 tomatoes, skinned
1 clove of garlic	and crushed
Thyme	2 tbsps. tomato purée
Rosemary	Madeira wine
A pinch of pepper	

Halve the trotters, wash well and leave them to soak for some hours in cold water. Drain them and put them in an earthenware casserole with the cut-up vegetables and the herbs. Cover with white wine and marinade for 3 days. Drain the trotters, parboil them, drain and add the marinade, the cut-up vegetables, the oil, the tomatoes and the tomato purée; cook over a low heat for 4 hours. Strain the sauce and flavour with Madeira wine. Dish the trotters up in a cocotte and serve with noodles.

MINCED TRIPE

3 tbsps. oil	Salt and pepper
2 onions	⅓ pint stock
1 clove of garlic	⅓ pint white wine or
1¾ lb. tripe	cider
¾ oz. flour	2 tbsps. tomato purée

Heat the oil and lightly fry the minced onions and garlic, then add the blanched and minced tripe and brown it lightly, stirring constantly. Sprinkle with flour, add seasonings, stir and moisten with the stock and the wine or cider; simmer for 2 hours. Add the tomato purée and simmer for another ¼ hour. Check the seasoning and serve very hot.

AARGAU SAUSAGE FRITTERS

½ cup potato purée	A pinch of salt
3 oz. butter	4 pairs of Vienna sausages
3 oz. flour	Egg white to glaze
1 egg yolk	Deep fat for frying

Mix the potato purée, butter, flour, egg yolk and salt to a smooth consistency, then leave to stand for 30 minutes. Skin and halve the sausages. Roll the potato mixture out thinly and cut into oblong pieces, wrap a sausage in each piece, join the edges with egg white and pinch in the ends of each roll to give a neat shape. Deep-fry or bake in a moderate oven (350° F., mark 4) (in the latter case, brush with egg yolk).

ÄPFELSCHNITTE
(BACON AND APPLE)

¾ lb. dried apples
1½ oz. fresh butter
1 tbsp. sugar

1¼ lb. lean bacon
1½ lb. diced potatoes
½ lb. smoked sausages

Soak the apples in cold water for 6–8 hours beforehand to let them swell. Melt the butter and sugar in a saucepan, add the soaked apples and the bacon and moisten with a little water, then cook for about 1 hour. Mix in the diced potatoes and the sausages and cook for another 25 minutes; add salt if necessary. Cut up the bacon and dish it up on top of the apples.

GLOBE ARTICHOKES WITH BEEF MARROW

2 lb. globe artichokes
Court-bouillon
Lemon juice

2 oz. beef marrow
1 pint Madeira sauce
(see page 263)

Peel the artichokes, removing the green leaves until only the white stalks remain; remove the "thistles" from the edge. Cut into 3 long pieces, removing any fluff that may have formed, and simmer for 4 hours in a court-bouillon to which some lemon juice has been added. Place in a vegetable dish. Add the lightly cooked, sliced bone marrow to the Madeira sauce and pour over the artichokes.

PÂTÉ DES PRINCES-ÉVÊQUES
(PRINCE-BISHOP'S PIE)

1 lb. pork meat
1 lb. veal meat
Red wine
1 large onion
2–3 carrots
1 clove of garlic

1 bay leaf
2 cloves
2 juniper berries
Salt
2–3 peppercorns

For the Pastry

1 lb. flour
4 oz. butter
Salt

¼ pint water (or ½ gill water and 1 egg)
1 egg to glaze

For the Filling

5 large white leeks
Lard
½ lb. veal
½ lb. pork
A little finely chopped parsley

Salt and pepper
2 truffles (optional)
4 gherkins
1 pint jellied stock

The meat should be weighed after all bones, skin and fat have been removed. Cut it into strips and marinade it in the wine mixed with the cut-up vegetables, herbs, etc., leaving it for 7 days in winter, 4 days in summer, and turning it each day. When the meat is ready, make the shortcrust pastry and divide it into 2 pieces, one twice as large as the other.

Next make the stuffing: chop the leeks very finely and cook them very gently in some lard for 1 hour. Add the minced veal and pork, the chopped parsley, salt, pepper, the chopped truffles (if used) and chopped gherkins; mix well. A more delicate flavour can be achieved by adding 2 calves' brains, blanched and chopped.

Roll out the larger piece of pastry ¼–⅜ inch thick and line a loaf tin with it, letting the pastry come a little way beyond the edge of the tin. Put in a layer of half the filling, then the marinaded meat and lastly the remaining filling. Roll out the remaining pastry and put it over the top of the pie, sticking the edges down with egg white. Fold the pastry projecting from the sides over on to the top of the pie. Decorate the top and brush it over with egg yolk. Cut 2 holes and put in each a little "chimney" of thin rolled cardboard. Bake in a hot oven (400° F., mark 6) for 2½ hours.

When the pie is cold, fill it up with the jellied stock, then remove the "chimneys." Leave in a cool place for 1–2 days and serve cut in slices. (A pie made with the above quantities will cut into about 30 slices.)

HOME-MADE JELLIED PORK

4 pig's trotters
2 pig's ears
1 pig's head
8–9 pints salted water
1 onion
2 cloves

1 bay leaf
Cooked carrot, hard-boiled egg and gherkin to garnish
3–4 egg whites
⅓ pint sharp white wine

In French Switzerland, after a pig has been killed and the ham has been salted, the blood puddings made and the lard rendered down, the remaining parts are often used to make jelly. This is a recipe for real home-made jellied pork platters, as made in peasant homes and country inns.

Free the trotters, ears and head of blood by soaking them in cold water for some hours, then simmer them for 3–4 hours in salted water, with the onion, cloves and bay leaf. Take out the meat, bone it, wrap it in a clean cloth and press it into an oblong loaf about 1½–2 inches thick. Put it in a press between two boards, with some weights on top, and leave till the next day; strain the jelly and leave in a cool place. The next day, cut the meat into slices, put on to platters and garnish with cooked carrot, hard-boiled egg and gherkin. Remove the fat from the jelly, clarify it with the egg whites and add the white wine, then strain through a cloth.

When it is cold, pour it over the meat to cover it and leave to set before serving.

GESCHNETZELTES
(ZÜRICH MINCED VEAL)

1½ lb. minced veal	1½ tbsps. paprika
3 oz. butter	¼ pint double cream
1 onion	¼ pint meat glaze or
4 oz. mushrooms,	brown sauce
washed and sliced	

Sauté the minced veal in the butter, then add the onion and brown it lightly. Take the meat out and add the sliced mushrooms, the paprika, cream and meat glaze. Simmer until reduced to a creamy consistency. Reheat the meat in the sauce, arrange on a dish and serve with savoury rice.

NEW POTATOES WITH ASPARAGUS

2 lb. asparagus	1 oz. butter
Salt and pepper	1 oz. flour
2 lb. new potatoes	A little cream

Wash and trim the asparagus, cut each stalk into 3 pieces and cook in salted water. Cook the unpeeled potatoes with a little salt, peel at once and cut into round slices about ¼ inch thick. Make a sauce with the butter, flour and asparagus liquor, season to taste and add a little cream. Mix with the vegetables and serve very hot.

TESSIN POTATO GNOCCHI

1½ lb. peeled and	2½ oz. butter
washed potatoes	1 tbsp. tomato purée
Salt and pepper	Red pepper (optional)
1 lb. flour	

Cook the potatoes in boiling salted water, drain and mash, then work in the flour to give a smooth mixture. Roll into small pieces, the size of your little finger, lay them on a clean cloth and let them " rest " for ½ hour. Boil them in salted water, stirring gently; as they rise to the surface, take them out with a draining spoon. Blend the butter, tomato purée (thinned with a little water) and salt and pepper to taste; if desired, add a little red pepper. Cover the gnocchi with this sauce.

" SWISS CREST " SALAD

2 lb. asparagus	½ lb. tomatoes
Salted water	Mayonnaise
5 oz. uncooked Grisons ham	

Wash and prepare the asparagus and cook in salted water; strain and cool. Divide into 4 equal portions and place on a large plate,

forming a cross. Fill the gaps between the arms of the cross with rolled slices of ham and surround with sliced ripe tomatoes. Fill the centre of the cross with mayonnaise. Serve cold.

TOMATOES STUFFED WITH APPLE AND CELERY

Cut a ¼-inch slice from the stem end of each of 6 large tomatoes; using a spoon, scoop out and keep the pulp. Sprinkle the tomato cups with 1 tsp. salt and ¼ tsp. pepper, then invert on a plate. Put 2 cups finely sliced celery in a bowl with 2 cups very coarsely grated unpeeled apples, ¼ cup lemon juice, ½ tsp. salt and 1 tsp. sugar. Combine ¼ cup sour cream, 3 tbsps. salad oil, 1 tbsp. horseradish, ½ tsp. salt and ¼ tsp. pepper. Drain the tomato pulp and coarsely chop enough of it to make 1¼ cups. Chill all these ingredients.

Combine the apple and sour cream mixtures, then add the tomato pulp. Use to fill the tomato cups, arrange these on a large dish and sprinkle with chopped chives. Garnish with watercress and radish roses.

CROÛTES AUX MORILLES
(CREAMED MUSHROOMS ON TOAST)

1 lb. morel mushrooms	8 slices of bread
⅛ pint cream	2 oz. butter
Juice of 1 lemon	Chopped parsley
Salt and pepper	

Wash the mushrooms several times, put them in cold water and bring to the boil, then immediately remove from the heat and drain. Cut the mushrooms up and simmer in the cream for about 20 minutes, until the liquid is reduced. Add the lemon juice and seasonings. Toast and butter the bread, spread with the mushroom mixture and garnish with chopped parsley.

TESSIN MUSHROOM RISOTTO

1–2 medium-sized	2 pints meat stock or
onions	diluted meat extract
2 oz. butter	2 small packets of
1 lb. rice	powdered saffron
1½ oz. dried mushrooms	Salt and pepper
soaked in tepid water	Grated cheese
to make them swell	

Chop the onions finely and lightly fry in the butter without letting them turn brown; remove with a skimming ladle. Put the rice into the same butter and stir gently to mix. Chop the drained mushrooms and add to the rice. Heat the stock, season with saffron, salt and pepper and pour over the rice. Stir and cook over a low heat until the rice is tender and has absorbed all the liquid—about 20 minutes. Serve with finely grated cheese.

ZÜRICH MUSHROOM TARTLETS
For the Pastry

7 oz. flour	1 egg
¼ lb. butter	1 tbsp. salted water

For the Filling

1 lb. mushrooms	2 tsps. flour
1½ oz. butter	¼ pint fresh cream
1 tbsp. finely chopped onions	Salt and pepper
	Juice of 1 lemon

Make the pastry, allow it to " rest," then roll out very thinly. Cut out tartlets with a buttered pastry cutter and bake " blind." Wash and chop the mushrooms and cook them in the butter, adding the chopped onions. Sprinkle in the flour, stir, add the cream, season, and add the lemon juice ; simmer for 5 minutes. Fill the hot tartlet cases with this mixture and serve very hot.

RAMEQUIN VAUDOIS
(CHEESE RAMEKIN)

12 oz. sandwich bread	1 pint boiling milk
1 lb. cheese	Salt and pepper
2 eggs	Grated nutmeg

Cut both the bread and the cheese in slices about ⅜ inch thick and arrange them alternately, échelon fashion, in a buttered au gratin dish. (The slices of cheese should project about ¼ inch beyond the bread slices.) Blend the eggs, milk and flavourings, and pour over the bread and cheese, then brown in a moderate oven (350° F., mark 4). The liquid will be absorbed by the bread and the top should take on an attractive golden-brown colour.

GLARON BACON " RÖSCHTI "

Wash, peel and grate 2 lb. potatoes, then squeeze in cloth to make as dry as possible. Heat a little oil or fat and lightly fry ½ lb. smoked streaky bacon, cut into thin fingers. Add the potatoes, mix and cook over a low heat, stirring frequently. Season with pepper and a very little salt.

BERNER RÖSCHTI
(BERNESE FRIED POTATOES)

Boil 2 lb. potatoes in salted water, without peeling them. When they are cold, skin them and cut into coarse strips. Heat 2 oz. butter in a frying pan, add the potatoes and cook on both sides till they become an even golden-brown.

Before serving arrange the potatoes in a flat, round cake, add another 2 oz. fresh butter and fry the outside of the cake to form a light, crisp crust. Turn the Röschti out on to a round plate

LE GÂTEAU AU FROMAGE DE PORRENTRUY
(PORRENTRUY CHEESE TART)
For the Pastry

8 oz. flour	4 oz. butter or lard
A pinch of salt	Water to mix

For the Filling

8 oz. grated Gruyère or Emmental cheese	Salt and pepper
	Grated nutmeg
¾ oz. flour	¼–½ pint milk (or half
3 eggs	cream and half water)

Make the shortcrust pastry and line a 9-inch flan ring with it. Mix all the ingredients for the filling and spread this over the pastry. Cook in a moderate oven (375° F., mark 5) for 25–35 minutes and serve hot.

In the Ajoie region, where people are fond of this cheese tart, it is the custom to eat it every Monday morning, on the stroke of ten o'clock, with a small glass of white wine. On market day the country people who have come into town have it for their midday meal.

OEUFS EN COCOTTE AUX ÉPINARDS
(BAKED EGGS AND SPINACH)

Wash some spinach, cook it in quickly boiling water, drain and plunge it into cold water. Drain it thoroughly, press out the cold water and chop very finely on a board with a large chopping knife. Add a little béchamel sauce, and reheat, then season well. Put some of the spinach into buttered cocotte dishes, then drop a raw egg into each and cover it with more béchamel sauce. Bake in a moderate oven (350° F., mark 3) until the eggs are cooked and the sauce lightly browned—20–25 minutes.

FONDUE ROMANDE

The most convenient number of people, when you are serving this dish, is 5–6. Allow for each person about 6 oz. of cheese (see notes below), ⅙ pint white wine and 2 tsps. potato flour, blended with 1 tsp. Kirsch. In Switzerland the cheese is prepared in a special pot of fire-proof earthware, but an ordinary strong saucepan can be used.

Rub the inside of the pan with a clove of garlic, then put in the grated cheese and the wine. Heat slowly, stirring with a wooden spoon. As soon as bubbles begin to form, add the potato flour blended with the Kirsch, then season with pepper and a little grated nutmeg.

The fondue is served at table in its pan, over a spirit lamp, the flame being adjusted so that the creamy mixture continues to " shiver "—not boil. Have a basket or plate of large cubes of bread; everyone then spears a piece of bread on a fork and twirls it two or three times in the hot melted cheese. According to the ritual, anyone who loses the bread from his fork must offer the company a bottle of wine. To accompany the fondue, serve if possible a white wine from the same region as the cheese, and some Kirsch.

Each canton, of course, claims to have the best recipe for Fondue. In the Jura they use half Gruyère and half Jura cheese (Noos or Chaux-d'Abel), and in addition to the garlic, they include 3 chopped shallots; with it they serve a sparkling white wine from Neuveville, and Kirsch from Ajoie. The Neuchâtel Fondue is made of equal quantities of Vacherin, Emmental and Gruyère cheeses, and served with Auvernier wine.

" PITZ "
(CHEESE-STUFFED TOMATOES—LOWER VALAIS)

92

2 lb. medium-sized tomatoes	A small bunch of fresh herbs, chopped
½ lb. grated cheese	½ cup sour cream
1–2 onions, chopped	Crumbled short pastry
Salt and pepper	

Cut the tomatoes in half and remove the seeds and cores. Mix the cheese, onions, salt, pepper and herbs. Fill the tomatoes with this mixture and pour sour cream on top. Line an oblong fireproof dish with the pastry, place the tomatoes in the dish, top with sour cream and bake in a hot oven (450° F., mark 8) until tender.

ST. GALL CHEESE BALLS

Mix well 4 egg yolks with 10 oz. grated cheese and add a beaten egg white. Shape the mixture into walnut-sized balls, roll them in flour, deep-fry and serve very hot with tomato sauce.

CHEESE TOAST WITH SCRAMBLED EGGS

Toast and butter 2 slices of bread for each person and keep them hot. Pour 1 cup white wine in a *fondue* dish, mix into it 1 oz. butter seasoned with chopped parsley and chives and a pinch of flour, also 10 oz. fatty, but not too salty, cheese, grated or chopped into fine pieces. Cook, stirring all the time. Break 6 eggs into a bowl and beat vigorously; pour them over the cheese

mixture when the latter begins to bubble and stir well in. Season lightly with pepper and spread the mixture on the bread. Serve very hot.

SOUFFLÉ AU FROMAGE
(CHEESE SOUFFLÉ)

2 oz. butter	4–6 egg yolks
2½ oz. flour	6 oz. grated cheese
¾–1 pint milk	Grated nutmeg
Salt	4 egg whites

Make a thick béchamel sauce with the butter, flour, milk and salt. Add the egg yolks, grated cheese and nutmeg and mix well. Whisk the egg whites very stiffly and fold lightly into the mixture. Pour into a buttered soufflé dish and bake in a moderately hot oven (400° F., mark 6) for 35–40 minutes. Put on a plate covered with a napkin and serve at once.

EGG RAGOÛT

93

6 eggs	1 onion, spiked with cloves
1¼ oz. fresh butter	
1½ oz. flour	Bay leaves
2½ cups meat stock	A little lemon juice

Hard-boil the eggs and keep warm. Heat the butter, stir in and brown the flour, dilute with stock and add the onion and bay leaves, then cook for at least 10 minutes. Add the lemon juice and the halved eggs.

BASLE SPINACH " FROGS "

94

16 large spinach leaves	Pepper and salt
1½ oz. butter	Grated nutmeg
1–2 minced shallots	1 egg
1 lb. minced lean pork	Cooking fat

Wash the spinach leaves and put them for 2–3 minutes into boiling salted water; drain and lay out on a wooden board. Mix the butter, shallots, pork, seasonings and nutmeg and bind with egg. Put some filling on each loaf and fold the edges together. Heat the fat in a frying pan and put in the stuffed leaves; baste frequently with the fat, and turn the " frogs " over once. Place in a vegetable dish and serve with béchamel sauce.

CHEESE TOAST À LA VAUDOISE

Cut slices off a round loaf. Spread one side of each with fresh butter, then cover with a ¼-inch slice of Jura or Gruyère cheese, cutting it a little smaller than the bread, since in the process of melting it is going to spread. Place the slices in a fireproof dish containing small knobs of butter and ½ cup La Côte wine. Put in a hot oven (450° F., mark 8) until the cheese melts into a smooth paste. Serve very hot, with freshly ground pepper.

CROÛTES AU FROMAGE FRIBOURGEOISES
(FRIBOURG FRIED CHEESE SLICES)

Allow a good slice of bread for each person. Fry it in butter and as soon as one side is golden, turn it and cover with a slice of Gruyère about ¼ inch thick. Cover the frying pan and cook until the cheese melts and spreads. Scatter the surface with some diced fried bacon and serve at once.

BÂTONS AU FROMAGE
(CHEESE FINGERS)

Cut some fingers of cheese about 1 inch thick, roll each in a piece of flaky pastry and seal well, then fry in deep oil until the batons are golden-brown. Serve hot or cold as an hors d'œuvre or after-dinner savoury.

If Gruyère cheese is used, add a little salt and pepper to the pastry, but this is not necessary with Cheddar cheese, which gives an equally good result.

KÄS-STANGE
(CHEESE STICKS)

Sift 2 cups flour into a large bowl with ¼ tsp. salt. Using a pastry blender, cut in 1 cup butter or margarine until the mixture is like coarse cornmeal. Blend in 1 egg, beaten with 2½ tbsps. milk. Wrap this dough in waxed paper and refrigerate for 1 hour.

Grate sufficient Swiss cheese to give 1½ cups (packed down). Start heating the oven to moderate (375° F., mark 5). Grease 2 baking trays. Roll out half the dough ⅛ inch thick on a lightly floured surface. Using a pastry wheel, cut into strips 5 inches by ½ inch. Twist the strips together in pairs, place on the trays and pinch the ends together. Repeat with the rest of the strips.

Brush the twists over with some beaten egg and sprinkle with ¾ cup grated cheese, then with 1 tbsp. caraway seeds and 1 tsp. salt. Bake for 15 minutes, or till golden. Treat the rest of the dough in the same way. Serve warm or cool, with soup or salad or as a nibbler.

The sticks will keep well in an airtight container.

POLENTA

1 pint salted water   1½ oz. butter
8 oz. maize flour   1½ oz. grated cheese

Bring the water to the boil and pour the maize flour in, mixing with a wooden spoon. Stirring continuously, cook for 30 minutes. When the mass comes away from the sides of the pan, blend in the butter and the grated cheese. Turn the mixture out on to a dish which has been rinsed in cold water. (In the Ticino a special round wicker dish or a wooden plank is used.) Serve sliced.

This Polenta may be served with tomato sauce, or it may be used as accompaniment to a stew or roast. Polenta is above all a country dish. In the old-fashioned houses, lacking in all "modern comforts," you will see it being cooked in a battered copper pan, on the hearth of an open fire or on the corner of an old wood-burning stove.

FLAN BERNOIS
(BERNESE HAM FLAN)

½ lb. flaky or puff pastry   ½ lb. tomatoes
Salt and pepper
½ lb. lean cooked ham   2–3 oz. grated cheese
½ lb. mushrooms   Prawns and ham to
A little butter   garnish

Line a Swiss roll tin with the pastry, and lay thin slices of ham over it. Slice the mushrooms and fry lightly in the butter. Cut the skinned tomatoes into thin slices and sprinkle with salt and pepper. Cover the ham first with a layer of mushrooms, then with a layer of tomatoes, and finally with a thin layer of grated cheese. Season, and cook in a hot oven (450° F., mark 8) until golden-brown—20 minutes. Garnish with prawns and rolled ham and serve hot.

SWISS CHEESE PIE

½ lb. bread dough   2 medium-sized onions,
3 oz. butter   chopped and fried in
½ lb. grated Gruyère cheese   butter
½ lb. Emmental cheese   2 eggs
1 cup cream   4 boiled and mashed potatoes

Knead the bread dough with the butter, roll out and use to fill a round baking tin. Mix the remaining ingredients thoroughly and cover the pastry in a 1-inch thick layer. Bake in a moderately hot oven (425° F., mark 7) for 30–35 minutes.

CÉRISES AU TAPIOCA
(CHERRY TAPIOCA)

2 oz. tapioca   1 lb. large ripe cherries
1 pint milk   A little brandy
Vanilla essence   Sugar
1 slice of lemon rind   Whipped cream

Soak the tapioca overnight in the milk flavoured with the vanilla and lemon rind. The following day cook it in a double saucepan until it thickens into a jelly; remove the lemon rind. Stone the cherries, put them into a fireproof dish, moisten with a little brandy, sweeten to taste and leave for an hour. Pour the tapioca mixture over the cherries and bake in a slow oven (325° F., mark 2) until cooked—25–30 minutes. Decorate and serve.

RHUBARB MOUSSE

Dice 1 lb. rhubarb and cook for a few minutes in very little water. Let it cool for a moment, then drain through a fine strainer. When cool, put into an enamelled fireproof casserole and add 5 oz. sugar and 3 eggs. Beat well over heat, but remove the mixture as soon as it is smooth and before it begins to boil.

POMMES AU TAPIOCA
(APPLE TAPIOCA)

2 oz. tapioca	1 oz. sugar
1 pint water	Rind of 1 lemon
4 cooking apples	Caster sugar
2 oz. raisins	Cream

Put the tapioca and water into a saucepan, bring to the boil and simmer until the mixture is thick and clear. Peel and core the apples and cut into thick slices. Stone the raisins. Put the apples and raisins into a buttered pie dish and sprinkle with the sugar and grated lemon rind. Pour the tapioca over the fruit and bake in a moderate oven (350° F., mark 3) for about 1 hour, until the pudding is set and the apples are cooked. Sprinkle with caster sugar and serve with cream.

MUESLI
(FRUIT AND ROLLED OATS)

Fruit as available	⅓ pint water
4 tbsps. rolled oats	Ripe dessert apples
4 good tbsps. sweet	Grated nuts
condensed milk	Bananas, grapes, etc.,
4 tsps. fresh lemon	to decorate
juice	Cream to decorate
Grated lemon rind	(optional)

Prepare the fruit as required. Put all the ingredients, except the apples and nuts, in a bowl, and mix to a thick cream. Wash and halve the apples, remove the stalks and flower end and grate the apple flesh directly into the rolled oats mixture, stirring this constantly to preserve the whiteness of the apples; the mixture should be light and creamy in consistency. Sprinkle the top with some grated nuts (or some rolled oats or wheat germ), decorate with apple quarters, sliced banana, seeded grapes or other fruit in season and if desired add some whipped cream.

FLAN DE PRUNES
(PLUM FLAN)

Line a plate with shortcrust pastry. Cut some large ripe plums into four, stone them and arrange these "fingers" of plum in overlapping circles on the pastry, beginning in the centre and working outwards. Sprinkle with sugar and put a few pieces of butter on the top. Bake in a moderately hot oven (400° F., mark 6), for 35–40 minutes, until pastry and plums are cooked.

A *Flan de Pommes* is made in the same way; cut the apples into fairly thick slices.

PETITS FLANS DE POMMES À L'ABRICOT
(APRICOT APPLE TARTLETS)

Make some flaky or puff pastry. Peel, wash and core some cooking apples and cut each apple in half lengthwise. Roll out the pastry to a thickness of ½ inch, and cut into squares, allowing one square to each half-apple. Place the half-apples on the pastry, then, with a sharp knife, cut into thin slices. (Do not separate the slices, as they will open slightly during the cooking.) Brush with apricot jam (first warming the jam a little, so that it will spread evenly). Bake in a hot oven (450° F., mark 8) for 30–35 minutes. When the flans are ready, the apple will be cooked and the pastry golden-brown and well risen round the edges. Re-glaze with apricot jam.

CHOCOLATE PEAR GÂTEAU

First make the chocolate sauce: mix equal parts of sugar syrup and melted plain chocolate, stirring over hot water, and blending until the mixture reaches the desired consistency—it will thicken as it cools.

Now soak a Genoese sponge with equal quantities of sugar syrup and Kirsch. Place on it some cooked halved pears, coat with the chocolate sauce and decorate with whipped cream.

BADEN CAKES

½ lb. caster sugar	1 tsp. baking powder
2 eggs	Grated rind of ½ a
1–2 tbsps. aniseed	lemon
½ lb. plain flour	2 tsps. lemon juice

Beat the sugar and eggs together until thick and pale in colour. Crush the aniseed, put through a fine sieve and add. Fold in the other ingredients and work lightly into a soft dough. Form into little rolls about the thickness of a finger and 3 inches long; pinch the ends together and curve round, then put on to a greased baking tray. (Alternatively, pipe the dough on to the tray to form horseshoes.) Cut 2 or 3 notches on each horseshoe, then bake in a moderate oven (350° F., mark 4) for 10–12 minutes. The tops should remain white, while the base is just coloured.

OBWALDEN HONEY CAKE

2½ cups honey
2½ cups sour cream or milk
A pinch of salt
7 oz. sugar
Juice and grated peel of 1 lemon
1 tbsp. ground cinnamon

A pinch of powdered cloves
A pinch of crushed aniseed
A little nutmeg
1 tbsp. bicarbonate soda
Flour

Pour the honey into a basin and mix in the cream or milk, salt, sugar, lemon and spices. Sieve in the bicarbonate and enough flour to make a firm dough. Form this into three slabs, put into a buttered tin and bake for ¾ hour in a moderate oven (350° F., mark 4). When done, brush over with diluted honey.

KIRSCHTORTE
(KIRSCH GÂTEAU)

For the Jap Cake Base

5 egg whites
4 oz. sugar
4 oz. ground almonds or hazelnuts

2 tbsps. flour
2 tbsps. potato flour or cornflour

For the Genoese Sponge Layer

4 eggs
6 oz. sugar
A pinch of salt
2½ oz. flour

3 oz. potato flour or cornflour
2 tsps. baking powder
Kirsch

For the Butter Cream

8 oz. butter
8 oz. icing sugar

Carmine colouring
Kirsch

To decorate

Whole almonds
Ground almonds

Icing sugar

Prepare 2 round 10-inch tins by lining with greased greaseproof paper. Make the Jap cake base by beating the egg whites very stiffly, adding the sugar, ground nuts and flours, and mixing lightly.

Divide the mixture into 2 equal parts, and spread each in one of the 2 round tins. Cook in a moderate oven (350° F., mark 4). Take off the paper from the base by moistening it with water, and, if necessary, finish drying the cakes in a slow oven. (These Jap cakes may be stored in an airtight tin.)

For the Genoese sponge, put the eggs, sugar and salt in a basin over hot water and beat until the mixture is light and thick (about 15 minutes). Add the mixed and sieved flours and baking powder, folding in delicately. Put into a greased and lined 10-inch cake tin and cook in a moderate oven (350° F., mark 4) for 40–45 minutes.

To make the butter cream, cream the butter and stir in the sieved icing sugar, then add a few drops of colouring to give a pale rose tint, then finally add the Kirsch and mix well.

To assemble the cake, spread one Jap cake with butter cream. Sprinkle the Genoese sponge with Kirsch to flavour and put on to the Jap cake.

Spread the top of the sponge thickly with butter cream and cover with the second Jap cake, pressing this in place with a plate, to keep the gâteau even and flat. Cover the top and sides with butter cream. Stick blanched and toasted almonds round the sides and dredge the top with lightly toasted ground almonds. Dust the surface generously with icing sugar, then, using the back of a knife, mark the sugar with a diamond pattern—the traditional decoration.

NILLON GÂTEAU

1 lb. shortcrust pastry
1 cup *nillon* (crushed nut kernels from which oil has been removed)
1 cup milk
1 cup water

Sugar to taste
A pinch of salt
1 tbsp. flour
3 tbsps. jam
½ cup nut oil

Line a round tin with the pastry. Grate the *nillon* finely, mix it with the liquids and add the remaining ingredients. Cover the pastry with the nutty mixture and bake in a moderate oven (350° F., mark 4) for about 40 minutes.

LECKERLI
(SMALL HONEY CAKES)

4 tbsps. water
7 tbsps. honey
9 oz. sugar
A pinch of salt
4 drops of lemon essence
2 tsps. ground cinnamon
1 tsp. ground cloves

1 tsp. grated nutmeg
1 tsp. ground ginger
1 lb. flour
1 tbsp. baking powder
6 oz. almonds
2 oz. candied peel
Glacé icing

Mix the water, honey, sugar and salt in a saucepan, heat to dissolve the sugar and pour this thick syrup into an ovenproof glass dish; leave until tepid. Stir in the lemon essence, spices and two-thirds of the mixed flour and baking powder and blend well. Add the rest of the flour, then the shredded almonds and the diced candied peel. Knead quickly to get a smooth dough, put this on a greased and floured baking tray, spreading it to a thickness of ⅛–¼ inch with a palette knife, and bake for about 25 minutes in a moderate oven (350° F., mark 4). Cut into squares and coat with glacé icing.

ZUPFE
(BERNESE HOLIDAY BREAD)

1 packet dry yeast	½ cup unblanched
1 cup milk	almonds, chopped
¼ cup sugar	¼ cup mixed red and
¼ cup butter	green Maraschino
1 tsp. salt	cherries, drained
1 egg	and halved
Flour	½ tsp. grated lemon
⅓ cup diced preserved	rind
citron	1 beaten egg to
1 cup chopped seeded	glaze
raisins	

Sprinkle the yeast into ¼ cup warm water and stir till dissolved. Put the scalded milk in a basin and stir in the sugar, butter and salt; leave till lukewarm; using a spoon, beat in 2 cups flour, then the yeast, egg and enough extra flour to make a soft dough—1½–1¾ cups.

Turn the dough on to a lightly floured surface, cover with a bowl and let it stand for 10 minutes, then knead until smooth—about 10 minutes. Place in a lightly greased bowl, turning it once to grease the whole surface. Cover and leave to rise in a warm place (80°–85° F.) till doubled in size—about 1½ hours.

Punch down the dough and again let it rise till it doubles its size, then again punch it down. Now, using the hands, work in the citron, raisins, almonds, cherries and lemon rind. Divide the dough in half, shape into 2 loaves, put into greased tins measuring about 9 by 5 by 3 inches and leave to rise till it is almost doubled in size—this should take about 30–40 minutes.

Meanwhile, start heating the oven to moderate (350° F., mark 5). Brush the loaves with beaten egg, then bake for 25–30 minutes, or until they sound hollow when tapped with the finger. Remove from the tins and cool on a rack.

FASTNACHTKUECHLI
(CARNIVAL FRITTERS)

2 eggs	1 oz. melted butter
5 tbsps. cream or milk	8 oz. flour
A pinch of salt	Deep fat for frying
½–1 oz. sugar	Icing sugar and cream

Mix the eggs, cream, salt, sugar and melted butter, then add flour till the mixture can no longer be stirred with a wooden spoon. Turn it on to a board and work in the rest of the flour, kneading till the dough is smooth and elastic. Cut it into 16 pieces. Roll each piece out as thinly as possible (the pastry ought to be as transparent as tissue paper) and leave to dry on a cloth.

Fry these pastry "leaves" in smoking-hot deep fat, pressing them down with the ends of two wooden spoons, so that when the fritters are cooked, they have a dimpled appearance. (In Switzerland a special 5-pointed star on a long handle is used to mark the fritters as they cook.) Drain the fritters, dust with icing sugar and pile up 7 or 8 at a time. Serve with whipped cream.

These fritters are a Shrove Tuesday Carnival speciality.

MADEIRA SAUCE

2 oz. butter	A bouquet garni
2 oz. flour	Salt and pepper
1 pint good brown stock	6 tbsps. Madeira wine

Make a brown roux with the butter and flour, stir in the stock, add the bouquet garni and seasoning and simmer for 15 minutes, to reduce a little. Before serving, remove the bouquet garni and add the wine.

PAINS D'ANIS
(ANISEED CAKES)

2 eggs	10 oz. flour
½ lb. sugar	2 tsps. baking powder
½ oz. aniseed	

Beat the eggs and sugar for 15 minutes, then gradually add the aniseed and the flour mixed with the baking powder. Knead quickly on a board. The dough should not be moist, but rather dry.

There are two ways of shaping the cakes. The first is to make rolls 2 inches long and nick each with a knife in 2 places, then shape into a semicircle. The other method is to roll out the dough ¼–⅜ inch thick and cut it with fancy cutters. Place the pieces on a buttered tin and leave to rest for 24 hours in a dry, airy place. When ready for cooking, the cakes should be dry and white on top but damp underneath. Bake in a moderate oven (350° F., mark 4) for about 15 minutes—the cakes should rise, but still remain white.

GAUFRETTES DE VALAIS
(WAFFLE CORNETS WITH CREAM)

½ cup sour cream	½ lb. flour
4 tbsps. milk	5 oz. sugar
2 tbsps. water	Grated peel of 1 lemon
1 tbsp. Kirsch	Juice of 1 lemon
Pinch of salt	Double cream

Mix all ingredients except the double cream and bake on a waffle iron. Form into cornets while hot and when cold fill with whipped cream.

95

Food in Yugoslavia is almost as varied as the character of the country itself; the influences of Turkey, Hungary, Italy and Greece can all be traced.

Fruit and vegetables grow in profusion in the sunny valleys and the wild strawberries, cherries and plums are second to none. Grapes and water melons, too, are abundant. The rich grazing lands yield meat of excellent quality and there is good fish to be had from the Adriatic.

The Yugoslavian people are hearty eaters and their dishes are often rich, solid and spicy, though the modern trend is to use rather less oil and spice. Goat's milk cheese is very popular, as are all stuffed vegetable dishes, such as vine leaves or peppers, which are served with sour cream. Bürek, the paper-thin pastry turnovers filled with curds, cheese or vegetables, are also served frequently. Cakes and sweet dishes vary from the Hungarian type, such as Dobos Torte and Moka Torte to the Turkish-style syrupy pastries and baklava.

Breakfast is an early meal, often eaten out of doors in the summer. It may consist of bread and coffee with fat bacon, curds, cheese or bürek and in bad weather a glass of slivovica helps to keep out the cold. Lunch is frequently composed of soup, a dish of Djuvetch, the characteristic thick, rich stew of tomatoes, paprika, potatoes and rice with meat or fish, or perhaps stuffed cabbage or vine leaves. Dinner is served fairly late and in the summer Yugoslavs love to eat their grilled meat or fish, kebabs and rice out of doors under the trees. The meal ends with coffee and fruit or cakes and pastries which are brought round on trays by itinerant vendors. Cheese is generally eaten at the beginning of the meal rather than the end and is often blended with onions or paprika and chives.

Yugoslavian table wines, which are now becoming very popular in this country, are good and plentiful and the country is famous for its delicious slivovica, or plum brandy.

Yugoslavia

CROATIAN BEAN SOUP

½ lb. haricot beans	3–4 tbsps. flour
2 large onions	Salt
1 oz. dripping	Pepper
2 pints light-coloured stock	¼ pint sour cream to garnish (optional)

Wash the beans and soak overnight. Boil them in the water in which they have been soaked and when soft rub through a hair sieve. Chop the onions and fry them in the dripping. When they are golden-brown, stir in the flour and continue to cook until the flour is also evenly browned, then add this onion and flour mixture to the sieved beans. Put all together into a saucepan, pour in the stock (the peasants frequently use stock in which bacon or ham has been boiled), add salt as required and simmer the soup for 1 hour. Stir a little pepper into the sour cream and add to the soup; reseason and reheat, but do not allow it to boil. Serve immediately.

This is a favourite dish with Croatian farm workers, who eat it with bread dumplings or boiled pork in the winter months.

JAGNJECA CORBA
(LAMB SOUP)

1 lb. lamb	2 tbsps. flour
Salt	A pinch of paprika
A little finely chopped parsley	pepper
1 large chopped onion	1 egg
1 tbsp. lard	A little vinegar

Cut the lamb into small squares, put into a pan of cold water, add a little salt and bring to the boil. Skim, then add the parsley and onion and continue cooking until the meat is tender. Meanwhile put the lard in a separate pan, add the flour and paprika and bring to the boil. Add this thickening to the soup, then stir in the egg and a little vinegar to taste.

KISELA CORBA
(SERBIAN SOUP)

2 lb. pork	A few peppercorns
1 parsnip	Paprika
1 celery head	2 tbsps. rice
1 carrot	2 egg yolks
1 large onion	2 tbsps. vinegar
Salt	1 cup sour cream

Cut up the pork, put in a saucepan and just cover with water; cook very slowly and remove the scum as it rises. Put in all the vegetables, previously prepared and cut small, together with salt, peppercorns and paprika to taste. Simmer slowly for about 2 hours; when all is thoroughly cooked stir in the rice and continue simmering for about 20 minutes. Beat up the egg yolks and pour them into a warmed tureen, stir in the boiling soup and then add 2 tbsps. vinegar and a cup of sour cream. Mix thoroughly to blend well and serve at once. Chicken, turkey or lamb can also be used in place of pork, or a mixture of meats can be used.

FISH DJUVETCH

2 lb. fish	Salt and pepper
½ lb. onions or leeks	2 lb. assorted vegetables,
A little fat	as available
1 oz. rice	¼ pint stock or water

Prepare the fish as required and cut it into slices. Chop the onions or leeks finely and fry them until they are soft and brown; add the rice and fry it lightly with the onions. Prepare and cut up the vegetables and add them to the rice and onion. Season and stir the mixture well and leave it cooking slowly for a few minutes. Put it in an earthenware dish, lay the slices of fish on the mixture and add the stock or water. Bake in a moderate oven (350° F., mark 4) for about 1½ hours.

BAKED FISH WITH DUBROVNIK SAUCE

Put slices of any kind of fish into an earthenware dish. Prepare the sauce in the following way. Melt ¼ oz. butter in a frying pan and in it sauté 1 oz. finely chopped onion and ½ lb. peeled and sliced tomatoes. When the onions and tomatoes are partly cooked, pour over them 1 wineglassful of white wine or cider and leave to simmer until the sauce thickens. When the sauce is ready, pour over, sprinkle with grated cheese and bake in a moderately hot oven (400° F., mark 6) for 20 minutes.

BRODET OD MORSKIH RIBA
(SAVOURY FISH STEW)

2 lb. fish (see note)	Chopped parsley
1 oz. seasoned flour	¼ pint vinegar
6 tbsps. olive oil	3 tsps. concentrated
2–3 onions, sliced	tomato purée or 1
1 clove of garlic	tin tomato juice

Prepare the fish and cut into 2-inch squares, coat with seasoned flour and fry in hot olive oil, then remove. Fry the onions until yellow and add the chopped garlic and parsley and the fish. Pour over the vinegar, tomato purée and sufficient water to cover, bring to the boil and simmer very gently for ½ hour, taking care not to break the fish. Serve hot with noodles or macaroni.

Note : The fish can be any one or a combination of tuna, eel, mackerel, or red mullet.

SERBIAN FISH

1 lb. fresh haddock fillet	2 tomatoes
3 tbsps. dry white wine	1 tsp. flour
1 medium-sized onion, finely chopped	1 tsp. paprika
	1 tsp. salt
1½ lb. potatoes	3 oz. bacon
1 oz. butter	¼ pint sour cream

Skin the fish and cut into cubes; place in a bowl with the wine and onion and marinade for 1 hour. Peel and slice the potatoes, place in an ovenproof dish, dot with pieces of butter and cover with the peeled and sliced tomatoes. Sprinkle with flour, paprika and salt and cook in a moderate oven (350° F., mark 4) till the potatoes are beginning to soften. Place the fish on the top, cover with the chopped bacon and return the dish to a moderately hot oven (425° F., mark 7) for 15 minutes. Reduce the heat to slow (325° F., mark 3), pour the sour cream over, cover the fish and cook for a further hour.

PITA
(MEAT PASTY)

This should strictly be made with the very thin pastry used by the Austrians for Apfel Strudel, but is quite successful made with a good flaky pastry. Roll out the pastry to fit a Yorkshire pudding tin and spread with a well-seasoned mixture of minced meat, lightly fried onion and a little stock. Cover with another layer of pastry, then repeat the layers. Bake the pasty in a hot oven (450° F., mark 8), until lightly browned.

LAMB ON SKEWERS

1 lb. lean lamb	Bay leaves
Oil and onion for marinading	1 large onion, cut in slices
Pieces of tender liver, kidney, etc.	Sliced tomatoes

Beat the lamb, cut it into small squares and marinade it in a little olive oil to which some finely chopped onion has been added. Impale all the meats, bay leaves, sliced onion and tomatoes alternately on skewers and grill under a fierce heat, turning the skewers frequently, until the meat is well cooked.

CEVAP
(MUTTON CHOPS WITH PAPRIKA)

6 mutton chops	Paprika
1½ oz. dripping	Tomato juice
3 onions or leeks	A little stock or water
Salt	

Fry the chops until they are brown on both sides. Lift them out and fry the finely chopped onions or leeks in the same fat. Add salt, paprika and tomato juice and a little stock or water. Return the chops to the pan and stew until tender.

MUTTON DJUVETCH (CASSEROLE)

1 lb. potatoes	1 lb. onions
1 lb. tomatoes	1 lb. neck of mutton
1 lb. cauliflower	Salt and pepper
2 oz. rice	2 tsps. paprika
1½ oz. dripping	½ pint water or stock

Prepare the vegetables, cutting the potatoes, tomatoes and cauliflower into small pieces. Add the rice (and any other vegetables you have left over) and mix well. Melt the dripping in a frying pan and slowly fry the chopped onions and the sliced meat. When the meat is half cooked, add the other vegetables, mix well, season and put the mixture into a casserole with the water; cook in a moderate oven (350° F., mark 4) for 1½ hours.

PORK AND VEAL DJUVETCH

¼ lb. chopped onions	1 cup rice
Butter or lard for frying	1 lb. tomatoes
	½ lb. sliced pork and veal mixed
Chopped parsley	
Seasonings	1 large cup stock or water

Fry the onions and when soft add the parsley, seasoning and rice; cook until the rice is clear, stirring well. Grease a fireproof dish and arrange in alternate layers of the rice mixture, thinly sliced tomatoes and meat, making the last layer of tomatoes. Pour in the stock or water, cover the dish and cook slowly in a moderate oven (350° F., mark 4) for about 2 hours, till all the liquid is absorbed—shake the dish gently from time to time so that the rice does not stick. Serve in the same dish.

PORK AND TOMATO DJUVETCH

1 lb. pork	1 cup olive oil
½ lb. onions	2 slices of fat bacon
2 cups cooked rice (measured after cooking)	Salt and pepper
	1 tsp. red paprika pepper
6 green peppers, chopped	2 lb. tomatoes

Cut the meat into small squares. Chop 3 of the onions and mix with the rice; add the chopped peppers and leave standing in a little oil. Meanwhile chop the remaining onion and fry with the meat and bacon. Add salt, pepper and paprika to taste. When the meat is brown and the onion quite soft, put half the rice mixture into an earthenware dish, then a layer of the meat mixture, and cover with the rest of the rice. Put the sliced tomatoes on top and pour over the oil, mixed with a little water. Cover and cook in a slow oven (325° F., mark 3) for 1½ hours.

Other vegetables such as aubergines and small marrows, may be included; parsnip and celery leaves are sometimes used for flavouring.

PORK AND ONION DJUVETCH

1 lb. onions	1 lb. pork, cut up small
1½ tbsps. lard	2–3 potatoes
Parsley	Seasoning
6–7 green peppers	1 cup rice
1 chilli (optional)	½ lb. tomatoes

Slice the onions and put them in a pan with the lard and some parsley; add the peppers and the chilli, if used. When these are partly cooked, add the pork and the potatoes and season to taste. Simmer for a while, then add the rice and the sliced tomatoes, stir well and put in a casserole. Bake in a moderate oven (350° F., mark 4) for 1½ hours.

PORK LOAF

1 oz. dripping	6 oz. rice
1 onion	4 green peppers
12 oz. minced pork	1 small tin of tomato
Seasoning	purée
1 egg	¼ pint water
2 oz. breadcrumbs	¼ pint sour milk

Melt the fat in a pan, fry the finely chopped onion and mix this with the meat, seasoning, egg and breadcrumbs. Mould the mixture into an oblong shape and put it into a well-greased baking tin. Half cook the rice in boiling salted water. Put a layer of rice at either side of the meat, place a few slices of green pepper over this and then add another layer of rice, and season; continue in this way, making the last layer rice. Mix the tomato purée with the water and sour milk and pour this over the meat and rice. Cover with a lid over greased paper and bake in a moderate oven (350° F., mark 4) for ¾ hour. Serve cut in slices, garnished with rice and peppers.

PORK WITH CELERY

1 lb. pork	¾ pint meat stock
Butter or lard	1 tbsp. flour
3 onions, chopped	Salt and pepper
1 lb. celery	

Cut the pork into small pieces and fry in hot fat with the chopped onions; add a little water and simmer very gently for about 15 minutes. Wash and peel the celery, cut in pieces and simmer with the meat, adding a little more water. Make a gravy with the meat stock, the flour and a little butter, season to taste and pour it over the meat.

If desired this dish can be cooked in the oven instead of on top of the stove.

SEKELIGULAS
(PORK AND SAUERKRAUT)

Cube 1½ lb. pork and slice ¼ lb. onions. Fry the onions in 1 oz. fat, add the pork and season with salt, pepper and paprika. Turn down the heat and allow to cook slowly in its own juice. When the meat is half cooked, slice and add 1 lb. tinned sauerkraut and the cabbage liquor. Pour in ½ pint cold water, bring to the boil and simmer gently until the pork is soft. Add ¼ pint sour cream, stirring well, and heat for 1–2 minutes. Serve hot with creamed potatoes.

CRIPULJA
(BEEF CASSEROLE)

1 lb. fat beef	A few haricot beans
¼ of a white cabbage	¼ of a red cabbage
1 small carrot	2 small onions
2 tomatoes	Salt
2 large potatoes	A few peppercorns
1 green pepper	1 small bottle of white
1 small parsnip	wine

Slice the meat and vegetables and lay them in alternate layers in a casserole, lightly salting each layer and adding the peppercorns. Pour the white wine over, cover the casserole closely and simmer for at least 2½ hours. Do not stir or the vegetables will break up. Serve in the casserole.

PECENI ZEC NA CREVNOME VINU
(RABBIT ROAST WITH RED WINE)

1 head of celery	Pepper and salt
1 carrot	1 wild rabbit
1 parsnip	Lard
1 red pepper	A small bottle of red wine
1 tomato	(not too sweet)
¼ of a white cabbage	2 tbsps. flour
White vinegar	

First make a vegetable soup with all the vegetable ingredients, adding vinegar, pepper and salt to taste. While this is simmering, clean the rabbit and put in a large dish; pour over it liquid from the vegetables and leave for 48 hours in a cool place. Three hours before the meal, remove the rabbit from the liquid and place in a roasting dish. Pour 1 small cup of melted lard over it and put in a moderate oven (350° F., mark 4). After 15 minutes start basting alternately with the vegetable liquid and red wine. Continue until the rabbit is cooked (when the flesh comes easily away from the bones).

Put 2 tbsps. lard in a saucepan with the flour and blend together, then add some of the rabbit liquor and stir until the mixture thickens. Pour in the sour cream, stir well, pour over the rabbit and serve at once.

CHEVAPCHICHI
(MEAT ROLLS)

These little rolls about the size of a man's thumb are made of minced raw meat (beef, mutton, veal or a mixture), well seasoned and bound with beaten egg. Grill rapidly, turning frequently; when nicely browned all over, serve on thick slices of new unbuttered bread, accompanied by thin slices or rings of raw onion and freshly ground black pepper.

EGG " PIGLETS "

10 eggs	A few black olives
Goose liver pâté	or truffles
Tomato-flavoured aspic	Ham and tongue
mayonnaise	salad

This is an amusing dish for a buffet table. Hard-boil 10 eggs and cut them in half lengthways, stuff them with goose liver pâté, put together and allow to cool thoroughly. Using the same filling mixture, shape the eggs into " piglets " and then coat them with a tomato-flavoured mayonnaise. Put in the eyes, etc., with pieces of olive or truffle. Serve with sliced ham and tongue.

PUNJENE PAPRIKE I PATZIDNANI
(STUFFED PEPPERS AND TOMATOES)

1 lb. pork	4 large green peppers
2 rashers of fat bacon	2 lb. smaller tomatoes
2 onions	1 tbsp. butter
2 tbsps. boiled rice	1 tbsp. flour
1 egg	½ pint milk
Salt	A little sugar
4 large tomatoes	

Mince the pork, dice the bacon and fry with 1 finely chopped onion. Mix in the cooked rice, then beat in the egg and salt to taste. Halve the large tomatoes and the peppers and scoop out the pulp and seeds, place the tomatoes and peppers side by side in a greased ovenproof dish and fill with the minced mixture.

Meanwhile, cut the smaller tomatoes into small pieces and simmer with 1 chopped onion until quite soft and pulpy, then strain. Melt the butter and blend with the flour, stir in the milk and strained tomato sauce, with salt to taste and a pinch of sugar and bring to the boil,

stirring all the time. Pour this over the stuffed tomatoes and peppers and cook in a slow oven (325° F., mark 3) for 45 minutes, covering the dish for the last half-hour.

SARMA OD VINOVOG LISCA
(STUFFED VINE LEAVES)

30–40 vine leaves	Dill and salt to taste
1 lb. veal or lamb	1 egg
2 tbsps. lard	1 tbsp. flour
1 minced onion	1 cup white wine
3 oz. rice, partly cooked	1 cup sour cream

Pour some fairly hot salted water over the vine leaves to soften them, then wash them well in cold water. Mince the meat and fry it in 1 tbsp. lard with the minced onions until cooked but not dry; remove it from the heat, stir in the half-cooked rice and add dill and salt to taste. Add the egg and mix thoroughly. Fill the leaves with this mixture and wrap closely, securing with fine string if necessary. Place in a dish, pour a little water over and cover the pan closely, then cook very slowly for 45 minutes.

Place 1 tbsp. lard in a saucepan with the flour and cook till brown, stirring well; add a little water and simmer, stirring until the mixture thickens. Add the wine and sour cream, pour this sauce over the stuffed vine leaves and serve at once.

STUFFED AUBERGINES—I

4 large aubergines	Salt and pepper
6 ripe tomatoes	2 tbsps. olive oil
1 tbsp. chopped parsley	1 cup stock
1 chopped onion	Parsley to garnish

Put the aubergines in water, boil for about 5 minutes, then drain and dry them, cut in half lengthways and take out some of the pulp. Add 4 skinned and chopped tomatoes, the parsley, onion, seasoning and aubergine pulp, then stuff the cases with this mixture. Pour the oil and stock over and around, put the remaining sliced tomato in between and bake in a moderate oven (350° F., mark 4) for about ½ hour, until tender. Garnish with parsley.

STUFFED AUBERGINES—II

4 aubergines	1 green pepper, finely
2 eggs	chopped
2 tbsps. breadcrumbs	Salt
2 tbsps. sour cream	Olive oil
A little finely chopped	1 lb. tomatoes
parsley	½ a parsnip
1 onion, finely chopped	

Simmer the aubergines until cooked, cut in half, remove the centres and mix with the beaten eggs, breadcrumbs, sour cream, parsley, onion and pepper; add salt to taste and a little oil. Fill the aubergines with this mixture, place the halves together again and put into a greased casserole. Make a sauce with the tomatoes cooked in their own juice with the parsnip, strain and pour over the aubergines. Cook in a slow oven (325° F., mark 2) for 45 minutes, covering the dish if necessary to prevent the top scorching.

STUFFED CABBAGE LEAVES

8–10 large outer leaves of cabbage	1 tsp. chopped parsley
	Stock
6 oz. raw meat	½ pint good brown
2 oz. rice	sauce
Salt and pepper	8–10 small slices
1 tsp. tomato sauce or ketchup	fried bacon

Wash and blanch the cabbage leaves and leave them soaking in hot water for a few minutes to soften them. Mince the raw meat and mix it with the uncooked rice. Add the seasonings, tomato sauce and parsley, form the mixture into 8–10 croquettes and wrap a cabbage leaf firmly round each one. Pack them into a saucepan or casserole, cover with stock and simmer for 1½ hours. Serve with the brown sauce poured round them and garnish with a slice of fried bacon on each cabbage roll. Podvarack (see next recipe) is an excellent accompaniment to this dish.

PODVARACK
(SAUERKRAUT AND ONIONS)

For two people take 1 lb. sauerkraut and 2 onions. Melt 1 oz. lard in a saucepan and add the chopped onions, fry until golden-brown, and then add the sauerkraut. Leave to simmer for ½ hour, stirring occasionally; serve hot.

PASULJ PREVRANAC
(ONIONS AND BEANS)

½ lb. beans (any kind)	2½ cups olive oil
2–3 onions, finely chopped	1 tsp. paprika and salt
	Pepper to taste
2 lb. small onions	

Partly cook the beans, drain and add some fresh water, then add the finely chopped onions and cook until soft; strain well. Meanwhile, peel and slice the remaining onions, cook in the hot oil in a saucepan, adding some paprika and pepper when the onions are nearly cooked, then remove from the heat. Grease an earthenware dish and put the onions in it, place a layer of beans over this, then add the rest of the onions and beans. Pour over any remaining oil and either simmer over a low heat or put in a slow oven (325° F., mark 3) for about 1 hour. This dish may be served hot or cold.

VARIVO OD KROMPIRA
(SAVOURY POTATOES)

8 large potatoes	1 tsp. red paprika
1 tsp. lard	Pepper and salt
1 onion	4 tbsps. vinegar
1 tbsp. flour	1 small bay leaf

Peel the potatoes and slice thickly. Put the lard in a saucepan, add the chopped onion and flour and fry lightly, then add the paprika and mix well. Add the potatoes and season to taste. Add to the mixture in the saucepan and leave to simmer for a short time. Mix the vinegar with a little cold water and add the bay leaf and add to the potato mixture; cook slowly until the potatoes are soft.

AUBERGINE AND PEPPER " CAVIARE "

Combine halved aubergines and cleaned seeded peppers in the proportion of 1 aubergine to 2–3 peppers. Put in a heatproof dish, cover and bake in a moderate oven (350° F., mark 3) until tender, then allow to cool. Skin and mince finely, together with a good-sized raw onion and 1–2 cloves of garlic, then mix well with 2–3 tbsps. salad oil, some salt and pepper and a very little vinegar. This " caviare " is very good eaten with roast meat, cold cuts or grills.

MAHUNE
(FRENCH BEANS)

Prepare and slice 2 lb. French beans, place in a little salted water and cook until soft. Melt 1 oz. butter, add 1 oz. flour, stir and brown lightly over a low flame. Add 1 garlic clove and 1 finely chopped onion, and brown slightly. Add the bean liquid gradually, stir well to make a smooth sauce and season. Pour over the beans, bring to the boil and cook for 3 minutes. Add 1 tsp. vinegar and 1 tbsp. sour cream and bring just up to the boil again.

SOUR CABBAGE

1 large cabbage	4 cloves
2 oz. lard, margarine or butter	1 tsp. salt
	3 tbsps. vinegar
1 pint water	2½ tbsps. sugar
2–3 peppercorns	

This popular dish somewhat resembles sauerkraut. Use a red cabbage if available; failing this, a white one will serve. Remove the outer leaves and the hard part of the stalk, shred very finely, put into a colander, pour boiling water over it and allow to drain. Melt the fat in a saucepan, stir in the shredded cabbage with the peppercorns, the cloves and the salt, pour in the vinegar, add a little water to prevent the cabbage from catching and simmer gently for about ½ hour, adding more water, if necessary. Add 2 tbsps. sugar, stir and simmer for another 20 minutes. Taste, and if necessary add a little more sugar. Serve very hot with any kind of meat.

POTATO NOODLES WITH CHEESE

1 lb. potatoes	1 tbsp. milk
½ lb. flour	A little butter
Salt	Grated cheese
1 egg	2 slices of bacon

Cook the potatoes and pass them through a fine sieve. Add the flour, salt, egg and milk and work the mixture with the fingers into a paste. Roll out to ½ inch thick and cut into strips ½ inch wide and about 2 inches long. Cook in boiling salted water—when they float on top of the water they are cooked enough. Put them on a hot dish with a very little butter and plenty of grated cheese. Serve garnished with the bacon, cut into small squares and fried.

DROBLJENAC OD BRASNA
(RICH BATTER PUDDING)

4 eggs (separated)	Grated rind of 1 lemon
2 oz. caster sugar	Salt
¾–1 pint milk	3 oz. lard
8 oz. flour	Icing sugar

Beat the egg yolks and sugar together, then add the milk, flour, lemon rind and salt and beat well. Fold in the stiffly beaten egg whites. Heat the lard in a Yorkshire pudding or meat tin and pour in the batter. Bake in a moderately hot oven (425° F., mark 7) for 20 minutes. Turn the pudding as for a pancake, and continue cooking for a further 15 minutes until well browned on both sides. Remove from the tin and when cold, break into small, irregular pieces. Sprinkle with icing sugar and serve with fruit sauce.

GIBANICA
(CREAM CHEESE " PIE ")

1 lb. flour	1 lb. cream cheese
Seasoning	4 oz. cream
Lard or margarine	A little milk
6–8 eggs	

Add a pinch of salt to the flour and mix to a smooth dough with a little water ; the dough should not be sticky and you should be able to roll it without difficulty. Divide into 20–30 pieces and roll these out as thin as possible.

Spread each piece with lard or margarine, putting one piece on top of another in pairs. Fry these in a greased frying pan until they begin to rise, then wrap each piece in a cloth.

In a separate bowl put the eggs, seasoning, cream cheese, cream, a little milk and 4 oz. of the lard or margarine and mix well together. Grease a tin approximately the size of your rolled-out dough and then place one piece in the tin, spread with the above filling and add another piece. Continue until all the pieces are used up, leaving the top piece plain. Spread the top with lard, and bake in a moderate oven (350° F., mark 4) for 15 minutes, until the top is a delicate brown.

OKRUGLJICE OD ŠLJIVA
(PLUM DUMPLINGS)

1 lb. boiled potatoes	1 egg
3 oz. butter	1 lb. plums
4 oz. flour	Sugar
Salt	1–2 oz. breadcrumbs

Sieve the potatoes while still hot, add 1 oz. of the butter and when this is melted, add the flour and salt and mix with egg and water to a stiff dough. Knead, roll out to ¼ inch thick and cut into 4-inch squares. Place a stoned plum in the centre of each, add 1 tsp. sugar, damp edges of pastry and bring together to form a ball. Place the dumplings in fast-boiling salted water for 5 minutes. Melt the remaining butter and fry the crumbs until golden. Strain the plum balls and serve them hot, sprinkled with the breadcrumbs.

FRUIT PURÉE

2 lb. apples	1 pint water
4–6 oz. sugar	2–3 tbsps. potato flour

Peel the apples and cut into small pieces, cook until quite soft, sieve and cook again with the sugar. Mix the potato flour in a teacupful of water and pour very slowly into the saucepan with the apples. Stir for a few minutes and simmer the mixture for a few minutes longer ; remove from the heat and allow to cool. Use as a sweet or to replace jam. Cranberries, black-currants and red-currants may also be made into purée.

LIKA NUT SPONGE

4 eggs	8 oz. seedless raisins
8 oz. granulated sugar	4 oz. flour
8 oz. ground hazel nuts	

Beat the eggs and sugar in a basin over hot water until thick and pale yellow. Fold in the nuts, raisins and flour and put into a buttered and floured 7-inch cake tin, then bake in a moderate oven (325° F., mark 3) for $1\frac{1}{4}$–$1\frac{1}{2}$ hours.

POTICA
(HOLIDAY YEAST CAKE)

99

$\frac{1}{4}$ cup lukewarm water	1 tsp. salt
1 packet dry yeast	$3\frac{1}{2}$–$3\frac{3}{4}$ cups flour
1 cup hot milk	2 egg yolks, slightly
$\frac{1}{4}$ cup granulated sugar	beaten
$\frac{1}{4}$ cup butter	

For the Filling

6 tbsps. single cream, scalded	2 tbsps. butter or margarine
2 cups ground walnuts	2 tbsps. fresh bread-
$\frac{2}{3}$ cup granulated sugar	crumbs
$\frac{1}{2}$ tsp. salt	2 egg whites
$\frac{1}{2}$ tsp. vanilla essence	

Put the warm water into a small bowl, sprinkle the dry yeast on it and stir until dissolved. Mix the milk, sugar, butter and salt; cool until lukewarm. Add 2 cups flour, beating well; beat in the yeast and egg yolks, then enough of the remaining flour to make a soft dough. Turn out the dough on to a lightly floured surface, cover with a bowl and let stand for 10 minutes; knead until smooth and elastic—8–10 minutes. Place the dough in a lightly greased bowl, turning it once to grease the surface, cover with clean towel and leave in a warm place (about 85° F.) to rise till doubled in size—about $1\frac{1}{2}$ hours. Punch it down, then let it rise till doubled—about 45 minutes. Meanwhile, grease 2 loaf tins measuring about 9 by 5 by 3 inches.

Make the filling as follows: Mix the scalded cream, walnuts, sugar, salt and vanilla. Melt the butter in a saucepan, add the breadcrumbs and sauté till golden, then add to the nut mixture. Keep back 2 tbsps. of the egg whites and beat rest till stiff, then fold into the nut mixture. Punch down the dough and divide into halves. On a lightly floured surface roll each half into an oblong measuring about 16 by 9 inches. Using a small spatula, spread on half the filling; starting from a short end, roll up Swiss-roll fashion and place in a loaf tin. Let the loaves rise till almost doubled—30–40 minutes. Meanwhile, start heating oven to moderate (375° F., mark 5). Brush the loaves with the 2 tbsps. egg white and sprinkle with sugar. Bake the loaves 35–40 minutes, or till they sound hollow when tapped with the finger. Remove from the tins and lay them on their sides on a rack to cool, out of the draught. Serve sliced.

SLATKO OD JAGODA
(STRAWBERRY PRESERVE)

2 lb. strawberries	$\frac{3}{4}$ pint water
2 lb. sugar	

Choose large strawberries, fully ripe but not soft. Boil the sugar with the water to make a syrup that will drop very slowly off a spoon. Skim well, then put it with the strawberries in a shallow, broad pan and cook very slowly, shaking gently but without stirring or the strawberries will break. Simmer until the fruit is absolutely transparent, then remove the pan from the heat and cover with a damp cloth wrung almost dry and press the lid well down over this, so that the steam cannot escape. Leave until quite cold, then put into sterilised jars and seal.

Middle East

THE Jewish year is studded with festivals and holidays, each one having its own rich assortment of customs, traditions and foodstuffs. Because the family plays such an important part in Jewish life, the majority of these celebrations centre round the home and Jewish women have the loving task of preparing the traditional foods and of seeing that the old customs are maintained.

The Jewish regulations governing foodstuffs are very strict and are supervised by an official religious body, which has the power to approve various products for Jewish consumption. Many rules govern the selection and preparation of food: animals must have cloven hoofs and chew the cud; all animals and birds must be without disease or deformity and must be ritually slaughtered; the hind quarters of beasts, even when slaughtered in the orthodox manner, are forbidden as food; meat, even from an orthodox butcher, must be *kashered*, that is, soaked in cold salt water at home before cooking, in order to remove all the blood; only fish with scales and fins may be eaten and milk or milk products must never be cooked or served with meat. Jewish ingredients are, in fact, divided into Meat, Milk and *Pareve*, or neutral, it being permitted to serve *Pareve* foods with either meat or milk. But in spite of these restrictions, or perhaps because of them—for necessity, as we know, is the mother of invention—Jewish cookery is rich, varied and interesting.

The Sabbath is the Jewish holy day and the Law lays down very firmly that no preparation of food may take place on that day; even the lighting and extinguishing of fires is forbidden. Traditional Sabbath recipes, therefore, are either for cold dishes that can be prepared on the previous day or for casserole meals that can be left to cook on the lowest possible heat for many hours.

One of the greatest of the Jewish feasts is Passover, which lasts for eight days, during which time no leaven except eggs may be used in any food, various dried beans and pulses are forbidden and food is cooked and eaten from special dishes and kitchen utensils which are reserved exclusively for Passover use. Yom Kippur, the Day of Atonement, is a fast day, the fast extending over the entire twenty-four hours. Other holidays include Succoth, lasting a week, Chanukah, lasting eight days, and Purim and each one has its special food customs. Many traditional ceremonies also take place in Jewish houses and such family festivals, which include births, confirmations and weddings, are the occasion for much rejoicing and the serving of many special dishes.

In Israel itself, because Jews from many countries have come to live there, food customs may vary, but basically the old Jewish traditions are adhered to. Fresh vegetables and grains, olives, fruit, honey, dates and nuts are all grown widely and with these natural products, meat, poultry and a plentiful supply of fish, the Israeli housewife has no lack of excellent raw materials to work with.

Israel

CHERRY SOUP WITH EGG DROPS
For the Soup

100

1 quart stemmed and stoned cherries	2 tbsps. sugar (more with sour cherries)
1 tbsp. lemon juice	A pinch of salt
1 quart cold water	

For the Egg Drops (Small Dumplings)

1 egg	A pinch of salt
¼ cup cold water	A pinch of nutmeg
3 tbsps. flour	

Beat egg well, add water, flour, salt and flavouring and beat vigorously till smooth. Bring the soup to a rapid boil and drop the egg mixture from the tip of a teaspoon into it. Cook for 5 minutes; the dumplings rise to the top when done.

To serve cold, cook the soup ingredients for 5 minutes, let it cool and transfer to the refrigerator for at least 2 hours. Just before serving, cook the egg drops in slightly salted fast boiling water. Drain well before adding to the soup. A spoonful of sour cream may be stirred into each plateful of soup. Serves 6–8.

UNCOOKED FRUIT SOUP

2 cups fruit pulp	Lemon juice
4 cups skimmed milk	4 tbsps. sour cream
Honey to taste	

Blend the first four ingredients, adjusting amount of lemon juice and honey to taste. Finally stir in the sour cream to thicken. Serve very cold.

GEFILLTE FISH

1 large haddock (pike or carp can also be used)	1 tbsp. breadcrumbs
	1 onion
	Chopped parsley
1 lb. onions	1 carrot
Parsley	Seasoning
2 eggs	1 tbsp. flour
Salt and pepper	Milk

Cut the fish into thick slices. Scoop out some of the flesh from each slice, leaving the pieces of fish in the same shape. Chop the flesh finely with the onions, parsley, eggs, seasoning and breadcrumbs. Press this stuffing into the holes left in the slices of fish. Put the pieces into a casserole with the onion, parsley, carrot and seasoning and cover with cold water. Bake in a moderate oven (350° F., mark 4) for an hour. Mix the flour to a smooth paste with cold milk; add some of the hot fish liquid and stir well. Pour this over the fish and return to the oven for 5 minutes. Serve hot. Alternatively the fish may be cooked until the water in which it was covered has been reduced to half. The fish is then removed to a cold place and the liquid strained into a separate bowl, where it will form a jelly. The fish is served cold, decorated with the jelly and the pieces of carrot.

BALUK PLAKKI

3 lb. any firm-fleshed fish	2 large onions
	4 large tomatoes
½ cup oil, butter or cooking fat	1 cup boiling water
	Parsley
Salt to taste	Lemon

Rub fish inside and outside with oil and salt lightly. Grill under a low heat turning when brown; then brown other side. Place in a baking dish, cover with sliced onions and tomatoes. Sprinkle lightly with salt and bake for 20 minutes at 400° F. (mark 6). Pour over boiling water and bake for 5–10 minutes longer, basting frequently. Serve either hot or cold, garnished with parsley and lemon. Serves 6.

BROWN FISH STEW

3 onions	2 small gingerbreads
½ pint cold water	¾ cup vinegar
3 lb. fish (salmon, mackerel, trout or similar fish)	6 oz. treacle
	Slices of lemon
	Chopped parsley
Seasoning	

Peel and slice the onions and cook in ½ pint of water in a casserole on the hotplate, until the onions are soft. Add the fish and seasoning, and cook for 20 minutes in the oven at 375° F. (mark 5). Meanwhile, melt the gingerbread in the vinegar and add the treacle to it. Pour this in with the fish. Shake the casserole to mix well and continue cooking for a further 15 minutes. Serve cold with slices of lemon and chopped parsley. The fish should be cooked the day before in order for it to become thoroughly cold.

PATLIJAN ALA NAZ
(SCALLOPED AUBERGINE WITH LAMB)

10 slices of aubergine, ½ inch thick	Salt to taste
	½ cup chopped parsley
1 lb. chopped lamb, mutton or beef	Pepper or paprika to taste
1 onion, minced or chopped	½ cup tomato purée
	1 cup water

Salt aubergine slices and drain dry as soon as softened. Combine chopped meat with onion and parsley and season to taste. Spread on each slice of aubergine and arrange in a well-greased baking dish. Top each piece with tomato purée diluted with water and bake for 1 hour at

325° F., mark 3. Put under the grill to brown on top, if desired, a few minutes before serving. Garnish with parsley or serve on toast, mashed potato or boiled rice. Serves 5.

STUFFED SHOULDER OF VEAL

1½ quarts fresh bread-crumbs	1 tsp. pepper
1¾ cups canned chicken broth	1 tsp. ground ginger
	1 egg, slightly beaten
½ cup melted chicken fat	4–4½ lb. boned shoulder of veal
1¼ cups chopped onions	2 tbsps. lemon juice
1 cup chopped parsley	1 large onion, sliced
3 or 4 oz. can sliced mushrooms	6 medium potatoes, peeled
1½ tsps. salt	1 tsp. paprika

Start heating oven to 325° F. (mark 3). In bowl, soak bread in broth. In ¼ cup fat, in pan, sauté chopped onions till tender. Drain soaked bread from broth, reserving both. To onion in pan add bread ; cook over medium heat, while stirring, 2 minutes.

Drain mushrooms, saving juice, and add to bread, with parsley, mushrooms, 1 tsp. salt, ¾ tsp. pepper, ¾ tsp. ginger and egg.

Combine ½ tsp. salt, ¼ tsp. pepper, ¼ tsp. ginger ; use to sprinkle surface and pocket of veal. Then stuff pocket with bread mixture and skewer.

Place stuffed veal in roasting pan ; brush with ¼ cup fat ; roast 1 hour. Combine broth, mushroom and lemon juices ; pour over meat ; top with onion slices. Place potatoes in pan ; sprinkle with paprika.

Continue roasting, while basting, 2 hours, or till tender, turning potatoes once. Remove skewers. Place meat and potatoes on heated serving dish. Serve with Pickled Beetroots (see below). Makes 6 servings.

PICKLED BEETROOTS

Cook 8 medium beets till tender ; peel, slice. Bring ½ cup water with ½ cup lemon juice, 2 tbsps. sugar, ½ tsp. salt to a boil ; stir in 2 tsps. horseradish. Pour over beets, refrigerate till needed.

CARROT TZIMMES

5 large carrots	Water
5 medium potatoes	1 small onion (optional)
3 medium sweet potatoes	2 tbsps. flour
2½–3 lb. beef brisket	2 tbsps. chicken fat or vegetable shortening
1 tsp. salt	
½ cup sugar or honey	

Cut carrots into thin rounds. Peel and cut

potatoes into quarters. Peel and cut the sweet potatoes into 1-inch thick rounds. Brown the meat in a casserole. Add the vegetables, salt and honey or sugar. Add water to cover, bring to the boil and simmer for about 3 hours, adding more boiling water as often as required during cooking until the meat is tender. Do not stir ; to prevent sticking, shake the casserole occasionally.

If an onion is used, it should be left whole and removed before it becomes too mushy.

When the liquid has been reduced by half, thicken by lightly browning flour in hot melted fat and stirring in some of the liquid from the tzimmes. Shake the casserole to distribute the thickening. Then bake in the oven for 30 minutes or till brown on top. Serves 6.

TURNIP TZIMMES

2 lb. brisket of beef	½ cup honey, brown sugar, syrup or black treacle
1 onion, diced	
2 lb. turnip (1-inch dice or cut into inch-square thin slices)	
	2 tbsps. hot melted fat, preferably chicken fat
Water to cover	
1 tsp. salt	2 tbsps. flour
A dash of nutmeg	

Brown the meat and onion in the casserole. When nicely browned, add the turnip and enough water to cover. Bring to the boil, skim well, then turn down heat to simmer. Add salt, sweetening and nutmeg. Cook over same heat for 1 hour, shaking dish occasionally to prevent burning. Should more liquid be required, add boiling water a little at a time. The turnip turns a golden-orange and looks most attractive.

This dish is done when the meat is tender enough to pierce with a fork. Lightly brown flour in melted fat and add, gently stirring in to distribute evenly. Cook 5 minutes longer. Serves 4–6.

CHOLENT

2 large sliced onions	8–10 medium potatoes, peeled and cut in halves or quarters
2 tbsps. chicken fat, or oil	
	2 tbsps. flour
½ lb. dried beans soaked till tender in cold water	Salt, pepper, paprika to taste
2 lb. brisket beef	Boiling water to cover

Sauté onions in hot fat in the bottom of a heavy pot with a tight-fitting lid. When light brown, add the prepared beans and potatoes and put the meat in the centre. Mix flour and seasonings and sprinkle over top. Add boiling water to cover, adjust lid and cook over heat for 3–4 hours. Lift lid to make sure no additional water is needed and then place the pot on an asbestos mat and simmer. The flame should be as low as possible without danger of being extinguished if the cholent is to cook slowly overnight and until noon of the following day.

SWEET-SOUR MEAT BALLS

1 lb. chopped beef
¼ cup brown or long grain rice
1 grated clove of garlic or ¼ tsp. garlic salt
1 grated onion
½ tsp. salt
2 eggs
1 tbsp. chopped parsley
4 tbsps. fat

For the Sauce

1 cup tomato soup
¼ cup cider vinegar
3 tbsps. brown sugar
1 cup finely cut celery
1 green pepper, chopped

Combine all the ingredients except the fat. Form into balls the size of walnuts and sauté in hot melted fat till browned on all sides. Add ingredients for sauce in the order listed. Cover and simmer for 20 minutes over moderate heat. Uncover and cook for 5–10 minutes longer. Serve with cooked spaghetti or noodles.

CHOPPED CALF'S OR OX LIVER

1 lb. liver
Fat for frying
¼ cup diced onion
Salt and pepper

Fry the slices of liver about 1 inch thick for 5–10 minutes or till light brown on both sides. Remove veins and skin. Put through mincer or chop to a smooth paste in a bowl.

Fry ¼ cup finely diced onion in ¼ cup hot melted fat till nicely browned, and add onion and fat to liver paste with salt and pepper to taste. Mix till smooth.

KIBBAS

For the Dough

8 oz. brown rice
1 pint boiling water
Salt
1 egg

For the Filling

1 lb. minced meat (preferably lamb)
2 tbsps. olive oil
2 tbsps. finely chopped onion
Fat for frying

Cook the rice in the boiling salted water, stirring occasionally until pasty and smooth. Stand it on one side until cool and then beat in the egg. Meanwhile brown the meat and onion in the olive oil. When the rice mixture is cool, divide it into eight and make each portion into a flat round cake. Divide the meat up between the rice cakes and roll up like a sausage roll, but make the rolls long and thin and pointed at each end. Fry the rolls until well browned on both sides and drain on crumpled paper.

LEMON STEW WITH LIVER BALLS

2½ lb. halibut or cod
1 onion
1 tbsp. oil
½ tsp. salt
¼ tsp. pepper
A little ginger
A pinch of cayenne pepper

For the Sauce

2 eggs
Juice of 3 lemons
1 tbsp. flour

Clean and cut the fish into medium-sized steaks. Chop the onion, leaving a quarter over for the liver balls, and fry it in oil. Place the fish in a casserole and add the onion, salt, pepper, ginger, cayenne and Liver Balls (see below) and a little water. Cover with a well-fitting lid, and cook in the oven for 40 minutes at 350° F. (mark 4). Beat the egg, add the lemon juice and flour and mix to a smooth paste. Add some liquid from the fish to this paste. Stir well and pour back into the stew. Cover and replace in the oven for a few minutes to finish cooking the sauce. Serve quite cold.

LIVER BALLS

¼ lb. fish liver
Salt and pepper
1 egg
¼ onion from stew
Breadcrumbs

Chop the liver finely, add the seasoning, beaten egg and onion. Form into balls, adding sufficient breadcrumbs to hold the mixture together, roll in flour and place on top of the fish.

PATLIJAN BOEREG
(AUBERGINE WITH CHEESE)

1 large aubergine
Salt
1 oz. flour
¼ pint oil
3 eggs
½ lb. cottage cheese
1 tsp. parsley
1 tbsp. lemon juice

Cut the aubergine into ¼-inch slices, without peeling. Sprinkle with salt and let stand for half an hour. Drain, dry, roll in flour and fry until browned on both sides. Use a fairly deep frying pan with a cover. When the aubergine is cooked, pour off the oil and take out half the aubergine, arranging the rest on the bottom of the pan. Beat up two eggs with the cheese and parsley and pour over the aubergine in the pan. Cover with the rest of the vegetable and cook, covered, for about 5 minutes. Beat the last egg very well and pour over the mixture in the pan.

Let cook uncovered until the egg is set. Garnish with parsley and lemon juice.

LATKES

6 medium-sized potatoes	1 tsp. salt
1 onion	Fat or oil for deep
2 eggs	frying
2 oz. flour	

Peel and grate potatoes into a mixing bowl. Squeeze out liquid. Peel and grate onion into potatoes. Add eggs, flour and salt and stir to make a smooth batter that will drop heavily from the spoon. Heat the fat in a heavy frying pan, drop the batter from a spoon into the hot fat, making pancakes 3 inches in diameter. Fry over moderate heat until brown on the underside, turn and brown other side. Lift out and drain off excess fat. The pancakes should be puffed and crisp.

VEGETABLE CASSEROLE

$\frac{1}{2}$ lb. diced green beans	Salt
$\frac{1}{2}$ lb. diced aubergine	4 oz. butter
$\frac{1}{2}$ lb. diced carrot	4 eggs
$\frac{3}{4}$ lb. sliced tomatoes	1 lb. cooked rice

Mix all the vegetables together in a well-buttered casserole and season with salt. Pour melted butter over the vegetables and cover with seasoned beaten eggs. Bake in a moderate oven (350° F., mark 4) until vegetables are tender and eggs cooked. Serve with the cooked rice.

PASSOVER BEET PRESERVES

3 lb. beetroot	2 tbsps. ground ginger
1 lb. honey	$\frac{1}{2}$ lb. blanched, chopped
1 lb. sugar	almonds

Cook beetroot in cold water to cover. When tender, skin and cut into thin strips or dice. Bring honey, sugar and ginger to the boil in a deep pot and add beetroot. Turn down heat and cook till the syrup is thick, approximately 30 minutes. Do not stir during cooking but shake the pot gently to prevent burning or sticking. Stir in chopped or slivered almonds and turn into jam jars or a stoneware crock. Store away from light to prevent discoloration.

POTATO MARASKA

6 small potatoes	1 egg
1 level dessertsp.	Pepper and salt
chopped parsley	

Peel and boil the potatoes. Drain off the water and mash them with the parsley, beaten egg, pepper and salt. Make into balls the size of large cherries. Place on a greased tin so that they do not touch each other. Bake in a moderate oven (375° F., mark 5) for 25 minutes.

CHALLAH

2 lb. flour	4 tbsps. fat
1 tbsp. salt	2 oz. yeast
1 tbsp. sugar	3 eggs
1 pint hot potato water	A pinch of saffron
or plain hot water	added to hot liquid

Sift flour and salt into a large mixing bowl and stand in a warm place. Dissolve sugar and fat in the hot liquid. When cooled to lukewarm, dissolve the yeast in some of the liquid and stir into the flour to make a sponge in the centre of the bowl. Cover and let rise for 30 minutes. Add slightly beaten eggs to the sponge and stir in remaining liquid and flour to make a dough. Turn out on a floured board and knead thoroughly until smooth and elastic. The dough should not stick to the hand or board. Return dough to the bowl, brush top with fat or dust with flour, cover with a clean cloth and let rise in a warm place until approximately double in bulk. Knead on floured board for 10 minutes and shape into coils for round loaves. Place on greased or floured baking sheet and let rise again till about double in bulk. Brush with egg yolk and water and bake for 15 minutes at 400° F. (mark 6); reduce heat to 375° F. (mark 5) and bake for 45 minutes or till nicely crusted and light brown on the bottom. Makes 2 loaves.

KATAIYIFF

1 lb. noodles	1 cup slivered almonds
Salt	or hazel nuts
4 tbsps. butter	1 cup honey

Cook the noodles in slightly salted water till tender and drain thoroughly. Pack into a shallow oblong dish and when cold and caked, turn out and cut into squares. Arrange on a well-greased baking sheet and cover each square with nuts. Pour honey over each piece and bake for 20–30 minutes at 350° F. (mark 4). Serve sprinkled with more nuts and honey.

PASSOVER INGERLACH

$\frac{3}{4}$ cup honey	1 cup matzo meal
$\frac{1}{2}$ lb. sugar	$\frac{1}{2}$ cup ground almonds
2 eggs, beaten till	or walnuts
creamy	1 tbsp. ground ginger

Mix honey and sugar in a deep saucepan, bring to the boil and cook for 10 minutes till it is a deep golden syrup. Remove from the heat. Combine other ingredients with a fork and stir into the syrup. Place over very low heat and cook for approximately 10 minutes, stirring constantly to prevent sticking or burning. The

101

mixture will be thick and sticky. Turn out on a wet slab and flatten to $\frac{1}{2}$ inch thickness with the bowl of a large spoon that has been dipped in cold water. Dust with sugar and ground ginger and cool for 10 minutes before cutting into 1-inch squares or diamond shapes. Makes approximately 30.

PURIM KICHLACH

102

1 cup sugar	3 tsps. baking powder
1 cup melted fat or salad oil	$\frac{1}{2}$ tsp. salt
	$\frac{3}{4}$ cup lukewarm water
4 eggs	or milk
4 cups sifted flour	$\frac{3}{4}$ cup poppy seed

Cream sugar and fat. Add one egg at a time, beating or stirring well after each addition. Sift dry ingredients and poppy seeds. Make a stiff dough with the two mixtures and a little of the liquid. Roll out on lightly floured board to $\frac{1}{4}$ inch thickness and cut into triangles $2\frac{1}{2}$ inches in size. Arrange on a greased and floured baking sheet, brush with egg yolk and sprinkle with a few poppy seeds. Bake for 12–15 minutes at 375° F. (mark 5). Makes 50–60 cookies.

MATZO KUGEL

3 matzos	$\frac{1}{4}$ cup raisins
Water	3 tbsps. fat
3 eggs, separated	3 cooking apples
$\frac{1}{2}$ cup sugar	Grated rind of 1 lemon
$\frac{1}{4}$ tsp. salt	$\frac{1}{4}$ cup chopped nuts
$\frac{1}{4}$ tsp. cinnamon	

Soak matzos in cold water and drain well. Beat egg yolks, sugar, salt and cinnamon. Stir in the matzos. Fold in stiffly beaten egg whites and raisins, and turn half the mixture into a heated, well-greased baking dish. Arrange thinly sliced apples on top, sprinkle with nuts and grated lemon rind. Cover with the rest of the matzo mixture. Dot with fat, sprinkle with more cinnamon and sugar, and bake at 350° F. (mark 4) for about 45 minutes or till nicely browned. Serve with apple sauce, wine sauce or stewed or fresh fruit.

HAMANTASHEN

$\frac{2}{3}$ cup fat	3 tbsps. milk or water
$\frac{1}{2}$ cup sugar	$\frac{1}{2}$ tsp. vanilla
1 egg	2 cups sifted flour

Cream fat and sugar. Add egg and continue creaming till smooth. Add liquid and flavouring and stir in sifted flour till a ball of dough is formed. Chill 2–3 hours or overnight.

Form balls of dough the size of a medium apple and roll out to 4–6 inches in diameter. On each round of dough place a ball of filling (see below) and bring edges together to form a triangle, pinching the seams together from top down to the corners. Brush tops with egg yolk and bake for 30–40 minutes at 350° F. (mark 4) till lightly browned.

A sweetened yeast dough may also be used, in which case the filled Hamantashen are left to double in size before baking.

HAMANTASHEN FILLINGS
POPPY SEED AND HONEY FILLING

2 cups poppy seed	$\frac{1}{4}$ cup sugar
1 cup water or milk	$\frac{1}{8}$ tsp. salt
$\frac{1}{2}$ cup honey	2 eggs

Combine poppy seed (large seeds should be scalded, drained and pounded) liquid, honey, sugar and salt in a saucepan. Cook over moderate heat till thick, stirring to prevent scorching. Let it cool before adding eggs, then beat thoroughly. If the addition of eggs makes the filling too thin, return to heat and stir for 1–2 minutes. Makes enough filling for 24 small or 12 or 14 large Hamantashen.

DRIED FRUIT FILLING

$\frac{1}{2}$ cup each seeded or seedless raisins, stoned prunes, dried apricots	$\frac{1}{2}$ cup dry bread or cake crumbs
A dash of salt	4 tbsps. honey

Combine ingredients and cook over boiling water till honey is melted. Stir well and allow to cool. If too thick to use as filling, add lemon juice ; if not thick enough, add more crumbs.

FRUIT STOLLEN

Kuchen dough (see page 283) or sour cream dough (see page 283)	$\frac{1}{4}$ cup candied fruit, diced fine
$\frac{1}{2}$ cup seeded raisins, cut or chopped	1 tbsp. citron, chopped fine
$\frac{1}{2}$ cup walnuts, chopped	3 tbsps. sugar
	3 tbsps. butter

For the Topping

2 tbsps. nuts	3 tbsps. icing sugar
1 tsp. citron	2 tbsps. water

After the dough has risen, pat or knead it into a rectangle. Combine raisins, nuts, candied fruit and citron. Spread over dough and sprinkle with sugar. Roll up, twist into a ring and place in a round buttered cake tin. If you prefer a long stollen, place the roll in a rectangular tin, without twisting. Brush the top with melted butter. Let rise till double in bulk. Bake at 375° F. (mark 5) for 30–40 minutes or till nicely browned. While the stollen is warm, brush again with melted fat and sprinkle with chopped nuts or decorate with citron, candied fruit or nuts. Pour a little thin icing over the top.

KUCHEN DOUGH

1 oz. yeast	½ cup melted fat mixed with 1 cup scalded milk
¼ cup lukewarm water	½ cup sugar
1 lb. flour	1 tsp. vanilla
1 tsp. salt	
2 eggs	

Let yeast stand in water for 3–5 minutes till softened. Sift together flour and salt into a mixing bowl and stir yeast mixture into the centre. Add the eggs, melted fat, milk, sugar and vanilla and stir till combined into a soft dough. Dust lightly with flour and cover with a towel. Let it rise till double in bulk.

BUTTER KUCHEN
(SOUR CREAM DOUGH)

6 oz. butter	2 oz. yeast
6 oz. sugar	⅛ pint warm milk
3 eggs	1 tsp. salt
½ pint sour cream	22 oz. flour (approx.)
1 tbsp. grated lemon rind	

Cream butter and sugar, add beaten eggs, sour cream, lemon rind, yeast dissolved in the warm milk, then the sifted flour and salt to make a dough. Turn out on a floured board and knead till soft and smooth. Place in a bowl, dust with flour and cover with a towel. Let rise overnight in a place free from draughts.

CHREMZLACH

3 tbsps. chicken or goose fat	4 eggs, separated
6 tbsps. hot water	¼ tsp. salt
1 lemon	1½ cups fat for deep frying
4 cups matzo meal (approx.)	

For the Filling

1½ cups cherry jam	2 tbsps. matzo meal
½ cup chopped almonds	

Mix fat, hot water, lemon juice and grated rind in a large bowl. Add matzo meal gradually to make a stiff, smooth batter. Beat egg yolks with sugar till creamy and stir in. Add salt to egg whites and beat stiff. Fold in beaten egg whites as soon as mixture is cool enough to handle. Add more water or lemon juice if the mixture seems too dry; it should be of a consistency that can be formed into balls after standing for 15–20 minutes.

Combine the ingredients for the filling and let stand for 10 minutes before using.

Form the batter into balls the size of medium apples; make a hole in the centre of each and insert a tablespoonful of filling. Mould the dough smoothly round the filling; flatten into a thick cake and fry in deep hot fat till lightly browned on both sides. Lift out and drain on paper. When all of the cakes are fried, arrange on a serving dish and cover with honey and slivered almonds, or sprinkle generously with sugar and cinnamon. Serve hot or cold. Makes 12–14.

TZIMMES OF DRIED FRUITS

½ lb. each prunes, dried apricots, peaches, pears, seeded raisins	½ cup honey
1 cup long grain rice (brown rice may be used)	½ tsp. salt
	½ tsp. cinnamon
	1 quart boiling water

Rinse dried fruits and drain well. Mix with rice and add the other ingredients in the order listed. Bring to the boil and then simmer (over an asbestos mat) for 15–20 minutes or until rice is tender and the liquid in the pan absorbed. Shake occasionally to prevent sticking, or add a little boiling water if necessary. Serve hot or cold.

LEKACH
(TRADITIONAL HONEY CAKE)

6 eggs	¼ tsp. ground cloves
½ lb. sugar	½ tsp. each allspice and cinnamon
1 cup honey	½ cup each raisins and chopped nuts
2 tbsps. salad oil	¼ cup finely cut citron
14 oz. flour	2 tbsps. brandy
1½ tsps. baking powder	
1 tsp. baking soda	

Beat the eggs, adding sugar gradually while beating until light and creamy. Stir in honey and oil. Sift together all dry ingredients and add nuts and fruit before combining with first mixture. Add brandy last. Bake in a rectangular tin, lined with greased paper (350° F., mark 4), for 1 hour. Invert tin and allow cake to cool before removing. Serve cut into squares or diamond shapes.

NUT AND RAISIN HONEY CAKE

2 eggs	2 tsps. baking powder
½ lb. sugar	½ tsp. baking soda
½ cup salad oil	⅛ tsp. salt
½ lb. honey	½ cup seedless raisins
2 tbsps. brandy	¼ cup chopped nuts
½ lb. flour	½ cup hot coffee

Beat eggs and sugar till smooth and creamy. Stir in oil, add honey and brandy and beat well with spoon. Sift dry ingredients together, add raisins and nuts and stir into creamy mixture, adding a little coffee to make a smooth batter. Pour into a greaseproof paper-lined baking tin (8 by 11 by 2 inches) and bake at 350° F. (mark 4) for 1 hour until browned at edges and light brown on top. Test by inserting a skewer in the centre. When cool, cut in diamond shapes.

CHEESECAKE
For the Crust
2 oz. butter   1 cup biscuit crumbs

For the Filling
1½ lb. cream cheese   1 tsp. vanilla
1 cup sugar   4 eggs

For the Topping
1 pint sour cream   ½ tsp. vanilla
2 tbsps. sugar

Melt butter and blend with crumbs; press firmly over bottom and sides of a cake tin with a removable base. Mix cheese, sugar and vanilla. Add one egg at a time, beating well. Turn the cheese mixture into the crumb-lined cake tin and bake at 350° F. (mark 4) for 35 minutes, or till firm in centre. Turn off heat and let the cake cool in the oven with the door open. When cold, pour over the sour cream mixed with sugar and vanilla. Return to the oven (preheated to 425° F., mark 7) and bake for 5 minutes only. The sour cream topping sets as the cake cools.

CHEESECAKE (WITH SOUR CREAM)
For the Crust and Topping
2 packets browned crumbs   1 tsp. cinnamon
¼ cup sugar   ¼ lb. butter

For the Cheese Filling
½ lb. cream cheese   A pinch of salt
½ lb. cottage cheese   1 cup sour cream
2 eggs   1 cup milk
1 cup sugar   1 tsp. vanilla
2 tbsps. cornflour

Mix the crumbs, sugar and cinnamon. Work in the softened butter until well mixed and use to line the bottom and sides of a well-buttered cake tin with removable base. Reserve a quarter of the crumb mixture to sprinkle on top.

Beat the cheeses together until smooth, then add one egg at a time, continuing to beat well. Mix the dry ingredients and add before stirring in the liquids. This makes a very loose batter which should be poured into the crumb-lined tin carefully. Sprinkle top with crumbs and

bake at 350° F. (mark 4) for 1 hour. Turn off heat and leave the cake in the oven until cool.

CHEESE KREPLACH
For the Dough
A pinch of salt   1 egg
Flour   1 tbsp. cold water

For the Cheese Filling
1 lb. cottage cheese   ¼ tsp. salt
2 egg yolks or 1 whole egg Sugar and cinnamon
2 tbsps. sour cream   to taste

Make a stiff dough from the sifted flour and salt, egg and water. Roll out ⅛ inch thick, cut into 2½ inch squares and fill each with the cheese mixture, pinch two points together to form triangle.

Drop turnovers into rapidly boiling water, one at a time, Cook, covered for 10 minutes. Uncover and simmer for 5 minutes. Drain. Dot with butter and brown under the grill. Serve with sugar, cinnamon and sour cream.

LEBKUCHEN
4 eggs   ¼ tsp. allspice
1 lb. brown sugar   ¼ cup shredded citron
14 oz. flour   ¼ cup chopped walnuts
1 tsp. baking powder   or almonds
2 tsps. cinnamon

Beat eggs and sugar till creamy. Sift dry ingredients and stir in with the chopped nuts and citron. Pat the dough to ½ inch thickness on a paper-lined baking sheet. Bake in a moderate oven (350° F., mark 4) for about 30 minutes. Cover with a thin icing made of icing sugar and water before cake is cool. Cut into squares or oblongs. Keep in an airtight jar for 1 week before serving.

STUFFED MONKEYS
6 oz. butter   ½ tsp. cinnamon
8 oz. flour   Salt
6 oz. demerara sugar   1 egg

For the Filling
½ lb. peel   2 yolks of eggs
½ lb. ground almonds   Vanilla essence
3 oz. butter   Salt

Rub the butter into the flour. Add the sugar, cinnamon and salt. Mix into a paste with the beaten egg. Turn the paste on to a board, roll it out and cut into two equal-sized pieces. Place one piece on a cake tray. Beat the butter, almonds and yolks together, mix in the chopped peel and vanilla. Spread this mixture on the piece of paste on the cake tray, cover with the other half of the paste, and brush over with yolk of egg. Place on the cake tray, bake in the oven at 350° F. (mark 4) for 30 minutes, leave to cool and cut into slices.

ALMOND PUDDING

8 eggs	$\frac{1}{2}$ lb. caster sugar
$\frac{1}{2}$ lb. ground sweet almonds	$\frac{1}{4}$ oz. ground bitter almonds

Beat the eggs for about 12 minutes. Add the sugar and beat again for another 12 minutes. Add the almonds and beat continuously for about $\frac{1}{2}$ hour. Turn the mixture into two pie dishes greased with olive oil. Bake in the oven for 1 hour with the setting at 350° F. (mark 4). When the pudding begins to leave the sides of the dish it is cooked.

Allow to cool in the pie dishes then turn out and serve cold, sprinkled with powdered sugar.

COOKING in the Lebanon owes a good deal to French influence, which is felt particularly in Beirut. The Arabs are, as a race, deeply interested in food and their country produces large quantities of fruit and vegetables of the finest quality, nuts, dairy produce and fish. In Syria meat is of a better quality than in the Lebanon, but the cuisine as a whole is of the traditional Arab variety in both countries. The Moslem rule forbidding alcohol is interpreted tolerantly and a typical meal will start with arak and the *meze* or appetisers that are so universally served throughout the Middle East, Turkey and Greece. These may consist of tiny fried pastries, pieces of cheese, black and green olives, smoked meat, gherkins, chilli peppers, onions, tomatoes, mussels, shrimps and pieces of fish grilled on skewers, meat balls, grilled liver, pieces of aubergine, salads of beans and cucumbers, yoghourt and nuts. After the *meze* comes a selection of dishes, followed by fruit and coffee, the latter often flavoured with spice. Cardamom is particularly popular in Syria and Jordan. Cooking in Jordan itself is much influenced by the nomad Arabs and here, too, a certain amount of wine and arak is drunk. Throughout the Levant a type of yoghourt called *Leben* is popular and used in most kinds of cooking, though never with fish.

It is interesting to note that many dishes are reserved for specific occasions and that some are served only at happy gatherings, such as weddings and birthdays. Coffee is served sweeter on joyous occasions than it is at funerals or farewell parties.

For centuries the bazaars of Baghdad have offered customers, along with the many different kinds of rice and lentils that form the staple diet of the people, a bewildering variety of spices, essences, dried leaves and flowers and aromatic seeds. It is these that give Iraqi cooking its particular character and flavour. Meat and game are plentiful and there is a profusion of fruit and vegetables, including all the familiar ones as well as more exotic pumpkins, okra and squashes.

Hospitality is spontaneous and widespread : extra food is always cooked for every meal and the Iraqi hostess is never put out of countenance by unexpected guests.

Coffee and sweet weak tea are drunk and there are many hot-weather drinks made from rosewater, almonds or yoghourt.

Food in Iran has changed little with the years. In the larger towns, of course, people have become more Westernised, but in the countryside the peasants, who are mostly Moslems, eat mainly dishes composed of mutton and rice and cook over charcoal fires, often in the open air. Bread ovens, too, are heated by charcoal, the thin rounds of bread being sold hot and fresh. Soured milk, cheese, nuts, vegetables and fruit all add interest to the staple diet of bread and rice ; soured milk is made into cooling drinks with the addition of soda water and other ingredients.

Persian sweetmeats are unduly cloying to Western palates : cakes are soaked in syrup, poppy seeds and dates are popular ingredients and the national sweetmeat, *Gaz*, is a kind of very sweet nougat, made from the resinous *manna* that is collected from the tamarisk tree. Both tea and coffee are drunk and some wine, notably *Shiraz*, is made.

Syria, Lebanon, Iraq and Iran

Lebanon

COUSA
(CREAM OF VEGETABLE MARROW SOUP)

Stew 3 medium-sized marrows in a little water until soft. Strain, measure and keep hot. With 2 cups of purée use 2 cups of hot milk thickened with 2 tbsps. of butter and 2 tbsps. of flour. When boiled, combine with marrow, season, reheat and serve.

FISH AND RICE

4 lb. fish	Onions
Salt	1 lemon
Oil for frying	Rice

Scale, clean and salt fish, and let stand for a while. Fry in oil, then chop onions finely and fry in the same oil as the fish. Place fish over onion and cook over low heat with 3 large cups of water. When cooked squeeze the juice of a lemon over it, simmer for 10 minutes more. Serve with rice cooked with the oil the fish was fried in.

STEW WITH MEAT AND VEGETABLES

1½ cups cubed mutton	1 large onion, minced
6 cups beans, aubergine or other vegetable	1 pint cold water
	4 medium tomatoes
1 tbsp. fat	Salt and pepper

Prepare the meat and vegetables; heat the fat in a saucepan and sear the meat, then add onion and fry until brown. Add the vegetable and stir all together. Cook for about 10 minutes, add the water, peeled and chopped tomatoes and seasoning. Stir well and allow to simmer slowly for 45 minutes until it is all tender. The stew should be served with plain rice.

Most vegetables may be used—green beans, aubergine, potatoes, haricot beans (soaked overnight before using), tomato, cauliflower, peas or artichokes. If chestnuts are used they should be cooked longer. Tomato should not be added to chestnut or cauliflower stew and the cauliflower should be divided into small pieces and fried before using.

RIZ BI DFEEN
(MUTTON, RICE AND CHICK PEAS)

3 cups rice	½ cup butter
Salt and pepper	2½ cups lean mutton
3 cups small onions	1 cup chick peas

Wash and drain rice, put in pan with salt, pour boiling water to cover it and leave to soak for 2 hours. Peel onions, leaving them whole. Fry in butter until light brown. Cut the meat into pieces the same size as the onions, add to the latter and let fry until brown, together with the chick peas which have soaked overnight. Season to taste, cover with water and simmer till the meat is tender. Drain rice and wash carefully in cold water. Put it on top of the other ingredients, adding water if necessary to bring the level of the liquid above the rice. Bring to the boil again and simmer till the rice is well cooked, adding more water if it seems too dry. Serve with yoghourt. Burghul or crushed wheat may be used instead of rice if wished. Enough for 8 people.

STUFFED SWEET PEPPERS

2 cups finely chopped meat	¼ tsp. cinnamon
	Small bunch parsley
2 medium onions	12 large green peppers
1 tbsp. butter	4 ripe tomatoes
Salt	1 tsp. dried mint
½ tsp. pepper	1 pint water

Fry meat until browned. Remove from pan. Cut the onions up finely and fry in the butter. Mix with meat and add seasoning, cinnamon and the finely chopped parsley. Cut the stems out of the peppers and dip them into boiling water, removing all seeds. Fill with fried meat, replace stems and set in a pan side by side, stem upwards. Peel tomatoes and cut in small pieces. Cover peppers with tomatoes, adding dried mint and a pinch of salt, and the water. Cook until the peppers are soft. Serve with rice.

MASBAHT EL DARWEESH
(THE DERVISH'S ROSARY)

3 cups potatoes	5 small minced onions
2 cups aubergine	2 tbsps. melted fat
2 cups tomatoes	1 tsp. salt
3 cups vegetable marrow	Flour
3 cups minced meat	1 pint water

Peel potatoes and other vegetables and cut them into pieces. Mix together in a baking dish with meat, onions, fat, salt and a sprinkling of flour. Pour the water over all and cook in a moderate oven (350° F., mark 4) until the meat and vegetables are tender and browned on top.

PATLIJAN IMAM BAYILDI
(THE FAINTING OLD MAN)

3 lb. of long aubergines, as small in size as possible	2 cups good tender meat, off leg of lamb if possible
¼ cup pine kernels	Cooking fat
Salt and pepper	Tomatoes

Prepare aubergines by peeling off the green round the stem, leaving the stem on. Fry one

91) Fondue (*right*), one of the most delicious of supper dishes, made with melted Swiss cheese.

92) From Switzerland, too, comes Pitz : bubbling hot tomatoes filled with cheese and herbs (*below*).

93 - 95

Three dishes from Switzerland.

93) Egg Ragoût (*right*), a savoury mixture of hard-boiled eggs in an onion-flavoured sauce.

94) These spinach "frogs" from Basle are stuffed with a minced meat mixture (*left*).

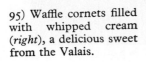

95) Waffle cornets filled with whipped cream (*right*), a delicious sweet from the Valais.

96) Savoury grilled meat rolls, served on new bread with onion slices (*left*).

97) Potato noodles (*right*) are served with grated cheese, butter and diced fried bacon.

98) Cream cheese pie, made with layers of pastry spread with a cheese-egg mixture and baked (*left*).

99) Potika (*right*), a delicious yeast cake with a filling of nuts and sugar.

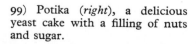

100 - 102

100) Cherry soup with egg drops, an unusual and refreshing Jewish dish (*right*).

101) Ingerlach (*below*), a sticky sweetmeat of honey and nuts, is a Passover speciality.

102) This poppy seed-filled Purim Kichlach is traditionally served in Jewish homes.

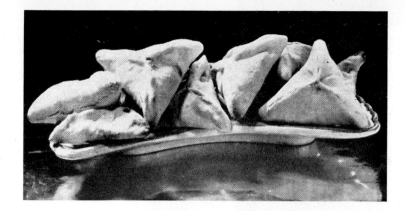

103) Little pastry turn-overs, filled with savoury spinach and baked, are a Middle Eastern dish (*left*).

104) Mjadarah is another Middle Eastern speciality, made with rice and lentils and garnished with fried onion (*right*).

105) Carabeige Aleppo (*left*), iced pastry cakes stuffed with nuts and sugar.

106 - 108

106) Ma'amool, little cakes from Arabia made with semolina dough and filled with nuts (*left*).

107) Shirini Pilau (*right*), a Persian dish of chicken and rice with raisins, nuts and orange peel.

108) Hodu Kabab (*left*), fried balls of lentils, eggs and meat, also from Persia.

109) In Turkey this savoury mixture of minced meat, onion and tomato (*left*) is served with eggs.

110) Halva (*above*), a Turkish sweet made from semolina, raisins and almonds and sprinkled with powdered cinnamon.

111) A typical, syrupy Turkish sweet, appropriately named " Lips of the Beauty " (*left*).

Indian and Pakistani dishes are shown on this and the opposite page.

112 - 114

112) Nargesi Kofte (*right*), hard-boiled eggs wrapped in a spiced meat mixture and simmered in gravy.

113) Kebabs Zeera, croquettes of lamb and onion, cumin-flavoured and served in a curry sauce (*above*).

114) Chicken Biryani (*left*) is seasoned and spicy and is mixed with rice, sultanas and saffron.

115) Fish curry, one of the most usual and delicious ways of cooking fish in India (*left*).

116) Kitchrie, a dish of spiced lentils and rice, with hard-boiled eggs and crisply fried onion (*right*).

117) Raitha (*left*) is a deliciously cool mixture of yoghourt, cucumber and other flavourings.

118) Gujrela, a Pakistani sweet made with rice, milk and grated carrot (*right*).

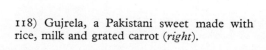

119) Seeni Sambol (*above*), a dish of curried prawns, popular in Ceylon.

120) Tender green chillies, stuffed with cheese and nuts are also from Ceylon (*left*).

121) Ceylon Pineapple curry, a piquant and unusual combination of flavours (*below*).

122) Chinese shrimp balls are fried golden-brown and served with mushrooms and bamboo shoots (*right*).

123) Chicken with Almonds (*below*), a famous and delicious Chinese dish, combining different flavours and textures.

124 - 126

124) Sweet and Sour Pork (*left*) is a classic Chinese dish, served with boiled rice or noodles.

125) A Chinese salad which includes tomatoes, cucumber and bean sprouts as well as lettuce and meat (*right*).

126) Litchies (*below*) soaked in sugar syrup, make a favourite Chinese dessert.

127) Japanese Tempura (*above*), a delicious mixture of fish and vegetables in a golden batter.

128) Crisply fried pork and apple balls, served with lettuce—another Japanese speciality (*below*).

129) O-Sushi, Japanese rice cakes, are garnished or stuffed with fish, meat or vegetables (*above*).

130) This Japanese steamed egg dish, Chawan Mushi (*left*), contains chicken, mushrooms and fish.

131) Maple Salad, from Japan, is a mixture of vegetables, prawns and egg, arranged in the shape of a leaf (*right*).

132) Indonesian Chicken Sour and Sweet, is served in a large hot bowl, with boiled rice (*above*).

133) Chicken is cooked with ginger, mushrooms and onions to make a favourite Indonesian dish (*left*).

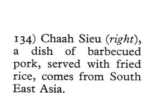

134) Chaah Sieu (*right*), a dish of barbecued pork, served with fried rice, comes from South East Asia.

135 - 137

135) Bamie, an Indonesian dish of pork and vegetables, noodles and strips of cooked egg (*left*).

136) Side dishes from Siam (*above*) include prawn pellets, sweet and sour pork and chicken with ginger.

137) Golden Threads, a Siamese sweet made with egg yolks and syrup (*left*).

by one in fat. Mince meat finely, turn it in some fat over the fire until half done. Season with salt and pepper to taste. Put in pine kernels and keep turning together on slow fire until kernels redden slightly. Place aubergines side by side on a flat baking dish, cut through each one from top to bottom, and fill with meat as full as it can hold, pressing in the meat a little. Add salt and pepper to taste.

Make tomato sauce with strained tomato juice, using as many as required to give a thick or thin sauce, according to taste. Season with salt and pour on to aubergines. Bake for ½ hour in moderate oven (350° F., mark 4). Pour on more sauce and serve in dish, to avoid breaking up the soft aubergines. Serve with rice. Makes 5 servings.

QUABLAMAH
(FRIED STUFFED MARROWS)

15–20 small marrows	Salt and pepper
3 cups minced meat	2 tbsps. pine kernels
Fat for frying	Tomato juice

Hollow out the marrows slightly. Fry the meat, seasoned to taste, until half done. Add pine kernels and continue cooking until the meat is done. Stuff the marrows with the meat mixture and fry the marrows in the same fat, adding more if necessary, and turning continuously until they are well browned. Place side by side in a baking dish, pour over tomato juice, seasoned to taste, to cover the bottom of the dish. Bake in a slow oven (325° F., mark 2) for ½ hour. Serve with plain rice in a separate dish. Makes 5 servings.

Potatoes and tomatoes may be stuffed in the same way.

MA'LOUBEH
(RICE, AUBERGINE AND MEAT CASSEROLE)

1 lb. minced mutton	2 cups rice
2 lb. aubergines	Salt
½ cup butter	Mixed spice

Simmer the meat with water until tender. Peel aubergines and cut each into two pieces; fry in butter until light brown. Wash and drain the rice. Pour the stock off the meat. In a round casserole arrange alternate layers of meat, aubergine and rice until all the ingredients are used up. Season the meat stock to taste with salt and spices, heat up and pour 4½ cups of stock over the ingredients in the casserole. More water should be added to the stock if necessary, or the amount may be made up with tomato juice. Cover the casserole and cook in a slow oven (325° F., mark 2) until the rice is tender and all the liquid absorbed. Turn out on to a hot dish to serve.

W.C.B.—19

FRIED MARROW STEW

4 lb. marrow	2 onions
Butter for frying	6 cups tomatoes
3 cups minced meat	Salt and pepper
¼ cup pine kernels	Cinnamon

Cut each marrow into two or three pieces lengthways. Fry the marrow in the butter, drain and then fry the meat with the onions and pine kernels. Divide the meat into two portions; put one over the bottom of a saucepan, cover with fried marrow, add the rest of the meat and finish with the remaining marrow. Sieve the tomatoes, mix the juice with salt, pepper, cinnamon and 1 teacupful of water, pour over the marrow and simmer gently until it is quite tender. Turn out on to a round dish to serve.

GREEN PEAS WITH MEAT

3 lb. green peas	½ an onion
1½ cups minced meat	½ a clove of garlic
Butter for frying	1 cup tomatoes
Salt and pepper	

Shell the peas; fry the meat with salt and pepper to taste. Chop the onion and garlic together and add to the meat. Add the peas, with more salt if required, and the tomatoes cut into small pieces. Cover with water and stew until tender. Serve with rice.

AUBERGINES WITH MEAT

2 cups minced meat	Fat for frying
¼ cup pine kernels	4 cups tomatoes
Butter for frying	1 tbsp. salt
2 lb. aubergines	1 teacupful water

Fry the meat and the pine kernels in the butter. Peel aubergines and cut them lengthwise; fry in the fat. Cut the tomatoes in slices and place over the bottom of a saucepan; season and add a layer of aubergines followed by one of the meat mixture. Continue until all ingredients are used up, seasoning each layer. Pour the water over and bake in a slow oven (325° F., mark 2) for about an hour. Serve with rice.

DA'UD PASHA
(SAVOURY MEAT BALLS WITH RICE)

2 cups lean meat	8 onions
Salt	8 tomatoes
3 tbsps. pine kernels	2 cups rice
Butter for frying	

Mince the meat several times or pound it in a mortar until it is almost like a paste. Add pine kernels and salt and mix well. Roll into balls the size of a large marble and fry in butter until brown. Remove from pan. Slice onions lengthways and fry in the same pan until golden.

Combine meat and onions in a thick pan, just cover with cold water, strain tomatoes over, season to taste and simmer for 1½ hours. Serve with boiled rice.

KIBBEH BI SSANIEH
(KOUBBEH IN A TRAY)
For the Koubbeh

4 cups lean mutton	5 cups burghul
2 tbsps. salt	(crushed wheat)
1 onion	1 cup butter for baking
½ tsp. pepper	

For the Filling

1 cup minced meat	Salt and pepper
½ cup pine kernels	Butter
1 onion	Cinnamon

To make the koubbeh, pound the meat well in a mortar with the salt. Put on one side and pound the onion with a little more salt and the pepper. Mix onion and meat and continue to pound together. Wash the burghul and squeeze dry; add to the meat and onion mixture and pound for at least an hour, until the mixture is quite smooth and like a paste. Spread half of this mixture evenly on a greased tray.

To make the filling, fry the minced meat, pine kernels and chopped onion, seasoned with salt and pepper, in the butter until well done and brown. Flavour with cinnamon and spread this mixture over the koubbeh on the tray. Cover with the remaining koubbeh, spreading it smooth and even. Cut with a knife into diamond shapes, pour over it the cup of melted butter and bake in a moderate oven (350° F., mark 4) for about 45 minutes or until well browned.

MEAT BALLS

1 chopped onion	1 egg
Salt	½ teacup flour
3 cups minced meat	Pine kernels
¼ tsp. pepper	½ cup butter

Chop the onion finely, sprinkle with salt and mix with the meat and pepper. Beat the egg and add to the meat, with enough flour to make a stiff dough. Roll the mixture into balls, stuffing each with a few pine kernels. Fry in butter to a good deep brown.

LEBEN IMMOU
(YOGHOURT WITH MEAT)

2 cups meat	5 cups yoghourt
Butter for frying	1 tsp. salt
1 cup chopped onion	Boiled rice
1 pint salted water	

Cut the meat into pieces and fry it with the butter. Add the onion and fry till soft, cover with the salted water and bring to the boil. Simmer until the meat is almost done and the liquid reduced to one cup. Pour in the yoghourt, add more salt if necessary and simmer until it thickens. Serve with boiled rice.

SMYRNA KEFTA
(MEAT AND CHEESE BALLS)

1½ cups marrow or	4 tbsps. cheese
aubergine	(grated)
5 large onions	Salt and pepper
¾ cup minced lean	2 eggs
meat (raw)	Deep fat for frying

Boil marrow and onions together in salted water until tender, drain and chop very small. Mix in all the other ingredients and bind with beaten egg. Roll into small balls, coat with flour and fry in deep fat. These are excellent hot or cold and make a good dish with salad or for picnics.

STUFFED VINE LEAVES

2 cups rice	1 sprig parsley
1 cup chick peas	Mint leaves
Salt	½ cup oil
1 large onion, chopped	1 cup lemon juice
fine	2 cups vine leaves
1 lb. chopped tomatoes	

Wash and drain rice, peel chick peas (which have been soaking overnight) and add to rice with 1 tsp. salt. Add the onion and tomatoes, chopped parsley and mint. Mix all together with the oil and half the lemon juice. Dip the vine leaves in hot water to make them pliable and roll each leaf round a heaped teaspoonful of the rice mixture. Place the rolls closely side by side in a pan and place a plate on top of them, to hold them down. Pour over 4½ cups boiling water and let them simmer for ½ hour. Remove the plate and continue to simmer until the rice is tender. Remove from the stove, pour over the rest of the lemon juice and let stand covered for ½ hour. Serve cold. This makes enough for 6 people.

FATAYER
(SPINACH TURNOVERS)

2 lb. spinach	Juice of 1 lemon
Salt	2 tbsps. oil
3 small onions	Bread dough (uncooked)

Wash spinach and chop finely, turn into a bowl and rub salt in with the fingers. Chop onions finely. Drain water from the spinach and squeeze dry, then mix with onions, lemon juice and oil. Roll the bread dough very thin, cut in rounds and fill with the spinach mixture, closing up to form a turnover. Bake in a moderate oven (350° F., mark 4) until brown. Chopped walnuts may be added to the filling if desired.

FRIED VEGETABLE TURNOVERS

2 cups spinach	3 tbsps. lemon juice
1 medium onion	A few walnuts
Salt	2½ cups flour
Cayenne pepper	Oil for frying
4 tbsps. olive oil	

Wash, chop and drain the spinach and mix with minced onion, seasonings, 3 tbsps. oil, lemon juice and chopped walnuts. Rub the flour with the remaining oil, 2 tsps. salt and make a dough with a little water. Roll this out and cut into rounds; fill with the spinach mixture and close up. Fry the turnovers in smoking hot fat until brown and crisp.

Endive, chard or sorrel may be used instead of spinach, or the turnovers may also be filled with fried minced meat, onions and pine kernels, or with cheese.

MTABBAL
(SEASONED AUBERGINE)

2 large round aubergines	¼ cup sesame seed oil
1 bulb of garlic (small)	Olive oil
1 tsp. salt	Pomegranate seeds
1-2 lemons, according to taste	Parsley

Grill the aubergines and then peel and clean them. Put a little salt with the garlic and pound it until soft. Mix the aubergines with the garlic and salt and pound together. Add sesame oil and lemon, mixing them well. Garnish with olive oil, sour pomegranate seeds and parsley.

HOUMOS BI TAHINI
(CHICK PEAS)

1 cup chick peas	Salt
½ tbsp. bicarbonate of soda	Olive oil
¼ cup sesame oil	Parsley
1 cup lemon juice	Chick peas

Soak chick peas overnight. The next day boil till tender in water and soda. Drain, pound very fine, add oil and lemon juice slowly, season and mix well. Pour on to plates, sprinkle with olive oil, parsley and a few whole boiled chick peas.

RICE AND SPINACH

½ large onion	2½ cups rice
½ cup oil	Salt and pepper
2 lb. spinach	2 pints water

Cut the onion finely and fry in the oil. Wash, chop and drain the spinach, then add to the onion and oil and stew well. Wash the rice and add to the spinach; season to taste. Pour over the water, bring to the boil quickly and then turn down heat and simmer until the rice is cooked.

TABBOULEH
(MINT AND PARSLEY SALAD)

1 cup burghul (fine crushed boiled wheat)	½-1 cup olive oil
½ cup mint leaves	2 tbsps. salt
1½ cups parsley	½ cup lemon juice
1 green onion	1 small tomato

Soak burghul until soft. It will require 2 hours in cold water or 1 hour in warm water. Wash parsley and mint leaves thoroughly and chop very fine. Cut the onion into small pieces and wash all carefully. Drain burghul and add. Pour over the oil, salt and lemon juice and mix all together. Chopped tomatoes may be added. This should be eaten using vine leaves, lettuce or cabbage leaves as scoops.

MJADARAH
(LENTILS AND RICE)

1½ cups lentils	1 onion
6 cups water	2 tbsps. olive oil
½ cup of rice	½ tbsp. salt

Put the lentils in the cold water and put the saucepan on the fire until the lentils are half cooked. Then add the rice to the lentils in the water, with salt. When the rice and lentils are quite cooked, chop the onion lengthwise; fry with the oil and brown well and then add to the lentils and the rice. Stir it to prevent sticking to the saucepan. Serve with more fried crisp onions. Serves 6.

MUGHLEY
(SPICE PUDDING)

4 tbsps. ground cinnamon	2 cupfuls washed, pounded and sifted rice
4 tbsps. pounded aniseed	
2 tbsps. pounded caraway seed	Sugar to taste
1 tbsp. pounded ginger	Nuts to decorate
6 pints water	

Sift spices together and mix gradually with a little cold water until a smooth paste is formed. Add 5 pints of water and boil for 30 minutes. Then mix the rice (pounded and sifted not too fine) to a smooth consistency with the remaining water. Pour the boiling spiced water gently over the rice, add sugar and keep stirring over a low heat until it thickens. Pour into bowls and when cool strew blanched almonds, walnuts and pistachios on top. This is a ceremonial pudding, served to celebrate the birth of a boy, and the above ingredients make about 25 portions.

CARABEIGE ALEPPO
(ICED ALMOND CAKES)

105

6 cups flour	Blanched almonds
3 cups butter	Sugar
Milk to mix	

For the Icing

1 lb. sugar	2 egg whites
¼ pint water	

Rub the flour and butter together until well mixed, then knead to a firm dough with a little milk. Form into small hollow cakes and stuff with a mixture of pounded nuts and sugar. Place on a greased baking sheet and bake in a moderate oven (350° F., mark 4) until slightly browned.

To make the icing, dissolve the sugar in the water and boil till it will spin a thread. Beat egg whites stiffly and pour the hot syrup over them, beating continuously. Cover the little cakes with this mixture.

SAREGHE BOURMA
(WALNUT WAFER BISCUITS)

3 cups flour	1 teacup sugar
1 oz. butter	30 walnuts
1 egg	

Rub fat into flour and mix to a stiff dough with the egg. Chop nuts roughly and mix with sugar. Roll out the dough thinly and sprinkle with the nut and sugar mixture. Cut into rounds, roll round the handle of a wooden spoon, remove from roller, place on a greased baking sheet and bake in a hot oven (450° F., mark 8) till golden-brown.

MA'AMOOL
(SEMOLINA CAKES)

106

4 cups semolina	1 tbsp. orange-flower
3 cups cooking fat	water
3 cups chopped walnuts	1 tbsp. rosewater
1 cup sugar	2 cups boiling water
A pinch of salt	Icing sugar

Sift the semolina ; heat the fat and add when nearly boiling. Mix well, cover and leave for 3 hours. Chop the walnuts finely and mix with the sugar and flavourings. Pour the boiling water over the semolina, adding more if necessary to make a stiff dough. Divide into pieces about the size of a small apple. Form these pieces of dough into hollow balls ; fill the hole with the

nut and sugar mixture and close up securely. Press the semolina balls well down into slightly greased, deeply fluted patty pans, so that the dough takes on the shape of the pan. Shake out, arrange on a greased baking sheet and bake in a moderate oven (350° F., mark 4) until slightly browned—about 25 minutes. Sprinkle icing sugar on top while still hot.

Iraq

LABANIYAH
(YOGHOURT SOUP)

1 lb. spinach	2 cloves of garlic
1 lb. finely chopped meat	Salt and pepper
Small handful of burghal	3 pints yoghourt

Wash and chop the spinach and put in a saucepan with the meat, burghal (crushed wheat), crushed garlic and salt and pepper to taste. Pour the yoghourt over and simmer gently until the meat is tender.

KUBBAT HALEB
(STUFFED RICE BALLS)

½ lb. rice	½ oz. minced blanched
3 pints water	almonds
1 tbsp. salt	Spice to taste
½ lb. minced mutton	2 eggs
1 oz. sultanas	Butter for frying
½ tsp. salt	

Simmer the rice in boiling salted water until soft and drain. Fry the meat, wash the sultanas and simmer for a few moments ; add to the meat with the almonds, ½ tsp. salt and spice. By now the rice should be cool and rather sticky. Make hollow balls with it, about 3 inches in diameter, put some of the stuffing in each hollow and close up the rice round it. Coat the balls in beaten egg and fry slowly in the hot butter until brown. Serve at once.

MAQLUB AL ABUFARWA
(LAMB AND CHESTNUT PILAU)

½ lb. rice	Salt and pepper
1 lb. chestnuts	Water
1 lb. lean lamb, cubed	Butter for frying

Wash and drain the rice. Peel the chestnuts by nicking the skins and cooking in boiling water for a few moments. Simmer the meat in salted water until tender. Drain the meat of any remaining liquid and fry in butter until brown. Add the chestnuts with 3 cups of water and bring to the boil. Stir in the rice and simmer for 20 minutes. Cover the pan tightly and leave over a very low heat, preferably on an asbestos mat, for ½ hour, until all the liquid has been absorbed.

Syria

HERB AND ONION OMELETTE

8 eggs	Salt and pepper
2 cups chopped parsley	Oil for frying
2 cups chopped onion	

Beat the eggs and add parsley, onions and seasoning. Grease a small omelette pan with oil and pour in one-quarter of the egg mixture. Cook until the underside is firm, turn and cook the other side. This quantity makes 4 omelettes.

MEHLI KHUBIZ
(BAKED FRUIT PUDDING)

8 slices white bread	1 lb. dried apricots
1 pint apricot juice	3 oz. sugar

Toast the bread and soak in the fruit juice. Meanwhile, cook the apricots, which have been soaking overnight, in a little water with sugar until they form a thick paste. Drain the bread slices and spread with the apricot purée. Arrange in a baking dish and bake in a slow oven (325° F., mark 2) until the bread is beginning to get crisp. Allow to cool and serve with yoghourt or whipped cream.

DATE AND WALNUT TART
8 oz. short pastry

For the Filling

3 eggs	Salt
3 oz. caster sugar	4 oz. chopped dates
3 oz. self-raising flour	4 oz. chopped walnuts

Line a flan tin with pastry and bake blind until cooked but not brown. Allow to cool. Beat the eggs and sugar together for 15 minutes, stir in the flour, salt, dates and nuts and pour into the flan case. Bake in a very slow oven (275° F., mark ½) until firm to the touch. Serve cold.

TAMRIAH
(DATE PUDDING)

2 lb. ripe dates	¼ lb. flour
3 oz. nuts	2 oz. butter

Stone the dates and mix thoroughly with the flour and nuts in a thick pan. Pour over the melted butter and leave on a low heat until all the butter is absorbed. Turn the cake over and brown on the other side. Continue to turn from time to time until both sides are nicely browned. Serve hot with cream or custard.

SAYADIAH
(FISH AND RICE CASSEROLE)

1½ lb. cod or haddock	3 cups water
Oil for frying	Salt
1 onion	1 tsp. allspice
3 cups rice	

Flake the fish and fry in the oil. Drain and in the same oil fry the onion, cut in rings, until the oil is well flavoured. Wash the rice, cover with boiling salted water and add the strained, onion-flavoured oil. Simmer for about 15 minutes, stirring occasionally, until all the liquid has been absorbed. Stir in the spice and allow the rice to steam for a few minutes. Put alternate layers of rice and fish in a greased casserole and bake in a moderate oven (350° F., mark 4) until brown. Turn out on to a round dish to serve.

BAKED AUBERGINE OMELETTE

3 aubergines	10 eggs
Salt and pepper	6 oz. grated cheese
Oil for frying	Butter

Peel and slice aubergines, sprinkle with salt and drain in a colander. Fry until golden-brown. Beat the eggs with salt and pepper and mix with the cheese. Chop the aubergines and mix them with the egg and cheese, pour into a shallow dish and bake in a moderately hot oven (425° F., mark 7) until a skin forms on top. Serve cut into squares and dotted with butter.

ROAST SHOULDER OF LAMB

1 shoulder of lamb	2 tsps. chopped parsley
½ lb. rice	Salt and pepper
2 tbsps. raw minced meat	Oil for roasting

With a sharp knife separate the skin from the meat, making a pocket. Wash and drain the rice and mix with the minced meat, parsley and seasoning. Stuff the pocket, leaving plenty of room for the rice to swell; sew up the opening. Roast for 3½ hours in a moderate oven (350° F., mark 4), basting frequently. Serve accompanied by broad beans.

MUTTON WITH MUSHROOMS

Oil for frying	½ lb. mushrooms
1½ lb. best end of neck of mutton	Salt and pepper
	1 cup water

Heat the oil and fry the meat until golden-brown. Peel the mushrooms and add to the meat with the salt, pepper and the water.

Cover the pan and simmer gently until the meat falls off the bone. Place the meat on a dish and keep hot while the liquor is reduced to a rich sauce. Pour over the meat and serve.

VEAL AND AUBERGINES

1½ lb shin veal	Oil for frying
3 aubergines	Salt
1 pint water	Pepper

Fry the veal in the oil until it is dark golden-brown on all sides. Add seasoning and half the water. Leave to simmer with the lid on. Peel and slice the aubergines, sprinkle with salt, drain and dry. Fry aubergine slices in oil until golden-brown; drain and reserve. When the meat is falling off the bone put alternate layers of aubergine and the boned veal in a hot casserole. Pour over the rest of the water and bake in a moderate oven (350° F., mark 4) until well done.

BROAD BEAN SALAD

2 lb. broad beans	2 cups of vinegar

Boil the broad beans in plenty of salted water. When the skins slip off, drain well, put them in a bowl and pour over the vinegar while they are still hot. Serve cold.

HREBAH
(ALMOND RING BISCUITS)

2 cups butter	3 cups flour
1 cup sugar	Blanched, slivered almonds

Clarify the butter, allow it to cool and beat with a wire whisk until it makes a thick white cream. Beat in the sugar gradually, then mix in the flour, working with the hands until a pliable dough is formed. Roll into 4-inch lengths, form into rings and flatten slightly. Stick almonds into the dough rings and bake in a slow oven (300° F., mark 1), so as to keep the biscuits as white as possible.

CHOZHAFFE
(CHILLED FRUIT SALAD)

4 oz. dried apricots	2 oz. pine kernels
4 oz. prunes	2 oz. pistachio nuts
4 oz. dried figs	2 tbsps. rosewater
Other dried fruit as available	Sugar syrup or fruit syrup to taste
2 oz. raisins	Ice
2 oz. almonds	

Wash the dried fruit, cover with cold water and leave to soak in a cool place for 24 hours. Blanch the nuts and add to the fruit, with the rosewater and enough syrup to sweeten. Keep in a cold place, preferably the refrigerator, until needed; serve with ice cubes floating in the juice.

Iran

COLD YOGHOURT SOUP

1 pint yoghourt	1 oz. raisins (stoned)
Salt and pepper	½ cucumber
1 tsp. mint	¼ pint water

Put the yoghourt into a cold bowl and beat very thoroughly with the seasoning and the mint, which has been finely chopped. Stir in the raisins, the peeled, diced cucumber and the water. Chill before serving.

PRUNE SOUP

½ lb. chopped spinach	2 oz. rice
¼ lb. stoned prunes	2 oz. lentils
½ lb. marrow, peeled	Salt and pepper
2 tbsps. finely chopped onion	Parsley

Cover all the ingredients with water and bring slowly to the boil. Let simmer for 4 hours. Rub through a sieve and return it to the fire, adding some chopped parsley. Serve hot.

STUFFED FISH

Use white fish, such as haddock or small cod, weighing about 2 lb.

For the Filling

4 oz. chopped nuts	2 oz. sultanas
4 tbsps. lemon juice	Chopped parsley
6 stoned prunes	

Clean the fish and wipe dry. Mix all the filling ingredients together and pack into the fish, securing with toothpicks. Arrange the fish on a grid over a baking pan containing a few inches of water. Cover with foil and bake in a moderate oven (350° F., mark 3) for an hour or until the fish is cooked.

SHIRINI PILAU
(CHICKEN PILAU)

2 good-sized chickens, cooked in aluminium foil until very tender	Pistachio nuts Raisins (seedless) Butter
1 orange	Salt
1 lemon	Rice

When the chickens are done, carve carefully,

10

using only good thick slices of breast. Keep the rest for some other dish. Put in the oven in covered dish to keep hot. Peel the orange. Boil it with the lemon for about 10 minutes or until the pith is soft. Cut the lemon and scrape out fruit and pith with a spoon so as not to pierce the skin. Scrape pith from orange skin. Shred both in very very fine slivers like thick threads about an inch long.

Peel the pistachios and shred. Wash and dry the raisins. Boil the rice with plenty of salt until the grains are only just done. Take off and drain at once, drying in a cloth if necessary. The grains must be clean and separate. Toss with a good piece of butter while hot. Mix the rice well with the nuts, raisins and shredded peel, and then bank some on a big dish. Arrange the chicken over it and cover the chicken completely with the remainder of the rice so that only a mound of rice shows. Keep hot by steaming until ready to serve.

THE SHAH'S PILAU

1½ cups Patna rice	4 onions
1 cup raisins	1 cup clear stock
3 tbsps. sugar	2 oz. butter
1½ lb. lean mutton	Salt and pepper
Olive oil	

Soak the rice in salted water for ½ hour and also soak the raisins in 2 cups of hot water, with the sugar. Cut the meat in small cubes and brown in a little oil. Fry the onions, chopped coarsely, in the same oil. Mix meat and onions and place in casserole. Drain rice and raisins, mix and spread on top of meat and onion mixture. Pour the stock over and dot with butter. Sprinkle with salt and pepper. Cook, uncovered, in a moderate oven (375° F., mark 5) for about 45 minutes, stirring occasionally and adding more stock if it appears too dry.

MUTTON PILAU

4 cups rice	½ pint sour milk curd
Butter	½ oz. cardamom
3 lb. mutton	½ oz. cinnamon
1½ lb. onions	½ oz. saffron
A large garlic clove	Juice of 2 lemons
Large piece ginger	Spinach leaves
¼ lb. almonds	Mint
Salt and pepper	Saffron

Cut the meat into pieces, wash and wipe. Slice the onions and fry in butter until slightly brown, then add meat and cook for 10 minutes. Add garlic, stir well and pour in 1½ pints water. Cook slowly until all the water has evaporated. Add milk, lemon juice, spices and seasoning.

When the meat is almost cooked remove from the fire and cover with spinach and mint leaves. Boil the rice in salted water until nearly cooked, drain and rinse. Spread half the rice in the bottom of a cooking pot, put the meat on top and cover with the remainder of the rice. Stud with almonds, sprinkle with saffron and cover the pot. Place on a low heat until the rice begins to steam, when the dish is ready to serve.

SHAMI KABAB
(RISSOLES)

1 lb. mutton	Butter
3–4 lb. cooked lentils	2 eggs
Mixed spices	

Cut the mutton into small pieces and cook with the lentils and enough water to moisten. When thoroughly cooked pound the mixture as smooth as possible, add eggs and spices, make into rissoles about ½ inch thick and fry in butter until brown. Serve with salad.

HODU KABAB
(MUTTON AND LENTIL BALLS)

¼ lb. mutton	A few raisins
½ pint lentils	¼ pint vinegar
½ oz. almonds	3 lemons
Saffron	1 lb. sugar
1 tsp. cloves	¼ lb. onions
1 tsp. cardamoms	1 lb. ghee or butter
1 inch cinnamon	6 eggs
A few prunes	

108

Cook lentils, mutton and spices together in enough water to cover. When cooked, pound lentils and meat together and add an egg. Boil and chop the other eggs, adding fruit and sliced almonds. Mix ingredients together, form into balls and fry in hot fat. Remove, fry the onions in the fat, pour in 1½ pints water, the vinegar, lemon juice and sugar. Return mutton balls to liquid and serve hot.

MUTTON STEW

1½ lb. breast of mutton or lamb	2 oz. dried peas
	2 oz. haricot beans
1 lb. potatoes	Seasoning
1 lb. tomatoes	

Soak the peas and beans overnight. In the morning cut the meat into small pieces, peel the tomatoes and add to the meat, with the soaked beans and peas and seasoning. Cover with plenty of water and bring to the boil. Skim and simmer for 5 or 6 hours. Half an hour before serving, add the potatoes, peeled and quartered. When the potatoes are cooked, strain off the soup; remove bones from the meat and mix meat with the vegetables. Serve soup and the meat and vegetable mixture separately. The soup may be thickened by stirring in some of the mashed potato if liked.

MUTTON WITH AUBERGINES

1 lb. mutton	$\frac{1}{2}$ lb. tomatoes
3 aubergines	Butter for frying
1 medium onion	Salt and pepper

Peel the aubergines and cut in thick slices. Cover with a little salt and leave for an hour. Drain and dry. Fry in butter until golden-brown, then put aside. In the same butter fry the onion, finely chopped, and the meat, cut into small pieces. Season, just cover with water and simmer until the meat is tender. Arrange the aubergines on top and cover with a layer of sliced tomatoes. Simmer very gently until the sauce is thick—about $\frac{3}{4}$ hour.

SAVOURY STUFFED QUINCES

4 quinces	Salt to taste
Minced cooked mutton or chicken	1 tbsp. honey
	1 oz. butter

Core the quinces, cover with boiling water and simmer for 20 minutes. Drain and stuff with the seasoned meat. Place in a shallow fire-proof dish, pour on the honey, dot with butter and bake in a moderate oven (375° F., mark 5) for 1 hour.

BAKED WALNUT OMELETTE

6 eggs	4 oz. chopped walnuts
Large handful of chopped chives	1 tbsp. currants
2 oz. white crumbs	Seasoning
	Butter

Beat the eggs and mix with the other ingredients, except the butter. Butter a round dish and let it heat in the oven for a moment. Pour in the egg mixture and cook in a moderate oven (400° F., mark 6) until set.

AUBERGINE SAUCE

1 large aubergine	$\frac{1}{8}$ tsp. each of paprika,
1 oz. butter for frying	coriander, turmeric
1 onion	and cinnamon
3 cloves of garlic	2 tbsps. tomato purée

Peel the aubergine, rub with salt and leave for 2 hours. Drain, wipe and fry in butter until dark brown. Mince the onion, add to the aubergine and fry; cover with water and boil for 15 minutes, by which time the aubergine will be soft and mushy. Add the tomato purée, crushed garlic and spices and simmer for 20 minutes, stirring frequently. Rub through a sieve and serve with fried chicken or meat and rice.

A similar sauce can be made using celery.

WALNUT SAUCE

1 lb. shelled walnuts	$\frac{1}{2}$ oz. brown sugar
2 chopped onions	Salt
1 oz. butter	Pepper
Small glass pomegranate juice	Allspice

Mince the walnuts and fry with the onions in the butter. When the onions are just coloured, pour in the juice and the sugar, stir well and simmer over a very low heat for 2 hours. Season with salt, pepper and allspice to taste. Serve with poultry or meat.

PRALINE CREAM

For the Praline

2 oz. blanched almonds	2 oz. caster sugar
browned in the oven	

For the Cream

$\frac{1}{4}$ lb. unsalted butter	$\frac{1}{4}$ pint double cream
3 eggs (separated)	Savoy biscuits
3 oz. caster sugar	

Make the praline by melting the sugar in a thick pan and when it is brown, stirring in the almonds. Pour the mixture on to a slab and when cold and hard, break it up and pound it finely. It will keep in an airtight container.

To make the cream, beat the butter until it is really light and creamy, which may take up to half an hour. Beat the egg yolks together and beat into the butter. Add the sugar and the praline mixture, beating continuously, and finally fold in the stiffly whipped egg whites and the whipped cream. Line a mould with Savoy biscuits and pour in the cream. Leave in a cold place until set and turn out to serve.

TURKISH cookery deserves to be more widely known than it is at present, for it is particularly nicely balanced between meat and vegetables, sweets and fruit and is far removed from the general conception of it as being composed largely of thick coffee, syrupy sweet pastries and a great deal of rice.

Each part of Turkey has its own specialities, but on the whole, lamb and mutton are the dominant meats, while vegetables and fruits are varied and interesting. Tomatoes, cucumbers, beans, aubergines, green peppers and okra are favourite summer vegetables—the Turks are said to have more than forty ways of cooking aubergines—and in the winter all the usual European vegetables abound. Pulses and rice form the background of many of the dishes, and cherries, apples, peaches, figs, grapes and melons are all widely used.

The Turks are jealous of their epicurean reputation; in Istanbul, drinking water is chosen with as much care as is devoted to wine in France; peaches and apples are ordered by name, for those from different areas have a different flavour and fragrance.

In Turkish cookery, sauces and gravies are rarely served separately, but all the ingredients of a dish are cooked together, so that the flavour of the one can pervade the other. A dish of mutton and beans cooked together is a standard Turkish winter meal, followed by dried fruit compote, but a formal dinner can start with as many as thirty or forty appetisers, served with raki, the anise-flavoured national drink.

Shish kebab, pilaff, dolmas—all these well-known dishes are of Turkish origin, while Turkish coffee has its own special niche in international cuisine.

Turkey

MARRIAGE SOUP

1 lb. mutton or lamb	1 cup flour
2 lb. mutton or lamb bones	Juice of 1 lemon
	3 egg yolks
1 onion	6 tbsps. melted butter (for garnish)
1 medium carrot	
1 tbsp. salt	1 tbsp. paprika
4 cups water	Dash of cayenne
6 tbsps. butter	

Add meat, bones, peeled onion, scraped carrot and salt to 4 cups of water. Cook over medium fire in covered pot until meat is tender (about 3 hours). Strain off the broth. Mince the meat, add it to the stock and set aside. Blend butter and flour in large saucepan over low flame, and stir constantly until mixture is light brown (about 3 minutes). Add meat stock gradually, stirring constantly. Simmer for about 5 minutes. Add lemon juice to beaten egg yolks, then gradually add about 2 ladles of the hot stock. Stir this mixture into the soup. Serve with garnish of melted butter to which paprika and cayenne have been added.

TRIPE SOUP WITH EGG SAUCE

4 lb. tripe	2 eggs
5 cups water	Juice of 2 lemons
Salt and pepper to taste	2 cloves garlic (optional)
Paprika	

Wash tripe well. Cook with the water over medium heat for 3 hours. Remove tripe (saving stock) and put through mincer or chop into small pieces. Season with salt and pepper and cook over low flame for 2 or 3 hours.

Sauce : Beat eggs well, gradually add lemon juice and beat again. Blend slowly with stock so as not to curdle the eggs. If desired, garlic may be added to sauce. Serve egg sauce with soup and sprinkle with paprika.

GHYUGHEJ BALIGHI
(SAVOURY BAKED FISH)

2 lb. striped bass or other fish	Paprika
	Salt to taste
2 medium onions	Juice of ½ lemon or lemon slices
½ cup olive oil	
¼ cup tomato paste	3 stalks chopped celery
1½ cups water	4 small carrots (diced)
3 cloves garlic (crushed)	½ tsp. chopped parsley

After cleaning fish, cut into 1-inch slices. Cut the onions into rings, and fry in a heavy pan in ⅛ cup of olive oil until light brown. Add tomato paste, 1½ cups of water, garlic, paprika, salt, juice of ½ lemon, remaining olive oil, celery and carrots. Cover and cook 25 minutes. Place fish in deep baking dish and cover with this sauce.

Bake in a moderately hot oven (400° F., mark 6) for 25 minutes. Garnish with parsley and lemon.

USSKUMRU BALIGHI KEBABI
(FISH KEBABS)

Mackerel	Fennel
Salt and pepper	Bay leaves
Parsley	

Get as many fresh mackerel as are desired and cut off the heads. If the fish are large, divide each one in 3 pieces ; if small, in 2 pieces. Wash and dry them in a cloth, sprinkle them with sufficient salt and pepper and a handful or two of chopped parsley mixed with fennel, and let them stand for an hour. Put them on skewers with a bay leaf between the pieces and grill, turning until cooked. Eels and grey mullets may be done in the same way.

SOMUN-BALIGHI KYUL BASSTISSI
(BROILED SALMON WITH SAUCE)

Salmon	Bay leaves
Salt	Lemon

For the Sauce (optional)

4 dozen almonds	Salt
2 garlic cloves	3 tsps. olive oil
2 oz. bread (crumbs only)	Lemon juice or vinegar

Cut from the tail end of a small salmon as many thin slices as are wanted and rub them with a little salt. Then cover a gridiron with some bay leaves, lay the slices of fish over and set it on a moderate charcoal fire. When nicely browned on both sides, dish it up and squeeze a lemon over. Alternatively, make a sauce : skin the almonds and pound them well in a mortar with the peeled garlic cloves. Add the piece of bread previously soaked in water, a little salt and 3 tsps. of olive oil. Pound them all together until they form a paste, then moisten it with lemon juice or wine vinegar and some water to form a smooth sauce, but not too thick. Pour it over the fish instead of lemon and serve hot. This sauce may be used with any kind of fried or broiled fish, if desired.

BAKED FISH

Fish	Parsley
Salt	½ teacup wine vinegar
1 teacup olive oil	4 tomatoes
4 sliced onions	

Get any fish you fancy, scale them and clean them well. If the fish is one large one, cut it in 3 or 4 pieces, sprinkle some salt over and let it stand for a little while. Put a teacupful of olive oil in a frying pan with 4 or 5 sliced onions, and a handful or two of chopped parsley. Put it on the fire and fry it golden-brown. Then lay half of it on the bottom of a rather deep baking dish and place the fish over, then the other half of the onions and parsley on top, with the oil that is left in the frying pan. Add ½ teacupful of wine vinegar and 1 of water, and the tomatoes cut in four crossways. Put into a moderate oven (375° F., mark 5) for 20 minutes or so. When nicely baked, dish it up and serve.

TAWUK KYUL BASSTISSI
(GRILLED CHICKEN)

Chicken	Cinnamon
Salt and pepper	Chicken broth

Split 1 or 2 chickens lengthways and remove the whole of the bones with a sharp knife. Cut the flesh in 4 or 5 pieces as you fancy and beat the thicker parts even with a rolling pin. Sprinkle them with sufficient salt and pepper, and a little cinnamon, and let them stand for 1 or 2 hours. Place them on a gridiron, set it on a moderate charcoal fire, and constantly turn them with a pair of tongs. When nicely browned, lay them in a stewpan and cover them with broth. Put the pan on a moderate charcoal fire and let simmer until tender. Dish up and serve hot.

CIRCASSIAN CHICKEN

1 chicken	1 tsp. salt
3 quarts water	Pepper
1 large onion	2 cups shelled walnuts
1 carrot	1 tbsp. paprika
1 bunch parsley	3 small slices white bread

Place chicken in pot containing 3 quarts of water and add onion, carrot, parsley, salt and pepper. Bring to a boil and skim foam off top. Cover and cook for 2 hours. (If pressure cooker is used, reduce water to 1½ pints and cooking time to 1 hour.) When tender, take from pot and allow to cool. (Save stock.) When cool, remove skin and bones and cut chicken into small pieces. Put walnuts through mincer twice, then add paprika. Press nuts and paprika between double layers of cheesecloth to get about 2 tbsps. of red oil to be set aside for garnishing. This is merely for decorating. Soak bread in chicken stock, squeeze dry and add to ground walnuts and paprika, mixing well. Put this bread-walnuts-paprika mixture through meat mincer 3 times, then add 1 cup of chicken stock and work into a paste. Divide paste in half and mix one half with minced chicken, blending it thoroughly. Spread other half of paste over the chicken mixture and decorate top with red walnut oil. Serve cold.

TAWUK DOLMASSI
(CHICKEN STUFFED WITH RICE)

Chickens	3 tbsps. pistachio nuts
Salt and pepper	1 tbsp. currants
Butter	Ground cinnamon
¾ lb. rice	Chicken broth

Thoroughly clean 2–3 chickens, sprinkle a little salt over, and let them stand for 10 minutes or so. Chop up the livers, hearts and the gizzards finely and put them in a frying pan with sufficient fresh butter. Then add ¾ lb. of well-washed rice, 2 or 3 tbsps. of pistachios, 1 tbsp. of currants, sufficient salt and pepper, and a little cinnamon. Stir round for a few minutes, then add a small teacup of hot water and keep stirring until the water is absorbed and the rice partly soft. Then stuff the chickens with it, sew them up, and fry them a nice brown in fresh butter. Place them in a stewpan, nearly cover them with broth, put the pan on a charcoal fire with the cover over, and let them simmer until the chickens are quite tender. Dish up and serve.

SIGHIR-ETI YAHNISSI
(STEAK WITH GARLIC)

5–6 lb. rump steak	3 lb. sliced potatoes
15 garlic cloves	Juice of 3 lb. tomatoes
¾ lb. fresh butter	Salt and pepper

Cut 5 or 6 lb. of rump steak into rather long pieces, ½ or ¾ inch thick, and tie them together, one over the other, with a piece of string to make 1 block of meat. With the point of a knife, make about 15 holes here and there and stick in each a peeled clove of garlic. Place the meat in a stewpan with about ¾ lb. of fresh butter, set it on a moderate charcoal fire with the cover over for about 3 hours, turning the meat every ½ hour. Then add 2 or 3 lb. of sliced potatoes partly fried in butter, and the juice of 2 or 3 lb. of ripe tomatoes with a little water and sufficient salt and pepper. Put the cover over the pan and let it simmer until the meat and potatoes are well done, then cut the string off the meat, dish up tastefully, and serve. Enough for 8 people.

KIZARTMA
(STEWED MUTTON)

Mutton	Butter
Salt	Onions
Curd	

Cut as much as is required of a leg of mutton in pieces the size of large eggs. Place them in a saucepan with sufficient salt and cover them with water. Set it on the fire and let it boil for 20 or 30 minutes. Skim it well, then take out the pieces of meat and rub them all over with curd. Fry them a rich brown in fresh butter and place them in a saucepan with sufficient onions, sliced thin and fried golden-brown in fresh butter. Add the liquor in which the pieces of mutton were boiled, put the cover over the pan, set it on a moderate charcoal fire until it forms a good thick gravy at the bottom and the meat is tender, then dish it up and serve.

This dish is generally made at public rejoicings on occasion of a marriage, etc.

ICHI DOLMUSH KUZU KEBABI
(WHOLE STUFFED ROAST LAMB)

Whole lamb	2–3 lb. rice
¾ lb. butter	Salt and pepper
3–4 chopped onions	Cinnamon
Pistachio nuts and currants	

This is not a very practical recipe for England, but it is the most characteristic Turkish dish for grand occasions.

Get the whole of a small lamb with the liver and the heart, and put in a large saucepan or iron pot without the liver and heart. Cover it with water, set it on the fire and let it boil for 10 or 15 minutes.

Chop up the liver very fine together with the heart. Put ¾ lb. of fresh butter in a stewpan with 3 or 4 chopped onions, put it on the fire and let them cook till nearly brown. Add the liver and the heart with a handful of skinned pistachios, and the same of currants, well cleaned. Stir until the liver begins to cook, then add 2 or 3 lb. of the best rice, well washed, sufficient salt, pepper and cinnamon. Keep stirring and add now and then a little of the liquor in which the lamb is boiled, until the rice is rather soft. Then stuff the lamb with this preparation and sew it up. Rub the lamb all over with some onion juice, place it in a baking tin and bake it in a moderately hot oven (425° F., mark 7) for 30 minutes, then at moderate (375° F., mark 5) for 25 minutes per lb. The meat should be well browned on both sides.

KUZU KIZARTMASSI
(LAMB WITH RICE)

Lamb	Lamb's heart
Curd	Pistachios
Butter	Currants
Onions	Mixed spice
Salt and pepper	Stock
Water	Rice
Lamb's liver	

This is elaborate, but good and typically Turkish.

Cut as much as is wanted of a leg or any other part of lamb in pieces the size of kidneys, then dip each piece in curd and fry them a nice brown in fresh butter. Place them in a stewpan with 2 or 3 sliced onions fried in butter, sufficient salt and pepper, and cover them with hot or cold water. Set it on a charcoal fire and let it simmer gently until it forms a good thick gravy at the bottom of the stewpan. While the meat is cooking, chop up the liver and the heart of a lamb together, then fry in fresh butter with a little salt. When they are cooked, add a handful of pistachios, skinned, 1 tbsp. of currants and a little mixed spice. Stir it with a wooden spoon for 5 minutes or so, then place it in a saucepan with some of the gravy of the lamb and 2 pints of stock. Set it on a charcoal fire with the cover over. When boiling, add 1 lb. of rice, well washed, stir it, put the cover over and let it boil until each grain is rather soft, but separate. Then take it off, wrap round the lid a wet cloth to prevent the steam from escaping, and put it by the side of the fire for 20 minutes or so. Each grain will then swell up and be well separated, and no moisture be left. Dish it up in the form of a dome, arrange the pieces of lamb over tastefully, and serve hot.

This is an excellent and attractive dish.

KABAK-BASSTISSI
(STEWED MEAT WITH VEGETABLE MARROW)

2 lb. mutton	5 courgettes
Salt	Lemon juice
3–4 sliced onions	Mint
Butter	Pepper or cinnamon

Cut 2 lb. of mutton or lamb in pieces about the size of walnuts. Put them in a stewpan with a little salt and cover them with water. Set pan on a charcoal fire. When scum begins to form, skim it well, and let it simmer till the meat is nearly tender. Put 3 or 4 sliced onions in a frying pan with sufficient fresh butter, and fry them slightly brown; then peel 4 or 5 vegetable marrows, cut each one in four crossways, take out the seeds, if present, and then slice ¾ inch thick. Lay some of the pieces of meat on the bottom of the stewpan, add some slices of vegetable marrow with part of the fried onions, then meat and vegetables in alternate layers until the whole is used up. Add the liquor in which the pieces of mutton were boiled and sufficient salt. If the liquor is not enough, add some broth. Set the stewpan on the fire and let it simmer until the vegetable marrow is tender. Then add the juice of 1 or 2 lemons with a little chopped mint. Let it simmer for 2 minutes longer and then take it off, dish it up, sprinkle a little pepper or cinnamon over, and serve hot.

TARABA
(MEAT BALLS IN SPINACH)

1 lb. spinach	Salt and paprika
1 lb. uncooked mutton	Butter
1 onion	Tomato sauce
1 shallot	Lemon juice

Wash the spinach and blanch it in boiling water for 1–2 minutes, then drain it. Make a forcemeat with the finely chopped mutton, onion and shallot, and season lightly with salt and paprika. Shape the mixture into tiny balls, and wrap each in two spinach leaves. Put the balls into a pan with some melted butter, tomato sauce and lemon juice, packing them closely, and keep in position by putting a plate on top. Simmer very gently for $1\frac{1}{2}$–2 hours.

TAS KEBAB
(POTTED LAMB)

2 lb. shoulder of lamb	1 large tin tomatoes
4 tbsps. butter	$\frac{1}{2}$ tsp. salt
2 onions (chopped)	$\frac{1}{4}$ tsp. pepper

Remove bone and cut lamb in 1-inch cubes. Cook in butter in heavy frying pan until browned. Add onions and brown, then add tomatoes, salt and pepper. Bring to boil, reduce heat and simmer for 45 minutes. Serve with pilav. (See recipe on p. 304).

CHOPPED MEAT WITH POACHED EGGS

1 lb. minced lamb or beef	1 tsp. chopped parsley
2 tbsps. butter	$\frac{1}{2}$ tsp. black pepper
1 large onion	Salt to taste
2 large tomatoes (peeled)	6 eggs

Place meat in pan with melted butter and sauté, stirring constantly, until meat has lost its moisture and is crumbly. Stir in chopped onion and continue stirring until onion turns light brown. Add tomatoes, peeled, seeded and cut into small pieces. Then add chopped parsley, pepper and salt. Mix well, cover and simmer for 15 minutes.

Hollow out 6 depressions in the meat and drop 1 egg in each. Sprinkle with salt and cook covered over low flame for 4 minutes.

SHISH KEBAB

2 lb. leg of lamb	3 sliced tomatoes
1 tbsp. olive oil	Bay leaves
Juice of $\frac{1}{2}$ lemon	Green pepper
Salt and pepper	Aubergine
1 sliced onion	

Cut meat into 1-inch cubes. Mix olive oil and lemon juice and rub into meat. Place in dish, sprinkle with salt and pepper, and cover with slices of onion and tomatoes and a few bay leaves. Place in refrigerator for 4 or 5 hours.

Arrange the meat on skewers alternately with tomatoes, onion, green pepper, sliced aubergine and an occasional bay leaf. Broiling over charcoal is the best way of cooking, but it may also be done over an open wood fire or under the grill.

BRAISED KEBAB

2 lb. lamb	Salt and pepper to taste
12 button onions	Few bay leaves
5 tbsps. butter	$\frac{1}{2}$ tsp. thyme
1 large tomato (peeled)	2 tbsps. water

Cut meat into small cubes and place in heavy frying pan with onions, butter, peeled tomato, salt, pepper, bay leaves, thyme and about 2 tbsps. water. Cook, tightly covered, over medium heat for 20 minutes, then decrease to low and continue cooking for another 2 hours.

MUHZIR KEBABI
(LAMB KEBABS)

Mutton	Cinnamon
Onions	Caul-fat
Salt and pepper	

Cut as much as is required of the best part of mutton in pieces the size of an egg. Then sprinkle 1 or 2 chopped onions over, with sufficient salt, pepper and cinnamon. Mix well together and let them stand for 1 or 2 hours. Thread the pieces of meat on the skewers and wrap them up with some thin caul-fat; place them before the fire and turn them gently. As soon as the meat begins to brown, baste it with the gravy that drops from it. Cook for about 20 minutes and serve hot.

JIGHER KEBABI
(LIVER KEBABS)

Liver	Wine vinegar
Caul-fat	Stock
Garlic	Salt and pepper

Cut into $1\frac{1}{2}$-inch dice as much sheep's or lamb's liver as required. Thread the pieces on skewers and wrap each one with a thin piece of caul-fat. Place them before a moderate fire and turn them slowly until the liver is nicely roasted (about 20 minutes). When cooked, dish it up.

Well pound 2 or 3 skinned cloves of garlic in a mortar, add $\frac{1}{2}$ teacup of wine vinegar, 2 of stock and a little salt and pepper. Stir it well with a wooden spoon and pour it over the liver. Put the cover on the dish and place it in a moderate oven (350° F., mark 4) or on a charcoal fire covered with ash for 5 minutes or so, and then serve.

TERBIYYELI KYUFTE
(MINCED MUTTON BALLS)

Mutton	Eggs
Onions	Lemon juice
Salt and pepper	

Mince very finely 2–3 lb. of the best part of raw mutton, with 2 or 3 peeled onions and a little salt and pepper. Make into balls the size of walnuts, put in a saucepan half full of water and set it on the fire until done. Beat up the yolks of 3 or 4 eggs with the juice of a lemon or two and a little salt. Pour it in a saucepan, put it on a slow fire, and keep stirring well until it begins to thicken. Add 3 or 4 tbsps. (1 at a time) of the liquor in which the balls of meat have been boiling. Stir it for 2 or 3 minutes longer, then dish the meat up. Pour this sauce over the meat and serve hot.

BROILED MEAT BALLS ON SPITS

2 lb. minced mutton (or lamb) mixed with beef	Salt and pepper to taste
	2 eggs
1 large onion	Olive oil

Mince the meat twice. Grate onion, add salt and let stand for 15 minutes. Then squeeze through cheesecloth. Add onion juice with eggs and pepper to meat and mix well. Shape into egg-sized balls and place on oiled skewers. Broil for 5 minutes each side over a flame-free charcoal fire or under the grill.

MEAT BALLS IN TOMATO SAUCE

1½ lb. minced mutton, lamb or beef	2 eggs
	Salt and pepper
1 large onion (grated)	1 tbsp. flour
1 tsp. chopped parsley	2 tbsps. butter
2½ slices dry wholewheat bread (soaked in water and squeezed dry)	2 medium tomatoes (or ¼ cup tomato paste)

Combine meat, grated onion, parsley, bread, eggs, salt and pepper. Shape into balls the size of walnuts, and dust with flour. Brown in a frying pan in melted butter. Add tomatoes (or tomato paste and 1 cup of water). Cover and cook over medium flame for 25 minutes. Serve hot.

LADY MEAT BALLS

1 lb. minced lean mutton or lamb	1 tsp. chopped dill
	⅛ tsp. pepper
3 large onions (diced)	Salt to taste
½ cup uncooked rice	½ cup flour
½ cup grated cheese	4 eggs
1 tsp. chopped parsley	¼ cup lard

Put meat through mincer, with onions. Boil rice until tender, then mix it with meat and onions, cheese, parsley, dill, pepper and salt. Knead mixture 5 minutes. Form into egg-sized ovals and roll in flour. Beat eggs until frothy and dip meat balls into egg. Fry on both sides in ¼ cup of lard.

SALONIQUE TOTI
(FRIED MEATS IN BATTER)

Put small pieces of liver, kidneys and brain on long metal skewers, alternating them with pieces of fat bacon and slices of egg plant. Dip in batter and fry in oil.

AADI PILAV
(PLAIN RICE PILAFF)

Pour 2 pints of water in a saucepan and put it on the fire. When boiling, throw in 1 lb. of the best rice, well washed, add salt to taste and boil it until the whole of the liquid is absorbed. Put in a saucepan ½ lb. of fresh butter and set it on the fire until it boils. Pour it all at once over the rice, put the cover over the pan, wrap a wet cloth round it to prevent the steam from escaping and keep it on the hob for ½ hour. Take the lid off and stir it once round with a fork. You will find that each grain is swollen and is well separated. Dish up in the shape of a dome and serve hot.

PILAV
(TOMATO RICE PILAFF)

2 cups uncooked rice	3½ cups liquid (water, meat stock or chicken broth)
4 medium tomatoes (or canned tomatoes)	
⅛ lb. butter	2 tsps. salt

Wash and drain rice well, then set aside. Cut peeled and seeded tomatoes into small chunks. Heat butter and tomatoes together until a tomato paste is obtained, then add liquid and salt and boil for 2 minutes. Add rice while liquid is boiling, stir once, cover and cook over medium heat without stirring again until rice has absorbed all the liquid. Turn flame very low and simmer for another 20 minutes. Remove from stove and leave covered for 30 minutes—do not stir.

When transferring rice to serving dish, use a flat serving spoon, handling the rice very gently, to keep it fluffy.

BOEREK

Turkish boerek can be made into very small rolls, triangles or other shapes and served as canapés ; when larger, they make a good appetiser, while a very large boerek makes the main dish of the meal.

Turkish boerek may be made of strudel pastry

which is on sale in some shops, or your own puff paste rolled thin as tissue paper.

Cut pastry into desired size and brush with melted butter. Place a teaspoon (or more) of filling on each piece of pastry, and roll up or fold over quickly, handling the dough as little as possible. Place on greased baking sheet and brush with melted butter. Bake in moderate oven (375° F., mark 5) until golden and crisp —25 minutes.

Cheese Filling for Boerek

½ lb. cheese (cream or   1 egg
    cottage cheese)   ¼ cup milk
2 tbsps. butter   ¼ cup chopped parsley

Soften cheese with fork, cream butter, and combine. Add egg, milk and parsley, and mix well. Makes enough for 6.

Other Fillings

Left-over cooked meat or chicken, chopped, and then mixed with 1 egg and a little chopped onion and parsley.

Chopped spinach and onion blended with a little milk and butter.

As a dessert—chopped nuts, cinnamon and sugar plus melted butter or honey syrup.

BANITZA
(SPINACH PIE)

A sort of mille-feuilles, or rich, wafer-thin pastry with cheese or other fillings. Ismet Inönü, President of Turkey, whose mother was a Bulgarian, has a special predilection for the Spinach Banitza, and when, as Ismet Pasha, he was attending a Conference at Lausanne, he gave careful instructions to the Chef at his hotel to make him this favourite dish. Greatly to his disappointment, the Banitza was served flat and long, like an Austrian Apfel Strudel, when it should have been high and round, like a mound. After further instructions had been given, however, a piping-hot Banitza was served, full of melted butter, with a delicious crackling pastry, and was greatly enjoyed by the various Turkish and Bulgarian delegates at the Conference.

3 lb. young spinach   1 bunch spring onions
1 lb. onions   ¾ lb. cheese
2 cups olive oil or butter   4 or 5 sheets strudel or
½ cup chopped dill   very thin puff pastry
1 cup chopped parsley   Salt

Remove the stalks of the spinach and wash the leaves in several waters, until they are completely free of any grit. Take the leaves and cut them up very finely. Mix in a bowl with chopped

W.C.B.—20

parsley, the dill and the spring onions, sprinkle with salt and set aside. Chop and fry the onions, mix with the other vegetables and the cheese, line a well-greased baking tin with 2 or 3 sheets of the pastry, spread the spinach and vegetables on top, shaping into a mound, cover with the rest of the sheets, brush with melted butter and bake in a moderate oven (350° F., mark 4) for about 30–45 minutes. These quantities will make enough for 5–6 people.

In Turkey and Greece ready-made pastry sheets can be bought, which are called Yufka in Turkey and Fillo in Greece. If ready-made pastry sheets are not obtainable they can be made at home, although it is a lengthy business and requires time and patience.

1 lb. flour   1 tsp. baking powder
1½ cups melted butter   1 tsp. salt
2 eggs   A little water

Sieve the dry ingredients, add the beaten eggs and some of the butter, then work to a stiff dough with a little water. Divide the dough into several pieces shaped like balls and leave under a damp cloth for ½ hour. Roll out each piece several times very thinly, brushing with melted butter every time. Cover and leave once more. Roll out again into separate sheets, brush with melted butter and lay out on a table, so that they do not touch each other. Leave while you make the stuffing.

SLASHED EGG PLANT

2 medium onions   ½ cup chopped parsley
    (chopped)   (optional)
4½ tbsps. butter   6 medium egg plants
½ lb. minced mutton,   (long and thin)
    lamb or beef   2 tbsps. butter for
2 medium tomatoes and   top of egg plant
    1 for garnish   (optional)
1 green pepper (optional)   1 cup meat stock or
1 tsp. salt   water
½ tsp. black pepper

Brown onions lightly in 2 tbsps. butter. Add meat and cook for about 10 minutes, stirring constantly. Add tomatoes (peeled and cut into small pieces), green pepper if desired, and salt. Cook until pepper and tomatoes are tender. Add black pepper, stir well and remove from stove. Chopped parsley may be added. Peel egg plants to within 1 inch of each end. Slash middle peeled portion crosswise to within 1 inch of each end (on one side of egg plant only). Sprinkle with salt, cover with water and set aside for 20 to 30 minutes. Pour off salted water, wash, dry and sauté on both sides in 2½ tbsps. butter to a very light brown. Remove carefully from frying pan with spatula and place in casserole, keeping slashed surfaces of egg plant on top. Insert knife blade carefully into slashes and stuff with meat mixture. Place a slice of tomato on top of each egg plant, dot each with a knob of butter if desired, add stock or water to casserole and bake in a moderate oven (350° F., mark 4) for about 30 minutes.

FASSULYA MUJMERI
(FRENCH BEANS WITH MINCED MEAT)

2 lb. French beans	4–5 tbsps. fried minced
Salt	meat
Flour	Pepper
4–5 eggs	Butter

Scald French beans with a little salt. When partly tender, put them on a board and chop them up. Place them in a basin, sprinkle some flour over, and rub them smooth with your hands. Then add 4 or 5 eggs, 4 or 5 tbsps. of fried minced meat, a little salt and pepper, and beat them up well with a fork. Put some fresh butter into the frying pan, set it on the fire until hot, then fry the mixture a tablespoonful at a time. When all are fried a golden colour, dish them up tastefully and serve hot.

BADINJAM-TAWASSI
(FRIED EGG PLANT)

Egg plants	Water
Salt	Butter
2–3 oz. flour	

Procure as many egg plants as are wanted, cut them in slices about ½ inch thick, sprinkle them with salt and let them stand about ½ hour. When the bitter juice is drawn from them, put 2 or 3 oz. of flour into a basin and mix with water to form a smooth batter, not too thick. Dip the egg plants in it and fry them in fresh butter until a golden colour, turning them over. When done, take them out with a slice, let them drain, dish up, and serve.

IMAM BAÏLDI
(STUFFED AUBERGINES—EGG PLANTS)

Remove the stalks of the aubergines, but do not skin them; blanch them in boiling water for 5–8 minutes. Cook ½ lb. chopped onions in some oil till they are golden in colour, then add 1 lb. quartered tomatoes and 1 clove of garlic. Season, and cook slowly till reduced to a pulp. Split the aubergines lengthways, remove a little pulp and mix with the stuffing. Fill each aubergine with some tomato and onion, put in a greased fireproof dish, pour a little of the mixture over them, and cook in a moderate oven (350° F., mark 3) for 1 hour.

DOLMAS
(STUFFED VEGETABLES)

1 lb. minced lamb or beef	1 tsp. chopped dill
(from fatty part of meat)	Salt and pepper
1 chopped onion	1 tbsp. tomato sauce
¼ cup uncooked rice	(optional)
1 tsp. chopped mint	

Place meat in bowl and add onion, rice, mint, dill, salt and pepper, and tomato sauce if desired. Knead well.

This stuffing may be used for a variety of dolmas, for example :

A. Egg Plant
B. Green Pepper
C. Tomato
D. Zucchini (Italian Squash)

These may be cooked separately or together, for assorted dolmas

E. Grape Leaf
F. Cabbage Leaf

These two are never cooked together

A. *Egg Plant Dolmas*

Choose a short round egg plant, since it is cooked upright in a saucepan. Cut off the stem-end and keep for a cover. Peel the egg plant lengthwise in strips, alternating peeled and unpeeled strips. Scoop out the inside, leaving a shell ½–1 inch thick. Fill with stuffing and replace with stem-end cover.

B. *Green Pepper Dolmas*

Slice through top of pepper but do not sever it, for it will serve as a cover. Remove seeds and membranes. Fill with stuffing and close cover.

C. *Tomato Dolmas*

Prepare and stuff same as green pepper dolmas.

D. *Zucchini Dolmas*

Clean the outside of zucchini and cut off one end to use as a cover. Scoop out the inside, leaving a ½-inch shell. Stuff and replace cover, fastening it with cocktail sticks.

Cooking Directions (Dolmas A–D)

2 tbsps. butter	1 cup water

When preparing dolmas, place egg plant and zucchini dolmas upright at bottom of saucepan, follow with a layer of green pepper dolmas, and top them with a layer of tomato dolmas. Add

2 tbsps. of butter and 1 cup of water, cover and cook over medium heat for 30–40 minutes, or until vegetables are soft. If any stuffing is left over, form into meat balls and place between stuffed dolmas in the saucepan.

E. *Grape Leaf Dolmas*

2 tbsps. butter	Yoghourt or lemon
1½ cups water	(optional)

Drop grape leaves into boiling water and boil for 5 minutes, then drain. Holding leaf in palm of hand, with top or glossy side of leaf down, cut off hard stem and place small portion of stuffing on broad end of inside of leaf. Fold ends of leave over stuffing and roll like a cigarette. Place grape leaf dolmas in saucepan in rows and add butter and water. Put a plate on top of dolmas to keep them in place, and cover the saucepan. Cook over medium heat for 35–40 minutes. May be served with yoghourt or lemon.

F. *Cabbage Leaf Dolmas*

2 tbsps. butter	2 cups water

Take outer leaves of a large head of cabbage and parboil for 5 minutes, then drain. Put spoonful of stuffing on each leaf and roll up. Place cabbage leaf dolmas in saucepan in rows and add butter and water. Put a plate on top of dolmas to keep them in place, and cover the saucepan. Cook over medium heat for 35–40 minutes.

VEGETABLE POT

1 lb. diced lamb	1 medium egg plant
2 medium onions (chopped)	¼ lb. okra
¼ cup butter	2 large green peppers
1½ cups water	Salt and pepper to
3 medium tomatoes	taste
2 small zucchini (Italian squash	½ lb. green beans

Prepare the meat. Sauté onions in butter in large saucepan until lightly browned. Add meat and ½ cup of water, and simmer until nearly tender. While meat is cooking, prepare vegetables as follows: Peel and slice tomatoes and zucchini. Peel 1-inch strips of skin from egg plant and cut into 2-inch segments. Trim okra by removing cone-shaped portions at top. Remove seeds from green peppers and dice them. When meat is nearly tender, add 1 cup of hot water, salt and pepper; then add beans, zucchini, egg plant, tomatoes, pepper and okra, in that order. Cover tightly and cook until vegetables are done (about 50 minutes). If necessary, hot water may be added during cooking.

HALVA
(MOULDED SWEET)

6 oz. sugar	Grated rind of 1
¼ pint water	orange
4 oz. butter	2 oz. ground almonds
4 oz. semolina	4–5 cardamom seeds
2 oz. seeded raisins	Powdered cinnamon

Put the sugar and water into a pan, and when the sugar has dissolved, bring to the boil; boil until the syrup thickens, then remove it from the heat. Melt the butter, put in the semolina and brown it, then add the raisins, orange rind, ground almonds and cardamom seeds. Finally add the syrup, and cook the mixture over a low heat, stirring all the time, until it is thick. Pour into wetted moulds, and when cold, turn out and serve sprinkled with powdered cinnamon.

TURKISH PUDDING

1 cup sugar	4 cups milk
4 tsps. cornflour	5 tsps. rosewater
6 tbsps. rice flour	4 almond macaroons

Mix sugar, cornflour and rice flour thoroughly in a 2-quart saucepan. Add milk and mix well. Cook over medium flame, stirring constantly for 10 minutes. Then, without stirring, cook slowly to allow flour paste to settle and caramelise. Occasionally test bottom of mixture with spoon for signs of caramelisation. When bottom layer becomes firm and sticks to spoon, turn flame slightly higher to speed up the process. When spoon gives off a caramel odour, the cooking is done. Remove from heat and add rosewater. Put macaroons in bottom of ovenglass dish and pour hot mixture over them, scraping caramelised bottom into pudding. The macaroons will quickly disintegrate and rise to form a crumb-like surface. Allow to cool and set (2–3 hours).

LIPS OF THE BEAUTY

7 tbsps. butter	1 tsp. salt
1¾ cups water	2 eggs and 1 egg yolk
1½ cups flour	1¼ cups vegetable shortening

Syrup

2½ cups sugar	1 tsp. lemon juice
3 cups water	

Make syrup of sugar, lemon juice and water boiled for 15 minutes. Set aside to cool. Heat butter in saucepan until it begins to change colour, then add 1¾ cups of water and bring to boil. Reduce flame, add flour and salt and continue cooking for 7 minutes, stirring constantly. Cool. When mixture is cool, add 2 whole eggs and 1 egg yolk one at a time, beating each in well. Then knead thoroughly. Divide dough into pieces the size of large walnuts, and shape into rolls, folded over to meet in the middle (to resemble lips, as suggested by the name of the recipe). Melt fat in pan, then place lip-shaped rolls in it and fry over high heat until golden-brown on both sides. Remove and drain off excess fat. Place hot rolls in cold syrup and leave for 15 minutes, then remove and serve.

TURKISH COOKIES

½ lb. unsalted butter   ½ lb. flour
½ lb. granulated sugar   ⅓ lb. blanched almonds

Place butter in mixing bowl and cream it well. Add sugar and sifted flour. Form into a paste, ½ inch thick, and cut into desired shapes. Place 1 almond on top of each cookie. Bake on greased pan in moderate oven.

YOGHOURT DESSERT

3 eggs   1 tsp. baking powder
1 cup sugar   1 tsp. grated lemon
1 cup yoghourt   or orange rind
1 cup flour   Whipped cream

Syrup

2½ cups sugar   3 cups water
1 tsp. lemon juice

Mix together 2½ cups of sugar and 3 cups of water and boil to syrup stage; add lemon juice and set aside to cool. Beat eggs with sugar until sugar dissolves. Add yoghourt, flour sifted with baking powder, and the fruit rind to the egg mixture and beat until smooth. Pour into greased baking pan and bake in a moderately hot oven (400° F., mark 6) for ½ hour. Remove pastry from oven and cut into desired shapes while still in pan. Immediately pour syrup over hot pastry. Cover pan and set aside until all syrup has been absorbed. Then transfer to dish and chill. Serve with whipped cream.

BAKLAVA

1 lb. unsalted butter   1 lb. chopped walnuts
1 lb. Boerek pastry

Syrup

2 lb. sugar   1½ cups water
Lemon juice

(For note on pastry, see BOEREK, pages 304–5.)

Melt butter. Place 1 sheet of pastry in well-buttered 11- by 17-inch baking tin, then spread with melted butter. Place second sheet on top of the first and butter again. Repeat until 6 layers of buttered pastry sheets have been built up, then sprinkle top sheet thickly with walnuts.

Place the rest of the sheets one on top of the other, buttering each generously. When finished, cut into diagonal sections across the pan and cut intersecting diagonals to form diamonds. Bake in moderate oven (350° F., mark 4) for 45 minutes. Excess butter may be drained off after baking.

Cook sugar and water to syrup, add a few drops of lemon juice, and pour hot over cooled baklava. Serve cold.

LALANGA
(FRIED PASTRIES)

Put into a basin 6 large tbsps. of flour, make a hole in the middle and put in an egg, a little salt, half a glassful of water or a little more, until you get a rather thick liquid. Fry this paste by pouring it in spoonfuls into very hot oil. Dip into cold syrup and arrange them on a dish, pouring remainder of syrup on top.

PUMPKIN DESSERT

4 lb. pumpkin   ½ cup water
1 lb. sugar   ½ cup ground walnuts

Pare pumpkin and cut into 1-inch slices. Place slices in cooking pot, sprinkling sugar in between layers. Add water, cover and cook over medium heat until tender. Cool in the pot, then remove to serving dish. Garnish with nuts and serve.

FARINA NUT PUDDING

1 cup sugar   1 cup farina
1 cup milk   ⅛ cup pine kernels
1 cup water   Cinnamon
⅛ cup butter

Mix together sugar, milk and water, then boil to syrup stage. Allow to cool. Melt butter in heavy saucepan, add farina and whole pinenuts; sauté over low flame until nuts turn light brown. Then pour cooled syrup gradually over hot farina and nut mixture, stirring until well mixed. Cover and cook until syrup is entirely absorbed, stirring frequently to keep farina from becoming lumpy. Remove from fire, wrap saucepan lid in dish towel, and replace on pan to draw excess moisture. Let stand ½ hour, then stir well, sprinkle with cinnamon, and serve.

RIZAKI UZUMU KHOSHABI
(RAISIN COMPOTE)

Take off the stalks of 1 lb. of raisins, wash and place them in a stewpan with 2 or 3 pints of water. Set it to boil until they are quite swollen up, then according to taste, add some powdered sugar and boil them for 1 or 2 minutes longer. Then take it off. When cold, pour all together into a glass bowl, add a few drops of any essence of flowers with some pieces of ice, and serve.

GHYULBE-SHEKER
(ROSE-PETAL JAM)

When the roses are in full bloom, gather about 1 lb. of the petals, pick out the large ones, and cut the white ends off with a pair of scissors. Put the small ones and the white ends in a very clean stewpan with ¾ pint of water and scald them. Pass the liquor through a piece of muslin or a sieve, squeeze the petals well and throw them away, then put the liquor in the pan with 3½ lb. white sugar, and stir them with a wooden spoon until the sugar is dissolved. Then add the large petals that you have picked out, stir and boil till rather thick. Try a little on a plate. If it sets, then remove it from the fire. When cold, fill the preserve jars, cover them in the usual way, and keep them in a rather cool place.

GHYULBE SHEKERI SHEMSIYYE
(CRYSTALLISED ROSE PETALS)

Procure 1 lb. of fresh rose petals, cut the white ends off with a pair of scissors and throw them away. Put the other parts in a basin with 2½ lb. of fine white sugar, and work it together with the hands until the rose petals are reduced to a pulp or paste. Put this into preserve jars or glass bowls, arrange them on a tray, and put them where the sun is powerful. When near sunset, put the covers over and take them in. The next day, uncover the jars and expose the preserve to the sun as before, and continue in this way until the top of the preserve is nicely crystallised. It is a delicate confection, and may be taken at breakfast or used with pastry. Violet petals may be done in the same way.

TURKISH COFFEE

A copper coffee pot with a long handle and without a lid is the correct utensil to use, when available.

For each cup of coffee use ¾ oz. very finely ground coffee, ¾ oz. sugar and a little more than ¼ pint water. Put all the ingredients in the coffee pot and stir till the mixture comes to the boil and becomes frothy. Remove from the heat, and when the froth has subsided, replace the pot on a brisk heat. Repeat the operation 3 times in all. Just before serving, add a little cold water to settle the dregs, together with a few drops of rosewater to perfume the coffee, if desired. (Milk is never added.)

INJIR KHOSHABI
(FIG SYRUP)

This Fig Syrup and the Flower Syrup which follows are typically Turkish and very popular drunk with candies.

Cut off the stalks of 2 lb. of figs, prick each one here and there with a wooden skewer, place them in a basin with 3 pints of hot water, and let them stand for 10 or 12 hours. Then pass the liquid through a sieve into a glass bowl, and add the figs with a few drops of orange-flower water and a few pieces of ice, and serve.

It is a refreshing and wholesome beverage.

MENEKSHE SHURUBI
(FLOWER SYRUP)

Procure 1 lb. of fresh-gathered violets, cut the stalks off, and put the leaves in a basin. Pour 2¼ pints of boiling water over them, immediately cover it, and let it remain for 12 or 15 hours. Then pass the liquor through a clean cloth into a stewpan, add about 3 lb. of crushed sugar, stir with a wooden spoon till the sugar is dissolved, and set it on a charcoal fire. Just as it commences to boil up, instantly remove it, and let it remain covered till nearly cold. Then pass it again through a cloth, bottle and cork it up until wanted.

Far East

THE dispensing of food has always been regarded as a sacred ritual throughout this great region, for it is believed that the food a man eats not only nourishes his body, but exalts his soul. Cookery is considered one of the fine arts and an essential accomplishment for every woman. Spices give subtle flavour to the most simple dishes, but always in true Indian cookery there is a very delicate balance of flavours, and the natural taste of each food is retained.

So vast an area, inhabited by a number of races of varying religions and cultures, has naturally developed many local dishes and food customs. The great majority of Hindus are still strict vegetarians, but if flesh foods are eaten, kid and chicken are the ones most commonly used, followed by mutton, beef being absolutely forbidden. Muslims, of course, avoid pork in all its forms, but may eat other meats. In the south and east, rice is the main cereal used; in the north and west chapattis and other breads made from wheat and maize are eaten. Lentils and vegetables are important, with fruit, and perhaps eggs and fish from local rivers and streams. Game and chicken are plentiful for those who can afford them and prawns and sea fish are available in the coastal regions. Mild curds or yoghourt and a kind of cottage cheese are widely eaten, being made into a variety of dishes with vegetables and flavourings. Even the plainest food is made varied and interesting by the use of titbits of contrasting tastes and textures—sweet and sour, salt and bland, nutty and hot, crisp and smooth.

In the north the Muslim religion predominates and kebabs, thick curries known as *kormas*, meat balls and rissoles and the two famous rice dishes, *pellao* and the richer *biryani* are popular.

The traditional way of serving a meal requires a Thali—a medium-sized round metal tray on which the rice, chapattis or other bread are set, the curries and various side dishes being ranged round in small metal bowls. The food is eaten with the fingers, with the aid of the piece of bread, and hands are washed both before and after the meal. If there is a sweet dish to round off the meal it will often take the form of a *hulwa* or *khir*. Delicious fresh fruits, especially mangoes, are of course abundant in many parts. Pan or betel-nut is often eaten after a meal, to sweeten the mouth.

To drink, the people of the south prefer coffee and those of the north, tea; in addition there is a wide choice of fruit juices, either plain or diluted with water or soda water, sherbets and variations of buttermilk, usually diluted with water and sweetened or salted.

In Ceylon, as on the Indian mainland, rice is the staple food and is accompanied by varied curries and side dishes. The curries often contain a large number of ingredients, including much coconut and the local vegetables and fruit. Sea-fish is abundant and there are good supplies of meat and poultry. Maldive fish—imported from the Maldive islands in dried and salted form—is powdered and added to curries. Curries in Ceylon are usually flavoured with mild condiments and not peppery or hot.

Tea, as one would expect in this tea-growing land, is drunk in large quantities.

India, Pakistan and Ceylon

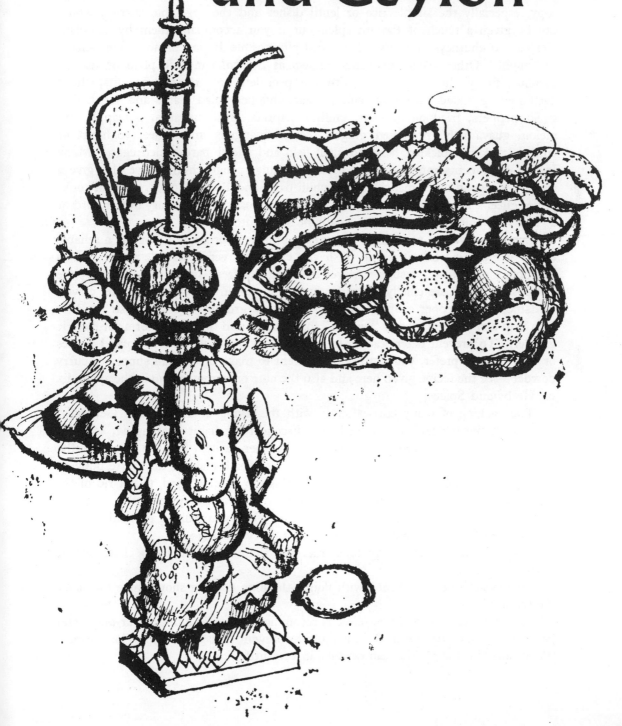

SOME NOTES ON INDIAN COOKING

MANY Indian and Pakistani dishes are quite possible for the English housewife to copy, especially the simple rice or lentil dishes and the vegetable curries, which can be given a touch of Eastern splendour if you accompany them by colourful pickles and chutneys and serve them with picturesque Indian breads—home-made or bought. Other accompaniments (known as *Sambals*) include plain or toasted coconut, finely chopped lemon (with the peel left on), roasted peanuts, sliced cucumber sprinkled with sugar and vinegar, chopped salad plants and vegetables, sweet peppers, fried onion rings, chillies, paprika, fresh bananas, pineapple and melon, guava jelly, preserved ginger, pickled mangoes and limes, yoghourt or curds, dried and pickled fish and shell fish, and sliced hard-boiled eggs. Many Indian condiments can be bought here, including mango chutney (we also give a recipe for a good mock mango relish), chilli paste and Bombay duck. Indian cooks prefer ghee, a rich clarified butter, for cooking purposes, but ordinary butter, lard or a good vegetable cooking fat may usually be substituted.

Curry powder and paste can be bought in prepared form and if you get a reliable brand and use it while it is still fresh you can make very palatable curries. You can obtain even better results however by using the fresh spices of which they are composed; these are chiefly coriander, turmeric, cumin seed, ginger, mace, cloves, cardamom and pepper. Spices should be freshly ground if possible, so the best plan is to buy them in seed or " whole " form and pound them in a mortar or electric grinder. To prevent deterioration, keep them in a dry place in well-corked bottles or tins. If you prefer, you can grind sufficient to make up a small supply of curry powder—see the recipe given here and also the note on *garam masala* in the appendix on Herbs and Spices.

The cooking of many curries starts with the frying of the spices. Generally, begin with the mustard seed (which has disconcerting habit of jumping, so don't be startled); add fenugreek last, as it burns rather easily. Fry the spices gently, turning them frequently, and avoid over-cooking, which makes a dish taste pungent and bitter. If you are using curry powder, this too is often fried, to get rid of the raw taste. The amount of either curry powder or individual spices and condiments can of course be varied to suit your own taste when you make a particular curry.

Here are some other notes about the art of curry-making :

Always cook curries slowly to extract the richness which is so characteristic of the dish.

Curries are rarely thickened with flour—the long cooking should give the sauce the required consistency.

In many recipes a sealed casserole is recommended. Use a thick flour-and-water paste, put round the rim of the casserole to prevent moisture escaping as steam—this means that the cooking can be done in very little liquid.

The coconut milk mentioned in many recipes means an infusion of the flesh, not the liquid found in the fresh nut ; see the recipe on p. 330.

If onions and garlic are fried as a preliminary step, do not allow them to brown unless this is specifically mentioned—to prevent browning, cover the pan with a lid and fry very slowly.

Although in this country we sometimes include apples (as a substitute for mangoes), sultanas, almonds, etc., these are not used in a true Indian curry, though they may appear in the accompanying rice or in pilaus and similar dishes. Another British habit which is not known in India is that of garnishing a dish of curry with rice—the two are always served separately.

The main ingredients of a curry should be so prepared that the curry can be eaten with a spoon.

If you desire a suitable drink to serve with curry, try iced lager or a light white wine.

The rice for curries must be carefully cooked, but it is by no means difficult to get a good result, with every grain separate, and we give some reliable directions. Unpolished rice is more nutritious than polished, and Patna rice is better than Carolina for curries, though either can be used.

SAMBOLS
(CURRY ACCOMPANIMENTS)

Coconut : Slice or grate fresh coconut and serve with chopped green and red peppers. Desiccated coconut may also be used.

Peppers : Red and green peppers can be parboiled, sliced, egg-and-crumbed and then fried, or they can be sliced and used raw.

Bananas : Use firm bananas ; slice them and sprinkle with salt, lemon juice and a little chilli powder.

Aubergine (Egg plant) : Boil until soft, then skin, mash the pulp and add a little finely chopped onion, 1–2 chopped chillies, a little coconut milk to moisten and salt to taste.

Cucumber : Fry a chopped onion and a clove of garlic in a little oil until soft but not coloured, then add the chopped cucumber with a little crumbled Bombay duck, a little curry powder, a squeeze of lemon juice and a little coconut milk. Simmer gently until the cucumber is just soft. Serve hot or cold.

Tomato : Skin and slice several tomatoes, mix with some fresh or pickled green chillies, cut lengthwise, a pinch of ground red chillies and a squeeze of lemon juice ; add salt to taste. Sprinkle with freshly grated or desiccated coconut and a little chopped onion.

Onions : Slice thinly and add lemon juice, seasonings and some chopped fresh (or pickled) chillies.

Potatoes : Cut several cold cooked potatoes into cubes and blend lightly with a few chopped green chillies, a little finely chopped onion or spring onion and some olive oil ; season to taste and add a little lemon juice.

Alternatively, mix some cold mashed potato with desiccated coconut, coconut milk, a little chopped onion and a few coarsely chopped red chillies ; add a little olive oil and lemon juice and season to taste.

Dried Peas : Soak the peas overnight, then simmer them until tender, drain and serve sprinkled with lemon juice and paprika pepper.

Eggs : Cut 2 hard-boiled eggs lengthwise into quarters and lightly blend with 1 finely chopped small-sized onion, 2 fresh (or pickled) green chillies, coarsely chopped, 1 tbsp. lemon juice and salt to taste ; sprinkle with fine desiccated coconut or fresh scraped coconut.

Bombay Duck : This is actually a fish (bummalo), which is sold salted and dried. It is a very popular accompaniment to many curries and is also often used as an ingredient. The smell when it is being prepared is rather unpleasant, but the taste is appetising and attractive.

Bake the pieces of " duck " in a hot oven or toast under the grill until crisp and brown ; if necessary, flatten during the cooking. Alternatively, fry the Bombay duck in hot fat and drain well before serving.

Break the Bombay duck into small pieces or crumble up and sprinkle over the curry at table.

Pickles and Chutneys : Very hot, pungent Eastern chutneys and pickles may be obtained, which are suitable for serving with curries. Mango chutneys, prepared in different ways to give a very sweet, a hot or a mild effect, are among the best-known and most usually served. Salted mangoes are served as an accompaniment to fish curries, and cut-up mangoes, both green and ripe, also mango sauce, are often included as ingredients in the actual curries. Other accompaniments listed by a firm specialising in Eastern foodstuffs include lime, green chillies, lemon, brinjal (aubergine), bamboo, sweet turnip and mustard pickles, tamarind chutney and guava jelly. The taste for some of these is only gradually acquired by the European palate ; others, such as guava jelly, appeal at once to most people.

Poppadums : These savoury wafer-like biscuits are usually purchased as they are laborious to make at home ; stored in an airtight tin, the " raw " product will keep for several months. The white variety are fairly mild, the red one very hot. To cook the poppadums, choose a frying pan much larger than the size of the raw article, as they expand considerably during cooking. Allow 1–2 per person. Place them one at a time in hot fat and fry for about 20–30 seconds, keeping them flat by holding under with a flat draining spoon. When crisp, drain and serve hot.

Alternatively, the poppadums may be heated through in the oven or under the grill.

To eat them, use as an accompaniment to rice or curry, or crumble them over the surface.

Chapattis (Phulkas) : Large, thin, round cakes, made from wholemeal wheat flour, with no leavening and little fat ; they are cooked on a girdle (see recipe).

Parathas are similar, but made with white flour and a little more fat, so that they are more flaky in texture ; they are usually shallow-fried, and can be stuffed with a savoury mixture.

Nan Roti is a slightly leavened baked bread.

Puris (Loochis) are made of wheat flour with fat included, and are deep-fried (see recipe).

RICE COOKERY

Rice is served in various forms in India and

Pakistan—plain boiled, as a curry accompaniment, as a pilau (pellao), or baked, as in a Biryani. Whatever the method, Patna or other long-grained rice gives the best results. Here are two methods of cooking it :

1. Allow ½ lb. Patna rice, 3 pints water and 1 tsp. salt for 4–6 persons. Put the washed rice in fast-boiling salted water and boil for 10 minutes, then drain it in a sieve and pour cold water through to get rid of the loose starch. Put the rice back into fresh boiling water and cook for 2–3 minutes, keep the pan uncovered throughout cooking. Drain the rice and serve (or keep it warm in a cool to moderate oven, covered with aluminium foil or a cloth).

2. Soak the rice for ¼–½ hour in cold water and drain. Put in a pan with fresh cold water, which should come about 1 inch above the rice. Add salt. Put the pan over a high heat, stirring occasionally to prevent sticking. Reduce the heat and cook gently until all the water is absorbed —about 20 minutes—by which time the rice should be tender. Remove from the heat, pour cold water over it, then strain thoroughly. Cover with a cloth and warm through (at a low heat) in the oven.

To Reheat Rice : Put in a pan of boiling salted water, stir and bring to the boil. Drain well before serving.

YELLOW RICE

½ lb. Patna rice	4 whole black peppercorns
2 tsps. salt	
6 cloves	½ tsp. saffron
1 stick of cinnamon	2 tsps. milk
3 bay leaves	A little melted butter

Place all the ingredients except the saffron, milk and butter in a saucepan with 1½ pints rapidly boiling water. When the rice is just tender, drain it through a sieve, but do not remove the spices from it. Mix the saffron with the hot milk. Place the rice in a dish, and pour a little melted butter over it, followed by the saffron and milk mixture. Serve with meat curries, etc.

RICE FOR PELLAO—I

2 onions	A little ground
2 oz. butter	cardamom
1 lb. rice	A few pieces of stick
Stock (preferably	cinnamon
chicken)	A few peppercorns
Salt to taste	A few sultanas
A few cloves	

Mince 1 onion, fry it in the hot butter until pale golden-brown, then add the uncooked rice and fry for about 5–6 minutes. Now add some stock, salt and the spices, adding more stock as the rice swells. When the rice is well cooked, put the pellao in a moderate oven (350° F., mark 4) for ½ hour to dry it off (or it may be dried by placing it in the saucepan over a very gentle heat—but Indian cooks generally find the oven more satisfactory). Slice the other onion, fry it with a few sultanas until golden-brown and crisp and sprinkle the mixture over the rice just before serving.

RICE FOR PELLAO—II

½ lb. Patna rice	1 inch cinnamon stick
6 oz. butter or ghee	2 bay leaves
2 small sliced onions	8 peppercorns
2 tbsps. stoned raisins	Salt
or sultanas	Stock or water
2 tbsps. blanched and	A few cooked peas
toasted almonds	1 tbsp. saffron water
Seeds from 3 cardamoms	

Wash and drain the rice. Put 2 oz. butter or ghee in a saucepan and when hot fry the onions till golden-brown. Now add the rice with the remaining fat and cook, stirring frequently, until the rice has absorbed most of the fat. Add the raisins, almonds, cardamoms, cinnamon, bay leaves, peppercorns and salt. Just cover with hot stock or water, cover the pan and simmer until the rice is tender and all the liquid absorbed. Add the peas and saffron water, stir lightly, put in a heatproof dish and dry off in a moderate oven (350° F., mark 4).

RICE PELLAO WITH PEAS

6 oz. Patna rice	2 small pieces of cin-
2 oz. fat	namon stick
4 cloves	1 tsp. salt
1 small tsp. caraway	4 oz. freshly shelled
seeds and ½ tsp.	peas
turmeric powder	½ pint hot water
(optional)	

Wash and soak the rice for ½–1 hour. Heat the fat in a heavy pan, put in the spices and fry for 1–2 minutes over a very low heat. Add the rice, salt and peas, mix and fry gently for a few minutes, stirring all the time. Add the hot water, mix well and bring to the boil quickly. Put on the lid and turn the heat very low, then cook on top of the stove, or, better still, in a moderate oven (350° F., mark 4) for ½ hour. Serve with meat or vegetable dishes.

Frozen or canned peas may if desired replace fresh ones ; canned peas, being already cooked, should be added after about 15 minutes to allow them time to heat through.

PINEAPPLE PILAU

¼ lb. sugar (preferably   1½ oz. cashew nuts
    brown sugar)   1½ cups Patna rice
1 teacup water   ½ tsp. ground coriander
1 small pineapple   ½ tsp. allspice
1½ oz. almonds

Simmer the sugar and water until syrupy. Add three-quarters of the pineapple, cut into thick chunks, and the nuts. Cook for about 10 minutes, until only a scant cupful of the syrup is left. Meanwhile cook the rice in plenty of boiling salted water until it is two-thirds dry, then drain it. Put the pineapple and nuts into the top half of a double boiler, add the rice and stir in the spices. Pour the syrup over, cover with a folded cloth and steam until the rice is tender. Turn on to a serving dish and garnish with the remaining raw pineapple, cut into very small pieces.

This can be eaten as a dish on its own, or with grilled or barbecued chicken or lamb kebabs.

BENGAL CURRY

4 oz. butter, margarine   A good pinch of saffron
    or dripping   1 tbsp. lemon juice
5–6 oz. thinly sliced   1–1½ lb. tender meat
    onion   or parboiled chicken,
1 clove of garlic   cut in pieces
2 tbsps. curry powder   1 tsp. salt
1 dessertsp. mixed spice   ¾ pint stock

Heat the fat, fry the onion and crushed garlic until well browned, then add the curry powder, spice, saffron and lemon juice and fry again for 5–10 minutes. Add the meat or chicken, salt and stock, and cook, stirring intermittently, for about ½ hour, by which time the stock should be partly absorbed and the curry thickened. Serve with boiled rice.

If the meat is not very tender, cook it first and fry it until lightly browned before adding it to the curry. Chicken should be boned before it is added.

MUTTON CURRY

1 lb. lean mutton   2 tbsps. garam masala
¼ pint yoghourt   ¼ tsp. chilli powder
½ tsp. salt   2 crushed garlic cloves
2 onions   ½ lb. skinned tomatoes
½ oz. ghee or butter   2 oz. creamed coconut

Cut the meat into small pieces, then leave to stand in the yoghourt and salt for ½ an hour. Fry the chopped onions in the fat and add the garam masala and chilli powder; cook for 2 minutes, then add the garlic, meat and sliced tomatoes. Bring to the boil and add the creamed coconut. Place in a casserole, seal and cook for 2½ hours in a very slow oven (275° F., mark ½).

MUTTON AND PINEAPPLE CURRY

1 small pineapple   Salt to taste
1 lb. cooked mutton   6 oz. rice
1 large onion   2 dessert apples
1 tbsp. ghee or butter   ¼ lb. seeded raisins
1 tsp. curry powder

Cut the pineapple in half lengthways and remove the inside, leaving the shell intact. Cut up the centre part. Cut the meat into cubes and chop the onion. Melt the ghee or butter and fry the onion until golden-brown, then add the curry powder, meat, cut-up pineapple and salt. Simmer together over a low heat for 30 minutes, then pile into the heated pineapple shell.

Cook the rice in boiling water and dry it. Meanwhile grate the apples coarsely. Add the apples and raisins to the rice and pile this round the pineapple.

CALCUTTA BEEF CURRY

1 lb. lean beef   1 oz. butter
1 pint water   ½ pint thick coconut
1 tbsp. ground cori-   milk
    ander seed   1 onion, sliced
1 tsp. ground turmeric   1 crushed clove of
1 tsp. ground chillies   garlic
A pinch of ginger   Salt
A pinch of black pepper   Lemon juice

Remove any fat from the meat, cut it into pieces and simmer in the water until just tender. Mix together the ground ingredients and pepper and make a paste with a little coconut milk. Fry the onion and garlic till tender and add the paste, then continue to fry for a further 3–4 minutes. Add the meat and a little stock, bring slowly to the boil and add the coconut milk, salt and lemon juice.

DRY BEEF CURRY

1 lb. beefsteak   A pinch of ground
1 tbsp. ground coriander   cinnamon
1 tsp. turmeric   2 oz. ghee or butter
1 bay leaf   1 finely chopped onion
2 cloves   1 crushed garlic clove
¼ tsp. chilli powder   1 tsp. curry paste
½ tsp. cumin seeds   ½ pint stock or water
Tamarind water   Salt to taste

Cut the beef into small pieces, removing any fat. Mix together the spices and tamarind water to form a paste. Melt the fat and fry the onion and garlic, then fry the spice mixture and curry paste very thoroughly, stirring well. Add the meat and cook it slowly for ½ hour, then add the stock and cook for 1½ hours. Season if necessary and reduce the stock—the meat should be almost dry. Serve with rice.

Dry curries are eaten very frequently in Southern India, though Hindus would make them of poultry or mutton rather than beef.

MADRAS MEAT CURRY

2 oz. chopped almonds	½ tsp. ground chillies
2 oz. butter or cooking fat	A very small piece of cinnamon stick
2 chopped onions	½ tsp. ground cloves
1 clove of garlic	2 tsps. flour
1 tsp. ground coriander seed	1 pint stock or water
1 tsp. black pepper	1 lb. meat (cut into small pieces)
½ tsp. ground cumin seed	2 tsps. turmeric powder
½ tsp. ground cardamom seed	1 tsp. sugar
	Salt to taste
	Juice of 1 lemon

Cover almonds with water, infuse for ¼ hour, then strain. Melt the fat and lightly fry the onions and garlic. Add the spices and flavourings (except the turmeric) and the flour, cook for 5 minutes, then add the stock and meat. Simmer till tender—1½–2 hours. Add the infusion of almonds, the turmeric, sugar and salt, and simmer for 15 minutes. Finally, add the lemon juice and serve with plain boiled rice.

LAMB VINDALOO

1 lb. lean lamb	2 tsps. turmeric
½ tsp. chilli powder	4 garlic cloves
8 peppercorns	3 tbsps. vinegar
½ tsp. pomegranate seeds	1½ oz. ghee or butter
¼ tsp. cumin	½ tsp. salt

Wipe the meat and cut into large pieces. Grind all the spices together and blend with the garlic and vinegar. Melt the fat and add the meat with the salt. Cook in a sealed casserole in a slow oven (300° F., mark 1) for 2 hours until tender.

Vindaloos, in which the meat is often marinaded in vinegar, are typical of Southern India and tend to be hotter than other types; they are often made of the richer meats.

PORK VINDALOO

2 oz. cooking fat	4 cloves of garlic, finely chopped
2 large onions, finely chopped	2 tbsps. vinegar
2 tbsps. curry powder (preferably special vindaloo mixture)	1 lb. fat pork, cut into 1-inch cubes
	Salt to taste

Heat the fat in a saucepan and fry the onions and garlic till the onion begins to change colour.

Add the curry powder and vinegar. (If vindaloo mixture is used, mix it to a paste with a little vinegar before adding it.) Stir well and cook for about 4 minutes over a low heat, taking care not to let it burn. Now add the meat and mix thoroughly, cover tightly and cook over a low heat until the pork is done. Watch constantly, and if necessary add a little water to form a thick, rich gravy. Add salt to taste.

BEEF VINDALOO

6 medium-sized onions	1 lb. rump steak
4 oz. butter or margarine	¼ pint vinegar
2 tbsps. curry powder	Salt

Slice the onions, and with the lid on brown them for 5 minutes in half the butter. Add the curry powder and continue to fry for a further 5 minutes. Cut the steak in pieces, removing any excess fat, and brown it slightly in the remaining butter; then add to the onions and curry powder. Gradually add the vinegar, with a pinch of salt, and simmer slowly for 2 hours, or cook in a slow oven. Garnish with gherkins sliced lengthwise and sliced olives. Serve with plain boiled rice.

BROWN BENGAL CURRY (ANGLO-INDIAN)

Fry 4 oz. onions in 4 oz. butter until nicely browned. Add 1½ lb. fresh rump steak which has been parboiled for 20 minutes in good strong stock and cut in small pieces. Add the meat stock, with a further ¾ pint stock or water, 2 tbsps. curry powder, 1 small tsp. salt and 1 tbsp. cream or milk; 1 tbsp. mango sauce or a slice of coconut is a great improvement. Stir constantly with a wooden spoon till all the stock is absorbed; when the butter separates from the stock, the curry is done.

Serve steaming hot with rice plentifully piled up in a separate dish.

TRIPE CURRY

2 lb. prepared honeycomb tripe	1 pint water in which 1 oz. desiccated coconut has been soaked overnight
2 tsps. butter	
2 chopped onions	
3 chopped garlic cloves	Juice of ½ a lemon
2 tbsps. curry powder or to taste (see over)	Pepper and salt

Cut the tripe into 1-inch squares, cover with cold salted water, bring to the boil and simmer until very tender; drain off the water. Heat the butter and fry the onions and garlic; add the curry powder, fry for a few minutes, then add the tripe, coconut water, lemon juice, salt and pepper. Simmer for 10 minutes.

To make the curry powder, mix together 10 dry pounded chillies, 2 tsps. pounded cumin seeds, 1 tsp. ginger and a good pinch each of powdered cinnamon and turmeric.

HUSAINI (STICK) CURRY

Cut meat or chicken into pieces about 1 inch square, and stick them on to wooden skewers, alternating them with pieces of onion and green ginger. (The skewers should not be longer than 3 or 4 inches and there should be one for each person to be served.) Soak the prepared skewered food for an hour or more in either sour milk or cream. Melt 2–3 oz. butter in a saucepan, add 1 medium-sized onion, chopped fairly finely, and fry until golden-brown. Add 2 tsps. turmeric powder, 1–2 pounded cloves of garlic, a pinch of ground cumin seed, 2 tbsps. coriander seed, roasted and ground, 1 clove, a tiny piece of cinnamon, 3 dried and pounded chillies and a little powdered ginger, if green ginger is not procurable. Fry all these spices, together with the onion, for a few minutes, then add the skewers of meat and fry them also. Add 1 breakfastcup of sour milk or a teacupful of sour cream (that in which the meat has been soaking can be used) and cook very slowly at the side of the stove.

LAMB KOFTA
(MEAT BALL CURRY)

1 lb. lamb	1 tsp. cumin seed
4 oz. butter or mar-	powder
garine	$\frac{1}{2}$ tsp. turmeric powder
2 large onions, sliced	$\frac{1}{4}$ tsp. ginger powder
1 full garlic, peeled and	1 tsp. allspice powder
finely minced	1 lb. tomatoes
2 tsps. chilli powder	2 tsps. salt
2 tsps. coriander powder	1 sprig of fresh mint

Mince the lamb. Heat the fat and fry the onions, remove 1 tbsp. onion when half done and set aside, but brown the remaining onions. Mix the garlic and all the powdered ingredients (using only half the allspice) and blend to a paste with 1 tbsp. water, then add to the browned onion. Add the tomatoes chopped, mix well and fry till soft. Remove 1 tbsp. of this mixture and set aside. Add 1$\frac{1}{2}$ cups hot water and the salt, and mix again. Allow this gravy to simmer for 10 minutes.

Add the onions and spice mixture that were set aside to the minced meat, with $\frac{1}{2}$ tsp. allspice powder and finely chopped mint. Knead thoroughly. Moisten the palm of your hand with water and form the mince mixture into balls

the size of a small walnut. Gently drop these, one at a time, into the slowly simmering gravy— do not stir. Simmer gently for $\frac{1}{2}$ hour, shaking the pan gently once or twice to mix the Koftas with the gravy.

Koftas are particularly popular in the Deccan and Central India; they may be made of many different ingredients, as in these recipes.

BEEF KOFTA

1 lb. finely minced beef	Pepper and salt
1 cup white breadcrumbs	1 egg to mix
2 tbsps. finely minced	Juice of $\frac{1}{2}$ a lime or
onion	lemon
2 minced garlic cloves	Egg and browned
1 pinch of powdered	breadcrumbs to
ginger, cinnamon and	coat
cloves	Fat for frying

Mix all the ingredients together, moistening with the slightly beaten egg and lemon juice. Form into small balls, dip in beaten egg and breadcrumbs, and fry.

To make the curry sauce, heat $\frac{1}{2}$ oz. fat, fry 2 tsps. chopped onion and 2 tsps. curry powder until the onion is soft, add $\frac{1}{2}$ pint stock and 2 tsps. powdered Bombay duck; bring to the boil and simmer till the sauce has thickened. Add the meat balls and simmer for 10 minutes.

SIMPLE MEAT KOFTA

6 small onions	2 oz. butter
1 lb. freshly minced meat	Salt
2 tbsps. curry powder	1 lb. tomatoes
1 clove of garlic	$\frac{1}{2}$ pint stock

Mince 3 onions and add to the meat, together with 2 tsps. curry powder; knead, divide into small portions, and roll into balls. Slice the rest of the onions, chop the garlic and fry in the butter till just turning golden-brown. Add remaining curry powder, some salt and the quartered tomatoes, add stock and leave to cook for a minute or two. Carefully add the meat balls, cover with a lid and cook very gently for 20–30 minutes, taking care not to break the balls. Serve with rice.

CHICKEN KOFTA

1 lb. chicken	$\frac{1}{2}$ tsp. chilli powder
2 small onions	$\frac{1}{2}$ tsp. salt
4 roasted red chillies	1 small egg
1 garlic clove	Fat for frying
$\frac{1}{2}$ tsp. ground coriander	

Mince the chicken, onions, chillies and garlic twice. Add the coriander, chilli powder and salt, mix thoroughly and bind with beaten egg. Shape into small balls, drop into hot fat and fry

until cooked through. Serve in curry sauce—see Beef Kofta recipe.

NARGESI KOFTE
(PAKISTAN " SCOTCH EGG ")

12

5 eggs	2 medium-sized onions
$\frac{1}{2}$ tsp. red chilli powder	About 3 cloves of garlic
$\frac{1}{2}$–1 tsp. salt	2 oz. ghee or butter
$\frac{1}{2}$ tsp. garam masala	$\frac{1}{2}$ tsp. turmeric powder
A few leaves of mint, finely chopped	$\frac{1}{2}$ tsp. coriander powder
1 lb. finely minced meat	2 tsps. tomato purée or tomato paste

Hard-boil 4 eggs and shell them. Mix 1 raw egg, half the chilli powder, half the salt, the garam masala and the mint very thoroughly with the minced meat. Wet your hands with water, take about a quarter of the meat and flatten it. Put an egg into the meat and cover it completely, making sure there are no cracks or uncovered spaces. Repeat with the remaining eggs. Put into a greased dish and bake in a hot oven (450° F., mark 8) for a few minutes, until brown—do not leave them in the oven too long or they will crack.

To make the gravy, mince or grate the onion and garlic finely. Fry them in the ghee or butter until light brown. Add the remaining chilli powder and salt, the turmeric and coriander, then the tomato purée ; continue to cook, stirring for 5 minutes, then add 1$\frac{1}{2}$ pints water. When the mixture boils, put in the nargesi kofte very carefully and let them cook for about 1 hour over a medium heat. The gravy should not be too thin or too thick. Take the kofte out, cut them into halves lengthways, and put them into a serving dish. Pour some gravy over them. Sprinkle with a pinch of garam masala and garnish with finely chopped mint.

MEAT KORMA

1 lb. beef or mutton	$\frac{1}{2}$ tsp. ground cumin
$\frac{1}{2}$ pint sour curds or yoghourt	$\frac{1}{2}$ tsp. ground chillies
2 garlic cloves, finely chopped	$\frac{1}{2}$ tsp. ground mustard
	1 oz. ghee or butter
$\frac{1}{2}$ tsp. ground ginger	1 onion, finely chopped
$\frac{1}{2}$ tsp. pepper	Stock or water if necessary
$\frac{1}{2}$ tsp. ground poppy seed	Salt
	Lemon juice

A Korma is a Muslim dish, rich and spicy, but not hot. The meat or poultry is very often marinaded in a mixture based on sour curds (yoghourt), known in Northern India as Dhye and in the South as Tyre.

Cut the meat into convenient-sized pieces and marinade in the curds or yoghourt with the

spices for $\frac{1}{2}$ hour or so. Heat the fat and fry the onion lightly. Add the marinade mixture and cook gently until the meat is tender. If possible, cook the curry without adding any stock or water—the curds will help to form a thick rich gravy. Just before serving add salt and lemon juice to taste. Serve with rice in some form—a pellao, kitchrie, etc.

CHICKEN KORMA
(CHICKEN CURRY)

1 roasting chicken (about 2 lb.)	$\frac{1}{2}$ tsp. chopped garlic
	1 bottle plain yoghourt
1 medium-sized onion	1 small piece of sliced ginger
$\frac{1}{2}$ lb. ghee or butter	
$\frac{1}{2}$ tsp. ground turmeric	1 tsp. cloves
3 tsps. coriander	Black pepper
$\frac{1}{2}$ tsp. ground chillies	Cumin seeds (whole)
Salt	

Divide the chicken into pieces.

Brown the sliced onion in the butter and then take it out. Put in the powdered spices, garlic and 1 cup water and cook for about 3 minutes, stirring. Add the chicken, mix it well with the spices, add a little water and cook for about 15–20 minutes with the lid on.

When the liquid is almost absorbed, stir the chicken, etc., for about 5 minutes, until golden-brown. Take the browned onion, crush it with a spoon and put it in the saucepan with the yoghourt and the rest of the spices. Add 1 cup of water and leave it on a very low heat. If the chicken is not quite tender by this time, add a little more water and cook for a little longer. It will take about 1–1$\frac{1}{2}$ hours in all. Serve with rice. 6 servings.

CHICKEN DOPYAZA

2 lb. skinned jointed chicken	Seeds of 1 cardamom
	1 tbsp. ground turmeric
1 tsp. ground ginger	1$\frac{1}{2}$ tbsp. ground cumin
1 tsp. salt	1 tbsp. ground coriander
2 lb. onions	$\frac{3}{4}$ pint yoghourt
1 crushed garlic clove	$\frac{1}{2}$ pint water
5 tbsps. ghee or butter	8 peppercorns

If possible, use an enamelled iron casserole. Wipe the chicken joints, prick with a fine skewer, rub in the ginger and salt and leave for $\frac{1}{2}$ hour. Roughly chop 1 lb. onions and crush the garlic. Fry the chopped onions in the fat until evenly browned, then add the garlic ; remove the onion and drain. Cook the cardamom seeds in the fat for a minute. Place the chicken in the fat with the turmeric, cumin, coriander and yoghourt, and cook until the yoghourt is almost absorbed. Pound the cooked onions (or pulp them in an electric liquidiser), add the water and pour over the chicken joints. Slice remainder of the onions thinly, put on top with the peppercorns, cover tightly and cook in a slow oven (325° F., mark 2) for 1 hour.

The name *dopyaza* means " twice onion " and, strictly speaking, in these curries, onions should be added in two different forms, at two stages of the cooking, as in this recipe. However, a number of authentic recipes do not use this method.

MEAT DOPYAZA

1 bottle of plain yog-hourt	1 tsp. each (whole) (black) peppers, cloves and cumin
1 lb. meat, cut in small pieces	½ lb. onions, sliced
3 or 4 red chillies (whole)	1 tsp. garlic, sliced
¾ lb. butter or mar-garine	1 small piece ginger, sliced
	Salt

Mix the yoghourt, meat, salt and all the spices together. Melt the butter in a fairly big saucepan and add all the other ingredients. Cook for about ½ hour, stirring from time to time. When all the liquid is absorbed, brown for a little while over a low heat. If the meat is not quite tender, add about 1 cupful of water and leave for another 10 minutes on a very low heat.

BENGAL CHICKEN CURRY

4 oz. butter	1 tbsp. curry powder
2 onions	2 tbsps. tomato paste
1 clove of garlic	Salt
1 chicken	1 tbsp. milk
¾ pint stock	Lettuce to garnish

Melt the butter and brown the sliced onions and chopped garlic. Cut up the chicken and add with the remaining ingredients. Simmer until most of the stock is absorbed—when the butter separates from the gravy, the curry is ready. Garnish with shredded lettuce and serve with a dish of boiled rice.

MADRAS CHICKEN CURRY

2 large onions	1 clove of garlic (pounded)
1 coconut	A little green ginger (pounded)
1 small chicken (or 1 pheasant, or 2 partridges)	1 heaped tbsp. curry powder
4 tbsps. butter	A little salt

Pound one onion and chop the other. Grate the coconut, soak in a breakfastcup of boiling water and then strain off the milk, squeezing it well to get out all the juice; add another ½ cup

of boiling water to the grated nut, and repeat the process, then discard the coconut. Cut the bird into pieces of equal size; the neck, back and giblets can all be used in the curry. Fry the chopped onions golden-brown in the butter, moisten the pounded garlic, onion, ginger and the curry powder with a little of the coconut milk, and add. Fry well, taking care not to let the mixture catch at the bottom of the saucepan, then add the bird and fry the pieces for a few minutes. Add the salt and the remainder of the coconut milk and cook slowly until the gravy is quite thick. It is essential to cook this curry slowly over a very low heat.

DECCAN DUCK CURRY

1 duck	A 2-inch piece of stick cinnamon
2 oz. butter or mar-garine	2 cardamoms
1 onion, sliced	1½ tbsps. curry powder
1 clove of garlic, crushed	Coconut milk
	Salt
2 cloves	Lemon juice

Divide the duck into joints. Melt the butter and fry the onion and crushed garlic till just tender. Pound together the cloves, cinnamon and cardamom seeds, add the curry powder and mix thoroughly. Add to the onion and continue to cook slowly for a further 5 minutes. Add the duck and sufficient water to form a thickish sauce; mix well, cover the pan and simmer till the duck is tender—this will take about 1½ hours. Add 2 tbsps. thick coconut milk, salt and lemon juice to taste, just before serving.

SEEK KEBAB
(SKEWERED CROQUETTES)

1 lb. minced beefsteak	1½ tsps. salt
1 medium-sized onion, finely chopped	½ tsp. ground ginger
	½ tsp. chilli powder
2 tsps. mixed herbs	A little oil
2 tsps. lemon juice	

Mix all the ingredients except the oil, form the mixture into small sausage-like shapes and put these on skewers. Brush the Kebabs over with oil, and grill, turning them frequently, until brown.

SHAMI KEBAB
(MINCED MEAT AND SPLIT PEA CAKES)

2 oz. split peas (yellow)	Salt and black pepper to taste
1 lb. minced meat	
2 onions	1 egg
4 cloves of garlic	4 oz. frying fat
1 pint water	

Clean and wash the split peas; mix with the

meat, chopped onions and garlic, salt and pepper, then boil with 1 pint water till the liquid is completely absorbed. Pass through the mincer twice and mix with the beaten egg. Take 1-oz. portions of the mixture to form small cakes and fry in a little fat until brown.

KEBAB ZEERA
(CUMIN-FLAVOURED CROQUETTES)

1 lb. lean lamb	2 tsps. cumin
1 onion	1 tbsp. chopped parsley
A pinch of cayenne	Salt
pepper	Fat for frying

Mince the lamb twice with the onion. Add the seasoning and blend thoroughly. Shape into sausages about 4 inches long and ¾ inch in diameter. Fry in shallow fat until evenly browned. Serve in a curry sauce.

This recipe is typical of the Eastern type of Kebab, consisting of minced ingredients formed into rissole-like shapes rather than chunks of meat grilled on skewers.

PARCHA SEEK KEBAB
(ROAST STUFFED MUTTON)

2 lb. best end of neck or breast of mutton	1 tsp. cardamom powder
1 large onion	1 tsp. cumin powder
1 clove of garlic	Salt and pepper
4 green chillies	Dripping
1 tsp. ground ginger	

Ask the butcher to bone and roll the meat. Mince the onion, garlic and chillies and mix with the rest of the ingredients, except the dripping. Unroll the meat, spread the mixture over it and re-roll, then secure with a skewer. Roast the meat with dripping in a moderately hot oven (425° F., mark 7) for about 1 hour. Leave to cool, and serve cut in slices.

The spicy stuffing in this recipe makes an agreeable change from the forcemeat generally used in this country.

INDIAN MUTTON CASSEROLE

¾ lb. lean mutton	1 carrot
1 tsp. made mustard	4 potatoes
1 tbsp. piquant table sauce	1 tsp. mixed herbs
	Rind of 1 lemon
3 oz. bacon	½ pint stock
1 small onion	

Spread the mustard over the sliced mutton and soak in the piquant sauce for 15 minutes. Fry the chopped bacon and onion in a flameproof, lidded casserole and add the meat, carrot, potatoes, herbs and thinly peeled lemon rind tied in muslin. Pour the stock over all and

simmer, tightly lidded, in a moderate oven (350° F., mark 3) for 2 hours. Serve with boiled rice and mango chutney.

DECCAN MEAT BURTAS

1 large onion, boiled	1 small tsp. salt
1 lb. cooked meat or fish	1 tsp. lemon juice
Cayenne pepper	2 oz. butter
Mace	

Pound the onion well. Next pound the meat or fish (underdone beef is the best), add as much pepper as will stand on a silver threepenny piece, the same quantity of mace, the salt and a few drops of lemon juice. (If preferred, use a smaller quantity of Cayenne.) Melt the butter in a saucepan, add all the ingredients, and cook very slowly for about ¼ hour. Serve on buttered toast or fried bread.

MUTTON PELLAO

2 lb. fat mutton	A little garlic
1 quart cold water	3 oz. butter
3 eggs	1 tbsp. curry powder
1 lb. potatoes	1 tsp. salt
½ tsp. saffron	¼ tsp. turmeric powder
1 lb. rice	2 oz. almonds
1 lb. onions	2 oz. raisins

Cut the mutton into small pieces, place in the cold water and cook until the meat is tender and the stock reduced by half. Boil the eggs and the potatoes, and soak the saffron in 1 tsp. hot water for 1 hour. Meanwhile, wash the rice well, parboil, drain, and spread on a tray to cool. Chop the onions and garlic and fry them in 2 oz. of the butter; add the curry powder, salt and turmeric, and continue cooking for 5 minutes. Strain the saffron water, add it to the onion, mix with the mutton stock, and pour this over the rice. Put into a saucepan alternate layers of rice, mutton, sliced hard-boiled eggs and potatoes, cover the saucepan with a well-fitting lid, and simmer slowly for 30 minutes. Blanch and slice the almonds, stone the raisins, and fry in 1 oz. butter. Serve the pellao piled on a hot dish, and garnish with the fried almonds and raisins.

CHICKEN PELLAO

Use a good-sized tender fowl (or young turkey or a similar amount of best end neck of mutton). Boil the fowl (or meat) with 1 lb. gravy beef and 2 cupfuls water; add 2 large onions, a little salt and a small pinch of ground ginger; when quite cooked and tender remove the meat and set it aside, then pour the stock into a bowl. Slice 1–2 large onions lengthways. Warm a pan and melt 4 oz. butter, put in the sliced onions and

13

fry till light brown, then set aside. Then take ½ lb. rice, which has been soaked and drained; fry the rice with the butter and onions; when all the butter is absorbed add a few cloves, 1–2 cardamoms, some chips of stick cinnamon, 2–3 peppercorns, a blade of mace and 1 tsp. salt. Mix up the whole and pour chicken stock over it till the rice is entirely covered. Close the saucepan immediately with a close-fitting cover and put on a slow heat. As the gravy becomes absorbed reduce the heat, shaking the saucepan occasionally or stirring the mixture with a wooden spoon to prevent burning.

Brown the boiled meat in a pan with some butter. When ready, serve on a hot dish and cover entirely with the rice pellao. Garnish with sliced hard-boiled egg and some large stoned raisins, or fried rolled bacon.

This dish takes time to make but is well worth the trouble. It is representative of the great variety of pellaos served for every kind of celebration and special occasion, especially in the Northern regions. Biryanis (see the two recipes on this page) are very similar.

MADRAS CHICKEN PELLAO

1 chicken	2-inches of cinnamon
3–4 shallots	Salt
4 oz. butter	4 oz. sultanas
1 lb. Patna rice, washed, soaked and drained	2 oz. blanched and halved almonds
6 cardamoms	Hard-boiled egg and fried onion garnish
6 cloves	

Boil the fowl till tender in just sufficient water to cover it, adding the shallots. Heat the fat and fry the spices and rice for about 5 minutes, stirring all the time. Add sufficient chicken stock to come an inch or so above the rice. Add salt, and simmer over a low heat till the water is absorbed and the rice cooked. Add the sultanas and almonds. Put a layer of rice on a flat dish, add the fowl (whole or jointed), then cover with rice and garnish.

MEAT BIRYANI

½ lb. onions, sliced	8 cardamoms
½ lb. ghee or butter	8 cloves
1 lb. meat from leg of lamb	2 bottles yoghourt
	1 lb. rice
6 cloves of garlic, sliced	Milk
2 medium-sized onions, minced	4 ground cardamoms
	2 tsps. ground saffron
1 piece fresh ginger, chopped	2 tsps. ground mace

Fry the onions in the ghee or butter and put in the meat, then add a little water, the garlic, minced onions, ginger, cardamoms and cloves. Cook well, then add the yoghourt, mixing well. Boil the rice separately in boiling water and when nearly cooked, strain and rinse with cold water. Spread the rice over the cooked meat in layers, sprinkling with milk and the ground spices. Cover with a damp cloth under the lid and cook in a moderate oven (350° F., mark 3) for about 45 minutes.

CHICKEN BIRYANI

2 lb. rice	½ oz. whole cumin seed
2 lb. chicken, cut up	3 oz. sultanas
1 clove of garlic	3 oz. seeded raisins
1 oz. whole coriander	1 grain of saffron mixed with 2 tsps. water
3 onions, halved	
2 tsps. salt	2 oz. browned salted almonds
¾ lb. margarine	
½ oz. whole black pepper	

Wash the rice and leave it in water for at least 3–4 hours before cooking. Boil the chicken in about 2 quarts water with the garlic, coriander seeds (tied in muslin), onions and salt, until fairly tender—about 2 hours—then remove from pan. Strain the broth and measure it—if less than 3 pints, make up with water.

Put the fat in a large saucepan, add the chopped cooked onions and fry gently over a low heat until brown; add 1 cup water and continue to cook until this evaporates. Add chicken and fry for a short time, then add the pepper and cumin seed and fry these for 2–3 minutes. Add the chicken broth and let it boil, then add the rice and sultanas and half of the raisins, mix well, and sprinkle in the saffron. Cover tightly and cook over very low heat until the water has completely evaporated. Pile in a dish and garnish with the remaining raisins and the almonds.

MULLIGATAWNY SOUP

1 oz. ghee or butter	1 tsp. coriander seeds
2 chopped onions	½ tsp. turmeric
1 garlic clove, crushed	A pinch of chilli powder
1½ pints rich meat stock	20 peppercorns
	3–4 fenugreek seeds
A little lemon juice or tamarind water	A few cumin seeds
	Salt
A tiny piece of fresh ginger	¾ pint coconut milk

Heat ½ oz. ghee in a thick pan and fry the onion and garlic. Add the stock and a little lemon juice or tamarind water, then simmer, uncovered, for 20 minutes. Prepare a *masala* by melting ½ oz. ghee and frying the ginger, turmerics, coriander, chilli and peppercorns for a few minutes, adding the fenugreek just at the

11

end. Add the cumin seeds to the stock and after a few minutes, add the *masala*. Simmer, stirring constantly, for a few minutes. Season with salt and cool slightly. Add the coconut milk and serve. (If you wish to reheat it do not allow it to boil.)

FISH CURRY

1 lb. filleted fish (e.g., cod or halibut)	2 oz. butter
	2 tsps. curry powder
2 small onions, sliced	Salt to taste
A little garlic	1 tomato, quartered

Prepare the fish in the usual way.

Fry the sliced onions and garlic in the fat. Stir in the curry powder and salt, then add the tomato and 1 tbsp. water, to make a thick paste. Put in the pieces of fish, seasoned with curry powder and salt, and fry them until brown. Pour in 1 teacupful warm water and let the curry cook in the pan with the lid on till the fish is tender when tested; take care not to let it get mashed. Serve with rice.

Lemon juice may be included if desired, and the tomato may be replaced by tomato paste, a little extra stock or water being added.

This is the most usual method of cooking fish in India. Good fish to use in this country are mackerel, fresh herring, eels, hake, cod, halibut, turbot, etc., mackerel being the best.

FISH MOLI

1 small onion	$\frac{1}{2}$ pint coconut milk
2 oz. butter	Salt to taste
A little green ginger	1 lb. fish
A few green chillies	$\frac{1}{4}$ tsp. turmeric
$\frac{1}{2}$ oz. flour	

Fry the sliced onion in the butter with the ginger and the chillies. Stir in the flour and cook slowly for 3 minutes; add the coconut milk and salt and stir slowly until the mixture comes to the boil. Add the fish and the turmeric. Let it simmer for 20 or 30 minutes, or until the fish is well cooked. Serve on a hot dish.

This is a Southern Indian dish, with a basis of coconut milk and rather mild seasonings and spices.

PRAWN AND POTATO CURRY

12 oz. fresh prawns	1 tsp. garam masala
$\frac{1}{2}$ lb. small new potatoes, sliced	$\frac{1}{4}$ tsp. chilli powder
1 chopped onion	3 medium-sized tomatoes, sliced
1 oz. butter	$\frac{1}{2}$ pint hot water
1 tsp. salt	1 tsp. lemon juice
$\frac{1}{2}$ tsp. ground turmeric	Chopped parsley

Shell the prawns and wash well. Prepare the potatoes. Fry the onion in the butter, add the salt and spices and fry for 2–3 minutes. Add the tomatoes and potatoes, fry a little longer and add the hot water; bring to the boil, lower the heat and cook for 15–20 minutes. Add the prawns, lemon juice and parsley and simmer for 1–2 minutes. Serve with rice and poppadums.

HINDUSTAN FRIED FISH

2 lb. fish	Wholemeal flour or breadcrumbs for coating
1 tsp. ground chillies	
$\frac{1}{2}$ tsp. turmeric powder	
1 onion, finely chopped	Fat for frying
Juice of 1 lemon	

Prepare the fish. Mix thoroughly the chillies, turmeric, onion and lemon juice. Rub this mixture over and into the fish, and allow it to stand for 30–45 minutes—the fish will then be well impregnated. Dip the fish in the flour or breadcrumbs and fry in hot fat.

FISH PELLAO

$1\frac{1}{4}$–$1\frac{1}{2}$ lb. filleted cod	2 onions
2 oz. ghee or butter	$\frac{1}{2}$ lb. Patna rice
1 tsp. turmeric	$1\frac{3}{4}$ pints water
$\frac{1}{2}$ tsp. chilli powder	2 bay leaves
1–2 tsps. garam masala	Tomatoes to garnish
2 tsps. lemon juice	

Skin the fish, wipe and cut into cubes. Melt half the ghee or butter and add the turmeric, chilli powder and garam masala; fry for 5 minutes and add the lemon juice. Cook the fish in this mixture for 10–15 minutes, then remove and place on a plate. Melt the remaining fat in a second pan and fry the sliced onions until pale golden-brown. Add the washed rice and continue frying for 3–5 minutes. Add the gravy mixture from the first pan, with the water and bay leaves, and cook for 20–30 minutes, by which time the liquid will be absorbed and the rice tender. Add the fish, stir gently and serve garnished with sliced raw tomato.

FISH BIRYANI

1 lb. fresh haddock fillet	$2\frac{1}{2}$ oz. ghee or butter
	Seeds from 2 cardamoms
3 tbsps. olive oil	3 cloves
A little flour	2 tsps. ground turmeric
1 tbsp. aniseed	1 tbsp. ground coriander
$\frac{1}{2}$ lb. Patna rice	Salt
$\frac{1}{2}$ pint yoghourt	1 skinned tomato
1 chopped onion	

Skin the fish and cut into pieces, rub lightly with oil and leave to stand for 15 minutes, then wipe to remove the excess oil. Meanwhile, fry the onion in $\frac{1}{2}$ oz. fat and pound with the cardamom seeds and cloves. Toss the fish in a little flour seasoned with some of the aniseed. Boil the rice for 10 minutes. Marinade the fish for ½ hour in ¼ pint yoghourt, well blended with the fried onion mixture. Put the fish and the marinade in a heavy fireproof casserole, sprinkle some of the turmeric over, add 1 oz. fat, some salt and half the coriander and put the rice on top. Pour on the rest of the yoghourt, dot with the remaining fat and coriander, turmeric and aniseed and add the sliced tomato. Cover with the lid and seal the edge with flour-and-water paste. Shake lightly, cook over a high heat for 4–5 minutes, then put in a very slow oven (275° F., mark ½) and cook for 35 minutes.

EGG KITCHRIE

½ pint dried peas or split peas	Salt and pepper
	Powdered mace
½ pint Patna rice	2 large onions
4 oz. butter	4 hard-boiled eggs

Soak the peas overnight in cold water. Cook them in boiling salted water until nearly soft, then add the rice, and simmer gently until both peas and rice are cooked—add extra boiling water if necessary. The rice should take about 10–15 minutes, but it must not be at all mushy. Drain, add half the butter, some salt and pepper and powdered mace to taste, and keep hot. Meanwhile peel and slice the onions thinly and fry in the remaining butter until they are soft and yellow. Cut the hard-boiled eggs in quarters, and mix them and the onions with the rice. Serve hot.

EGG CURRY WITH GREEN PEAS

3 oz. cooking oil or dripping	A little chopped garlic
	1 cup coconut milk or stock
4 tsps. minced onion	
½ tsp. salt	6–8 hard-boiled eggs
1 tsp. ground turmeric	½ pint shelled young peas
1 tsp. ground chillies	
½ tsp. ground ginger	

Melt the fat and fry the onion, cooking it until brown. Add the condiments and spices and the coconut milk or stock. Cover and simmer for about 10 minutes, then add the eggs and green peas, and continue to simmer until the peas are tender.

Extra vegetables, cooked meat, etc., may be added if desired.

VEGETABLE BURTAS

Parboil 2 carrots, 1 large onion and 1 pint fresh peas. Chop the carrots and onions, or put them through a mincer. Put 2 oz. butter or margarine in a saucepan, add the minced or chopped vegetables, pepper, salt and a pinch of mace, and cook slowly for 15 minutes. Cayenne pepper and a little curry powder may also be added, if liked. When the vegetables are thoroughly cooked, add 1 tsp. cornflour blended with a little cold stock or milk, and continue to cook for another 8–10 minutes. Serve on crisp biscuits or toast.

If preferred, tomatoes can be used instead of, or in addition to, the peas.

POTATO BURTAS

½ lb. potatoes	½ an onion, sliced very fine
Salt and pepper to taste	
	1 green chilli, sliced

Boil the potatoes; when soft, cool and mash them; sprinkle with salt and pepper and mix in the onion and the chilli. Shape into a flat round cake and mark it into quarters, but do not separate the quarters. Serve cold, as a relish with curry and rice or with cold meat.

KITCHRIE
(RICE AND LENTIL DISH)

6 oz. rice	3–4 cloves
2 oz. lentils	A small piece of cinnamon stick
2½ oz. butter	
1½ pints water	1 bay leaf
Pepper and salt	1 or 2 sliced onions
Peppercorns	1 hard-boiled egg
A little cardamom	

Wash the rice and lentils, then fry in 1½ oz. butter for 6–8 minutes. Add the water, pepper, salt and other spices and cook thoroughly, adding more water if necessary, until the grains are soft. Finish cooking on a very low heat, to dry off any surplus moisture; put it into a moderate oven (350° F., mark 4) for ½ hour or so, stirring it from time to time to separate the grain. Meanwhile, fry the onions in the remaining fat and cut the egg in quarters. Place the rice and lentils on a hot dish and garnish with the crisp fried onions and quartered egg.

VEGETABLE CURRY—I

1 cauliflower, cut in large pieces	1 tbsp. turmeric
	1½ tbsps. mild curry powder
6 tomatoes	
6–8 small potatoes, quartered	½ tsp. salt
	2 oz. butter
¼ lb. peas	6 small onions
¼ lb. French beans, sliced	½ a garlic bulb
	½ pint stock

Place the raw vegetables on a large plate. Mix the spices and salt and sprinkle over the vegetables. Melt the butter in a heavy pan and sauté the finely shredded onions and garlic. Add the vegetables, then a little stock, cover, bring to the boil and simmer until tender. Serve with dry boiled rice.

VEGETABLE CURRY—II

½ lb. prepared mixed vegetables
1 oz. fat
1 onion
1 clove of garlic
½ tbsp. ground coriander
½ tsp. ground turmeric
½ a bay leaf
A pinch of salt
2–3 cloves
A pinch of ground cumin seed
¼ tsp. ground ginger
A little mustard seed
Tamarind water or weak vinegar
A little stock

Dice the vegetables. Melt the fat and fry the thinly sliced onion and the garlic. Make a paste of the other ingredients with the tamarind water or vinegar and fry it for 5 minutes, then add the vegetables and stock and simmer until cooked.

DRY VEGETABLE CURRY

½ lb. potatoes, peeled
¼ lb. peas
1 small cauliflower
1 lb. onions
½ lb. tomatoes
1 clove of garlic
2 oz. butter
1 tbsp. curry powder
Salt

Cut the potatoes into ½-inch slices; shell the peas, divide the cauliflower into florets, and cut up the onions, tomatoes and garlic. Melt the butter, sprinkle in the curry powder, add the vegetables and some salt, and cook in their own juice over a moderate heat, until tender—stir now and again to prevent sticking. Serve the curry with a dish of boiled rice.

BHUJIA
(DRY POTATO AND GREEN PEA CURRY)

1 lb. potatoes
1½ lb. green peas
3 oz. oil or margarine
½ tsp. cumin seeds
7 oz. chopped onions
1 full garlic (cleaned and chopped)
½ tsp. turmeric powder
6 oz. fresh tomatoes
1 tsp. ginger powder
2 tsps. coriander powder
Salt
½ tsp. chilli powder

Peel the potatoes and cut into 1-inch cubes. Shell the peas. Pour the oil into a saucepan and when hot add the cumin seeds, followed by the chopped onions. As the onions are just turning golden, add the chopped garlic and the turmeric powder; stir well and allow to brown. Now add the chopped tomatoes and cover the pan until these are cooked. Next add the ginger powder, coriander powder and salt to taste; lower the heat and allow to cook to a thin paste.

Now add the potatoes and green peas and mix well. Add 1 cup water, mix and cover with the lid; simmer over a low heat until the vegetables are cooked. Add the chilli powder and remove from the heat. Serve garnished with fresh coriander leaves, if available.

DECCAN LENTIL CURRY

½ lb. lentils
1 small onion
2 red chillies
1 bay leaf
A 1-inch piece of stick cinnamon
3 cloves
2 whole cardamoms
1 oz. fat
1 clove of garlic
½ tsp. ground turmeric
¼ tsp. ground cumin seed
A pinch of ground chillies
A pinch of ground ginger
2 tsps. ground coriander
Tamarind water or vinegar
¼ pint tomato juice

Cook the lentils with the finely chopped onion, the chillies, bay leaf, cinnamon, cloves and cardamoms in salted water until they are soft but not mushy. Melt the fat in a saucepan and fry the finely chopped garlic. Meanwhile mix the turmeric, cumin, ground chillies, ginger and coriander to a paste with a little tamarind water or vinegar; fry for 5 minutes in the fat, add the tomato juice and lentil mixture and continue cooking for 15–20 minutes. The curry will vary in thickness according to the amount of liquid added: if it is too liquid, boil it rapidly for a short time to reduce it.

PUMPKIN CURRY

1 lb. pumpkin
2 small onions, sliced
2 oz. butter
½ tsp. curry powder
Salt to taste
½ lb. tomatoes

Peel the pumpkin and slice thickly. Fry the sliced onions in the fat till brown. Add the curry powder and salt and mix well. Add the cut-up tomatoes, pour in a little water and stir to form a thick, rich paste. Put in the pumpkin pieces and add a little water if necessary—pumpkin is very watery. Let the curry simmer over a very gentle heat, stirring occasionally, but take care not to mash the pumpkin pieces. Remove from the heat when the gravy becomes thick.

MARROW CURRY

1 lb. prepared marrow
2 large onions
1½ oz. butter
2 tsps. curry powder
2 tsps. turmeric powder
2 tsps. salt
2 large tomatoes
2 tsps. lemon juice

Cut the marrow into cubes. Slice the onions and fry them in the melted butter until they are golden-brown. Stir in the curry powder, turmeric and salt, add the sliced tomatoes and cook for a few minutes. Add the marrow, stir all well together and cook gently for 15–20 minutes; then shake the pan over heat without the lid until the marrow is dried. Sprinkle on the lemon juice, cook for another minute, serve very hot.

STUFFED GREEN PEPPERS

6 green peppers	1 tsp. piquant table sauce
1 lb. haddock	1 tsp. vinegar
2 oz. butter	2 sprigs of mint, chopped
2 large onions, finely minced	2 slices of stale bread
Pepper	1 egg
½ tsp. salt	Breadcrumbs
1 lb. tomatoes, peeled	Fat for frying

Carefully cut round the green peppers and remove the stalks; scoop out the seeds. Boil the fish and remove the bones and fins. Heat the butter in a saucepan and fry the onions until half done—do not brown. Add the fish, pepper and salt, mix thoroughly; then add the chopped tomatoes and fry well. When fairly dry, remove from the heat, add the sauce, vinegar and chopped mint and allow to cool. Soak the bread in water, squeeze out and combine with the fish mixture. Stuff the green pepper cases with this mixture and coat the top with beaten egg and breadcrumbs. Fry in a little butter, placing crumbed side down; turn over and fry the other side for a minute.

RAITHA
(YOGHOURT AND CUCUMBER)

117

½ a cucumber, peeled and sliced thin	½ green pepper or 2 small green chillies
1 tsp. sugar	¼ tsp. pepper
1 tbsp. vinegar	½ tsp. salt
2 chopped tomatoes	2 bottles plain yoghurt
½ small chopped onion	Chopped parsley

Place the sliced cucumber in a bowl, sprinkle with sugar and vinegar and leave to marinade for 10 minutes. In another bowl mix lightly the chopped tomatoes, green pepper and onion; strain off the liquid from the tomatoes and season with pepper and salt. Add the bottles of yoghourt and mix. Combine the two mixtures and garnish with chopped parsley.

BHINDI MASALA
(STUFFED OKRA)

1 lb. okra (bhindi)	1 tsp. ground cumin
½ oz. ghee or butter	¼ tsp. ground turmeric
1 small onion, very finely chopped	¼ tsp. ground chillies
	A few pomegranate seeds
1 tsp. ground coriander	

Chop a small piece from the broad end of the okra, then wipe the vegetable with a damp cloth. Melt a knob of fat in a shallow pan, add the onion and cook for 5 minutes. Add the coriander, cumin, chilli and turmeric; crush a few pomegranate seeds and add to the other spices, then cook for 2–3 minutes. Slit the centre of the okra lengthwise, open out and stuff each piece with the spice mixture. Add a little more fat to the pan and arrange the stuffed okra in a single layer over the base. Sauté gently for a few minutes, but do not brown it. Cover the pan with a lid or with aluminium foil. Reduce the heat to the lowest mark and cook till the okra is tender but still crisp.

BEANS IN AKNI

2 lb. green beans	1½ tsps. crushed coriander seeds
1 small finely chopped onion	1½ tsps. crushed fennel seeds
1 crushed garlic clove	3 tbsps. lemon juice
⅛ tsp. powdered ginger	2 oz. butter
2 pints water	

Break the beans in pieces, or slice. Now prepare the "akni." Put the onion, garlic, ginger, coriander and fennel in a muslin bag, place in water, bring to the boil, simmer for 15 minutes, cool and remove the spices. Just cover the beans with the akni liquid and simmer until tender. Drain off the liquor and toss the beans in lemon juice and melted butter. Serve hot.

Akni can be kept for a short time and used for stock.

FOOGATH OF BEANS

Soak ½ lb. haricot or butter beans overnight, then cook till tender; drain well. Heat 2 oz. fat and lightly fry the following for 3–4 minutes: 1 onion, 2 finely sliced cloves of garlic, 6 thin slices of fresh or pickled green ginger, and 2–3 fresh or pickled chillies, finely chopped. When the onion is cooked, add the beans, 1 tbsp. desiccated coconut and salt to taste.

KOOTU
(VEGETABLE STEW)

¾ lb. French beans	2 onions, cut in eighths
¾ lb. carrots	½ pint stock or potato water
1 small cauliflower	
1 oz. ghee or butter	¼ of a fresh coconut
1 large onion, finely chopped	1 tsp. chilli powder
	Salt

Break the beans in half, scrape and slice the carrots and divide the cauliflower into sprigs. Melt the fat and sauté the chopped onion and then add the carrots, beans, cauliflower and other onions; stir and "sweat" slowly for minutes. Gradually add the stock. Cook till tender with the lid off the pan. Grind or mince the coconut with the chilli powder and add to the vegetables; season with salt and bring to simmering point. Serve hot.

SUKKE
(SPICY POTATO DISH)

1 lb. potatoes	A small piece of
¼ a small fresh coconut	tamarind
3 roasted red chillies	1½ oz. ghee or butter
1 tsp. turmeric	2 chopped onions
6 bay leaves	½ lb. tomatoes
¼ tsp. coriander seeds	½ tsp. mustard seeds
3–4 fenugreek seeds	Salt

Boil the potatoes in their skins, drain, peel and cut into cubes. Grind or mince the flesh from the coconut and add the pounded chillies and turmeric. Fry the bay leaves, coriander seeds, tamarind and lastly the fenugreek seeds for a minute or two in 1 oz. fat. (Fenugreek seeds burn easily.) Sauté the onions in ½ oz. fat, until tender, and add to the potato. Add the coconut mixture to the cooked potatoes with the skinned chopped tomatoes and reheat. Remove from the heat and season with mustard seeds and salt.

PEAS AND CARROTS

8 spring onions	¼ tsp. chilli powder
1 tsp. mixed herbs	(optional)
2 tsps. ghee or butter	½ lb. carrots, cut up small
1 tsp. turmeric	¼ pint water
1 tsp. garam masala	1 packet frozen peas
1 tsp. salt	2 tsps. lemon juice

Slice the onions and fry with the herbs in the ghee or butter. Add the turmeric, garam masala, salt and chilli powder, then the carrots, and fry gently for a minute. Add the water, cover, and cook for about 10 minutes, then put in the peas, and continue cooking until cooked and dry. Add the lemon juice just before serving.

DHAL
(LENTIL PURÉE)

4 oz. red lentils	1 medium-sized onion
½ pint cold water	Fat for frying
Pepper and salt	1 oz. butter or dripping

Wash the lentils—there is no need to soak them—put them into the cold water, add pepper and salt, and allow them to cook steadily, adding more water if they get too dry. Meanwhile, chop the onion finely and fry it. When the lentils are tender, remove them from the heat and stir vigorously. Add the dripping and

the fried onion to the lentils and stir over the heat to blend well. Serve with curry.

CURRY POWDER

1 oz. turmeric	2 oz. cumin seed
½ oz. coriander seed	1½ oz. fenugreek
½ oz. red chillies	½ oz. powdered ginger
½ oz. black pepper	¼ oz. poppy seed

The strength of curry powder is a matter of individual taste and it is often more satisfactory to mix your own rather than to use the bought variety.

If not already powdered, crush the ingredients in a pestle and mortar and mix them all well together. Sieve to remove any imperfectly crushed seeds and pound these again, then add to the mixture. Stored in an airtight jar, curry powder will keep quite satisfactorily. This recipe is for a powder of medium strength; a hotter one can be made by increasing the quantity of chillies.

PUSTHOLES AND SAMOSAS
(PASTIES)

These pasties or puffs are the Eastern equivalent of the sandwich; they are made in various sizes and shapes, with savoury or sweet fillings. Pustholes often have a curry filling, and samosas usually have a type of freshly made chutney.

Pastry for Indian Pasties

2 oz. butter	Sour milk, milk or milk
½ lb. fine white flour	and water
¼ tsp. salt	Fat for frying

Rub the fat into the flour, add the salt and make into a paste with the liquid, using rather less than ¼ pint. Knead until the pastry feels soft and velvety, and is extremely pliable, then roll it out to the thickness of a penny. Cut 2-inch rounds and place a spoonful of filling in each. Wet the edges and fold one half over the other, press down, and fry in fat till golden-brown. Drain on kitchen paper.

Mince Curry Filling for Pustholes

2 oz. fat	2 whole cardamoms
12 spring onions, or one medium-sized onion	A 2-inch stick of cinnamon
1 clove of garlic	1 heaped dessertsp. curry powder or paste
½-inch piece green ginger	½ lb. finely minced lean mutton or beef
2 whole cloves	Salt and lemon juice

Melt the fat and lightly fry the chopped onions, garlic, ginger and spices. Add curry powder or paste, mix, and cook for 2–3 minutes. Add meat, mix well, cover, and simmer until the meat is cooked—10–20 minutes. Watch carefully, and if necessary add a very little water. Add salt and lemon juice.

VEGETABLE SAMOSA

½ lb. potatoes   ½ lb. self-raising flour
½ lb. green peas   1 oz. butter
Salt and pepper to taste   ½ lb. fat for frying

Peel and dice the potatoes and boil with the peas; when cooked, strain and add salt and pepper. Mix the flour, a pinch of salt and the butter, add the water and make into a pastry dough. Roll out the pastry ⅛ inch thick and cut into 3-inch circles. Add 2 tsps. of the potato and pea mixture, fold over the pastry and seal the edges. Fry in deep fat till golden-brown.

CHAPATTIS
(INDIAN GIRDLE CAKES)

½ lb. wholemeal flour   ¼ lb. ordinary white
Water   flour

Take a large deep dish and knead the flour in it with water to make a soft dough, and meanwhile heat a girdle. Take small pieces of the dough and roll them first into small balls, the size of an apple, then flatten them with a rolling-pin on a pastry board or marble slab into thin discs the size of a pancake. Cook them on a greased girdle on both sides; press the cake gently with a clean cloth before taking it off the girdle till it is full of air like a balloon. It will puncture automatically—when the air has escaped, put the chapatti into a clean basket, to keep it warm. It should really be served hot direct from the girdle.

Chapattis are eaten with curries as a substitute for rice or as a second course after rice and curry.

In England they may be bought at shops stocking Eastern foods or from Indian restaurants.

PURIS
(INDIAN FRIED BREAD)

4 oz. plain wholemeal   Pepper and salt
   flour   4 tbsps. water
A knob of ghee or   Fat for frying
   butter

Place the flour in a small bowl and rub in the fat; season with pepper and salt. Gradually work in just sufficient water to give a pliable dough and knead well. If time permits, cover and leave for an hour. Roll out wafer-thin between sheets of silicone paper, then cut rounds about 3 inches in diameter; if not to be fried at once, cover lightly with a damp cloth. Fry in hot fat, one or two at a time—drop the raw *puri*

into the fat by slithering it on to the side quickly, hold it down with a wide draining slice, lightly press to distribute the air, which causes the characteristic balloon shape. Turn once, remove carefully, drain on absorbent paper and serve at once. Allow 4–6 per person.

COCONUT MILK FOR USE IN CURRIES, ETC.

Fresh coconut gives a richer and more mellow result, but the desiccated nut is quite satisfactory. Grate the flesh and pour over it enough boiling water to cover. Infuse for 20–30 minutes (or 1 hour in the case of desiccated coconut), then squeeze the liquid out through a fine strainer. A thinner milk may be obtained by using the grated coconut a second time.

The coconut may be dried slowly and used in curry or as a separate accompaniment.

MOCK MANGO CHUTNEY (HOT)

1½ lb. sugar   2 oz. chillies
3 pints vinegar   ½ lb. ground ginger
5 lb. apples   2 oz. mustard seed
1 lb. chopped dates 1 dessertsp. ground
2 oz. raisins   cinnamon
2 oz. currants   3 bay leaves
2 oz. garlic cloves 4 oz. salt

Make a syrup with the sugar and vinegar. Peel, core and slice the apples and put them in a preserving pan with the dates, dried fruit and the garlic, pour the vinegar syrup over them and boil till they are tender. Allow to become quite cold, then add the remaining ingredients. Bring slowly to the boil and simmer for ½ hour, stirring all the time. Add more salt if required. Allow to become cold before bottling. Store for about six months before using.

ORIENTAL CHUTNEY

2½ lb. dried apricots   2 oz. salt
1½ lb. dried peaches   ¼ lb. garlic
1½ lb. stoned dates   1 oz. ground cloves
2 lb. sultanas   1 oz. cinnamon
1½ lb. seedless raisins ¼ tsp. cayenne pepper
1½ lb. currants   2 pints vinegar
6½ lb. Demerara sugar

Mince or cut into small pieces the apricots, peaches and dates. Wash all the dried fruits. Cover with water and stew until tender and thick. Add the rest of the ingredients and boil rapidly, stirring well, for about ½ hour, or until the contents of the pan are thick. Taste and add more salt if required. Put into hot jars, cover and store 6 months before using.

If dried apricots are not available, use twice the quantity of fresh fruit, and a little less water.

HOT INDIAN CHUTNEY

3 lb. apples	4 oz. salt
3 lb. marrow	½ oz. chillies
2 lb. plums	½ oz. cloves
3 lb. tomatoes	½ oz. white peppercorns
2 lb. onions	2 oz. mustard seed
½ lb. shallots	½ oz. bruised root ginger
½ lb. garlic	3 pints vinegar
2 lb. sugar	

Boil the apples until beginning to soften. Chop the rest of the fruit and vegetables and sprinkle with sugar and salt. Leave to stand for 12 hours. Tie the spices in a bag, then place all the ingredients in a pan and bring to the boil and simmer gently for about 8 hours. If possible this chutney should be stored for several months before using; this ensures that the flavour of the ingredients matures fully.

For a less pungent chutney, use only ¼ lb. garlic.

SHAHI TUKREY
(FRIED BREAD SWEET)

½ lb. ghee or lard	1¼ lb. sugar
6 slices bread, 1 inch thick	1 tsp. saffron, crushed and soaked in a little milk
1 cup milk and 1 cup water	
2 tbsps. blanched and sliced almonds	2 tbsps. sliced pistachio nuts

Heat the fat in a large frying pan and then fry pieces of bread till light brown; remove. In the same pan, bring the milk and water to the boil; add the sugar and boil for 10 minutes. Arrange the browned pieces of bread in the same pan (not placing one on top of the other). Pour the saffron on the slices and cook over a low heat till the moisture is absorbed. Sprinkle with chopped nuts and cardamoms to decorate and serve in a flat dish.

COPHERA HALVA
(COCONUT PASTE CAKES)

½ lb. desiccated coconut (medium grade)	1 pint milk
½ lb. caster sugar	Ground pistachio nuts
	Sugar syrup

Put the coconut, sugar and milk into a saucepan and cook over a low heat until the mixture turns a pinkish brown and is *very* thick. Turn into a greased tin and flatten with a palette knife. Make a separate paste with the ground pistachio nuts, adding sugar syrup until of a spreading consistency. Spread a layer of this mixture over the coconut candy and allow both to set firm. When set, cut into fancy shapes and serve with 4 o'clock tea.

KELA HALVA
(BANANA SWEET)

6 ripe bananas	2 oz. walnuts or almonds, chopped
4 oz. granulated sugar	
½ pint water	A few cardamoms
4 oz. ghee or butter	Saffron for colouring

Mash the fruit to a pulp and place in a saucepan with the sugar and water; stir over a low heat until the sugar has dissolved, then boil rapidly for 5 minutes. Take off the heat and gradually stir in the melted fat. Replace on the heat and stir constantly until the mixture begins to form a firm ball in the pan—about 10–15 minutes. Stir in the chopped nuts and crushed cardamom seeds, colour if desired with saffron, and turn on to a flat dish. When cool, cut into 1½-inch squares.

KHIR
(MUSLIM SWEET RICE)

½ lb. Patna rice	A few bruised cardamom seeds
2 pints milk	
1 small can evaporated milk	1 clove
	3 oz. seeded raisins
¼ lb. sugar	2 oz. shredded almonds
Grated rind of ½ a lemon	1½ tbsps. rosewater

Wash the rice and simmer in milk until it is quite thick and tender. Add the evaporated milk and sugar and stir. Add the lemon rind, cardamom seeds, clove, raisins and almonds and cook very slowly for a further 15 minutes. Just before serving, add the rosewater.

GUJRELA
(PAKISTAN CARROT SWEET)

1 lb. carrots	2 tbsps. rice
½–1 oz. almonds	Sugar to taste
3 pints milk	

118

Peel and wash the carrots and then grate them, leaving out the hard core. Soak the almonds in hot water. Put the milk on a very slow heat for 2 hours. Boil the rice separately and add the carrots and boiled rice to the milk. Cook till they are well done and the mixture is thickened. Add sugar, and sprinkle with chopped skinned almonds.

BOMBAY PUDDING

Boil 2½ tbsps. semolina in 1 pint milk until it becomes thick; stir in 2 oz. fresh butter, then pour on to 2–3 plates and let it get cool and firm.

Dust over with flour and fry in lard, butter or dripping. Cut into three-cornered pieces as you would a teacake, and serve with a thin sauce of sherry or lemon juice and sugar.

SOJI HULWA
(SEMOLINA PUDDING)

A few cloves	4 oz. ghee or butter
A pinch of cardamom	1 cup of semolina
A pinch of cinnamon	2 cups of sugar
1 oz. cleaned raisins	1½ cups of water
1 oz. chopped almonds	Almonds and cream

Fry the spices, raisins and chopped almonds in the hot ghee or butter then sprinkle in the semolina and fry until brown, stirring the whole time. Add the sugar and water, mix, cover and lower the heat, then simmer gently, stirring frequently, for 10–15 minutes, until quite dry. Serve hot on a flat dish, decorated with whole almonds and accompanied by cream.

GALAB JAMUN
(SWEET SEMOLINA CAKE)

½ lb. semolina	2 lb. sugar
¼ lb. milk powder	1 quart water
¼ lb. ground almonds	Inner seeds of 6
2 eggs	cardamoms
Oil for deep frying	A few sprigs of saffron

Mix semolina, milk powder and ground almonds. Add 1 tbsp. warm water and the eggs, and knead into a dough and knead well for 10–15 minutes. Add some more water gradually, but do not make the dough too soft. Form into small rolls about 2 inches long and fry in deep boiling oil until golden-brown. Drain well and while hot drop them into the hot syrup made by boiling the sugar, water, cardamoms and saffron together until a heavy syrup is formed.

Ceylon

DRIED PRAWN CURRY

This is typical of the many delicious fish curries which are popular in Ceylon. Wash and soak about ½ lb. dried prawns for 3 hours, then grind thoroughly into a paste. Mix in 1 tbsp. rice flour and shape into small round balls. Fry in oil until nicely browned, then fry about 15 green chillies in the same oil. Make a curry sauce which includes coconut milk and some small pieces of coconut, and add the chillies and prawn balls.

GINGER-CURRIED SHRIMPS

Put into a large pan 1¼ pounds cleaned raw shrimps, 1 medium-sized onion, sliced, 2 cloves of garlic, sliced, ⅛ tsp. cayenne, ⅛ tsp. ground turmeric, 1½ tsps. salt, 2 cinnamon sticks, 2 pieces of green ginger and 1 cup milk; cover and simmer for 10 minutes.

Heats 2 tbsps. salad oil in a small frying pan and sauté 1 medium-sized sliced onion till tender; stir in 2 tbsps. lime juice and 1 tsp. sugar.

Stir 1 tsp. cornflour into ¼ cup milk, then pour into the shrimp mixture, stirring. Add the sautéed onion and cook till thickened. Serve over hot fluffy rice, with Egg and Onion Sambol.

FRESH PRAWN CURRY

1 pint prawns or 1 doz.	Salt
Dublin Bay prawns	1 tsp. sugar
2 oz. butter	1 tsp. ground cloves
1 onion	1 tsp. ground cinnamon
1 clove of garlic	2 oz. coconut, infused
1 tbsp. flour	½ pint stock
2 tsps. turmeric powder	1 tsp. lemon juice

Shell the prawns. Melt the butter and add the finely chopped onion and garlic; fry them lightly, then add the flour, turmeric, 1 tsp. salt, sugar, cloves and cinnamon. Cook gently for 10 minutes, then add the strained coconut infusion and the stock. Simmer gently for 10 minutes, add the cooked prawns and lemon juice and reseason as necessary. Cook for a further 10 minutes, then serve with rice.

SEENI SAMBOL
(PRAWN SAMBOL)

Fat for frying	A few cloves
2 large onions, chopped	A small piece of
Curry leaves	cinnamon stick
2 bulbs of garlic, chopped	2 ripe tomatoes
A few slices of ginger,	½ cup milk
chopped	A little tamarind
A little chilli powder	1 tsp. sugar
A few cardamoms	Salt

Heat 1 tbsp. fat and lightly fry a little of the onion with the curry leaves. Mix the remaining onion, garlic, ginger, prawns and chilli powder. Fry all together with the cardamoms, cloves and cinnamon, for about 5 minutes, stirring all the time. Now add the tomatoes and cook for a few minutes longer; add the milk and cook for about ½ hour over a low heat. Dissolve the tamarind in a little water and add to this; lastly, add 1 tsp. sugar and salt to taste.

EGG AND ONION SAMBOL

Arrange in a salad bowl 1 large onion, thinly sliced, 1 medium-sized cucumber, thinly sliced, and 1 large green pepper, sliced into rings ⅛ inch thick. Toss in a dressing made of ⅓ cup lemon juice mixed with ⅓ cup cold water, 1 tsp. sugar, ½ tsp. salt and ½ tsp. pepper. Chill. Just before serving, toss the salad well and garnish with 3 halved hard-boiled eggs. Serves 6.

DRY POTATO CURRY

1 lb. potatoes	3 tbsps. butter
2 tsps. chilli paste	2 sliced onions
Salt to taste	Lemon juice

Cook the potatoes in their skins, peel and cut into rounds; add the chilli paste and salt. Heat the butter and cook the onions till soft, add the potatoes and cook over a low heat for 10 minutes. Stir well, and finish cooking over a very low heat, until quite dry. Sprinkle with lemon juice.

POTATO BURTHA

1 small green pepper	Juice of ½ lemon
1 onion	Salt and pepper
1 lb. cold mashed potato	

Slice the pepper very thinly and grate the onion as finely as possible. Mix with the potato, lemon juice and seasonings until the mixture is quite smooth. Serve cold.

Burthas can be made with almost any cooked vegetable such as marrow, aubergine, tomato, etc.

STUFFED CHILLIES

½ doz. tender green chillies	2 tsps butter
¼ lb. cheese	1 tsp. sugar
1 tsp. mustard	Salt to taste
	Chopped cashew-nuts

Boil the chillies in salted water for a few minutes, split them lengthwise and remove the seeds. Make a paste with all the ingredients except the nuts; add the nuts and fill the chillies with this mixture. Alternatively, pipe the filling to make it look more attractive, and top each chilli with half a cashew-nut.

CHICKEN CURRY

Fat for frying	2 tsps. curry powder
1 onion	1 good tsp. chilli powder
Curry leaves (omit if necessary)	½ tsp. turmeric powder
2 cardamoms	2 ripe tomatoes
A piece of cinnamon stick	Salt
2 cloves	2 tsps. vinegar
4 good-sized pieces of chicken	Milk or yoghourt
	Lemon juice if required

Melt 1 tbsp. fat and fry to a light brown colour the onion, curry leaves, cardamoms, cinnamon and cloves. Mix the chicken with the curry powder, chilli powder and turmeric and fry all for about 10 minutes. Add the tomatoes, salt to taste and vinegar, cover and cook over a low heat till the chicken is done, then add the yoghourt or milk and taste for salt and acid; if necessary, add a little lemon.

Note : " Curry leaves " are from a purely local herb, unobtainable in this country.

YELLOW RICE

2 cups rice	3–4 cloves and cardamoms
1 onion, finely chopped	½ tsp. turmeric powder
Ghee or butter	3½ cups milk and water, salted
A few curry leaves	Eggs or potatoes to garnish
A piece of cinnamon stick	

Wash the rice and leave to drain. Fry the onion in the fat with the curry leaves, cinnamon, cloves, cardamoms and turmeric, then add the rice and fry all for a few minutes longer. Add sufficient salted liquid to come about 1¼ inches above the rice. Cook over a good heat till the liquid boils, then cover the pan, reduce the heat and cook for about 10 minutes. If all the water has evaporated before the rice grains are cooked, add a little more liquid, cover and cook for a further 5 minutes on a very low heat. Before dishing up, remove all the curry leaves, etc.; decorate with hard-boiled eggs which have been lightly fried and cut in halves or quarters, or with potatoes, cut in fine strips and fried.

PINEAPPLE CURRY

½ oz. fat	1 tsp. dry mustard
1 tbsp. sliced onions	A pinch of turmeric powder
1 pineapple or 1 tin of pineapple rings	Ground cinnamon and cumin to taste
2 tsps. crushed Bombay duck	Salt to taste
6 pounded chillies	

Melt the fat and fry the onions; add the pineapple juice and then the rest of the ingredients and simmer for 10–15 minutes.

BANANA PUFFS

Sieve 2 cups flour, 2 tsps. sugar and ½ tsp. salt into a bowl; rub in ½ cup butter, then blend in ½ cup buttermilk and knead lightly. Cut 1 large ripe banana into ½-inch cubes and toss with ¼ cup flaked coconut and 1 tsp. lime juice.

Put the dough on a lightly floured surface and roll out about ¼ inch thick; using a 2¾-inch cutter, cut into about 24 rounds. Put on half the rounds, 1 tbsp. of the banana mixture, brush the edges of the pastry with lightly beaten egg white, then top each with a second round; press the edges together with a fork.

Heat 1½ inches salad oil in a large pan to 360° F., then fry 5 or 6 puffs at a time until golden, turning them once; drain on a paper towel. Serve warm or cold.

In recent years, Chinese food has become extraordinarily popular in Western countries and Chinese restaurants are springing up in every town. The larger number of these restaurants offer Cantonese cooking, for the Cantonese have always been much more addicted to travel than other Chinese people. It is Cantonese food therefore that has become accepted as typically Chinese. There are, however, four other distinct types of cooking. Fukien is famous for soups, for fish and for spring rolls ; Shantung for Peking Duck and wine sauces ; Honan for sweet and sour dishes and carp ; Szechuan for the use ot spices and hot peppers.

Traditional Chinese cookery is a complicated art, brought to a fine point of perfection through the centuries. The Chinese have always been epicureans, but they are also thrifty and capable of producing delicious dishes from unpromising material. Chinese dishes are blended with great care and precision and the texture of food is considered almost as important as its flavour. Bamboo shoots, water chestnuts, celery and all crisp raw or lightly cooked vegetables help to give subtlety to the various dishes. This short cooking-time for vegetables and, indeed, all foods, lends great interest to the dish.

Chinese meals generally consist of rice or noodles, with soup and an assortment of different dishes, carefully chosen to complement each other, from which the eater may make his own selection. A typically Chinese table setting would consist of the rice bowl on its own saucer, in front of the guest ; a soup bowl, a tiny wine cup hardly bigger than a thimble, a small bowl for condiments, a porcelain spoon and a pair of chopsticks. Each diner has his own bowl of rice and larger bowls and dishes containing soup and five or more different selections of food are placed in the middle of the table for everyone to help himself. At a dinner party the host and hostess may have an extra pair of particularly long chopsticks, with which they will pick out special titbits to place on a guest's plate.

Wine is drunk during the meal, served warm in tiny cups. Chinese wines are distilled from rice or millet and rice wine is very similar to a medium dry sherry. In fact, sherry makes a very acceptable substitute if you are anxious to serve a typically Chinese meal. If you prefer to offer wine, a dry white wine such as Graves goes best with Chinese food.

Tea is, perhaps, the national drink of China, served in handleless porcelain cups, without milk or sugar. There are three main categories of tea ; green, black and oolung all of which are available in many different types. Chinese tea is often scented with petals of jasmine, chrysanthemum or other fragrant flowers ; it should be made with freshly boiling water and never served too strong, as this is apt to give it a faintly medicinal or herbal taste and destroy the aroma which is so much esteemed by the Chinese who inhale the bouquet much as a connoisseur of wine does.

China

SOME NOTES ON CHINESE COOKING

THE English housewife who is anxious to prepare an authentic Chinese meal at home, must be prepared to go to some trouble, for the Chinese themselves spare no pains to achieve their subtle and delicate results.

There are four main methods of preparing food in China.

1. *Sautéeing.* The pan is oiled, preferably with peanut oil and made very hot. If meat and a green vegetable are to be used, the vegetable is cooked first for a minute, until it turns bright green. It is then put aside while the pan is reheated and oiled and the meat sautéed. Soya sauce or other liquid is added when the meat is half done. The vegetable is returned to the pan when the meat is nearly cooked and the mixture is stirred constantly for half a minute or so, seasonings being added just before the dish is ready. The liquid may be thickened with cornflour if desired. Meat should be sliced, shredded or diced small for sautéeing; vegetables are sliced crosswise or diagonally and all ingredients should be prepared before cooking starts and added to the pan according to the length of time they take to cook. They should all be cooked and ready together. Soya sauce should not be added to white meats, as it makes them brown.

2. *Red cooking.* This is a type of slow stewing in soya sauce.

3. *Deep frying.* The food, cut into medium-sized pieces, is generally marinated for a short time before frying. It may also be dipped in batter.

4. *Steaming.* Food is placed in tiers of perforated containers—often bamboo baskets—over boiling water so that the steam actually touches the food. Containers, plates and water must all be hot before the food is put in.

Cooking utensils include the *kuo*, a kind of frying pan with a rounded bottom; several sharp, heavy knives to use for chopping and mincing; a thick chopping block and a cutting board. Chopsticks are used not only for eating but for numerous culinary processes, such as whisking, draining, mixing and so on.

COLD CELERY HORS D'ŒUVRE

6 stalks of celery	½ tsp. sugar
1 tsp. soya sauce	1 tsp. sesame seed oil
½ tsp. salt	

Cut the celery into sections about ½ inch wide and 1½ inches long; blanch them in boiling water for 1 minute, then drain. Arrange on a serving plate and leave in a cold place for at least an hour. Mix the other ingredients, making sure that the sugar has dissolved. Half an hour before serving the hors d'œuvre pour the sauce over the celery and allow it to marinade. Serve cold.

MUSHROOM SOUP

1 small clove of garlic	2 pints chicken and
Oil for frying	pork stock
4 oz. mushrooms	Sesame oil
1½ oz. salted ginger	Salt

Crush the garlic, put it in a hot oiled pan and cook for a few seconds, then remove. Cook the peeled mushrooms in the pan for 5 minutes. Add the ginger and stock and simmer gently for 2 hours. Remove the ginger, add the salt and a few drops of sesame oil and stir well.

If salted ginger is not available, substitute ordinary root ginger.

BEEF CHOWDER

2 quarts beef stock	½ lb. minced beefsteak
5 oz. rice	Sesame oil
1 oz. noodles	1 tsp. soya sauce
Oil for frying	Salt and pepper
1 oz. fresh ginger,	1 beaten egg
finely chopped	Spring onions to garnish

Place the beef stock and rice in a saucepan and cook slowly for 2½ hours. Fry the rice and noodles in the hot oil for a few seconds, then remove the noodles. Add the ginger and the minced meat separately to the rice mixture and cook for about 10 minutes. Just before serving, season the chowder with sesame oil, soya sauce and salt and pepper. Place a little of the beaten egg in each of 4 bowls and pour the chowder over; garnish with spring onions, sliced into fine " curls."

EGG FLOWER SOUP

2 pints chicken stock	½ tsp. salt
6 eggs	2 finely chopped spring
2 tbsps. soya sauce	onions
1 tsp. vinegar	

Heat the chicken stock in a saucepan. Meanwhile beat the eggs well and then pour in a thin stream into the soup, stirring all the time. Add the soya sauce, vinegar and salt to taste and simmer for about 1 minute. Serve garnished with the chopped spring onions.

BEEF AND WATERCRESS SOUP

3–4 oz. watercress	2 pints chicken broth
½ lb. lean beef	(made up with water
1 tbsp. soya sauce	if necessary)
1 tsp. oil	½ tsp. sesame seed oil
1 tsp. salt	

Wash the watercress very thoroughly, discard the hard stems and leave to drain. Finely dice the beef, put into a bowl and mix well with the soya sauce, oil and salt, then allow it to stand for about 30 minutes. Bring the chicken broth to the boil, add the watercress, stir well and when it comes to the boil again add the sesame oil and the meat. Simmer until the meat is cooked—15–20 minutes—and serve very hot.

BIRDS' NEST SOUP

3 oz. dried birds' nest	2 egg whites
1 tbsp. sherry	1 tbsp. cornflour
1 pint chicken stock	1 small tsp. monosodium
1 pint ham stock	glutamate
3 oz. cooked chicken	1 oz. chopped ham to
meat	garnish

Soak the birds' nest in boiling water for 6 hours, drain, then add the sherry and ½ pint

hot water to it and simmer for ½ an hour. Add the two kinds of stock and simmer for 15 minutes. Mince the chicken and beat it up with the egg whites, then add this to the boiling soup, whisking all the time. Blend the cornflour with a little water, and stir in this and the monosodium glutamate. Simmer for a further 10–15 minutes and garnish with the ham.

TING WAR GAI LAP TONG
(BIRDS' NEST SOUP WITH CHICKEN)

2 oz. dried birds' nest	Stock
10 oz. chopped raw chicken	Salt and pepper
2 oz. bamboo shoots	Sesame oil
2 oz. button mushrooms	Soya bean sauce
2 oz. Chinese ham	

Soak the birds' nest in hot water for 3–4 hours, put it in a saucepan of boiling water and boil for 5 minutes, then drain and put into a basin, with 6 oz. of the chopped chicken. Put the basin in a steamer and steam for 6 hours. Remove the chicken and discard it. To the remaining 4 oz. chicken add the diced bamboo shoots, button mushrooms and ham. Put the birds' nest in a saucepan, cover with stock, boil for 5 minutes and add the bamboo shoots, mushroom, chicken and ham. Season with salt and pepper and add sesame oil and soya bean sauce to taste.

CHICKEN NOODLE SOUP

3 oz. raw chicken meat	Salt
2 oz. bamboo shoots	1 tbsp. vesop (a con-
3 oz. ham	centrated vegetable
2 pints chicken stock	extract)
1 oz. egg noodles	1 tbsp. sherry

Slice the chicken, bamboo shoots and ham into matchstick strips, then simmer them in the stock for 10 minutes. Add the noodles and salt and simmer for a further 5 minutes. Add the vesop and sherry and boil gently for 3 minutes.

SOLE SAUTÉED IN EGG

1½ lb. fillet of sole	2 tbsps water
3 eggs	2 spring onions,
Salt	finely chopped
2 tbsps. cornflour	2 slices of ginger,
4 tbsps. oil	finely chopped
1 tbsp. sherry	

Cut the fish into pieces about 1½ inches long. Beat the eggs lightly and add ¼ tsp. salt. Slowly fold in the cornflour and mix together till it is smooth. Dip the fish pieces in this mixture till they are well covered. Heat the oil and when it is very hot, sauté the fish for 2 minutes on one side and 1 minute on the other.

To the remaining egg mixture, add ½ tsp. salt, the sherry, water, onion and ginger; blend well, add to the fish and cook for about 2 minutes, or until the sauce thickens, stirring constantly and turning the fish two or three times. Serve very hot on a shallow platter.

FOO YUNG LOONG HAR
(LOBSTER OMELETTE)

4 oz. lobster meat	4 eggs, well beaten
½ oz. onions	Salt and pepper

Chop the lobster and onions into small pieces. Place the onions in a hot oiled pan and cook for ½ minute; add the lobster and cook for 2 minutes. Season with salt to taste. Add the beaten eggs, mix all together thoroughly and cook for 1 minute. Add a little pepper, then shake the omelette over frequently, so that each side will be properly done; cook for 1 minute.

SUBGUM CHOW GOONG YUE CHU
(FRIED SCALLOPS WITH MIXED VEGETABLES)

7 fresh scallops	¼ oz. Wun Yee (lichen)
3 oz. onions	if available
1 small stick of celery	Stock
2 oz. water chestnuts	Pepper
3 oz. bamboo shoots	Cooking sherry
2 oz. cucumber	Sesame oil
½ oz. mushrooms	Soya sauce

Remove the shells from the scallops and clean thoroughly. Cut all the vegetables, etc. (except the lichen) into fine pieces, put in a hot oiled pan and cook for 1 minute. Cover with soup stock, cover the pan and cook for 1 minute. Take out the vegetables and place in a dish. Place the scallops in a hot oiled pan, add a little pepper and sherry and cook for 1 minute. Add the vegetables to the scallops and cook for 2 minutes. Add a little water, sesame oil and soya sauce and cook for a further minute.

FRIED PRAWNS

10 large prawns	1 spring onion, cut
2 oz. butter	in 1-inch pieces
1 tbsp. chopped parsley	½ tsp. sugar
1 tbsp. finely shredded	1 tbsp. white wine
fresh ginger	1 tbsp. soya sauce
1 tsp. salt	

Fry the prawns lightly in the hot butter. Add remaining ingredients and cook for 5 minutes.

FRIED SHRIMPS IN BATTER

1 lb. shrimps	6–8 tbsp. flour
2 egg whites	Oil for deep frying

Shell the shrimps but leave the tails on; split the shrimps, taking care not to cut them all the way through. Make a batter of the egg whites and flour. Heat the oil; when it is ready dip the shrimps into the batter and then drop them one by one into the oil. When they are brown and float to the top, they are ready. Serve hot.

SHRIMP BALLS

1 lb. shrimps	1 egg
2 tsps. sugar	Deep fat for frying
1 tbsp. ginger juice	2 medium-sized mush-
2 tsps. white wine	rooms
1 tsp. salt	1 oz. bamboo shoots
1 oz. cornflour	2 tbsps. butter
6 large water chest-	1 lettuce, finely
nuts, peeled and	shredded
finely chopped	1 tbsp. soya sauce

Chop the shrimps finely. Combine the sugar, ginger juice, wine, salt and cornflour. Add half this mixture to the shrimps and chestnuts and stir in the beaten egg. Drop by spoonfuls into deep hot fat and fry until golden-brown. Drain. Slice the mushrooms and bamboo shoots and fry them in the butter with the shredded lettuce; add the remainder of the flavouring mixture and all the soya sauce. Put in the fried shrimp balls and serve very hot.

CHINESE COLD CHICKEN

Steam a chicken until it is tender, cut the flesh into small pieces and arrange on a dish lined with sliced cucumber and tomatoes. Serve with oyster sauce.

BRAISED CHICKEN WITH MUSHROOMS

A 3-lb. chicken	1 tsp. salt
15 dried mushrooms,	2½ cups water
soaked	⅓ tsp. sugar
1 medium-sized bamboo	⅛ tsp. pepper
shoot	2 onion stalks, cut
2 water chestnuts	into 1-inch pieces
1 tbsp. soya sauce	2 tsps. cornflour mixed
Oil for deep frying	with 3 tbsps. water
5 slices of fresh ginger	

Cut the chicken in half and rub inside and out with soya sauce. Slice the mushrooms, bamboo shoot and water chestnuts into shreds. Put about 1 inch oil into a deep frying pan and when it is very hot fry the chicken on each side for 2 minutes; drain the chicken and set aside. Drain off the oil. In the oily pan sauté the ginger with the salt for 1 minute; add the water, mushrooms, onions, water chestnuts, bamboo shoot, sugar, pepper and onion. Place the chicken in this mixture, cover, lower the heat and simmer for 15 minutes. Remove the chicken, chop into pieces 1½ inches by 1 inch and arrange on a serving dish. Stir the thickening into the gravy and when it is clear and thick pour the whole mixture over the chicken and serve at once.

FRIED HONEY PIGEONS

2 young and tender	Honey
pigeons	½ pint sesame oil

Dress the pigeons, sprinkle inside with salt and rub in honey well all over the outside. Heat the oil and fry the pigeons until they are brown and cooked, drain thoroughly and sprinkle with pepper. Serve with spring onions or garlic.

CHICKEN WITH ALMONDS

¾ lb. raw chicken	Salt
4 tbsps. oil	
4 oz. blanched almonds	2 tsps. cornflour
2 oz. mushrooms	2 tsps. sugar
1 green pepper	1 tbsp. soya sauce
1 carrot	2 tsps. sherry
1 bamboo shoot	½ pint water
1 onion	6 oz. boiled rice

Cut up the chicken into cubes. Heat a little oil and fry the almonds until golden-brown. Cut up the vegetables. Cook the onion in 2 tbsps. of oil until it is transparent; fry the chicken until it begins to brown; add the rest of the oil and some salt and cook, stirring occasionally, for 5–6 minutes.

Blend the cornflour, salt, sugar, soya sauce, sherry and water, bring to the boil, stirring all the time, and pour over the chicken. Add the almonds and make very hot. Serve at once, with the boiled rice.

FRIED SAVOURY NOODLES WITH CHICKEN

1 lb. Chinese noodles	1 breakfastcupful
¼ lb. white cabbage	shredded cooked
1 dozen water chestnuts	chicken
4 oz. bean sprouts	1 breakfastcupful
1 oz. bamboo shoots	shelled shrimps
Sesame oil	1 tbsp. soya sauce

Cook the noodles for 5 minutes in plenty of boiling water; strain and hold under cold running water to separate them; drain and spread out on a flat dish. Cut the cabbage, water chestnuts, bean sprouts and bamboo shoots into thin strips. Heat some oil and quickly fry together the vegetables, chicken and shrimps; add the soya sauce and mix well. Fry the noodles separately in 2 tbsps. hot oil

for 5 minutes, put them on a hot dish and pile on top the vegetable, shrimp and chicken mixture.

DONG GOO MAN ARP
(STEWED DUCK WITH MUSHROOMS)

½ young duck, about	Soya sauce
2 lb.	A little sherry
1 oz. dried mushrooms,	A small clove of garlic
soaked	Stock
Salt, pepper and sugar	Sesame oil

Remove the backbone from the duck, then cut the flesh into pieces 1½ inches long and ½ inch wide. Place the duck in a hot oiled pan with the mushrooms, add a little salt, pepper, sugar, soya sauce and sherry to taste and cook for 3 minutes. Place the duck in a dish. Put the garlic in a hot oiled pan and cook for 5 minutes. Add the duck and enough stock to cover and cook for 45 minutes. Add a little water and sesame oil and cook for a further minute.

SIMMERED DUCK

1 fat duck	Several slices of fresh
1 pint Chinese wine	ginger
2 oz. dried tangerine	Salt
skin	Lettuce and spring
2 spring onions, sliced	onions to garnish

Singe and clean the duck well, put it into a casserole with the wine and other ingredients and simmer gently for 3 hours. Leave until it is quite cold, then carefully strip the meat from the breast, wings and legs and cut into equal-sized strips. Line a serving dish with shredded lettuce, lay the neck of the duck in the centre and pile the strips of duck on this. Garnish with more salad and a few spring onions.

ROAST DUCK—I

1 duck	1 tsp. sugar
1 garlic clove	Seasoning
1 tbsp. soya sauce	2 tbsps. honey
2 tbsps. sherry	A little water

Clean and wash the duck. Mix the pressed and chopped garlic with the soya sauce, sherry, sugar and seasoning. Rub the inside of the duck with this mixture; if any remains it may be incorporated in the sauce. Place the duck in a roasting tin, breast side up, put into a moderately hot oven (400° F., mark 6) and roast, uncovered, for ½ hour. Drain any fat from the tin and rub the bird with the honey, mixed with a little water. Continue roasting for about ½ hour, with the temperature raised to 425° F. (mark 7);

baste with the honey mixture from time to time.

Make a sauce by draining any excess fat from the pan, mixing in a little flour and adding a little stock and the remains of the marinade; season to taste. The duck may be served garnished with watercress and orange slices and surrounded by boiled rice (see recipe).

ROAST DUCK—II

To ensure that the skin of the duck has the crisp and evenly coloured effect so much appreciated by the Chinese, make sure that the trussing has been competently done and that the skin is dry and tight. Dissolve 2 tsps. honey in ½ pint hot water, cool and rub this dressing well into the skin. Hang the bird, after trussing and dressing, for 3 hours. Cook over a clear charcoal fire until the skin is a rich brown colour. The skin is then carved off entirely and served separately from the flesh of the bird.

SWEET AND SOUR PORK

124

1 lb. pork (ribs)	½ cupful vinegar
2 tbsps. cornflour or flour	1 tbsp. soya bean sauce
½ cupful water	2 tsps. sugar
½ tsp. salt	½ lb. Chinese or English pickles
1 lb. lard or oil	

Chop the pork into neat medium-sized pieces. Make a mixture of cornflour or flour, water and ½ tsp. salt, drop the pork pieces in it and mix well. Fry the meat in a saucepan of heated lard or oil until each piece is brown, then drain well. To the remaining cornflour mixture add the vinegar, soya bean sauce and sugar; place in a saucepan and bring to the boil, then cook for a few minutes, stirring it well on a slow heat. Add all the fried pork pieces and the pickles, cut up small and stir together quickly for 1–2 minutes.

CHAR SHIU
(ROAST LOIN OF PORK)

This has a subtle flavour and bears little outward resemblance to its British counterpart. For four servings, use about 1 lb. of fillet pork. Season with salt and pepper, a little soya sauce, a pinch of sugar and a dash of brandy or sherry, then roast in a little fat for 30–40 minutes, putting 2 tbsps. in the pan to provide moisture. When the meat is cooked, slice it into thin pieces about 2 inches long and serve on a bed of vegetables (bean shoots or shredded semi-fried spring greens or mixed vegetables) and pour on the gravy.

TUNG-PO PORK
(STEAMED PORK WITH VEGETABLES)

1 lb. pork	1½ lb. spinach
2 tbsps. soya bean sauce	2 lettuce hearts
1 tbsp. sherry	Pork fat for frying
1 tsp. sugar	

Put the pork into a pan of boiling water and simmer for 20 minutes; pour off the water into a basin and add to the pork the soya bean sauce, sherry and sugar. Simmer very slowly, turning all the time, until the meat is well browned, then continue cooking slowly for a further 20 minutes; from time to time, as necessary, add some of the water which was drained off.

Leave the meat to get cold, cut it into long slices and arrange in a basin, with the rind at the bottom. Put into a steamer and steam for an hour. Finely shred the spinach and the lettuce and fry them in hot pork fat. Heap the fried vegetables on the pork and turn it out on to a hot fireproof dish, so that the vegetables are covered with the pork, rind uppermost. Serve very hot.

FOO YUNG YOOK
(MINCED PORK OMELETTE)

½ oz. onion	3 oz. minced pork
3 eggs, well beaten	Pepper

Chop the onion into small pieces, place in a hot oiled pan and cook for ½ minute. Add the minced pork and cook for 4 minutes. Add the eggs and a little pepper and cook all together for 1½ minutes; shake the omelette over frequently while cooking, so that each side will be cooked properly.

CHOW MEIN

2 oz. very fine vermicelli	3 sticks of celery, finely chopped
⅓ pint sesame oil	½ a tin of bean sprouts
½ lb. lean diced pork	Salt and pepper
1 bunch of chopped spring onions or 2 onions	2 tbsps. soy sauce
½ a crisp cabbage finely shredded	3 eggs

Cook the vermicelli in boiling salted water. Meanwhile heat most of the oil and fry the meat; add all the remaining ingredients except the eggs and cook for 5 minutes. Drain the vermicelli and mix with the other ingredients. Beat the eggs and scramble them in a separate pan with a little oil, then break into small pieces, lightly mix into the Chow Mein and serve hot.

KU LU YU
(FRIED PORK AND VEGETABLES)

½ lb. lean pork
1 egg
1 tsp. soya sauce
White rice wine or sherry
Pepper
Peanut oil or lard for frying
Green peppers

Bamboo shoots
Leeks
Any other crisp, stalky vegetables available
Garlic to taste
Red peppers to taste

For the Sauce

2 tbsps. white vinegar
1½ oz. granulated sugar
1 tbsp. tomato sauce

1 tbsp. bean flour or cornflour

Cut the pork into pieces about ½ inch thick by 1 inch square. Mix all the sauce ingredients together, with enough water to form a thin batter. Beat the eggs well and add the soya sauce, a little rice wine or sherry and some pepper. Dip the pieces of meat into the sauce then into the mixture, stirring well to coat them. Fry the meat in the hot fat for about 2 minutes and drain. Fry all the vegetables in the hot fat for about 30 seconds, then add the meat, stir the meat and vegetables well together and continue cooking for another 20 seconds, adding a few extra drops of oil if necessary. Meanwhile cook sauce in a separate pan till thickened and add to the meat and vegetables. Sauté over a good heat, shaking the pan quickly; add a few spoonfuls of white rice wine or sherry at the last moment. Serve hot.

Note: Bamboo shoots must be previously prepared by boiling 3–4 hours, unless tinned ones are used.

CANTONESE TRIPE

1 lb. cooked tripe
2 oz. sesame oil
2 onions
1 clove of garlic
1 tbsp. sherry

¼ pint water
1 tbsp. soya sauce
4 small mushrooms
2 tomatoes

Cut the tripe into thin strips about 2 inches long and fry lightly in the hot oil with the chopped onions and garlic. Add the sherry, water, soya sauce, sliced mushrooms and tomatoes, simmer for 30 minutes and serve hot.

PORK MEAT BALLS

4–8 oz. minced lean pork
1 tsp. chopped spring onion
Salt and pepper to taste

1 tsp. soya sauce
1 egg
2 tbsps. cornflour
Sesame oil for frying

Mix the pork with the onion, salt, pepper and soya sauce; bind with the egg and shape into small balls. Coat each ball with cornflour and fry in smoking hot fat. Serve piled in a hot dish.

CHUN GUIN
(PANCAKE ROLLS)

6 oz. pork
4 large onions
4 large sticks of celery
1 large leek
½ oz. mushrooms
2 oz. bamboo shoots
4 oz. crabmeat
Salt and pepper

Oil
Sugar
Soya sauce
Stock
3 oz. flour
1 oz. cornflour
1½ eggs, beaten up
A piece of pork fat

Chop the pork, onions, celery, leek, mushrooms, bamboo shoots and crabmeat very finely. Mix, add salt to taste, place in a hot oiled pan and cook for 2 minutes. Add a little sugar and pepper, a little soya sauce and a little stock, then cook for 8 minutes. When ready, place in a dish and leave until needed. Mix thoroughly the flour, cornflour, a little salt and the eggs, then add some water little by little, stirring all the time, until the mixture is reduced to a very thin paste. Well grease a small frying pan with a piece of pork fat, then heat the pan. Pour a little of the batter into the pan so that it just covers the bottom and cook for 2 minutes over a very low heat. Turn out the pancake, then place a little of the vegetable mixture in the middle of it; roll the pancake round the filling and secure the ends with a little beaten egg. Repeat until all the ingredients have been used. Place the pancake rolls in a large saucepan of boiling oil and cook for 3 minutes. Drain well.

TIM-SHUN-YOK-KOW
(SWEET AND SOUR MEAT BALLS)

3 large green peppers, seeded
4 pineapple slices
1 lb. minced beef
Soya sauce
Salt and pepper
Seasoned salt, if available
1 tbsp. flour

2 tbsps. butter
1 cup chicken broth
½ cup juice from pineapple
¼ cup vinegar
2 tbsps. cornflour
1 tbsp. sugar
Boiled rice (see recipe)

Wash the peppers and cut each into 6 pieces; cook in boiling water to cover for 3 minutes, then drain. Cut each pineapple slice into 6 pieces; drain.

Combine the meat, 2 tsps. soya sauce, ¾ tsp. salt, 1 tsp. seasoned salt, ¼ tsp. pepper and blend well. Shape the mixture into 16 small balls and roll them in the flour.

Heat the butter and brown the balls on all sides over a medium heat; cover and simmer for 5 minutes, remove to a hot dish and keep warm. Add to the butter ½ cup chicken broth, the green peppers and pineapple pieces; cover and simmer for 8 minutes. Meanwhile, combine the remaining broth, pineapple juice, vinegar, cornflour, sugar, 2 tsps. soya sauce and ½ tsp. salt; add to the green pepper mixture and stir constantly till the sauce is thickened and clear. Pour the pepper mixture over the meat balls and serve hot, with the rice.

NGOW YOOK SOONG FAN
(STEAMED MINCED BEEF WITH RICE)

¼ lb. minced lean beef	A few drops of
3 water chestnuts	cooking sherry
1 oz. bamboo shoots	2 tsps. cornflour
2 large mushrooms	A little water
½ oz. *chung chow* (preserved parsnips in bundles), if available	A little sugar and salt
	Soya sauce
½ tsp. powdered ginger	4 oz. rice
A few drops of sesame oil	1 egg

Mix all the ingredients except the soya sauce, rice and egg; chop very fine, then mix together with a little soya sauce. Place the rice in a jar, together with 1½ gills boiling water, cover the jar, stand it in a saucepan of boiling water and steam for 30 minutes. Place the beef, etc., on top of the rice, replace the cover and steam for a further 8 minutes. Break the egg, place on top of the beef and cook for a further 5 minutes. Serve hot. Sufficient for one person.

FRIED LIVER

1 lb. liver	A few small onions,
2 tsps. cornflour	finely sliced
2 tbsps. sherry	6 oz. bamboo shoots
3–4 pieces of fresh ginger	2 tsps. soya sauce
1 oz. dried mushrooms	Sesame oil for frying

Cut the liver into small pieces and mix with the cornflour, sherry and ginger. Soak the mushrooms in hot water until soft, then cut into small pieces. Cut the bamboo shoots into strips. Heat the sesame oil, fry the liver quickly over a good heat and add the vegetables. Keep stirring until every piece is golden-brown, then pour in the soya sauce and serve hot.

MINCED KIDNEY

1 lb. pig's kidney	1 tsp. sesame seed oil
1 tbsp. oil for frying	1 tsp. soya sauce
1 finely chopped onion	1 tsp. lemon juice

Wash the kidney well and remove the membrane, white veins and core, then soak it in water for 1 hour, changing the water once or twice. Place in a pan with 1 pint fresh water, bring to the boil and boil for 5 minutes; remove from the water and drain. Heat the frying oil in a pan and sauté the chopped onion until it browns, then remove and drain well. Mince the kidney and combine with the onion. Mix the sesame seed oil, soya sauce and lemon juice and add to the kidney.

FRIED COS LETTUCE

1 cos lettuce	1 tsp. salt
½ oz. oil	1 clove of garlic

Wash and drain the lettuce, break the leaves into small pieces and fry quickly in the hot oil. Season with salt and crushed garlic before serving.

STUFFED MUSHROOMS

6 large mushrooms	2 tbsps. chicken
2 tbsps. oil	stock
1 tsp. salt	2 tsps. cornflour
⅛ tsp. pepper	Soya sauce

For the Stuffing

¼ lb. minced pork	2 tsps. soya sauce
½ tbsp. oil	1 tbsp. cornflour
½ tsp. salt	2 finely chopped
¼ tsp. pepper	spring onions

Make the stuffing by mixing all the ingredients, then fill the mushroom caps with this mixture. Heat the oil and seasonings in a heavy pan, then add the mushrooms and the chicken stock. Turn down the heat, cover the pan and cook slowly for 20 minutes. Remove the mushrooms on to a flat serving plate and keep hot. Mix the cornflour, a little soya sauce and a little water and add to the juices in the pan; when the sauce is thick and smooth, pour it round the mushrooms.

TURNIP SALAD

Thinly slice the required number of fresh young turnips, sprinkle thickly with salt and then rinse in cold water. Add some thinly sliced onions, sprinkle with sugar and stir in soya sauce to taste. Just before serving, pour over the salad a little hot sesame oil.

This is a very popular family dish.

EGG AND SPINACH

½ lb. spinach	½ tsp. salt
1 oz. sesame oil	4 eggs

Wash and pick the spinach carefully, cutting out any coarse stems or veins; drain well.

Heat a little of the oil until it smokes and fry the spinach quickly for 3 minutes. Remove the spinach from the pan and chop it very finely, adding the salt. Beat the eggs and mix them thoroughly with the spinach. Heat the remaining oil until it is smoking hot and quickly fry the egg and spinach mixture for 3 minutes. Serve very hot.

MIXED SALAD

25

½ lb. tomatoes	1 tbsp. salad oil
¼ lb. cucumber	2 tsps. sugar
2–3 lettuce leaves	Cold chicken or other
½ lb. bean sprouts	leftover meat
4 tbsps. vinegar	

Peel the tomatoes, remove the seeds and chop in small pieces. Prepare and chop the cucumber and lettuce. Mix all the vegetables together and pour the vinegar, oil and sugar over them. Chill until ready to use. Serve on thinly sliced meat.

BOILED RICE (CHINESE STYLE)

½ lb. Patna rice	1 clove of garlic
6–7 spring onions	Seasonings
1 green pepper	1 tbsp. soya sauce
1 thick slice of	1 egg
cooked ham	½ cup finely chopped
Nut oil	parsley

Cook the rice the day before in plenty of salted boiling water ; drain, rinse and dry. Cut the spring onions, green pepper and ham into small pieces of about the same size. Melt a little nut oil and lightly fry the mashed and chopped garlic, spring onions, green pepper, ham and seasonings for about 3 minutes. Put in the rice and the soya sauce, heat through, mix in the beaten egg and cook lightly. Add the parsley and serve.

EIGHT-JEWEL RICE PUDDING

1 lb. rice	½ lb. dragons' eyes (or
2 pints water	dates)
4 oz. caster sugar	20 cumquats (Chinese
6–8 oz. candied fruits	oranges)
(4 different types, if	2 oz. raisins
possible)	12 blanched almonds

Simmer the rice in 1½ pints of the water until nearly soft. Add the sugar and the remaining ½ pint water and simmer for a further 15 minutes. Oil the inside of a large pudding basin and arrange a few of the candied and other fruits and nuts at the base to make an attractive pattern. Carefully add a 2-inch layer of rice and then another layer of fruit and nuts, cut into equal-sized pieces ; repeat, then finish with a layer of rice. Cover the top of the basin

with greaseproof paper and steam for about 2 hours.

This is almost the only Chinese sweet which is anything like an English pudding.

DATE AND NUT BALLS

6–8 dates, stoned	1 oz. walnuts, chopped
¼ pint water	very finely
1 oz. lard	½ oz. sugar
2 oz. rice flour	A little oil

Wash the dates and simmer gently in the water until this has all evaporated. Sieve the dates, add to the lard and flour, mix well and knead until it is a pliable dough. Form into a roll 1 inch in diameter and cut off about 10 pieces ½ inch wide ; flatten each piece out thinly. Toss the chopped nuts and sugar in a little hot oil and sauté for 2 minutes. Divide this mixture between the rounds of dough, placing some on each and bringing up the edges to form balls. Roll the balls in flour, place on squares of greaseproof paper and steam for 15 minutes. Serve very hot.

ALMOND COOKIES

3 oz. flour	A pinch of salt
¼ tsp. baking powder	2 oz. sugar
2 tbsps. oil	½ an egg
1 oz. ground almonds	10 blanched almonds
¼ tsp. almond essence	

Sieve the flour and baking powder, add the oil and mix well. Add the rest of the ingredients (except the whole almonds), mix and knead together. Shape into 10 balls, press flat, making rounds ½ inch thick, and place on a greased baking tray. Place an almond on each cookie and bake in a moderate oven (350° F., mark 4) for 15 minutes, or until golden-brown.

HONEYED PEARS

Wash 4–6 sound pears. Cut about 1 inch off the top of each and carefully remove the core without cutting right through the flesh. Fill the holes with honey and cinnamon (allow 2 tsps. honey and ¼–½ tsp. ground cinnamon for each pear), replace the tops and steam the fruit for ½–1 hour, according to size and ripeness. Serve hot.

LITCHIES IN SYRUP

Make a sugar syrup with 4 oz. sugar and ½ pint water, then leave 1 lb. peeled litchies to soak in this for about ½ hour.

126

Chinese Gooseberries may be treated in the same way ; peel and slice first.

ALTHOUGH the area of Japan is only small, the length of the country from north to south means that it enjoys a very varied climate, with a difference of as much as two months in temperature between the extremes. It follows that Japanese food also varies from the produce of frigid zones to sub-tropical fruits, fish and vegetables.

Because Japan is comparatively small, transportation is not difficult and this ensures a wide variety of food all over the country. Fish, perhaps, is the universal favourite, and both shell fish and ordinary fish form a large part of the Japanese diet. Fruit and vegetables are also grown in variety and profusion and the Japanese hostess is always anxious to serve the first spring vegetables to her guests. Japanese hospitality is famous, and when there are guests at the table, a great many different dishes are served, including soup, raw fish with horseradish, both hot and cold meats and fish, salads and boiled rice. The usual drink is saké, or rice wine, which is served through-out the meal. Until recently, each guest was served separately on a small, low, individual tables, but nowadays it is becoming more usual to present the various dishes on one larger table. Small bowls and dishes are used and the Japanese hostess uses matching porcelain for each different course. At informal meals, fewer courses are served.

Perhaps the most characteristic aspect of Japanese food is the manner of presenting it. Enormous importance is attached to the appearance of a dish, which is often decorated with flowers and leaves and must always be a pleasure to the eye as well as the palate.

Japanese cooking also adheres to the general rule of smallness and extreme delicacy. All foods are cut into thin strips and pieces, so that cooking times are short and the natural crispness and fragrance of the ingredients are preserved as far as possible. Seasonings are added during cooking and rarely at table, except when a special sauce or dressing is served. Food is eaten with chopsticks out of the thin porcelain bowls and platters and saké drunk from tiny, stemmed porcelain wine cups.

In these Japanese recipes the use of soya sauce has been indicated, but the true Japanese " shoyu " gives a more authentic flavour. For saké and mirin, whisky and sherry may be substituted.

Korean food has something in common with both Japanese and Chinese cooking. Many different dishes—up to twelve or more—are offered to the guest and the preparation of meals takes much time. Korean housewives like to use a great deal of spice and seasoning, but our recipes have been adapted slightly for Western taste. Rice provides the staple cereal; soups are very popular and vegetables of all kinds, including the more exotic ones, are widely used. Beef, pork and chicken are the most usual meats and there is a plentiful supply of fish, both dried and fresh. Dessert is generally fresh fruit, but chestnuts, cinnamon, honey and ginger are used in sweetmeats.

Japan, Korea

and the Philippines

Japan

CHICKEN AND MUSHROOM SOUP

½ lb. chicken meat	3 mushrooms
Salt	4 cups seasoned stock
Cornflour	1 lemon

Slice the skinned chicken into 10 pieces, salt and allow to stand for 30 minutes. Coat with cornflour, drop into boiling salted water and cook until tender ; set aside. Wash the mushrooms, after trimming off the ends of the stems. Slice each mushroom into 3–4 and boil for a few minutes over a low heat in the stock. Allow 2 pieces of chicken and a few slices of mushroom for each bowl of soup ; add a piece of lemon rind and pour in the heated soup.

BUTA-GIRU—I
(PORK AND VEGETABLE SOUP)

1 pint stock made from pork pieces	Onions to taste
½ lb. potatoes, sliced	2 tbsps. soya bean paste
½ lb. carrots, sliced	Seasonings

Make a soup of the vegetables and stock ; when cooked, add bean paste and season.

BUTA-GIRU—II
(PORK AND VEGETABLE SOUP)

¼ lb. pork	A few string beans
Salt	4 cups chicken soup stock
1 spring onion	
1 small bamboo shoot	1 cup bean sprouts
A few dried mushrooms	Monosodium glutamate

Cut the meat into 2-inch slices and salt it. Slice the onion, bamboo shoot and soaked mushrooms into pieces 1½ inches long, cut the string beans into fine strips. Bring the stock to the boil, add all the vegetables and the meat and boil again ; add 1 tsp. salt and 1 tsp. monosodium glutamate, then skim. Add the onion, remove from the heat and serve.

EGG CUSTARD SOUP

8 eggs, beaten	Monosodium glutamate
5½ cups seasoned stock	¼ lb. spinach
Soya sauce	Salt
Sugar	Lemon

Mix eggs, 1½ cups stock, 1½ tsps. soya, ⅔ tsp. sugar and ⅔ tsp. monosodium glutamate ; beat again and strain. Pour the mixture into a square mould and steam gently for 40 minutes ; unmould and chill, then divide into small squares. Cook the washed spinach in boiling salted water, rinse, drain and cut into pieces 1½ inches long. Put 1 square of custard in each soup bowl and on top of it a strip of spinach ; pour the heated remaining stock over carefully and add a small piece of lemon peel.

OYSTER SOUP

8 oz. oysters	½ tsp. red pepper or tabasco sauce
1¼ pints good fish stock	
2 tsps. cornflour	

Wash the oysters and add to the boiling fish stock. When the oysters are cooked, add the cornflour, mixed with a little cold water, then add the seasoning and cook for a few minutes until thickened.

HORS D'ŒUVRE

Arrange a selection of the following items, or similar ingredients, on lettuce leaves on a large platter and serve while the guests are waiting for *sukiyaki* to be cooked.

Fresh Ginger : Cut into convenient-sized pieces and soak in vinegar with a little salt, sugar and red colouring.

Lima Beans : Boil, peel and soak in sugar syrup.

Shrimps : Mince some fresh raw shrimps finely. Add egg whites with white wine and monosodium glutamate to taste (allow 2 egg whites to 1 lb. shrimps). Make this paste into balls about ¾ inch in diameter and put them all at once into a pan of boiling water ; when they rise to the surface they are cooked. Remove at once and put on skewers, alternately with cubes of cucumber.

Squid (*cuttlefish*) : Wash and clean, leaving only the meaty part ; salt this, then grill over an open fire. When cooked, brush the surface with egg yolk, slice and sprinkle with a green-coloured herb or spice, for example, marjoram or edible seaweed.

White Fish : Skin, then slice or cut into convenient-sized pieces, salt and leave for 2–3 hours, then marinate overnight in a mixture of vinegar and edible seaweed. Cut into small pieces to serve.

ISEEBI-NO-AMARU
(LOBSTER IN SOYA SAUCE)

1 lobster	4–5 tbsps. saké
3–4 tbsps. soya sauce	2 tbsps. sugar

Put the lobster into a sauce made from the other ingredients and cook over a very low heat, turning it frequently, for about 20 minutes.

If preferred, remove the lobster meat, cook as above, then return it to the shell.

GLAZED GRILLED FISH

Soak 4–5 fish fillets for 2 hours in stock to which has been added 2 tbsps. mirin (Japanese sweet rice wine) and $1\frac{1}{2}$ tbsps. soya sauce. Grill, basting several times with the marinade mixture. Boil 1 tbsp. soya sauce and $1\frac{1}{2}$ tbsps. mirin together until thickened, then pour over the fish to serve.

FRIED SALMON BALLS

5 oz. canned salmon	2 eggs, beaten
2–3 lb. potatoes	Monosodium glutamate
1 small carrot, cooked	Cornflour
1–3 oz. dried mushrooms (soaked until soft)	Frying oil
	Soya sauce
	Vinegar
$\frac{1}{2}$ oz. fresh ginger	Sugar
Salt	

Mince the salmon, mash the cooked potatoes; cut the carrot and dried mushrooms into strips. Add the minced ginger, 1 tsp. salt, the eggs and some monosodium glutamate. Form into 1-inch balls, coat with cornflour and fry in the hot oil. Mix 3 tbsps. soya sauce, $2\frac{1}{2}$ tbsps. vinegar and 2 tsps. sugar with a little monosodium glutamate. Serve as a sauce in separate bowls and dip the fish balls into it when eating. Lettuce is the usual accompaniment.

NAMBANMUSHI
(STEAMED SOLE IN SAKÉ)

1 sole	6 oz. spring onion
Salt	1 tbsp. sugar
2 tbsps. saké	3 eggs, beaten
1 tsp. shoga (vegetable ginger) or other seasoning	2 tsps. soya sauce
	Oil for frying

Skin the fish, sprinkle with $\frac{1}{2}$ tsp. salt, and leave for 5–10 minutes, then wipe off the salt with a cloth. Fillet the fish and score lightly. Mix the saké and grated ginger and marinade the fish in this for about 20 minutes. Chop the spring onions, mix the eggs, 1 tsp. salt, soya sauce and $\frac{1}{2}$ tsp. sugar well. Heat the oil and fry the onions till soft, then add the egg mixture and cook until just set; divide into portions, one for each person. Put one portion of egg and onion mixture on top of each piece of fish, enclose in aluminium foil and steam for 15 minutes.

BOILED WHITE FISH FILLET

1 lb. fish (sea bream, sole, sea perch)	Soya sauce
	Mirin
Saké	

Allow 1 piece of fish per person. Mix 4 tbsps. saké, 4 tbsps. soya sauce and 3 tbsps. mirin in a saucepan and bring to the boil. Add the fish and cover with a plate which fits inside the pan on the fish, then put on the saucepan lid. (This prevents evaporation.) Boil over a good heat; if the contents boil over, remove only the saucepan lid. Pour the liquor from the pan over the fish when serving.

CUCUMBER AND CRAB SALAD

1 lb. cucumber	Soya sauce
Salt	Sugar
Vinegar	Monosodium glutamate
$\frac{1}{2}$ can of crabmeat	1 oz. fresh ginger

Slice the unpeeled cucumbers as thinly as possible, salt and allow to stand for 20 minutes; squeeze to remove the liquid. Add 1 tbsp. vinegar and gently squeeze again. Break the crabmeat apart into small pieces. Mix 3 tbsps. vinegar, $\frac{1}{2}$ tsp. salt, $1\frac{1}{2}$ tsps. soya sauce, 1 tbsp. sugar and some monosodium glutamate. Add the cucumbers and crabmeat and mix well, divide into equal portions and place in individual dishes. Garnish with a few finely cut strips of ginger.

LOBSTER, TEMPURA STYLE

$\frac{1}{2}$ pint good fish stock	4 oz. flour
4 tbsps. soya sauce	8 oz. water
4 tbsps. dry cooking sherry	Salad oil
	1 cupful Patna rice
1 lobster (or 1 tin)	Ground ginger
1 egg	

First prepare the sauce by simmering the fish stock, soya sauce and sherry for 10 minutes and allowing it to cool. Prepare the lobster and cut the flesh into chunks. Beat the egg lightly, whisk in the flour, and add the water. Heat the salad oil to 300° F., dip the lobster chunks into the batter mixture and fry in the hot oil till golden-brown. Meanwhile cook the rice in plenty of boiling salted water until tender. Serve the lobster on top of the mound of rice, pour the sauce over, and sprinkle with a little ground ginger.

Prawns, shrimps, scallops, etc., or any white fish (cut into small fingers) may be cooked in the same way.

This is a somewhat simplified tempura recipe. More elaborate ones include a variety of vegetables, such as radishes, onions, carrots, celery, French beans, green peppers and sweet potatoes. All these vegetables are sliced or cut into pieces about $\frac{1}{4}$–$\frac{3}{8}$ inch wide and $1\frac{1}{2}$–2 inches long, then dipped into batter in little bundles, fried with the fish and served on a large platter or in a small dish. Each guest helps himself to some of the various items and dips the pieces into his own bowl of tempura sauce before eating.

An alternative way of making tempura sauce

is to heat together ½ cup soya sauce, ½ cup water, 2 tsps. sugar, ½ tsp. salt, 2 tbsps. sherry or white wine and 2 tbsps. drained pickled horseradish or 2 tsps. ground ginger ; bring to the boil, stir then cool.

FISH AND VEGETABLE TEMPURA

127

Any white fish, scampi, carrots, onions, sweet potatoes, French beans, radishes, etc., can be used. Wash and peel the vegetables and cut into long, thin strips (about ¼–⅜ inch wide). Cut fish into strips of about the same length, but slightly thicker ; leave prawns or shrimps whole.

Make a batter as follows : Break 1 egg into a bowl, add about ½ tsp. sugar, ½ cup milk and 1 cup flour. Stir slightly but do not over-mix, which would result in too heavy a mixture. A little water can be added if the batter is too stiff. Dip the fish pieces and the vegetable strips (in little bundles) in the batter and fry in deep oil.

KANOKOYAKI
(SHRIMP AND SPINACH OMELETTE)

5 eggs	½ tsp. salt
4 tbsps. dashi (see below) or stock	A little spinach
	2 tbsps. shrimps
4 tbsps. sugar	Vinegar to taste
2 tsps. soya sauce	

Mix the eggs, dashi or stock, sugar, soya and salt well. Cook the spinach. Blanch the shrimps and season with vinegar and a little sugar. Heat a pan and grease it lightly. Put in half the egg mixture, followed by half the spinach and half the shrimps. Cook until just set, then add the other half of the shrimps, spinach and egg. This makes a kind of " sandwich " of the ingredients. When all is set, slice across.

Dashi is a light, clear fish stock or bouillon, much used as a basis for soups, etc., made as follows :

1 scant cup flaked dried fish (Katsoubushi)	5 cups water
	1 tsp. soya sauce
1 square inch dried seaweed (Kombu)	2 tsps. salt

Clean the Kombu and bring to the boil in the water. Remove Kombu and add fish to the boiling water. Remove from heat immediately and let it steep for a few minutes. Strain and add seasonings.

TONKATSU
(FRIED PORK)

½ lb. pork fillet or leg per person	Seasonings
	Egg and breadcrumbs
Flour	Oil for frying

Cut the pork into strips, roll them in flour and season with pepper and salt, then dip in beaten egg and breadcrumbs ; fry in oil until well done.

Serve with Buta-giru (see recipe on p. 346).

BUTA-NO-KAKUNI
(PORK IN SOYA SAUCE)

1 lb. lean pork	Sugar
5 tbsps. saké	5 tbsps. water
A little spring onion	2 tbsps. stock
Salt	A little ground ginger
Potato flour	Beetroot
Oil	3 oz. bean sprouts
2 tbsps. soya sauce	

Cut the meat into 1-inch cubes. Mix the saké, onion and salt. Dip the meat in potato flour and brown it in the hot oil. Mix the soya sauce, 2 tbsps. sugar, water, saké, stock and seasonings as desired and bring to the boil. Add the meat and cook on a very low heat until it is tender. About 5 minutes before the meat is done, add the beetroot, with more liquid if necessary. Cook the sprouts separately but serve on the same dish.

FRIED PORK AND APPLE BALLS

128

1 lb. pork	Salt
¼ of a spring onion or ordinary onion	Monosodium glutamate
	Salad oil for frying
3 dried mushrooms	1 lettuce
½ an apple	Soya sauce
1 egg	Vinegar
Saké	Mustard

Mince the pork and the onion. Soften the dried mushrooms in cold water and cut into ⅛-inch cubes. Peel the apple and cut up like the dried mushrooms. Mix all together and add the egg, ⅔ tbsp. saké, 1 tsp. salt and some monosodium glutamate. Mix well, make about 15 patties and fry in deep fat.

Place on lettuce leaves and serve with a side dish of equal parts of soya sauce and vinegar with monosodium glutamate and a little mustard.

SUKIYAKI

1 aubergine	1 bunch of watercress
6 leeks	1½ lb. topside or entre-côte steak
2 large mild onions	
3 medium-sized carrots	A piece of beef fat
4 large mushrooms	2 oz. bean sprouts
A few sticks of celery	2 tsps. monosodium glutamate
¼ of a cabbage	
2 oz. bean curd, if available	2 tsps. sugar
	¼ pint soya sauce
A small tin of bamboo shoots	¼ pint fish stock
	4 tbsps. saké (or other white wine)
2 oz. Japanese vermicelli, if available	3 eggs

Sukiyaki means literally " roasted on a plough-share," and Japanese farmers say that from time immemorial meat has been cooked on the blades of a plough. The modern interpretation of this is a heavy iron casserole or an electric hot-plate, which may be put on the table, so that the dish is cooked in front of your guests. Everything must, of course, be completely prepared beforehand—the raw vegetables look very attractive arranged on a platter. In Japan, the meat used is specially prepared to disperse the fat throughout the flesh, and is then sliced very finely.

Each person has chopsticks and a bowl into which a raw egg has been broken ; this is beaten up with the chopsticks, and each piece of food is then dipped in egg—the hot food cooks the egg, and the egg cools the boiling food.

Prepare the vegetables, slicing the aubergine, leeks, onions, carrots, mushrooms and celery. Leave the cabbage in one piece and cook till almost done, then slice it. Cut the bean curd in small squares, slice the bamboo shoots, wash the watercress, and soak the vermicelli in hot water for a minute or two. The meat should be sliced as thinly as possible and beaten flat, then cut into small pieces. Heat a heavy casserole, put in the fat trimmed from the meat, and heat till smoking hot, then add the vegetables, bean sprouts and vermicelli, and stir them round. Lay the meat on top, covering the vegetables completely, then sprinkle with monosodium glutamate and sugar, and add the soya sauce, stock and saké. Leave to cook for 20 minutes over quite a good heat, or until the meat is done to your taste ; turn the slices over at half-time. Serve as already described.

The casserole may be refilled as the food is eaten out of it. Add extra sugar, soya sauce, etc., as desired ; if the gravy becomes too salty, add broth or water to thin it down. The vegetables used can be varied according to season, tastes and the number of people eating. This is a fine dish for a cool evening.

GRILLED CHICKEN AND MUSHROOMS

2 dried mushrooms, soaked	Soya sauce
	Saké
2–3 oz. bamboo shoots	Salt
A 4-inch piece of spring onion	Sugar
	1 egg
½ lb. minced chicken meat	Monosodium glutamate
	1 tsp. poppy seeds

Mince the soaked mushrooms with the bamboo shoots and onion. Add the chicken meat, 1 tbsp. soya sauce, 2 tbsps. saké, ½ tsp. salt, 2 tsps. sugar, the egg and some monosodium glutamate. Mix

well and form into a large square 1 inch thick. Put on a baking sheet, sprinkle with poppy seeds and bake in a moderate oven (350° F., mark 4) until the chicken is tender. Cut into small squares.

ROAST CHICKEN

10 oz. chicken meat	Salad oil
Soya sauce	1 lemon
Mirin (sweet rice wine)	

Cut the chicken into ¼-inch slices and marinade in 1 tbsp. soya sauce and 1½ tsps. mirin for 1 hour. Heat 1 tbsp. oil and fry the chicken, removing the pieces and dipping into the marinade twice during the course of frying. Serve with a slice of chicken between two thin slices of lemon.

NA MESHI
(GREEN RICE)

4 cups rice	1 bunch of parsley or edible chrysanthemum leaves
Salt	
Monosodium glutamate	

Cook the rice as described below. Meanwhile cook the greenstuff in boiling water until tender, taking care to retain the green colour ; rinse in cold water and squeeze dry. Cut into short pieces, sprinkle with ⅔ tsp. salt and some monosodium glutamate and mix with the cooked rice. Serve in large, covered rice bowls, if possible.

BOILED RICE—JAPANESE STYLE

Put the rice and water in a deep pan and mix well. Cover and bring to the boil over a strong heat ; when it boils, turn the heat as low as possible and simmer for 3 minutes. Bring again to the boil over a rather higher heat and as the water reduces, turn the heat lower. When the water is nearly absorbed (after about 20 minutes) turn the heat up for 1–2 seconds and remove the pan from the heat still covered ; allow to stand for 7 minutes.

O-SUSHI
(RICE CAKES)

Boil some rice in the usual fashion. Prepare a sauce of vinegar, sugar and salt whilst it is cooking, using 2 tsps. sugar to 1 tbsp. vinegar. The rice should be dried and cooled quickly and the juice is shaken over it whilst it cools.

Form the rice into small flat rolls or cakes and garnish with any of the following : boiled prawns ; smoked salmon ; raw fish ; tinned fish ; anchovy fillets ; ham or any cold meat, thinly sliced ; a thin omelette seasoned with salt

129

and sugar; edible seaweed, or any salad vegetable.

Place the garnish on top of or around the rice cakes. Alternatively, cylindrical cakes can be made with a filling in the centre and a thin layer of egg, seaweed, etc., around the outside.

SAVOURY RICE

½ lb. cooked chicken	¾ lb. boiled rice
½ lb. mushrooms	½ tsp. sugar
½ lb. tinned bamboo shoots	½ pint chicken stock
	½ tbsp. soya sauce
2 oz. butter or oil	

Cut the chicken into ½-inch squares. Slice the mushrooms and bamboo shoots thinly and fry in butter for 2 minutes. Add the chicken, mushrooms and bamboo shoots to the rice, sprinkle in the sugar, add the stock and stir gently. Cover the pan and simmer very gently for 30 minutes, till the stock is absorbed. Add the soya sauce, mix well and serve.

BLACK NOODLES

1 lb. soya bean flour	1 egg yolk
1 tsp. salt	Cold water

Mix the flour, salt and egg yolk with enough cold water to make a thick paste; leave for 30 minutes. Roll out paper-thin and fold in a roll about 14 inches long, then cut into ⅛-inch strips or slices. Throw into boiling water, boil for 5 minutes, drain and serve.

CHAWAN MUSHI
(STEAMED EGG DISH)

30

3 eggs	5 pieces of dried mush-
Soya sauce	room
1 tbsp. salt	4–5 pieces of white
Monosodium glutamate	fish
2½ cups stock	A few shrimps
2 oz. chicken, sliced	Watercress

Beat the eggs well. Add 1 tsp. soya sauce and some monosodium glutamate and salt to the stock and mix with the eggs. Divide between 5 cups, adding to each some pieces of chicken, mushroom and fish, a few shrimps and some watercress. Cover and steam briskly for 3–4 minutes, then for 10–15 minutes over a low heat.

MAPLE SALAD

31

½ lb. radishes	Vinegar
1 small carrot	½ lb. prawns
¼ lb. cucumbers	3 eggs
Salt	Sugar
A few dried mush-	1 oz. butter
rooms (soaked)	Monosodium glutamate

Peel the radishes and carrot and cut into 1½-inch strips; cut the cucumbers in the same manner, without peeling. Salt and allow to stand until they become soft, then press out the liquid. Slice the dried mushrooms into thin strips. Mix the cucumbers, carrot, radishes and mushrooms with 1½ tbsps. vinegar. Slice the prawns lengthwise.

Beat the eggs, add 1 tsp. salt, 1 tbsp. sugar and 1 oz. butter and scramble them, stirring all the time. Force this egg mixture through a sieve while hot and allow to cool; mix in 2 tbsps. vinegar.

Add 1½ tbsps. vinegar to the drained vegetables, mix well and squeeze. Add the vegetables, the prawns and a little monosodium glutamate to the egg mixture, stirring gently. Arrange the salad on individual plates, preferably in the form of a maple leaf. (The colours of these foods are chosen to suggest the autumn colouring of the Japanese maple.)

BOILED WATERCRESS

Chop 4–6 bunches of watercress coarsely, put in a saucepan, bring to the boil and simmer in its own juice till tender—about 10 minutes. Drain well, stir in 2 tsps. soya sauce and serve as a green vegetable.

PICKLED LETTUCE, CUCUMBER AND TURNIP

2 lettuce hearts	1 turnip
1 cucumber	1 tsp. salt

Cut the lettuces in half; peel the cucumber and turnip and slice thinly lengthwise. Sprinkle with the salt and leave for 2 days. This is eaten as a separate vegetable course with rice.

Korea

SPINACH SOUP

¼ lb. beef	1 tsp. salt
2 spring onions	A pinch of pepper
1 clove of garlic	6 cups fresh spinach
1 tbsp. prepared sesame	(approx. 1 lb.)
seed (see below)	7 cups of water
4 tbsps. soya sauce	

Slice the beef thinly and cut into 1-inch squares. Add the chopped onions (including the tops), chopped garlic, prepared sesame seed, soya sauce, salt and pepper and mix well. Cook for a few minutes, until the meat is coloured. Add the water and cook until the meat is tender. Wash the spinach well. Just before serving the soup, add the spinach and continue to cook only until this is tender.

To prepare sesame seed, wash 1 cup white

sesame (first removing any sand found among the seeds), put in a heavy frying pan and brown very gently, stirring constantly. When the seeds are brown and rounded, remove at once from the heat, add 1 tsp. salt and mash the seeds until pulverised.

EGG SOUP

¼ lb. beef, thinly sliced
4 tbsps. soya sauce
A pinch of pepper
1 tbsp. prepared sesame seed
1 tbsp. oil
7 cups water
6 spring onions (green part)
3 eggs
Salt

Cut the beef into 1-inch squares. Add 2 tbsps. soya sauce, the pepper, prepared sesame seed and the oil. Cook until meat is well coloured.

Add the water and remaining soya sauce and cook until the meat is almost tender. Cut the onion tops into 1½-inch lengths, add to the soup and cook until tender. Just before serving, add the slightly beaten eggs all at once and stir. Season and serve immediately.

SALTED FISH

1 lb. mackerel or perch
¼ cup soya sauce
3 tbsps. water
1 tbsp. sugar
¼ tsp. pepper
1 spring onion
1 clove of garlic
½ tsp. candied ginger

Skin, bone and clean the fish, then cut into pieces 1 inch square and ¼ inch thick. Add the soya sauce, water, sugar and pepper. Cut the onion (including the top), the garlic and the ginger diagonally into thin pieces and add to the fish. Mix well and cook until the fish is tender.

This is a salty relish and is eaten in small amounts with rice.

SALTED BEEF SQUARES

½ lb. beef
¾ cup soya sauce
1 spring onion
1 clove of garlic
A pinch of pepper
1 tbsp. oil
2 tbsps. prepared sesame seed
¼ cup water
3 tbsps. sugar
1 tbsp. pine nuts

Chop the beef finely. Combine 3 tbsps. soya sauce, the chopped onion (including the top), chopped garlic, pepper and 1 tbsp. sesame seed and mix well with the beef. Shape the mixture into 4 flat squares ½ inch thick and press each until firm; sprinkle with the remaining sesame seed. Fry the squares slowly until done in the centre, then cut into 1-inch squares and put into a saucepan. Add the remaining soya sauce, water and sugar and cook until the beef is dark brown. Remove from the liquid and arrange attractively on a plate, then sprinkle the top with chopped pine nuts.

This is a very salty relish, eaten in small amounts with rice.

PIQUANT LIVER

½ lb. liver
2 tbsps. soya sauce
1 clove of garlic
A pinch of pepper
1 tbsp. prepared sesame seed
1 tsp. oil
1½ tbsps. sugar
1 large onion
½ cup water
Salt

Cut the liver into very thin slices 1½ inches long and 1 inch wide. Combine the soya sauce, chopped garlic, pepper, sesame seed, oil and sugar and add to the liver. Cut the onion into quarters and then cut each quarter into 4 slices crosswise; add to the liver. Cook for 5 minutes, add the water and cook until tender. Season to taste with salt.

VEGETABLE PORK SALAD

¼ lb. pork
1 tsp. chopped ginger
1 tsp. chopped garlic
1 tbsp. chopped spring onion
1 turnip
Salt
Oil
1 small round onion
½ cup mushrooms
1 small carrot
2–3 sticks of celery or ½–1 lb. fresh spinach
1 hard pear
2 tbsps. soya sauce
2 tbsps. sugar
¼ tsp. pepper
2 tsps. vinegar
1 tsp. pine nuts

Boil pork until tender and cut in fine strips 2 inches long. Add the chopped ginger, garlic and spring onion. Wash and peel the turnip and cut into 2-inch strips, add 1 tsp. salt and let it stand for 10 minutes; drain and fry in a small amount of oil. Cut the onion and mushrooms into pieces of the same size as the turnip and fry in a small amount of oil. Wash and peel the carrot, cut into 2-inch strips and boil for 2–3 minutes in a small amount of water, then drain. Wash the celery and cut into 2-inch pieces, add 1 tsp. salt and let it stand for 10 minutes; drain well and fry in a small amount of oil for a few minutes, or until a bright green colour. (If spinach is used, wash well and cook only until it is tender.) Wash and peel the pear and cut into 2-inch pieces.

Combine the pork, vegetables and pear. Combine the soya sauce, sugar, pepper and vinegar and mix lightly with the pork and vegetable mixture. Arrange the salad on a plate and sprinkle the top with chopped pine nuts.

FRIED BEEF BALLS

½ lb. beef	1 tbsp. prepared sesame
3 tbsps. soya sauce	seed
¼ tsp. salt	3 tbsps. oil
A pinch of pepper	3 tbsps. flour
1 spring onion	2 eggs
1 clove of garlic	Oil for frying

Mince the beef. Add the soya sauce, salt, pepper, chopped onion (including the top), chopped garlic, sesame seed and oil. Mix well and shape into flattened balls 1½ inches in diameter. Roll in flour and slightly beaten egg and fry in a small amount of oil until tender. Serve with vinegar-soya sauce (see below).

VINEGAR-SOYA SAUCE

6 tbsps. soya sauce	1 tbsp. chopped pine
6 tbsps. vinegar	nuts
2 tbsps. sugar	

Combine the soya sauce, vinegar and sugar, mix well and put 2 tbsps. of the sauce into individual dishes. Chop the pine nuts finely and sprinkle over the top of each dish.

The vinegar-soya sauce is served individually because each person dips morsels of all fried foods into it before eating them.

RICE AND MUSHROOMS

2 cups rice	2 tbsps. soya sauce
1 cup thinly sliced	A pinch of pepper
mushrooms	1 tbsp. oil
1 cup thinly sliced	2 tsps. prepared sesame
onions	seed
½ cup minced lean	3 cups cold water
beef	½ tsp. salt

Pick over the rice carefully and wash it well. Mix the mushrooms, onions, beef, the soya sauce, pepper, oil and sesame seed and cook for 2 minutes, stirring well. Add this meat mixture to the rice, with the cold water and salt. Cover tightly and bring quickly to the boil; reduce the heat as low as possible and steam for 30 minutes, without stirring or removing the lid.

RICE AND BEAN SPROUTS

2 cups rice	2 tsps. prepared sesame
3 cups cold water	seed
1 green onion	1 tsp. oil
1 clove of garlic	1 cup prepared bean
2 tbsps. soya sauce	sprouts

Pick over the rice carefully, wash well and add the cold water. Combine the chopped green onion (including the top), chopped garlic, sesame seed, soya sauce, oil and bean sprouts and cook all together for 2 minutes, stirring well. Combine the bean sprout mixture and the rice, cover tightly and bring quickly to the boil. Reduce the heat as low as possible and steam for 30 minutes. Do not stir or remove the lid while cooking.

FRIED POTATO, ONION AND CARROT

1 medium-sized potato	¾ cup flour
1 medium-sized onion	¼ cup water
1 medium-sized carrot	1 tsp. salt
2 eggs	2 tbsps. oil

Cut the vegetables in pieces 1½ inches long and shred lengthwise very finely. Beat the eggs slightly with a fork, add the flour, salt and water and beat well. Add the vegetables and mix lightly. Drop by teaspoonfuls in an oblong shape on to a heated and oiled frying pan. Fry slowly in a small amount of oil until light brown on both sides. Serve with vinegar-soya sauce.

BEETS IN SOYA SAUCE

6 large beetroots	1 tsp. oil
2 tbsps. soya sauce	2 tbsps. vinegar
1 tsp. prepared sesame	1 tsp. sugar
seed	1 tsp. salt

Cut off and keep the beet tops. Wash, peel and cook the beets. When they are almost done, add the beet tops cut into 2-inch lengths and cook until tender; drain. Cut the beets into pieces 1 inch long, ¼ inch wide and ¼ inch thick, combine with the tops and add the soya sauce, sesame seed, oil, vinegar, sugar and salt. Mix lightly.

KEEM-CHEE
(CUCUMBER PICKLE)

3 large cucumbers	½ tsp. chopped red
1½ tbsps. salt	chilli pepper
1 spring onion	½ cup water
½ clove of garlic	

Wash the cucumbers and cut into 1½-inch lengths without peeling; cut each piece in half lengthwise and remove the seeds. Add 1 tbsp. salt to the cucumbers, mix well and leave to stand for 15 minutes. Cut the onion (including the top) into 1½-inch lengths and shred each piece lengthwise very finely. Chop the garlic and red chilli pepper into fine pieces.

Wash the salt from the cucumbers. Add the onion, garlic, red pepper, ½ tbsp. salt and water, mix well and leave to mature. In warm weather 2 days are sufficient, but in cold weather a week is required.

This and similar pickles made of raw vegetables are served at practically all meals; they are a good source of vitamins.

The Philippines

KARI-KARI
(CURRIED SHRIMPS)

½ lb. raw shrimps   Stock
3 tbsps. lard   2 cups coconut milk
2 cloves of garlic   2 medium-sized egg-
1 onion   plants
1 tsp. curry powder 1 small red pepper
Salt to taste

Shell the shrimps. Heat the lard and sauté the chopped garlic and finely sliced onion, then add the curry powder, shrimps and salt. When these are cooked, add the eggplants, sliced crosswise, some stock and the coconut milk in which a little red pepper has been crushed. Stir the mixture until it boils and serve hot.

KALDERETA
(MEAT STEW)

2¼ lb. goat's meat or Paprika pepper and salt
  pork   to taste
2 cloves of garlic   Flour to thicken
1 cup olive oil   ½ cup chopped ham
1 large onion   1 tin pimientos
8 tomatoes   1 tin garden peas
1 lb. potatoes   Sliced hard-boiled eggs

Prepare the meat and cut into pieces. Heat the oil and brown the garlic. Add the onion and tomatoes, then the meat and seasonings. When it is partly cooked, transfer the mixture into a deeper vessel, then add enough stock to cover and cook until the meat is tender. Add the potatoes, cut in cubes, and continue cooking. When they are cooked, thicken the stock and add ham, pimientos and peas. Garnish with egg.

LUMPIA
(FRIED MEAT PASTIES)

½ lb. raw shrimps   ½ lb. minced pork
1 lb. bamboo shoots Salt and pepper
1 onion   ½ lb. garbanzo beans
½ lb. potatoes   ½ cup raisins
Lard for frying   Monosodium glutamate
½ lb. water chestnuts Lumpia wrappers (see
2 cloves of garlic   below)

Pound the shrimps into a paste. Cut the bamboo shoots into slices about the size of matchsticks. Chop the onion coarsely. Cut the potatoes into chips and fry them. Cut the water chestnuts into the same size as the fried potatoes. Melt 3 oz. lard in the hot frying pan and sauté the garlic in this. When it is nicely cooked add the cut-up ingredients and meat. When the mixture is half cooked, add the bamboo shoots and season well with salt; add

W.C.B.—23

the garbanzo beans and some more salt, then add the fried potatoes and raisins and season with pepper and monosodium glutamate. When all this is well cooked, remove from the heat.

Take a tablespoonful at a time of this mixture, put on a lumpia wrapper and place a piece of water chestnut or raw carrot in the centre; fold the wrapper securely around this and fry in deep hot fat until crisp; serve hot.

Lumpia wrappers are paper-thin sheets of a flour-and-water pastry, which can be bought ready prepared. As a substitute, use very thin-rolled shortcrust pastry.

STUFFED CAPON

1 large capon   ⅓ cup raisins
1 slice of ham   4 tbsps. butter
2½ lb. minced pork Salt and pepper
1 small tin devilled 1 tsp. monosodium
  ham   glutamate
1 small tin potted meat 2 raw eggs
1 onion, chopped fine 2 hard-boiled eggs
½ cup grated mild   5–10 stuffed green
  cheese   olives
⅓ cup sweet pickles Butter for roasting

Prepare the capon (see below); chop up the ham very fine and add the minced pork, devilled ham, potted meat, onion, cheese, sweet pickles, raisins, butter, a little seasoning and monosodium glutamate. Add the raw eggs and mix thoroughly. Stuff the capon with this mixture. Cut hard-boiled eggs into 6 wedges each and put them at either side of the capon; push the olives into the stuffing. Sew up the capon and spread the whole surface of the bird with butter. Extra stuffing can be put in the tin alongside the capon. Roast for 30 minutes in a moderately hot oven (400° F., mark 6), then decrease to moderate (350° F., mark 4) and cook for 30–45 minutes longer.

To Bone and Prepare the Chicken : Slice down the back, running the knife along the carcase inside the skin and flesh to free from the bones. Work the flesh free of all the bones, thus removing the legs, wings, etc. The bones can be removed joint by joint; try to strip all the meat off them. Soak the boned chicken overnight in a mixture of lime juice and 1 tbsp. soya sauce.

ADOBONG MANOK
(FRIED CHICKEN)

Soak a chicken in 1 cup vinegar and ½ cup water, with 3 cloves of garlic and salt and pepper to taste. Heat 6 tbsps. lard in a frying pan and cook the mixture until the chicken is tender and the garlic brown.

THROUGHOUT South East Asia, Malaya and Indonesia, rice forms the staple food of the people served, of course, with an enormous variety of different sauces, spices and relishes. The climate is tropical and often humid and rice, maize and cassava are the basic food crops, with the sago palm in the Moluccas. Soya beans, groundnuts and potatoes are also plentiful; fruit includes bananas and pineapples. Coffee, sugar and cocoa are all exported and coconuts also form an integral part of the economics of the area, providing fresh food as well as copra for export.

Indonesian food at its best is delicious and has given rise to the well-known *Rijstafel* of Holland. Rice is served with literally dozens of different side dishes, which include such things as rich soups, dried shrimp and ginger, fish of all kinds, curries, bananas fresh or fried, peanuts, coconut and so on. The spices for which this district is so famous add interest and piquancy to all the dishes. In England, these spices may be difficult to obtain and ginger makes a good substitute, while a couple of drops of aniseed oil can take the place of anise.

The Thai are not lavish in their daily menus; a large proportion of the population eats two meals a day, both consisting of rice with meat, fish or a sauce to flavour it. The peasants usually eat glutinous rice with a little *kapi* sauce, making a small ball of rice with their fingers and dipping it into the relish. They prefer to eat on the floor, which is covered with spotlessly clean mats and this mode of eating is also favoured by many educated Thai, though the more Westernised people generally eat sitting at table and using Western type cutlery.

Sea-fish, including squids, crabs, shrimps, prawns and turtles are plentiful. The *platoo* is a small fish, something like a mackerel, which is very popular; it is sold in small baskets already cooked, each basket containing three or four fish. Fresh-water fish are also abundant.

Grapefruit and other citrus fruit, custard apples, mangoes and melons are among the numerous fruits that grow freely. Strawberries and grapes can also be grown quite successfully. *Durian* is an unusual fruit, with a distinctive perfume and *lumyai* is another fruit, which resembles the Chinese lichi. Most vegetables grow well and poultry farming flourishes. Pork is the most usual meat and is served frequently.

Many different fruit drinks are made, and a local spirit is distilled from rice or palm sap.

Three sauces which are used with rice are: *Nampla,* a watery fish sauce often sprinkled on fruit; *Kapi,* a peppery fish paste, made with small shrimps; and *Namprik,* a cooked sauce with the consistency of thick gravy.

Malaya, Siam, Indonesia

MALAY CHINESE SPINACH SOUP

1 onion	1 oz. flour
2 bacon rashers	Seasoning to taste
1 oz. butter	¼ pint evaporated
2 lb. spinach	milk
1 quart boiling water	Croûtons to garnish

Sauté the chopped onion and bacon in the fat for 15 minutes, then add the spinach and water; cook gently until tender, then sieve. Add the flour, mixed to a smooth paste with a little cold water, season and boil well. Beat in the milk and serve with croûtons.

SOTOH WITH NASI IMPIT
(SOUP WITH RICE CUBES)

1 lb. beef, mutton or chicken	2 tbsps. vinegar
	Salt
2 tsps. ground coriander	2 tbsps. butter or cooking fat
½ tsp. ground cinnamon	
½ tsp. ground nutmeg	4 shallots, finely sliced
¼ tsp. ground cloves	¼ of a small cabbage
¼ tsp. pepper	1 tsp. chopped parsley
1 tsp. ground ginger	1 tsp. chopped spring onions
1 tsp. sugar	
1 tbsp. soya sauce	Rice cubes (see below)

Wash the meat and cut into small pieces. Put with the mixed spices and sugar in a saucepan and cover with water; bring to the boil and simmer gently for 1 hour. Add the soya sauce, vinegar and salt to taste and again simmer for ½ hour. Melt the fat in a frying pan and fry the shallots golden brown, then put them with the fat into the soup. Slice the cabbage very finely and cook in boiling salted water until almost tender, then drain it. Five minutes before serving the soup, sprinkle in the chopped parsley and spring onions. Garnish with the rice cubes and cooked cabbage strips and hand pickled chillies separately.

RICE CUBES FOR SOUP GARNISH

Wash 1½ cups rice until the water is clear, then put the rice with ¼ tsp. salt and 3½ cups water into a saucepan and boil until the water has almost evaporated, stirring occasionally. Turn the heat low, lid the pan and cook until the rice is done—15–20 minutes. Put a damp cloth on a wetted tray, spread the rice on it, fold the cloth over and press well. Turn the rice out on to a wetted tray, spread it out evenly and again press well with a damp cloth, smoothing the top. Leave to cool for about 1½ hours, then cut into small cubes (or any shape desired), dipping the knife in hot water to prevent it sticking. Just before the soup is to be served,

fry the rice cubes in deep hot fat for 1–2 minutes, until slightly browned. Drain on kitchen paper and sprinkle with salt.

MUSHROOM SOUP

½ pint chicken stock	½ a beaten egg
2 tsps. pork	1 saltspoonful mono-sodium glutamate
1 cupful button mushrooms	

Boil the chicken stock, add the minced pork and the washed and roughly cut-up mushrooms and cook until tender, then add the egg and the monosodium glutamate (2 servings).

MALAYAN FISH STEW

1 lb. white fish	Milk
2 oz. butter	½ cup cooked rice
2 oz. flour	Salt and pepper
2 tsps. curry powder	1 tsp. lemon juice
2 tsps. chutney	2 hard-boiled eggs, sliced
3 slices of pineapple	

Poach the fish in a little water, then flake it, removing any bones. Keep the fish stock. Melt the butter and add the flour to make a roux; cook for a few minutes. Add the curry powder, chutney and pineapple. Add enough milk to the fish stock to make 1 pint; bring to the boil and pour on to the roux, stirring all the time. Cook for a few minutes. Add the cooked rice, flaked fish, salt, pepper and lemon juice, then the sliced eggs.

FISH CURRY

1 lb. fish	1 tbsp. butter
1 red pepper	½ tsp. salt
½ lb. onions	1 tsp. turmeric powder
¼ oz. root ginger	¾ pint coconut milk

Wash the fish and cut it into serving pieces. Cut the red pepper into fine strips and skin and slice the onions. Fry these lightly with the ginger in the butter, add the salt and turmeric and fry for a few minutes longer. Pour in the milk and bring to the boil. Lay the fish in the mixture and simmer gently for 15 minutes, until tender. Remove the ginger and serve the fish immediately.

SOUR FISH CURRY
(A NORTHERN THAI DISH)

Uncooked fish	Chillies (or 3–4 pepper-corns or red peppers)
Lard or cooking fat	
1 onion	Citrons, limes or a lemon
1 piece ginger	Spring onion

Cut the fish into small pieces about 1 inch square. Fry the onions. Add a very little ginger and chilli finely chopped and mashed into the browned onions. Put in the fish and cook until tender. Pour the juice of the lemon over the fish. Turn out on to a warm dish, season with the remainder of the chopped ginger and pepper, garnish with slices of lime or lemon and add a little spring onion. Serve hot, cooked rice with this.

Note : The ginger and chilli can be omitted and the fish cooked with only the onion and squeezed juice of lemon.

FISH MOOLIE
(CURRY)

1 lb. fish	A piece of cinnamon
1 large onion	A few small slices of
1 small coconut	green ginger
1 tbsp. butter	1 clove of garlic,
½ oz. saffron powder	sliced
A few curry leaves	4 green chillies
(optional)	

Cut the fish and the onions into large slices. Scrape the coconut, mix with a cup of hot water and strain through a wire strainer ; add another cup of hot water to the coconut to give a second cup of coconut milk—keep the two separate. Brown the onion in the fat, add the saffron, the second cup of milk, the fish and all the flavourings and cook for 15–20 minutes. Add the first cup of coconut milk and simmer for 15 minutes. Serve hot.

FRIED FISH WITH GINGER SAUCE

1½ lb. (approx.) filleted	1 tbsp. olive oil
white fish	¼ pint water
1 cup flour	Fat for frying
1 tsp. salt	

Clean and dry the fish and remove the skin. Mix the flour, salt and olive oil and add water to form a thick, smooth batter. Heat the fat, dip the fish in the batter and fry till golden-brown ; drain on crumpled kitchen paper and serve accompanied by ginger sauce.

This is a particularly good way of serving the cheaper types of white fish, such as cod and haddock.

OTAK-OTAK
(STUFFED TROUT)

2 trout	½ cup of milk
¼ tsp. coriander seed	Butter for frying
Pepper and salt	Cabbage leaves
Chopped onion and	Oil for frying
garlic	Red pepper, tomatoes
1 egg	and lettuce to garnish

Beat the fish gently with a wooden meat-beater to loosen the skin, then carefully take out the flesh, damaging the skin as little as possible.

Remove all the bones and chop the flesh, mix with the ground coriander, seasoning, onion and garlic, egg and milk and fry in the butter, without allowing the mixture to become dry. Fill the fish skins with this stuffing, wrap each fish in cabbage leaves and steam for about 20 minutes. Finally, fry the fish brown in hot olive oil and serve garnished with small pieces of pepper, tomato and lettuce.

NGA-BAUNG-DOKE
(CABBAGE LEAVES STUFFED WITH FISH)

1 lb. cod or other white	1 tbsp. flour
fish	1 tbsp. thick coconut
½ tsp. turmeric powder	milk (made from de-
1 tbsp. salt	siccated nut)
8 medium-sized onions	1 tbsp. good cooking oil
4 garlic cloves	15–20 large pieces of
A small piece of fresh	cabbage leaf (these
ginger (or 1 tsp.	replace the banana
ground ginger)	leaves that would be
1–2 dried red chillies	used in Burma)

Rub the cleaned fish thoroughly with a mixture of half the turmeric and half the salt, then cut into pieces about 3 by 1½ inches. Pound 3 of the onions with the garlic, ginger and chillies and mix with a paste made by combining the flour, coconut milk, oil and remaining salt and turmeric. Add the remaining onions, finely sliced. Trim the cabbage leaves into 6-inch squares and on each place a spoonful of the spice paste and one or two pieces of fish, topped by another layer of paste and some more fish. Fold the leaf over and secure with a cocktail stick. Steam in a double saucepan for 15–20 minutes.

If desired, the fish and paste filling may be " sandwiched " between nasturtium leaves before being encased in the cabbage leaves.

HO MOK

½ lb. white fish	A green pepper, red pepper,
3–4 pieces of	chilli or peppercorns
ginger	Cabbage leaves or lettuce
A small onion	leaves
Salt	

Cut up all the ingredients into very small pieces and pound together. Wrap cabbage or lettuce leaves round small individual portions. Tie with cotton or string, or fasten the package with a toothpick. Steam until tender. Remove the string and serve with hot, cooked rice. Garnish with parsley.

Notes : Chopped vegetables such as celery and sprouts can be included in the fish mixture. In place of the fish, chopped liver is often used, mixed with the above ingredients. In Thailand, the mixture is wrapped in banana leaves which are not eaten with the fish, but if cabbage or lettuce is used, the whole can then be eaten.

FISH SAMBAL

About 1 lb. cooked fish (cod, or other white fish or herring)
2 green chillies
A small piece of fresh ginger
2–4 garlic cloves
A small piece of saffron
6 small onions
3 fresh red chillies
½ a fresh coconut
½ tsp. cumin seeds
Oil for frying
Salt

Remove all bones from the fish. Pound the garlic, saffron, red chillies and cumin; slice the green chillies, ginger and onions. Make ¾ pint coconut milk in the usual way. Fry the sliced ingredients in the oil, then add the ground ingredients, put in the fish and fry well. Add salt to taste and mix in the coconut milk. Simmer for 5–10 minutes, stirring.

LAPIS ŒDANG
(FRIED PRAWNS)

1½ lb. large prawns
1 tsp. vinegar
Salt and pepper
1 tsp. soya sauce
3 eggs
1 tsp. sugar
Oil for deep frying
2 large onions, sliced and fried till brown
1 tbsp. butter
1 tbsp. flour
3 potatoes, chipped and fried with onions
2 tbsps. tomato sauce

Shell and wash the prawns, then rub them with salt and pepper. Dip the prawns into the lightly beaten eggs, then fry them in hot oil until cooked.

To prepare the sauce, heat the butter in a pan and fry the flour brown. Put in the tomato sauce, vinegar, soya sauce, sugar, onions and a little water and add salt to taste. Lastly put in the prawns and cook for a few minutes, till done. Serve with the potato chips.

KUNG YAM
(SHRIMP SALAD)

1 good cup grated fresh or canned flaked coconut
2 garlic cloves, minced
3 shallots, chopped
1 cup single cream
2 large green peppers, chopped
2 lb. shrimps, shelled and deveined
2 apples, peeled and coarsely grated
2 cups boiling water
½ cup broken pecan nuts
2 tsps. salt
¼ cup soya sauce
1 large bay leaf
Lettuce leaves
1 tbsp. olive oil

Combine the coconut and cream, bring to the boil then cool for 30 minutes; drain off the cream and chill it. Meanwhile, put the shrimps into the boiling water with the salt and bay leaf, cover and cook for about 5 minutes. Drain, split in halves lengthwise and chill.

Heat the olive oil in a frying pan and sauté the garlic and shallots till golden. Combine the peppers, apples, pecans, garlic mixture, soya sauce and cream; toss together, then chill for ¾ hour. Arrange the lettuce on a large platter and place on it the shrimps, then the apple mixture. Makes 6 servings.

UDANG BUMBU DENDENG
(SPICED FRIED SHRIMPS)

1 cup peeled fresh shrimps
A pinch of salt
1 tsp. ground ginger
1 tsp. vinegar
½ tsp. *laos* powder (if available)
1 tsp. coriander powder
1 tsp. sugar
¼ tsp. garlic powder
Fat for deep frying

Split the shrimps down the back. Combine the vinegar and all the flavourings and marinade the shrimps in this mixture for about 2 hours. Deep-fry, and serve at once.

CURRIED DUCK

1 duck, about 3–4 lb.
A small piece of fresh ginger (or 1 tsp. ground ginger)
1 tbsp. salt
1 tsp. powdered saffron
3 tbsps. Chinese soya sauce
1 cup good cooking oil
10 medium-sized onions
5 peppercorns
15 garlic cloves
2–3 curry leaves or bay leaves
5–10 dried chillies

Cut the cleaned duck into 8 pieces, and rub these over thoroughly with a mixture of salt, saffron and soya sauce; put aside for an hour.

Pound half the onions with the ginger, 8 garlic cloves and the chillies, if used. Heat the oil and put in the peppercorns, curry leaves and pounded ingredients. Add the duck, brown and simmer for 5 minutes, then add just enough water to cover it and simmer for 2 hours. Slice the remaining onions and garlic and put over the duck about ½ hour before serving.

WOOD-PIGEON WITH CUCUMBER

1 large wood-pigeon
2 tsps. flour
1 small cucumber
Salt to taste
3 green chillies
1 oz. lard
1 tbsp. wine vinegar or ¼ pint cider
1 large garlic clove, sliced
2 tsps. sugar
1 small onion, sliced
1 tbsp. Chinese soya sauce
A few crushed coriander leaves (if available)

Clean and joint the pigeon. Slice the cucumber without peeling ; slice the chillies, remove the seeds and cut the flesh into neat pieces. Mix the vinegar or cider, sugar, soya sauce, flour and salt. Heat the lard and fry the garlic and onion till golden-brown. Add the bird and fry, stirring, for about 2 minutes, then put in all the other ingredients except the chillies and coriander leaves and stir again. Continue to cook gently until the bird is tender. Dish up and garnish with the coriander leaves and green chillies.

KAI PRIAO WAN
(CHICKEN SOUR AND SWEET)

32

Heat 2 tbsps. fat in a large pan and sauté 3 crushed garlic cloves till golden. Add 1½ chicken breasts, thinly sliced, 5 chicken livers, quartered, and 2 large carrots, sliced ½ inch thick. Cook over a moderate heat, stirring for 5 minutes. Now add 1 large cucumber, peeled, split lengthwise, then sliced crosswise ⅛ inch thick, 3 small tomatoes, peeled and cut into eighths, 1 large onion, cut into ¼-inch wedges and ½ cup canned condensed chicken broth, undiluted. Cover and simmer until tender.

Meanwhile, combine 1 tbsp. flour, 2 tbsps. sugar, ¼ cup soya sauce and ¼ cup vinegar. Pour this over the chicken and vegetables, stirring ; cook till thickened.

Serve in a large hot bowl, with hot boiled rice and noodles. Makes 6 servings.

CHICKEN WITH GINGER AND MUSHROOMS

33

Meat cut from 2 legs of chicken	3 cloves of garlic, chopped
Chicken giblets	1 tbsp. soya bean sauce
½ cup black mushrooms	Fish sauce
4 spring onions	2 tsps. caster sugar
3 tbsps. finely shredded ginger	1 tbsp. vinegar
	Pepper
Salt	Coriander leaves, if
1 tbsp. chopped onion	available
2 tbsps. lard	

Cut chicken meat and giblets into small pieces. Put the mushrooms into hot water and let stand for some time ; when soft, wash and trim. Cut the spring onions into small pieces and soak in cold water. Squeeze the ginger in salted water to get rid of some of its hot taste ; wash and drain well. Fry the chopped onion in the lard until soft, add the chopped garlic and stir for a while. Add the soya bean sauce, ginger and chicken, stirring all the time, then add the other ingredients and season to taste with fish sauce, sugar, vinegar and pepper. Take care not to overcook the chicken or it will be tough.

Decorate with coriander leaves, if available, and serve with boiled rice.

KANF PED KAI
(CHICKEN CURRY)

1 chicken	1 tsp. *makrut* leaves,
Curry paste (see p. 365)	when obtainable
7 cups coconut milk (made from 1 large nut)	¼ cup fresh green chillies
	½ cup *horapa* leaves
2 tbsps. fish sauce	(when obtainable)

Cut the chicken meat into small pieces and break up the bones. Put the coconut milk into a large pan and heat, stirring, until it comes to the boil ; boil for 5 minutes. Pour off half the boiled coconut milk and simmer the other half for a further 15 minutes. Put in the chicken and cook for 10 minutes. Add the curry paste, fish sauce, *makrut* leaves and the remaining coconut milk, and cook, stirring, for a few minutes longer. Add the green chillies and the *horapa* leaves.

SOTO AJAM
(CHICKEN BOUILLON)

1 chicken	2 potatoes
Onions and garlic to taste	2 cooked carrots
Oil for frying	1–2 sticks of celery
Salt and pepper	1–2 cooked leeks
Ground ginger to taste	4 meat cubes
3 pints water	A little red pepper
2 eggs	A little lemon juice

Cut up the chicken. Fry the onions and garlic in the oil without browning, then boil the chicken until tender with the onions, garlic, salt, pepper, ginger and water. Hard-boil the eggs and slice ; cut up the peeled potatoes and fry them ; cut the carrots into small pieces and slice the celery and leeks finely. To add extra flavour, mix in a sauce made by dissolving the meat cubes in boiling water and adding red pepper and lemon juice. To serve, put into each soup cup a spoonful of chicken meat, cut up small, a few slices of egg, and some of the various vegetables. Pour hot chicken broth over all and serve very hot.

AJAM PANGGANG BOEMBOE KETJAP
(BARBECUED CHICKEN WITH SPICED KETCHUP)

1 chicken	1 small tsp. *sambal œlek*
Butter for frying	2 tbsps. soya sauce
2 onions	Juice of ½ a lemon
1 clove of garlic	Salt to taste
1 tbsp. sugar	

Cut the chicken in half. Melt the butter in a shallow saucepan or lidded frying pan. Slice the onions and fry with the garlic in the butter.

Add the sugar, *sambal*, soya sauce, lemon juice and salt and put in the halved chicken. Cover the pan and cook slowly for about 2 hours, then remove the lid and simmer until the oil from the butter comes to the top. Just before serving, place the pan under the grill until the chicken is crisp on top. Serve with boiled rice.

SATE AJAM
(SKEWERED CHICKEN)

Cut a chicken into small pieces and fix these on to cocktail sticks. Mix some ground black pepper, salt and ketchup, pour over the chicken, and steam until the chicken is tender, then brown under a grill just before serving. Serve on the skewers, accompanied by a sauce made as follows : Mince or pound together 1 stewed red pepper and 2–3 fried cloves of garlic, mix with 4 tbsps. peanut butter and a meat cube dissolved in a little boiling water, and add lemon juice to taste. Serve accompanied by yellow rice.

CHICKEN LIVERS

¼ lb. chicken livers	½ tsp. ground ginger
2 cloves of garlic	1 tsp. grated lemon
1 large onion	rind
2 green peppers	1 tsp. sugar
1 oz. blanched almonds	1 tsp. salt
2 tbsps. oil for frying	1 tbsp. vinegar

Wash the livers and cut up finely. Crush the garlic and chop the onion, peppers and almonds. Heat the oil and add all the ingredients except the livers and vinegar. Put in the meat and fry for a few minutes, then add the vinegar and 1 cup of water ; simmer gently until all the ingredients are tender. Serve with rice. Sufficient for 2 servings.

CHICKEN WITH YELLOW RICE

1 chicken	¾ lb. small onions
A bouquet garni	2 tbsps. butter
2 tsps. ground turmeric	A few seeded raisins
2 cups Patna rice	1 egg

Boil the chicken with the bouquet garni in about 1½ pints water until tender. Remove the chicken and bouquet garni from the stock ; joint the chicken and keep it hot. Make the chicken stock up to 2 pints with water, add the turmeric and bring to the boil. Put in the washed rice, cover and simmer gently until all the stock has been absorbed.

Meanwhile, fry the finely chopped onions in the butter and add the raisins. Beat the egg, add it to the onion mixture and fry like an omelette, then roll it up and cut into strips. Put the rice on to a dish, lay the joints of chicken on it and sprinkle the omelette strips on top.

An alternative method of preparing yellow rice is given in the next recipe.

NASI KUNING
(YELLOW RICE)

1 lb. Patna rice	Celery leaf or watercress,
1½ pints coconut milk or milk and water	fresh red chillies, 1 onion (sliced), fried black soya beans, ½ a
1 tsp. turmeric powder	cucumber (sliced), and carrot or radish " flow-
½ tsp. salt	ers " to garnish
2 eggs	

Wash the rice. Bring the coconut milk to the boil, add the rice and seasonings and cook until the milk is absorbed, stirring once or twice to prevent burning ; leave on a low heat for about 5 minutes. Now steam the rice until it is cooked. Meanwhile make an omelette with the eggs and cut it into strips. Put the yellow rice into a dish and decorate with the omelette strips, etc. Serve as an accompaniment to roast chicken, etc., with mixed pickles as a side dish.

CHICKEN STEW

1 cut-up chicken	2 tsps. paprika
2 diced onions	2 tsps. *sambal œlek*
Fat for frying	(or ground red chillies
½ cup water	mixed with tomato
1 cup coconut milk	purée)
1 tsp. ground ginger	1 tsp. sugar

Fry the chicken and the diced onions in the fat until well browned. Add the water, while continuing to cook, and when this has evaporated add the coconut milk, ginger, paprika, *sambal œlek* and sugar and mix well. Turn heat very low, cover the pan and simmer for about 1 hour, or until the meat is so well cooked that it will easily fall away from the bone ; if necessary, add another cup of coconut milk. Serve with rice.

MAW GWOOH CHOW GHUY PIEN
(MUSHROOM BRAISED VELVET CHICKEN)

4–6 chicken breasts	¼ cup mushroom liquor
1 tbsp. cornflour	1 can white button
1 tsp. salt	mushrooms
¼ tsp. white pepper	1 slice of fresh ginger
1 tsp. soya sauce	1 garlic clove (if desired)
2 tbsps. vegetable oil	

Slice the chicken breasts thinly. Mix together 1 tsp. cornflour, ½ tsp. salt, the pepper, soya sauce and vegetable oil. Coat the chicken slices with this mixture and allow to stand for 1 hour. Mix the remaining cornflour and salt with the mushroom liquor, then cook over a gentle heat, stirring continuously. Add the mushrooms and heat thoroughly. Chop the ginger and garlic finely and fry in a little vegetable oil; add the chicken and fry for about ½ minute. Pour on the mushroom mixture and continue frying until the chicken is just cooked—take care not to overcook the chicken. Serve at once.

HUNG YEN SO KAI
(CHICKEN WITH CHOPPED ALMONDS)

3 lb. cockerel or capon	1 tsp. *vietsin*
Cornflour or tapioca starch	1 tsp. light soya sauce
	1 egg
A little water	4 oz. chopped almonds
1 tsp. rock salt	Deep fat for frying

Take all the chicken flesh off the bones with a sharp knife or chopper; cut it in very thin slices (as for Wiener Schnitzel). Mix 1 tbsp. cornflour or tapioca starch with a little water and add the rock salt, *vietsin*, soya sauce and lightly beaten egg. Pour over the chicken slices and mix so that every piece is coated with the mixture. Spread some cornflour on a baking tin or tray and lay the pieces of chicken on it. Sprinkle the chopped almonds over the chicken, then turn the pieces over to coat them with the cornflour. (Both sides of the chicken may be coated with nuts if preferred.)

Fry in deep fat (this should not be too hot, or it may darken the nuts too much—they should be an attractive golden-brown when the chicken is ready). Serve on a dish garnished with sliced cucumber and tomato and some very small pieces of red chilli.

This dish is either served as part of a Chinese meal, or as a main course with rice and vegetables or potato chips. Pork fillets may be cooked in the same way.

DEVILLED HEN
(INDO-MALAYAN)

1 chicken, about 3–4½ lb.	1 large onion, minced
Salt	2 oz. butter or lard
10 dried red chillies	1 inch fresh ginger
5 peppercorns	1 garlic clove
4 cloves	Thick and thin milk
½ inch turmeric	made from ½ a
1 tsp. anise	coconut
A 2-inch piece of stick cinnamon	1½ oz. tamarind paste
	2 tsps. vinegar
1 cardamom pod	

Clean the fowl and cut in pieces, wash and sprinkle with a little salt. Grind together the next seven ingredients. Fry the minced onion in the fat in a saucepan till browned, then add the sliced ginger and garlic and fry for a minute

or two. Add the ground ingredients and fry for a further 2 minutes, then add the chicken pieces. Lid the pan tightly and cook for about 15 minutes, stirring occasionally. Add the thin coconut milk, lid the pan and cook for a further 15 minutes, then put in the tamarind juice (or a little vinegar). After half an hour add the thick coconut juice and boil for 10 minutes, unlidded. Add the vinegar and cook for a further 15 minutes over a low heat.

If an old fowl is used, allow longer cooking time.

BOEBOE AYAM
(RICE AND CHICKEN)

¼ of a chicken	5 oz. rice
½ lb. pork bones	1 tsp. *vietsin*
2½ pints stock	½ tsp. pepper
1 oz. onions, sliced finely	2 tsps. salt
	3 stalks Chinese celery
1½ tbsps. lard	(optional)

Cook the chicken with the pork bones in the stock. Take the flesh from the chicken and cut into cubes. Fry the onion in the lard until golden-brown, then remove and keep aside. Fry the rice in 1 tsp. lard for about 5 minutes. Bring the stock to the boil and add the rice, *vietsin*, pepper and salt; continue boiling until the rice is cooked, then add the cubed chicken. Serve garnished with the crisp fried onions and Chinese celery.

HOT CURRY

1 shredded coconut	Nampla or other
½ lb. beef	sauce flavouring
1 onion	A little butter or
A little garlic	lard
Curry powder or paste	5–6 leaves of bai
Potatoes (other vegetables can be added as desired)	lapah (a herb similar to mint)
Salt	

Cover the shredded coconut with water and squeeze to make coconut milk. Do this three times. Heat the second squeezing to the boil, add the beef cut into small pieces. Cook for half an hour. Brown the onion in a pan with a little fat, mix in the garlic and the curry paste or powder (about 1 tsp. of curry paste or a dessertsp. of powder). Add the beef removed from the coconut milk. Stir over the heat for a short time. Return the mixture into the coconut milk and add the potatoes cut in small cubes. Add other vegetables, if desired. Add salt, bai lapah and sauce.

Cook gently until done and serve with a dish of hot, cooked rice.

134

CHAAH SIEU
(BARBECUED PORK)

1 lb. lean loin of pork	1 tsp. sugar
½ tsp. salt	1 tsp. sherry
¼ tsp. pepper	2 tbsps. soya sauce

Cut the pork along the grain into strips about 2 inches wide. Mix the salt, pepper and sugar and rub into the pork slices; allow to soak for about 2 hours. Heat the oven to moderate (350° F., mark 4). Rub the sherry and soya sauce into the pork and roast for 10 minutes; turn the slices of pork over, raise the temperature to hot (450° F., mark 8) and roast the meat for about 15 minutes, basting it with the juices in the baking tin. Cut each slice against the grain into ¼-inch pieces. Dish up and serve with fried rice (see below).

CHOW FAAHN
(FRIED RICE TO SERVE WITH CURRY, ETC.)

½ cup sliced barbecued pork (see previous recipe)	1 tsp. salt
	¼ tsp. pepper
3 eggs	4 spring onions
Oil	2 tbsps. soya
4 cups cold boiled rice	sauce
(cooked a day beforehand)	

Dice the pork and beat the eggs. Heat a little oil in a frying pan, add the cooked rice and fry until hot, stirring and pressing out all lumps. Add the salt, pepper, onions, and pork and mix thoroughly. Make a hollow in the centre of the rice, pour in the beaten eggs and scramble these; when semi-cooked stir in the rice. When well mixed, sprinkle with soya sauce and serve.

GOLDEN PORK

¾–1 lb. lean pork	2 oz. fresh ginger
4 oz. onions	2 oz. cooking oil
2 oz. garlic	Salt to taste

Cut the pork into 1-inch squares. Pound the onions, garlic and ginger together, then put the mixture in a muslin square and squeeze out the juice. Mix this juice with the pork, oil and salt, then put in a hot saucepan and cook slowly. When the pork is nearly done, take out half of the pieces and pound them. Mix with the pounded onions, garlic and ginger and put back in the pan. Cook until golden-brown.

PORK SAMBAL

1½ lb. pork	4–5 garlic cloves
A few anise seeds	Fat for frying
A few dried chillies	A little ground cinnamon
3 large onions	A little lime juice

Cut up the pork. Grind the anise and chillies

together. Slice the onions and garlic and fry them, then add the ground ingredients and the pork, bring to the boil and cook for 15 minutes, or till the pork is done. Just before removing from the heat, add the lime juice.

BAMIE
(PORK AND NOODLES)

135

2 lean pork chops	Fat for frying
⅓ of a cabbage, shredded	1 tsp. ground ginger
A small quantity of celery tops	1 small can of shrimps
2 diced onions	½ large packet of egg noodles
1 clove of garlic	1 egg for omelette

Dice the pork chops and cook in 1 cup salted water for 15 minutes. Use this water to blanch the cabbage and celery tops for a few minutes. Fry the onions and garlic; when browned, remove from the pan and mix in the ground ginger. Drain the shrimps and wash well. Cook the noodles for 10 minutes and rinse. Fry the pork in the fat; when slightly browned add the cabbage and celery tops and continue to fry, stirring all the time. Add the onions and mix well, then add the shrimps and noodles.

Make an omelette and when it is cooked cut it in strips. Place the noodle mixture on a large platter and garnish with the omelette strips. Serve with soya sauce. Mushrooms or ham may also be included.

SWEET PORK

1 whole coconut	Salt
Pork suitable for stewing	Sugar
2–3 small pieces of ginger	Pepper

Scrape and make one cup of coconut milk from one whole coconut. Cut the pork into small pieces or thin slices. Cook until tender in plain water sufficient to cover the meat well, add a little salt and pepper. Now add the coconut milk with a little sugar. Do not make it too sweet. Chop the ginger and add to the coconut milk and pork. Mix in a small teaspoonful of cornflour tot hicken. Simmer for a few minutes. Serve with a pepper sauce.

NAM PRIK
(THIN SAUCE)

4 oz. dried shrimps	1 small onion
4 oz. peanuts	1 hard-boiled egg
6–7 peppercorns	A little salt

Roast the shrimps and the peanuts in the oven. Keep them a good colour and do not burn. The shrimps should be crisp. Pound the shrimps, nuts and peppercorns together with a little pinch of salt. Mash the egg yolk and onion with the mixture. Pound in a mortar with a pestle if available. Mix in a little water until the sauce is the consistency of gravy. Put in a jar for storing.

PEPPER SAUCE

Roasted, dried chillies   A little vinegar

Roast the chillies. Crush finely and mix with a little vinegar. The small pieces of pork are dipped into the sauce and eaten as a side dish with the rest of the meal.

If desired, chopped celery can be added to the pork while cooking—this greatly adds to the flavour.

MANGO AND PORK SALAD

2 large green mangoes	1 tbsp. dried salted
Salt and pepper	shrimps, finely
2 tbsps. lard	pounded
1 tbsp. each of finely	1 tbsp. roasted peanuts,
shredded garlic and	partly pounded
shallots	1 tbsp. fish sauce
½ cup lean pork, finely	1 tsp sugar
chopped	A little shredded chilli

Shred the mangoes into long even strips, mix with about 1 tsp. salt to remove some of the sour taste, wash and squeeze gently to free the flesh from water, then put into a large bowl.

Heat the lard and fry the shredded shallots and garlic separately; when crisp remove from the pan. In the remaining lard fry the pork until done. Add the shrimps, peanuts, fish sauce and sugar and stir well. Just before serving, add the fried ingredients to the mango in the large bowl, mix well and season to taste, adding more nampla and sugar if required. Put in a serving dish and place the fried shallots and garlic and the shredded chilli on top. Serve with cooked rice.

PORK AND PINEAPPLE CURRY—I

4 pork chops	A few dried shrimps (or
1 pineapple	a little anchovy paste)
2–3 fresh red chillies	A few small onions
A small piece of saffron	2–3 garlic cloves
2 tsps. coriander	1 small coconut
1 oz. almonds	Fat or oil for frying

Trim the chops; cut the pineapple into pieces. Grind or pound the chillies, saffron, coriander, nuts and shrimps and lastly add the onions and garlic. Scrape and grate the coconut and make two successive infusions of coconut milk. Fry the ground ingredients well, add the meat and cook well, then add the pineapple and lastly the second (thinner) coconut milk. A few minutes before serving add the first (thick) coconut milk.

The original recipe also includes local herbs such as lemon grass, and candle nuts instead of the almonds.

PORK AND PINEAPPLE CURRY—II

1 lb. pork	1 tbsp. grated lemon
2 oz. butter	rind
1 clove of garlic	1 tsp. coriander powder
1 medium-sized	2 oz. blanched almonds
onion	½ pint water
2 red chillies	1 small tin of pineapple
1 tbsp. shrimp or	chunks
anchovy paste	¼ tsp. saffron
1½ oz. fresh ginger	

Cut the pork into small pieces and sauté in the butter with the crushed garlic, chopped onion and sliced chillies. Mix together the fish paste, chopped ginger, lemon rind, coriander powder and chopped almonds; add this to the pork mixture and continue frying gently for a few minutes. Add the water and cook until the meat is tender. Finally, add the pineapple chunks and saffron and cook for a few minutes longer. Serve very hot.

If you cannot obtain the fresh ginger (also called green ginger) or the coriander powder, use root ginger and ¼ oz. coriander seed; tie them in a muslin bag, and remove when the curry is cooked.

BEEF CURRY

1 lb. beef	2 tsps. salt
2 large onions	½ tsp. saffron
2 garlic cloves	½ tsp. ground chillies
A small piece of fresh	2 tbsps. oil
ginger (or 2 tsps.	2 tsps. Chinese soya
ground ginger)	sauce

Cut the meat into 2-inch strips. Pound the onions, garlic and ginger. Mix the salt, saffron and chilli powder. Heat the oil in a saucepan and put in all the seasonings; add the meat and cook until brown. Add water to cover and simmer for ½ hour, or until tender. Serve with boiled rice.

Mutton or pork may be used instead of beef.

MANDALAY MEAT CURRY

1 lb. stewing steak or	½ lb. tomatoes
mutton	¼ pint milk
1 medium-sized onion	2 tsps. lemon juice
1 clove of garlic	Seasoning
1 oz. butter	2 tsps. sugar
2 tbsps. curry powder	

Cut the meat into cubes. Cut up the onion and garlic and fry in the butter for 3–4 minutes, then add the curry powder and fry for about

2 more minutes. Now add the cut-up tomatoes and cubed meat, with just enough water to cover, and simmer very gently for about 1½ hours, till the meat is tender. Stir in the milk and lemon juice. Season well and add the sugar. Serve with plain boiled rice.

CURRIED TRIPE, MALAY STYLE

1 lb. tripe	1 onion
1 tbsp. vinegar	1 clove of garlic
1 tbsp. coriander seed	2 oz. coconut infused
1 tsp. turmeric powder	in boiling water for
A pinch of cumin	15 minutes
½ tsp. ground mustard	1 tsp. mango chutney
½ tsp. pepper	Stock
1 oz. fat	Salt to taste

Wash the tripe and cut into convenient-sized pieces; cover with cold water and simmer until tender. Make a paste with the vinegar, spices and pepper. Melt the fat and fry the chopped onion and garlic. Add the curry paste, mix thoroughly and cook for 3–4 minutes. Add the strained coconut infusion, chutney, tripe and enough stock to make a thick gravy. Season with salt, heat thoroughly and serve.

BANANA CURRY

4 large unripe bananas	1 green chilli, sliced
1 tsp. salt	1 tbsp. Bombay
A pinch of ground saffron	duck
or turmeric	¼ tsp. fenugreek
2 tbsps. oil or butter	A 1-inch piece of
2 breakfastcups coconut	cinnamon
milk (extracted from	A 1-inch piece of
½ lb. desiccated coco-	*rampe*, if available
nut)	3–4 curry leaves, if
1 tbsp. small onions,	available
sliced	1 sprig of fennel

Skin the bananas (which should be as green as possible), cut them lengthwise and then in half. Rub the pieces with the salt and saffron or turmeric, then fry them in the oil or butter. Pour the coconut milk into a saucepan with the remaining ingredients and bring to the boil. Simmer for 30 minutes, then add the bananas and simmer until the gravy is thick.

FRIKADEL GORENG
(MEAT BALLS)

1¼ lb. potatoes, boiled	8 oz. minced meat
Salt	(pork, beef or chicken)
2 oz. butter	3–4 eggs (depending on
2½ large onions, sliced	size
¾ tsp. pepper	Deep fat for frying
¾ tsp. grated nutmeg	

Mash the potatoes, add salt to taste. Melt the butter and fry the onions, pepper, nutmeg and meat for about 5 minutes. Add this to the mashed potatoes, then mix with the eggs; if sufficiently moist, add another egg. (The best way to test is to fry one of the meat balls.) Shape into balls and fry in deep fat until the meat is cooked through.

VEAL AND TONGUE JELLY

2 sheep's tongues	1 tbsp. chopped parsley
Salt and peppercorns	½ tsp. dried herbs
1 lb. neck of veal	2 hard-boiled eggs

Wash the tongues well and stew gently with the peppercorns until the skin can easily be removed. Cut the veal into small pieces and cook either by stewing very slowly or in the oven in a casserole, with the parsley and herbs and enough cold water to cover the meat. Arrange the cut-up hard-boiled eggs in the bottom of a basin or mould, mix the pieces of tongue and veal together and put in, adding a layer of cold vegetables if liked. Strain the gravy and dissolve in it ½ oz. gelatine to ½ pint gravy. (Although veal stock sets in a jelly, it is too soft to allow the mould to be turned out.) Keep cold in a refrigerator for at least 3 hours before serving. Dip the mould into very hot water for a minute before turning out. Serve with a salad.

BURMESE BEEF CURRY

1 lb. beef	1 tsp. turmeric powder
2 fairly large or 3	½ tsp. red pepper
medium-sized onions	2 tsps. powder paprika
3 cloves garlic	(optional)
(optional)	½ tsp. powdered ginger
6 tbsps. good cooking	or small piece fresh
oil	ginger

Trim the meat, remove all fat and cut into pieces about an inch square, but they should not be too thick. Grate the onions or chop very fine, crush garlic; if fresh ginger is used cut very finely. Mix all ingredients together. Mix the onions and other ingredients first, then rub well into the meat. Allow it to stand for a few minutes then add ¾–1 cup of water, bring to the boil and simmer till cooked. The curry is ready when not only is the meat tender, but all the water has evaporated and only the oil is left.

SATAY
(SKEWERED MEAT WITH SATAY SAUCE)

Use fatty beef, mutton or chicken meat cut into thin slices or little chunks; flatten out and thread on a thin skewer, then roast or grill over a hot fire. The best results are obtained if the meat is basted with oil while cooking. The meat on the skewer is then dipped into the satay sauce prior to eating.

SATAY SAUCE

1 lb. ground nuts	Juice of ½ a lemon
2 tsps. chilli powder	Salt to taste
1 tbsp. sugar	¾ cup fat
¾ cup water	

Make the fat very hot. Mix the nuts, chilli powder and sugar and pour into the fat; stir for 5 minutes. Add the water, lemon juice and salt and cook for 10 minutes. If the mixture is too thick, add a little more water.

KORMAK
(CURRIED BEEF)

2 lb. beefsteak	1 tsp. ground carda-
4 cloves of garlic	mom powder
2 tsps. powdered ginger	4 oz. butter
4 tsps. ground coriander	1 lb. onions
2 tsps. cumin powder	2 cups milk and the
½ tsp. ground cloves	juice of 1 lemon

Cut the meat in half, wash and dry well. Pound the garlic, mix with the ginger and rub well into the meat; add the other spices, mixed with a little water, and leave for 20 minutes. Melt the fat in a saucepan, put in the meat and keep it moving for 2 minutes. Fill the pan a quarter full with water and let it boil for 10 minutes, then add the quartered onions, turn the heat low, and simmer for 15 minutes with the lid on. Add the milk (soured by the addition of the lemon juice) and simmer till the meat is tender. If the gravy has not thickened at this stage, remove the meat, keep it hot and boil the gravy until it is sufficiently reduced. Serve with rice, accompanied by chutney and diced cucumber, pineapple and tomato.

SATE KAMBING
(GRILLED LAMB)

1 lb. lamb	1 clove of garlic
¾ tsp. coriander	Salt and pepper
1 onion	Tamarind or lemon juice

For the Sauce

1 teacup peanuts	Tamarind or lemon
1 onion	juice
1 clove of garlic	1 leaf *daon djeruk purut*
3 red chillies	and a little *sereh*, if
½ tsp. ground ginger	available
A little *laos*, if available	

Cut the meat into 1-inch squares. Mince the coriander, onion and garlic, then mix them with the meat, seasoning and tamarind juice; thread on skewers (4 or 5 pieces to each) and roast.

Serve with the sauce, ketchup, fried onion rings and tamarind juice or a little vinegar. To make the sauce, mince the peanuts, fry with the chopped onion, garlic, chillies, ginger and *laos* and add a little water; add the tamarind or lemon juice and the other flavourings, if available.

SIMPLE MEAT CURRY

1 lb. beefsteak, finely chopped	1 tsp. shrimp paste
1 oz. lard	Grated rind of
1 pint stock	1 lemon
1 tsp. curry paste (see below)	1 green pepper

Brown the meat in the lard, then add the stock and cook until the meat is tender. Fry the curry paste in the lard and stir in the shrimp paste and lemon rind. Add the meat and stock and simmer for 20 minutes. Cut up the green pepper and add a few minutes before serving.

SIAMESE CURRY PASTE

5 large dried chillies	½ tsp. grated lemon rind
1 tsp. salt	1 tsp. peppercorns
2 tsps. caraway seeds (optional)	2 tbsps. chopped shallots
2 tsps. chopped coriander roots (or seeds)	1 tbsp. chopped garlic
	1 tbsp. shrimp paste

De-seed the chillies and pound them with the salt. Add the rest of the ingredients and pound the mixture until it becomes a fine paste.

PRAWN PELLETS (SIDE DISH)

¼ of a clove of garlic	A little lard
1 Pacific king prawn (raw and minced)	¼ tsp. cayenne pepper
Pepper	2 tsps. *vesop*

Chop the garlic very finely and mix it with the minced prawn and a pinch of pepper. Make into balls, drop into hot fat and fry until golden-brown, shaking the pan as you do so, then add the cayenne and *vesop*.

Failing Pacific king prawn, use 2 oz. frozen scampi.

FRIED MEAT BALLS (SIDE DISH)

½ lb. pork (or beef and pork mixed)	Grated nutmeg
2 cloves of garlic	1 egg
A few finely chopped chives	A little *vesop*
Coriander	Flour
	Lard for frying

Mince the meat finely with the garlic and chives, then add the coriander and nutmeg.

136

Beat in the egg and add the *vesop*. Form into small balls, roll in flour and fry in the hot fat till brown.

CHICKEN AND GINGER (SIDE DISH)

1 clove of garlic	½ tsp. monosodium
2 tbsps. lard	glutamate
2–3 oz. raw chicken	1 tbsp. chicken broth
1 tsp. yellow soya beans	1 tbsp. thinly sliced
½ tsp. *vesop*	fresh ginger
½ tsp. sugar	1 tsp. spring onions or
1 tsp. vinegar	chives

Chop the garlic and fry in the hot lard till brown, then add the chicken, cut into small pieces; fry for a short time, then add the soya beans, flavourings and broth and cook gently for 5–10 minutes. Add the ginger; lastly, just before serving, add some chopped spring onions or chives. Serve as one of several side dishes.

If fresh ginger is unobtainable, flavour the dish with a piece of root ginger, which should be added with the beans, etc., and removed before serving.

GINGER SAUCE

4 oz. chopped mushrooms	¼ pint water
(or 7–8 dried mushrooms)	1 tbsp. soya sauce
4 tbsps. vinegar	1 oz. ground ginger
2 tbsps. finely chopped	1 tbsp. cornflour
onion	blended with a
2 oz. sugar	little water

Put all the ingredients except the cornflour in a saucepan and boil for 5 minutes. Stir in the blended cornflour and simmer for a few minutes, until cooked.

SWEET AND SOUR PORK (SIDE DISH)

½ a clove of garlic	¼ pint chicken stock
1 tsp. lard	1 tsp. cornflour blended
2 tbsps. cut-up raw	with 2 tsps. water
pork	¼ tsp. monosodium
2 tsps. vinegar	glutamate
2 tsps. sugar	1 small tomato
2 tsps. *vesop*	1 tbsp. cucumber chunks
1 tbsp. chopped onion	

Chop the garlic finely and fry it in the lard till brown, then add the pork, vinegar, sugar, *vesop*, chopped onion and stock and boil all together until tender. Add the blended cornflour and the monosodium glutamate. At the last minute add the cut-up tomato and the cucumber chunks.

SAMBAL GORENG OMELETTE—I

Pound or grind together 2 large onions, 2 garlic cloves, ½ tsp. sugar, a few dried shrimps (or a little anchovy paste), 1 fresh chilli, 1 oz. almonds or other nuts and herbs as desired (the original calls for various local ones), with salt to taste. Fry in a little oil, adding 1 tsp. tamarind paste mixed with a little water, or 2 tsps. vinegar. Stir in ½ cup coconut milk and 1–2 cut-up fresh chillies. Meanwhile make a large omelette from 4–5 eggs and cut into strips; add it to the fried mixture and serve.

SAMBAL GORENG OMELETTE—II

Butter or oil for frying	Salt to taste
1 garlic clove, crushed	1 tsp. tamarind paste
2 finely chopped onions	mixed with a little
2 tsps. grated lemon rind	water or 2 tsps.
¼ tsp. chilli powder	vinegar
1 tsp. shrimp or anchovy	4–5 eggs
paste	½ cup coconut milk
½ tsp. sugar	

Heat the fat and fry all the ingredients except the eggs and milk; mix well and cook until golden-brown. Beat the eggs, add the milk and pour over the fried mixture, then cook as for an omelette.

SAMBAL GORENG TELOR
(EGGS IN RED PEPPER SAUCE)

1 tbsp. chopped onion	1 tsp. crushed red
1 clove of garlic	pepper
Butter for frying	½–1 tsp. paprika
1 cup coconut milk	½ tsp. *laos* powder
1 cup stock	(if available)
Salt to taste	4 hard-boiled eggs

Sauté the chopped onion and garlic in the butter. Add the other ingredients (except the eggs) and bring to the boil, stirring occasionally. Add the eggs and continue cooking and stirring for 3 minutes. Remove from the heat and halve the eggs, then serve hot.

SERNOONMAKIN

4 oz. semolina	5 tbsps. good cooking
4 oz. sugar	oil
4 oz. desiccated coconut	Poppy seeds
A pinch of turmeric	1 pint water
powder	

Heat the semolina over a low gas till it begins to darken in colour, then let it cool. Be very careful not to burn the semolina. Pour ½ pint boiling water over the desiccated coconut and allow it to stand for a while, strain and keep the liquid. Pour another ½ pint boiling water over the same coconut, stir well and allow to stand and strain. Add the two liquids together and make up to 1 pint. Let it get cold. Take 1 tbsp. oil, then heat and add the turmeric and cook gently till the raw smell of the turmeric has disappeared. When the semolina has cooled add the sugar and all the oil and mix thoroughly, lastly add the coconut, mix well and cook over medium heat, till the mixture is thick and leaves the side of the pan. The mixture should be stirred all the time during cooking. Now put into a baking tin, sprinkle with poppy seed and bake in a moderate oven (400° F., mark 6) till it is set and the top is browned. When cold, cut into diamond shapes.

EGGS WITH MUSHROOM AND PEPPER SAUCE

Hard-boil 2 eggs; when cold slice into quarters and arrange in a small dish. To make the sauce, slice 2 or 3 mushrooms and $\frac{1}{2}$ a red pepper. Put these on to the hot-plate of an electric cooker or a heavy frying pan, and allow them to burn slightly on each side. Put into a small bowl and add $\frac{1}{2}$ tsp. *vesop* and $\frac{1}{2}$ tsp. lemon juice, a little sugar and a pinch of monosodium glutamate to enhance the flavour. Pour this sauce over the eggs, and serve.

FRIED RICE WITH EGGS

$\frac{1}{2}$ a clove of garlic	2 tsps. chopped onion
2 tsps. lard	1 tbsp. tomato paste
1 tbsp. raw pork	3 cups cooked rice
2 tsps. *vesop*	1 egg
$\frac{1}{2}$ tsp. garam masala	Cucumber (optional)

Chop the garlic and fry it in the lard, add the cut-up pork and fry for a minute or two; now add the *vesop*, garam masala, onion and tomato paste, and continue stirring and cooking for about 3 minutes. Add the cooked rice, and stir till hot. Serve with a fried egg on top, and accompanied by sliced peeled raw cucumber, if available. Sufficient for 2 servings.

SWEETENED NOODLES (MEE)

Vermicelli	Sliced bean curd (soya)
Lard for frying	celery or crisp lettuce
2–3 onions	leaves, tomato paste
A very little garlic	or a sauce for flavour-
Pork meat or chicken	ing and colouring
meat	Spring onions
Shrimps	

Moisten the vermicelli in a little water in a hot skillet or pan. In a clean pan, fry the prepared onions and garlic in hot fat, until brown. Chop the meat into small pieces, and add to the hot fat and onions. Add shrimps and sliced bean curd. Add the cooked vermicelli with some tomato paste or sauce, mixing well. Cut through the vermicelli with spoon and toss to separate the strands. Serve with celery or crisp lettuce leaves. Decorate with spring onions. This dish is often eaten sprinkled with caster sugar instead of the tomato paste, and slices of lime or lemon squeezed over.

CRISP NOODLES (MEE)

Vermicelli (amount as required)	Pepper (green, red or crushed peppercorns)
Prawns	Kapi
Chillies	Soya bean sauce
A little garlic	Spring onions
Frying fat	

Wash the vermicelli in moderately hot water. Chop into lengths desired. Chop the prawns, chillies, garlic. Mix with a little pepper. Now fry the vermicelli in deep, hot fat. Lift, drain, mix with the prepared ingredients. Serve on a flat dish with Kapi and soya bean sauce. Hot roasted peanuts may be added to the mixture at the last, or served separately. Decorate with spring onions.

In the same way, bean shoots may also be included or even a little chopped celery.

KAPI SAUCE

This is a paste made with tiny shrimps. Use butter, red pepper, onions, shrimps and chillies when possible. Chop the onions, red peppers and chillies and shell the shrimps. Mash them together into a smooth paste. This is best done with a pestle and mortar. This paste is much used for flavouring.

THANAT
(BURMESE SALAD)

1 small cauliflower	4 tbsps. good cook-
1 small cabbage	ing oil
2 small aubergines	1 tbsp. sesame seeds
1 bunch spring onions	A pinch of turmeric
$\frac{1}{2}$ lb. French beans	powder
1–2 medium onions	

Cut the aubergines into 1–$1\frac{1}{2}$-inch wide lengths. Break up the cauliflower into medium-size pieces and string the beans. Cut the cabbage lengthwise 1–$1\frac{1}{2}$ inches wide (do not shred). Trim the spring onions to about 4 inches in length. Boil each vegetable separately in a mixture of 1 part vinegar to 3 parts water, to which a little salt has been added. When cooked (do not let the vegetables get too soft), remove, drain and place on a dish without mixing the different vegetables together. Heat the oil, add a pinch of turmeric powder, and fry the sliced onions in the oil, till the onions are crisp. Add a little salt to the sesame seeds and heat, shaking the pan continuously to avoid burning ; when the aroma begins to rise, remove from the pan immediately. Pour sufficient of this cooked oil over the vegetables, and garnish with sesame seeds and fried onions.

MARROW FRITTERS

1 marrow	Salt to taste
A batter mixture of flour and water	Cooking oil

Cut the marrow into small strips about 2 inches long and $\frac{3}{8}$ inch wide and mix with the batter, which can be coloured with a little turmeric. Take a spoonful at a time and fry in the hot oil.

Sliced onions and shredded cabbage may be treated in the same way. In the case of onions, fry them slowly so as to get them crisp.

GANG CHUD

Butter or lard	Kapi for flavouring or other sauce
2–3 slices onion	
Vegetables in season	

Put a little fat in a pan. Add the onion slices. Fry until lightly brown then add the prepared vegetables. Cover with salted water and simmer till tender. Flavour with Kapi or other seasoning.

Other soups can be made as above, but fish or prawns may be used instead of the vegetables, or included with them.

Note : Soups are not eaten at the beginning of a meal. They are served with the other dishes and eaten at the same time. Individual bowls are placed on the table and Gang Chud is served hot with the other dishes.

PRAWN AND CUCUMBER SALAD

A little cucumber	1 tsp. *vesop*
1–2 oz. prepared prawns	$\frac{1}{2}$ tsp. sugar
Cold pork, cut into small slices	$\frac{1}{2}$ tsp. lemon juice
	1 tsp. chopped mint

Peel the cucumber, then slice from the end as though you were sharpening a pencil ; mix with the prawns and pork. Mix the *vesop*, sugar and lemon juice, and toss the other ingredients in this mixture. Sprinkle with the chopped mint.

BHOONEE KITCHREE
(RICE AND LENTILS—INDO-MALAYAN)

$\frac{1}{2}$ lb. rice	A few peppercorns
$\frac{1}{2}$ lb. lentils	A few cloves
2 oz. butter	A small piece of stick cinnamon
1–2 onions	
A few slices of green ginger	1–2 bay leaves
	Salt to taste

Wash the rice and the lentils. Melt the butter

in a saucepan and fry the sliced onions till golden. Remove them from the pan, then cook the rice and lentils in the fat until it is all absorbed. Add the ginger and other seasonings and flavourings, cover with hot water, lid the pan and simmer very slowly until the water is completely absorbed ; stir occasionally with a wooden spoon and shake the pan to prevent burning. Serve very hot, with the fried onions scattered over the top.

PINK DAWN SALAD

1 cup rice	1 packet frozen shrimps or prawns
1 tsp. salt	
4 hard-boiled eggs	3 bananas
4 small ripe tomatoes	2 tbsps. tomato paste
1 tbsp. olive oil	2 tbsps. mayonnaise
1 tbsp. lemon juice	Paprika

Cook the rice in boiling salted water until tender, then drain it and hold it under running water ; spread it on a tray to dry and cool. Shell the hard-boiled eggs and cut in half ; skin the tomatoes and slice them. Mix the oil and lemon juice and toss the shrimps in this dressing. Peel the bananas, and cut into chunks.

If possible, serve this salad on a green dish. Put the rice in the centre and arrange the shrimps, bananas and eggs around it. Place the tomatoes round these, then make a small hollow in the centre of the rice and in it place a bowl filled with a mixture of tomato paste and mayonnaise. Sprinkle the rice with paprika.

GADO-GADO
(MIXED VEGETABLE SALAD)

2–3 cabbage leaves	2 eggs
$\frac{1}{2}$ lb. bean sprouts	1 *tahu*, if available
2 tomatoes	Prawn fritters, if available
$\frac{1}{2}$ a cucumber	2 onions
$\frac{1}{2}$ a lettuce	A little butter
2 boiled potatoes	

For the Sauce

1 tsp. powdered chillies	2 tbsps. sugar
	Salt to taste
2 tsps. butter	$\frac{1}{2}$ a jar of peanut butter
1$\frac{1}{2}$ teacupfuls water	1$\frac{1}{2}$ tbsps. lemon juice

Cook the cut-up cabbage and bean sprouts separately. Slice the tomatoes, cucumber, lettuce, potatoes and eggs. Fry the sliced *tahu* and onions and the prawn fritters.

For the sauce, fry the chilli powder in fat for a few seconds, add 1 teacupful water, the sugar, salt and peanut butter and stir until well mixed. Add the remaining water and the lemon juice and boil for a few minutes. To serve, put the

cabbage on a plate and on it place the bean sprouts, then the lettuce, etc. Serve with the sauce.

SAMBAL KELAPA
(HOT SAUCE WITH SHREDDED COCONUT)

1 tbsp. *sambal œlek*	1 tsp. sugar
½ tsp. shrimp sauce	1 tsp. *laos* powder
½ tsp. salt	½ tsp. garlic powder
2 tbsps. shredded coconut	A little butter

Combine all the ingredients and sauté in a frying pan in a little butter.

SALAD GULONG
(STUFFED SALAD PANCAKES)
For the Stuffing

2 turnips	1 oz. butter or cooking
2 sticks of celery	fat
½ a small bunch of	A little chicken stock
spring onions	1 tsp. sugar
2 bamboo shoots	¼ tsp. pepper
1 cucumber	Salt to taste
1 lettuce	1 cup prawn meat
1 large onion	1 cup crab meat
1 tsp. cornflour	Made mustard
1½ tsps. soya sauce	Blackcurrant jelly
1 cup chicken meat	Chilli sauce

For the Pancakes

1 cup flour	1½ cups salted water
1 tsp. cornflour	A little cooking fat
1 egg	

First prepare the stuffing. Clean and peel all the vegetables as necessary. Cut the turnips, celery, spring onions, bamboo shoots and cucumber into fine strips about 1 inch long; shred the lettuce finely; slice the large onion finely. Mix the cornflour, soya sauce and chicken meat and fry in the hot fat in a saucepan until slightly browned, then add the sliced onion and stir well; next add the turnips and again mix well. Pour in the stock, with the sugar, pepper and salt, and simmer for 10 minutes. Add the celery, bamboo shoots and spring onions and simmer until quite tender. Lastly, put in the prawns and crab meat and simmer until cooked—about 10 minutes. Put in a dish and leave to cool.

Now make the pancakes. Mix the flour and cornflour, make a well in the centre and drop in the egg. Stir lightly, gradually adding half the salted water and gathering in the flour slowly. Beat with a wooden spoon until quite smooth and free from lumps, add the remaining water and stir well, then leave in a cool place for 15 minutes. Heat a pan until very hot and grease

W.C.B.—24

it with a little cooking fat. Pour in sufficient mixture (about 3 tbsps.) to cover the base of the pan thinly and cook over a low heat until set; loosen the edges and turn out on to a wooden board to cool. Cook the rest of the mixture.

Brush a little of the mustard, jelly and chilli sauce in the middle of each pancake, then put on 1 tsp. shredded lettuce, place 1 tbsp. stuffing mixture on this and cover with 1 tsp. cucumber. Fold the pancake in at both sides and roll it up neatly. Repeat until all are filled. The pancakes may now be served as a cold dish; if they are required hot, fry them in cooking fat until golden-brown.

CUSTARD IN YOUNG COCONUT

½ cup very thick coconut milk	1½ cups sugar (preferably palm or maple)
3 young coconuts	Vanilla essence (optional)
1½ duck's eggs	

First make some very thick coconut milk; mix 3–3¾ lb. shredded coconut with ½ cup luke-warm water, squeeze with the hands, then put in a thin cloth and squeeze out the milk.

Remove the husks from young coconuts, cut off and keep the top of the shell and pour out the water. Beat the eggs well until light, add the sugar and beat again, then add the thick coconut milk and beat well. Flavour with a little vanilla, if desired. Pour the mixture into the coconut shells and put in a moderate oven (350° F., mark 4) or steam until cooked; test with a knife. Serve cold.

Pumpkins can be used as substitute for young coconuts, provided you can get tiny ones.

SANKHAYA
(COCONUT CUSTARD)

1 cup coconut milk (as above)	1 cup brown sugar
	2–3 eggs

Mix the sugar in the coconut milk until it is well dissolved. Blend in the beaten eggs. A pumpkin or coconut can be used as a container. Clean the pumpkin or coconut and scoop out most of the inside that is not needed. Leave a sufficient thickness in the container to hold the custard.

The top of the container should be sliced off neatly, near the top. This piece can be used as a lid. Strain the custard through a sieve or cloth into the container, replace the lid and place on a plate inside a steamer. Steam until the custard is well set.

This coconut custard is delicious served ice-cold with iced fruit. It is often served hot, together with glutinous rice.

GOODANG KASTURL
(FRIED RICE DUMPLINGS)

Mix 1 breakfastcup cooked rice and 1 tbsp. brown sugar, then beat in 1 egg. Mix 2 oz. ground rice with enough thick coconut cream to give a thin paste. Shape the rice and sugar mixture into dumplings, leave for about ½ hour, then dip them in the ground rice paste and fry in very hot deep fat until golden-brown. Drain and serve at once.

ROTTIE KOEKOES
(STEAMED BREAD)

5 eggs	1 large spoonful
Sugar	soda water
Flour	A few drops of
Juice of 1 lemon	vanilla essence

Weigh the eggs, then weigh out the same weight of sugar and of flour. Beat the eggs with the sugar for ½ hour, or until they are very fluffy. Add the lemon juice, soda water, vanilla and flour. Put a cloth into the bottom of a steamer and place the dough on top of the cloth. (If any other method of steaming is used, place a cloth over the top of the lid, to ensure that no steam escapes.) Steam for 1 hour, remove from the heat, and leave to stand for 15 minutes. Eat either cold, or warm with butter—it is delicious for breakfast.

SERIKAYA
(BANANA PUDDING)

1 vanilla pod	4 oz. sugar
½ pint milk	3 bananas
3 eggs	

Infuse the vanilla pod in the milk until this is well flavoured, then take it out and beat in the eggs, sugar and sliced bananas. Pour into a basin or dish and steam for 30–40 minutes, until set. Turn out and serve either hot or cold.

SULTAN'S KEP

Pour 1 cupful of sago into plenty of boiling water. Turn off the heat and leave to stand for 5–6 minutes, until the sago is cooked. Drain it, then rinse it under running cold water and drain again. Put it into a wetted 1-pint mould and leave in a cold place to set. Turn out and serve with coconut milk and, if desired, with golden syrup diluted with milk.

SARIKAUJI
(COCONUT CUSTARD)

Break open 2 coconuts and grate the flesh, then add a little water and squeeze the coconut to give ½ pint thick cream; strain this carefully. Beat 8 egg yolks with 4 oz. sugar until thick. Gradually add the coconut cream. Pour the mixture into a greased pudding basin or mould and cover with greaseproof paper. Steam in a double boiler until the custard sets, and when cool, chill in a refrigerator.

Alternatively, bake in a slow oven (300° F., mark 1) as for an ordinary baked egg custard.

KANOM MAW GENG
(BAKED COCONUT)

1 coconut	Lukewarm water
2 eggs	A little fat
1 cup brown sugar	1 onion (optional)

Shred the coconut and pour ½ a cup of lukewarm water over the shreds. Squeeze to make one cup of coconut milk. Beat the eggs, add the sugar, pour in the coconut milk. Put into a covered dish. Bake in a moderate oven (350° F., mark 4) till well set. It can be served either in the dish or turned out. Sometimes glutinous rice is served with the coconut custard.

The onions are fried till dark brown and are used to garnish the custard. (These are optional.)

RICE BISCUITS

Wash glutinous rice in cold water 2–3 times, then steam it till tender and dry it off. Make some rings out of cardboard, 2–3 inches across and about ¾ inch deep and place on a baking tray. Put in a dessertspoonful of rice in the centre of the ring. Spread with a fork, lightly and evenly. Lift the rings and dry off the rice in a warm oven or on the oven top. When dry, finish by frying in a deep, hot fat. Cool the biscuits on top of a wire tray or sieve. Store for use.

These can be eaten with butter and jam or used as cookies with tea and coffee.

These biscuits make an ideal accompaniment to Foi T'ong (see below).

FOI T'ONG
(" GOLDEN SHREDS " SWEET)

Lightly blend some egg yolks and let them drain through a fine sieve. Make a syrup with 8 oz. sugar and ½ pint water and boil to 230° F. Put some of the prepared yolk into a forcing bag, using a nozzle with a very fine hole, and let it drop through into the hot syrup. Cook for a few minutes, then collect the threads and lay them on a flat plate, folding up into a square or oblong shape.

If the shreds are left in the syrup until quite hard, they may be formed into little round cakes.

13

CARAMELLED BANANAS

Peel some bananas, cut each into 4 long pieces, and boil in a sugar syrup (about 1 pint syrup for 1 lb. bananas). When the bananas are cooked, remove from the syrup, and simmer this until it has caramellised. Roll the pieces, two at a time, in the caramel until completely coated; serve with cream.

BANANA NUN
(BANANA AND COCONUT SWEET)

½ pint coconut milk   Salt
Sugar   1 banana

Stir the coconut milk over a good heat until it reduces and thickens; add sugar and salt to taste and leave to cool. Add the cut-up banana and leave to infuse for an hour or two before serving.

Pumpkin can also be served in the same way.

BABIN
(COCONUT SWEETMEAT)

½ lb. sugar   4 oz. desiccated coconut
½ pint water   4 oz. glutinous rice powder

Dissolve the sugar in the water and boil for 5 minutes; mix with the coconut and rice powder and put into a greased square tin about 1 inch deep. Put into a pre-heated hot oven; turn the oven to moderate (350° F., mark 4) as you put the cake in and cook for ½ hour. Turn the oven off and leave the cake to cool in the oven; cut into small pieces just before serving.

Ordinary rice flour cannot be used in this recipe—you must use glutinous rice powder, which can be obtained from Oriental shops or the food departments of big stores.

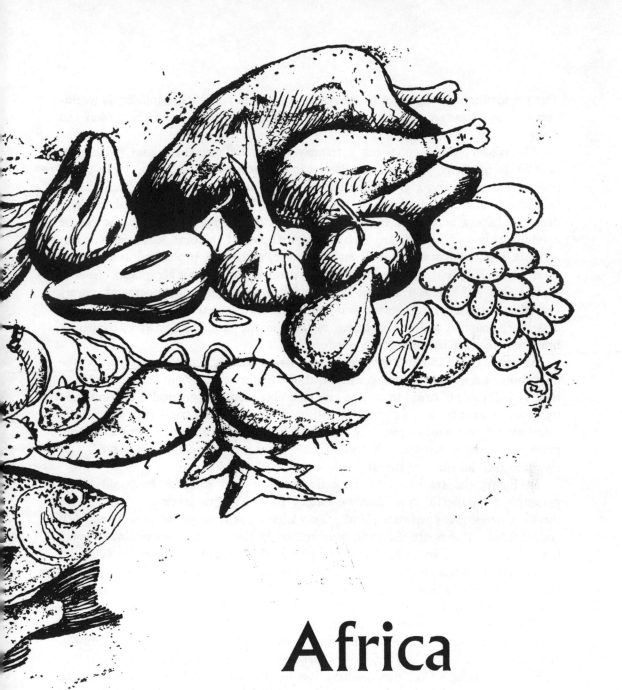

Africa

THE predominating religion of North Africa is Moslem; and its hospitality is world-famous; any stranger who comes to the door is made welcome and given food and drink.

The cookery of Morocco has extremely varied and ancient origins, which are derived from many parts of the East. It is wheat-based and the staple cereal preparation is *Kuskus*, a granular mixture of flour and water which is steamed and used much as rice is used in Eastern countries. On the whole, Moorish cookery does not have a very wide range, but it makes interesting and subtle use of the condiments and spices that are such an essential part of the best Moroccan cuisine.

Pork and carnivorous animals and birds are, of course, prohibited as food and even fish such as eels, that are thought to be carnivorous, are not acceptable. Lamb, mutton, kid and chicken are the most widely used meats; potatoes and purely vegetable dishes are rarely served and fruit is generally eaten raw. Cooking is often done over charcoal and the food sent to table in the same earthenware, copper or brass pots that are used for cooking it.

All meals begin and end with ceremonial hand-washing and the guests sit on the floor round a low table. Food is eaten with the fingers of the right hand, which also hold a small piece of bread to act as a kind of edible scoop. The meal is accompanied by water or mint tea and followed by coffee. Breakfast often consists of soup and a sweet pastry; main meals generally begin with a pastry dish and go on to fish, chicken, perhaps a mutton Kuskus and fresh fruit. Mint tea and coffee are served with sweetmeats at all times of the day.

In Egypt, the traditions of domestic harmony and gracious hospitality have persisted. Wonderful fruit and vegetables grow in abundance and everywhere there are dense groves of date palms. Very little meat is eaten but poultry and fish are plentiful. Pulses are the main protein food of the country and in almost every house, beans, baked in an earthenware jar with butter, garlic and other flavourings, are served for breakfast, the alternative being an enormous pancake served with sour cream. In addition to beans the diet of the labourers and peasants includes plenty of fresh salads, fruit, vegetables and cheese. Yoghourt is universally popular.

Algeria is an agricultural country, growing cereals of every kind, supporting large flocks and herds and producing much wine. Fruit and vegetables are plentiful, especially dates, figs and olives and excellent quality olive oil is made locally.

Ethiopia, being a Christian country, does not share the food customs that prevail throughout most of North Africa. The most widely eaten cereals are millet and barley and in some parts of the country a fermented barley porridge forms the main food. Beef and mutton, kids and small game animals are plentiful. Meat is usually served in the form of a highly spiced stew, called a *wat* or *zegeni* and onions are much used as flavourings. The Ethiopians drink *tedj* or *mies*, a sort of honey mead, *Talla*, a barley beer or Araqi, a fierce spirit. Coffee grows well and is a popular drink.

North Africa

ZEILOOK
(VEGETABLE SOUP)

6 small egg plants (auber-   1 small leek
gines), cut in thick   1 tsp. red pepper
slices   1 tsp. cumin
4 courgettes   Approx. ½ pint olive
3 large tomatoes, skinned   oil
½ tbsp. chervil

Fry the egg plant in oil until very well done, then set it aside. Cook first the courgettes, then the tomatoes in the same oil. Pound the cooked egg plant, courgettes and tomatoes (reserving a few slices of egg plant). Pound together the chervil and an equal amount of leek with the red pepper, cumin and 2 tbsps. oil. Mix all the ingredients together and cook for about 20 minutes.

Serve hot or cold in a soup plate, with the slices of egg plant arranged on top. This will keep for 2 days, and is enough for 3 persons.

FUL SUDANI SOUP
(SUDAN GROUNDNUT SOUP)

1 lb. fresh peanuts   Stock
Flour   1 tsp. butter
2 teacups milk   Cream, if liked

Shell and clean the nuts, place in the oven and when slightly roasted take out and leave to cool. Remove the brown skin, i.e., blanch the nuts, then grind them very finely. Mix with a little flour and the milk, then add the mixture to some good stock. Season to taste and slowly bring to the boil. Add the butter and a little cream before serving.

FARIK
(CHICKEN AND MEAT SOUP)

1 boiling chicken   Salt
½ lb. shin veal   Pepper
1 lb. barley   4 hard-boiled eggs
1 onion

This soup is a meal on its own, and is particularly suitable for supper.

Simmer the chicken, the shin of veal (cut into about 8 pieces, the barley, onion, salt and pepper in a panful of water for 4–6 hours, until the chicken meat falls off the bone. Remove the bones, put the meat back into the soup and add the sliced eggs.

SHTON MAKALLI
(FRIED WHITEBAIT)

7 oz. whitebait   1 pint olive oil
5 tbsps. semolina

Roll the fish in the semolina and fry in the boiling oil, shaking the pan, until they are slightly browned all over. Serve seasoned with salt or lemon, as preferred.

SHTON
(WHITEBAIT OMELETTE)

4–5 oz. whitebait   ½ tsp. salt
4 beaten eggs   ½ tsp. pepper
1 handful chopped parsley   8 tbsps. olive oil

Prepare the whitebait. Mix together the eggs, parsley, salt and pepper. Cook the fish in the oil with 2 tbsps. water, then pour in the egg mixture and stir gently until the egg is set. Enough for 2 persons.

HUT MAMAR
(BRAISED FISH)

3 lb. fish   1 tsp. salt
1 leek   2 tsps. red pepper
1 tbsp. chervil, chopped   ¾ pint olive oil (approx.)
small   6 oz. stalks of parsley
1 tsp. cumin   5 tbsps. lemon juice

Cut the fish into 3-inch squares. Crush the leek in a mortar with the chervil and cumin and mix with the salt, red pepper and oil. Cover the bottom of a deep earthenware dish with the parsley stalks, lay the pieces of fish over them, then pour the sauce over, adding 8 tbsps. water and then the lemon juice. Cook for about ½ hour with the lid on, then grill for 15 minutes. Serve in the same dish.

This dish can be allowed to cool and then heated up again for a few minutes before serving. Enough for 5 persons.

BAKED FISH

2 lb. turbot, cod or   2 oz. blanched almonds
halibut   or pistachio nuts
Salt and pepper   Tomato sauce (see
1 cup oil   below)
2 oz. raisins

Wash the fish well and slash diagonally with a knife; put into a well-greased baking tin and sprinkle well with salt and pepper. Pour most of the oil over it, put it into a moderately hot oven (400° F., mark 6) and cook, basting occasionally. Meanwhile, fry the nuts and raisins in a little oil.

Tomato Sauce : Wash 1 lb. tomatoes and cut them into quarters, put into a saucepan with some salt and pepper, and the oil in which the nuts and raisins were fried. Cover the pan and cook until the tomatoes are reduced, then strain the mixture. Rinse out the pan, put the sauce back in it and reduce it (uncovered) until very thick.

Put the fish on to a serving dish and just

before serving pour the sauce over; sprinkle the nuts and raisins on top.

SAMAK MESLOOK
(FISH BRAISED WITH TOMATOES)

3 lb. filleted fish	2 tsps. cumin
10 tomatoes, cut in half and seeded	3 tsps. red pepper
	1 tsp. salt
1 large tsp. chopped chervil	½ tsp. powdered saffron
	½ pint olive oil
1 large tsp. chopped garlic	Juice of 1 lemon

Lay the fish in a flat cooking dish and cover with the tomatoes. Pound the chervil and garlic and mix with the other ingredients (except the lemon). Pour over the fish and tomatoes, cover and cook for about ¾ hour, or until the fish is cooked. Pour the lemon juice over all and serve in the same dish. Enough for 6 persons.

DEJAJ MACFOOL MA MATISHA
(BRAISED CHICKEN WITH TOMATOES)

1 chicken, cut in four	½ an onion, finely chopped
2 pieces of cinnamon bark	1½ tsps. powdered saffron
5 onions, sliced	½ tsp. pepper
7 tomatoes, cut in half and seeded	½ tsp. ground ginger
	½ tbsp. chopped parsley
1 tsp. salt	½ pint olive oil

Spread the pieces of chicken in a flameproof casserole with the cinnamon bark, cover with the sliced onion and then with the tomatoes. Mix all the other ingredients well to make a sauce, then pour this over the chicken. Simmer for 1½ hours, or until the chicken is tender. Serve in the same dish, first removing the cinnamon bark.

SFA MERDUMA
(CHICKEN WITH KUSKUS)

About 1 lb. *kuskus*	2 oz. finely chopped parsley
1 raw chicken	
1 tsp. salt	3 small pieces of saffron bark
1 tsp. saffron	
1 tsp. pepper	1 tbsp. finely chopped chervil
1 tsp. ground ginger	
2 large onions, finely chopped and par-boiled for 2 minutes	1 lb. butter
	3 tsps. caster sugar

To make the *kuskus*, see p. 380. Cut the chicken into small chunks. Put all the ingredients except the *kuskus*, half the butter and the sugar in a deep saucepan with 1 pint water and boil for about ½ hour. Then put a steamer lined with muslin on the top of the cooking pan and fill with the *kuskus*. Let this steam for ¼ hour, then take it off and leave it to dry in another dish for ¼ hour. Steam it again for 5 minutes, then remove and add the remaining butter, mixing well.

When the chicken is done, spread some *kuskus* on a large plate to a depth of about 2 inches. Pile the pieces of chicken on the *kuskus* in a cone shape and pour a little cooking liquid over. Cover with the remaining *kuskus* and sprinkle lightly with sugar.

TREED
(CHICKEN IN PASTRY)

1 whole chicken, cleaned	1 tbsp. chopped parsley
	3 pieces of cinnamon bark
2 tsps. salt	
1 pinch of saffron	3 large onions
1 tsp. ground ginger	1 pint olive oil
1 tsp. pepper	1¾ lb. flour
1 tbsp. chopped chervil	

Simmer the chicken with 1 tsp. salt, the saffron, ginger, pepper, chervil, parsley, cinnamon bark, onions and a scant ¾ pint olive oil.

Make the pastry by kneading the flour with a very little water, adding more as necessary; work it very thoroughly. Make the dough into about 40 balls the size of a small egg; with an oiled hand flatten each ball of dough over an oiled dish until it is very thin and about 8 inches across. Heat a griddle or electric hot-plate and oil slightly. Put the dough sheet by sheet on the hot-plate, when it will immediately dry. Turn it over to dry the other side, and then take it off. Put about 30 of these sheets of pastry on a plate, overlapping each other and making a circle about 18 inches across.

When the chicken is cooked, take out the cinnamon bark and put the chicken with the onion on to the pastry; cover all with the remaining sheets of pastry, pour a very little of the liquid from the cooking pot over all and serve immediately.

This is a very ancient Arab dish.

DEJAJ MESLOOK
(BOILED CHICKEN WITH POTATOES)

1 cleaned chicken	3 tsps. salt
½ a leek	A little more than 1 pint olive oil
½ tbsp. chervil	
½ tbsp. cumin	1¾ lb. skinned and sliced potatoes
½ tbsp. red pepper	
½ tbsp. saffron	

Cook the chicken together with the pounded leek and chervil, cumin, red pepper, saffron, 1 tsp. salt, about ¾ pint olive oil and 1¼ pints water until tender. Meanwhile, cook the potato slices in the remaining olive oil with 2 tsps. salt until slightly browned. When the chicken is done, take it out and brown it in the oil in which the potatoes were cooked. Put the potatoes into the cooking liquor, and baste the chicken also with some of the liquor. Spread some of the potatoes over a deep plate and arrange the chicken on top ; put the rest of the potatoes all round, pour the broth over all and serve.

FRACH BIL LOOZ
(STUFFED PIGEONS)

3 pigeons	$\frac{1}{2}$ tbsp. finely chopped
5 tbsps. ground almonds	parsley
1 tbsp. raisins, stoned	1 tbsp. caster sugar
1 tsp. ground cinnamon	$\frac{3}{4}$ pint olive oil (approx.)

Clean the pigeons. Mix the dry ingredients well with a little water, stuff the birds with this and sew up, then cook them with the giblets in a covered pan, basting with the oil, until they are done. Serve in a flat dish with the oil in which they have been cooked.

FRACH BIL HAMUS
(CHICKEN STEW)

1 raw chicken, cut into 6 pieces	5 small onions, cut up coarsely
$\frac{1}{2}$ tsp. saffron	5 oz. butter
1 tsp. ginger	7 tbsps. chick peas
1 tsp. pepper	1 large onion, sliced
1 tbsp. chopped parsley	2 tbsps. raisins
1 tsp. salt	

Put all, except the sliced onion and the raisins, into a pot with almost 1 quart water and boil for 1 hour. Add the sliced onion and raisins and continue to cook until the chicken is tender. Serve the whole in a deep dish.

LEMA MA'AMARA
(STUFFED BRAISED CHICKEN)

1 chicken	1$\frac{1}{2}$ tbsps. parsley, finely
3 tbsps. *kuskus*	chopped
4 tbsps. caster sugar	3 pinches salt
2 tsps. ground cinnamon	3 pinches of powdered saffron
3 tbsps. sultanas	$\frac{3}{4}$ pint olive oil

Clean the chicken. For the stuffing, put the *kuskus* over the heat in a dry dish, keeping it moving until very dry, then mix with the sugar, cinnamon, sultanas, 1 tbsp. parsley, a pinch of salt, a pinch of saffron and almost $\frac{1}{4}$ pint olive oil. Stuff the chicken with this, taking care that the neck and breast are filled, then sew up. Put the chicken in a saucepan with the neck and liver, add $\frac{1}{2}$ pint olive oil and a little more than $\frac{1}{2}$ pint water and bring to the boil. Cook the chicken

for 1$\frac{1}{4}$ hours or until nearly tender, then add the remaining parsley. Baste the chicken with a mixture of the remaining saffron, salt and 3 tbsps. water, cover and continue to cook until the bird is tender.

DEJAJ MAHAMMARA
(ROAST CHICKEN)

1 chicken	2 tbsps. butter
$\frac{1}{2}$ tbsp. chervil	1 tsp. cumin
$\frac{1}{2}$ tbsp. leek	1 tsp. red pepper

Prepare the chicken. Pound the chervil and leek together in a mortar and mix with the butter, cumin and red pepper to make a paste. Roast the chicken on a turning spit, spreading the paste over it with a knife. When the chicken is nearly cooked, make some cuts in the breast and put in more of the paste.

This dish can be served hot or cold.

MAKALLI
(CHICKEN WITH CITRON PEEL)

1 chicken	1 tsp. ground ginger
1 leek	A little more than $\frac{1}{2}$ pint olive oil
1 preserved citron	
$\frac{1}{2}$ tsp. powdered saffron	6 stoned olives
$\frac{1}{2}$ tsp. salt	

Clean the chicken and put it with neck and liver in an earthenware dish. Pound together in a mortar the leek and half the citron peel. Mix well with a tbsp. water, the saffron and salt ; spread this over the chicken. Add the ginger, olive oil and 1 pint water and simmer for 1 hour, or until the chicken is nearly tender, basting it occasionally with the liquid. Add the olives and remaining chopped citron peel and heat up for a few minutes before serving.

This is a dish much eaten in Fez.

CHICKEN
(ETHIOPIAN STYLE)

Poultry is consumed extensively in Ethiopia, and chicken has much the same place in the national menu as roast beef in England. It is invariably served on ceremonial occasions and feast days. A favourite way of preparing it for a family dish is as follows :

Plunge the dead chicken into boiling water as soon as it is killed, so that it can be plucked very closely. After all the feathers have been removed put it once again into boiling water and skin it. Cut open the breast and draw it, then wash the carcase thoroughly inside and out. Now cut up the chicken into 12 pieces, including the upper part of the head, after removing the eyes but leaving in the brain. Rub each with pea flour.

Wash again, piece by piece, put into boiling water and allow to simmer.

Make a sauce of melted butter seasoned with pepper, salt and spices to taste and add some cut-up onions, stirring well until the pieces of onion are soft and have almost disappeared. To this mixture add, drop by drop, the water in which the chicken has been simmering, stirring all the time so that the sauce is quite smooth. Then place the chicken, piece by piece, into the sauce, which must be just sufficient to cover it entirely. Stir gently and constantly so that the sauce does not become lumpy.

Meanwhile, boil 2–4 eggs for about 4 minutes and shell them. Add them to the saucepan containing the chicken, taking care that they do not break up, then simmer all together until the chicken is quite tender. Arrange the chicken, eggs and sauce in a dish and serve with potatoes or cabbage or any seasonal vegetables.

BRAISED OX TONGUE

Blanch the ox tongue in boiling water, then rinse it in cold water. Crush a garlic clove with some salt; peel 4 onions; scrape a carrot and put all these in a saucepan with a bouquet garni and some seasoning. Add the tongue, cover with cold water, bring to the boil and simmer, covered, for 2–3 hours. Remove the tongue from the pan, skin it and keep hot while boiling up and reducing the liquor. Put the tongue back in the saucepan, add ½ glass white wine and a few cut-up mushrooms and cook until tender. Serve with the sauce poured over it.

ROAST KID

Plunge the joint into a bowl of boiling water for about 10 minutes, then wipe dry before putting it in the baking tin. Make one or two incisions in the skin and slip in a leaf of mint or a " tooth " of onion. Put in a moderate oven (350° F., mark 4) and cook, basting well; it is a good plan to have a tin of hot water at the bottom of the oven, so that the steam from it keeps the meat tender. Serve with mint sauce or fruit chutney and plenty of green vegetables.

BISSARA
(BEEF AND BROAD BEAN STEW)

4 tbsps. oil	6 cloves of garlic
1 lb. beef, cut up	Salt
¾ lb. broad beans	1 tsp. coriander seed

Heat the oil in a saucepan and cook the beef until brown on all sides. Add the broad beans, garlic, coriander seed and salt to taste, cover

with hot water, put the lid on and cook in a slow oven (300° F., mark 1) for 4 hours.

To serve, pour into a dish the liquor and the broad beans (which will have cooked almost to a purée) and arrange the pieces of meat on top. This may be served with rice pilaff or a purée of potatoes.

MISSAA
(BAKED AUBERGINES AND MEAT)

Peel about 4 aubergines and slice them, put into a colander, sprinkle liberally with salt and leave to drain; when well drained, fry in smoking-hot oil, then drain again. Fry a chopped onion in the oil; when it is brown add ½ lb. minced meat and fry this until lightly coloured. Put half the sliced aubergines in an ovenproof dish and add the meat, seasoning it to taste; finish with a further layer of aubergine, pour on 1 cup tomato juice or water and cook in a moderate oven (350° F., mark 4) for 1½–2 hours, until well cooked and slightly crisp on top.

QUALEEMA
(TONGUE AND BEEF SAUSAGES)

2 ladles tongue, cut into pieces	3 tbsps. red pepper, " awaze "
2 ladles fat beef	½ ladle chopped red onions
1 tsp. powdered black pepper	1 sheep's intestine, cleaned and washed
1 tbsp. powdered ginger	½ ladle butter
1 tbsp. salt	

Chop the raw tongue and meat into very small pieces and mix with the black pepper, ginger, salt, red pepper and onions. Tie one end of the intestine with thread and fill with the meat mixture. Cut it into 6–8 inch lengths and tie both ends of each piece with thread. Heat the butter in a frying pan and cook the stuffed pieces over a low heat for a long time.

Note : A " ladle " equals 10 tbsps.; 1 tbsp. equals 3 tsps. in the Ethiopian kitchen.

MACFOOL BIL CROOMBE
(BRAISED BEEF AND CABBAGE)

2 lb. beef (with fat and bone) cut in small chunks	1 tsp. cumin
	1 tbsp. red pepper
1 leek	¾ pint olive oil
1 tbsp. chervil	1½ tsps. salt
½ tsp. saffron	3 cabbage hearts
	2 lemons

Cook the beef in 1 quart water with the leek and chervil, pounded together, the saffron, cumin, red pepper, oil and 1 tsp. salt; simmer slowly until the meat is tender. Cut the hearts of 3 cabbages (about 6 inches across) into 12 pieces each; boil these in another pan for

¼ hour, adding ½ tsp. salt. When the meat is done, remove it to a deep ovenproof dish. Spread the half-cooked cabbage over it, then pour over all the liquid in which the meat was cooked. Put in a slow oven (300° F., mark 1) and cook for ¼ hour with the lid on, then remove the lid and raise the heat until the cabbage is slightly browned. Pour the juice of 2 lemons over and serve in the same dish. Enough for 5 persons.

EL KEFTA
(MEAT BALLS IN SPICY SAUCE)

About 2 lb. mutton (one quarter of it should be fat)
2 tsps. chopped parsley
1½ tbsps. finely chopped chervil
7 oz. butter
1 finely chopped onion
½ tsp. powdered saffron
½ tsp. pepper
½ tsp. ground ginger
½ tsp. cumin
1 tsp. red pepper
A pinch of salt

Mince the meat. Mix the parsley and ½ tbsp. chervil with the minced meat and roll into balls about the size of a marble. Heat together the butter, 2 tbsps. chopped onion, the remaining chervil, the saffron, pepper, ginger, cumin, red pepper, salt and ½ pint water until the butter is melted; put in the meat balls and cook for about ¼ hour. Serve the meat balls in a deep dish in the liquid in which they were cooked.

MUTTON KUSKUSU

1½ lb. mutton, cut in 6 or 7 pieces
2 onions, thickly sliced
2 tsps. pepper
2 tsps. ground ginger
1 tsp. powdered saffron
1 tbsp. chopped parsley
12 oz. butter
4 tsps. salt
1¼ lb. kuskus (see below)
2 peeled courgettes
10 small carrots, halved
10 small turnips, halved
2 tbsps. raisins, stoned

Cook the meat, onions, pepper, ginger, saffron, parsley, 5 oz. butter and 2 tsps. salt together in 1½ pints water. Wash the kuskus by running a little water over it—this will cause it to swell a little. When the meat has cooked for about 1 hour, line a steamer with muslin and put in the kuskus, half at first and the remainder after a few minutes, then steam for ¼ hour; remove from the heat, mix the kuskus with 2 tsps. salt and 1 tbsp. water and leave to dry.

Halve the courgettes lengthwise, discard the core and cut the flesh into about 6 pieces. Add a little more water to the meat saucepan and put in the carrots, turnips, raisins and courgettes. Simmer until the courgettes are cooked, then take them out and put the kuskus to steam again for 10 minutes. Mix the hot kuskus in another dish with the remaining 7 oz. butter and arrange in a ring round a flat dish; put the meat in the middle covered by all the vegetables. Pour over the dish some of the meat juices, but not enough to soak through the kuskus. Enough for 6 persons.

TO MAKE KUSKUS

Sieve 1 lb. flour. Sprinkle 1 tbsp. of water over half of it and work it well in, rubbing continually between the hands. Continue adding a small amount of flour and a sprinkling of water until all the flour is used up. Break up the larger lumps now and again and work in this way for 20 minutes or so, rubbing the mixture between the hands until it forms grains resembling large semolina in appearance. Be very careful not to add too much water. Sieve to ensure uniform-sized grains, then leave to dry.

Semolina, though it has smaller grains, may be used as a substitute for kuskus.

DFINA
(EGYPTIAN STEW)

1½ lb. sorrel
Oil for frying
½ lb. beef
1 calf's foot
3 cloves of garlic
Salt and pepper
6 onions
½ lb. white beans
1 egg per person (in the shell)

This dish is most practicable for people with a solid-fuel stove, so that the stew can be left to cook overnight in the oven.

Wash the sorrel and blanch it in boiling water; press it well down in a colander and drain thoroughly, then fry it in a little very hot oil. Cut the beef into cubes; blanch the calf's foot; crush the garlic with some salt; chop the onions; wash the beans well and also wash the eggs. Put all these ingredients into an earthenware dish or a casserole with the fried sorrel and some seasoning. Cover the whole with water, lid tightly and leave all night in a very slow oven (lowest possible setting).

SEFRITO
(BRAISED VEAL)

1 tbsp. oil
1 cup boiling water
Juice of 1 lemon
½ tsp. paprika
Saffron (optional)
Salt
1 lb. veal

Heat the oil in a stewpan, add the boiling water, lemon juice, paprika, saffron and salt, then put in the veal (whole or sliced) and half cook it on a low heat for about 20 minutes, with the lid off the pan. Cover and leave it to cook for another hour. When the veal is cooked place it on a hot dish in the oven. Then make a sauce by reducing the liquid in which the meat was boiled. Adjust the seasoning, strain and pour over the meat.

QUAAH
(SPICED KEBABS)

9 oz. lean mutton and 9 oz. fat
1 leek
2 small onions
1 tbsp. chopped chervil
1 tsp. salt
1 tsp. cumin
1 tsp. ground ginger
1 tsp. pepper
1 tsp. red pepper

Cut the meat in pieces about 1 inch square and $\frac{1}{4}$ inch thick. Pound together the leek, 1 onion, the chervil and some salt and mix with the meat and fat. Chop the other onion finely and mix with the meat, adding the cumin, ginger, pepper and red pepper. Put the meat on to skewers, alternating fat and lean pieces, and grill for 10 minutes. Serve on the skewers.

This dish is a speciality of Marrakesh.

KEBAB EMSHARMEL
(GRILLED MEAT WITH EGGS)

Kebabs made as in previous recipe
7 oz. butter
$\frac{1}{2}$ tsp. saffron
$\frac{1}{2}$ tsp. pepper
$\frac{1}{2}$ tsp. ground ginger
$\frac{1}{2}$ tsp. cumin
1 tsp. red pepper
1 tsp. chervil, chopped finely
1 onion, chopped small
2 lemons
5 eggs

Remove the meat from the skewers. Mix the butter, saffron, pepper, ginger, cumin, red pepper, chervil and 1 tbsp. chopped onion. Add 1 pint water and cook for $\frac{1}{2}$ hour, stirring occasionally. Put in the meat and 2 tbsps. lemon juice and cook gently for 5–10 minutes longer. Break the 5 eggs separately into the mixture and cook again for a few minutes, until the eggs are set. Serve in the same dish.

SAMBOUSEK
(MEAT PASTIES)

$\frac{1}{2}$ lb. self-raising flour
2 oz. melted butter
$\frac{1}{4}$ pint warm water
2 tsps. salt
A pinch of baking powder
1 medium-sized onion
Oil for frying
$\frac{1}{2}$ lb. leftover or raw meat, minced
Beaten egg to glaze

Put the flour on a slab and add the melted butter, working it well in; add the warm water, salt and baking powder and knead the paste well. It should be rather more sticky than a bread dough.

Chop the onion and fry it in a little oil until it is golden, then add the minced meat and brown it well. Remove it with the onion, straining off the oil. Roll out the paste as thinly as possible, cut it into large rounds, put a spoonful of the mixture into each round and fold over into halves, sealing the edges well. Paint over with beaten egg. Caraway seeds may be sprinkled on top if desired to give a more finished appearance. Put the sambousek on to well-greased baking sheets, and cook in a hot oven (450° F., mark 8) till golden. They are best eaten hot, but may be served cold if preferred.

LERRNIB
(STEWED HARE)

1 hare, cut in 6 pieces
1 tsp. salt
1 tsp. saffron
$\frac{1}{2}$ tsp. ground ginger
$\frac{1}{2}$ tsp. pepper
2 tsps. saffron wood
2 tbsps. finely chopped parsley
1 tsp. *ras el hanoot* (see below)
3 small onions, cut fairly small
Approx. $\frac{1}{4}$ pint olive oil
A handful finely cut onion tops or stalks
7 oz. sultanas

Cook the pieces of hare with the salt, saffron, ginger, pepper, saffron wood, parsley, *ras el hanoot*, onions, olive oil and almost 1 pint water until the hare is tender—if necessary, add a little more water to keep the meat just covered. Add the onion and sultanas and cook for 20 minutes longer, then put the meat into a deep dish and pour the sauce over it.

Ras el hanoot is a mixture of pepper, curry powder, cinnamon, saffron wood and other powdered spices and herbs, which can be bought ready prepared in Morocco. It may be replaced by a mixture of available spices to suit your own taste.

MACFOOL MA ASEL
(MUTTON AND ONION STEW)

2 lb. mutton, cut in small chunks
1 tsp. salt
1 tsp. pepper
1 tsp. ground ginger
$\frac{1}{2}$ tsp. powdered saffron
$1\frac{1}{2}$ tsps. chopped chervil
3 pieces of cinnamon bark
4 small and 4 large onions
$\frac{1}{2}$ pint olive oil
1 tbsp. ground cinnamon
$\frac{1}{2}$ tbsp. chopped parsley
4 tbsps. sugar (or liquid honey)

Mix the mutton with the salt, pepper, ginger, a pinch of saffron, 1 tbsp. chervil, the cinnamon bark, the small onions cut in pieces, the olive oil and nearly 1 quart water. Simmer for 1 hour, or until the meat is almost cooked, then take out the cinnamon bark and spread the meat in a flameproof casserole. Slice the large onions and cover the meat with them. Mix the remaining ingredients (except the sugar) with the meat liquor and pour over the onions and meat. Cook for ½ hour, then sprinkle the sugar or honey over all. Grill for 15 minutes, until browned; serve in the same dish. Enough for 5 persons.

JILBANA BIL GUB
(MEAT STEW WITH PEAS)

2 lb. lean, boned mutton, cut in 3-inch squares	¾ pint olive oil (approx.)
	Peel of 1 citron
	"Chokes" of 20 artichokes
1 tbsp. salt	
1 tsp. saffron	1 lb. peas
2 tsps. ground ginger	1 lemon
1 tbsp. leek, cut small	

Put the mutton, salt, saffron, ginger, leek, olive oil and 2¼ pints water into a deep cooking pot. After cooking for 1 hour, put in the citron peel, in 2 pieces. When the meat is nearly cooked, take out the citron peel and put in the artichokes and peas and continue cooking until all is well done; put into a deep serving dish. Cut the citron peel small, mix it with the juice of the lemon and sprinkle over the meat.

DULAA
(SAFFRON BRAISED LAMB)

4½ lb. shoulder of lamb with ribs and shoulder blade	3 tsps. pepper
	2–3 small pieces of saffron bark
½ tbsp. salt	2 onions
½ tsp. powdered saffron	1 tbsp. chervil (uncut)
3 tsps. ground ginger	¾ pint olive oil

Take out the shoulder joint from the meat and break the ribs. Mix the salt, saffron, ginger and pepper with 6 tbsps. water and work this well into the meat. Add the saffron bark, 1 onion, quartered, with the chervil, olive oil and 1¼ pints water. Simmer for 1 hour, then add the other onion, cut into 6 pieces. Cook gently for ½ hour longer, when the meat should be cooked and all but a small quantity of the liquid boiled away. Put into a serving dish with the remaining liquor (removing the saffron bark).

HAMINE EGGS

This is a delicious version of hard-boiled eggs. In Egypt there are special shops selling them; there, after the eggs have been cooked for 3 or 4 hours, they are put under the ashes of a fire and left for as long as 8 hours—this makes them as creamy as butter.

Here is a simplified method of preparing them at home. Put the brown outside skins of some onions into a saucepan of cold water with the eggs and boil for 2 hours, or as long as possible. The onion skins turn the shells of the eggs and the whites brown. Shell and halve the eggs and serve hot or cold with lemon wedges, salt, pepper and mixed spices.

PILAFF EGYPTIAN

Heat 1 tbsp. oil in a shallow saucepan, then add 1½ cups water and a generous sprinkling of salt. When it comes to the boil, add 1 cup well-washed rice. Put the lid half on the pan and cook for about 20 minutes on a low heat. When all the water has been absorbed, take off the lid and fork the rice gently, then let it continue to cook in the steam for a few minutes.

Serve with meat, fish, vegetables or tomato sauce.

STUFFED VEGETABLES

Tomatoes, marrows, aubergines, leeks, vine leaves or cabbage leaves	Oil for frying
	½ lb. rice
	1 tbsp. chopped parsley
	Salt and pepper
4 oz. minced meat	Juice of 1 lemon

Prepare the vegetables (see below). Fry the meat in a little oil until just brown. (If leftover cooked meat is used, omit this step.) Wash and drain the rice, mix with the meat and parsley and season well. Three-quarters fill each vegetable or leaf, put in a saucepan with sufficient water to come half-way up the vegetables, add the lemon juice and 1 tbsp. oil and stew gently for 2 hours. Place on a hot dish with the cooking liquor poured over them; stuffed marrows should be cut in slices.

Tomatoes : Cut a slice off the top and scoop out the pulp; replace the top slice after the tomato has been filled.

Marrow : Use a large marrow; scrape off the outside skin, cut off one end and scoop out the seeds from the middle.

Aubergines : Put the unpeeled aubergines into a little oil and water, cook gently until nearly done, then scoop out the middle and mix this flesh with the filling.

Leeks : Cut into 4-inch lengths, remove the coarse outer leaves, then gently pull out the central leaves, leaving a tube.

Vine and Cabbage Leaves : Blanch in hot water for a few seconds to make them pliable.

TAFIFA
(SAVOURY PUMPKIN)

Cut a piece of pumpkin weighing about 2½–3 lb. into 2-inch squares, then wash these well. Cut up some leftover meat. (The amount will vary according to what is available, but about 2–4 oz. would be sufficient for this amount of pumpkin.) Fry the meat lightly in a little hot oil, then add ½ a garlic clove, crushed with a little salt, and 1–2 shallots. Add about ½–¾ lb. shredded cabbage and the pumpkin pieces and season well with salt and pepper. Cover and cook gently over a low heat for 2½ hours, adding a little water if required.

HALELAM
(SEMOLINA " RISSOLES " WITH VEGETABLES)

1 lb. semolina	¾–1 lb. tomatoes
Salt and pepper	½ lb. brown lentils
Oil for frying	½ lb. shelled broad beans

Mix the semolina with some salt and enough water to make a stiff paste, then roll into little finger-shaped pieces. Quarter the tomatoes and fry them in hot oil, then keep them hot. Fry the semolina fingers, seasoning them with salt and pepper.

Boil the lentils and the broad beans separately, mix all together and serve if desired with fried sausages.

BUTTER BEANS IN TOMATO SAUCE

1 lb. tomatoes	Meat trimmings
Salt and pepper	1 shallot
1 lb. butter beans	

Wash and quarter the tomatoes, put into a saucepan, season and stew, covered, until soft, then sieve them.

Rinse the saucepan and put in the beans, the sieved tomato sauce and seasonings to taste; simmer gently uncovered. Brown the meat trimmings and finely chopped shallot in a little oil and add the contents of the frying pan to the beans and tomato sauce. Cook gently until the beans are just tender and the liquid is reduced to a thick sauce. Serve as an accompanying vegetable with meat.

FOUL MADUMNAS
(EGYPTIAN BEANS)

1½ lb. dried broad beans	Juice of 2 lemons
4 hard-boiled eggs	Salt and pepper
½ cup cooking oil	

Soak the beans for 24 hours. The following day, boil them in a covered pan with just enough water to cover; add more hot water as necessary until the beans are tender, then let the water reduce until there is very little left. Serve the beans in the remaining liquor, accompanied by separate dishes of roughly chopped hard-boiled eggs, oil, lemon juice, salt and pepper—mix a little of these flavourings with the beans in your plate.

The Arabs are very fond of this dish; they sit in a circle in the street round a pot of foul on a fire. They dip pieces of bread into the beans, or they make sandwiches of it with the native bread.

FILAFIL
(FRIED BEAN BALLS)

2 lb. broad beans	Black pepper
1 clove of garlic	1 large onion, chopped
Salt	Oil for frying

Boil the broad beans, remove the skins and rub the beans through a sieve, then put them back into the saucepan. Crush the garlic with some salt and add it to the purée, with some black pepper and the onion. Keep the mixture warm. Heat the oil. Form the bean mixture into balls the size of a half-crown and fry them in the smoking oil until they are a dark golden-brown in colour.

This may be served as a *mese* (aperitif) with drinks.

FRENCH BEANS IN TOMATO SAUCE

1 large onion	1 lb. French beans
A little oil for frying	1 lb. tomatoes
Leftovers of meat	Salt and pepper

Chop the onion, heat the oil in a saucepan and brown the onion in it. Add the meat, cut into small pieces, and let it brown. Meanwhile prepare the French beans by slicing them and removing the strings; put into the saucepan. Peel and quarter the tomatoes, add to the beans and season well. Put on the lid and stew gently on top of the stove or in a moderate oven (350° F., mark 4) for several hours.

Serve the beans in their own liquor as an accompanying vegetable or with pilaff Egyptian (see p. 382).

Peas and marrows may also be cooked in this way.

HOT AUBERGINES AND TOMATOES

4 aubergines	4 tomatoes
Salt	1 clove of garlic
Fat for frying	Pepper

Peel the aubergines, cut them in long slices, sprinkle lightly with salt and put in a colander, press a plate well down on them and leave to drain. Heat a little fat in a frying pan and when it is smoking, fry the aubergines till they begin to shrivel; remove them from the pan and drain well.

Cut the tomatoes into slices, put a layer of them in an ovenproof dish, then add a layer of aubergines, another layer of tomatoes and so on. Sprinkle with the garlic crushed with some salt, season with pepper and cook in a moderate oven (350° F., mark 4) for 30–40 minutes.

POTATO ALECHA (FASTING)
(POTATO AND ONION MASH)

1 ladle red onions	5 green peppers
1 ladle oil	2 tsps. salt
2 ladles potatoes	2 tsps. spices

Chop the onions into small pieces and brown them in a clay pot on the fire. Stir constantly. Add the oil. Wash, peel and quarter the potatoes and add them to the pot. Cut the green peppers in halves; remove the seeds and add the flesh to the potatoes. When the potatoes are cooked, add the salt, then the spices.

MIXED VEGETABLE ALECHA (FASTING)
(VEGETABLE MASH)

1 ladle of cabbage	1 ladle carrots
1 ladle red onions	2 tsps. salt
2 ladles oil	3 large tomatoes
3 ladles potatoes	8 green peppers

Wash the cabbage and take the leaves apart, then boil it. Chop the onions into small pieces and cook in the oil without browning. Wash, peel and slice the potatoes and carrots and add to the mixture with the salt; when they are well done, add some warm water. Cut the cooked cabbage into large pieces and add it; stir gently to prevent the potatoes from mashing. Plunge the tomatoes into hot water, peel, remove the seeds and chop the flesh into small pieces. Add a little more water to prevent the alecha from burning, then add the tomatoes. Wash the green peppers, cut in halves and take out the seeds; add to the alecha. Season with salt if necessary and continue to cook until all the vegetables are tender.

CHESTNUT PRESERVE

Shell 2 lb. large chestnuts. To do this, score across the rounded side of each nut with a sharp knife, spread in a baking tin and put in a slow oven for 10–15 minutes, then peel off the shell and inner skins as soon as the nuts are cool enough to handle. Boil the chestnuts in a little water and drain. Now cook them in 6 tbsps. orange-flower water with 2 lb. sugar and a few drops of vanilla essence, stirring occasionally, until quite soft. To test, drop a little of the mixture into cold water—if it goes solid, the preserve is ready. Pot at once in warmed jars, and cover when cold.

RAIFF OF CHEESE
(CHEESE PASTIES)

12–15 sheets of pastry	1 egg
7 oz. ewe's milk cheese	½ pint olive oil (approx.)

Make the pastry sheets as described on p. 385.

Pound the cheese in a mortar. Fold 2 tsps. cheese in a sheet of pastry, making a pasty about 4 inches across. Seal the edges of the pastry with a beaten egg, then brown on both sides in hot oil.

RAIFF
(SEMOLINA " SCONES ")

1 lb. 2 oz. coarse semolina	3 tbsps. butter or honey
1 tsp. salt	

Put a handful of the semolina in a small bowl of water and let it stand for 2 hours, until it thickens. Knead the rest of the semolina into a dough with 1 cup of the semolina water from the bowl, 1 cup fresh water and the salt. Roll out to about ½ inch thick, then cut into about 20 rounds the size of the top of a tumbler. Put these rounds on a dry griddle or hot-plate over the heat, turning them until the outside is dried and very slightly browned and they have puffed up to 1 inch thick, then split them and spread with butter or honey. Serve at once.

RICE BRAEWATS
(FRIED RICE PASTRIES)

½ lb. flour	¼ pint milk
5 oz. rice	1 tsp. salt
2½ oz. sugar	1 tbsp. orange water
1½ tsps. cinnamon	¼ pint olive oil (approx.)

Make about 20 sheets of pastry with the flour, as for *Treed* (p. 377), making them about 9 inches across. Cook the rice well in a little water, add the sugar and cinnamon and stir over the heat for ¼ hour; then put in the milk and salt and cook for a further 10 minutes, adding the orange water and stirring until the mixture forms a thick paste. Put it into a dish to cool. Roll small tbsps. of this mixture in a sheet of pastry, making a roll or packet about ½ inch thick and 3½ inches long. Brown the pastries in hot oil on both sides and serve at once on a hot dish.

These pastries are eaten for breakfast.

ALMOND BRAEWATS (PASTIES)

½ lb. flour	2 tsps. ground cinnamon
4 tbsps. blanched almonds	½ pint olive oil (approx.)

With the flour and a little water make 12–15 sheets of pastry as described in the recipe for *Treed* (p. 377). Fold each sheet into a strip about 3 inches wide. Pound the almonds and cinnamon together in a mortar. Take 1 tsp. of the almond mixture and shape into a flat triangle with sides about 2 inches long; wrap this in a strip of pastry, retaining the triangular shape.

Repeat until all the mixture has been used. Cook the pastries in hot olive oil, browning them on both sides. Drain and serve at once.

MILLET BREAD

Several varieties of bread are made by Ethiopians, but the kind that is most generally eaten throughout the country is called *tef* and is made from millet.

The millet flour is mixed with yeast and made into an extremely thin dough, then baked on a kind of flat girdle. When it is cooked the surface looks rather like a honeycomb. After being baked the *tef* is folded over two or three times, rather like an omelette or pancake, and is then ready for the table.

KHUBZ EL JARADE
(LOCUST BREAD)

An unusual " bread " is sometimes made from the eggs of the locust, which are squeezed from the female insect's body and mixed with an equal amount of flour before being baked in small loaves, but this is only made rarely, on the occasion of a swarm of locusts—something which fortunately occurs only once in every nine or ten years.

MAHANSHA
(" SNAKE " PASTRIES)

18–20 sheets of pastry
½ lb. ground almonds
4 oz. caster sugar
½–1 oz. ground cinnamon
2 tsps. orange water
2½ tbsps. butter melted and beaten up until cheesy

Make pastry sheets about 10 inches across, as described below. Mix the almonds, sugar, cinnamon, orange water and 1 tbsp. butter in a mortar and knead this mixture into a dough. Smear a little butter over a griddle or hot-plate. Put 2 sheets of pastry on the griddle, end to end. Roll some of the almond mixture into a long rope ½ inch in diameter, fold this in the pastry sheets and curl it round like a snake. Put the griddle over the heat, adding the remaining butter, and brown the roll slightly on each side—about 15 minutes. Repeat until all the mixture is used.

TO MAKE MOORISH PASTRY

Knead some coarse semolina with water into a dough, adding a little plain flour from time to time, and continue kneading until the dough is very elastic—this may take 45 minutes. When the dough is ready, throw it quickly on to a hot griddle, removing at once so as to leave on the hot-plate only a small transparent patch of dough. The lumps of dough must never rest for any length of time on the griddle, and experts work

W.C.B.—25

with a kind of bouncing movement, never letting go of the main lump of dough.

Continue making " dabs," touching each other, until there is a patch of dough some 12 inches in diameter, which should come off the hot-plate in one transparent sheet—2 lb. semolina with about 2 oz. flour is enough to make about 30 sheets of this pastry.

MAAMOULE
(NUT PASTRIES)

1 lb. almonds or walnuts
6–8 oz. granulated sugar
5 oz. butter
6 oz. self-raising flour
½ cup water
Icing sugar

Remove the shells or skins of the nuts, chop the nuts up finely and mix with the sugar. Melt the butter but do not allow it to boil. Sieve the flour on to a marble slab, pour the melted butter into the middle and work with the hands as for dough, then add the water and knead well until smooth and slightly moist—it must cling together well. Roll out the pastry, cut it into large rounds and put 1 heaped tsp. of the nut-and-sugar mixture into each; roll up into " sausages " about 3 inches long. Lay those on well-greased baking sheets and cook in a hot oven (450° F., mark 8) for about 10 minutes. As soon as they come out of the oven dip them into icing sugar and leave to cool on a wire rack.

MAKROUD
(DATE AND SEMOLINA SWEET)

Chop ½ lb. stoned packet dates, then fry in a little hot oil until very soft. Pound with ¼ lb. caster sugar, ½ tsp. ground cinnamon and ½ tsp. ground ginger.

Fry 1 lb. semolina in some hot (not smoking) oil until the grains are just beginning to turn colour. Put a layer of half the fried semolina at the bottom of a flat dish, cover with a layer of the dates, then add the rest of the semolina. Cut into diamond shapes and fry in smoking hot oil, put at once into a bowl of honey or sugar syrup and serve immediately.

YOGHOURT SALAD

1 pint yoghourt
3 cloves garlic
1 tbsp. vinegar
1 small cucumber
Salt
Chopped mint

Beat the yoghourt until smooth. Pound the garlic with the salt and mix with the vinegar. Stir this into the yoghourt. Peel and dice the cucumber and stir all together, chill and sprinkle with mint.

Finely shredded lettuce may be substituted for cucumber if preferred.

WITH the improved methods of husbandry introduced by the Europeans, the great tracts of Kenya, Tanganyika and Uganda can grow a very wide range of crops, though the Africans' own dishes still tend to be based largely on the starchy cereals, vegetables and fruits, particularly maize, sweet potatoes and bananas, with a fair amount of groundnuts and coconut and the occasional feast of beef, pork or chicken. The Arab and Indian communities have, of course, kept their own traditional dishes, which have to some extent influenced the cuisine of the towns. Europeans can enjoy a slightly modified version of their familiar cookery, though the range of meats is restricted; mutton in particular is scarce and poultry is represented chiefly by chickens. Fish is plentiful on the coast but not inland, though frozen products are becoming more common. Dairy products, especially in Kenya, are good and plentiful and there is an abundance of fruit and vegetables, with both temperate and tropical varieties, ranging from strawberries and apples to pineapples, mangoes and avocado pears.

As with so many African countries, the area of the Rhodesias is so vast that it is almost impertinent to generalise about the food and cookery of its peoples. The native Africans rely very largely on mealies (maize), pawpaws, yams, bananas, pumpkins and groundnuts. They cannot usually afford chickens or meat as a daily food, much as they may like them. As this is an inland region, fresh fish is lacking away from the rivers, but the native people eat it in dried form.

For the Europeans living in Northern and Southern Rhodesia, meat (chiefly beef and pork) is fairly plentiful and there are of course various tinned meat and fish products as well as some deep-frozen ones. Corn-on-the-cob, rice and pumpkin are called in to supplement the vegetables. Fruits like grenadillas or passion fruit, pineapples, guavas, loquats and mulberries replace apples and plums, currants and raspberries; peanuts appear instead of almonds and walnuts. The cookery is naturally enough mainly British in type with a fairly strong Afrikaans strain.

Nyasaland is essentially a tropical country and the native dishes are based on such typically African products as yams, bananas, mangoes and groundnuts, with rice taking quite a prominent place. There is abundant fish from Lake Nyasa, as well as chicken, eggs and a certain amount of beef and mutton.

The European is apt to find the meat somewhat tough, so suitable cooking methods have to be evolved; one trick is to wrap the meat in pawpaw leaves and leave it for twenty-four hours before cooking, to tenderise it. Chickens are small and need fattening before they are worth eating; the local eggs, too, are rather sub-standard. As in the other East African territories, canned and frozen foods are available and the European housewife has evolved various recipes based on local products, such as Iced Banana Soup, Chicken and Pawpaw or Mango and Banana Pie.

East Africa

CREAM OF CORN SOUP

One cup of cold stock or cold water	Salt and pepper
2 cups grated green corn	2 tbsps. cream or evaporated milk
2 small onions	1 egg yolk
1 tbsp. corn cut from cob	Lettuce

Add the liquid to the 2 cups of grated corn and bring it to the boil, skimming off the husk as it rises to the surface. Add the onions, the corn cut from the cob and salt and pepper to taste. Boil up again and stir in the cream. Put the beaten egg yolk into a basin and pour the soup over, stirring all the time. Add to each plate some shredded lettuce. Sufficient for 2 servings.

GROUNDNUT SOUP

1 lb. fresh peanuts	Stock
2 teacups milk	½ dessertsp. butter
Flour	Cream if liked

Shell and clean nuts, place in the oven. When slightly roasted take out and leave to cool.

Remove brown skin by rubbing between the hands and then grind very finely. Mix with a little flour and about 2 teacups of milk then add the mixture to a good stock. Season to taste and put on the fire, slowly bring to the boil. When ready add the butter and a little cream if liked and serve.

FISH COOKED IN " TUI "

1 cup coconut cream (see below)	3 cloves
1 cup fish stock	Salt and pepper
1 lb. white fish	1 tbsp. butter
4 peppercorns	1 tbsp. flour

Simmer the fish in the liquids with the flavourings until done. Thicken the liquid with a little butter and some blended cornflour and pour over the fish.

TUI YA NAZI
(COCONUT CREAM)

Grate the coconut flesh and pour over ½ cup of water, then squeeze it through a piece of muslin or cheese cloth. The thick, creamy liquid is an essential ingredient of a good curry and gives a most delicious flavour to fish or vegetables cooked in it. It is also very good with fruit salad.

BUCK FILLETS

Wrap the fillet round with plenty of bacon rashers and sprinkle with herbs. Cook in a casserole with a little fat and water and some vegetables to flavour.

Any buck meat should be cooked with plenty of fat ; a leg can be slashed and pieces of bacon put in each cut.

SAVOURY PORK NOODLES

3 lb. lean pork fillet	1 tbsp. sugar
3 or 4 large onions	2 tsps. piquant table sauce
A little fat for frying	½ lb. strong Cheddar cheese
2 garlic cloves	
Salt	1 or 2 chillies
Black pepper	1 packet flat noodles
2 tsps. lemon juice	
4 skinned tomatoes	

Dice the pork removing the sinews. Chop the onions and fry with the pork using very little extra fat. Add the crushed garlic, salt, pepper, chillies, lemon juice, tomatoes, sugar and piquant sauce and simmer gently until tender. Grate the cheese and stir into the mixture ; do not cook after the cheese has been added. Cook the noodles in boiling salted water, after breaking them into short lengths, and fold gently into the pork mixture.

BREEDIE ZIMBABWE

1 lb. stewing steak or mutton cut small	1 tbsp. sultanas
	1 tsp. sugar
½ lb. onions	Salt and pepper
½ oz. dripping	1 tsp. chopped green pepper
1 lb. tomatoes or green beans	
	1 small chopped chilli

Stew the meat gently until tender. Brown the onions in the dripping. Peel and slice the tomatoes. Add all the ingredients except meat to the onions and cook gently until a thick sauce is obtained. Stir in the meat. Serve with peas, rice and mango chutney.

MATABELE FRIED CHICKEN

1 broiling chicken about 3 lb.	1 clove of garlic
	2 tbsps. finely chopped chervil, chives or spring onions
Seasoning	
Olive oil	
1 sweet red pepper	12 oz. rice
3 rashers of bacon	2 rounds of pineapple, diced
1 large onion	

Divide the chicken into joints and soak in the seasoned olive oil. Make some stock from the chicken carcase. Prepare the red pepper, removing the seeds and white pith, then cut into thin strips. Dice the bacon and the chicken liver and slice the onion thinly. Pour 1 tbsp. olive oil into a frying pan and add the diced bacon, red pepper, onion and garlic ; cover and cook gently for 15 minutes. Drain and keep warm, returning the oil to the pan and adding 1 tbsp. more oil.

Fry the rice until it starts to brown, stirring gently with a wooden spoon. Skim the chicken stock and add a little at a time to the rice so that the grains absorb the stock before more is added. Add the chicken liver after the rice has been cooking for about 10 minutes; when the rice is fully cooked stir in the other ingredients and keep warm. Add a further 1 tbsp. oil to the pan and cook the chicken pieces gently for about 20 minutes or until just golden and tender—allow longer for the legs and thighs. Turn the rice mixture on to a large dish and arrange the chicken pieces on it. Sprinkle with chopped chervil and diced pineapple and serve with green salad. In Rhodesia a usual complement to this dish is avocado salad, served individually on cos lettuce leaves.

HAM KARIBA

2 avocado pears	½ cup chopped peanuts
Lemon juice	Mayonnaise
2 hard-boiled eggs	Salt and pepper
3 tomatoes	Cayenne
½ onion	1 lb. sliced cooked ham
Lettuce	Chopped parsley

Cut the avocado pears into thin strips and dip into the lemon juice; chop the hard-boiled eggs; skin and slice tomatoes; chop the onion and some of the lettuce. Mix all those and the peanuts with some of the mayonnaise, adding seasoning to taste. Pile the mixture on slices of ham, folding each slice into a cornet, lay on a lettuce leaf and sprinkle with parsley.

SAMBUSA

1 lb. meat	5 grains cardamom
6 cloves of garlic	2 tsps. powdered cumin
2 lemons	seeds
2 lb. onions	1 tsp. powdered cin-
3 chillies	namon
1½ lb. ghee for frying	1 tsp. white pepper

For the Pastry

2 lb. wheat flour	Salt to taste
1½ oz. rice flour	

Mince the meat. Prepare onions and cut into small square pieces. Put minced meat into a pan with salt, crushed garlic, cumin powder, pepper, chillies, cardamom and lemon juice. Cook slowly stirring from time to time until all the liquid has been absorbed. Remove from the heat. Put the prepared onions into a pan with some salt and cook very slowly about 20–25 minutes. Add the meat, mix thoroughly and cook together (about 5 minutes). Remove from the heat.

To make the pastry sieve the wheat flour into a bowl. Make a soft but not sticky dough with the water and a little salt. Knead very thoroughly. Roll out the pastry on a prepared board until it is as thin as paper, using rice flour to prevent it sticking. Cut into strips 12 inches long and 2 inches wide. Place a tablespoonful of the meat in one corner of each strip. Fold over and over in a triangular shape. Fry in hat deep ghee until golden-brown. Drain and serve hot.

MTABAK

½ lb. meat	2 eggs
½ lb. onions	A pinch of cardamom
1 tsp. powdered cumin	6 cloves of garlic
seeds	1 lemon
½ tsp. cinnamon	1 lb. ghee

For the Pastry

1 lb. wheat flour	Rice flour
Saltt o taste	

Prepare meat and pastry as for Sambusa above, but cut the pastry into squares on a floured board. Place the meat mixture in the middle, cover with finely chopped hard-boiled eggs and fold the pastry over, sides to middle, keeping the square shape. Fry in deep hot fat.

MSANIF

1 lb. meat	1 lb. ghee
1 lb. onions	6 cloves of garlic
2 lemons	5 crushed cardamoms
1½ lb. flour	2 chillies
1 tsp. pepper	Salt to taste

Prepare meat and seasonings as for Sambusa. Sieve flour into a basin. Add salt and sufficient water to make a batter, mix carefully to avoid lumps. Heat a frying pan, pour in a tablespoonful of ghee and allow to become hot. Pour in one tablespoonful of batter, when just set put prepared meat in the middle and cover with another spoonful of batter. Allow to set, turn it over and brown on the other side. Drain and serve hot.

NUT FRICASSÉE

1 oz. butter	3 oz. cashew nuts
2 sticks celery	Salt
1 medium-sized onion	2 tbsps. cream
2 oz. flour	Cooked carrots and
1 pint milk	green peas

Melt the butter, cut the celery and onion into small pieces and fry. Stir in the flour, add the whole nuts and salt to taste, and allow to cook very gently with the lid on for 15 minutes. Add the cream. Make a border of peas in a serving dish, pour the mixture into the centre and garnish with the cooked carrot.

SAVOURY AVOCADO MOUSSE

2 cups of avocado pulp	$\frac{1}{2}$ cup boiling water
1 tsp. salt	$\frac{1}{2}$ cup mayonnaise
A few drops of onion juice	$\frac{1}{2}$ tbsp. gelatine soaked in half cup cold water
2 tsps. piquant table sauce	$\frac{1}{2}$ cup double whipped cream

Mash the avocado with a silver fork and add the salt, onion juice and sauce. Mix the cream with the mayonnaise and add gelatine dissolved in boiling water and slightly cooled. Add the avocado pulp and put the mixture into a mould. Turn out and serve on lettuce with tomato wedges and mayonnaise.

CURRIED AUBERGINE

Slice 2 medium-sized onions and fry in a little fat till golden-brown. Add 2 tsps. curry powder and 1 tbsp. flour, cook for a few minutes and then slowly add 2 cups stock or milk. Peel thinly 2–3 aubergines and cut into dice, add to the curry sauce and simmer all together until the aubergines are soft. Serve with rice (preferably boiled in thick coconut cream with 1–2 cloves and a stick of cinnamon).

GREEN MEALIES AND TOMATOES

Boil some green corn cobs; when cooked, cut the grains off. Make the same quantity of thick tomato pulp by mincing the tomatoes first and frying them in with a little butter till thick; add sugar and salt to taste. Butter a pie dish, put in a layer of tomato pulp, then a layer of mealies, then more tomato pulp and mealies, finishing with a last layer of tomato pulp; put small pieces of butter on each layer. Sprinkle some breadcrumbs and a little parsley on top and bake in a moderate oven (375° F., mark 5) until hot through and lightly browned.

KENYA GROUNDNUT QUENELLES

Mash 2 tbsps. cooked root vegetables (e.g., turnip, parsnip, carrot) and mix with 2 good cups groundnut flour. Add 1 egg, salt, pepper and other flavourings or seasonings if desired. Heat some oil for deep frying. Roll the quenelles in fine breadcrumbs and drop one by one into the oil; fry till golden-brown and drain well. Serve hot.

SWEET CORN WITH EGGS

Put some sweet corn in a shallow dish and sprinkle with grated cheese. Make hollows in the corn and break an egg into each. Bake in a slow oven until the eggs are set (300° F., mark 1).

SAVOURY CORN AND CARROT CUSTARD

Boil a corn cob and some carrots together until tender. Take the corn kernels off the cob; chop up the carrots. Put all into an ovenproof dish and pour over the mixture an egg custard, seasoned with salt and pepper. Put little dots of butter on top and bake in a slow oven (325° F., mark 2) till set.

SWEET POTATOES

1$\frac{1}{2}$ lb. medium-sized sweet potatoes	$\frac{2}{3}$ cup caster sugar
	1$\frac{1}{2}$ tbsps. butter

Scrub the potatoes, place in a saucepan and cover with boiling water. Cover the pan and boil gently until the potatoes are tender. Drain off water, skin the potatoes, halve lengthwise and place in a shallow greased baking tin. Put the sugar, water and butter into a saucepan and stir over a slow heat until the sugar is dissolved. Bring to the boil and boil for 5 minutes, then pour over the potatoes. Bake in a medium hot oven (350° F., mark 4) about 20 minutes, until pale brown. These are particularly delicious with hot ham, baked.

EGG PLANT (AUBERGINES)

Baked : Marinate for 15 minutes in French dressing, then drain, put in an ovenproof dish and spread with soft butter. Bake in a moderate oven for 15 minutes (375 F., mark 5) or until tender, turning once. Sprinkle with lemon juice.

Fried : Dip in batter or in flour, egg and crumbs and fry in deep fat. Fried egg plant is delicious cut in thin strips instead of slices.

Sautéed : Dredge with flour and sauté slowly in butter until crisp and brown.

Scalloped : Cut the egg plant into cubes and cook in a small amount of boiling water; drain, cook 1 onion in butter until yellow and add a little chopped parsley. Put the egg plant in a buttered pie dish, and add the onion and parsley, cover with buttered crumbs and bake in a moderate oven (375° F., mark 5).

SADZA SUKKANAUKKA
(SAVOURY MEALIES)

2 cups fine mealie (maize) meal	2 medium onions
4 cups water	2 medium-sized tomatoes
3 tbsps. cooking oil	Chopped parsley

Mix the mealie meal and water and cook slowly

in a thick-bottomed pan, continually stirring to avoid lumps. Chop the onions and fry brown in the oil. Skin the tomatoes, cut into small sections, add both to the meal and mix all together. Serve in a vegetable dish, smoothing the top or shape into balls. This is delicious whether hot or cold and may be served with a green salad.

CORN AND CABBAGE SALAD

This is made with fresh corn in Tanganyika, but is equally good made with the tinned variety.

Soak a cabbage in iced water, then shred the heart very finely. Mix 1 tbsp. lemon juice with 1 tbsp. salad oil and some seasoning and toss cabbage in it. Mix 1 medium-sized tin of corn with a little mayonnaise, arrange on a dish and surround with the cabbage. Garnish with young radishes. This salad is very good with cold ham.

COCONUT FINGERS

4 oz. butter	1 tsp. baking powder
6 oz. flour	3 eggs
4 oz. caster sugar	A little milk
3 oz. coconut, grated	Desiccated coconut
2 oz. cornflour	

Rub the butter into the flour. Add all the dry ingredients and mix to a thick paste with the eggs and milk. Roll out, cut into fingers, brush with egg and sprinkle some desiccated coconut ove them. Bake for 15 minutes in a moderate oven (350° F., mark 4).

COCONUT CAKE FEATHER

1½ cups flour	½ cup milk
⅞ cup sugar	1 tsp. lemon essence
4 tsps. baking powder	½ cup fresh grated
4 tbsps. melted butter	coconut
1 egg	

Sift together the flour, sugar and baking powder. Add the melted butter and beaten egg to the milk, then add to the dry ingredients and mix well. Add the lemon essence and coconut and put into a greased tin. Bake in a moderate oven (375° F., mark 5) until it is firm and lightly coloured. Sprinkle with caster sugar before serving.

COCONUT ICE

4 cups granulated sugar	1 cup grated coconut
1 cup milk	Cochineal

Have ready 2 wetted bowls. Boil the sugar, milk and coconut together for 15 minutes. Divide into 2 bowls, then colour one half with cochineal. Beat both mixtures with a wooden spoon until quite thick. Pour the white mixture on a flat dish and spread the pink over it. Cut into squares before it is quite stiff.

COCONUT CREAM DESSERT

Grate a coconut and extract the milk from the flesh (see p. 330). Add 3 tsps. caster sugar and a tbsp. gelatine and beat for a few minutes. Beat 3 egg whites stiff with ¼ pint of cream then whisk the whole together. Chill thoroughly.

MOONSHINE PUDDING

24 grenadillas	¾ oz. gelatine
½ lb. sugar	1 egg white

Scoop out the grenadillas and boil with enough water to make a pint when strained. Add the sugar and gelatine and bring to the boil. Strain into a basin and when beginning to set beat it for 20 minutes until light and frothy. Add the well-beaten egg white to the mixture and put into a mould to set. Serve with cream.

PINEAPPLE PUDDING

2 oz. butter	2 oz. sugar
2 tbsps. flour	2 eggs
¾ pint milk	Fresh or tinned pineapple

Melt the butter in pan and stir in the flour till smooth. Add milk gradually, stir in 1 oz. sugar and boil for 3 minutes. Beat the egg yolks, add the sliced or diced pineapple. If fresh fruit is used, stew with a little water, then drain. Pour the flour mixture on to the pineapple, put into an ovenproof dish and bake in a slow oven (325° F., mark 3) until set. Whip the whites of eggs and add 1 tbsp. sugar and whip again, then pile on the pudding and return to the oven to brown. Serve with cold coconut cream or ordinary cream.

GUAVA PLATE PIE

6 oz. shortcrust pastry	1 pint milk (or tinned
½ lb. guavas	evaporated milk)
3 oz. sugar	1 lime
3 eggs	

Line a pie plate with pastry and decorate the edge. Stew the guavas with 1 oz. of the sugar. Make a custard with the eggs, milk and remaining sugar; when cool add juice and grated rind of lime. Sieve guavas to remove the pips, put the pulp over the pastry and cover with the custard. Bake in a moderate oven (350° F., mark 4) for 40 minutes.

PAWPAW PUDDING

Peel some pawpaws and cut into thin strips,

put in a pie dish and sprinkle with sugar and ground cinnamon. Add the juice of 1 lemon and cover with breadcrumbs. Put a little butter over the top, cover with a lid and bake in a moderate oven (350° F., mark 4). Serve with a sweet sauce or fresh cream.

LEMON PUNCH

Juice of 6 lemons	½ cup mashed straw-
Juice of 3 oranges	berries
1 quart water	½ cup crushed pine-
Sugar syrup to	apple
sweeten	Orange slices to garnish

Mix fruit juices, add the water, sweeten to taste with syrup, then add the crushed fruit and garnish with very thin slices of oranges.

PINEAPPLE PUNCH

Take the skin off the pineapple, cut the flesh into small pieces and place in a glass bowl. Pour over the pineapple 1 pint water in which is dissolved 1 heaped cup sugar and allow to stand for 2–3 days. Strain off the liquid through muslin, bottle, cork firmly and keep for 10 days to a month. The longer it is stored the better. Add more sugar if preferred sweet. Dilute to make a pineapple drink, adding a few pieces of cut pineapple.

GRENADILLA FILLING FOR VICTORIA SANDWICH

3 tbsps. icing sugar	1 tbsp. strained grena-
2 good tsps. butter	dilla juice
2 tsps. cornflour	

Cook all together in a double saucepan till thick. Leave to get cold, and spread between the sandwich cake layers.

Grenadilla Icing : Boil 1½ tsps. juice, then let it cool a little and add enough icing sugar to make a thick icing.

CRYSTALLISED GREEN FIGS

Cut some unripe figs in half, cover with water and boil until soft. Pour off the liquid and boil it up with sugar in the proportion of 2 cups sugar to 1 cup liquid—continue until syrupy. Pour over the figs and leave till next day. Boil the figs in the syrup till transparent and leave for 2 days in the syrup, then take out and roll them in sugar.

PAWPAW AND PINEAPPLE JAM

Skin 1 medium-sized pawpaw (not quite ripe) and remove pips ; peel 1 medium-sized pine-apple. Put both through a mincer, add the juice of 1 lemon and measure the quantity. Add an equal quantity of sugar and boil for about 20 minutes, till a little will set when tested on a cold plate.

GUAVA JELLY

Cut the guavas in halves, put into a preserving pan, cover with water and cook until mushy. Strain all night through a jelly bag. To each pint of juice, add ¾ lb. sugar and the juice of 1 lemon. Boil in the usual way till a little of it will jell on a plate. (It is essential to add the lemon juice to ensure a set.)

KEI APPLE JELLY

Put some kei apples in a saucepan with enough water to float them. Simmer slowly till they are pulpy, then rub through a sieve. To every pint of pulp add 1 lb. sugar and cook slowly, skimming well, until the mixture jells when tried on a cold plate. Bottle while hot. Serve with game and cold meat.

SUBSTITUTES FOR APPLE SAUCE

Pawpaw with lemon juice ; unripe mango and lemon juice ; chow-chow and cloves—any of these makes a good substitute for apple sauce.

KENYA CRYSTALLISED WATER MELON

Peel and halve a water melon, remove the soft flesh from the centre, with all the seeds, then cut the firm pink flesh into strips and weigh them. Prick the pieces all over with a sharp fork and put into a large jar or basin. Mix 2½ tsps. lime juice with 1 quart cold water and pour over the melon, taking care to cover all the strips. Cover with a plate, weight this down and leave for 24 hours. Make a syrup with 1 lb. sugar and 1 pint water to every 1 lb. melon. Bring the syrup to the boil and meanwhile wash the melon thoroughly to remove the lime flavour. Put the melon into the syrup, add sufficient ginger to give a good flavour and cook until the melon is clear and most of the syrup is absorbed. Drain the melon, arrange the pieces on a flat tray, cover with muslin and dry in the sun or in a cool oven.

KASHATA YA LOZI (ALMOND SWEETMEAT)

1 lb. almonds	A few drops essence
1 lb. sugar	5 grains cardamom

If fresh almonds are used, blanch them and dry preferably in the sun for one day. Pound them well. Prepare a syrup with the sugar and water and cardamom. Cook it till it becomes thick and sticky, then add the ground almonds. Pour into a greased tray, spread about ½ inch thick. When cold cut in pieces.

MKATE WA MAYAI

6 eggs	A few drops of vanilla essence
½ lb. sugar	A little ghee or butter
½ lb. flour	2 oz. currants

Beat the eggs and sugar till fluffy, then add the flour and essence gradually. Pour in a greased tin or pan and bake in a moderate oven (350° F., mark 4). Put the currants on top when mixture has set and continue to bake until done.

BANANA LOAF

2 oz. butter	3 well-mashed bananas
6 oz. light brown sugar	8 oz. flour
1 egg	1 tsp. baking powder
½ tsp. bicarbonate of soda	(omit if self-raising flour is used)
2 tbsps. milk	½ tsp. ground cinnamon

Cream the butter and sugar, beat in the egg, then add the soda, dissolved in the milk, the bananas and finally the flour, baking powder and cinnamon sieved together. Put in a greased tin and bake in a moderate oven (350° F., mark 4) for 45 minutes.

BANANA AND NUT CAKE

½ cup fat	1 cup mashed bananas
½ cup sugar	1 cup chopped walnuts or pecans
2 eggs, well-beaten	
1 tsp. bicarbonate of soda	1¾ cups flour sifted with 1 tsp. baking powder
4 tbsps. cream	

Cream the fat and sugar and add the eggs. Dissolve the soda in the cream and add to the first mixture. Stir in the remaining ingredients. Put into a greased loaf or tube tin and bake in a moderate oven (350° F., mark 4) for 45 minutes. Alternatively, bake in 2 round layer cake tins for 30–40 minutes.

This cake can be served plain or with caramel, chocolate or vanilla icing; if made in layers fill as desired. It improves with keeping; the banana flavour is more pronounced after a day or so.

COFFEE GROUNDNUT CAKE (KENYA)

Mince ½ lb. groundnuts (shelled, but with the brown inner skin still on) twice, to grind them really fine. Beat together ½ lb. caster sugar and 8 egg yolks until the mixture is almost white. Whisk the 8 egg whites very stiffly. Add the nuts and about 2 doz. coffee beans, ground to a powder, to the egg yolk mixture. Fold in the egg whites, put into a greased sandwich tin and bake in a moderate oven (350° F., mark 4) until firm. When cool, cut in half and fill with coffee butter cream.

CHOCOLATE GROUNDNUT COOKIES (KENYA)

4 oz. butter	3 tsps. cocoa powder
1 cup sugar	1 tsp. baking powder
1 egg	1 cup groundnuts, shelled and broken into small pieces
1¼ cups flour	
A pinch of salt	

Cream the butter and sugar, beat in the egg, then add the flour, salt, cocoa and baking powder. Stir in the nuts, to give a fairly stiff mixture. Place in spoonfuls on a greased baking sheet, spacing them fairly well apart, and bake in a moderate oven (350° F., mark 4) until lightly browned.

THE people of West Africa have had to be ingenious and resourceful in making the most of the ingredients available in a region not particularly blessed from the point of view of climate. Some of their dishes, however, such as Groundnut Chop, Palm Oil Chop and Ashanti Chicken, are so good that they have been adopted by the European residents.

The staple foods are manioc or cassava, made into Foofoo and other dishes, maize in various forms, and such starchy vegetables and fruits as yams, cocoyams, sweet potatoes and bananas

The yams of West Africa are a root vegetable, very large, often weighing about 4 lb. each. The flesh is much drier than that of the potato but it can be cooked in the same ways. For mashed yam, peel, dice, boil, then mash with plenty of milk and butter and an egg if available. Yam chips can also be made, but as the flesh is so dry, the smaller they are cut the better the result. The traditional native way of cooking yam, cocoyam and cassava is to boil them, either alone or mixed, and then pound them in a wooden bowl with a heavy stick until they form a sticky dough, which is eaten with stews and soups.

The Africans enjoy fish, chickens and meat, but flesh food is often scarce and dear, especially in the remoter parts. Meat, when obtainable, mostly takes the form of pork and beef, either fresh or salted, but such " extras " as porcupine are also eaten. Fish and shell fish are obtainable on the coast and to a certain extent inland in smoked and dried form. Eggs are widely used but are smaller than in Europe.

Tropical fruits such as guavas, pawpaws, etc., are of course plentiful. European-type vegetables are scarce, but the native people eat a number of unusual greenstuffs. Spices and flavourings such as chillies, garlic and red pepper are lavishly used. Peanuts or groundnuts, which appear constantly in all kinds of dishes, are rich in fat and protein, iron and certain vitamins, so they form a valuable addition to the diet. On the whole, however, the native food tends to be starchy, lacking in protein and somewhat monotonous. Food is boiled or stewed, pot-roasted, fried (often in palm oil) or baked in rather primitive ovens outside the towns.

For gala occasions such as weddings, richer fare is enjoyed, including various meat and vegetable stews, chicken dishes, a type of pilaff known as Jollof Rice, the palm oil and groundnut chops already mentioned and *couscous*, which was originally borrowed from the Arabs. Palm wine is the typical celebration drink.

Western influences are making themselves felt and the town dwellers at any rate are adopting European table customs and some foodstuffs and methods of cooking. At the same time, the Europeans living in West Africa have learnt to contrive colourable imitations of some of their own favourite dishes by adapting and combining local ingredients.

West Africa

PORK AND GROUNDNUT SOUP

1 lb. groundnuts	Pepper and salt
½ lb. pork	2 small aubergines
A little flour	1 tomato
Lard for frying	2 onions

Roast the nuts till light brown, rub off the skins and grind the nuts to a paste. Cut the meat into small pieces, flour and fry in lard for 10 minutes. Add salt, cover with 1 quart boiling water and cook for ½ hour. Take out some of the stock and mix with the groundnut paste, then add the whole to the stock and meat. Mince aubergines, tomato and onions, add to the mixture and boil for ½ hour.

COCONUT SOUP

2 oz. shredded coconut	½ pint milk
1 quart stock (preferably chicken)	Salt and pepper
2 oz. flour	Pinch of ground mace

Simmer the coconut in the stock for 1 hour. Sieve, thicken with the flour, boil up and add the milk, seasonings and mace. Reheat and serve with fried bread.

GHANA GROUNDNUT SOUP

8 oz. peanut butter (or roasted groundnuts ground to a paste)	Seasoning to taste
1 large onion	1½ pints chicken stock
6 medium-sized tomatoes	Hard-boiled eggs and okra to garnish

Simmer all the ingredients until tender, pass the soup through a fine sieve and season to taste. Garnish with slices of hard-boiled egg and okra.

GHANA AVOCADO HORS D'ŒUVRE

Avocado pears	Seasoning
Lime juice	Mayonnaise
Crayfish	Lettuce leaves

Cut the avocado pears in half lengthwise and remove the stones. Sprinkle with lime juice. Shred the crayfish, season and add mayonnaise. Stuff the avocado, chill and serve on lettuce leaves, with the crayfish heads to garnish.

FANTE FANTE
(GHANA FISH STEW)

1 lb. fresh fish	1 onion
¼ tsp. red pepper	2 aubergines
½ tsp. salt	3 tbsps. fish stock
2–3 tomatoes	2 tbsps. olive oil

Cut fish into even-sized pieces and season with salt and pepper. Slice the tomatoes, onion and aubergines finely. Put the fish and vegetables into a casserole and add the stock and olive oil. Cook in a slow oven (325° F., mark 3) for 45 minutes. Serve with rice and other vegetables.

NIGERIAN FRESH FISH STEW

1 lb. fresh fish	2 large tomatoes
Crayfish, as desired	½–¾ pint boiling water
4–6 peppers	1 tbsp. palm oil
1 small onion	Seasoning

Prepare the fish and crayfish. Add the finely minced peppers, onion and tomatoes to the water and lastly put in the crayfish. Leave this to cook for a short time, then add the palm oil; stir well and season. Add the prepared fish (whole or cutlets) and reduce the heat, to prevent the fish breaking up. Cook gently until the fish is well done but not overcooked.

SPICED FRESH FISH

1 lb. fresh fish	6 peppercorns
½ pint vinegar	Salt
6 cloves	

Put the fish in a deep dish and bake till cooked through. Put the vinegar in a saucepan with the spices and salt to taste and boil for 10 minutes, strain the liquid over the fish and allow to cool. Serve cold with salad.

ACRAS
(FISH BALLS)

3 oz. salt fish	3 oz. flour
2 tomatoes	1 tsp. baking powder
6 small onions	Milk
Pepper	Fat for deep frying

Boil the fish for 10 minutes, skin and bone it, then pound finely in a mortar. Add the chopped tomato, onion and pepper, mix well and add the flour and baking powder. When thoroughly blended, add milk to make a stiff paste. Form into balls and fry in deep fat.

CHICKEN CURRY

1 chicken	1–1½ tbsps. curry powder
1 oz. butter	Salt and pepper
2 chopped onions	1½ pints stock (chicken if possible) or 1 bouillon cube dissolved in water
4 chopped tomatoes	
1 small tin of tomato paste	
2 cloves of garlic, chopped	Flour to thicken (optional)
1 red pepper, chopped	Hard-boiled eggs

Joint the chicken and fry in the butter. Add the onion, tomatoes, tomato paste, garlic, red pepper, curry powder and seasonings and fry for a few minutes. Add the stock and simmer for 1–2 hours. Thicken with flour if desired. Add 2–3 sliced hard-boiled eggs before serving. Serve with boiled rice and a variety of side dishes in small bowls. These can include bananas, red peppers, oranges and avocado, all cut up very small; groundnuts, small chips, fried bread cubes and fried onion and banana can also be served.

This curry is usually served buffet style.

FRIED FISH AND RED PEPPER SAUCE (GHANA)

Herrings, mackerel or other fish	$\frac{1}{4}$–$\frac{1}{2}$ tsp. cayenne pepper
2 tbsps. olive oil	$\frac{1}{4}$ tsp. salt
4 tomatoes, cut up	A pinch of grated nutmeg
1 onion, chopped	Parsley to garnish

Fry or grill the fish in the usual way. Heat the oil, add the tomatoes, onion and pepper and cook slowly for 15–20 minutes. Add the salt and nutmeg. Pour this sauce over the fish and garnish with parsley.

FRIED CHICKEN (GHANA)

1 small frying chicken	$\frac{1}{2}$ lb. rice
Seasoning	Sweetcorn
Oil or lard for frying	Red peppers

Clean the chicken and cut into pieces. Season and fry in hot fat until golden-brown. Arrange the fried chicken on a platter of boiled rice and surround with cooked sweetcorn, garnish with sliced red peppers.

PALM OIL CHOP

1 chicken	1 small tin prawns
1$\frac{1}{2}$ cups palm nuts	12 okras
1 cup groundnuts	4 hard-boiled eggs
2 onions	2–3 large green peppers
Seasoning	4–5 aubergines
1 lb. spinach	

Prepare the chicken, cutting it into joints. Wash the palm nuts, cover with cold water and boil for 1 hour. Strain off the water, crush the nuts, return to the pan with enough fresh water to cover, mix well, strain carefully and put on the heat; boil for about $\frac{1}{2}$ hour. Grind the groundnuts well, mix with a little water to make a paste and add to the soup little by little, taking care not to make it too thick.

Leave to simmer slowly. Add the chicken to the soup with the onions, pepper and salt and continue cooking until the chicken is cooked and the palm oil floats on top of the soup; skim carefully and keep simmering gently. Mean-while, cook the spinach in another saucepan, strain, chop finely and add to the soup.

The prawns, okras and aubergines are cooked in separate pans. When the soup is ready all the ingredients are mixed together with the hard-boiled eggs in a casserole. Crush the green peppers and serve in a separate dish. Hand round coconut, fried bananas, pawpaw, pine-apple, orange and ground ginger as side dishes.

GOLDEN CHICKEN STEW

1 chicken	Turnips and potatoes
Carrots	$\frac{1}{2}$ lb. groundnuts
Seasoning	

Joint the chicken and stew till tender with the vegetables and seasoning. Pound the nuts to a paste with a little water. Ten minutes before serving thicken the stew with the groundnut paste and stir thoroughly; serve hot.

GHANA GROUNDNUT MEAT STEW

$\frac{1}{2}$–1 lb. mutton or beef	8 oz. groundnuts
3 large tomatoes, finely chopped	3 pints stock
6 small onions, finely chopped	1 tsp. red pepper (or chopped fresh red pepper)
2–3 aubergines, finely chopped	2 tsps. salt

Cut the meat into $\frac{1}{2}$-inch cubes. Chop the tomatoes, onions and aubergines, finely. Roast the nuts to enable the skins to be removed, chop and grind the nuts into a smooth paste. Put the meat and stock into a saucepan and simmer for 1 hour, add the vegetables, the nut paste, blended with some of the stock and the seasonings and simmer for another hour.

Serve with rice and with side dishes, which could consist of chopped onion, tomato, red and green peppers, banana, orange, avocado pear, desiccated coconut and chopped groundnuts. The side dishes are served in small bowls round the stew and the rice is garnished with parsley and rings of pepper.

White fish, such as cod or haddock, may also be used in this stew.

CHICKEN GROUNDNUT STEW (NIGERIAN)

2$\frac{1}{2}$–3 lb. chicken	$\frac{1}{2}$ pint (approx.) hot chicken stock or water
1 large onion	
1 tbsp. margarine or cooking oil	3–4 tomatoes
	1 chilli
6 heaped tsps. peanut butter or 2 lb. roast and ground nuts	$\frac{1}{4}$ tsp. ground cumin or curry powder

Cut the chicken into pieces. Fry chopped onion slowly in the fat until pale golden-brown.

Remove the pan from the heat, add the peanut butter or groundnuts and enough liquid to give the consistency of thin cream. Add the tomatoes, chilli, pepper, curry powder and sections of chicken, put the lid on the pan and simmer for $1-1\frac{1}{2}$ hours; season to taste.

Serve with plain boiled Patna rice and with side dishes; these can be rings of green pepper, mango chutney, sliced banana and hard-boiled eggs. Spinach or marrow are good vegetables to serve with it.

Roast or boiled chicken can be heated through in this type of curry sauce.

NIGERIAN JOLOFF RICE

This consists of raw salt pork, beef and chicken cooked together with onions, tomatoes, tomato purée, seasonings and herbs; oil and rice are also included. Serve on a long dish with dressed, boiled cabbage and peas.

This dish is always eaten at weddings and at Christmas.

GHANA JOLLOF RICE

2 tbsps. olive oil	$\frac{1}{4}$ tsp. cayenne pepper
$\frac{1}{2}$ lb. minced meat	Salt and pepper
1 large chopped onion	2 tsps. tomato purée
2 large chopped tomatoes	$\frac{1}{2}-\frac{3}{4}$ pint stock
8 oz. rice	

Heat the oil and sauté the meat, onion and tomatoes. Add the rice and seasonings, stir in the stock and cook slowly over a low heat with the lid on until the rice is thoroughly cooked. A tomato sauce can be served as accompaniment.

PALM NUT HASH

40 palm nuts	Potatoes
1 lb. stewing steak	Seasoning
Onions, carrots, turnips, tomatoes	Fat for frying

Boil the palm nuts until cooked, drain, pound, cover with fresh water and mix well, then strain into a saucepan. Fry the meat, onions, carrots and turnips golden-brown and add to the palm nuts. Season and simmer gently for 2 hours, skimming off the grease as it rises. Add potatoes half an hour before serving. Chicken can be used instead of meat.

BANANA STEAK

$\frac{3}{4}$ lb. beefsteak	2 bananas
Pepper and salt	Sugar
Grated nutmeg	2–3 rashers of bacon

Split the steak in half without cutting it right through, put in a baking dish, season with pepper, salt and nutmeg. Cut the bananas in pieces, lay them inside the steak, sprinkle with sugar and close up the steak. Lay the bacon on top and secure with skewer or cocktail sticks. Add a little water and bake in a moderate oven (375° F., mark 5) for about $\frac{1}{2}$ hour, basting occasionally. Serve with parsley.

HAM AND PINEAPPLE HOT-POT

1 lb. potatoes	$\frac{1}{4}$ lb. sliced cooked ham
Thin slices of pineapple	1 finely chopped onion
Brown sugar	A little stock
Pepper and salt	

Arrange the ingredients in layers in a greased dish, with a little brown sugar on the pineapple. Add enough stock to keep it moist and bake in a moderate oven (350° F., mark 4) for about $1\frac{1}{2}$ hours.

Remove the lid for the last $\frac{1}{2}$ hour to brown the potatoes.

CURRIED MEAT PATTIES (GHANA)

8 oz. cooked minced meat or flaked fish	1 tsp. curry powder
10 oz. cooked potato	$\frac{1}{2}$ tsp. piquant table sauce
1 egg	Stock or brown sauce to bind
Fat for frying	
1 onion, grated	Egg and breadcrumbs for coating
Salt and pepper	

Mix the meat and potato and add the beaten egg. Heat the fat and fry the onion and curry powder, then add to the meat. Add the other ingredients, form into round cakes, coat with egg and breadcrumbs and fry until golden-brown.

Fish may be used in the same way.

ASHANTI FOWL

1 fowl	4 onions
1 lb. sausages	Salt and pepper
$\frac{1}{2}$ lb. breadcrumbs	3 eggs
4 tomatoes	

Carefully bone the chicken. Make a stuffing of the other ingredients, using egg to bind. Fill the chicken, reconstructing its shape. Pot-roast until tender and serve either hot or cold.

FREJON
(NIGERIAN BEAN PURÉE)

Pick and wash some black beans (if available) or haricot-type white beans and cook in either coconut milk or water till soft. Either pound or sieve the beans well, then return them to the coconut milk, flavour as desired and cook until the purée is the consistency of cream soup. If it is left for any time before eating, stir it up, as the bean paste tends to settle. This is traditionally eaten on Good Friday.

Frejon Soup : Add crayfish, pepper, salt, tomatoes, etc., to the sieved bean and coconut mixture and re-cook until the added ingredients are done.

Sweet Frejon : Make the frejon according to the above instructions, but make it somewhat thinner and add only sugar to taste. Chill and serve in individual dishes as a sweet.

NIGERIAN MOYINMOYIN
(STEAMED BEAN CAKES)

2 tbsps. groundnut oil	1 tsp. cayenne pepper
3 cups powdered black-eyed beans	(optional)
1 small tin tomato purée	A pinch of ground ginger
1 tbsp. grated onions	Pieces of fish, prawns or meat (optional)
Salt to taste	

Warm the oil and ½ pint water together. Put all the other ingredients in a mixing bowl and mix in the oil and water very gradually. (The secret is to blend thoroughly till the mixture is smooth and is of a thick but runny paste consistency.) Wrap in individual leaves or pieces of foil, allowing 3–4 tbsps. each. Place in a pudding basin and steam in a small amount of water until cooked and solid—about 1–1½ hours. (When the special leaves are used, they turn brown by the time the Moyinmoyin is cooked.)

This dish is often eaten on Saturdays.

SPINACH AND ONION

Remove the stems and wash the spinach thoroughly, cook until soft, strain and add a pinch of salt. Fry some sliced onions in lard and add the spinach and a little pepper. Fry all together and serve in a hot dish, garnished with hard-boiled egg.

TATALE
(SAVOURY FRITTERS)

2 bananas	¼ tsp. cayenne pepper
1 tbsp. ground rice	½ tsp. salt
1 tbsp. flour	A pinch of ground ginger
1 onion, grated	Oil for frying

Mash the bananas, add all the other ingredients and mix well. Add 1 tsp. cold water and leave to stand for 10–15 minutes. Fry in hot oil in tablespoonfuls until golden-brown. Serve with grilled bacon or ham and tomatoes or beans.

EGG AND YAM FRITTERS (NIGERIAN)

1 slice of raw white yam	Salt
1 pepper, finely chopped	1 egg
1 tomato, finely chopped	Deep fat for frying
¼ onion, finely chopped	

Grate the yam, add the pepper, tomato, onion and salt to taste. Add the beaten egg and mix all together. Form into small balls and fry in the hot fat. Drain well and serve hot.

Grated potato could be substituted for the yam.

WEST AFRICAN PUMPKIN OMELETTE

Stew the pumpkin until tender, mash with butter and season with salt, pepper and a little sage. Fry like an omelette in bacon fat, and serve with bacon for breakfast.

NIGERIAN YAM CHIPS

Cut peeled yam into strips 4 inches long and ¼ inch thick and fry in hot oil. Serve with fried fish.

NIGERIAN YAM CRISPS

Slice peeled yam and cut each slice into very thin, almost transparent slices or grate into large shreds. Soak in salted water, then drain and fry in hot oil for a minute or so.

FRUIT SALAD—I

1 pineapple or melon	1 grapefruit
½ pint sugar syrup	2–3 tbsps. whisky
1 orange	Cream or ice cream

Cut the top off the pineapple or melon, then remove and dice the flesh. (If pineapple is used, soak it overnight in sugar syrup.) Mix the sugar syrup with the diced fruit and the grapefruit segments, then add the whisky. Put in the fruit shell and serve with cream or ice cream.

FRUIT SALAD—II

Slice a pineapple from the end downwards, scoop out the flesh from the centre and cut in slices. Mix with pieces of pawpaw, water melon and segments of orange and grapefruit; if necessary sweeten with honey. Pile the fruit into the hollowed pineapple and decorate with black grapes. Serve on a bed of ice cubes.

NIGERIAN PAWPAW FOOL

Prepare pawpaw and sieve to a pulp. Add an equal quantity of custard and sweeten to taste. Chill before serving.

GUAVA AND LIME CUPS

1 packet lime jelly	1 medium-sized orange
1 small tin guavas	per person

Make up the lime jelly and allow to stand until almost set. Meanwhile prepare orange cups by cutting the tops off the oranges in a " waterlily " fashion and removing the pulp with a teaspoon.

Whisk the jelly when it is almost set and carefully spoon a little into each orange cup ; add a layer of orange pulp and chopped guava and fill up with the remaining jelly. Chill thoroughly.

GHANA BANANA FRITTERS

4 bananas	2 tbsps. flour
¼ tsp. salt	Oil for frying
¼ tsp. grated nutmeg	Sugar
½ an egg	

Mash the bananas well, adding the salt and nutmeg. Add the beaten egg and sifted flour and leave standing for 10–15 minutes. Put in tablespoonfuls into the hot oil and fry for 2–3 minutes on each side until golden-brown. Drain well and serve hot, sprinkled with sugar.

Lemon juice can be served with the fritters if desired.

BAKED BANANAS

Peel 6 ripe bananas and lay in a pie dish. Cover with a syrup made from 3 tbsps. sugar, the juice of a lime and some water. Bake in a slow oven (300° F., mark 1) and serve with coconut cream.

SCALLOPED BANANAS

Cover the base of a buttered dish with a thick layer of sliced bananas, sprinkle with 2 tbsps. sugar and moisten with lemon juice. Then add a layer of breadcrumbs and repeat until the dish is full, pour a little melted butter over and bake in a moderate oven (375° F., mark 5) till lightly browned.

BANANA CAKE

½ cup butter	1 tsp. bicarbonate of soda
1 cup caster sugar	2 cups flour
3 ripe bananas	A pinch of salt
4 beaten eggs	2 tsps. baking powder
4 tbsps. sour milk	1 tsp. vanilla essence

Cream the butter and sugar, add the mashed bananas, the eggs and the milk with the soda dissolved in it. Add the remaining ingredients and beat well. Put into a greased tin and bake in a moderate oven (350° F., mark 4). Open the oven door and allow the cake to cool there before taking it out.

GROUNDNUT CAKES

4 oz. butter	4 oz. flour
4 oz. sugar	½ tsp. baking powder
2 eggs	1½ oz. chopped groundnuts

Cream the butter and sugar ; beat in the eggs separately. Sieve the flour and baking powder

and add 1 oz. of the nuts, add all to the egg mixture and fold in lightly. Put into small greased tins and sprinkle with the remaining nuts. Bake in a hot oven (450° F., mark 8) for 10–15 minutes.

GHANA BANANA AND NUT CAKE

4 oz. butter	1 cup mashed banana
6 oz. sugar	2 oz. chopped nuts
2 eggs	1 tsp. lemon juice
8 oz. flour	Water to mix

Cream the fat and sugar and add the beaten eggs. Add half the flour, the banana, and then the rest of the flour and the nuts, with the lemon juice and sufficient water to give a soft dropping consistency. Put into a lined 7-inch cake tin and bake in a moderate oven (350° F., mark 4) for 30–40 minutes.

COCONUT PUDDING

½ lb. grated coconut	¼ lb. sifted sugar
4 egg whites	Juice and grated rind
1 oz. butter	of ½ lemon

Mix the coconut, butter, sugar, lemon juice and grated rind. Whisk the egg white stiffly and fold into mixture. Put into a dish and bake in a moderate oven (350° F., mark 4) until risen and set.

SWEET POTATO PIE

12 tbsps. boiled and mashed sweet potato	Grated nutmeg
	Grated lemon rind
3 tbsps. sugar	Milk
1 tbsp. butter	Pastry

Mix the potatoes, eggs, sugar, butter, flavouring and milk to make a batter. Pour into a pie dish, cover with pastry and bake in a moderately hot oven (400° F., mark 6) until lightly browned.

SWEET POTATO PUDDING

8 tbsps. boiled and mashed sweet potato (boil for 30 minutes)	2 tsps. sugar
	2 tbsps. evaporated milk

Beat up the potatoes and add the sugar and milk. Put into a greased dish and bake in a moderately hot oven (400° F., mark 6).

SWEET POTATO BREAD

1 cup mashed sweet potatoes	1 egg
	2 tsps. baking powder
1 cup cornmeal	½ tsp. salt
1 cup flour	Milk or water to mix

Mix quickly into a dough with the liquid. Make into small loaves or scones and bake in a hot oven (450° F., mark 8).

138) From Fez comes Makalli (*above*), a dish of braised, spiced chicken garnished with olives and citron.

139) South African lamb chops are grilled with apricots until the meat is tender and the fruit brown (*below*).

140) Boontjie Bredee (*above*), a hearty mutton stew with green beans, comes from Cape Province.

141) Honder Pastei, a delicious Boer chicken pie with vegetables, egg and ham (*left*).

142) South African pineapple, baked with a peach, almond and rum filling and served flambé (*right*).

143) Chicken à la King (*above*), creamy and delicious, is a classic American recipe.

144) Chinese food is popular in America and Chicken Chop Suey (*above*) is a transatlantic version of this dish.

145) Ham Supreme (*above*), ham slices and tomato, grilled together and served with potato croquettes and corn.

146) Corned Beef Hash is fried crisp and brown with onion and potato (*above*).

147) The custom of serving savoury mixtures with different " dippers " (Nibbler Dunks, *right*) is an established one.

148) Virginia Chicken Salad combines chicken with crunchy endive and apple and a lemony dressing (*below*).

9) Lemon Meringue Pie (*right*), world-wide favrite with its eamy filling and sp top.

150) Strawberry Shortcake (*above*), deliciously buttery and filled with fresh fruit and cream.

151) Another of America's favourite desserts (*below*), Pineapple Upside-down Cake, served warm with cream.

152) French-Canadian Pea Soup, hot and appetising, is a traditional recipe (*above*).

153) Creamy Canadian Salmon à la King is served in patty shells, on toast (*above*) or with rice.

154) Halibut fillets (*above*) baked in the Canadian way with onion and tomato.

155) Tender Canadian steak, stuffed with tongue and smothered with onions (*left*).

156) One of Canada's many salads (*left*), Cabbage Slaw, with apple, celery and peppers.

157) Popular Canadian cookies include Peanut butter cookies, date bran muffins and Matrimonia cake (*below*).

158) From Mexico comes this bowl of spicy fish soup (*left*), served with fried bread and lemon.

159) Stuffed cornmeal pancakes with chilli sauce and a fried egg, a version of the Mexican Enchiladas (*below*).

160) Bunuelos (*above*), crisp, flaky
Mexican pancakes, sprinkled with
sugar and cinnamon.

161) Glorietta (*below*) a dish of
savoury rice with eggs and
bananas, traditional in Argentina

162) Flan de café (*above*), little coffee custards with brazil nuts and egg white, an Argentine dish.

163) Argentine Empanadas, sweet pastry turnovers filled with meat and fruit (*below*).

164) Crabes farcies (*above*), served hot and spicy in the Caribbean.

165) Beef Cutlets, a West Indian dish of thin, savoury beef slices served with mashed potato (*right*).

166) The Zombie's Secret (*left*), an unusual West Indian salad, served with coffee - flavoured whipped cream.

167) Corroboree Curry Hot-pot, a savoury Australian dish of beef, vegetables and fruit (*above*).

168) From Australia come Boojanga Nests (*left*), crisply fried potato cups filled with egg and cheese.

169) Murrumbidgee Favourites (*right*), sweet, fruit-filled turnovers, an Australian speciality.

170) Mussel Cocktail (*left*), a delicious hors d'œuvre, using the famous New Zealand mussels.

171) Wellington Lamb Stew, a New Zealand dish making good use of tender meat and vegetables (*above*).

172) Fudge Cake (*right*), one of New Zealand's, favourite cakes, rich, sweet and easy to make.

173) South Sea fish, baked with
butter and spices and wrapped
in foil instead of leaves (*above*).

174) Teriyaki (*left*) a
South Sea Island dish
of spiced beef cubes,
grilled with pineapple.

LIME CAKE

3 tbsps. sugar	1½ cups flour
2½ tbsps. butter	2¼ tsps. baking powder
2 eggs	A few chopped ground-
Juice of 1 lime	nuts

Cream the sugar and butter, add the well-beaten eggs and the lime juice, then the flour and baking powder. Pour into a lined cake tin, sprinkle the chopped groundnuts on top and bake in a moderate oven (375° F., mark 5).

BANANA JAM

12 large bananas	6 sweet oranges
Sugar	4 lemons

Peel the bananas and slice into thin rounds. Add ¾ lb. preserving sugar for each lb. bananas. Add the juice and pulp of the oranges and lemons and boil for ¾ hour.

ATWIMO
(GHANA TWISTED CAKES)

4 oz. butter	¼ tsp. grated nutmeg
3 oz. sugar	Milk or water if necessary
1 egg	Oil for frying
6 oz. self-raising flour	Caster sugar
A pinch of salt	

Cream the fat and sugar, add the egg and beat well. Sieve flour, salt and nutmeg and fold into the mixture to form a stiff dough, adding liquid if necessary. Roll out ¼ inch thick, and cut into diamond shapes. Make a slot in the centre of each and pull one corner through, then fry in hot oil until golden-brown. Drain well and sprinkle with caster sugar.

PINEAPPLE JAM

2 limes	1¼ lb. pineapple
1¼ lb. sugar	¼ pint water

Peel the limes thinly and put the peel into a muslin bag. Squeeze out the juice and add, with the fruit, to a syrup made of the sugar and water. Boil about 1 hour until pineapple is soft and clear. Bottle in hot, dry jars.

EWE ANYATA
(LIME TOFFEE)

Boil up ¼ lb. sugar, 1 cup water, 1 tsp. fresh lime juice and a pinch of ground ginger until deep brown. Pour on to a wetted marble slab and as soon as it can be handled, pull with the hands until white and opaque. Cut into small pieces.

COCOA SYRUP

Boil together 2 cups sugar, ¼ cup cocoa and a cup boiling water for 5 minutes. When cold, add 1 tsp. vanilla essence then bottle. When using, add the required quantity of hot milk.

To speak of " South African cookery " calls up a picture of solid good fare of both British and Dutch origin, with an admixture of French Huguenot delicacies and Eastern-type dishes borrowed from the Malay, Indian and Arab communities. Few people would wish to imitate the limited diet of the non-Europeanised native, based as it is on mealies, white beans and similar foods, varied by local greenstuff, root vegetables, marrows and a little meat, and washed down with native beer or a sour milk drink.

Meats include mutton, beef, venison and other game, pork and bacon ; besides being cooked in all the familiar ways, they are used by the Afrikaners to make various highly spiced sausages and Sassaties, a type of kebab. Biltong, the famous dried meat of the Boer fighters, is made from venison, beef, or mutton and eaten uncooked. Well-made biltong has the power of retaining its nutriment and flavour for many years. In fact, the old ladies of the veldt claim that biltong aged for ten years or more has definite medicinal properties, especially if it has been made from beef and it is the custom in some households to nourish the sick with finely grated biltong. Good biltong is not made in the sun, in fact, it never comes in direct contact with the sun. The farmers who know the real art of preparing it hang the meat in strips from the rafters of large and airy rooms, through which a continual draught of air plays. And there it remains until it is properly cured.

Poultry and game birds are abundant. Fish and shell fish are plentiful round the coasts, and can be bought inland in salted or deep-frozen form. Cereals and wheat grow well in many parts ; dairy produce is of good standard ; vegetables and fruits are abundant, while spices of excellent quality are plentiful for those who want to make curries, pickles or chutneys.

The meals follow the normal European pattern, but people seem to eat more heartily and there is more emphasis on snacks like elevenses and the tea-time meal. South African women devote much care and thought to their cooking ; home baking and preserving in particular are a matter of great pride and they have some first-rate recipes. Fritters, doughnuts and waffles are especially popular, reflecting the continental rather than the British influence.

South Africa

ENGELEGTE
(CAPE PICKLED FISH)

2 good-sized soles (filleted)	6 large chillies
Fat for frying	Salt
6 large onions	1 oz. mango relish
2 oz. curry powder	1 quart vinegar

Fry the fish brown in lard, butter or olive oil, drain and cool. Slice 4 onions and fry until brown, add 1 oz. curry powder, 2 chillies, cut fine, 2 tsps. salt and the mango relish. Lay the fish in a jar and spread over each layer some of this mixture. Cut the rest of the onion in rings and boil in the vinegar very gently until tender with the remaining curry powder and a little salt; pour over the fish, leave to cool, then cover well. The fish will be fit for use in 2–3 days, but will keep for months.

HADDOCK KEDGE

1 lb. smoked haddock	1 cup seedless raisins or sultanas
2 cups cooked rice	
2 chopped hard-boiled eggs	2 oz. melted butter
	Pepper

Cook the smoked haddock, flake and remove all bones and skin. Combine with the rest of the ingredients, put in a greased dish and reheat.

SOUTH AFRICAN BŒUF À LA MODE

Choose a good-sized round of beef, lard it with pork or bacon fat and season well. Put some fat bacon at the bottom of a large pan, put in the meat and add 2–3 bay leaves, a few peppercorns, a few cloves and 3–4 slices of lemon. Pour over the meat a good ½ cup of South African red wine, cover the pan closely and cook very slowly for 4–5 hours, until tender; baste frequently.

Use the remaining liquid in the pan to make a sauce to serve with the meat. Boiled potatoes and white cabbage are the usual accompaniment.

STUFFED HAM ROLLS

1½ cups apple rings	1 tomato
½ cup rice	2 tsps. chopped parsley
A little lemon juice or rind	Salt and pepper
1 tbsp. seedless raisins	10 pieces of ham
	Mustard sauce

Cook the apple rings until nearly tender. Wash the rice well, cook in briskly boiling water for 10 minutes with some lemon juice or rind added, then rinse, drain and allow to dry. Drain the apple rings, chop small and mix with the rice, raisins, peeled chopped tomato, parsley, salt and pepper. Divide the mixture into 10 parts and put one portion on each slice of ham; roll up and skewer. (To prevent the ham breaking when rolled, do not put it in a

refrigerator.) Place in a fireproof dish, pour some mustard sauce over, cover and heat through in the oven. Serves 5.

BOBOTIE
(MEAT CURRY)

2 lb. cooked lamb or mutton	2 tsps. caster sugar
	Salt to taste
1 thick slice of bread	8 almonds, finely chopped
½ pint milk	
2 medium-sized onions, sliced	A handful of raisins or sultanas
1 apple, sliced	2 eggs
1 oz. butter	Pepper
2 tbsps. curry powder	

Mince the meat finely. Soak the bread in the milk, beat the lumps out with a fork and drain off any surplus milk. Fry the onions and apple in the butter, add the curry powder, sugar, a little salt, almonds, raisins and 1 well-beaten egg, then the meat. Mix well, stirring over the heat for a few minutes, then put into a well-buttered dish. Beat the second egg, add the rest of the milk strained off the bread, which should not be less than a quarter of a pint. Add salt and pepper to taste and pour over the mixture, then bake gently in a moderate oven (350° F., mark 4) until the custard is set.

The same mixture, put into an open shortcrust flan and served cold, makes an excellent picnic dish.

LAMB CHOPS WITH APRICOTS

Put some chops to grill. Arrange over them some soaked or stewed dried apricots, brushed over with butter, and cook until the fruit browns slightly and the meat is tender.

SWARTSUUR
(DUTCH MUTTON STEW)

3 lb. neck of mutton	½ oz. brown sugar
1 large onion	6 cloves
A few peppercorns	Salt and pepper
2 oz. tamarind or ½–¾ pint mild-flavoured vinegar	4 oz. flour (approx.)
	1 egg

Bone the meat and cut into convenient-sized pieces. Put in a large pan with the onion and peppercorns, cover with cold water, bring to the boil and simmer gently until tender.

Meanwhile soak the tamarind in ¾ pint warm water for about 20 minutes, squeeze well, then mix with the sugar and cloves and put aside.

Strain 1 breakfastcup of the mutton broth into a separate saucepan, season, bring to the boil and stir in the flour, adding enough to give a thick paste. Continue to cook, stirring, until the flour is thoroughly cooked—about 10 minutes. Let the dough cool, then work in the beaten egg. Break off small pieces of dough, shape them lightly into dumplings and put into the stew, with the spiced tamarind juice or the vinegar. Cook for a further 10–15 minutes, until the dumplings are light and fluffy.

BOONTJIE BREDEE
(CAPE PROVINCE BEAN STEW)

140

3 lb. ribs of mutton | 2 tbsps. dripping or fat
Flour | Plenty of green beans
Pepper and salt | 6 potatoes
3 onions

Cut the mutton into small pieces, flour each piece thoroughly and season with pepper and salt; skin the onions, chop them up finely and fry them golden-brown in the dripping or fat; then add the meat and the green beans, cut in small pieces; add a little water, also the potatoes, peeled and halved, then stew gently for at least 3–4 hours.

Tomatoes, a green chilli, a small cauliflower and other vegetables may be added; also peeled, cored and sliced quince (previously parboiled in water and sugar, if the fruit is acid and hard).

GALANTINE OF SHEEP'S HEAD
(CAPE DUTCH RECIPE)

Take a well-cleaned sheep's head and feet, put them into a deep saucepan and cover them with cold water. Add a few bay leaves, 2 tsps. coriander seeds, 1 tbsp. allspice and 4 cloves, tied up in a piece of muslin, then boil for some hours, till the bones can be taken out. Skin the tongue and lay it in a mould; fill up with the rest of the meat and pour in a sauce made by boiling up 1 pint of broth with 1 small cupful of vinegar, 1 small sliced onion, 1 tsp. turmeric and a little salt. Leave in the mould till next day, then turn out.

SASSATIES
(GRILLED MARINADED MEAT)

Cut 3 lb. mutton in small, thin, round pieces and put in a dish with pieces of fat in between.

Soak ½ cup dried apricots overnight, boil them and press through a sieve. Slice 3 large onions with a piece of garlic and fry in 2 tbsps. dripping. Mix together the apricots, onions, some cayenne pepper, 6 lemon or orange leaves (when available), 1 tbsp. salt and 3 tbsps. vinegar and boil all together for a minute. Let it cool, then pour over the raw meat and leave to soak overnight in the sauce. Grill (or fry) the meat, boil up the sauce again and pour over the cooked pieces of meat. Serve with rice.

FRIKKADELS
(RISSOLES)

2 lb. minced mutton | 1 egg (beaten)
(preferably raw) | ¼ grated nutmeg
A little chopped onion | Salt and pepper
1–2 slices white bread | Egg and crumbs to
soaked in milk | coat
1–2 tbsps. tomato sauce | Deep fat for frying

Mix the ingredients well, shape into balls, egg and crumb and fry in hot fat.

GESMOORDE HOENDER
(BRAISED CHICKEN)

Joint a young chicken and lightly fry the pieces in 2–3 oz. butter in a saucepan until golden-brown. Take out and keep hot. Thinly slice 1–2 large onions and fry until they too are golden-brown. Put the chicken back in the pan, add ¼ pint or so South African dry white wine (or water), salt, pepper, 1–2 green chillies and a little grated nutmeg. Cover and simmer very slowly until the chicken is tender.

HOENDER PASTEI
(BOER CHICKEN PIE)

141

A 3-lb. ready-to-cook | 2 hard-boiled eggs
chicken | 1 oz. butter
3 cups water | 1 oz. flour
1 tbsp. salt | 1 cup chicken broth
1 tsp. whole allspice | 2–3 tbsps. sherry
1 tsp. peppercorns | 1 tbsp. lemon juice
2 bay leaves | 1 tsp. sugar
3 carrots, 2 celery | A pinch of ground mace
stalks, 2 medium- | A pinch of pepper
sized onions | 1 egg yolk
5–6 sprigs of parsley | Shortcrust pastry
2 oz. thinly sliced ham | Egg to glaze

This delicious pie can be prepared early in the day, kept in a cool place and baked just before it is required.

Quarter the chicken, put in a large pan with the water, salt, allspice, peppercorns and bay leaves, vegetables, cut into large pieces, and the parsley sprigs, tied together. Simmer, covered, for ½ hour, or until the vegetables are tender, but not over-done. Take out the vegetables and chicken and strain the broth. Cut the vegetables up small; cut the meat from the chicken bones in large chunks. Put into a baking dish alternate layers of chicken, vegetables, quarter-slices of ham, folded over, and sliced hard-boiled egg.

Melt the butter and gradually stir in the flour, broth, sherry, lemon juice, sugar, mace and pepper. Cook until the sauce is thick and smooth. Beat the egg yolk well and slowly stir into the sauce. Heat gently, stirring, till thick, but do not boil. Pour this sauce over the chicken and vegetables. Cover the pie with shortcrust pastry, then, using a sharp knife, cut a short line from the centre towards each of the four corners and fold each pastry triangle back, leaving an open square. Put the pie into the refrigerator, if it is not to be baked at once. Brush the pastry over with beaten egg to glaze and bake in a moderately hot oven (425° F., mark 7) for 25 minutes.

MEAT AND FRUIT CURRY

1 cup apple rings	2 lb. stewing steak
$\frac{1}{2}$ cup prunes	$\frac{1}{2}$ cup seedless raisins
2 onions	2 tsps. lemon juice
1 oz. oil or cooking fat	Salt to taste
1 tbsp. curry powder	Chopped nuts (optional)

Wash and soak the apple rings and prunes for an hour or two, then chop the apple rings, removing any core and stone and chop the prunes. Brown the onions in the oil or fat, add the curry powder, cook for a few minutes, then add about 1 cup water and simmer. Add the chopped meat (from which all the fat has been removed), fruit, lemon juice and salt. Stir for a while, cover and simmer for 2–3 hours, adding water if necessary. Just before serving add the nuts. Serve with dry boiled rice and chopped banana.

SETTLERS' MEALIE BREAD

Scrape off and mince the kernels from 4–5 corn cobs. Add 1 tsp. salt, 1 tsp. baking powder, a knob of butter (about the size of a walnut) and mix well. Pour into a well-greased dish, seal and steam for 1 hour or longer. Slice and serve hot with a generous amount of butter. Any leftover cold bread may be sliced and fried to serve with eggs and bacon.

MEALIE FRITTERS

Scrape the kernels from a fresh corn cob, mix with $\frac{1}{2}$ cup flour, 1 egg, and salt and pepper to taste. Heat some fat until very hot and drop in spoonfuls of the mealie mixture; fry until golden-brown on both sides, drain well and serve at once with fried bacon.

For sweet fritters, omit the seasoning and serve with sugar or golden syrup and ground cinnamon.

APRICOT CHUTNEY

4 lb. fresh apricots	2 pints vinegar
2 lb. raisins	4 oz. salt
4 oz. root ginger	2 cloves of garlic
2 lb. sugar	4 oz. chopped chillies

Stone the apricots and stone and cut up the raisins. Peel the ginger and pound it to a smooth paste. Boil the fruit and sugar together until thick, then add the remaining ingredients and cook for a further 10 minutes. Pot and seal.

KOESISTERS
(SWEET FRITTERS)

1 lb. flour	2 eggs
1 tbsp. baking powder	$\frac{1}{8}$ pint milk
A pinch of salt	Deep fat for frying
2 oz. butter	Syrup to dip Koesisters

Sieve the flour, baking powder and salt together and rub in the butter well. Add the well-beaten eggs, then add the milk and form into a dough. Roll out $\frac{3}{4}$ inch thick and cut into 2-inch squares. Drop 3–4 Koesisters at a time into the hot deep fat—when they are cooked they pop up to the surface; turn them over and cook for a minute longer, lift out quickly and immediately dip them into a bowl of very cold syrup. Lift out and allow the excess syrup to drain off on a wire cake rack (with grease-proof paper underneath to catch the syrup). Provided the syrup was kept very cold and the Koesisters were dunked when very hot, they should glisten with the frying fat and be impregnated with syrup so that they have a golden glazed appearance. Eat them cold as biscuits with coffee.

To make the syrup, put 1 lb. sugar and $\frac{1}{2}$ tsp. ground ginger in a saucepan, add $\frac{1}{2}$ pint water and stir until the sugar is dissolved. Boil until quite thick—about 8 minutes; do not stir during this time. Leave to get cold, then put some of the syrup in two or three different bowls as it warms up very quickly from the hot Koesisters, and to give a good glaze it should be kept as cool as possible.

MELKTERT
(DUTCH MILK TART)

2 cups milk	1 tbsp. ground almonds
$\frac{1}{2}$ tsp. butter	A few drops almond essence
1 stick of cinnamon	4 eggs
1 cup sugar	Short or sweet pastry
$\frac{1}{2}$ cup flour	Flaked almonds
A pinch of salt	

Scald the milk, butter and cinnamon. Mix the sugar, flour and salt together and make into a smooth paste with a little cold milk. Add to the hot milk (removing the cinnamon), bring to the boil and cook for 5 minutes, stirring constantly. Remove from the heat and add the ground almonds, essence and beaten egg yolks. Fold in the stiffly beaten egg whites. Line a deep pie plate with the pastry, pour the filling in and sprinkle with flaked almonds. Put in a hot oven (450° F., mark 8) and cook for 5 minutes, then reduce to moderately hot (400° F., mark 6) and cook for 25 minutes longer. Serve immediately.

BAKED PINEAPPLE

1 large pineapple	¼ cup sugar
1 large ripe peach	Butter
½ cup blanched almonds	1 oz. brandy
4 oz. light rum	

Cut off and retain the top of the pineapple. Scoop out the flesh, taking care not to puncture the skin; discard any tough or pithy flesh and cut the rest into ½-inch cubes. Skin and stone the peach and cut into ½-inch cubes. Shred the almonds and mix with the pineapple and peach, pour the rum over the mixed fruit and almonds, sprinkle with sugar and toss lightly.

Put the fruit back into the pineapple shell in layers, dotting each layer with butter. Replace the top of the pineapple and bake in a moderate oven (350° F., mark 4) until the fruit is tender—about 20–30 minutes. Place on a platter, pour 1 oz. warm brandy over the pineapple and set it alight.

RUGENKUCHEN
(DUTCH CAKES)

½ lb. butter	A good pinch of ground
½ lb. sugar	cinnamon
3 eggs	Rind of 1 lemon
½ lb. flour	3 tbsps. rum or brandy
1 tsp. baking powder	Halved glacé cherries
A good pinch of ground	or chopped blanched
cloves	almonds (if desired)

Grease and flour a cake tin. Cream the butter and sugar, add the beaten eggs and the sieved flour and baking powder alternately, then add the other ingredients. Bake in a moderate oven (350° F., mark 4) for 1 hour.

MANDELKOEK
(ALMOND CAKE)

1 lb. blanched almonds	12 oz. caster sugar
1 oz. blanched bitter	10 eggs, separated
almonds	8 tbsps. pounded
A little rosewater	macaroon biscuits

Pound the two kinds of almonds together, adding about 2 tsps. rosewater. Beat the sugar and egg yolks together until fluffy. Whisk the egg whites stiffly. Add the egg whites and the almonds alternately to the egg yolk mixture, putting in only a small amount at a time, then stir in the pounded macaroons. Put the mixture into a well-buttered tin and bake in a very slow oven (275° F., mark ½) for about 1 hour.

OUBLIETYES
(FRENCH HUGUENOT WAFERS)

12 oz. flour	6 oz. caster sugar
1 tsp. sieved powdered	⅛ pint South African
cinnamon	red wine
6 oz. butter	1 large or 2 small eggs

Sieve the flour and cinnamon together. Cream the butter, add the sugar and beat until white and frothy. Add the whisked egg, beating it in well. Add the wine and finally the flour, handling all the ingredients lightly. Pour dessertspoonfuls of the mixture into a waffle iron or greased pan, to make light, thin wafers, and cook until brown and crisp. Roll them up like a pancake while still hot.

MOSBOLLETJES
(YEAST BUNS)

2 lb. flour	4 oz. sugar
½ pint raisin *most* (see	⅛ oz. aniseed
below)	1 egg
4 oz. butter	A little milk to glaze
½ pint warm milk	Caster sugar to dredge

Mix one-third of the flour with the raisin *most* to a soft sponge and set to rise in a warm place for 8 hours. Heat the butter and milk until lukewarm; add this and the rest of the flour to the sponged dough and knead well. Leave to rise for another 8–10 hours. Add the sugar and aniseed, mixing well, break off pieces of the dough, shape into buns and pack close together in a baking tin, so that they will rise high rather than spreading sideways. Leave to prove until double the original size. Brush over with egg and milk and bake in a hot oven (450° F., mark 8) for 20–30 minutes. Sprinkle with caster sugar.

To make the raisin *most*, mince ½ oz. raisins finely, put in a jar and add ½ pint lukewarm water. Leave in a warm place until the raisins begin to ferment—about 3–4 days; they will rise to the top when ready. Strain before using.

The
Americas

FOOD in the United States, just as food in most places, ranges from the sublime to the better left unmentioned. Each region has its favourite foods—from Pecan Pie in the south to the very distinctive, tiny shrimp found on the north-west coast.

People debate endlessly and tirelessly on the relative merits of corn bread with sugar and without, and have been known to come almost to blows over the question of adding tomatoes to clam chowder!

California begins its meals with the salad courses (and wins honours for excellent salads), the rest of the country has it with the entrée, or later as a separate course. And thus it goes all across the country.

To-day, busy homemakers are using many of the " convenience foods " which crowd the supermarket shelves. Frozen foods, refrigerated breads and cookies, cake mixes, packaged foods that are semi-prepared are welcomed for their time-saving quality. Many homemakers add their special touches to such foods to make them more their own creation. But the time-honoured recipes are still used and loved and we trust this will always be true.

The following recipes are only a sampling of popular American dishes. We hope that some of them will become favourites of your own family.

Notes :

All Purpose Flour : For recipes requiring " all purpose flour " use plain white flour.

Cake Flour : Special American cake flour is now being imported into this country and is available at a few food stores and grocers. It costs three to four times as much as other flours.

New Orleans Creole Cookery

Louisiana, with New Orleans, its chief city, was colonised by the French, ceded to Spain, ceded back again less than half a century later, and finally sold by Napoleon to the United States of America. Like the other States of the South, it has long had a large Negro population. All these peoples, and the good supplies of semi-tropical foodstuffs, helped to form its great cookery tradition.

Whenever New Orleans cookery is mentioned, you are bound to hear references to Gumbos, Jambalayas, Calas and Pralines, so here are some brief notes on these exotic-sounding mysteries.

Gumbos (or Gombos) : Originally this type of soup or stew contained the vegetable known as Gumbo or Okra. A *Gombo file* contains *file* powder, that is, the dried and powdered tender young leaves of the sassafras tree which imparts a distinctive flavour and also thickens the soup.

Jambalayas : These rice dishes are said to be of Spanish origin, and certainly they somewhat resemble *paellas*.

Calas, a type of rice fritter eaten at breakfast.

Pralines are a sort of nut and sugar sweetmeat, but not necessarily made only of almonds as in French cookery—coconut, pecans and peanuts are also used.

U.S.A

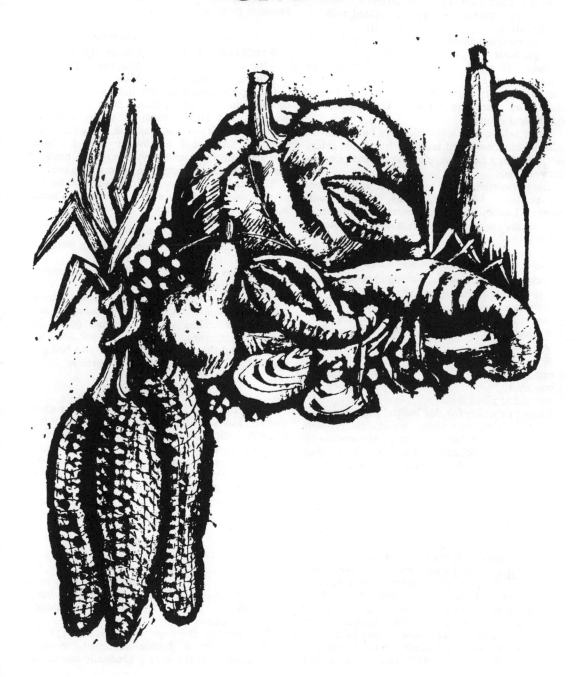

BOSTON CLAM CHOWDER

3 oz. shucked raw soft-shell clams, with the strained liquid
2 cups cold water
$\frac{1}{4}$ lb. diced salt pork (or 2 tbsps. butter or margarine)
2 sliced medium onions
2 tbsps. flour

$\frac{1}{4}$ tsp. celery salt
$\frac{1}{4}$ tsp. pepper
2 tsps. salt
3 cups diced, pared potatoes
3 cups scalded milk
$1\frac{1}{2}$ tsps. salt
1 tbsp. butter or margarine

Snip off necks of clams; cut fine with scissors; leave soft parts whole. Place clams (necks and soft parts) in saucepan with liquid. Add water; bring to the boil. Drain, reserving liquid and clams.

Sauté salt pork in large saucepan until golden; add onions, cook until tender. Stir flour, celery salt, pepper, 2 tsps. salt, clam liquid and potatoes into onions.

Cook, covered, for 20 minut es or ntil potatoes are tender. Add milk, clams, $1\frac{1}{2}$ tsps. salt, butter. Ladle into big soup bowls—or into mugs if you are serving out of doors. (Makes 8 servings.)

PENNSYLVANIA DUTCH CHICKEN-CORN CHOWDER

2 ready-to-cook chickens, 3–4 lb. each, cut into eighths
3 quarts cold water
3 medium onions, minced

1 cup chopped celery
$2\frac{1}{2}$ tsps. salt
$\frac{1}{4}$ tsp. pepper
$1\frac{1}{4}$ tsp. nutmeg
10 ears fresh corn

For the Rivels (tiny Dumplings)

1 egg
$\frac{1}{2}$ cup milk
1 cup sifted plain flour

2 hard-boiled eggs
Chopped parsley

Early in the day (or day before) place chickens in Dutch oven, with water, onions, celery, salt, pepper and nutmeg. Cover; simmer 2–$2\frac{1}{2}$ hours, or until chickens are fork-tender, adding water if needed. Remove chickens from broth; refrigerate separately till fat solidifies on broth. With knife, split corn kernels, cutting lengthwise on ears; cut off kernels; refrigerate.

About 45 minutes before serving, remove fat from chicken broth. If necessary, add water to make 10 cups. Add corn; cover and simmer till corn is tender. Remove chicken meat from bones, cut it into $1\frac{1}{2}$-inch chunks. Make batter for dumplings; in small bowl, beat 1 egg till light in colour; add milk; then beat in flour until mixture is smooth. Now add chicken to broth mixture; bring to simmer, then let batter fall into it from a large serving spoon, making each rivel the size of a cherry stone by using a knife to stop the flow of batter. Simmer 2–3 minutes, or until *rivels* are cooked. (Or cook 4 oz. fine noodles in simmering broth as label directs.) Stir in chopped hard-boiled eggs and top with parsley. Makes 10–12 main dish servings.

This chowder is a favourite for Sunday School summer picnics.

FISH AND BACON CHOWDER

6 rashers of bacon
$\frac{1}{2}$ lb. white fish
$\frac{1}{2}$ lb. sliced potatoes

1 large onion
Salt and pepper
Milk

Cut up the bacon and fry lightly. Put a layer of bacon in a casserole, then a layer of fish, then potatoes and sliced onion. Season well and continue the layers until all the ingredients are used up. Add milk to cover by about 1 inch, and bake in a moderate oven (375° F., mark 5) for about 1 hour, or until the potatoes are cooked.

This dish can be cooked in a saucepan on top of the oven: it takes about $\frac{1}{2}$ hour, but needs watching.

PRAWN CHOWDER

$\frac{1}{2}$ oz. butter
1 onion
5 potatoes
Salt and pepper

$\frac{1}{2}$ pint boiling water
$\frac{3}{4}$ pint milk
2 packets frozen prawns

Melt the butter and fry the onion lightly without browning. Add the sliced potatoes, salt, pepper and boiling water. Simmer gently for about 15 minutes, or until the potatoes are cooked. Add the milk and prawns and bring to the boil. Garnish with chopped parsley.

FRIED CLAMS

Beat 1 egg with 2 tbsps. water. Drain 1 quart shelled, raw soft-shell clams, removing any bits of shell; dip into egg, then into dried breadcrumbs, corn meal or fine cracker crumbs. Shallow-fry at 365° F. until nicely browned on all sides. Drain on paper towels. Serve with tartare or chilli sauce or chutney.

Alternatively, heap on toast and serve with lemon wedges, or with tartare or chilli sauce in lettuce cups.

CHIP-TUNA CASSEROLE

2 cans solid-pack tuna (2 cups)
2 tbsps. flour
$\frac{1}{2}$ tsp. salt
A little pepper

2 cups milk
$\frac{1}{3}$ cup sherry or 2 tsps. piquant table sauce
1 cup crumbled potato crisps

Start heating the oven to moderate (375° F., mark 5). Into a double saucepan, measure 2 tbsps. oil from the tuna; gradually stir in the flour, salt, pepper and milk and cook, stirring, until smooth and thickened; add the sherry or sauce.

Cover the bottom of a greased 1½ quart casserole with ¼ cup potato crisps. Add one-third of the tuna, in chunks, then one-third of the sauce. Repeat, making 3 layers; top with the rest of potato crisps. Bake, covered, for 20 minutes, then uncover and bake for 10 minutes, or until brown.

SOUTHERN CRAB CAKES

3 cups flaked fresh or canned crab meat	1 tbsp. mayonnaise
	2 tsps. chopped parsley
1½ tsps. salt	Flour
1 tsp. dry mustard	1 egg, slightly beaten
½ tsp. pepper	2 tbsps. water
1 egg yolk	Dried breadcrumbs
2 tsps. piquant table sauce	Butter or bacon fat

Mix the crab meat, salt, mustard, pepper, egg yolk, piquant sauce, mayonnaise and parsley; press the mixture firmly into 8 small cakes and chill well.

Dip the cakes into the flour, then into the combined egg and water, then into the crumbs. Melt a little butter or bacon fat in a frying pan and quickly sauté the cakes over a high heat until golden.

Serve with potato salad, coleslaw or chipped potatoes, or put into hot toasted rolls for lunch or supper.

HOOSIER FRIED CHICKEN

A 2–3 lb. ready-to-cook chicken, cut up	3 tsps. salt
	¾ tsp. pepper
¾ cup flour	Fat or salad oil
3 tsps. paprika	Parsley

Wash and wipe the chicken pieces dry. Mix the flour, paprika, salt and pepper in a paper bag, drop in the chicken, 2 or 3 pieces at a time, and shake until coated. In a large deep pan place ½ inch fat and heat till a drop of water sizzles in it. Brown the chicken pieces, turning them now and again. As the meatier pieces brown, slip in the less meaty pieces. When all have browned, reduce the heat and cook, covered, for 20–25 minutes, or till the large pieces are fork-tender; turn them once. Uncover the pan and re-crisp the chicken over a moderate heat for about 10 minutes, turning the pieces once. Heap the chicken in a napkin-lined large wooden bowl and garnish with parsley. Makes 4–6 servings.

In the Farm Belt and in Delaware, cooks serve this with mashed potatoes.

In Kansas they simmer the browned chicken in sweet or sour cream.

In New York they simmer the chicken until tender (as for fricassee) before frying it.

In Connecticut they serve it with cream gravy, to which is added a little sugar.

Along the Gulf Coast they rub the chicken with lemon before frying it, and eat it with beans and rice.

In North Carolina they eat it with cream gravy and hot scones.

In Kentucky they serve it with griddle cakes.

In Virginia they enjoy it with waffles and cream gravy.

In Georgia they like it with rice, hominy grits or with candied sweets.

In Alabama they dip the chicken pieces in egg, then in flour or fine corn meal before frying, to ensure a crispy crust.

And in most of the South they often let the chicken stand in milk or buttermilk before frying it.

CHICKEN TERRAPIN, PHILADELPHIA STYLE

2 tbsps. butter or margarine	1 cup parboiled sweetbreads, in chunks
2 tbsps. flour	2 egg yolks, beaten
1 cup single cream	¼ cup sherry
¾ tsp. salt	Chopped fresh dill or parsley
¼ tsp. pepper	
2 cups cooked (or canned) chicken chunks	Hot boiled rice or buttered toast

In a double saucepan melt the butter, add the flour and blend; gradually stir in the cream, salt, pepper. Add the chicken and sweetbreads and cook over boiling water till thickened. Now stir in the egg yolks and sherry. Garnish with dill or parsley and serve with the hot rice or buttered toast. Makes 4–6 servings.

CHICKEN WITH OYSTERS

A 3 lb. ready-to-cook chicken, cut into eighths	¼ tsp. powdered dried sage
1¼ tsp. salt	1 pint shelled oysters, drained
½ tsp. pepper	1 cup double cream
¼ cup butter	½ tsp. dried basil
½ cup milk	

In the fall, when the wonderful New England oysters are just coming into season, Yankees like to smother their chicken in a kind of oyster stew.

Start heating the oven to moderate (375° F., mark 5). Sprinkle the chicken with ¾ tsp. salt and ¼ tsp. pepper. Heat the butter in a large pan and sauté the chicken pieces (covered) for 10 minutes, turning them once. Put into a baking dish measuring about 12 by 7½ by 2 inches, pour the milk over the top; sprinkle with ½ tsp. salt, ¼ tsp. pepper and the sage; cover with aluminium foil and bake for 1¼ hours. Uncover the dish, add the oysters, then the cream and basil, cover and bake for 15 minutes, or until the sauce is hot. Serve in soup plates with a fork and spoon. Makes 6 servings.

TEXAS BARBECUED CHICKEN

½ cup butter or margarine	2 garlic cloves, minced
¼ cup granulated sugar	¼ cup minced onion
¼ tsp. cayenne pepper	¼ cup lemon juice
½ tsp. prepared mustard	¼ tsp. liquid hot pepper seasoning
1 cup salad oil	2 ready-to-cook
1 14 oz. bottle ketchup	chickens, about 3 lb.
⅓ cup piquant table sauce	each

Early in the day, make the barbecue sauce. In a small saucepan, melt the butter, stir in the sugar, then the rest of the ingredients except the chickens. Simmer, uncovered, stirring occasionally, for 20 minutes; refrigerate.

About 2½ hours before dinner, start the fire. When the coals are glowing, rub the whole chickens with salt and pepper; then mount them on the spit and cook for about 1 hour, or until tender, basting frequently with the sauce and turning now and then (if the spit is not of the revolving type). Serve half a chicken per person, handing the rest of the hot sauce separately.

West Coast Barbecued Chicken: In a small bowl, combine ½ cup honey, ⅓ cup prepared mustard, 2 tbsps. lemon juice and 1 tsp. salt; pour over whole chickens and refrigerate for 2 hours. Then cook as above, basting alternately with the honey sauce and ¼ cup melted butter.

New England Barbecued Chicken: In an uncovered small saucepan, simmer 1 cup water with ½ cup tarragon vinegar, 1 tbsp. sugar, 2 tsps. hickory smoked salt, ½ tsp. pepper, ½ tsp. dry mustard, 1 tsp. paprika, ¼ cup butter or margarine and 2 garlic cloves, minced, for 10 minutes. Use to baste the chickens, while cooking as above.

CHICKEN À LA KING

⅓ cup butter or margarine	A dash of pepper
¼ lb. mushrooms	½ cup single cream
5 tbsps. flour	2 cut-up cooked or canned chickens
½ tsp. salt	1 cut-up pimiento
1⅓ cups chicken broth (canned if necessary)	Sherry to taste

In a double saucepan over direct heat, melt the butter, add the mushrooms and sauté for 5 minutes. Stir in the flour, salt, pepper and pimiento till smooth. Place over boiling water and slowly stir in the broth and cream; cook, stirring until thickened. Add the chicken and sherry and heat well.

Serve on or with :

Toast, waffles, baking powder biscuits (scones), split hot corn muffins, pancakes, toasted split muffins (English type).

Mashed potatoes, baked potatoes, cooked broccoli or asparagus, grilled pineapple slices.

Buttered noodles, with croûtons, almonds, or poppy seeds added; Chinese Chow-mein noodles.

Boiled rice, tossed with chopped parsley or chutney.

Scrambled eggs or omelette.

Turkey may be used in the same way.

CHICKEN CHOP SUEY

A 3½–4½ lb. ready-to-cook chicken, cut up (or 3 cups firmly packed, cut-up canned or cooked chicken)	1½ cups raw rice (or 2⅔ cups packaged pre-cooked rice)
	1 medium-sized onion, sliced
6 cups boiling water	1½ cups sliced celery
3 chicken bouillon cubes	¼ cup soy sauce
	A 1 lb. can of bean sprouts (drained)
6 whole black peppers	3 tbsp. cornflour

The day before put the chicken in a pan with the water and bouillon cubes, cover and simmer for 3–4 hours, or until fork-tender; cool quickly by putting in the refrigerator at once. Cut the meat from bones and refrigerate the meat and the broth.

About ½ hour before serving, cook the rice and keep hot. Measure the broth (there should be about 6 cups); reserve 1 cup. In the rest of broth, cook the peppers, onion and celery (uncovered) for 10 minutes, or until tender but still crunchy. Add the soy sauce, chicken and bean sprouts (rinsed in cold water). Cook for 3–4 minutes. Mix the cornflour with the remaining 1 cup broth and add to the chicken mixture; cook, stirring, until smooth and slightly thickened. Serve at once on hot rice. Serves 8.

To vary, substitute turkey or 3–4 cups cooked veal or pork, in thin strips, for the chicken.

Chow-mein Style: Serve the chicken on a deep heated platter, garnished with cooked spring onions. Substitute canned chow-mein noodles for the rice.

CHICKEN-TAMALE PIE

¼ cup butter or margarine
1 medium onion, chopped
1 clove garlic, chopped
4 cups cooked-chicken meat (in large pieces)
2–3 tsps. chilli powder
1 cup stoned sliced ripe olives
½ tsp. coriander
A 10 oz. can tomato purée
3½ tsps. salt
½ tsp. pepper
6 cups chicken broth
2 cups cornmeal

In 1 tbsp. melted butter in a large pan, sauté the onion and garlic until tender. Add the chicken, chilli powder, olives, coriander, tomato purée, 1½ tsps. salt, pepper and ½ cup chicken broth. Cover and simmer for 15 minutes. Bring 5½ cups chicken broth to the boil and add 2 tsps. salt; slowly stir in the cornmeal. Add 3 tbsps. butter and cook, stirring constantly, for about 5 minutes. Butter a 3-quart casserole and line it with half the cornmeal mush. Pour in the chicken mixture and cover with rest of mush. Bake for 1¼ hours in a slow oven (300° F., mark 1). 6 hearty servings.

Versions of this dish are popular in Texas, Nevada and Tennessee.

NEW ENGLAND CHICKEN PIE

A 4½ lb. ready-to-cook chicken
3 cups hot water
Salt
¾ cup cooked shredded carrots
¾ cup frozen peas (thawed)
An 8 oz. can onions
3 tsps. chopped parsley
¾ lb. pastry for 10-inch double-crust pie
3 tbsps. butter
3 tbsps. flour
¼ tsp. pepper
1 cup single cream
¾ cup milk or chicken broth

Simmer the quartered chicken in the water with 1 tbsp. salt for 2–2½ hours or till tender, adding more water if necessary. Cut the chicken meat into chunks. In a bowl combine 3 cups chicken, the carrots, peas, drained onions and parsley. Make up the pastry. Start heating oven to moderately hot (425° F., mark 7). Line a 10-inch pie plate with half the pastry extending it 1 inch over the edge. Roll the other half of pastry into an oblong 14 inches by 8 inches, then cut into 12 strips 14 inches by ½ inch. Melt the butter, stir in the flour, 1½ tsps. salt and some pepper. Cook, stirring, for 2–3 minutes; remove from the heat and stir in the cream and milk. Cook, stirring, till thickened; remove from heat. Spoon the chicken into the pie plate and pour on the sauce. Moisten the rim of the bottom crust with water; to it attach one end of a pastry strip, press, twist strip across filling, attach to rim on opposite side and press. Repeat with 5 strips, 1¼ inches apart. Place the other 6 strips across

the first ones. Turn up the bottom crust overhang over the rim and the ends of the strips; press firmly to seal strips to rim; flute the edge.

Bake in the moderately hot oven for 10 minutes, then reduce the heat to moderate (350° F., mark 4) and bake for 45 minutes. Serve hot, cut into wedges. Makes 6–8 servings.

In the South, variations on the chicken pie theme include a sweet potato crust; a rolled rich scone mixture crust; a topping of tiny rich scones.

A MAN'S BARBECUED CHICKEN

2 tsps. salt
¼ tsp. pepper
1½ cups tomato juice
¼ tsp. cayenne pepper
¼ tsp. dry mustard
1 bay leaf
4½ tsps. piquant table sauce
¾ cup vinegar
1 tsp. sugar
3 minced garlic cloves
3 tbsps. butter, margarine or salad oil
2 ready-to-cook chickens, about 3½ lb. each, halved or quartered
3 medium-sized onions, thinly sliced

Early in day or day before : Make a barbecue sauce by combining, in a saucepan, the salt, pepper, tomato juice, cayenne, mustard, bay leaf, piquant sauce, vinegar, sugar, garlic and butter. Simmer, uncovered, for 10 minutes. Refrigerate.

About 2¼ hours before serving : Start heating the oven to moderate (350° F., mark 4). Arrange the chicken pieces, skin side up, in a single layer in a shallow open pan. Sprinkle lightly with salt and pepper and pour in just enough hot water to cover bottom of pan. Arrange sliced onions on chicken, tucking a few pieces under wings and legs. Bake, uncovered, for ½ hour; turn over and bake for ½ hour.

Remove chicken from oven; pour off all but ¾ cup liquid. Arrange the chicken skin side up; pour on the barbecue sauce, then bake in a moderate oven (350° F., mark 4), basting often with the sauce, for 1 hour, or until fork can be inserted easily into legs. Makes 4–6 servings.

SOUTH-WESTERN ARROZ CON POLLO

A 4 lb. ready-to-cook chicken, cut up
½ cup flour
½ cup fat
1 large onion, minced
1 can of tomatoes (2 cups)
2 small cans of pimientos, cut up
2 beef bouillon cubes
1 small jar of stuffed olives
2 cups raw rice
1 tbsp. salt
¼ tsp. pepper
½ lb. fresh pork sausages
1 package frozen peas (thawed)

In a paper bag, shake the chicken pieces with the flour till coated. In hot fat, sauté the chicken, a few pieces at a time, until golden on all sides;

set aside. In same fat in a large saucepan, sauté the onion until golden. Drain the tomatoes and add enough water to tomato liquid to make 2¼ cups. To the onion, add the tomato liquid, tomatoes, pimientos with their liquid, bouillon cubes, olives with their liquid, rice, salt, pepper, and fresh pork sausages, cut into ½-inch pieces. Place the chicken on top and simmer, covered, for 30 minutes, occasionally lifting the rice with a fork to prevent its sticking. Then uncover and add the peas. If any liquid is left in, cook, uncovered, for a further 10 minutes. If mixture seems dry, cook it covered, instead of uncovered. Makes 8 generous servings.

The cuisine of the South-west has been influenced by the Spanish tradition and by Mexico.

KANSAS CHICKEN CHEESE
(PRESSED CHICKEN)

2 ready-to-cook chickens, about 4 lb. each	2 bay leaves
	¼ tsp. whole cloves
	1 tsp. dried savory
5 cups water	10 parsley sprigs
1 beef bouillon cube	1 garlic clove
1 tbsp. vinegar	¾ cup minced onion
1 carrot, peeled and sliced	¼ tsp. whole black peppers
1 cup sliced celery	1 tbsp. salt
Green celery tops	3 tbsps. chopped parsley
1 leek, halved lengthwise (optional)	Lettuce
	Mayonnaise

The day before, place the halved chickens in a saucepan with the rest of ingredients, except the chopped parsley, lettuce and mayonnaise. Cover and simmer for 1½ hours, or until tender. Remove the chickens from the liquid; skim the fat from the broth and strain this through a fine sieve into a saucepan; boil down, uncovered, until only 2 cups remain. Meanwhile, remove the chicken meat from the bones, chop it very fine and refrigerate. Add the chicken to the 2 cups of concentrated broth and simmer for 10 minutes, then stir in the chopped parsley. Turn the mixture into a loaf tin measuring about 9 by 5 by 3 inches. Weight down by placing another tin on top of mixture, and refrigerate overnight.

To serve, loosen the chicken from the tin with a spatula, turn out and slice. Garnish with lettuce, cranberry jelly slices or tart fruit jelly and hand mayonnaise separately. Serves 8.

East Coast Pressed Chicken : Make as above but substitute 1 cup sherry for 1 cup of the water and omit the bouillon cube and vinegar; leave the chicken in large pieces. In cutting, make slices ¾ inch thick.

ADAMS CASSEROLE FROM ILLINOIS

6 cups crumbled corn bread	3 tbsps. chopped parsley
½ tsp. mixed dried herbs	5 cups cooked or canned chicken, in small or large pieces
1 tsp. celery seeds	¼ cup butter or margarine
⅛ tsp. pepper	
Salt	¼ cup flour
¼ cup minced onion	2 cups chicken broth
½ cup melted butter or margarine	2 eggs, well beaten
	1 quart milk

Start to heat oven to moderate (375° F., mark 5). In a large bowl combine the corn bread, herbs, celery seeds, pepper, ¾ tsp. salt, onion, parsley and ½ cup melted butter, tossing the ingredients together with a fork. Spread a layer at the bottom of a buttered baking dish measuring about 13 by 9 by 2 inches. Arrange the chicken evenly over the top. In a large pan melt ¼ cup butter, then stir in the flour and 1½ tsp. salt until smooth; stir in the broth and heat. Combine the beaten eggs and milk, add to the sauce and cook until slightly thickened, stirring. Pour this sauce over the chicken and bake for 45 minutes. Makes 8–10 servings.

In Iowa they put the corn bread mixture on top, instead of underneath the chicken.

GEORGIA COUNTRY CAPTAIN

½ cup salad oil	1 green pepper, coarsely chopped
2 garlic cloves, halved	
2 medium-sized onions, thinly sliced	1 can of tomatoes (3½ cups)
½ cup plain flour	1 cup raw rice
Salt	¼ cup currants
¼ tsp. pepper	2 tbsps. butter or margarine
A 3½ lb. ready-to-cook chicken, cut up	⅓ cup blanched almonds
1 tbsp. curry powder	Chopped parsley
½ cup chopped celery	

Heat the oil in a large pan and sauté the garlic and onions over a medium heat until tender but not brown; remove from the oil. Meanwhile combine the flour, 1 tsp. salt and pepper in a paper bag and coat the chicken pieces in this, one at a time. Fry the chicken in the hot oil until golden, turning once. (Cook in 2 batches, if necessary.) Now add the garlic and onions, 2 tsps. salt, curry powder, celery, green pepper and tomatoes, cover and simmer for 45 minutes, or until chicken is tender. Meanwhile cook the rice, add the currants and toss lightly. In melted butter in a small pan over medium heat, brown the blanched almonds. When the chicken is done, arrange it at one end of a heated platter, with the rice at the other end. Remove the

garlic from the sauce, spoon some over the chicken and hand the rest separately. Sprinkle with almonds and parsley.

This is an American version of a dish evolved for Anglo-Indians!

CALIFORNIA CHICKEN FRICASSEE

A 3-3½ lb. ready-to-cook chicken, cut into eighths
3 cups water
Salt
1 carrot, peeled
1 onion, sliced
1 celery stalk, sliced
6 whole black peppers
6 whole allspice
¼ cup flour
3 tbsps. butter
1 egg yolk, slightly beaten
½ cup single cream
1 tbsp. lemon juice
1 tsp. sugar
¼ tsp. pepper
1 lemon, sliced
2 tbsps. chopped parsley

Put the chicken in the water in a large saucepan with 1 tbsp. salt, the carrot, onion, celery, peppers and allspice, cover and simmer until tender—about 1 hour. Arrange the chicken on a large heated platter and keep warm. Strain the broth. In a double saucepan, melt the butter and stir in the flour until smooth, then add 2 cups strained chicken broth. Cook the sauce over boiling water, stirring, until thickened. Combine the egg yolk, cream and lemon juice; add to sauce, stirring constantly, cool for 1 minute and season with 1 tsp. salt, the sugar and pepper. Pour some of the sauce over the chicken and garnish with lemon slices and parsley. Hand rest of sauce, with more chopped parsley. Serves 4–6.

In the Deep South they add green peppers to their chicken fricassee.

COWBOY STEW (TEXAS)

5 lb. tenderloin of beef
5 lb. sweetbread
4 sets of brains
3 lb. calf liver
3 calf kidneys
1 calf heart
1 lb. suet
1 large onion
2 whole small hot green peppers (or dry hot chillies)

Cut steak, liver, heart and kidney in cubes about ¾ inch in size. Cut suet in small pieces and use to braise all of the above separately until a little brown. Season with salt and pepper. After taking the membrane from sweetbreads, cut in small pieces and put all these meats in a large vessel. Cover with water and cook slowly for 3–4 hours, then put in the brains, the whole onion and hot peppers and allow to cook for 1½ hours more. Then take out the onion, as it is for seasoning only.

Do not add any flour or thickening of any kind

—the juices from the meat should make a good, thick gravy. If you need to add any water, be sure it is boiling hot and be careful not to add too much. Serves about 30 people.

TENNESSEE BRUNSWICK STEW

4 cups water
1¼ lb. chuck steak, cut in 1-inch cubes
½ a ready-to-cook broiler-fryer (1½ lb.)
5 tsps. salt
2 medium-sized potatoes, peeled
2 medium-sized onions, peeled
½ cup raw rice
½ package frozen okra (canned okra could be used)
1 can of creamy-style corn
1 can of tomatoes (2½ cups)
1 tbsp. sugar
½ tsp. pepper
A pinch of cayenne pepper
½ tsp. celery seeds

Early in the day, put the water, chuck steak, chicken and 2 tsps. salt in a large pan and simmer, covered, for 2 hours or until meat is tender; remove steak and chicken from the broth. Skin and bone the chicken; cut the meat into small pieces; set aside 1 cup chicken broth (use rest as desired). Refrigerate all.

About 2 hours before serving, boil the potatoes and onions for about 20 minutes or until partially cooked; drain. In the pan, combine 1 cup chicken broth, the chicken, steak, rice, okra, corn, tomatoes, sugar, 3 tsps. salt, peppers and celery seeds; add the diced potatoes and chopped onions and simmer, covered, for 1½ hours. Serve at once or refrigerate and reheat next day. Makes 6–8 servings.

The original Brunswick Stew used squirrel instead of steak and chicken, but town-dwelling Americans have modified it to suit modern conditions.

STEAK EROS

¼ lb. fillet steak
Salt and pepper
¼ lb. butter
1 tsp. piquant table sauce
Chopped parsley

Beat the steak and flatten it out to a very thin shape; salt and pepper to taste. Heat the butter in a pan till brown, add the sauce and cook the steak in this. Sprinkle with parsley.

POT-ROAST

3 tbsps. fat or salad oil
4–5 lb. boned rump steak
2 tsps. salt
¼ tsp. pepper
1 tbsp. water
1 sliced small onion
A pinch of dill seeds

Heat fat in a heavy saucepan over medium heat and brown the meat well on all sides, turning it as it browns and sprinkling it with some salt and pepper. This may take 15–20 minutes.

Add the water, onion and dill seeds, cover tightly and simmer (do not boil) over low heat, turning it occasionally to cook it evenly throughout. Allow about 4–4½ hours, or until fork-tender. If needed, add a few tablespoonfuls hot water during cooking.

When meat is done, dish it up on a heated platter, and keep it warm while making gravy in the saucepan. Serve with mashed potatoes.

Let the host carve the pot-roast; or serve it sliced. Pass the gravy in a bowl and have piquant table sauce or horseradish, mustard or chilli sauce. Serves a family of 4 for two meals.

NEW ENGLAND BOILED DINNER

Use half a brisket. About 45 minutes before the meat is done, skim excess fat from the top of the liquid. Add 6 peeled medium potatoes, 6 peeled carrots, 6 peeled white turnips and simmer, covered, for 15 minutes. Add a cabbage and simmer until all the vegetables are just tender-crisp. Serve the sliced meat on platter, with the vegetables. Pass chilli sauce, mustard, pickles or horseradish.

BROWN BEEF STEW

⅓ cup flour
¼ tsp. pepper
½ tsp. celery salt
1¾ lb. boned chuck steak or bottom round, cut into 1½-inch cubes
¼ cup fat or salad oil
¼ cup minced onion
1 minced garlic clove (optional)
3¾ cups boiling water
½ tsp. salt

4 tsps. meat-extract or 4 beef bouillon cubes
½ tsp. piquant table sauce
1 doz. small white onions
1 doz. pared small carrots, whole or halved lengthwise
½ packet frozen peas
5 hot boiled potatoes
Chopped parsley

In a bowl, combine the flour, pepper, celery salt. Drop in the meat, a few pieces at a time, and toss until well coated. Reserve the leftover flour.

Slowly fry the floured meat in hot fat in a deep saucepan, a few pieces at a time, brown it on all sides—15–20 minutes. Remove pieces as they brown. To the fat, add the minced onion, garlic and simmer until just tender. Stir in the remaining flour until blended. Slowly stir in the boiling water, meat extract, salt and piquant sauce, then add the meat. Simmer, covered, over low heat for about 2 hours, or until meat is fork-tender. Add whole onions and carrots and simmer, covered, for about 15 minutes. Add

the peas and simmer, covered, for about 5 minutes or until vegetables are tender. Meanwhile mash and season the potatoes.

Serve the stew in the pot or transfer to a casserole; heap potatoes in ring on top of stew. Or serve it on a heated platter with the vegetables heaped around it. Sprinkle with parsley. Makes 4–6 servings.

CABIN CASSEROLE

4 lean chops
1 oz. dripping
1 rasher of bacon
4–5 large onions

4–5 large tomatoes
Salt
Curry powder

Fry the chops lightly in the dripping with the chopped bacon. Place the sliced onions and tomatoes in alternate layers in a greased casserole, sprinkling each layer with salt and curry powder. Lay the browned chops on top, cover tightly and bake in a moderate oven (375° F., mark 5) for ¾ hour. Remove the lid and cook for a further 30 minutes. Serve very hot.

HAM SUPREME

2 centre-cut slices of lean ham
1 tin of sweet corn
¼ cup minced green pepper

Hot potato croquettes
3 firm tomatoes
¼ cup minced onion
Salt and pepper
Parsley

Cut the ham into ½-inch slices, then into rounds slightly larger than the sliced tomatoes. Heat the corn, draining off any excess of liquid, season and add a little butter. Put the corn into a grill pan, set the rack on top and grill the slices of ham gently, turning once. When done, put a slice of uncooked tomato on top of each piece of ham, and on each of these 1 tbsp. of mixed green pepper and onion, well seasoned. Continue cooking under the grill until slices of tomato are hot through, then serve on a hot dish with the corn in centre and rounds of ham and tomato around, alternating with freshly fried potato croquettes. Garnish with parsley.

HAM 'N' PEACHES

3 lb. piece of corner gammon
1 tsp. ground ginger
1 tsp. paprika pepper
6 oz. Demerara sugar

Lard
½ pint rich gravy
1 wineglassful Madeira
Peaches to garnish

Remove the skin from the gammon. Cover over the fat with a mixture of ginger, paprika and sugar. Place the ham in an earthenware casserole, pour some melted lard over to baste and put on the lid. Bake in a moderate oven (325° F., mark 3) for 2–2½ hours. When the ham is tender, remove the excess fat, add the gravy and Madeira and continue to cook for a further 15 minutes. Serve on a dish surrounded by the peaches, which can be poached around the meat for the last 5 minutes.

PEACH-BRAISED HAM

1 gammon hock	2 oz. brown sugar
1 onion	Peaches in syrup
1 carrot	2 cloves
1 bay leaf	½ oz. cornflour
6 peppercorns	Parsley and celery hearts

Soak the ham for 12–24 hours. Simmer gently in water with the vegetables and herbs, allowing 20 minutes to the lb. Allow to cool slightly in the liquid. Remove the brown skin carefully and press brown sugar over the fat. Strain the juice from some tinned or stewed peaches and add a little of the ham stock and 2 cloves, heat gently in a pan and thicken with a little cornflour; some cider may be added. Braise the ham in the oven, basting with this liquid for ½ hour before serving. The peach halves may be placed round the ham 10 minutes before bringing from the oven. Strain the basting liquid and serve with the ham, accompanied with the parsley, peaches and braised celery hearts.

PHILADELPHIA SCRAPPLE

Half a pig's head	Stock
2 pig's feet	Wholemeal flour
½ lb. onions	Coarse oatmeal
¼ lb. carrots	Sugar
2 oz. turnips	Breadcrumbs
Salt, pepper, paprika	Fat for frying

Prepare the head and feet. Cover with cold water, add the vegetables, salt and peppers and boil until tender. Remove the meat and put it through a mincing machine. To each 1 lb. of meat, allow 1 pint stock, 4 oz. wholemeal flour and 4 oz. oatmeal; mix together, and cook in a double saucepan for 1–2 hours until the meat is cooked. Add seasoning and sugar to taste, put into wetted moulds and set to cool.

To serve the scrapple, cut in slices, toss in breadcrumbs and fry until golden-brown.

SWEETBREADS MARYLAND

1 medium-sized pair of sweetbreads	A little white pepper and cayenne
2 tbsps. butter	1 cup cream
2 tbsps. flour	½ cup cooked mushrooms
½ tsp. salt	

Soak the sweetbreads in cold water for 30 minutes, drain, then plunge them into boiling water to which has been added 1 tbsp. of lemon juice or vinegar, a little parsley and some celery; simmer for 15 minutes and add some salt before they are done. Drain, put into cold water, and remove the tough parts and skin.

Meanwhile make a sauce in the usual way with the butter, flour, seasonings, cream and chopped mushrooms. Add the sweetbreads and serve at once.

STEWED OXTAIL

2 tbsps. butter	Salt and pepper
1 tbsp. chopped onion	2 cups stewed tomatoes
1 tbsp. chopped green pepper	(or tinned ones)
	2 slices of lemon
2 rather small oxtails	½ tsp. ginger
Flour	Stock or water

Heat the butter, add the chopped onion and green pepper and fry gently for a few minutes. Wash the oxtails, previously cut into suitable-sized pieces, and cover with boiling water. Leave for a few moments, then throw this water away and drain and dry the pieces of tail; roll each one in seasoned flour and brown in the butter with the onions and green pepper. When nicely coloured, add the remaining ingredients, with as much stock or water as desired—about 2 cups is sufficient, as the tomatoes and the other ingredients supply liquid. Cover the pot closely and stew gently for 3–4 hours until the meat falls away from the bones.

CORNED BEEF HASH

2 cups chopped corned beef	Salt
	A pinch of pepper
2–3 cups chopped cooked potatoes	⅓ cup single cream
	2 tbsps. fat or salad oil
6 tbsps. minced onion	

Chop the corned beef and cold potatoes separately, then put in a mixing bowl—don't chop them too fine or the hash will be close-textured. Toss in the onion, add salt, pepper and the cream and mix well. Melt the fat in a frying pan, tip the pan and run the fat right round the sides so that the whole surface is well greased. Put in the hash, spreading it evenly, and cook over a low heat without stirring until light brown on the underside—30–40 minutes.

With a spatula or palette knife loosen the hash from the sides of the pan and make a cut across the centre of the hash, at right angles to the handle. Tilt the pan slightly and fold one half of the hash over the other, then gently tip it out on to a platter. Serve with a chilli, tomato orp iquant sauce, or piccallili. This quantity serves 4–5.

146

Variations : Bake or sauté the hash ; or slice, then grill, sauté or bake brown on both sides ; or use as a hot sandwich spread. It may also be served with poached eggs, or grilled tomatoes or savoury mustard sauce.

BARBECUED FRANKS—PICNIC STYLE

¾ cup ketchup	1 tsp. sugar
1 tbsp. piquant table sauce	A dash of tabasco
	1 cup water
1 tsp. chilli powder	8–12 frankfurters
½ tsp. salt	

Combine all the ingredients except the frankfurters in a saucepan and bring to the boil ; reduce the heat and simmer for 15–20 minutes. Put the frankfurters in a casserole, pour the sauce over and bake, uncovered, for 30 minutes in a moderate oven (350° F., mark 4) ; turn them occasionally.

Serve in toasted split rolls ; on hot fluffy rice, buttered noodles or creamy mashed potatoes ; or with baked or boiled potatoes.

Picnic-style : Let the sauce simmer 15–20 minutes. Put some grilled frankfurters in split rolls and spoon on some sauce.

" BEST EVER " HAMBURGERS

1 lb. minced chuck steak	2 tbsps. minced onion
1 tsp. salt	¼ tsp. monosodium
¼ tsp. pepper	glutamate

Toss the meat lightly with the other ingredients. (Some cooks prefer to shape the unseasoned meat into flat cakes, then to sprinkle seasonings on both sides of them before cooking—this eliminates too much handling.)

With the help of a kitchen fork, and using as little pressure as possible, divide the meat, gently shape and flatten loosely into 4 thick patties, about 3½ inches by ¾ inch, or into 8 thin patties, 3 inches by ½ inch. Cook in one of these ways :

Fried : Heat 2 tbsps. fat or salad oil in a frying pan or on a griddle. Cook patties until done to your family's taste. As a general guide, allow about 4–8 minutes over a medium heat, turning once, for thick patties ; if patties are thin, allow about 2–6 minutes, turning once. Do not flatten or " spank " patties with a spatula —it presses out the juices.

Pan-Broiled : Heat a heavy frying pan or griddle till sizzling hot. If you are afraid the meat will stick, rub the surface lightly with fat or salad oil or sprinkle with salt. Brown the patties on both sides, then cook over a medium heat for about same time as above.

Grilled : Pre-heat the grill for 10 minutes. Arrange thick patties on the cold grill rack. (If you can, line the grill pan with aluminium foil, corners turned under, to catch the dripping and save washing-up.) Grill for about 8–12 minutes, turning once.

After turning the patties, you may top them with one of the following, then complete cooking :

Cheese slice, a little prepared mustard.

Ketchup, or chilli, soy or barbecue sauce.

Grated cheese or ¼ cup crumbled blue cheese, mashed with ¼ cup soft butter or margarine, ½ tsp. dry mustard, 1 tsp. salt, 2 tsps. piquant sauce.

HAMBURGER SPREADS

Spread the cooked hamburgers with a mixture of 2 tbsps. melted butter or margarine and one of the following :

2 tbsps. minced stuffed or ripe olives.

2 tbsps. ketchup or prepared mustard.

2 tbsps. crumbled blue cheese or grated sharp cheese. Add chilli sauce if you wish.

2 tbsps. chilli sauce, 1 tsp. prepared mustard, a pinch of chilli powder.

¼ tsp. salt, a pinch of dried thyme.

1 tbsp. horseradish, a pinch of garlic salt.

2 tbsps. chopped dill pickle or pickle relish, plus a little minced onion or garlic.

2 tbsps. prepared mustard, chopped parsley.

Soy or barbecue sauce or French dressing.

¼ cup canned crushed pineapple or apple sauce or apple jelly, plus a pinch of nutmeg.

1 tsp. chopped parsley, 1 tsp. minced onion, a dash of piquant sauce, salt.

3 tbsps. lemon or orange juice, a pinch of nutmeg.

BARBECUED HAMBURGERS

Shape the hamburger mixture into 4 large patties. Brown these in 1 tbsp. hot fat or salad oil in a frying pan, turning to cook both sides.

Combine 1 cup ketchup, 1 sliced onion, ¼ cup vinegar, 1 tbsp. sugar, ½ tsp. dry mustard, pour over the patties and simmer, covered, for 20 minutes.

HAMBURGER GO-BETWEENS

Shape the hamburger mixture into 8 thin patties. Place one of the fillings below on half of them, then top with the remaining patties, press edges together and cook till done.

Blue Cheese : Combine ¼ cup crumbled blue cheese, 2 tbsps. mayonnaise, 1 tbsp. piquant sauce, ½ tsp. dry mustard.

Chilli-Cheese : Mix 1 cup grated processed cheese, 1 tbsp. piquant sauce, ¼ cup chilli sauce.

Chilli-Onion : Use sautéed onions.

Relish : Top thin onion slices with prepared mustard, then with pickles or chilli sauce.

Stuffing : Mix 2 tbsps. melted butter or margarine with 1¼ cups fine fresh breadcrumbs, ½ tsp. dried thyme, a little minced onion, 1 tsp. lemon juice.

Tomato-Cheese : Top thin tomato slices with onion salt, then with grated cheese.

HAMBURGER TOSS-INS

Bacon-Wrapped : Wrap thick patties in bacon slices, securing each with cocktail sticks, then grill.

Bohemian Burgers : Increase minced onion to 3 tbsps. Toss the patties in 3 tbsps. minced dill pickle, ½ cup minced pickled beets and 1 cup finely chopped, cooked potatoes. Fry the patties.

Cheeseburgers : Toss in 1 cup (¼ lb.) grated processed cheese ; add ¼ cup water.

Chip Burgers : Toss in 1 cup crushed potato chips.

Devilled Burgers : Increase minced onion to 3 tbsps. Add 1½ tsps. prepared mustard, ¼ cup ketchup or chilli sauce, 2 tsps. horseradish, 1½ tsps. piquant sauce.

Extra-Juicy : Add ¼ cup undiluted evaporated milk or water.

Jumbo Burgers : Increase onion to ¼ cup ; add 1¾ cups fresh breadcrumbs, 1 beaten egg, ¼ cup milk.

Herb Burgers : Add ¼ tsp. each dried marjoram and thyme ; increase onion to ¼ cup ; add ¼ cup minced celery, 1 tsp. chopped parsley, ½ tsp. garlic salt. After cooking, top with 2 tbsps. melted butter or margarine, mixed with 3 tbsps. lemon or orange juice and a pinch of nutmeg.

Moreburgers : Add 1 cup wheat flakes, cracker crumbs, cooked rice or ½ cup uncooked rolled oats ; also add ½ cup milk or tomato juice, plus a little prepared mustard, horseradish or ketchup.

Mushroom Burgers : Add ½ cup chopped mushrooms.

Nut Burgers : Toss in ½ cup chopped walnuts.

HOME-MADE CORNED BEEF AND CABBAGE

4–5 lb. brisket of beef	1 garlic clove
3 onion slices	2 green pepper rings
4 cloves	1 stalk of celery
6 whole black peppers	1 carrot
1 bay leaf	A few sprigs of parsley
½ tsp. dried rosemary	1 green cabbage

Place the brisket in a large, deep saucepan and cover with cold water. Add the onion slices, studded with cloves, the whole peppers, bay leaf, rosemary, garlic, pepper rings and celery, carrot and parsley, tied in a bunch. Cover, bring to the boil and reduce the heat ; simmer for 4–5 hours, or until fork-tender.

Wash the cabbage, cut into quarters and trim off the core, leaving enough to hold cabbage intact. About ½ hour before the meat is done skim excess fat from top of liquid, arrange cabbage on meat and simmer, covered, for 25–30 minutes, or until cabbage is tender-crisp.

To serve, slice the meat and put on a platter, with the cabbage round it. Makes 8 servings.

DEVILLED EGGS

6 hard-boiled eggs	½ tsp. prepared mustard
¼ cup melted butter or mayonnaise	1 tsp. minced onion
	½ tsp. curry powder (optional)
¼ tsp. salt	
A little pepper	

Halve the shelled eggs lengthwise. Using a teaspoon, carefully remove the yolks, putting into a small bowl ; set the whites aside. Mash the yolks until very fine and crumbly, then blend in the butter and other ingredients.

Generously refill the hollows in the egg whites with the yolk mixture, slightly rounding the top. If desired, garnish with strips of pimiento, ripe or green olives, parsley, watercress or capers.

Serve as hors d'œuvres ; as salad, on lettuce or other greenstuff ; as garnish for chicken, meat, fish or vegetable salad ; or with a cold meat platter.

ITALIAN-STYLE PIZZA

2 lb. white bread dough	A 6-oz. can tomato paste (⅔ cup)
½ lb. sliced mushrooms	⅛ tsp. garlic salt
2 tbsps. butter	½ lb. Mozzarella or Cheddar cheese, grated
1–2 lb. fresh pork sausage-meat or sausages	
½ cup minced onions	Grated Parmesan or Cheddar cheese
An 8-oz. can tomato sauce	Chopped parsley
¼ tsp. orégano	

Let the dough rise in a warm place (about 85° F.) until light—30–60 minutes.

Meanwhile, sauté the mushrooms in the butter until tender, then remove. Fry the sausage-meat until the pink colour disappears (if using sausages, fry until lightly browned, then slice). Remove the sausages and pour off all the dripping, except 1 tbsp. Sauté the onions until tender, add the tomato sauce and paste, orégano and garlic salt.

Divide the dough into 4 parts. Flatten each piece and pat into the bottom of 4 pie plates (9-inch or 10-inch size). Alternatively, divide dough in half, roll out into 2 oblongs 12 by 8 inches, and place on baking sheets. Brush the dough over with olive oil or sausage dripping. Arrange half the Mozzarella cheese on the dough and cover with tomato mixture. Top with the rest of the cheese and sausage. Sprinkle with grated Parmesan cheese, parsley and sautéed mushrooms. Bake in a hot oven (450° F., mark 8) for 15–20 minutes. Serve hot, cut into wedges. Makes 8 servings.

NIBBLER DUNKS

147 " Dunking " is an established American custom. For any informal buffet-type party savoury " dips " are very popular. Guests help themselves to the bite-size snippets of toast, etc., and dip them into one of several soft, piquant mixtures.

Heap one or more dips or dunks (recipes below) in attractive bowls and garnish with paprika, chopped chives or parsley, or a few carrot, celery or green pepper strips. Serve on a tray, with two or more of these " dippers " :

Crispbread ; Melba toast ; pumpernickel strips ; crisp rolls, cut into chunks ; toast fingers ; breadsticks ; crisp crackers ; potato crisps ; raw carrot sticks or slices ; celery chunks, hearts or sticks ; radishes ; spring onions ; cucumber fingers ; sprigs of raw cauliflower ; avocado pear chunks (dipped into lemon juice and heaped in the avocado shell) ; fresh or canned pineapple chunks ; shelled shrimps or prawns (mounted on cocktail sticks, if desired) ; chunks of lobster or tuna ; chicken chunks.

ANCHOVY-CELERY COCKTAIL DUNK

An 8-oz. packet of cream cheese
A dash of paprika
½ tsp. celery seeds
2 tsps. minced onion
1 tbsp. lemon juice
2 tsps. anchovy paste
2 tbsps. cream

Cream the cheese until smooth, add the remaining ingredients and blend until fluffy.

BLUE-CHEESE DUNK

Mix 2½ oz. blue cheese with ½ lb. cottage cheese, a little grated onion and ⅓ cup yoghourt.

GARLIC-CHEESE DUNK

Combine a 6-oz. packet of soft cheese with ⅔ cup yoghourt and a little garlic juice.

CHILLI-CHEESE DUNK

Use an electric blender if available. Blend 2 cups cottage cheese with 2 tbsps. chilli sauce and a dash of onion salt until the cheese is very smooth.

AVOCADO-CREAM CHEESE DUNK

1 medium-sized avocado pear
2 3-oz. packets soft cream cheese
½ tsp. minced onion
1 tbsp. lemon juice
⅛ tsp. salt
2 tbsps. milk

Halve the avocado lengthwise and remove the stone, then scoop out the pulp, saving one shell. Mash the pulp, add the cheese and rest of ingredients and serve in the avocado shell.

CHEESY EGG DUNK

A 6-oz. packet of soft cream cheese (preferably chive-flavoured)
2 tbsps. mayonnaise
1 tsp. prepared mustard
¼ tsp. salt
½ tsp. piquant table sauce
⅛ tsp. pepper
2 chopped hard-boiled eggs
3 tbsps. milk

Combine all the ingredients.

CLAM AND CHEESE DUNK

1 garlic clove
2 tsps. lemon juice
An 8-oz. packet cream cheese
½ tsp. salt
A dash of pepper
1½ tsps. piquant table sauce
A 7½-oz. can of minced clams, drained
¼ cup clam broth

Rub a small mixing bowl well with the halved garlic. Blend the remaining ingredients well in the bowl. If a thinner dunk is desired, add more clam broth.

TANGY SALMON DUNK

1 cup flaked canned salmon or tuna
½ lb. cottage cheese
⅓ cup yoghourt
¼ cup pickles, finely chopped
4 bacon rashers, crisply fried, then crumbled

Combine all the ingredients.

TUNA-CHEESE DUNK

1 can flaked tuna (1 cup)
3 3-oz. packages of cream cheese
¼ cup dry white wine
1 tbsp. mayonnaise
2 tbsps. chopped parsley
¼ cup well-drained sweet pickle
1 tsp. grated onion
A dash of tabasco
¼ tsp. salt
¼ tsp. garlic salt

Drain the tuna, blend with the cream cheese, then with the remaining ingredients.

GRILLED CHEESE SANDWICHES

Cover some rounds of bread with cheese slices or cheese spread. Spread with prepared mustard, devilled ham, or barbecue sauce, top with more bread, then toast on both sides.

AVOCADO DIP

Halve 2 pears, remove the stones and mash the flesh in a basin. Then add 1 finely chopped onion, 1 skinned chopped tomato and 1 chopped and crushed clove of garlic; season with salt, pepper, chilli pepper and 1 tbsp. vinegar.

DOUBLE-DECKER SANDWICHES

For each sandwich lightly toast 3 bread slices.

Spread each slice lightly with butter or margarine, mayonnaise, cooked salad dressing or Russian dressing.

Choose one of the sandwich combinations below. Place the lower-layer ingredients on first toast slice; cover with second toast slice, buttered side up; put upper-layer ingredients on second slice, then top with third toast slice, buttered side down.

Fasten slices together at corners with cocktail sticks. Cut into triangles and garnish with potato crisps, celery, olives, pickles, etc.

Ham or Luncheon Meat, Cheese, Tomato and Lettuce

Lower layer : Ham slices, processed cheese.

Upper layer : Thin tomato slices and lettuce.

Cheese, Bacon, Tomato and Lettuce

Lower layer : Gruyère cheese slices, crisp bacon.

Upper layer : Thin tomato slices, lettuce.

Bacon, Tomato and Lettuce

Lower layer : Sautéed bacon rashers.

Upper layer : Thin tomato slices, lettuce, processed cheese slices.

Chicken and Egg Salad

Lower layer : Sliced chicken.

Upper layer : Egg salad.

Sardine, Tomato, Bacon and Gherkins

Lower layer : Sardines sprinkled with lemon juice.

Upper layer : Tomato slices, crisp bacon, gherkins.

Chicken, Tomato, Tongue and Coleslaw

Lower layer : Chicken, thin tomato slices.

Upper layer : Tongue slices, spread with mustard, coleslaw. If desired, spread top slice with chilli sauce.

Frankfurter, Tomato and Pickle

Lower layer : Tomato slices.

Upper layer : Split hot frankfurters, sliced pickles.

Tuna Salad, Egg and Tomato Slices, Bacon and Lettuce

Lower layer : Tuna salad, hard-boiled egg slices.

Upper layer : Thin tomato slices, crisp bacon, lettuce.

Crab Salad, Tomato, Egg Salad and Lettuce

Lower layer : Crab salad, thin tomato slices.

Upper layer : Egg salad, lettuce.

Turkey, Bacon or Ham, Tomato and Lettuce

Lower layer : Turkey and crisp bacon or ham slices.

Upper layer : Thin tomato slices, lettuce.

CHICKEN SALAD EXOTIC

4–5 cups cooked chicken, in large chunks

2 tsps. grated onion

1 cup celery, cut slantwise

1 cup minced green peppers

¼ cup single cream

1 tsp. salt

⅔ cup mayonnaise or cooked salad dressing

⅛ tsp. pepper

2 tbsps. vinegar

⅔ cup slivered toasted almonds or chopped pecans

2 cups halved and seeded green grapes or orange sections

Combine the chicken, onion, celery and peppers. Mix the cream with the mayonnaise, salt, pepper and vinegar, then toss with the chicken. Refrigerate till required, then garnish with toasted almonds and grapes.

To serve, arrange the salad on lettuce or other greenstuff on a platter.

If desired, ring the salad with any of the following : Sliced hard-boiled egg, asparagus tips, avocado pear slices, cheese-stuffed celery, ripe and stuffed olives, pickled peaches, pineapple chunks, spiced prunes, spoonfuls of cranberry jelly.

Turkey may be used in the same way.

VIRGINIA CHICKEN-APPLE SALAD

5 cups cooked chicken in chunks

2 cups unpeeled, cubed apples

Lemon juice

2 cups sliced celery

⅔ cup sliced stuffed olives

½ cup slivered almonds

⅓ cup salad dressing

½ cup double cream, whipped

2 tsps. salt

1 lettuce

Endive

Unpeeled, cored apple rings and wedges

148

Combine the chicken, cubed apples (dipped in and out of ½ cup lemon juice), celery, olives and almonds. Blend the salad dressing, whipped cream, 2 tbsp. lemon juice and salt, then toss with the chicken and refrigerate. At serving time, heap the salad on a bed of lettuce and endive. Dip the apple rings and wedges in lemon juice; lay the rings round the salad and the wedges on top; tuck some endive in each ring and on top of salad. Serves 8–12.

In Virginia on occasion they use *chowchow* instead of apples.

In New Orleans they garnish their salad with olives, capers and hard-boiled eggs.

In Texas they serve their salad in balls, rolled in chopped parsley and nested in lettuce.

In Maine they like to add chopped hard-boiled eggs and prepared mustard to taste.

JELLIED TOMATO SALAD

3¾ cups tomato juice	1 oz. unflavoured
1 stalk of celery	powdered gelatine
1 small onion, sliced	About 1½ cups chopped
2 lemon slices	mixed raw vegetables
1 small bay leaf	or mixed cooked or
1 tsp. salt	canned vegetables
⅛ tsp. pepper	(optional)
¼ cup vinegar	

Combine 3 cups tomato juice, the celery, onion, lemon, bay leaf, salt and pepper and simmer (uncovered) for 10 minutes ; strain. Meanwhile sprinkle the gelatine over the remaining cold tomato juice and vinegar and leave to soften ; stir in the hot mixture until dissolved. (If adding vegetables, chill the tomato mixture, stirring occasionally, till it reaches the consistency of unbeaten egg white, then fold in the vegetables.) Pour into 6–8 individual moulds and refrigerate till firm. To serve, unmould on to lettuce.

WINTER-PEAR WALDORF

2 cups diced, peeled	1 tsp. sugar
pears ; or 1 cup	½ cup mayonnaise
each diced pears	1 cup thinly sliced
and unpeeled red	celery
apples	½ cup broken walnuts
2 tbsps. lemon juice	or shredded coconut

Toss the fruits with the lemon juice, sugar and 1 tbsp. mayonnaise. Just before serving, add the celery, walnuts and the rest of the mayonnaise and toss again. Serve on lettuce and top with French dressing.

WALDORF SALAD

For pears, substitute 2 cups diced unpeeled red apples and ½ cup sultanas or raisins.

CAESAR SALAD

1 garlic clove	¼ cup crumbled blue
¾ cup salad oil	cheese
2 cups ¼-inch bread	1 tbsp. piquant sauce
squares	¾ tsp. salt
1 large head each cos	¼ tsp. freshly ground
and round lettuce	black pepper
¼ cup grated Parmesan	1 egg
cheese	¼ cup lemon juice

Quarter the garlic, drop into ¼ cup oil and set aside. Put the bread squares in a shallow pan

and " toast " in a slow oven (300° F., mark 1) for 20 minutes or until golden, tossing them often with a fork. Tear the lettuce into bite-size pieces and put into a salad bowl. Refrigerate all these ingredients.

Sprinkle the lettuce with the cheeses ; drizzle on ½ cup salad oil mixed with the piquant sauce, salt and pepper, then toss gently until every leaf glistens. Break the whole raw egg on to the lettuce, pour the lemon juice over all and toss until the egg specks disappear. Now remove the garlic from the ¼ cup flavoured oil and pour over the bread squares ; toss, then sprinkle over the salad. If desired, add 8 cut-up anchovies. Toss the salad and serve at once.

OLD-FASHIONED POTATO SALAD

4 cups diced, cooked	1 cup mayonnaise
potatoes	1 tbsp. vinegar
1½ cups sliced celery	2 tsps. prepared
½ cup cut-up spring	mustard
onions	½ tsp. celery seeds
¼ cup sliced radishes	1½–2 tsps. salt
2 tbsps. chopped	⅛ tsp. pepper
parsley	

Combine all the ingredients and refrigerate for several hours. Serve on lettuce and garnish with tomato or hard-boiled egg wedges, sliced olives, grated carrots or pickles. Makes 6 servings.

PICKLED BEETS

½ tsp. dry mustard	6 tbsps. vinegar
1 tbsp. sugar	¼ cup water
½ tsp. salt	2 cups cooked or can-
½ tsp. ground cloves	ned beets, drained
½ a garlic clove	and sliced

Combine the mustard, sugar, salt, cloves and garlic ; slowly stir in the vinegar and water. When the mixture is smooth, pour it over beets and refrigerate until well chilled. Remove the garlic and serve with meat or fish. Makes 6 servings.

Note : Add a pinch of fennel if desired.

BOSTON BAKED BEANS

12 oz. brown beans	A pinch of ground
2 sliced stalks of celery	cloves
or ¼ tsp. celery salt	2 tbsps. molasses or
1 sliced carrot	black treacle
1 large quartered onion	2 tsps. salt
2 oz. brown sugar	1 tsp. dried mustard
1 tbsp. malt vinegar	12 oz. salt pork, cut up
A pinch of ground	Pepper to taste
cinnamon	

Wash the beans, cover with 1 pint water and

soak overnight. Place in a pan with a little over ½ pint water and all the other ingredients except the salt pork and the pepper. Boil with the lid on for 1 hour. Place the pork in a casserole, pour the beans and the liquid over and sprinkle well with pepper. Cook with the lid on in a slow oven (325° F., mark 3) for 6–8 hours, until tender; uncover during last hour of cooking. It may be desirable to add a little water at this stage of the cooking, since the beans tend to absorb a lot of moisture.

A CORN ROAST
(PICNIC OR BARBECUE PARTY)

Wedges of Cheddar cheese   Potato crisps
(Guests munch while corn roasts)
Corn roasted in husks
Tray of " fixin's "
Spiced apple turnovers
Hot coffee   Lemonade

Start the fire about 1 hour ahead so that you'll have a bed of glowing coals. About 10 minutes before eating, place the first round of fresh corn, in husks, on grill over coals. (If you wish, plunge the corn into salted cold water first.) Roast, turning often, until husks are steaming hot —about 10 minutes. Husk and sample one cob to test. Act accordingly, then pass the fixin's— soft butter, salt, pepper, mustard or ketchup, etc. It's best to allow at least 4 ears corn per person.

" BEST-EVER " BOILED CORN FOR A BARBECUE

Husk some garden-fresh corn cobs, and boil at once in a pot on a grill over hot coals just as you would on your indoor range. For easy eating, break each ear of corn in half. Don't boil the corn more than 5 or 10 minutes; cook the second batch while the first is being eaten; use tongs for removing or turning the cobs.

Drain the corn well and put into a hot dish, covered with a napkin. Allow 4 or more cobs per person if the corn is the *pièce de résistance*. Serve with plenty of soft butter or margarine (and if possible a brush to spread it on the corn), plain, garlic or onion salt, and freshly ground black pepper.

SUCCOTASH

1½ cups hot cooked (or canned) whole-kernel corn	1½ cups hot cooked or canned green beans or green limas
2 tbsps. butter	Salt and pepper
½ cup single cream	

Combine all the ingredients, adding salt and pepper to taste, then heat. Makes 6 servings.

SUMMER CORN

¼ cup minced onion	A little pepper
2 tbsps. butter	½ tsp. sugar
2 cups cooked whole-kernel corn, removed from the cob	1 tsp. lemon juice
	¼ cup minced water-cress

Cook the onion in the butter until tender. Add the corn and remaining ingredients and heat. Serves 3.

CORN FRITTERS, SOUTHERN STYLE

1 cup flour	¼ cup milk
1 tsp. baking powder	2 tsps. salad oil
1 tsp. salt	2½ cups cooked (or canned) whole-kernel corn
2 eggs	

Sift the flour with the baking powder and salt. Beat the eggs, add the milk and salad oil, then stir in the flour mixture; add the corn and drop by tablespoonfuls into fat heated to 365° F. Fry for 3–5 minutes, turning once. Makes 5 or 6 servings.

WEST VIRGINIA CORN PUDDING

8–12 corn cobs	1¼ cups single cream
1½ tsp. salt	

Heat the oven to moderate (350° F., mark 4). Husk the corn, then split the kernels by running a sharp knife down each cob lengthwise. Then, with the back of the knife, scrape out kernels until you have 2 cups corn pulp. Combine with salt and cream, pour into a buttered 1½-quart casserole and bake for 1 hour. Serve piping hot, with butter. (1 cup milk and ¼ cup melted butter can be substituted for the cream.)

LEMON CHIFFON PIE

A 9-inch baked pie shell	¼ cup lemon juice
	⅓ cup cold water
1½ tsps. gelatine	4 egg whites
Granulated sugar	¼ tsp. salt
4 egg yolks	½ cup double cream, whipped
1 tbsp. grated lemon rind	

Combine the gelatine and ⅓ cup sugar. In the top part of a double saucepan, beat the egg yolks, stir in the lemon rind and juice, the water, then the gelatine mixture. Cook over boiling water, stirring, for 5 minutes or till thickened; remove from the heat. Beat the egg whites with the salt till fairly stiff; gradually add ½ cup sugar, beating until stiff, and fold in the lemon mixture. Turn into the shell and refrigerate until set.

To serve, spread whipped cream over the pie and garnish with blueberries, sliced strawberries or bananas.

FRESH APPLE PIE

12 oz. flaky pastry
⅔–¾ cup granulated sugar (or half granulated and half brown sugar)
1–2 tbsps. flour (if fruit is very juicy)
⅛ tsp. salt
1–2 tsps. lemon juice
½ tsp. grated lemon rind
¼ tsp. grated nutmeg
½ tsp. ground cinnamon
6–7 cups thinly peeled, cored and thinly sliced cooking apples (2 lb.)
1 tbsp. butter

Start heating the oven to moderately hot (425° F., mark 7). Make the pastry and line a 9-inch pie plate with half of it. Roll out the top crust. Combine all the filling ingredients except the apples and butter (the amount of sugar depends on the tartness of the apples). Place half the apples in the lined pie plate, "sharp" edges facing inward, and sprinkle with half the sugar mixture. Top with the rest of apples, heaping them up in the centre, then with the rest of the sugar mixture; dot with butter. Put on the top crust and glaze if desired. Bake for 40–50 minutes, or until the filling is tender and the crust nicely browned. Especially nice served warm.

LEMON MERINGUE PIE

149

A baked pie shell
1 cup granulated sugar
¼ cup cornflour
⅛ tsp. salt
1¼ cups warm water
Grated rind of 1 lemon
¼ cup lemon juice
3 egg yolks, slightly beaten
1 tbsp. butter or margarine
Pie meringue (see below)

In a double saucepan, combine the sugar, cornflour and salt. Slowly stir in the water, then the lemon rind and juice, egg yolks and butter. Cook, stirring, until smooth and thick enough to mould when dropped from spoon; cool thoroughly. Start heating the oven to moderate (350° F., mark 4). Spoon the filling into the cooled pie shell and top with meringue, then bake for 12–15 minutes.

PIE MERINGUE
For 8-inch Pie

2 egg whites
¼ tsp. salt (scant)
4 tbsps. caster sugar

For 9-inch Pie

3 egg whites
¼ tsp. salt
6 tbsps. caster sugar

Have the eggs at room temperature. (The whites beat to a greater volume when not too cold.) Start heating the oven to moderate (350° F., mark 4). Place the whites in a medium-sized bowl and add the salt; using an electric mixer at high speed or an egg beater, beat until frothy throughout (do not wait until whites begin to stiffen).

Add the sugar, a little at a time, beating well after each addition. Continue beating until stiff peaks are formed. To test, slowly withdraw the beater and hold it up; the meringue should form pointed peaks that are so stiff they stand upright and do not curl over. Using a spoon, place mounds of meringue around edge of pie filling; spread the meringue so that it touches the inner edge of the crust all round to prevent shrinking. Heap the rest of the meringue in the centre, then push it out to meet the meringue border. Using the back of the spoon, pull up points on the meringue, to make an attractive top. Bake for 12–15 minutes. Cool on a rack, away from draughts. To cut meringue neatly when serving the pie, first dip a sharp knife into water, then shake off any excess drops.

PILGRIM PUMPKIN OR SQUASH PIE

An unbaked 9-inch pie shell
1 cup granulated sugar
½ tsp. salt
1½ tsps. ground cinnamon
½ tsp. ground ginger
½ tsp. grated nutmeg
½ tsp. allspice
½ tsp. ground cloves
1½ cups canned pumpkin
1⅔ cups undiluted evaporated milk
2 eggs, well beaten

Refrigerate the pie shell for several hours. Start heating oven to moderately hot (425° F., mark 7). Combine the sugar, salt and spices and add the pumpkin, milk and eggs; beat till smooth. Pour into the shell and bake for 15 minutes; reduce the heat to moderate (350° F., mark 4) and bake for 35 minutes, or until the filling is set. Cool.

To serve, top each wedge with whipped cream, with honey, chocolate curls or drained canned crushed pineapple in the centre; or top with spoonfuls of ice cream; or top with whipped cream cheese and chopped nuts.

STRAWBERRY SHORTCAKE

150

2 cups flour
3 tsps. baking powder
¾ tsp. salt
3–5 tbsps. granulated sugar
1 tsp. grated lemon or orange rind (optional)
½ cup fat
1 egg, beaten
About ⅓ cup milk
Butter or margarine
4 cups sweetened sliced or crushed strawberries
1 cup double cream (optional)

Start heating the oven to hot (450° F., mark 8). Sieve the flour, baking powder, salt and sugar into a mixing bowl and add the rind.

Using a pastry blender or 2 knives, scissor-fashion, cut the fat into the flour mixture until it resembles corn meal. Add the egg, then enough milk to make an easily handled dough.

For a large shortcake, roll or pat the dough into a ½-inch thick round, to fit a greased 9-inch tin. Bake at 450° F., mark 8, for 15–20 minutes, or until done.

For individual shortcakes, roll or pat the dough ½ inch thick and cut into 3-inch rounds; place 1 inch apart on a baking sheet and bake for 12–15 minutes, or until done.

To serve, split the hot shortcake and butter well; fill with some of the strawberries, top with the rest of the berries, then with whipped cream. Alternatively, omit the cream and hand cream or yoghourt separately. Serves 6–8.

MAPLE NUT WHIP PIE

Bake an 8-inch pie shell with a high fluted edge. Sprinkle ½ oz. unflavoured gelatine over ¼ cup cold water and stir till dissolved. In a double saucepan, thoroughly beat 3 egg yolks with ¾ cup maple syrup. Cook over boiling water, stirring, till slightly thickened—about 5 minutes. Add the gelatine mixture and stir till dissolved. Pour into a large bowl and refrigerate, stirring occasionally, till it has consistency of unbeaten egg white. Now whip 1 cup double cream till stiff. Beat 3 egg whites with ½ tsp. salt till stiff but not dry; fold in 1 tbsp. icing sugar.

Fold the whipped cream into the gelatine mixture, then fold in the beaten egg whites and ¾ cup broken walnuts or other nuts. Pour into the cold pie shell and refrigerate until set— about 2 hours. Sprinkle ¼ cup broken walnuts around the edge before serving.

APPLE BROWN BETTY

⅓ cup melted butter or margarine
2 cups fresh bread-crumbs
6 cups sliced, peeled and cored cooking apples
½ tsp. grated nutmeg
½ cup granulated or brown sugar
¼ tsp. ground cinnamon
1 tbsp. grated lemon rind
2 tbsps. lemon juice
¼ cup water

Start heating the oven to moderate (375° F., mark 5). Toss the butter with the crumbs and arrange one-third of this mixture in a greased 1½-quart casserole. Cover with half the apples and half the combined sugar, nutmeg, cinnamon and lemon rind. Cover with one-third of the crumbs, the rest of the apples and the rest of the sugar mixture. Spoon on the combined lemon juice and water, then top with remaining crumbs.

Bake, covered, for ½ hour; uncover and bake for ½ hour longer, or until the apples are done.

Serve warm, with thin cream or with whipped cream sprinkled with cinnamon or grated cheese. Makes 6 servings.

OHIO PUDDING

4 oz. plain flour
2 tsps. baking powder
½ tsp. ground cinnamon
1 tsp. mixed spice
A pinch of salt
2 oz. fresh bread-crumbs
2 medium-sized carrots
1 potato (about ¼ lb.)
3 oz. Demerara sugar
4 oz. cleaned currants
4 oz. cleaned sultanas
2 oz. cleaned raisins
3 oz. chopped mixed peel
Milk to mix

Sieve together the flour, baking powder, cinnamon, mixed spice and salt; add the bread-crumbs. Mince or grate the carrots and potato and mix these with all the remaining ingredients, adding sufficient milk to give a stiff dropping consistency. Place in a greased 1½-pint pudding basin and steam for about 2½ hours.

DEVIL'S FOOD CAKE

2 cups flour
1 tsp. bicarbonate of soda
¾ tsp. salt
1⅓ cups granulated sugar or 1½ cups brown sugar
2 medium-sized eggs, unbeaten
½ cup soft fat
3 squares unsweetened chocolate, melted
1¼ cups milk, minus 2 tbsps.
1 tsp. vanilla essence or ¼ tsp. peppermint essence

Start heating the oven to moderate (350° F., mark 4). Grease, then line with waxed paper, the bottoms of 2 cake tins measuring 9 inches across and 1½ inches deep. Sieve the flour, soda and salt 3 times. In a large electric-mixer bowl, with mixer at medium speed, mix the fat with the sugar, then with the eggs, until very light and fluffy—about 4 minutes altogether. Mix in the chocolate. At low speed beat in alternately, until just smooth, the flour mixture (add a quarter at a time) and the mixed milk and vanilla, in thirds. Turn into the tins and bake at 350° F., mark 4, for 25–30 minutes, or until a fine skewer inserted in the centre comes out clean. Place (in the tin) on a rack and cool for 10–15 minutes, then turn out and finish cooling.

Fill and ice with American Frosting or Mocha Butter Cream.

AMERICAN FROSTING OR ICING

1 lb. loaf sugar
¼ pint water
A pinch of cream of tartar
2 egg whites

Dissolve the sugar in the water, add the cream

of tartar and boil rapidly until a temperature of 240° F. is reached. Meanwhile, whisk the egg whites stiffly. Pour the sugar syrup in a thin stream on to the egg whites and continue whisking until the mixture thickens sufficiently to hold " peaks "—if it does not thicken enough it will slide off the cake. Quickly put the icing on the cake and add any decorations before it sets.

MOCHA BUTTER CREAM

⅓ cup butter   ¼ cup milk or top-of-
A pinch of salt   the-milk
3 cups sieved icing sugar   1½ tsps. vanilla essence

Cream the ingredients to a smooth spreading consistency.

To make a Chocolate Nut Cream Filling, add some chopped nuts and chocolate powder to the above mixture.

MARSHMALLOW TREATS

Toast marshmallows until " gooey " and crisp. Place on biscuits, crackers or thin gingerbread slices, top with a piece of sweet chocolate, then cover with another biscuit or thin gingerbread slice, sandwich style.

SUNDAE TOPPINGS

Top Vanilla Ice Cream with :
Apple purée, warmed, with a sprinkling of grated nutmeg or cinnamon.
Canned apricots and a sprinkling of plain or toasted coconut.
Banana slices and a sprinkling of nutmeg.
Crème de menthe.
A dusting of cocoa.
Coconut, tinted green, with lemon wedges.
Coconut, tinted pink, with lime wedges.
Cranberry juice cocktail and melon balls.
Canned whole cranberry sauce, mixed with drained canned crushed pineapple.
Dates, dried figs or raisins, chopped, then soaked in brandy.
Hot fudge sauce with crumbled biscuits.
Frozen grape-juice concentrate, slightly thawed ; seedless grapes and a sprinkling of cinnamon.
Crumbled macaroons or chocolate wafers.
Maple syrup, warmed, with a sprinkling of salted almonds, peanuts, etc.
Prepared mincemeat, heated.
Frozen orange or tangerine juice concentrate, slightly thawed, with a sprinkling of grated chocolate.
Orange marmalade, or berry or apricot jam, heated.
Peanut brittle, crushed.

Fresh or canned peach slices and a sprinkling of cinnamon.
Stoned stewed prunes and a sprinkling of ground cloves.
Frozen strawberries or raspberries, slightly thawed.

Top Chocolate Ice Cream with :
Canned crushed pineapple.
Chocolate sauce and crumbled biscuits.
Honey, mixed with crunchy peanut butter.
Grated orange rind mixed with sugar.
Hard peppermint candy, crushed.
Peanut brittle, crushed.
Marshmallow cream, thinned to sauce consistency, with grated chocolate.
Toasted shredded coconut.

Top Coffee Ice Cream with :
Peanut brittle, crushed.
Prepared mincemeat, warmed.
Custard sauce and shaved chocolate.
Sliced peaches and custard sauce.
Maple syrup and a few salted nuts.

Top Orange or Lemon Water Ice with :
Grated orange rind, mixed with sugar.
Whipped cream, plus drained crushed berries.
Slightly thawed frozen raspberries or orange juice concentrate.
Canned crushed pineapple and mint sprigs.
Seedless grapes and cut-up oranges or pineapple.
Crème de menthe or *triple-sec.*

LOVELIGHT CHIFFON LAYER CAKE

2 eggs, separated   1 tsp. salt
1½ cups granulated sugar   ⅓ cup salad oil
2¼ cups flour   1 cup milk
3 tsps. baking powder   1½ tsps. vanilla essence

About 1 hour ahead, set out the separated eggs.

When ready to make the cake, start heating the oven to moderate (350° F., mark 4). Choose 2 sandwich tins 8–9 inches across and 1½ inches deep ; grease generously, then dust with flour.

Beat the egg whites until frothy ; gradually beat in ½ cup sugar and continue beating until the mixture is stiff and glossy enough to stand in peaks.

Into a large electric-mixer bowl, sieve the remaining 1 cup sugar, the flour, baking powder and salt ; pour in the oil and half the milk. With mixer at medium speed, beat for 1 minute, scraping sides and bottom of bowl as needed. Add the remaining milk, the egg yolks and vanilla ; beat for 1 minute.

Fold the beaten egg whites into the batter,

turn into the tins and bake for 30–35 minutes. Cool in the tins on wire racks for about 10 minutes. Remove from tins and cool on racks. Fill with clear orange filling (see below) and ice with American frosting or cover with the same orange mixture.

CLEAR ORANGE FILLING

1 cup granulated sugar	2 tbsps. grated orange
3 tbsps. cornflour	rind
½ tsp. salt	¾ cup orange juice
1 cup boiling water	2 tbsps. butter

Combine all the ingredients in a saucepan and bring to the boil, stirring occasionally; turn the heat down and boil gently for 1 minute, stirring. Allow to cool, then beat with an egg beater and fill layers and cover the top of the cake; use as desired.

To make Lemon Filling, substitute grated lemon rind and use ½ cup lemon juice.

SPICY GINGERBREAD

2½ cups flour	½ cup soft fat
1½ tsps. bicarbonate of	½ cup granulated sugar
soda	1 medium-sized egg,
½ tsp. ground cloves	unbeaten
1 tsp. ground cinnamon	1 cup molasses
1 tsp. ground ginger	1 cup hot water
¾ tsp. salt	

Start heating the oven to moderate (350° F., mark 4). Grease a 9-inch tin about 2 inches deep, then line with waxed paper. Sieve the flour, soda, cloves, cinnamon, ginger and salt. In a large bowl, with electric mixer at medium speed, mix the fat with the sugar, then with the egg, until very light and fluffy—about 4 minutes altogether. Beat in the molasses. At low speed, beat in alternate additions of the flour mixture and the hot water; add the flour in about 4 portions and the water ⅓ cup at a time; beat until just smooth. Turn the mixture into the tin and bake for 50–55 minutes, or until a fine skewer inserted in the centre comes out clean. Cool on a rack.

OLD-FASHIONED POUNDCAKE

3 cups flour	1 cup granulated sugar
1½ tsps. baking powder	1 tsp. vanilla essence
⅛ tsp. salt	3 eggs, unbeaten
¼–½ tsp. mace	½ cup milk
1 cup soft butter	

Start heating the oven to moderate (350° F., mark 4). Grease a 3-quart ring mould on bottom and sides. Sieve the flour, baking powder, salt and mace 3 times. In a large electric-mixer bowl, with mixer at medium speed, mix the butter with the sugar and vanilla, then with the eggs, until very light and fluffy—about 4 minutes altogether. Then, at low speed, beat in the flour mixture alternately with the milk in small amounts, beating well after each addition. Turn into the ring mould and bake for 50–60 minutes, or until a fine skewer inserted in the centre comes out clean. Cool on a rack. If desired, dust with icing sugar before serving. Leave for a day before eating.

FROSTED FRUIT PYRAMID

For this you need a selection of fruits, for example, green and black grapes, clementines, dessert dates, green and red-skinned apples. Leave the apples whole; leave some clementines whole but cut 2–3 of them into segments; divide the grapes into small bunches. Dip all the fruits into egg white and then into caster sugar, making sure that the whole surface of each is thoroughly coated, leave overnight for the frosting to become firm. The next day, build the fruit up into a pyramid, using a silver cake board as a base and securing the layers of fruit with cocktail sticks. Decorate the base of the pyramid with sections of clementine and sprays of frosted fern. This makes an excellent centre-piece for a formal table.

UPSIDE-DOWN CAKE

1¼ cups flour	5 Maraschino cherries
2 tsps. baking powder	⅓ cup soft fat
¼ tsp. salt	½ cup granulated
3 tbsps. butter or mar-	sugar
garine	1 egg, unbeaten
½ cup brown sugar	1 tsp. vanilla essence
(packed down)	½ cup syrup drained
A No. 2 can of pine-	from pineapple
apple chunks	

151

Start heating the oven to moderate (350° F., mark 4). Sieve the flour, baking powder and salt. Melt the butter in an 8-inch square aluminium cake tin over a low heat; remove from heat and sprinkle with brown sugar. Meanwhile drain the pineapple chunks, reserving the syrup. Arrange 6 pineapple chunks to form a small daisy pattern over the sugar coating; repeat, making 5 daisies in all. (Any extra chunks may be placed between daisies and at edges of tin.) Place a drained Maraschino cherry in the centre of each daisy.

In a large electric-mixer bowl, with mixer at medium speed, mix the shortening with the granulated sugar, then with the egg and vanilla, until very light and fluffy—about 4 minutes altogether. At low speed, beat in alternately, until just smooth, flour mixture (add one-third at a time) and the pineapple syrup (add half at a time). Spread the batter carefully over the pineapple " daisies," keeping the design intact. Bake the cake for 1 hour, or until a fine skewer inserted in the centre comes out clean. Remove from oven and cool on a cake rack for 10 minutes ; then, with a spatula, loosen the cake from sides of the tin. Invert a serving plate on to the tin, then, with one hand under the tin, the other on top of the plate, turn both until the cake rests, fruit side up, on the serving plate ; remove the tin. If the fruit sticks to the tin, lift off with a spatula and return it to its place on the cake. Serve the cake warm, topped with cream, whipped cream, or vanilla ice cream. Makes 6–8 servings.

BROWNIES

¾ cup sifted cake flour	2–2½ squares unsweet-
½ tsp. baking powder	ened chocolate,
¾ tsp. salt	melted
1 cup granulated sugar	1 cup chopped walnuts,
½ cup soft fat	almonds, pecans,
2 eggs, unbeaten	Brazil nuts, pistachio
1 tsp. vanilla essence	nuts or peanuts

Start heating the oven to moderate (350° F., mark 4). Grease an 8-inch square tin about 2 inches deep. Sieve the flour, baking powder and salt. Gradually add the sugar to the fat, mixing until very light and fluffy. Add the eggs and vanilla and mix till smooth. Mix in the chocolate, flour mixture and nuts. (If desired, save half of nuts to sprinkle on top of batter before baking.)

Turn mixture into tin and bake for 30–35 minutes, or until done. Cool slightly, cut into 16 squares or bars, then sprinkle with icing sugar if desired. Store in the tin.

LEMON WAFERS

1½ cups flour	Granulated sugar
½ tsp. salt	1 egg, beaten
½ tsp. bicarbonate of soda	2 tsps. lemon rind
½ cup butter	1 tbsp. lemon juice

Sieve the flour, salt and baking soda ; in a small bowl, with the mixer at medium speed, cream the butter, ¾ cup sugar, egg and lemon rind, then beat well. With mixer at low speed, beat in the flour mixture little by little ; add the lemon juice and refrigerate for ½ hour.

Meanwhile start heating the oven to moderate (375° F., mark 5). Grease 2 baking sheets. Shape the dough, by tablespoonfuls, into balls ; roll these in 3 tbsps. granulated sugar till coated, place 2 inches apart on the greased sheets and

press each ball down till flat and round. Bake for 10–12 minutes, or till pale gold ; remove and cool on rack. Makes about 25.

POPOVERS

1 cup flour	2–3 eggs
¾ tsp. salt	1 cup milk
1 tbsp. fat (optional)	

Grease 8 large (or 12 medium-sized) custard cups or dariole moulds ; place on a baking sheet. Start heating the oven to moderate (375° F., mark 5). Into a mixing bowl, sieve the flour and salt. Using a pastry blender or 2 knives, scissor-fashion, cut in the fat until the mixture resembles corn meal.

In a small bowl, beat the eggs slightly, then beat in the milk. Add to the flour mixture and beat until smooth. Fill the cups one-third full and bake for 50 minutes. Remove from the oven, quickly cut a slit in the side of each popover to let out steam, and return them to the oven for 10 minutes. Promptly remove the popovers from the cups so that the bases do not steam and soften. Serve at once.

BAKING POWDER BISCUITS (SCONES)

2 cups flour	6–7 tbsps. fat
3 tsps. baking powder	About ⅔–¾ cup milk
1 tsp. salt	

Start heating the oven to hot (450° F., mark 8). Sieve the flour, baking powder and salt. Using a pastry blender or 2 knives, scissor-fashion, cut in the fat until the mixture is like coarse corn meal.

Make a well in the centre and pour in ½ cup milk. Using a fork, mix lightly and quickly. Add enough milk to form a dough just moist enough to leave the sides of bowl and cling to the fork in a ball. Turn on to a lightly floured surface and knead : pick up the side of the dough furthest from you ; fold over towards you ; with the palms, press down, pushing the dough away lightly ; turn dough part-way round and repeat 6 or 7 times, working gently. Lightly roll the dough out from the centre, lifting the rolling pin as you get near the edges. Roll it out ½–¾ inch (¼ inch for thin, crusty scones). Cut out with a floured 2-inch biscuit cutter—do not twist the cutter—and cut the biscuits as close together as possible ; between cuttings, dip the cutter into flour. Using a spatula, lift the biscuits on to an ungreased baking sheet ; place about 1 inch apart for crusty biscuits, nearly touching for soft-sided ones. Lightly press the dough trimmings together, then roll and cut as before. Brush the biscuit tops over with milk.

melted butter or margarine, or single cream. Bake for 12–15 minutes or until a delicate brown. Serve hot. Makes about 20 2-inch biscuits.

BOSTON BROWN BREAD

1 cup unsifted whole-wheat flour	1½ tsps. bicarbonate of soda
1 cup unsifted rye flour	¾ cup molasses
1 cup yellow corn meal	2 cups buttermilk or sour milk
1½ tsps. salt	

Grease and flour a 2-quart mould. Combine the flours, corn meal, soda and salt. Stir in the molasses and buttermilk, turn into the mould and cover tightly. Place on a trivet in a deep saucepan, add enough boiling water to come half-way up the sides of the mould, then cover the pan and steam for 3½ hours, or until done. Remove from the mould to a cake rack.

Serve hot with baked beans, boiled tongue, etc.

FLUFFY SPOON BREAD

1 quart milk	2 tbsps. butter or margarine
1 cup corn meal (yellow or white)	4 eggs
1½ tsps. salt	

In a double saucepan, heat the milk; gradually stir in the corn meal mixed with the salt and cook, stirring, until smooth and thick. Cover and cook till mushy. Meanwhile, start heating the oven to moderately hot (425° F., mark 7). Remove the mush from the heat and add the butter. Beat the eggs till well blended and slowly stir into the mush. Pour into a well-greased 1½-quart casserole and bake, uncovered, for 50–55 minutes.

Serve from the casserole, spooning some on to each plate. Eat instead of bread, with lots of butter or margarine. Makes 4 or 5 servings.

SKILLET CUSTARD CORN BREAD

2 tbsps. butter or margarine	3–4 tbsps. granulated sugar
1⅓ cups yellow corn meal	1¼ tsps. salt
⅓ cup flour	2 cups milk
1 tsp. bicarbonate of soda	2 eggs, unbeaten
	1 cup buttermilk or sour milk

Start heating the oven to moderately hot (400° F., mark 6). Place the butter in a 9-inch iron frying pan or a 9-inch square baking tin, and heat in the oven. Meanwhile sieve the corn meal, flour, soda, sugar and salt into a bowl. Stir in 1 cup milk and the eggs, then the buttermilk. Pour into the pan or tin, then pour 1 cup milk over the top of the corn mixture but do not stir. Bake for 35 minutes.

When cooked, the bread has a layer of custard, and should be eaten with a fork. Serve it straight from the pan, cutting it into wedges. Put a lump of butter on each wedge, or serve a tart jelly or jam separately. Makes 6 servings.

DROP SCONES OR PANCAKES, AMERICAN STYLE

1¼ cups flour	1¼ cups milk
2½ tsps. baking powder	3 tbsps. melted butter, margarine or fat, or salad oil
2 tbsps. sugar	
¾ tsp. salt	
1 egg	

Set a griddle over a low heat to warm up. Into a medium-sized bowl or wide-mouthed pitcher sift the flour, baking powder, sugar and salt.

In a small bowl, beat the egg well and add the milk and butter; slowly stir into flour mixture, mixing only until the dry ingredients are wet.

When the griddle is hot enough to make a drop of cold water dance, lightly grease. Drop on the batter from the pitcher or a large spoon, lightly spreading each cake with the back of the spoon into a round about 4 inches in diameter. (Do not crowd the cakes or they will be difficult to turn—cooking about 3 cakes at a time is usually safe.)

Cook over low heat until the rim of each cake is full of broken bubbles and the underside golden-brown. Using a broad spatula, loosen and turn each cake and brown on the other side. (Turn only once.)

When the pancakes are done, remove to a heated platter or plates, stacking about 4 in each pile. Serve at once, with butter and maple, or corn syrup, molasses, shaved maple sugar, etc. Makes about 12 cakes.

OLD-FASHIONED FUDGE

2 cups granulated sugar	2 tbsps. white corn syrup
1 cup milk or ½ cup evaporated milk and ½ cup water	2 tbsps. butter or margarine
½ tsp. salt	½ tsp. vanilla essence
2 squares unsweetened chocolate	½ cup chopped nuts

Grease a loaf tin measuring about 9 by 5 by 3 inches. Combine the sugar, milk, salt, chocolate and corn syrup in a saucepan and stir over a low heat until the sugar dissolves; cook gently, stirring occasionally, to 238° F. or until a little mixture dropped into cold water forms a soft ball. Remove from the heat and drop in the butter, but do not stir. Cool, without stirring, to 110° F., or until the outside of the pan feels lukewarm to the hand. Add the vanilla. With an electric mixer at medium speed, or with a spoon, beat until the candy loses its gloss, and a small amount dropped from the spoon holds its shape ; add the nuts. Turn the mixture into the tin, but don't scrape the pan—the bits on the sides may be sugary. Cool and cut. Makes 1¼ lb.

Créole Cookery

CRÉOLE FISH IN COURT-BOUILLON

2 lb. cod or other fish, cut in steaks
1 large onion
1 green pepper
2 oz. butter
4 tomatoes
Juice of ½ lemon
Parsley, marjoram, crushed bay leaf and a little allspice
1 wineglassful claret
Salt and cayenne pepper
1 lemon

Prepare the fish. Mince the onion and the seeded green pepper and fry in butter until lightly coloured. Add the chopped tomatoes, herbs and allspice and cook for a few minutes, then stir in the lemon juice and claret, with a little water to thin the sauce if necessary. Season with salt and cayenne. Lay the fish in the sauce, cover and cook very gently for about 30 minutes, or until the fish is tender. Dish up and pour the sauce over the fish. (It should be of the consistency of thin cream.) Garnish with lemon slices.

"Court-bouillon," as used in New Orleans, means a sauce rather than the thin liquor used for cooking fish.

LA MÉDIATRICE
(THE PEACE-MAKER—OYSTER DISH)

Dip some oysters in flour, brush over with beaten egg yolk, season well and fry in deep fat for 3–4 minutes, until light gold. Drain well and pile into a prepared loaf or bread rolls. Garnish with sliced gherkins, put on the lid and serve at once.

To prepare the bread case, cut the top off a sandwich or similar loaf, scoop out the crumb, pour in a little melted butter and heat through in the oven.

The story behind the name given to this delicious dish is that when erring husbands were coming home in the small hours, they would buy a loaf straight from the baker's oven, have it filled with freshly fried oysters and present it as a peace-offering.

LOUISIANA CHICKEN PILAU

A 3 lb. ready-to-cook chicken
8 cups cold water
4 stalks of celery, sliced
1 large onion, sliced
6 parsley sprigs
Salt
6 rashers of bacon
1 large green pepper, chopped
¾ cup chopped onion
A can of whole okras, if available
Pepper
2½ cups rice
3 large tomatoes

Early in the day, or the day before, put the quartered chicken in a large covered pan with the water, celery, onion, parsley and 2 tbsps. salt and simmer for 1 hour, or until tender. Put the chicken in a large bowl, strain the chicken broth over it, cool and refrigerate until needed.

Cut the rashers into thirds and sauté till golden in a deep frying pan or saucepan ; drain on paper towels. Set aside 2 tbsps. of the bacon fat. In rest of the bacon fat sauté the green pepper, onion and okra (if used) with 1 tsp. salt and ¼ tsp. pepper ; cook for 3 minutes, stirring occasionally. Put into a dish. Pour into the pan 5 cups chicken broth and add the rice, 1 tsp. salt and ¼ tsp. pepper. Top with the onion mixture, cover and simmer for 15 minutes. Add the tomatoes, cover and simmer till the liquid is absorbed—15 minutes.

Meanwhile cut the chicken quarters in half, skin and, if desired, bone. Heat the chicken in the rest of the chicken broth. Remove a few of the okras from the rice mixture, then toss the rice together with the onion mixture and tomatoes. Pile in a hot dish and garnish with the sautéed bacon and the okras. 6 servings.

GOMBO AUX HERBES
(HERB GUMBO)

2–3 lb. brisket of veal
¾ lb. lean ham or gammon
A mixture of green vegetables, including young cabbage leaves
1 large onion
Butter or lard for frying
Thyme, marjoram and bay leaf
½ a red chilli
1 clove
A little allspice
Salt and pepper

Trim the fat from the veal and the ham and cut the meat into small cubes. Prepare the vegetables. Remove the midrib from the cabbage leaves, then parboil the leaves with the other greens (which might consist of equal amounts of turnip tops, spinach, radish tops, watercress and parsley). Drain well, retaining the water. Chop the onion. Heat the fat in a saucepan and brown the meat with the onion. Chop all the green vegetables finely, add them to the saucepan and cook until well browned, then put in the boiling

vegetable liquor, the herbs, chilli, spices and seasonings, bring to the boil and simmer for 1 hour. Serve with boiled rice.

CHICKEN CHANTECLAIR

Marinate a 3 lb. chicken for 24 hours in good claret with some chopped carrot, shallots, celery and 2 minced garlic cloves. Drain, season and sauté in butter, then stew in the wine with some strips of bacon and dried mushroom. Serve sprinkled with tarragon leaves.

LES GRILLADES
(STEAK IN TOMATO AND ONION SAUCE)

Despite its name, this dish is not a grill—the French word has become altered in meaning through its sojourn in Louisiana.

Cut some steak from the round of beef into pieces about 4 inches square, beat well and season with pepper and salt. Heat 1–2 tbsps. butter in a deep frying pan or wide saucepan and fry 2 chopped onions until golden in colour. Add ½ lb. cut-up tomatoes, crushing them with a wooden spoon ; season with salt, pepper and a little cayenne pepper and cook for about 10 minutes. Put in the steaks, add a little hot stock or water to thin the sauce mixture, cover the pan and simmer for about ½ hour, or until the steak is tender. From time to time add a little liquid as required and turn the meat over. To serve, put the steaks on a hot dish and pour the sauce over. Plain boiled rice or boiled hominy (Indian corn meal) makes a good accompaniment.

Slices of veal or gammon, cut rather less than ½ inch thick, may be cooked in the same way, and leftover cold meat may be reheated for 10 minutes in the same sort of sauce.

JAMBALAYA WITH SAUSAGES

½ lb. rice	4 tomatoes
1 large onion	1 lb. sausages
1 clove of garlic	1 small chilli
2 oz. butter	Salt and cayenne pepper

Cook the rice in boiling salted water until tender, drain and dry so that each grain is separate.

Chop the onion and garlic and fry in 1½ oz. butter until light golden-brown, add the sliced tomatoes and cook for several minutes. Grill or fry the sausages and cut into 2-inch lengths.

Put the rice, tomato mixture, sausages and any remaining butter into a pan and add the salt, cayenne pepper and the finely chopped chilli. Mix lightly, add an extra knob of butter, cover and cook over gentle heat for about 20 minutes.

W.C.B.—28

Crab meat, prawns or Dublin Bay prawns may be substituted for the sausages.

CANDIED SWEET POTATOES

6 medium-sized sweet potatoes	½ cup dark corn syrup or molasses
¼ cup butter or margarine	2 tbsps. water
	¼ cup brown sugar

Scrub the sweet potatoes, but do not peel ; cook in boiling water for 15 minutes ; cool, peel and halve lengthwise.

Heat the butter, corn syrup, water and sugar in a frying pan or shallow baking tin. Arrange the potatoes on top, cut sides down, and cook uncovered over a very low heat, basting occasionally, for about 1 hour, or until the potatoes are tender and well glazed. Makes 6 servings.

HOMINY

Soak ½ pint hominy overnight in cold water. Drain, put into 1 quart cold water with 1 tsp. salt, bring to the boil and simmer for 3–4 hours, until it is of the consistency of thick starch. Serve hot with meat. Hominy may also be eaten as a breakfast dish with milk or cream and sugar.

The slightly coarser meal known as grits (gru) is not soaked ; after being washed in cold water it is put into cold salted water (1 quart water and 1 tsp. salt to 1 cup grits) and brought to the boil, then simmered for 1 hour. It may be eaten in the same way as the hominy (saccamité) described above. It may also be spread out on a dish about ½ inch thick and, when cold, cut into small rounds which are seasoned, floured, dipped in beaten egg yolk and fried in hot butter, to eat with meat or bacon.

CALAS
(BREAKFAST RICE FRITTERS)

3 cups water	½ cup sugar
½ cup rice	3 tbsps. flour
Just under 1 oz. yeast	Lard or oil for deep
3 eggs	frying

Boil the water in a pan and add the rice ; cook until very soft and mushy, then allow to cool. Mix with the yeast, dissolved in warm water, and leave to rise overnight. The next day add the well-beaten eggs, sugar and flour, beat well to form a thick batter, then leave to rise again for about 15 minutes. Heat the fat or oil, drop the mixture in 1 tbsp. at a time and fry till golden. Drain well, sprinkle with sugar and serve very hot.

A COMPLETELY distinctive national cuisine takes centuries to grow up, so it would be unreasonable to expect it of a comparatively young country like Canada. Canadian territories were at first mainly colonised by two large groups which took with them their ready-made traditions—the French and the British. More recently, of course, the United States has exerted an ever-increasing influence, while other contributions come from the original Red Indian inhabitants and from the newest immigrants from Central Europe, who cling to their own familiar cookery traditions.

Side by side with this gradually emerging " national " cuisine are the various regional specialities. Because Canada is such an immense country the climatic conditions vary considerably. In the early years this had a great influence on the foods available and on the dishes that could be produced from them—fish chowders on the east coast, bison, elk and venison meat inland, seal liver in the north, salmon in the west—and in many cases the regional dishes based on local products are still jealously guarded.

Canadians eat a great deal of fruit and often include it in savoury dishes, serving pineapple, for instance, with bacon and ham and cranberries with turkey. They grow first-class apples, peaches and strawberries (with the additional boon of delicious wild strawberries), grapes and melons; native fruits include blueberries, Saskatoon berries and chokeberries.

There is a wide range of vegetables, including sweet corn, sweet potatoes and wild rice; many of them are served raw, alone or in salads. Salads indeed, are one of the delights of the Canadian table, featuring imaginative and unusual combinations of ingredients.

Canadians enjoy good meat, bacon, poultry and game; dairy products are plentiful; and excellent fish abounds. Other specialities are the various breads, cakes and puddings made with corn (maize); the cakes and cookies and the pancakes which are so delicious served with maple syrup.

French Canadians have clung very tenaciously to their ancestral cookery traditions as they have to their religion and language and they still live a life which is somewhat apart from the rest of the country. A few of their recipes are included here, including the famous French Canadian Pea Soup.

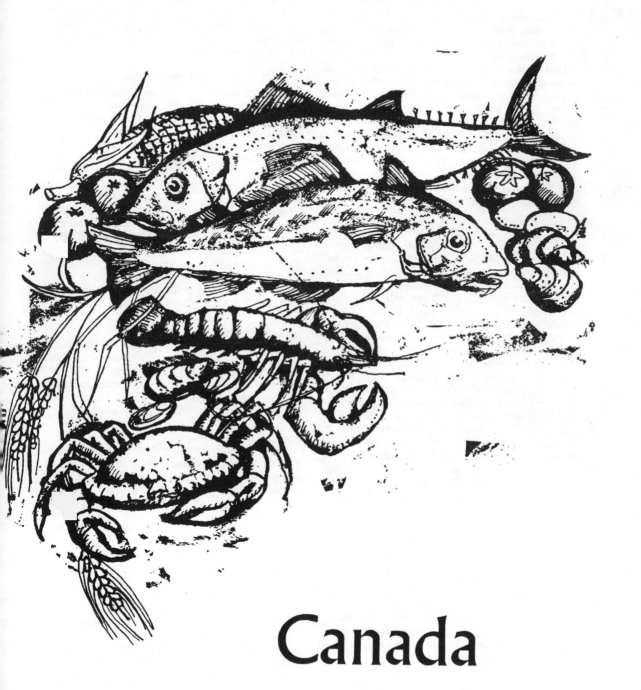

Canada

152

FRENCH CANADIAN PEA SOUP

1 lb. dried whole or split peas	1 small turnip
1 lb. bacon	Seasoning
3 pints water	Parsley

Soak peas in cold water overnight. Soak bacon in separate water overnight. Strain peas, cover with clean, cold water, bring to boil and strain. (This will help to prevent the formation of scum during cooking.) Place peas and bacon in large pan with 3 pints water, add prepared turnip and seasoning. Bring to boil, simmer gently for 2–3 hours, until tender. Remove bacon and either serve separately, or mince or dice finely and serve added to the soup. Garnish with parsley and serve with crisp rolls.

ST. LAWRENCE CHOWDER

2 oz. bacon fat	$\frac{2}{3}$ pint boiling water
2 onions, chopped	1 large can tomatoes
4 tbsps. carrots, finely chopped	3 $7\frac{1}{2}$-oz. tins minced clams
4 tbsps. celery, finely chopped	1 tsp. salt
	$\frac{1}{4}$ tsp. thyme
2 medium potatoes, peeled and diced	A dash of pepper
	Cream crackers

Melt fat in a saucepan, add the onions, carrots and celery, cover pan and cook over very low heat 10 minutes. Add potatoes with boiling water and cook 15 minutes or until vegetables are nearly tender. Cut the tomatoes into pieces, add and bring to boiling point only. Stir in the clams and seasonings and simmer gently 10 minutes. Correct seasoning and serve with cream crackers. Yields 4 hearty servings.

SALMON BURGERS

1 can ($15\frac{1}{2}$ oz.) salmon	1 tbsp. finely chopped onion
$2\frac{1}{2}$ oz. soft breadcrumbs	
$\frac{1}{2}$ tsp. salt	1 egg, well beaten
$\frac{1}{8}$ tsp. pepper	Fat for frying

Empty contents of can into bowl. Flake the salmon, mash the bones and mix with the salmon liquid. Add the breadcrumbs, salt, pepper and onion and mix lightly. Add egg and mix well. Shape into 8 patties and fry until browned on one side. Turn and brown the other side. Makes 8 salmon burgers. Serve with fluffy mashed potatoes, green peas and raw tomato slices.

BAKED MACKEREL WITH FAT PORK

Wash and clean as many mackerel as required. Take some slices of fat pork, lay them at the bottom of a pan, cover with the mackerel and add more slices of pork on top. Season with plenty of salt and pepper. If the pork is not fat enough, add some more fat such as pork dripping. Cover, put in a slow oven (325° F., mark 2) and bake slowly for 1 hour.

LAKE TROUT WITH DRESSING

2 lb. lake trout fillets	1 tsp. mixed poultry seasoning
2 tsps. salt	$\frac{1}{2}$ medium onion, minced
4 breakfastcups dry breadcrumbs	4 tbsps. butter

Wipe the fillets with a damp cloth. Sprinkle with 1 tsp. of salt and place them in a buttered baking dish. Mix the breadcrumbs, seasoning and remaining salt. Heat the butter, lightly fry the onion and stir into the breadcrumbs. Arrange the stuffing over the fish and cover. Bake in a moderately hot oven (400° F., mark 6), allowing 10 minutes per lb. of fish. Remove the cover after 10 minutes' baking, to allow stuffing to brown.

Poultry seasoning is the same as used in forcemeat stuffing, sage, thyme, etc.

SALMON À LA KING

1 cup ($15\frac{1}{2}$ oz.) salmon	$1\frac{1}{2}$ cups liquid (liquid from canned salmon plus milk)
$\frac{1}{3}$ cup chopped celery	
$\frac{1}{2}$ cup chopped green pepper	1 cup canned mushrooms, sliced
$\frac{1}{4}$ cup butter, melted	2 tbsps. chopped pimiento
$\frac{1}{4}$ cup flour	
$\frac{1}{2}$ tsp. salt	
1 tsp. garlic salt (optional)	

Drain salmon, and save liquid. Break salmon into bite-sized chunks. Combine celery and green pepper in melted butter and cook over low heat until vegetables are tender. Blend in flour and salt. Add combined salmon liquid and milk gradually. Cook and stir until the sauce is thick and smooth. Add the salmon, mushrooms, pimiento and, if desired, garlic salt. Heat thoroughly. Serve in patty shells, toast cups or on cooked rice. Makes 6 servings.

TUNA BAKE WITH CHEESE SWIRLS

3 tbsps. chopped onion	1 can condensed chicken soup with rice
$\frac{1}{2}$ small green pepper, chopped	
3 tbsps. fat	$\frac{2}{3}$ pint milk
1 tsp. salt	A 7 oz. can tuna, flaked
6 tbsps. plain flour	1 tbsp. lemon juice

Cook the onion and pepper in the hot fat till golden, then add salt and flour and blend together. Add soup and milk, then cook, stirring often till thick. Add flaked tuna, lemon

15

juice. Pour into greased dish. Cover with swirls (below). Bake in a hot oven (450° F., mark 8) for 15 minutes, then reduce the heat to 425° F. (mark 7) for 15 minutes. Serve with salad. (6 portions.)

CHEESE SWIRLS

9 oz. plain flour	¼ pint milk
½ tsp. salt	3 oz. grated cheese
¾ tsp. baking powder	

Sift flour, salt, baking powder until it resembles coarse crumbs. Add milk all at once and mix with a fork. Turn out on a floured surface, knead gently for ½ minute. Roll out ¼ inch thick and sprinkle with the cheese. Roll as for Swiss roll and cut in ½-inch slices. Place cut side down on hot tuna mixture.

BAKED HALIBUT FILLETS

54

1 tbsp. fat	1 small piece of bay
1 tsp. chopped onion	leaf
2 tomatoes	6 halibut fillets
1 green pepper, sliced	Juice of 1 lemon
Salt	Hollandaise sauce
Pepper	

Melt the fat, add the onion and cook slowly until soft. Arrange the tomatoes, peeled and sliced thickly, in the bottom of a shallow baking dish. Overlap with slices of green pepper. Sprinkle with the onion and seasonings. Cover with the fish fillets; sprinkle with the lemon juice and seasoning and cover. Bake in a moderate oven (350° F., mark 4) for 20–30 minutes until the fish is tender and flakes easily. Remove the cover, pour the hollandaise sauce over and brown under the grill.

HOLLANDAISE SAUCE

3 dessertsps. butter	A dash of cayenne pepper
2 yolks of eggs	2 tbsps. boiling water
¼ tsp. salt	1 tbsp. lemon juice

Cream the butter and add the beaten yolks. Add the seasoning and water. Cook over water, boiling very gently until the sauce is thick; stir constantly. Remove from the heat and add lemon juice. Serve at once with fish steaks, baked or grilled fish, hot asparagus or broccoli.

OYSTER STEW

1 pint light cream	¾ tsp. salt
2 tbsps. fine cracker	A dash of pepper
crumbs	Parsley
1 pint oysters	Green onions or
2 tbsps. butter	chives

Heat the cream and crumbs in the top of a double boiler. Add the juice from the oysters, the seasoning and the butter. when the cream is hot Cook until the oysters are plump and the edges begin to curl. Serve at once. Sprinkle with chopped green onions, chives or parsley.

STUFFED STEAK

155

1 slice of round steak	Chopped parsley
Salt and pepper	Butter
¼ lb. chopped boiled	Chopped onions
tongue	Mushroom sauce

The slice of steak must be not less than ½ inch thick and neatly shaped, trimmings being used for stock or gravy. Cut the slice of steak into halves, crosswise. On the lower half, sprinkle salt, pepper, chopped parsley and a few small bits of butter. Put the chopped tongue in the centre and cover the whole thing with the other half of the steak, fastening them securely together by deep stitches, using thin string and a trussing or big darning needle for the job. Cover the top with a thick layer of finely chopped onions, bits of butter, salt and pepper. Put the steak in a tin, add a cup of either water or stock to it and small cut-up pieces of the beef fat or suet. Bake in a moderately hot oven (400° F., mark 6) for ¾ hour, basting 3 or 4 times. When done, remove string and serve with a rich mushroom sauce.

GASPÉ BOILED DINNER

Put a large piece of lean salt pork into a black iron pot. Cover with cold water and boil for one hour. Drain and add fresh water, boil again. About half an hour before the pork is ready, add some peeled whole potatoes and dumplings the size of an egg. Place these on top of the potatoes but take care the water does not boil over the dumplings or they will be heavy. Boil for 20 minutes, or longer, or until the potatoes are cooked. Serve with molasses.

TORTIÈRE
(PORK PIE)

2 lb. veal and lean	½ tsp. nutmeg
shoulder of pork	A dash of mace and
Water	cayenne pepper
1 onion	¼ tsp. celery salt
1 clove of garlic	Pastry (as in recipe
1 tsp. salt	for Pork and Veal
¼ tsp. pepper	Pie)

Chop the meat finely and place in a saucepan with the water, seasonings and any bones and trimmings. Cover the saucepan and simmer for about 1 hour, until the meat is tender, adding water, if necessary, as the meat cooks. The mixture should be thick. As an alternative, brown the meat, onions and some bacon before adding the water. Remove the bone, season if necessary and allow the mixture to cook. Prepare the pastry (see next recipe) and line 2 8-inch tins. Fill with the meat mixture and add a top crust which has been slit to let the steam escape. Bake in a moderately hot oven (425° F., mark 7) for 40 minutes. Serve hot with chilli sauce or other relishes.

PORK AND VEAL PIE

Filling

1 lb. pork, minced	1 tsp. salt
½ lb. veal, minced	¼ tsp. black pepper
3 oz. salt pork, minced	2 tsps. gelatine
2 cups (6) onions, minced	1¼ cups highly seasoned stock or bouillon
¼ tsp. ground allspice	

Pastry Dough

1 cup flour	⅛ tsp. salt
⅓ cup butter	½ egg
1½ tbsps. lard	1 tsp. milk

Mix minced meats together. Put in a heated pan with onions and let meat brown in its own fat. Add allspice, salt and pepper. Prepare pastry dough by cutting butter, lard and salt into flour and working with finger-tips. Add egg and milk and allow to chill for 1 hour. Roll out and line bottom and sides of buttered baking dish, leaving enough dough to cover pie. Put the mixture in dish, cover with remaining dough and cut out a hole in centre of the top crust. Bake in a moderately hot oven (425° F., mark 7), lowering the heat if the crust browns too quickly. Cook for 1½ or 2 hours and when the pie is done remove it from the oven. Mix gelatine with bouillon and pour through hole in crust. Let the pie cool and chill so gelatine sets. Cut in thick slices to serve. Can also be eaten hot.

GAME

Game is protected in Canada and may be shot only during the hunting season. The amount of game which may be taken home by the hunter is regulated by the government. Deer or venison is likely to be the most common. Moose, bear and buffalo are less common. Buffalo meat is available in the shops in Alberta when the size of the herds in one of the national parks is reduced by the government. The meat is usually roasted or grilled.

GRILLED VENISON STEAK

Rub each steak with a cut clove of garlic and softened butter. Grill quickly, unless the steaks are very thick. Turn once. Season with salt and pepper. Flavour the drippings with a little sherry and pour over the steaks.

ELK WITH SOUR CREAM SAUCE

Lard the underneath of the joint with fat ham or bacon. Fry in butter till coloured and moisten with a pint of sour cream, pepper, 2 cloves, bay leaf and ½ pint of white wine. Braise slowly for 3 hours, basting frequently with the sauce. Skim off the fat from the sauce, squeeze in the juice of ½ a lemon and a little coarse pepper from the pepper-mill.

WILD RICE

This is a superb accompaniment to game but expensive for everyday eating.

1 cup wild rice	1½ tsps. salt
2 cups cold water	

Wash the rice in several waters and place in a saucepan with the cold water and salt. Cover and bring slowly to the boil once, reduce heat and stir with a fork so that it does not stick. Boil without stirring for about 30–40 minutes or until the rice is tender. Drain and shake gently over the heat to dry. Season with salt, pepper and butter.

As a variation, add sautéed mushrooms and a little chopped parsley to the cooked rice ; chicken stock may be used instead of plain water.

APPLE AND TUNA SALAD

A 7-oz. can tuna fish	2 tbsps. lemon juice
2 cups unpeeled diced red apple	1 cup celery, diced
	½ cup salad dressing

Drain the tuna fish ; rinse in lukewarm water, drain again, flake and chill. Sprinkle the apples with the lemon juice to prevent discoloration and combine with the tuna, celery and salad dressing.

SCALLOPED POTATOES

2 tbsps. flour	1 medium onion, sliced or chopped
2 tsps. salt	
⅛ tsp. pepper	2 tbsps. butter
6 medium potatoes, thinly sliced	⅔ pint milk

Mix the flour, salt and pepper. Arrange one-third of the potatoes in a greased casserole, sprinkle with half the flour mixture and dot with half the butter. Add half the onion. Cover with another third of the potatoes and add the remaining flour mixture, butter and onion. Top with remaining potatoes. Pour milk over the top. Cover and bake in a moderate oven (350° F., mark 4) until milk comes to a gentle boil, about

45 minutes. Uncover and continue baking until potatoes are tender and top is lightly browned—30–35 minutes longer. (Total time 75–78 minutes. Makes 6–8 servings.)

Variations : Add sliced ham or chunks of sausage or frankfurters between the potato.

SALAD PLATTER

Cottage cheese	Tomato wedges
Lettuce	Celery hearts
Asparagus tips, cooked	Green pepper rings
Turnip sticks	Sprigs of parsley
Carrot sticks	

Pile cottage cheese into a lettuce cup. Arrange vegetables attractively around cheese. Garnish with green pepper rings and sprigs of parsley. Serve at a buffet lunch or supper with a choice of dressings in side dishes.

WALDORF SALAD

Mix lightly together diced unpared apple (red skin is most eye-appealing) with half as much diced celery. Sprinkle with a little lemon juice. Add some broken walnut halves (as many as you desire). Toss with mayonnaise or salad dressing to moisten and chill. Serve on crisp lettuce or in apples scooped out to form cups. Garnish with Maraschino cherries.

POTATO BALLS

2 lb. potatoes	1 beaten egg
4 oz. breadcrumbs	Egg and breadcrumbs
½ tsp. nutmeg	Fat for deep frying
Salt and pepper	

Cook the potatoes in boiling salted water. Mash the potatoes thoroughly and stir in the breadcrumbs and seasonings. Bind with the beaten egg. Shape the mixture into nut-sized pieces. Egg and breadcrumb the balls, and deep-fry until they are a golden-brown colour. Drain on absorbent paper before serving.

SCRAPPLE

Heat to boiling point, ⅛ pint water in a saucepan. Mix 4¾ oz. corn meal and 1 tsp. salt with 1½ gills cold water. Pour the mixture into the boiling water, stirring constantly, and cook until thickened, stirring frequently. Cover, and continue to cook over a low heat for 1 minute. Pour the cooked corn meal into a greased loaf pan and cool. Cover to prevent a crust from forming, and chill overnight. When it is firm and cold, cut into ¼-inch slices, dip in flour and sauté in bacon fat or butter, until crisp and nicely browned on both sides. Serve hot for breakfast, with butter and syrup, honey or jelly or to accompany crisp bacon or small sausages. For a crisper crust, dip the slices in cornmeal, then sauté. Wonderful on a chilly morning !

CABBAGE SLAW

1 small cabbage, finely shredded	½ green pepper, diced
1 tsp. salt	½ tsp. caraway seeds
1 medium red apple (diced but not peeled)	Salad dressing or mayonnaise to moisten
2 sticks chopped celery	

Combine above ingredients and toss lightly with a fork. Serve immediately in lettuce cups.

QUICK BAKED BEANS

1 medium-sized onion, minced	1 tbsp. molasses
4 strips of bacon, diced	2 oz. maple syrup
2 large tins baked beans (with pork)	½ tsp. dry mustard

Sauté the onion in the bacon fat until it is yellow and the bacon crisp. Stir in the remaining ingredients, and pour into a greased 1½-quart casserole. Bake uncovered in a moderate oven (350° F., mark 4) until the beans are brown and bubbly—about 45 minutes. Serve hot.

STIR 'N' STIR PASTRY

½ lb. vegetable fat	1 level tsp. salt
2 oz. butter	¾ gill cold water
12 oz. flour	

Cream the vegetable fat and the butter thoroughly. Gradually add the sieved flour and salt, creaming well after each addition. Add the water, and mix thoroughly. The mixture will be sticky at first and will be rather difficult to stir. When rolling out this pastry, use plenty of flour on the board. The dough can be kept in the refrigerator for 10 days at least. After storing it in this way, allow it to stand at room temperature to soften before rolling out.

GRILLED CHEESE SANDWICHES

For each serving, place sliced American processed cheese between 2 slices of bread. Spread butter over the outside of both bread slices. Brown lightly on both sides in a heavy frying pan and serve immediately, garnished with paper-thin slices of dill pickle.

EGG SALAD

6 hard-boiled eggs	Salt
2 or 3 small green onions	Mayonnaise or salad dressing
1 or 2 large stalks celery	

156

Cut eggs, onions and celery into medium-sized pieces. Season to taste. Add dressing to moisten. Toss lightly with two forks.

Egg salad may be served on crisp greens. It may also be used to stuff tomatoes, hollowed-out cucumber halves, celery or sliced ham rolls.

WALNUT PIE

2 eggs	2 tbsps. soft butter
4 oz. Demerara sugar	$\frac{1}{2}$ tsp. vanilla essence
6 oz. molasses or	4 oz. halved walnuts
maple syrup	7–8 inch raw pastry shell

Beat the eggs lightly. Add the sugar, molasses, butter and vanilla, blend well, then stir in the walnuts. Pour into the pastry case and bake in a moderately hot oven (425° F., mark 7) for 10 minutes ; reduce to moderate (350° F., mark 4) and bake for a further 30 minutes. Serve cold or slightly warm. Hand whipped cream separately. As an alternative to molasses or maple syrup, use either golden syrup, black treacle or half and half.

APPLE PIE

4 or 5 sour Canadian-grown apples	$\frac{1}{2}$ cup sugar
	$\frac{2}{3}$ tsp. salt
1 tsp. nutmeg or cinnamon	1 tsp. lemon juice and a few gratings
1 tsp. butter	of lemon rind

Plain Pastry

$1\frac{1}{2}$ cups pastry flour	$\frac{1}{2}$ tsp. salt
$\frac{1}{3}$–$\frac{1}{2}$ cup shortening	$\frac{1}{4}$ tsp. baking
Iced water to make a stiff dough	powder

Mix and sift the dry ingredients ; rub in half the shortening. Add the iced water and roll out the dough on a floured board. Put the remaining shortening on $\frac{2}{3}$ of top in small pieces. Fold pastry, pat and roll out ; repeat several times.

Combine all the filling ingredients and place in a small earthenware baking dish, then add hot water to prevent apples from burning. Cover closely and bake 3 hours in a slow oven (325° F., mark 2) when apples will be a dark red colour. Brown sugar may be used instead of white sugar, a little more being required. Cool and bake between two crusts of the pastry.

BLUEBERRY PIE

Pastry	A pinch of salt
$\frac{3}{4}$ lb. fresh blueberries (bilberries), washed	2 tbsps. plain flour
	1 tbsp. lemon juice
3 oz. sugar	1 tbsp. butter
$\frac{1}{4}$ tsp. cinnamon	

Line a 9-inch pie plate with pastry. Mix the sugar, cinnamon, salt and flour, sprinkle some on the bottom of the pie. Alternate the layers of berries and sugar mixture, finishing with the berries. Add the lemon juice and dots of butter. Cover with a top crust or lattice of pastry. Bake in a moderately hot oven (400° F., mark 6) for 30 minutes.

MAPLE CREAM SAUCE

1 cup maple syrup (8 fl. oz.)	1 tbsp. butter
	$\frac{1}{2}$ tsp. vanilla
8 tbsps. cream	essence

Boil the syrup and cream to the soft ball stage (230° F.). Add butter and vanilla and beat until it is of the consistency of cream. Serve with ice cream or sponge puddings.

PEANUT BUTTER COOKIES

4 oz. peanut butter	1 egg
4 oz. butter	3 oz. chopped raisins
Grated rind of 1 orange	4 oz. plain flour
3 oz. soft brown sugar	$\frac{3}{4}$ tsp. baking powder
4 oz. caster sugar	

Cream peanut butter, butter and orange rind with the sugars till light and fluffy. Beat in the egg, add the raisins and stir in the sieved flour and baking powder. Pinch off small pieces of dough, roll each into a small ball the size of a walnut and place on an ungreased baking sheet. Dip a fork in flour and press lines criss-cross fashion on each ball. Bake in a moderate oven (350° F., mark 4) 12–15 minutes till golden.

RUM AND BUTTER TARTLETS

5 oz. currants	$\frac{1}{2}$ tsp. rum essence
$1\frac{1}{2}$ oz. butter	1 egg, well beaten
2 oz. cream or top of the milk	Pastry for unbaked tart cases
$7\frac{1}{2}$ oz. soft brown sugar	

Pour boiling water over the currants and allow them to stand until soft, then drain. Melt the butter, add the cream, sugar, rum essence and prepared currants. Blend in the egg, then fill the tart cases. Bake in a moderate oven (375° F., mark 5), until pastry and filling are a light golden-brown.

SUNNY CORN BREAD

$4\frac{3}{4}$ oz. cornmeal	1 egg
4 oz. flour	$1\frac{1}{2}$ gills (8 oz.)
2 oz. granulated sugar	milk
$\frac{1}{2}$ tsp. salt	2 oz. butter
2 tsps. baking powder	

Sieve the dry ingredients together into a bowl. Add the egg, milk and butter and beat with the beaten egg until smooth—about 1 minute. Do not overbeat. Bake in a greased 8-inch square pan or in a greased bun tray in a moderately hot oven (425° F., mark 7) for 25 minutes. Serve warm with butter or covered with creamed chicken, fish or meat. In Canada it is eaten as a breakfast hot bread with butter and maple syrup.

DATE AND NUT MERINGUES

2 egg whites	6 oz. stoned dates
6½ oz. caster sugar	3 oz. chopped walnuts
1 tsp. cornflour	

Whisk the egg whites until stiff. Add the sugar and cornflour. Place in the top of a double boiler and cook for 7 minutes, stirring constantly. Add the dates and nuts. Drop in teaspoonfuls on a buttered baking sheet. Bake in a slow oven (300° F., mark 1) for 30 minutes or until golden-brown. Makes 12 large meringues.

BAKED FRESH PEARS

4 fresh pears	2 tbsps. maple syrup
6 tbsps. orange juice	

Cut the pears in half lengthwise, remove the core and place cut side up in a casserole. Fill the centres with the orange juice. Drizzle with maple syrup and bake in a moderate oven (350° F., mark 4) for 20 minutes, or until the pears are tender, when tested with the point of a knife.

As a variation, omit the orange juice and bake the pears in enough maple syrup to cover. Add a sprinkling of ginger.

MAPLE SYRUP FUDGE

1 cup maple syrup	½ cup single cream
2 cups sugar	1 cup chopped walnuts
2 tbsps. butter	

Combine all the ingredients in a saucepan with the exception of the nuts. Stir over the heat until the sugar is dissolved. Boil gently without stirring to the soft ball stage or 238° F. on the candy thermometer. Cool to lukewarm and beat until the colour changes and the candy begins to set. Stir in the chopped nuts and turn into a buttered pan. When firm, mark into squares.

MAPLE SYRUP CREAM

¾ pint milk	2 egg yolks, beaten
3 tbsps. cornflour	2 tbsps. butter
½ tsp. salt	2 egg whites
20 tbsps. maple syrup	

Heat the milk in the top of a double boiler. Combine the cornflour, salt and 16 tbsps. syrup;

add to the hot milk and stir until thick. Add a little hot mixture to the beaten egg yolks and stir into the cornflour. Cook over boiling water until the mixture thickens again. Add the butter and cool slightly. Beat the egg whites with the remaining 4 tbsps. maple syrup until stiff. Fold into the mixture. Serve cold.

FRYING PAN COOKIES

6 oz. brown sugar	1½ oz. chopped walnuts
2 well-beaten eggs	20 chopped red Mara-
12 oz. chopped dates	schino cherries
¼ tsp. salt	1 oz. rice crispies
1 tsp. vanilla essence	1½ oz. coconut

Beat the sugar and eggs together; add the chopped dates. Place the mixture in a slightly greased frying pan and cook for 10–12 minutes, stirring constantly. Remove the mixture from the heat; add the salt, vanilla, chopped nuts, cherries and cereal and mix thoroughly. Cool the mixture until lukewarm, shape into balls and then roll each in coconut. Makes approximately 40 cookies.

BLUEBERRY CAKE

1½ breakfastcups flour	3 oz. butter
1 breakfastcup sugar	½ breakfastcup milk
2 eggs	2 tsps. baking
½ tsp. lemon flavouring	powder
1 breakfastcup blueberries	A pinch of salt

Beat the eggs until light. Cream the butter. Gradually add the sugar. When the mixture is very creamy, add the eggs. Sift the flour, salt and baking powder together. Add the flour alternately with the milk to the creamed butter. Add the lemon flavouring.

Butter a medium-sized loaf tin. Half fill it with blueberries and pour the mixture over them. Bake in a moderate oven (375° F., mark 5) for about 40 or 50 minutes.

Blackberries can also be used for this cake.

PORK CAKE

1 lb. salt pork	2 tsps. ground cinnamon
1 pint boiling water	2 tsps. ground nutmeg
1 breakfastcup	1 lb. currants
molasses	1 lb. raisins
1 breakfastcup jam	½ lb. candied peel
4 breakfastcups flour	½ lb. chopped nuts
1 tsp. bicarbonate of	2 beaten egg yolks
soda	2 stiffly beaten egg
1 tsp. ground cloves	whites
1 tsp. ground ginger	1 tsp. grated lemon rind

Clean and pick over the fruit. Mince or dice the pork very finely, discarding any bits of lean meat. Cover with boiling water and leave to stand for 5 minutes. Add the molasses, jam and bicarbonate, and stir until the molasses is well dissolved. Add the egg yolks, sift the flour with the spices and add this to the cake mixture alternately with the fruit and nuts. When these ingredients are well blended, add the finely chopped peel and the lemon rind. Lastly, fold in the stiffly beaten egg whites.

Line two oblong cake tins, roughly 8 inches by 3 inches, with greaseproof paper and pour the cake mixture into them. Bake in a very slow oven (275° F., mark ½) for 2½ hours.

The cakes are better stored for a week or two before eating.

MATRIMONIAL CAKE

4½ oz. rolled oats	6 oz. butter, melted
5 oz. plain flour	1 tsp. bicarbonate of
1 tsp. lemon flavouring	soda
9 oz. soft brown sugar	Date filling (below)

Mix the flour with rolled oats. Add the lemon flavouring, sugar and melted butter, stir with a fork. Add the bicarbonate of soda. Press half of this mixture on the bottom of a well-greased 13- by 9-inch oblong pan. Spread with the cooled date filling and cover with the remaining crumb mixture, patting lightly. Bake until lightly browned, in a moderate oven (375° F., mark 5) for 45 minutes. Cut into finger lengths or squares to serve.

DATE FILLING

8 oz. stoned dates	1 tsp. lemon flavouring
3 dessertsps. soft brown sugar	Water to cover the mixture

Place the above ingredients in a saucepan and bring to the boil, then simmer gently until thick and smooth. Cool.

NANAIMO BARS
First Part

4 oz. butter	1 tsp. vanilla essence
1½ oz. caster sugar	6 oz. graham wafers
3 tbsps. cocoa	2¼ oz. coconut
1 beaten egg	2 oz. chopped nuts

Second Part

2 oz. butter	2 tbsps. custard powder
9 oz. icing sugar	3 tbsps. hot water

Third Part

2 oz. plain chocolate	1 oz. icing sugar
3 tbsps. butter	

Place the butter, sugar and cocoa in the top of a double boiler. Stir until blended. Add the egg and vanilla and cook for 1 minute. Remove from the heat. Make the wafers into crumbs. Add these with the coconut and walnuts. It is quite a stiff mixture. Pat into a greased 9- by 5-inch pan and place in the refrigerator for ½ hour. Cook the second part together. Spread over the first part and return to the refrigerator for a further ½ hour. Melt the chocolate and butter. Add the icing sugar and spread over the top of the second layer. Let it stand until firm, then cut into bars.

DATE BRAN MUFFINS

3½ oz. sieved plain flour	2 tbsps. soft shortening
½ tsp. salt	3 tbsps. caster sugar
3 tsps. baking powder	1 beaten egg
2 oz. bran	4 oz. chopped dates
½ pint less 3 tbsps. milk	

Start heating the oven to moderately hot (400° F., mark 6). Grease well about 12 2½-inch muffin pan cups. Sieve the flour, salt, baking powder. Soak the bran in the milk for 5 minutes. Meanwhile, in a small bowl, beat the shortening and sugar until light, add the beaten egg, stir until smooth. Add to the bran mixture and stir. Add the flour mixture and dates, stirring only until just mixed, no longer. Fill the muffin cups two-thirds full. Bake for 25 minutes, or until done. Makes 12 muffins.

DATE CAKE

6 oz. flour	About 12 dates, stoned and chopped
4 oz. rolled oats	
6 oz. brown sugar	¼ pint water (good
5 oz. butter or margarine	measure

Mix the dry ingredients and rub in the fat. Cook the dates with the water until soft. Place half the crumble mixture at the bottom of an 8-inch square greased tin, cover with dates, and then add remaining crumble mixture. Press well down and bake in a moderate oven (375° F., mark 5) for 1¼ hours; allow to cool slightly before turning it out.

SUGAR AND CREAM PIE

Make enough flaky pastry for a 9-inch pie.

Line a 9-inch baking dish with flaky pastry. Fill it ¾ full with maple sugar. Sprinkle 2 oz. of sifted flour over this. Moisten the sugar and flour with fresh cream. Do not add too much cream or the sugar will become soggy. Add some blanched and chopped walnuts and a chunk of butter. Cover with a lattice-work of flaky pastry. Bake in a hot oven (450° F., mark 8) until the pastry is a light golden colour.

HONEY DROPS

8 oz. butter (or part butter and part homogenised cooking fat)
7 oz. soft brown sugar
2 eggs
4 tbsps. honey
1 tsp. vanilla
14 oz. plain flour
1 tsp. bicarbonate of soda

Mix the fat, soft brown sugar and eggs together thoroughly. Stir in the honey and vanilla. Sieve the flour and baking soda together and add to the mixture. Stir. Chill until firm, several hours or overnight. Heat oven to moderate (350° F., mark 4). Roll dough into balls the size of walnuts. Place on an ungreased baking sheet. Bake for 10–12 minutes or until almost no imprint remains when touched lightly with the finger. When slightly cooled, put together in pairs with apricot or other jam.

Makes approximately 2–3 dozen pairs of cakes, depending on size.

RELATIVELY little is known in England about Mexican cuisine, its long development, its almost unique raw materials and its vivid contrast to other basic cuisines. It has much in common with its neighbours in Central and South America but its own character remains strong and unmistakable.

Maize, the cereal upon and around which Mexican cuisine is built, is essentially a cultivated plant ; in its wild state it is little better than a grass and cannot be used for food. Its original cultivation was said to be the work of the great Quetzalcoatl, the plumed serpent god of the ancient Maya civilisation.

Mexico is the home of many foodstuffs which, since the Spanish conquest, have found their way all over the world. These include tomatoes, beans, vanilla, potatoes, aubergines, pumpkins, avocados, chocolate, chillies in many forms and both cashews and peanuts. Many herbs and spices grow in both wild and cultivated forms and the Mexican makes much use of orégano (wild marjoram), wild mint, wild celery, black sage, bay leaves, coriander, cumin, anise and cloves.

Sauce-making in Mexico is a fine art and was already highly developed by the sixteenth century. Sauces were devised especially to complement different meats and vegetables, the most famous of all being *Mole*. There are several variations of *Mole* : one *Il Gran Mole*, traditionally calls for five kinds of chillies, almonds, pecans, peanuts and avocados, raisins, peppercorns, cinnamon, cloves and chocolate—a list of twenty-seven ingredients in all.

The backbone of Mexican diet consists of maize, beans and chilli. The maize is ground and made into flat, thin cakes called *tortillas*, which are eaten in many ways. Filled with a mixture of meat, beans and chilli they become *tacos* and can be eaten either as they are or crisply fried and they are sometimes smothered in sauce and served as *enchiladas*. The Mexican will roll his own *tacos*, choosing the filling from various bowls of meat, sauce and vegetables. There is a real art in the rolling, so that the filling does not fall out of one end while the *tacos* are being eaten. Tortillas can be used as a kind of edible scoop for eating thick bean soups or meat stews and are even served as a sweet, combined with sugar, nuts and spices.

Fruit juices, chocolate and barley water flavoured with cinnamon are among the favourite Mexican soft drinks ; several kinds of spirits are distilled and Mexican beer has a very high reputation.

Mexican dishes are traditionally cooked in clay casseroles or pots. The variety of ingredients used is very wide and many dishes are most complicated in preparation, great imaginative use being made of a large range of herbs and condiments.

Mexico and
Central America

CALDO TLALPENO
(CHICKEN AND PEA SOUP)

Chick peas   Sliced avocado
Chicken broth   (optional)
Boiled chicken   Chopped onions
Chile chipotle

Simmer the chick peas in rich chicken broth until tender. To serve, add a whole piece of boiled chicken, *chile chipotle* (see page 450) and, if liked, sliced avocado and chopped onions.

SOPA DE QUESO
(CHEESE SOUP)

Chicken stock   Strong cheese
Sliced green *chile poblano*

With the chicken stock boil the sliced green *chile poblano* (see page 455). Before serving, melt the cheese into the boiling mixture.

The Mexican cook uses either Oaxaca or Chihuahua cheese.

FISH SOUP

158

1 lb. white fish head   1 chilli in vinegar
1 lb. white fish fillets   A pinch of ground
2 bay leaves   cinnamon
2 medium-sized onions   Fresh herbs (thyme,
1 garlic clove   marjoram, bay leaf,
6 oz. small peas   parsley, etc.)
Oil for frying   Salt and pepper
¾ lb. tomatoes   1 small tin mushrooms
4 oz. olives   Fried croûtons

Boil all the fish in 5 pints water with the bay leaves, 1 onion and the garlic. When cooked, take the bones out and shred the fish; strain the liquid. Cook the peas separately. Chop the other onion and fry for a while. Grill, chop and sieve the tomatoes, and add. Simmer until the mixture has thickened a little, then add the liquid in which the fish was boiled, the olives, chopped chilli, cinnamon and the fresh herbs. Let it simmer for 5 minutes; take out the herbs, season with salt and pepper and put in the fish, peas and the chopped mushrooms together with their juice. Cook for a few minutes and re-season if necessary. Serve with little squares of fried bread. Some people like lemon with it.

APPLE SOUP

3 sweet apples   Salt and pepper
2 tsps. flour   1 tsp. parsley,
4 oz. butter   chopped very
½ lb. tomatoes   finely
1 medium-sized onion   1 small glass of
3 pints chicken or beef broth   dry sherry

Peel and dice the apples and put into a quart of water with a spoonful of salt (this is to prevent discoloration). Brown the flour in the butter, add the tomatoes and onion which should be grilled, minced and sieved, then simmer until slightly thickened. Add the broth, salt and pepper, boil for 10 minutes and reseason if necessary. Drain the apples well and put them in with the parsley. When they are cooked, take the soup from the heat and pour in the sherry; serve immediately.

HUACHINANGO À LA VERACRUZANA

Fish fillets   Flour
Salt and pepper   Fat for frying
Lemon juice

For the Sauce

1 tomato   Fat for frying
Chopped onion   Parsley
Chopped garlic   Olives

Sprinkle salt, pepper and lemon juice over the fillets. Dredge in flour and fry until golden-brown. To make the sauce: toast a large tomato over an open flame, peel and mince. Add finely chopped onion and garlic and fry the mixture. When it is well fried, add the fish, cover with water and cook over a low heat for 15 minutes. Serve hot with chopped parsley and green olives.

CEVICHE
(RAW FISH SALAD)

Mackerel   Lemon juice

For the Sauce

Tomatoes   Olive oil
Onions   Vinegar
Chillies   Olives
Parsley   Avocado pear
Coriander

Chop the fish into small squares and cover with lemon juice. Let it pickle for at least 4 hours. For the sauce, chop tomatoes, onions and *chiles serranos*; add parsley or coriander and toss fish and sauce together with a dressing of 3 tbsps. olive oil to 1 tbsp. vinegar. Green olives may be added, and then the whole garnished with sliced avocado pear.

ZIHUATANEJO APPETIZER

2 lb. raw mackerel or crab   4 oz. olives (whole)
1 cup of lemon juice   2 bay leaves (ground)
Salt   or ¼ tsp. orégano
½ cup olive oil   ½ tsp. chilli powder
1 lb. tomatoes, chopped   1 cup white wine
2 large onions, chopped   Avocado to garnish

Cut the fish into small pieces and let it stand in the lemon juice with salt for 4 hours. Drain and mix together with the other ingredients. Garnish with sliced avocado.

SALVADOR SPANISH HADDOCK

1 3-lb. fresh haddock	3 large onions, sliced
1 clove of garlic, crushed	1½ lb. tomatoes, peeled and sliced
1 tsp. salt	2 tbsps. chopped parsley
½ tsp. pepper	¼ pint olive oil
3 tbsps. lemon juice	

Take an oval casserole, with a lid, and rub the inside with oil; put the fish in and rub in the garlic, salt, pepper and one-third of the lemon juice. Leave for 15 minutes. Cover the fish with layers of onion, tomato and parsley; pour over it the oil and remaining lemon juice. Cover the dish and bake in a moderate oven (350° F., mark 4) for 30 minutes, basting from time to time. Take the lid off and cook for a further 20 minutes till done, basting frequently.

FISH TEA

This bouillon is served as the equivalent of beef-tea or broth, and is thought to be very nourishing. It is made by boiling up fish heads, tails, etc., with a flavouring of fresh thyme, ground black pepper and salt, and straining the liquid. When serving it, float some sprigs of fresh thyme on top.

EL GRAN MOLE
(TURKEY IN SAUCE)

1 small turkey	Salt and pepper
Fat for frying	

For the Sauce

(A)	12 chiles mulato	6 chiles pasilla
	8 chiles ancho	
(B)	1 tortilla	Fat
	½ cup blanched almonds	1 tbsp. peanuts
		1 cup raisins
(C)	1 cup sesame seeds	10 coriander seeds
	3 cloves	1 oz. plain chocolate
	8 peppercorns	5 cloves garlic
	10 cumin seeds	

Brown the turkey on all sides in fat. Reserve the fat and put the turkey in a deep saucepan. Just cover with water, season to taste and simmer until tender. Meanwhile clean and mince the ingredients marked (A); brown the tortilla in a frying pan without fat, then add fat and sauté it with the rest of the ingredients marked (B).

Pound together the ingredients marked (C) and when they have formed a paste, add the sautéed tortilla, etc., the chillies and 5 cloves of garlic. Fry this mixture in the turkey fat until it has thickened. Then add turkey stock slowly until the desired consistency is reached. Cut the cooked turkey into convenient pieces and simmer in this sauce for 30 minutes.

COSTA RICAN CASSEROLE OF GUINEA FOWL

A 4-lb. guinea fowl	1 tsp. paprika pepper
4 rashers of fat bacon, chopped	1 large onion, chopped
2 oz. flour	½ pint boiling water
1 tsp. salt	½ pint red wine

Cut the bird into joints and chop the liver. Fry the bacon slowly in the casserole, add the pieces of bird and brown. Add the flour, stir well, then add all other ingredients. Cover lightly and simmer very gently for 2 hours, or until the bird is tender.

LA OLLA PODRIDA
(SAVOURY POT)

½ lb. each pork, chicken, veal, beef	½ tsp. pepper
1 tsp. salt	1 pinch wild or cultivated celery
⅛ tsp. each ground cinnamon, allspice, nutmeg, cloves	1 wineglass sherry
	Shortcrust pastry
	Flour

Cut the meats into cubes, add the seasonings and spices and mix well. Line a greased baking pan with pastry rolled ⅜ inch thick. Pour in the meat, dredge with flour and add water to cover. Cover with a top crust, bake in hot oven (450° F., mark 8) for 12 minutes and continue baking in a slow oven (300° F., mark 1) for 2–3 hours. When the meat is done, lift top crust and add the sherry.

ROAST SUCKING PIG

A sucking pig, prepared for roasting	2½ tsps. salt
	½ tsp. sage
Salt and pepper	½ tsp. pepper
2 loaves of stale bread	A generous pinch wild or cultivated celery or ¼ tsp. celery salt
1 onion, chopped	
1 garlic clove, chopped	
1 cup seeded raisins	Chicken broth
1 pinch mint	Fat for frying

Rub the inside of the pig with salt and pepper. Make the stuffing. Remove the crusts from the bread, slice, moisten in hot chicken broth and squeeze out the surplus moisture, then fry in hot fat. When the mass leaves the pan easily, add the other ingredients and mix well. Stuff the pig, sew together and roast until well done.

Do not baste, but occasionally prick the skin so it will not blister.

When the pig is done, pour a glass of red wine over it and put a red apple in its mouth.

The above stuffing may also be used with roast turkey or loin of pork.

CHILE CON CARNE

1 lb. beef	4 slices of onion,
3 garlic cloves	finely minced
2 tbsps. lard	Salt
$\frac{1}{4}$ cup flour	A pinch of orégano
$\frac{1}{2}$ lb. red peppers or	Hot water
2 tbsps. chilli powder	

Cut the meat into $\frac{1}{2}$-inch cubes. Fry the garlic in the lard until brown, then remove. Sprinkle the flour over the meat, then brown this in the hot lard. Make a thin paste of the peppers or chilli powder. (If red peppers are used, remove the seeds, veins, stems and skins by soaking in hot water.) Pour this paste and the other ingredients over the meat, cover with hot water and simmer until the meat is very tender and the sauce thickened.

COCIDO
(STEW)

In Mexico, as in Spain and probably in every Spanish-speaking country, *cocido* is a most important dish. It is a generous affair, for it is soup, meat and vegetables in one, and is meant to last for several meals, getting more savoury with each reheating.

1 lb. fresh pork	2 onions
2 lb. beef	1 stalk of celery
3 slices of bacon	2 summer squash
1 cup of chick peas	1 apple
2 corn on the cob	1 pear
2 large potatoes	1 tsp. salt
2 sweet potatoes	A generous pinch
$\frac{1}{2}$ head of cabbage	of orégano
1 turnip	A pinch of cumin
1 bunch of carrots	

Cut the meat into large cubes and wash the other ingredients as necessary, but do not peel them. Start with the meat, the peas, tied in a cheesecloth bag, and add the corn, cut into small lengths, the potatoes, cabbage and turnip, covered with water. Later add the other vegetables, and lastly the fruit, all whole. Then add the salt, orégano and cumin. The stew should simmer slowly for 3–4 hours—if the fruit gets done, take it out.

The soup may be served first and then the rest.

For the second day's serving, cut the corn from the cob, run everything through a mincer and fry in lard until it leaves the pan.

For both servings, two sauces may be offered; here are the recipes:

Sweet Sauce

1 onion	2$\frac{1}{2}$ tbsps. sugar
2 tbsps. lard	$\frac{1}{2}$ tsp. salt
2 tomatoes	3 tbsps. vinegar

Chop the onion very finely and fry in lard until it begins to brown. Add the tomatoes, seasonings and vinegar and fry until the mixture leaves the pan. Serve hot.

Piquant Sauce

$\frac{1}{2}$ an onion	$\frac{1}{2}$ tsp. salt
2 tomatoes	3 tbsps. vinegar
2 pods red chilli pulp	1 tbsp. of oil

Chop the onion, mash the tomatoes and add the salt, chilli, vinegar and oil. Beat until smooth and serve cold.

CARNE ADOBADA
(SPICED MEAT)

1 pork loin, cut into	4 garlic cloves, mashed
strips	1 tsp. salt
12 red chillies (pulp and	$\frac{1}{8}$ tsp. orégano
seeds) or substitute	

Prepare the meat. Add the seasonings to the chilli pulp and soak the meat in this mixture—3 minutes is usually enough, but the longer it stays the stronger it gets. Take the meat strips out and hang in a cool place to dry. Serve roasted or fried.

If chilli powder is used, add water enough to make a paste.

ASADITO
(LITTLE ROAST)

2 lb. veal, lamb or	1 small can tomatoes
mutton ribs	1 onion
2 tbsps. flour	2 tbsps. rice
3 tbsps. lard or fat	1$\frac{1}{2}$ tsps. salt
from meat	$\frac{1}{8}$ tsp. pepper
3 cups boiling water	

Cut the meat into small pieces, coat with flour and brown in the hot fat. Add the water, tomatoes and chopped onion, simmer for 1 hour, then add the rice and seasonings and simmer for another hour, or until the meat is tender.

Instead of rice, chicos (green corn cut from the cob) may be used. Chicos should be partially cooked separately and added when the meat has cooked for an hour; they require only 30 minutes' cooking.

CHILLI CROQUETTES

1 lb. round steak	½ cup seedless raisins
2 tbsps. lard	6 green chillies, chopped
½ cup sugar	½ cup vinegar or red wine
¼ tsp. cloves	3 eggs
½ tsp. cinnamon	Flour
½ tsp. salt	Deep fat for frying

Stew the steak and mince it. Brown in the hot lard. Add the sugar, spices, salt, raisins, chillies and liquid. Mix thoroughly and mould into egg-shaped croquettes.

Beat the egg whites very stiff. Add the yolks and beat. Roll each croquette in flour, then in the beaten egg and fry in deep fat until well browned. Serve very hot.

ALBONDIGAS
(MEAT BALLS)

1 lb. chopped meat (half beef, half pork)	2 hard-boiled eggs
Chopped onion	½ cup of raisins
Salt and pepper	1 can tomato soup
Some chopped herbs	Dry mustard or a chilli
½ cup rice, boiled	A few olives

Put the meat in a bowl. Form a hollow with a fork and add a little chopped onion, salt, pepper and herbs. Mix together thoroughly with the boiled rice. Form the mixture into tiny balls, putting a small piece of boiled egg and a few raisins in the centre of each. Heat the tomato soup with the same amount of water; add a pinch of dry mustard or a chilli to flavour. When the soup comes to the boil drop the meat balls in carefully and cook for 10 minutes. Serve with olives.

PORK WITH MARROW

1½ lb. pork (cut in pieces)	1 cup minced garlic cloves
1 lb. marrow (cut in cubes)	1 tbsp. chilli powder
1 large chopped onion	1 cup cooked corn kernels
1 cup sieved tomato	1 cup grated cheese

Cook the pork until tender. Add the chopped marrow and other ingredients together (except the cheese). Bring to the boil and cook until the marrow is tender but not too soft. Cover with cheese and serve.

FRESH TOMATO RELISH

Several hours before serving chop 2 lb. tomatoes, 2 medium-sized green peppers and 2 medium-sized onions; drain slightly. Add 2 tsps. salt, 1 tsp. dry mustard, 1 tsp. celery

seeds, ¼ cup vinegar and ¼ cup salad oil. Mix and refrigerate. Makes 1 quart.

PANAMA RADISH SALAD

3 bunches of radishes, sliced	1 tsp. chopped mint
1 small onion, finely chopped	2 tbsps. olive oil
1 large tomato, peeled and chopped finely	2 tbsps. lemon juice
	½ tsp. salt
	¼ tsp. black pepper

Prepare the vegetables and mint and mix together. Blend the oil, lemon juice, salt and pepper well together, and pour over the vegetables.

SAINTS' SAUCE (FOR FISH)

Mash and sieve 6–8 pickled walnuts and mix with ¾ cup mayonnaise, 2 tbsps. yoghourt, salt, pepper and a little allspice to taste. Whip together.

Serve with cold halibut steak, crab or lobster, etc., and add a garnish of lemon.

CHILES RELLENOS
(STUFFED CHILLIES OR GREEN PEPPERS)

Chilli or green peppers	Cloves
Minced pork	Black pepper
Lard	Saffron
Garlic	Blanched almonds, raisins, capers and olives
Tomatoes	
Parsley	Fat ham
Vinegar	Beaten egg

For the Sauce

Garlic	Tomato
Parsley	

Toast and peel the peppers, remove seeds and veins. Cook the pork in the lard with a little garlic until browned. Add chopped tomatoes and parsley and continue to fry for 5 minutes; add a little water and simmer for a short time. Then add a dash of vinegar, the well-ground spices and the rest of the ingredients chopped up, except the egg. Simmer until all is well cooked and almost dry. Fill the peppers with the mixture, roll in flour and beaten egg and fry. Serve covered with a sauce made by frying the garlic, parsley and tomatoes together. Slices of banana or apple can be added to this dish.

A variation is to fill the peppers with cottage cheese and pour sour cream over the finished dish.

CHILES EN NOGADA
(PEPPERS WITH NUT SAUCE)

Follow the previous recipe for *Chiles Rellenos*

but serve with the following sauce instead of the garlic, parsley and tomato sauce.

Walnuts	Vinegar
Garlic	Salt
Black pepper	Pomegranate seeds
Breadcrumbs	Lettuce

Soak the walnuts for several hours and then mince finely. Mince the garlic, pepper and breadcrumbs which have previously been soaked in vinegar. Season to taste and mix with the walnuts. Arrange the peppers on a serving dish and cover with the sauce, sprinkling pomegranate seeds over the top. Serve with fresh lettuce.

STUFFED PEPPERS WITH CHEESE

4 green peppers	2 tbsps. raisins
1 tbsp. dripping	1 oz. butter
1 lb. minced meat	1 oz. flour
1 onion	2 cups milk
Salt	1 oz. grated cheese

Parboil the peppers until slightly soft. Peel and remove veins and seeds, opening them lengthwise. Melt the dripping in a pan and fry the minced meat and chopped onion. When cooked, add salt and the raisins. Stuff the peppers, fastening with cocktail sticks.

Make a cheese sauce by melting the butter in pan, blending in a little flour. Add the milk and boil, until it thickens, then stirring in the grated cheese. Pour the sauce over the peppers and bake in a moderate oven (350° F., mark 4) for 30 minutes.

EGGS À LA MEXICANA

1 chilli	Fat for frying
1 small onion	2 eggs
1 small tomato	

Chop the chilli, onion and tomato very fine and fry them all together. Beat the eggs thoroughly, pour over the mixture and scramble in the usual way. 1 serving.

TORTA DE HUEVO
(EGG FRITTERS)

3 eggs	1 pinch orégano
2 tsps. flour	A pinch of mint
½ tsp. salt	Deep fat for frying
½ tsp. baking powder	

Beat the whites stiff, add the yolks and beat again. Stir the flour, baking powder, salt, orégano and mint lightly into the eggs. Drop by teaspoonfuls into deep fat and fry; drain and serve with chilli sauce. 2 servings.

Mexican cookery includes an enormous number of sauces, generally with chilli as a basic ingredient, which are served with tortillas, meat, poultry—in fact, with almost everything. The exact amount of the ingredients used depends very largely on the cook; most of the quantities given in the following recipes are capable of variation according to taste.

CHILE CHIPOTLE
(CHILE SAUCE)

| Chile | Olive oil |
| Salt | Onion |

Toast the chile, peel and remove veins. Pound it into a paste with salt, olive oil and finely chopped onion.

SALSA RANCHERA
(FARMHOUSE SAUCE)

Green peppers	Garlic
Green tomatoes	Onions
Red tomatoes	Lard

Boil the peppers for a few minutes, remove the veins and mince together with the tomatoes, which have been peeled, garlic and onions. Fry the mixture in a little lard until it is thick and serve with fried eggs and tortillas.

SALSA VERDE
(GREEN SAUCE)

Green tomatoes	2 chillies
1 onion	2 tbsps. olive oil
1 tbsp. coriander	Salt and pepper

Skin the tomatoes, chop the onion and mix with the coriander, chopped, toasted chillies, oil and seasoning. The mixture may be served raw or cooked for a few minutes. It may also be made with ordinary tomatoes.

GUACAMOLE
(AVOCADO PEAR SAUCE)

3 avocado pears	1 tbsp. coriander
2 tomatoes	2 tbsps. olive oil
1 chopped onion	Salt and pepper
1 chilli pepper	

Peel and mash the avocados with a wooden spoon, leaving the stones in the mixture (this prevents discoloration). Skin and mince the tomatoes, onion and chilli and mix with the avocados and the rest of the ingredients. This makes a good sauce for meat, or may be served as an appetiser with drinks.

SALSA BARRACHA
(BEER SAUCE)

This simple sauce is made by boiling several

chillies, straining through a sieve and thinning the mixture with *pulque* or, since this is not readily available, a light beer.

RAJAS
(CHEESE AND PEPPER SAUCE)

Green peppers   Cheese
Fat for frying

Remove veins and seeds from the peppers, toast them, slice about ¾ inch thick and fry until tender. Sprinkle crumbled fresh cheese over the hot peppers and serve with meat. Sour cream can be added instead of the cheese.

MASA

Masa is dough made from finely ground, specially treated corn. It is the basic ingredient for making most of Mexico's corn-based foods. To make *masa* add 1 tbsp. of slaked lime to about 4 quarts of boiling water. Add 2 lb. of clean, dry corn and let the water come to the boil again, and then spoon out a few kernels. If the skin peels off readily, remove the corn from the heat. You may have to let it boil 4 or 5 minutes before the skin will peel off easily, but the corn should by no means cook. Drain off the lime water and wash the corn in several changes of fresh cold water; then drain it again. At this point, the prepared corn is either ground wet to make *masa* directly, or it is dried and then ground to make *masaharina* or *masa* flour.

TORTILLAS

Use equal parts of *masa* flour and water and let the dough stand for 20 minutes before using it. It should be firm but pliable, rather like clay of a good consistency for modelling. To turn *masa* into tortillas, you will probably want to try patting it between your hands in traditional style. Make a flattened little ball of *masa* about the size of a walnut, dip your hands in water and shake them nearly dry, and then pat the ball of dough back and forth between your hands with quick, light strokes, until you have an almost paper-thin, evenly shaped round.

If this proves impossibly difficult—and it is an acquired art—make walnut-sized balls of *masa* and flatten them slightly. Place a flattened ball between two sheets of waxed paper, and then use a plate to press the ball evenly and firmly into a large, thin circle. Peel off the top sheet of paper, turn the tortilla over, and peel the bottom sheet off carefully until the tortilla drops on to your hand or directly on to a hot griddle.

To bake the tortillas, heat a heavy, ungreased griddle over high heat, or use an electric frying pan set at 420° F. (or its highest setting). Cook the tortillas rapidly until the underside is dry and may be beginning to blister, flip them over (they may puff up, but they will settle back into flatness again) and cook until the second side is well done and beginning to blister. Stack the hot baked tortillas one on top of another inside the fold of a napkin, to keep them hot. Serve sprinkled with salt and rolled into a cylinder, or spread with butter and a sprinkle of salt or dipped into any spicy sauce, or with beans or meat spooned on and the tortilla rolled up.

TACOS

A *taco* is a hot tortilla rolled up around meat, beans or crushed green chillies, with or without added chopped fresh onions and tomatoes.

ENCHILADAS

Heat half an inch of oil in a small, deep pan and fry tortillas, one by one, for half a minute—they should be hot and pliable, but not at all crisp. As the tortillas come out of the frying pan, dip them into hot chile sauce, add a stuffing of coarsely grated good cheese, mixed with a good handful of very finely chopped raw onion. Roll them up tightly and arrange them side by side on a platter. When the platter is filled, pour any remaining sauce over the enchiladas and sprinkle them with any remaining cheese-and-onions. Reheat for just a few minutes. Add, if you like, a few bands of sour cream; garnish with radish roses and strips of avocado.

A variation on the enchilada theme is called Envueltos. Here, the sauce may be a plain thick tomato sauce, or it may have chile in it, and the stuffing is chicken or sausage or quite frequently strips of avocado.

The enchilada pie.—One of the very pleasant variations on the enchilada theme is a casserole dish called, according to your wish, Aztec Pudding or Tortilla Pudding or Cuauhtemoc or Moctezuma Pudding. Here, layers of tortillas are alternated with layers of sauce and strips of chile or cheese or chicken or meat, and the whole affair is baked.

ENCHILADAS
(A SIMPLIFIED VERSION)

1 pint water	2 eggs
4 oz. cornmeal	Fat for frying
1½ oz. butter	

Boil the water, sprinkle in the corn meal, stir in the butter and cook for 1–2 minutes. Remove

159

from the heat, then beat in the eggs, and make pancakes in the usual way. (Failing corn meal, make an ordinary pancake mixture.)

Fill each pancake with a savoury mixture of cooked chicken or pork, chopped red or green chillies, a little grated onion, salt and pepper to taste, then roll up and put in an ovenproof dish ; cover with tomato purée, grated cheese and sour cream and cook in a slow oven (325° F., mark 3) for about 15 minutes. Alternatively, pile up pancakes and filling and top with a fried egg.

MEXICAN DESSERTS

Almost all of the desserts and sweetmeats served in Mexico were invented during Colonial times by nuns in the many communities located all over Mexico. Depending on their ingenuity and the wealth of the nunnery, the dishes were sometimes overwhelmingly spectacular.

" The dessert with less sweet and more egg " should be worth trying because of its name alone. We are told to make a clear sugar syrup with 2½ lb. sugar, add 15 egg yolks and 2½ lb. ground almonds and boil to the consistency of thick caramel ; then add ½ pint wine and some ground cinnamon. The mixture is served when set.

EMPANADAS
(TURNOVERS)

2 cups flour	⅓ cup milk
1 tsp. baking powder	Filling as desired
½ tsp. salt	(see below)
1 pinch coriander	Deep fat for frying
½ cup lard	

Mix and sift the dry ingredients, cut in the lard and add the liquid. Roll out to ⅛ inch thickness and cut into 4-inch rounds. Fill with fruit or other mixture, moisten the edges with cold water, fold one half over the other and press the edges together. Fry in deep fat until brown and drain on paper.

Empanadas are filled with various mixtures. The imagination may go on for ever, making new combinations. Mincemeat makes one very desirable filling.

MANGO CREAM

2 mangoes	1 cup double cream,
1 orange	whipped
½ cup sifted icing	⅓ cup coarsely chopped
sugar	toasted pecans

Peel the mangoes and cut the flesh away from the stones. Peel and section the orange. Combine the mangoes, orange sections and sugar. Using a potato masher, mash the fruits or blend in an electric blender. Fold in the whipped cream and pecans and spoon into sherbert glasses ; refrigerate till well chilled. If desired, garnish with more whipped cream and pecan halves. Makes 6 servings.

PASTEL DE ELOTE
(CORN CAKES)

12 ears of corn	1 cup cottage cheese
1 tsp. cinnamon	1 dozen eggs
1½ cups sugar	1 small pat of butter

Separate the grains of corn from the cob and beat in a blender until smooth and soft. Mix with the cinnamon, sugar and cottage cheese and add the egg yolks one by one. Beat the egg whites until stiff and add little by little to the mixture. Pour into greased tins and put pieces of butter on the top. Bake in a moderate oven (350° F., mark 4) for 45 minutes.

BUNUELOS
(PANCAKES)

Sift 3 cups of flour, 1 tbsp. sugar, 1 tsp. baking powder, 1 tsp. salt together and break 4 eggs into the mixture. Add 1 cup of milk and ¼ cup of melted butter and beat the mixture, adding as much water as is necessary to make a dough that is easily handled. Knead the dough well and form into small balls. Cover the balls with a cloth and leave for 20 minutes ; then sprinkle some flour on a board and roll out each ball into a very thin round pancake. After letting these stand for an additional 5 minutes, fry them in deep hot oil until they are golden-brown, crisp and flaky. Drain on absorbent paper and dip into a mixture of sugar and cinnamon or serve covered with thin honey. Mexicans often break them into a soup bowl and add a syrup made with brown sugar and cinnamon.

CALABAZA EN PILONCILLO
(PUMPKIN SWEET)

Take a large pumpkin and cut it into pieces, without peeling. Remove the seeds and place the pieces into a bowl of cold water. Sprinkle in some lime water and let it stand for about an hour. Drain off the water and add 1½ lb. brown sugar to each 2 lb. of pumpkin, with the rind of 4 oranges cut into chunks and about 3½ oz. of stick cinnamon. Let the mixture boil until the pumpkin is soft and the syrup is stringy, then cool.

The classic way to serve this is with cold milk in deep bowls.

Another version of this dish is to punch a hole

160

into a large pumpkin and to pour in as much rum as it will hold. Do this the night before you plan to serve it. Then, in the morning, cook it as above.

CALABAZA EN MIEL
(PUMPKIN HONEY)

Wash a small pumpkin (about 5 lb.) and cut into chunks, leaving the seeds and fibres. Arrange the chunks in a deep, heavy pan with a tight-fitting lid. Pack brown sugar (about 2 lb.) firmly around the chunks and tuck in slices of 2 whole unpeeled oranges. (In Mexico, guavas and other fruits are also added.) Tie a large stick of cinnamon, 10 whole cloves and 1 tsp. aniseeds in a square of cheesecloth and bury it in the middle of the fruit.

Add $\frac{1}{2}$ cup water and cook over very low heat for an hour or until the pumpkin is tender and darkly glazed. Remove the pumpkin and cook the syrup a few minutes longer if it is not thick and heavy. Pour the syrup over the pumpkin.

In Mexico, this is sometimes eaten at breakfast in a deep bowl with cold milk.

DULCE DE CALABAZA EN TACHA
(BAKED PUMPKIN)

Wash and weigh a pumpkin, cut a deep wedge out of the top and for every 2 lb. of pumpkin, put $1\frac{1}{2}$ lb. brown sugar and 2 sticks of cinnamon into the hole. Replace the wedge and place the entire thing into an ovenproof dish. Cook in a very slow oven (250° F., mark $\frac{1}{4}$) until a toothpick stuck into the shell goes easily through the flesh. Serve by simply breaking apart at the table.

CAJETA
(SWEET MILK SPREAD)

Probably the most popular of sweet substances in Mexico is *cajeta* in all of its many forms and flavours. This is a rich and golden caramel-like sauce made from goat's milk in Celaya and from cow's milk in other areas. The cow's milk mixture is called *leche quemada* or "burned milk," which is not at all an accurate description of its flavour. It may be served on small plates and eaten with spoons, but the best way is to spread it on hard-crusted rolls.

To prepare *leche quemada*, scald 2 quarts milk and add 1 lb. granulated sugar. Dissolve $\frac{1}{4}$ tsp. bicarbonate of soda in 1 tbsp. water and stir this into the milk and sugar mixture. Boil slowly, stirring constantly, until the syrup is caramel-tan in colour and about as thick as sweetened condensed milk. This should take from $\frac{1}{2}$–1 hour.

Variations are flavoured with sherry, quince or sweet potatoes and pineapple, lemons, guavas or grape juice.

CAJETA ALMENDRADA
(ALMOND MILK SWEET)

Soak almonds in hot water until you can peel them. Mince and mix with a small amount of milk. Bring the mixture to the boil and add a small amount of sugar. Continue boiling the nuts and milk and sugar until the sugar dissolves. Remove from the heat, pour into a serving dish and garnish with sliced toasted almonds.

SOPA
(BREAD PUDDING)

6 thin slices of bread, toasted brown	1 cup seeded raisins
	1 cup grated cheese
6 thin slices of bread fried in deep fat	

For the Sauce

$\frac{1}{3}$ cup brown sugar	2 cups of water
$\frac{1}{2}$ tsp. cinnamon	A pinch of cloves

In a deep buttered baking dish arrange a layer of toasted bread, a layer of fried bread, a layer of chopped raisins and some grated cheese. Repeat.

Bring the sauce ingredients to the boil and pour on the bread in the dish; add water, if necessary, to cover.

Bake in a slow oven (300° F., mark 1) until firm and well browned—about 1 hour.

CAPIROTADA or TORREJAS
(FRIED BREAD SWEET)

$2\frac{1}{2}$ cups bread cubes	3 oz. almonds
1 egg	3 oz. peanuts
Deep fat for frying	3 oz. pine nuts, chopped
$\frac{1}{4}$ cup sugar	$\frac{1}{2}$ cup citron, finely chopped
1 tsp. cinnamon	

For the Sauce

2 cups sugar	1 cup water
$\frac{1}{8}$ tsp. cream of tartar	$\frac{1}{2}$ tsp. cinnamon

Brown the bread cubes thoroughly in the oven. Separate the egg, beat the white until stiff and add the yolk, then beat again. Dip the bread cubes into the egg and fry in deep fat, drain and pile on a hot dish. Sprinkle with cinnamon and sugar sifted together and add the nuts and citron. Combine sauce ingredients, heat gradually to boiling point and boil until the syrup "threads." Pour over the bread while still hot.

ATOLE

Even beverages are made out of corn in Mexico. One such beverage is atole.

Mix together $\frac{1}{2}$ cup cornflour and 2 cups cold water. Cook over medium heat, stirring constantly, until thickened and clear. Add $\frac{3}{4}$ cup sugar and stir; then add, slowly, and stirring with a wire whisk, 1 quart of hot milk. Remove from the heat and add any of the following : a shake of powdered cinnamon and a few drops of orange flower water; or $\frac{1}{2}$ cup sweetened strawberry juice (or puréed thawed frozen strawberries) and a drop or two of cochineal; or 4 generous tbsps. of peanut butter; or $1\frac{1}{2}$ cups sweetened guava juice. You could use guava jelly, but in that case use much less sugar when making the atole.

CHOCOLATE

To make the perfect cup of hot chocolate, take a $\frac{1}{2}$–1 oz. tablet of chocolate for every cup of water, add a little ground cinnamon if desired and place together on the heat. Whisk the hot chocolate when it begins to boil and continue to whisk until the mixture foams. When it does, remove from the heat and allow to subside. Do this 3 times. Then remove, and whisk thoroughly until the drink is frothy and foamy. Sweeten as desired. Serve and drink in the traditional way—one sip of the magical health-giving " drink of the Gods " alternated with one sip of cold milk.

GALLETAS DE NUEZ
(NUTTY CAKES)

Mix $10\frac{1}{2}$ oz. finely minced pecans with $10\frac{1}{2}$ oz. granulated sugar. Add 2 eggs and mix lightly, taking extreme care not to touch the mixture with your hands. Drop forkfuls of the mixture carefully on to a greased baking sheet and bake in a moderate oven (350° F., mark 4) for 12 minutes. Do not open the oven during the cooking time or the mixture will all run together.

GLOSSARY OF MEXICAN COOKERY TERMS

Albóndiga en chile	Ball of ground meat and eggs in chilli sauce.
Arroz	Rice.
Barbacoa mexicana	Pit barbecue of mutton or goat.
Cabrito al asador	Broiled young kid.
Calabaza de tacha	Pumpkin baked with brown sugar.
Caldo	Broth.
Ceviche	Pickled fish in chilli and tomato sauce.
Chicharrón	Cracklings.
Chilaquiles	Stale tortillas fried and cooked in hot chilli and tomato sauce.
Chile ancho ; chile mulato ; chile pasilla	Hot peppers. Hot pepper sauce. (Tabasco, etc.)
Chile jalapeño	Medium-sized green chilli pickled.
Chile poblano	Green chile used for chiles rellenos. Green peppers may be substituted.
Chiles rellenos en nogada	Stuffed green pepper with walnut and pomegranate seed sauce.
Cocada	Concentrated coconut candy.
Cochinita	Roasted suckling pig.
Dulce de nuez	Walnut confection.
Enchilada	Tortillas with chilli sauce and meat.
Entremés	Hors d'œuvre.
Frijol	There are over 60 beans to choose from in Mexico. The favourites are : frijol nero (black bean), frijol bayo and frijol canario.
Frijoles de olla	Pot beans.
Garbanzo	Chick pea.
Gusano de maguey	Edible maguey (century plant) worms.
Guacamole	Avocado sauce.
Manchamanteles	A soupy chilli sauce ; literally, tablecloth-spotter.
Metate	Stone mortar and pestle for grinding.
Mole poblano	No few lines can define this. A special chilli sauce invented in Puebla, traditionally used with turkey, but can be used with any meat.
Nopal	Prickly pear cactus leaf.
Quesadilla de flor de calabaza	A tortilla dish prepared with yellow squash blossoms.
Sangrita	Tomato and orange juice seasoned with chilli and always accompanied by tequila.
Sopa de medula	Bone marrow soup.
Sopa de tortillas	Tortilla soup ; similar to chilaquiles.
Tacos	Tortilla filled with anything.
Tamales	Corn meal, filled with any number of things, wrapped in the corn husk and steamed.
Tuna	Prickly pear.
Zapotes	Tropical, avocado-like, rich, creamy fruit.

ALTHOUGH South America includes many nations and covers a vast area, there is a great deal in common between the various countries when it comes to cooking. It derives very largely from Spanish and Portuguese cuisine, but as is usual in really hot climates, a much larger amount of spice and pepper is used.

The Argentine is a great agricultural country, producing maize, cotton and coffee as well as an abundance of fruit and particularly grapes. Cattle rearing is, however, perhaps the most important industry and large quantities of beef and mutton of excellent quality are produced. This means, of course, that Argentine and indeed most of South America, eats a great deal of meat, either plainly grilled with salt or made into rich and interesting stews, combined with apricots and peaches. A whole sheep or goat is sometimes roasted on a spit in a hearty version of the barbecue.

Brazilian cookery has both influenced and been influenced by that of Portugal. The country is fertile and there is a plentiful supply of fruit, meat and fish. Bananas grow in countless varieties and are used either ripe or unripe in many dishes, sweet and savoury, being frequently combined with beef. Brazilian coffee is world-famous ; Brazil nuts, too, are used extensively at home as well as being exported. A typical Bahian meal will start with *Vatapa*, a porridge-like cake of bread, okra, dried shrimps, coconut, nuts, spices and oil, followed by fish, crab or oysters, a spicy stew with rice and a coconut sweet. Brazilian aguardiente is drunk, often with fruit juice or coconut milk.

Chile's famous Central Valley, which lies between two long mountain ranges, has some of the best agricultural soil in South America. Its vineyards in season are heavy with clusters of grapes and its fruit orchards laden with plums, peaches, apples, citrus fruits, olives, nuts and figs.

Although many of Chile's fruits came originally from Europe, America abounded in wild fruits before the arrival of the Spanish settlers. Some of these fruits are the particular gift of Chile to the world. Chile is renowned for her wines, but few know that the strawberry was first cultivated when the Chilean species from the south of the country was introduced into Europe.

South America

Argentine

VERMICELLI SOUP

3 oz. butter or dripping   A pinch of saffron
1 large onion, minced   2 pints chicken stock
1½ tbsps. parsley, chopped   A pinch of chilli
2 oz. vermicelli   powder
1 lb. tomatoes, peeled   Salt and pepper
    and sliced   1½ oz. grated cheese

Heat the fat in a saucepan, fry the onion and parsley for 3 minutes, then add the vermicelli and fry for 2 minutes till lightly browned—be careful not to burn it. Add the tomatoes and saffron and cook gently for 5 minutes. Pour on the stock, bring to the boil and simmer for about 15 minutes, till the vermicelli is tender. Add the chilli powder, salt and pepper to taste, and sprinkle with cheese before serving.

SOPA À LA REINA
(QUEEN'S SOUP)

Place the yolks of 4 eggs in a terrine, add 1 cup hot milk and stir in ¼ lb. melted butter and 1½ pints boiling chicken stock. Serve with diced bread browned in butter and sprinkled with grated cheese.

CARBONADO
(MINCED BEEF STEW)

1½ lb. beef   2 pears, peeled and sliced
2 oz. butter   2 peaches, peeled and
4 medium-sized   sliced
    onions, sliced   4 plums, peeled and
1 large tomato, peeled   sliced
    and sliced   4 medium-sized potatoes,
1 tsp. salt   cut in ½-inch dice
¼ tsp. pepper   2 oz. seedless raisins
¼ pint meat stock

Mince the beef. Heat the butter in a casserole, fry the onions till brown, add the tomato and fry for 2 minutes. Add the minced beef, stir well and brown for 2 minutes. Add the salt, pepper and stock, cover and cook very gently for 1 hour. Now add the fruit and potatoes and cook again till tender. Just before serving add raisins. This is a delicious and unusual dish.

CHURRASCO
(GRILLED STEAK)

An almost universal dish in Argentine, especially in small restaurants which specialise in the cookery of the country. It is a thick beefsteak which is salted, placed on an almost red-hot flat iron and fired till it is about to burn, then turned over and cooked on the other side. It is served without the addition of more salt, so that it retains the appetising " singed " flavour.

ASADO
(ARGENTINE BARBECUE OR ROAST)

The true *asado* must be cooked in the open to yield its full savour. It is made by taking a section of the ribs of a sheep or an ox and skewering it on a long metal spike, like that of an iron hurdle. Then a wood fire is lit on the ground and when this has passed its early and smokier stages, the spike is driven into the ground at an angle, so that the meat hangs over the embers and is slowly roasted, the fire being fed carefully to keep a certain heat.

The *criollo*, the true Argentine, pours a strong garlic sauce over the meat at intervals, but when the *asado* is eaten, the flavour of garlic is indiscernible, leaving only a pleasant savouriness in the meat. He eats the resulting roast in his fingers, having hacked the piece of his choice from the appetising joint. And if there is anyone who thinks that less primitive ways of cooking meat can compare with this one for fullness of flavour and tenderness, let him try.

PUCHERO
(NATIONAL DISH OF ARGENTINE)

2 lb. beef cut in pieces   4 cobs of sweet corn
   2 inches by 3 inches   4 potatoes
1 boiling fowl, jointed   2 onions
1 calf's foot, split in 4   4 pieces of pumpkin
Boiling water   each cut 3 inches
1½ tsps. salt   square
4 carrots   4 oz. bacon, cut in
4 sweet potatoes   1-inch squares
2 tomatoes   8 slices liver sausage

This is a substantial dish for 6 or 8 people. Take a large pot and half-fill it with boiling salted water. Put in the beef, fowl and calf's foot, bring to the boil and skim. Simmer for 1½ hours. Now add everything else, add more water if necessary and simmer till the vegetables are tender. Serve in 3 dishes—one for the meat, one for the vegetables and one for the soup.

LOCRO DE CHOCIO DESGRANADO
(THICK CORN STEW)

1 dozen heads corn   1 little diced pumpkin
   on the cob or 2 tins   1 chopped onion
   whole corn   2 tbsps. dripping
½ lb. stewing beef   1 chopped green pepper
A little stock   2 peeled tomatoes
3 blanched carrots   Salt and pepper

Clean the corn on the cob and separate from

the cob with a knife. Place in a saucepan, with the diced meat, a little stock, sliced carrots and diced pumpkin and cook until tender. Meanwhile sauté the onion in the dripping, add the chopped green pepper, tomatoes, salt and pepper and cook for about 20 minutes. Pour this sauce over the meat.

EMPANADAS FRITAS
(FRIED PASTIES)
For the Pastry

1 lb. flour	Salt and pepper
4 oz. suet	Oil for frying
1 egg	

For the Filling

8 oz. fat	2 oz. raisins
½–¾ lb. onions	2 oz. green olives
1 green pepper	2 hard-boiled eggs
1 lb. minced meat	Salt and pepper
1 tsp. chopped chillies	1 tbsp. sugar

Place the fat in a saucepan and sauté the chopped onions; when brown add the chopped green pepper and the minced beef, pressing this with a fork to cook thoroughly; add the chillies, raisins, olives, chopped eggs, salt, pepper and sugar. Make a rather firm pastry with all the ingredients. Knead it well and leave to rest for a little while, wrapped in a floured cloth. Roll out thinly, fold in two, re-roll and cut into rounds with a pastry cutter. Put about 1 tbsp. filling in each round and fold over as for Cornish pasties. Fry in very hot cooking oil.

ESTOFADO
(BRAISED BEEF)

2 lb. stewing beef	½ lb. Spanish-type sausages
1 cup oil	1 glass of white wine
1½ oz. butter	1 tbsp. mushrooms
1 onion	A handful of parsley
4 cloves of garlic	Thyme
4 peeled and sliced tomatoes	2 bay leaves
	Salt and pepper
1 tbsp. tomato purée	2 tbsps. stock

Brown the meat in very hot oil. Add the butter, chopped onion and chopped garlic and sauté for a few minutes. Add the peeled and sliced tomatoes, tomato purée, chopped sausages, white wine, mushrooms, herbs, seasonings and stock. Cover the saucepan, reduce the heat and cook until the meat is tender—about 2 hours.

CROQUETAS DE CARNE
(MEAT CROQUETTES)
Sauté 1 chopped onion in 2 tbsps. oil, with 3 chopped cloves of garlic; when brown add ½ lb. raw minced meat, pressing with a fork and stirring to cook thoroughly. Add ½ cup grated cheese, salt and pepper, orégano and powdered nutmeg. Pour in a cup of milk gradually, alternating with 2 tbsps. flour, stirring all the time to avoid lumps. Cook this mixture for about 4 minutes over a low heat, then leave it to cool. Shape into meat balls, roll in beaten egg and breadcrumbs and fry in oil.

GUISO TRIFON
(RAGOÛT)

½ cup cooking oil	Salt and pepper
2 chopped onions	1 bay leaf
1 lb. veal chops	1 pint stock
4 oz. bacon	1 small white cabbage
3 Spanish-type sausages	½ lb. rice

Sauté the onions in the oil; when brown, add the meat, sauté for a few minutes, add the bacon, sausages and seasonings, pour in the stock and cook for about 1 hour. Add the cabbage and cook for 20 minutes, then add the rice and cook for another 20 minutes.

SALPICON
(MEAT SALAD)
Leftover of any cooked meat can be used for this cold dish. Slice the meat very thinly, cut some boiled potatoes in small dices, add a few lettuce leaves, 1 thinly sliced onion, 1 thinly sliced green pepper and 1 boiled egg (the white and the yellow chopped separately). Prepare a salad dressing with ½ cup of wine vinegar, 2 tbsps. oil, salt and pepper to taste. Add to the mixture and decorate with 1–2 sliced tomatoes.

HUMITA EN CHAIA
(STUFFED CORN LEAVES)

2 dozen corn cobs	A little milk
1 onion, chopped	4 oz. raisins
¼ lb. butter	Salt and pepper
2 peeled and sliced tomatoes	1 tsp. sugar
	Stock
1 green pepper, chopped	Some pumpkin

Carefully remove the leaves from the corn cobs and wash and dry them. Clean the corn cobs and grate off the grains. Sauté the chopped onion in butter, add the tomato and green pepper and cook for about 20 minutes, then add the grated corn, stirring continuously. Should the mixture be too thick, pour in a little milk. Add the raisins, season and leave to cool. For each *humita* place two leaves of corn in the form of a cross, with the wider part in the centre;

put in 1 tbsp. of the mixture, fold the leaves over and tie with strips taken from one of the leaves. Cook in stock with pumpkin (or other vegetables if preferred) for about ½ hour.

ROPA VIEJA
(SLICED MEAT WITH VEGETABLES AND EGGS)

Leftovers of roast beef or other cooked meat can be used for this. Slice the meat, boil 2 potatoes, peel 1 tomato, chop 1 onion, 1 green pepper and some parsley. Sauté the onion in 2 tbsps. oil, add the sliced tomato and chopped pepper and cook for a short time. Add the meat, potatoes and parsley, season and simmer for a few minutes. Stir in 3 beaten eggs and cook for about 4 minutes. Serve with sliced bread fried in butter.

RICE WITH CHICKEN GIBLETS

1 onion	A little saffron
2 oz. butter	Salt and pepper
4 chopped giblets	2 teacups stock
2 carrots	6 tbsps. rice
1 tbsp. chopped mushroom	1 chopped pimiento
1 bay leaf	

Sauté the chopped onion in the butter; when brown add the chopped giblets and cook for about 5 minutes. Blanch and slice the carrots and mushroom and add to the giblets, with a bay leaf, saffron and seasoning. Pour in the stock, bring to the boil, reduce the heat and simmer for another 25 minutes until the rice is tender. (If necessary add more stock.) Garnish with pimiento.

PASTEL CHOCOANO
(CHICKEN AND EGG PIE)

1 lb. minced chicken (or any other meat)	Salt and pepper
	3 egg yolks
1 chopped onion	2 tbsps. sugar
2 tbsps. oil	2 egg whites
2 dried peaches	2 oz. flour
2 oz. green olives	2 hard-boiled eggs
1 tbsp. raisins	Ground cinnamon
1 egg, beaten	

Sauté the meat and the chopped onion in the oil, add the diced peaches, the olives and raisins and cook about 4 minutes; stir in egg and seasoning.

Beat separately the 3 egg yolks with sugar and the 2 egg whites with salt. Mix them carefully, then add the flour. Turn half this mixture into a buttered fireproof dish and bake in a moderate oven (350° F., mark 4) for about 10 minutes. Put the meat on top, add the 2 sliced hard-boiled eggs and sprinkle with ground cinnamon. Cover

with remaining egg mixture and cook in a hot oven (450° F., mark 8) until brown.

STUFFED CHICKEN

1 chicken	4 tbsps. bread, soaked in milk and squeezed
1 onion	
1 oz. butter	Salt and pepper
1 green pepper	Nutmeg
1 tin whole corn	Melted butter
2 eggs	

Prepare the chicken. Sauté the chopped onions in the butter, add the chopped green pepper and corn and cook for a few minutes. Stir in the eggs and bread and season with salt, pepper and grated nutmeg. Fill the chicken with this mixture and sew up the opening; tie up the legs and spread with melted butter. Cook in a moderate oven (350° F., mark 4) for about 1½ hours. Serve with a green salad.

MINCE AND POTATO PIE

2 chopped onions	1 tsp. salt
2 tbsps. oil	Pepper
1 lb. minced beef	1 hard-boiled egg
3 peeled tomatoes	1 lb. potatoes
2 oz. black olives	2 oz. butter
1 tbsp. raisins	1 egg

Sauté the onions in the oil and when brown add the minced beef, pressing it with a fork to cook it thoroughly. Add the tomatoes, olives, raisins and seasonings and cook for about 15 minutes over a low heat. Add the chopped egg and transfer the mixture to a fireproof dish.

Boil the potatoes separately, mash them, mix with butter and 1 egg and season. Put a thick layer over the meat and bake in a hot oven (450° F., mark 8) until lightly browned.

CARBONADA CRIOLLA
(BEEF AND FRUIT STEW)

1 chopped onion	1 sliced blanched carrot
2 chopped cloves of garlic	Warm stock or water
	1 lb. diced pumpkin
½ cup oil	½ cup peas
1 lb. stewing beef	1 diced potato
2 peeled tomatoes	4 dried peaches or 2 fresh ones
Thyme	
4 oz. butter	1 peeled and chopped plum
1 corn on the cob	1 peeled and sliced apple

Sauté the chopped onion and garlic in the oil; when brown, add the meat, cut into 1-inch cubes, the tomatoes and thyme and cook for a short time. Add the butter, corn, carrot and stock and cook for about 1 hour. Add the pumpkin, peas, potato, peaches, plum and apple, cover the saucepan and cook for another ½ hour.

EMPANADAS SANTIAGUENAS
(MEAT TURNOVERS)
For the Filling

1 lb. onions, chopped	1 lb. lean minced veal
Dripping	2 tsps. vinegar
1 tsp. chopped chillies	2–3 hard-boiled eggs
Salt	

For the Pastry

1 lb. flour	½ lb. suet
2 tsps. salt	Water to mix

Sauté the onions in the dripping and add half the chillies. Place the meat in a basin, pour some boiling water over and strain. Transfer it to a plate, season with salt and add the remaining chillies and the vinegar. Leave to stand.

Make a rather stiff pastry, knead it and then leave for 15 minutes wrapped in a floured cloth. Take a small piece and knead into balls; roll these out one at a time, to form rounds. Place a little meat, onion mixture and chopped egg in each and fold over as for Cornish pasties. Prick the top with a fork and bake in a hot oven (450° F., mark 8) for about 12 minutes.

STUFFED AUBERGINES

6 medium-sized aubergines	A handful of
1 chopped onion, sautéed	chopped parsley
for 1–2 minutes in hot oil	Salt and pepper
A slice of bread soaked in	1 egg
milk	Breadcrumbs

Cut off the aubergine ends and boil in salted water without overcooking. Drain them, cut lengthwise and carefully take out all the flesh. Chop this and add the onion, bread, parsley, salt and pepper; bind with the egg and fill the aubergines with this mixture. Arrange in a fireproof dish, sprinkle some breadcrumbs and a little more oil over them and cook in a moderate oven (350° F., mark 3) for about 15 minutes.

HUEVOS AL COLCHON
(SAVOURY FRIED EGGS)

6 slices of bread	Salt and pepper
½ cup oil	Grated nutmeg
2 chopped onions	1 tsp. sugar
4 peeled tomatoes	6 eggs
2 green peppers	1 tbsp. butter

Fry the bread in the oil, then sauté the onions in the same oil. Add the peeled tomatoes and chopped green peppers, season with salt, pepper, nutmeg and sugar and cook until the liquid is reduced. Fry the eggs in the butter. On top of each slice of bread place a layer of sauce and a fried egg.

STUFFED POTATOES

Select 8 medium-sized potatoes. Boil, cut off the top and remove the inside flesh. Soak a little bread in milk, then squeeze it. Place in a bowl together with 1 egg, some chopped parsley, 1 chopped garlic clove and 1 tbsp. grated cheese; mix well and use to fill the potatoes. Sprinkle with breadcrumbs and fry in very hot oil.

MAZAMORRA
(MAIZE PORRIDGE)

1 lb. white maize	½ tsp. bicarbonate
4 pints water	of soda

Place the maize in a saucepan with the water and cook over a low heat for about 3 hours, stirring frequently with a wooden spoon; after the first hour add the bicarbonate of soda. The grains should be tender and creamy. Serve hot with sugar or honey, or if preferred cold, with sugar and a little milk.

GLORIETTA
(SAVOURY RICE AND BANANAS)

161

Heat a little fat in a saucepan then add 2 breakfast cups washed rice; when the rice has absorbed the fat and looks pale yellow, add 4 breakfast cups boiling water and boil rapidly for 10 minutes; lower the heat to a mere glimmer, cover the rice with greased greaseproof paper and leave until the water is absorbed and the rice is cooked—do not stir, but shake the pan from time to time. Meanwhile fry 1 egg and 1 banana for each person. Pile the rice in a very hot dish, arrange the bananas and eggs on it, and garnish the latter with a mixture of finely chopped raw onion, chopped tomato and chopped parsley.

FLAN DE CAFÉ
(COFFEE CUSTARD)

162

Scald 3 cups milk with 1 cup single cream, then add 6–8 tbsps. instant coffee and 2 tsps. grated orange rind, stir well and cool for 10 minutes. Meanwhile, slightly beat 4 eggs with 1 egg yolk and ½ cup granulated sugar. (If using an electric mixer, set it at a low speed.) Now slowly add the coffee mixture, then 1 tsp. vanilla essence, 1 tsp. almond essence and ½ tsp. salt; blend well. Strain through a fine strainer into 6 custard cups. Sprinkle with grated nutmeg, place the cups in a shallow baking tin and fill the tin with cold water up to ¾ inch from the top of cups. Bake in a slow oven

(325° F., mark 2) for 1 hour, or until a knife inserted in the centre comes out clean. Cool, then chill.

Just before serving remove the custards from the cups, using a small spatula, and arrange upside-down on a serving dish. Sprinkle with 1 cup chopped Brazil nuts. Beat 1 egg white quite stiffly then beat in 3 tbsps. guava jelly until stiff. Swirl this over the nuts.

PASTELITOS DE DULCE
(LITTLE JAM PUFFS)

1¼ lb. flour	Quince jam
6 oz. butter	Oil for frying
1 small cup water	Hot vanilla-flavoured
A pinch of salt	sugar syrup
Melted butter	

Place the flour on board and add the salt, 6 oz. butter and water to make a soft dough. Knead, leave to rest for a little and roll out rather thinly. Spread with melted butter, sprinkle with flour and fold in two. Re-butter, sprinkle with flour and fold again, then flatten with the rolling pin and cut into 5-inch squares. Take half the squares and place on each 1 tbsp. jam thinned with a little water; moisten the edges and cover with another square, pressing the edges. Fry in very hot oil. Dip the pastelitos in hot syrup and cook for 2 minutes. To make the syrup, put 1 lb. sugar in saucepan, cover with water, add some vanilla essence and boil for 5 minutes.

(SWEET EMPANADAS)
For the Filling

2 oz. butter	1 tbsp. chives, finely
1 large onion, finely	chopped
chopped	1 large green pepper,
2 large tomatoes,	seeded and finely
peeled and chopped	chopped
1 large pear, finely	12 oz. raw minced meat
chopped	2 tbsps. sugar
2 large peaches, finely	½ tsp. salt
chopped	⅛ pint dry white wine

For the Pastry

8 oz. flour	6 oz. butter
A pinch of salt	2 egg yolks, beaten
2 tsps. ground	4 tbsps. dry white wine
cinnamon	2 tbsps. milk
2½ oz. sugar	Egg to glaze

Make the filling first. Heat the butter in a large saucepan and fry the onion till transparent. Add the tomatoes, stir well and simmer gently for 5 minutes, then add everything else, stir well,

cover and cook gently for 15 minutes. Leave to cool.

For the pastry, sieve the flour and salt, add a pinch of the cinnamon and ½ oz. sugar. Add the butter and mix till the mixture looks like breadcrumbs. Mix half the egg yolk with the wine, add, then add the milk gradually till the mixture begins to stick together. Form it into a firm dough, roll it out and then cut into rounds the size of a saucer. Put an equal amount of filling on each, moisten the edges and turn the pastry over to form half circles; seal well. Brush the tops with egg and sprinkle with 2 oz. sugar and the rest of the cinnamon. Bake in a hot oven (450° F., mark 8) for 15 minutes.

Brazil

CANJA
(CHICKEN SOUP)

1 fowl	Tomatoes
1 tbsp. butter	Parsley
1 tbsp. chopped onion	½ cup rice
Salt	

Cut up an old fat fowl. Fry in butter, add chopped onion, when golden-brown cover with water, season with salt, add tomatoes and parsley. Simmer gently until tender. Strain the broth. Remove bones and skin from chicken and cut up the meat. Cook the rice in broth and when it is nearly tender, add chicken and salt if required. Simmer until broth is yellow and not too thick. Skim fat from surface before serving.

MAYONNAISE DE CAMARRAO E LINGUADO
(SHRIMP AND FLOUNDER MAYONNAISE)

Melt 2 tbsps. butter in a large frying pan, add ⅓ cup lemon juice, ¼ cup chopped parsley, 1 tbsp. sugar, 1 tsp. salt, 6 whole peppercorns and 2 bay leaves; bring to the boil.

Place 2 flounder fillets (about ½ lb. each) in the mixture in the pan, cover and simmer for 5 minutes. Cool, then refrigerate.

Combine ⅓ cup lemon juice, 2 tbsps. chopped parsley, ¼ tsp. seasoned salt and 2 dozen large shrimps (cooked and deveined). Refrigerate this mixture also.

Halve 3 hard-boiled eggs lengthwise and top each with ¼ tsp. mayonnaise, then with a rolled anchovy fillet with a caper centre.

Slice 1 dozen of the marinaded shrimps and add 1 cup shredded round lettuce and ¼ cup mayonnaise. Arrange 6 beds of cos lettuce leaves round the edge of a large platter. Cut

163

each fish fillet into thirds and lay one piece on each lettuce bed. Top with sliced shrimp mixture and ½ cup mayonnaise. Garnish each piece of fish with 2 pieces of pickled gherkin and 2 whole shrimps.

In the centre of the platter, arrange the egg halves, 6 gherkin slices, 6 pickled beet slices and 12 stoned ripe olives; garnish with celery leaves.

COLD FISH SALAD

1½–2 lb. lightly poached white fish (haddock, flounder, etc.)
½ cup olive oil
1 cup white wine vinegar
A dash of pepper
½ tsp. salt
2 bay leaves
1 tsp. sugar
1 tbsp. tomato purée
2–3 garlic cloves, crushed
6 medium-sized onions, very thinly sliced

Marinade the fish overnight in a mixture made by combining all the ingredients except the onion rings; arrange the onions on top of the fish. The next day, drain the fish and serve cold, with tomato and potato salad.

BACALHAU FRITO À BAIANA
(FRIED CODFISH)

First wash and skin the fish, then dip it in batter. Fry in oil with chipped potatoes. Take out the fish with the potatoes, and in the same oil, cook some onions, chopped parsley, plenty of pepper and a little crushed garlic. When the onions are soft, thicken the sauce with a little flour. Put back the fish and the potatoes and finish cooking. There must be plenty of pepper in this dish.

CODFISH BALLS

Soak the codfish overnight; next day boil until tender. Remove bones and put fish through a mincer. Add some boiled and mashed potatoes. Mix with 2 eggs or more, chopped onion and chopped parsley. Shape into balls. Fry in boiling fat until brown.

FISH AND TOMATOES

Melt 2 oz. fat in a saucepan and add some chopped onion, some tomatoes, cut into small pieces, and 4 red peppers. Prepare 1 large or 2 small white fish, season with salt and lemon juice, slice and put on top of the vegetables. Add some chopped parsley and cover with greaseproof paper or metal foil (the original recipe calls for banana leaves). Cook over a very gentle heat until the fish is done but not broken up. Blend some butter, flour and fish liquor, boil up and pour over the fish.

COD PIE

1½ lb. cod fillet
Olive oil
A clove of garlic
Chopped parsley
1 small onion
1 lb. cooked potatoes
1 oz. butter
1 cup milk
Salt and pepper
3 eggs
Garnish
(see below)

Cook the cod fillet and flake it, removing any skin or bone, then put it through a mincer. Heat some oil in a deep frying pan and fry the chopped garlic, parsley and sliced onion. Add the fish and fry this, then take it from the heat and stir in the creamed potatoes, butter, milk and seasonings. When the mixture is cold, separate the eggs and whisk the whites stiffly. Fold these into the yolks and then into the cod mixture. Bake in a moderately hot oven (425° F., mark 7) for 15–20 minutes. When the pie is done, decorate the top with sliced hard-boiled eggs, sliced tomatoes, olives and grated cheese, etc., as desired.

UNCOOKED SAUCE FOR FRIED FISH

1 tsp. cumin seed
3 cloves of garlic, finely chopped then pounded
1 tsp. chopped parsley
A pinch of saffron
½ tsp. salt
¼ tsp. black pepper
¼ pint vinegar
4 tbsps. water
2 tbsps. tomato sauce (optional)

Pound the cumin seed to a powder, add the other ingredients and stir well.

While the fried fish is still hot, turn it for a few seconds in the sauce; pour the rest of the sauce over the hot fish on the serving dish.

DUCK WITH ORANGE

Prepare the duck the day before it is required and season it with salt, pepper and a little lemon juice, ½ cup white wine and ½ cup water. Just before cooking the duck, cover it with butter or sliced bacon; roast in a moderately hot oven (425° F., mark 6) for 1–1½ hours; baste well and often. When it is cooked, cut it up, and place the portions on a dish surrounded by 4 oranges, peeled and sliced.

Remove the grease from the liquid in which the duck was soaked, add the juice of 2 oranges, heat, stirring well, and serve separately as a sauce.

GALINHA DE MOLHA PARDO
(CHICKEN STEW)

For this you require a freshly killed chicken, as the blood should be kept (add a cupful of vinegar to prevent clotting). Cut the chicken into pieces and brown lightly in hot lard, then add 1 tsp. sugar and a little chopped onion and fry together. Add 2 tsps. flour, stirring it well in, with half a bay leaf, some chopped parsley, salt and 1 pint warm water. Bring to the boil, then simmer gently for about 1 hour. Just before serving, stir in the blood and vinegar gradually. Serve with boiled rice.

VATAPA
(BRAZILIAN CHICKEN)

Boil a large chicken until tender, adding salt, minced onion, garlic and half a bay leaf. Drain carefully, take the meat from the bones and cut up. Melt about 2 oz. fat in a saucepan and add the chicken pieces, with onion, garlic, salt and spices to flavour, then fry until browned. Add some of the chicken broth and as many as possible of the following ; a few prawns, fried and minced peanuts, some black pepper, a cupful of palm or olive oil and the milk of a fresh coconut. Thicken slightly with cornflour and cook for a few minutes longer.

CHICKEN AND MUSHROOMS

1 cup chicken broth	4 egg yolks
1 cup milk or thin cream	$\frac{1}{2}$ green pepper
2 oz. butter	$\frac{1}{2}$ red pepper
2 oz. flour	1 cup mushrooms
Salt and pepper	1 tsp. lemon juice
3 cups cooked chicken	

Melt the butter, add the mushrooms and shredded green pepper. Cook for 5 minutes over a slow heat to prevent butter from burning, add flour and seasoning, mix well, then add cold chicken stock and milk. Stir constantly until creamy. Set dish over hot water, add chicken slices, red pepper and lemon juice and cook until hot. Then add well-beaten egg yolks. Serve on toast, if preferred. .

FEIJOADA COMPLETA
(BRAZILIAN BLACK BEANS)

1 lb. salt pork	1 lb. sausages
1 salted tongue	2 lb. black beans
1 lb. dried meat	Onion, tomato, parsley,
$\frac{1}{4}$ lb. bacon	bay leaf

Wash and soak the meats overnight and wash and soak the beans in a separate bowl. Next day drain the water off the meats and add to the beans, cover with water and boil until beans are tender—from 3–4 hours. Fry onions, tomatoes, parsley and bay leaf and add to bean pot ; boil until the broth thickens. Before serving remove the salt meats on to a separate

dish, mash the beans a little to thicken the broth and serve in a tureen. Serve with rice. Peel and cut some oranges and serve on separate plates.

STUFFED PIMIENTOS

Choose even-sized pimientos and simmer them for about 5 minutes in boiling water. Take off the tops and remove the seeds. Fill with a very highly seasoned mixture of minced or finely cut up cooked chicken, chopped cooked onions, chopped garlic and freshly chopped herbs. Sprinkle with oil or dot with shavings of butter and bake in a moderately hot oven (425° F., mark 6) until heated through and browned.

BRAZILIAN-STYLE LIVER

1 lb. lambs' or calves' liver	Pepper
	2 large onions
1 clove of garlic (crushed)	Fat for frying
	Boiled rice
$\frac{1}{4}$ pint vinegar	

Slice the liver thinly and marinade it overnight in the vinegar with the garlic and pepper. Slice the onions and fry them in hot fat until brown. Take them out and keep hot while the liver is fried on both sides. Take this out also and pour the strained vinegar into the pan. When it is simmering and almost boiling, add the liver. Dish the liver up on the boiled rice with the onions and pour the sauce over.

PORCO RECHEIADO
(ROAST STUFFED PORK)

$\frac{1}{4}$ cup salad oil	$\frac{1}{2}$ tsp. pepper
1 cup chopped onion	4–5 lb. pork shoulder, boned
1 garlic clove, minced	
$\frac{1}{2}$ cup chopped green pepper	$2\frac{1}{2}$ cups cold cooked rice
3 cups diced fresh tomatoes	2 lb. whole white onions
$\frac{2}{3}$ cup sultanas or raisins	6 carrots, cut in halves
$\frac{1}{4}$ cup sliced ripe olives	Butter
$2\frac{1}{2}$ tsps. salt	Parsley or watercress
1 tsp. chilli powder	(optional)

Heat the salad oil in a frying pan and sauté the onion, garlic and green pepper, till tender. Add the tomatoes, sultanas or raisins, olives, $1\frac{1}{2}$ tsps. salt, chilli powder and $\frac{1}{4}$ tsp. pepper, cover and simmer for 5 minutes, stirring occasionally.

Sprinkle the inside of the pork joint with 1 tsp. salt and $\frac{1}{4}$ tsp. pepper. Toss the cold cooked rice in a bowl with $\frac{1}{2}$ cup of the tomato mixture, then use to fill the pocket in the pork

and skewer securely. (Cover the remaining tomato mixture and set aside.) Arrange the stuffed pork on a wire trivet in a roasting pan, put into a slow oven (325° F., mark 2) and roast for 1 hour, then remove the dripping from the pan. Cover the pork with the rest of the tomato mixture and cover with foil. Continue roasting for 1½–2 hours longer; remove the foil.

Meanwhile cook the whole onions and halved carrots till just tender; season and keep warm.

Place the roasted pork on a large heated platter and remove the skewers. Arrange the buttered, cooked whole onions and carrots around and garnish with parsley or watercress. Serve with dry boiled rice.

CHEESE BALLS

Mix 3 eggs, 3 soupspoonfuls flour, 1 soupspoonful of milk and 1 tsp. of salt. Beat well and add 6 oz. grated cheese. Fry spoonfuls of the mixture in hot fat.

CROQUETTE DE MILHO

2 oz. butter or margarine	Pepper
½ an onion, chopped	1 cup milk
Salt	1 tbsp. cornflour
2–3 tomatoes	1–2 eggs
1 tin of sweet corn, minced	3 tbsps. flour
	1 tsp. baking powder
1 cup sweet corn liquor	Breadcrumbs
1 lemon	Fat for frying

Melt the fat in a saucepan, add the onion, salt, tomatoes (skinned and seeded), corn and corn liquor; stir in a little lemon juice, some pepper, the milk and cornflour. When the mixture has the consistency of mashed potato, remove the pan from the heat and let it cool a little. Beat the egg whites until stiff, add to the mixture, followed by the yolks, and stir well. Add the flour and baking powder, mix and cook again until stiff. Shape into small cakes, roll them in breadcrumbs and fry in hot fat until golden-brown.

BRAZILIAN SALAD

½ lb. skinned tomatoes	Juice of 1 lemon
1 celery heart	2 tsps. cream
4 oz. pineapple pieces	Cayenne pepper
1 good lettuce heart	

Slice the tomatoes, cut up the celery heart and mix together with the pineapple pieces. (Although fresh pineapple should be used if possible, well-drained tinned pineapple can be substituted.) Shred the lettuce heart and mix this with the other ingredients, reserving some

pineapple for decorating the salad. Put it into a glass dish and pour over the lemon juice, cream and some cayenne pepper, blended well together.

FRIED CABBAGE

Wash a large cabbage, separating the leaves. Pile several leaves on each other, roll up tightly and slice with a sharp knife, to give fine shreds. Blanch with boiling water, drain and put into a frying pan containing a generous amount of hot pork dripping. Fry quickly, sprinkle with salt and serve at once.

DULCE COCADA
(COCONUT SWEET)

1 large coconut	½ lb. sugar
4 eggs	¼ pint cream

Shell the coconut and scrape away the brown skin. Break the nut, reserving the milk, and grate or finely shred it. Beat the eggs well with the sugar and stir in the cream. Add to the coconut, with some of the milk, and put into a greased fireproof dish. Bake in a slow oven (325° F., mark 2) for about 45 minutes, or until set. Put aside to get cold (or chill it in a refrigerator) before serving.

BANANA PIE

Slice 6 bananas and fry them lightly in butter. Place them in a fireproof dish and cover them with either (a) a syrup made with ½ cup sugar and ¼ cup water, to which are added 2 beaten egg yolks flavoured with vanilla, or (b) an ordinary custard made with either eggs or custard powder. Now make a stiff meringue of egg whites and fine sugar, and pour it over the custard. Bake for about 15 minutes in a moderate oven (350° F., mark 4). Decorate with small pieces of crystallised or fresh fruit.

BANANA FRITTERS

Peel some bananas, halve them lengthways and marinade in some liqueur or rum. Dip in liqueur-flavoured batter (using the same flavour as in the marinade), and fry in hot fat. Sprinkle with sugar and serve at once.

COCONUT PIE

Shortcrust pastry	A little grated nutmeg
2 eggs	1 pint hot, but not
1 cup grated coconut	boiling, milk
4 oz. caster sugar	

Line a pie plate with shortcrust pastry and bake it lightly. Beat the eggs, add the other ingredients, mix thoroughly and pour into the dish. Bake in a moderate oven (350° F., mark 4) for about ½ hour, or until the filling is set.

BANANA SPONGE CAKE

½ cup butter	2 tsps. bicarbonate of
2 cups sugar	soda
1½ cups mashed bananas	2 tsps. vanilla essence
3 cups plain flour	2 eggs
2 tsps. baking powder	

Cream the butter well, add the sugar a little at a time, stir in the mashed bananas and beaten eggs. Sift the flour and baking powder and mix with the rest. Dissolve the soda in a little water, and add to the mixture, with the vanilla essence. Mix everything well and bake in a deep oblong tin which has been very well greased, for about 50 minutes in a moderate oven (350° F., mark 4).

BANANA PUDDING

8 eggs	Grated lemon rind
14 oz. cooked bananas, passed through a sieve	9 oz. sugar
3½ oz. butter	Cinnamon

Beat the eggs with the sugar. Add slowly, banana, butter, lemon rind and cinnamon, stirring carefully. Cook in buttered pudding dish in a moderately hot oven (425° F., mark 7).

PAVE
(LAYERED SPONGE BISCUITS)

2 packets savoy biscuits	8 tbsps. powdered
8 oz. butter	chocolate
8 oz. sugar	Port wine
8 egg yolks	

Mix butter, sugar and eggs. Then add chocolate which has been dissolved in 2 spoonfuls of water. Arrange a layer of biscuits dampened with a little port wine and a layer of the above mixture and so on until all the biscuits are finished, then cover with a layer of the mixture and sprinkle with chopped toasted almonds. Leave until the following day and then serve.

Chile

SOPITA AROMATIZADA
(HERB-FLAVOURED SOUP)

4 slices of stale bread	1 egg
Colouring (see below)	Salt and cayenne
1 tsp. vinegar	Mutton broth
2 sprigs of mint	Grated cheese

Cut the slices of bread in half and fry in the colouring till quite crisp, then put them in the bottom of a casserole or tureen. Pour in the vinegar and place the slightly crushed sprigs of mint on top. Beat the egg slightly, add the seasoning and pour it over the toast. Pour in sufficient boiling broth to serve the required number of portions, cover the casserole and let the soup simmer for 2 minutes. Sprinkle with grated cheese and serve immediately.

Note : Colouring is made by heating 1 cup beef suet in a frying pan and adding ½ a chopped onion, 3 chopped red peppers and ⅓ tsp. cayenne.

CONGRIO EN FUENTE À LA CHILENA
(CASSEROLED CONGER EEL)

2½ lb. conger eel	A little ground cumin
Salt and pepper	seed
Olive oil	4 tomatoes
2 tbsps. butter	4 potatoes
2 tbsps. lard	2 ears of corn
2 chopped onions	Croûtons
2 minced garlic cloves	Sliced hard-boiled egg
A little marjoram	

Cut the eel into individual portions, season with salt and pepper and brown slightly in olive oil. Heat the butter and lard in a saucepan and add the chopped onion, garlic cloves, marjoram and ground cumin. When the onions are soft, add the peeled and thinly sliced tomatoes, the peeled and sliced potatoes, and the kernels and cream of the grated corn, cover and cook until the potatoes are done, then season to taste. Put half this vegetable mixture in a casserole, lay the fish on this and add the remaining sauce. Cover and cook in a slow oven (325° F., mark 2) until the fish is done. Garnish with croûtons and sliced egg and serve hot.

CAZUEIA
(CHICKEN AND VEGETABLE STEW)

1 fowl	Salt and pepper
2 quarts water	1 tsp. cumin seed
1 summer squash, diced	1 mashed garlic clove
Pieces of pumpkin, diced	Chopped leaves of
¼ lb. of string beans	1 celery stalk
2 ears of corn, cut into lengths	2 tbsps. minced parsley
2 chopped onions	1 tbsp. rice
1 green pepper, chopped	1 egg, beaten slightly
½ cup peas	¼ lb. potatoes
1 large carrot, diced	1 egg yolk, beaten
1 tbsp. colouring (see above)	slightly
	1 tbsp. vinegar

Simmer the fowl in the water until tender.

Add the vegetables (except the potatoes), the colouring, seasonings, spices, herbs and rice and cook until tender. Then add the beaten egg, cook for 5 minutes and skim. Bone the fowl. Boil the potatoes and make into a paste with the egg yolk and the vinegar; put this in a tureen and pour over it the broth and the pieces of boned fowl.

EMPANADAS AL HORNO
(MEAT PASTIES)

1 lb. flour	Deep fat for frying
$\frac{1}{4}$ lb. lard	Caster sugar
$\frac{1}{4}$ tsp. salt	(optional)

For the Filling

A little fat	2 chillies (if a " hot "
2 medium-sized onions,	taste is preferred)
cut very finely	A good pinch of
1 lb. finely cut up	marjoram
chicken (or other	1 tsp. chopped
light-fleshed bird	parsley
or veal)	Flour to thicken
Salt	2 hard-boiled eggs
$\frac{1}{2}$ breakfast cup cleaned	Olives
and stoned raisins	

The sauce is best made the day before the pasties are required.

Heat the fat and fry the onions slightly, add the meat, salt and sufficient water to cover and simmer for 1 hour. Now add the raisins, the chillies, if used, the marjoram and parsley and cook until the meat is tender. Thicken slightly with flour and water and cook for another 5 minutes; allow to cool.

Now prepare the pastry by stirring the flour and salt into the hot lard. When it has cooled, roll half of it out thinly. At intervals of 3 inches over the pastry put 2 tsps. sauce plus a slice of hard-boiled egg and a stoned olive. Cover with the remaining pastry, thinly rolled, pat gently round the mounds of filling and cut round the shapes with a pastry wheel. Fry in boiling fat. Reshape the odd pieces of pastry and repeat the process until all the pastry is used up. Serve hot, sprinkled, if desired, with caster sugar.

CARNE DE CHILE
(FRIED MUTTON SLICES)

Cold mutton	1 tsp. vinegar
2 well-beaten eggs	Salt and cayenne
3 tbsps. flour	Lard
1 tbsp. mustard	Broth or hot milk
1 tsp. olive oil	1 tbsp. butter

Slice the meat. Make a batter of the eggs, flour, mustard, oil, vinegar, salt and cayenne. Soak the slices of meat in this batter for a few minutes, then fry them in hot lard. Pour the remaining batter into the hot milk or hot broth, add the butter and heat to make a sauce which is poured over the fried meat just before serving.

SALPICON
(A CHILEAN SALAD)

2 cups cold veal, lamb	2 heads of lettuce,
or chicken, diced	shredded
2 hard-boiled eggs,	2 tbsps. chopped
sliced	parsley
1 tsp. onion juice	Well-seasoned French
A few mint leaves,	dressing
minced	

Mix all the ingredients and add the French dressing. Toss until well mixed and serve on crisp lettuce leaves.

HUMITAS DE CHOCIO
(CORN " PARCELS ")

12 ears of corn	1 chopped tomato
Cornhusks	Salt and pepper
1 chopped onion	1 tbsp. sugar
3 tbsps. butter	

Grate the corn from the cobs and save the cobs. Pour boiling water over the largest cornhusks and allow to soften. Fry the onion in the butter until brown, then add the tomato, grated corn and seasoning; allow to cool. Take the cornhusks from water and spread out flat. Put 3 tbsps. corn mixture in the centre of each husk, roll, tie each end with a strip of cornhusk and trim the ends neatly. Place the stripped corn cobs in a deep saucepan and pour just enough boiling water over them to cover. Lay the *humitas* on top of the cobs, cover tightly and cook for 30 minutes. Take the *humitas* from the pan and untie the ends without opening the husks. Sprinkle the *humitas* with sugar and stack on a platter.

STUFFED POTATOES

1 onion	About $\frac{1}{2}$ lb. cold cooked
1 oz. butter	meat or chicken,
1 tsp. chopped parsley	minced
$\frac{1}{4}$ tsp. chopped thyme	1 egg yolk
1 tbsp. rich stock	1 lb. mashed potatoes
1 hard-boiled egg,	Cornflour
chopped	Olive oil for deep
A few raisins	frying

Fry the chopped onion in the butter and add the herbs and stock. Add the hard-boiled egg, raisins and minced meat or chicken. Cool this mixture a little and roll into small balls, using a little flour on the hands and board. Add the egg yolk to the hot mashed potatoes and beat well. Cover the meat balls with the potato and form into egg-shaped croquettes; roll them in cornflour and fry in hot oil.

CAJEYA DE ALMENDRA
(ALMOND CAKES)

2 cups sugar	5 egg whites
1 cup water	¾ cup chopped almonds

Cook the sugar and water together until a thread may be spun when a little of the syrup is dropped from a spoon. Beat the egg whites stiff and add the syrup a little at a time, beating constantly. Beat with an egg beater until the mixture thickens slightly; add the finely chopped nuts. Pour into small paper cups and bake in a moderate oven (350° F., mark 3) for 12–15 minutes. Allow to cool and serve with fruit.

Bolivia

CAMARONES AL HORNO
(PRAWN SAVOURY)

1 lb. prawns	2 tsps. aji salt
½ oz. lard or margarine	¼ pint (approx.) white sauce
1 small onion, finely chopped	1 small egg
2 tsps. finely chopped parsley	A little white wine (optional)
1 tomato	Breadcrumbs

Shell the cooked prawns. Melt the fat and fry the onion, parsley and tomato, with the aji salt (which may be replaced by 2 tsps. piquant table sauce); cook very slowly for about 20 minutes, stirring constantly. Mix the creamy white sauce with the contents of the pan, then add the well-beaten egg and the prawns with a little white wine. Transfer to an ovenproof dish, cover the top with breadcrumbs and bake in a slow oven (325° F., mark 2) for 25 minutes.

STUFFED AVOCADOS

6 avocado pears	1 medium-sized lettuce
4 oz. cooked chicken, shrimps or fish, finely chopped	¼ pint mayonnaise sauce
	Salt and pepper to taste
	1 hard-boiled egg, sliced

Cut the avocados in half and remove the large seed. Mix the meat or fish and lettuce with the mayonnaise and season to taste. Pile on the avocados and garnish with the egg.

BOLIVIAN CORN ON THE COB

Strip 1 dozen corn cobs and crush the grain in a basin. Heat a little fat and mix with the corn; add 4 well-beaten eggs, a little salt, a little grated cheese and a little aniseed and mix well. Put into a greased ovenproof dish and cook in a slow oven (325° F., mark 2) until set.

HUMITA EN CHALA
(STUFFED CORN LEAVES)

These are made in a similar way to the Argentine version, but the filling consists of the grated corn kernels, 2 tbsps. aji salt (or piquant table sauce), 1 tsp. ordinary salt, 1 tbsp. sugar, a few aniseeds, 2 tomatoes (peeled and mashed), 4 eggs, 1 small glass brandy, 4 oz. melted lard and a little milk to mix, if required. After placing some of this mixture on each leaf, add a thin slice of cheese, then fold over and secure. Bake in a greased dish in a moderate oven (350° F., mark 4) for about 20–25 minutes.

EMPANADAS BOLIVIANAS
(BOLIVIAN PASTIES)

1 lb. flour	2 tsps. salt
4 oz. lard	3 egg yolks
1 tsp. sugar	1 cup tepid water

For the Filling

1 lb. stewing steak	½ lb. cooked green peas
3 tbsps. lard	1 tbsp. aji salt (or 1 tbsp. piquant table sauce)
1 large onion	
2 tomatoes	
1½ tbsps. powdered gelatine	Seasoning
	A few sultanas
2 teacupfuls good stock	A few olives
3 cooked potatoes	Hard-boiled egg

Begin making the filling 12 hours beforehand. Chop the meat. Heat the lard and fry the chopped onion and tomatoes, then add the gelatine (previously dissolved in ½ cupful water) and the stock. Add half the chopped meat, bring to the boil, then put aside in a cool place for 12 hours. The next day add the rest of the meat (raw), the potatoes, peas, salt or sauce and seasoning to taste.

Sieve the flour; melt the lard, add the sugar and salt and leave to get slightly cool, then stir gradually into the flour, together with egg yolks and water.

Roll out, cut into saucer-like rounds and put on each a portion of meat filling, a few sultanas, an olive and a few pieces of egg. Fold over envelope fashion, rolling the edges to keep the filling from oozing out. Bake in a moderately hot oven (425° F., mark 7) for 15 minutes. Serve hot or cold.

Venezuela

HALLACAS
(MEAT PIES)
For the Filling

2 oz. suet or dripping	8 oz. raw beef or veal,
1 large onion, sliced	minced
1 red or green pepper,	2 oz. seedless raisins
seeded and finely	2 oz. stoned green olives
chopped	2 hard-boiled eggs,
Salt and pepper	chopped

For the Pastry

4 oz. flour	2 oz. butter
A pinch of salt	2 small eggs
2 oz. lard	

Make the pastry in the usual way, roll out $\frac{1}{8}$ inch thick and cut into 8 saucer-sized rounds.

For the filling, heat the suet and fry the onion till brown; add the chopped pepper, salt and pepper and fry for 2 minutes. Now add the meat, raisins, olives and chopped eggs; cook gently for 4 minutes, then leave to cool. Put an equal amount of pastry filling on each round, moisten the edges and put another round on top; seal tightly. Bake in a moderately hot oven (425° F., mark 7) for 15 minutes.

Colombia

CUCHUCO
(BARLEY SOUP)

1 lb. meat bones	8 oz. fresh green peas
4 pints water	8 oz. cabbage, finely
1 large onion, chopped	chopped
1 bay leaf	2 tsps. salt
3 peppercorns	$\frac{1}{2}$ tsp. pepper
1 lb. barley	

Place the bones in the 4 pints water, add the onion, bay leaf and peppercorns and simmer, covered, for 2 hours. Wash the barley and place in another pot, cover with water, bring to the boil, strain, cover again with water and cook for 3 minutes; strain and add to the strained bone stock. Bring to the boil, add the vegetables and seasonings and simmer gently until the soup thickens and the barley is cooked.

Peru

HUANCAINA PAPAS
(POTATOES WITH CHEESE AND ONION SAUCE)

6 large potatoes	1 medium-sized onion
1 cup cottage cheese	(or 4–5 shallots),
$\frac{1}{2}$ cup milk	thinly shaved
Juice of 1 lemon	1 hard-boiled egg yolk,
Salt and pepper	mashed
A little paprika	

Bake the potatoes in a moderately hot oven (400° F., mark 6) for about $\frac{3}{4}$–1 hour. Alternatively, boil them whole and unpeeled in salted water. Peel the potatoes, cut into chunks and serve with a sauce made by combining the remaining ingredients. This should be served either cold or just slightly warm—but not hot.

Uruguay

DULCE DE LECHE
(MILK SWEET)

This is another dish which is widely spread through South America. Mix 2 pints milk, $1\frac{3}{4}$ lb. sugar and a little vanilla essence, then simmer over a very low heat, stirring constantly to prevent burning. After about an hour the mixture should have the consistency of cream or thick pea soup. It may be eaten as a sweet or spread on bread.

PUCHERO
(BEEF STEW)

Boil some water in a large saucepan and put in some beef, in large pieces, a boiling fowl, some whole corn cobs, thickly sliced carrots, leeks, chick peas, Spanish-type sausages and a good-sized piece of boiling bacon. Season to taste (according to the saltiness of the bacon). Cook for at least 3 hours over a low heat. About 20 minutes before serving add some potatoes and cook until these are done. Serve with cabbage.

ALBONDIGAS
(MEAT BALLS)

Mince some beef very finely (it is best to put it twice through the mincer). Add some finely chopped raisins and olives and season with salt, pepper and a pinch of sugar. Mix well and shape into very small balls. Egg-and-crumb, then simmer for about 10 minutes in a sauce made by simmering together chopped tomatoes, minced onion, chopped parsley and chopped garlic. Add a little water and simmer for a further 30 minutes, but take care the meat balls do not break up.

THE West Indies, exotic and fruitful, offer a variety of interesting and unusual dishes based on the products of the islands and the seas surrounding them. Bananas, citrus fruits and pineapples grow freely everywhere and the colourful market stalls offer peppers, tomatoes, spices, avocados, pomegranates and passion fruit, as well as the more unusual yams and breadfruit. Beef, mutton and goat's meat are all available and pork is both popular and plentiful. Chickens and eggs are sold in the markets and the warm seas round the islands offer a plentiful supply of fish, ranging from barracuda and shark to crayfish and prawns.

Despite the fact that a distinctive pattern of living and eating is common to all the West Indian islands, there are, nevertheless, real differences between them.

Bermuda has a slightly American atmosphere, while Barbados remains staunchly British and St. Lucia and Dominica, French. Jamaican and Barbados rum, molasses and cane sugar are world-famous and Dominica exports enormous quantities of lime juice and pulp, as well as vanilla. From Trinidad comes angostura bitters—originally invented as a remedy for stomach complaints, but now a popular ingredient in drinks and even in cooking.

West Indian cooking has its roots in many cultures—English, French, Spanish and African. The diet of the West Indian negro population is starchy, based as it is on cassava, yams, sweet potatoes and similar vegetables ; meat is not of a very high quality and the spicy and hot sauces add interest and colour. At its best West Indian and Créole cooking compares favourably with that of other regions and the local housewives take great pride in their skill.

The Caribbean

AVOCADO PEAR SOUP

1 tbsp. butter	½ a large pear
1 tbsp. flour	1 tsp. salt
¼ pint milk	A dash of piquant table
1 pint white stock	sauce (optional)
A piece of green pepper	

Melt the butter and stir in the flour without browning. Add the milk gradually and then cook the mixture until it is like a thick white sauce. Stir in the stock and add the green pepper. Just before serving, stir in the peeled pear, which should be either pounded or sieved. Warm the soup for a few minutes, but do not boil, which causes a bitter taste. Season, strain and serve at once.

PEANUT SOUP

1 lb. peanuts	1 oz. flour
1 onion	2 cups milk
2 sticks of celery	A pinch of salt
2 cups white stock	A pinch of cayenne pepper
2 oz. butter	

Mince the peanuts; cook them slowly with the chopped onion and celery in the stock. In another saucepan melt the butter, add the flour, stir till smooth, then add the milk. Combine the mixtures, season with salt and pepper and cook for 5 minutes. Rub through a strainer and serve hot. Makes 6 helpings.

JAMAICAN PUMPKIN SOUP

¼ lb. salt pork (minced)	1 lb. pumpkin (peeled
4 pints water	and seeds removed)
1 tsp. thyme	1 tsp. pepper
1 bay leaf	½ tsp. grated nutmeg
1 tsp. salt	

Cook the pork in the water with the thyme and bay leaf for 30 minutes. Add the pumpkin, salt and pepper, cook for 15–20 minutes, then sieve. Add the nutmeg, reheat and serve. Makes 6 helpings.

PEA SOUP

½ cup split peas	A small pinch of bicar-
1 lb. stewing meat or	bonate of soda
salt beef	1 lb. "ground pro-
2 tbsps. oil or butter	visions," i.e., root
1 bunch "finity"	vegetables
(soup seasoning)	2 tsps. salt—less if
1 onion, chopped	salted meat is used
2–3 blades of chives,	¼ tsp. black pepper
chopped	Dumplings, if desired
2 pints water	

Pick and wash the peas and soak overnight. Wash and cut up the meat. (Soak salt meat for at least ½ hour before cutting up.) Heat the oil until smoking, lightly fry the seasonings, onion and chives, and set on one side. Brown any lean meat, but not salt beef. Put the water, meat, peas and bicarbonate of soda to cook in a covered pot; when boiling, skim well and add the prepared seasonings. Simmer until the peas are thoroughly softened and broken down—stirring if necessary. Peel and wash the root vegetables, cut into neat slices or dice, add to the soup with the salt and pepper (and dumplings, if used) and cook until soft—about 30 minutes. 6 servings.

DUMPLINGS

4 oz. flour	2–3 tbsps. lard (or fat
2 tbsps. breadcrumbs,	pork or suet)
if liked	1 tsp. baking powder or
Pinch of salt	¼ tsp. baking soda

Sift the flour. Chop suet or fat pork if used. Mix all the dry ingredients and fat and add enough cold water to mix to a stiff dough. Knead lightly and form into balls. Put into boiling water or soup and cook for 30 minutes. This makes 8 medium-sized dumplings.

OXTAIL SOUP

1 small oxtail	2 tbsps. toasted crumbs
(jointed)	Seasoning (cayenne
½ gill white beans	pepper, chopped
1 small bunch of	onion, salt)
carrots	1 tbsp. sherry

The day before the soup is required, put the oxtail, beans and carrots in enough cold water to cover, boil until tender, then add the breadcrumbs; leaving the lid off the pot, boil until the meat is cooked. Put aside in a cool place. The following day, skim off the fat and add sufficient cold water to make the required quantity of soup; add the seasoning and sherry just before serving.

SANCOCHE
(PICKLED MEAT SOUP)

¾ lb. pickled meat (e.g.,	About 1½ lb. vegetables
a thick slice of salt	Herbs (e.g., parsley,
beef, thick slices of	chives)
salt pork, or pickled	½ tsp. salt
pig's tail)	¼ tsp. pepper
1 tbsp. butter or oil	Dumplings, if liked
1 quart water	

Soak and cut up the meat. Peel and cut the vegetables into chunks or thick slices. Peel, cut up and lightly fry the seasonings in the butter. Mix all the ingredients and simmer till soft—about 1 hour. Serves 4–6 people.

The vegetables would include plantains or

bananas, *tamias* (replaced by potatoes), sweet potatoes, cassava, pumpkin, okras, callaloo (replace by spinach), green figs, etc.

CORN SOUP

2 corn cobs	1 large onion, chopped
1 oz. butter	Salt and pepper
1 oz. flour	$\frac{1}{2}$ pint cream or milk

Cook the corn cobs in boiling water until tender, then drain (keeping the liquor) and scrape off the corn kernels; pound and sieve these. Heat the butter, stir in the flour and add the onion, seasonings and sufficient corn liquor to make a thick soup. Stir in the corn and simmer for about 10 minutes, then add the cream or milk and reheat (stirring), but do not boil.

FISH FRITTERS AND FLOATS

Shred any cold cooked fish. Make a thick batter with egg, flour and water and mix in the fish—the mixture should have a thick consistency. Drop spoonfuls into a frying pan containing some smoking hot fat and fry on both sides; place on a dish in the oven while you make the " floats."

Mix some self-raising flour and salt to taste with cold water to give a thick, smooth paste—it should drop easily from the spoon. Drop spoonfuls into boiling fat and fry both sides till golden-brown. The mixture puffs up into light, bready fritters. Serve on the same dish as the fish fritters, garnish with parsley, and serve at once.

These are very quick and easy to make. Bacon fat for frying improves the flavour.

WHITE FISH STEW

2 snappers or white fish	Salt and black pepper
1 large onion	2 cups water
2 tbsps. sweet oil	2 eggs
2–3 small tomatoes	Juice of 2 limes
1 small piece of green ginger	1 tbsp. flour
2–3 pimiento seeds	Chopped parsley

Prepare the fish. Slice the onion very thinly, put into a deep saucepan with the sweet oil and sauté well. Then put in the tomatoes and green ginger, also sliced thinly, and the pimiento. Season with salt and black pepper. Sauté all together, then add the water, put in the fish, and cook again until it is well done. While the fish is cooking, mix the well-beaten eggs and the lime juice. Take out the fish, mix the flour to a smooth paste with a little water and thicken the gravy, then put in the egg and lime juice mixture,

stirring continually until all the froth disappears. Pour the sauce over the fish, sprinkle with chopped parsley and serve.

FRIED FISH—WEST INDIAN STYLE

6 fillets of white fish	2 large lemons
4 tsps. red peppers	Coconut oil
4 oz. salt	

Prepare the fish. Crush the peppers and blend with the salt. Coat the fish thoroughly with this mixture, lay it in a flat dish and squeeze over it the juice of 1 lemon; marinate for 2 hours. Heat the coconut oil in a heavy iron pan, put in the fillets and brown on both sides. Squeeze more lemon juice over the fillets, cover tightly and reduce the heat. Cook until the flesh shows a tendency to flake. Serve with cut lemon. Makes 6 helpings.

CODFISH BALLS

1 lb. salt codfish	A pinch of pepper
3 lb. potatoes	Juice of onion
2 eggs	Breadcrumbs
1 tbsp. butter	Deep fat for frying

Soak the fish for 3–8 hours, shred, then simmer for 10 minutes. Boil the potatoes and when cooked mash with a fork. Add the fish, 1 beaten egg, butter, pepper and onion juice; mix well. Roll into balls, dip in egg and breadcrumbs and fry in deep fat. Makes 6 helpings.

CODFISH BREAKFAST—BERMUDA STYLE

2 lb. salt cod	6 ripe bananas
6 medium-sized potatoes	3 avocado pears

Soak the codfish for 3–8 hours, drain off the water, shred the fish and simmer slowly for 10–15 minutes. Boil and mash the potatoes. Make into a ring on a plate and place the drained cooked fish in the middle. Serve with bananas and sliced avocado pears. Makes 6 helpings.

SALT COD ACCRATS

4–8 oz. dried salt cod	$\frac{3}{4}$ pint warm water
1 clove of garlic	8 oz. flour
1 small onion	Salt
$\frac{1}{2}$ a chilli pepper	Fat for deep frying
$\frac{1}{4}$ oz. yeast	

Les Accrats are fritters, usually made from a yeast batter with salt fish, meat or vegetables, and they are very popular in the West Indies.

Soak the cod for 12 hours, changing the water frequently. Remove the skin and bone and flake the fish finely. Pound the garlic, sliced onion, sliced chilli pepper and flaked cod in a mortar.

To make the batter, cream the yeast with a little of the tepid water, then stir in the remaining water. Sieve the flour and salt into a basin and gradually add the yeast liquid to make a batter. Add the pounded fish, beat all together, cover and leave in a warm place for about 2 hours to rise.

Fry spoonfuls of the mixture in hot fat until golden-brown, drain and serve.

SALT FISH FRITTERS

Fritter batter	Pepper to taste
$\frac{1}{2}$ lb. salt fish	Oil for deep frying
2–3 blades of chives	

Prepare a plain batter (page 38). While it is standing, thoroughly scald the fish, then bone, skin and pound or flake it. Chop the chives very finely, add to the batter with the fish and pepper, and drop spoonfuls of the mixture into smoking-hot oil. Turn as required and cook until golden-brown—about 2–3 minutes.

SALT FISH IN CHEMISE

$\frac{1}{2}$ lb. salt fish	1 small tomato, chopped
2 tbsps. oil	A little thyme
$\frac{1}{4}$ tsp. pepper	2 tsps. flour
1–2 blades of chives, chopped	$\frac{1}{2}$ pint water
	2 eggs
$\frac{1}{2}$ an onion, chopped	

Scald the fish, remove the skin and bone and flake the flesh finely. Heat the oil and lightly fry the seasonings, without browning. Add the flour and water, then the fish, and simmer for 10 minutes. Place the mixture in a greased fireproof dish and break the eggs over it. Steam or bake until the eggs are set, and serve at once.

SALT SALMON WITH COCONUT

1 lb. salt salmon	1 small onion
$\frac{1}{2}$ a coconut, grated	$\frac{1}{2}$ a green pepper

Wash and parboil the salmon, pour away the water, put the fish in a shallow pan and simmer it gently with the coconut milk till tender. Add the sliced onion and pepper and cook for a little longer. Leave the pepper in long enough to flavour the dish.

CUBAN STUFFED FISH

For this you need a fairly substantial fish, such as a small cod. Remove the backbone, dividing the fish into an upper and a lower (belly) part. Simmer the top part in a little water with a flavouring of onion, garlic, parsley and finely chopped green pepper, lift it from the pan as soon as it is cooked. Meanwhile season the lower part of the fish with salt, pepper, lemon and a little oil. Sandwich the two parts of the fish together with a stuffing made as follows: Soak some breadcrumbs in the fish cooking liquor and mix with 3 chopped hard-boiled eggs, 2 beaten raw eggs, some chopped raisins and olives; cook over a low heat until dry. Bake the stuffed fish gently in a moderate oven (350° F., mark 4) until lightly browned all over—about $\frac{3}{4}$–$1\frac{1}{4}$ hours, according to size; if necessary, cover the fish with foil or greaseproof paper for the first part of the cooking time, to prevent it becoming too dry.

CRABES FARCIES
(STUFFED CRABS)

Cook the crabs in the usual way, take out and chop the meat and wash and dry the shells. Make the stuffing as follows: Soak some bread in milk and squeeze it moderately dry. Mix with some chopped fat bacon, 1 finely chopped garlic clove, some chopped chives, a chopped red chilli and salt to taste. Brown the mixture lightly in a little butter, put into the shells, sprinkle with breadcrumbs and bake in a moderately hot oven (400° F., mark 6) for 20–25 minutes.

CALLALOO

1 lb. callaloo (dasheen)	1 green chilli
20 okras	$\frac{1}{4}$ lb. salt pork
1 clove of garlic	Pepper and salt
1 onion	3 crabs

Wash the callaloo leaves and shred, taking out any coarse stems. Prepare the okras and cut in rounds. Chop the garlic, onion and chilli. Cut the salt pork in 2-inch lengths. Put all the ingredients except the crabs into a large saucepan with the seasonings. Just cover with boiling water and simmer very gently until all are tender, adding extra water if needed—it should take about 3 hours. Half an hour before serving, add the crab meat, cut very small. Serve very hot, with rice.

CRAB GUMBO

6 crabs	A piece of parsley or thyme
3 large tomatoes	
1 onion	6–7 okras (gumbos or lady's fingers)
1–2 blades of chive	
$\frac{1}{4}$ red pepper (without seeds)	2 tbsps. butter
	Salt to taste
1 bay leaf	

Scald and thoroughly wash the crabs, remove the claws and take the flesh from the shell, discarding the gall bladder. Cut the body flesh into four. Scald and skin the tomatoes, if liked.

164

Wash and cut up the seasonings and slice the okras. Melt the butter and brown the crabs. Add the seasonings and when brown put in the okras. When all are well browned, add the bay leaf and enough water to cover—2–2½ pints. Cover the pan and simmer for 1 hour. When cooked the mixture should be like thick soup. Serve in a hot tureen, with rice.

Strictly speaking, no gumbo dish can be made without the succulent vegetables that give it its name. They may be bought in tinned form in some shops in this country.

WEST INDIAN PEPPERPOT

1 small cabbage	A sprig of thyme
2 large handfuls of spinach	2 lb. mutton
	½ lb. salted pork
1 lettuce	1 lobster or crab
3 onions	Salt and cayenne pepper

For the Dumplings

4 oz. flour	¼ tsp. baking powder
1 oz. fat	Water to mix

Cut all the vegetables small and stew with the mutton and pork in 3 quarts of water until the meat is tender. Add dumplings and, half an hour before serving, the meat from the crab or lobster with plenty of seasoning.

QUAILS, CUBAN STYLE

After cleaning the birds rub them with salt, pepper and lemon. Put some finely chopped bacon and ham into a large frying pan and fry lightly with some sliced onion and a little grated nutmeg. Put in the quails and fry for a few minutes, then add about ½ cup good stock; when this is absorbed, after a few minutes, add the same amount of sherry, then cover and cook gently until tender. Thicken the gravy slightly with flour, simmer for a few minutes longer and serve with the quails arranged on a bed of the onions and bacon, with the gravy poured over.

CRÉOLE SAUTÉ OF LAMB

2 lb. neck or shoulder of lamb	1 oz. flour
	½–¾ pint stock
2 onions	A pinch mixed herbs
1½ oz. butter	Seasoning
2 tsps. curry powder	Cooked Patna rice

Cut the lamb into neat pieces, removing most of the fat. Lightly brown the finely chopped onions in the butter, then add the lamb pieces; brown all together. Sprinkle with the curry powder and the flour, stirring well, gradually add the hot stock and a pinch of herbs or a few fresh ones, season to taste and cook for 1 hour, or until the meat is tender. Serve with boiled rice which has been rinsed, drained and reheated in a warm oven.

MEAT AND OLIVES

Any kind of cooked meat	A little fat
	Chopped onions
Orange juice	Stoned and quartered olives
A dash of wine	
Salt and pepper	A little stock

Cut the meat into strips and sprinkle with orange juice, wine, salt and pepper. Heat the fat and fry the onions and olives lightly, then add the seasoned meat; when this is golden-brown add a little stock or water and simmer until the meat is tender. Serve with any kind of vegetable and hard-boiled eggs.

POULET COCOTTE AUX BANANES
(CHICKEN AND BANANA CASSEROLE)

Brown the chicken in a fireproof casserole in butter and season well. Add a few shallots and some diced gammon, cover and simmer gently, adding a little water as required to prevent burning. Peel some unripe bananas, halve lengthwise, then crosswise, and put in boiling water until tender; drain well and add to the chicken about 15 minutes before the dish is to be served. Garnish with chopped parsley.

POULET AU RIZ CRÉOLE
(CRÉOLE CHICKEN AND RICE)

Put the chicken in a pan with just enough water to come two-thirds of the way up the bird; add sliced turnips, carrots and onions, a bouquet garni and plenty of pepper and salt. Bring to the boil and simmer until tender. Strain the stock and in it cook 1 cupful rice, until the stock is absorbed and the rice dry and tender.

BAKED COW HEEL

1 cow heel	Grated nutmeg
1 onion	A little mace
1 tomato	1–2 cloves
1 shallot	1 tbsp. butter
2 pimiento seeds	A little vinegar and
1 red pepper	lime juice
Salt	Breadcrumbs
1 wineglass sherry	

Cut up the heel, put into sufficient water to cover and boil till the bones drop out. Season with the onion, etc. Add the sherry, nutmeg, mace, cloves, butter, vinegar and lime to taste. Put the mixture into a pie dish, sprinkle with breadcrumbs and bake in a moderate oven (350° F., mark 4) until browned.

TURTLE STEAK

1½ lb. turtle steak	Tomatoes, onions, pep-
Lime juice	per, salt and a little
¼ lb. lard	lime juice to season
Breadcrumbs	1 tbsp. sherry

Rub the steak well with lime juice, then scald with boiling water, drain off the water and slice the meat. Put it in a frying pan with a little lard and brown—the heat of the pan will draw water from the steak, so pour this off continually, but keep it. When all the water has been drawn off, put the seasonings into the frying pan with the turtle liquor and cook till the steak is brown and tender, adding more lard as necessary. The gravy should be thickened with breadcrumbs, and the sherry is added just before serving.

CORN MEAL ARRAPE
(MEAT AND CORN MEAL BALLS)

1 lb. 5 oz. corn meal	2 tsp. salt
2 oz. flour	3 tsp. baking powder
1 oz. butter	Water to bind
1 oz. lard	Fat for frying

For the Filling

½ lb. beef	Seasonings to taste
1 oz. fat pork	(chives, parsley, etc.)
½ tsp. salt	2 tbsp. oil

Clean the beef and brown with the fat pork, seasonings and salt ; cover and stew for ½ hour, then mince or chop finely. Mix the corn meal, flour, fat, salt and baking powder with the fingertips until it resembles breadcrumbs, then mix in water to give a soft dough. Roll into balls, flatten these till ⅛–¼ inch thick and cut into 2- or 3-inch rounds with a cup or cutter. Put about 1 tbsp. meat mixture on one round, damp the edges and cover with a second round ; pinch the edges together and fry in smoking-hot oil till golden-brown. Drain and serve hot.

LIVER CRÉOLE

1 lb. liver	1 green pepper (seeds
½ tsp. salt	removed)
Flour	1 onion
3 tbsps. oil	1 bay leaf
1 lb. tomatoes	6 peppercorns

Coat the liver with seasoned flour. Heat the oil in a pan and brown the liver. Crush the tomatoes ; remove the seeds from the pepper ; slice the onion. Add the remaining ingredients to liver, cover and simmer slowly for 15 minutes.

Uncover and continue cooking slowly till the liver is tender and the sauce thickened. Makes 6 helpings.

DAUBE DE PORC
(BRAISED PORK)

Fillet of pork is suitable for this typically Créole dish. Brown it in butter or lard, adding a few shallots. When it is well browned on all sides, add about 1 tbsp. water, cover the casserole and cook very gently in a slow oven (320° F., mark 2) until tender ; turn it occasionally, to prevent its catching. Peeled aubergines may be added 20 minutes before serving.

CARNE VINHO E ALHOS
(PIQUANT PORK TITBITS)

Cut some pork into squares about 1 inch thick and place in a jar filled with vinegar, with 2 whole heads of garlic and some crushed parsley, chives, etc. Leave to soak for 3 days. When ready to use, take out the pork and fry in its own fat until crisp. Serve on pieces of dry bread done in the same fat.

This is a delicious dish that is traditionally eaten by the Portuguese in Trinidad on Christmas morning.

PICADILLO
(PIQUANT MINCE)

½ lb. chopped onions	2 oz. raisins
½ lb. tomatoes	½ oz. capers
1 finely chopped green	9–10 stoned and halved
pepper	olives
1¼ lb. minced beef	A dash of sherry
2 oz. blanched almonds	

Fry the onions, then add the tomatoes and green pepper, and finally the meat. Stir and fry gently for a few minutes, then add the almonds, raisins, capers and olives. Cover the pan and cook very slowly, adding a dash of sherry when the meat is almost done. Allow about 1½–1¾ hours. When it is quite cooked serve very hot with salad and rice, fried bananas and fried eggs.

JUG JUG
(HOT MEAT MOULD)

¼ lb. fresh or salt beef	2–3 blades of chives
¼ lb. lean pork	Thyme and parsley
Salt and pepper	½ cup cornflour (good
1 pint pigeon peas	measure)
1 small onion	

Clean, cut up and season the beef and pork. (If salt beef is used it should be soaked.) Stew the pork for 20 minutes, then add the beef, peas, onion, chives and herbs and stew for another $\frac{1}{2}$ hour, or until the peas are soft. Strain off and keep the water. Mince or chop the meat and peas.

Take $\frac{1}{2}$ pint of the meat broth, add the meat and peas and stir in the cornflour. Cook for 15–30 minutes, stirring all the time. Pour into a buttered basin, turn out and serve hot.

BŒUF CRÉOLE

3 lb. rump of beef	1 chilli
Fat bacon slices	2 lb. onions
Salt and pepper	2 lb. tomatoes

Put the beef in an earthenware casserole and cover with a few slices of fat bacon. Season with salt and pepper and 1 chilli, chopped finely. Cover the meat entirely with a layer of sliced onions and another of tomatoes. Cover closely and simmer for 4 hours—no extra liquid must be added.

BEEF CUTLETS

1½ lb. fillet of beef	1 egg
Tomato, onion, all-spice, black pepper and salt to season	Breadcrumbs
	Oil for frying

Early in the day cut the beef into thin slices, season and cover until ready to cook. Beat the egg, dip the beef in it and coat with bread-crumbs. Fry in hot oil and serve at once round a dish of mashed potatoes, with slices of lime or lemon.

SALT BEEF WITH RED PEAS

1½ lb. salt beef	Thyme
½ pint red peas	Shallot
Seasoning	1 tbsp. butter
Allspice	Dumplings
Pimiento seeds	

Soak the beef in cold water overnight. Put into fresh water, bring to the boil, and cook slowly. Meanwhile boil the peas separately; when cooked, put into the pot with the beef and season with salt and pepper, pimiento seeds, thyme and shallot. Shortly before serving put in the butter and some small dumplings. Put on the lid, and when the dumplings are cooked, serve immediately.

STEWED OXTAIL

Joint the tail, season with onion, tomato, thyme and pepper and let it stand for an hour before cooking. Brown it in hot fat, put in a saucepan, cover with plenty of water and let simmer for 4 hours. When it is nearly cooked, add chochos or turnip and carrot, or some butter beans. Thicken the broth with a little flour if desired.

BEEF BALLS

1 lb. beef	Salt and pepper
2 onions	1 egg
1–2 tomatoes	Deep fat for frying

Put the beef, onions and tomato through the mincer and season with salt and pepper. Beat the egg well, add to the beef mixture, mix well and form into balls; fry in deep fat and serve with gravy if liked.

LES ACHARDS
(VEGETABLE HORS D'ŒUVRE)

Wash and peel as many different vegetables as available and cut them up very small. A usual mixture would be carrots, French beans, cabbage, cauliflower and the " cabbage " or heart of the palm-tree or coconut palm. Soak all the vegetables separately in salted water for 24 hours, then drain thoroughly and put them in a deep dish, still in their separate heads. Pour over a dressing made with boiling oil, sliced onions, a good pinch of saffron and salt, pepper and chilli pepper to taste. Leave in this marinade for a further 48 hours.

ROUGAILS
(HORS D'ŒUVRE)

Tomato : Peel some tomatoes and pound them with small red chillies, lemon juice, a little olive oil and salt to taste, working the mixture into a smooth paste. This may be eaten with bread or rolls, or used as a condiment during the meal.

Aubergine : Boil or grill the aubergines and peel them, then use as above.

Shrimps : Boil, shell and pound the shrimps with the other ingredients.

MOORS AND CHRISTIANS
(BLACK BEANS AND RICE)

2 cups black beans, soaked overnight in 6 cups water	1 onion, peeled and halved
4 cups water	1 large garlic clove, minced
Salt and pepper	Boiled Patna rice
Chopped parsley	

Obviously it was the contrast in colour between the beans and the white rice that gave this dish its imaginative name. It is hearty, peasant-type fare, eaten by the workers on the plantations or the fishermen when they return from work.

Drain the soaked beans and put in a large saucepan with the fresh water, seasoning to taste, garlic and onion. Cover and cook very gently over a low heat for 2 hours, or until soft. Drain and sprinkle generously with freshly chopped parsley. Serve with the rice.

165

CARROTS IN SAUCE

Cubans have a very individual way of cooking carrots. Scrape the carrots and cut into rounds, then simmer in a little well-salted water. When just cooked, put in a saucepan with some butter, a pinch of sugar, a little milk and some chopped parsley. Simmer for a moment or two, then add a little flour and a pinch of nutmeg; simmer gently, stirring until the sauce thickens. Serve at once.

TOMATES FARCIES AU RIZ
(RICE-STUFFED TOMATOES)

First make the stuffing. Fry a little chopped onion in butter, add some washed rice and mix well, moisten with stock and cook for about 20 minutes, until the rice is done. Add grated Parmesan cheese to taste, a little butter, ground chillies, salt and pepper and stuff some large tomatoes. Sprinkle with a little more grated cheese, pour some melted butter over and cook in a moderate oven (350° F., mark 4) for about 20 minutes.

STUFFED GRAPEFRUIT SALAD

¼ cup olive oil	2 cups fresh pineapple,
2 tbsps. cider vinegar	cut in ¾-inch chunks
3 tbsps. lime juice	1½ cups fresh rasp-
1 tbsp. sugar	berries
½ tsp. salt	2 oranges
½ tsp. pepper	12 Maraschino cherries
3 large grapefruit	

Mix the oil, vinegar, lime juice, sugar, salt and pepper; blend well and refrigerate. Cut each grapefruit in half and remove the pith. Using a grapefruit knife, carefully scoop the flesh from each half. Cut the flesh into ¾-inch chunks. Mix the pineapple and grapefruit chunks, add the olive oil mixture and toss well. Then gently mix in the raspberries. Heap the fruits in the grapefruit shells; arrange these on a large serving plate, and garnish with segments of oranges and Maraschino cherries. Makes 6 servings.

Failing grapefruit, avocados may be used for the salad.

AUBERGINE ACCRATS

3 medium-sized auber-	1 tbsp. finely chopped
gines	chilli
2 oz. flour	Seasoning
1 egg	Oil for deep frying

Peel the aubergines, cut in thick slices and cook in boiling water until tender; drain and rub through a sieve. Add the beaten egg to the aubergine purée and gradually beat in the sifted flour. Continue beating for some minutes, then add the chopped chilli and seasoning. Drop spoonfuls of the mixture in hot oil and fry until golden-brown. Drain and serve.

PUMPKIN FRITTERS

Make 1 cup thick batter and grate into it some raw pumpkin until the mixture is fairly stiff. Fry spoonfuls in hot fat and sprinkle with sugar and mixed spice.

MASHED PUMPKIN

Boil, mash with some butter, salt and pepper and put neatly into a dish. Alternatively boil with rice, a shallot, some tomatoes, butter and a little salt pork.

CANDIED SWEET POTATOES

Wash the potatoes and cook them in their skins until tender, then peel and slice. Put 1 tbsp. brown sugar into a thick saucepan and caramelise it, then add a further ½ lb. sugar, 2 tbsps. melted butter and a little water. Either simmer the potatoes in this for 5 minutes, or dip them in, season and bake in a moderate oven (350° F., mark 4) for about 15 minutes, until brown, basting them occasionally.

Serve with roast pork, fried chicken, etc.

COO-COO

3–4 okras	1 cup corn meal
1 tsp. salt	Butter
¾ pint water or	
milk and water	

Wash and slice the okras, add the salt and boil them in half the liquid. When the okras are soft enough to be mashed, mix the corn meal with the rest of the liquid, stir this paste into the boiling mash and continue to cook, stirring all the time, until the mixture is thick and smooth. Turn out into a well-buttered mould or basin. Serve as a vegetable.

WEST INDIAN HOT SAUCE

Recipes for this are innumerable, but here is one fairly representative version.

Mix peeled, seeded and chopped tomatoes, chopped white onions, chopped and seeded fresh red chillies, 1–2 garlic cloves (crushed or chopped), 2 cloves, a few peppercorns, a little salt and a good squeeze of lime (or lemon) juice, using sufficient to fill a 1 lb. jam jar or similar container, packing it tightly. Fill up with good quality vinegar, seal and leave for at least a week before using.

WEST INDIAN RELISH FOR FISH

1 tsp. dry mustard	A touch of garlic
1 tbsp. butter	Juice of 1 lime
1 tbsp. chilli sauce	Salt
1 tbsp. grated onion	¾ tsp. angostura bitters

Mix all the ingredients together and bottle the sauce.

JAMAICA PONE

½ pint corn meal	1 tbsp. butter
A pinch of salt	A few currants (optional)
Sugar to taste	Ground cinnamon
Milk of one coconut	

Mix the corn meal, salt and sugar with milk from the coconut and add the butter. The mixture should be of the consistency of pancake batter. A few currants may be added if liked. Bake in a well-buttered pie dish in a moderate oven (350° F., mark 4) for about 1 hour. Sprinkle the top with cinnamon.

ST VINCENT ARROWROOT PUDDING

Mix 2 tbsps. arrowroot with a little cold milk until smooth; add this to 1 pint boiling milk, stirring all the time. Sweeten to taste, add 3 well-beaten eggs and a few drops of vanilla essence, cook gently till it thickens. Serve hot or cold.

CONKEYS

4 oz. mashed, cooked pumpkin	3 beaten eggs
	¼ pint milk
½ lb. maize, flour or oatmeal (fine or medium)	2 oz. sugar
	5 oz. butter

Mix all the ingredients well, and either steam the whole quantity in a basin for 2–3 hours, or wrap dumpling-size quantities in greaseproof paper and steam for 1 hour.

COCONUT BISCUITS

1 large coconut	1½ cups flour
1½ breakfastcups granulated sugar	Salt
3 tbsps. butter	3 level tsps. baking powder
2 beaten eggs	

Remove the brown skin from coconut and grate finely. To this add the sugar and fat; mix well. Beat the eggs thoroughly and stir into mixture; lastly add the flour into which has been sifted the baking powder and ½ tsp. salt. Drop in teaspoonfuls on a greased baking sheet and bake in a moderate oven (375° F., mark 5) till light brown, then turn over and bake on the other side. Cool the biscuits and as soon as crisp, place in an air-tight tin. These biscuits will keep fresh for weeks; if they lose their crispness, they may be reheated in the oven.

TULOONS
(COCONUT SWEETS)

1 breakfastcup molasses	2 breakfastcups fresh grated coconut
2 oz. sugar	Nuts if desired
Flavouring, e.g., orange peel or preserved ginger or vanilla	

Boil the molasses and sugar with the chosen flavouring until the syrup will form a long thread when dropped from the spoon. Remove the orange peel, etc., then beat in the coconut. When the mixture thickens, drop in spoonfuls on to a wetted baking sheet and leave to set. If they tend to spread, shape them before they are cold.

COCONUT PUDDING

2 eggs	1 cup grated coconut
2 tbsps. sugar	

Stir the yolks of eggs and sugar together. Butter a pie dish, put in the coconut, add the egg yolks and sugar and bake in a moderate oven (350° F., mark 4) until set. Make a meringue with the egg whites and pile on to the pudding; return it to the oven and brown slightly.

RUM OMELETTE

Beat 2 eggs and 2 tsps. sugar for 10 minutes; add 1 tsp. mixed spices and 1½ tbsps. old rum. Beat again for a minute or two, then pour into a hot buttered frying pan and cook. Sprinkle sugar on top and serve at once.

BAKED PINEAPPLE

For this you need a large ripe pineapple. Cut off the top and scoop out the flesh, leaving an unbroken "case." Cut the pineapple flesh into cubes and soak them for several hours in rum or brandy, then put them back in the case and bake in a moderate oven (350° F., mark 4) until tender—30–40 minutes.

GROUND NUT MOLASSES PIE

6 oz. shortcrust pastry	¼ pint milk
8 tbsps. molasses	¼ tsp. salt
¼ oz. butter	5 oz. chopped, toasted nuts
1–2 eggs	
4 oz. sugar	½ tsp. vanilla essence, if liked
¼ oz. flour	

Line a large enamelled plate or a pie dish with the pastry and set aside on ice. Heat the molasses and butter to boiling point and leave to cool. Whisk the eggs and gradually beat in the sugar and flour. Stir in the milk, salt and then the molasses. Add the chopped nuts and essence and pour the mixture into the pastry case. Put into a moderately hot oven (425° F., mark 7). After 10 minutes reduce the heat to moderate (350° F., mark 4) and cook until the filling is set and the pastry crisp and golden-brown—20–30 minutes.

RICEYCOCO

Boil 2 tbsps. rice with 1 small piece of stick cinnamon in cold water until tender. Grate 1 small coconut, put it in muslin, squeeze out all the milk and add to the boiling rice. Heat, but do not let it come to the boil. Serve with brown sugar and milk, as a porridge.

THE ZOMBIE'S SECRET

166

3 avocados, stoned and cut into 1-inch squares
1 large banana, thinly sliced
1 package cream cheese, cubed
2 tbsps. grated coconut
2 tbsps. sugar
1 tbsp. powdered cinnamon
2 tsps. strong coffee
½ pint double cream

Combine the avocados, banana and cheese, sprinkle with coconut, sugar and cinnamon, then chill. Stir the coffee into the whipped cream and pour over the fruit just before serving.

JAMAICAN GISADAS
(CUSTARD TARTS)

6 oz. flaky pastry
2 eggs
½ pint fresh coconut milk
1 cup grated coconut
1 tbsp. brown sugar
Nutmeg

Line deep patty pans with the thinly rolled pastry. Beat the eggs and add ½ pint fresh coconut milk, sugar and a cupful of grated coconut. Pour into the pastry cases and grate a little nutmeg on each. Bake in a moderate oven (350° F., mark 4) until the pastry is golden-brown and the custard firm.

CRÉOLE BANANAS

2 eggs
1 cup white bread-crumbs
4 bananas, cut up
½ cup fine sugar
1 large lemon
½ an orange
1 oz. butter
1 cup milk
Apricot or strawberry jam sauce

Beat the eggs well and add the bananas, breadcrumbs and sugar. Squeeze and strain the juice of the lemon and half-orange and add, then grate in the rind of half the lemon, with the melted butter and milk. Mix, mashing down the banana pieces. Turn the mixture into a buttered and sugared mould and put into a large dish half-filled with water. Cook in a slow oven (300° F., mark 1) for 1½ hours, replenishing the water as necessary. When cooked, turn out on to a hot dish. (Run a knife round the edge of the mould to loosen the pudding.) Serve hot with the hot jam sauce.

This is reputed to have been a favourite pudding of the Empress Josephine, who came, of course, from Martinique.

BANANA FRITTERS

3 ripe bananas
1 egg
1 tbsp. sugar
3 tbsps. flour
½ tsp. baking powder
Lard for frying

Mash the banana to a pulp. Beat the egg and sugar together, add the bananas, then the flour and baking powder. Fry in the lard, dropping it in by spoonfuls. Sprinkle with granulated sugar and serve.

BANANAS WITH CLARET

4–6 bananas
Butter for frying
½ lb. sugar
¼ pint claret
Grated nutmeg

Peel the bananas and fry in the butter until light brown, keeping them whole. Make a thick syrup by slowly dissolving the sugar in the claret. Add the bananas to this, flavour with nutmeg, cover and cook gently for about 20 minutes. Lift out the bananas, boil up the syrup, pour over and serve hot.

BARBADOS BANANAS—I

Grease a pie dish thickly with butter. Cover with a layer of bananas, sliced lengthwise and add a layer of Barbados brown sugar; repeat alternate layers of bananas and sugar to fill the dish. Cover with shreds of butter and bake in a moderate oven (350° F., mark 4) until the bananas are soft. Turn out on to a hot dish, pour a glass of rum or brandy over, set light to this and serve at once; hand thick cream separately.

BARBADOS BANANAS—II

Peel 6 bananas, which should be under- rather than over-ripe. Slice each banana in half lengthwise and coat each piece generously in Demerara sugar. Have ready a well-buttered fireproof dish and lay the fruit in this. Pour over them a large glassful of Jamaican rum, sprinkle lavishly with more sugar and add small pieces of butter on top. Bake in a moderately

hot oven (400° F., mark 6) for about 25 minutes. Serve hot, with the thin fan-shaped wafers usually served with ices.

BANANA WHIP

Crush a banana well. Beat an egg white to a stiff froth, flavour with vanilla essence and sweeten to taste. Beat in the banana gradually, add a pinch of salt, and serve with pudding or cake as a sauce.

BIZCOCHO DE ESPECIES
(SPICECAKE)

14 oz. sifted flour	11 oz. dark brown
3 tsps. baking powder	sugar
1 tbsp. ground cinna-	6 eggs, unbeaten
mon	1 cup milk
1 tbsp. ground cloves	½ cup sweet Madeira
1 tbsp. grated nutmeg	Icing sugar
8 oz. butter	

Lightly grease a 9-inch angel-food tube pan. Sift together the flour, baking powder, cinnamon, cloves and nutmeg. Cream the butter, gradually adding the brown sugar, and beat until well blended. Add the eggs one at a time, with 1 tbsp. flour mixture, and beat well. Add the remaining flour mixture and the milk alternately, then add wine. Beat well, pour into the tube pan and bake in a moderate oven (350° F., mark 4) for 1 hour, or until a skewer inserted in the centre comes out clean.

Cool the cake in the pan for 10 minutes; remove from the pan and invert on a wire rack. When the cake is cool, sprinkle the top with icing sugar. This cake keeps nicely and improves in flavour when it is stored in a cake tin.

SPONGE ROLL WITH COCONUT FILLING

Make an ordinary Swiss roll. Have 3 egg whites ready beaten, to which has been added sugar to taste, dry grated coconut and almond essence. Spread this mixture on the sponge cake, and then roll it up. This must be done as quickly as possible, while the cake is still hot.

PEANUT BUNS

2 oz. roasted peanuts	4 oz. flour
4 oz. butter	¼ tsp. baking powder
4 oz. sugar	2 eggs

Remove the brown inner skins from the nuts and pound or grind them finely. Cream the butter and sugar. Sieve the flour and baking powder together, then beat the flour and eggs alternately into the creamed mixture. Fold in the ground nuts. Butter some small patty or queen cake tins, half-fill with the mixture and

W.C.B.—31

bake in a hot oven (450° F., mark 8) until golden-brown.

PANETELA
(SPONGE CAKE)

6 eggs	Grated rind of 1 lemon
1 cup sugar	1 cup flour

Beat the egg yolks to a cream, then add the sugar and lemon rind, beating all the time. When thoroughly blended, add the flour, a little at a time, and then the egg whites, beaten till stiff. Pour mixture into a greased tin and bake in a moderate oven (350° F., mark 4) until firm and golden-brown.

ORANGE WINE

4 quarts sweet orange	5 pints brown sugar
juice	5 pints strong rum
1 quart lime juice	

Mix together. Put into a stone jar and leave it for 3 days. Add the whites and the washed shells of 2 eggs (remove the inner membrane from the shells). Add ½ pint fresh milk. Mix well and leave for another 3–4 days. Strain and bottle.

PONCHE DE CREMA

2 oz. cornflour	1½ pints rum
1½–2 pints milk	Wine, if liked
6 eggs	Vanilla essence to taste
½ lb. sugar	Angostura bitters

Mix cornflour with a little milk, boil the remainder and add to the cornflour; stir the two together over the heat for 7 minutes. Cool and add the beaten eggs. " Swizzle " and cook again until the eggs thicken, but avoid boiling or the mixture will curdle. Add the sugar, with the rum, wine and vanilla essence, and stir until dissolved. Keep in a cool place till required. Add some crushed ice and a little angostura bitters before serving.

FRUIT CUP

4 oranges (juice and	Sugar to taste
pulp)	2 tangerines (juice and
1 cup grated pineapple	pulp)
1 grenadilla (juice and	1 glass sherry
pulp)	Ice
¾ pint water	

Mix in the order given, using plenty of ice and serve. A grated apple greatly improves the flavour.

When frozen this makes a delicious ice. Just before it is fully frozen, add as much cream as desired. Stir once or twice and serve.

Australasia

AUSTRALIA does not lay claim to many national recipes. The pioneers were too busy carving a new life out of their tough and beautiful land to have time to devote much attention to gastronomy. Time was pressing and the function of food was not to excite a jaded palate, but to fill an empty stomach and provide energy for a new day.

Inevitably, Australian cookery is basically English in character, though special dishes have been evolved which use local products such as the delicious lamb and mutton, various types of exotic fish, vegetables and fruit, such as yams, taro and soursop, grenadilla, loquat and passion fruit, and even the indigenous kangaroo sometimes finds himself in the pot. In general, Australian food is of excellent quality, plainly cooked and generously served. Meat is abundant and Australian fruit is world-famous.

The Australian has a large appetite and is quite capable of facing an enormous steak with fried eggs for breakfast on a blazing hot morning. Australian women take a great pride in their baking and there is always a wonderful selection of scones, cakes and pastries at tea-time. The Australian national drink must surely be tea.

The influx during recent years of " New Australians " from various European countries has brought with it many unusual recipes and customs and native Australians, particularly in the big cities, are themselves more sophisticated and interested in cooking as a fine art. Australian wines are very good indeed and with all the natural advantages, Australia should one day be a gourmet's paradise. But for some time to come, it seems likely that the world's idea, however mistaken, of Australian national cuisine will be restricted to carpet-bag steak, damper bread and billy tea !

Australia

SHELL FISH

Australia rejoices in excellent prawns and a variety of good shell fish, including oysters, and these are eaten in a number of different ways. Probably the most popular ways of serving prawns is in some type of salad—sometimes the rather elaborate American style. Oysters are used in soups, sauces, stuffings, fritters and so on. Pipis, which resemble clams, are served in a similar way; we give below a recipe for a favourite dish using this shell fish.

PIPI PANCAKES

Chop the shelled pipis rather small and add them to a fritter batter. Heat some shallow fat and drop in tablespoonfuls of the pipi mixture; fry until lightly browned on both sides and serve at once.

OYSTERS AND BUTTERED EGGS

Beard a dozen oysters and cut up into about 3 pieces each. Beat 4 eggs and add the oysters, put into a pan containing 1–2 oz. hot butter, season to taste and cook until the mixture is set but still creamy. Pile up on slices of hot buttered toast.

ROAST CHICKEN WITH RICE AND SULTANA STUFFING

A 3–4 lb. chicken	A little ground cinnamon
6 oz. rice	A little grated nutmeg
1 onion	Salt and pepper to taste
2 oz. butter	Fat for roasting and basting
3 oz. sultanas	

Prepare the chicken in the usual way. Put the washed rice and finely chopped onion into 1 quart boiling salted water and cook until tender; drain. Heat the butter, add the rice, sultanas and seasonings and cook, stirring well. Put into a basin and leave till cold, then use to stuff the chicken. Roast as usual, basting as required.

COLONIAL GOOSE

4 lb. hogget shoulder or leg (from lamb 1 year old)	1 medium-sized apple, chopped
1 sheep's kidney	1 medium-sized tomato, chopped
2 rashers of bacon	1 tsp. salt and pepper
6 oz. breadcrumbs	1 egg
1 tsp. mixed herbs	1 oz. butter, melted
1 small onion, chopped	

Have the meat boned and remove any surplus fat; skin and chop the kidney and chop the bacon. Combine all other ingredients to make a stuffing and then add the chopped kidney and bacon. Stuff the meat, roll and tie up securely. Tie up one end with string to look like the head of a goose, and shape the joint to represent the body. Cook as for roast lamb in a moderate oven (375° F., mark 5) allowing 30 minutes to the lb. and 30 minutes over. Serve hot or cold.

FRUIT AND WINE STUFFING FOR TURKEY

2 oz. raisins	1 small onion, chopped
2 oz. prunes	4 oz. breadcrumbs
$\frac{1}{8}$ pint Australian burgundy	1 tbsp. chopped parsley
3 oz. butter	1 tsp. salt
$\frac{1}{2}$ a head of celery, chopped	Pepper

Soak the raisins and the cut-up prunes overnight in the wine. The following day, melt the butter and gently sauté the celery and onion. Add the breadcrumbs, parsley, seasoning, fruit and finally the wine in which it was soaked. Use this to stuff the neck-end of the bird.

CORROBOREE CURRY HOT-POT

1 lb. braising steak	$\frac{1}{2}$ pint stock
2 onions	1 tbsp. flour
2 cooking apples	Salt
2 tomatoes	Brown sugar
1 tbsp. dripping	Parsley
2 tsps. curry powder	3 hard-boiled eggs
2 oz. sultanas	2 packets of potato
1 oz. seeded raisins	crisps

Cut up the meat and slice the onions, apples and tomatoes. Heat the dripping in a pan, add the meat, onion and apple, and fry until golden-brown. Add the tomatoes and curry powder and cook for a few minutes longer. Place the mixture in a casserole, add the dried fruit, and barely cover with stock. Lid the casserole and cook in a moderate oven (350° F., mark 4) for $1\frac{1}{2}$ hours. Blend the flour with a little extra water and stir into the casserole. Season to taste with a little salt and brown sugar, garnish with parsley and sliced egg, surround the casserole with potato crisps, and serve at once.

CARPET-BAG STEAK

Choose a piece of the very best rump or fillet steak, weighing $1\frac{1}{2}$–2 lb.; it must be at least 2 inches thick. Slit the steak through its thickness so that it opens like a book. Fill with a dozen raw oysters taken from their shells, cover these, if desired, with finely sliced mushrooms and sprinkle with a very little salt and some cayenne pepper. Sew up with fine white string, so that neither the filling nor the juice can escape. Rub

167

the steak over on both sides with olive oil or melted butter and grill under a quick flame for 5 or 6 minutes on each side. When the meat has browned, finish cooking in a hot oven (450° F., mark 8) for a further 10 minutes or so—according to the extent of " rareness " desired.

ROAST MARINADED BEEF

Choose a medium-sized piece of sirloin, prepared for rolling, but keep it flat while marinading it. Pour over it 2 wineglasses Australian red wine and 1 glass vinegar, then leave for 2 days; turn it over from time to time. Drain the meat, cover it with a rich forcemeat, roll up and tie or skewer firmly. Roast in the usual way, basting with the marinade liquor, to which 1 tsp. mixed spice should be added. Serve the beef with the strained gravy and with red-currant jelly.

GLAZED HAM AND PINEAPPLE LOAF

A 12-oz. can of spiced ham	2 tsps. butter
½ a cup of finely cut pineapple pieces	2 tsps. Demerara sugar

Mix together the pineapple, butter and sugar in the bottom of an ovenproof dish. Remove the meat from the can without breaking it and place it in the centre of the fruit. Bake in a moderate oven (350° F., mark 4) for 20 minutes, basting often.

Serve hot, with jacket potatoes, green peas and carrots, or cold with green salad.

SPICY MUTTON CASSEROLE

Bone a small leg of mutton and rub it all over with a mixture of ½ tsp. ground cinnamon and ½ tsp. grated nutmeg. Slice a large onion and spread half of it at the bottom of a deep dish, then put in the meat and add the rest of the onion, a few cloves, a crushed clove of garlic and a bay leaf. Pour over it 1 large cup of Australian wine (or vinegar) sweetened with 1 large cup brown sugar. Leave for a day, turning the meat over from time to time. Transfer the mutton to a casserole, with the liquor and a little water, and cook in a slow oven (325° F., mark 2) for at least 2 hours, or until the meat is tender.

SHEEP'S TONGUES IN ASPIC

Skin 3 boiled sheep's tongues and slice them, then arrange in a mould. Pour over them 1 pint hot seasoned stock in which 1 tbsp. gelatine has been dissolved. Leave to set; to serve, turn out and garnish with sliced cucumber or other salad plants.

KANGAROO

To have an Australian section with no mention of kangaroo would leave most readers feeling slightly cheated, and yet it is no use pretending that many of us will be able to use this exotic meat. Even in its native country, probably only a small proportion of people eat it more than once or twice in a lifetime.

The long, thick tail may be made into soup, rather after the manner of oxtail soup, though there is more fat to skim from the surface of the cold stock. (Incidentally the soup is now available in this country in tinned form.) Other recipes describe how to curry or fricassee the jointed tail.

The actual kangaroo meat is much less fatty than that of the tail—indeed, some people liken it to the flesh of the hare. For interest's sake we give one recipe.

BUSHMAN-STYLE KANGAROO

Slice 1 lb. very fat bacon and line the bottom of a saucepan with it, then add about 3 lb. kangaroo meat, neatly sliced; sprinkle with pepper and salt and lay over the meat some sliced onions. Cover closely and fry for about 10 minutes, to extract some of the bacon fat, then reduce the heat to the lowest possible point and cook for about 2 hours; take care the meat does not burn. Pour in 1 pint boiling water and simmer gently for 20–25 minutes. Thicken the gravy with blended flour and pour over the hot meat before serving.

TASMANIAN CREAMED RABBIT

Cook 1 or 2 young rabbits in a very little water, adding salt, pepper, a few cloves, a small pinch of grated nutmeg, a few peppercorns, a small onion and, if possible, a bacon bone. When the meat is tender, take it from the bones and cut up very small. Mix with it a little finely chopped cooked bacon. Make a rather thick white sauce, using some of the rabbit liquor and the grated rind and strained juice of 1 lemon. Reheat the rabbit and bacon mixture in the sauce and serve hot.

BRAIN AND WALNUT SANDWICHES

These are a speciality of the district round Canberra, the sheep-farming area, from which a great deal of mutton is exported.

The brains should be cooked, allowed to cool, well seasoned with salt, pepper and lemon juice and mixed with a few chopped walnuts, if liked, before being used as a sandwich filling.

168

BOOYANGA NESTS

2 lb. potatoes	Salt and pepper
Deep fat for frying	4 eggs

Have ready 2 strainers, one about 4 inches in diameter and the other 2 inches. Shred the raw potatoes, then place a quarter of the pulp in the large strainer, and press the small one lightly on top. Deep-fry the potato, held between the 2 strainers, then remove the strainers, leaving a hollow "nest" of cooked potato; drain, sprinkle with salt and pepper, and keep warm. Repeat with remaining potato. Poach or fry the eggs and place one in each nest. Garnish, and serve at once.

To vary the flavour, the nests may be lined with melted cheese before the eggs are placed inside.

BARBECUE SAUCE

1 large onion, finely chopped	$\frac{1}{2}$ cup tomato sauce
1 oz. butter	$\frac{1}{2}$ tbsp. prepared mustard
2 tbsps. vinegar	1 cup water
2 tbsps. brown sugar	2 sticks of celery, chopped
Juice of 1 lemon	
2 tbsps. piquant table sauce	Salt and cayenne pepper

Fry the chopped onion in the butter until brown. Add the remaining ingredients and simmer for 30 minutes. Serve with any kind of barbecued meat or chicken.

CREAMED TOMATOES ON TOAST

1 lb. tomatoes	Salt and pepper
1–2 eggs	Hot buttered toast
2–4 tbsps. fresh cream	

Peel and quarter the tomatoes and simmer them in their own juice until cooked. Add the well-beaten eggs, the cream and seasonings to taste and cook, preferably over boiling water, until the mixture thickens. Serve at once on the hot toast.

MASHED PUMPKIN

Slice and peel the pumpkin (or part of a large one), then cut up small. Cook in a very little water until tender and drain well. If time permits, sieve the purée; otherwise, mash it very well, adding seasoning to taste and some butter; reheat if necessary and serve as a vegetable with meat.

AUSTRALIAN FRUIT SALAD

This is popular in Brisbane, where much fruit is grown. The salad will include such fruits as mango, pawpaw, oranges, bananas and pine-apple, and passion fruit is essential. These fruits are coarsely grated and mixed together.

Tinned mangoes are obtainable over here, and passion fruit can be bought at any green-grocer specialising in tropical fruit.

PAVLOVA CAKE

3 egg whites	$\frac{1}{2}$ pint double cream (whipped and flavoured)
6 oz. caster sugar	
1 bare tsp. vanilla essence	A 16-oz. tin pineapple, peaches or apricots
1 bare tsp. vinegar	Glacé cherries and angelica to decorate
2 tsps. cornflour	

Beat the egg whites till very stiff, then add the sugar gradually, continuing to beat until it has dissolved. Fold in the vanilla, vinegar and corn-flour. Spread the mixture in an 8-inch round on greaseproof paper placed on a baking tray, making the sides higher than the centre, to form a shell. Bake for 1 hour in a slow oven (300° F., mark 1). The Pavlova should be crisp on the surface but still soft in the centre. Cool and remove carefully on to a flat cake tray or board, fill with cream and arrange the drained fruit on top. Decorate with cherries and angelica and serve cut in wedges. 8 servings.

PINEAPPLE PAVLOVA

A meringue case	$\frac{1}{2}$ tsp. grated lemon rind
3 egg yolks	A can of pineapple pieces
1 tbsp. sugar	$\frac{1}{2}$ cup strained pineapple syrup
$\frac{1}{2}$ tbsp. butter	
1 tsp. lemon juice	

Make the meringue case as above. Put all the other ingredients in a saucepan (keeping back a few pieces of pineapple for decoration) and cook over a low heat, stirring, until quite thick. Cool, then pour the mixture over the meringue case and decorate the Pavlova with the remaining pineapple.

COOTAMUNDRA CREAM

3 eggs	1 small can of passion-fruit pulp
2 tsps. sugar	
2 tsps. gelatine	Whipped cream, halved grapes or glacé cherries for decoration
$\frac{1}{4}$ pint hot water	
Juice of 1 lemon	
$\frac{1}{4}$ pint milk	

Beat the egg yolks, place the yolks and sugar in a basin and beat lightly. Dissolve the gelatine in the water and add to the mixture, with the lemon juice and milk; stir in the passion-fruit pulp. Leave to stand until on the point of setting, then whisk well. Lastly, fold in the stiffly beaten egg whites, then pour the mixture into a glass dish or individual glasses and chill well. Serve with whipped cream, decorated with halved grapes or glacé cherries.

GOVERNMENT HOUSE PUDDING

4 eggs	4 bananas
1 pint milk	½ pint whipped cream
Sugar to taste	

Make a baked custard with the eggs, milk and sugar, cooking it in a large dish so that this is only three-quarters full. Leave the custard to get quite cold, then cover it with a layer of mashed bananas and a final layer of whipped cream.

SUNSHINE DESSERT

4 tbsps. cornflour	A 1-lb. can of halved
1 pint milk	apricots
1 egg	4 oz. marshmallows and
2 tbsps. sugar	1 tbsp. milk
Lemon essence	

Blend the cornflour with a little of the cold milk and put the remainder of the milk on to heat. Pour some heated milk on to the blended mixture, then return this to the pan and stir, still boiling. Cook for 2 minutes and allow to cool a little. Mix the egg yolk with the sugar, add to the cornflour and cook without boiling. Stir in a few drops of lemon essence and transfer to a deep ovenproof dish.

Strain the juice from the apricots and place them on top of the cornflour mixture. Place the cut-up marshmallows in a pan with the milk and melt over a gentle heat. Beat the egg white stiffly, pour the marshmallow in gradually and fold in. Pour the mixture on to the apricots and place under a grill until golden-brown.

ALMOND LOAF

6 oz. butter or	½ tsp. salt
margarine	1 tsp. baking powder
6 oz. sugar	1–2 lb. mixed dried
2 eggs	fruit
Almond essence	4 oz. almonds
12 oz. flour	Milk to mix

Cream the fat and sugar and beat in the eggs and a few drops of essence. Sieve the dry ingredients and add the fruit and chopped nuts (reserving about 1 oz. unchopped for top of cake). Combine the dry and the creamed ingredients, and mix with the milk to give a soft, dropping consistency. Put into a lined loaf tin and place the halved nuts neatly over top. Bake in a slow oven (325° F., mark 3) for about 3 hours.

LAMINGTONS

This is a type of cake widely eaten in Australia, but unknown over here. Cut a Madeira cake that is several days old into neat pieces about ½ inch thick. Dip each piece into a mixture of cocoa and cold water (unsweetened) or into half-set jelly, drain on a fork and toss immediately in desiccated coconut. Leave spread out on a plate until the coating has set. Decorate with whipped cream.

TASMANIAN DATE BROWNIES

2 cups sugar	4 cups flour
2 cups water	2 tsps. mixed spice
2 tbsps. dripping	1 tsp. bicarbonate of soda
1 lb. dates (stoned)	A pinch of salt

Cook the sugar, water, dripping and dates gently together for about 5 minutes, then leave to cool. Sieve together the dry ingredients and beat into the date mixture. Spread the mixture in a flat greased baking tin and bake in a slow oven (325° F., mark 3) until brown and set. Leave in the tin until cool, and do not cut until the next day. Serve sliced and buttered.

BUSHMAN'S BROWNIES

4 cups flour	1 cup dripping or
1 tsp. bicarbonate of	butter
soda	1 cup sugar
1 tsp. cream of tartar	1 cup currants
1 tsp. mixed spice	1 cup raisins (stoned)
1 tsp. ground cinnamon	Milk to mix

Sieve together the dry ingredients, then rub in the fat. Add the sugar, fruit and enough milk to give a fairly stiff mixture. Grease a flat baking tin generously, spread the cake mixture in it and bake in a moderate oven (350° F., mark 4) for about 1 hour, until brown. Cut up when cold.

MURRUMBIDGEE FAVOURITES

½ lb. flaky pastry	2 oz. raisins
1 banana	2 oz. sultanas
1 cooking apple	1 egg
(grated)	1 tbsp. granulated
Juice of 1 lemon	sugar

Make the pastry. Mash the banana and mix well with the apple, lemon juice, raisins and sultanas. Roll out the pastry thinly, and cut into triangles with approximately 4-inch sides. Place a spoonful of the fruit filling on to each triangle, brush the sides with a little beaten egg and fold the three corners into the centre. Brush with egg and sprinkle with granulated sugar. place on a greased tray, and bake in a moderately hot oven (400° F., mark 6) until golden-brown. Makes 20.

169

NOT surprisingly, the great national dish of New Zealand is roast lamb. It is served with roast potatoes and two or three vegetables, often including roast pumpkin or Kumara. That is how New Zealand men like their food—no frills, no foreign touches, although, as in Australia, new immigrants from Europe and Asia are introducing their own ideas.

The supply of food is good; beef, mutton and dairy produce are, of course, excellent. Fruit is also of good quality and there is a great variety—besides the usual apples, pears, cherries and plums, the climate is excellent for the growing of passion fruit, Chinese gooseberries, pomegranates and peaches. Towards the north there are orchards of oranges and lemons, grapefruit (the flesh is more orange in colour and sweeter than that of the Trinidad or Jaffa fruit, but that may partly be the difference between fruit ripened in ships and fruit ripened on the tree). Bananas, mangoes and pawpaw remind you that the northern-most part of the country is sub-tropical. Tree tomatoes are a fruit peculiar to New Zealand—they look a bit like tomatoes with a rather tough skin and have a distinctive flavour. They are delicious with sugar and cream. We include a recipe for interest although it is unlikely that they would be available here.

New Zealand women are proud of their baking—and quite justly! The preference being for plainly served meat dishes, their creativeness is lavished on puddings and cakes. The housewife proudly produces three or four cakes for the unexpected guest and, of course, Pavlova cake for the party. The recipe for the latter is a subject of endless and occasionally acrimonious discussion.

One thinks of New Zealand as a rich agricultural country; but an odd phenomenon is that the land is short of iodine, despite the long coast-line, and goitre was endemic there until the iodized salt came into general use some years ago.

The Maoris had their own methods of cooking, making use of the natural hot springs. They wrapped food in leaves, placed it in flax baskets and lowered it into the gently steaming and bubbling pools. Alternatively, they dug a hole in the ground, made a fire in it and covered it with stones. When the stones were really hot, the food, wrapped in wet leaves, was placed on the stones, covered with wet sacks and left to cook. This method of cooking is still sometimes found in the Pacific islands, but progress being what it is, the Maoris now generally use electric stoves.

New Zealand

MUSSEL SOUP

1 pint fish stock	1 pint milk
1/2 lb. mussels	Salt and pepper
2 oz. butter	Chopped parsley
1 1/2 oz. flour	

To make the fish stock, cover some fish heads with water, add 1 onion, 1 carrot, a pinch of mixed herbs and some peppercorns. Simmer for 30 minutes; strain. Cut the mussels into small pieces, cover with water and simmer for 5 minutes; put through a food blender or sieve if desired. Melt the butter, add the flour and cook slowly for 3 minutes; add enough milk to make a thick sauce. Blend the mussels with the sauce and thin to the required consistency with milk and stock. Season and garnish with chopped parsley. 6 servings.

TOHEROA SOUP

This is a speciality of New Zealand, particularly of the North Island. *Toheroa* is a large shell fish rather like a clam, native to that part of the world; it is possible to obtain *toheroas* over here in tinned form. Drain the liquor from the fish and mince the latter. Make a roux with 2 oz. butter and 2 oz. flour and add the liquor, made up to 1 pint with court-bouillon. Stir in 1 pint milk, the minced fish and 1 tsp. curry powder; season with salt and pepper to taste.

PUMPKIN AND CHEESE SOUP

Place 4 cups stock or water in a saucepan and add 2 cups uncooked sliced pumpkin. Wash 1/2 cup lentils and add. Season with salt and pepper and cook for 3/4 hour. Push through a colander, mashing through all the pumpkin and the lentils; return the soup to the saucepan and add 2–3 oz. grated cheese. Serve piping hot with toast croûtons.

OYSTER COCKTAIL

1 1/2–2 dozen oysters	Lemon juice
Tomato sauce	Salt and pepper
Piquant table sauce	

Into each glass put 4–6 oysters (removed from their shells), 1 tbsp. tomato sauce and 1 tsp. each of piquant table sauce and lemon juice, mixed and seasoned with salt and freshly ground pepper. Chill before serving.

MUSSEL COCKTAIL

170 Prepare some canned Castlerock mussels by removing the outside lips, inner tongue and white core. Cut them up into small pieces and divide between individual glasses. Make a cold sauce from 1 tin unsweetened condensed milk

(or cream), 1 cup of tomato sauce, 1 cup of tomato juice, 1 tsp. piquant table sauce and seasoning to taste; stir thoroughly and pour over the mussels in the glasses.

OYSTER SOUP

12 oysters	2 cups milk
1 tbsp. butter	Salt
1 tbsp. flour	Cayenne pepper

Beard the oysters and save the liquid. Melt the butter, add the flour and seasoning and stir until free of lumps. Gradually add the milk and the oyster liquid and simmer for 5 minutes; add the oysters. Leave for a few minutes and then serve in a hot tureen. If too thick add more milk. A little whipped cream and a teaspoon of chopped parsley may be added. When making a larger quantity use less butter in proportion.

OYSTER FRITTERS

4 oz. flour	Seasoning
1 egg	1 dozen oysters
1/2 pint milk	Deep fat for frying

Make a batter in the usual way with the flour, egg, milk and seasoning. Mince the oysters and add to the batter mixture. Fry spoonfuls in the deep fat.

COLD MUSSELS

Take a can of Castlerock mussels and prepare in the normal way, removing the outside lips, inner tongue and white core. Place in a shallow dish, pour the liquid from the tin over them, add extra vinegar and seasoning if desired and serve cold, with bread and butter.

WHITEBAIT AND BREADCRUMB FRITTERS

4–6 oz. whitebait	2 large tbsps. fine, soft
2 eggs	white breadcrumbs
1/2 tsp. salt	Butter for frying
Pepper	

Wash the whitebait and dry in a cloth. Beat the eggs, add the other ingredients and blend well. Heat a knob of butter in a frying pan. Drop tablespoons of the mixture into the fat, and fry on both sides. Serve hot with lemon slices 4–6 servings.

MUSSELS WITH RICE

Cook 3 oz. rice. While it is cooking, fry 3 large, finely diced onions in 1/4 cup olive oil until tender. Chop 24 prepared cooked mussels into 1/2-inch cubes. Heat in a large pan 1/4 cup olive oil and 1 cup vinegar. Add alternately the rice, shell fish and onions, stirring with a wooden spoon. Add salt and pepper, a pinch of cayenne and a pinch of mixed spice. Cook gently for 10 minutes to blend the flavours. If desired, the vinegar may be added little by little at the same time as the seasoning. Serve alone, sprinkled with chopped parsley.

Scallops or (in New Zealand) *pipis* may be used in place of mussels.

STUFFED LOIN OF HOGGET

Loin of hogget	½ tsp. mixed herbs, dried
(1-year-old lamb)	1 tsp. chopped parsley
1 tomato, chopped	1 egg
1 apple, chopped	1 oz. suet
1 onion, chopped	Salt and pepper
4–6 oz. breadcrumbs	

Bone the lamb. Combine the other ingredients to make a stuffing, lay this along the loin, roll up and tie. Roast in a moderate oven (350° F., mark 4) for 2–2½ hours.

ROAST CROWN OF HOGGET

To prepare crown use a full loin, with the rib bones separated a little at top and bottom, and the tops trimmed as for cutlets; roll the loin into a circle, so that the trimmed bones stand upright and the chops form a complete circle; tie with a thick string, or skewer firmly. Cover each bone tip with a thick piece of pork fat and cook the crown standing upright in a slow to moderate oven (325°–350° F., marks 2–3) for 2–2½ hours.

To serve, remove the pork fat from bones and replace by cutlet frills; remove the string. Fill the centre with boiled new potatoes garnished with parsley butter, or with green peas and diced carrots, or with other vegetable; garnish between the chops. To carve, cut each chop separately.

CRUMBED CHOPS

Dip some lamb chops in egg, beaten up with a little water, salt and pepper, and then in breadcrumbs. Put in really hot fat in a roasting tin and bake in a moderate oven (350° F., mark 4) for 45 minutes.

SMOTHERED CHOPS

6 leg chops	1 green pepper,
Salt and pepper	sliced thinly
1 lemon, sliced very	6 sliced tomatoes or
thinly with rind	2 cans of tomato
2 onions, sliced thinly	purée

Wipe and trim the chops, dust with seasonings and lay them in a baking dish. Cover with lemon slices, then with onion and green pepper; cover with tomato and season. Bake (uncovered) in a moderate oven (350° F., mark 4) for 1½ hours. Thicken the gravy. Garnish with parsley.

CREAMED HAM PIE

2 cups minced cooked ham	½ pint white sauce
1 small can garden peas	Shortcrust pastry

Mix the ham with the drained peas and white sauce. Place in a greased pie dish, cover with pastry and bake in a moderately hot oven (400° F., mark 6) until the pastry is browned.

WELLINGTON PIE

1 lb. New Zealand	1 tbsp. chopped parsley
lamb	A little stock or water
2 lambs' kidneys	Salt and pepper
2 skinned tomatoes	8 oz. shortcrust pastry
4 small potatoes	Egg or milk to glaze
2 tsps. chopped onion	

Cut the lamb into thin slices. Skin and slice the kidneys. Slice the tomatoes and potatoes and fill the pie dish with alternate layers of meat and vegetables, adding to each layer a little chopped onion, parsley and seasoning. Add a little stock. Cover the pie with shortcrust pastry, decorate and glaze with a little egg or milk. Bake in a moderately hot oven (400° F., mark 6) for ½ hour, and then in a moderate oven (350° F., mark 3) for another hour.

WELLINGTON LAMB STEW

A large breast of lamb,	Seasoning
boned	6 oz. rice
1 oz. cooking fat	A large packet frozen
¾ lb. thinly sliced	peas
onions	¾ lb. sliced mushrooms
½ lb. diced carrots	⅛ pint red wine
1 pint stock or water	

Cut the lamb in pieces and brown in the melted fat in a pan with the onions. Add carrots, stock or water and seasoning, cover and cook over a low heat until tender (about 1½ hours).

Add the rice, then ten minutes later, the peas, mushrooms and wine. Cover again and simmer until the vegetables are ready (about 30 minutes). Stir occasionally; if the rice should stick, add a little hot water or stock.

CORN FRITTERS

Sift 4 oz. flour, ½ tsp. baking powder and a pinch of salt; add 1 beaten egg and ¼ pint milk and beat. Add the drained contents of an 11-oz. can of whole kernel corn. Put spoonfuls into hot fat, fry until browned on both sides and serve immediately.

171

ROAST PUMPKIN

Peel the pumpkin thickly, cut into pieces and roast round the joint, as for potatoes, for $\frac{3}{4}$–1 hour. This is a very popular New Zealand vegetable.

CANDIED KUMARA
(SWEET POTATO)

Boil kumaras until almost cooked, peel and cut into thick slices. Brush with melted butter and brown sugar, then bake in a moderately hot oven (425° F., mark 7) for 15 minutes.

SILVER BEET

This is a vegetable like celery, with leaves resembling spinach. The stems and leaves are generally cooked separately, as the stems require a longer time.

LEMON DELICIOUS

$\frac{1}{2}$ cup sugar	1 cup milk
1 tbsp. butter	Juice and rind of
2 eggs, separated	1 lemon
1 tbsp. flour	

Mix the sugar and butter well. Add the egg yolks, flour, milk, lemon juice and grated rind. Beat the egg whites stiffly and fold into the mixture. Cook in a soufflé dish in a baking tin of water in a slow oven (325° F., mark 2) for $\frac{3}{4}$ hour. The top should set as a very light sponge with a custard sauce underneath.

PAVLOVA CAKE

3 egg whites	1 tsp. vinegar
6 oz. sugar	Whipped cream
1 tsp. vanilla essence	Fruit

This cake, although it originated in Australia, is now very popular in New Zealand and a number of different versions are made.

Beat the egg whites stiffly, then add the sugar a spoonful at a time, still beating. Fold in the vanilla essence and vinegar. Wet a piece of greaseproof paper and lay it on a baking tin, pile the mixture on this, hollowing the centre slightly and bake in a very slow oven (275° F., mark $\frac{1}{2}$) for 2–3 hours. When cold, pile with whipped cream and fruit—passion fruit and pineapple are both excellent.

PASSION-FRUIT CREAM

2 tsps. gelatine	1 tbsp. sherry
$\frac{1}{2}$ pint milk	Pulp of $\frac{1}{2}$ dozen
$\frac{1}{2}$ cup sugar	passion fruit
$\frac{1}{4}$ pint double cream	(or an 8-oz. can)

Soak the gelatine in a little of the milk. Bring the remaining milk to the boil and add the sugar, pour on to the gelatine and stir. Allow to cool until almost setting. Beat the cream stiffly, add the sherry, passion fruit and gelatine mixture and beat until smooth, then pour into a mould. (The pips of the passion fruit need not be removed—they can safely be eaten.)

FUDGE CAKE

$\frac{1}{4}$ lb. sugar	$\frac{1}{2}$ lb. chopped nuts
$\frac{1}{4}$ lb. butter	$\frac{1}{2}$ lb. crushed biscuits
1 tbsp. cocoa	(semi-sweet)
1 egg, beaten	

Heat the sugar, butter and cocoa together, until melted. Add the egg and cook gently till thick, then pour on to the nuts and biscuits. Press the mixture into a tin, allow to set and then cut into fingers.

ROROI
(MAORI KUMARA PUDDING)

This recipe is perhaps the only Maori pudding known.

Take some very fresh kumaras or sweet potatoes, straight from the garden if possible, wash and then grate. Put in a shallow baking dish and sprinkle with sugar. Over the top spread some broad slices of sweet potato, to keep the mixture from hardening in the oven. Bake in a moderate oven (350° F., mark 4) for 1 hour. When cooked, this is similar to a steamed pudding, and may be served with cream or other sauce or accompaniment. When cold, it may be sliced up like bread and spread with butter.

BAKED PUDDING

3 oz. fat	A pinch of salt
3 tbsps. sugar	About $\frac{1}{4}$ pint milk
1 egg	3–4 oz. dried fruit—
$\frac{1}{2}$ lb. flour	currants, sultanas,
1 tsp. baking powder	raisins and peel

Cream the fat and sugar together, add the egg (unbeaten), then beat all together. Sift the flour, baking powder and salt and fold into the mixture. Add just sufficient milk to make a soft heavily dropping batter; stir in the dried fruits. Put the mixture into a greased dish or tin and bake in a moderate oven (375° F., mark 5) for 20–30 minutes.

This pudding is usually served hot, with ice cream.

TREE TOMATOES

Peel the fruit and cut in halves. Mix equal quantities (about 2 tbsps. of each) of golden syrup, honey and water, pour over the tree

172

tomatoes and allow to stand for ½–1 hour. Serve with cream or milk.

AFGHANS

7 oz. butter	2 oz. cornflakes
3 oz. sugar	½ tsp. vanilla essence
6 oz. flour	Chocolate icing
1 tbsp. cocoa	Walnuts, shelled

Cream the butter and sugar and add the flour, cocoa, cornflakes and vanilla essence. Pile in small heaps on a greased baking sheet and bake in a moderate oven (350° F., mark 4) for 15–20 minutes. When cool, ice with chocolate icing and decorate each with a walnut half.

ANZAC BISCUITS

4 oz. butter	8 oz. sugar
1 tbsp. golden syrup	3 oz. desiccated coconut
1 tsp. bicarbonate of soda	4 oz. rolled oats
	1 oz. chopped walnuts
2 tbsps. water	A pinch of salt
3 oz. plain flour	

Melt the butter and syrup in a saucepan and add the soda dissolved in the water. Mix all the other ingredients in a bowl, add the liquids and mix together. Put on a greased tray in dessert-spoonfuls, leaving room for them to spread. Cook for 15–20 minutes in a moderate oven (350° F., mark 4).

ALTHOUGH customs and habits vary from island to island in the Pacific, nevertheless there is inevitably an overall similarity in the methods of preparing and serving food and in the food itself, since the local produce is largely the same in each island. Bananas and breadfruit grow everywhere and with taro, yams and tapioca form the staple food of the inhabitants. Large quantities of coconut provide most of the fat in the native diet and fish, shell fish and octopus are widely used. Pork is the favourite meat and chicken is also popular.

The mainstay of the Hawaiian diet was *poi*, a pasty mass made from the cooked, mashed taro root, served with salty and piquant sauces and relishes, often derived from seaweed or dried fish. The Samoans also rely upon taro for their staple vegetable food, but do not make it into *poi*, preferring to bake or boil it. Sea water is used as an ingredient in sauces and coconut and breadfruit dishes. Fruit is eaten and enjoyed before it is fully ripe.

The old method of cooking was in an *imu* or underground oven and this is still used when a feast or *luau* is being prepared. First of all a deep hole is dug and is lined with round, porous stones. These are heated very thoroughly, by lighting a fire of branches in the pit which is then lined with *ti* leaves and banana stalks. The food to be cooked—pig, potatoes, chicken, fish, bananas and so on—is wrapped in leaves and placed in the *imu*. More leaves and stalks cover the packages of food, then more hot stones and finally a layer of soil or sand. The whole thing is left undisturbed all day, until the food is thoroughly cooked. A typical *luau* will include such foods as :

Lomi lomi salmon : Shredded salt salmon, tomatoes and green onions chopped fine, covered with crushed ice and served in small dishes.

Opihi : A shell fish.

Poi : Pounded taro root, mixed with water to the consistency of thick cream.

Haupia : Cornflour pudding made with coconut cream.

Kulolo : Baked coconut and taro pudding.

Chicken luau : Chicken cooked in coconut cream with taro leaves. Fresh fruit is served and coconut milk drunk.

Everyday food is considerably less elaborate and consists generally of two main meals, both often including bananas, breadfruit and coconut in one form or another, with fish, shell fish or turtle served at the main meal. Leftovers from the two main meals are frequently eaten as snacks at other times of day.

South Sea Islands

AVOCADO PEAR SOUP

2 tsps. butter	2 pints stock
1 tsp. flour	1 pear
½ pint milk	Seasonings

Cream the butter and flour together until quite smooth, then stir in the milk slowly, cook until thickened, stirring all the time. Add the stock and keep hot. Mash the pear smoothly and add to the stock, but do not allow to boil. Adjust the seasoning and strain before serving.

FIJIAN TOMATO SOUP

¾ cup rice	½ tsp. salt
⅓ cup chopped onion	1 tbsp. chopped parsley
2 tbsps. dripping	1 tsp. sugar
2 cups cut-up tomato	⅛ tsp. paprika
2–3 slices red pepper	

Wash the rice, add to 3 cups boiling water and boil for 30 minutes. Cook the onion in a pan with the dripping till tender but not brown; add the tomatoes and pepper and simmer for 10 minutes. Rub the mixture through a strainer into the boiling rice and water. Add the salt, pepper and sugar and sprinkle the parsley and paprika on top of the soup when serving.

PEANUT SOUP

Roast ¾ lb. peanuts, shell and skin them and put through the mincing machine. Then to each cup minced peanuts add 2 cups milk and pepper and salt to taste; simmer gently and serve with fried bread croûtons.

PEANUT BUTTER SOUP

Blend 1 tbsp. melted butter, 1 tbsp. grated onion, 1 tbsp. flour, and salt and pepper to taste, then add 2 heaped tsps. peanut butter. Pour 1 pint hot milk slowly over this and cook for 20 minutes.

LOLO OR COCONUT CREAM

Take a ripe coconut and grate all the white flesh. To make a rich cream, pour a teacupful of hot water over the grated coconut and squeeze the mixture well in the hands, then strain off the liquid through muslin.

To be used with fish or vegetables the lolo may be slightly salted. It may be heated but should not be boiled, as this spoils the creaminess. It may be iced for use with cold sweets.

COCONUT SOUP

Make a stock of bones and vegetables and thicken slightly. Strain and add lolo to taste, but do not re-boil or it will curdle. Excellent results can be obtained by the addition of coconut cream to any fish or shell-fish soup.

FISH BAKED IN LOLO

Clean, scale and gut the fish, then rub it well with lime juice and salt. Simmer some thick lolo until it becomes a thickish sauce and leave to cool. When the sauce is sufficiently cooled, pour it over the fish and bake in a moderate oven (375° F., mark 5) until tender.

PRAWN SOUP

To make this, use the heads, tails, etc., left after the prawns have been shelled. Simmer them in water with a little onion, salt, pepper and any other pieces of fish heads, tails and bones that may be available. When the stock is well flavoured, strain it through a fine sieve. Mix with plenty of thick lolo, reheat very gently, add ½ tsp. of anchovy essence and serve hot.

FISH IN LOLO SAUCE

Cut 3–4 lb. of any firm white fish into cubes or fillets. Soak in lemon or lime juice and leave in the refrigerator for 12 or more hours.

Make 6–8 breakfastcups of lolo from 3 whole coconuts, flavour with a little salt, pepper, 1–2 finely chopped chillies and 1 grated onion, put this mixture into a saucepan and slowly bring to the boil, then chill—the sauce will thicken as it cools. Drain off the lime or lemon juice from the fish and pour the sauce over the fish 1–2 hours before it is to be served.

FISH IN EGG AND LEMON SAUCE

Prepare about 2 lb. fish. Cook 2 sliced onions in enough water to cover the fish; when they are done, put in the fish and cook until tender. Take a little of the fish liquor, mix with 2 well-beaten eggs, add the juice of 4 good-sized lemons, then stir into the fish and reheat without boiling. Remove from the heat, cool and leave in a cold place till set.

KADAVU FISH

¼ pint cooked rice	1 egg
2 tbsps. butter	2 tbsps. milk
1 tbsp. flour	1 finely chopped onion
2 cups cooked and flaked fish	1 tbsp. chopped parsley
	Salt and pepper

Grease a mould (or small moulds) and line with cooked rice. Melt the butter, add flour and stir till smooth. Mix in the flaked fish, beaten egg, milk, onion, parsley and salt and pepper, stir well and cook for a few minutes.

Fill the lined moulds with the mixture and cover with more rice. Put in a shallow pan of water and cook in a moderate oven (350° F., mark 4) for ½ hour. Turn out and serve at once. Tomato sauce goes well with this dish.

FIJIAN BAKED FISH

1 lb. white fish	Salt and pepper
1 tbsp. minced onion	1 cup tomato purée
½ cup grated cheese	2 tsps. chopped parsley

Place the fish in a buttered fireproof dish. Mix the onion, cheese, salt and pepper into the tomato purée and pour over the fish. Bake in a moderate oven (350° F., mark 4) until the fish is cooked. Garnish with the parsley.

FISH WITH ONIONS

Lightly fry 1 sliced onion, add ½ cup water, some pepper and salt and boil till the onion is well cooked. In a separate pan, fry the fish, browning both sides lightly, pour off the fat, then add the onion and liquid, cover the pan and simmer slowly for 10 minutes.

PICKLED FISH

3 lb. fish	3 large onions
Flour	½ pint vinegar
Salt	1 tbsp. cornflour
Fat for frying	1 tbsp. curry powder

Cut the fish into neat pieces, dry, sprinkle with a little flour and salt and fry. Cut up the onions and boil until soft; strain off the water, cover the onions with vinegar and boil up again. Mix the cornflour and curry powder and use to thicken the onions and vinegar. Place alternate layers of fish and onion mixture in a dish and serve cold.

ISLAND FRIED FISH

2 lb. white fish fillets	½ tsp. salt
⅓ cup soya sauce	¼ tsp. pepper
⅓ cup flour	1 large can of pineapple
⅓ cup cornflour	chunks
About ⅔ cup milk	½ cup sugar
1 egg	Cooking oil
2 tsps. baking powder	

Wash the fish, pat dry and cut into pieces about 1½ inches square. Marinate in the soya sauce for 20–30 minutes, turning once or twice. Combine the flour, cornflour, milk, egg, baking powder and seasonings to make a batter, about the consistency of very thick cream. Pour the pineapple and its syrup into a saucepan, stir in the sugar and heat very gently and thoroughly. Pour the cooking oil into a heavy saucepan to a depth of 1½ inches and heat to 375° F. When ready, drain the fish of surplus soya sauce, dip quickly into the batter, drain a little, and plunge it into the hot oil. Add as many pieces as you can at one time—but be sure that the temperature of the oil stays at 375° F. The fish will cook in 1–2 minutes, when the crust will be crisp and golden; remove to a pan lined with absorbent paper and keep in a warm oven until all the fish is ready. Mix 1 tbsp. cornflour with ¼ cup water, add to the pineapple and cook until the syrup has thickened. Arrange the pineapple in the sauce on a hot dish and place the fish carefully on top.

RAW FISH PICKLED IN LIME JUICE

1 fish about 2 lb.	Coconut cream
1 chopped onion	2 tbsps. olive oil
Salt and pepper	2 tbsps. vinegar
Limes	1 lettuce
4 cloves of garlic	2 tomatoes
6 gherkins	2 hard-boiled eggs
6 olives	

Wash the fish well, bone and skin it, then cut into small cubes. Place it in a pie dish with the chopped onion, sprinkle with 3 tsps. salt and a little pepper and mix well. Squeeze fresh lime juice over the fish until they are covered; place in a refrigerator for 4 hours, then drain. Mince the garlic, cube the gherkins, halve the olives, mix with the fish, add the oil and vinegar. Cover with coconut cream and serve with lettuce, tomato and egg.

SOUTH SEAS FISH IN FOIL

6 trout or any white	Juice of 1 lemon
fish (½–¾ lb.)	½ tsp. ground ginger
6 tbsps. melted butter	½ lb. fresh spinach
2 tsps. soya sauce	leaves, washed

173

Clean and wash the fish. (If using frozen fish, thaw according to directions.) Stir the melted butter, soya sauce and lemon juice together and brush on to the fish, inside and out. Sprinkle the inside of each fish generously with the ginger and then dust lightly on top. Wrap each fish in foil in this way: Place a few spinach leaves on a square of aluminium foil, lay a seasoned serving of fish on spinach and place a few leaves on top; wrap in foil, turning the ends in and folding it securely. Place on a shallow baking tray and cook in a moderate oven (350° F., mark 4) for 30–40 minutes. Bring to the table in the foil. If you prefer, wrap several pieces of spinach-covered fish in one large piece of foil and remove from the foil to a hot serving platter.

Note : The foil is used as a substitute for the

large leaves of various tropical plants. The leaves or husks of sweet corn could also be used.

POLYNESIAN FISH

3 lb. halibut or cod steak cut $\frac{3}{4}$ inch thick	A generous pinch of marjoram
$\frac{1}{3}$ cup lime juice	$\frac{1}{2}$ a can of shrimp soup
$\frac{1}{4}$ cup melted butter	$\frac{1}{2}$ cup sour cream
$\frac{1}{2}$ tsp. salt	3–4 onions, with tops, sliced thinly
$\frac{1}{4}$ tsp. freshly ground pepper	$\frac{1}{2}$ cup shrimps

Wash the fish, pat dry, cut into 6 serving-size pieces and trim as required. Place in a shallow ovenproof baking dish. Pour the lime juice over the top and allow to soak for a few minutes on each side, then discard the juice. Pour the butter over the fish and sprinkle with seasonings. Grill for about 10 minutes, basting once with the butter. Remove from the heat and baste again with pan juices ; set aside to cool slightly. Mix the soup and sour cream together and spoon on top of each piece of fish. Bake for 30 minutes in a slow oven (325° F., mark 3). Serve in the baking dish and garnish with onions and shrimps. Makes 6 servings.

LOMI LOMI SALAD
(SHREDDED SALMON)

$\frac{3}{4}$ lb. salmon	4 ripe tomatoes (about
$1\frac{1}{2}$ tbsps. salt	$1\frac{1}{2}$ lb.)
3 tbsps. lemon juice	4 medium-sized onions

Wash the salmon, pat dry, rub with the salt and sprinkle lemon juice on both sides ; cover and place in the refrigerator for 12–24 hours, turning it once. The lemon juice will " cook " the salmon. Remove the bones and skin from the fish and cut it into pieces $\frac{1}{4}$–$\frac{1}{2}$ inch in size, or pull it apart with your fingers—in this way you will be sure to feel and remove any small bones. Peel and chop the tomatoes and add to the salmon. Wash and trim the onions and slice very thinly, using the tender part of the stem. Add more lemon juice and salt to taste, cover and again place in the refrigerator for several hours. Serve very cold on lettuce or watercress. Alternatively, stuff tomatoes with the mixture. Serve as a first course for lunch or supper. Serves 6. See also recipe on p. 505.

CURRIED PRAWN OR CRAB

Prepare the prawns or crab and cook in lolo made from 1 coconut, adding curry powder, salt and pepper to taste.

CRAB OMELETTE

Slice 1 large onion and mash 2 cloves of garlic ; fry these together until light brown, then add the meat of a crab and cook for about 5 minutes. Beat 4 eggs well, add 1 cup water and stir into the mixture in the pan. Turn carefully and when the egg is cooked dish up, sprinkle with pepper and salt and garnish with parsley.

PRAWNS COOKED IN LOLO

2 coconuts	2–3 chopped chillies
1 grated onion	2 lb. shelled uncooked
Salt	prawns

Make 4 breakfastcups of thick lolo from the coconuts, mix with the onion, salt and chillies. Bring slowly to the boil, add the prawns and simmer gently for 15 minutes. Serve the prawns with or without the sauce.

COCONUT SAUCE FOR FISH

Grate a coconut and pour on 1 cup water. Peel a lemon and cut into slices, add $\frac{1}{2}$ a finely chopped onion and pound all together. Pour off the thick milk and strain it, then add lemon mixture, salt to taste, and a little finely chopped chilli.

CHICKEN LUAU
(CHICKEN FEAST)

A $2\frac{1}{2}$ lb. chicken, cut up	1 cup hot milk
Flour	4 oz. shredded coconut
$\frac{1}{2}$ cup butter or mar- garine	2 lb. spinach, washed
	2 tbsps. minced onion
Salt	

Lightly dust the chicken with flour. Heat the butter in a large pan and cook the chicken until evenly browned ; add 1 tsp. salt and 1 cup water, cover and simmer for about 30 minutes, or until tender. Meanwhile, pour the milk over the coconut ; let it stand for 15 minutes, then simmer for 10 minutes. Cut the spinach into large pieces, cook with the onion and $\frac{1}{2}$ tsp. salt in $\frac{1}{4}$ cup water for about 5 minutes, then drain. Add to the chicken with the coconut, and simmer for 3 minutes. Makes 8 servings.

CHICKEN PORTELLO
(CHICKEN IN COCONUTS)

6 fresh coconuts	Salt and pepper
6 bacon rashers, diced	1 clove of garlic, minced
$1\frac{1}{2}$ cups cut fresh corn— 3 ears	6 small tomatoes, peeled and cut into sixths
3 onions, sliced	
$1\frac{1}{2}$ cups chopped green pepper	4 cups cooked or can- ned chicken chunks

With a long nail or ice-pick, puncture 3 indentations at one end of each coconut ; drain the milk from these holes. From the punctured end of each coconut, saw off about 1½ inches to make a lid. Using a sharp knife, remove the coconut meat from each lid in large chunks, then peel and grate it. Sauté the bacon in a large pan until crisp; mix in the corn, ¼ cup grated coconut, the onions, green pepper, 1 tsp. salt, ¼ tsp. pepper and the garlic; cook until tender. Sprinkle the tomatoes with salt and pepper, and add with the chicken to the corn mixture; cook for 5 minutes. Start heating the oven to moderate (350° F., mark 4). Spoon the chicken mixture into the coconut shells, top with the lids and wrap each coconut completely in foil. Place the coconuts in a baking tin with 1 inch water and bake for 1¼ hours. Serve in the shells, topped with grated coconut. Makes 6 good servings.

CASSEROLED CHICKEN

Strip the meat from the bones and roll it in flour, then fry brown in butter. Put into casserole with 1 finely chopped medium-sized onion, 2 tbsps. rice, a little green chilli and about 1 pint coconut cream. Cook for 1–1½ hours in a moderate oven (350° F., mark 4).

TAVEUNI
(CHICKEN MOULD)

Butter a pudding mould and line it with an inch-thick layer of boiled and well-seasoned rice. Fill the centre with 2 cups of finely chopped chicken, 1 tbsp. butter, ½ cup breadcrumbs, 1 beaten egg and enough chicken stock to moisten well; add salt, pepper, finely chopped parsley and a small minced onion. Mix well and put into the mould, cover with a thick layer of rice, cover with greaseproof paper, tie down and steam for 40 minutes. Turn out on a hot dish and garnish with parsley.

YASAWA
(FRIED CHICKEN BALLS)

Mince some cold cooked chicken as finely as possible; add a quarter of its weight in breadcrumbs and 1 tsp. chopped parsley, with pepper and salt to taste, and beaten egg to mix. Form into small balls, dip into more beaten egg and roll in breadcrumbs, then fry in lard or dripping until brown all over. Serve with boiled rice.

ROAST SUCKING PIG

Order a young pig and get the butcher to clean it well. Scrape and wash it and slash the skin. Rub the incisions and the inside of the pig with peeled fresh ginger or with preserved ginger root, then sprinkle generously with salt and soya sauce. If a European-type stuffing is used, do not put in too much, or the flesh will split during the cooking; sew up the belly opening if the pig has been stuffed. Truss with the front legs skewered backwards and the hind legs drawn forward, put into a large roasting tin, back uppermost, brush over with oil and sprinkle with salt. Cook in a moderate oven (350° F., mark 4), allowing 30 minutes per pound and basting every 15 minutes.

The native way of cooking a whole pig is to wrap it in aromatic leaves (replaced here by the ginger and soya sauce) and lay it on previously heated stones in a trench oven; vegetables like taro, sweet potatoes or green bananas are often included. More aromatic leaves and more hot stones are packed on top and the whole is left undisturbed for some hours.

CUTLETS AND BANANAS

Dip the cutlets in egg and breadcrumbs and place in a baking dish lined with buttered paper; place a roll of bacon on each cutlet. Cook in a moderate oven (350° F., mark 4) for 15 minutes. Before serving dip some peeled bananas in egg and breadcrumbs, add to the cutlets and finish cooking.

HAWAIIAN MEAT ROLLS

1 lb. minced steak	1 lb. potatoes
½ cup shredded pineapple	1 tsp. butter
	½ cup self-raising flour
1 tsp. minced onion	1 tbsp. chopped parsley
1 tbsp. tomato sauce	1 egg
Salt and pepper	

Combine the meat, pineapple, onion and tomato sauce, season with salt and pepper and cook over a low heat until the meat changes colour. Cook the potatoes, drain, mash and mix with the butter, flour, parsley and beaten egg. Turn on to a floured board, roll out ¼ inch thick and cut into 3-inch squares. Place a spoonful of meat mixture on each square, moisten the edges and fold over; press the edges lightly with a fork. Place on a greased baking tray and brush with the remaining egg mixture. Bake in a moderately hot oven (425° F., mark 7) for 15–20 minutes. Serve piping hot.

TERIYAKI, MAINLAND STYLE
(GRILLED SKEWERED BEEF)

1 can pineapple chunks	1 lb. sirloin of beef, cut in ¾-inch slices
⅓ cup soya sauce	
1 clove of garlic, minced	1 small jar of small stuffed olives
¾ tsp. ground ginger	

Drain the juice from the pineapple and mix

174

with the soya sauce, garlic and ginger ; add the beef and let it stand for 1 hour. Cut the beef into $\frac{3}{4}$-inch cubes. Place alternate pieces of beef and pineapple on wooden skewers and put an olive at the end of each skewer. Grill, turning once, for 10–12 minutes. Makes about 2 doz. ; allow 2–3 per person.

This is a dish of Japanese origin.

PORK AND PINEAPPLE PACKAGES

2 lb. fresh pork shoulder (with some fat left on), cut into 2-inch pieces
$\frac{1}{2}$ tsp. ground ginger
1 can pineapple chunks, drained
$1\frac{3}{4}$ tsps. onion or garlic salt
2 seeded and quartered green peppers
$1\frac{1}{8}$ tsps. pepper
8 small potatoes

Start heating the oven to moderate (350° F., mark 4). Put the pork on waxed paper, then sprinkle with onion salt, pepper and ginger. Cut 8 pieces of foil about a foot square. Put on each some pork, pineapple, green pepper and potatoes, gather the foil together at the top, arrange in a shallow baking tin and cook for 2 hours (makes 8).

EGG PLANT SAUCE

Peel and cut 2 small egg plants and 2 small onions into small pieces, add $\frac{1}{4}$ tsp. salt and a little water and cook till soft ; drain well. Add 1 tbsp. butter, 2 tbsps. curry powder, $\frac{1}{8}$ tsp. allspice, 1 tsp. ground cinnamon and a pinch of ground nutmeg. Mix well and simmer for $\frac{1}{4}$ hour. Serve with steak or cold meats.

FAI 'AI
(BAKED COCONUT CREAM)

Make lolo from 2 coconuts, add a little salt and bake in a moderate oven (350° F., mark 4) for about an hour. Very good with vegetables.

VEGETABLE OMELETTE

Make a thick purée of spinach, beetroot or carrots and form into a flat oval shape on a hot dish. Make a plain omelette and place it on the purée. Sprinkle with grated cheese or coconut.

SWEET POTATO PILHI
(SWEET POTATO PUDDING)

Grate 6 large sweet potatoes and add the white flesh of 2 grated coconuts and coconut cream made from 2 coconuts. Mix all together, put in a well-greased meat dish and bake in a hot oven (450° F., mark 8) for 45 minutes. Serve with meat.

A small quantity of the cooked pilhi may be taken and put into a saucepan and more coconut cream mixed into it ; when the cream has thickened it is ready to serve.

PUMPKIN PILHI
(BAKED PUMPKIN PUDDING)

1 medium-sized pumpkin
1 breakfastcup flour
1 teacup sugar
3 coconuts

Peel and cook the pumpkin and drain in a colander overnight. The next day mash the pumpkin, sift in the sugar and flour and add the milk squeezed from the grated coconuts. Mix all together, put in a well-greased baking tin and bake in a moderately hot oven (400° F., mark 6) for about 1 hour. Serve as a vegetable.

PLUM MUDDER
(BANANA DUMPLINGS)

Grate some green bananas and add salt to taste. Drop by tablespoonfuls into boiling water or milk and poach for 20–30 minutes. Eat as an accompaniment to roast duck, pork or other meat, or with sugar or jam.

BRAISED STUFFED CUCUMBER

2 long, thin cucumbers
1 tbsp. soya sauce
$\frac{1}{2}$ cup minced pork
1 tsp. salt
$\frac{1}{2}$ cup dry breadcrumbs
$\frac{1}{4}$ tsp. sugar
$\frac{1}{8}$ tsp. peeled and shredded ginger root, or $\frac{1}{4}$ tsp. powdered ginger
$\frac{1}{4}$ tsp. monosodium glutamate
1–2 tbsps. cooking oil
1 tbsp. red wine vinegar

Wash, peel and trim the cucumbers ; cut across into slices about $1\frac{1}{2}$ inches thick and hollow out the centre. Mix the pork with the remaining ingredients, except the oil, and pack into the cucumbers. Heat the oil in a saucepan, stand the stuffed cucumbers in the oil and cook gently until tinged with brown, then turn and brown the other end. Add $\frac{1}{4}$ cup water, cover, turn the heat low and continue cooking for 8–10 minutes longer. The cucumbers should be tender but not soft, and the pork done through. Makes 6 servings.

STUFFED NASTURTIUM FLOWERS

4 tbsps. finely grated cheese
$\frac{1}{2}$ tsp. finely chopped parsley
2 tbsps. finely chopped gherkins
Enough salad cream to mix
1 tsp. anchovy essence French dressing
2–3 doz. nasturtium flowers

Mix together all the ingredients except the flowers. Fill each nasturtium with a little of the mixture, pressing the petals down to close each flower completely. Arrange on a glass plate, pour some French dressing over them and leave on ice until required. They should be served very cold.

AUBERGINES IN LOLO

4 medium-sized aubergines	1 grated onion
	2–3 chopped chillies
Salt	5–6 breakfast cups lolo

Peel the aubergines and slice thickly. Arrange in layers in a casserole, sprinkle each layer with salt, onion and chopped chillies. Add enough lolo to cover. Bake in a slow oven (325° F., mark 3) until the aubergines are soft.

PAULISAMI
(LOLO IN DALO LEAVES)

6 ripe brown coconuts	Salt and pepper
1 large coarsely grated onion	70 dalo leaves
	Breadfruit leaves
1 thinly sliced lime or small lemon	

This is an example of the dishes offered when chiefs gather together for discussions and when important personages are being entertained.

From the 6 coconuts make about 12 breakfastcups of thick lolo, using 1 breakfastcup of water to each coconut; squeeze through a cloth. Flavour the cream with the onion, lime slices, salt and pepper. Moisten 6 of the dalo leaves and shape each into a cornet shape—like the old-fashioned grocer's bag. Fill each leaf with lolo and fold over the pointed top to keep in the cream. Arrange all 6 on one of the breadfruit leaves, shiny side up. Make a round package, tucking the edge of the leaf in carefully and securing it with the stem pushed through the midrib. Repeat this process until all the leaves and coconut are used up. Bake the paulisami for about 1 hour, or until tender.

Sea water is often mixed with the coconut to vary the flavour.

BANANA AND CARROT SALAD

Slice 3 bananas and mix with 2 minced raw carrots and ¼ cup salted peanuts; bind with mayonnaise.

BANANA AND PEANUT SALAD

Cut some bananas in halves, slice each half into three, sprinkle with lemon juice, roll in chopped peanuts and place in a salad bowl with alternate layers of crisp lettuce. Serve with French dressing.

SUVA SALAD

Peel a cucumber and cut into 2-inch pieces; scoop out some of the inside to form cups. Dice ½ cup tomatoes, ½ cup cucumber and a little onion and mix with ¼ cup French dressing. Fill the cucumber cups with this and serve on lettuce leaves.

LIME SALAD DRESSING

4 tbsps. olive oil	2 tbsps. fresh lime juice
5 drops of tabasco sauce	A few grains of cayenne
⅓ tsp. pepper	¼ tsp. salt
1 tsp. celery salt	2 tsps. sugar

Mix all the ingredients and chill. Shake thoroughly before using.

PINEAPPLE PICKLE

Cut 7 lb. pineapple into small pieces, leaving out the core. Mix 3½ pints vinegar with 3 lb. brown sugar and 1 tbsp. each of cloves, peppercorns and broken cinnamon stick (tied in muslin). Boil for 10 minutes, add the fruit and cook till tender, then strain off the syrup and boil for 10 minutes longer. Bottle when cold.

PUMPKIN HONEY

Cut up 3 lb. pumpkin, boil until soft and rub through a colander. Put the pulp back into the saucepan with 3 lb. sugar, 6 oz. butter and grated rind and juice of 3 lemons; boil for ½ hour, stirring constantly. Bottle when cold.

BANANA JAM

2 lb. bananas, peeled and cut small	Grated rind and juice of 2 lemons
1½ lb. white sugar	

Mix all the ingredients together and boil rapidly, stirring constantly. When dark red in colour, the jam is cooked.

PINEAPPLE JAM

Allow the juice of ½ lemon and 1 lb. white sugar to each large pineapple. Cut the pineapple in very small cubes, squeeze the lemon juice over it, add the sugar and leave for 24 hours. Boil well for about 1 hour, or until it will set.

COCONUT PIE

1 coconut	1 cup sugar
1 tbsp. flour	¾ cup milk
1 tbsp. butter	4 oz. shortcrust pastry
1 egg white	

Grate the coconut flesh. Beat the egg white, add dry ingredients and butter and mix in the milk. Line a 7-inch pie plate with pastry, pour in the coconut mixture and bake in a moderately hot oven (425° F., mark 7) till brown and set.

COCONUT FRITTERS

1 cup flour	2 tbsps. butter
1½ tsps. baking powder	2 egg yolks
2 tsps. sugar	2 tbsps. coconut milk
1 cup grated coconut	Deep fat for frying

Sieved together the flour and baking powder and add the sugar and coconut. Add the butter and mix thoroughly with a fork. Add the egg yolks and coconut milk and mix all together. Turn on to a floured board and toss lightly until the dough looks smooth. Roll out ½ inch thick, cut into strips measuring about 2 by 1 inch and fry in deep fat until golden-brown.

TAPIOCA BANANAS

Fry some ripe bananas in butter; when cooked, mash well and add equal quantity of cooked sweetened tapioca and a little coconut cream. Make into a mould and put in a cool place to set.

BANANAS STUFFED WITH COCONUT

Peel some bananas and cut a small slit in the sides. Fill with freshly grated coconut, add some sugar and cook for ¾ hour in a small quantity of water. When cold, serve with iced lolo.

LOTE
(BANANA MOULD)

Mix 1 breakfastcup water with the juice of 6 lemons and sugar to taste; bring to the boil and slice into it 3–4 ripe bananas. Simmer until the bananas are soft, then stir in a little cornflour blended to a paste with cold water and simmer for 10 minutes. Pour into a mould, chill and serve with thick coconut cream.

BANANA ROLLS

Make some shortcrust pastry, roll out and cut into 4-inch squares. Place ½ a banana on each square, sprinkle with sugar, coconut and nutmeg and roll up, sealing the ends well. Place in a baking tin, dot with butter, sprinkle with sugar, prick well and bake in a slow oven (300° F., mark 1). Serve with cream or custard.

BAKED GRAPEFRUIT PUDDING

2¼ cups grapefruit sections	3 tsps. baking powder
	¼ tsp. salt
¾ cup brown sugar	1 egg
1½ cups flour	⅓ cup milk
4 tbsps. melted butter	

Free the grapefruit sections of pips and pith and lay them in a buttered dish. Mix the sugar and 1 tbsp. each of flour and butter, then sprinkle over the fruit. Sift the remaining flour, baking powder and salt, add the butter and mix well with a fork. Beat the egg and add milk to make ½ cup of liquid; add to the flour mixture. Turn out on to a floured board and knead lightly until smooth. Roll out ¼ inch thick and cut to fit the dish. Place on top of the grapefruit and bake in a hot oven (450° F., mark 8) for 25 minutes. Turn upside down on to a hot dish to serve.

LOLO SPONGE

3 eggs	1½ tsps. baking powder
1 teacup sugar	2 tbsps. cocoa
1 cup flour	1 cup lolo

Beat the eggs and sugar and add the flour, baking powder and cocoa, then the lolo. Cook in a moderate oven (350° F., mark 4) for about 20–25 minutes.

PINEAPPLE SNOW PUDDING

3½ cups canned pine-apple juice	¼ cup lemon juice
	1½ cups double cream
3 envelopes unflavoured gelatine	1½ cups flaked coconut
6 tbsps. granulated sugar	4 cups halved fresh strawberries (or frozen strawberries, thawed)
⅛ tsp. salt	
2 tsps. grated lemon rind	4 canned pineapple slices, quartered

Mix 1 cup pineapple juice, the gelatine and sugar; let stand for 5 minutes, then set the bowl in boiling water and stir till the gelatine is dissolved. Combine the remaining pineapple juice, the salt, lemon rind and lemon juice, then stir in the gelatine mixture. Refrigerate till it resembles unbeaten egg white. Beat the gelatine mixture till fluffy. Whip the cream; quickly fold it, and ¾ cup coconut, into the gelatine. Pour into a 2-quart mould and refrigerate till set.

Unmould the pudding on to a large serving dish. Sprinkle the top with some coconut and strawberries and arrange some quartered pineapple, strawberries and the rest of the coconut round the base. Hand the remaining pineapple and strawberries separately. Makes 8 servings.

KAIVITI GINGERBREAD

Lolo from 4 coconuts	2 tsps. ground cinnamon
2 small cups sugar	2 tsps. bicarbonate of soda dissolved in ½ cup warm milk
3 eggs	
4 small cups flour	
6 tsps. ground ginger	¾ cup golden syrup

Beat the lolo and sugar and add the eggs. Sift in the dry ingredients, then add the soda and milk and finally the syrup. Bake in a moderate oven (350° F., mark 4) for about 35–40 minutes.

ICE CREAM ALOHA

Place a ball of vanilla ice cream in each dessert dish or coconut shell and circle with banana slices.

TROPICAL TREASURE CAKE

Make and bake 2 Victoria sandwich cakes 8 inches in diameter; cool. Make a fluffy white cake frosting, using pineapple juice instead of water. Cover an inverted plate with strips of waxed paper. Lay one cake layer on them and spoon over it 1 cup canned crushed pineapple; spread a thin layer of frosting over this. Put the second cake layer on, then spoon on 1 cup canned crushed pineapple. Frost the entire cake with the rest of the frosting. Sprinkle the top and sides of the cake with 1 cup flaked coconut, then decorate the top with 1 cup canned crushed pineapple, thoroughly drained. Lift cake on to clean plate.

FRUIT PUNCH

Combine about 2 pints chilled canned pineapple juice (unsweetened), 1 pint chilled ginger ale and some Maraschino cherries and juice. Makes 8–10 glassfuls.

POI SUPPER

(A SOUTH SEAS MENU)

The following three dishes together with sweet potato may be used on the same menu and called a " poi supper." If canned poi is available, it should be served also. The meal may be finished off with slices of fresh pineapple.

LOMI LOMI SALMON

1 lb. salt salmon
3–5 ripe tomatoes
Crushed ice
1 large round onion or a bunch of green onions

Soak the salmon in water for a short time. If the salmon is very salty, repeat this process two or three times. Drain salmon and shred into very fine pieces and put in a basin, discarding all bones and skin. Cut up the tomatoes in fine pieces and add to the salmon. Do the same with the onion and then add crushed ice. Mix this with the hands. If green onions are used, be sure to use all the onion tops—the bits of green make this dish more attractive. The amount of crushed ice should be equal to the amount of the other ingredients. This is served while the ice is still solid. See also recipe on p. 500.

Canned salmon may be substituted if the salted variety is not available.

LAU-LAU

Freshly washed spinach or taro leaves
2–3 oz. fat pork
2–3 oz. stewing beef
Salt
Ti leaves or aluminium foil

To each lau-lau allow 3–6 leaves of spinach, one piece each pork and beef. Sprinkle with a little salt. Roll the spinach and meat in ti leaves (usually three per lau-lau) or wrap in aluminium foil. Place lau-laus in a steamer. Steam for about 5 hours (or it can be cooked in a pressure cooker for $1\frac{1}{2}$ hours). About $1\frac{1}{2}$ hours before the lau-lau are done, sweet potatoes may be placed in with the lau-laus and steamed with them.

CHICKEN LUAU

1 chicken, cut in slices
2 cups cooked taro or 1 packet frozen spinach, cooked
Cream from 1 coconut
Grated coconut

Brown the cut up chicken in a little butter in a large skillet or a medium-sized pan. Add enough water to cover and simmer until tender. Cook the spinach or taro and add to the chicken. Add salt to taste. Cook for 5 minutes. Add the coconut cream (a cream soup can be used as a substitute) and stir until it is well blended. The gravy will be a little watery, but thickening can be added.

To make this dish really elegant, remove all the bones and cut the meat into bite-size pieces.

What the

THE world drinks water, of course, when it is safe to drink and, frequently, when it isn't. But when he can afford it, man likes to drink something more interesting and exciting, that something depending on the resources of his country. Briefly the main drinks are beer, wine, spirits, tea, coffee, cocoa, fruit juice, natural mineral waters and synthetic drinks.

In Europe, the chief drinks are wine, beer and spirits made from fermented or distilled barley or potatoes, and mineral waters; imported tea, coffee and cocoa are drunk in large quantities.

Asia is largely a tea-drinking continent, with some wines and spirits from a variety of fruit and cereals.

Coffee, with wine as a close second, is the chief drink in North Africa, particularly in Algeria, Morocco and Tunisia. Further south, in Central Africa, drinks are made from fermented millets and other grains.

South America is best known for its coffee, which is also drunk in North America in addition to spirits from distilled rye and other grains. Fruit juice and synthetic drinks of the cola type are also popular.

Alcoholic drinks are extremely widespread and the pleasure they give is apparently universal. Almost anything containing sugar or starch can be fermented to produce a drink.

Although the best beers come from malted barley, beer is also made from other grains and from other foods in different parts of the world. The sap of the toddy-palm in the East, the sap of the cactus in Mexico, and even various flowers in India are fermented to make beer. Cider and perry are similarly made from apples and pears.

World drinks

Grapes make the best wine, but other fruit, flowers and vegetables are used. There is some gentle snobbery in sophisticated countries about the place of origin of various wines. According to the wine-snob other wines do not have the cachet—nor, to the connoisseur, the bouquet—of French and German wines, although Italian wines are becoming fashionable, and very drinkable wines are produced in Commonwealth countries, America, Eastern Europe and other parts of the world. The fortified wines, sherry and port are, of course, in a category of their own.

Spirits are distilled from fermented liquids and there are many of them, each with its distinctive characteristic. Brandy comes from wine, rum from sugar cane, whisky from barley and gin from various grains and potatoes flavoured with juniper berries. Scandinavian Aquavit is made from sawdust, of all things; Hungarian Slivovitz from plums; Ouzo is a Greek brandy, flavoured with aniseed. Liqueurs are spirits flavoured with fruit or herbs and often heavily sweetened.

Tea, which originated in China, spread to Java, Ceylon, India and Japan and was later introduced to Europe; it is now even growing in popularity in America. Tea-making is a great cause for misunderstanding between nations. The British have strong feelings about boiling water, not shared even by the originators of the drink, the Chinese. Green tea is popular in the East but generally disliked in other parts. Maté is a South American drink made from the leaves of a native shrub, which resembles tea, but is more stimulating. Various other herbal teas, or tisanes, are drunk in other parts of the world—for example, the mint tea of North Africa.

Coffee was discovered in Arabia (or, according to some stories, Ethiopia) and gradually spread over Africa, Europe and South America—it grows particularly well in the last-named region. It is the main drink in many countries and the methods of making it are even more varied and argued about than tea.

Cocoa originated in South America, where it was adopted by the Spaniards. The Aztecs considered the beverage to have magical curative powers and only the noblest of the aristocracy was allowed to drink it. The servants who prepared it were put to death if they were caught tasting it. The best cocoa comes from Venezuela, though much is also grown in Africa.

Fresh, bottled and canned fruit juice is popular in most Western countries, particularly the United States, but for some reason has never really " caught on " in Britain; most of the British actually seem to prefer the synthetic soft drinks and the comminuted " squashes."

Then there are natural and the artificial mineral waters. Mineral waters from springs all over the world are drunk, sometimes for their supposed healthful properties and sometimes because the local water supply is not pure; internationally known are Evian, Perrier, Vichy and Appollinaris. By aeration and the addition of mineral salts, imitations can be produced from ordinary water.

We cannot hope to mention all the drinks enjoyed throughout the world, but here are a few alcoholic ones, unfamiliar to Europeans as a whole.

Arrak : A particularly fierce spirit distilled from rice ; also spirits distilled from other sources, e.g., toddy-palm ; India and other Eastern countries.

Ava or Kawa : Fermented from the roots of a kind of pepper plant ; South Sea Islands.

Cajuada : Fermented from cashew nuts ; West Africa.

Cape Smoke : Crude spirit drunk by Africans ; South Africa.

Julep : Used to be drunk in England, but is now associated with the Southern States of the U.S.A. There are various recipes based on whisky (Scotch or Bourbon), brandy or rum, with mint, crushed ice and sugar.

Kwass : Made from rye flour, malt and mint ; Russia.

Mescal : A spirit distilled from the American aloe—drunk in Central and South America and Mexico.

Okolehao : Made from molasses, rice and taro, fermented and distilled ; Hawaii.

Pirau : Maori drink made from fermented corn ; New Zealand.

Pulque : Fermented from aloes ; can be distilled to give *tequila* ; Mexico.

Saké : Fermented from rice ; Japan.

Samshu : Fermented from rice and yeast ; China.

Tembo : A very potent East African drink made from a special type of long green banana ; the fruit is fermented for a month or two in a hole dug in the ground and lined with banana leaves.

Tequila : A Mexican drink, distilled from the American aloe.

Van der Hum : A South African liqueur made from Cape brandy and flavoured with tangerines.

Zubrowka : Vodka in which *Zubrowka* grass has been soaked, adding a little colour and taste.

THE word " cereal " has two or three meanings. Scientifically, it means the grasses that are grown for food. They have been selected and bred to produce larger seeds and now do not much resemble the plants first grown in Egypt and Arabia thousands of years ago. Cereals grow all over the world and even within the Arctic Circle, although the Eskimos themselves are not crop-growers. The amount of cereal in the Asian and African diet is far higher than in the prosperous Western countries.

In the notes on " The World's Food " we gave a list of the main cereals, to which we might add barley—probably the oldest cereal, it is not now much used for human food, but is important for cattle fodder and for making into malt for brewing. Oats are still important in Germany, North America and Britain. In addition to the familiar wheat, rice, rye and maize, there are such lesser known cereals as *adlay*, grown in Spain and Portugal, and *quinoa* in South America.

In the kitchen, " cereals " also means tapioca and arrowroot, which are root products ; sago, derived from the pith of a tree trunk and even soya-bean flour, which is really a legume, and a very valuable source of protein in some parts of the world.

Another meaning nowadays given to the word " cereals " is the processed and packaged form, as eaten at breakfast with milk ; they make a good meal and save work. The importance of all cereals is that they give lots of cheap calories and have a subdued taste—if any. Their cooking possibilities are endless.

We give below fuller notes on some of the more important cereals.

Wheat : The most important wheat product is bread, of which there are many varieties—see the next section.

Another popular wheat product is pasta, which originated in Italy. It is made from a very hard wheat flour, kneaded with oil and water, sometimes with an egg added. It is rolled out very thinly and hung up to dry before being made into *cannelloni, ravioli* and so on. Pasta is also produced commercially in a wide variety of shapes—tubes, ribbons, stars, shells and circles. Some are coloured green, some have a meat filling, some, the smaller ones like *vermicelli* and *stelline*, go into soups, and some are served with sauces.

The pasta is boiled from 5–20 minutes, depending on the size. Whatever the method of serving—and there are many delicious recipes—grated Parmesan cheese adds a tang to the dish.

Rice : Rice goes with lots of dishes. The way of eating it depends on the variety, and there are many types available. Patna rice is a thin grain, it does not absorb much liquid and boils into the dry, fluffy rice associated with curries. Italian rice is rather thicker, absorbs more liquid and is suitable for risotto. We doubt whether this theory covers Carolina rice in milk pudding—we think this is a British invention !

Good washing, fast boiling, quick rinsing and thorough draining are the secret

Cereals
and Breads

of dry, fluffy rice. For fried rice, cook in butter with onions, herbs, saffron, etc. The risotto and pilaff (or pilau) eaten in Mediterranean and Near East countries are creamy, not dry ; the rice is fried, unwashed, with onion, garlic and other ingredients, then simmered in a well-flavoured stock with vegetables, meat, chicken or fish.

Rice has now joined the ranks of " convenience " foods in the form of instant rice, which is commercially cooked and dried and merely needs soaking in hot water. Not a great time-saver, but a help if you cannot cook rice well.

Maize : Half the total world crop of maize grows in America, where corn-on-the-cob is particularly popular. Maize meal and hominy grits are other maize products in the States but almost unknown here. Maize meal is used in Italy in polenta, a sort of porridge. The grain, freed from all bran, is also ground into cornflour, which is practically pure starch. This is the basis of custard and blancmange powders. Maize, or corn oil, is used for salad dressings.

Millet : Because millet grows in poor, arid regions, its social status is low. Irrigation, almost synonymous with education and progress, means that wheat, which has a higher prestige value, can be grown, while millet is then neglected. It is not as nice to eat, anyway, but it is a pity to despise it, for its food value is high. The grains are generally husked, soaked and boiled into porridge. It is very rarely prepared commercially, as it is mostly eaten by the more backward peasants of Africa or Asia.

BREAD AROUND THE WORLD

THE best cereal for bread-making is wheat. The type of wheat determines the kind of flour, strong or weak, which in fact partly determines the sort of bread. How much of the wheat grain is used governs whether the bread is fine and white or coarse and dark. The popular demand is for white bread and it has been so all through history—white bread was highly prized even by the ancient Egyptians.

In various countries, wheat flour is eked out by adding potato flour, maize, barley, oats, rye, ground cassava or bean meal. In Europe, maize is often added to wheat flour in times of scarcity and it makes a good loaf. Some of the other cereals are also used by themselves, but they do not produce a true bread as we know it.

Basically, bread dough is made of flour and water and it can be baked unleavened, but is usually leavened by fermentation. Other ingredients can be added—milk, sugar, fat, eggs, dried fruits, wheat grains, poppy or caraway seeds. The dough can be baked in any number of shapes and sizes.

In Britain and most Western countries, several varieties of white, wheatmeal and wholemeal bread are available. French bread, crusty outside, white and soft inside, is baked two or three times a day and the housewife buys it fresh for every meal.

In Northern Europe, rye bread is commonly eaten. In Finland, for example, the bread is made mostly from rye, although wheat bread is available in some towns and is used for special occasions. Rye bread does not rise in the same way as wheat bread and is darker in colour—almost black if the whole grain is milled. Sour rye bread is popular. It is fermented with a piece of old dough which has gone sour, in much the same way as yoghourt and other fermented milks are made.

Crispbreads, originally, from Sweden, are made from either rye or wheat flour; they contain less water than ordinary bread. There are also *pretzels* and other varieties which could almost be termed biscuits.

In India, Pakistan and other Eastern countries, *chapattis* are made from whole wheat flour; water, salt and sometimes oil, are added and the dough is kneaded. It is rolled into very thin rounds and cooked in a flat iron pan. *Puris* are a little more extravagant; more oil is added, they are broken into smaller pieces and dropped into hot ghee or vegetable oil. A cheaper bread than either of these, *rotla*, is made from cornflour, which is kneaded with water, patted into rounds $\frac{1}{4}$ inch thick and cooked over the fire in a pan greased with ghee. (Incidentally, the flat or slightly curved iron pan, plate or griddle is used for breadmaking in most countries—oven-baked bread is not so general outside Europe.)

In Central America, the Mayan Indians make *tortillas*. The maize grains are treated with lime-water, ground into a dough and cooked on a hot iron plate; the result is a flat bread eaten daily by the Indians throughout the district, particularly in Mexico and Guatemala. The Central Americans of Spanish extraction eat more wheat bread. The Mestizos, Spanish-Indians, eat *rosquillas* prepared from maize flour and cheese. The Central American or Caribbean negro makes his own kind of pancake from wheat flour and fat.

There are many varieties of bread in Africa. *Injera*, the staple food in Ethiopia, for example, is made from a peculiar cereal called *teff* which has pin-head size seeds that are surprisingly high in food value. The dough of flour and water is fermented with a piece of old dough and allowed to sour before being cooked over the fire in the ubiquitous curved iron pan. The roots and stem of a plant called *enseta* are fermented for months, the fibres removed and the remaining dough baked into another sort of bread.

The story of bread is endless and fascinating and we cannot hope to cover it completely in these brief notes.

WE have listed below some fruit and vegetables that are uncommon or unknown in this country : a few of them may occasionally be available at specialised shops.

Alligator Pear	Another name for Avocado Pear : see below.
Annona	A name given to a number of tropical fruits, such as the Custard Apple, Cherimoya and Soncoya.
Avocado Pear	Found in many varieties, growing in tropical and sub-tropical climates. It is pear-shaped, usually green and weighs about $\frac{1}{2}$ lb. It contains a great deal of oil and can be served, halved and stoned, with salt and pepper or a French dressing.
Barberry	Many varieties. In the West, they were once used in pies and drinks, but are less popular now. In the East they are sometimes dried.
Blueberry	A small blue-black berry similar to the bilberry, grown in North America and used for pies and preserves.
Breadfruit	This looks rather like a pineapple, but the flesh is white and rather tasteless. It grows in most tropical countries, and is the staple food in some Pacific islands.
Bush Apple	A native of Australia, this resembles a plum rather than an apple.
Cape Gooseberry	Grown in tropical and sub-tropical countries and is rather like a cherry. It makes excellent preserves.
Chinese Gooseberry	A delicious fruit with a brownish, hairy skin and green flesh. It is often served cut in half sprinkled with sugar and scooped out with a teaspoon.
Crab Apple	There are many varieties. A red, yellow or greenish fruit. Not much used in the U.K. except for crab apple jelly.
Cranberry	A hard berry, growing on a small shrub. It is very acid, but has a pleasant flavour when added to sauces, relish, preserves and puddings. It is popular in the United States, particularly as cranberry sauce with roast turkey on Thanksgiving Day.
Custard Apple	Several varieties grow in the tropics. It is green or brownish in colour, with yellow pulpy flesh. It is rather large and has a knobbly skin.
Durian	A native of Thailand. A delicious fruit with a rather curious scent.

Fruit and Vegetables

Grenadilla	Passion fruit, the fruit of the passion flower (the English variety does not fruit). It has a tough purplish skin which is wrinkled when ripe. Inside there is a green liquid pulp with black seeds. It has a delicious flavour.
Goumi	Orange-coloured fruit, native to China.
Guava	The South African guava is about the size of an apple, with pink flesh and numbers of seeds. It is made into jelly and also guava cheese. The guava in Australia and New Zealand is quite a different fruit—a small, red-skinned berry with white flesh.
Jackfruit	Similar to breadfruit, it grows in East Africa, sometimes to an enormous size. This can be eaten raw or cooked, and the seeds can be roasted like chestnuts. In India, it is frequently added to curries.
Kumquat	A miniature orange, growing mainly in China and Japan. It is delicious preserved in syrup, like ginger.
Lime	Citrus fruit, similar to a lemon but smaller. It is yellow when really ripe, but green when imported into England. The juice is used to make cordial.
Litchi or Lychee	A Chinese fruit, about the size of a large gooseberry with a reddish-brown granulated shell and white flesh.
Lumyai	A native of Thailand. A fleshy golden fruit encased in a hard shell.
Loquat or Japanese Medlar	A yellowish fruit, the size of a plum, growing originally in China and Japan, and now in other warm countries. A bit tasteless, but it makes a pleasant jelly.
Mango	This grows in tropical countries, particularly Malaya and the West Indies. It is roughly pear-shaped and orange in colour. Some mangoes are delicious, others are really unpleasant to eat. They are usually made into preserves, particularly mango chutney.
Mangosteen	This has a brown rind and pink flesh and grows in the East and West Indies, India and Ceylon. It must be eaten soon after picking, or it loses its flavour.
Mirabelle	A small, golden plum and very sweet. Popular in France and Germany.
Monstera	The long, cone-shaped fruits of a climbing plant which grows in Mexico, Madeira, etc. Unusual and very good flavour.
Pawpaw, Papaya	A native of South America, now grown in most tropical countries and used as an important food in some. The varieties differ in colour and size. When ripe they can be eaten like a melon with sugar or boiled as a vegetable.

Persimmon . .	.	This grows in China, Japan and the United States and can be made into preserves. Some varieties are not very pleasant to eat.
Pomegranate .	.	This grows in Eastern countries and round the Mediterranean, particularly Spain. It is about the size of a grapefruit, with a tough rind and juicy flesh.
Quince . .	.	A round, yellow fruit not used much in England now, except in quince jelly.
Sloe . .	.	A small plum used on the Continent for jam and jelly making, and in this country for sloe jam and for flavouring a cordial made with gin.
Tamarind. .	.	Originally an Indian tree, the best now grow in the East Indies. The leaves, flowers and fruits are all eaten. The fruit is imported into England to make sauces and chutneys.
Ugli . .	.	This is a large fruit, a cross between a grapefruit and a mandarin orange. It is called a Tangelo in the United States.

VEGETABLES AND CEREALS

Adzuki . .	.	A bean grown in China and Japan. It can be cooked in the pod or the beans can be dried and ground into a sort of flour.
Alga Mar .	.	A seaweed, popular in Chile.
Aubergine or Egg Plant		There are many varieties, the purple-skinned one being the most usual in this country. It can be eaten in many ways, e.g., baked, fried, stuffed, in fritters and moussaka.
Bamboo Shoots	.	Mostly grown in tropical and sub-tropical climates in the East. The very young shoots are about 2 inches wide and yellowish. They can be obtained canned in this country.
Bean Shoots .	.	Small beans, frequently soya beans, are allowed to sprout for a few days and the little shoots are eaten. Popular in China and very typical of Chinese cooking in this country.
Brinjaul . .	.	A West Indian egg plant.
Capsicum. .	.	Peppers, available in many varieties. The two main types are hot, such as chilli, and sweet. The latter are becoming popular in this country. They are generally green, but sometimes they are red when ripe. Cayenne pepper is made from chillies, and paprika made from the seeds of the sweet pepper.

Carob . . .	Eaten in most Mediterranean countries, sometimes called locust bean. The whole pod is edible.
Coco Yam . .	This is a tropical plant. The roots are ground to make taro flour.
Dhal . . .	A variety of pulse, resembling split peas and lentils, popular in India. It is made into a sort of thick pease pudding.
Glutinous Rice . .	A species of rice grown largely in Siam but not widely available in England.
Gumbo . . .	A plant native to South America. The pods are known as okra and bania. There is also another plant by the same name in Africa and India.
Gourds . . .	These are grown all over the world. They are known as pumpkins and marrows in this country. Eaten as a vegetable, pudding or soup.
Kuchay . . .	A Chinese garlic.
Okra . . .	A bean, very popular in the United States and parts of Africa and India. Sometimes called quimbobo.
Soya Bean . .	Grown in the East, Africa and America. An important food in China. Can be eaten fresh as a vegetable or dried and pounded to a flour.
Succotash . .	Lima beans and sweet corn, cooked and then mixed together. Popular in the United States.
Sweet Potato . .	A tuber, like a large potato. It grows mainly in the tropics and sub-tropics. It can be cooked as a vegetable and is particularly delicious when roasted. In the tropics, it is frequently made into a pudding with spices, sugar and milk.
Truffle . . .	A fungus. It adds flavour to food, and is much used in pâté in France.
Wild Rice . .	This is not really rice but a grass with seeds resembling rice and cooked in the same way.
Yam . . .	Many varieties of this tuber are grown in the tropics. A staple food in some countries.

HERBS and spices have been used to flavour food throughout the history of the world. Whole economies were founded on the spice trade, exploration was initiated, wars were fought and fortunes were made. The explanation for the great importance of spices was that, before the days of preserving and processing, food was apt to be dull and monotonous, particularly in the winter, and as far as meat was concerned, frequently bad. Herbs and spices both alleviated the monotony and covered up the putrefaction.

Here is a " dictionary " of the most commonly used of these and similar flavourings :

Allspice . . . The Jamaican pepper, or pimento. Small dried berries of the pimento tree, very aromatic, not quite as hot as peppercorns. Used for pickling.

Angelica . . . An aromatic plant of which the green stems are sold in candied or crystallised form.

Anise . . . A plant of the fennel family, grown in China and in Mediterranean countries. The berries are much used in Oriental cooking and as a flavouring for sweets and liqueurs in the West. Aniseeds are the seeds of this plant.

Asafœtida . . . A kind of resinous gum of vegetable origin used by some Indians as a flavouring to replace onion and garlic.

Badian . . . A type of anise grown in China and India.

Basil . . . A herb with a flavour resembling cloves, native of the East Indies, but now grown in Europe.

Bay . . . A type of laurel tree, the leaves of which are a very popular flavouring.

Borage . . . A flavouring herb used to flavour drinks ; has a faintly cucumber flavour.

Capers . . . The pickled buds of a bush grown in Southern Europe.

Caraway . . . Seeds of a plant grown mostly in Holland and Germany and used in bakery and confectionery.

Cardamoms . . Spicy seeds of a plant grown in the East, particularly Malabar ; related to ginger.

Cayenne . . A very hot condiment produced from the pods and seeds of capsicums ; it is not really a pepper.

Chillies . . . Small red or orange capsicums ; both the seeds and the pods are very pungent. There are Chinese, Japanese, Indian and several African varieties ; large quantities also grown in Mexico.

Cinnamon . . The bark of a kind of laurel tree growing in the East, the finest coming from Ceylon. Used in both " stick " and ground form.

Herbs and Spices

Cloves	.	.	.	The dried flower-buds of a kind of myrtle tree, the finest coming from Penang, but the greatest quantity from Pemba and Zanzibar. Used in whole or ground form.
Coriander	.	.	Seeds of a plant resembling parsley; very aromatic, used to flavour confectionery, cordials, gin, etc., and sometimes included in curry powder and mixed spice.
Cubeb	.	.	Dried berries with a faint camphor taste, used in Oriental cookery. The shrub is a native of Java, but now grows in China and Africa as well as the East Indies.
Cumin	.	.	Seeds resembling caraway seeds but with a faint aniseed flavour. Used on the Continent in cheese and bread, and occasionally for making curry powder.
Dill	.	.	A plant that somewhat resembles fennel; the seeds taste rather like caraway. Used for flavouring pickles and sauces on the Continent and in America.
Fennel	.	.	A member of the cow-parsley family. The feathery leaves add a pleasant flavour to fish dishes; the seed is also used as a spice.
Fenugreek	.	.	The seed is used in the East and Near East. It is sometimes ground and added to curry powder.
Garam Masala	.	.	A flavouring made by mixing 1 tsp. ground cloves, 1 tsp. cinnamon powder, 1 tsp. ground black pepper, 1 tsp. cumin seeds and 1 tsp. ground cardamom seeds.
Ginger	.	.	The roots of a tree, originally a native of China and the East Indies, but now grown in other tropical countries. Used in whole and ground form, and also preserved in syrup and crystallised.
Horseradish	.	.	A hardy plant, the thick roots of which are scraped and used to make a pungent sauce or cream eaten with roast beef.
Mace	.	.	The red outer covering of the nutmeg (see opposite). Used in " blade " and ground form.
Marjoram	.	.	An aromatic plant native to certain Mediterranean countries. Has an excellent flavour either fresh or dried.
Mint	.	.	There are several varieties of this popular herb, of which garden or spearmint is the best known. Peppermint oil and essence are obtained from a similar plant.
Mustard	.	.	A plant of the same family as the cabbage; that grown in England is the best. There are two varieties with white (or yellow) seeds and with black ones. The latter produce the true mustard flavour, but the yellow seed helps to develop the flavour of the black.

Nutmeg	A native of the Moluccas, this tree is now grown in other East Indian Islands, in Africa and the West Indies. The fruits contain a single spicy seed, which is usually bought whole and grated as required.
Orégano	A kind of marjoram, with a flavour between that and sage.
Paprika	The bright red pods and seeds of a type of capsicum, sold in ground form; it is less pungent than other peppers. Hungary produces the finest paprika.
Pepper	The aromatic, " hot " seeds of a tropical plant; both white and black types come from the same source, the white being the riper fruit, with the dark rusk removed. Sold in whole form (peppercorns) or ground. Many products called pepper are not really from pepper trees but from capsicums—see Cayenne, Paprika.
Poppy Seeds	Greyish-black seeds of a special type of poppy; largely used on the Continent to flavour bread and cakes.
Rosemary	A herb that gives meat, particularly lamb, a delicious flavour.
Saffron	The dried and powdered stigmas of a flower of the crocus family. Saffron adds a deep yellow colour as well as a slightly bitter flavour to rice and curries.
Sage	The leaves of this herb have a strong, bitter-sweet flavour. It is used in sausages, stuffings, etc., in fresh or dried form.
Sesame	The seeds of a plant widely grown in India, Egypt, China and other regions. They are used as a flavouring and also pressed to produce oil. Very popular in India.
Tabasco	A pungent, hot, red sauce made from a special capsicum first grown in Tabasco, Mexico; used to flavour meat dishes.
Tarragon	A pungent herb, used in sauces and vinegar, giving a flavour rather like aniseed.
Thyme	A shrubby herb; the fragrant leaves are widely used in meat dishes as part of a *bouquet garni*.
Turmeric	The root of an East Indian plant of the ginger family, grown particularly in China and Zanzibar. It has a faintly bitter taste and is bright yellow. It is an important ingredient in Indian curry powder, is included in mustard pickles and is sometimes used as a substitute for saffron.
Vanilla	The dried seed pods of a type of orchid, used in sweet dishes. They may be used to flavour sugar, infused in milk, etc. The commercially prepared vanilla essence is even more widely used.

CHEESE is among the foods that are older than history. As soon as a pastoral civilisation evolved and mammals were tamed to provide a handy meat supply, it would occur to man to take advantage of their milk. Very vexing it must have been for the primitive housewife that she couldn't save the milk from the times of plenty to the inevitable lean periods, or even from day to day. But sooner or later it was discovered that milk, put into a skin for easy transport as the tribes pursued their nomadic life, turned into a pleasant food resembling yoghourt, as a result of the accidental shaking it received. With some attention, this fermented milk could then be produced at will. The next step must have occurred when the milk was put into an animal's stomach, suitably sewn up; a fresh stomach retains traces of rennin, which would clot the milk into cheese. The first example of processing food, that is, treating it to lengthen its life, had then been taken.

Probably Asiatic nomads wandering into Europe brought the habit of cheese-making with them. It has been a favourite food ever since, becoming more sophisticated with civilisation, and there are now innumerable varieties. The milk used can be that of the cow, goat, ewe, reindeer, buffalo, camel, llama, mare or yak; it is clotted by the addition of rennet, or it can first be soured and then clotted. Extra cream can be added or the milk skimmed; the whey may be allowed to drain away naturally or pressed out; the amount of salt added, the temperature, the bacteria and other local differences combine to produce the wide range of modern cheeses. Many of them are unique and cannot be produced except in their own districts. Some can be imitated in other parts of the world, though the imitations are rarely identical with the original.

Hard cheese, such as Cheddar, is treated by heating the curd, salting and pressing it. Semi-hard cheese, such as Stilton and Gorgonzola, is not pressed; the whey is allowed to drain away, or just lightly pressed out by hand. The cheeses in this category, like Roquefort, can be inoculated with mould to produce bluish veins. Soft cheese is not heated or salted at all and is not intended to be kept for long. Cottage cheese and Cambridge cheese are soft. Cream cheese should be made from cream, although the name is sometimes inaccurately used for Cottage cheese which is made from skimmed milk.

This classification varies a little depending on the source of information, some lists not using the term " semi-hard."

Europe has developed the art of cheese-making to a high degree. We in England are justifiably proud of the quality of our best cheeses, but France produces a far greater variety and Italy is not far behind. It would be impossible in this short chapter to mention more than a few, so we shall leave out most of those already well known in Great Britain and mention some of the more out-of-the-way cheeses. For instance, Norway has a goat's milk cheese, Gjetöst or Gietöst, firm in texture

Cheeses

and light brown in colour. Mysöst, made from whey, is found more or less throughout Scandinavia. In Spain the most popular cheese is the hard Manchego, made on small farms from ewe's milk, as it has been for many centuries ; Villalon is a soft cheese also made from ewe's milk. In Portugal, Serra is made from ewe's or goat's milk (or a mixture).

Moving eastwards in Europe, we find that the cheese in Greece is mostly the soft kind. One rather salty type, called Feta, is also available in other parts of the Balkans. Most of these countries produce, among other cheeses, a kind that resembles the Italian Cacciocavallo—even its name is similar, in forms like Katschkawalj. Turkey tends to prefer yoghourt, but even so has a fair amount of cheese. Tribesmen in neighbouring countries such as Iraq still produce cheese in the traditional way by hand ; Roos and Meira are two of the varieties.

In Egypt and other Arabic countries, buffalo milk is often used. Domiati, for instance, is a soft, white cheese which can either be eaten fresh or pickled in a brine solution and kept for some months. Further East, cheese is not so popular ; very little is eaten in India, for instance, except where European influence has encouraged it, though curds are a favourite foodstuff.

In Australia and New Zealand an enormous amount of cheese is produced, largely for export, most of it of the Cheddar type. In North America also the cheeses resemble the European ones, though with more variety, depending on the country from which the local farmers originally came. In the States, the main types are American Cheddar, Blue cheese (like Roquefort), Camosun (like Gouda), Chantelle (like Bel Paese), Mysöst, made from whey, and Swiss cheese (like Gruyère). Canada produces mainly Cheddar cheese, although there are small quantities of other kinds.

In Central and South America the cheeses naturally have Spanish and Portuguese names ; Queso gruyère o Emmenthal Argentino is an exotic example.

We might add, as an afterthought for those interested in etymology, that the word is almost the same in many European languages, starting with *caseus* in Latin —*käse*, *queijo*, *queso*, *kaser* and cheese are obviously related. *Fromage* and *formaggio* seem to be odd men out.

Weights
and Measures

Weights
and Measures

W.C.B.—34

THE usual tables of weights and measures can be found in many reference books including ordinary dictionaries. Here are just a few figures which may be useful when you are trying foreign recipes.

Weight

1 kilogram (1000 gm.)	=2·2 lb.
100 gm.	=about $3\frac{1}{2}$ oz.
1 oz.	=28 gm.
1 lb.	=a little under $\frac{1}{2}$ kilogram

Capacity

1 litre (10 decilitres or 1000 millilitres)	=1·76 Imperial pints, i.e., about $1\frac{3}{4}$ pints
1 fl. oz.	=28 ml.
1 Imperial pint	=0·57 litres or just over $\frac{1}{2}$ litre
1 Imperial gall.	=4.55 litres or just over $4\frac{1}{2}$ litres
1 Imperial pint	=20 fl. oz.
1 American pint	=16 fl. oz.
1 cup (British Standard)	=10 fl. oz.
1 cup (American)	=8 fl. oz.

Comparison of Cup Measures

	British Standard Cup	American Type Cup
Flour	5 oz.	4 oz.
Sugar	8 oz.	$6\frac{1}{2}$ oz.
Fat	8 oz.	$6\frac{1}{2}$ oz.
Fresh breadcrumbs .	3 oz.	$2\frac{1}{2}$ oz.
Grated cheese . .	4 oz.	$3\frac{1}{2}$ oz.
Currants, sultanas, etc. .	6 oz.	5 oz.

Advice on obtaining Ingredients

It has become a great deal easier in recent years to obtain unusual ingredients for foreign dishes both in London and in the Provinces; in London almost anything from all over the world can be bought in Soho, while throughout the country there are an increasing number of Health Food Shops, Delicatessens, and high-class Grocers such as W. H. Cullen which stock unusual foods.

The following is a list of the main shops in London where foreign ingredients for this book can be bought:—

Harrods—Knightsbridge, S W 1:
Selfridges—Oxford Street, W 1: } Both these stores have a very wide selection of unusual groceries, and will send non-perishables on mail order.

Fortnum and Mason—Piccadilly, W 1

Jackson's of Piccadilly, W 1

Del Monico—66 Old Compton Street, W 1: Ingredients for all Continental dishes.

Dine's Food Store—191 Shepherd's Market, W 1: Indian and African foods, both tinned and fresh.

Continental Food Store—Old Compton Street, W 1: Fruit and Vegetables, particularly out of season.

Schmidt's—41 Charlotte Street, W 1: German Food.

Leon's—6 Marylebone High Street, W 1: American and Jewish Food.

Likewise, in the United States there is a wide selection of Specialty Foods Shops in most of the major cities, and again there is an ever increasing number of Health Food Shops and Delicatessens:

Atlanta, Georgia
Cloudt's Food Store and Village Kitchen—1937 Peach Tree Road, N.E.
Colonial Stores
Matthews Supermarkets

Boston, Massachusetts
Cardulo's Gourmet Shop—6 Brattle Street, Cambridge
Ellis Provisions—Newbury Street, Boston
Sage's—60 Church Street, Cambridge
Savenore's—Kirkland Street, Cambridge

Chicago, Illinois
Conte-di-Savoia—555 West Roosevelt
Stop and Shop, Gourmet Department—1600 Washington Street
Kuhn's Delicatessan (German)—351 North Lincoln
Diamond Trading Company (Oriental)—1108 North Clark

San Francisco, California
Simon Brothers,—California Street

Cannery Gourmet and Liquor—2801 Leavenworth
Norman D. Lane in City of Paris—Union Square
Goldberg Bowen Gourmet Foods—Sutter, California and Fox Plaza
Washington, D.C.
Le Gourmet,—3318 "M" Street, Georgetown
What in the World—5441 MacArthur Boulevard, N.W.
Magruder's—5626 Connecticut Avenue, N.W.
Karl's Caterers, Inc—5018 Connecticut Avenue, N.W.
Safeway International—1110 "F" Street, N.W.
New York, New York
Bloomingdale's—Lexington and 59th Street
Charles and Company—340 Madison Avenue
Manganaro Brothers (Italian)—Ninth Avenue at 37th Street
Java-Indian Condiment Company (Indian)—440 Hudson Street
Murray's (Jewish)—2429 Broadway
Russ and Dauters (Jewish)—179 East Houston
Nyborg & Nelson (Scandinavian)—937 Second Avenue
Old Denmark—135 East 57th Street
New International Importing Company (Greek)—517 Ninth Avenue

House of Yemen (Arab and Middle Eastern)—370 Third Avenue
In Austalia most ingredients can be purchased at major Supermarkets, Department Store Foodhalls. There are Specialist Continental Delicatessens and a few Health Food Stores but some of the more very exotic ingredients might be fairly difficult to obtain:
Adelaide
David Jones (S.A.) Ltd.—44 Rundle Street, Adelaide
Brisbane
Myers Ltd.—270 Brunswick Street, Fortitude Valley
Canberra
David Jones Ltd.—Civic Centre, Canberra
Hobart
Bay Supermarket Ltd.—201 Sandy Bay Road, Sandy Bay
Melbourne
Georges Ltd.—Collins Street, Melbourne
Perth
Boans Pty. Ltd.—425 Wellington Street, Perth
Sydney
Daivd Jones Ltd.—Market Street, Sydney

ACKNOWLEDGMENTS

WE should like to thank the following for their kind help in the preparation of this book :

The High Commissioner for Ceylon ; The High Commissioner for Rhodesia and Nyasaland ; The High Commissioner for New Zealand ; The High Commissioner for Nigeria ; The Chilean Embassy ; The Czechoslovak Embassy ; The Icelandic Embassy ; The Imperial Ethiopian Embassy ; The Japanese Embassy ; The Luxembourg Embassy ; The Mexican Embassy ; The Peruvian Embassy ; The Legation of the Rumanian People's Republic ; The Tunisian Embassy ; Anglo-Argentine Society (Madame Herminia Gutierrez) ; Anglo-Austrian Society ; Anglo-Brazilian Society ; Anglo-Hellenic League ; Anglo-Spanish Society ; Association of Ceylon Women in the U.K. ; Brazilian Chamber of Commerce and Economic Affairs ; Brazilian Government Trade Bureau (Mr. P. J. Pullen) ; Ceallaigh Cain, Cookery Editor of *Mexico—This Month* ; *The Czechoslovak Woman* ; The East Africa Office ; Federation of Women Zionists of Great Britain and Ireland ; Good Housekeeping Institute of the U.S.A. ; Montreal Star-Standard Bureau ; Norwegian National Tourist Office ; Swedish Institute for Cultural Relations.

We should like to thank the following for their help in providing colour photographs:

The Australian Recipe Service	464.
The Danish Agricultural Producers	65, 80, 81.
Christian Délu	32, 112, 113, 160, 305, 352, 369, 384, 385.
The Dutch Dairy Bureau	145.
The Flour Advisory Bureau	48, 49, 161, 240.
Good Housekeeping	33, 64, 128, 129, 144, 176, 177, 192, 193, 224, 225, 241, 257, 272, 273, 304, 320, 321, 336, 337, 353, 368, 416, 417, 432, 433, 465, 480, 481.
The Swiss Cheese Centre	256.

COLOUR PLATES

Index

The following abbreviations, which appear in this Index, indicate the country or district of origin of the various recipes.

A : Austria ; Au : Australia ; B/L : Belgium and Luxembourg ; Br.I : British Isles ; C : Canada ; Car : Caribbean ; Cen.Am : Central America and Mexico ; Ch : China ; Cz : Czechoslovakia ; D : Denmark ; EA : East Africa ; F : France ; G : Germany ; Gr : Greece : H : Holland ; Hu : Hungary ; I : Israel ; I/P/C : India, Pakistan and Ceylon ; It/M : Italy and Malta ; J/K : Japan, Korea and the Philippines ; ME : Middle East (Syria, Lebanon, Iraq and Iran) ; M/S/I : Malaya, Siam and Indonesia ; NA : North Africa ; N/F : Norway and Finland ; NZ : New Zealand ; P : Portugal ; Pol : Poland ; R : Russia ; R/B : Rumania and Bulgaria ; S : Spain ; SA : South Africa ; S.Am : South America ; SS : South Seas ; Sw : Switzerland ; Swe : Sweden ; T : Turkey ; USA : United States ; WA : West Africa ; Y : Yugoslavia.